The Heritage Guide to the Constitution

Library of Congress Cataloging-in-Publication Data

The Heritage guide to the constitution / edited by Matthew Spalding, Executive Editor, David F. Forte, Senior Editor ; foreword by Edwin Meese III, Chairman of the Editorial Advisory Board. -- Fully revised second edition.
        pages cm
    Summary: "Everything you thought you knew about the Constitution and more-broken down, spelled out, and expounded upon. The Heritage Foundation presents its updated Guide to the Constitution, the preeminent and invaluable reference (with clause-by-clause analyses) for policy-makers and students alike. With laws deconstructed, addendums unveiled, this guide proves to be the most comprehensive authority on our country's framework"-- Provided by publisher.
    ISBN 978-1-62157-268-8 (hardback)
    1. United States. Constitution. 2. Constitutions--United States. 3. Constitutional law--United States. I. Spalding, Matthew, editor. II. Forte, David F., editor. III. Heritage Foundation (Washington, D.C.) IV. Title: Guide to the Constitution.
    KF4527.H47
    2014
    342.7302'3--
    dc23
                2014027849

Published in the United States by
Regnery Publishing   The Heritage Foundation
A Division of Salem Media Group   214 Massachusetts Avenue NE
300 New Jersey Avenue NW   Washington, DC 20002
Washington, DC 20001   (202) 546-4400
www.Regnery.com   www.heritage.org

Manufactured in the United States of America

10 9 8 7 6 5 4 3

Books are available in quantity for promotional or premium use. For information on discounts and terms, please visit our website: www.Regnery.com.

THE HERITAGE GUIDE
TO THE
CONSTITUTION
FULLY REVISED SECOND EDITION

David F. Forte
Senior Editor

Matthew Spalding
Executive Editor

EDITORIAL ADVISORY BOARD

CONTENTS

CONTRIBUTORS

William B. Allen
Professor of Political Philosophy
Michigan State University

Albert W. Alschuler
Julius Kreeger Professor Emeritus of Law
and Criminology
Northwestern University Law School

Dennis W. Arrow
Professor of Law
Oklahoma City University School of Law

John S. Baker, Jr.
Professor Emeritus
Louisiana State University Law Center

Rachel E. Barkow
Segal Family Professor of Regulatory Law
and Policy
New York University School of Law

William Baude
Neubaurer Family Assistant Professor of Law
University of Chicago Law School

Herman Belz
Professor Emeritus of History
University of Maryland

Thomas Berg
James L. Oberstar Professor of Law and
Public Policy
University of St. Thomas School of Law

David E. Bernstein
George Mason University Foundation Professor
George Mason University School of Law

Joseph Bessette
Alice Tweed Tuohy Professor of Government
and Ethics
Claremont McKenna College

G. Robert Blakey
William J. and Dorothy K. O'Neill Chair in
Law Emeritus
Notre Dame Law School

Gerard V. Bradley
Professor of Law
Notre Dame Law School

James L. Buckley
Senior Judge
United States Court of Appeals, District of
Columbia Circuit

Michael A. Carrier
Distinguished Professor of Law
Rutgers School of Law—Camden

Lee Casey
Partner
BakerHostetler

Eric Chiappinelli
Frank McDonald Endowed Professor of Law
Texas Tech University School of Law

Roger Clegg
President & General Counsel
Center for Equal Opportunity

Charles Cooper
Chairman
Cooper & Kirk, PLLC

Douglas Cox
Partner
Gibson, Dunn & Crutcher LLP

Robert Delahunty
Associate Professor
University of St. Thomas School of Law

Brannon P. Denning
Professor of Law
Cumberland School of Law, Samford University

John G. Douglass
Professor of Law
University of Richmond School of Law

Daniel L. Dreisbach
Professor of Justice, Law, and Society
School of Public Affairs, American University

Donald Dripps
Warren Distinguished Professor of Law
University of San Diego School of Law

John C. Eastman
Henry Salvatori Professor of Law &
Community Service
Chapman University School of Law

Einer Elhauge
Carroll and Milton Petrie Professor of Law
Harvard Law School

James W. Ely, Jr.
Milton R. Underwood Professor of
Law Emeritus
Vanderbilt University Law School

David Engdahl
Professor Emeritus
Seattle University School of Law

Trent England
Vice President for Strategic Initiatives
Oklahoma Council of Public Affairs

Richard A. Epstein
James Parker Hall Distinguished Service
Professor Emeritus of Law
The University of Chicago

Edward Erler
Professor Emeritus
California State University San Bernadino

John Feerick
Norris Professor of Law
Fordham University School of Law

David F. Forte
Professor
Cleveland Marshall School of Law

Matthew Franck
Director, William E. and Carol G. Simon
Center on Religion and the Constitution
Witherspoon Institute

Charles Fried
Beneficial Professor of Law
Harvard Law School

Richard W. Garnett
Professor of Law
Notre Dame Law School

Todd Gaziano
Senior Fellow in Constitutional Law
Pacific Legal Foundation

Michael J. Gerhardt
Samuel Ashe Distinguished Professor in
Constitutional Law
University of North Carolina at Chapel Hill
School of Law

Andrew S. Gold
Professor of Law
DePaul University College of Law

Eric Grant
Senior Counsel
Hicks Thomas LLP

Michael S. Greve
Professor of Law
George Mason University School of Law

Arthur Hellman
Sally Ann Semenko Endowed Chair
University of Pittsburgh School of Law

James C. Ho
Partner
Gibson, Dunn & Crutcher LLP

John Inazu
Associate Professor of Law and Political Science
Washington University

Erik M. Jensen
Schott-van den Eynden Professor
Case Western Reserve Law School

Patrick Kelley
Professor of Law Emeritus
Southern Illinois University School of Law

Gary Kepplinger
Retired
Government Accountability Office

Orin S. Kerr
Fred C. Stevenson Research Professor of Law
George Washington University

Vasan Kesavan
Investment Analyst
Valinor Management

Charles Kesler
Dengler-Dykema Distinguished Professor of
Government
Claremont McKenna College

Adam Kurland
Professor of Law
Howard University

Tadahisa Kuroda
Deceased

Joan L. Larsen
Counsel to the Associate Dean for Student and
Graduate Activities
University of Michigan Law School

Gary Lawson
Philip S. Beck Professor of Law
Boston University School of Law

Andrew D. Leipold
Edwin M. Adams Professor of Law
University of Illinois College of Law

Robert Levy
Chairman of the Board of Directors
Cato Institute

Nelson Lund
University Professor
George Mason University School of Law

Earl Maltz
Distinguished Professor
Rutgers School of Law—Camden

Calvin Massey
Daniel Webster Distinguished Professor of Law
University of New Hampshire School of Law

Forrest McDonald
Distinguished University Research Professor
Emeritus
University of Alabama

John McGinnis
George C. Dix Professor in Constitutional Law
Northwestern University School of Law

Thomas W. Merrill
Charles Evans Hughes Professor of Law
Columbia Law School

Tiffany J. Miller
Associate Professor
University of Dallas

Paul Moreno
William and Berniece Grewcock Chair in
Constitutional History
Hillsdale College

Andrew P. Morriss
D. Paul Jones, Jr. & Charlene Angelich Jones
Chairholder of Law
University of Alabama School of Law

Thomas Nachbar
Professor of Law
University of Virginia School of Law

John Copeland Nagle
John N. Matthews Professor of Law
Notre Dame Law School

Robert G. Natelson
Senior Fellow in Constitutional Jurisprudence
Independence Institute

Erin O'Connor
Milton R. Underwood Chair in Law
Vanderbilt University Law School

Mackubin Owens
Professor of National Security Affairs
Naval War College

Bruce Peabody
Professor of Political Science
Fairleigh Dickinson University

Anthony Peacock
Professor, Department of Political Science
Utah State University

Terence Pell
President
Center for Individual Rights

Richard Peltz-Steele
Professor of Law
University of Massachusetts School of Law

Ronald J. Pestritto
Charles and Lucia Shipley Chair in American
Constitution
Hillsdale College

James Pfiffner
University Professor of Public Policy
George Mason University

Saikrishna B. Prakash
David Lurton Massee, Jr., Professor of Law
University of Virginia School of Law

Stephen B. Presser
Raoul Berger Professor of Legal History
Northwestern University School of Law

Claire Priest
Professor of Law
Yale Law School

Robert J. Pushaw, Jr.,
James Wilson Endowed Professor of Law
Pepperdine School of Law

Michael D. Ramsey
Hugh and Hazel Darling Foundation
Professor of Law
University of San Diego Law School

Michael B. Rappaport
Hugh and Hazel Darling Foundation
Professor of Law
University of San Diego Law School

Paul Rosenzweig
Founder
Red Branch Consulting

Ralph Rossum
Department of Government
Claremont McKenna College

Ronald D. Rotunda
Doy & Dee Henley Chair
Chapman University School of Law

Stephen E. Sachs
Assistant Professor of Law
Duke University School of Law

Stephen Safranek
General Counsel and Corporate Secretary
Wiss, Janney, Elstner Associates, Inc.

Stephen Saltzburg
Wallace and Beverley Woodbury University
Professor of Law
The George Washington University Law
School

Peter W. Schramm
Senior Fellow
John M. Ashbrook Center

J. Gregory Sidak
Chairman
Criterion Economics, L.L.C.

Jeffrey Sikkenga
Associate Professor of Political Science
Ashland University

Bradley Smith
Josiah H. Blackmore II/Shirley M. Nault
Designated Professor of Law
Capital University Law School

Loren Smith
Judge
United States Court of Federal Claims

David Smolin
Harwell G. Davis Professor of Constitutional
Law
Cumberland School of Law,
Samford University

Matthew Spalding
Associate Vice President and Dean of
Educational Programs
Hillsdale College

Andrew Spiropoulos
Professor of Law
Oklahoma City University School of Law

Milena Sterio
Associate Professor of Law
Cleveland Marshall College of Law

William J. Stuntz
Deceased

Paul Taylor
Chief Counsel
House Judiciary Subcommittee on the
Constitution and Civil Justice

George Thomas
Board of Governors Professor of Law
Rutgers School of Law—Newark

Daniel Troy
Senior Vice President and General Counsel
GlaxoSmithKline

Michael Uhlmann
Professor
Claremont Graduate University

Paul Verkuil
Chairman of the Administrative Conference
of the United States
Benjamin N. Cardozo School of Law

Adrian Vermeule
John H. Watson, Jr. Professor of Law
Harvard Law School

Eugene Volokh
Gary T. Schwartz Professor of Law
University of California, Los Angeles School
of Law

David Wagner
Professor
Regent University School of Law

Bradley C. S. Watson
Chairman, Politics Department
Saint Vincent College

Ryan Williams
Associate in Law
Columbia University School of Law

John Yoo
Emanuel S. Heller Professor of Law
University of California Berkeley School of
Law

Ernest A. Young
Alston & Bird Professor of Law
Duke University School of Law

Todd Zywicki
University Foundation Professor of Law
George Mason University School of Law

Preface

*T*he *Heritage Guide to the Constitution* is intended to provide a succinct and accurate explanation of each clause of the Constitution as understood by the framing generation and as applied in contemporary law. While the *Guide* provides a reliable reference for lawmakers and policymakers and is useful for the trained jurist, it is written to be accessible and helpful for informed citizens and students of the Constitution as well.

To create such a unique line-by-line analysis of our supreme law, the editors engaged scholars and experts to elucidate each clause of the Constitution, from the Preamble to the Twenty-seventh Amendment. Each contributor was asked to write a brief essay on a particular clause with two objectives. First, the article was to provide a description of the original understanding of the clause, as far as it can be determined. If within the standard of original understanding there are credible and differing interpretations, they were to be noted and explained. (The concept of "originalism" is discussed in the introductory essay, "The Originalist Perspective.") Second, the article was to provide an explanation of the current state of the law regarding the clause and, where appropriate, to give brief explanations of the historical development of current doctrine. At the end of each essay, the authors have added cross-references to other clauses in the Constitution, suggestions for further research, and a listing of significant cases concerning that clause. (An index of referenced cases is provided in Appendix A.)

Many individuals deserve acknowledgment for their ideas, comments, and substantive contributions in the long process of compiling this book. The project began in conversations between Dr. David F. Forte, Dr. Matthew Spalding, and then–Vice President Adam Meyerson of The Heritage Foundation and continued with the steady guidance of Edwin Meese III, the Ronald Reagan Distinguished Fellow in Public Policy. Executive Vice President Phil Truluck understood the importance of this unique scholarship and strongly supported the project from the beginning.

Mr. Meese acted as the Chairman of this project's Editorial Advisory Board, which included distinguished scholars who read and commented on the essays as they were produced and edited. The Editorial Advisory Board for the second edition is made up of Gary S. Lawson of Boston University School of Law, John O. McGinnis of Northwestern University School of Law, Michael B. Rappaport of the University of San Diego School of Law, and Ronald D. Rotunda of Chapman University School of Law.

Numerous individuals contributed to the project working under Dr. Spalding. In the production of the second edition, Julia Shaw was invaluable as Assistant Executive Editor for the project, tracking essays through the process, checking case citations, and generally keeping a very complicated project organized. Ashlea Varndell assisted the project's management, and Michael Kelsey supported the project throughout as a Research Fellow at Heritage and then Hillsdale College. Student researchers Renee Davis of the University of Dallas and John Brooks of Hillsdale College supported the project while interning at The Heritage Foundation. Heritage's then–Vice President for Communications and Marketing Genevieve Wood played a vital role in the publication of the *Guide*, and Joshua Shepherd assisted with its production and marketing. Initial line editing was done by Jan Smith.

Several researchers also supported the project, working under Dr. Forte: Jon Beckman, Meggan Decker, Daniel Dew, Megan Dillhoff, Nathan Guinn, Matthew Hebebrand, Kevin McConnell, Anthony Miranda, Ryan Mulvey, Brandon Piteo, Benjamin Pruett, Colin Ray, Peter Reed, Christopher Stuart, and John Clay Sullivan.

As the revisions for the second edition began, the editors engaged a number of scholars to review relevant scholarly literature that had been published since the first edition: Kurt T. Lash of the University of Illinois College of Law, Gary S. Lawson of Boston University School of Law, Robert G. Natelson of the Independence Institute, Michael B. Rappaport of the University of San Diego School of Law, Ronald D. Rotunda of Chapman University School of Law, and Eugene Volokh of the UCLA School of Law. Other scholars, including some who were also contributors, provided valuable commentary on a number of particular articles.

Throughout, we have used *The Chicago Manual of Style* and *The Bluebook: A Uniform System of Citations* as style guides. For the text of the Constitution, we used the National Archives' transcription of the document in its original form. For *The Federalist Papers* we used the 2006 Signet Classics edition, edited by Clinton Rossiter with an introduction and notes by Charles Kesler, which is taken from the first edition of the collected essays published in 1788 by J. and A. McLean.

Founded in 1973, The Heritage Foundation is a research and educational institution whose mission is to formulate and promote public policies based on the principles of free enterprise, limited government, individual freedom, traditional American values, and a strong national defense. Governed by an independent Board of Trustees, The Heritage Foundation is an independent, tax-exempt institution.

The *Heritage Guide to the Constitution* was made possible by two self-made entrepreneurs and generous philanthropists who made endowments to The Heritage Foundation. Born in Italy, Henry Salvatori founded the Western Geophysical Company, one of the most successful oil-exploration and contracting enterprises in the world. B. Kenneth Simon was a U.S. Marine during the Second World War before founding and building a thriving business to distribute, design, and contract the manufacture of packaging materials. Later in life, both men dedicated their time and considerable fortunes to strengthening the underpinnings of American liberty and constitutionalism.

THE MEANING OF THE CONSTITUTION

*T*he Constitution of the United States has endured for over two centuries. It remains the object of reverence for nearly all Americans and an object of admiration by peoples around the world. William Gladstone was right in 1878 when he described, in *Life and Public Services,* the U.S. Constitution as "the most wonderful work ever struck off at a given time by the brain and purpose of man."

Part of the reason for the Constitution's enduring strength is that it is the complement of the Declaration of Independence. The Declaration provided the philosophical basis for a government that exercises legitimate power by "the consent of the governed," and it defined the conditions of a free people, whose rights and liberty are derived from their Creator. The Constitution delineated the structure of government and the rules for its operation, consistent with the creed of human liberty proclaimed in the Declaration.

Justice Joseph Story, in his *Familiar Exposition of the Constitution of the United States* (1840), described our founding document in these terms:

> We shall treat [our Constitution], not as a mere compact, or league, or confederacy, existing at the mere will of any one or more of the States, during their good pleasure; but, (as it purports on its face to be) as a Constitution of Government, framed and adopted by the people of the United States, and obligatory upon all the States, until it is altered, amended, or abolished by the people, in the manner pointed out in the instrument itself.

By the diffusion of power—horizontally among the three separate branches of the federal government and vertically in the allocation of power between the central government and the states— the Constitution's Framers devised a structure of government strong enough to ensure the nation's future strength and prosperity but without sufficient power to threaten the liberty of the people.

The Constitution and the government it establishes "has a just claim to [our] confidence and respect," George Washington wrote in his *Farewell Address* (1796), because it is "the offspring of our choice, uninfluenced and unawed, adopted upon full investigation and mature deliberation, completely free in its principles, in the distribution of its powers uniting security with energy, and containing, within itself, a provision for its own amendment."

The Constitution was born in crisis, when the very existence of the new United States was in jeopardy. The Framers understood the gravity of their task. As Alexander Hamilton noted in the general introduction to *The Federalist*,

> [A]fter an unequivocal experience of the inefficacy of the subsisting federal government, [the people] are called upon to deliberate on a new Constitution for the United States of America. The subject speaks its own importance; comprehending in its consequences nothing less than the existence of the Union, the safety and welfare of the parts of which it is composed, the fate of an empire in many respects the most interesting in the world.

Several important themes permeated the completed draft of the Constitution. The first, reflecting the mandate of the Declaration of Independence, was the recognition that the ultimate authority of a legitimate government depends on the consent of a free people. Thomas Jefferson had set forth the basic principle in his famous formulation:

> We hold these truths to be self-evident, that all men are created equal, that they are endowed by their Creator with certain unalienable Rights, that among these are Life, Liberty, and the pursuit of Happiness. That to secure these rights, Governments are instituted among Men deriving their just powers from the consent of the governed.

That "all men are created equal" means that they are equally endowed with unalienable rights. Nature does not single out who is to govern and who is to be governed; there is no divine right of kings. Nor are rights a matter of legal privilege or the benevolence of some ruling class. Fundamental rights exist by nature, prior to government and conventional laws. It is because these individual rights are left unsecured that governments are instituted among men.

Consent is the means by which equality is made politically operable and whereby arbitrary power is thwarted. The natural standard for judging if a government is legitimate is whether that government rests on the consent of the governed. Any political powers not derived from the consent of the governed are, by the laws of nature, illegitimate and hence unjust.

The "consent of the governed" stands in contrast to "the will of the majority," a view more current in European democracies. The "consent of the governed" describes a situation in which the people are self-governing in their communities, religions, and social institutions and into which the government may intrude only with the people's consent. There exists between the people and limited government a vast social space in which men and women, in their individual and corporate capacities, may exercise their self-governing liberty. In Europe, the "will of the majority" signals an idea that all decisions are ultimately political and are routed through the government. Thus, limited government is not just a desirable objective; it is the essential bedrock of the American polity.

A second fundamental element of the Constitution is the concept of checks and balances. As James Madison famously wrote in *The Federalist* No. 51,

> In framing a government which is to be administered by men over men, the great difficulty lies in this: you must first enable the government to control the governed; and in the next place oblige it to control itself. A dependence on the people is, no doubt, the primary control on the government; but experience has taught mankind the necessity of auxiliary precautions.

These "auxiliary precautions" constitute the improved science of politics offered by the Framers and form the basis of their "republican remedy for the diseases most incident to republican government." (*The Federalist* No. 10)

The "diseases most incident to republican government" were basically two: democratic tyranny and democratic ineptitude. The first was the problem of majority faction, the abuse of minority or individual rights by an "interested and overbearing" majority. The second was the problem of making a democratic form of government efficient and effective. The goal was limited but energetic government. The constitutional object was, as the late constitutional scholar Herbert Storing said, "a design of government with the powers to act and a structure to make it act wisely and responsibly."

The particulars of the Framers' political science were catalogued by Madison's celebrated collaborator in *The Federalist*, Alexander Hamilton. Those particulars included such devices as representation, bicameralism, independent courts of law, and the "regular distribution of power into distinct departments," as Hamilton put it in *The Federalist* No. 9; these were "means, and powerful means, by which the excellencies of republican government may be retained and its imperfections lessened or avoided."

Central to their institutional scheme was the principle of separation of powers. As Madison bluntly put it in *The Federalist* No. 47, the "preservation of liberty requires that the three great departments of power should be separate and distinct," for, as he also wrote,

> The accumulation of all powers, legislative, executive, and judiciary, in the same hands, whether of one, a few, or many, and whether hereditary, self-appointed, or elective, may justly be pronounced the very definition of tyranny.

Madison described in *The Federalist* No. 51 how structure and human nature could be marshaled to protect liberty:

> [T]he great security against a gradual concentration of the several powers in the same department consists in giving to those who administer each department the necessary constitutional means and personal motives to resist encroachments of the others.

Thus, the separation of powers frustrates designs for power and at the same time creates an incentive to collaborate and cooperate, lessening conflict and concretizing a practical community of interest among political leaders.

Equally important to the constitutional design was the concept of federalism. At the Constitutional Convention there was great concern that an overreaction to the inadequacies of the Articles of Confederation might produce a tendency toward a single centralized and all-powerful national government. The resolution to such fears was, as Madison described it in *The Federalist* No. 39, a government that was "neither wholly federal nor wholly national" but a composite of the two. A half-century later, Alexis de Tocqueville would celebrate democracy in America as precisely the result of the political vitality spawned by this "incomplete" national government.

The institutional design was to divide sovereignty between two different levels of political entities, the nation and the states. This would prevent an unhealthy concentration of power in a single government. It would provide, as Madison said in *The Federalist* No. 51, a "double security … to the rights of the people." Federalism, along with separation of powers, the Framers thought, would be the basic principled matrix of American constitutional liberty. "The different governments," Madison concluded, "will control each other, at the same time that each will be controlled by itself."

But institutional restraints on power were not all that federalism was about. There was also a deeper understanding—in fact, a far richer understanding—of why federalism mattered. When the delegates at Philadelphia convened in May 1787 to revise the ineffective Articles of Confederation, it was a foregone conclusion that the basic debate would concern the proper role of the states. Those who favored a diminution of state power, the Nationalists, saw unfettered state sovereignty under the Articles as the problem; not only did it allow the states to undermine congressional efforts to govern, it also rendered individual rights insecure in the hands of "interested and overbearing majorities." Indeed, Madison, defending the Nationalists' constitutional handiwork, went so far as to suggest in *The Federalist* No. 51 that only by way of a "judicious modification" of the federal principle was the new Constitution able to remedy the defects of popular, republican government.

The view of those who doubted the political efficacy of the new Constitution was that good popular government depended quite as much on a political community that would promote civic or public virtue as on a set of institutional devices designed to check the selfish impulses of the majority. As Herbert Storing has shown, this concern for community and civic virtue tempered and tamed somewhat the Nationalists' tendency toward simply a large nation. Their reservations, as Storing put it, echo still through our political history.[1]

It is this understanding, that federalism can contribute to a sense of political community and hence to a kind of public spirit, that is too often ignored in our public discussions about federalism. But in a sense, it is this understanding that makes the American experiment in popular government truly the novel undertaking the Framers thought it to be.

At bottom, in the space left by a limited central government, the people could rule themselves by their own moral and social values and call on local political institutions to assist them. Where the people, through the Constitution, did consent for the central government to have a role, that role would similarly be guided by the people's sense of what was valuable and good as articulated through the political institutions of the central government. Thus at its deepest level popular government means a structure of government that rests not only on the consent of the governed but also on a structure of government wherein the views of the people and their civic associations can be expressed and translated into public law and public policy, subject, of course, to the limits established

---

1   Herbert J. Storing, "The Constitution and the Bill of Rights," in Joseph M. Bessette, ed., *Toward a More Perfect Union: Writings of Herbert J. Storing* (Washington, D.C.: The AEI Press, 1995).

by the Constitution. Through deliberation, debate, and compromise, a public consensus is formed about what constitutes the public good. It is this consensus on fundamental principles that knits individuals into a community of citizens. And it is the liberty to determine the morality of a community that is an important part of our liberty protected by the Constitution.

The Constitution is our most fundamental law. It is, in its own words, "the supreme Law of the Land." Its translation into the legal rules under which we live occurs through the actions of all government entities, federal and state. What we know as "constitutional law" is the creation not only of the decisions of the Supreme Court, but also of the various Congresses and of the president.

Yet it is the court system, particularly the decisions of the Supreme Court that most observers identify as providing the basic corpus of "constitutional law." This body of law, this judicial handiwork, is, in a fundamental way, unique in our scheme, for the Court is charged routinely, day in and day out, with the awesome task of addressing some of the most basic and most enduring questions that face our nation. The answers the Court gives are very important to the stability of the law so necessary for good government. But as the constitutional historian Charles Warren once noted, what is most important to remember is that "however the Court may interpret the provisions of the Constitution, it is still the Constitution which is the law, not the decisions of the Court."[2]

By this, of course, Warren did not mean that a constitutional decision by the Supreme Court lacks the character of binding law. He meant that the Constitution remains the Constitution and that observers of the Court may fairly consider whether a particular Supreme Court decision was right or wrong. There remains in the country a vibrant and healthy debate among the members of the Supreme Court, as articulated in its opinions, and between the Court and academics, politicians, columnists and commentators, and the people generally about whether the Court has correctly understood and applied the fundamental law of the Constitution. We have seen throughout our history that when the Supreme Court greatly misconstrues the Constitution, generations of mischief may follow. The result is that, of its own accord or through the mechanism of the appointment process, the Supreme Court may come to revisit some of its doctrines and try, once again, to adjust its pronouncements to the commands of the Constitution.

This recognition of the distinction between constitutional law and the Constitution itself produces the conclusion that constitutional decisions, including those of the Supreme Court, need not be seen as the last words in constitutional construction. A correlative point is that constitutional interpretation is not the business of courts alone but is also, and properly, the business of all branches of government. Each of the three coordinate branches of government created and empowered by the Constitution—the executive and legislative no less than the judicial—has a duty to interpret the Constitution in the performance of its official functions. In fact, every official takes a solemn oath precisely to that effect. Chief Justice John Marshall, in *Marbury v. Madison* (1803), noted that the Constitution is a limitation on judicial power as well as on that of the executive and legislative branches. He reiterated that view in *McCulloch v. Maryland* (1819) when he cautioned judges never to forget it is a constitution they are expounding.

The Constitution—the original document of 1787 plus its amendments—is and must be understood to be the standard against which all laws, policies, and interpretations should be measured. It is our fundamental law because it represents the settled and deliberate will of the people,

---

2   Charles Warren, *The Supreme Court in United States History*, 3 Vols., (Boston: Little, Brown, and Co., 1922–1924), 470–471.

against which the actions of government officials must be squared. In the end, the continued success and viability of our democratic republic depends on our fidelity to, and the faithful exposition and interpretation of, this Constitution, our great charter of liberty.

★ ★ ★ ★ ★

I have been honored to have been associated with this unique project from the very beginning when it was envisioned and undertaken by Matthew Spalding under the auspices of the Henry Salvatori endowment at The Heritage Foundation. The esteemed members of the Editorial Advisory Board—Gary Lawson of Boston University School of Law, John O. McGinnis of Northwestern University School of Law, Mike Rappaport of the University of San Diego School of Law, and Ronald Rotunda of the Chapman University School of Law—assured the accuracy and analysis of the numerous articles in the Guide. Working with Dr. David Forte of Cleveland Marshall School of Law and Dr. Spalding of Hillsdale College, these scholars closely vetted each article to produce a work of enduring value.

Edwin Meese III
Honorary Chairman of the Editorial Advisory Board

Introduction to the Constitution

$\mathcal{T}$he United States Constitution is central to American life. The Declaration of Independence asserts the ends of American government: equal rights and the consent of the governed for the sake of life, liberty, and the pursuit of happiness. But the Constitution is the fundamental act of lawgiving which orders our politics, secures our rights, and defines our nation. It creates the institutions and practical arrangements by which we express our consent and govern ourselves. The development, design and structures of constitutionalism in the United States are important not because these concepts are old, or even exclusively ours, but because they form the basic architecture of American liberty.

The Road to Philadelphia

In 1774, after Parliament had shut down the Massachusetts legislature and closed the port of Boston in response to the Boston Tea Party, itself the culmination of various colonial protests against a decade of onerous British laws, the First Continental Congress advised Massachusetts to form an independent colonial government. In May 1776, a year after the first hostilities at Lexington and Concord, the Second Continental Congress charged the colonies to develop "such Government as shall, in the opinion of the Representatives of the People, best conduce to the happiness and safety of their Constituents in particular, and America in general." These steps led to the development of constitutions for many of the colonies, the first being the one John Adams wrote for Massachusetts in 1780. Roundly skeptical of monarchs and overbearing leaders, these constitutions increased the power of the legislature to the diminishment of the executive. Most state legislatures appointed a one-term governor largely excluded from the legislative process, with minimal veto powers and negligible appointive authority.

At the same time, the colonies together began the process of creating the first constitution of the United States. Resolving to declare American independence in July 1776, the Second Continental Congress also called for the drafting of a plan to unify the colonies as a confederation. There had been attempts at national union before, such as Benjamin Franklin's Albany Plan in 1754 proposing a governing body and an independent executive for the purposes of handling defense, trade, and the western lands. But with the coming of independence and the exigencies of war, there was a new urgency to regularize the common identity of the colonies. Proposed in 1777 and ratified in 1781, the Articles of Confederation—under which the nation won the Revolutionary War, formed diplomatic relations with major nations around the world, settled land claims, and began western expansion through the Northwest Ordinance—is an important bridge between the government of the Continental Congress and that of the current United States Constitution.[1]

From its inception, the Articles of Confederation was plagued with inherent weaknesses that ultimately made it unworkable. Because of the colonies' distaste for British central authority, and based on their successful experience as united colonies, the Articles created a "Confederation and perpetual union" of sovereign states: "Each state retains its sovereignty, freedom and independence, and every power, jurisdiction, and right, which is not by this Confederation expressly delegated to the United States, in Congress assembled." On paper, Congress had the power to make war and peace, regulate coinage, create a postal service, borrow money, and establish uniform weights and measures. Yet Congress lacked authority to impose taxes to cover national expenses or enforce requests on the states. Moreover, there was no independent executive or judiciary. Because all thirteen states had to ratify amendments, one state's refusal prevented structural reform; nine of thirteen states had to approve important legislation or treaties, which meant that five states could thwart any major proposal.

By the end of the war in 1783, it was clear that the new system had become, as George Washington observed, "a shadow without the substance." States were imposing punitive tariffs and refusing to protect property or enforce contracts. Weakness in international affairs and in the face of continuing European threats in North America, the inability to enforce a peace treaty with Great Britain, and the failure to collect enough taxes to pay foreign creditors intensified the drive for a stronger national government.[2] An immediate impetus to re-evaluate the Articles was an armed revolt in 1786–1787 called Shays' Rebellion. A group of farmers, objecting to a state law requiring that debts be paid in specie and to increasing farm and home foreclosures resulting from the law, took up arms in protest and attacked a federal armory in Springfield, Massachusetts. It was put down eventually by local militia, but the federal government proved helpless and unable to defend itself or quell the uprising.

In 1785, representatives from Maryland and Virginia, meeting at George Washington's Mount Vernon home to discuss interstate trade, requested a gathering of all the states to discuss trade and commerce. The next year, delegates from several states met at a conference in Annapolis, Maryland,

---

1   See Edmund S. Morgan, *The Birth of the Republic, 1763–89* (Chicago: University of Chicago Press, 1956) for a concise history of colonial and British policies during the American Revolution.

2   For a detailed account of the defects and downfall of the Articles of Confederation, see Vol. 1, Bk. II, Ch. IV of Joseph Story's *Commentaries on the Constitution of the United States*, 3 vols. (Boston: Hilliard, Gray, and Company; Philadelphia: P. H. Nicklin and T. Johnson, 1833). The classic work on this period is John Fiske's *The Critical Period of American History 1783–1789* (Boston and New York: Houghton, Mifflin, 1888), but a more popular and recent work is *The Perils of Peace: America's Struggle for Survival After Yorktown* (New York: HarperCollins, 2007) by Thomas Fleming.

to discuss commercial issues. The Annapolis meeting was not a success as an insufficient number of states sent delegates, but James Madison and Alexander Hamilton persuaded that conference to issue a call for a general convention of all the states "to render the constitution of government adequate to the exigencies of the union." From May 25 to September 17, 1787, delegates met in Philadelphia at the same statehouse (now called Independence Hall) from which the Second Continental Congress a decade earlier had issued the Declaration of Independence.

The Constitutional Convention

John Adams once described the Constitutional Convention as "the greatest single effort of national deliberation that the world has ever seen." There were not only leaders in the fight for independence, such as Roger Sherman and John Dickinson, and leading thinkers just coming into prominence, such as James Madison, Alexander Hamilton, and Gouverneur Morris, but also prominent figures, such as Benjamin Franklin and George Washington. Patrick Henry and Samuel Adams, both of whom considered a strong national government antithetical to republican principles, did not attend the convention. Notably absent as well were John Jay, who was then the Secretary of Foreign Affairs, and John Adams and Thomas Jefferson, who were both out of the country representing the new nation. Their absence was providential: the attendance of both strong-willed figures might have made it impossible for the convention to make the compromises that proved essential to their work. Every state was represented except for Rhode Island, which opposed any major change in the Articles of Confederation fearing that a stronger national government would injure its lucrative trade.

As their first order of business, the delegates unanimously chose Washington as president of the convention. Though he had initially been hesitant to attend the convention, Washington pushed the delegates to adopt "no temporizing expedient" and instead to "probe the defects of the Constitution [i.e., the Articles of Confederation] to the bottom, and provide radical cures." While they waited in Philadelphia for a quorum, Washington presided over daily meetings of the Virginia delegation to consider strategy and a set of reform proposals to be presented at the outset of the convention. Although he contributed to formal debate only once, at the end of the convention, Washington was actively involved throughout the three-and-a-half-month proceedings.

The convention had three basic rules: voting was to be by state, with each state, regardless of size or population, having one vote; proper decorum was to be maintained at all times; and the proceedings were to be strictly secret. To encourage free and open discussion and debate, the convention shifted back and forth between full sessions and meetings of the Committee of the Whole, a parliamentary procedure that allowed informal debate and flexibility in deciding and reconsidering individual issues. Although the convention hired a secretary, the best records of the debate—and thus the most immediate source of the Framers' intentions—are the detailed notes written by James Madison, which were not published until 1840 in keeping with the pledge of secrecy.[3]

As soon as the convention agreed on its rules, Edmund Randolph, on behalf of the Virginia delegation, presented a set of fifteen resolutions, known as the Virginia Plan, which set aside the

---

3   *The Records of the Federal Convention of 1787* (New Haven and London: Yale University Press, 1966), edited by Max Farrand, gathers into three volumes all the records written by participants of the Constitutional Convention, including the extensive notes taken throughout by James Madison.

Articles of Confederation and created a new national government with separate legislative, executive, and judicial branches. The plan was largely the work of the young James Madison, who came to the convention extensively prepared and well-versed in the ancient and modern history of republican government. The delegates generally agreed on the powers that should be lodged in a national bicameral legislature but disagreed on how the states and popular opinion should be reflected in it. Under the Virginia Plan, population would determine representation in both houses of Congress, giving the advantage to larger, more populous states.

To protect their equal standing, delegates from less-populous states rallied around William Paterson's alternative New Jersey Plan, which would preserve each state's equal vote in a one-house Congress with slightly augmented powers. After the delegates rejected the New Jersey Plan, Roger Sherman proffered what is often called "the Great Compromise" (or the Connecticut Compromise, after Sherman's home state), under which a House of Representatives would be apportioned based on population and each state would have an equal vote in a Senate. A special Committee of Eleven (one delegate from each state present at the time) elaborated on the proposal, and the convention then adopted it. As a precaution against having to assume the financial burdens of the smaller states, the larger states exacted an agreement that revenue bills would originate in the House, where the more populous states would have greater representation.

In late July, a Committee of Detail (John Rutledge of South Carolina, Edmund Randolph of Virginia, Nathaniel Gorham of Massachusetts, Oliver Ellsworth of Connecticut, and James Wilson of Pennsylvania) reworked the resolutions of the amended Virginia Plan into a draft constitution. The text now included a list of the key powers of Congress, a "necessary and proper" clause, and a number of prohibitions on the states. Over most of August and into early September, the convention carefully worked over this draft and then gave it to a Committee of Style (William Johnson of Connecticut, Alexander Hamilton of New York, Gouverneur Morris of Pennsylvania, James Madison of Virginia, and Rufus King of Massachusetts) to polish the language. The literary quality of the Constitution, most prominently the language of the Preamble, is due to Morris's work. The delegates continued revising the final draft until September 17 (now celebrated as Constitution Day), when they signed the Constitution and sent it to the Congress of the Confederation, and the convention officially adjourned.

Some of the original fifty-five delegates had returned home over the course of the summer and were not present at the convention's conclusion. Of the forty-one who remained, only three delegates—Edmund Randolph and George Mason of Virginia and Elbridge Gerry of Massachusetts—opposed the Constitution in its completed form and chose not to sign. Randolph, who had introduced the Virginia Plan, thought that the Constitution was not sufficiently republican and was wary of its single executive. Mason and Gerry, who later supported the Constitution and served in the First Congress, were concerned about the lack of a declaration of specific rights. Despite these objections, George Washington thought that it was "little short of a miracle" that the delegates had agreed on the new governing document.[4]

---

4   Of the books on the Constitutional Convention, Clinton Rossiter's *1787: The Grand Convention* (New York: Macmillan, 1966) is very readable and comprehensive, while Catherine Drinker Bowen's *Miracle at Philadelphia: The Story of the Constitutional Convention, May to September 1787* (Boston: Little, Brown, 1966) is more popular and narrative. A more recent work is *The Summer of 1787: The Men Who Invented the Constitution* (New York: Simon & Schuster, 2007) by David O. Stewart.

Reading the Constitution

The Constitution begins with a preamble, or introductory clause, asserting the authority—"We the People"—that establishes the document and "ordains" or orders it into effect. This is very different from the opening of the Articles of Confederation, which speaks in the name of individual states, and represents an important shift (strongly opposed by some) in the understanding of the constitutional sovereignty underlying the document. The Preamble then proclaims the ends or purposes for which the Constitution is formed.

After the Preamble, the rest of the Constitution—being a practical document to create a framework of law—describes the powers, procedures, and institutions of government. The Constitution is divided into seven parts, or articles, each dealing with a general subject. Each article is further divided into sections and clauses. The first three articles create three distinct branches of government: the legislature, the executive, and the judiciary. These three branches correspond to the three primary functions of governing: to make laws, to execute and enforce the laws, and to uphold (judge or adjudicate) the rule of those laws by applying them to particular cases.

The Constitution creates three branches of government of equal "rank" in relation to each other. No branch is higher or lower than any other, and no branch controls the others; each has independent authority and unique powers. The order—legislature, executive, judiciary—is important, however, moving from the most to the least "democratic" (that is, from the most to the least directly chosen by the people). The Constitution lodges the basic power of government in the legislature not only because it is the branch most directly representative of popular opinion, but also because the very essence of governing according to the rule of law is centered on the legitimate authority to make laws.

The Constitution creates a government of *delegated* and *enumerated* powers. Despite the popular term "states' rights," no government (federal, state, county, or local) actually possesses any *rights* at all. Recall from the Declaration of Independence that *persons* are endowed with unalienable rights. Governments possess only *powers*, which in legitimate governments are derived from the consent of the governed. In particular, governments have only those powers that are given (or delegated) to them by the people. The concept of enumerated (or listed) powers follows from the concept of delegated powers, as the functional purpose of a constitution is to write down and assign the powers granted to government. The delegation of powers to government and a written agreement as to the extent (and limits) of those powers are critical elements of limited constitutional government.

The status of the states within the constitutional system is defined in Article IV, which requires that every state give its "Full Faith and Credit" to the laws and decisions of every other state and that citizens of each state enjoy all privileges and immunities of citizenship in every other state—both of which are conducive to establishing the rule of law. It also provides for the admission of new states to the union as *states*, not *colonies*, on an equal footing with the original thirteen—an exceedingly important distinction responsible for America's successful growth as a nation of states rather than as a colonial empire. Finally, Article IV stipulates that the United States will guarantee to each state a republican form of government and protect the states from invasion and, upon request, domestic violence.

Article V provides a process for amending the Constitution. Here we see the American concept that the Constitution is fundamental law that can be changed, thus allowing for constitutional reform and adaptation, but only by a popular decision-making process and not by ordinary legislation or judicial decree. Neither an exclusively federal nor an exclusively state action, the amendment process is a shared responsibility of both Congress and the states representing the American people.

Article VI ensures that America's legal system—especially the federal and state courts—is centered on the United States Constitution. It begins by recognizing the debts that existed prior to the Constitution, which is to say it recognizes that the United States existed before the United States Constitution. More important, it makes the Constitution and the laws and treaties made pursuant to it the "supreme Law of the Land." Finally, Article VI bans religious tests for office and instead binds all federal and state officeholders, by oath, to the Constitution.

Article VII requires the Constitution to be ratified by state conventions rather than state legislatures, again pointing to the document's legitimacy in the sovereignty of the people acting in their state capacity. It also dates the Constitution in "the Year of our Lord" 1787 and "of the Independence of the United States of America the twelfth," thereby locating the document in time according to the religious traditions of Western civilization and the birth of the United States as proclaimed in the Declaration of Independence.

Auxiliary Precautions

In addition to the formal provisions of the document, there are three important but unstated mechanisms at work in the Constitution: the extended republic, the separation of powers, and federalism. These "auxiliary precautions" constitute improvements in the science of politics developed by the Founders and form the basis of what they called in *The Federalist* No. 10 "a republican remedy for the diseases most incident to republican government."

The effect of representation—of individual citizens being represented in the government rather than ruling through direct participatory democracy—is to refine and moderate public opinion through a deliberative process. Extending the Republic, literally increasing the size of the nation, would take in a greater number and variety of opinions, making it harder for a majority to form on narrow interests contrary to the common good. The Founders also knew, as Madison explained in *The Federalist* No. 48, that "the accumulation of all powers, legislative, executive, and judiciary, in the same hands, whether of one, a few, or many, and whether hereditary, self-appointed, or elective, may justly be pronounced the very definition of tyranny." In order to distribute power and prevent its accumulation, they created three separate branches of government, each performing its own functions and duties and sharing a few powers—as when the president shares the legislative power through the veto—so that they would have an incentive to check each other.

And although national powers were clearly enhanced by the Constitution, the federal government was to exercise only delegated powers, the remainder being reserved to the states or the people. While they harbored no doctrinaire aversion to government as such, the Framers remained distrustful of government in general and of a centralized federal government in particular. "The powers delegated by the proposed Constitution to the federal government are few and defined," Madison wrote in *The Federalist* No. 45. "Those which are to remain in the State governments are numerous and indefinite." In the same way that the separation of powers works *within* the federal and state constitutions, federalism is the basic operational structure of American constitutional government as a whole and provides the process by which the two levels of government check each other.

Debating the Constitution

On September 28, 1787, according to the rules of the Constitution, Congress sent the document to the states to be ratified not by state legislatures but by conventions that were elected by the people of each state.

Those who had concluded that the government under the Articles of Confederation was weak and ineffective, who had advocated a convention to substantially rework the structure of the national government, and who then had supported the new constitution were called "Federalists," while those who opposed changing that structure and then opposed the ratification of the new constitution became known as "Anti-Federalists." Made up of diverse elements and various individuals, the Anti-Federalists generally held that the only way to have limited government and self-reliant citizens was through a small republic, and they believed that the Constitution gave too much power to the federal government relative to the states. They were especially suspicious of executive power, fearing that the presidency would evolve into a monarchy over time. At the same time, they warned of judicial tyranny stemming from the creation of independent, life-tenured judges. While the Anti-Federalists failed to prevent ratification of the Constitution, their efforts led directly to the creation of the first ten amendments to the U.S. Constitution. Many of their concerns and warnings, whether or not they justified opposition to the Constitution, were prescient in light of modern changes in American constitutionalism.[5]

During the ratification debate in the State of New York, Hamilton, Madison, and John Jay wrote a series of newspaper essays under the pen name of Publius (a figure from Roman republican history) to refute the arguments of the Anti-Federalists. The eighty-five essays, mostly published between October 1787 and August 1788, were later published in book form as *The Federalist* (also known as *The Federalist Papers*). The initial essays (Nos. 2 through 14) stress the weaknesses of the Confederation and the advantages of a strong and permanent national union. The middle essays (Nos. 15 through 36) argue for energetic government, in particular the need for the government to be able to tax and provide for national defense. The last essays (Nos. 37 through 85) describe the branches and powers of the new government and explain the "conformity of the proposed Constitution to the true principles of republican government." These essays are the leading presentation of the Federalist position.[6]

The first state convention to ratify the Constitution was Delaware's, on December 7, 1787; the last convention of the thirteen original colonies was that of Rhode Island, on May 29, 1790, two-and-a-half years later. Although there was strong opposition in Massachusetts, Virginia, New York, and North Carolina, in the end no state convention decided against ratifying the new constitution. With the ratification by the ninth state convention—New Hampshire, on June 21, 1788—Congress

---

5   For an introduction to Anti-Federalist thought, see Herbert J. Storing's *What the Anti-Federalists Were For: The Political Thought of the Opponents of the Constitution* (Chicago: University of Chicago Press, 1981); an accessible selection of leading Anti-Federalist writings is *The Essential Antifederalist* (Lanham, MD: Rowman & Littlefield Publishers, Inc., 2nd ed. 2001), edited by William B. Allen and Gordon Lloyd.

6   There are many editions of *The Federalist Papers*. The Signet Classics edition (New York, 2003) is edited by the late Clinton Rossiter and has been updated with an extended introduction and notes by Charles R. Kesler.

passed a resolution to make the new constitution operative and set dates for choosing presidential electors and the opening session of the new Congress.[7]

A Bill of Rights

There had been some discussion at the Constitutional Convention of a bill of rights, but the proposal was rejected on the grounds that there was no need for a bill of rights in a *federal* constitution of limited powers (unlike the *state* constitutions of extensive reserved powers) and that enumerating rights would imply powers not delegated. The lack of a bill of rights like that found in most state constitutions, however, became a rallying cry for the Anti-Federalists in the ratification debate, and the advocates of the Constitution agreed to add one in the first session of Congress.

When Congress convened in March 1789, Representative James Madison took charge of the process. Only eighteen months before, as a member of the Philadelphia convention, Madison had opposed a bill of rights, but he wanted above all for the new constitution to be ratified and, if possible, have the widest possible popular support. If that meant adding a bill of rights, then Madison would draft the language himself to make sure that these early amendments did not impair the Constitution's original design.[8]

Based largely on George Mason's Declaration of Rights written for the Virginia Constitution of 1776, seventeen amendments were quickly introduced. Congress adopted twelve, and President Washington forwarded them to the states for ratification. By December 15, 1791, three-fourths of the states had ratified ten amendments, now known collectively as the Bill of Rights (the first two proposed amendments concerning the number of constituents for each representative and the compensation of congressmen, were not ratified).

The First Amendment guarantees *substantive* political rights involving religion, speech, press, assembly, and petition, recognizing certain areas that are to be free from federal government interference. Likewise, the Second Amendment guarantees an individual right to keep and bear arms. The next six amendments deal with more *procedural* political rights, mostly restraints on criminal procedure that regulate the exercise of government's law enforcement power so that it is not arbitrary or excessive.

The Bill of Rights also includes important property protections. The Second Amendment prohibits confiscation of arms, and the Third Amendment prohibits the lodging of troops in any home. The Fourth Amendment prohibits unreasonable searches and seizures of persons, homes, papers, and effects, and the Eighth Amendment prohibits excessive bail and fines, as well as cruel and unusual punishment, an additional protection of property in one's person. Most significantly, of course, the Fifth Amendment says that no person shall "be deprived of life, liberty, or property, without due process of law; nor shall private property be taken for public use, without just com-

---

7   For a two-volume collection of Federalist and Anti-Federalist speeches, articles, and letters during the struggle over ratification of the Constitution (focusing on debates in the press and correspondence, and the debates in the state-ratifying conventions of Pennsylvania, Connecticut, Massachusetts, South Carolina, Virginia, New York, and North Carolina), see *The Debate on the Constitution*, 2 vols. (New York: Library of America, 1993), edited by Bernard Bailyn.

8   The story of the creation of the Bill of Rights is told in Robert A. Goldwin's *From Parchment to Power: How James Madison Used the Bill of Rights to Save the Constitution* (Washington, DC: AEI Press, 1997).

pensation." In this sense, the protection of property is both a substantive and a procedural right guaranteed by the Constitution.

The Ninth and Tenth Amendments briefly encapsulate the twofold theory of the Constitution, and address the confusion (which was Madison's concern) that may arise in misreading the other amendments to imply unlimited federal powers. The purpose of the Constitution is to protect *rights* that stem not from the government but from our human nature and thus belong to the people themselves, and to limit the *powers* of the national government to those delegated to it by the people through the Constitution.

Amending the Constitution

There have been only seventeen additional amendments besides the Bill of Rights to the Constitution. A disputed Supreme Court decision (*Chisholm v. Georgia*, 1793) led to enactment of the Eleventh Amendment (1795), which limits the jurisdiction of the federal judiciary with regard to suits against states. The election of 1800, which was decided by the House of Representatives because of a tied electroal vote, led to enactment of the Twelfth Amendment (1804), which provided for separate balloting for president and vice president. The Civil War was followed by enactment of the Thirteenth, Fourteenth, and Fifteenth Amendments (ratified in 1865, 1868, and 1870, respectively), which abolished slavery; conferred citizenship on all persons born or naturalized in the United States and established the rule that a state cannot "deprive any person of life, liberty, or property, without due process of law"; and made clear that the right of citizens to vote cannot be denied or abridged on account of race, color, or previous condition of servitude.

There were four amendments during the Progressive era, at the beginning of the twentieth century. The Sixteenth Amendment (1913) gave Congress the power to levy taxes on incomes, from any source, without apportionment among the several states, and so was born the modern income tax. The Seventeenth Amendment (1913) provided for the direct election of senators by popular vote. The Eighteenth Amendment (1919), the so-called prohibition amendment, prohibited the manufacture, sale, or transportation of intoxicating liquors. (This failed experiment in social reform was repealed by the Twenty-first Amendment in 1933.) The Nineteenth Amendment (1920), completing a political movement that had started much earlier, extended to women the right to vote.

The remaining amendments have dealt with the executive and elections. The Twentieth Amendment (1933) cut in half the "lame-duck" period between presidential elections and the inauguration of the new executive; the Twenty-second Amendment (1951), following in the wake of Franklin Roosevelt's four terms, limited presidents to two terms (the tradition until Roosevelt); the Twenty-third Amendment (1961) gave the District of Columbia electors in the electoral college system; the Twenty-fourth Amendment (1964) abolished poll taxes, which were used to deny persons the right to vote in presidential and congressional primaries and elections; and the Twenty-fifth Amendment (1967) established the procedure (in the wake of the Kennedy assassination) for presidential succession.

With the military draft of eighteen-year-old males during the Vietnam conflict, the Twenty-sixth Amendment (1971) lowered the voting age to eighteen, and the most recent change was the Twenty-seventh Amendment, which provided that any pay raise Congress votes itself would not take effect until after an intervening congressional election. It was ratified finally in 1992, 203 years after James Madison wrote and proposed it as part of the original Bill of Rights.

Arguing the Constitution

Written after ratification but before any source material on the Constitutional Convention was available, the first histories of the American Founding (most prominently those of John Marshall, David Ramsay, and Mercy Otis Warren) covered the period leading up to the Constitution but skipped over its framing. Justice Joseph Story's three-volume *Commentaries on the Constitution of the United States* (1833), for instance, focuses on colonial history, the deficiencies of the Articles of Confederation, and the text of the Constitution but has only a few sentences on the Philadelphia convention.[9] This changed in 1840 with the posthumous publication of James Madison's notes of the Constitutional Convention debates, as can be seen for instance in George Bancroft's ten-volume *History of the United States of America*, the last volume of which relies extensively on Madison's notes.[10] The first political group to take advantage of Madison's notes were the abolitionist opponents of slavery, who argued that Madison's notes proved that the Constitution was a pro-slavery bargain between North and South and as such a counterrevolution against the Declaration of Independence.

The debate over slavery in theory and practice created a constitutional crisis in the United States. Some, like Senator John C. Calhoun of South Carolina, had denied the principle of human equality in the Declaration and had gone so far as to embrace slavery as a "positive good." Alexander Stephens, the vice president of the Confederacy, argued that slavery would be the cornerstone of their new nation. Chief Justice Roger B. Taney argued for the Supreme Court in *Dred Scott v. Sanford* that slaves were property under the U.S. Constitution and "had no rights which the white man was bound to respect." Senator Stephen Douglas of Illinois hoped to solve the problem by turning to "popular sovereignty" and allowing territories and new states to decide for themselves whether to endorse slavery. Abraham Lincoln held that slavery violated the Declaration of Independence and recalled the nation to the Founders' Constitution and the principles it enshrined in order to place slavery once again on "the road to ultimate extinction." He maintained that the Constitution was made to secure the principles proclaimed in the Declaration of Independence and that those principles and the Constitution, properly understood, were perfectly compatible. His achievement, in the midst of civil war, was to preserve the constitutional republic while restoring its dedication to the timeless principles that form its central idea.

In the years after the Civil War and with the rise of American industrialization, some concluded that the original constitutional system had failed completely and that America needed fundamental social and political reform appropriate for the modern age. Having studied with or been influenced by political thinkers in England, France and especially Germany, these "progressive" thinkers set out

---

9   John Marshall, *The Life of George Washington*, 5 vols. (London: Printed for R. Phillips, 1804–1807); David Ramsay, *The History of the American Revolution*, 2 vols. (Philadelphia: Printed and sold by R. Aitken [et] Son, 1789); *History of the United States*, 3 vols. (Philadelphia: Published by M. Carey, 1816–1817); Mercy Otis Warren, *History of the Rise, Progress, and Termination of the American Revolution*, 3 vols. (Boston: Printed by Manning and Loring for E. Larkin, No. 47, Cornhill, 1805); Story, *Commentaries on the Constitution of the United States.*

10 George Bancroft, *History of the United States of America, From the Discovery of the American Continent* (Boston: Little, Brown, and Co.), numerous editions of eight or ten volumes, 1854–1878.

to create a movement in the United States that for the first time self-consciously aimed at changing the principles and practices of American constitutionalism.

This "revolt against formalism" took many forms, in theology, history, law and politics, and social policy.[11] In the academy, progressives held that there were no self-evident truths but only historical values, and they repudiated any concepts of natural right or natural law—that is, ideas of right and law grounded in a fixed or enduring nature. Scholars like James Allen Smith and most famously Charles Beard argued that the Constitution represented the triumph of moneyed elites protecting their economic interests in the face of a populist revolution. Progressive historians asserted that the democratic forces of the American Revolution, having produced an idealistic Declaration of Independence, were later defeated by reactionary forces that produced an antidemocratic constitution, an interpretation that is widely portrayed as the key dynamic of American political history. The Constitution's focus on controlling and restricting government power and moderating democratic opinion was viewed as misguided and a serious barrier to the extensive government thought necessary for progress. As a result, the practical aim of the progressives was to make the Constitution flexible and pliable by replacing the original constitutional system of individual rights and limited government with a "living" Constitution of evolving rights and unlimited government capable of easy growth and adaptation in changing times.[12]

The judiciary would play the central role in legitimizing this new constitutionalism through innovative and forward-looking interpretations of the Constitution. Oliver Wendell Holmes (who served on the Supreme Court from 1902 to 1932) famously argued that the life of the law was nothing more than experience, and that the key factor in the development (and interpretation) of the law was a consideration of "the felt needs of the time." According to this outcome-oriented jurisprudence, later called "legal realism," judging is not distinct from legislating but merely a different form of it, filling in the "gaps" created by general laws. Judges determine not only what the Constitution says

---

11 See *Social Thought in American: The Revolt Against Formalism* (New York: Viking Press, 1949) by Morton G. White. Ronald J. Pestritto and William J. Atto's *American Progressivism: A Reader* (Lanham, MD: Lexington Books, 2008) is a good collection that runs the gamut of progressive thought, from political principles to Social Gospel writings to foreign policy speeches. It also includes a fine introductory essay explaining the basic views of the Progressives. An honest and comprehensive overview from a historian sympathetic to the reform efforts of the period is Eric F. Goldman's *Rendezvous with Destiny: A History of Modern American Reform* (New York: Alfred A. Knopf, 1952). Several recent works have delved more deeply into the progressive rejection of the American Founding. A good introduction to this scholarship is *The Progressive Revolution in Politics and Political Science: Transforming the American Regime*, edited by John Marini and Ken Masugi (Lanham, MD: Rowman & Littlefield, 2005), with essays on the progressive critique of American constitutionalism, as well as on progressive ideas in theory and practice. An important volume that treats Woodrow Wilson as a political thinker as well as a politician, Ronald J. Pestritto's *Woodrow Wilson and the Roots of Modern Liberalism* (Lanham, MD: Rowman & Littlefield, 2005) reveals Wilson's progressive philosophy, derived from nineteenth-century German thought, and its profound and continuing influence on progressive liberalism in America.

12 The argument for relativism is made clearly in John Dewey, "The Future of Liberalism," Address to the 24th annual meeting of the American Philosophical Association on December 28, 1934, and is reflected in Carl L. Becker, *The Declaration of Independence: A Study in the History of Political Ideas* (New York: Harcourt, Brace, 1922); J. Allen Smith, *The Spirit of American Government* (New York: Macmillan, 1907); Charles A. Beard, *An Economic Interpretation of the Constitution of the United States* (New York: Macmillan, 1913). For the general progressive constitutional argument, see also Frank J. Goodnow, *Politics and Administration* (London, New York: Macmillan, 1900) and Charles Merriam, *American Political Ideas: Studies in the Development of American Political Thought 1865–1917* (New York: Macmillan, 1920).

about certain questions but also, in effect, what policies will best harmonize the document's presumptions with popular opinion.[13]

The response to the claims of progressive constitutionalism came in several forms. The economic interpretation of the Constitution was refuted by the historians Robert Brown and Forrest McDonald.[14] More mainstream academics attempted to forge an historical consensus that emphasized the Lockean principles of classical liberalism as the foundation of American constitutionalism[15] while another group of historians (preeminently J. G. A. Pocock and Bernard Bailyn) argued that the American Founding was not Lockean at all but instead posited a republican synthesis of radical Whig ideology that defined the origins of the American Revolution.[16] Over time, these historical debates turned academic attention increasingly to a direct reconsideration of the Founders' ideas and political thought, seen for instance in the early essays of the historian Douglas Adair and the seminal work of Martin Diamond to revive *The Federalist Papers*—in particular Madison's *Federalist No. 10*—as the political theory of the Constitution.[17] The progressive interpretation was later revived by scholars such as Merrill Jensen, while Gordon Wood developed an adaptation of the republican synthesis. The intellectual efforts of Adair and Diamond have been matured and expanded by the students of Leo Strauss and in particular the Claremont school of thought led by Harry Jaffa and Charles Kesler.[18] Constitutional historians and practitioners also argued against the progressives. Contemporary scholars such as Edward Corwin and Andrew McLaughlin defended traditional constitutionalism as a means to order and restrain government, as did numerous jurists such as William Howard Taft and George Sutherland.[19] Scholars associated with the National Association for Constitutional Government (NACG) and its publication *Constitutional Review* made informed

---

13 For an assessment of modern legal thought as it develops out of progressivism, see Bradley C. S. Watson, *Living Constitution, Dying Faith: Progressivism and the New Science of Jurisprudence* (Wilmington, DE: ISI Books, 2009).

14 Robert E. Brown, *Charles Beard and the Constitution* (Princeton: Princeton University Press, 1956), and Forrest McDonald, *We the People: The Economic Origins of the Constitution* (Chicago: University of Chicago Press, 1958).

15 For examples of early scholarship on the importance of Locke to the Founding, see Merle Curti, "The Great Mr. Locke: America's Philosopher, 1783–1861," *Huntington Library Bulletin 11* (1937); Louis Hartz, *The Liberal Tradition in America: An Interpretation of American Political Thought Since the Revolution* (San Diego: Harcourt Brace Jovanovich, 1955).

16 Bernard Bailyn, *The Ideological Origins of the American Revolution* (Cambridge, MA: Harvard University Press, 1967). For a broader argument concerning the historical origins of the American Founding, see J. G. A. Pocock's *The Machiavellian Moment: Florentine Political Thought and the Atlantic Republican Tradition* (Princeton: Princeton University Press, 1975).

17 Trevor Colbourn, ed., *Fame and the Founding Fathers: Essays by Douglas Adair* (Indianapolis: Liberty Fund, 1998); Martin Diamond, "Democracy and The Federalist: A Reconsideration of the Framers' Intent," *American Political Science Review* 52 (March 1959).

18 Merrill Jensen, *The Articles of Confederation: An Interpretation of the Social-Constitutional History of the American Revolution, 1774–1781* (Madison: University of Wisconsin Press, 1940); Gordon S. Wood, *The Creation of the American Republic, 1776–1787* (Chapel Hill: University of North Carolina Press, 1969); Harry V. Jaffa, *How to Think About the American Revolution* (Durham, NC: Carolina Academic Press, 1978) and *Original Intent and the Framers of the Constitution* (Washington, DC: Regnery Gateway, 1994); Charles Kesler, ed., *Saving the Revolution: The Federalist Papers and the American Founding* (New York: Free Press, 1987).

19 Edward S. Corwin, "The 'Higher Law' Background of American Constitutional Law," 42 *Harvard Law Review* 149, 365 (1928 and 1929); Andrew McLaughlin, *The Foundations of American Constitutionalism* (New York: New York University Press, 1932); William Howard Taft, *Popular Government: Its Essence, Its Permanence and Its Peril* (New Haven: Yale University Press, 1913) and *Liberty Under Law: An Interpretation of the Principles of Our Constitutional Government* (New Haven: Yale University Press, 1922); George Sutherland, *Constitutional Power and World Affairs* (New York: Columbia University Press, 1919).

arguments against progressivism and affirmed constitutional government.[20] Although challenged and debated, the broad contours of the progressive interpretation still form the leading arguments opposing the traditional views of American constitutionalism.[21]

The progressive constitutional view came into maturity during the New Deal. At first, the Supreme Court struck down many of Franklin Roosevelt's New Deal programs—regulating agriculture, manufacturing, labor, transportation—as unconstitutional. But eventually two justices modified Supreme Court doctrine and allowed New Deal initiatives to be approved. The process was fully concretized when Roosevelt was able to appoint new justices who dramatically changed the direction of the Supreme Court. In this way the Constitution was changed not by the process of amendment but by the *interpretation* on the part of judges, amounting to what some have called a constitutional revolution.[22] Traditional arguments against progressive and New Deal constitutionalism became even more focused in the scholarship responding to the activist decisions of the Warren Court, laying the groundwork for what came to be called broadly "originalism" and calling for a revival of a traditional constitutionalism of the American founders, or what then-Attorney General Edwin Meese in a series of important speeches criticizing liberal jurisprudence referred to as a jurisprudence of original intention.[23] In recent years, these calls have led to a robust body of originalist scholarship and, with the founding of the Federalist Society in 1982, a growing number of originalist law students, lawyers and jurists.[24]

Matthew Spalding

---

20 Johnathan O'Neill, "Constitutional Conservatism During the Progressive Era: The National Association for Constitutional Government and Constitutional Review," in Joseph Postell and Johnathan O'Neill, eds., *Toward an American Conservatism: Constitutional Conservatism During the Progressive Era* (New York: Palgrave MacMillan, 2013).

21 For an overview of the interpretive debate concerning the American Founding, see Alan Gibson's *Interpreting the Founding: Guide to the Enduring Debates Over the Origins and Foundations of the American Republic* (Lawrence, KS: University Press of Kansas, 2006), which discusses six approaches that have dominated the study of the American Founding: the progressive, Lockean-liberal, republican, and Scottish enlightenment interpretations, as well as the multiple traditions approach and the modern social history view.

22 A good overview of constitutional history including the New Deal shift is *The American Constitution: Its Origins and Development* (New York: W. W. Norton & Company, 1991) edited by Alfred Hinsey Kelly, Winfred Audif Harbison, and Herman Belz.

23 Address by Attorney General Edwin Meese, "Address to the D.C Chapter of the Federalist Society Lawyers Division," Washington, D.C. (Nov. 15, 1985), reprinted in 19 U.C. Davis L. Rev. 22 (1985).

24 The Federalist Society for Law and Public Policy Studies (fed-soc.org) is dedicated to advancing constitutional principles throughout the legal community. A national membership organization of law students, law school faculty, and lawyers, it has established chapters at every one of America's accredited law schools, and lawyers chapters may be found in many cities across the United States. It sponsors campus lectures, debates (many of which are posted on its website), conferences, and legal practice groups.

A Note on the
Originalist Perspective

*W*ritten constitutionalism implies that those who make (the legislature), adjudicate (the courts), and enforce (the executive) the law ought to be guided by the meaning of the United States Constitution—the "supreme Law of the Land"—as it was understood by those who wrote and ratified the Constitution and its amendments. As Chief Justice John Marshall said in *Marbury v. Madison* (1803), "The powers of the legislature are defined, and limited; and that those limits may not be mistaken, or forgotten, the constitution is written. To what purpose are powers limited, and to what purpose is that limitation committed to writing, if these limits may, at any time, be passed by those intended to be restrained?"

Nonetheless, by a long and complicated development in American legal thought—including the influence of progressivism, pragmatism, sociological jurisprudence, and legal realism—the view of the appropriate place of the original Constitution in our law came to be seriously eroded over the course of the last century. In its stead grew a theory of the Constitution as a "living document" with no fixed meaning, subject to changing interpretations according to the "spirit of the times," or more particularly, by the views of the judges who decide the cases. That looser standard came to dominate constitutional interpretation particularly during the second half of the twentieth century.

Confronting the theory of the "living Constitution," a number of scholars began disputing the grounding of much of the modern Supreme Court's jurisprudence, particularly in the areas of religion, criminal procedure, and abortion. In 1985, Attorney General Edwin Meese III delivered a series of speeches challenging the then dominant view of constitutional jurisprudence. He called for judges to embrace a "jurisprudence of original intention." Meese's effort took what had been a growing dispute among academics and historians and thrust it into national prominence. The Attorney General's call changed the way the Senate and the public looked at the Supreme Court. It derailed the then standard "non-interpretivist" methodology of parsing the Constitution—that is, the idea that Constitutional principles behind the text can be modified and freely adapted to modern problems and sensibilities. Meese's speech encouraged new research into virtually every clause of the Constitution.[1] It affected the way many judicial opinions are written. It would help to make Justice Antonin Scalia's name a household word.

In point of fact, Attorney General Meese had given impetus to what was already in train. The cases dealing with criminal procedure (and the incorporation of the Bill of Rights into the Fourteenth Amendment), the Establishment Clause, and abortion had already engendered an outpouring of historical investigation—most of it to dispute but some also to defend the respective majority opinions. In sum, scholars and Supreme Court justices were already "doing" originalist research by the time Attorney General Meese gave the project new momentum.

While scholars were researching into the original understanding of particular clauses of the Constitution, the debate over originalism as a *theory of interpretation* grew apace. Many believe that Robert Bork provided the opening salvo in his 1971 article "Neutral Principles and Some First Amendment Problems,"[2] followed in 1976 by Justice William Rehnquist's critique "The Notion of a Living Constitution" and the next year by Raoul Berger's broadside *Government by Judiciary*. The growing corpus of historical investigations into original intent, as well as the articulate attacks on the freewheeling methods of interpretation being employed by judges, impelled a counterattack by the defenders of the status quo. Paul Brest, who actually coined the term "originalism," put forward an articulate critique of originalism in 1980. Thus, by the time Attorney General Meese had made the issue one of national import, the contest had already been joined.[3]

In part, because of Brest's critique and that of H. Jefferson Powell, among others, the theory of originalism underwent internal modifications and renewed rigor. As has often been reported, originalism evolved from notions of the "original intent" of the Framers, to that of the ratifiers, to "original meaning," and to "original public meaning" (the last the most espoused, though there remain prominent academic defenders of "original intent"). Today, there are many different schools of originalist theory, even among those espousing "original public meaning," as well as critics. Although a few critics of originalism continue to echo Justice William J. Brennan's unfounded and calumnious criticism of Attorney General Meese's position as "little more than arrogance cloaked as humility,"[4] most critics take the theory as a serious intellectual rather than political enterprise.

Originalism in the literature today is in fact the major interpretive theory with which all sides contend. True, Ronald Dworkin continued to embrace a theory of interpretation that included non-textual underlying moral principles. And John Hart Ely's "representative reinforcing" model, seeking to expand access to and accountability of the political branches, also continues to have adherents,

---

1   Several of Attorney General Meese's speeches are reprinted in Steven G. Calabresi, ed., *Originalism: A Quarter-Century of Debate* (Washington, D.C.: Regnery Publishing, 2007).

2   Robert H. Bork, *Neutral Principles and Some First Amendment Problems*, 47 Ind. L.J. 1 (Fall 1971).

3   William H. Rehnquist, *The Notion of a Living Constitution*, 54 Texas Law Review 693 (1976); Roaul Berger, *Government by Judiciary: The Transformation of the Fourteenth Amendment*, Foreword by Forrest McDonald (2nd ed.) (Indianapolis: Liberty Fund, 1997); Paul Brest, *The Misconceived Quest for the Original Understanding*, 60 B.U. L. Rev. 204 (1980).

4   Justice William J. Brennan Jr., The Constitution of the United States: Contemporary Ratification, Address at Georgetown University (Oct. 12, 1985) reprinted in 19 U.C. Davis L. Rev. 2, 7 (1985).

arguably including Justice Stephen Breyer. But it is originalism that frankly occupies pride of place as the focus of interpretive debate among academics.

As noted, some originalists responded to their critics by developing what has been termed the "New Originalism" or the "Doctrine of Original Public Meaning." Other originalists differentiated between "constitutional interpretation" and "constitutional construction," and some developed the idea of "original methods originalism," which includes not only the Framers' meaning of the text, but also their method of interpreting the text.[5]

The term the "New Originalism" argues that originalism governs the adjudication of cases under the provisions of the Constitution when provisions are not ambiguous or unclear. Where meaning runs out, however, New Originalists argue that judges must engage in "construction" as opposed to interpretation. Justice Scalia has rejected the concept of construction. Other academics, also rejecting the idea of construction, have developed the idea of "original methods originalism," which suggests that the meaning of the text is fixed not only by the meaning of words but also by the interpretive methods the Framers expected to apply.[6]

Among the many contributors to the development of an originalist theory of interpretation, the following authors have been particularly prominent (this is but a partial listing): Lawrence A. Alexander, Jack M. Balkin, Randy E. Barnett, Stephen G. Calabresi, Robert N. Clinton, Frank Easterbrook, Jeffrey Goldsworthy, Kurt T. Lash, Gary S. Lawson, Thomas B. McAffee, Michael W. McConnell, Gary L. McDowell, John O. McGinnis, Robert G. Natelson, Michael Stokes Paulson, Michael J. Perry, Roger Pilon, Saikrishna B. Prakash, Stephen B. Presser, Michael B. Rappaport, Ronald D. Rotunda, Richard B. Saphire, Antonin Scalia, Guy Seidman, Lawrence B. Solum, Lee J. Strang, Clarence Thomas, and Keith E. Whittington.

As complex as an originalist jurisprudence may be, the attempt to build a well-grounded non-originalist justification of Supreme Court decisions (excepting the desideratum of following *stare decisis*) is still short of success. At the same time, those espousing originalism have profited from the criticism of nonoriginalists, and the originalist enterprise has become more nuanced and self-critical as research into the Founding period continues to flourish.

Indeed, it is fair to say that this generation of scholars knows more about what went into the Constitution than any other since the time of the Founding. To borrow from Thomas Jefferson, in a significant sense "we are all originalists" now.

This is true of both "liberal" and "conservative" judges. For example, in *United States Term Limits, Inc. v. Thornton* (1995), Justices John Paul Stevens and Clarence Thomas engaged in a debate over whether the Framers intended the Qualifications Clauses (Article I, Section 2, Clause 2 and Article I, Section 3, Clause 3) to be the upper limit of what could be required of a person running for Congress. In *Wallace v. Jaffree* (1985), Justice William H. Rehnquist expounded on the original understanding of the Establishment Clause (the First Amendment), which Justice David Souter sought to rebut in *Lee v. Weisman* (1992). Even among avowed originalists, fruitful debate takes place. In *McIntyre v. Ohio Elections Commission* (1995), Justices Thomas and Scalia disputed whether the anonymous pamphleteering of the Founding generation was evidence that the free

---

5   Lawrence B. Solum, *Originalism and Constitutional Construction*, 82 Fordham L. Rev. 453 (2013).

6   See, e.g., John O. McGinnis and Michael B. Rappaport, *Original Methods Originalism: A New Theory of Interpretation and the Case Against Construction*, 103 N.W. L. Rev. 751 (2009).

speech guarantee of the First Amendment was meant to protect such a practice. The entire set of opinions, both majority and dissenting, in *District of Columbia v. Heller* (2008) was an extended foray into the original understanding of the Second Amendment.

Originalism is championed for a number of fundamental reasons. First, it comports with the nature of a constitution, which binds and limits any particular generation from ruling according to the passion of the times. The Framers of the Constitution of 1787 knew what they were about, forming a frame of government for "ourselves and our Posterity." They did not understand "We the People" to be merely an assemblage of individuals at any one point in time but a "people" as an association, indeed a number of overlapping associations, over the course of many generations, including our own. In the end, the Constitution of 1787 is as much a constitution for us as it was for the Founding generation.

Second, originalism supports legitimate popular government that is accountable. The Framers believed that a form of government accountable to the people, leaving them fundamentally in charge of their own destinies, best protected human liberty. If liberty is a fundamental aspect of human nature, then the Constitution of 1787 should be defended as a successful champion of human freedom. Originalism sits in frank gratitude for the political, economic, and spiritual prosperity midwived by the Constitution and the trust the Constitution places in the people to correct their own errors (and to expand the kinds of persons who constitute "the People").

Third, originalism accords with the constitutional purpose of limiting government. It understands the several parts of the federal government to be creatures of the Constitution and to have no legitimate existence outside of the Constitution. The authority of these various entities extends no further than what was devolved upon them by the Constitution. "[I]n all free States the Constitution is fixd," Samuel Adams wrote, "& as the supreme Legislative derives its Power & Authority from the Constitution, it cannot overleap the Bounds of it without destroying its own foundation."[7]

Fourth, it follows that originalism limits the judiciary. It prevents the Supreme Court from asserting its will over the careful mix of institutional arrangements that are charged with making policy, each accountable in various ways to the people. Chief Justice John Marshall, overtly deferring to the intention of the Framers, insisted that "that the framers of the constitution contemplated that instrument, as a rule for the government of courts, as well as of the legislature." In words that judges and academics might well contemplate today, Marshall said in *Marbury v. Madison*,

> Why otherwise does it direct the judges to take an oath to support it? This oath certainly applies, in an especial manner, to their conduct in their official character. How immoral to impose it on them, if they were to be used as the instruments, and the knowing instruments, for violating what they swear to support!

Fifth, supported by recent research, originalism comports with the understanding of what our Constitution was to be by the people who formed and ratified that document. It affirms that the Constitution is a coherent and interrelated document, with subtle balances incorporated throughout.

---

7   Samuel Adams, "Massachusetts House of Representatives, Circular Letter to the Colonial Legislatures, 11 Feb. 1768," in *The Founders' Constitution*, eds., Philip B. Kurland and Ralph Lerner (Chicago: University of Chicago Press, 1987), 632-33.

Reflecting the Founders' understanding of the self-motivated impulses of human nature, the Constitution erected devices that work to frustrate those impulses while leaving open channels for effective and mutually supporting collaboration. It is, in short, a remarkable historical achievement, and unbalancing part of it could dismantle the sophisticated devices it erected to protect the people's liberty. Originalism includes the constitutional amendments, many of which have significantly changed the content of the Constitution of 1787. In sum, originalism is not about what the nonoriginalists call "framer worship" and instead is about giving effect to whatever is legally placed into the Constitution. In fact, further originalist research since the time of Mr. Meese's speech has led many to contend that incorporation of the Bill of Rights to limit the states was in fact intended by the framers of the Fourteenth Amendment.

Sixth, originalism, properly pursued, is not result-oriented, whereas much nonoriginalist writing is patently so. If evidence demonstrates that the original meaning of the commerce power, for example, was broader than we might wish, then the originalist ethically must accept the conclusion. If evidence shows that the commerce power was to be more limited than it is permitted to be today, then the originalist can legitimately criticize governmental institutions for neglecting their constitutional duty. In either case, the originalist is called to be humble in the face of facts. The concept of the Constitution of 1787 as a good first draft in need of constant revision and updating—encapsulated in vague phrases such as the "living Constitution"—merely turns the Constitution into an unwritten charter to be developed by the contemporary values of sitting judges.

Discerning the Founders' original understanding is not a simple task. There are the problems of the availability of evidence; the reliability of the data; the relative weight of authority to be given to different events, personalities, and organizations of the era; the relevance of subsequent history; and the conceptual apparatus needed to interpret the data. Originalists differ among themselves on all these points and sometimes come to widely divergent conclusions. Nevertheless, the values underlying originalism do mean that the quest, as best as we can accomplish it, is a moral imperative.

How does one go about ascertaining the original meaning of the Constitution? All originalists begin with the text of the Constitution, the words of a particular clause. In the search for the meaning of the text and its legal effect, originalist researchers variously look to some or all of the following (with debated priority):

- The evident meaning of the words.
- The meaning according to the lexicon of the times.
- The meaning in context with other sections of the Constitution.
- The meaning according to the Framer who suggested the language.
- The elucidation of the meaning by debate within the Constitutional Convention.
- The historical provenance of the words, particularly their legal history.
- The words in the context of the contemporaneous social, economic, and political events.
- The words in the context of the Revolutionary struggle.
- The words in the context of the political philosophy shared by the Founding generation or by the particular interlocutors at the Convention.
- Historical, religious, and philosophical authority put forward by the Framers.
- The commentary in the ratification debates.

- The commentary by contemporaneous interpreters, such as Publius in *The Federalist Papers.*
- The subsequent historical practice by the Founding generation to exemplify the understood meaning (e.g., the actions of President Washington, the First Congress, and Chief Justice Marshall).
- Early judicial interpretations.
- Evidence of long-standing traditions that demonstrate the people's understanding of the words.

As passed down by Sir William Blackstone and later summarized by Justice Joseph Story, similar interpretive principles guided the Framing generation itself. It is the legal effect of the words in the text that matters, and its meaning is to be determined by well-known and refined rules of interpretation, supplemented where helpful by the understanding of those who drafted the text and the legal culture within which they operated. As Chief Justice Marshall put it,

> To say that the intention of the instrument must prevail; that this intention must be collected from its words; that its words are to be understood in that sense in which they are generally used by those for whom the instrument was intended; that its provisions are neither to be restricted into insignificance, nor extended to objects not comprehended in them, nor contemplated by its framers;—is to repeat what has been already said more at large, and is all that can be necessary. (*Ogden v. Saunders*, Marshall, C. J., dissenting (1827))

Marshall's dialectical manner of parsing a text, seeking its place in the coherent context of the document, buttressed by the understanding of those who drafted it and the generally applicable legal principles of the time are exemplified by his classic opinions in *Marbury v. Madison, McCulloch v. Maryland* (1819), *Gibbons v. Ogden* (1824), and *Barron v. Baltimore* (1833). Both Marshall's ideological allies and his enemies, such as Alexander Hamilton and Thomas Jefferson, utilized the same method of understanding.

Originalism does not remove controversy or disagreement, but it does cabin it within a principled constitutional tradition that makes real the Rule of Law. Without that, we are destined, as Aristotle warned long ago, to fall into the "rule of men."

With its format of brief didactic essays, the work that follows does not seek to be a thorough defense of originalism against its critics, nor does it choose which strains of originalism or which authorities are to be accorded greater legitimacy than others. But it does respect the originalist endeavor. Each contributor was asked to include a description of the original understanding of the meaning of the clause, as far as it can be determined, and to note and explain any credible and differing originalist interpretations.

It is within this tradition that this volume is respectfully offered to the consideration of the reader.

David F. Forte

The Constitution of the United States

The Constitution of the United States

WE THE PEOPLE of the United States, in Order to form a more perfect Union, establish Justice, insure domestic Tranquility, provide for the common defense, promote the general Welfare, and secure the Blessings of Liberty to ourselves and our Posterity, do ordain and establish this Constitution for the United States of America.

Preamble

ARTICLE. I.

Section. 1.

All legislative Powers herein granted shall be vested in a Congress of the United States, which shall consist of a Senate and House of Representatives.

Legislative Powers

Section. 2.

The House of Representatives shall be composed of Members chosen every second Year by the People of the several States, and the Electors in each State shall have the Qualifications requisite for Electors of the most numerous Branch of the State Legislature.

House of Representatives

No Person shall be a Representative who shall not have attained to the Age of twenty five Years, and been seven Years a Citizen of the United States, and who shall not, when elected, be an Inhabitant of that State in which he shall be chosen.

Requirements of Office

[Representatives and direct Taxes shall be apportioned among the several States which may be included within this Union, according to their respective Numbers, which shall be determined by adding to the whole Number of free Persons, including those bound to Service for

Changed by Section 2 of the Fourteenth Amendment

a Term of Years, and excluding Indians not taxed, three fifths of all other Persons.] The actual Enumeration shall be made within three Years after the first Meeting of the Congress of the United States, and within every subsequent Term of ten Years, in such Manner as they shall by Law direct. The Number of Representatives shall not exceed one for every thirty Thousand, but each State shall have at Least one Representative; and until such enumeration shall be made, the State of New Hampshire shall be entitled to chuse three, Massachusetts eight, Rhode-Island and Providence Plantations one, Connecticut five, New-York six, New Jersey four, Pennsylvania eight, Delaware one, Maryland six, Virginia ten, North Carolina five, South Carolina five, and Georgia three.

When vacancies happen in the Representation from any State, the Executive Authority thereof shall issue Writs of Election to fill such Vacancies.

Speaker
Impeachment

The House of Representatives shall chuse their Speaker and other Officers; and shall have the sole Power of Impeachment.

Section. 3.

Senate
Changed by the Seventeenth Amendment

The Senate of the United States shall be composed of two Senators from each State, [chosen by the Legislature thereof] for six Years; and each Senator shall have one Vote.

Immediately after they shall be assembled in Consequence of the first Election, they shall be divided as equally as may be into three Classes. The Seats of the Senators of the first Class shall be vacated at the Expiration of the second Year, of the second Class at the Expiration of the fourth Year, and of the third Class at the Expiration of the sixth Year, so that one third may be chosen every second Year; [and if Vacancies happen by Resignation, or otherwise, during the Recess of the Legislature of any State, the Executive thereof may make temporary Appointments until the next Meeting of the Legislature, which shall then fill such Vacancies.]

Changed by the Seventeenth Amendment
Requirements of Office

No Person shall be a Senator who shall not have attained to the Age of thirty Years, and been nine Years a Citizen of the United States, and who shall not, when elected, be an Inhabitant of that State for which he shall be chosen.

Role of Vice President

The Vice President of the United States shall be President of the Senate, but shall have no Vote, unless they be equally divided.

The Senate shall chuse their other Officers, and also a President pro tempore, in the Absence of the Vice President, or when he shall exercise the Office of President of the United States.

Impeachment

The Senate shall have the sole Power to try all Impeachments. When sitting for that Purpose, they shall be on Oath or Affirmation. When the President of the United States is tried, the Chief Justice shall preside: And no Person shall be convicted without the Concurrence of two thirds of the Members present.

Judgment in Cases of Impeachment shall not extend further than to removal from Office, and disqualification to hold and enjoy any Office of honor, Trust or Profit under the United States: but the Party convicted shall nevertheless be liable and subject to Indictment, Trial, Judgment and Punishment, according to Law.

Section. 4.

The Times, Places and Manner of holding Elections for Senators and Representatives, shall be prescribed in each State by the Legislature thereof; but the Congress may at any time by Law make or alter such Regulations, except as to the Places of chusing Senators.

Elections

The Congress shall assemble at least once in every Year, and such Meeting shall [be on the first Monday in December,] unless they shall by Law appoint a different Day.

Changed by Section 2 of the Twentieth Amendment

Section. 5.

Each House shall be the Judge of the Elections, Returns and Qualifications of its own Members, and a Majority of each shall constitute a Quorum to do Business; but a smaller Number may adjourn from day to day, and may be authorized to compel the Attendance of absent Members, in such Manner, and under such Penalties as each House may provide.

Each House may determine the Rules of its Proceedings, punish its Members for disorderly Behaviour, and, with the Concurrence of two thirds, expel a Member.

Rules of Proceedings

Each House shall keep a Journal of its Proceedings, and from time to time publish the same, excepting such Parts as may in their Judgment require Secrecy; and the Yeas and Nays of the Members of either House on any question shall, at the Desire of one fifth of those Present, be entered on the Journal.

Neither House, during the Session of Congress, shall, without the Consent of the other, adjourn for more than three days, nor to any other Place than that in which the two Houses shall be sitting.

Adjournment

Section. 6.

The Senators and Representatives shall receive a Compensation for their Services, to be ascertained by Law, and paid out of the Treasury of the United States. They shall in all Cases, except Treason, Felony and Breach of the Peace, be privileged from Arrest during their Attendance at the Session of their respective Houses, and in going to and returning from the same; and for any Speech or Debate in either House, they shall not be questioned in any other Place.

Privilege from Arrest

No Senator or Representative shall, during the Time for which he was elected, be appointed to any civil Office under the Authority of the United States, which shall have been created, or the Emoluments whereof shall have been encreased during such time; and no Person holding any Office under the United States, shall be a Member of either House during his Continuance in Office.

Section. 7.

All Bills for raising Revenue shall originate in the House of Representatives; but the Senate may propose or concur with Amendments as on other Bills.

Revenue Bills

Presentment Clause Every Bill which shall have passed the House of Representatives and the Senate, shall, before it become a Law, be presented
Veto to the President of the United States: If he approve he shall sign it,
but if not he shall return it, with his Objections to that House in
which it shall have originated, who shall enter the Objections at
large on their Journal, and proceed to reconsider it. If after such
Reconsideration two thirds of that House shall agree to pass the
Bill, it shall be sent, together with the Objections, to the other
House, by which it shall likewise be reconsidered, and if approved
by two thirds of that House, it shall become a Law. But in all such
Cases the Votes of both Houses shall be determined by yeas and
Nays, and the Names of the Persons voting for and against the
Pocket Veto Bill shall be entered on the Journal of each House respectively. If
any Bill shall not be returned by the President within ten Days
(Sundays excepted) after it shall have been presented to him, the
Same shall be a Law, in like Manner as if he had signed it, unless
the Congress by their Adjournment prevent its Return, in which
Case it shall not be a Law.

Every Order, Resolution, or Vote to which the Concurrence of
the Senate and House of Representatives may be necessary (except
on a question of Adjournment) shall be presented to the President
of the United States; and before the Same shall take Effect, shall be
approved by him, or being disapproved by him, shall be repassed by
two thirds of the Senate and House of Representatives, according to
the Rules and Limitations prescribed in the Case of a Bill.

Section. 8.

Enumerated Powers of The Congress shall have Power To lay and collect Taxes, Duties,
Congress Imposts and Excises, to pay the Debts and provide for the common
Spending Defence and general Welfare of the United States; but all Duties,
Imposts and Excises shall be uniform throughout the United States;

To borrow Money on the credit of the United States;

Commerce To regulate Commerce with foreign Nations, and among the
several States, and with the Indian Tribes;

Naturalization To establish an uniform Rule of Naturalization, and uniform
Laws on the subject of Bankruptcies throughout the United States;

To coin Money, regulate the Value thereof, and of foreign Coin,
and fix the Standard of Weights and Measures;

To provide for the Punishment of counterfeiting the Securities
and current Coin of the United States;

To establish Post Offices and post Roads;

To promote the Progress of Science and useful Arts, by securing
for limited Times to Authors and Inventors the exclusive Right to
their respective Writings and Discoveries;

Inferior Courts To constitute Tribunals inferior to the supreme Court;

To define and punish Piracies and Felonies committed on the
high Seas, and Offences against the Law of Nations;

War Power To declare War, grant Letters of Marque and Reprisal, and make
Rules concerning Captures on Land and Water;

To raise and support Armies, but no Appropriation of Money to that Use shall be for a longer Term than two Years;

To provide and maintain a Navy;

To make Rules for the Government and Regulation of the land and naval Forces;

To provide for calling forth the Militia to execute the Laws of the Union, suppress Insurrections and repel Invasions;

To provide for organizing, arming, and disciplining, the Militia, and for governing such Part of them as may be employed in the Service of the United States, reserving to the States respectively, the Appointment of the Officers, and the Authority of training the Militia according to the discipline prescribed by Congress;

To exercise exclusive Legislation in all Cases whatsoever, over such District (not exceeding ten Miles square) as may, by Cession of particular States, and the Acceptance of Congress, become the Seat of the Government of the United States, and to exercise like Authority over all Places purchased by the Consent of the Legislature of the State in which the Same shall be, for the Erection of Forts, Magazines, Arsenals, dock-Yards, and other needful Buildings;—And **District of Columbia**

To make all Laws which shall be necessary and proper for carrying into Execution the foregoing Powers, and all other Powers vested by this Constitution in the Government of the United States, or in any Department or Officer thereof. **Necessary and Proper Clause**

Section. 9.

The Migration or Importation of such Persons as any of the States now existing shall think proper to admit, shall not be prohibited by the Congress prior to the Year one thousand eight hundred and eight, but a Tax or duty may be imposed on such Importation, not exceeding ten dollars for each Person.

The Privilege of the Writ of Habeas Corpus shall not be suspended, unless when in Cases of Rebellion or Invasion the public Safety may require it. **Habeas Corpus**

No Bill of Attainder or ex post facto Law shall be passed. **Ex Post Facto Laws**

No Capitation, or other direct, Tax shall be laid, [unless in Proportion to the Census or enumeration herein before directed to be taken.] **Changed by the Sixteenth Amendment**

No Tax or Duty shall be laid on Articles exported from any State.

No Preference shall be given by any Regulation of Commerce or Revenue to the Ports of one State over those of another; nor shall Vessels bound to, or from, one State, be obliged to enter, clear, or pay Duties in another.

No Money shall be drawn from the Treasury, but in Consequence of Appropriations made by Law; and a regular Statement and Account of the Receipts and Expenditures of all public Money shall be published from time to time. **Appropriations**

No Title of Nobility shall be granted by the United States: And no Person holding any Office of Profit or Trust under them, shall, without **No Titles of Nobility** the Consent of the Congress, accept of any present, Emolument, Office, or Title, of any kind whatever, from any King, Prince, or foreign State.

Section. 10.

Restrictions on States

No State shall enter into any Treaty, Alliance, or Confederation; grant Letters of Marque and Reprisal; coin Money; emit Bills of Credit; make any Thing but gold and silver Coin a Tender in Payment of Debts; pass any Bill of Attainder, ex post facto Law, or Law impairing the Obligation of Contracts, or grant any Title of Nobility.

No State shall, without the Consent of the Congress, lay any Imposts or Duties on Imports or Exports, except what may be absolutely necessary for executing it's inspection Laws: and the net Produce of all Duties and Imposts, laid by any State on Imports or Exports, shall be for the Use of the Treasury of the United States; and all such Laws shall be subject to the Revision and Controul of the Congress.

No State shall, without the Consent of Congress, lay any Duty of Tonnage, keep Troops, or Ships of War in time of Peace, enter into any Agreement or Compact with another State, or with a foreign Power, or engage in War, unless actually invaded, or in such imminent Danger as will not admit of delay.

ARTICLE. II.

Section. 1.

Executive Power

The executive Power shall be vested in a President of the United States of America. He shall hold his Office during the Term of four Years, and, together with the Vice President, chosen for the same Term, be elected, as follows:

The Electoral College

Each State shall appoint, in such Manner as the Legislature thereof may direct, a Number of Electors, equal to the whole Number of Senators and Representatives to which the State may be entitled in the Congress: but no Senator or Representative, or Person holding an Office of Trust or Profit under the United States, shall be appointed an Elector.

[The Electors shall meet in their respective States, and vote by Ballot for two Persons, of whom one at least shall not be an Inhabitant of the same State with themselves. And they shall make a List of all the Persons voted for, and of the Number of Votes for each; which List they shall sign and certify, and transmit sealed to the Seat of the Government of the United States, directed to the President of the Senate. The President of the Senate shall, in the Presence of the Senate and House of Representatives, open all the Certificates, and the Votes shall then be counted. The Person having the greatest Number of Votes shall be the President, if such Number be a Majority of the whole Number of Electors appointed; and if there be more than one who have such Majority, and have an equal Number of Votes, then the House of Representatives shall immediately chuse by Ballot one

Changed by the Twelfth Amendment

of them for President; and if no Person have a Majority, then from the five highest on the List the said House shall in like Manner chuse the President. But in chusing the President, the Votes shall be taken by States, the Representation from each State having one Vote; A quorum for this purpose shall consist of a Member or Members from two thirds of the States, and a Majority of all the States shall be necessary to a Choice. In every Case, after the Choice of the President, the Person having the greatest Number of Votes of the Electors shall be the Vice President. But if there should remain two or more who have equal Votes, the Senate shall chuse from them by Ballot the Vice President.]

The Congress may determine the Time of chusing the Electors, and the Day on which they shall give their Votes; which Day shall be the same throughout the United States.

No Person except a natural born Citizen, or a Citizen of the United States, at the time of the Adoption of this Constitution, shall be eligible to the Office of President; neither shall any Person be eligible to that Office who shall not have attained to the Age of thirty five Years, and been fourteen Years a Resident within the United States.

Requirements of Office

[In Case of the Removal of the President from Office, or of his Death, Resignation, or Inability to discharge the Powers and Duties of the said Office, the Same shall devolve on the Vice President, and the Congress may by Law provide for the Case of Removal, Death, Resignation or Inability, both of the President and Vice President, declaring what Officer shall then act as President, and such Officer shall act accordingly, until the Disability be removed, or a President shall be elected.]

Changed by the Twenty-fifth Amendment

The President shall, at stated Times, receive for his Services, a Compensation, which shall neither be increased nor diminished during the Period for which he shall have been elected, and he shall not receive within that Period any other Emolument from the United States, or any of them.

Before he enter on the Execution of his Office, he shall take the following Oath or Affirmation: — "I do solemnly swear (or affirm) that I will faithfully execute the Office of President of the United States, and will to the best of my Ability, preserve, protect and defend the Constitution of the United States."

Oath of Office

Section. 2.

The President shall be Commander in Chief of the Army and Navy of the United States, and of the Militia of the several States, when called into the actual Service of the United States; he may require the Opinion, in writing, of the principal Officer in each of the executive Departments, upon any Subject relating to the Duties of their respective Offices, and he shall have Power to grant Reprieves and Pardons for Offences against the United States, except in Cases of Impeachment.

Commander in Chief

Reprieves and Pardons

He shall have Power, by and with the Advice and Consent of the Senate, to make Treaties, provided two thirds of the Senators

Treaty Power

Nominations and Appointments present concur; and he shall nominate, and by and with the Advice and Consent of the Senate, shall appoint Ambassadors, other public Ministers and Consuls, Judges of the supreme Court, and all other Officers of the United States, whose Appointments are not herein otherwise provided for, and which shall be established by Law: but the Congress may by Law vest the Appointment of such inferior Officers, as they think proper, in the President alone, in the Courts of Law, or in the Heads of Departments.

Recess Appointments The President shall have Power to fill up all Vacancies that may happen during the Recess of the Senate, by granting Commissions which shall expire at the End of their next Session.

Section. 3.

State of the Union He shall from time to time give to the Congress Information of the State of the Union, and recommend to their Consideration such Measures as he shall judge necessary and expedient; he may, on extraordinary Occasions, convene both Houses, or either of them, and in Case of Disagreement between them, with Respect to the Time of Adjournment, he may adjourn them to such Time as he shall think proper; he shall receive Ambassadors and other public Ministers; he **Take Care Clause** shall take Care that the Laws be faithfully executed, and shall Commission all the Officers of the United States.

Section. 4.

Impeachment The President, Vice President and all civil Officers of the United States, shall be removed from Office on Impeachment for, and Conviction of, Treason, Bribery, or other high Crimes and Misdemeanors.

ARTICLE. III.

Section. 1.

Judicial Power The judicial Power of the United States shall be vested in one supreme Court, and in such inferior Courts as the Congress may from time to time ordain and establish. The Judges, both of the **Tenure** supreme and inferior Courts, shall hold their Offices during good Behaviour, and shall, at stated Times, receive for their Services a Compensation, which shall not be diminished during their Continuance in Office.

Section. 2.

Jurisdiction, Cases, and Controversies The judicial Power shall extend to all Cases, in Law and Equity, arising under this Constitution, the Laws of the United States, and Treaties made, or which shall be made, under their Authority; — to all Cases affecting Ambassadors, other public Ministers and Consuls; — to all Cases of admiralty and maritime Jurisdiction; — to Contro- **Changed by the Eleventh Amendment** versies to which the United States shall be a Party; — to Controversies between two or more States; — [between a State and Citizens of another State; —] between Citizens of different States; — between Citizens of the same State claiming Lands under Grants of different States, [and between a State, or the Citizens thereof, and foreign States, Citizens or Subjects.]

Changed by the Eleventh Amendment
Original Jurisdiction

In all Cases affecting Ambassadors, other public Ministers and Consuls, and those in which a State shall be Party, the supreme Court shall have original Jurisdiction. In all the other Cases before mentioned, the supreme Court shall have appellate Jurisdiction, both as to Law and Fact, with such Exceptions, and under such Regulations as the Congress shall make.

Appellate Jurisdiction

The Trial of all Crimes, except in Cases of Impeachment, shall be by Jury; and such Trial shall be held in the State where the said Crimes shall have been committed; but when not committed within any State, the Trial shall be at such Place or Places as the Congress may by Law have directed.

Trial by Jury

Section. 3.

Treason against the United States, shall consist only in levying War against them, or in adhering to their Enemies, giving them Aid and Comfort. No Person shall be convicted of Treason unless on the Testimony of two Witnesses to the same overt Act, or on Confession in open Court.

Treason

The Congress shall have Power to declare the Punishment of Treason, but no Attainder of Treason shall work Corruption of Blood, or Forfeiture except during the Life of the Person attainted.

ARTICLE. IV.

Section. 1.

Full Faith and Credit shall be given in each State to the public Acts, Records, and judicial Proceedings of every other State. And the Congress may by general Laws prescribe the Manner in which such Acts, Records and Proceedings shall be proved, and the Effect thereof.

Relations Among the States

Section. 2.

The Citizens of each State shall be entitled to all Privileges and Immunities of Citizens in the several States.

Privileges and Immunities

A Person charged in any State with Treason, Felony, or other Crime, who shall flee from Justice, and be found in another State, shall on Demand of the executive Authority of the State from which he fled, be delivered up, to be removed to the State having Jurisdiction of the Crime.

Extradition

[No Person held to Service or Labour in one State, under the Laws thereof, escaping into another, shall, in Consequence of any Law or Regulation therein, be discharged from such Service or Labour, but shall be delivered up on Claim of the Party to whom such Service or Labour may be due.]

Changed by the Thirteenth Amendment

Section. 3.

Admission of New States
New States may be admitted by the Congress into this Union; but no new State shall be formed or erected within the Jurisdiction of any other State; nor any State be formed by the Junction of two or more States, or Parts of States, without the Consent of the Legislatures of the States concerned as well as of the Congress.

Territories
The Congress shall have Power to dispose of and make all needful Rules and Regulations respecting the Territory or other Property belonging to the United States; and nothing in this Constitution shall be so construed as to Prejudice any Claims of the United States, or of any particular State.

Section. 4.

Republican Form of Government
The United States shall guarantee to every State in this Union a Republican Form of Government, and shall protect each of them against Invasion; and on Application of the Legislature, or of the Executive (when the Legislature cannot be convened), against domestic Violence.

ARTICLE. V.

Procedures for Amending the Constitution
The Congress, whenever two thirds of both Houses shall deem it necessary, shall propose Amendments to this Constitution, or, on the Application of the Legislatures of two thirds of the several States, shall call a Convention for proposing Amendments, which, in either Case, shall be valid to all Intents and Purposes, as Part of this Constitution, when ratified by the Legislatures of three fourths of the several States, or by Conventions in three fourths thereof, as the one or the other Mode of Ratification may be proposed by the Congress; Provided that no Amendment which may be made prior to the Year One thousand eight hundred and eight shall in any Manner affect the first and fourth Clauses in the Ninth Section of the first Article; and that no State, without its Consent, shall be deprived of its equal Suffrage in the Senate.

ARTICLE. VI.

All Debts contracted and Engagements entered into, before the Adoption of this Constitution, shall be as valid against the United States under this Constitution, as under the Confederation.

Supreme Law of the Land
This Constitution, and the Laws of the United States which shall be made in Pursuance thereof; and all Treaties made, or which shall be made, under the Authority of the United States, shall be the supreme Law of the Land; and the Judges in every State shall be bound thereby, any Thing in the Constitution or Laws of any State to the Contrary notwithstanding.

The Senators and Representatives before mentioned, and the Members of the several State Legislatures, and all executive and judicial Officers, both of the United States and of the several States, shall be bound by Oath or Affirmation, to support this Constitution; but no religious Test shall ever be required as a Qualification to any Office or public Trust under the United States.

Oath to Support Constitution

No Religious Test

ARTICLE. VII.

The Ratification of the Conventions of nine States, shall be sufficient for the Establishment of this Constitution between the States so ratifying the Same.

Ratification

Done in Convention by the Unanimous Consent of the States present the Seventeenth Day of September in the Year of our Lord one thousand seven hundred and Eighty seven and of the Independence of the United States of America the Twelfth In witness whereof We have hereunto subscribed our Names,

Attest William Jackson, Secretary

G°. Washington – Presidt
and deputy from Virginia

Delaware
  Geo: Read
  Gunning Bedford jun
  John Dickinson
  Richard Bassett
  Jaco: Broom

Maryland
  James McHenry
  Dan of St Thos. Jenifer
  Danl. Carroll

Virginia
  John Blair
  James Madison Jr.

North Carolina
  Wm. Blount
  Richd. Dobbs Spaight
  Hu Williamson

South Carolina
  J. Rutledge
  Charles Cotesworth
    Pinckney
  Charles Pinckney
  Pierce Butler

New Hampshire
  John Langdon
  Nicholas Gilman

Massachusetts
  Nathaniel Gorham
  Rufus King

Connecticut
  Wm. Saml. Johnson
  Roger Sherman

New York
  Alexander Hamilton

New Jersey
  Wil: Livingston
  David Brearley
  Wm. Paterson
  Jona: Dayton

Pennsylvania
  B Franklin
  Thomas Mifflin
  Robt. Morris
  Geo. Clymer
  Thos. FitzSimons

Georgia
William Few
Abr Baldwin

Jared Ingersoll
James Wilson
Gouv Morris

Amendments to the Constitution of the United States of America

The First Ten Amendments— the Bill of Rights— Were Ratified Effective December 15, 1791

AMENDMENT I

Religion, Speech, Press, Assembly, and Petition

Congress shall make no law respecting an establishment of religion, or prohibiting the free exercise thereof; or abridging the freedom of speech, or of the press; or the right of the people peaceably to assemble, and to petition the Government for a redress of grievances.

AMENDMENT II

Right to Bear Arms

A well regulated Militia, being necessary to the security of a free State, the right of the people to keep and bear Arms, shall not be infringed.

AMENDMENT III

Quartering of Troops

No Soldier shall, in time of peace be quartered in any house, without the consent of the Owner, nor in time of war, but in a manner to be prescribed by law.

AMENDMENT IV

Searches and Seizures

The right of the people to be secure in their persons, houses, papers, and effects, against unreasonable searches and seizures, shall not be violated, and no Warrants shall issue, but upon probable cause, supported by Oath or affirmation, and particularly describing the place to be searched, and the persons or things to be seized.

AMENDMENT V

Grand Juries, Double Jeopardy, Self Incrimination, Due Process

No person shall be held to answer for a capital, or otherwise infamous crime, unless on a presentment or indictment of a Grand Jury, except in cases arising in the land or naval forces, or in the Militia, when in actual service in time of War or public danger; nor shall any person be subject for the same offence to be twice put in jeopardy of life or limb; nor shall be compelled in any criminal case to be a witness

Taking of Property

against himself, nor be deprived of life, liberty, or property, without due process of law; nor shall private property be taken for public use, without just compensation.

AMENDMENT VI

In all criminal prosecutions, the accused shall enjoy the right to a speedy and public trial, by an impartial jury of the State and district wherein the crime shall have been committed, which district shall have been previously ascertained by law, and to be informed of the nature and cause of the accusation; to be confronted with the witnesses against him; to have compulsory process for obtaining witnesses in his favor, and to have the Assistance of Counsel for his defence.

Criminal Court Procedures

AMENDMENT VII

In Suits at common law, where the value in controversy shall exceed twenty dollars, the right of trial by jury shall be preserved, and no fact tried by a jury, shall be otherwise re-examined in any Court of the United States, than according to the rules of the common law.

Trial by Jury in Civil Cases

AMENDMENT VIII

Excessive bail shall not be required, nor excessive fines imposed, nor cruel and unusual punishments inflicted.

Bail, Cruel and Unusual Punishments

AMENDMENT IX

The enumeration in the Constitution, of certain rights, shall not be construed to deny or disparage others retained by the people.

Other Rights of the People

AMENDMENT X

The powers not delegated to the United States by the Constitution, nor prohibited by it to the States, are reserved to the States respectively, or to the people.

Powers Reserved to the States, or the People

AMENDMENT XI

(Ratified February 7, 1795)

The Judicial power of the United States shall not be construed to extend to any suit in law or equity, commenced or prosecuted against one of the United States by Citizens of another State, or by Citizens or Subjects of any Foreign State.

Suits Against States

(Ratified June 15, 1804)

AMENDMENT XII

Election of the President

The Electors shall meet in their respective states and vote by ballot for President and Vice-President, one of whom, at least, shall not be an inhabitant of the same state with themselves; they shall name in their ballots the person voted for as President, and in distinct ballots the person voted for as Vice-President, and they shall make distinct lists of all persons voted for as President, and of all persons voted for as Vice-President, and of the number of votes for each, which lists they shall sign and certify, and transmit sealed to the seat of the government of the United States, directed to the President of the Senate; — the President of the Senate shall, in the presence of the Senate and House of Representatives, open all the certificates and the votes shall then be counted; — The person having the greatest number of votes for President, shall be the President, if such number be a majority of the whole number of Electors appointed; and if no person have such majority, then from the persons having the highest numbers not exceeding three on the list of those voted for as President, the House of Representatives shall choose immediately, by ballot, the President. But in choosing the President, the votes shall be taken by states, the representation from each state having one vote; a quorum for this purpose shall consist of a member or members from two-thirds of the states, and a majority

Superseded by Section 3 of the Twentieth Amendment

of all the states shall be necessary to a choice. [And if the House of Representatives shall not choose a President whenever the right of choice shall devolve upon them, before the fourth day of March next following, then the Vice-President shall act as President, as in case of the death or other constitutional disability of the President. —] The person having the greatest number of votes as Vice-President, shall be the Vice-President, if such number be a majority of the whole number of Electors appointed, and if no person have a majority, then from the two highest numbers on the list, the Senate shall choose the Vice-President; a quorum for the purpose shall consist of two-thirds of the whole number of Senators, and a majority of the whole number shall be necessary to a choice. But no person constitutionally ineligible to the office of President shall be eligible to that of Vice-President of the United States.

(Ratified December 6, 1865)

AMENDMENT XIII

Section. 1.

Prohibition of Slavery

Neither slavery nor involuntary servitude, except as a punishment for crime whereof the party shall have been duly convicted, shall exist within the United States, or any place subject to their jurisdiction.

Section. 2.
Congress shall have power to enforce this article by appropriate legislation.

AMENDMENT XIV

(Ratified July 9, 1868)

Section. 1.

All persons born or naturalized in the United States, and subject to the jurisdiction thereof, are citizens of the United States and of the State wherein they reside. No State shall make or enforce any law which shall abridge the privileges or immunities of citizens of the United States; nor shall any State deprive any person of life, liberty, or property, without due process of law; nor deny to any person within its jurisdiction the equal protection of the laws.

Citizenship

Privileges and Immunities

Due Process

Equal Protection

Section. 2.

Representatives shall be apportioned among the several States according to their respective numbers, counting the whole number of persons in each State, excluding Indians not taxed. But when the right to vote at any election for the choice of electors for President and Vice-President of the United States, Representatives in Congress, the Executive and Judicial officers of a State, or the members of the Legislature thereof, is denied to any of the male inhabitants of such State, [being twenty-one years of age,] and citizens of the United States, or in any way abridged, except for participation in rebellion, or other crime, the basis of representation therein shall be reduced in the proportion which the number of such male citizens shall bear to the whole number of male citizens twenty-one years of age in such State.

Apportionment

Superseded by Section 1 of the Twenty-sixth Amendment

Section. 3.

No person shall be a Senator or Representative in Congress, or elector of President and Vice-President, or hold any office, civil or military, under the United States, or under any State, who, having previously taken an oath, as a member of Congress, or as an officer of the United States, or as a member of any State legislature, or as an executive or judicial officer of any State, to support the Constitution of the United States, shall have engaged in insurrection or rebellion against the same, or given aid or comfort to the enemies thereof. But Congress may by a vote of two-thirds of each House, remove such disability.

Disqualification for Rebellion

Section. 4.

The validity of the public debt of the United States, authorized by law, including debts incurred for payment of pensions and bounties for services in suppressing insurrection or rebellion, shall not be questioned. But neither the United States nor any State shall assume or pay any debt or obligation incurred in aid of insurrection or rebellion against the United States, or any claim for the loss or emancipation of any slave; but all such debts, obligations and claims shall be held illegal and void.

Debts Incurred During Rebellion

Section. 5.

The Congress shall have the power to enforce, by appropriate legislation, the provisions of this article.

(Ratified February 3, 1870)

AMENDMENT XV

Section. 1.

Suffrage—Race The right of citizens of the United States to vote shall not be denied or abridged by the United States or by any State on account of race, color, or previous condition of servitude —

Section. 2.

The Congress shall have the power to enforce this article by appropriate legislation.

(Ratified February 3, 1913)

AMENDMENT XVI

Federal Income Tax The Congress shall have power to lay and collect taxes on incomes, from whatever source derived, without apportionment among the several States, and without regard to any census or enumeration.

(Ratified April 8, 1913)

AMENDMENT XVII

Popular Election of Senators The Senate of the United States shall be composed of two Senators from each State, elected by the people thereof, for six years; and each Senator shall have one vote. The electors in each State shall have the qualifications requisite for electors of the most numerous branch of the State legislatures.

When vacancies happen in the representation of any State in the Senate, the executive authority of such State shall issue writs of election to fill such vacancies: *Provided,* That the legislature of any State may empower the executive thereof to make temporary appointments until the people fill the vacancies by election as the legislature may direct.

This amendment shall not be so construed as to affect the election or term of any Senator chosen before it becomes valid as part of the Constitution.

(Ratified January 16, 1919)
Repealed by the
Twenty-first Amendment

AMENDMENT XVIII

Prohibition

Section. 1.

After one year from the ratification of this article the manufacture, sale, or transportation of intoxicating liquors within, the importation thereof into, or the exportation thereof from the United States and all territory subject to the jurisdiction thereof for beverage purposes is hereby prohibited.

Section. 2.

The Congress and the several States shall have concurrent power to enforce this article by appropriate legislation.

Section. 3.

This article shall be inoperative unless it shall have been ratified as an amendment to the Constitution by the legislatures of the several States, as provided in the Constitution, within seven years from the date of the submission hereof to the States by the Congress.

AMENDMENT XIX

(Ratified August 18, 1920)

The right of citizens of the United States to vote shall not be denied or abridged by the United States or by any State on account of sex.

Suffrage—Sex

    Congress shall have power to enforce this article by appropriate legislation.

AMENDMENT XX

(Ratified January 23, 1933)

Section. 1.

The terms of the President and the Vice President shall end at noon on the 20th day of January, and the terms of Senators and Representatives at noon on the 3d day of January, of the years in which such terms would have ended if this article had not been ratified; and the terms of their successors shall then begin.

Lame-duck Amendment

Section. 2.

The Congress shall assemble at least once in every year, and such meeting shall begin at noon on the 3d day of January, unless they shall by law appoint a different day.

Section. 3.

If, at the time fixed for the beginning of the term of the President, the President elect shall have died, the Vice President elect shall become President. If a President shall not have been chosen before the time fixed for the beginning of his term, or if the President elect shall have failed to qualify, then the Vice President elect shall act as President until a President shall have qualified; and the Congress may by law provide for the case wherein neither a President elect nor a Vice President shall have qualified, declaring who shall then act as President, or the manner in which one who is to act shall be selected, and such person shall act accordingly until a President or Vice President shall have qualified.

Presidential Succession

Section. 4.

The Congress may by law provide for the case of the death of any of the persons from whom the House of Representatives may choose a President whenever the right of choice shall have devolved upon them, and for the case of the death of any of the persons from whom the Senate may choose a Vice President whenever the right of choice shall have devolved upon them.

Section. 5.
Sections 1 and 2 shall take effect on the 15th day of October following the ratification of this article.

Section. 6.
This article shall be inoperative unless it shall have been ratified as an amendment to the Constitution by the legislatures of three-fourths of the several States within seven years from the date of its submission.

(Ratified December 5, 1933)

AMENDMENT XXI

Section. 1.
Repeal of Prohibition The eighteenth article of amendment to the Constitution of the United States is hereby repealed.

Section. 2.
The transportation or importation into any State, Territory, or Possession of the United States for delivery or use therein of intoxicating liquors, in violation of the laws thereof, is hereby prohibited.

Section. 3.
This article shall be inoperative unless it shall have been ratified as an amendment to the Constitution by conventions in the several States, as provided in the Constitution, within seven years from the date of the submission hereof to the States by the Congress.

(Ratified February 27, 1951)

AMENDMENT XXII

Section. 1.
Limit on Presidential Terms No person shall be elected to the office of the President more than twice, and no person who has held the office of President, or acted as President, for more than two years of a term to which some other person was elected President shall be elected to the office of President more than once. But this Article shall not apply to any person holding the office of President when this Article was proposed by Congress, and shall not prevent any person who may be holding the office of President, or acting as President, during the term within which this Article becomes operative from holding the office of President or acting as President during the remainder of such term.

Section. 2.
This article shall be inoperative unless it shall have been ratified as an amendment to the Constitution by the legislatures of three-fourths of the several States within seven years from the date of its submission to the States by the Congress.

AMENDMENT XXIII

(Ratified March 29, 1961)

Section. 1.

The District constituting the seat of Government of the United States shall appoint in such manner as Congress may direct:

    A number of electors of President and Vice President equal to the whole number of Senators and Representatives in Congress to which the District would be entitled if it were a State, but in no event more than the least populous State; they shall be in addition to those appointed by the States, but they shall be considered, for the purposes of the election of President and Vice President, to be electors appointed by a State; and they shall meet in the District and perform such duties as provided by the twelfth article of amendment.

Presidential Electors for the District of Columbia

Section. 2.

The Congress shall have power to enforce this article by appropriate legislation.

AMENDMENT XXIV

(Ratified January 23, 1964)

Section. 1.

The right of citizens of the United States to vote in any primary or other election for President or Vice President, for electors for President or Vice President, or for Senator or Representative in Congress, shall not be denied or abridged by the United States or any State by reason of failure to pay poll tax or other tax.

Prohibition of the Poll Tax

Section. 2.

The Congress shall have power to enforce this article by appropriate legislation.

AMENDMENT XXV

(Ratified February 10, 1967)

Section. 1.

In case of the removal of the President from office or of his death or resignation, the Vice President shall become President.

Presidential Succession

Section. 2.

Whenever there is a vacancy in the office of the Vice President, the President shall nominate a Vice President who shall take office upon confirmation by a majority vote of both Houses of Congress.

Vice Presidency

Section. 3.

Whenever the President transmits to the President pro tempore of the Senate and the Speaker of the House of Representatives his written declaration that he is unable to discharge the powers and duties

Incapacity to Perform Duties of Office

of his office, and until he transmits to them a written declaration to the contrary, such powers and duties shall be discharged by the Vice President as Acting President.

Section. 4.

Whenever the Vice President and a majority of either the principal officers of the executive departments or of such other body as Congress may by law provide, transmit to the President pro tempore of the Senate and the Speaker of the House of Representatives their written declaration that the President is unable to discharge the powers and duties of his office, the Vice President shall immediately assume the powers and duties of the office as Acting President.

Thereafter, when the President transmits to the President pro tempore of the Senate and the Speaker of the House of Representatives his written declaration that no inability exists, he shall resume the powers and duties of his office unless the Vice President and a majority of either the principal officers of the executive department or of such other body as Congress may by law provide, transmit within four days to the President pro tempore of the Senate and the Speaker of the House of Representatives their written declaration that the President is unable to discharge the powers and duties of his office. Thereupon Congress shall decide the issue, assembling within forty-eight hours for that purpose if not in session. If the Congress, within twenty-one days after receipt of the latter written declaration, or, if Congress is not in session, within twenty-one days after Congress is required to assemble, determines by two-thirds vote of both Houses that the President is unable to discharge the powers and duties of his office, the Vice President shall continue to discharge the same as Acting President; otherwise, the President shall resume the powers and duties of his office.

(Ratified July 1, 1971)

AMENDMENT XXVI

Section. 1.

Suffrage—Age The right of citizens of the United States, who are eighteen years of age or older, to vote shall not be denied or abridged by the United States or by any State on account of age.

Section. 2.

The Congress shall have power to enforce this article by appropriate legislation.

(Ratified May 7, 1992)
Proposed September 25, 1789
as part of the original
Bill of Rights
Congressional Compensation

AMENDMENT XXVII

No law, varying the compensation for the services of the Senators and Representatives, shall take effect, until an election of representatives shall have intervened.

THE HERITAGE GUIDE TO
THE CONSTITUTION

PREAMBLE

We the People of the United States, in Order to form a more perfect Union, establish Justice, insure domestic Tranquility, provide for the common defense, promote the general Welfare, and secure the Blessings of Liberty to ourselves and our Posterity, do ordain and establish this Constitution for the United States of America.

≈

*T*he Preamble was placed in the Constitution more or less as an afterthought. It was not proposed or discussed on the floor of the Constitutional Convention. Rather, Gouverneur Morris, a delegate from Pennsylvania, who as a member of the Committee of Style actually drafted the near-final text of the Constitution, composed it at the last moment. It is likely that the Committee assigned him to do so, inasmuch as such preambles were common practice in the era.

Nevertheless, it was Morris who gave the considered purposes of the Constitution coherent shape, and the Preamble was the capstone of his expository gift. The Preamble does not, in itself, have substantive legal meaning. The understanding at the time was that preambles are merely declaratory and are to be read as defining rather than granting or limiting power—a view sustained by the Supreme Court in *Jacobson v. Massachusetts* (1905).

The Preamble has considerable potency, however, by virtue of its specification of the purposes for which the Constitution exists. It identifies the legal power—the union—called into existence by the Constitution and distills the underlying values that moved the Framers during their long debates in Philadelphia. As Justice Joseph Story put it in his celebrated *Commentaries on the Constitution of the United States* (1833), "its true office is to expound the nature, and extent, and application of the powers actually conferred by the Constitution." Alexander Hamilton, in *The Federalist* No. 84, went so far as to assert that the words "secure the blessings of liberty to ourselves and our posterity" were "a better recognition of popular rights than volumes of those aphorisms which make the principal figure in several of our State bills of rights."

An appreciation of the Preamble begins with a comparison of it to its counterpart in the compact the Constitution replaced, the Articles of Confederation. There, the states joined in "a firm league of friendship with each other, for their common defence, security of their Liberties, and their mutual and general welfare" and bound themselves to assist one another "against all force offered to, or attacks made upon them, or any of them, on account of religion, sovereignty, trade, or any other pretence whatever." The agreement was among states, not people, and the safety and liberties to be secured were the safety and liberties of the states.

The very opening words of the Constitution, "We the People of the United States," presume the language of the Declaration of Independence, in which the "unanimous declaration of the thirteen united States" declared the sense of "one people." It was therefore at striking variance with the prevailing norm, in that the word "people" had not been used in documents ranging from the Articles of Confederation drafted in 1777 and the 1778 treaty of alliance with France to the 1783 Treaty of Paris recognizing American independence, and the phrase "the United States" was followed by a listing of the states ("viz., New-Hampshire, Massachusetts-bay, Rhode-Island and Providence Plantations," and so on down to Georgia).

The new phraseology was necessary, given the circumstances. The Constitutional Convention had provided that when the popularly elected ratifying conventions of nine states had approved the Constitution, it would go into effect for those nine, notwithstanding whether any of the remaining states ratified. Inasmuch as no one could know which states would and which would not ratify, the Convention could not list all thirteen. Moreover, states' names could scarcely be added to the Preamble retroactively as they were admitted. Even so, the phraseology set off howls of protest from a number of opponents of ratification, notably Patrick Henry. Henry charged that the failure to follow the usual form indicated an intention to create a "consolidated" national government instead of the system that James Madison described in *The Federalist* No. 39 as being "neither a national nor a federal constitution, but a composition of both." Henry's assertion in the Virginia ratifying convention was

promptly and devastatingly rebutted by Governor Edmund Randolph: "The government is for the people; and the misfortune was, that the people had no agency in the government before... If the government is to be binding on the people, are not the people the proper persons to examine its merits or defects?" Randolph made clear that the "people" and not the "states" acting through their established governments were the ratifying authority, a deliberate move on the part of the drafters of the Constitution. We should also note that George Washington's "letter of transmittal" which reported the Convention's work to the Confederation Congress specifically referred to the drafted "consolidation of our Union," meaning that Henry spoke accurately but not quite to the point.

The Preamble's first-mentioned purpose of the Constitution, "to form a more perfect Union," was likewise subjected to misreading by Anti-Federalists. "More perfect" may strike modern readers as a solecism or as an ambiguous depiction, for "perfect" is now regarded as an absolute term. At the time of the Framing, however, it had no such connotation. For example, Sir William Blackstone, in his widely read *Commentaries on the Laws of England*, could assert that the constitution of England was perfect but steadily improving. Thus a more perfect union was simply a better and stronger one (one that is more perfected or brought to completion) than had pre-existed the Constitution. Yet a New York Anti-Federalist who wrote under the pseudonym Brutus professed to believe that, to carry out the mandate, it would be "necessary to abolish all inferior governments, and to give the general one compleat legislative, executive and judicial powers to every purpose." Madison disposed of that exaggerated fear in *The Federalist* No. 46 by demonstrating that "the powers proposed to be lodged in the federal government, are as little formidable to those reserved to the individual States as they are indispensably necessary to accomplish the purposes of the Union; and that all those alarms which have been sounded of a meditated and consequential annihilation of the State governments must, on the most favourable interpretation, be ascribed to the chimerical fears of the authors of them."

In the second stated objective, to "establish Justice," the first word is "establish," clearly implying that justice, unlike union, was previously nonexistent. On the face of it, that implication seems hyperbolic, for the American states and local governments had functioning court systems with independent judges, and trial by jury was the norm. But Gouverneur Morris chose the word carefully and meant what he wrote; he and many other Framers thought that the states had run amok and had trampled individual liberties in a variety of ways. The solution was twofold: establish an independent Supreme Court and, if Congress decided, a federal judiciary superior to those of the states and prohibit outright egregious state practices. Moreover, the third and fourth purposes presuppose justice, or just rule, as that for which security against domestic turmoil or foreign invasion is required.

The third avowed purpose, to "insure domestic Tranquility," was in a general sense prompted by the longstanding habit of Americans to take up arms against unpopular government measures and was more immediately a response to Shays' Rebellion in Massachusetts (1786–1787) and lesser uprisings in New Hampshire and Delaware. The most important constitutional provisions directed toward that end give Congress ultimate control over the militias (see Article I, Section 8) and guarantee each state a republican form of government and protection against domestic violence (see Article IV, Section 4). One should bear in mind that two rebellions broke out during the first decade under the Constitution, the Whiskey Rebellion (1794) and Fries's Rebellion (1799), both of which were speedily crushed without the shedding of blood.

The fourth purpose, to "provide for the common defense," is obvious—after all, it was by this means the United States came into being. But the matter cannot be dismissed lightly. For the better part of a century Americans had been possessed by a fear of "standing armies," insisting that armed forces adequate to defend the nation would also be adequate to enslave it. Besides, ordinary Americans could believe that, since the War for Independence had been won over the best fighting force in Europe under the aegis of the Confederation, further provision was unnecessary as well as dangerous. Anti-Federalists clearly thought along those lines. By and large, those who agreed had seen little of the fighting during the war, whereas veterans of actual combat and people who had served in Congress or the administration during the darkest hours of the war knew differently. They expected that other wars would occur and were determined to be prepared to fight them. The Framers did, however, take fears of standing armies into account, hence their commitment to civilian control of things military, and, for many, the right to bear arms.

The fifth purpose, to "promote the general Welfare," had a generally understood meaning at the time of the Constitution. The concept will be developed fully in the discussion of the Spending Clause of Article I, Section 8, but a few comments are germane here. The salient point is that its implications are negative, not positive—a limitation on power, not a grant of power. By definition "general" means applicable to the whole rather than to particular parts or special interests. A single example will illustrate the point. In the late 1790s Alexander Hamilton, an outspoken advocate of loose construction of the Constitution as well as of using the Necessary and Proper Clause to justify a wide range of "implied powers," became convinced that a federally financed system of what would soon be called internal improvements—building roads, dredging rivers, digging canals—was in the national interest. But, since each project would be of immediate advantage only to the area where it was located, none could properly be regarded as being in the general welfare. Accordingly, Hamilton believed a constitutional amendment would be necessary if internal improvements were to be undertaken. James Madison, in his second term as president, would veto a congressional bill on precisely that ground.

The sixth purpose of the Constitution is to "secure the Blessings of Liberty to ourselves and our Posterity." In broad terms the securing of liberty is a function of the whole Constitution; for the Constitution makes possible the establishment of a government of laws, and liberty without law is meaningless. Special provisions, however, in Article I, Sections 9 and 10 and in

Article III were designed to prevent specific dangers to liberty about which history had warned the Framers. Those in Section 9 were drawn from the example of English history: the prohibitions against suspending the writ of habeas corpus, against bills of attainder and ex post facto laws, and against granting titles of nobility. In addition, Article III, Section 2, guaranteed trial by jury in criminal cases, and Section 3 defined treason extremely narrowly and prohibited corruption of the blood to protect innocent relatives from being punished. These are protections of individual liberty, not the liberty of states as under the Articles of Confederation. What the Preamble conveys is a clear sense that the purpose of this form of government entails certain consequences of liberty, and logically rejects consequences that are contradictions to liberty itself, such as the liberty to enslave others, a problem patently evident to many of the Framers themselves, but one which was abided so that the entire enterprise of republican government would not be derailed at its start.

To the extent that liberty confirms the right of consent for rational beings capable of choice, it depends for its continued existence as well as its efficacy on what James Wilson called the equal, honest, and impartial administration of the laws. The provision for the rule of law is crucial to curbing the excesses of liberty—a strengthening of liberty's "blessings"—and therefore central in fostering moral virtue.

The restrictions in Article I, Section 10, apply to the state governments and were born of more recent history. The states are forbidden, among other things, to issue paper money, to make anything but gold and silver legal tender, or to pass bills of attainder, ex post facto laws, or laws impairing the obligation of contracts. All these mischievous kinds of laws had in fact been enacted by the states since the Declaration of Independence.

That brings us back to another point about the "general Welfare" and enables us to arrive at a broader understanding of the Preamble than is possible through a provision-by-provision analysis. Some historians have argued that the philosophy or ideology of the Constitution was at variance with that of the Declaration; indeed, several have described the adoption of the Constitution as a counter-Revolution. But consider this: the Declaration refers to God-given rights to life, liberty, and the pursuit of happiness. The Preamble introduces a document whose stated purpose is to secure the rights of life and liberty. And what of happiness? Once again the word "Welfare" is crucial: in the eighteenth century the definition of welfare included well-being, but it also and equally encompassed happiness.

The Preamble as a whole, then, declares that the Constitution is designed to secure precisely the rights proclaimed in the Declaration. The Constitution was therefore not the negation of the Revolution; it was the Revolution's fulfillment. What the Declaration sets forth as the reason for the people acting *in* the Revolution has been repeated in the Preamble as *the end* for which the people exist as a people. And this end, most notably, is promised not just to the people, but to "posterity." In that sense, it emphatically endorses the transcendent moral purpose of both the Revolution and the move to "ordain and establish" the Constitution. The Preamble is far more a statement of the people's duties than their hopes, duties by which they are honor bound to hold the government both politically and legally accountable.

Forrest McDonald and William B. Allen

See Also

Article I, Section 8
Article I, Section 9
Article I, Section 10
Article III, Section 2
Article III, Section 3
Article IV, Section 4 (Guarantee Clause)

Significant Case

Jacobson v. Massachusetts, 197 U.S. 11 (1905)

Suggestion for Further Research

Peter Charles Hoffer, *For Ourselves and Our Prosperity: The Preamble to the Federal Constitution in American History* (New York: Oxford University Press, 2013).

ARTICLE I

Legislative Vesting Clause

All legislative Powers herein granted shall be vested in a Congress of the United States, which shall consist of a Senate and House of Representatives.

(ARTICLE I, SECTION 1)

~

*M*uch of the greatness of the United States Constitution can be attributed to the elegant pen of Gouverneur Morris, who, as leader of the Committee on Style, fashioned the text into a coherent and practical symmetry. Because of his writing, the document's first three articles lay out the structure of the separation of powers, each dealing with the powers of the legislature, the executive, and the judiciary respectively.

The economical wording of the Legislative Vesting Clause performs three critical constitutional functions. First, it defines the Congress as "a Senate and House of Representatives." Thus, when the Constitution elsewhere refers to "Congress," as it frequently does, it refers to a specifically defined institution consisting of two subsidiary houses or "branches." In establishing two legislative chambers, the House and the Senate, the Framers paid heed to a requirement championed by the respected voice of Baron de Montesquieu, who opined that liberty could be preserved only if two branches of the legislature, chosen from different constituencies, could check each other. Similarly, in his influential *Thoughts on Government* (1776), John Adams declared that "[a] single assembly is liable to all the vices, follies, and frailties of an individual."

The clause thus reflects a particular suspicion of what James Madison called the "impetuous vortex" of the federal legislative power. As Alexander Hamilton explained in *The Federalist* No. 22, unlike the Congress under the Articles of Confederation, the Congress under the Constitution would have such greater powers that it was necessary that it be divided for the sake of the people's safety. In *The Federalist* No. 62, Madison agreed, stating that having a Senate "doubles the security to the people by requiring the concurrence of two distinct bodies in schemes of usurpation or perfidy, where the ambition or corruption of one, would otherwise be sufficient."

Thus, no bill can become a law without the assent of both branches of Congress, which respond to different constituencies. In sum, the Legislative Vesting Clause represents a kind of separation of power of the legislative houses within a larger separation of powers among legislative, executive, and judicial institutions.

Second, and more substantively, the trio of clauses that begin each of the first three Articles of the Constitution—the Legislative Vesting Clause, the Executive Vesting Clause (Article II, Section 1, Clause 1), and the Judicial Vesting Clause (Article III, Section 1)—allocates classes of governmental power to different, and differently selected and responsive, federal actors. The "executive Power" is vested in the President, the "judicial Power" is vested in the life-tenured federal courts, and "[a]ll legislative Powers herein granted" are vested in Congress. By vesting different classes of power in different institutions, the Constitution clearly contemplates that there are types of governmental powers that, as Madison put it in *The Federalist* No. 48, "may in their nature be legislative, executive, or judiciary." This is not to say, however, that one can neatly and easily place every particular exercise of governmental power into a legislative, executive, or judicial category. Indeed, Madison, in *The Federalist* No. 37, wrote that "[e]xperience has instructed us that no skill in the science of government has yet been able to discriminate and define, with sufficient certainty, its three great provinces—the legislative, executive, and judiciary.... Questions daily occur in the course of practice…which puzzle the greatest adepts in political science." Moreover, according to Madison, some overlap is necessary to make the separation of powers work. The "partial agency" of one branch in the workings of the others was essential. *The Federalist* No. 47.

Third, all legislative powers that are granted are vested in Congress, but Congress is not vested with all legislative powers. Rather, the Constitution vests in Congress only those particular legislative powers "herein granted" and directs us to the other provisions in the Constitution to determine the precise content of the federal legislative power. The Legislative Vesting Clause thus does not itself serve as a font of powers, but rather functions as a designation of who must exercise the legislative powers granted elsewhere in the Constitution. Once a particular substantive power is properly labeled legislative (for example, the power over interstate commerce), then the Legislative Vesting Clause makes clear that it is Congress that is to exercise that particular power.

The Constitution, however, does not directly circumscribe the line that separates legislative from executive or judicial power. If a law is so precise and unambiguous that it leaves nothing to the discretion of executive or judicial actors, then enforcement by the executive and application by the judiciary are mechanical tasks, and no one could complain that executive or judicial actors are somehow exercising legislative power vested exclusively in Congress. But few laws are or can be crafted so precisely. It is commonplace for executive and judicial actors to need to *interpret* enacted laws in the course of their duties. Indeed, some measure of discretion in the interpretation and application of laws is the essence of the executive and judicial powers. But can the formal exercise of executive or judicial interpretation ever become so extensive in shaping the meaning of a law that the executive or judicial actor in reality becomes the lawmaker?

The scheme of American constitutional government requires answers to the question where the legislative power ends and the executive and judicial powers begin, but those answers have been, and remain, notoriously elusive. For example, is it possible for Congress to enact a law so vague that, in substance, it impermissibly allows executive or judicial actors to usurp the legislative function that is vested exclusively in Congress? Or is the only purely "legislative" power vested in Congress simply the power to enact a law through the processes required by Article I, Section 7, so that all acts of interpretation, even "interpretation" of an utterly vacuous enactment, is a permissible exercise of executive or judicial power so long as it is performed by an executive or judicial actor? These are chief among those questions that "puzzle the greatest adepts in political science"— both in the eighteenth century and today.

There are some contexts in which the Constitution specifically enumerates a congressional power to designate subsidiary lawmakers. The Territories and Property Clauses (Article IV, Section 3, Clause 2), which gives Congress power to make "all needful Rules and Regulations respecting the Territory or other Property belonging to the United States," has long been construed to give Congress general governmental power over federal possessions, including the power to create territorial legislatures with independent lawmaking authority, and the same reasoning might allow Congress to designate executive officers as the effective authorities over federal property. Similarly, the Enclave Clause (Article I, Section 8, Clause 17) has long been understood to grant equivalent power with respect to the District of Columbia. Outside of those contexts that specifically authorize delegation of legislative authority to non-congressional lawmakers, however, the question whether law interpretation can ever impermissibly morph into law making looms large.

The Supreme Court's first major encounter with this question, which is often described as the question of *legislative delegation*, remains among its most instructive. *Wayman v. Southard* (1825) involved a challenge, as an impermissible delegation of legislative power, to a congressional statute authorizing federal courts to make changes to the rules for such matters as serving process and executing judgments. Congress's enumerated legislative power, under the Necessary and Proper Clause, surely allows it to make laws "for carrying into Execution" the judicial power by specifying forms of process and the manner of execution of judgments. In a lengthy *dictum*, Chief Justice

John Marshall, for a unanimous Court, noted that "[i]t will not be contended that Congress can delegate to the Courts, or to any other tribunals, powers which are strictly and exclusively legislative." But, as the Chief Justice also noted, some powers are not, in their nature, exclusively legislative. The fact that Congress could properly legislate in the area of *judicial* procedure did not mean that the *courts* could not exercise it as well. This point is crucial to an understanding of the Constitution's essential structure and to the lines drawn by the document among the various governmental powers.

The Constitution divides and allocates governmental *powers*, not governmental *functions* or *actions*. There may be some *actions*—such as the passage of a bill, the direction of troops in battle, or the entry of a criminal judgment—that are uniquely the exercise of legislative, executive, or judicial *powers*, respectively. But other *actions* can easily fall within scope of more than one of the three vested constitutional *powers*. For example, Congress has the *power* of establishing in law the right of persons to present claims against the government. But it can vest the *action* of adjudicating those claims in the courts (as part of its judicial power of deciding cases), or in the executive branch (as part of its power to execute the laws faithfully), or in itself as part of its own legislative power by passing private bills for the relief of individuals. Thus, in terms of the actions that fall within them, the legislative, executive, and judicial powers are thus partially overlapping rather than mutually exclusive categories.

Chief Justice Marshall's point was that so long as the action in question falls within the power vested in the actor who performs it, it is constitutional even if could also have been performed by some other actor under that actor's vested power. Thus, reasoned the Court in *Wayman*, if the courts could promulgate rules of procedure under their "judicial Power," it would not constitute a delegation of legislative power for Congress to channel that power through a statute, even if the statute provided no clear guidelines. Because this discussion was *dictum*, it was not necessary for the Court to determine precisely which procedural rules had to be fixed by Congress and which could be set by courts under a

vague authorization from Congress; as Marshall noted, "there is some difficulty in discerning the exact limits within which the legislature may avail itself of the agency of its Courts" in such matters. Similarly difficulty arises when Congress seeks to "avail itself" of the aid of the executive in implementing statutes, perhaps by having agencies pass regulations or conduct adjudications to fill out the meaning of a statute, as when the First Congress provided for the payment of military pensions "under such regulations as the President of the United States may direct" and required licensed Indian traders to be governed "by such rules and regulations as the President shall prescribe." Marshall explained that "[t]he difference between the departments undoubtedly is, that the legislature makes, the executive executes, and the judiciary construes the law; but the maker of the law may commit something to the discretion of the other departments, and the precise boundary of this power is a subject of delicate and difficult inquiry...."

As for how to resolve this "delicate and difficult inquiry" when necessary, Marshall wrote: "The line has not been exactly drawn which separates those important subjects, which must be entirely regulated by the legislature itself, from those of less interest, in which a general provision may be made, and power given to those who are to act under such general provisions, to fill up the details." Moreover, the line may well need to be drawn in different places depending upon the subject matter of the legislation; more vagueness, for example, may be permissible when Congress grants authority to the President in military or foreign affairs than in other areas.

Courts and scholars have spent two centuries trying to improve upon, or avoid, Chief Justice Marshall's distinction between "important" matters and matters of "less interest" as the touchstone for determining the kind and quality of discretion that Congress can permissibly vest in executive or judicial actors without crossing the line into a delegation of legislative authority. It is unclear whether there has been improvement. The more common solution has been avoidance.

Until the New Deal, there were many cases raising challenges to statutes as delegations of legislative authority. In all of those cases the

Court treated the challenges as constitutionally serious, but in only two did it find a statute unconstitutional. Most of those cases involved so-called "conditional legislation," in which the effective date or precise terms of a statute depended upon factual or policy determinations by executive actors, such as making tariffs or tariff rates dependent upon findings by the President about the activities of other countries. For example, in *J. W. Hampton, Jr. & Co. v. United States* (1928), the Court upheld a statute authorizing the President to adjust tariff rates to "equalize the ... costs of production" in the United States and the exporting country. In oft-quoted language, the Court set out what remains the governing standard, noting that a statute vesting even very broad discretion in executive or judicial actors is constitutional if "Congress shall lay down by legislative act an intelligible principle to which the person or body ... is directed to conform." The Court found the principle of equalizing costs of production to be intelligible, and its application therefore an exercise of executive rather than legislative power, because such an allocation of responsibility between the President and Congress was consistent with "common sense and the inherent necessities of ... governmental co-ordination."

Seven years later, in *Panama Refining Co. v. Ryan* (1935) and *A.L.A. Schechter Poultry Corp. v. United States* (1935), the Court found an absence of "intelligible principle[s]" in two provisions of the National Industrial Recovery Act, and for the first and only times in the nation's history found statutes to be unconstitutional delegations of legislative authority. The sheer scope of power over national affairs granted by the statute was unprecedented, and many scholars have speculated that this feature of the statute played a role in the decisions.

Since 1935, the Court has never invalidated a statute on delegation grounds. A possible exception is *Clinton v. New York* (1998), which held that when Congress gave the President a limited line-item veto power, it violated the Presentment Clause (Article I, Section 7, Clause 2). While the majority opinion did not expressly rely upon delegation concerns, those issues were extensively briefed, were invoked by three dis-

senting Justices who thought the statute easily constitutional on delegation grounds, and may have shaped somewhat the majority's Presentment Clause holding. But in all other assertions of an unconstitutional delegation of legislative power, the Court has found validating "intelligible principle[s]" in statutes requiring agencies to determine "excessive profits," to grant licenses as "public interest, convenience, or necessity" require, to set "fair" and "equitable" prices, and to prohibit corporate structures that "'unfairly or inequitably' distribute voting power among security holders." In *Mistretta v. United States* (1989), the Court all but declared the delegation doctrine non-justiciable (that is, a dispute incapable of being resolved by the courts), when it upheld an open-ended grant of authority to the United States Sentencing Commission to set ranges for criminal sentences by explaining that "our jurisprudence has been driven by a practical understanding that in our increasingly complex society, replete with ever changing and more technical problems, Congress simply cannot do its job absent an ability to delegate power under broad general directives." Justice Antonin Scalia dissented on grounds narrowly tailored to the specific powers conferred upon the Sentencing Commission, but he agreed with the otherwise unanimous majority's view that courts should not generally try to place enforceable limits on the kind and quality of discretion that Congress grants to other actors.

Indeed, in 2001, Justice Scalia authored a unanimous opinion in *Whitman v. American Trucking Ass'ns, Inc.*, which upheld, with relatively little discussion, a statute instructing the Environmental Protection Agency to set an ambient air quality standard "which in the judgment of the Administrator ... is requisite to protect the public health" with "an adequate margin of safety." Justice Clarence Thomas indicated a willingness to reconsider the Court's lax delegation doctrine in an appropriate case, but no other current Justice has echoed those sentiments. Indeed, the votes on the merits in delegation cases in the Supreme Court from 1989 to 2012 were 53–0 against the challenges.

Notwithstanding the strong signals from the Supreme Court that delegation challenges will not be well received, lower courts judges continue to find delegation problems with statutes at a rate that some might find surprising given the seeming clarity of the doctrine. Some Justices, on hard-to-predict occasions, invoke delegation concerns as a reason to construe statutes in order to avoid having those statutes raise constitutional issues, as did a plurality of the Court in *Industrial Union Dep't, AFL-CIO v. American Petroleum Inst.* (1980). Justices Scalia and Ruth Bader Ginsburg, neither of whom is noted for sympathy for delegation challenges, employed delegation concerns in this fashion in their dissent from the majority in *Reynolds v. United States* (2012).

The consequences of the Court's reluctance to police the boundaries of the legislative, executive, and judicial powers cannot be overstated. In modern times, Congress routinely enacts statutes that place the vast bulk of responsibility for promulgating binding norms in administrative agencies (and derivatively in courts that review the decisions of administrative agencies), to the point that agencies are, by any relevant measure, far more important instruments of governance than is Congress.

When he was an academic in 1980, then-Professor Scalia urged courts to reinvigorate the delegation doctrine. As a Justice, he abandoned that position because, as he explained in his dissenting opinion in *Mistretta*, "while the doctrine of unconstitutional delegation is unquestionably a fundamental element of our constitutional system, it is not an element readily enforceable by the courts. Once it is conceded, as it must be, that no statute can be entirely precise, and that some judgments, even some judgments involving policy considerations, must be left to the officers executing the law and to the judges applying it, the debate over unconstitutional delegation becomes a debate not over a point of principle but over a question of degree." Those who wish for the Court to take delegation concerns more seriously thus need to convince at least some Justices that a test for drawing the line among legislative, executive, and judicial powers can be found that is no more troubling than other tests employed by the Court in other contexts. A return to the first principles articulated by Chief Justice Marshall

in *Wayman v. Southard* might be a productive place to start.

Gary Lawson

See Also

Article I, Section 8, Clause 17 (Enclave Clause)

Article II, Section 1, Clause 1 (Executive Vesting Clause)

Article III, Section 1 (Judicial Vesting Clause)

Article IV, Section 3, Clause 2 (Territories Clause; Property Clause)

Suggestions for Further Research

Larry Alexander & Saikrishna Prakash, *Reports of the Nondelegation Doctrine's Death Are Greatly Exaggerated*, 70 U. Chi. L. Rev. 1297 (2003)

Douglas H. Ginsburg, *Delegation Running Riot*, 1 Reg. 83 (1995)

Gary Lawson, *Delegation and Original Meaning*, 88 Va. L. Rev. 327 (2002)

Gary Lawson, *Discretion as Delegation: The "Proper" Understanding of the Nondelegation Doctrine*, 73 Geo. Wash. L. Rev. 235 (2005)

Eric A. Posner & Adrian Vermeule, *Nondelegation: A Post-Mortem*, 70 U. Chi. L. Rev. 1331 (2003)

Michael B. Rappaport, *The Selective Nondelegation Doctrine and the Line Item Veto: A New Approach to the Nondelegation Doctrine and Its Implications for* Clinton v. City of New York, 76 Tul. L. Rev. 265 (2002)

David Schoenbrod, Power Without Responsibility: How Congress Abuses the People Through Delegation (1993).

Significant Cases

Wayman v. Southard, 23 U.S. (10 Wheat.) 1 (1825)

J. W. Hampton, Jr. & Co. v. United States, 276 U.S. 394 (1928)

Panama Refining Co. v. Ryan, 293 U.S. 388 (1935)

A.L.A. Schechter Poultry Corp. v. United States, 295 U.S. 495 (1935)

Industrial Union Dep't, AFL-CIO v. American Petroleum Inst., 448 U.S. 607 (1980)

Mistretta v. United States, 488 U.S. 361 (1989)

Skinner v. Mid-America Pipeline Co, 490 U.S. 212 (1989)

Clinton v. City of New York, 524 U.S. 417 (1998)

Whitman v. American Trucking Ass'ns, Inc., 531 U.S. 457 (2001)

Reynolds v. United States, 132 S. Ct. 975 (2012)

House of Representatives

The House of Representatives shall be composed of Members chosen every second Year by the People of the several States...

(ARTICLE I, SECTION 2, CLAUSE 1)

*T*hree issues—length of terms, equal versus proportional representation of states, and method of selection—dominated the Constitutional Convention's debate over the makeup of the House of Representatives. Each of those issues was resolved in the language of Article I, Section 2.

The two-year term of office for the House was a straightforward compromise between those who preferred annual elections and those who favored a longer, three-year term. The original Virginia Plan envisaged that both branches of the federal legislature would be directly or indirectly accountable to "the People." In the end, however, in the "Great Compromise," the Convention determined that the states would be represented in the Senate and the people in the House of Representatives. During the debate over equal or proportional state representation in the House, several delegates, notably James Wilson, James Madison, and George Mason, argued for population as the just basis of apportionment. That later became conflated with the related but distinct question on the manner of selection of representatives.

What the Framers intended in providing for election "by the People" can be better understood in terms of the alternatives that they rejected. The Committee of the Whole vigorously debated and discarded a counter resolution that the House be selected by "the State Legislatures, and not the People." Elbridge Gerry suggested that Members be selected by state legislatures from among

candidates "nominated by the people." Another compromise, proposed by Charles Cotesworth Pinckney, provided for the House to be selected "in such manner as the legislature of each state shall direct." Against these proposals, Madison and Wilson argued that selection by the people was necessary to link citizens directly to the national government and to prevent the states from overpowering the central authority. Article I, Section 2 secured direct popular election of the House.

The scope of the phrase "by the People," however, was neither debated nor defined at the Convention. It appears to have meant the direct popular election with a relatively broad right of suffrage as determined by the states' own practices. Madison described electoral accountability to the people as "the republican principle." *The Federalist* No. 10. Responding to charges that the House would not represent "the mass of the people," Madison argued in *The Federalist* No. 57 that "[t]he electors are to be the great body of the people of the United States. They are to be the same who exercise the right in every State of electing the corresponding branch of the legislature of the State." Leading Anti-Federalists, such as Melancton Smith and the anonymous Brutus, used the term in a similar fashion, affirming the broadly accepted meaning. Thomas Jefferson defined "the People" as no particular class but, rather, "the mass of individuals composing the society."

The Constitution does not, however, require Representatives to be elected by districts. In the beginning, many states chose their Representatives on an at-large basis. Congress, however, used its authority to regulate the "Times, Places and Manner" of choosing its Members (Article I, Section 4, Clause 1) to require single-member districting in the Apportionment Act of 1842.

Comments at both the Convention and at state ratifying conventions indicate substantial support for the general proposition that Representatives within each state should be apportioned in districts in a manner roughly equal to population. Although every state admitted to the Union between 1790 and 1889 had an original state constitution providing for district apportionment based on population, none adopted absolute equality of population for each district. Geography, history, and local political boundaries cut against equally populated districts. Thus, in the Northwest Ordinance of 1787, Congress provided for up to one Representative per 500 persons, but based on townships and counties. Furthermore, besides the celebrated compromise providing each state with equal representation in the Senate, the Constitution specifically grants each state, no matter how small its population, one Representative in the House.

There was a limit, however, to what the states could do in fashioning congressional districts. The Framers did, in fact, disapprove of the infamous "rotten boroughs" of Great Britain, districts with no more than a few inhabitants that nevertheless held seats in Parliament equal, in some cases, to large cities. But they decided to address inequities in representation by leaving it to Congress's discretion to "alter" the "Times, Places and Manner" of choosing Members. (Article I, Section 4.) Madison argued that this authority was a necessary safeguard against state-created inequalities in federal representation. In fact, in the Apportionment Act of 1872, Congress required states to provide for congressional districts with "as nearly as practicable an equal number of inhabitants," but this language was dropped from reapportionment acts after 1911.

Until 1962, Article I, Section 4 was indeed held to be the sole constitutional remedy to malapportionment. However, in the early twentieth century, rural state legislators in many states had simply stopped redistricting in order to avoid transferring power to more populous urban areas. In 1962, the Supreme Court held in *Baker v. Carr* that redistricting questions were justiciable in the courts. In *Wesberry v. Sanders*, decided in 1964, the Court held that Article I, Section 2 mandated that congressional districts be equal in population "as nearly as is practicable." In doing so, the Court relied heavily on statements made at the Convention in favor of representation according to population. These comments, however, were made during debate over the proportional representation of the states in Congress, not the manner in which Representatives would be selected according to the first paragraph of Article I, Section 2. Nevertheless, later that year, in *Reynolds*

v. Sims, the Court extended the doctrine of "one person, one vote" to state legislatures, based on the Equal Protection Clause of the Fourteenth Amendment. In *Lucas v. 44th General Assembly of Colorado*, decided the same day as *Reynolds*, the Court applied the equal population rule to overturn a state districting plan that the state's voters had specifically approved, including a majority of voters in those parts of the state underrepresented by the plan.

The Court has since held to the principle of precise mathematical equality when congressional districting is at issue. Most notably, *Karcher v. Daggett* (1983) struck down a New Jersey plan in which the average district population variation was 726 people, or 0.1384 percent, a difference well within the margin of error in the census count. State redistricting plans, scrutinized under the Fourteenth Amendment rather than Article I, have been granted more leeway. The Court has upheld state legislative districts with population variances up to 10 percent with no state justification at all. *Gaffney v. Cummings* (1973). Variations to nearly 20 percent are permissible where the state demonstrates a rational basis for its plan, such as drawing districts to follow municipal lines. *Mahan v. Howell* (1973). Consideration of group or economic interests is not, however, an accepted justification. *Swann v. Adams* (1967).

The Court has also applied the "one person, one vote" rule to local governments. *Avery v. Midland County* (1968). In a few limited circumstances, however, where the entity in question does not exercise "a traditional element of governmental sovereignty," as in the case of a water storage district, the Court has not required the "one person, one vote" rule. *Ball v. James* (1981).

In recent years, the reapportionment decisions have drawn renewed scholarly attention. Critics claim that they have inhibited the formation of regional government consortiums to deal with metropolitan-wide problems; removed traditional constraints on gerrymandering, such as adherence to political jurisdictions or geographic regions; and imposed a particular theory of representation on the states and Congress that is not grounded in the Constitution. Critics also note that equal population does not correspond to an equal number of voters, due to differing numbers of children, immigrants, and other nonvoters in a district. Thus votes are still not weighted equally. Further, birth rates, death rates, and the migration of persons in and out of districts during the decade between redistricting means that virtually all districts always have greater "malapportionment" than that permitted by the Court in *Karcher*. Nonetheless, the standard of "one person, one vote" remains Supreme Court doctrine, and there is little evidence that the Court is prepared to reassess its jurisprudence in the area.

Bradley Smith

See Also

Article I, Section 2, Clause 3 (Allocation of Representatives)

Article I, Section 3, Clause 1 (Senate)

Article I, Section 4, Clause 1 (Election Regulations)

Article IV, Section 4 (Guarantee Clause)

Amendment XIV, Section 2 (Apportionment of Representatives)

Suggestions for Further Research

Gordon E. Baker, The Reapportionment Revolution: Representation, Political Power and the Supreme Court (1966)

Robert G. Dixon, Jr., Democratic Representation: Reapportionment in Law & Politics (1968)

Grant M. Hayden, *The False Promise of One Person One Vote*, 102 Mich. L. Rev. 113 (2003)

Michael W. McConnell, *Voting Rights, Equality, and Racial Gerrymandering: The Redistricting Cases: Original Mistakes and Current Consequences*, 24 Harv. J.L. & Pub. Pol'y 103 (2000)

James L. McDowell, *"One Person, One Vote" and the Decline of Community*, 23 Legal Stud. F. 131 (1999)

Scott A. Reader, *One Person, One Vote Revisited: Choosing a Population Basis to Form Political Districts*, 17 Harv. J.L. & Pub. Pol'y 521 (1994)

Significant Cases

Baker v. Carr, 369 U.S. 186 (1962)

Lucas v. 44th General Assembly of Colorado, 377 U.S. 713 (1964)

Reynolds v. Sims, 377 U.S. 533 (1964)

Wesberry v. Sanders, 376 U.S. 1 (1964)

Swann v. Adams, 385 U.S. 440 (1967)

Avery v. Midland County, 390 U.S. 474 (1968)

Gaffney v. Cummings, 412 U.S. 735 (1973)

Mahan v. Howell, 410 U.S. 315 (1973)

Ball v. James, 451 U.S. 355 (1981)

Karcher v. Daggett, 462 U.S. 725 (1983)

Elector Qualifications

...the Electors in each State shall have the Qualifications requisite for Electors of the most numerous Branch of the State Legislature.
(**Article I, Section 2, Clause 1**)

~

*A*t the Constitutional Convention, the Framers debated whether the electors of the House of Representatives should be limited to freeholders, or whether they should incorporate state voting laws by requiring that whoever the state decides is eligible to vote for "the most numerous Branch of the State Legislature" is also eligible to vote for the House of Representatives. The majority of the delegates preferred to defer to the states and approved the Elector Qualifications Clause. As James Wilson summarized in records of the Convention, "It was difficult to form any uniform rule of qualifications for all the States." Unnecessary innovations, he thought, should also be avoided: "It would be very hard & disagreeable for the same persons, at the same time, to vote for representatives in the State Legislature and to be excluded from a vote for those in the Natl. Legislature."

Thus, the Constitution gives authority for determining elector qualifications to the states. The Seventeenth Amendment adopted the same qualifications language to apply to the popular election of United States Senators. This authority is superseded only insofar as the Constitution itself forbids the denial of equal protection and the exclusion of voters on specific grounds, such as race (Fifteenth Amendment), sex (Nineteenth Amendment), failure to pay a poll tax or other tax (Twenty-fourth Amendment), and, for those eighteen years old or older, age (Twenty-sixth Amendment).

Article I, Section 4 allows Congress to "make or alter such [state] Regulations" regarding "the Times, Places and Manner of holding Elections for Senators and Representatives," but, as a textual matter, Congress's power is about "holding Elections"—not about who votes, which is the express focus of Section 2. Both Alexander Hamilton and James Madison believed the two clauses to be independent in this way. Hamilton, in *The Federalist* No. 60, said of Article I, Section 4 that the national government's "authority would be expressly restricted to the regulation of the *times*, the *places*, and the *manner* of elections. The qualifications of the persons who may choose or may be chosen...are defined and fixed in the Constitution, and are unalterable by the [national] legislature." (Emphasis in original.) In *The Federalist* No. 52, Madison wrote of Article I, Section 2, "[t]o have left it [the definition of the right of suffrage] open for the occasional regulation of the Congress, would have been improper...." Hamilton and Madison believed that generally the state constitutions, and certainly not Congress, would determine who could vote.

The Supreme Court has applied the Equal Protection Clause of the Fourteenth Amendment to invalidate certain state regulations that excluded classes of voters from the franchise. In *Kramer v. Union Free School District No. 15* (1969), the Court declared that it was unconstitutional to limit school district elections to property holders or to those who had children enrolled in the district schools.

The Court has also upheld congressional regulation of federal elections over contrary state laws. In *Oregon v. Mitchell* (1970), a decision of limited precedential value, five Justices in a highly fractured series of opinions voted to uphold federal legislation—passed prior to the adoption of the Twenty-sixth Amendment, which was ratified a little over six months after the Court's decision—that required the states to allow eighteen-year-olds to vote in federal elections. While it is true that in this case a majority of the Justices did vote to uphold a statute that dictated who could vote in federal elections, only one of the five Justices who did so—Justice Hugo L. Black—

relied on Article I, Section 4 (power of Congress to regulate the times, manner, and places of elections). The other four relied on interpretations of Congress's enforcement authority under the Fourteenth and Fifteenth Amendments. In *City of Boerne v. Flores* (1997), the Court ruled that Congress may not assert authority under Section 5 of the Fourteenth Amendment "to enforce" the amendment by prohibiting state actions not closely related to violations of the amendment. The Court has not yet directly applied this principle to congressional statutes regulating suffrage.

Accordingly, it would seem that reliance on Article I, Section 4 to trump Article I, Section 2 lacks textual support, and only Justice Black endorsed it in 1970. In sum, the general rule seems to be that Congress may pass laws superseding the states' determination of elector qualifications only when confronted with a deliberate denial of either a specific constitutional guarantee of the right to vote or of equal protection under the Fourteenth Amendment.

In *Tashjian v. Republican Party of Connecticut* (1986), the Supreme Court, by a 5–4 majority, used the First Amendment to restrict the application of the Elector Qualifications Clause in primary elections. In that case, a Connecticut law that required a closed primary conflicted with a Connecticut Republican Party rule that permitted independent voters to vote in Republican primaries for federal and statewide offices. The Court said that the Connecticut law violated freedom of association. Similarly, the Court struck down California's blanket open primary law in *California Democratic Party v. Jones* (2000), but the Court upheld Oklahoma's more moderate form of a closed primary law, which prevented voters registered with other parties to cross over to vote in another party's primary. *Clingman v. Beaver* (2005).

The majority in *Tashjian* also held that the implementation of party rules—that established different qualifications for voting in congressional elections than in elections for the more numerous house of the state legislature—did not violate the Elector Qualifications Clause (or the Seventeenth Amendment). Primaries are subject to these clauses, the Court said, but the purpose of those clauses is satisfied "if all those qualified to participate in the selection of members of the more numerous branch of the state legislature are also qualified to participate in the election of Senators and Members of the House of Representatives." There is no need for "perfect symmetry." Justice John Paul Stevens, joined by Justice Antonin Scalia, dissented: "The Court nevertheless separates the federal voter qualifications from their state counterparts, inexplicably treating the mandatory 'shall have' language of the clauses as though it means only that the federal voters 'may but need not have' the qualifications of state voters."

Roger Clegg

See Also

Article I, Section 4, Clause 1 (Election Regulations)
Amendment XIV, Section 1 (Equal Protection)
Amendment XV (Suffrage—Race)
Amendment XVII
Amendment XIX (Suffrage—Sex)
Amendment XXIV (Poll Taxes)
Amendment XXVI (Suffrage—Age)

Significant Cases

United States v. Classic, 313 U.S. 299 (1941)
Carrington v. Rash, 380 U.S. 89 (1965)
Kramer v. Union Free School District No. 15, 395 U.S. 621 (1969)
Oregon v. Mitchell, 400 U.S. 112 (1970)
Tashjian v. Republican Party of Connecticut, 479 U.S. 208 (1986)
City of Boerne v. Flores, 521 U.S. 507 (1997)
California Democratic Party v. Jones, 530 U.S. 567 (2000)
Clingman v. Beaver, 544 U.S. 581 (2005)

Qualifications for Representatives

No Person shall be a Representative who shall not have attained to the Age of twenty five Years, and been seven Years a Citizen of the United States, and who shall not,

when elected, be an Inhabitant of that State in which he shall be chosen.

(ARTICLE I, SECTION 2, CLAUSE 2)

~

*W*hen Edmund Randolph of Virginia presented the Virginia Plan at the beginning of the Constitutional Convention, he suggested among other things that Representatives should meet certain qualifications. It was some time, however, before the delegates turned to the issue. When they had completed their consideration, the Framers had opted for only a few restrictions.

The Framers considered and rejected property, wealth, and indebtedness qualifications. On republican grounds, the Framers cut loose from the British practice of multiple qualifications and limitations. As Justice Joseph Story wrote in his *Commentaries on the Constitution of the United States* (1833),

> Among the American colonies antecedent to the revolution, a great diversity of qualifications existed; and the state constitutions, subsequently formed, by no means lessen that diversity. Some insist upon a freehold, or other property, of a certain value; others require a certain period of residence, and citizenship only; others require a freehold only; others a payment of taxes, or an equivalent; others, again, mix up all the various qualifications of property, residence, citizenship, and taxation, or substitute some of these, as equivalents for others.

But unlike the Elector Qualifications Clause (Article I, Section 2, Clause 1), which left the decision as to who could vote for U.S. Representatives with the respective states' determination of who could vote for the most numerous body of the state legislature, the Framers settled on three defined qualifications for Representatives. First, they must be a minimum of twenty-five years of age so that the office-holders would possess some modicum of life's experience to season their judgment. Second, a Representative must be a U.S. citizen for seven years, a compromise among widely different views, but seemingly long enough to prevent foreign nations from infiltrating the halls of Congress with persons holding alien allegiances. Third, the Member of the House must be an inhabitant of the state in which he is chosen, a change from "resident," which word might, according to James Madison, "exclude persons absent occasionally for a considerable time on public or private business." Although a Representative must be an inhabitant of the state in which he is chosen, according to the Constitution, he need not be an inhabitant of the district from which he is elected. When the Constitution was before the state ratifying conventions, delegates paid little attention to the issue of qualifications, and although disputes occasionally arose over the seating of a Member of the House, the clause attracted no judicial attention for nearly two centuries.

Judicial involvement in the clause did not occur until the latter part of the twentieth century. The question of whether the House of Representatives could, through Article I, Section 5, Clause 1, add to or define for itself what constituted "qualifications" reached the Supreme Court in *Powell v. McCormack* (1969). Finding that an elected Representative, Adam Clayton Powell, Jr., had engaged in serious misconduct, the House refused to seat him, even though Powell had met the formal qualifications of Article I, Section 2, Clause 2. In its decision, the Supreme Court held that Congress had no constitutional authority to alter the qualifications for Representatives as stated in the Constitution. So far as Congress was concerned, the constitutional qualifications were fixed. The Congress could not validly exclude Powell.

The *Powell* decision left open the question whether the states could add to the qualifications stated in the Constitution. Were the qualifications in the Constitution a floor on which the states could erect other requirements, or were they the sum of all qualifications, brooking no alteration from any source?

This issue came to a head in the 1990s when a popular movement to limit the terms of Members of Congress swept the country. In *United States Term Limits v. Thornton* (1995), the Court struck down those attempts. The Court ruled that the qualifications in the Constitution were in fact exclusive and could not be added to or altered.

In his opinion for the majority, Justice John Paul Stevens reaffirmed the historical argument in *Powell* that Congress did not have the power to alter the qualifications. He then extended that rationale to reach the issue *Powell* had not decided: whether any given state could impose additional qualifications. The Court held that the historical record demonstrated that the qualifications were exclusive in relation to the states as well. Stevens argued that Framers and early commentators, such as John Dickinson, James Madison, and Justice Joseph Story, thought that the states could not add additional qualifications, that the federal government was a creature of the people and not of the states, and that, consequently, the Members of the House of Representatives were accountable to the people and not to the states. He added that after ratification of the Constitution, the states retained the power to add certain qualifications for voters, such as property, but had no power to add qualifications for Representatives beyond what the Constitution prescribed. Quoting earlier cases and Alexander Hamilton, Stevens' central argument was "that the people should choose whom they please to govern them."

Justice Clarence Thomas, speaking for the four-person dissent, developed a contrary history and argued that the federal government was created by the people, not as a whole, but of the several states. Whatever powers not given to the federal government were thus retained by the states. Consequently, the states retained the power to add qualifications to Representatives elected within their respective jurisdictions. As Thomas noted, the text of the clause limits the power of Congress, not that of the states. In addition, neither in the Constitutional Convention nor in the state ratifying conventions was there a statement that the states could not add qualifications. The Court's majority, on the other hand, stated that creating qualifications for federal Representatives did not derive from the states and there was, consequently, no such power that was retained by the states.

Joseph Story argued that the phrasing of the Qualifications Clause for Representatives and the similar clause for Senators (Article I, Section 3, Clause 3) had to be exclusive of other qualifications: "It would seem but fair reasoning upon the plainest principles of interpretation, that when the constitution established certain qualifications, as necessary for office, it meant to exclude all others, as prerequisites. From the very nature of such a provision, the affirmation of these qualifications would seem to imply a negative of all others."

Story admitted that Thomas Jefferson had a different view, believing that the Constitution chose "the middle way," by mandating "some disqualifications"—those dealing with age, state residency, and U.S. citizenship—while allowing the states to impose other, non-uniform disqualifications that are otherwise constitutional. But Story dismissed Jefferson's view with the same argument that Justice Stevens was to use, namely, that adding qualifications was not "reserved" to the states when the Constitution was adopted.

Nonetheless, commentators have noted that the Court's analysis in *Powell* and *Thornton* retains some problematical elements, for the Constitution does permit the addition of further qualifications or disqualifications from those stated in the Qualifications Clauses. For example, Article I, Section 6, Clause 2 disqualifies anyone while he holds any other federal office from becoming a Member of Congress. If the Senate impeaches someone, it can impose a disqualification from becoming a Member of Congress (Article I, Section 3, Clause 7). Senators or Representatives who meet the minimum requirements of age, U.S. citizenship, and state residency are still disqualified from serving if they refuse to take the constitutional oath of office (Article VI, Clause 3).

Moreover, the Constitution specifically refers to Senators and Representatives in forbidding the states from imposing any religious test for any federal office (Article VI, Clause 3). Textually, this would be an unnecessary prohibition if the Qualifications Clauses by themselves excluded states from imposing additional qualifications. Historically, states have imposed various requirements besides those listed in the Qualifications Clauses, such as disqualifying state judges from running for Congress, and the Supreme Court has upheld them if they are reasonable and do not violate specific guarantees, such as free speech. Lastly, beginning in 1842, Congress has passed legislation requiring states to elect Members of Congress by district, even though there is no such requirement in the Constitution. Even Justice Story had earlier opined that such an act was improper.

In the wake of *U.S. Term Limits v. Thornton,* there have been several challenges to state and federal laws on the basis that they constitute improper additional qualifications under Article I, Section 2, Clause 2, but few have been successful. However, in *Campbell v. Davidson* (10th Cir. 2000), a circuit court struck down a Colorado statute that prevented those who are ineligible to vote, such as felons, unregistered voters, and people residing outside the congressional district, from running for office. The court quoted *Thornton* in stating that election procedures could not "provide States with license to exclude classes of candidates from federal office."

Most courts have distinguished between election procedures and qualification requirements. Thus, requiring a certain percentage of signatures in order to run for office is not a qualification, nor are filing fees, nor is the requirement that persons who are federal employees not run for office "in a partisan election" while they are employed. Another court declared the residency qualification is fulfilled on the day of election.

David F. Forte, Ronald D. Rotunda, and
Stephen Safranek

See Also

Article I, Section 6, Clause 2 (Incompatibility Clause)
Article VI, Clause 3

Suggestions for Further Research

Roderick Hills, *A Defense of State Constitutional Limits on Federal Congressional Terms*, 53 U. Pitt. L. Rev. 97 (1991)

David Hays Lowenstein, *Congressional Term Limits and the Constitution*, in *The Politics and Law of Term Limits* 125–140 (Edward H. Crane & Roger Pilon eds., 1994)

Ronald D. Rotunda, *Rethinking Term Limits for Federal Legislators in Light of the Structure of the Constitution*, 73 OR. L. REV. 561 (1994)

Ronald D. Rotunda & Stephen Safranek, *An Essay on Term Limits and a Call for a Constitutional Convention*, 80 MARQ. L. REV. 227 (1996)

STEPHEN SAFRANEK, THE CONSTITUTIONAL CASE FOR TERM LIMITS (1993)

Significant Cases

Powell v. McCormack, 395 U.S. 486 (1969)

United States Term Limits, Inc. v. Thornton, 514 U.S. 779 (1995)

Biener v. Calio, 361 F.3d 206 (3d Cir.), cert. denied, 543 U.S. 817 (2004)

Campbell v. Davidson, 233 F.3d 1229 (10th Cir. 2000)

Cartwright v. Barnes, 304 F.3d 1138 (11th Cir. 2002)

Merle v. United States, 351 F.3d 92 (3d Cir. 2003)

Texas Democratic Party v. Benkiser, 459 F.3d 582 (5th Cir. 2006)

Three-fifths Clause

Representatives and direct Taxes shall be apportioned among the several States which may be included within this Union, according to their respective Numbers, which shall be determined by adding to the whole Number of free Persons, including those bound to Service for a Term of Years, and excluding Indians not taxed, three fifths of all other Persons.

(ARTICLE I, SECTION 2, CLAUSE 3)

~

The three-fifths rule for counting slaves is often misunderstood. When the Constitutional Convention debated the issue of how to count population for the purposes of representation, the Southern delegates to the Convention would have been pleased if nonvoting slaves had been counted as full persons. That way, the Southern states would have had a greater representation in the House of Representatives. In contrast, some Northern delegates resisted counting slaves at all. Why, asked Elbridge Gerry, "shd. the blacks, who were property in the South, be in the rule of representation more than the cattle & horses of the North?" Among other things, counting slaves provided an incentive to import still more slaves.

Nor was the three-fifths rule new at the Convention. It was derived from a mechanism adopted in 1783 to apportion requisitions (the national government's only revenue source under the Articles of Confederation) among the states. That rule was intended to provide rough equality between the North and the South, and when the idea first appeared at the Convention, no one suggested that another fraction would be more appropriate. Indeed, the rule was included in a June 11 motion, made by James Wilson of Pennsylvania and seconded by Charles Pinckney of South Carolina, suggesting that a compromise had already occurred behind the scenes.

By itself, however, the three-fifths compromise for representation was not enough. Facing deadlock at the Convention, Gouverneur Morris (representing Pennsylvania) moved on July 12 to add a "proviso that taxation shall be in proportion to Representation" (later limited to direct taxation), the purpose of which, wrote James Madison, was to "lessen the eagerness on one side, & the opposition on the other, to the share of Representation claimed by the [Southern] States on account of the Negroes." Morris subsequently said he meant his motion only "as a bridge to assist us over a certain gulph," but tying apportionment to both taxation and representation turned out to be crucial. Slaves were to be counted as less than whites for representation, which was not in the interests of the South. Slaves were, however, also to be counted as less than whites for measuring a state's apportioned direct-tax liability, and that was a benefit to the South. A fuller account of how the Framers handled this sensitive matter requires looking as well at the Direct Taxes Clause (Article I, Section 9, Clause 4) and at other clauses of the Constitution dealing with slavery (Article I, Section 9, Clause 1; Article IV, Section 2, Clause 3; and Article V).

Furthermore, the compromise protected the integrity of the census, as Madison explained in *The Federalist* No. 54, "the States should feel as little bias as possible to swell or to reduce the amount of their numbers.... By extending the rule to both [taxation and representation], the States will have opposite interests which will control and balance each other and produce the requisite impartiality."

The three-fifths rule does not directly affect litigation today, but it affects how scholars interpret the apportionment requirement for direct taxes. It has been argued, for example, that the clauses dealing with direct taxation should be ignored because they are tainted by slavery, or because, with slavery ended, there is no longer reason to honor any part of the compromise. In light of the entire history that led to the Revolution and the Constitution, however, it would go too far to assume that in a world without slavery, the Founders would have been indifferent to the dangers of national taxation.

Furthermore, understood in context, the three-fifths apportionment rule was not necessarily proslavery in principle, for even though slaves were property under the laws of the Southern states, the Constitution itself acknowledged that they were persons. In addition, by tying both representation and direct taxation to apportionment, the Framers hoped to remove any sectional benefit, and thus any proslavery taint, from the special counting rule. In fact, the slave states despised having to give in and accept the Direct Taxes Clause as part of the price of obtaining the three-fifths counting rule.

No one at the time knew that the direct tax requirement would be weakened by Supreme Court interpretation, and few understood that the three-fifths rule would yield such extraordinary political dividends for the slave states. Many scholars have pointed out that the three-fifths rule provided Southern States significant political advantages in the House of Representatives and the Electoral College, and thus also in the choice of President and the appointment of members of the Supreme Court until the election of Abraham Lincoln and the coming of the Civil War. But at the Constitutional Convention, the Framers believed that they had crafted a workable compromise.

Erik M. Jensen

See Also

Article I, Section 8, Clause 1 (Taxation Clause; Uniformity Clause)

Article I, Section 9, Clause 1 (Migration or Importation Clause)

Article I, Section 9, Clause 4 (Direct Taxes)

Article II, Section 2, Clause 3 (Recess Appointments Clause)

Article IV, Section 2, Clause 3 (Fugitive Slave Clause)

Article V (Prohibition on Amendment: Slave Trade)

Suggestions for Further Research

Bruce Ackerman, *Taxation and the Constitution*, 99 COLUM. L. REV. 1 (1999)

ROGER H. BROWN, REDEEMING THE REPUBLIC: FEDERALISTS, TAXATION, AND THE ORIGINS OF THE CONSTITUTION 195–197 (1993)

James Oakes, *"The Compromising Expedient": Justifying A Proslavery Constitution*, 17 CARDOZO L. REV. 2023 (1996)

Erik M. Jensen, *The Apportionment of "Direct Taxes": Are Consumption Taxes Constitutional?*, 97 COLUM. L. REV. 2334 (1997)

Garrett Epps, *The Antebellum Political Background of the Fourteenth Amendment*, 67 LAW & CONTEMP. PROBS. 175 (Summer 2004)

Ralph A. Rossum, Taking the Constitution Seriously: Akhil Reed Amar's Biography of America's Framing Document, 57 SYRACUSE L. REV. 289 (2007)

Enumeration Clause

The actual Enumeration shall be made within three Years after the

first Meeting of the Congress of the United States, and within every subsequent Term of ten Years, in such Manner as they shall by Law direct.

(**Article I, Section 2, Clause 3**)

~

This section, as amended by Section 2 of the Fourteenth Amendment, requires, for the purpose of apportioning the House of Representatives, that a census be taken of the whole number of persons in the nation. Congress has followed the Constitution's command, even extending the census into territories and appending long lists of additional inquiries, although it is questionable as to what power Congress possesses to ask non-apportionment-related questions.

The central question regarding the original meaning of this section is whether the Constitution requires that this census consist only of an actual counting of individuals or whether the national government may rely on estimates of the national population to apportion the House. There was no direct discussion at the Constitutional Convention regarding whether there should be an actual count. The Committee of Detail's draft of the section stated that the number of inhabitants "shall…be taken in such manner as…[Congress] shall direct." That phrasing was modified to "as they shall by Law direct," and the Committee of Style subsequently added the phrase "actual Enumeration."

Those who contend that this section allows the use of estimates of the population argue that this phrase "actual Enumeration" likely means the most accurate possible calculation. When this phrase, so defined, is read together with the words "in such Manner as they shall by Law direct," they conclude that the Framers intended to grant Congress complete discretion to choose whatever method of census taking they thought would result in the most accurate calculation of population, including the use of estimating methods. Alternatively, the word "actual" refers to the first census to be conducted three years after the meeting of the first Congress, as opposed to the less formal enumeration the Framers relied upon in apportioning the first and second Congresses.

Those who maintain that the phrase "actual Enumeration" means actual counting of individuals as opposed to the use of estimating methods argue, as Justice Antonin Scalia did in *Department of Commerce v. United States House of Representatives* (1999), that the words mean "counting 'singly,' 'separately,' 'number by number,' 'distinctly.'" The distinction between actual counting and estimating was well known and thoroughly discussed both in debates in eighteenth-century English politics and in controversies between the American colonies and England. Indeed, the participants in these debates used the precise terms at issue; those who criticized the use of estimates in calculating population figures demanded instead that an enumeration—an actual count—be taken.

In *The Federalist* No. 36, Alexander Hamilton, in attempting to reassure his audience that the population figures upon which taxation would be based would not be subject to political manipulation, stated that "an actual census or enumeration of the people must furnish the rule, a circumstance which effectually shuts the door to partiality or oppression." The Census Act of 1790, establishing the first census, required an actual counting; census takers were required to swear an oath to "truly cause to be made, a just and perfect enumeration and description of all persons resident within [their] districts."

The Supreme Court, after avoiding the constitutional question in previous cases challenging the use of advanced statistical methods, decided the question of whether an actual counting is required in *Utah v. Evans* (2002), a case involving the use of a methodology that infers that households not actually counted in the census have the same population characteristics as their geographic neighbors that were counted. Justice Stephen Breyer, writing for the majority, concluded that the Framers "did not write detailed census methodology into the Constitution," and therefore methods, such as the one used in this case, that are based on inference and not actual counting are constitutionally valid. Justice Clarence Thomas, writing in dissent, lamented the Court's decision. He concluded: "Well familiar with methods of estimation, the Framers chose to make an 'actual Enumeration' part of our constitutional structure. Today, the Court undermines their decision, leaving the basis of our representative government vulnerable to political manipulation."

Andrew Spiropoulos

See Also

Article I, Section 9, Clause 4 (Direct Taxes)

Amendment XIV, Section 2 (Apportionment of Representatives)

Suggestions for Further Research

Margo Anderson & Stephen E. Fienberg, *Census 2000: Politics and Statistics*, 32 U. Tol. L. Rev. 19 (2000)

Stephen Kruger, *The Decennial Census* (February 29, 2012), at http://papers.ssrn.com/abstract=1985554 or http://dx.doi.org/10.2139/ssrn.1985554

Thomas R. Lee, *The Original Understanding of the Census Clause: Statistical Estimates and the Constitutional Requirement of an "Actual Enumeration,"* 77 Wash. L. Rev. 1 (2002)

Nathaniel Persily, *The Law of the Census: How to Count, What to Count, Whom to Count, and Where to Count Them*, 32 Cardozo. L. Rev. 755 (2011)

Significant Cases

Wisconsin v. City of New York, 517 U.S. 1 (1996)

Dep't of Commerce v. United States House of Representatives, 525 U.S. 316 (1999)

Utah v. Evans, 536 U.S. 452 (2002)

Allocation of Representatives

The Number of Representatives shall not exceed one for every thirty Thousand, but each State shall have at Least one Representative; and until such enumeration shall be made, the State of New Hampshire shall be entitled to chuse three, Massachusetts eight, Rhode-Island and Providence Plantations one, Connecticut five, New-York six, New Jersey four, Pennsylvania eight, Delaware one, Maryland six, Virginia ten, North Carolina five, South Carolina five, and Georgia three.

(Article I, Section 2, Clause 3)

~

*I*n Philadelphia, the Framers spent untold hours discussing the basis of representation for the new government and then fell to haggling over the number of Representatives to be elected from each state for the House of Representatives. A majority of delegations set the initial size of the House at a modest sixty-five Members, defeating James Madison's wish to have it doubled. They wished to leave Congress the flexibility to set numbers in the future, making sure that Congress would not allow for more than one Representative for every 30,000 persons, a last-minute modification of the original floor of 40,000 persons.

At the ratifying conventions, the Anti-Federalists were extremely exercised over the clause. George Mason, for example, inveighed against the small number of Representatives during the debates at the Virginia ratifying convention. James Madison accurately summarized their objections in *The Federalist* No. 55:

> [F]irst, that so small a number of representatives will be an unsafe depositary of the public interests; secondly, that they will not possess a proper knowledge of the local circumstances of their numerous constituents; thirdly, that they will be taken from that class of citizens which will sympathize least with the feelings of the mass of the people, and be most likely to aim at a permanent elevation of the few on the depression of the many; fourthly, that defective as the number will be in the first instance, it will be more disproportionate, by the increase of the people, and the obstacles which will prevent a correspondent increase of the representatives.

Madison spent much time rebutting these objections. "Nothing can be more fallacious than to found our political calculations on arithmetical principles," he declared. He assured his audience that Congress would increase the number of Representatives as the population grew; that the Senate would not stand in the way; that there was more danger in a cabal of the few forming in a large assembly than in a small one; that there were sufficient checks against corruption within the Constitution; and that Representatives needed knowledge only over subjects they could legislate upon, namely, commerce, taxation, and the militia.

Behind the debate between the Federalists and the Anti-Federalists lay different understandings of the future course of American republicanism. The Anti-Federalists did not believe that the country could grow and still remain republican, a proposition rebutted in Madison's classic argument in *The Federalist* No. 10. At the Constitutional Convention, Madison resisted any built-in increase to the numbers of Representatives, arguing that population growth would "render the number of Representatives excessive." Nathaniel Gorham of Massachusetts responded, "It is not to be supposed that the Gov't will last so long as to produce this effect. Can it be supposed that this vast Country including the Western territory will 150 years hence remain one nation?"

In response to Anti-Federalist objections, Congress sent twelve amendments to the states for ratification, the first of which changed the method of calculating the number of Representatives. Instead of there being no more than one Representative for 30,000 people, the amendment would have required at least one Representative for 30,000, or later, 40,000 and 50,000 as the population grew. But the amendment failed to achieve ratification, the only one of the original twelve never to have been approved by the states. The Federalist vision of the Union prevailed.

It was not clear whether the Allocation of Representatives Clause required the *national average* district population to be not less than 30,000, or whether a state's average district population had to be at least that number. Interestingly, President George Washington vetoed Congress's first apportionment plan because eight states would have had

average district populations of less than 30,000, which he thought in violation of this Clause.

True to Madison's prediction, Congress nonetheless dutifully increased the number of Representatives as the population grew. By 1833, Justice Joseph Story would write in his *Commentaries on the Constitution of the United States* that the dire predictions of the Anti-Federalists "have all vanished into air, into thin air." After the Civil War, Southern representation increased with the ending of slavery and the three-fifths rule. Congress, however, failed to enforce Section 2 of the Fourteenth Amendment, written to compel the Southern states to enfranchise blacks or lose representation. Finally, in 1929, after being unable to make a reapportionment of seats among the states after the census of 1920, Congress decided to cap the number of Representatives at 435.

Since 1790, Congress has applied five different methods of apportioning Representatives among the states. The present "Hill Method," with its complex formula determining when a state may gain or lose a seat, has been in use since 1940. It has been twice challenged before the Supreme Court. In *Franklin v. Massachusetts* (1992), the Court upheld the inclusion of federal military and civil personnel and their dependents in the apportioned populations. In *United States Department of Commerce v. Montana* (1992), the Court unanimously approved the "Hill Method" in the face of a challenge by Montana, which had lost one seat in favor of Washington after the 1990 census.

Although under the Equal Protection Clause of the Fourteenth Amendment, the population for each Congressional district *within* each state must be the same, *Wesberry v. Sanders* (1964), populations of districts *among* the states do not have to be. State average district populations vary considerably from the national average. For example, after the 2000 Census, Wyoming had an average district population that was 23.44 percent smaller than the national average while Montana's was 39.94 percent larger.

A federal court turned aside claims that, under this clause, allocating seats by voting age population, rather than numerical population, should be required. *Kalson v. Paterson* (2008). And the clause does not compel the government to treat Puerto Rico as a state for purposes of representation, for the clause only applies to actual states, not territories. *Igartúa v. U.S.* (2010).

David F. Forte

See Also

Article I, Section 2, Clause 1 (House of Representatives)

Amendment XIV, Section 1 (Equal Protection)

Amendment XIV, Section 2 (Apportionment of Representatives)

Suggestions for Further Research

David P. Currie, *The Constitution in Congress: The Second Congress 1791–1793*, 90 Nw. U. L. Rev. 606 (1996)

Paul H. Edelman, *Getting the Math Right, Why California Has Too Many Seats in the House of Representatives*, 59 Vand. L. Rev. 297 (2006)

David B. Goldin, *Number Wars: A Decade of Census Litigation*, 32 U. Tol. L. Rev. 1 (2000)

Jeffrey W. Ladewig, *One Person, One Vote, 435 Seats: Interstate Malapportionment and Constitutional Requirements*, 43 Conn. L. Rev. 1125 (2011)

Significant Cases

Wesberry v. Sanders, 376 U.S. 1 (1964)

Franklin v. Massachusetts, 505 U.S. 788 (1992)

United States Department of Commerce v. Montana, 503 U.S. 442 (1992)

Kalson v. Paterson, 542 F.3d 281 (2d Cir. 2008)

Igartúa v. United States, 626 F.3d 592 (1st Cir. 2010)

Executive Writs of Election

When vacancies happen in the Representation from any State, the Executive Authority thereof shall issue Writs of Election to fill such Vacancies.

(**Article I, Section 2, Clause 4**)

~

*A*lthough the phrasing of the Executive Writs of Election Clause varied until the Committee of Style established its final wording, there was no dispute among the Framers as to the necessity of having vacant House seats filled by special election. James Madison wrote in *The Federalist* No. 52, "As it is essential to liberty that the government in general should have a common interest with the people, so it is particularly essential that the branch of it under consideration [the House] should have an immediate dependence on, and an intimate sympathy with, the people. Frequent elections are unquestionably the only policy by which this dependence and sympathy can be effectually secured." The House of Representatives is unique in that it is the only part of the federal government that is required by the Constitution's text to be composed only of those who are elected.

The clause vests the governor with the responsibility of calling such special elections to fill vacant House seats. Justice Joseph Story wrote of the clause that "[i]t is obvious, that such a power ought to reside in some public functionary" and that the Constitution vests such power with "the State Executive, which is best fitted to exercise it with promptitude and discretion." In fact, the clause combined the principles of those who did not want to see "the people" unrepresented in any part of the government with those who desired to continue to support state authority over the electoral process.

The Seventh Circuit Court of Appeals has ruled that the clause imposes a mandatory duty on governors to issue writs of election to fill vacancies in the United States House of Representatives. *Jackson v. Ogilvie* (1970). More specifically, the court held that in performing that duty, the governor has the discretion to choose one day of the week over another on which to issue writs of election, but he does not have the discretion to decide against issuing the writs of election altogether. The Sixth Circuit Court of Appeals has also held the clause imposes a mandatory duty, leaving only the possibility that a governor could avoid such duty when the time remaining on the congressional term "is truly de minimus." *American Civil Liberties Union of Ohio, Inc. v. Taft* (2004). The rule had been articulated earlier in *United States Term Limits, Inc. v. Thornton* (1995), when Justice Clarence

Thomas for the four-person dissent indicated that the clause prescribes an affirmative duty on the state executive to issue a writ whenever a vacancy occurs.

Paul Taylor

See Also

Article I, Section 4, Clause 1 (Election Regulations)

Amendment XVII (Vacancies in the Senate)

Suggestion for Further Research

Paul Taylor, *Proposals to Prevent Discontinuity in Government and Preserve the Right to Elected Representation*, 54 Syracuse L. Rev. 435 (2004)

Significant Cases

Jackson v. Ogilvie, 426 F.2d 1333 (7th Cir. 1970)

United States Term Limits, Inc. v. Thornton, 514 U.S. 779 (1995) (Thomas, J., dissenting)

ACLU of Ohio, Inc. v. Taft, 385 F.3d 641 (6th Cir. 2004)

Speaker of the House

The House of Representatives shall chuse their Speaker and other Officers....

(**Article I, Section 2, Clause 5**)

~

A "Speaker of the House" has been an organic part of the Anglo-American legislative process for centuries—at least since 1377, when the Rolls of Parliament first noted it. As with his power to dissolve Parliament, the King sought to control Parliament by influencing the choice of the Speaker once Parliament was in session. During Tudor times, because the King had to consent to the nomination of the Speaker, the Tudors were able to use the threat of a veto to gain the ability to nominate the person whom the Commons would choose.

After the Tudors, the process of selecting the Speaker of the House of Commons slowly transitioned into a process completely controlled by the House. Throughout the seventeenth and eighteenth centuries, as the House of Commons fought for independent legislative power, Parliament pursued and eventually won the right to select the Speaker without hindrance from the Crown. Not since the late seventeenth century has a monarch, for political reasons, dared to challenge the House of Common's selection of a Speaker.

Until the eighteenth century, the Speaker had much power in deciding what issues would be brought to the floor of Parliament. He also was able to interpret House proceedings and positions to the King. After Parliament gained control over the choice of Speaker, the position devolved into an umpire simply refereeing the manner of debate.

Prior to American independence, the selection of the Speaker in colonial legislative houses closely mirrored the earlier British process. Though colonial assemblies chose their speakers, the royally appointed governors sought to control the result. As trouble grew between America and Britain, the Speaker became a spokesman of the various assemblies' positions against the actions of Parliament and the Crown's agents, mimicking the period leading to the Glorious Revolution in England (1688).

Under Article IX of the Articles of Confederation (1781), the Congress of the United States had the power "to appoint one of their number to preside, provided that no person be allowed to serve in the office of president more than one year in any term of three years."

At the Constitutional Convention, however, the Framers drew not only on their own history but more directly on the model of the Massachusetts Constitution of 1780, which provided that "the House of Representatives...shall choose their own Speaker, appoint their own officers, and settle the rules and order of proceeding in their own House." The language in the Massachusetts Constitution emphasizing "their own" was to declare the legislature free from the kind of gubernatorial control under which colonial assemblies had struggled. The more succinct language of Article I, Section 2, Clause 5 of the Constitution carried the same meaning and clearly established the House's power to choose its leadership free from the executive and Senate power. The Speaker was now an internal House of Representatives officer, relieved of the burden of pleasing the Crown (or Executive) as a prerequisite for assuming the Speakership.

Without Constitutional specification, the Speaker of the House gained duties and powers as the issues of the day required them to be granted. The first Speaker of the House, Frederick Muhlenberg, led a House of Representatives that was devoid of parties and was attempting to construct the Republican institutions of which the Constitution was the source. But even during this early stage, the Speaker obtained an important role in the first session of Congress: the ability to appoint Members of the House to committees. Later, during his time as Speaker, Henry Clay demonstrated the extraordinary power that an active Speaker could assume, skillfully filling committees to build support for the war against England in 1812.

By the early twentieth century, the Speaker, described contemporaneously as an "autocrat," was the second most powerful person in Washington. The Speaker possessed the power to appoint members and chairmen of all committees, and he also controlled the timing and content of bills brought before the House. But in a Republican revolt against Speaker Joseph Cannon in 1910, the Speaker's power was reduced, and chairmen came to be appointed primarily by reason of seniority. Thereafter, the chairmen of the various committees became the center of power until the mid-1970s, when the House restored many of the Speaker's prerogatives.

The House of Representatives elects its Speaker as the first order of business at the start of each two-year term or when a Speaker dies or resigns during the legislative term. The practice is customary, for it occurs before the House formally adopts its rules of procedure for the legislative term. Until 1839, the House elected the Speaker by ballot, but since that time the election has been by roll call. The party caucuses, however, predetermine the result by meeting and selecting the candidates to be voted upon. The successful candidate must obtain a majority of the votes cast. Only when party discipline breaks down, or a third party has sufficient

strength, is there the possibility for multiple ballots. In 1923, for example, when the Progressive Party held a number of seats, the House took nine ballots before electing Frederick Gillett, a Republican.

Unlike British practice and unlike the President Pro Tempore of the Senate, the Speaker of the House is the primary legislative leader of the body. As the leader of the majority party, the Speaker declares and defends the legislative agenda of the majority party. However, the Speaker traditionally refrains from debating or voting in most circumstances and does not sit on any standing committees in the House.

The House also elects its other officers such as the Clerk, Sergeant-at-Arms, Chief Administrative Officer, and Chaplain, whereas the Speaker appoints the Historian of the House, the General Counsel, and the Inspector General.

David F. Forte

See Also

Article I, Section 3, Clause 5 (President Pro Tempore)
Article II, Section 2, Clause 3 (Recess Appointments Clause)
Article II, Section 3 (Convening of Congress)

Suggestions for Further Research

Judith Bentley, Speakers of the House (1994)

Richard S. Beth & Valerie Heitshusen, *Speakers of the House: Elections 1913–2013*, CRS Report RL30857 (2013)

Mary P. Follett, The Speaker of the House of Representatives (reprint, Burt Franklin 1974) (1902)

Hubert Bruce Fuller, The Speakers of the House (reprint, Arno Press 1974) (1909)

Matthew N. Green, The Speaker of the House: A Study of Leadership (2010)

Douglas B. Harris, *The Rise of the Public Speakership*, 113 Pol. Sci. Q. 193–212 (Summer 1998)

Valerie Heitshusen, *The Speaker of the House: House Officer, Party Leader, and Representative*, CRS Report 97-780 (2011)

Asher C. Hinds, *The Speaker of the House of Representatives: Origin of the Office, Its Duties and Powers*, 3 Am. Pol. Sci. Rev. (May 1909)

Dell G. Hitchner, *The Speaker of the House of Representatives,* 13 Parliamentary Affairs 185 (Spring 1960)

Alfred T. Zubrov, Speakers of the House, 1789–2002 (2002)

Impeachment

The House of Representatives...shall have the sole Power of Impeachment.

(Article I, Section 2, Clause 5)

～

$\mathcal{I}$n the debates in the Constitutional Convention, the delegates were attempting to craft a mechanism that would allow for the disciplining of a President who abused his constitutional responsibilities without creating a weapon by which the President would be prevented from carrying them out. At bottom, it was a question of how to refine and make effective the separation of powers.

Article II, Section 4 states that the President, Vice President, and "all civil Officers of the United States"—which includes judges—can be impeached. Members of Congress can be expelled by their own respective body. (*See* Article I, Section 5, Clause 2.)

Early on, some delegates expressed the apprehension that those serving in the federal government would be disinclined to monitor each other. Accordingly, John Dickinson proposed "that the Executive be made removeable by the National Legislature on the request of a majority of the Legislatures of individual States." James Madison opposed the idea because it would subject the executive to the "intrigues" of the states. After defeating Dickinson's proposal, the members of the Convention also turned aside George Mason's and Gouverneur Morris's initial fears that the impeachment power might render the executive the servant of the legislature. Instead, the Framers opted for the procedure that had been followed by the English and by the constitutions of most of the states. The appropriate place of bringing charges of impeachment, which

power is analogous to the bringing of criminal charges by a grand jury, is in the lower house of the legislature. Just as the grand and petit juries are popular institutions, so it made sense to have the branch closest to the people charged with this indictment-like power.

The Constitution does not specify how impeachment proceedings are to be initiated. Early in our history, a Member would rise on the floor of Congress and propose an impeachment, which would then be assigned to a committee. In recent years, Members of the House Judiciary Committee have initiated the proceeding and then made recommendations for the whole House's consideration. If the House votes an impeachment resolution, the Chairman of the Judiciary Committee recommends a slate of "managers," whom the House subsequently approves by resolution, and who then become prosecutors in the trial in the Senate.

For a time there was legislation enabling the Attorney General to appoint a "special prosecutor" with the power to recommend impeachments to Congress, but dissatisfaction with the power of such an unchecked independent counsel led to the expiration of the authorizing statute. Even the most famous "independent counsel," Judge Kenneth Starr, who recommended the impeachment of President William Jefferson Clinton to Congress, had consistently argued against the practice of appointing such independent counsels.

There have not been many instances of impeachment over the years—a few dozen in all, mostly of corrupt federal judges. The most notable impeachments—Justice Samuel Chase, and Presidents Andrew Johnson and William Jefferson Clinton—have ended in acquittals by the Senate. There were proceedings and hearings at the House Judiciary Committee and a bill of impeachment reported to the House against President Richard M. Nixon. Nixon resigned before the full House could vote on the impeachment charges against him.

The near-unanimous view of constitutional commentators is that the House of Representatives' "sole power" of impeachment is a political question and therefore not reviewable by the judiciary. The House is constitutionally obligated to base a bill of impeachment on the standards set out in Article II. (*See* Article II, Section 4.) However, the fact that the Constitution's text grants the House the "sole power," and the fact that such a review is not clearly within the Article III power of the federal judiciary, indicate that this responsibility is the House's alone. The Supreme Court has found that the Senate's "sole power" to try impeachments is not justiciable. *Nixon v. United States* (1993).

That leaves the question of whether the clause imposes an affirmative duty on the House to monitor the conduct of those subject to impeachment, and, when evidence of impeachable offenses is manifest, to initiate proceedings. It has been the general American practice regarding criminal law to grant considerable discretion to prosecutors, so that by analogy one could argue that the House has complete discretion to decide whether to initiate impeachment proceedings. On the other hand, Alexander Hamilton argued in *The Federalist* No. 77 that the nation would find "republican" safety from a presidential abuse of power by the mode of his election and by his "being at all times liable to impeachment." There is no doubt that the Framers saw impeachment as a part of the system of checks and balances to maintain the separation of powers and the republican form of government. The implication is that when the President (or other impeachable official) has committed an impeachable offense, the Members of the House, bound by the oaths they take to uphold the Constitution, are under a particular obligation to deal with the miscreant's offenses, irrespective of whether their bill of impeachment may or may not lead to a conviction in the Senate.

Stephen B. Presser

See Also

Suggestions for Further Research

Michael J. Gerhardt, The Federal Impeachment Process: A Constitutional and Historical Analysis (2d ed. 2000)

Michael J. Gerhardt, *Rediscovering Nonjusticiability: Judicial Review of Impeachments after Nixon*, 44 Duke L.J. 231 (1994)

Stephen B. Presser, *Would George Washington Have Wanted Bill Clinton Impeached?*, 67 Geo. Wash. L. Rev. 666 (1999)

Ronald D. Rotunda, *An Essay on the Constitutional Parameters of Federal Impeachment*, 76 Ky. L.J. 707 (1988)

Jonathan Turley, *Congress as Grand Jury: The Role of the House of Representatives in the Impeachment of an American President*, 67 Geo. Wash. L. Rev. 735 (1999)

Significant Case

Nixon v. United States, 506 U.S. 224 (1993)

Senate

The Senate of the United States shall be composed of two Senators from each State, chosen by the Legislature thereof for six Years; and each Senator shall have one Vote.
(Article I, Section 3, Clause 1)

≈

*T*he formulation of the Senate was the result of the famous Connecticut Compromise (sometimes called the "Great Compromise") at the Constitutional Convention, which provided for proportional representation of the states in the House and equal representation of the states in the Senate. Each state was to have two Senators, who would be elected by its state legislature, serve for staggered six-year terms, and vote individually. By these devices, the Framers intended to protect the interests of the states as states.

Equal representation of all states in the Senate ensured that the ability of the smaller states to protect their interests would not be seriously impaired. Combined with the bicameral system created by the Constitution, it required that all legislation would have to be ratified by two independent power sources: Representatives of the people in the House and Representatives of the states (regardless of their respective size) in the Senate.

The mode of election impelled Senators to preserve the original federal design and to protect the interests not only of their own states, but, concomitantly, of the states as political and legal entities within the federal system. As Alexander Hamilton declared during the New York ratifying convention in 1788,

> When you take a view of all the circumstances which have been recited, you will certainly see that the senators will constantly look up to the state governments with an eye of dependence and affection. If they are ambitious to continue in office they will make every prudent arrangement for this purpose, and, whatever may be their private sentiments of politics, they will be convinced that the surest means of obtaining a re-election will be an uniform attachment to the interests of their several states.

On first blush, per capita voting seems, as Luther Martin argued in the Constitutional Convention, to depart "from the idea of the States being represented in the second branch." However, the Framers knew from their experiences with block voting under the Articles of Confederation that states had often gone unrepresented because of an evenly divided delegation. They also appreciated that per capita voting could often represent a state's interests better than block voting, even if occasionally that state's Senators split their vote. Because their six-year terms of office were to be staggered, and because they were elected by state legislatures which, as James Madison observed in *The Federalist* No. 63, were continuously "regenerate[d]" by "the periodical change of members," a state's two Senators would end up

representing somewhat different political moods and sentiments. Elected by shifting majorities in the state legislature, the two Senators, voting per capita, would be able to reflect more accurately the shifting political sentiments of the people in their home states than if they were required to vote as a block.

The Seventeenth Amendment profoundly altered Article I, Section 3 by providing for direct election of the Senate. Several interrelated factors explain its ratification: (1) legislative deadlocks over the election of Senators brought about when one party controlled the state assembly or house and another the state senate; (2) scandals brought on by charges of bribery and corruption in the election of Senators; (3) the growing strength of the Populist movement, with its deep-seated suspicion of wealth and influence and its penchant for describing the Senate as "an unrepresentative, unresponsive 'millionaires club,' high on partisanship but low in integrity"; (4) deadlocks in state legislatures that often left states with no elected Senate representation for years; and (5) the rise of Progressivism and its conviction that the solution to the problems of democracy was more democracy—in this case, popular election of Senators.

Ralph Rossum

See Also

Suggestions for Further Research

Jay S. Bybee, Ulysses at the Mast: Democracy, Federalism, and the Sirens' Song of the Seventeenth Amendment, 91 Nw. U. L. Rev. 500 (1997)

George H. Haynes, The Election of Senators (1906)

George H. Haynes, The Senate of the United States: Its History and Practice (2 vols. 1938)

Ronald D. Rotunda, *The Aftermath of Thornton*, 13 Constitutional Commentary 201, 206–10 (1996)

Ralph A. Rossum, Federalism, the Supreme Court, and the Seventeenth Amendment: The Irony of Constitutional Democracy (2001)

Senatorial Classes and Vacancies Clause

Immediately after they shall be assembled in Consequence of the first Election, they shall be divided as equally as may be into three Classes. The Seats of the Senators of the first Class shall be vacated at the Expiration of the second Year, of the second Class at the Expiration of the fourth Year, and of the third Class at the Expiration of the sixth Year, so that one third may be chosen every second Year; and if Vacancies happen by Resignation, or otherwise, during the Recess of the Legislature of any State, the Executive thereof may make temporary Appointments until the next Meeting of the Legislature, which shall then fill such Vacancies.

(ARTICLE I, SECTION 3, CLAUSE 2)

~

*W*ell before the delegates to the Constitutional Convention had reached "the Great Compromise" that accorded the states equal votes in the Senate, they had already decided much about the upper house. They determined that the state legislatures would choose the Members of the Senate from their respective states; that it would have fewer Members than the lower house; and that the Members of the Senate would serve longer terms. By these mechanisms, the delegates integrated the states into the national legislative process, "protected" and "preserved" the states, provided for a forum to represent "the great mercantile interest," and made the Senate's membership more "permanent," in order to modify the more "transient impressions" that would influence the House. They perceived the Senate to be a more deliberative body. The House of Representatives, the Framers thought, would initiate most legislation, whereas the Senate was to be a corrective and a refinement of what emanated from the House. James Madison in *The Federalist* No. 62 confirmed the goal of stability: the Senate "ought

to hold its authority by a tenure of considerable duration" to give it "firmness."

Various delegates suggested terms ranging from three to nine years. Madison argued for a longer term "to give to the Govt. that stability which was everywhere called for." Most delegates seemed to support a term of seven years, but after Alexander Hamilton proposed a complex system of rotation, Hugh Williamson of North Carolina suggested a term of six years "as more convenient for Rotation then 7 years." After some hesitation, the delegates agreed to six-year staggered terms.

But longer terms were not the only structural mechanism used to bolster Senate stability; the Senate was also divided into three "classes" and only one class stood for re-election every 2 years. James Wilson explicitly connected the longer six-year terms and the overlapping classes as two structural mechanisms working toward the same end: "[t]he qualities of stability and consistency will be expected chiefly from the senate; because the senators continue longer in office; and because only a part of them can be changed at any one time."

The first Senate was able to reach a quorum on April 6, 1789, and immediately counted the electoral ballots that elected George Washington as President. On May 13, they divided themselves into three geographically balanced classes, with no two Senators from the same state in the same class. Then, the Senate resolved that "three papers of an equal size, numbered 1, 2, and 3, be, by the Secretary, rolled up and put into a box," and drawn by three Senators representing the previously assigned classes. The class drawing "1" would vacate at the end of two years, "2" at the end of four, and "3" at the end of six. New states' Senators would be allocated among the classes. Thus began the institution of staggered terms by which the Senate continues to be elected, now through the terms of the Seventeenth Amendment.

With time, the overlapping terms of Senators—especially when contrasted with the two-year life cycle of the House—created a sense of continuity that is unique in our legislative system. As Senator (and future President) James Buchanan stated in 1841, "This was the very same body, constitutionally, and in point of law, which had assembled on the first day of its meeting, in 1789. It had existed, without any intermission, from that day until the present moment....It never dies; and it was the sheet-anchor of the Constitution, on account of its permanency."

As a "continuing body," the Senate does not need to re-enact its procedural rules every two years. It is thus, practically speaking, an exception to the rule that one legislature cannot bind a future legislature, for the Senate is the same legislature. This allows such continuing parliamentary practices to become entrenched, some through tradition and some like the filibuster, which carries with its own protection: a motion to do away with the filibuster can itself be filibustered.

The clause also allows state governors to "make temporary Appointments until the next Meeting of the Legislature, which shall then fill such Vacancies." At the Convention, only James Wilson had objected to granting governors the power to make appointments to the Senate if there were a sudden vacancy and the legislature was not in session. He thought the device contrary to the principle of the separation of powers. Edmund Randolph, however, declared that the provision was "necessary in order to prevent inconvenient chasms in the Senate," and the Convention agreed. This provision was modified by the Seventeenth Amendment, which now, in the case of a vacancy, requires governors to "issue writs of election to fill such vacancies."

David F. Forte

See Also

Article I, Section 3, Clause 1 (Senate)

Article I, Section 3, Clause 3 (Qualifications for Senators)

Amendment XVII (Popular Election of Senators)

Suggestions for Further Research

Aaron-Andrew P. Bruhl, Burying the "Continuing Body" Theory of the Senate, 95 Iowa L. Rev. 1401 (2010)

Daniel Wirls & Stephen Wirls, The Invention of the United States Senate (2004)

2 Collected Works of James Wilson 829, 853 (Kermit L. Hall & Mark David Hall eds., 2007) (1790–1791)

Significant Case

McGrain v. Daugherty, 273 U.S. 135 (1927)

Qualifications for Senators

No person shall be a Senator who shall not have attained to the Age of thirty Years, and been nine Years a Citizen of the United States, and who shall not, when elected, be an Inhabitant of that State for which he shall be chosen.

(Article I, Section 3, Clause 3)

~

*T*he Framers understood that the frequent elections for Members of the House meant that Congress as a whole could be subject to the dangers of faction unless a "responsible" Senate were added to the legislature. Publius argued in *The Federalist* No. 63 that the role of the Senate ensures that "the cool and deliberate sense of the community" prevails in Congress over the potential tyranny of momentary passions. In *The Federalist* No. 62, he explained that the more advanced age of Senators and their longer period of citizenship would make them better suited for the "senatorial trust, which, requiring greater extent of information and stability of character, requires at the same time that the senator should have reached a period of life most likely to supply these advantages." Before the Constitutional Convention settled on a required nine-year citizenship compromise, Gouverneur Morris had pressed for a fourteen-year period of citizenship. It would take at least that long, Morris argued, for foreigners to learn the American Constitution and its system of laws. James Madison, Benjamin Franklin, and James Wilson opposed a period of such length, arguing that it would make the Constitution too "illiberal."

The age, residency, and citizenship requirements for the Senate have not, themselves, been the subject of judicial dispute. The clause makes it clear that one must be a resident of the state at the time of election, but the Senate has adopted the practice of receiving into its membership Senators who attain the minimum age or length of citizenship subsequent to their election but prior to assuming office.

In the aftermath of the Civil War, both Houses of Congress did occasionally deny individuals their seats if they could not swear that they had never been disloyal to the union. The question of Congress's power to consider qualifications in addition to those stated in Article I remained open until 1969, when Chief Justice Earl Warren wrote in *Powell v. McCormack* that "in judging the qualifications of its members Congress is limited to the standing qualifications prescribed in the Constitution."

The question whether states could add to the Constitution's list of requirements was the focus of *United States Term Limits v. Thornton* (1995). Previously, both the House and the Senate had seated Members who were not in compliance with an additional state requirement. For example, in 1856 the Senate seated Lyman Trumbull from Illinois, even though, as a sitting state judge, Trumbull was forbidden by the Illinois Constitution from serving in any other state or federal office. A 1970 circuit opinion by Justice Hugo L. Black in *Davis v. Adams* upheld a lower court's determination that the state of Florida could not require a candidate for Congress to resign his state office prior to assuming his federal candidacy. In writing for the Court in *Thornton*, Justice John Paul Stevens concluded that "the Framers intended the Constitution to be the exclusive source of qualifications for members of Congress, and that the Framers thereby 'divested' States of any power to add qualifications."

Ronald Pestritto

See Also

Suggestion for Further Research

John C. Eastman, *Open to Merit of Every Description? An Historical Assessment of the Constitution's Qualifications Clauses*, 73 Denv. U. L. Rev. 89 (1995)

Significant Cases

Powell v. McCormack, 395 U.S. 486 (1969)

Davis v. Adams, 400 U.S. 1203 (1970)

United States Term Limits, Inc. v. Thornton, 514 U.S. 779 (1995)

Vice President as Presiding Officer

> The Vice President of the United States shall be President of the Senate, but shall have no Vote, unless they be equally divided.
>
> (Article I, Section 3, Clause 4)

$\sim$

*T*he only regular responsibility that the Constitutional Convention assigned to the office of the Vice President (other than the duty to receive the tally of electoral votes for President) was to preside over the Senate and to cast tie-breaking votes. Because this role seemed to give the Vice President some legislative responsibility, George Mason argued during the Convention that this was a violation of the separation of powers, that "it mixed too much" the executive and legislative powers. But Roger Sherman responded: "If the Vice President were not to be President of the Senate, he would be without employment." The Anti-Federalists echoed Mason's concern, that the Vice President would be an agent of executive subversion of the legislature. John Adams intentionally signed Senate documents as "John Adams, Vice-President." The Anti-Federalist William Maclay responded, "Sir, we know you not as Vice-President within this House. As President of the Senate only do we know you, as President of the Senate only can you sign or authenticate any Act of that Body."

Allowing the Vice President to preside over the Senate, and to vote in case of a tie, solved two important problems. First, it allowed that body—at all times—to come to a definitive resolution, because the President of the Senate would break tie votes. Second, it preserved the equality of the states in the Senate. As Justice Joseph Story noted in his *Commentaries on the Constitution of the United States* (1833), should a Senator have been chosen to preside over the body, and should that Senator cast the tie-breaking vote, a state would, in effect, increase its representation.

Alternatively, if the Senator as presiding President would be allowed to vote only in case of a tie, a state would end up losing half its representation during normal votes. *The Federalist* No. 68. There have been over two hundred occasions when the Vice President has had to cast a tie-breaking vote, but most occurred early in the history of the Republic. In fact, the first Vice President, John Adams, cast the highest number of such votes, twenty-nine in all, including the Decision of 1789, confirming the President's authority to remove executive officers.

Early in the Republic the Vice President took seriously his constitutional duty of presiding over the Senate, and John Adams and Thomas Jefferson did much to shape the presider's role. Rarely, however, does the Vice President sit in modern times. The President Pro Tempore of the Senate is the formal substitute, but normally a junior Member of the Senate is assigned to sit in the chair. The ambiguity in the constitutional position of the Vice President has led to a debate among commentators as to whether to site the office in the legislative or executive branches. The consensus among the Framers seems to have been that his constitutional duties lay in the legislative branch unless and until he succeeded to the Presidency. Significantly, the Vice President's salary, his expenses, and his staff are still paid for out of the Senate's budget. Nonetheless, under the broad discretion that the Constitution leaves to each branch to develop its own structure, the political influence of Vice Presidents in the executive branch has increased as modern Presidents have delegated many functions to their Vice Presidents.

Peter W. Schramm

See Also

Article II, Section 1, Clause 3 (Electoral College)
Article II, Section 1, Clause 6 (Presidential Succession)
Amendment XII (Electoral College)
Amendment XXII (Presidential Term Limit)
Amendment XXV (Presidential Succession)

Suggestions for Further Research

Richard Albert, *The Evolving Vice Presidency*, 78 Temp. L. Rev. 811, 813 (2005)
David P. Currie, *The Constitution in Congress: The First Congress and the Structure of Government, 1789–1791*, 2 U. Chi. L. Sch. Roundtable 161 (1995)
MARK O. HATFIELD, VICE PRESIDENTS OF THE UNITED STATES, 1789–1993 (1997)
PAUL C. LIGHT, VICE-PRESIDENTIAL POWER: ADVICE AND INFLUENCE IN THE WHITE HOUSE (1984)
L. EDWARD PURCELL, VICE PRESIDENTS: A BIOGRAPHICAL DICTIONARY (4th ed., 2010)
Glenn Harlan Reynolds, *Is Dick Cheney Unconstitutional?*, 102 Nw. U.L. Rev. 1539 (2008)

President Pro Tempore

The Senate shall chuse their other Officers, and also a President pro tempore, in the Absence of the Vice President, or when he shall exercise the Office of President of the United States.

(**ARTICLE I, SECTION 3, CLAUSE 5**)

⁓

*T*o maintain the appropriate ordering of the legislative process in the Senate, the Constitution provided for the appointment of a temporary presiding officer when the Vice President was absent from the body. As with Article I, Section 2, Clause 5, vesting the appointment of the Speaker and other officers in the House of Representatives, this clause avoids any inference that the Appointments Clause (Article II, Section 2, Clause 2) might apply to legislative officers. It is, in other words, another carefully drafted provision to protect the separation of powers.

At first, the Senate elected a President Pro Tempore each time the Vice President absented himself from the chair, the office ending upon the return of the Vice President. In 1792, John Adams began the custom of vacating the presidential chair shortly before the end of each day's session, permitting the Senate to elect a President Pro Tempore who would be in place in case the Vice President died or assumed the functions of the President of the United States. The Senate codified that practice by resolution in 1876.

In 1890, the Senate adopted the procedure that continues today of electing a President Pro Tempore who holds the office until replaced. By custom, the Senate elects the Member of the majority party who is senior in terms of length of service. By statute, the office is third in succession to the presidency after the Vice President and the Speaker of the House of Representatives.

The President Pro Tempore is not a legislative leader. He supervises the Senate and makes procedural rulings while in the chair. Like the Vice President, the President Pro Tempore does not actually preside over many sessions of the Senate. He appoints substitutes from the Members to sit in the chair when he steps down. Often the daily roster of substitutes includes younger Senators in order to acquaint them with the procedures of the Senate. Unlike the Vice President, the President Pro Tempore does not vote to break tie votes, but rather votes as a Senator from his own state.

When there was no Vice President because of death or succession to the Presidency, the President Pro Tempore occupied the "office" of the Vice President to oversee the Senate staff and to perform the other administrative duties of the Vice President, but he did not thereby succeed to the *constitutional* office of the Vice President.

In recent decades, the Senate has created the ceremonial office of Deputy President Pro Tempore, available to Senators who were former Presidents or Vice Presidents. Hubert Humphrey is only person to have held the post under those terms (though Senator George Mitchell was given the post while President Pro Tempore John Stennis was ill). In addition, the Senate has established the honorary position of President Pro Tempore Emeritus for a senator of the minority party who had earlier served as President Pro Tempore.

"Other Officers" of the Senate include the majority and minority leaders who have the primary responsibility of directing the flow of legislation, party secretaries, the Sergeant at Arms and Doorkeeper, Chaplain, Secretary of the Senate, Chief Clerk, and Executive Clerk.

David F. Forte

See Also

Article I, Section 2, Clause 2 (Qualifications for Representatives)

Article I, Section 2, Clause 5 (Speaker of the House)

Article I, Section 3, Clause 4 (Vice President as Presiding Officer)

Article II, Section 2, Clause 2 (Appointments Clause)

Suggestion for Further Research

Richard C. Sachs, The President Pro Tempore of the Senate: History and Authority of the Office (2001)

Trial of Impeachment

The Senate shall have the sole Power to try all Impeachments. When sitting for that Purpose, they shall be on Oath or Affirmation. When the President of the United States is tried, the Chief Justice shall preside: And no Person shall be convicted without the Concurrence of two thirds of the Members present.

(Article I, Section 3, Clause 6)

⁓

*T*he essential powers and procedures for Senate impeachment trials are set forth in this clause. The Framers vested the Senate with the "sole Power to try Impeachments" for several reasons. First, they believed Senators would be better educated, more virtuous, and more high-minded than Members of the House of Representatives and thus uniquely able to decide responsibly the most difficult of political questions. Second, the Framers vested the Senate rather than the judiciary with the authority to try impeachments because they favored, as Alexander Hamilton explained in *The Federalist* No. 65, a "numerous court for the trial of impeachments." He believed such a body would be well suited to handle the procedural demands of an impeachment trial, in which it, unlike judges, should "never be tied down by such strict rules, either in the delineation of the offense by the prosecutors or in the construction of it by the judges, as in the common cases serve to limit the discretion of courts in favor of personal security." Hamilton explained further that "[t]he awful discretion which a court of impeachments must necessarily have, to doom to honor or infamy the most confidential and the most distinguished characters of the community forbids the commitment of the trust to a small number of persons."

There are three special requirements for impeachment trials. The requirement that Senators be on Oath or Affirmation in impeachment trials was plainly designed to impress upon them the extreme seriousness of the occasion. The requirement for the Chief Justice to preside over presidential impeachment trials underscores the solemnity of the occasion and aims to avoid the possible conflict of interest of a Vice President's presiding over the proceeding for the removal of the one official standing between him and the presidency. Moreover, the supermajority requirement was designed to facilitate serious deliberation and to make removal possible only through a consensus that cuts across factional divisions. This requirement's impact is apparent in the fact that the Senate has convicted only seven of sixteen people impeached by the House. It was instrumental in Andrew Johnson's trial, as the majority fell one vote short of removing him from office. In President William Jefferson Clinton's trial, there was never a question of his removal so long as all forty-five Democrats in the Senate uniformly opposed his ouster.

In addition to the requirements in the Constitution's text, three significant questions have arisen about Senate authority to try impeach-

ments. The first concerns the minimum the Senate must do once the House impeaches someone. This question arose after the House's first impeachment in 1797. One day after the House impeached Senator William Blount, the Senate expelled him by a vote of 25–1. Blount claimed the Senate lacked authority to try him because Senators were not impeachable and, in any event, he no longer occupied an office from which he could be removed. The Senate voted to dismiss the impeachment resolution against the expelled Blount for lack of jurisdiction. Subsequently, many Senators have construed this vote as supporting their authority to dismiss an impeachment without a full-scale trial.

The second question concerns the extent of the Chief Justice's authority (or the Vice President's in ordinary impeachment trials) as presiding officer to render unilateral rulings. In the first presidential impeachment trial in 1868, Chief Justice Salmon Chase claimed the authority to decide certain procedural questions on his own, but the Senate challenged several of his rulings and overruled him at least twice. In President Clinton's impeachment trial in 1999, Chief Justice William H. Rehnquist ruled on some procedural questions, but the Senate never challenged, much less overruled, any of these rulings.

A third question revolves around the procedures the Senate must employ in impeachment trials. Because the Constitution both provides the Senate with the "sole power to try impeachments" and empowers each house "to determine the Rules of its Proceedings," the Senate has formulated its own special impeachment trial procedures (first written down by Thomas Jefferson when he was Vice President). In President Andrew Johnson's impeachment trial, the Senate formulated an additional set of rules that have largely remained intact ever since and were followed by the Senate in President Clinton's impeachment trial.

In 1936, the Senate amended these rules to include Rule XI, which allows the appointment of a small number of Senators to operate as a trial committee to gather evidence and take testimony. The Senate has used trial committees on only three occasions, in the 1980s, to assist with fact-finding regarding impeachment articles approved by the House against three federal district judges. Before the Senate and in federal court, all three judges challenged the legitimacy of trial committees. They argued the Senate's "power to try impeachments" imposed on the full Senate the obligation to conduct a full trial. The Senate countered that it had complete authority over how to fashion proceedings and that Senators' political accountability was the only check on this authority. Ultimately, the Supreme Court accepted the Senate's arguments in *Nixon v. United States* (1993) on the principal ground that the Senate's power to try impeachments included the nonreviewable final discretion to determine how to conduct its trials. The Court did not address the propriety of judicial review of the Senate's possible deviation from any explicit safeguard required by the Constitution for impeachment trials.

The Senate settled some other procedural questions raised in the 1980s, including the applicability of the Fifth Amendment Due Process Clause to and the requisite rules of evidence and burden of proof for impeachment trials. The Senate ruled that adopting a uniform rule on these questions was impractical because it lacked the means for enforcing any such rule against Senators. It decided that each question was a matter for the Senators to decide for themselves.

The Constitution fastens the responsibility of trying impeachments upon the Senate. Yet some Senators have doubted whether they have the requisite competence to try impeachments. Rule XI was adopted as a response to poor attendance and preparation by Senators in impeachment trials in the early twentieth century. Yet even in the 1980s, some Senators claimed that they had not bothered to prepare before voting, and such proceedings diverted their energies away from legislative business of greater concern to their constituents. Others argued the proceedings restored their confidence in the Senate's institutional competence to conduct them. In any event, the Framers of the Constitution vested that task in the Senate and nowhere else.

The last question is the continuing debate over how effective impeachment is as a remedy for executive or judicial misconduct. After the acquittal of President Clinton, some commentators have wondered whether impeachment is a meaningful option for dealing with a popular President's misconduct. Some believe that Clinton's acquittal strengthened the presidency because it makes it less likely future Presidents will face serious impeachment attempts for private misconduct. Others think Clinton's acquittal reflects an appropriate compromise that was consistent with the structure: he had been impeached by the House and therefore disgraced for his misconduct but not removed from office.

Nonetheless, it remains clear that impeachment remains an effective remedy for egregious judicial misconduct. Every official thus far impeached and removed from office has been a federal judge. This includes former federal district judge Thomas Porteous, whom the House impeached and the Senate voted to remove from office in 2010 on the basis of four articles of impeachment. One of those articles was based on misconduct that had begun before he assumed his federal judgeship and that, by his failing to disclose to the Senate in his confirmation proceedings, had included "knowingly [making] material false statements about his past to both the United States Senate and the Federal Bureau of Investigation in order to obtain the office of United States District Court Judge." The Senate went further to make Porteous the fourth official whom it not only removed but also disqualified from holding future federal offices and pensions.

Michael J. Gerhardt

See Also

Article I, Section 2, Clause 5 (Impeachment)

Article I, Section 3, Clause 7 (Punishment for Impeachment)

Article I, Section 5, Clause 2 (Expulsion Clause)

Article II, Section 4 (Standards for Impeachment)

Article III, Section 1 (Good Behavior Clause)

Suggestions for Further Research

Raoul Berger, Impeachment: The Constitutional Problems (1974)

Charles L. Black, Impeachment: A Handbook (1998)

Rebecca Brown, *When Political Questions Affect Individual Rights: The Other* Nixon v. United States, 1993 Sup. Ct. Rev. 125

Michael J. Gerhardt, The Federal Impeachment Process: A Constitutional and Historical Analysis (2d ed. 2000)

Peter Charles Hoffer & N.E.H. Hull, Impeachment in America, 1635–1805 (1984)

Buckner F. Melton, Jr., The First Impeachment: The Constitution's Framers and the Case of Senator William Blount (1998)

Richard A. Posner, An Affair of State: The Investigation, Impeachment and Trial of President Clinton (1999)

William H. Rehnquist, Grand Inquests: The Historic Impeachments of Justice Samuel Chase and President Andrew Johnson (1992)

Ronald D. Rotunda, *An Essay on the Constitutional Parameters of Federal Impeachment*, 76 Ky. L.J. 707 (1988)

Significant Cases

Powell v. McCormack, 395 U.S. 486 (1969)

Hastings v. United States, 802 F. Supp. 490 (D.D.C. 1992), *rev'd and remanded* Order No. 92-5327 (D.C. Cir. March 2, 1993); 837 F. Supp. 3 (D.D.C. 1993)

Nixon v. United States, 506 U.S. 224 (1993)

Punishment for Impeachment

Judgment in Cases of Impeachment shall not extend further than to removal from Office, and disqualification to hold and enjoy any Office of honor, Trust or Profit under the United States: but the Party convicted shall nevertheless be liable and subject to Indictment, Trial, Judgment and Punishment, according to Law.

(**Article I, Section 3, Clause 7**)

∼

*T*he Punishment for Impeachment Clause sets forth the scope and nature of the punishments that the Senate may impose in impeachment tri-

als. In fashioning this clause, the delegates to the Constitutional Convention deliberately distinguished impeachment in this country from the British system by limiting the punishments in the federal Constitution to those typically found in state constitutions, that is, removal and disqualification, in contrast to the House of Lords' practice of imposing any punishment, including death, in an impeachment proceeding.

Since ratification, four troublesome questions have arisen under this clause. The first was whether the Senate may impose the sanctions of removal and disqualification separately and, if so, how. The Senate claims that it may impose these sanctions by separate votes: (1) removal, involving the ouster of an official from the office he occupies at the time of his impeachment trial, and (2) disqualification, barring the person from ever serving again in the federal government. In 1862, 1913, and 2010, the Senate took separate votes to remove and disqualify judges West Humphreys, Robert Archbald, and Thomas Porteous, respectively. For each judge, a supermajority first voted to convict followed by a simple majority vote to disqualify. The Senate defended this practice on the ground that the clause mentioning disqualification does not specify the requisite vote for its imposition, although Article II, Section 4 mentions removal as following conviction. The Senate in 1862, 1913, and 2010 considered that the supermajority requirement was designed as a safeguard against removal that, once satisfied, did not extend to the separate imposition of disqualification.

The second question involves the proper sequence of impeachment and criminal proceedings. It is clear from practice and judicial interpretation that officials other than the President may be convicted and even imprisoned before impeachment. The question is whether a sitting President, though not singled out in the text of the Constitution, is immune from trial and conviction in the ordinary courts before impeachment and removal from office. The provision that a convicted official is "liable and subject to Indictment, Trial, Judgment and Punishment, according to Law" gives rise to two constructions. Alexander Hamilton in *The Federalist* No. 69 construed the clause as requiring that a President would first be impeached and removed from office and "would afterwards be liable to prosecution and punishment in the ordinary course of law." The argument, made by many of President William Jefferson Clinton's defenders during his impeachment and trial, is that prosecuting Presidents poses a unique risk not applicable to prosecuting the leaders of other branches because the executive branch is the only federal branch overseen by a single individual and thus prosecuting its leader—the President—uniquely risks paralyzing the entire branch he oversees.

The counter-arguments seem at least as strong. First, the clause could be read not as requiring that impeachment precede prosecution, but as reflecting an expectation that impeachments generally might but are not required to precede prosecutions. In other words, the Constitution merely provides that these proceedings are mutually exclusive. Second, the President is not above the law, and a President is subject to the same legal requirements and burdens as any citizen, as implied by two unanimous Supreme Court decisions: *United States v. Nixon* (1974) (the President is not immune to subpoenas for evidence in a federal criminal trial) and *Clinton v. Jones* (1997) (the President is not immune from civil litigation based on his personal, unofficial conduct). Third, several judges have been prosecuted (and even imprisoned) before being impeached. Indeed, several courts rejected their efforts to bar their prosecutions before being impeached. On the other hand, an impeachable offense (such as abuse of office) may not be a crime. If an impeachable offense had to be first enacted into a criminal code, then the House of Representatives would not have the "sole" power to impeach because a criminal law would first have to be passed and therefore approved by the other branches of government.

The third question involves the interpretation of the provision that "Judgment in Cases of Impeachment shall not extend further than to removal from Office, and disqualification to hold and enjoy any Office of honor, Trust or Profit under the United States." Throughout President Clinton's impeachment proceedings,

Members of Congress considered whether this language permitted the Congress to impose a sanction against him short of impeachment and removal, such as a resolution passed by the House or Senate denouncing him for his misconduct. The congressional and academic debates at the time remain the most extensive yet on the legitimacy of censure.

There are strong arguments against censure. First, the Constitution does not explicitly authorize censure. Second, the vesting of the impeachment power in Congress arguably implies the exclusion of other means by which to punish officials who have committed impeachable offenses. Third, the use of censure would undermine the Framers' objective to narrow the range of permissible sanctions in an impeachment trial. Fourth, allowing censure could upset the delicate system of checks and balances by making it easier for Congress to harass or embarrass a President. Fifth, censure conceivably constitutes a bill of attainder (a legislative imposition of a punishment that only a court should have been authorized to impose after a trial).

There are also arguments supporting censure. First, the relevant text seems to imply that "lesser" punishments than removal or disqualification are permissible. Second, other clauses of the Constitution (including the Speech and Debate Clause, the First Amendment's freedom of speech guarantee, and the vesting of power in the House and the Senate to keep journals of their respective proceedings) empower Members of Congress to enter critical comments about public figures into the congressional record. While a "censure" consisting of mere words may or may not be thought a meaningful punishment, such expression could be easily accomplished outside of the impeachment process as a matter of collective speech of Senators and Representatives. Third, historical practices support censure. The House and Senate have passed over a dozen such resolutions, including resolutions condemning Presidents James K. Polk and Andrew Jackson. Hence, the debates over censure, like those over the other questions about the appropriate sanctions the Senate may impose for presidential misconduct, are likely to persist until historical practice resolves the matter.

Michael J. Gerhardt

See Also

Article I, Section 2, Clause 5 (Impeachment)
Article I, Section 3, Clause 6 (Trial of Impeachment)
Article II, Section 4 (Standards for Impeachment)
Article III, Section 1 (Good Behavior Clause)

Suggestions for Further Research

RAOUL BERGER, IMPEACHMENT: THE CONSTITUTIONAL PROBLEMS (1974)

Arthur Bestor, *Impeachment*, 49 Wash. L. Rev. 255 (1973) (reviewing R. BERGER, IMPEACHMENT: THE CONSTITUTIONAL PROBLEMS (1973))

CHARLES L. BLACK, IMPEACHMENT: A HANDBOOK (1998)

MICHAEL J. GERHARDT, THE FEDERAL IMPEACHMENT PROCESS: A CONSTITUTIONAL AND HISTORICAL ANALYSIS (2D ED. 2000)

RICHARD A. POSNER, AN AFFAIR OF STATE: THE INVESTIGATION, IMPEACHMENT AND TRIAL OF PRESIDENT CLINTON (1999)

Ronald D. Rotunda, *An Essay on the Constitutional Parameters of Federal Impeachment*, 76 KY. L.J. 707 (1988)

EMILY FIELD VAN TASSEL, IMPEACHABLE OFFENSES: A DOCUMENTARY HISTORY 1787 TO THE PRESENT (1999)

Significant Cases

United States v. Isaacs, 493 F.2d 1124 (1974)
United States v. Nixon, 418 U.S. 683 (1974)
Nixon v. Fitzgerald, 457 U.S. 731 (1982)
Clinton v. Jones, 520 U.S. 681 (1997)

Election Regulations

The Times, Places and Manner of holding Elections for Senators and Representatives, shall be prescribed in each State by the Legislature thereof; but the Congress may at any time by Law make or alter such Regulations, except as to the Places of chusing Senators.

(**ARTICLE I, SECTION 4, CLAUSE 1**)

∼

*T*he purpose of this provision of the Constitution was twofold. First, it made clear the division of responsibility with respect to the conduct of the election of federal Senators and Representatives. That responsibility lay primarily with the states and secondarily with Congress. Second, the clause lodged the power to regulate elections in the respective legislative branches of the states and the federal government, not with the executive or judicial branches.

Opponents to the Constitution hotly contested the clause during the ratification debates. The concern of the Anti-Federalists was that the default prerogatives to Congress would result in Members of Congress manipulating election laws so that they could stay in office indefinitely. Alternatively, Congress might alter the times and places of elections so as to make it extremely difficult to vote, undermining the franchise. On the other hand, defenders of the clause argued that if Congress did not retain residual power to control federal elections, state officials might effectively destroy Congress by failing to make rules for the election of its Members. As Alexander Hamilton remarked in *The Federalist* No. 59, "every government ought to contain within itself the means of its own preservation." Hamilton argued that the provision was a reasonable compromise that gave Congress default powers that would be exercised "whenever extraordinary circumstances might render that interposition necessary to its safety." In addition, the fact that Congress as a whole, and not any single house of Congress, was authorized to make or alter regulations under the clause meant that a national consensus between the people's or "democratic" branch of the legislature and the Senate, representing the states, would have to take place before any changes could occur.

The Framers of the Constitution drew upon British precedents and state practices in their understanding of what constituted the "Times, Places and Manner of holding Elections," but in a more precise way. British and state practice had subsumed the qualifications of electors and candidates, and the times and places of elections, in the phrase "manner of elections." The Framers, on the other hand, thought the elements of elections should be more particularly delineated. As Hamilton's discussion in *The Federalist* Nos. 59–61 made clear, the "Times, Places and Manner" provisions of the Election Regulations Clause were to be taken literally. They referred to states having the primary power of determining the dates, the locations, and the conditions under which elections for federal Senators and Representatives would be held. Congress had only a secondary power in this regard and had no power to alter the location states chose for selecting Senators. This last, James Madison argued at the Constitutional Convention, was reserved to the state legislatures, which alone had the sovereign right to determine where to convene to elect Senators.

However, there were some additional restrictions. In response to the complaint that the federal government might attempt to manipulate the places elections took place to benefit "the wealthy and the well-born," Hamilton remarked in *The Federalist* No. 60 that securing the rich such a preference could only be done by "prescribing qualifications of property either for those who may elect or be elected. But this forms no part of the power to be conferred upon the national government. Its authority would be expressly restricted to the regulation of the *times*, the *places*, and the *manner* of elections. The qualifications of the persons who may choose or be chosen...are defined and fixed in the Constitution, and are unalterable by the legislature."

Since ratification of the Constitution, there have been many legal developments that have altered the provisions of Article I, Section 4, the most significant of which came after the Civil War. The Fifteenth Amendment (1870) prohibited voter discrimination on the basis of race. The Enforcement Act of 1870 had some beneficial effect in curbing the abuse of the electoral process, particularly in the South, but with its evisceration in *United States v. Reese* (1875) and *United States v. Cruikshank* (1876), Southern states were able effectively to disenfranchise black citizens.

The Voting Rights Act of 1965 resurrected tough legal prohibitions on racial discrimination in voting and transformed Southern politics and American politics in the process. The most important and controversial of the act's original provisions, Sections 4 and 5, required states predominantly in the South (covered by Section 4) to seek "preclearance" (under Section 5) from the federal Department of Justice or U.S. District Court for the District of Columbia for any new voting practices or procedures postdating November 1, 1964. The constitutionality of these provisions was upheld in *South Carolina v. Katzenbach* (1966). The 1970 Voting Rights Act proposed to reduce the voting age in national, state, and local elections to eighteen. In *Oregon v. Mitchell* (1970), the Court upheld this provision as it applied to national elections but disallowed it as it applied to state and local elections. The Twenty-sixth Amendment effectively overruled this latter holding. The scope of the Voting Rights Act's coverage has increased over the decades and continues to impose significant constraints on states covered by the act, particularly when it comes to redistricting.

In addition to statutory constraints, Congress and the people have altered the electoral process through the amending process. The Seventeenth Amendment altered the manner of conducting the elections of Senators by requiring their popular election. The Nineteenth Amendment prohibited voter discrimination on the basis of sex. The Twenty-fourth Amendment prohibited poll taxes in federal elections, and as mentioned above, the Twenty-sixth Amendment gave eighteen-year-olds the right to vote.

Despite Alexander Hamilton's assurance that Congress would regulate elections only in "extraordinary circumstances," congressional intervention has been significant. In 1842, Congress required the election of Members of the House of Representatives by district. Repealed in 1929, the single-Member district rule was restored by Congress in 1967. Also, until 1929 Congress required that each district's territory be compact and contiguous with substantially the same number of inhabitants. *Wood v. Broom* (1932).

In recent decades, the Supreme Court has stepped into the electoral process. In *Wesberry v.*

Sanders (1964), the Supreme Court determined that, despite congressional practice, Article I, Section 2, Clause 1 mandated that the "one person, one vote" formula be applied to each congressional district. Critics of the Court's decision have noted that it ignored the language of Article I, Section 4, Clause 1, which appeared to leave questions of reapportionment and redistricting to the legislative, not judicial, branch of government. Under the Fourteenth Amendment's Equal Protection Clause, the Court has also indicated that gerrymandered districts can be an indication of an unconstitutional, racially motivated redistricting plan. *Shaw v. Reno* (1993). However, the Court has not yet required, as a constitutional matter, that districts be compact and contiguous. *Shaw v. Reno* and *Miller v. Johnson* (1995) also highlighted the potential conflict between the demands of the Voting Rights Act for the creation of "safe minority seats" and the constitutional prohibition on redistricting in which race is the predominant factor motivating the redistricting. The passage of the 2006 Voting Rights Act has raised the further constitutional question of whether jurisdictions covered by Section 5 of the act should still have to seek preclearance from the federal Department of Justice for changes to their electoral practices, which the 2006 Voting Rights Act extended through 2031.

Beginning with the Tillman Act in 1907, Congress has imposed a growing number of restrictions on elections and campaign financing. The most significant piece of legislation has been the 1971 Federal Election Campaign Act, amended in 1974. It was this legislation that was at issue in the Supreme Court's seminal decision, *Buckley v. Valeo* (1976), which, in the face of a First Amendment challenge, set the ground rules for campaign finance legislation, generally disallowing restrictions on expenditures by candidates, but permitting restrictions on contributions by individuals and corporations. The Bipartisan Campaign Finance Reform Act of 2002, which amended FECA, sought to impose further restrictions on "soft money" contributions and electioneering communications, such as issue advertisements by corporations and unions, but these latter provisions were deemed unconstitutional restrictions on political speech in *Citizens United v. Federal Election Commission* (2010).

Anthony A. Peacock

See Also

Article I, Section 2, Clause 1 (Elector Qualifications)
Article I, Section 2, Clause 2 (Qualifications for Representatives)
Article I, Section 3, Clause 1 (Senate)
Article I, Section 3, Clause 3 (Qualifications for Senators)
Article I, Section 5, Clause 1 (Qualifications and Quorum)
Article II, Section 1, Clause 2 (Presidential Electors)
Amendment XIV (Equal Protection)
Amendment XV (Suffrage—Race)
Amendment XVII (Popular Election of Senators)
Amendment XIX (Suffrage—Sex)
Amendment XXIV (Poll Taxes)
Amendment XXVI (Suffrage—Age)

Suggestions for Further Research

Ward E.Y. Elliott, The Rise of Guardian Democracy: The Supreme Court's Role in Voting Rights Disputes, 1845–1969 (1974)

Robert G. Natelson, *The Original Scope of the Congressional Power to Regulate Elections*, 13 U. Pa. J. Const. L. 1 (2010)

Anthony A. Peacock, Deconstructing the Republic: Voting Rights, the Supreme Court, and the Founders' Republicanism Reconsidered (2008)

Bradley A. Smith, Unfree Speech: The Folly of Campaign Finance Reform (2001)

Significant Cases

United States v. Reese, 92 U.S. 214 (1875)
United States v. Cruikshank, 92 U.S. 542 (1876)
Wood v. Broom, 287 U.S. 1 (1932)
Smith v. Allwright, 321 U.S. 649 (1944)
Wesberry v. Sanders, 376 U.S. 1 (1964)
South Carolina v. Katzenbach, 383 U.S. 301 (1966)
Powell v. McCormack, 349 U.S. 486 (1969)
Oregon v. Mitchell, 400 U.S. 112 (1970)
Beer v. United States, 425 U.S. 130 (1976)
Buckley v. Valeo, 424 U.S. 1 (1976)
Karcher v. Daggett, 462 U.S. 725 (1983)

Thornburg v. Gingles, 478 U.S. 30 (1986)

Shaw v. Reno, 509 U.S. 630 (1993)

Miller v. Johnson, 515 U.S. 900 (1995)

United States Term Limits, Inc. v. Thornton, 514 U.S. 779 (1995)

Georgia v. Ashcroft, 539 U.S. 461 (2003)

McConnell v. FEC, 540 U.S. 93 (2003)

League of United Latin American Citizens v. Perry, 548 U.S. 399 (2006)

Northwest Austin Municipal Utility District No. 1 v. Holder, 557 U.S. 193 (2009)

Citizens United v. Federal Elections Comm'n, 558 U.S. 310 (2010)

Meetings of Congress Clause

The Congress shall assemble at least once in every Year, and such Meeting shall be on the first Monday in December, unless they shall by Law appoint a different Day.

(ARTICLE I, SECTION 4, CLAUSE 2)

~

*E*ver mindful of federalism and the separation of powers, the delegates to the Constitutional Convention believed that the scheduling of congressional sessions was a significant issue. There was no thought given to the British model, in which the executive called Parliament to meet. The Framers did allow the President to convene Congress in a special session for "extraordinary Occasions" (Article II, Section 3), but they fixed the date of Congress's regular sessions to keep it free from executive control.

James Madison submitted that the "Legislature shall meet on the first Monday in December in every year" and the delegates added a provision to allow for a different date "appointed by law" (thus permitting the possibility of executive veto). At first, the delegates argued over the date on the basis of convenience or for extrinsic concerns. Gouverneur Morris moved to substitute May for December because the United States would likely legislate in response to Europe's measures, which were generally planned during

the winter and would likely arrive in the United States by spring. Madison changed his mind and stated that he also preferred May because the season would be more agreeable to traveling to and from the capital. In contrast, James Wilson and Oliver Ellsworth argued that requiring the legislature to assemble in December would be more convenient for private business, because most of the Members would be involved with agriculture during the spring and summer.

Edmund Randolph, however, turned the debate to concerns for the structural integrity of the polity. He noted that the state elections would better coincide with the December date, and the vote to require assembly in the month of May did not pass. The issue was not closed, however. Madison was in favor of annual meetings, but of leaving the date to "be fixed or varied by law." Gouverneur Morris and Rufus King believed yearly meetings were not necessary, for there would not be enough legislative business for Congress to deal with annually.

Nathaniel Gorham of Massachusetts focused the delegates' attention once again on the structural needs of the new government. He argued that the time should be fixed to prevent disputes from arising within the legislature, and to allow the states to adjust their elections to correspond with the fixed date. A fixed date also corresponded to the tradition in the states of having annual meetings. Finally, Gorham concluded that the legislative branch should be required to meet at least once a year to act as a check upon the executive department.

Ultimately, Article I, Section 4, Clause 2 bound legislative discretion and placed the requirement for annual legislative sessions "beyond the power of faction, and of party, of power, and of corruption," according to Justice Joseph Story in *Commentaries on the Constitution of the United States* (1833). In practice, prior to the passage of the Twentieth Amendment in 1933, each numbered Congress existed from March 4 of the odd-numbered year to March 3 of the next odd-numbered year, but the regular sessions began on the first Monday in December and generally lasted well into spring.

Such an arrangement did not become controversial until the sixth Congress, elected in 1798 and controlled by Federalists, met in its second session in December 1800, after it was clear that Jefferson had won the presidency. Its sweeping legislative program embittered the new President, who sought the following year, with his new Republican majority, to undo what that previous Congress had wrought.

David F. Forte

See Also
Article II, Section 3 (Convening of Congress)
Amendment XX (Presidential Terms)

Qualifications and Quorum

Each House shall be the Judge of the Elections, Returns and Qualifications of its own Members, and a Majority of each shall constitute a Quorum to do Business; but a smaller Number may adjourn from day to day, and may be authorized to compel the Attendance of absent Members, in such Manner, and under such Penalties as each House may provide.
(**Article I, Section 5, Clause 1**)

$\sim$

*T*he tradition of permitting a legislative body to judge its own elections, returns, and qualifications was fairly uniform throughout England and America. Parliament had begun wresting control over elections from the Chancery (which was beholden to the crown) in the mid-sixteenth century. By 1624, the Parliament's privilege of examining the election returns was undisputed.

At the time of the Constitutional Convention, eight states had similar clauses in their state constitutions and the Framers approved the provision without debate. According to Justice Joseph Story in his *Commentaries on the Constitution of the United States* (1833), it was a necessary attribute of the separation of powers. If that

power, Justice Story wrote, were "lodged in any other, than the legislative body itself, its independence, its purity, and even its existence and action may be destroyed, or put into imminent danger." Further, Story declared, the power allowed each House to "sustain the free choice of its constituents." The only objections to the clause in the state ratifying conventions were by those who wanted the power to judge elections to reside with the state legislatures, as it had under the Articles of Confederation.

The power to judge elections extends to investigations of fraud. It includes the power to subpoena witnesses and to impose punishment for perjury. There have been a number of noteworthy cases decided by the House or the Senate under the clause.

In 1793, the Senate investigated the qualifications of Albert Gallatin, a rival to Alexander Hamilton and his economic theories, when the Pennsylvania state legislature elected him to the U.S. Senate. Born in Switzerland, Gallatin had been in the United States for thirteen years, but it was unclear whether he had been a resident of Pennsylvania for the requisite nine years. Two Senate committees, dominated by Federalists, found against him, and he was barred from the seat.

During the Civil War, the Senate judged whether James H. Lane of Kansas was entitled to be a Senator even though he accepted a Brigadier General's commission shortly after arriving in Washington. Lane was apparently in violation of the Incompatibility Clause (Article I, Section 6, Clause 2). Even though the Senate Judiciary Committee found against Lane, the full Senate nonetheless accepted his credentials.

In 1935, West Virginia elected Rush D. Holt as Senator even though he would not be thirty years of age for another seven months. Holt promised he would not present himself to take the oath until his thirtieth birthday. He did so, and the Senate engaged in a long and contested investigation, eventually seating Holt on the ground that the requirement of thirty years of age applied only when the candidate took office.

The manner in which the House and Senate decided qualification cases suggests that the power was unreviewable in the courts. And in

Morgan v. United States (1986), then-Circuit Judge Antonin Scalia declared that the House's determination as to which of two candidates had been elected was nonjusticiable under this clause, a position supported in dicta by previous Supreme Court cases. However, when the House of Representatives sought to expand the definition of "qualifications" beyond those expressly listed in Article I, Section 2, Clause 2 that it was judging under this clause, then the Court not only found the issue justiciable, but struck down the action by the House. *Powell v. McCormack* (1969).

The second section of the Qualifications and Quorum Clause, dealing with the numbers necessary to constitute a quorum, caused more concern. All agreed that the two-thirds requirement under the Articles of Confederation had been a major hindrance. Nathaniel Gorham, however, objected to even a simple majority, as it might cause a "great delay" in the legislature's business. Most of the debate revolved around the fear of factions. John Mercer of Maryland thought that "[s]o great a number will put it in the power of a few by seceding at a critical moment." George Mason answered that by having a quorum set at less than a majority would "allow a small number of members of the two houses to make laws." The attempt to fix a specific number of votes for a quorum failed and the majority provision remained in the text. The provision allowing day-to-day adjournment by a smaller number permits the business of each house to lie over without the need of continually calling for a quorum.

The convening of the House and the Senate of the First Congress in 1789 was in fact delayed until a quorum of Members arrived in New York to begin the business of the new government. For some decades after the Constitution, the House of Representatives did not pass legislation unless a full quorum of the House approved the bill. Those present but not voting could prevent a quorum. In 1890, the House changed its rules to determine that a quorum is satisfied if a majority of Members are present, even if they withhold their votes on a particular bill. The Supreme Court upheld that procedure in *United States v. Ballin* (1892), and later found that the procedure was the "almost universally accepted common-

law rule." *FTC v. Flotill Products, Inc.* (1967). It continues to the present. Some concern has been raised over how Congress could constitutionally meet and reach a quorum in the event of a catastrophe that killed or left Members of Congress from gathering. The House would likely be unable to correct the Constitutional requirement of a majority quorum through the clause that allows it to change its proceedings (Rules Clause, Article I, Section 5, Clause 2). Like the Twenty-fifth Amendment, which sought to regularize presidential succession, a Constitutional amendment may be the only solution to solve the potential problem for Congress to be able to operate during a national emergency.

The third and final part of the clause, authorizing each house "to compel the attendance of absent members," introduced by John Randolph and James Madison, also passed without debate. It was an additional guard against the power of a minority to abuse the quorum process. Justice Story declared that the provision did away with any apprehension that a minority could "subvert the fundamental principle of a republican government" by intentionally preventing the formation of a quorum. Under current practice, fifteen Members of the House or a majority of the Senate may order the Sergeant at Arms of each respective chamber to compel the attendance of absent Members. By motion of the requisite number of Members of the House or of the Senate, the Sergeant at Arms is authorized to make arrests of recalcitrant Members with the aid of police, an event that has occurred a number of times during the history of Congress.

David F. Forte

See Also

Article I, Section 2, Clause 2 (Qualifications for Representatives)

Article I, Section 5, Clause 2 (Rules Clause)

Article I, Section 6, Clause 2 (Incompatibility Clause)

Amendment XXV (Presidential Succession)

Suggestion for Further Research

Congressional Quarterly's Guide to Congress (Mary Cohn ed., 4th ed. 1991)

Paul E. Salamanca & James E. Keller, *The Legislative Privilege to Judge the Qualifications, Elections, and Returns of Members*, 95 Ky. L.J. 241 (2007)

Adrian Vermeule, *The Constitutional Law of Congressional Procedure*, 71 U. Chi. L. Rev. 361 (2004)

Significant Cases

United States v. Ballin, 144 U.S. 1 (1892)

Reed v. County Commissioners of Delaware County, 277 U.S. 376 (1928)

Barry v. United States ex rel. Cunningham, 279 U.S. 597 (1929)

FTC v. Flotill Products, Inc., 389 U.S. 179 (1967)

Powell v. McCormack, 395 U.S. 486 (1969)

Roudebush v. Hartke, 405 U.S. 15 (1972)

Morgan v. United States, 801 F.2d 445 (U.S. App. D.C. 1986)

Rules Clause

Each House may determine the Rules of its Proceedings ...
(ARTICLE I, SECTION 5, CLAUSE 2)

~

*T*he Constitution grants the House and the Senate the power to determine the rules of their respective proceedings. In *A Familiar Exposition of the Constitution of the United States* (1840), Justice Joseph Story wrote that without this power, "it would be utterly impracticable to transact the business of the nation at all, or at least, to transact it with decency, deliberation, and order. Without rules, no public body can suitably perform its functions. If rules are made, they are mere nullities, unless the persons on whom they are to operate, can be compelled to obey them." Consequently, the Rules Clause has been interpreted by the Supreme Court to grant each House broad discretion in determining the rules of its own internal operations.

In *United States v. Ballin* (1892), the Supreme Court was asked to determine the constitutionality of a House rule that allowed the Speaker of the House to count for purposes of a quorum Members whom he ascertained were part of a cabal

that was simply refusing to answer a quorum call in an attempt to deny the House a quorum and stop legislative business. In upholding the rule's constitutionality, the Court stated that "[n]either do the advantages or disadvantages, the wisdom or folly, of such a rule present any matters for judicial consideration. With the courts the question is only one of power. The Constitution empowers each house to determine its rules of proceedings." The Court continued that "[i]t is no objection to the validity of a rule that a different one has been prescribed and in force for a length of time. The power to make rules is not one which once exercised is exhausted. It is a continuous power, always subject to be exercised by the House, and, within the limitations suggested, absolute and beyond the challenge of any other body or tribunal." In *NLRB v. Canning* (2014), the Supreme Court held that for purposes of the Recess Appointments Clause (Article II, Section 2, Clause 3), the Senate has the power under the Rules Clause to determine when it is in session.

While the *Ballin* Court emphasized that neither house could constitutionally adopt rules that "ignore constitutional restraints," insofar as a House or Senate rule affects only its internal operations, the courts have held that challenges to such rules are nonjusticiable under two separate doctrines.

First, as the Supreme Court observed in *Allen v. Wright* (1984), "[t]he law of Article III standing is built on a single basic idea—the idea of separation of powers." Under current standing rules, it is unlikely a federal legislator could establish standing to challenge the constitutionality of a House or Senate rule when the body as a whole has already rejected such a challenge; unless, as the Supreme Court stated in *Raines v. Byrd* (1997), the challenged rule has "completely nullified" the votes of federal legislators.

Second, as the Supreme Court stated in *Baker v. Carr* (1962), under the political question doctrine a court will not hear a case if sufficient separation of powers concerns are raised, and such is the case when there is a "textually demonstrable constitutional commitment of the issue to a coordinate political department...or the impossibility of a court's undertaking independent resolution without expressing lack of the respect due coordinate branches of government." The Rules Clause would seem to constitute a "textually demonstrable constitutional commitment" of the rulemaking power to each house under the Constitution.

David F. Forte

See Also

Article 1, Section 5, Clause 1 (Qualifications and Quorum)

Suggestions for Further Research

Paul Taylor, *Proposals to Prevent Discontinuity in Government and Preserve the Right to Elected Representation*, 54 SYRACUSE L. REV. 435 (2004)

Significant Cases

United States v. Ballin, 144 U.S. 1 (1892)
Baker v. Carr, 369 U.S. 186 (1962)
Allen v. Wright 468 U.S. 750 (1984)
Raines v. Byrd, 521 U.S. 811 (1997)
National Labor Relations Board v. Noel Canning, 573 U.S.___ (2014)

Expulsion Clause

Each House may . . . punish its Members for disorderly Behaviour, and, with the Concurrence of two thirds, expel a Member.
(ARTICLE I, SECTION 5, CLAUSE 2)

$\sim$

*A*lthough the original proposal to give each house of Congress the power to expel lacked a supermajority requirement, James Madison, pointing out the danger that a majority faction could abuse its power by expelling Members of the minority, successfully moved to insert the two-thirds rule. Unlike the exclusion power of Article I, Section 5, Clause 1, there are no judicially enforceable constitutional standards limiting the use of the expulsion power other than the supermajority requirement. *In re Chapman*

(1897). Moreover, the courts generally regard disputes arising from the procedural rules of Congress as nonjusticiable (not amenable to judicial review), unless Congress "ignores constitutional restraints or violates fundamental rights." *United States v. Ballin* (1892). *Powell v. McCormack* (1969), for example, assumed that the case would be nonjusticiable if two-thirds of the House had "expelled" Congressman Adam Clayton Powell instead of "excluding" him.

The Expulsion Clause stands as the analog to the impeachment clauses. It is the only constitutional mechanism by which a sitting Member of Congress can be removed from office. Alexander Hamilton assumed that Members of the legislature could be impeached, and some comments in the ratifying conventions presumed the same. Some scholarly commentary suggest that the various ways in which the Constitution refers to the term "officer" may indicate that Members of the legislature could be impeached, but historical practice has been to the contrary. In 1797, the Senate expelled William Blount, but it later refused to convict him on a bill of impeachment because it concluded that there was a lack of jurisdiction. Subsequent interpretation of the Senate's action, supported in particular by Justice Joseph Story, has found the Senate's action dispositive: Members of Congress may be expelled by their own respective body, but they cannot be impeached. Story's position is supported at least in part by the text of the Constitution. The existence of the specific removal provisions for Members of Congress negates any inference that impeachment exists as an alternative removal mechanism.

Since 1789, the Senate has had nine expulsion proceedings out of which fifteen Senators were expelled, most of them early in the Civil War on grounds of supporting the rebellion. The House has also proceeded against twenty-nine of its Members but has expelled only five, two for corruption and three for supporting the rebellion.

More frequent have been instances when each house has punished its respective Members by a simple majority. Punishments have included censure (or the somewhat lesser "denouncement"), reprimand, loss of seniority, removal from committee or subcommittee chairmanship, and fine. Each house sets its own procedures for punishments less than expulsion. Conviction is by a simple majority. There have been a total of nine Senators and twenty-three House members censured. Censure in the House is more formal. The censured Member must rise while the Speaker reads aloud the actions for which he is being rebuked. In addition, when a Member of Congress is convicted of a crime, he is expected to refrain from voting unless and until his conviction is overturned or he is re-elected.

One important recent development is the establishment of the Office of Congressional Ethics, an internal entity charged with reviewing allegations of misconduct and recommending action to the House Ethics Committee. The Senate has not taken similar action.

David F. Forte

See Also

Article I, Section 5, Clause 1 (Qualifications and Quorum)

Suggestions for Further Research

Ittai Bar-Siman-Tov, *Lawmakers as Lawbreakers*, 52 Wm. & Mary L. Rev. 805 (2010)

Anne M. Butler & Wendy Wolff, United States Senate Election, Expulsion, and Censure Cases, 1793–1990 (1995)

Josh Chafetz, *Leaving the House: The Constitutional Status of Resignation from the House of Representatives*, 58 Duke L. J. 177 (2008)

Josh Chafetz, *Congress's Constitution*, 160 U. Pa. L. Rev. 715 (2012)

Laura Krugman Ray, *Discipline Through Delegation: Solving the Problem of Congressional Housecleaning*, 55 U. Pitt. L. Rev. 389 (1994)

John C. Roberts, *Are Congressional Committees Constitutional?: Radical Textualism, Separation of Powers, and the Enactment Process*, 52 Case W. Res. L. Rev. 489 (2001)

Ronald D. Rotunda, *An Essay on the Constitutional Parameters of Federal Impeachment*, 76 Ky. L.J. 707 (1988)

Significant Cases

United States v. Ballin, 144 U.S. 1 (1892)

In re Chapman, 166 U.S. 661 (1897)

Powell v. McCormack, 395 U.S. 486 (1969)

House Journal

Each House shall keep a Journal of its Proceedings, and from time to time publish the same, excepting such Parts as may in their Judgment require Secrecy; and the Yeas and Nays of the Members of either House on any question shall, at the Desire of one fifth of those Present, be entered on the Journal.

(**Article I, Section 5, Clause 3**)

              ~

*T*he requirement to publish a journal of each house's proceedings occasioned little debate either in the Constitutional Convention or at the ratifying conventions. The British provenance of the practice was well established. The official House of Lords Journal and House of Commons Journal had begun in the early sixteenth century, but the "Parliament Rolls of Medieval England" stretched back much further into the thirteenth century. Parliament's journals, however, merely summarized the activities of each house: the recording of bills proposed, votes counted, and bills passed. Only beginning in 1771 was there a concerted effort to have the actual debates set down, which Parliament finally acceded to in 1803.

Although Justice Joseph Story stated in his *Commentaries on the Constitution of the United States* (1833), "The object of the whole clause is to ensure publicity to the proceedings of the legislature, and a correspondent responsibility of the members to their respective constituents," the Framers in fact did not require the recording of debates but only the basic proceedings as had been the previous British practice. In fact, the official journals of each house contain a list of the bills and resolutions that are introduced, but they do not normally include the text. Instead, in the early decades of the republic, newspaper reporters, either from the galleries or more frequently from the floor, attempted to record or summarize debates for their publications.

Moreover, there was a provision for secrecy in the clause, which stirred much controversy. At the Constitutional Convention, Oliver Ellsworth unsuccessfully moved to have the secrecy option deleted, while at the Virginia ratifying convention, Patrick Henry railed, "The liberties of a people never were, nor ever will be, secure, when the transactions of their rulers may be concealed from them." Others feared that, even aside from the secrecy provision, the permission to publish a journal "from time to time" would allow either branch of Congress to conceal its doings. James Madison assured his fellow Virginians that the discretion was only to allow flexibility for the purposes of accuracy and convenience.

The secrecy provision applies to whether the House or the Senate will have its daily proceedings accessible to the public. Both history and judicial opinion have determined that each house possesses complete discretion over what proceedings shall be secret. *Field v. Clark* (1892). For the first twenty years of the country, secret sessions were frequent. Beginning with the War of 1812, however, both houses have kept most of their proceedings open to the public. The Senate is most likely to hold secret sessions, but over the last seventy-five years, it has done so only during debates over impeachment, classified information, and national defense. The Senate did keep its committee sessions closed, however, until the 1970s.

In 1834, Joseph Gales and William Seaton began the commercially published *Annals of Congress.* Its formal title is *The Debates and Proceedings in the Congress of the United States.* Part of *The Annals* consisted of reports of the First Congress from Thomas Lloyd, a shorthand writer, who published his record of debates in *The Congressional Register,* but whose product has been termed "incomplete and unreliable." Unfortunately, Lloyd was often intoxicated when he took notes, and a later comparison of his notes to what he published in *The Congressional Register* show "only slight resemblance" between the two. *The Annals* also compiled selected paraphrased remarks of the Members of Congress in their speeches and debates gathered from newspaper accounts. The project took twenty-two years to complete, and when finished, covered the years from 1789 to 1824. Congress began underwriting the project in 1849. Meanwhile, in 1824, Gales and Seaton attempted to record contemporaneous debates and publish them in the *Register of the Debates in Congress,* which continued until 1837. Both publications reported Members' remarks in the third person.

A competitive private publication, *The Congressional Globe,* began in 1833. Published by Francis Blair and John C. Rives, it did not at first attempt to include debates verbatim, but only summaries. Reportedly, as Gales and Seaton were Whigs, and Blair and Rives Democrats, partisanship marred the objectivity of *The Globe's* editing. Later, *The Globe* attempted to record Members' statements verbatim and in the first person. The publication continued until 1873, at which time Congress initiated *The Congressional Record.* The now official *Record* reports the debates on the floor of each House nearly verbatim, and it can also include undelivered remarks and documents. A federal judge has held that the rules allowing a Member of Congress to edit his remarks before publication are unreviewable by the courts. *Gregg v. Barrett* (1985).

Media access continues to be a major method for the political accountability of the House and Senate. In the very early years, as noted, newspaper reporters normally had free access to the floor to report on or record the statements of the Members. In recent years, radio and television have increased the public's access to Congress's proceedings.

David F. Forte

See Also

Article I, Section 6, Clause 1 (Speech and Debate Clause)

Suggestions for Further Research

N. David Bleisch, *The Congressional Record and the First Amendment: Accuracy Is the Best Policy,* 12 B.C. Envtl. Aff. L. Rev. 341 (1985)

James H. Huston, *The Creation of the Constitution: The Integrity of the Documentary Record,* 65 Tex. L. Rev. 1 (1986)

Richard J. McKinney, *An Overview of the Congressional Record and Its Predecessor* Publications, in 46 Law Libr. Lights 16 (Winter 2002)

Elizabeth Gregory McPherson, *Reporting the Debates of Congress*, 28 Q. J. of Speech 141 (1942)

Seth Barrett Tillman, *The Annals of Congress, the Original Public Meaning of the Succession Clause, and the Problem of Constitutional Memory* (2011), at http://papers.ssrn.com/sol3/papers.cfm?abstract_id=1524008

Significant Cases

Field v. Clark, 143 U.S. 649 (1892)

Gregg v. Barrett, 771 F.2d 539 (D.C. Cir. 1985)

Adjournment

Neither House, during the Session of Congress, shall, without the Consent of the other, adjourn for more than three days, nor to any other Place than that in which the two Houses shall be sitting.

(**Article I, Section 5, Clause 4**)

~

*D*ividing the legislative department into two chambers was one of the most important checks on the legislative power that the Framers devised. At the same time, the Framers believed that it was vital to the affairs of the nation that one house not be permitted to keep Congress as a whole from meeting and performing its functions. Under this clause, neither house can use its power to adjourn to another time or to another place in order to check the actions of the other legislative chamber. If the two houses cannot agree on a time of adjournment, then pursuant to Article II, Section 3, Clause 1 the President can "adjourn them to such Time as he shall think proper." At the Virginia ratifying convention, James Monroe and George Mason worried that the clause might give the Senate the power to prevent House Members from returning home, but James Madison opined that the President's power to resolve the dispute would prevent the Senate from keeping the House hostage to its will. Since the time of the First Congress, the two chambers have always reached agreement, and the President has never had to intervene.

At the Constitutional Convention, Rufus King raised a different concern. He worried that the two houses of Congress could actually move the seat of government merely by agreeing upon the place to which they would adjourn. The Convention decided that Congress could by law establish the seat of government (see Article I, Section 8, Clause 17), but the Framers left Congress the option of making temporary moves in the face of exigencies. Thus, during the yellow-fever outbreaks in the 1790s, the three departments moved from Philadelphia to Trenton. Of course, during the War of 1812, the government fled from Washington.

Congress has followed the text of the Adjournment Clause. Either house may adjourn or recess for up to three days on its own motion. Longer adjournments or recesses, or adjournments sine die, ending a session require the concurrent resolution of both houses. An adjournment of whatever length ends the "legislative day," requiring much legislative business to be recommenced when the chamber reconvenes. In the Senate, introduced bills must lie over one legislative day before they can be considered. Recesses do not interrupt the legislative process.

A decision by Congress to adjourn is also part of each house's power to "determine the Rules of its Proceedings" (Article I, Section 5, Clause 2). As Thomas Jefferson wrote in 1790, "Each house of Congress possesses this natural right of governing itself, and, consequently, of fixing its own times and places of meeting, so far as it has not been abridged by . . . the Constitution." The Supreme Court earlier held in *United States v. Ballin* (1892) that when it comes to the constitutional power of each house to determine the rules of its proceedings, "[n]either do the advantages or disadvantages, the wisdom or folly, of such a rule present any matters for judicial consideration. With the courts the question is only one of power. The constitution empowers each house to determine its rules of proceedings." Consequently, courts can be expected to defer to the political branches the question of whether or not Congress is adjourned or in session.

The issue of what constitutes an adjournment directly implicates the President's power to "fill up all Vacancies that may happen during the Recess of the Senate" (Article II, Section 2, Clause 3). The validity of the President making recess appointments is covered in Article II, Section 2, Clause 3 (Recess Appointments Clause).

David F. Forte

See Also

Article I, Section 4, Clause 2 (Meetings of Congress Clause)

Article I, Section 5, Clause 2 (Rules Clause)

Article I, Section 8, Clause 17 (Enclave Clause)

Article II, Section 2, Clause 3 (Recess Appointments Clause)

Article II, Section 3 (Convening of Congress)

Significant Case

United States v. Ballin, 144 U.S. 1 (1892)

Compensation Clause

The Senators and Representatives shall receive a Compensation for their Services, to be ascertained by Law, and paid out of the Treasury of the United States.

(Article I, Section 6, Clause 1)

~

*T*he Framers of the Constitution included the Compensation Clause (also known as the Ascertainment Clause) in an attempt to structure the incentives facing Senators or Representatives in desirable ways. Two questions were critical: Would federal legislators be paid at all? If so, would they be paid by their respective states, or by the federal government?

First, as to whether federal legislators would be paid, the Constitutional Convention feared that

unpaid legislators would turn to corruption to supplement their incomes. As Justice Joseph Story wrote in his *Commentaries on the Constitution of the United States* (1833), "they might be compelled by their necessities, or tempted by their wants, to yield up their independence, and perhaps their integrity, to the allurements of the corrupt, or the opulent." Thus, supporters of the federal legislative salary argued that providing no salary would not attract candidates motivated only by a sense of duty, but would instead permit only wealthy candidates, creating a de facto legislative plutocracy.

The second question involved the source of the payment. Under the Articles of Confederation, the states, rather than Congress, had paid the salaries of delegates to Congress. Most of the delegates to the Convention, by contrast, hoped that requiring federal legislators to be paid according to federal law, and out of federal funds rather than state funds, would make them less beholden to state governments. As Edmund Randolph put it, "if the States were to pay the members of the National Legislature, a dependence would be created that would vitiate the whole system."

Modern controversies over the Compensation Clause have focused on different questions. Who should be able to change the level of legislative compensation, and how may the changes be made? The leading case is the 1988 decision of the Court of Appeals for the District of Columbia Circuit in *Humphrey v. Baker*. Under the mechanism for legislative compensation then in place, established by the Federal Salary Act of 1967, a "Quadrennial Commission" would make recommendations for salary increases to the President, who in turn had statutory authority to recommend increases to the Congress. The presidential recommendations became effective as law unless Congress enacted a joint resolution of disapproval within thirty days. After this procedure brought about a legislative pay raise effective in 1987, Senator Gordon Humphrey and five Members of the House sued the Secretary of the Treasury, claiming that the Salary Act violated both the Compensation Clause and the nondelegation doctrine. Relying heavily on precedent, the Court of Appeals rejected both claims. It read the Salary Act as fully complying with the clause, because the procedure that produced the pay increase (namely the delegation to the President followed by the disapproval option) was itself "ascertained" by statute, the clause was satisfied. *Humphrey*'s capacious reading of the clause suggests that Congress has broad flexibility in designing schemes of legislative compensation, subject to the restrictions of the Twenty-seventh Amendment, which now prevents a sitting Congress from giving itself a pay raise to take effect during its term. In *Schonberg v. Federal Election Commission* (2011), the U.S. District Court for the District of Columbia held that the Compensation Clause only indicates the procedure by which compensation is determined, and it does not limit what Congress may define as compensation.

Adrian Vermeule

See Also

Article II, Section 1, Clause 7 (Compensation)
Article III, Section 1 (Judicial Compensation Clause)
Amendment XXVII (Congressional Compensation)

Suggestions for Further Research

Articles of Confederation, Article V

L. Anthony Sutin, *Check, Please: Constitutional Dimensions of Halting the Pay of Public Officials*, 26 J. Legis. 221 (2000)

Adrian Vermeule, *The Constitutional Law of Official Compensation*, 102 Colum. L. Rev. 501 (2002)

Adrian Vermeule, *Selection Effects in Constitutional Law*, 91 Va. L. Rev. 953 (2005)

Significant Cases

Pressler v. Simon, 428 F. Supp. 302 (D.D.C. 1976) (three judge court), *aff'd sub nom.* Pressler v. Blumenthal, 434 U.S. 1028 (1978)

Humphrey v. Baker, 848 F.2d 211 (D.C. Cir. 1988)

Schonberg v. Federal Election Commission, 792 F. Supp. 2d 20 (D.D.C. 2011)

Privilege from Arrest

The Senators and Representatives...shall in all Cases, except Treason, Felony, and Breach of the Peace, be privileged from Arrest during their Attendance at the Session of their respective Houses, and in going to and returning from the same ...

(Article I, Section 6, Clause 1)

～

*T*he Privilege from Arrest Clause provides a Member of Congress a privilege from civil arrest only, but not from other civil processes. Even the privilege from civil arrest would be valid only while Congress is in session.

Civil arrest is the physical detainment of a person, by lawful authority, to answer a civil demand against him. At the time the Constitution was adopted, civil arrests were common. *Long v. Ansell* (1934). Following long-standing English practice, the Framers almost certainly saw the immunity as a method of protecting the legislative process. Today, civil arrest is rarely, if ever, practiced, so this clause is virtually obsolete and has little contemporary application.

The Supreme Court interpreted the language "in all Cases, except Treason, Felony, and Breach of the Peace" to encompass all crimes. *Williamson v. United States* (1908). Tracing the origins of the clause to parliamentary privilege, the Court found this identical language was used to qualify Parliament's privilege from arrest so that the members of Parliament were not immune from criminal prosecution. The Court concluded that the Framers' use of the identical phrase, without any explanation, indicated that Congress's privilege was to have the same limitation regarding criminal actions as did the parliamentary privilege from which the language was borrowed. The clause, therefore, does not provide any Member of Congress with any immunity from criminal prosecution.

The Supreme Court, applying the Framers' intent, later declared that the clause also did not provide any privilege from civil process. *Long v. Ansell*. Hence, civil litigants can compel Members of Congress to appear in a court of proper jurisdiction to defend against civil actions. Furthermore, the Court has so narrowly interpreted the clause that Members of Congress may even be compelled by subpoena to testify in criminal and civil actions while Congress is in session.

David F. Forte

See Also

Article I, Section 6, Clause 1 (Speech and Debate Clause)

Suggestion for Further Research

Louis S. Raveson, *Unmasking the Motives of Government Decisionmakers: A Subpoena for Your Thoughts?*, 63 N.C. L. Rev. 879 (June 1985)

Significant Cases

Williamson v. United States, 207 U.S. 425 (1908)
Long v. Ansell, 293 U.S. 76 (1934)

Speech and Debate Clause

... for any Speech or Debate in either House, [Senators and Representatives] shall not be questioned in any other Place.

(**Article I, Section 6, Clause 1**)

~

*T*he right of legislators to speak their minds with impunity while engaged in legislative work was acknowledged by the British Bill of Rights of 1689, written into the Articles of Confederation, and, after the Revolution, guaranteed by state constitutions as well as by the Speech and Debate Clause. James Wilson, one of the principal architects of the Constitution, explained in his *Lecture on Law* (1791) the purpose of the clause:

> In order to enable and encourage a representative of the publick to discharge his publick trust with firmness and success, it is indispensably necessary, that he should enjoy the fullest liberty of speech, and that he should be protected from the resentment of every one, however power-

ful, to whom the exercise of that liberty may occasion offence.

In his *Commentaries on the Constitution of the United States* (1833), Justice Joseph Story wrote that in England the privilege was "strictly confined to things done in the course of parliamentary proceedings, and [did] not cover things done beyond the place and limits of duty." To illustrate this limitation, he noted that although a libelous speech delivered in the House of Commons was privileged, if a Member republished that speech elsewhere, the libeled party was free to bring him to court. He then added that "the same principles seem applicable to the privilege of debate and speech in congress."

Although the only early case to deal with the privilege was concerned with a virtually identical provision of a state constitution, rather than the Speech and Debate Clause itself, the Massachusetts Supreme Court agreed that the privilege was limited to actions taken by a legislator "in the exercise of the functions of [his] office." *Coffin v. Coffin* (1808). This view of the scope of the privilege is consistent with that of another delegate to the Constitutional Convention, Charles Pinckney, who later observed in remarks in the U.S. Senate that the Framers "knew that in free countries very few privileges were necessary for the undisturbed exercise of legislative duties... they therefore not only intended, but did confine their privileges within the narrow limits mentioned in the Constitution."

Over the past fifty years, the Supreme Court has reaffirmed that the purpose of the clause is to protect the independence of Congress when exercising the legislative responsibilities assigned to it by the Constitution, *Eastland v. United States Servicemen's Fund* (1975); and it will interpret the clause broadly to that effect. *United States v. Johnson* (1966). The Court has also consistently limited its application to activities that are "clearly a part of the legislative process." *United States v. Brewster* (1972).

An activity is deemed to be within the legislative sphere only if it is "an integral part of the deliberative and communicative processes by which Members participate in committee and

House proceedings with respect to the consideration and passage or rejection of proposed legislation or with respect to other matters which the Constitution places within the jurisdiction of either House." *Gravel v. United States* (1972). Thus, the Court has held that the clause protects such acts as voting, the conduct of committee hearings, the issuance and distribution of committee reports, the subpoenaing of information required in the course of congressional investigations, and even the reading of stolen classified materials into a subcommittee's public record. *Doe v. McMillan* (1973). Conversely, speech and debate immunity will not protect Members engaged (even in their official capacities) in such non-legislative activities as negotiations with federal agencies, the issuance of press releases and newsletters, and the delivery of speeches in their home districts. *Gravel v. United States*; *Hutchinson v. Proxmire* (1979).

If a Member's actions meet the "legislative process" test, his immunity is absolute; and that is so even if he has acted contrary to law. Accordingly, although the government may prosecute a Member for a criminal act, such as accepting a bribe in exchange for a vote, it may not pursue the case if proof of the crime "depend[s] on his legislative acts or his motive for performing them." *United States v. Brewster*. Thus, the government may not prove that the Member voted a particular way on the House floor in exchange for a bribe; the government, however, may prove (by other means) that the Member *promised* to vote a particular way in exchange for the bribe. The former (the vote) requires proof of what happened on the House floor whereas the latter (the promise to vote) does not.

Members must be shielded not only from the consequences of litigation, but from its burdens because engagement in litigation of any kind "creates a distraction and forces Members to divert their time, energy, and attention from their legislative tasks." *Eastland v. United States Servicemen's Fund*. Consequently, a Member may immediately appeal a trial court's denial of a Member's motion to dismiss a case based on a claim of speech and debate immunity so that the Member may be spared the burden of a trial if his motion proves to be valid. *Helstoski*

v. Meanor (1979). Circuit courts are divided on the extent of the distraction that is prohibited by the clause. The District of Columbia Circuit put a stop to the FBI's non-consensual search of a Member's files containing legislative and non-legislative materials because such a search will "disrupt the legislative process" irrespective of the use to which such documents may be put. *United States v. Rayburn House Office Bldg.* (2007). The Ninth Circuit disagrees, however, and it has ruled that the clause permits such searches. *United States v. Renzi* (2011).

A circuit split also exists with respect to informally gathered information, such as that secured in meetings with constituents. The Tenth Circuit holds that such information is unprotected because it is not gathered "in the course of a formal committee action." *Bastien v. Office of Campbell* (2004). The Third and Ninth Circuits, however, conclude that such fact-finding is essential to the legislative process and therefore it is covered by the clause. *Gov't of Virgin Islands v. Lee* (1985); *Miller v. Transamerican Press, Inc.* (1983). The Ninth Circuit notes in *Renzi* that the clause's protection does not apply where the fact-finding involves criminal activities.

The limitations on the protections accorded Members of Congress by the Speech and Debate Clause prompted one Member also to assert the much broader privilege of "qualified immunity" from a common law defamation suit for activities he engaged in "within the scope" of his legislative duties. The D.C. Circuit, however, declined to accord Members of Congress the same kind of immunity for official acts as is enjoyed by members of the executive branch. *Chastain v. Sundquist* (1987).

Although the Speech and Debate Clause speaks only of "Senators and Representatives," in order to effect its purpose the Court in *Gravel* declared that it applies "not only to a Member but also to his aides insofar as the conduct of the latter would be a protected legislative act if performed by the Member himself." An aide who carries out congressional instructions that are found to be unlawful, however, is responsible for his acts even though the legislators who issued the instructions continue to be protected. *Powell v. McCormack* (1969); *Doe v. McMillan*.

In *Eastland*, the Supreme Court acknowledged that the clause may shield Members from civil or criminal liability "even though their conduct, if performed in other than legislative contexts, would in itself be unconstitutional or otherwise contrary to criminal or civil statutes." The risk of such abuse, however, "was the conscious choice of the Framers' buttressed and justified by history." While state legislators may receive similar protection under state constitutions or common law, the clause does not protect them from prosecution for the commission of federal crimes. *United States v. Gillock* (1980). Errant Members nevertheless remain subject to disciplinary action by their respective houses for "disorderly behavior"—and, of course, by their constituents on election day.

James L. Buckley

See Also

Article I, Section 1 (Legislative Voting Clause)

Article I, Section 5, Clause 2 (Rules Clause; Expulsion Clause)

Suggestions for Further Research

2 The Founders' Constitution 318–45 (Philip P. Kurland & Ralph Lerner eds., 1987)

2 Ronald D. Rotunda & John E. Nowak, Treatise on Constitutional Law: Substance and Procedure §§8.6 to 8.9 (5th ed. 2012)

Significant Cases

Coffin v. Coffin, 4 Mass. 1 (1808)

United States v. Johnson, 383 U.S. 169 (1966)

Powell v. McCormack, 395 U.S. 486 (1969)

Gravel v. United States, 408 U.S. 606 (1972)

United States v. Brewster, 408 U.S. 501 (1972)

Doe v. McMillan, 412 U.S. 306 (1973)

Eastland v. United States Servicemen's Fund, 421 U.S. 491 (1975)

United States v. Powell, 423 U.S. 87 (1975)

Helstoski v. Meanor, 442 U.S. 500 (1979)

Hutchinson v. Proxmire, 443 U.S. 111 (1979)

United States v. Helstoski, 442 U.S. 477 (1979)

United States v. Gillock, 445 U.S. 360 (1980)

Miller v. Transamerican Press, Inc., 709 F.2d 524 (9th Cir. 1983)

Gov't of Virgin Islands v. Lee, 775 F.2d 514 (3d Cir. 1985)

Chastain v. Sundquist, 833 F. 2d 311 (D.C. Cir. 1987)

Bastien v. Office of Campbell, 390 F.3d 1301 (10th Cir. 2004)

United States v. Rayburn House Office Bldg, 497 F.3d 654 (D.C. Cir. 2007)

United States v. Renzi, 651 F.3d 1012 (9th Cir. 2011)

Sinecure Clause

No Senator or Representative shall, during the Time for which he was elected, be appointed to any civil Office under the Authority of the United States, which shall have been created, or the Emoluments whereof shall have been encreased during such time …

(Article I, Section 6, Clause 2)

~

*D*etermined to avoid corruption and self-dealing in the legislative process, the Framers kept all appointive powers out of the hands of Congress (Article II, Section 2, Clause 2). But corruption could come not only from self-dealing but also from the blandishments of the executive. Consequently, in order to prevent a repetition of the British Crown's practice of "buying" support by creating offices and sinecures to give to members of Parliament, Robert Yates proposed to the Constitutional Convention a ban on Members of Congress from "any office established by a particular State, or under the authority of the U. States … during the term of service, and under the national Government for the space of one year after its expiration."

All the delegates in Philadelphia agreed that no Member of Congress should serve in an appointive position while he was sitting, but Nathaniel Gorham, James Wilson, and Alexander Hamilton wanted no bar at all once a person was no longer in Congress. Hamilton argued that since passion drives all men, the executive should be able to satisfy the desires of the better qualified men by inducing them to serve in appointive offices.

James Madison proposed a solution that sought to reconcile the divergent concerns of the Framers: "that no office ought to be open to a member, which may be created or augmented while he is in the legislature." For some time, the delegates debated whether this idea was too restrictive or not restrictive enough. Madison responded that "the unnecessary creation of offices, and increase of salaries, were the evils most experienced, & that if the door was shut agst. them, it might properly be left open for the appointt. of members to other offices as an encouragmt. to the Legislative service." Eventually, the delegates accepted Madison's view, but they deleted the prohibition from holding state office (the state might need the Member's services) and the one-year bar after leaving office (it was not long enough to be of any significant effect). They also limited the bar to "civil" offices so that the military could have the service of all when the country was in danger.

The result was the Sinecure Clause, also known as the Emoluments Clause or the Ineligibility Clause. As adopted, the relatively limited bar of this clause reinforces the separation of powers and the federal structure of the union. Of the separation of powers, Madison famously wrote in *The Federalist* No. 51: "Ambition must be made to counteract ambition. The interest of the man must be connected with the constitutional rights of the place." The clause puts an obstacle to the President's ability to shift a Member of Congress's ambition from the legislative to the executive. Of the federal structure of the union, Madison had warned of "the unnecessary creation of offices"—obviously beyond what was appropriate for the central government—that could occur if the clause were not adopted.

The clause establishes a number of formal requirements: (1) It applies to those Members who have actually taken their seats, not to those who were elected but not yet sworn in. (2) "Appointed" means at the moment of nomination for civil office, not at the time of approval. (3) The bar cannot be evaded by resignation from Congress. In a written opinion of Attorney General Benjamin Brewster in 1882, the clause

applies for the term "for which he was elected," not the time during which the Member actually holds office. (4) "Civil office" is one in which the appointee exercises an authoritative role. It does not apply to temporary, honorific, advisory, or occasional postings. *United States v. Hartwell* (1868). (5) "Emoluments" means more than salary, *McLean v. United States* (1912), but it is unclear how much more. In 1937, the Senate approved the appointment of Hugo L. Black to the Supreme Court even though Congress had passed legislation significantly augmenting the pensions of Supreme Court justices during the Senate term in which Black served. Later, under Presidents Lyndon B. Johnson and James Earl Carter, the Department of Justice opined that it did not matter when Congress passed legislation increasing the salary for an office, so long as the former Member of Congress was nominated before the salary increase went into effect. The courts dismissed suits contesting the appointments of Justice Black and Judge Abner Mikva on lack of standing grounds. *Ex parte Levitt* (1937); *McClure v. Carter* (1981).

In his *Commentaries on the Constitution of the United States* (1833), Justice Joseph Story, even in his panegyric, was hesitant about the clause: "It has been deemed by one commentator an admirable provision against venality, though not perhaps sufficiently guarded to prevent evasion." For well over a century, Presidents and their attorneys general had rigorously followed the formal requirements of the clause. In 1973, however, despite the evident textual commands of the Sinecure Clause, Congress and the executive devised an effective stratagem to avoid its limitations. Termed the "Saxbe fix," it copied an idea invented during the Taft administration. President Richard M. Nixon appointed Senator William Saxbe to be Attorney General even though Saxbe had been a Senator when Congress voted to raise the Attorney General's salary from $35,000 to $60,000. Under an opinion from acting Attorney General Robert H. Bork, Congress "fixed" the violation of the clause by returning the salary to the $35,000 level.

Presidents Gerald R. Ford (appointing Representative Robert Casey of Texas to the Federal Maritime Commission), Carter (appointing Senator Edmund Muskie as Secretary of State), and William Jefferson Clinton (appointing Senator Lloyd Bentsen as Secretary of the Treasury) went further and utilized "temporary Saxbe fixes," persuading Congress to reduce the salary of a position to which a Member had been appointed but only until the date when the Member's term would have ended. Only under Attorney General Edwin Meese III did the Department of Justice eschew this end run around the formal requirements of the Sinecure Clause. In 1987, the Office of Legal Counsel issued an opinion that Senator Orrin Hatch would be ineligible for nomination to the Supreme Court because Congress had raised the salaries for Associate Justices during Hatch's term. President Ronald Reagan chose to nominate Judge Robert H. Bork, whom the Senate did not approve. Under President Clinton, however, the Office of Legal Counsel declared that the Ineligibility Clause of the Constitution would not bar the appointment of Representative Bill Richardson to serve as United States Ambassador to the United Nations or of Senator William Cohen to serve as Secretary of Defense.

In 2008, Congress once again utilized the "Saxbe fix." It passed the Secretary of State Emoluments Act retroactively reducing the salary of the Secretary of State so that Hillary Clinton, who had voted for the increase while Senator, could take the cabinet post. At the same time, however, Congress, perhaps aware of the doubtful constitutionality of the practice, provided that, "Any person aggrieved by an action of the Secretary of State may bring a civil action in the United States District Court for the District of Columbia to contest the constitutionality of the appointment and continuance in office of the Secretary of State on the ground that such appointment and continuance in office is in violation of article I, section 6, clause 2, of the Constitution." Act of Dec. 19, 2008, § 1(b)(1)–2). Apparently in response, the Office of Legal Counsel affirmatively declared that salary rollback was a valid constitutional means of complying with the Sinecure ("Ineligibility") Clause.

In fact, a foreign service officer did bring suit alleging that Hillary Clinton's appointment violated the Constitution. The district court dismissed the suit on standing grounds, holding that the foreign service officer failed to allege any action by the Secretary of State that "aggrieved" him. *Rodearmel v. Clinton* (2009).

In reflecting on the Sinecure Clause, Justice Story had also written, "It has sometimes been [a] matter of regret, that the disqualification had not been made co-extensive with the supposed mischief; and thus to have for ever excluded members from the possession of offices created, or rendered more lucrative, by themselves." He was writing at a time when many saw the Sinecure Clause as too weak. Before 1850, over thirty amendments had been proposed to strengthen the prohibition. Yet Justice Story was unsure of the merit of the proposals: "Perhaps there is quite as much wisdom in leaving the provision, where it now is." The upshot is that fidelity to the Constitution by any of the branches of the government remains as much a function of internal commitment as it is of external constraint.

David F. Forte

See Also

Article II, Section 2, Clause 2 (Appointments Clause)

Suggestions for Further Research

Appointment to Civil Office, 17 Op. Att'y Gen. 365 (1882)

Appointment of Senator as Federal Judge, 33 Op. Att'y Gen. 88 (1922)

Member of Congress–Appointment to Civil Office Prior to Pay Increase, 42 Op. Att'y Gen. 381 (1969)

Memorandum for Attorney General Eric Holder from David Barron, Assistant Attorney General, Office of Legal Counsel, *Validity of Statutory Rollbacks as a Means of Complying with the Ineligibility Clause* (May 20, 2009), http://www.justice.gov/olc/2009/ineligibility-clause.pdf

Memorandum Opinion for the General Counsel, Immigration and Naturalization Service, 3 Op. O.L.C. 286 (1979)

Note: The Ineligibility Clause's Lost History: Presidential Patronage and Congress, 1787–1850, 123 HARV. L. REV. 1727 (2010)

John F. O'Connor, *The Emoluments Clause: An Anti Federalist Intruder in a Federalist Constitution*, 24 HOFSTRA L. REV. 89 (1995)

Michael Stokes Paulsen, *Is Lloyd Bentsen Unconstitutional?*, 46 STAN. L. REV. 907 (1994)

Significant Cases

United States v. Hartwell, 73 U.S. (6 Wall.) 385 (1868)

McLean v. United States, 226 U.S. 374 (1912)

Ex parte Levitt, 302 U.S. 633 (1937)

McClure v. Carter, 513 F. Supp. 265 (D. Idaho 1981), *aff'd*, 454 U.S. 1025 (1981)

Rodearmel v. Clinton, 666 F. Supp. 2d 123 (2009)

Incompatibility Clause

...no Person holding any Office under the United States, shall be a Member of either House during his Continuance in Office.

(ARTICLE I, SECTION 6, CLAUSE 2)

~

*T*he Constitution establishes several limitations on a person's ability to serve in Congress. For example, Article I, Sections 2 and 3 limit the class of persons eligible to serve in Congress by imposing age, citizenship, and residency requirements. The Incompatibility Clause of Article I, Section 6 imposes a further limitation: it forbids federal executive and judicial officers from simultaneously serving in Congress.

The Framers of the Constitution understood the Incompatibility Clause primarily as an anticorruption device. Painfully familiar with the system of "royal influence," whereby the English kings had "purchased" the loyalty of members of Parliament with appointment to lucrative offices, the Framers sought to limit the corrupting effect of patronage and plural office holding in the new Republic. Drawing on examples provided by the bans on plural office holding contained in contemporaneous state constitutions and in the Articles of Confederation, the Framers crafted a ban on dual office holding, which Alexander Hamilton described

in *The Federalist* No. 76 as an important guard "against the danger of executive influence upon the legislative body."

It is easy, in modern times, to underestimate the importance of the Incompatibility Clause. There has been very little litigation involving its meaning, perhaps because its commands are relatively clear. Yet the clause serves a vital function in the American system of separated powers. By preventing joint legislative and executive office holding, the clause forecloses any possibility of parliamentary government in America, and thus preserves a hallmark of American constitutional government: the independence of the executive and the Congress.

Beyond this vital structural function, what is perhaps most interesting about the clause is what it does not, by its terms, prohibit. Neither the clause itself nor any other constitutional provision expressly prohibits joint service in the federal executive and judiciary, or joint service in federal and state office. The latter issue is largely handled as a matter of state constitutional law, which generally forbids most forms of dual federal–state office holding. As for the question of simultaneous service in federal executive and judicial offices, the constitutionality of the practice might be suggested not only by the lack of a textual prohibition, but by a few prominent examples of such service in the early days of the Republic, such the simultaneous service of Chief Justices John Jay, Oliver Ellsworth, and John Marshall in judicial and executive posts. Nonetheless, examples of joint service in the executive and the judiciary have been rare in American history, and a strong tradition has developed disfavoring the practice. Moreover, some might argue that general separation of powers principles render the practice constitutionally suspect.

What little litigation the clause has generated has centered on two questions: its justiciability and its application to service by Members of Congress in the military reserves. In *Schlesinger v. Reservists Committee to Stop the War* (1974), the Supreme Court held that citizens who had filed a civil action to challenge the reserve membership of some Members of Congress were asserting only "generalized grievances about the conduct of government" and therefore lacked standing to sue.

Schlesinger did not, however, decide that the Incompatibility Clause could never be enforced in court. Instead, one might read the case to leave open the possibility of judicial enforcement if a sitting Member of Congress who was also an Officer of the United States were to take official action that adversely affected an individualized private interest. On this view, it was only the plaintiff's lack of a sufficiently concrete and particularized injury that led to the result in *Schlesinger.*

In *United States v. Lane* (2006), the U.S. Court of Appeals for the Armed Forces adopted this view. *Lane* was an appeal of a recusal motion filed by an airman who had been convicted by court-martial of a cocaine offense. Senator Lindsay Graham, a lieutenant colonel in the Air Force Reserves, sat on the Air Force Court of Criminal Appeals that reviewed the airman's conviction. The airman filed a motion to recuse Senator Graham on the ground that his service on the court violated the Incompatibility Clause.

Applying Article III standing principles, the Armed Forces Court of Appeals held that the airman had standing. The court reasoned that the "fact that a Member of Congress sat as a judge in this criminal case" carried "direct liberty implications" for the airman that distinguished his case "from other abstract circumstances where the Incompatibility Clause might be implicated."

The court in *Lane* also rejected a theory under which the Incompatibility Clause would always be nonjusticiable, no matter who the plaintiff. On this theory, compliance with the clause is only a condition for service in Congress, not a disqualification from service in the other branches; and enforcement of this condition rests with Congress alone. This was the litigating position of the United States in *Schlesinger.* Brief of Petitioner, *Schlesinger v. Reservists Committee to Stop the War* (1974). The Office of Legal Counsel has also endorsed this view. 1 Op. Off. Legal Counsel 242 (1977) ("exclusive responsibility for interpreting and enforcing the Incompatibility Clause rests with Congress").

Although the United States advanced this "congressional commitment" theory in *Lane*, the court was not persuaded. The court noted that if the government's position were accepted, "Members of Congress could serve as the heads of departments and regulatory agencies, simultane-ously participating in the passage of legislation and in the execution of the laws" and yet "no citizen could cite the Incompatibility Clause in challenging a governmental decision bearing directly on the life, liberty, or property of the citizen." In other words, the court believed that leaving the clause to congressional enforcement alone posed too great a risk that the clause would go under-enforced.

On the merits, the court in *Lane* held that the position of judge on the Air Force Court of Criminal Appeals is an "office of the United States and cannot be filled by a person who simultaneously serves as a Member of Congress." The Court therefore concluded that the review panel was not properly constituted, invalidated the prior proceedings, and returned the trial record for a new review proceeding.

Joan L. Larsen

See Also

Suggestions for Further Research

Members of Congress Holding Reserve Commissions, 1 Op. O.L.C. 242 (1977)

Steven G. Calabresi & Joan L. Larsen, *One Person, One Office: Separation of Powers or Separation of Personnel?*, 79 Cornell L. Rev. 1045 (1994)

Daniel H. Pollitt, *Senator/Attorney-General Saxbe and the "Ineligibility Clause" of the Constitution: An Encroachment upon the Separation of Powers*, 53 N.C. L. Rev. 111 (1974)

Saikrishna Bangalore Prakash, *Why the Incompatibility Clause Applies to the Office of the President*, 4 Duke J. Const. L. & Pub. Pol'y 143 (2009)

David J. Shaw, *An Officer and a Congressman: The Unconstitutionality of Congressmen in the Armed Forces Reserve*, 97 Geo. L.J. 1739 (2009)

Seth Barrett Tillman, *Why Our Next President May Keep His or Her Senate Seat: A Conjecture on the Constitution's Incompatibility Clause*, 4 Duke J. Const. L. & Pub. Pol'y 107 (2009)

Seth Barrett Tillman & Steven G. Calabresi, *The Great Divorce: The Current Understanding of Separation of Powers and the Original Meaning of the Incompatibility Clause*, 157 U. Pa. L. Rev. 134 (2008)

Russell Wheeler, Extrajudicial Activities of the Early Supreme Court, 1973 Sup. Ct. Rev. 123

Significant Cases

Schlesinger v. Reservists Committee to Stop the War, 418 U.S. 208 (1974) No. 72-1188

United States v. Lane, 64 M.J.1 (2006)

Origination Clause

All Bills for raising Revenue shall originate in the House of Representatives; but the Senate may propose or concur with Amendments as on other Bills.

(**Article I, Section 7, Clause 1**)

~

*C*onsistent with the English requirement that money bills must commence in the House of Commons, the Framers expected that the Origination Clause would ensure that "power over the purse" would lie with the legislative body closer to the people. Under the Articles of Confederation, the national government could not tax individuals, and the Origination Clause was one of several provisions meant to cabin the national revenue power created under the Constitution. The clause was also part of a critical compromise between large and small states, helping to temper the large states' unhappiness with equal representation in the Senate by leaving the power to initiate tax bills with the House of Representatives, where the large states had greater influence.

The final version of the clause was much weaker than the form proposed by Elbridge Gerry of Massachusetts, which would have required all "money bills" (including appropriations) to originate in the House and would have given the Senate no power to amend. Gerry feared that the Senate would become an aristocratic body because of its small size, its selection by legislatures rather than by election, and its six-year term of office. "It was a maxim," he said, "that the people ought to hold the purse-strings."

The strongest proponents of national power opposed the clause in any form. As James Wilson of Pennsylvania explained at the Constitutional Convention, "If both branches were to say yes or no, it was of little consequence which should say yes or no first." What survived the contentious debates was closer to Wilson's vision than to Gerry's. The clause was restricted to bills for raising revenue, and the Senate was given the amendment power (which, Gerry thought, gutted the provision of any real effect).

Even in weakened form, however, the Origination Clause was not meaningless. James Madison, no supporter of the clause at the Convention, gave it a generous interpretation in *The Federalist* No. 58: "The House of Representatives cannot only refuse, but they alone can propose the supplies requisite for the support of the government.... This power over the purse may, in fact, be regarded as the most complete and effectual weapon with which any constitution can arm the immediate representatives of the people, for obtaining a redress of every grievance, and for carrying into effect every just and salutary measure."

As it turned out, the Origination Clause has had little effect. For one thing, many revenue bills have their intellectual genesis in the Treasury Department, not in Congress. Furthermore, Elbridge Gerry's fears were well founded: the Senate's power to amend is generally understood in practice to be so broad that the Senate can replace the entire text of a bill that technically originates in the House.

The understanding that the clause is a nullity reflects practice, however, not doctrine. In its most recent Origination Clause case, *United States v. Munoz-Flores* (1990), a divided Supreme Court rejected the argument that origination issues are nonjusticiable political questions. The Court held that a plaintiff with standing may pursue a claim that a revenue statute improperly originated in the

Senate. In *Munoz-Flores*, however, the Court did not reach the larger issues, concluding that a bill to impose a user's fee, where raising revenue was a secondary concern, was not a "bill for raising revenue." The Supreme Court has affirmed that, consistent with Congress's "uniform action," the term "bills for raising revenue" is "confined to bills to levy taxes in the strict sense of the words, and has not been understood to extend to bills for other purposes which incidentally create revenue." *United States v. Norton* (1875). That distinction is an easier one to state than to apply, however. The Supreme Court's decision in *National Federation of Independent Business v. Sebelius* (2012)—namely, that the so-called individual mandate penalty, applicable to those who after 2014 do not acquire health insurance, will really be a tax—illustrates the categorization difficulties. The issue in *NFIB* was not the Origination Clause, of course, but the result in the case may have many spillover effects.

The larger issues await another case where a taxpayer subject to an unquestioned revenue statute can raise serious questions about the statute's origin.

Erik M. Jensen

See Also

Article I, Section 7
Article I, Section 8, Clause 1 (Taxation Clause)

Significant Cases

United States v. Norton, 91 U.S. 566 (1875)
Millard v. Roberts, 202 U.S. 429 (1906)
Rainey v. United States, 232 U.S. 310 (1914)
United States v. Munoz-Flores, 495 U.S. 385 (1990)
National Federation of Independent Business v. Sebelius, 132 S. Ct. 2566 (2012)

Presentment Clause

Every Bill which shall have passed the House of Representatives and the Senate, shall, before it become a Law, be presented to the President of the United States: If he approve he shall sign it, but if not he shall return it, with his Objections to that House in which it shall have originated, who shall enter the Objections at large on their Journal, and proceed to reconsider it. If after such Reconsideration two thirds of that House shall agree to pass the Bill, it shall be sent, together with the Objections, to the other House, by which it shall likewise be reconsidered, and if approved by two thirds of that House, it shall become a Law. But in all such Cases the Votes of both Houses shall be determined by yeas and Nays, and the Names of the Persons voting for and against the Bill shall be entered on the Journal of each House respectively.

(**ARTICLE I, SECTION 7, CLAUSE 2**)

⁓

*T*he Presentment Clause is commonly viewed as a provision that protects the President's veto power, an association reinforced by the clause's name. Yet, the Presentment Clause has a broader function: The clause prescribes the exclusive method for passing federal statutes, indicating that all bills must pass both houses of Congress and be subject to the President's veto. Thus, with some justification, one might call the provision the Lawmaking Clause.

The Presentment or Lawmaking Clause was often debated during the Founding, but the discussions generally focused on issues not relevant to current interpretive controversies. In the Constitutional Convention, the principal focus was on how difficult it should be for Congress to override the President's veto and on whether the President should possess the veto alone or should share it with the judiciary in a council of revision. During the ratification debates, the Federalists sought to justify the veto and bicameralism as devices for restraining the legislature from invading executive power and for limiting the enactment of hasty and unwise legislation.

The Presentment Clause ultimately drafted by the Convention was one of the most formal provisions in the Constitution. The Framers apparently feared that factions would attempt to depart from the constitutional method for passing laws and therefore they spelled out that method in one of the document's longest provisions. The clause describes the specifics of the lawmaking process, including that the President's veto can be overridden by two-thirds of both houses. In the Pocket Veto Clause that immediately follows (Article I, Section 7, Clause 2) the President has ten days to decide whether to veto a bill and congressional adjournments may not deprive the President of his ability to veto measures. The Framers even mentioned (in the Pocket Veto Clause) that Sundays should not be counted in the ten-day period, and James Madison had the phrase "after it shall have been presented to him" inserted into the clause to "prevent a question whether the day on which the bill be presented, ought to be counted or not as one of the ten days." Moreover, to preclude Congress from bypassing the President by calling a bill by another name, Madison also persuaded the Convention to take the extraordinary step of adding a second Presentment Clause that required submission to the President of "Every Order, Resolution, or Vote to which the Concurrence of the Senate and House of Representatives may be necessary." (Article I, Section 7, Clause 3.) Clearly, the Framers believed that lawmaking was so important that they could not take any chances that the Congress might try to circumvent the President's role in the legislative process.

There are two ways that the Presentment Clause might be violated. First, Congress might pass statutes that authorize the legislative Houses or the President to take legislative-type actions without conforming to bicameralism and presentment. Second, Congress or the President might take legislative-type actions on their own initiative without statutory authority. The Framers' efforts have largely proved successful in preventing this second type of Presentment Clause violation. Thus, Congress has rarely if ever attempted to pass laws without either the approval of both houses or presentment to the President. In addition, the President's assertions of the constitutional authority to take legislative-type actions in the domestic sphere have been relatively rare and, when they do occur, have often been restrained by the courts. *Youngstown Sheet & Tube Co. v. Sawyer* (1952); but see *In re Debs* (1895).

The Constitution has been less successful, however, in preventing Congress from authorizing departures from bicameralism and presentment through the enactment of legislation, such as through statutory delegations of administrative discretion to the executive. These statutes raise complex questions and therefore may sometimes be constitutional. Still, as a general matter, it seems unlikely that the Framers would have allowed Congress to bypass the bicameralism and presentment requirements simply by passing legislation.

One important statutory departure from the traditional lawmaking process was the legislative veto, in which Congress usually granted each house the authority to nullify administrative actions taken by the executive. One might view the legislative veto from several different perspectives, but in each case the veto is unconstitutional. If the legislative veto is conceptualized as executive power, then it is unconstitutional because the legislators who wield it are not executive officials. If the veto is viewed as involving the power to pass legislation, then it clearly violates the Presentment Clause, because the veto does not conform to the requirements of bicameralism or presentment. Finally, the veto might be viewed as an exercise of the power of an individual house, but such powers are either mentioned in the Constitution, such as the power of each house to pass legislative rules, or might be inferred because they are traditionally possessed by legislative houses, as with the power of investigation. The legislative veto, however, falls under neither category. The Supreme Court has largely conformed to the Constitution's original meaning and held legislative vetoes to be unconstitutional. *INS v. Chadha* (1983); *Metropolitan Washington Airports Authority v. Citizens for the Abatement of Aircraft Noise* (1991).

The most common departure from bicameralism and presentment has involved the statutory delegation to the executive of administrative discretion. Although such delegations certainly do not conform to the Presentment Clause, there is a plausible originalist argument that these delegations are constitutional either under the Necessary and Proper Clause or because they confer executive power rather than legislative power. Nonetheless, many originalists reject these arguments and conclude that broad delegations are constitutionally problematic because they give to the executive either legislative or nonexecutive power. The Supreme Court, however, currently holds that these delegations are constitutional, based in part on the nonoriginalist argument that the modern administrative state requires them. *Mistretta v. United States* (1989).

More recently, the Supreme Court has reviewed a different departure from the traditional lawmaking process—the conferral of cancellation authority on the executive—and held it to be unconstitutional as a violation of the Presentment Clause. *Clinton v. City of New York* (1998). In 1995, Congress enacted the Line Item Veto Act, which despite its name, did not provide the President with veto authority, but instead authorized him to cancel certain spending provisions. This cancellation authority was similar to an ordinary delegation of administrative authority in that it conferred discretion on the executive, subject to a statutory standard, to take certain actions. Cancellation authority, however, differs from an ordinary delegation since it is generally narrower. Whereas an ordinary delegation allows the executive to promulgate a rule of his choosing, cancellation authority permits him only to accept or reject a statutory rule. For example, in the appropriation law area, ordinary delegations under traditional appropriation laws permit the President to spend any sum between the amount appropriated and zero, whereas cancellation authority only permits him the choice to spend the appropriated amount or to cancel the appropriation and spend nothing.

Reviewing the cancellation authority provided by the Line Item Veto Act, the Supreme Court found it unconstitutional. In the Court's view, cancellation authority was similar to the power to repeal a law, because the authority could eliminate an appropriation. The exercise of cancellation authority therefore needed to conform to the Presentment Clause. Of course, if cancellation authority is similar to repealing an appropriation, then the executive's authority under a traditional appropriation to decide how much to spend is similar to enacting an appropriation, because the executive can "legislate" the amount that should be spent. Under the Court's reasoning, then, ordinary delegations may also logically violate the Presentment Clause, but the Court continues regularly to permit such delegations. The Court has yet to resolve this double standard whereby cancellation authority is unconstitutional even though such authority is generally narrower than ordinary delegations.

Several other matters raise questions under the Presentment Clause. First, some have argued that the clause defines a "Bill" as a provision relating to a single subject; consequently, if Congress were to combine two separate subjects in a measure, that would really be two bills and the President could therefore exercise a kind of item veto by vetoing one of the bills, while approving the other. Historical and structural evidence reveals, however, that the original meaning of a "Bill" was a measure that included whatever provisions Congress placed within it. Second, the Line Item Veto Act provided that the President would receive cancellation authority only as to bills that he signed but that he would lack such authority if he vetoed the bill, a provision that arguably places an unconstitutional burden on the President's veto power. Third, it has been argued that the Presentment Clause requires that Congress pass bills under a majority voting rule, but the clause's language, which simply refers to every bill "which shall have passed" the legislative houses, combined with its structure and history, indicates that each house can employ supermajority rules to govern the passage of bills.

Finally, in response to the recent practice of a President signing a bill but then ordering that a portion of it not be enforced, two arguments have been made. The broader one claims that the President has a duty to veto all unconstitutional laws, rooted in the Executive Vesting Clause (Article II, Section 1, Clause 1), the Presidential Oath of Office Clause (Article II, Section 1, Clause 8), and the Take Care Clause (Article II, Section 3).

A narrower argument maintains that, if the President asserts a claim strong enough to support not enforcing a provision as unconstitutional, then this claim will also require that he veto a law containing the provision.

Michael B. Rappaport

See Also

Article I, Section 1 (Legislative Vesting Clause)

Article I, Section 7, Clause 2 (Pocket Veto)

Article I, Section 7, Clause 3 (Presentment of Resolutions)

Article I, Section 8, Clause 18 (Necessary and Proper Clause)

Article II, Section 1, Clause 1 (Executive Vesting Clause)

Article II, Section 1, Clause 8 (Presidential Oath of Office)

Article II, Section 3 (Take Care Clause)

Suggestions for Further Research

Dan T. Coenen, *The Originalist Case Against Congressional Supermajority Voting Rules*, 106 Nw. U. L. Rev. 1091 (2012)

Gary Lawson, *Delegation and Original Meaning*, 88 Va. L. Rev. 327 (2002)

John O. McGinnis & Michael B. Rappaport, *The Rights of Legislators and the Wrongs of Interpretation: A Further Defense of the Constitutionality of Legislative Supermajority Rules*, 47 Duke L.J. 327 (1997)

Saikrishna B. Prakash, *Deviant Executive Lawmaking*, 67 Geo. Wash. L. Rev. 1 (1998)

Saikrishna B. Prakash, *Why the President Must Veto Unconstitutional Bills*, 16 Wm. & Mary Bill of Rts. J. 81 (2007)

Michael B. Rappaport, *The President's Veto and the Constitution*, 87 Nw. U. L. Rev. 736 (1993)

Michael B. Rappaport, *The Selective Nondelegation Doctrine and the Line Item Veto: A New Approach to the Nondelegation Doctrine and Its Implications for* Clinton v. City of New York, 76 Tul. L. Rev. 265 (2002)

Michael B. Rappaport, *The Unconstitutionality of "Signing and Not Enforcing,"* 16 Wm. & Mary Bill of Rts. J. 113 (2007)

Michael B. Rappaport, *Veto Burdens and the Line Item Veto Act*, 91 Nw. U. L. Rev. 771 (1997)

J. Gregory Sidak & Thomas A. Smith, *Four Faces of the Item Veto: A Reply to Tribe and Kurland*, 84 Nw. U. L. Rev. 437 (1990)

Significant Cases

In re Debs, 158 U.S. 564 (1895)

Youngstown Sheet & Tube Co. v. Sawyer, 343 U.S. 579 (1952)

INS v. Chadha, 462 U.S. 919 (1983)

Mistretta v. United States, 488 U.S. 361 (1989)

Metropolitan Washington Airports Authority v. Citizens for the Abatement of Aircraft Noise, 501 U.S. 252 (1991)

Clinton v. City of New York, 524 U.S. 417 (1998)

Pocket Veto

If any Bill shall not be returned by the President within ten Days (Sundays excepted) after it shall have been presented to him, the Same shall be a Law, in like Manner as if he had signed it, unless the Congress by their Adjournment prevent its Return, in which Case it shall not be a Law.

(**Article I, Section 7, Clause 2**)

~

*I*n order to ensure the vitality of the separation of powers, the Framers gave the executive, as James Madison wrote in *The Federalist* No. 47, a "partial agency" in the legislative process. Under Article II, Section 3, Clause 1, the president can propose measures to Congress, and under Article I, Section 7, Clause 2, the president can approve or veto bills that the Congress must present to him. If he does veto the bill, he must return it to Congress, which may then override his veto by a two-thirds vote. By these devices, the Framers set themselves squarely against any absolute veto by the president. But what happens if the president refuses to approve or to return the bill to Congress? What happens if Congress adjourns, preventing a return of the bill?

In order to solve these two problems, the Framers crafted the Pocket Veto Clause. If the president refuses to approve or return the bill within ten days (not including Sunday), the bill automatically becomes law. If, in the interim, Congress has adjourned, the bill dies and the legislation must be reintroduced and passed again when Congress reconvenes. Later termed by Andrew Jackson the "Pocket Veto," the clause has been the subject of much controversy between the president and Congress.

There is an ambiguity as to what kinds of adjournment the clause covers: (1) *sine die* adjournment when a Congress comes to an end, and a newly elected Congress must convene, (2) intersession adjournment between two sessions of the same Congress, and (3) intrasession adjournments when Congress takes a break within a session. There is virtually unanimous agreement that the president may pocket veto a bill when Congress adjourns *sine die*. Although some members of Congress have disputed the validity of intersession and intrasession pocket vetoes, Congress as a whole has acquiesced in these kinds of presidential pocket veto.

As a model for the veto power, the Framers used the constitution of the state of New York of 1777 but omitted the section that would have prohibited intersession pocket vetoes ("that if any bill shall not be returned...within ten days after it shall have been presented, the same shall be a law, unless the legislature shall, by their adjournment, render a return of the said bill within ten days impracticable; in which case the bill shall be returned on the first day of the meeting of the legislature after the expiration of the said ten days.")

Other parts of the Constitution refer to adjournments of differing lengths, but the Framers did not particularize which adjournments would or would not affect a pocket veto. Textually, therefore, it seems that the clause permits the president to exercise a pocket veto any time the Congress as a whole adjourns.

On the other hand, advocates for the view that the clause applies only to *sine die* adjournments hold that the purpose of the Pocket Veto Clause was to permit the president and Congress to continue to engage in the legislative process

if at all practicable. Just as the president is not permitted to veto a law simply by not signing it, so should he not be permitted to veto a law simply because Congress has recessed for a few days. The advocates for greater congressional authority assert that an intrasession adjournment (and perhaps even an intersession adjournment) does not "prevent a return" as the clause states it. It merely postpones the return until Congress reconvenes. Further, many holding this view have also asserted that so long as Congress appoints an agent to receive the return while it is adjourned, the president may not pocket veto the legislation at all.

President James Madison exercised the first pocket veto during an intersession, Andrew Jackson exercised the first pocket veto after a final adjournment (prompting an objection from Henry Clay), and Andrew Johnson exercised the first intrasession vetoes (rejecting five bills). In response to Johnson's action, the Senate passed a bill regulating the presidential return of bills, excluding intrasession recesses from the definition of adjournment. The bill never made it through the House. That action typifies the history of the dispute. From time to time, members of Congress have sought legislation limiting the president's use of the pocket veto, but none of these efforts has ever ripened into law.

Meanwhile, the use of the pocket veto accelerated, bolstered by several attorney general opinions stating that both intersession and intrasession pocket vetoes are constitutional. By 1929, 479 bills had been pocket vetoed, about one-fourth during intersession adjournments but only eight during intrasession breaks. In that year, the Supreme Court decided *The Pocket Veto Case*. During a five-month intersession adjournment, President Calvin Coolidge had pocket vetoed a bill that would have given entitlements to a group of Indian tribes. The tribes sought to claim their rights, asserting that the president's veto was invalid and that therefore the bill had become law. The Court unanimously upheld the president's action. It found no constitutional distinction among the various types of adjournment. The president, the Court declared, could not return a bill to a Congress that was not actually sitting. It was Congress's choice whether to adjourn before the ten-day period could run its course. Further, the Court found "no substantial basis" for the view that a bill constitutionally could be returned to an adjourned house "by delivering it, with the President's objections, to an officer or agent of the House." In *Wright v. United States* (1938), however, the Court held that a three-day recess by a single house while the other remained in session did not meet the clause's definition of adjournment.

Beginning with President Franklin D. Roosevelt's tenure, presidential power increased and so did the use of the pocket veto. From 1930 until 1972, seventy-six bills fell to vetoes during intrasession breaks and 143 others during intersession adjournments. Presidents accompanied many vetoes with messages explaining the reason for the rejection. The high point of the congressional attack on Roosevelt's expansive use of the pocket veto came in 1940. Congress passed a bill that would have revived all legislation previously pocket vetoed during non–*sine die* adjournments of Congress. Congress passed the measure as a means of asserting that Roosevelt's pocket vetoes had not been valid. The bill was "returned" as a regular veto by President Roosevelt, and the House failed to override. Subsequently, Congress fell back into acquiescence.

The congressional counterattack was renewed during President Richard M. Nixon's administration, this time through the courts. In *Kennedy v. Sampson* (1974), a federal court declared an intrasession pocket veto invalid and held that the disputed legislation was validly enacted. Two years later another dispute, *Kennedy v. Jones* (1976), produced an agreement between Congress and the president limiting the use of the pocket veto to *sine die* adjournments.

President Ronald Reagan, however, renounced that agreement and made pocket vetoes during intersession adjournments, even though Congress had appointed an agent to receive a "return" of the legislation as a standard veto subject to being overridden. One of President Reagan's pocket vetoes resulted in a suit by members of Congress. In *Barnes v. Kline* (1985), a panel of the D.C. Circuit, over a dissent by Judge Robert Bork, held that members of Con-

gress possessed standing to bring the suit and that the issue was "justiciable," that is, capable of judicial resolution rather than being left to the political branches to decide. The court then held that the Constitution forbids intersession pocket vetoes when Congress has appointed an agent to receive a return. The *Barnes* court distinguished *The Pocket Veto Case* by stating that appointing an agent would be valid if it "would not occasion undue delay or uncertainty over the returned bill's status."

The Supreme Court vacated the decision as moot, as the law at issue had expired by its own terms. Following the action by the Supreme Court, the Department of Justice declared its opinion that the president's pocket veto power extends to any adjournment of longer than three days. President George H. W. Bush and President William Jefferson Clinton each used a pocket veto once. President George W. Bush's administration asserted that the president was entitled to exercise a pocket veto with as little as a three-day recess of the house in which the bill had originated. President Barack Obama has exercised two pocket vetoes, each accompanied by a regular veto of the same bill at the same time. Each time when it returned from its recess, the House of Representatives attempted to override his "regular" veto, solely to show its disapproval of the pocket veto. The overrides failed.

Repeated attempts in Congress to pass legislation stating its view of the pocket veto power continue to fall short of passage. Thus far, anytime Congress has treated a pocket veto as a regular veto and has scheduled an override vote, the attempt has failed. When presidents now exercise the pocket veto, they typically do so, as did President Obama, with a "protective return": a message declaring the objections to the bill so that if, perchance, a court holds the pocket veto invalid, the bill will be treated as vetoed in the regular manner, rather than becoming law by default. Observers have noted that the purposes of the pocket veto and the return veto are so inconsistent that presidents who use the device of the "protective return" are committing constitutional self-contradiction.

David F. Forte

Suggestions for Further Research

Butler C. Derrick Jr., *Stitching the Hole in the President's Pocket: A Legislative Solution to the Pocket-Veto Controversy*, 31 Harv. J. Legis. 371 (1993)

Robert Neal Webner, *The Intersession Pocket Veto and the Executive-Legislative Balance of Powers*, 73 Geo. L.J. 1185 (1985)

Significant Cases

The Pocket Veto Case, 279 U.S. 655 (1929)

Wright v. United States, 302 U.S. 583 (1938)

Kennedy v. Sampson, 511 F.2d 430 (D.C. Cir. 1974)

Kennedy v. Jones, 412 F. Supp. 353 (D.D.C. 1976)

Barnes v. Kline, 759 F.2d 21 (D.C. Cir. 1985)

Presentment of Resolutions

Every Order, Resolution, or Vote to which the Concurrence of the Senate and House of Representatives may be necessary (except on a question of Adjournment) shall be presented to the President of the United States; and before the Same shall take Effect, shall be approved by him, or being disapproved by him, shall be repassed by two thirds of the Senate and House of Representatives, according to the Rules and Limitations prescribed in the Case of a Bill.

(**ARTICLE I, SECTION 7, CLAUSE 3**)

~

*I*n August 1787 following the submission of the draft by the Committee of Detail, James Madison noted that Congress could evade the possibility of a presidential veto by simply denominating a "bill" as a "resolution." Although his motion to insert the words "or resolve" after the word "bill" in the Presentment Clause (Article I, Section 7, Clause 2) was defeated, the following day Edmund Randolph proposed a freestanding clause with more exacting language, and the Convention approved it. Even before the posthumous publication of Madison's Convention record, Justice Joseph Story took a view similar to Madison's: "[C]ongress, by adopting the form of an order or resolution, instead of a bill, might have effectually defeated the president's qualified negative in all the most important portions of legislation." *Commentaries on the Constitution of the United States* (1833). Nearly all commentators have agreed with that interpretation.

Nonetheless, not all resolutions of Congress require presidential approval because not all are intended to be law. Generally, joint resolutions do require presentment to the President as they are designed to have the force of law. They differ from bills only in that they usually deal with a single subject, such as a declaration of war. Congressionally proposed amendments to the Constitution are also styled as joint resolutions, but they are not presented to the President. Under the form of the amending process in Article V that has been followed in all cases except the Twenty-first Amendment, Congress proposes and three-quarters of the legislatures of the several states approve. Thus, no presidential involvement is necessary for a joint resolution proposing an amendment to the Constitution. *Hollingsworth v. Virginia* (1798).

Concurrent resolutions, passed by both houses, apply only to subjects affecting the procedures of both houses, such as fixing the time for adjournment, or to express "the sense of Congress" on an issue of public policy, or to set revenue and spending goals. Concurrent resolutions are not "law" and are not presented to the President. Similarly, simple resolutions (sometimes just known as resolutions) do not have the force of law and apply only to the operations of a particular branch of Congress dealing with its internal procedures, imposing censure on a Member, setting spending limits for particular committees, or expressing the viewpoint of one house on a public issue. A bill of impeachment passed by the House of Representatives could technically be seen as in the form of a simple resolution (as might also be Senate approval of treaties and presidential appointments), although it may not officially be designated as such. The Senate's resolution to convict is similar.

For many decades, Congress attempted to use a simple or concurrent resolution (or, at times, so has even a committee within one house) to "veto" executive actions. Congressional expression of disapproval would not go to the President for his signature or veto. In *INS v. Chadha* (1983), the Supreme Court invalidated the use of a resolution by one house (or by extension, a concurrent resolution by both houses) to "veto" an executive action as violative of the Presentment of Resolutions Clause.

By the time of *INS v. Chadha,* there were 295 various types of legislative vetoes in 195 different statutes. Congress initiated the device in 1932, giving President Herbert Hoover the authority to reorganize the executive branch, subject to the approval of Congress. Other versions of the legislative veto became more numerous as the administrative state grew, particularly in the 1940s.

Despite the *Chadha* decision ruling legislative vetoes unconstitutional, legislative vetoes still occur in pieces of legislation. By one scholar's count, between the date of the Court's decision in *Chadha* and 2005, 400 legislative veto-type provisions had been enacted or instituted. Most of these provisions are informal and concern a power of a committee or subcommittee to require its approval before an executive action may go forward. These kinds of arrangements were not directly addressed by the *Chadha* case and have continued ever since.

Often, a President will object to a formal legislative veto in a congressional enactment in his signing statement, citing *Chadha*. Signing statements, however, do not reach "vetoes" that are the result of amicable relationships between members of executive agencies and Members of Congress at the legislative committee and sub-committee levels. An executive agency will agree, for example, not to exceed a budgetary limit except by permission of a particular Congressional committee. As a result, through informal agreements, committees maintain an even stronger veto-type power over executive action. An example of an early informal agreement to allow committee-level vetoes occurred with the "Baker Accord" of 1989, when Secretary of State James Baker allowed certain committees and party leaders the ability to block aid sent to the Nicaraguan Contras.

Some legislation that *Chadha* purportedly struck down is still seen by some as being legitimate. In particular, many in Congress argue that the War Powers Act of 1973 is still in force, though the central component of the legislation is a legislative veto. After *Chadha*, there were proposals to change the War Powers Act from a concurrent resolution from both houses that does not require presentment to a joint resolution of disapproval. Those proposals failed.

David F. Forte

See Also
Article I, Section 7, Clause 2 (Presentment Clause)
Article V

Suggestion for Further Research

Congressional Quarterly's Guide to Congress (Mary Cohn ed., 4th ed. 1991)

Louis Fisher, Cong. Research Serv., RS22132, Legislative Vetoes After Chadha (2005), at http://www.loufisher.org/docs/lv/4116.pdf

Gary Lawson, Comment, *Burning Down the House (and Senate): A Presentment Requirement for Legislative Subpoenas Under the Orders, Resolutions, and Votes Clause,* 83 Tex. L. Rev. 1373 (2005)

David A. Martin, *The Legislative Veto and the Responsible Exercise of Congressional Power,* 68 Va. L. Rev. 253 (1982)

Seth Barrett Tillman, *A Textualist Defense of Article I, Section 7, Clause 3: Why* Hollingsworth v. Virginia *Was Rightly Decided, and Why* INS v. Chadha *Was Wrongly Reasoned,* 83 Tex. L. Rev. 1265 (2005)

Darren A. Wheeler, *Actor Preference and the Implementation of* INS v. Chadha, 23 BYU J. Pub. L. 83 (2008)

Significant Cases

Hollingsworth v. Virginia, 3 U.S. (3 Dall.) 378 (1798)
INS v. Chadha, 462 U.S. 919 (1983)

Taxation

The Congress shall have Power
to lay and collect Taxes, Duties,
Imposts and Excises.
(ARTICLE I, SECTION 8, CLAUSE 1)

~

*T*he first power that the Constitution grants
to Congress in Article I, Section 8 is the power to
tax. The Articles of Confederation had granted
Congress only the power to seek "requisitions"
(requests) from the states, which Alexander
Hamilton called "this *ignis fatuus* [will-o'-the-
wisp] in finance" in *The Federalist* No. 30. Most
of the leading figures at the Constitutional Convention, including William Paterson, author of
the New Jersey Plan that was most protective
of the states, believed that the new government
should have an independent power to tax. But
many important Anti-Federalists balked at the
idea. At the Convention, the Virginia Plan made
no provision for an independent taxing power,
but based representation on the states' "quotas
of contributions" and enabled Congress to "call
forth the force of the Union against any member
of the Union failing to fulfil its duties under the
articles thereof." The New Jersey Plan avoided the
Virginia Plan's recipe for confrontation between
the federal government and the states by specifying that Congress be independently "authorized
to pass acts for raising a revenue, by levying a
duty or duties" on imports, stamps, and postage, with congressional acts as "supreme law,"
enforceable against individuals.

In the ratification debates, most delegates
presumed that Congress would seek to apply
"direct taxes" rather than excises as the main
basis of obtaining revenue. And the Anti-Federalists expressed much apprehension over that
power. At the Virginia ratifying convention, for
example, George Mason argued that Congress's
ability to lay direct taxes was "at discretion,
unconfined, and without any kind of controul"
and would lead to "consolidated Government."
After Pennsylvania succeeded in ratifying the
Constitution, the *Pennsylvania Packet* printed
"The Dissent of the Minority of the Convention,"
which stated Congress's power to levy direct taxes

on "land, cattle, trades, occupations, etc. to any
amount" would force people to pay even the most
oppressive taxes or have their property seized
because "all resistance will be in vain." In Massachusetts, one delegate noted that raising taxes for
"the general welfare" meant it could cover "any
expenditure whatsoever" and that such a "universal, unbounded" power should not be given
by a free people to its government, and he argued
rather for a limited grant of revenue "adequate to
all necessary purposes."

The Federalists answered these charges by
claiming that duties on imports would normally
be sufficient for federal needs and that direct
taxes would only be used during great emergencies, like war, in which relying on requisitions
from the states would be dangerously slow and
risk national security. Additionally, the United
States could borrow money with greater ease if it
had what Edmund Randolph at the Virginia ratifying convention called the "full scope and complete command over the resources of the union,"
which the Federalists argued was also essential
to national security because Congress otherwise
would have to borrow money to finance wars.

Still, Massachusetts, South Carolina,
New York, New Hampshire, Virginia, as well
as delegates from an unofficial convention in
Harrisburg, Pennsylvania, all supported the Constitution on the basis that it would be amended,
and each of those states proposed amendments
that would require Congress to requisition the
states for their portion of a federal direct tax and
let the federal government raise those taxes itself
only after a state failed to act. But when James
Madison proposed a set of amendments to the
First Congress, he and the Federalist majority left
the federal taxing power as it was.

Nonetheless, the Framers did not leave the
taxing power unbounded. The Constitution
placed a number of limitations on it: "direct"
taxes must be apportioned according to population (Article I, Section 9, Clause 4); other taxes
must be "uniform" throughout the United States
(Article I, Section 8, Clause 1); and Congress cannot tax exports (Article I, Section 9, Clause 5). As
Alexander Hamilton put it in his 1791 "Report
on Manufactures," "These three qualifications
excepted, the power to raise money is plenary,

and indefinite; and the objects to which it may be appropriated are no less comprehensive...." Hamilton's second claim—set off, appropriately enough, by a semicolon—concerns what has been called the "spending power" (Article I, Section 8, Clause 1), the subject of enormous interpretive controversy, but which can be seen as an additional limitation on the taxation power ("to pay the Debts and provide for the common Defence and general Welfare of the United States"). The interpretation of the first portion of Article I, Section 8, Clause 1, the power to tax, has been more limited.

The most important dispute surrounding the clause was whether the taxing power could be used for any purpose other than raising revenue. The first Congress had little difficulty justifying an import tax that also protected domestic industry from foreign competition. The first section of the first tariff act (4 July 1789) declared that "it is necessary for the support of government, for the discharge of the debts of the United States, and the encouragement and protection of manufactures, that duties be laid on goods, wares and merchandise imported." Though the duties and their protective impact were modest, there is little doubt that the act's purpose was protective, and nobody in Congress objected on constitutional grounds.

The tariffs of 1824 and 1828 were even more protective, and produced a new set of constitutional objections. John C. Calhoun and his allies now claimed that Congress could tax imports only for revenue, not to regulate trade. The American colonists made the opposite comparison during the Imperial Conflict of the 1760s based on their understanding of the unwritten constitution that governed England and the colonies: Parliament could impose taxes to regulate imperial trade as part of its sovereign imperial power, but not to raise revenue. The last required a mechanism of consent on the part of the governed.

In two letters of 1828 to Joseph C. Cabell, Madison took the same principle as had the colonists and stated that under the commerce power, Congress could regulate trade with foreign nations including by means of taxation, and that Congress did not need a separate power

of taxation to do so. Justice Joseph Story supported Madison's position in his *Commentaries on the Constitution of the United States* (1833). Subsequently, Congress reduced tariffs to minimize protection after the Nullification crisis of 1832–1833. The Republicans restored protection in 1861, and the United States remained a high-tariff country almost continuously until the Second World War. The Supreme Court did not rule on the constitutionality of a protective tariff until 1928, upholding it in *J. W. Hampton, Jr. & Co. v. U.S.*

The principle that a delegated power of Congress implies the necessary means (confirmed by the Necessary and Proper Clause, Article I, Section 8, Clause 18) came to be applied to internal taxes as well, beginning with the Civil War.

In 1866 Congress imposed a tax on state banknotes, which had been the nation's only form of paper currency since the demise of the Second Bank of the United States in 1836. The 1866 tax meant to drive state banknotes out of existence (the constitutionality of which the Supreme Court had upheld in *Briscoe v. Bank of Kentucky* in 1837). In *Veazie Bank v. Fenno* (1869) the Court upheld the tax on state banknotes. The Court recognized that the taxing power could not be "exercised for ends inconsistent with the limited grants of power in the Constitution." But, reading the Constitution's grant of power "to coin money [and] regulate the value thereof" broadly enough to include the issuing of national banknotes, the Court found that Congress could stamp out state rivals.

In doing so, the Court affirmed that the power to tax even as a means to execute a delegated power was subject to constitutional limitations. Although the Court rejected the argument that the 1866 tax was a "direct" tax, it did admit that, "There are, indeed, certain virtual limitations, arising from the principles of the Constitution itself. It would undoubtedly be an abuse of the power if so exercised as to impair the separate existence and independent self-government of the States." This principle would later spawn a host of "intergovernmental tax immunity" cases.

McCulloch v. Maryland (1819) held that a state did not have the sovereign power to tax a federal instrumentality. Concomitantly, in

Collector v. Day (1871), the Court found that a federal tax on the income of a state judge violated the Constitution because the federal and state governments are "separate and distinct sovereignties, acting separately and independently of each other, within their respective spheres." The argument was that the tax on the wages of the state judge was really a tax on the state. After a number of decades dealing with the implications of the intergovernmental tax immunity doctrine, the Supreme Court reversed course in *Helvering v. Gerhardt* (1938), holding that the federal government could tax the income of state employees. Earlier *Pollock v. Farmers' Loan & Trust Co.* (1895) had held that the tax on the interest of a state or municipal bond is a tax on the state or municipality. For some time after *Gerhardt*, the federal government continued to exempt interest from state issued bonds from federal taxation. Finally, in *South Carolina v. Baker* (1988), the Court formally overruled *Pollock* and held that such interest has no immunity from federal taxation, effectively ending, for constitutional purposes, state immunity from federal taxation. The federal government, by statute however, exempts from federal income tax the interest of state and municipal bonds in some circumstances.

The question still remained, when the federal government does not use a tax as a means to effectuate a delegated power, but only as a tax designed to obtain revenue, what constitutional limits apply? In the 1860s a French chemist invented a cheap butter substitute called "oleomargarine." American dairy farmers lobbied for a ten-cent per pound tax to drive oleo out of the market. In 1886, Congress enacted a milder two-cent tax, and required manufacturers and sellers to purchase federal licenses and clearly to package and label their product as "oleomargarine." President Grover Cleveland reluctantly signed the bill. He noted that if he had been truly convinced that the revenue aspect was simply a pretext "to destroy...one industry of our people for the protection and benefit of another," he would have vetoed it. The Supreme Court unanimously upheld the oleomargarine tax as akin to excises on tobacco or alcohol. *In re Kollock* (1897). Chief Justice Melville Fuller declared, "The act before us is on its face an act for levying taxes, and although it may operate in so doing to prevent deception in the sale of oleomargarine as and for butter, its primary object must be assumed to be the raising of revenue."

In 1902, Congress amended the 1886 act and adopted a prohibitive ten-cent tax on artificially colored oleo, and reduced the tax on the less palatably looking uncolored or naturally colored oleo to one-quarter cent. Though many Members of Congress objected to this use of the taxing power for unenumerated ends, Maryland Representative William H. Jackson had no such qualms. He replied, "This government, sir, is all powerful; this government is the people, and the people can do anything with their government that they desire.... This is an age of progress." In *McCray v. United States* (1904), the Supreme Court upheld the new tax. Justice Edward White observed that Congress's power to enact such an excise "is so completely established as to require only statement." The Court, Justice White observed, had unanimously upheld the 1886 oleo tax as a revenue measure, even though "it may operate in so doing to prevent deception in the sale of oleomargarine." The amount of the tax was not for the Court to judge. However, Justice White warned that a tax "so extreme as to be beyond the principles which we have previously stated, and where it was plain to the judicial mind that the power had been called into play not for revenue, but solely for the purpose of destroying rights which could not be rightfully destroyed consistently with the principles of freedom and justice upon which the Constitution rests," would be unconstitutional. After *McCray*, the federal tax power was applied to limit the manufacture and sale of phosphorous matches, opium, and other narcotics.

In the progressive era, Congress attempted to expand its regulatory powers principally via the interstate commerce clause rather than the taxing power. However, when the Court held that Congress could not prohibit the interstate shipment of goods produced by child labor, *Hammer v. Dagenhart* (1918), Congress swiftly countered by enacting a prohibitive tax on the profits of manufacturers who used child labor. In *Bailey v. Drexel Furniture Co.* (1922), the Court struck down the act. The "tax," the Court argued, was in reality a criminal penalty. It required "knowing" violation of the act; was notably heavy (ten percent of net profits) without regard to the extent of the infraction; and the Department of Labor (not the Department of the Treasury) collected part of the tax. "A Court must be blind not to see that the so-called tax is imposed to stop the employment of children within the age limits prescribed. Its prohibitory and regulatory effect and purpose are palpable. All others can see and understand this," Chief Justice William Howard Taft wrote. "How can we properly shut our minds to it?"

On the same day, the Court unanimously struck down the Futures Trading Act of 1921 by which Congress had attempted to steer commodity futures trading to certain markets by enacting a prohibitory tax on trades in unregulated markets. *Hill v. Wallace* (1922). But reversing the order of the attempt to ban child labor, Congress then enacted a revised version of regulating commodity markets by using the commerce power, which the Court upheld in *Board of Trade of City of Chicago v. Olsen* (1923).

The Court continued to scrutinize tax measures that Congress was attempting to use for regulatory rather than income purposes. In 1933, the Court voided the Agricultural Adjustment Act of 1933, which provided subsidies to farmers from taxes on the processors of food and fiber. *United States v. Butler* (1936). Justice Owen Roberts' opinion focused on the agricultural processing tax as an attempt to achieve the unconstitutional end of regulating agricultural production, and "the expropriation of money from one group for the benefit of another," rather than for any public purpose.

The Court also held the Bituminous Coal Conservation Act of 1935 unconstitutional, which attempted to regulate coal production through heavy taxes that were rebated to producers who agreed to production limits and labor provisions. *Carter v. Carter Coal Company* (1936). Subsequently, Congress uncoupled the taxing provisions from the spending provisions in the Agricultural Adjustment Act and other acts, and never again did the Court hold that a purported tax was not a tax within the meaning of the Constitution.

Finally, in 2012 the Court made a curious inversion of the *Bailey* decision when it upheld the "individual mandate" of the 2010 Patient Protection and Affordable Care Act, which imposed a "penalty" on non-indigent persons who did not purchase health insurance. Members of Congress and President Barack Obama sedulously denied that the mandate was a tax, but the Court, speaking through Chief Justice John Roberts, upheld it as such: "The reasons the Court in *Drexel Furniture* held that what was called a 'tax' there was a penalty support the conclusion that what is called a 'penalty' here may be viewed as a tax."

Paul Moreno

See Also

Article I, Section 8, Clause 1 (Spending Clause)

Article I, Section 8, Clause 1 (Uniformity Clause)

Article I, Section 8, Clause 3 (Commerce with Foreign Nations)

Article I, Section 8, Clause 3 (Commerce Among the States)

Article I, Section 8, Clause 18 (Necessary and Proper Clause)

Article I, Section 9, Clause 4 (Direct Taxes)

Article I, Section 9, Clause 5 (Export Taxation Clause)

Article I, Section 10, Clause 2 (Import-Export Clause)

Article IV, Section 3, Clause 2 (Property Clause)

Suggested Readings

Robert E. Cushman, *The National Police Power Under the Taxing Clause of the Constitution*, 4 Minn. L. Rev. 247 (1920)

James Willard Hurst, A Legal History of Money in the United States, 1774–1970 (1973)

R. Alton Lee, A History of Regulatory Taxation (1973)

Edward Stanwood, American Tariff Controversies in the Nineteenth Century, 2 vols. (1903)

Frank W. Taussig, The Tariff History of the United States (8th ed. 1967)

Stephen B. Wood, Constitutional Politics in the Progressive Era: Child Labor and the Law (1968)

Significant Cases

McCulloch v. Maryland, 17 U.S. (4 Wheat.) 316 (1819)

Briscoe v. Bank of Kentucky, 36 U.S. (11 Pet.) 257 (1837)

Veazie Bank v. Fenno, 75 U.S. (8 Wall.) 533 (1869)

Collector v. Day, 78 U.S. (11 Wall.) 113 (1871)

Pollock v. Farmers' Loan & Trust Co., 157 U.S. 429, *aff'd on reh'g,* 158 U.S. 601 (1895)

In re Kollock, 165 U.S. 526 (1897)

Schollenberger v. Pennsylvania, 171 U.S. 1 (1898)

McCray v. United States, 195 U.S. 27 (1904)

Hammer v. Dagenhart, 247 U.S. 251 (1918)

Bailey v. Drexel Furniture Co., 259 U.S. 20 (1922)

Hill v. Wallace, 259 U.S. 44 (1922)

Bd. of Trade of the City of Chicago v. Olsen, 262 U.S. 1 (1923)

J. W. Hampton, Jr. & Co. v. United States, 276 U.S. 394 (1928)

United States v. Butler, 297 U.S. 1 (1936)

Carter v. Carter Coal Co., 298 U.S. 238 (1936)

Helvering v. Gerhardt, 304 U.S. 405 (1938)

Graves v. New York *ex. rel.* O'Keefe, 306 U.S. 466 (1939)

South Carolina v. Baker, 485 U.S. 505 (1988)

National Federation of Independent Business v. Sebelius, 132 S. Ct. 2566 (2012)

Spending Clause

The Congress shall have Power ... to pay the Debts and provide for the common Defence and general Welfare of the United States ...

(ARTICLE I, SECTION 8, CLAUSE 1)

 ~

*A*lthough, taken as whole, Article I, Section 8, Clause 1 is the source of congressional authority to levy taxes (*see* Taxation Clause), it permits the levying of taxes for two purposes only: to pay the debts of the United States, and to provide for the "common Defence and general Welfare" of the United States. Taken together, these purposes have traditionally been held to imply and constitute the "Spending Power."

As a matter of original meaning, there is reason to doubt whether the federal spending power flows from this clause. On its face, the clause grants only the power to tax, and any inference of a spending power from the clause's language about the "general Welfare" leaves unexplained where Congress obtains the power to spend borrowed money or the proceeds from land sales. It is more plausible to locate the federal spending power in the Necessary and Proper Clause, or perhaps even the Territories and Property Clauses of Article IV. Nonetheless, modern law has settled on the Taxation Clause as the source of federal spending authority, though a more accurate description would be to entitle the clause as "The General Welfare Clause."

Even so, many legal scholars and jurists today believe that the two purposes of the Spending Clause (to pay the debts of the United States and to provide for the common defense and "general Welfare" of the United State) are so broad as to amount to no limitation at all. The contemporary view is that Congress's power to provide for the "general Welfare" is a power to spend for virtually anything that Congress itself views as helpful. To be sure, some of the Founders, most notably Alexander Hamilton, supported an expansive spending power during the Constitutional Convention; but such proposals, including an explicit attempt to authorize spending by the federal government for internal improvements, were rejected by the Convention. Hamilton continued to press his case by arguing during George Washington's administration for an expansive interpretation of the clause (which Washington adopted). In his "Report on Manufactures" (1791), Hamilton contended that the only limits on the tax-and-spend power were the requirements that duties be uniform, that direct taxes be apportioned by population, and that no tax should be laid on articles exported from any state. The power to raise money was otherwise "plenary, and indefinite," he argued, "and the objects to which it may be appropriated are no less comprehensive."

Hamilton's broad reading met with opposition from many of the other Founders. James Madison repeatedly argued that the power to tax and spend did not confer upon Congress the right to do whatever it thought to be in the best interest of the nation, but only to further the ends specifically enumerated elsewhere in the Constitution, a position supported by Thomas Jefferson.

There was also a third interpretation, recognized later even by Alexander Hamilton. According to this intermediate view, the "common Defence and general Welfare" language is not, as Madison contended, a shorthand way of limiting the power to tax and spend in furtherance of the powers elsewhere enumerated in Article I, Section 8; but it does contain its own limitation, namely, that spending under the clause be for the "general" (that is, national) welfare and not for purely local or regional benefit. President James Monroe later adopted this position—albeit with more teeth than Hamilton had been willing to give it—in his 1822 message vetoing a bill to preserve and repair the Cumberland Road. Monroe contended that Congress's power to spend was restricted "to purposes of common defence, and of general, national, not local, or state, benefit."

There are relatively few examples from the early Congresses of debate over the scope of the spending power, but the few that do exist are enlightening. The First Congress refused to make a loan to a glass manufacturer after several Members expressed the view that such an appropriation would be unconstitutional, and the Fourth Congress did not believe it had the power to provide relief to the citizens of Savannah, Georgia, after a devastating fire destroyed the entire city. The debates do not reflect whether Congress thought such appropriations unconstitutional because they did not further other enumerated powers (Madison's position) or because they were of local rather than national benefit (Monroe's position), but they reflect a rejection of the broad interpretation of the spending power originally proffered by Hamilton.

On the other hand, Congress approved some appropriations for apparently local projects, but it can be argued that those projects were of general benefit or specifically tied to other enumerated powers, and hence within the authority conferred by Article I, Section 8. At the same time it was denying a request to fund the dredging of the Savannah River, for example, Congress approved an appropriation for a lighthouse at the entrance of the Chesapeake Bay. Both measures were important for navigation, but the lighthouse was of benefit to the coastal trade of the entire nation (and hence to interstate commerce), while the dredging operation was primarily of local, intrastate benefit to the people of Georgia and hence fell on the "local" rather than the "general" side of the public welfare line.

Congress approved various appropriations to fund a road across the Cumberland Gap, but it rejected as unconstitutional a larger appropriation for internal improvements of which the Cumberland Gap road project was a part. Congress accepted the view that it had no power under the Constitution to open roads and canals in any state; its power to fund the Cumberland Road was the result of the compact with Ohio "for which the nation receive[d] an equivalent," namely, Ohio's promise not to tax for five years any lands sold by the federal government in Ohio. Moreover, as George Washington had repeatedly urged while President, the opening of a road across the Cumberland Gap was strategically necessary to keep the western territories allied with the coastal states (rather than with the foreign powers that controlled the Mississippi river region at the time), something critically important to the security of the entire nation and not just the people of Ohio. The Cumberland Gap road was an example of a local project that directly benefited the nation. Appropriations for other local projects such as public education and local roads and canals, the "general" benefit of which was less direct, were viewed as unconstitutional, and a proposal in Jefferson's 1806 State of the Union Address to amend the Constitution to permit funding for such internal improvements was never adopted.

In sum, although Alexander Hamilton and other leaders of the Federalist Party argued for an expansive reading of the spending power, their reading was, on the whole, rejected both by Congress and, after the election of 1800, by the executive. Indeed, the differing views on the scope of federal power was a principal ground upon which the 1800 presidential-election contest between Jefferson and incumbent Federalist President John Adams was waged. As Jefferson would note in an 1817 letter to Albert Gallatin, the different interpretations of the Spending Clause put forward by Hamilton on the one hand, and Madison and Jefferson on the other were "almost the only landmark which now divides the federalists from the republicans." Jefferson won that election, and, save for a brief interlude during the one-term presidency of John Quincy Adams, every President adopted the more restrictive interpretation of spending power until the Civil War.

President Madison vetoed as unconstitutional an internal improvements bill that Congress passed at the very end of his presidency. President Monroe also rejected the expansive Hamiltonian view of the Spending Clause (albeit on slightly different grounds than Madison had), vetoing various attempts at internal improvement bills during most of his two terms. But in the last year of his presidency, finding the line between "general" welfare and local welfare a hard one to define, Monroe signed a few bills to fund surveys for some local internal improvement projects. He thus opened a gate through which flowed a flood of spending on local projects during the administration of President John Quincy Adams.

Adams's resurrection of the Hamiltonian position became the focus of the next presidential election, contributing to Adams's defeat at the hands of Andrew Jackson, who promptly put to rest "this dangerous doctrine" by vetoing a $200 million appropriation for the purchase of stock in the Maysville and Lexington Turnpike Company and for the direct construction of other "ordinary" roads and canals by the government itself. So strong was his veto message that for four years Congress did not even try to pass another such bill, and when in 1834 it passed an act to improve the navigation of the Wabash River, Jackson again responded forcefully, rejecting as a "fallacy" the contention that the Spending Clause conferred upon Congress the power to do whatever seemed "to conduce to the public good."

In 1847 and 1857, Presidents James K. Polk and James Buchanan, respectively, vetoed subsequent congressional efforts to fund internal improvements. Polk vetoed a bill strikingly similar to much of the pork-barrel legislation to which we have grown accustomed in modern times. It provided $6,000 for projects in the Wisconsin territory—constitutionally permissible because of Congress's broader powers over federal territories—but it also included $500,000 for myriad projects in the existing states. Polk contended that to interpret the Spending Clause to permit such appropriations would allow "combinations of individual and local interests [that would be] strong enough to control legislation, absorb the revenues of the country, and plunge the government into a hopeless indebtedness."

Similarly, in his message vetoing the college land grant bill, President Buchanan took it as a given that the funds raised by Congress from taxation were "confined to the execution of the enumerated powers delegated to Congress." The idea that the resources of the federal government—either taxes or the public lands—could be diverted to carry into effect any measure of state domestic policy that Congress saw fit to support "would be to confer upon Congress a vast and irresponsible authority, utterly at war with the well-known jealousy of Federal power which prevailed at the formation of the Constitution."

Thus, while there were clearly voices urging for an expansive spending power before the Civil War, the interpretation held by Jefferson, Madison, and Monroe is the one that prevailed for most of the first seventy years after adoption of the Constitution.

Modern-day jurisprudence on the Spending Clause begins with the New Deal-era case of *United States v. Butler* (1936). In that case, both parties relied upon the Hamiltonian position, despite the history recounted above. Both the majority and dissenting opinions of the Court facially accepted the correctness of Hamilton's position even though the majority ruled that the particular tax and regulatory program at issue in the case was unconstitutional because its purpose was to regulate and control agricultural production, "a matter beyond the powers delegated to the federal government"—a holding much more in line with Madison's interpretation of the spending power than Hamilton's.

Moreover, the Hamiltonian position purportedly adopted by the Court was not the expansive view that Congress could do whatever it deemed to be in the public interest, but the much more limited view that the limits on spending were contained in the Spending Clause itself and not in the remainder of Article I, Section 8. "While, therefore, the power to tax is not unlimited," Justice Owen J. Roberts wrote, "its confines are set in the clause which confers it, and not in those of Section 8 which bestow and define the legislative powers of the Congress." In other words, the only limitation on Congress's power to tax and spend was that the spending be for the "general Welfare"—the position actually advocated by James Monroe. What really makes *Butler* a departure from the early interpretation of the clause, then, was that it gave Congress virtually unlimited discretion to determine what was in the "general Welfare"—a holding that, practically speaking, is much more in line with the expansive Hamiltonian position than with the positions advocated either by Monroe or by Madison and Jefferson.

Since *Butler* and until *NFIB v. Sebelius* (2012) the courts have treated whatever limitation the clause might impose as essentially a nonjusticiable political question. In the case of *South Dakota v. Dole* (1987), for example, the Supreme Court noted that "the level of deference to the congressional decision is such that the Court has more recently questioned whether 'general welfare' is a judicially enforceable restriction at all." Instead, the courts have focused not on the constitutionality of spending programs themselves, but on whether various conditions imposed on the receipt of federal funds—conditions designed to achieve ends concededly not within Congress's enumerated powers—were constitutionally permissible.

In *South Dakota v. Dole*, the State of South Dakota challenged the constitutionality of a federal statute conditioning states' receipt of a portion of federal highway funds on the state's raising its minimum drinking age to twenty-one. *Dole* upheld the federal spending restriction and the Court adopted a four-prong test to assess the constitutionality of spending conditions: (1) the spending power must be in pursuit of the "general Welfare," a requirement that the Court left to Congress's judgment to satisfy because, in its view, "the concept of welfare or the opposite is shaped by Congress"; (2) whether the conditions imposed were unambiguous (so the states know what they are agreeing to); (3) whether they were related to the particular national projects or programs being funded (thus far, the Court

has not invalidated a spending restriction on the grounds that it is too unrelated to the programs being funded); and (4) whether there are other constitutional provisions that provide an independent bar to the conditional grant of federal funds. For example, Congress could not impose as a condition that a state receiving federal funds for its welfare programs require welfare recipients to waive their Fourth Amendment rights.

Dole also added another test: "Our decisions have recognized that in some circumstances the financial inducement offered by Congress might be so coercive as to pass the point at which 'pressure turns into compulsion.'" The Court then briefly announced that there was no coercion because states that refused to raise their drinking age to twenty-one would "lose a relatively small percentage of certain federal highway funds."

Of these requirements, only the requirement that the condition be unambiguous has received much play in the courts. Yet that requirement is more an issue of legislative drafting than of actual limits on Congress's spending power. The Court has thus far been highly deferential to Congress in its assessment of the other requirements, which at least offer some prospect of limiting Congress's spending power should the Court decide to put some teeth into them. Yet the facts of *South Dakota v. Dole* itself demonstrate just how little teeth those requirements have. The Court concluded in that case that conditioning receipt of federal highway funds on a state's adoption of a drinking age of twenty-one was sufficiently related to the funding program. Eighteen-year-old residents of states that had a drinking age of twenty-one would drive to border states where the drinking age was eighteen to procure their liquor, the argument went. When driving back, the drivers had an increased risk of drunk driving on the highways paved by federal funds, and that was a sufficient connection for the Court.

Both Justices William J. Brennan, Jr., and Sandra Day O'Connor dissented. Justice O'Connor noted in her *South Dakota v. Dole* dissent: "If the spending power is to be limited only by Congress' notion of the general welfare, the reality…is that the Spending Clause gives 'power to the Congress…to become a parliament of the whole people, subject to no restrictions save such as are self-imposed.' This…was not the Framers' plan and it is not the meaning of the Spending Clause."

The Supreme Court had also been suggesting since its decision in *Butler* that the spending power could not be used to "coerce" action that, because of constitutional principles of federalism, were properly left to the States. But in the 75 years following *Butler*, the Court never held that a congressional spending program violated the coercion principle until its decision in the 2012 health care case, *NFIB v. Sebelius*. In that case, the Court held (by a vote of 7–2) that Congress's threat to withhold *all* existing Medicaid program funds from states that chose not to participate in the significant expansion of that program mandated by the 2010 Affordable Care Act was unduly coercive, a "gun to the head" of the states, and "economic dragooning" that left "the States with no real option but to acquiesce in the Medicaid expansion." But the Court then severed that penalty from the rest of the statute, leaving the expanded Medicaid spending program in place. As a result, the other coercion problem inherent in the Act was permitted to stand, and states were still left with an unpalatable choice: either participate in the expansion demanded by Congress or decline to participate and watch billions of dollars in tax revenues flow from the state's own citizens to fund Medicaid programs in other states. And the Court did not even consider that such massive transfers of tax revenues from non-participating to participating states might not qualify as spending in the "general" welfare.

Thus, while the Court has recently restored some limits to other powers delegated to Congress (such as the Commerce Clause), the spending power remains virtually unlimited in contemporary jurisprudence, contrary to the evident views of most of the Constitution's Framers. This does not prevent Congress from adopting on its own a view of its power to spend that is more in accord with those of the Founders, of course, but the spending power appears to be one whose limits the Court will not enforce.

John C. Eastman

See Also

Article I, Section 8, Clause 1 (Taxation)

Article I, Section 8, Clause 1 (Uniformity Clause)
Article I, Section 8, Clause 3 (Commerce Among the States)
Article I, Section 8, Clause 17 (Enclave Clause)
Article I, Section 8, Clause 18 (Necessary and Proper Clause)
Article I, Section 9, Clause 4 (Direct Taxes)
Article I, Section 9, Clause 5 (Export Taxation Clause)
Article IV, Section 3, Clause 2 (Territories Clause; Property Clause)

Suggestions for Further Research

Lynn A. Baker, *Conditional Federal Spending After Lopez*, 95 Colum. L. Rev. 1911 (1995)

Erwin Chemerinsky, *Protecting the Spending Power*, 4 Chap. L. Rev. 89 (2001)

John C. Eastman, *Restoring the "General" to the General Welfare Clause*, 4 Chap. L. Rev. 63 (2001)

David E. Engdahl, *The Spending Power*, 44 Duke L.J. 1 (1994)

Gary Lawson & Guy Seidman, The Constitution of Empire: Territorial Expansion and American Legal History 23–32 (2004)

Celestine Richards McConville, *Federal Funding Conditions: Bursting Through the Dole Loopholes*, 4 Chap. L. Rev. 163 (2001)

Robert G. Natelson, *The General Welfare Clause and the Public Trust: An Essay in Original Understanding*, 52 U. Kan. L. Rev. 1 (2003)

Jeffrey T. Renz, *What Spending Clause? (Or the President's Paramour): An Examination of the Views of Hamilton, Madison, and Story on Article I, Section 8, Clause 1 of the United States Constitution*, 33 J. Marshall L. Rev. 81 (1999)

Significant Cases

United States v. Butler, 297 U.S. 1 (1936)
South Dakota v. Dole, 483 U.S. 203 (1987)
National Federation of Independent Business v. Sebelius, 132 S. Ct. 2566 (2012)

Uniformity Clause

…all Duties, Imposts and Excises shall be uniform throughout the United States….
(Article I, Section 8, Clause 1)

~

*A*mong the unsatisfactory aspects of the Confederation government were its inability to regulate interstate and foreign commerce and its weak powers of taxation. The Constitution cured these defects, but thereby created a new danger: the greatly strengthened national government might abuse its powers by oppressing politically weaker groups and strangling the economic activity that the Framers hoped to promote.

At the Constitutional Convention, the Uniformity Clause was initially joined with what is now the Port Preference Clause (Article I, Section 9, Clause 6), which forbids Congress to give preferences "by any Regulation of Commerce or Revenue" to the ports of one state over those of another. Along with other provisions restricting congressional power over taxes and commercial regulations, these two were designed to forestall economically oppressive discrimination. The Port Preference Clause limits both the commerce and taxing powers, whereas the Uniformity Clause applies to the taxing power alone. Their common origin, however, is a sign of their common purpose: each was meant to prevent geographic discrimination that would give one state or region a competitive advantage or disadvantage in its commercial relations with the others.

Because the goods and activities that can be taxed are distributed unequally through the country, virtually all duties, imposts, and excises have nonuniform effects. A tax on oil production, for example, will affect certain regions more severely than others. Because the Constitution expressly empowers Congress to levy these taxes, it must also permit some of the nonuniform effects that inevitably accompany them. The principal challenge in interpreting the Uniformity Clause is to distinguish between the kind of nonuniformity that is forbidden by the Constitution and the inevitable nonuniform effects that accompany legitimate duties, imposts, and excises.

In its earliest exposition, the Supreme Court declared that a tax is uniform if it "operates with the same force and effect in every place where the subject of it is found." *Edye v. Robertson* (1884). This rule correctly recognized that the Uniformity Clause was meant to forbid geographically nonuniform taxes without outlawing all geographically nonuniform effects. But the formula is inadequate, because it does not describe the limits on Congress's discretion to define the "subjects" of taxation. Suppose, for example, that Congress chose to define the subject of an excise tax as "oil produced in Alaska." The rule would be formally satisfied, but the most flagrant geographic discrimination would be possible.

In *United States v. Ptasynski* (1983), a unanimous Court concluded that: (1) any tax in which the subject is defined in nongeographic terms satisfies the Uniformity Clause, and (2) where the subject is defined in geographic terms, the tax will be scrutinized for "actual geographic discrimination."

The first part of this test creates a very large safe harbor for discriminatory taxes, which can almost always be framed without using overtly geographic terminology (for example, "oil whose production might affect caribou populations"). Nor is it clear that the second part of the test puts any real limit on Congress's power to impose discriminatory and oppressive taxes, for the Court nowhere defined "actual geographic discrimination." In fact, the Court went out of its way to emphasize that review of statutes using geographic terminology would be highly deferential. With no promise of effective judicial enforcement, the Uniformity Clause has, at least for the present, apparently been rendered nugatory, save for Congress's own sense of its obligations under the Constitution.

Nelson Lund

See Also

Suggestions for Further Research

Richard A. Epstein, Takings: Private Property and the Power of Eminent Domain 289–293 (1985)

Nelson Lund, Comment, *The Uniformity Clause*, 51 U. Chi. L. Rev. 1193 (1984)

Significant Cases

Edye v. Robertson, 112 U.S. 580 (1884)

Knowlton v. Moore, 178 U.S. 41 (1900)

United States v. Ptasynski, 462 U.S. 74 (1983)

Borrowing Clause

The Congress shall have Power... To borrow Money on the credit of the United States....

(Article I, Section 8, Clause 2)

$\sim$

*T*he power to borrow money is essential to the existence and survival of a national government. In the Founding era, political leaders expected that in peacetime Congress would craft the federal government's budget so that revenues equaled or surpassed expenditures. Indeed, the Treasury Department strictly complied with a policy of earmarking all revenues for particular government programs. Nonetheless, the nation could not successfully defend itself militarily without the power to borrow quickly and extensively when the need arose. The Framers therefore drafted the Borrowing Clause without an express limitation.

The Borrowing Clause, however, has a practical corollary. The terms upon which a nation could borrow money depended upon its credit standing. President George Washington's Farewell Address (1796) captures the general sentiment of the times:

> As a very important source of strength and security, cherish public credit. One method of preserving it is to use it as sparingly as possible, avoiding occasions of expense by cultivating peace, but remembering also that timely disbursements to prepare for danger frequently prevent much greater disbursements to repel it; avoiding likewise the accumulation of debt, not only by shunning occasions of expense, but by vigorous exertions in time of peace to discharge the debts which unavoidable wars may have occasioned, not ungenerously throwing upon posterity the burden which we ourselves ought to bear.

Although Federalists and Republicans agreed on the need to maintain the public credit, they diverged considerably on how the borrowing power should be implemented. Indeed, the core differences in the visions of the Federalists and Republicans in the Founding era relate to contrasting views of this power. Alexander Hamilton sought to assure a strong central government by interpreting the Borrowing Clause as authorizing Congress to charter the First Bank of the United States (established in 1791), which maintained federal control over the federal monetary reserves and issued debt instruments that circulated like money. Hamilton viewed the issuing of federal debt instruments as an essential stimulant to commerce, providing a source of capital to a capital-poor society, and equally important for revenue collection purposes. The Constitution, however, did not expressly authorize Congress to charter corporations, and the constitutionality of the bank was widely debated.

Thomas Jefferson dismantled much of Hamilton's program. To the Jeffersonian Republicans, a balanced budget reflected a popular desire to limit the size and power of the federal government and to protect states' rights. Jefferson repealed Hamilton's internal taxes (which provided security for the federal debt) and appointed Albert Gallatin as Secretary of the Treasury with a mandate to pay down the federal debt. With a few exceptions, subsequent administrations also prioritized balancing the federal budget, and Andrew Jackson successfully paid down the federal debt in 1835. In this, the early presidents were following the advice of George Washington in his Farewell Address.

Wartime exigencies and economic crises led the country toward the modern interpretation of the Borrowing Clause. A financial emergency that threatened national security during the War of 1812 led to the bipartisan acceptance of the need for federal government control of its reserves through the (Second) Bank of the United States, which was held constitutional in Justice John Marshall's opinion in *McCulloch v. Maryland* (1819).

The policy dealing with incurring and repaying debt, however, remained relatively consistent from 1789 until 1917. Congress borrowed money to pay for wars and to sustain the economy during a recession, but it began paying it down upon the return to peace and financial stability. In 1917 Congress granted the Department of the Treasury standing borrowing authority, but for many years Congress continued to manage the incurrence and repayment of debt in substantially the same manner as before. After World War II, changed attitudes, including the influence of economic thinkers such as John Maynard Keynes and the expansion of government-funded entitlements as well as a large standing military force produced sustained peacetime deficits and very few periods of debt reduction. The past few decades have been punctuated by failed attempts at spending and debt limits, and the federal debt has reached unprecedented levels. One attempt, granting the President a line-item veto power, was struck down by the Supreme Court in *Clinton v. City of New York* (1998)

With respect to a federal currency, the Report of the Committee of Detail (debated at the Constitutional Convention) had given Congress the power to "borrow money, and emit bills on the credit of the United States." The delegates voted to strike the power to "emit bills," which strongly suggests that Congress was not authorized to borrow by means of issuing paper money, although it is clear that interest-bearing debt instruments were permissible. The Union's financial crisis during the Civil War, however, led to the attempt by the federal government to issue and make legal tender a paper-money currency, which was held constitutional in *The Legal Tender Cases* (1871). Sixty years later, financial problems during the Great Depression led Congress to define what constitutes legal tender. In 1933, a congressional joint resolution prohibited the enforcement of gold clauses in both contracts between the government and individuals and in private contracts, thereby making Federal Reserve notes the exclusive legal tender. The Supreme Court held the resolution constitutional in *The Gold Clause Cases* (1935).

Legal disputes dealing with the Borrowing Clause today involve two issues. The most litigated issue involves the principle of intergovernmental-taxation immunity. The Supreme Court has held that the Supremacy Clause (Article VI, Clause 2) prohibits state and municipal governments from directly or indirectly taxing the interest income on federal government debt and thereby interfering with the federal government's power under the Borrowing Clause. *See State of Missouri ex rel. Missouri Insurance Co. v. Gehner* (1930).

The clause also implicitly requires Congress to maintain the public credit. The Supreme Court has invoked the clause in treating the government like a private party in its contractual dealings by vesting Congress with the power to contract against subsequent repudiation or impairment of its obligations by future Congresses. In *Perry v. United States* (1935), the Court cautioned that the power to borrow money is a power vital to the government, upon which in an extremity its very life may depend. The binding quality of the promise of the United States is of the essence of the credit that is so pledged. Though having this power to authorize the issuance of definite obligations for the payment of money borrowed, Congress has not been vested with authority to alter or destroy those obligations. However, in *United States v. Winstar Corp.* (1996), the Court held, among other things, that contractual obligations of the government would be enforced unless doing so blocked the exercise of one of the government's essential sovereign powers.

Because the Constitution imposes no express limits on the borrowing power, the political branches must decide the issue. As in the Founding era, the question of the extent to which the government should run deficits and maintain a large federal debt are at the essence of contrasting views about the proper scope of the federal government.

Claire Priest

See Also

Article I, Section 8, Clause 5 (Coinage Clause)
Article I, Section 10, Clause 1
Article VI, Clause 2 (Supremacy Clause)
Amendment XIV, Section 4 (Debts Incurred During Rebellion)

Suggestions for Further Research

ALBERT S. BOLLES, THE FINANCIAL HISTORY OF THE UNITED STATES, 1774–1885 (vols. 1–3, reprinted 1969) Kenneth W. Dam, *The Legal Tender Cases,* 1981 SUP. CT. REV. 367 (1981)

Anita S. Krishnakumar, *In Defense of the Debt Limit Statute,* 42 HARV. J. ON LEGIS. 135 (2005)

JAMES MACDONALD, A FREE NATION DEEP IN DEBT: THE FINANCIAL ROOTS OF DEMOCRACY (2003)

JAMES D. SAVAGE, BALANCED BUDGETS AND AMERICAN POLITICS (1988)

Significant Cases

Scope of the Borrowing Clause:
McCulloch v. Maryland, 17 U.S. (4 Wheat.) 316 (1819)
Maintaining the Public Credit:
Perry v. United States, 294 U.S. 330 (1935)
United States v. Winstar Corp., 518 U.S. 839 (1996)
Authority to Determine Legal Tender:
Bronson v. Rodes, 74 U.S. (7 Wall.) 229 (1868)
Veazie Bank v. Fenno, 75 U.S. (8 Wall.) 533 (1869)
The Legal Tender Cases, 79 U.S. (12 Wall.) 457 (1871), overruling in part Hepburn v. Griswold, 75 U.S. (8 Wall.) 603 (1870)
Julliard v. Greenman, 110 U.S. 421 (1884)
Clinton v. City of New York, 524 U.S. 417 (1998)
Treasurer of New Jersey v. U.S. Dep't of Treasury, 684 F.3d 382 (3d Cir. 2012)
The Gold Clause Cases:
Norman v. Baltimore and Ohio R.R., 294 U.S. 240 (1935)
Nortz v. United States, 294 U.S. 317 (1935)
Perry v. United States, 294 U.S. 330 (1935)
Intergovernmental Taxation Immunity:
State of Missouri ex rel. Missouri Ins. Co. v. Gehner, 281 U.S. 313 (1930)
New Jersey Realty Title Ins. Co. v. Division of Tax Appeals, 338 U.S. 665 (1950)

Commerce with Foreign Nations

The Congress shall have Power ... To regulate Commerce with foreign Nations. ...
(ARTICLE I, SECTION 8, CLAUSE 3)

~

$\mathcal{E}$ven before the Constitutional Convention, James Madison had long argued that exclusive power over foreign commerce should be vested in the national government. Under the Articles of Confederation, the states had the power to raise tariffs against goods from others states and from foreign nations, creating, as Madison put it, "rival, conflicting and angry regulations." Thus, Great Britain had been able to use its power over duties and tariffs to monopolize trade in its favor without the United States government having the ability to respond.

At Philadelphia, there was unanimity that one of the general powers of the new government should be to regulate foreign commerce. Even Anti-Federalist Luther Martin, who later left the Convention to oppose the Constitution, had no doubts about it. In fact, in *The Federalist* No. 42, one of Madison's arguments for lodging the power to regulate commerce among the states with Congress was that "without this supplemental provision, the great and essential power of regulating foreign commerce, would have been incomplete, and ineffectual."

Some delegates, particularly from the South, wanted any regulation of foreign commerce to be effective only through a supermajority vote in Congress, but Madison successfully countered that a supermajority would cripple the government if it were necessary to retaliate against discriminatory tariffs from a foreign country.

Although Madison undoubtedly believed that the power to regulate foreign commerce was exclusive to the federal government, the proposition is not obvious from the text. Elsewhere, the Constitution denies the states certain powers over foreign commerce (no treaties or other agreements and no tariffs except under very limited circumstances). The text of the Commerce Clause does not differentiate between Congress's power "to regulate" foreign commerce from its power over interstate commerce, and some Justices on the Supreme Court have opined that Congress's power to regulate interstate commerce is coextensive with its power over foreign commerce. Nonetheless, a number of other opinions have held that Congress's power over foreign commerce is qualitatively greater than its power to regulate commerce among the states, because it is part of the federal government's complete sovereign power over foreign relations, in which the states have no standing. *Brolan v. United States* (1915). *In Board of Trustees of University of Illinois v. United States* (1933), the Court stated: "In international relations and with respect to foreign intercourse and trade the people of the United States act through a single government with unified and adequate national power." And in *Japan Line, Ltd. v. County of Los Angeles* (1979), the Court declared that "[f]oreign commerce is preeminently a matter of national concern." As early as 1827 in *Brown v. Maryland*, Chief Justice John Marshall held that both the Import-Export Clause and the Commerce with Foreign Nations Clause precluded a state from burdening an imported good with a tax or license so long as the good remained in the ownership of the importer and "in the original form or package," though, later, the Court permitted states to prohibit dangerous or noxious foreign goods. *Compagnie Francaise de Navigation a Vapeur v. Louisiana Board of Health* (1902).

The courts have affirmed Congress' extensive power over foreign commerce. According to Professor Louis Henkin, the foreign commerce clause was originally the "basis for Congressional regulation of maritime and admiralty affairs and its control of immigration." Subsequently, the clause has been the basis for extending American criminal jurisdiction abroad. Foreign commerce "includes both goods and services," *United States v. Clark* (2006), and the regulation of foreign commerce "includes the entrance of ships, the importation of goods, and the bringing of persons into

the ports of the United States." *United States ex rel. Turner v. Williams* (1904). There must always be some nexus between the United States and the foreign commercial activity, but the nexus need not be extensive. For example, Congress's power over foreign commerce does not turn on whether Americans are transporting American goods or even whether the voyage includes an American port, so long as the goods are being transported in American flag ships. *Pacific Seafarers, Inc. v. Pacific Far East Line, Inc.* (1968).

Unlike Congress's power over commerce "among the several states," federalism concerns are not as present in its control over foreign commerce. Today, the Court allows the states less power to tax foreign commerce than they have to tax interstate commerce. In *Complete Auto Transit, Inc. v. Brady* (1977), the Supreme Court declared that a state tax affecting interstate commerce would be valid only if it were: (1) nondiscriminatory, (2) applied to an interstate activity that had a "substantial nexus" with the state, (3) apportioned fairly, and (4) connected to services that the state provided. Later, in *Japan Line*, the Court added two further considerations to taxation of a foreign instrumentality: (1) the danger of multiple taxation and (2) the danger that the tax may damage the need for federal uniformity. Even though the Court has been somewhat more generous in recent years in permitting state taxation that involves foreign commerce, the rules continue to suggest a greater federal constitutional interest in foreign commerce than in commerce among the states, where the background principles of federalism still have some presence.

David F. Forte

See Also

Article I, Section 8, Clause 3 (Commerce Among the States; Commerce with the Indian Tribes)
Article I, Section 10, Clause 1 (State Treaties)
Article I, Section 10, Clause 2 (Import-Export Clause)

Suggestions for Further Research

Albert S. Abel, *The Commerce Clause in the Constitutional Convention and in Contemporary Comment*, 25 MINN. L. REV. 432 (1941)

Anthony J. Colangelo, *The Foreign Commerce Clause*, 96 Va. L. Rev. 949 (2010)

Louis Henkin, Foreign Affairs and the United States Constitution (2d ed. 1996)

Saikrishna Prakash, *Our Three Commerce Clauses and the Presumption of Intrasentence Uniformity*, 55 Ark. L. Rev. 1149 (2003)

Significant Cases

Brown v. Maryland, 25 U.S. (12 Wheat.) 419 (1827)

Compagnie Francaise de Navigation a Vapeur v. Louisiana Board of Health, 186 U.S. 380 (1902)

Buttfield v. Stranahan, 192 U.S. 470 (1904)

United States *ex rel.* Turner v. Williams, 194 U.S. 279 (1904)

Brolan v. United States, 236 U.S. 216 (1915)

Bd. of Trustees of University of Illinois v. United States, 289 U.S. 48 (1933)

Pacific Seafarers, Inc. v. Pacific Far East Line, Inc., 404 F.2d 804 (D.C. Cir. 1968)

Michelin Tire Corp. v. Wages, 423 U.S. 276 (1976)

Complete Auto Transit, Inc. v. Brady, 430 U.S. 274 (1977)

Japan Line, Ltd. v. Cnty. of Los Angeles, 441 U.S. 434 (1979)

Container Corp. of America v. Franchise Tax Bd., 463 U.S. 159 (1983)

Itel Containers Int'l Corp. v. Huddleston, 507 U.S. 60 (1993)

United States v. Clark, 435 F.3d 1100 (9th Cir. 2006)

Commerce Among the States

The Congress shall have Power... To regulate Commerce... among the several States....

(Article I, Section 8, Clause 3)

$\sim$

*T*he Commerce Among the States Clause (or, "the Commerce Clause") operates both as a power delegated to Congress and as a constraint upon state legislation. No clause in the 1787 Constitution has been more disputed, and none has generated as many cases.

To this day, the debate over the extent of the commerce power centers on the definitions of "to regulate," "commerce," and "among the several States."

The narrowest definition of "to regulate" is to "make regular," that is, to facilitate the free flow of goods, but not, except in cases of danger, to prohibit the flow of any good. Some scholars and a number of Supreme Court Justices have supported that narrow definition. In fact, in 1886, the House Judiciary Committee declared that a proposed bill that would have prohibited the sale of oleomargarine was against the original intent of the Framers. The Committee reasoned that the purpose of the Commerce Clause was to prevent state barriers to commerce, not to give Congress the power to do the same.

Nonetheless, the Supreme Court has never formally accepted a limited view of what "to regulate" means. From the beginning, Chief Justice John Marshall in *Gibbons v. Ogden* (1824) saw the power to regulate as coextensive with the other delegated powers of Congress. He declared: "This power, like all others vested in Congress, is complete in itself, may be exercised to its utmost extent, and acknowledges no limitations, other than are prescribed in the constitution." In other words, "to regulate" is descriptive of the essential and core Congressional power to legislate. The manner in which Congress decides to regulate commerce, Marshall said, is completely at the discretion of Congress, subject only to the political check of the voters. Its exercise, therefore, is nonjusticiable. This power, as it later turned out, includes the power to prohibit the transportation of articles, as well as to control their exchange and the manner of transportation. In *Champion v. Ames* (1903), the Supreme Court (5–4) upheld a congressional ban on the interstate transportation of lottery tickets over the dissent on Chief Justice Melville Fuller, though all states at that time had prohibited such lotteries.

Even if "regulation" is a political question, the definition of "commerce," however, is not up to Congress. It has an objective quality and is determinable by the courts. For many scholars such as Randy Barnett, Richard Epstein, and Raoul Berger, commerce means the trading, bartering, buying, and selling of goods, and they include the incidents of transporting those goods within the definition. Commerce would not include manufacturing or agriculture. Robert Pushaw and Grant Nelson assert a somewhat broader view, believing that commerce means "any market-based activity" having an economic component. Jack Balkin suggests a much more expansive concept, namely that the term "commerce" in the eighteenth century meant all forms of social and economic intercourse between persons, including but not limited to "traffic," which was then the term for trade. The transportation of goods is not literally part of the exchange of goods, Balkin observes, but it would be part of commerce as intercourse.

Justice Clarence Thomas has embraced the limited definition of commerce as trade: "At the time the original Constitution was ratified, 'commerce' consisted of selling, buying, and bartering, as well as transporting for these purposes." He noted that the etymology of the word *com-merce* meant "with merchandise." *United States v. Lopez* (1995). Much of the modern Supreme Court's jurisprudence, however, regards commerce as comprising "economic activity" generally.

In *Gibbons v. Ogden,* Chief Justice Marshall declared that commerce is more than "traffic," that is, more than mere trade. It is "commercial intercourse," which includes both trade and the manner in which trade is carried on. Thus, he held that the government, under the definition of commerce as he affirmed, had the right to prescribe the rules of navigation for trade.

Though Marshall's notion of commerce was relatively narrow, his conception of the third term of the clause, "among the several States," was quite broad. Some commentators have defined "among the several States" as the trading and movement of goods between two or more states. But Chief Justice Marshall thought "among" had a wider purview than would the word "between:" "Comprehensive as the word 'among' is, it may very properly be restricted to that commerce which concerns more States than one." Although this was a broader concept, Marshall nonetheless saw that there is some commerce that Congress cannot reach: "The enumeration presupposes something not enumerated; and that something, if we regard the language or the subject of the sen-

tence, must be the exclusively internal commerce of a State." Purely local activities (i.e., commerce that does not concern "more States than one"), therefore, remain outside of the reach of Congress under the Commerce Among the States Clause.

After *Gibbons v. Ogden*, there was little occasion for the Supreme Court to investigate the breadth of federal commerce power until the late nineteenth century and the advent of national economic legislation. (However, the Court considered many cases involving the so-called dormant commerce power: the power of the states to enact legislation that affects interstate commerce when Congress is silent, i.e., has not enacted any legislation.) From 1895 on, the Court experimented with differing notions of the commerce power until 1938, when it signaled that it was abdicating any serious role in monitoring Congress's exercise of this delegated power.

In *United States v. E.C. Knight Co.* (1895), the Supreme Court declared that the Sherman Antitrust Act could not constitutionally be interpreted to apply to monopolies in manufacturing, for "commerce" did not reach manufacturing. "Manufacture is transformation—the fashioning of raw materials into a change of form for use.... The buying and selling and the transportation incidental thereto constitute commerce." Any effect manufacturing has on commerce was merely "indirect" and could not be reached under the commerce power.

This qualitative distinction between manufacturing and commerce held for forty years, but the Court was not ungenerous in otherwise upholding federal regulatory legislation. If companies engaged in price-fixing and marketing schemes, the Court held them to be "in commerce" and subject to Congress's power to regulate commerce. *Addyston Pipe & Steel Co. v. United States* (1899). In an expansionary gloss to the qualitative distinction, the Court also held that goods in the "stream of commerce," such as cattle at the Chicago stockyards and slaughterhouses on the way from farm to nationwide distribution, also fell under the commerce power. *Swift & Co. v. United States* (1905); *Stafford v. Wallace* (1922). Beyond manufacturing, the Court had earlier declared that insurance contracts were not items of trade and therefore could not be reached by Congress under the commerce clause. *Paul v. Virginia* (1869).

In *Champion v. Ames*, the Court added a new perspective on the commerce power. It eschewed any scrutiny on whether the purpose of congressional regulation of interstate commerce had to be focused on the regulation of goods in commerce, in this case, lottery tickets. So long as the good traveled across state lines, the Court held, Congress could regulate or prohibit it, even if Congress's purpose was moral. The dissenters pointed out unsuccessfully that legislation to regulate morals had been traditionally left to the states under their police power. Soon thereafter, on this basis, the Court upheld the Pure Food and Drug Act, *Hipolite Egg Co. v. United States* (1911); legislation restricting interstate prostitution, *Hoke v. United States* (1913); and even personal immorality connected with interstate commerce, *Caminetti v. United States* (1917) (crossing a state line with a paramour, when no money exchanged hands). These cases stood for what later came to be called the "jurisdictional element" test, namely, that Congress could regulate the transportation and disposition of any item that travelled across state lines, and it was not clear that the item even had to be commercial.

Thus, outside of the "jurisdiction" test, the Court applied a limiting qualitative test to legislation, the purpose and effect of which was to regulate manufacturing, as in the laws regulating child labor, *Hammer v. Dagenhart* (1918), and railroad retirement plans, *Railroad Retirement Board v. Alton Railroad* Co. (1935). Manufacturing was not, in its nature, "commerce," even though it might have an effect on commerce. Similarly, regarding commerce "among the several States," the Court balked if Congress sought to regulate goods after their interstate transportation had come to rest, *A.L.A. Schechter Poultry Corp. v. United States* (1935), or before transportation had begun, *Carter v. Carter Coal Co.* (1936).

As limited as the Court's use of the qualitative test was, an alternative test had begun to develop that would have approved even more congressional legislation. Traditionally ascribed to the opinion of Justice Charles Evans Hughes in the *Shreveport Rate Case* (1914), which permitted federal regulation of intrastate railroad rates

to harmonize with interstate railroad rates, this quantitative test asserted that Congress could regulate a local activity, even manufacturing, if that local activity had a "substantial" effect on interstate commerce (i.e., "commerce which concerns more States than one" when the concern was "substantial"). Although Hughes' language in the case could be read as referring, not to Congress's power under the Commerce Clause, but rather to the Necessary and Proper Clause (Article I, Section 8, Clause 18), the case became symbolic of a turn towards an expansion of congressional legislative power under the Commerce Clause itself. Over the next two decades, a minority of Justices continued to argue in favor of a quantitative test. The dispute between those espousing a qualitative version of the power and those supporting a quantitative interpretation increased during the 1930s as more extensive federal regulatory legislation came before the Supreme Court.

In 1935, Justice Benjamin N. Cardozo, concurring in the unanimous opinion in *Schechter*, suggested a test that would allow the government to regulate local activities if they had a proximate or foreseeable effect on interstate commerce: "The law is not indifferent to considerations of degree. Activities local in their immediacy do not become interstate and national because of distant repercussions." The following year, in striking down the Bituminous Coal Conservation Act in *Carter v. Carter Coal* Co., the Court seemingly accepted Cardozo's proximate cause test. (Cardozo dissented from the decision on procedural grounds.) Writing for the majority, Justice George Sutherland declared: "The word 'direct' implies that the activity or condition invoked or blamed shall operate proximately—not mediately, remotely, or collaterally—to produce the effect. It connotes the absence of an efficient intervening agency or condition."

A year later, in *NLRB v. Jones & Laughlin Steel Corp.* (1937), Chief Justice Hughes, in upholding the National Labor Relations Act's regulation of factory working conditions, clearly rejected the qualitative test. But he filled his opinion with overlapping justifications, some sounding in the quantitative test language, or again a possible use of the Necessary and Proper Clause, but the proximate cause language was prominent. The commerce power could not reach activities that were "indirect and remote," he wrote. Federal power could reach those activities that have a "close and intimate effect" on interstate commerce. An industry organized on a national level had such an effect, he declared. Soon, however, Justice Cardozo died, and other Justices retired. By 1941, in *United States v. Darby*, it was clear that the new majority rejected the qualitative test and the causal tests in *Schechter, Carter,* and *Jones & Laughlin*. Instead, the Court fully embraced a very expansive quantitative test and, as events were to show, these Justices were able to find that any local activity, taken either separately or in the aggregate, *Wickard v. Filburn* (1942), always had a sufficiently substantial effect on interstate commerce to justify congressional legislation. By these means, the Court turned the commerce power into the equivalent of a general regulatory power.

The Court invoked newly expanded interpretation of the commerce power to approve wider federal criminal legislation as well as major social reforms such as the Civil Rights Act of 1964. But in *United States v. Lopez* and *United States v. Morrison* (2000), the Supreme Court limited Congress's power under the Commerce Clause for the first time since in the 1930s. In *Lopez*, Chief Justice William H. Rehnquist wound his way among the Court's precedents to strike down a federal law that had criminalized the possession of a gun near a school. He declared that the commerce power extended to: (1) "the use of the channels of interstate commerce"; (2) the regulation of "instrumentalities of interstate commerce, or persons or things in interstate commerce"; and (3) a local commercial activity having a "substantial relation" to interstate commerce. Rehnquist emphasized two points in his opinion. First, possessing a gun is not a commercial activity, and the effects prong of the commerce power only applies when the regulated activity is commercial. Second, he insisted that the rule of *substantial* effects must be observed. In his opinion, Chief Justice Rehnquist did not overrule any prior case.

Justice Stephen G. Breyer, for the dissent, agreed that there are limits to the commerce power—it does not grant a general federal police power. But he could not express what those limits were. He argued that there is a sufficient connection between guns near schools, the impact on the educational process, and the eventual connection to the nation's economy to justify the regulation, but he could not, under his formula, put forward any activity that could not thus be reached by Congress under the Commerce Clause. Concurring with the majority, Justice Thomas suggested that, upon the proper occasion, the Court should reexamine some of its more expansionary precedents dealing with the "affects" test, implying that he would revive the qualitative test instead.

Subsequent to the decision, Congress amended the law, requiring that the particular gun found in possession near to a school must be shown to have traveled in interstate commerce, thus validating the law under the "jurisdictional element" test. Later, Justice Thomas urged that, even while the "substantial effects" remains current Supreme Court doctrine, it should be applied to limit the "jurisdictional element" test. Thus, Thomas would require that any item travelling across state lines could only be regulated if it could be shown to have exerted a substantial effect on interstate commerce. *Alderman v. U.S.* (2011) (Thomas, J., dissenting).

In *United States v. Morrison*, the Court struck down a suit for damages for rape, even though the suit would have been permitted under the Violence Against Women Act. Here, Chief Justice Rehnquist explained *Lopez* by emphasizing that noneconomic activities (violence against women, or violence against men, or violence in general) could not be aggregated to establish a substantial connection to interstate commerce. Moreover, Rehnquist asserted that it was the Court's independent duty to determine whether a regulated activity is commercial and whether it substantially affects commerce, even if Congress has explicitly found otherwise, a position that the Court earlier adopted in *Jones & Laughlin*. As Justice Hugo Black had earlier noted in *Heart of Atlanta Motel v. United States* (1964): "whether particular operations affect interstate commerce sufficiently to come under the constitutional power of Congress to regulate them is ultimately a judicial rather than a legislative question, and can be settled finally only by this Court."

However, a majority of the Supreme Court reaffirmed the expansive scope of the commerce power in *Gonzales v. Raich* (2005). In that case, the Court found that the federal Controlled Substances Act (CSA) preempted a California law that legalized marijuana—in this case, totally locally home-grown marijuana— for medicinal uses. The Court found that marijuana was a commercial product, albeit illegal, and, citing *Wickard v. Filburn*, found that the aggregate effect of home-grown marijuana substantially impacted the federal government's legitimate policy of controlling certain illegal substances.

Thus, the line that the Court has drawn is between an activity that is "commercial" or economic and one that is not. Non-economic activities cannot be aggregated to show a substantial effect on commerce, but economic activities, no matter how small or local, can be so aggregated. In *National Federation of Independent Business v. Sebelius* (2012), by a narrow majority, the Supreme Court added an additional line: the government may not aggregate the economic affects of a commercial *inactivity* (a decision not to buy insurance) to find that there is a substantial effect on commerce. In fact, for the first time since *Gibbons*, the Court glossed the meaning of "to regulate." Congress, the Court declared, has the power to regulate an activity, but an inactivity, by its nature, does not yet exist and cannot be regulated.

As noted earlier, lurking behind the debate over the commerce power and occasionally hinted at in some of the Court's opinions is the Necessary and Proper Clause. In *Gibbons v. Ogden,* Chief Justice Marshall noted that there may be some "internal concerns" with which it may be "necessary to interfere, for the purpose of executing some of the general powers of the government." Thus, even if the commerce power in and of itself cannot reach particular local activities, Congress may still be able to regulate them if to do so has an appropriate connection to commerce. As Marshall said five years before *Gibbons* in *McCulloch v. Maryland* (1819):

> Let the end be legitimate [for example, the protection of interstate com-
merce], let it be within the scope of the constitution, and all means which are appropriate, which are plainly adapted to that end, which are not prohibited, but consist with the letter and spirit of the constitution, are constitutional.

As Marshall stated it, the required connection between the regulation of the local activity and the protection of Congress's policy on interstate commerce may produce a connection similar to what later became the proximate cause test devised by Justice Cardozo in *Schechter* and developed by Justice Sutherland in *Carter v. Carter Coal.*

One should also recall Marshall's limitation, again from *McCulloch v. Maryland*, on the uses of the Necessary and Proper Clause (*see* Article I, Section 8, Clause 18 for a fuller explication):

> Should Congress, in the execution of its powers, adopt measures which are prohibited by the constitution; or should Congress, under the pretext of executing its powers, pass laws for the accomplishment of objects not entrusted to the government; it would become the painful duty of this tribunal, should a case requiring such a decision come before it, to say that such an act was not the law of the land.

It would follow that Congress could regulate a local activity only if its purpose comports with its delegated power to regulate commerce and the regulation is plainly adapted to its interstate commerce purpose.

The "substantial effects test" could be recast as falling under the Necessary and Proper Clause. But in his concurrence in *Gonzales v. Raich*, Justice Antonin Scalia separated the Necessary and Proper Clause from the substantial effects test. He rejected the substantial effects test as "incomplete," and he thus found that locally grown marijuana could *not* be reached directly under the commerce power. Rather, he argued, "The regulation of an intrastate activity may be essential to a comprehensive regulation of interstate commerce even though the intrastate activity does not itself 'substantially affect' interstate commerce." He decided therefore that prohibiting locally grown marijuana was "necessary and proper" to the integrity of Congress's overall regime of regulating controlled substances. In dissent, Justice Thomas argued against the use of the Necessary and Proper Clause in this case. He declared that punishing persons who had grown their own marijuana for their own medicinal purposes was not "plainly adapted" to maintaining the coherence of the federal controlled substances program. Nor was it "proper" for the federal government to prohibit a non-economic activity under the guise of protecting interstate commerce.

The second constitutional role of the Commerce Clause is to act as an extrinsic restraint on state legislation that may impede or intrude upon interstate commerce. The Supreme Court has built up a prodigious amount of case law commentary on the Commerce Clause when it is in its "dormant" state.

The traditional view is that the Constitution grants Congress plenary power over interstate commerce. Justice Scalia agrees that Congress has *plenary* power (it can control all aspects of interstate commerce), but denies that it has *exclusive* power. Thus, he believes that the states can enter the field until Congress acts. *Tyler Pipe Industries v. Washington State Department of Revenue* (1987). But for the majority of Justices, the Commerce Clause operates as a limit on the legislative powers of the states *even when Congress has not acted*.

If Congress has legislated upon a subject within its commerce power, then, due to the Supremacy Clause (Article VI, Clause 2), any state law to the contrary falls. Congress may even consent to state regulation that directly regulates interstate commerce. *Prudential Insurance Co. v. Benjamin* (1946). But the question remains. To what extent may a state legislate upon a subject that impacts interstate commerce in the absence of congressional action? Does it matter if the state law discriminates against interstate commerce, either in purpose or effect?

It was inevitable that the states, even in the honest exercise of their police powers, would trench on interstate commerce. How far the states can even incidentally intrude upon interstate commerce has been the subject of scores of Supreme Court cases, often with inconsistent holdings. A detailed treatment of that complicated history is beyond the scope of this essay, but in 1970 in *Pike v. Bruce Church, Inc.*, the Court consolidated its dormant Commerce Clause jurisprudence into the following test: "Where the [state] statute regulates evenhandedly to effectuate a legitimate local public interest, and its effects on interstate commerce are only incidental, it will be upheld unless the burden imposed on such commerce is clearly excessive in relation to the putative local benefits."

A few decades ago, some scholars opined that the *Pike* test was a codification of an *ad hoc* balancing test. More recent scholarship, however, has indicated that the Supreme Court rarely, if ever, decides a dormant Commerce Clause case on balancing grounds since it would be attempting to compare incommensurables. Rather, the *Pike* test describes a series of separate standards by which a state statute can be determined to be within its constitutional powers.

Those determinative principles for state statutes are as follows:

1. The statute must have a "legitimate" and "public" purpose. It must be within the state's police power, and not designed either to regulate interstate commerce as such, or to discriminate against out-of-state economic interests in favor of private in-state interests in the same market. If, however, the state is acting as a "market participant" similar to a private entity, the dormant Commerce Clause is not a bar to its economic decisions even if they impact or discriminate against interstate commerce, though the Privileges and Immunities Clause of Article IV may be a constraint.

2. The effect on interstate commerce must be "incidental" rather than the primary purpose of the statute.

3. The interest must be "local." It must regulate elements that are

peculiar to the state, such as its harbors, and not impose a pattern of "multiple inconsistent burdens" with other states' conflicting laws on an interstate enterprise.

4. The statute must "regulate even-handedly," that is, its impact may not be discriminatory absent compelling reasons.

5. The statute must "effectuate" its local public interest. If there is little evidence of such a result, the court may infer that the interstate impact was intentional and hence unconstitutional, after all.

If a state statute survives all these criteria, it will be upheld unless the burden imposed on interstate commerce is "clearly excessive" in relation to the asserted local benefits. This last clause is indeed a balancing test (weighted in favor of the state), but the Court rarely, if ever, reaches it, preferring to decide the issue on one of the antecedent principles.

Justice Scalia does not believe the Court should be monitoring the states' impact on interstate commerce, outside of discrimination against interstate commerce or creating multiple inconsistent burdens. *CTS Corp. v. Dynamics Corp. of America* (1987) (Scalia, J., dissenting). He believes that the Constitution gives the power to Congress to cure (or approve of) any excessive state action by legislation. Justice Thomas would rather use the Import-Export Clause to strike down state discriminations against interstate commerce. *Camps Newfound/Owatonna, Inc. v. Town of Harrison* (1997) (Thomas, J., dissenting).

David F. Forte

See Also

Suggestions for Further Research

Albert S. Abel, *The Commerce Clause in the Constitutional Convention and in Contemporary Comment*, 25 Minn. L. Rev. 432 (1941)

Jack M. Balkin, *Commerce*, 109 Mich, L. Rev. 1 (2010)

Randy E. Barnett, *New Evidence of the Original Meaning of the Commerce Clause*, 55 Ark. L. Rev. 847 (2003)

Randy E. Barnett, *The Original Meaning of the Commerce Clause*, 68 U. Chi. L. Rev. 101 (2001)

Raoul Berger, *Judicial Manipulation of the Commerce Clause*, 74 Tex. L. Rev. 695 (1996)

Barry Cushman, Rethinking the New Deal Court: The Structure of a Constitutional Revolution (1998)

Brannon P. Denning, *Why the Privileges and Immunities Clause of Article IV Cannot Replace the Dormant Commerce Clause Doctrine*, 88 Minn. L. Rev. 384 (2003)

Richard A. Epstein, *The Proper Scope of the Commerce Power*, 73 Va. L. Rev. 1387 (1987)

Barry Friedman & Genevieve Lakier, *"To Regulate," Not "To Prohibit": Limiting the Commerce Power*, 2012 Sup. Ct. Rev. 255 (2013)

Robert J. Pushaw & Grant S. Nelson, *A Critique of the Narrow Interpretation of the Commerce Clause*, 96 Nw. U. L. Rev. 695 (2002)

Martin H. Redish & Shane V. Nugent, *The Dormant Commerce Clause and the Constitutional Balance of Federalism*, 1987 Duke L.J. 569 (1987)

Donald H. Regan, *The Supreme Court and State Protectionism: Making Sense of the Dormant Commerce Clause*, 84 Mich. L. Rev. 1091 (1986)

Ronald D. Rotunda, *The Doctrine of the Inner Political Check, the Dormant Commerce Clause, and Federal Preemption*, 53 Transp. Prac. J. 263 (1986)

Significant Cases

McCulloch v. Maryland, 17 U.S. (4 Wheat.) 316 (1819)

Gibbons v. Ogden, 22 U.S. (9 Wheat.) 1 (1824)

Cooley v. Bd. of Wardens, 53 U.S. (12 How.) 299 (1851)

Paul v. Virginia, 75 U.S. (8 Wall.) 168 (1869)

United States v. E.C. Knight Co., 156 U.S. 1 (1895)

Addyston Pipe & Steel Co. v. United States, 175 U.S. 211 (1899)

Champion v. Ames, 188 U.S. 321 (1903)

Swift & Co. v. United States, 196 U.S. 375 (1905)

Hipolite Egg Co. v. United States, 220 U.S. 45 (1911)

Hoke v. United States, 227 U.S. 308 (1913)

Shreveport Rate Case, 234 U.S. 342 (1914)

Caminetti v. United States, 242 U.S. 470 (1917)

Hammer v. Dagenhart, 247 U.S. 251 (1918)

Stafford v. Wallace, 258 U.S. 495 (1922)

A.L.A. Schechter Poultry Corp. v. United States, 295 U.S. 495 (1935)

Railroad Retirement Bd. v. Alton Railroad Co., 295 U.S. 330 (1935)

Carter v. Carter Coal Co., 298 U.S. 238 (1936)

NLRB v. Jones & Laughlin Steel Corp., 301 U.S. 1 (1937)

United States v. Darby, 312 U.S. 100 (1941)

Wickard v. Filburn, 317 U.S. 111 (1942)

Prudential Ins. Co. v. Benjamin, 328 U.S. 408 (1946)

H.P. Hood & Sons v. Du Mond, 336 U.S. 525 (1949)

Dean Milk v. Madison, 340 U.S. 349 (1951)

Heart of Atlanta Motel v. United States, 379 U.S. 241 (1964)

Katzenbach v. McClung, 379 U.S. 294 (1964)

Pike v. Bruce Church, Inc., 397 U.S. 137 (1970)

Hughes v. Alexandria Scrap Corp., 426 U.S. 794 (1976)

Hunt v. Washington State Apple Advertising Comm'n, 432 U.S. 333 (1977)

Philadelphia v. New Jersey, 437 U.S. 617 (1978)

Reeves, Inc. v. Stake, 447 U.S. 429 (1980)

Kassel v. Consolidated Freightways Corp. of Delaware, 450 U.S. 662 (1981)

Minnesota v. Clover Leaf Creamery Co., 449 U.S. 456 (1981)

South-Central Timber Development, Inc. v. Wunnicke, 467 U.S. 82 (1984)

CTS Corp. v. Dynamics Corp. of America, 481 U.S. 69 (1987)

Tyler Pipe Industries v. Washington State Dep't of Revenue, 483 U.S. 232 (1987)

United States v. Lopez, 514 U.S. 549 (1995)

Camps Newfound/Owatonna, Inc. v. Town of Harrison, 520 U.S. 564 (1997)

United States v. Morrison, 529 U.S. 598 (2000)

Gonzales v. Raich, 545 U.S. 1 (2005)

Alderman v. U.S., 131 S. Ct. 700 (2011)

National Federation of Independent Business v. Sebelius, 132 S. Ct. 2566 (2012)

Commerce with the Indian Tribes

The Congress shall have Power... To regulate Commerce... with the Indian Tribes....

(**ARTICLE I, SECTION 8, CLAUSE 3**)

～

*T*he Commerce Clause grants Congress power to regulate commerce between the United States and three forms of sovereign entities: the states, foreign nations, and the Indian tribes. The Supreme Court has long assumed that the Indian Commerce Clause, along with the Treaty Clause (Article II, Section 2, Clause 2) granted Congress "plenary and exclusive power" over Indian affairs, a position recently affirmed in *United States v. Lara* (2004). For Justice Joseph Story, the power to regulate trade and commerce with the Indian tribes passed naturally from the Crown to the federal government after the Revolution and, he argued in his *Commentaries on the Constitution of the United States* (1833), this clause confirmed that proposition. In *Worcester v. Georgia* (1832), Chief Justice John Marshall confirmed the supremacy of federal authority over the states in regard to the Indians. In the late nineteenth century, the Supreme Court went even further. It asserted that the power over the Indian tribes was an attribute of sovereignty, unencumbered by the delegated powers doctrine of the Constitution. *See, e.g., United States v. Kagama* (1886).

But recent scholarship has cast serious doubt upon the proposition that the Framers intended the power to be exclusively in the hands of Congress.

At the Constitutional Convention, there were several different drafts describing how the Indians should be incorporated into the Constitution. Finding a single formula was not easy, because Indians resided within the states as well as within the United States. To begin with, during the colonial era, it is evident that the Colonies exercised concurrent jurisdiction with the Crown over Indians. During the drafting of the Articles of Confederation, the delegates had difficulty drawing an acceptable line between state and national jurisdiction over Indian affairs, but all seemed to agree that there had to be some degree of concurrency. The final formulation read: "The United States, in Congress assembled, shall also have the sole and exclusive right and power of regulating the trade and managing all affairs with the Indians not members of any of the States; provided that the legislative right of any State within its own limits be not infringed or violated."

The drafting of the Indian Commerce Clause was no less difficult. The Framers did not take up the regulation of Indians until August 18, when James Madison proposed Congress "regulate affairs with the Indians as well within as without the limits of the U. States." The Committee of Detail revised Madison's proposal to grant Congress the power "to regulate Commerce with foreign Nations, and among the several States, and with Indians, within the Limits of any State, not subject to the laws thereof," an echo of the Articles of Confederation. Working out the final details, the Committee of Eleven simply added "and with Indian Tribes" to the Commerce Clause, shunting aside the wording of previous proposals. Neither the final formulation, nor previous drafts, asserted exclusive congressional power in so many words.

Robert Natelson argues that the entire drafting history and the debate in the Convention demonstrate that the Framers intended the power over Indians to be concurrent with the states. Elsewhere in the Constitution, exclusive federal jurisdiction is sometimes declared in explicit terms, as in Article I, Section 8, Clause 17 (Enclave Clause), or through prohibitions placed upon the states (Article I, Section 10). Nonetheless, the Constitution contains other provisions, such as the Treaty Clause (Article II, Section 2, Clause 2) and the Property Clause (Article IV, Section 3, Clause 2) granting significant power over Indian affairs. And in case of any conflict with state law, there remains the force of the Supremacy Clause (Article VI, Clause 2).

Notwithstanding what might have been the understanding of the Framers, Congress has asserted plenary jurisdiction over the Indians. For the first century following the ratification of the Constitution, Congress regulated Indian affairs through the Trade and Intercourse Acts and through treaties. Tribes had juridical existence, not as foreign states, but as "domestic dependent nations," *Cherokee Nation v. Georgia* (1831), and were entitled to rights in property and self-rule, subject to the will of Congress, *Johnson v. McIntosh* (1823). The Supreme Court declared Indians as "wards" in a trust relationship with the United States government. *Cherokee Nation v. Georgia; United States v. Kagama* (1886).

Federal policy toward the Indians has developed through a number of phases, punctuated by treaties (until 1871), legislation, and conflict, but it has sought to reject state incursions into federal authority. Expansion of lands for settlement and Indian removal from east of the Mississippi dominated congressional attention until 1850. Thereafter, the government attempted to move the western tribes to reservations, which it followed, beginning in 1887, with a policy of assimilation. In 1924, Congress granted citizenship to all Indians born in the United States who had not been made citizens under a prior treaty. In the Indian "New Deal" beginning in 1934, the government ended the assimilation policy and sought to reorganize and maintain tribal structure. In the 1950s, however, federal policy veered again, this time toward ending tribal status and integrating the Indians into the political structure as individuals. In 1953, Congress began allowing some states to extend their jurisdiction to Indian areas within their borders, but beginning in 1968, policy once again reversed when the Indian Civil Rights Act extended constitutional guarantees to Indians in relation to their own tribal governments. At the same time, Congress sought to expand the areas of Indian local self-rule. Under the Indian Gaming Regulatory Act (1988), Indian tribes throughout the country have been able to establish gambling institutions on their lands under compacts entered into with the states.

The Supreme Court has been highly deferential to congressional control of relations with the Indian tribes, and the Court closely monitors under the Supremacy Clause any state legislation affecting the Indians. Furthermore, the Court has increasingly required the executive to abide by specific undertakings found in the laws and treaties dealing with the Indians, particularly in upholding Indian monetary claims.

There were few hesitations in Supreme Court opinions according deference to Congress until

United States v. Lara (2004), a case in which the Court rejected a double jeopardy claim by an Indian, who had been convicted in a tribal court of violence against a policeman and was subsequently charged for the same offense in a federal court. In concurring, Justice Clarence Thomas declared that he could not locate congressional plenary authority over Indian affairs in the Treaty Clause or the Indian Commerce Clause.

David F. Forte

See Also

Article I, Section 8, Clause 3 (Commerce with Foreign Nations; Commerce Among the States)
Article II, Section 2, Clause 2 (Treaty Clause)
Article IV, Section 3, Clause 2 (Property Clause)
Article VI, Clause 2 (Supremacy Clause)

Suggestions for Further Research

Sarah H. Cleveland, *Power Inherent in Sovereignty: Indians, Aliens, Territories, and the Nineteenth Century Origins of Plenary Power over Foreign Affairs*, 81 Tex L. Rev. 1 (2002)

Matthew L.M. Fletcher, *The Supreme Court and Federal Indian Policy*, 85 Neb. L. Rev. 121, (2006)

Matthew L.M. Fletcher, *The Supreme Court's Indian Problem*, 59 Hastings L.J. 579 (2008)

Gerard N. Magliocca, *The Cherokee Removal and the Fourteenth Amendment*, 53 Duke L.J. 875 (2003)

Robert G. Natelson, *The Original Meaning of the Indian Commerce Clause*, 85 Denv. U. L. Rev. 201 (2007)

Nell Jessup Newton, *Federal Power Over Indians: Its Sources, Scope, and Limitations*, 132 U. Pa. L. Rev. 195 (1984)

Saikrishna B. Prakash, *Against Tribal Fungibility*, 89 Cornell L. Rev. 1069 (2004)

Mark Savage, *Native Americans and the Constitution: The Original Understanding*, 16 Am. Ind. L. Rev. 57 (1991)

Significant Cases

Johnson v. McIntosh, 21 U.S. (8 Wheat.) 543 (1823)
Cherokee Nation v. Georgia, 30 U.S. (5 Pet.) 1 (1831)
Worcester v. Georgia, 31 U.S. (6 Pet.) 515 (1832)
Ex parte Crow Dog, 109 U.S. 556 (1883)
United States v. Kagama, 118 U.S. 375 (1886)
Talton v. Mayes, 163 U.S. 376 (1896)

Lone Wolf v. Hitchcock, 187 U.S. 553 (1903)
United States v. Creek Nation, 295 U.S. 103 (1935)
Seminole Nation v. United States, 316 U.S. 286 (1942)
Williams v. Lee, 358 U.S. 217 (1959)
McClanahan v. Arizona State Tax Comm'n, 411 U.S. 164 (1973)
Morton v. Mancari, 417 U.S. 535 (1974)
Oliphant v. Suquamish Indian Tribe, 435 U.S. 191 (1978)
Santa Clara Pueblo v. Martinez, 436 U.S. 49 (1978)
United States v. Wheeler, 435 U.S. 313 (1978)
United States v. Mitchell, 445 U.S. 535 (1980)
Montana v. United States, 450 U.S. 544 (1981)
United States v. Mitchell, 463 U.S. 206 (1983)
California v. Cabazon Band of Mission Indians, 480 U.S. 202 (1987)
Brendale v. Confederated Tribes and Bands of Yakima, 492 U.S. 408 (1989)
Nevada v. Hicks, 533 U.S. 353 (2001)
United States v. Lara, 541 U.S. 193 (2004)

Naturalization

The Congress shall have Power... To establish an uniform Rule of Naturalization....
(Article I, Section 8, Clause 4)

∼

*F*ew powers are more fundamental to sovereignty than the control over immigration and the vesting of citizenship in aliens (naturalization). According to the Declaration of Independence, "obstructing the Laws for the Naturalization of Foreigners" was one of the grievances that led the American colonists to break with Britain.

Under the Articles of Confederation, each state retained authority over the naturalization of aliens. This resulted in widely varying state practices, which James Madison in *The Federalist* No. 42 called a "fault" and "defect" of the Confederation. At the Constitutional Convention, there was virtually no opposition to moving the naturalization power from the states to the new national government, and in the ratification debates only a handful of Anti-Federalists even raised the issue.

Madison seemed to speak the sentiment of most when at the Convention he expressed his wish "to invite foreigners of merit & republican principles among us. America was indebted to emigration for her settlement & prosperity."

Congress passed the first "uniform Rule of Naturalization" under the new Constitution in March 1790. It allowed "any alien, being a free white person" and "of good character" who had resided in the United States for two years to become a "citizen of the United States" by taking an oath in court "to support the constitution of the United States." Although Alexander Hamilton had argued in *The Federalist* No. 32 that the power to establish "'an uniform rule of naturalization.' . . . must necessarily be exclusive; because if each State had power to prescribe a distinct rule, there could not be a uniform rule," some states continued to naturalize foreigners even after Congress had acted. In 1795, Congress claimed exclusive authority over naturalization by establishing new conditions—"and not otherwise"—for aliens "to become a citizen of the United States, or any of them." In *Chirac v. Lessee of Chirac* (1817), the Supreme Court affirmed that "the power of naturalization is exclusively in congress," notwithstanding any state laws to the contrary.

Individual naturalizations following Congress's "uniform Rule" were not the only avenues to citizenship for those who were not American citizens by birth. The incorporation of the Louisiana Territory and Florida into the Union in the first decades of the nineteenth century raised the issue of whether the national government through treaty or law could vest citizenship collectively. A federal circuit court in 1813 and then the Supreme Court in *American Insurance Co. v. 356 Bales of Cotton, Canter* (1828) upheld collective naturalization. Moreover, in 1848 the Treaty of Guadalupe Hidalgo, which ended the Mexican-American War, offered the Mexican inhabitants of the territories ceded to the United States the option of maintaining their Mexican citizenship or, if they made no such request, becoming American citizens.

From the beginning, American naturalization law and practice assumed that a free citizen of one country had the right to transfer his allegiance to another if the latter allowed: hence, the provision of the 1795 law that required the new citizen to "absolutely and entirely renounce" any previous allegiance. However, this essential element of social-contract theory—that political communities are the free association of individuals to promote their mutual security and happiness—violated settled European norms. Sir William Blackstone had written in *Commentaries on the Laws of England* that the "natural allegiance" owed by all those born within the sovereign's domain could not be "forfeited, cancelled, or altered" by any act of the subject himself, including moving to another country and "swearing allegiance to another."

This conflict of views on the legitimacy of voluntary expatriation led to considerable conflict between the new nation and both Britain and France, especially when the latter two nations captured on the high seas and impressed into their naval service former nationals who had moved to the United States. This was one of the American grievances that led to the War of 1812. As late as the 1860s, the British government refused to recognize the American naturalization of former Irish subjects. In response, Congress passed the Expatriation Act of 1868, which declared that "the right of expatriation is a natural and inherent right of all people, indispensable to the enjoyment of the rights of life, liberty, and the pursuit of happiness."

Key criteria for citizenship of the Naturalization Act of 1795 remain part of American law. These include: (1) five years of (lawful) residence within the United States; (2) a "good moral character, attached to the principles of the Constitution of the United States, and well disposed to the good order and happiness of the United States"; (3) the taking of a formal oath to support the Constitution and to renounce any foreign allegiance; and (4) the renunciation of any hereditary titles.

Current law, which is much more detailed than the first naturalization statutes, also requires competency in the English language and excludes those who advocate world communism or the violent overthrow of the government of the United States. Also, current law prohibits discrimination in naturalization on the basis of race, sex, or marital status. Federal agencies have expanded the elements of the oath to require a solemn commitment "to support and defend the Constitution and the laws of the United States against all enemies, foreign and domestic;...to bear true faith and allegiance to the same; and...to bear arms on behalf of the United States when required by the law, or...to perform non-combatant service in the Armed Forces of the United States when required by the law" (with exceptions for conscientious objectors).

Federal law and regulations establish procedures, administered by the U.S. Department of State, by which Americans can voluntarily renounce their citizenship. In addition, federal law lists a variety of acts that shall result in the loss of citizenship if "voluntarily perform[ed]...with the intention of relinquishing United States nationality." These include obtaining naturalization in a foreign state; declaring allegiance to a foreign state; serving in the armed forces of a foreign state as an officer or when the foreign state is engaged in hostilities against the United States; and, in some cases, serving in governmental office in a foreign state.

Prior to several important Supreme Court decisions in the last half of the twentieth century, federal law had also required loss of citizenship for, among other acts, voting in a foreign election; deserting during wartime; leaving the country during wartime to evade military service; and, for those who acquired dual nationality at birth, voluntarily seeking or claiming the benefits of foreign nationality and residing in the foreign state for three years continuously after the age of twenty-two.

Although the Supreme Court in *MacKenzie v. Hare* (1915) upheld Congress's power to expatriate, in 1958 the Court began to cut back on Congress's power in a number of closely decided cases. Although it upheld expatriation (removal of citizenship) for voting in a foreign election, *Perez v. Brownell* (1958), it explicitly overruled that decision less than a decade later, in *Afroyim v. Rusk* (1967), ruling that a naturalized American citizen who relocated to Israel and voted in an election for the Israeli Knesset could not lose his citizenship as a result. It also overturned expatriations for desertion from the military during

wartime, *Trop v. Dulles* (1958), and for service by a dual national in the Japanese army during World War II, *Nishikawa v. Dulles* (1958). In 1963, in *Kennedy v. Mendoza-Martinez*, the Court ruled that a citizen could not be expatriated for fleeing the country during wartime to evade military service. The following year, it extended the limits on expatriation to naturalized citizens who returned to their native countries and resided there for at least three years, *Schneider v. Rusk* (1964).

In *Rogers v. Bellei* (1971), however, the Court did uphold a statute that provided that a person who acquires United States citizenship by being born abroad to an American citizen shall lose that citizenship unless he resides in the United States continuously for five years between the ages of fourteen and twenty-eight. The Court did not backtrack on its earlier cases that held, in general, that Congress cannot take away citizenship granted by the Constitution under Section 1 of the Fourteenth Amendment, which provides that all persons who "are born or naturalized in the United States" are U.S. Citizens. That clause, the Court has held, does not allow Congress to take away that which Section 1 has granted. Bellei gained U.S. citizenship outside of the United States, the Court held, and hence Section 1 did not protect him. In 1978, however, Congress removed from federal law the continuous-residency requirements that had been upheld in *Rogers v. Bellei*.

Finally, in *Vance v. Terrazas* (1980), the Court clarified its decision in *Afroyim* by holding that it was not enough to show that an individual voluntarily committed an act that Congress determined was inconsistent with American citizenship. It was necessary also to show independently that the individual "intended to relinquish his citizenship." Given the broad language of the more recent cases, it seems that no involuntary expatriations are lawful. The one exception, which applies only to naturalized Americans, is the denaturalization (and deportation) of those who became citizens through fraud or illegality. It has been applied most notably in recent decades to former Nazis who engaged in war crimes during World War II and later lied about their wartime activities either when they entered the United States as "displaced persons" or when they applied for citizenship.

Until recent decades, American public policy consistently prohibited dual citizenship. Most notably, since 1795, Congress has required that all candidates for naturalization formally renounce allegiance to their native land and any other foreign power. That requirement remains a part of national law and is an integral element of the citizenship oath. Also, as noted above, the Treaty of Guadalupe Hidalgo required the residents in the ceded lands to choose between Mexican and American citizenship. The rationale for such policies is that citizenship demands undivided loyalty to one country.

Yet today there are millions of American citizens who are also citizens of other countries. Many are naturalized American citizens whose native countries do not recognize the renunciation of loyalty that their native citizens make in the American citizenship oath. Others are the offspring of one American parent and one foreign parent, deriving citizenship from both sides, or foreign-born children adopted by American parents. Others are those who are natural born U.S. citizens who later become citizens of a foreign country. Because the courts now prohibit the government from expatriating those who maintain an active citizenship in a foreign nation (some American citizens have even held political office in other countries), dual citizenship has become a fact of American life.

Joseph M. Bessette

See Also

Article IV, Section 2, Clause 1 (Privileges and Immunities Clause)

Amendment XIV, Section 1 (Citizenship)

Suggestions for Further Research

Leonard Dinnerstein & David M. Reimers, Ethnic Americans: A History of Immigration (4th ed. 1999)

James H. Kettner, The Development of American Citizenship, 1608–1870 (1978)

Arthur Mann, The One and the Many: Reflections on the American Identity (1979)

Significant Cases

Chirac v. Lessee of Chirac, 15 U.S. (2 Wheat.) 259 (1817)

American Ins. Co. v. 356 Bales of Cotton, Canter, 26 U.S. (1 Pet.) 511 (1828)

Boyd v. State of Nebraska, 143 U.S. 135 (1892)

MacKenzie v. Hare, 239 U.S. 299 (1915)

Nishikawa v. Dulles, 356 U.S. 129 (1958)

Perez v. Brownell, 356 U.S. 44 (1958)

Trop v. Dulles, 356 U.S. 86 (1958)

Kennedy v. Mendoza-Martinez, 372 U.S. 144 (1963)

Schneider v. Rusk, 377 U.S. 163 (1964)

Afroyim v. Rusk, 387 U.S. 253 (1967)

Rogers v. Bellei, 401 U.S. 815 (1971)

Vance v. Terrazas, 444 U.S. 252 (1980)

Bankruptcy Clause

The Congress shall have Power...To establish...uniform Laws on the subject of Bankruptcies throughout the United States....

(Article I, Section 8, Clause 4)

~

*T*he Bankruptcy Clause of the Constitution is one of Congress's several delegated powers in Article I, Section 8 that were designed to encourage the development of a commercial republic and to temper the excesses of pro-debtor state legislation that had proliferated under the Articles of Confederation. Both state legislation and state courts tended to use debtor-creditor laws to redistribute money from out-of-state and urban creditors to rural agricultural interests. Under the Articles of Confederation, the states alone governed debtor-creditor relations, and that led to diverse and contradictory state laws. It was unclear, for instance, whether a state law that purported to discharge a debtor of a debt prohibited the creditor from trying to collect the debt in another state. Pro-debtor state laws also interfered with the reliability of contracts, and creditors confronted still further obstructions in trying to use state courts to collect their judgments, especially when debtors absconded to other states to avoid collection.

A coherent and consistent bankruptcy regime for merchants was also required for the United States to flourish as a commercial republic. The Bankruptcy Clause helped to further the goals of uniformity and predictability within the federalist system. As James Madison observed in *The Federalist* No. 42, "The power of establishing uniform laws of bankruptcy is so intimately connected with the regulation of commerce, and will prevent so many frauds where the parties or their property may lie or be removed into different States, that the expediency of it [i.e., Congress's power to regulate bankruptcy] seems not likely to be drawn into question." The Framers were so convinced of the need for a national power over bankruptcy that, as Madison suggests, there was little debate over the issue and little opposition to the Bankruptcy Clause at the Constitutional Convention. Although state law continued to govern most routine debtor-creditor relations, Congress had the authority to override state laws dealing with insolvency.

Following ratification of the Constitution, the mercantile northeastern states spearheaded the movement for a national bankruptcy law. The first bankruptcy law was passed under the Federalists in 1800, but it lasted only until 1803. Other bankruptcy laws existed from 1841 to 1843 and from 1867 to 1878. The first permanent bankruptcy law was enacted in 1898 and remained in effect, with amendments, until being replaced with a comprehensive new law in 1978, the essential structure of which continues today.

Subsequent to the ratification of the Constitution, it remained unclear where the line between the state and federal power should be drawn. English law relied upon a traditional distinction between "bankruptcies" on one hand and "insolvency" on the other. Under English law, only merchants and traders could be declared "bankrupt," which enabled them to have their debts discharged upon the satisfaction of certain requirements. By contrast, nonmerchants had to seek refuge under "insolvency" laws, which did little more than to release a debtor from debtor's prison but did not discharge the debtor from his indebtedness. Thus, many understood

the Constitution's grant of power to Congress to regulate "bankruptcies" as creating federal power to regulate only with respect to merchants and traders and not with respect to those individuals traditionally subject to "insolvency" laws, which remained under state control. Others argued that this traditional distinction had disappeared by the mid-eighteenth century, such that by the time of the Constitution, the terms became interchangeable so as to give Congress the power to regulate all insolvent debtors. In 1819, the Supreme Court held in *Sturges v. Crowninshield* that the use of the term bankruptcy in the Constitution did not limit Congress's jurisdiction, thereby permitting Congress to regulate both of these realms. In *Ogden v. Saunders* (1827), the Court further restricted the states' concurrent power, prohibiting discharge of debts owed to citizens of another state, but permitting discharge of debts owed to a citizen of the same state so long as the law operated prospectively so as not to impair contract obligations.

Still, the original understanding of the Bankruptcy Clause placed several clear constraints on Congress's authority to regulate on the subject of debtor-creditor relations. First, Congress's power under the Bankruptcy Clause is limited to the adjustment of the debts of insolvent debtors and their creditors and does not extend to the general regulation of debtor-creditor law. Previous bankruptcy laws required that the debtor be insolvent as a condition for bankruptcy, but the current Bankruptcy Code contains no such limitation. Second, Congress's bankruptcy power was limited to the adjustment of relations between a debtor and its creditors and does not extend to the protection or benefit of third parties, except to the extent that such protection is ancillary to the adjustment of the debts of an insolvent debtor. This original limitation is also ineffective today.

The Bankruptcy Code thus represents a tenuous accommodation between federal and state law. Most of the nonbankruptcy law that governs debtor-creditor relations remains state law, and federal bankruptcy law honors these state-law substantive entitlements, unless federal law and policy expressly preempt them. Moreover, the Bankruptcy Code expressly incorporates some elements of state law into the Code itself, such as in the treatment of a debtor's property exemptions. This interaction between state and federal law guarantees that creditors and debtors will be treated differently depending on the state that determines their rights.

At the same time, any bankruptcy legislation enacted by Congress must also be "uniform...throughout the United States." In *Hanover National Bank v. Moyses* (1902), the Supreme Court held that this "personal" nonuniformity in treatment among individuals was permissible, so long as "geographical" uniformity was preserved. Thus, debtors and creditors in different states may receive different treatment, so long as the debtors and creditors within the same state are treated the same. The "uniformity" requirement does, however, forbid "private" bankruptcy laws that affect only particular debtors.

Courts have also had to consider the contours of this power to make uniform bankruptcy legislation in light of the Eleventh Amendment's protection of states against private suit. In *Central Virginia Community College v. Katz* (2006), the Supreme Court found that a bankruptcy trustee's proceeding to set aside the debtor's preferential transfers to state agencies is not barred by sovereign immunity. This implies that the power of Congress to enact bankruptcy legislation gives them the power to abrogate state sovereign immunity protected by the Eleventh Amendment. In dissent, Justice Clarence Thomas argued this was inconsistent with the Constitution's "text, structure, or history."

In administering the bankruptcy system there are additional restraints placed on bankruptcy courts by the separation of powers and the nature of the judicial power under Article III. As currently designed, bankruptcy courts are units of the United States District Court and bankruptcy judges are so-called "Article I" judges, appointed for a term of years rather than for good behavior and lacking many of the formal protections for judicial independence under Article III. In *Granfinanciera, S. A. v. Nordberg* (1989), the Supreme Court held that Seventh Amendment jury trial rights are preserved in bankruptcy. In *Stern v. Marshall* (2011), the Court addressed the related question of when a party is entitled to have its case heard by an Article III district court judge rather than a bankruptcy judge. The case involved a state law counterclaim to a proof of claim filed in a bankruptcy case. That counterclaim was a "core" proceeding under the Bankruptcy Code, which authorized the bankruptcy court to render a final judgment. However, that statutory grant was unconstitutional, the Court found, and a bankruptcy judge lacked the power to enter a final judgment because it violated the right to have the claim heard by an Article III judge.

Todd Zywicki

See Also

Article I, Section 8, Clause 3 (Commerce Among the States)
Article I, Section 10, Clause 1 (Obligation of Contract)
Article III
Article IV, Section 1 (Full Faith and Credit Clause)
Amendment V (Takings Clause)
Amendment VII (Right to Jury in Civil Cases)
Amendment XI (Suits Against a State)

Suggestions for Further Research

Peter J. Coleman, Debtors and Creditors in America: Insolvency, Imprisonment for Debt, and Bankruptcy, 1607–1900 (1999)

Frank R. Kennedy, *Bankruptcy and the Constitution,* in Blessings of Liberty: The Constitution and the Practice of Law, 131–74 (1988)

Judith Schenck Koffler, *The Bankruptcy Clause and Exemption Laws: A Reexamination of the Doctrine of Geographic Uniformity,* 58 N.Y.U. L. Rev. 22 (1983)

Kurt H. Nadelmann, *On the Origin of the Bankruptcy Clause,* 1 Am. J. Legal Hist. 215 (1957)

Thomas E. Plank, *The Constitutional Limits of Bankruptcy,* 63 Tenn. L. Rev. 487 (1996)

David A. Skeel, Jr., Debt's Dominion: A History of Bankruptcy Law in America (2001)

Charles Jordan Tabb, *The History of the Bankruptcy Laws in the United States,* 3 Am. Bankr. Inst. L. Rev. 5 (1995)

Charles Warren, Bankruptcy in United States History (1935)

Significant Cases

Sturges v. Crowninshield, 17 U.S. (4 Wheat.) 122 (1819)

Ogden v. Saunders, 25 U.S. (12 Wheat.) 213 (1827)

Hanover National Bank v. Moyses, 186 U.S. 181 (1902)

Louisville Joint Stock Land Bank v. Radford, 295 U.S. 555 (1935)

Northern Pipeline Construction Co. v. Marathon Pipe Line Co., 458 U.S. 50 (1982)

Granfinanciera, S.A. v. Nordberg, 492 U.S. 33 (1989)

Central Virginia Community College v. Katz, 546 U.S. 356 (2006)

Stern v. Marshall, 131 S. Ct. 2594 (2011)

Coinage Clause

The Congress shall have Power... To coin Money, regulate the Value thereof, and of foreign Coin....

(ARTICLE I, SECTION 8, CLAUSE 5)

~

*C*ongress's power to coin money is exclusive. Article I, Section 10, Clause 1 (State Coinage) does not allow the states to "coin Money; emit Bills of Credit; [or] make any Thing but gold and silver Coin a Tender in Payment of Debts...." Whereas the prohibitions on the states are clear and detailed, Congress's grant of power under the Coinage Clause is open-ended.

Nonetheless, certain elements are clear. First, this clause grants Congress the authority to "coin money" from precious metals such as gold and silver. Under the Articles of Confederation, the power to coin money was a concurrent power of Congress and the states. To create a more standardized monetary system and reduce the costs of running mints, the Constitution granted this power to Congress exclusively. The elimination of the states' power to coin money and the exclusive grant to Congress provoked controversy because the power to coin money was traditionally understood as a symbol of political sovereignty.

Second, this clause authorizes Congress to regulate the value of the coins struck domestically and to set the value of foreign coins. Under the Articles, Congress held the former power but not the latter. The Constitution gave both powers to Congress to encourage domestic and foreign commerce by preventing the states from attaching disparate valuations to circulating coins.

Beyond these simple issues, however, the scope of the federal government's powers under the Coinage Clause is unclear. In particular, although the Coinage Clause empowers Congress to coin money from precious metals, it is not clear whether the federal government could also issue paper money. Linguistic and conceptual usage during the Founding era distinguished between several different concepts: the power to "coin" specie money (i.e., money backed by gold or silver), the power to borrow money through the issuance of interest-bearing "notes," and the issuance of "Bills of Credit." Unlike coined money, whose value was inherent in the metal that composed the coin, and unlike "notes" that accrued interest, a bill of credit was non–interest-bearing paper money issued on the good credit of the United States with no tangible backing in precious metal.

Under the Articles of Confederation, both the federal and state governments were guilty of rampant issuing of bills of credit to finance the Revolutionary War, which led to extensive inflation. In response to this Revolutionary history, Article I, Section 10 of the Constitution expressly prohibits the states from issuing bills of credit. With respect to Congress's power, however, the issue is not as clear. At the Constitutional Convention, it was proposed to give the federal government the power to "emit bills on the credit of the United States," but the Framers defeated this language as being too prone to abuse. As a result, the Constitution's monetary clauses expressly grant Congress the power to coin money and to borrow money by issuing "notes" (i.e., interest-bearing government bonds), but not to issue bills of credit. Given the Framers' general hostility to paper money (James Madison, for instance, bemoaned its "pestilent effects" under the Articles), it is likely that the Framers' intended to prohibit the federal government from issuing bills of credit, just as they expressly barred the states from doing so. Moreover, the Constitution itself created a government of enumerated powers; thus, absent an express grant, Congress lacked the power to act. In fact, both those who spoke for and those who spoke against the proposed language to grant this power to the federal government understood that striking the language amounted to a prohibition on Congress's power to issue paper money.

The monetary system that prevailed throughout most of the eighteenth and nineteenth centuries up until the Civil War comprised a hodgepodge of different types of money. Circulating money consisted of specie; coins minted by the government; privately minted coins; certain foreign coins; and paper banknotes issued by state-chartered private banks and backed by those institutions. Congress regulated the weight of gold and silver required to be contained in coins, but these ratios were often manipulated for political purposes. There were also several private mints, which stamped coins whose value reflected their intrinsic weight in specie. The dominant form of circulating money for most of this period was currency issued by state-chartered private banks and redeemable in gold or silver from the banks. Privately stamped "token" money, often made of copper, also circulated as an instrument for low-value exchange.

In general, the federal government did not issue fiat money (paper money not backed by specie) prior to the Civil War. Issuances were usually short-lived and were intended to be temporary solutions for government finance needs during a war or to shore up the bank system during a crisis. They were receivable for payment of government obligations and taxes, but the federal government did not declare these issuances to be legal tender for private debts, although they did circulate for private transactions to some degree. Issuances usually were interest-bearing and of relatively large denominations that discouraged the circulation of the notes as money. The federal government issued large denomination interest-bearing notes at the outset of the War of 1812, but subsequent issuances declined in denomination and did not pay interest. The government also issued interest-bearing notes in response to the Panic of 1837. Notwithstanding the Framers' opposition to paper money and principles of constitutional interpretation that suggest that Congress is barred from issuing paper money, in *Veazie Bank v. Fenno* (1869), the Supreme Court held that the federal government's issuance of bills

of credit to fund government operations was a valid exercise of the Necessary and Proper Clause.

To fund the Civil War, Congress also passed the Legal Tender Act of 1862. Unlike earlier issuances that were used to pay government obligations (as well as the paper money issued by the Confederate government), Civil War "greenbacks" (for which redemption in gold was "postponed") were for the first time declared legal tender for all debts, public or private. Even if the federal government had the authority to issue bills for payment of government obligations, it was a distinct question whether the federal government could also force private individuals to accept them for private contracts, an issue *Veazie Bank* specifically did not reach.

The Framers believed that in prohibiting the authority of the federal government from issuing bills of credit, they also were prohibiting their recognition as legal tender by definition. Moreover, they also separately and expressly barred the states from recognizing anything as legal tender other than gold or silver, which was generally understood as further evidence of the Framer's hostility to legal tender laws. Even those at the Constitutional Convention who supported Congress's power to issue bills of credit opposed granting the power to declare them legal tender.

In a series of nineteenth-century cases dubbed *The Legal Tender Cases*, the Supreme Court addressed the federal government's power to order its bills of credit to be accepted as legal tender for all debts, public and private. In *Hepburn v. Griswold* (1870), the Court held it violated the Obligation of Contract Clause for Congress to retroactively alter contract terms by permitting payment in "greenbacks" of an obligation incurred in gold dollars. Greenbacks were not immediately redeemable in gold. Following a dramatic change in membership, however, just one year later in the *Knox v. Lee* (1871), the Court expressly overruled *Hepburn* and upheld the Legal Tender Act as applied to both prospective and retrospective debts. Pointing to the crisis occasioned by the Civil War, *Knox* upheld the power to declare paper money to be legal tender.

In *Julliard v. Greenman* (1884), the Supreme Court extended *Knox*, upholding the validity of legal tender laws during peacetime. The Court held that the federal government's monetary power was inherent in its sovereignty; thus it was not necessary for the Constitution to enumerate this power. Justice Stephen Field's blunt dissent declared, "If there be anything in the history of the Constitution which can be established with moral certainty, it is that the Framers of that instrument intended to prohibit the issue of legal tender notes both by the general government and by the States; and thus prevent interference with the contracts of private parties." The Court used the recognition of Congress's expansive discretion on monetary issues in *The Legal Tender Cases* to support the federal government's invalidation of gold clauses in private contracts in the 1930s.

Robert Natelson has contested some parts of the traditional understanding of the original meaning of the Coinage Clause. He argues that legal tender and paper money laws are in fact consistent with the original understanding of that clause. He cites the history of legal tender laws and the setting of coin values in England and colonial America to establish the familiarity and popularity of these measures among the ratifiers of the Constitution. In light of this history, he argues the public meaning of "coin Money" included the power to issue paper currency at the federal level and that "regulate the Value thereof" included the power to establish legal tender.

Todd Zywicki

See Also

Article I, Section 8, Clause 2 (Borrowing Clause)

Article I, Section 8, Clause 18 (Necessary and Proper Clause)

Article I, Section 10, Clause 1 (State Coinage)

Article I, Section 10, Clause 1 (Obligation of Contract)

Suggestions for Further Research

Kenneth W. Dam, *The Legal Tender Cases*, 1981 Sup. Ct. Rev. 367 (1981)

Robert G. Natelson, *Paper Money and the Original Understanding of the Coinage Clause*, 31 Harv. J.L. & Pub. Pol'y 1017 (2008)

Bernard H. Siegan, The Supreme Court's Constitution: An Inquiry into Judicial Review and Its Impact on Society (1987)

James B. Thayer, *Legal Tender*, 1 Harv. L. Rev. 73 (1887–1888)

Richard Timberlake, Gold, Greenbacks, and the Constitution (1991)

Thomas F. Wilson, The Power "to Coin" Money: The Exercise of Monetary Powers by the Congress (1992)

Significant Cases

Craig v. Missouri, 29 U.S. (4 Pet.) 410 (1830)

Bronson v. Rodes, 74 U.S. (7 Wall.) 229 (1868)

Veazie Bank v. Fenno, 75 U.S. (8 Wall.) 533 (1869)

Hepburn v. Griswold, 75 U.S. (8 Wall.) 603 (1870), *overruled in part by* The Legal Tender Cases (Knox v. Lee) 79 U.S. (12 Wall.) 457 (1871); *sub nom.* The Legal Tender Cases (Julliard v. Greenman), 110 U.S. 421 (1884)

Weights and Measures

The Congress shall have Power To ... fix the Standard of Weights and Measures....

(Article I, Section 8, Clause 5)

~

*T*he Articles of Confederation was the immediate source that gave the central government "the sole and exclusive right and power of ... fixing the Standard of Weights and Measures throughout the United States." Article IX, Section 4. More remotely, the power to establish national standards of weights and measures resided in the English Crown or Parliament from the late eleventh century, although it appears that official standards were frequently ignored throughout England. The phrase itself dates from the late fourteenth century.

By the time of the Constitutional Convention, it appears that the Weights and Measures Clause was not an attempt to remedy a situation in which various standards obtained in various parts of the country. A customary uniformity already existed.

Rather, the purpose in granting this power was to facilitate domestic and international commerce by permitting the federal government to adopt and enforce national measurement standards based upon the prevailing consensus.

The clause excited no controversy among the Framers or in the ratifying conventions. During their respective tenures as Secretary of State, Thomas Jefferson and John Quincy Adams, as well as a House committee, produced extensive studies calling for congressional adoption of uniform standards. The reports by the House and Adams rejected adopting the metric system of France and proposed no federal enforcement mechanism, leaving the application of the standards to the executives of the several states. Congress itself did not adopt any systems of weights or measures, although the Treasury Department established standards for the pound, yard, gallon, and bushel for customs purposes and, beginning in the 1830s, sent complete sets of weights and measures to each state.

A question then arises as to what use the clause had in light of Congress's power to regulate commerce among the states. The answer would seem to be that the clause would have allowed Congress to set and enforce the standards for weights and measures even for intrastate trade. In fact, however, Congress chose the Commerce Clause or the Necessary and Proper Clause whenever it wanted to regulate the standards of goods permitted in intrastate as well as interstate trade.

In the face of official congressional inaction, many states defined standard measures for trade purposes. No Supreme Court case has explicitly held that the states are free to establish such standards in the absence of congressional action, although Justice Oliver Wendell Holmes intimated as much in *Massachusetts State Grange v. Benton* (1926). Justice Robert Cooper Grier, on circuit, was perhaps more dubious of the states' power. *The Miantinomi* (1855).

Congress has acquiesced in (though never authorized) the use of the traditional English system of weights and measures in nonbusiness activities. In 1866, Congress authorized, but did not mandate, the use of the metric system and, since 1975, the metric system has been the "preferred system" for trade and commerce. The Office of Weights and Measures within the Commerce Department's National Institute of Standards and Technology publishes standards for English and metric weights and measures.

Eric Chiappinelli

See Also

Article I, Section 8, Clause 1 (Uniformity Clause)

Article I, Section 8, Clause 3 (Commerce with Foreign Nations)

Article I, Section 8, Clause 3 (Commerce Among the States)

Article I, Section 8, Clause 8 (Patent and Copyright Clause)

Article I, Section 8, Clause 18 (Necessary and Proper Clause)

Amendment X (Reserved Powers of the States)

Suggestions for Further Research

David P. Currie, *Weights & Measures*, 2 Green Bag 2d 261 (1999)

Louis A. Fischer, History of the Standard Weights and Measures of the United States (1925)

Lewis V. Judson, Weights and Measures Standards of the United States (1976)

Significant Cases

The Miantinomi, 17 F. Cas. 254 (C.C.W.D. Pa. 1855) (No. 9521)

Massachusetts State Grange v. Benton, 272 U.S. 525 (1926)

Counterfeiting

The Congress shall have Power... To provide for the Punishment of counterfeiting the Securities and current Coin of the United States....
(Article I, Section 8, Clause 6)

$\sim$

*I*n England, counterfeiting was a treasonous act. The American colonies differed widely in their attitude towards counterfeiting. New York, for example, applied the death penalty, while Connecticut limited punishment to six months in jail. During the Revolution, the British counterfeited state and continental paper scrip to depreciate the currency.

At the Constitutional Convention, Gouverneur Morris voiced concern that "[b]ills of exchange…might be forged in one State and carried into another." Another delegate feared that the counterfeiting of "foreign paper" might embarrass foreign relations. Consequently, when Oliver Ellsworth moved to allow Congress the power to punish "counterfeiting the securities and current coin of the U. States," it was unanimously approved. Yet in light of the Necessary and Proper Clause, it is not clear why there was a need for this power to be defined in the Constitution at all. Justice Joseph Story later declared in his *Commentaries on the Constitution of the United States* (1833) that "this power [to provide for the punishment of counterfeiting] would naturally flow, as an incident, from the antecedent powers to borrow money, and regulate the coinage; and, indeed, without it those powers would be without any adequate sanction."

Nonetheless, there are three reasons why a separate delegated power to punish counterfeiting is appropriate. First, the Framers took pains to undo the British law on treason, which included counterfeiting and was often punished by parliamentary bills of attainder. Thus, the Constitution defines the crime of treason in terms that leave Congress no power to expand it. The Constitution also prohibits bills of attainder. But the Framers did want authority over the remaining formerly treasonous crime of counterfeiting to be left in the hands of the national legislature. Otherwise, having denied Congress the power to define treason, it might be inferred that the Constitution also denied Congress the power to legislate against counterfeiting.

Second, the Framers lodged all the incidents of the foreign-affairs power in the national government. Counterfeiting of foreign securities was a serious breach of international comity. The clause empowers Congress to deal with an important element of the nation's international obligations.

Third, the clause betokens federal supremacy in the field of monetary policy. In *The Federalist* No. 42, James Madison includes the power over

counterfeiting as among those powers "which provide for the harmony and proper intercourse among the States." The implication is that, like commerce, the power over counterfeiting is exclusive and plenary. Justice Joseph Story was explicit: "this power would seem to be exclusive of that of the States, since it grows out of the Constitution, as an appropriate means to carry into effect other delegated powers, not antecedently existing in the States."

In the hands of the judiciary, however, the power became limited and eventually superfluous. In *Fox v. Ohio* (1847), the Supreme Court upheld an Ohio law that punished the "passing" or "uttering" of counterfeited money. The Court reasoned that the actual act of counterfeiting was an offense directed at the federal government, whereas uttering counterfeited money was a "private harm" within a state's police power. Moreover, the Court noted, England had distinguished between the two offenses, making counterfeiting a treasonous offense, but the passing or "uttering" of counterfeit coin was neither "treason nor misprision of treason." As the Supreme Court of South Carolina explained in *State v. Tutt* (1831): "The offence against the Government of the United States consists in discrediting its currency. That against the State in defrauding its citizens. The offence against the State is certainly of the more palpable and dangerous character." The result is that although the federal government has exclusive power to punish the actual act of counterfeiting, states have the concurrent power to punish the passing of counterfeited currency. The federal and state governments possess concurrent power to punish the possession of devices for making counterfeited money. *Baender v. Barnett* (1921).

In cases upholding the right of Congress to punish counterfeiting coinage, *United States v. Marigold* (1850), and counterfeiting foreign currency, *United States v. Arjona* (1887), the Court justified Congress's power under the Coinage Clause, the Necessary and Proper Clause, the Commerce Clause, and the Counterfeiting Clause. In practical terms, there seems little if any activity that can be reached under the Counterfeiting Clause that could not also be reached by other congressional powers. The Court, however, does apply the First Amendment as a limit to legislation passed under

≈

the Counterfeiting Clause. In *Regan v. Time, Inc.* (1984), the Court struck down a portion of the statute permitting limited reproduction of United States currency "for philatelic, numismatic, educational, historical, or newsworthy purposes" as being content-based.

Congress passed the first anti-counterfeiting statute in 1790. The current federal prohibition on counterfeiting is found in 18 U.S.C. §§ 470–513 (2004), which generally provides for an unspecified fine or imprisonment of not more than twenty years, or both, for its violation.

David F. Forte

See Also

Article I, Section 8, Clause 3 (Commerce Among the States)

Article I, Section 8, Clause 5 (Coinage Clause)

Article I, Section 8, Clause 18 (Necessary and Proper Clause)

Article I, Section 10, Clause 1 (State Coinage)

Suggestion for Further Research

Nathan K. Cummings, *The Counterfeit Buck Stops Here: National Security Issues in the Redesign of U.S. Currency,* 8 S. Cal. Interdisc. L.J. 539 (1999)

Lynn Glaser, Counterfeiting in America (1968)

Kenneth Scott, Counterfeiting in Colonial America (1957)

Significant Cases

State v. Tutt, 18 S.C.L. (2 Bail.) 44 (1831)

Fox v. Ohio, 46 U.S. (5 How.) 410 (1847)

United States v. Marigold, 50 U.S. (9 How.) 560 (1850)

United States v. Arjona, 120 U.S. 479 (1887)

Sexton v. California, 189 U.S. 319 (1903)

Baender v. Barnett, 255 U.S. 224 (1921)

Regan v. Time, Inc., 468 U.S. 641 (1984)

Post Office

The Congress shall have Power...To establish Post Offices and post Roads....

(**Article I, Section 8, Clause 7**)

*U*nder the Articles of Confederation, Congress possessed the power to establish and regulate post offices. The Framers easily transferred the power into the Constitution and gave Congress the additional authority to establish postal roads. At the Constitutional Convention, Benjamin Franklin (who had been appointed Postmaster General in 1775 by the Second Continental Congress) suggested that, in addition to establishing post roads, Congress should have the "power to provide for cutting canals where deemed necessary," and James Madison sought to enlarge the power "to grant charters of incorporation where the interest of the U.S. might require & the legislative provisions of individual States may be incompetent." However, the Founders turned aside these extensions on the ground that such powers were already assumed in the power to regulate trade.

Following the adoption of the Constitution, the Act of September 22, 1789 (1 Stat. 70) established (at first temporarily) a post office and created the Office of the Postmaster General. By that time, seventy-five post offices and over 2000 miles of post roads already existed. What was originally thought to be a rather simple and benign power soon turned controversial; there was disagreement over whether this power merely enabled Congress to direct where post offices should be located and on what roads mail should be carried, or whether it authorized Congress to construct and maintain roads and post offices within the states. Thomas Jefferson and James Monroe doubted whether the clause granted Congress the power to construct roads, whereas many in Congress asserted that it did have such power. In fact, most congressional enactments merely designated post roads, but in 1833, Justice Joseph Story declared in his *Commentaries on the Constitution of the United States* that the words "to establish" encompass a power to create roads as well as to designate them. Story maintained, however, that once built, a post road is subject to the laws of the state. In 1845, in the case of *Searight v. Stokes,* Chief Justice Roger B. Taney held that mail carriages were immune to state road taxes on the Cumberland Road (part of the National Road), but, over the dissent of Justice

Peter V. Daniel, he specifically avoided the question of the power of Congress to construct post roads.

Story's view has stronger textual support than does Jefferson's. The power "to establish an uniform Rule of Naturalization, and uniform Laws on the subject of Bankruptcies" (Article I, Section 8, Clause 4), and the power of Congress to "establish" inferior federal courts (Article III, Section 1) clearly contemplate the creation of such laws and courts, respectively. Congress would seem to have a similar creative power in establishing post roads.

A second point of contention was the question whether Congress could delegate the designation of post offices (most of which were in existing institutions, such as general stores or inns) and post roads. The First Congress debated the issue and resolved it with the Postal Service Act of 1792, which provided a detailed list of post offices and post roads, keeping the power in Congress's hands and becoming a principal means for Members to patronize their home districts until the Postal Reorganization Act of 1970. That Act transformed the Post Office Department, which had been a tax-subsidized cabinet-level federal agency, and turned it into the United States Postal Service, an independent federal agency with a specific mandate to "conduct affairs...on a business-like basis."

Congress's power under the Post Office Clause is consequential. It has been the source, supported by the Necessary and Proper Clause, of much federal criminal legislation. The Supreme Court has consistently interpreted this clause broadly. In *Ex parte Jackson* (1877), the Court held that congressional power over the mail is indeed far-reaching, including the right to determine what can and cannot be mailed:

> The validity of legislation prescribing what should be carried, and its weight and form, and the charges to which it should be subjected, has never been questioned.... The power possessed by Congress embraces the regulation of the entire Postal System of the country. The right to designate what shall be carried necessarily

involves the right to determine what shall be excluded.

In *In re Rapier* (1892), the Court held that Congress has exclusive jurisdiction over the mail, which includes the right to prohibit the circulation of materials that are immoral and injurious, such as lottery tickets. The Court in *Brennan v. United States Postal Service* (1978) reaffirmed the federal government's monopoly over the postal system; and in *United States Postal Service v. Council of Greenburgh Civic Ass'ns* (1981), the Court upheld a federal law prohibiting the placing of unstamped mail in home mailboxes.

During World War I, the government's power to ban incendiary and disloyal material figured largely in prosecutions under the Espionage Act of 1917. *See Masses Publishing Co. v. Patten* (1917). Later cases dealt with laws prohibiting the mailing of obscene material. *Roth v. United States* (1957); *United States v. Reidel* (1971). Meanwhile, lower courts added that regulations governing what materials could be mailed are subject to First Amendment scrutiny. *See United States v. Handler* (D. Md. 1974). The Supreme Court has confirmed that, like all other delegated powers, the post office power is subject to extrinsic restraints such as the First Amendment. For example, in *Postal Service v. Council of Greenburgh Civic Ass'ns*, the Court acknowledged the broad sweep of the Post Office Clause, all the while holding that its broad power cannot be exercised in a way that abridges the rights protected under the First Amendment. The Court has also held that the Tenth Amendment may also be a limitation on the postal power. *Bond v. United States* (2011).

Another area of contention relevant to the Post Office Clause is the franking privilege, which exempts all federal governmental officials from paying postage when conducting official business. The frank itself is a reproduction of the Member's signature, which is affixed to the mailed item in lieu of a stamp. Members of the House of Commons and Members of the Continental Congress enjoyed the privilege. The First Congress retained the privilege in 1789. The Act of 1895, 28 Stat. 601, 622 § 85, restricted the use of the privilege only for correspondence on "official business," to be interpreted by the Post Office Department, which would issue advisory opinions on whether a contemplated mailing could be franked. By 1971, after the Postal Reorganization Act, the Post Office had relinquished any responsibility to give advisory opinions. This led to a number of lawsuits by disgruntled candidates who ran against incumbent Members who used their franking privileges in mass mailings to constituents. Abuses became more flagrant, and the Franking Act of 1973, Pub. L. No. 93–191, 39 U.S.C. § 3210, was enacted to limit "official business" to "cover all matters which directly or indirectly pertain to the legislative process...." The Act also laid out a noninclusive list of what constitutes official business, and established two special commissions, the House Commission on Congressional Mailing Standards and the Select Committee on Standards and Conduct of the Senate, to provide advisory opinions as to whether certain business is official or not.

The major controversy that raged over the post office power in the nineteenth century (following the Second Great Awakening) was whether Sunday deliveries ought to be discontinued in honor of the Sabbath. Congress had mandated seven-day delivery in 1810. Ultimately, the Sabbatarians failed. Sunday mail deliveries were too important to the people. The post office (usually in the general store) was usually the only place open on Sunday. It was the place to go to obtain the latest news (virtually all newspapers were delivered by mail), and to socialize around the issues of the day. In other words, the post office and its Sunday deliveries were too much of a civic association of the republic to give way to religious law. The federal government maintained Sunday deliveries until 1912.

The Postal Service has not fared well since the Reorganization Act of 1970. Competition from private carriers, the expansion of the internet, and a poorly constructed pension system have brought the agency near financial collapse. Because of its severe financial difficulties, both the Postal Service and proposed legislation contemplate ceasing most Saturday deliveries.

David F. Forte

See Also

Article I, Section 8, Clause 4 (Naturalization)

Article III, Section 1 (Inferior Courts)

Suggestions for Further Research

Anuj C. Desai, *The Transformation of Statutes into Constitutional Law: How Early Post Office Policy Shaped Modern First Amendment Doctrine*, 58 HASTINGS L.J. 671 (2007)

Darrell E. Issa, *The Postal Reform Act: A Plan for an Affordable, Sustainable Postal Service*, 38 J. LEGIS. 151 (2012)

RICHARD R. JOHN, SPREADING THE NEWS: THE AMERICAN POSTAL SYSTEM FROM FRANKLIN TO MORSE (1995)

PATRICK REEBEL, UNITED STATES POST OFFICE: CURRENT ISSUES AND HISTORICAL BACKGROUND (2003)

Amy Zelcer, Mail and Wire Fraud, 49 AM. CRIM. L. REV. 985 (2012)

Significant Cases

Searight v. Stokes, 44 U.S. (3 How.) 151 (1845)

Ex parte Jackson, 96 U.S. 727 (1877)

In re Rapier, 143 U.S. 110 (1892)

Masses Publishing Co. v. Patten, 244 F. 535 (S.D.N.Y. 1917), *rev'd* 246 F. 24 (2d Cir. 1917)

Roth v. United States, 354 U.S. 476 (1957)

United States v. Reidel, 402 U.S. 351 (1971)

United States v. Handler, 383 F. Supp. 1267 (D. Md. 1974)

Brennan v. United States Postal Service, 439 U.S. 1345 (1978)

United States Postal Service v. Council of Greenburgh Civic Ass'ns, 453 U.S. 114 (1981)

Bond v. United States, 131 S. Ct. 2355 (2011)

Patent and Copyright Clause

The Congress shall have Power...To promote the Progress of Science and useful Arts, by securing for limited Times to Authors and Inventors the exclusive Right to their respective Writings and Discoveries....

(ARTICLE I, SECTION 8, CLAUSE 8)

~

There is little direct evidence about the Patent and Copyright Clause's original meaning. The clause neither represented a legal tradition of great historical and practical significance to the Framers, such as the availability of habeas corpus (*see* Article I, Section 9, Clause 2), nor was it one of the great structural innovations of the Constitution that attracted so much attention because of its gravity and novelty. Rather, the clause appears to have been largely an afterthought.

The clause was neither the subject of much debate during the Constitutional Convention nor was it a major topic of discussion during the ratification debates. James Madison, in his wrap-up of "miscellaneous powers" in *The Federalist* No. 43, devoted only a single paragraph to the clause, justifying it both on the need to provide a national, uniform standard of intellectual property regulation as well as on the merits of the protection itself. "The copyright of authors," Madison wrote, "has been solemnly adjudged in Great Britain to be a right of common law. The right to useful inventions seems with equal reason to belong to the inventors." On this point Madison was mistaken; the House of Lords had decided in 1774 that copyright was not a common-law right, and invention patents had always been granted as a matter of political discretion, not legal right. In the very same breath as he extolled a natural-rights view of intellectual property, however, Madison also struck upon an incentives-based approach, justifying intellectual property regulation by its contribution to the public, as well as private, benefit. Madison concluded, "The public good fully coincides in both cases with the claims of individuals." He did not address the question of what to do in cases in which the public's good is not served by extending intellectual property rights.

In the end, no one appears to have objected seriously to the clause. George Mason and Thomas Jefferson (privately to Madison), along with a few other Anti-Federalists, raised concerns over the granting of state-sanctioned monopolies, which the Framers certainly disfavored as a general matter. But no one took the clause to authorize federal trade monopolies, and such objections were rebuffed by Federalists (in Jefferson's case by Madison himself) by reference to the value of granting copyright and patents and the need for national uniformity, which no one appears to have questioned. What little direct evidence we have about the circumstances of the clause's adoption has been of little help in resolving the disputes that have arisen, many of them quite recently, over its meaning.

The clause's text, too, has been of limited help in resolving modern disputes over its meaning. Although some commentators have developed complex textual arguments about the clause, courts have been wary of applying the many limits potentially to be mined from its wording. In *Graham v. John Deere Co.* (1966), the Court discussed the limits of Congress's power under the clause. It declared that Congress may not grant patents "without regard to the innovation, advancement or social benefit gained thereby" or "whose effects are to remove existent knowledge from the public domain or to restrict free access to materials already available." More generally, the Court opined that the patent system as adopted must "promote the Progress of...useful Arts." In *Feist Publications, Inc. v. Rural Telephone Service Co.* (1991), the Court stated that because the clause permits copyright protection only for creative works, facts cannot be copyrighted. But neither *Graham* nor *Feist* involved actual challenges to Congress's power; neither case required the Court to apply the limits it had found in the clause. In fact, the Court has been deferential to Congress. Thus, although the Court has frequently repeated its statement in *Graham* that "[t]he clause is both a grant of a power and a limitation," at the same time it has explained that "it is generally for Congress, not the courts, to decide how best to pursue the Copyright and Patent Clause's objectives." *Eldred v. Ashcroft* (2003).

Indeed, with one early exception, the Court has deferred to Congress's view of its own powers under the clause. For example, in *Eldred*, the Court upheld not only Congress's extension of the duration of copyrights to almost five times what it was in the 1790 copyright act, it also ruled that the requirement that copyrights be for "limited Times" did not prevent Congress from extending the copyright term for a work already under protection. Similarly, in *Golan v. Holder* (2012), the Court upheld section 514 of the Uruguay Round Agreements Act (which extended protection to some works previously in the public domain), eliding the Court's pronouncement in *Graham* as dicta and rejecting a narrower interpretation of the clause as authorizing only copyright grants that promote the creation of new works. Rather, the Court deferred to Congress's possible interpretation that the withdrawal of works from the public domain could, on the whole, "promote the diffusion of knowledge." The early exception to the pattern of deference was in the *Trade-Mark Cases* (1879), in which the Court held that the clause did not provide authority for federal trademark legislation. Even that limit was eventually circumvented by Congress's use of the commerce power as authority for trademark legislation.

Although the history of the clause's adoption has not featured prominently in the Court's jurisprudence, history has. Indeed, Justice Ruth Bader Ginsburg (echoing Justice Oliver Wendell Holmes, Jr.) wrote in *Eldred* that, when it comes to interpreting the clause, "a page of history is worth a volume of logic." In a series of cases, the Court referred to early congressional practice under the clause in interpreting the clause's reach. In *Burrow-Giles Lithographic Co. v. Sarony* (1884), the Court held that protection for photographs was within the clause even though the clause limits copyright to "Writings" and "Authors," in part because the first Congress granted copyright protection to other graphical works (such as maps and charts). The Court later extended this logic to allow protection for sculptures as well. Similarly, in both *Eldred* and *Golan*, congressional practice under the clause figured prominently in the Court's interpretation, including both the extension of copyright terms for existing works and in the protection of works previously in the public domain.

It is possible that, given the strongly deferential approach taken by the Court in *Eldred* and *Golan*, the Court will permit virtually any grant under the clause. The prohibition against copyright in facts contained in *Feist*, for instance, could just as easily be characterized as

dicta as was the prohibition against recapture of the public domain contained in *Graham*. Should the Court encounter legislation seeming to exceed the clause's limits, proponents of such measures might rely on other constitutional powers, such as the power to regulate interstate commerce and, because some of new grants might be intended to bring the United States into compliance with international intellectual property conventions, the treaty power (raised but not relied upon by the Court in *Holder*). Such reliance on other clauses has been the subject of much debate by commentators but little action by courts. The Court's decision in *National Federation of Independent Business v. Sebelius* (2012) striking the "individual mandate" provisions of the Patient Protection and Affordable Care Act of 2010 as beyond the power to regulate interstate commerce but upholding them as an exercise of the taxing power suggests that the powers enumerated in Article I, Section 8 are indeed alternative rather than exclusive and that, should the Court's deference to Congress's interpretation of the Patent and Copyright Clause run out, legislation pursuant to other powers is a potential avenue.

Just as proponents of broader exclusive rights have looked to other parts of the Constitution, so too have their opponents. In *Harper & Row Publishers, Inc. v. Nation Enterprises* (1985), the Court acknowledged the possibility that copyright legislation might result in so heavy a burden on speech as to run afoul of the First Amendment. In *Eldred v. Ashcroft*, the Court held that copyright term extension did not call for heighted First Amendment scrutiny because "the traditional contours of copyright protection" include protection for the expressive interests normally guaranteed by the First Amendment, prompting the question of whether some copyright protection (such as the removal of works from the public domain) might deviate far enough from those traditional contours to require heighted First Amendment scrutiny. In *Golan*, the Court clarified that those "traditional contours" with First Amendment significance are limited to the idea/expression dichotomy and the fair use defense and that removal of works from the public domain, for instance, presents no serious First Amendment problem.

Even given the seemingly broad discretion the Court has given Congress with regard to patent and copyright laws, with the ever-increasing importance of information to the economy, it is likely that constitutional challenges to intellectual property laws will continue.

Thomas Nachbar

See Also

Article I, Section 8, Clause 3 (Commerce Among the States)

Article I, Section 9, Clause 2 (Suspension of Habeas Corpus)

Article II, Section 2, Clause 2 (Treaty Clause)

Amendment I (Freedom of Speech and of the Press)

Suggestions for Further Research

BRUCE W. BUGBEE, GENESIS OF AMERICAN PATENT AND COPYRIGHT LAW (1967)

Jane C. Ginsburg, No "Sweat"? Copyright and Other Protection of Works of Information after Feist v. Rural Telephone, 92 COLUM. L. REV. 338 (1992)

Adam Mossoff, *Who Cares What Thomas Jefferson Thought About Patents? Reevaluating the Patent "Privilege" in Historical Context*, 92 CORNELL L. REV. 953 (2007)

Thomas B. Nachbar, *Intellectual Property and Constitutional Norms*, 104 COLUM. L. REV. 272 (2004)

Tyler T. Ochoa & Mark Rose, *The Anti-Monopoly Origins of the Patent and Copyright Clause*, 84 J. PAT. & TRADEMARK OFF. SOC'Y 909 (2002)

EDWARD C. WALTERSCHEID, THE NATURE OF THE INTELLECTUAL PROPERTY CLAUSE: A STUDY IN HISTORICAL PERSPECTIVE (2002)

Significant Cases

In re Trade-Mark Cases, 100 U.S. 82 (1879)

Burrow-Giles Lithographic Co. v. Sarony, 111 U.S. 53 (1884)

Graham v. John Deere Co., 383 U.S. 1 (1966)

Harper & Row Publishers, Inc. v. Nation Enterprises, 471 U.S. 539 (1985)

Feist Publications, Inc. v. Rural Telephone Serv. Co., 499 U.S. 340 (1991)

Eldred v. Ashcroft, 537 U.S. 186 (2003)

Golan v. Holder, 132 S. Ct. 873 (2012)

Inferior Courts

The Congress shall have Power... To constitute Tribunals inferior to the supreme Court....
(ARTICLE I, SECTION 8, CLAUSE 9)

$\sim$

While the Constitutional Convention agreed that the new central government should include a permanent judiciary, there was disagreement over its size. The original proposal (the Virginia Plan) called for "one or more supreme tribunals" as well as "inferior tribunals." (In English and American usage at that time, "supreme" and "inferior" were normally used to indicate different breadths of geographic or subject matter competence, rather than appellate hierarchy; Virginia, for example, had four "supreme" courts, with a complex of relations among them.) Many of the delegates, however, believed it would be sufficient to have a single national court, empowered to review certain state court judgments. By successive amendments, those delegates succeeded first in reducing the number of "supreme" courts to one and then in eliminating the reference to "inferior" courts.

The latter vote was very close, however; James Madison moved as a compromise "that the National Legislature be empowered to institute inferior tribunals." Madison repeated his earlier argument that "unless inferior tribunals were dispersed throughout the Republic with *final* jurisdiction in *many* cases" (the words are emphasized in Madison's own notes), there would be docket overload and oppressive expense. The delegates' approval of this compromise resulted in three separate but related constitutional provisions: the Inferior Courts Clause in Article I, granting Congress power (and discretion) to constitute "inferior" tribunals; the phrase in Article III alluding to "such inferior Courts as the Congress may from time to time ordain and establish"; and the Appellate Jurisdiction Clause in Article III, Section 2, Clause 2, which provides that judgments may be excluded by Congress from Supreme Court review.

Some commentaries and judicial opinions have maintained that the Inferior Courts Clause of Article I implies congressional discretion to determine how much of the subject-matter jurisdiction authorized by Article III should actually be vested in federal courts. The Framers, however, specified in the Constitution itself the subject-matter extent of "the judicial Power of the United States" and directed in mandatory language that it "shall be vested" in the national judiciary (to consist of the one "supreme" and whatever "inferior" courts Congress might establish). Indeed, the Framers specifically voted down a succession of proposals that would have empowered Congress to exclude subject matters from the inferior courts; with regard to the "supreme" court, though, they included the Appellate Jurisdiction Clause, so that if Congress did create "inferior" courts, these could be given "final jurisdiction in many cases," as Madison had urged.

Yet the Necessary and Proper Clause (Article I, Section 8, Clause18) gave Congress a discretion to distribute jurisdiction among whatever courts it established. Barely a week before finalizing the scope of subject-matter jurisdiction, the delegates had approved the Necessary and Proper Clause, which the Committee of Detail had devised, in part, for the very purpose of empowering Congress to organize the judicial branch. It must have been obvious that, if inferior tribunals were created at all, this Necessary and Proper Clause would enable Congress to distribute the jurisdiction prescribed by Article III without diminishing the collective competence of the federal judiciary as a whole. It logically follows that Congress may constitute specialized tribunals for admiralty, bankruptcy, claims, tax, or diversity cases, for example, so long as it makes one or another federal tribunal available for each subject matter on the Article III list.

There are intrinsic limits, however. In 1818, the United States rebuffed British pressure to participate in an international tribunal to deal with the slave trade on the high seas. President John Quincy Adams (with the unanimous support of his cabinet) decided "that it would be repugnant to the article in the Constitution concerning the organization of the judicial power." On the other hand, one commentator has suggested that Congress's power to "constitute" inferior tribunals under this clause (Article I, Section 8, Clause 9) would allow it to confer jurisdiction over federal claims even in state courts. In contrast, the power of Congress "to ordain and establish" inferior courts to the Supreme Court in Article III, Section 1 refers only to the power to establish a federal court system.

Congress's power to organize the judicial branch goes beyond constituting inferior courts and distributing the Article III subject-matter jurisdiction. Congress also may designate some courts for trials, others for appeals, and (if it chooses) some for both; it may facilitate, restrict, or preclude appellate review, and prescribe its procedural course; and it may legislate rules of evidence and practice.

As to the latter, ever since the Justices affirmed the argument of Attorney General Edmund Randolph regarding process and service in *Chisholm v. Georgia* (1793), it has been understood that, where Congress is silent, federal courts can establish procedures of their own, but that legislation regarding procedure prevails by virtue of the Supremacy Clause. Congressional discretion over procedural matters is not unlimited, however. If its power were really derived from the Inferior Courts (Tribunals) Clause (which contains no intrinsic limit), Congress could even dictate procedures impeding the judiciary or impairing the independence at which the judicial tenure and salary guarantees of the Constitution are aimed. Because this power actually comes from the Necessary and Proper Clause, however, laws regarding the judiciary must satisfy the requirement that they be "necessary and proper for carrying into Execution the . . . Powers vested by this Constitution in [the judicial] department. . . ." This intrinsic limit leaves ample discretion to Congress as to whether and how to assist, but if judges find a procedure enacted by Congress incompatible with the independent performance of their own constitutional duties, it would seem that they are bound by their oaths to disregard it.

While the judges of inferior federal courts have the same tenure and compensation guarantees as Supreme Court Justices, it may not necessarily follow that they must be nominated or appointed in the same political manner. Lower federal court judges might be considered "inferior Officers," whose appointment Congress is empowered by the Appointments Clause to vest "in the President alone, in the Courts of Law, or in the Heads of Departments." In any event, Congress has not yet attempted to dispense with either presidential appointment or Senate confirmation for life-tenured inferior court judges.

The Judiciary Act of 1789, drafted in the first Congress by a Senate committee—half of whose Members had participated at the Constitutional Convention—established a federal court system very different from that which is familiar today. Reflection on that system helps one understand how much discretion the Constitution gives Congress regarding judicial system design. Single-judge district courts heard admiralty matters, tried civil "forfeiture" proceedings (a category which, at the time, embraced federal question claims), and exercised concurrent jurisdiction over minor federal crimes. Three-judge circuit courts were the principal federal tribunals; they tried diversity cases and most federal crimes, heard cases removed from state courts, and could review most of the single-judge district courts' decisions. Supreme Court Justices spent most of their time presiding at the several circuit courts. They gathered only briefly twice each year to try matters within the Supreme Court's scant original jurisdiction and to hear a few appellate cases. However, Supreme Court review was not available for any criminal case (unless by habeas corpus) or for civil cases that had begun in a district court. Except for federal question cases from state courts, no other case could reach the Supreme Court unless the amount in controversy exceeded a sum that very few Americans at that time could hope to earn in a year.

Supreme Court review of inferior federal courts was rare. Statistics confirm that most federal court litigation began and ended in the circuit courts. The establishment thus conformed to Madison's model of "inferior tribunals . . . dispersed throughout the Republic with final jurisdiction in many cases. . . ." This decentralization was consistent with Alexander Hamilton's prediction in *The Federalist* No. 78 that the judiciary could "take no active resolution whatever" and "may truly be said to have neither Force nor Will, but merely judgment." Some scholars, however, argue that "inferior to the supreme Court" in the clause textually demands that the Supreme Court not be shorn of power to review decisions of the lower federal courts, believing that a decentralized judiciary could become a political organ in competition with the executive and the legislature.

The decentralized framework of 1789, with slight modifications, was still in place when Alexis de Tocqueville visited America in 1831. Tocqueville described the practice of judicial review in this distinctly nonhierarchical judicial system as "one of the most powerful barriers ever erected against the tyranny of political assemblies." He observed that when any judge, from constitutional conviction, "refuses to apply a law in a case, it loses at once part of its moral force," prompting other litigants to contest it, too. Then, should other judges reach the same conclusion, the force of that law would be further diminished; but, Tocqueville observed, "it is only gradually, under repeated judicial blows, that it finally succumbs." Thus the accumulation of independent judgments, rather than any central, authoritative pronouncement, safeguarded the Constitution. At the same time, the consequences of an ill-considered ruling would probably be confined to the particular parties and case.

Not everyone was pleased with the decentralized judiciary. James Wilson, a participant at the Convention who became one of the original Associate Justices, criticized the federal judiciary as "a very uncommon establishment," and urged in his law lectures that instead it "should resemble a pyramid. . . . [O]ne supreme tribunal should superintend and govern all others." By 1801, this argument had persuaded the Federalist Congress to remodel the judicial branch; but the Federalist overhaul was repealed by Thomas Jefferson's Republicans the next year. Jefferson's own Congress, however, soon enacted some piecemeal revisions that gradually, but significantly, began to pyramid the judicial branch: justices' circuit-riding duties were reduced, enabling them to focus on appellate work; restrictions on appellate review were relaxed; and a process was enacted for certifying to the Supreme Court any question of law over which the two or more judges presiding at a Circuit Court proceeding disagreed. Thus did the wish for uniform resolution of legal questions begin to eclipse the original conception of conscientious, oath-bound, and independent adjudication of each litigant's case.

Nonstatutory developments—like the increasing availability of Supreme Court opinions once official publication started in 1817, and the widespread respect gained by Chief Justice John Marshall—helped make the centralization of judicial authority seem safe and desirable. Soon another development occurred, however, which nobody could have foreseen.

A decade before the American Revolution, English legal scholar Sir William Blackstone had written that a judge is "not delegated to pronounce a new law, but to maintain and expound the old one." A few years earlier, Baron de Montesquieu had seen English judges as "no more than the mouth that pronounces the words of the law, mere passive beings, incapable of moderating either its force or its rigour." That is why, in discussing the separation of powers, Montesquieu put aside the judiciary as "next to nothing" and focused on the three political elements— executive, commons, and lords. During the early decades of the nineteenth century, however, the possibility that judges might actually revise the law by their decisions began to be recognized; and some frankly embraced the potential. Before long, new appointees brought this new instrumentalism to the Supreme Court.

Gradually, instrumentalist jurisprudence operating in an increasingly hierarchical system made the federal judiciary a different institution from what the Framers had conceived. This combination enabled judges to make effective throughout the nation their honorably held, but not always predominantly shared, opinions on controversial questions of public policy linked to some constitutional phrase or ideal.

Harmonization of legal opinion may be a beneficial effect of a hierarchical judiciary in certain areas, but its persistence in whole or in part is at Congress's option. A pyramided

judicial branch is not constitutionally ordained, although not prohibited either. Circuit courts can, and often do, develop Constitutional doctrine before it is concretized by the Supreme Court. But centralized judicial decision of controversial public issues, under the rubric of constitutional generalities, frequently stirs vigorous dissent. At times, Members of Congress have urged that categories of jurisdiction be stripped from the judicial branch as a whole. The Framers refused to allow that, of course; when a divestment law was actually enacted in 1867, inferior courts ignored it and proceeded with the forbidden cases anyway. *See Beckwith v. Bean* (1878). In contrast, laws that de-pyramid by making exceptions to Supreme Court appellate jurisdiction are valid because of the Appellate Jurisdiction Clause, so long as the excepted cases have access to the inferior federal courts structured by Congress for carrying into execution the federal judicial power.

David Engdahl

See Also

Article I, Section 8, Clause 18 (Necessary and Proper Clause)

Article III, Section 1 (Inferior Courts)

Article III, Section 2, Clause 2 (Appellate Jurisdiction Clause)

Suggestions for Further Research

Steven G. Calabresi & Gary Lawson, *The Unitary Executive, Jurisdiction Stripping, and the Hamdan Opinions: A Textualist Response to Justice Scalia*, 107 Colum. L. Rev. 1002 (2007)

Robert N. Clinton, *A Mandatory View of Federal Court Jurisdiction: A Guided Quest for the Original Understanding of Article III*, 132 U. Pa. L. Rev. 741 (1984)

David E. Engdahl, *Intrinsic Limits of Congress' Power Regarding the Judicial Branch*, 1999 BYU L. Rev. 75 (1999)

David E. Engdahl, *What's in a Name? The Constitutionality of Multiple "Supreme" Courts*, 66 Ind. L.J. 457 (1991)

Doni Gewirtzman, *Lower Court Constitutionalism: Circuit Court Discretion in a Complex Adaptive System*, 61 Am. U. L. Rev. 457 (2012)

Eugene Kontorovich, *The Constitutionality of International Courts: The Forgotten Precedent of Slave-Trade Tribunals*, 158 U. Pa. L. Rev. 39 (2009)

James E. Pfander, *Federal Supremacy, State Court Inferiority, and the Constitutionality of Jurisdiction-Stripping Legislation*, 101 Nw. U. L. Rev. 191 (2007)

Ronald D. Rotunda, *Congressional Power to Restrict the Jurisdiction of the Lower Federal Courts and the Problem of School Busing*, 64 Geo. L.J. 839 (1976)

Gordon G. Young, *A Critical Reassessment of the Case Law Bearing on Congress's Power to Restrict the Jurisdiction of the Lower Federal Courts*, 54 Md. L. Rev. 132 (1995)

Significant Cases

Chisholm v. Georgia, 2 U.S. (2 Dall.) 419 (1793)

Sheldon v. Sill, 49 U.S. (8 How.) 441 (1850)

Ex parte Yerger, 75 U.S. (8 Wall.) 85 (1868)

Beckwith v. Bean, 98 U.S. 266 (1878)

Lockerty v. Phillips, 319 U.S. 182 (1943)

Plaut v. Spendthrift Farm, Inc., 514 U.S. 211 (1995)

Jinks v. Richland Cnty., 538 U.S. 456 (2003)

Piracy and Felonies

The Congress shall have Power... To define and punish Piracies and Felonies committed on the High Seas....

(Article I, Section 8, Clause 10)

$\sim$

*T*he need to strengthen the national government to protect against piracy and avoid the then current situation of each of the thirteen states treating the offense of piracy differently was an issue for the United States at the time of the Founding. For millennia, pirates have been referred to as *hostis humani generis*—"enemies of all humankind." Under "the law of nations," it was a crime of universal jurisdiction, but a state could choose only to enact proscriptions against various forms of "municipal or statutory piracy" that only applied within its jurisdiction. At the time of independence each of the new states enacted new piracy statutes, but not each of

them dealt with universal jurisdiction piracy. For example, Connecticut's statute only dealt with municipal piracy, while Pennsylvania's statute referenced the law of nations and, therefore, had universal jurisdiction.

Under Article IX of the Articles of Confederation, Congress had "the sole and exclusive right ... [and] States shall be restrained from... appointing courts for the trial of piracies and felonies committed on the high seas; and establishing courts for receiving and determining finally appeals in all cases of captures."

There were several problems with this provision. The Articles of Confederation did not set up a system of federal courts, so when Congress did pass an ordinance appointing courts under the piracy provision of the Articles, it provided that cases be tried by "the justices of the supreme or superior courts of judicature, and judge of the Court of Admiralty of the... states."

The other problem with the piracy provision under the Articles is that it allowed Congress to appoint courts but did not allow it to declare what was a piracy or other maritime felony. In fact, the ordinance Congress passed specifically allowed the states to use their own common law for the substantive crimes and causes of action to be brought against those accused of piracy. This allowed each of the states to prosecute piracy differently. And, as already stated, not all of the states' piracy statutes had universal jurisdiction.

These problems were recognized immediately, but attempts at reform under the Articles proved impossible. Thus, at the Constitutional Convention, there was little discussion of the provision, for the delegates understood the difficulties that had beset the Confederation Congress. The delegates therefore accorded Congress the power to "define and punish Piracies and Felonies committed on the High Seas."

Almost immediately, in 1790, Congress undertook the task. It defined piracy as murder or robbery on the high seas, or any other crime committed on the high seas that would be punishable by death under United States law, if committed on land. In 1819, Congress passed the predecessor to the present-day piracy statute. It removed any nexus to the territory of the United States from the definition of piracy and instead conceived of piracy as a truly universal crime defined by the law of nations. The current piracy statute, enacted in 1909 and based on the 1819 statute, can be found in 18 U.S.C. § 1651: "Whoever, on the high seas, commits the crime of piracy as defined by the law of nations, and is afterwards brought into or found in the United States, shall be imprisoned for life."

The reference to the "law of nations" in section 1651 was subject to a constitutional challenge in 1820. In *United States v. Smith* (1820), Justice Joseph Story opined that the crime of piracy had a definite meaning in international law, and that consequently, Congress's definition of piracy was sufficiently precise. Justice Story also concluded that the crime of piracy under the law of nations consisted of acts of robbery at sea.

No additional piracy cases have been litigated before the Supreme Court since 1820. However, piracy cases may end up before the Supreme Court in the near future, in light of recent controversy over the definition of piracy. While the first Supreme Court case limited the crime of piracy to robbery on the high seas, more recently, the courts have expanded the definition of piracy in light of contemporary customary international law.

In 2010, two new piracy cases litigated in federal courts raised novel issues regarding the definition of piracy. *United States v. Said* (2010), involved the pirates who approached a U.S ship on a small skiff. Although one of the pirates fired a shot at the ship, no pirates boarded or attempted to board it. Instead, pirates were apprehended by the crew of the ship and subsequently taken to Virginia for a criminal prosecution. The pirates moved for dismissal of the count of piracy against them, alleging that their acts did not constitute piracy under section 1651 because they did not board or take control of the victim vessel. The district court granted the motion to dismiss, concluding that the definition of "piracy" in the 1820 Supreme Court *Smith* case as "robbery or forcible depredations committed upon the sea" was still valid, and that due process considerations did not allow a construction of the piracy statute to include other actions. The court, in effect, decided that attempted piracy was not a crime under the law of nations, either in 1820 or today.

In the second case, *United States v. Hasan* (2010), pirates mistook a military vessel, the U.S.S. *Nicholas*, for a merchant ship. After an initial exchange of fire between the pirates and the crew of the U.S.S. *Nicholas*, the pirates fled in their vessel but were captured and brought to the United States for prosecution. These pirates similarly moved for dismissal of the piracy count under section 1651, arguing that the facts in the indictment were insufficient to constitute the crime of piracy. The court denied the motion, concluding that in light of developments in American piracy law, and of more recently drafted international treaties and customary law, piracy must be defined according to "contemporary customary international law." The court found that customary international law had evolved on the subject of maritime piracy and had changed since 1820 when the United States Supreme Court decided the *Smith* case. Finally, the court concluded that contemporary customary international law did not require an actual robbery on the high seas as a prerequisite for a piracy conviction under section 1651.

The defendants in the *Hasan* case appealed their conviction and sentence of life imprisonment to the Fourth Circuit Court of Appeals. The Fourth Circuit affirmed the conviction in *United States v. Dire* (2012) and vacated the decision in *Said*. The appellate judges concluded that when Congress enacted section 1651 and provided for piracy to be defined by the "law of nations," it had contemplated that the definition of piracy would evolve as the law of nations evolved. The Fourth Circuit thus opined that limiting the definition of piracy to robbery on the high seas would "render it incongruous with the modern law of nations and prevent [the federal courts] from exercising universal jurisdiction in piracy cases."

In a third case, *United States v. Shibin* (2012), pirates attacked and hijacked a German vessel and a United States yacht. The defendant was not directly involved in the attack; rather, he subsequently served as a hostage negotiator for the pirates and received a share of the ransom money. He was convicted under section 1651 and sentenced to life imprisonment. The district court, as in the *Hasan* case, opined that the crime of piracy under section 1651 encompassed acts other than just robbery at sea. At this writing, the case is pending appeal.

Finally, in *United States v. Ali* (2012), the D.C. District Court held that universal jurisdiction over the crime of piracy did not extend to the crime of conspiracy to commit piracy. This was the first case in United States history in which the government asserted universal jurisdiction over a crime of piracy that had no connection to the United States or its citizens. The defendant in *Ali* allegedly assisted the pirates both before and after their crime. He, in fact, provided interpretation services after the hostages were already in the pirates' custody in order to negotiate their ransom. One of the counts that the defendant was charged with included conspiracy to commit piracy. The court reasoned that because of the exceptional nature of universal jurisdiction, federal courts could only rely upon it when the precise conduct in question was not universally cognizable. Moreover, the court held that universal jurisdiction over piracy only applied on the high seas and not in foreign countries. It concluded that the universal jurisdiction over piracy included acts that aided or abetted the crime, but not conspiracy to commit the crime. Under this view, pirate negotiators have a form of immunity when acting on behalf of (and aiding and abetting for profit) those pirates who actually board the vessel.

In U.S. federal courts today, piracy now includes acts committed on the high seas other than robbery. It is thus likely that an unsuccessful attempt to rob a ship on the high seas would fall under the statute.

Milena Sterio

See Also

Article 1, Section 8, Clause 10 (Offenses Against the Law of Nations)

Suggestions for Further Research

Anthony J. Colangelo, *The Legal Limits of Universal Jurisdiction*, 47 Va. J. Int'l L. 149, 150 (2006)

Tara Helfman, *Marauders in the Courts: Why the Federal Courts Have Got the Problem of Maritime Piracy (Partly) Wrong*, 62 Syracuse L. Rev. 53, 57 (2012)

Eugene Kontorovich, *The "Define and Punish Clause" and the Limits of Universal Jurisdiction*, 103 Nw. U. L. Rev. 149 (2008)

Eugene Kontorovich, *Discretion, Delegation, and Defining in the Constitution's Law of Nations Clause*, 106 Nw. U. L. Rev. 1675 (2012)

Milena Sterio, *The Somali Piracy Problem: A Global Puzzle Necessitating a Global Solution*, 59 Am. U. L. Rev. 1449 (2010)

U.N. Convention on the Law of the Sea, opened for signature Dec. 10, 1982, 1833 U.N.T.S. 397 (entered into force November 16, 1994, without U.S. ratification)

Significant Cases

United States v. Smith, 18 U.S. (5 Wheat.) 153 (1820)

United States v. Hasan, 747 F. Supp. 2d 599 (E.D. Va. 2010)

United States v. Said, 757 F. Supp. 2d 554 (E.D. Va. 2010)

United States v. Dire, 680 F.3d 446, 450 (4th Cir. 2012)

United States v. Shibin, No. 2:11–cr–033, *slip op. at* 14 (E.D. Va. Apr. 16, 2012)

United States v. Ali, CRIM. 11-0106, 2012 WL 2870263 (D.D.C. July 13, 2012); *opinion vacated in part*, CRIM. 11-0106, 2012 WL 3024763 (D.D.C. July 25, 2012)

Offenses Against the Law of Nations Clause

The Congress shall have Power ... To define and punish Piracies and Felonies committed on the high Seas, and Offences against the Law of Nations....

(Article I, Section 8, Clause 10)

⁓

*T*he power of Congress to define "offenses against the law of nations" encompasses three subjects: 1) piracies and 2) felonies committed on the high seas, and 3) offenses against the law of nations. At the time of the framing, piracy was the only universal crime contrary to the law of nations, and Congress quickly dealt with it in a

1790 statute. (*See* Piracy and Felonies Clause) But although piracy is defined by the law of nations, "felonies committed on the high seas," such as murder, must be specifically defined by Congress. *United States v. Furlong* (1820). Determining the grounds on which Congress can define offenses against the law of nations, however, has been more difficult.

The inability of the government to conduct foreign affairs effectively under the Articles of Confederation led the Continental Congress to pass a resolution in 1781 asking the states to "provide expeditious, exemplary and adequate punishment…for the infractions of the immunities of ambassadors and other public ministers, authorized and received as such by the United States in Congress assembled." Leaving the issue in the hands of the states, however, impelled Edmund Randolph, in his opening speech to the Constitutional Convention in 1787, to emphasize that this was one of the major defects of the Articles of Confederation.

At the Constitutional Convention, the Article I, Section 8, Clause 10 went through a number of redactions. At one point, Gouverneur Morris thought the term "define" too rigid (as applied to piracy and felonies), because it was "limited to preexisting meaning." He thought "designate" might give Congress more discretion. But other delegates insisted that "define" was broad enough to be "applicable to the creating of offenses also," as the Supreme Court would later affirm in *Furlong*.

Gouverneur Morris then later argued that Congress should also have the power to "define" offenses against the law of nations, but James Wilson expressed a concern. "To pretend to define the law of nations which depended on the authority of all the Civilized Nations of the World, would have the look of arrogance, that would make us look ridiculous." But Gouverneur Morris thought that Congress must be given the discretion to make specific what may be ambiguous. He responded: "The word define is proper when applied to offenses in this case; the law of nations being often too vague and deficient to be a rule." This time, Morris's position prevailed and was later supported by Justice Joseph Story in the seminal case of *United States v. Smith* (1820): "Offences, too, against the law of nations, can-

not, with any accuracy, be said to be completely ascertained and defined in any public code recognized by the common consent of nations." Story continued, "[T]here is a peculiar fitness in giving the power to define as well as to punish; and there is not the slightest reason to doubt that this consideration had very great weight in producing the phraseology in question."

The question of the range of discretion possessed by Congress in defining what is an offense against the law of nations has continued to be debated. In the main, the judiciary has regarded Congress's power as limited by what is objectively part of the law of nations, but has accorded discretion to Congress in making such a determination. In *United States v. Arjona* (1887), the Court declared that Congress need not formally define an offense as "against the law of nations" in a statute that criminalized counterfeiting foreign securities, so long as it was punishing an action that was in fact contrary to customary international law. The Court stated, "[I]f the thing made punishable is one which the United States are required by their international obligations to use due diligence to prevent, it is an offense against the law of nations." However, the Court insisted, "Whether the offense as defined is an offense against the law of nations depends on the thing done, not on any declaration to that effect by congress."

Similarly, in *Ex parte Quirin* (1942), the Court upheld Congress's statutory establishment of military commissions to try enemy aliens when it "incorporated by reference…all offenses which are defined as such by the law of war," itself a part of the law of nations.

In *Sosa v. Alvarez-Machain* (2004), the Court was forced to confront its own power in defining offenses against the law of nations. The case dealt with the meaning of the Alien Tort Statute, which Congress had enacted as part of the Judiciary Act of 1789. The statute read, "The district courts shall have original jurisdiction of any civil action by an alien for a tort only, committed in violation of the law of nations, or a treaty of the United States." The Court concluded that the Alien Tort Statute did not grant the courts any new causes of action, but only allowed for jurisdiction to hear individual suits based on common law violations of the law of nations that existed at the time of the founding, such as infringement of safe conducts, diplomatic immunity, or piracy. Because the Supreme Court later rejected the idea of a "federal common law" (*Erie v. Tompkins* (1938)), the Alien Tort Statute has only limited scope: there remains but a "narrow class of international norms" that the Court could recognize and enforce. In concurrence in *Sosa*, Justice Antonin Scalia insisted that the courts could enforce such rules, but not on its own cognizance of them. Rather, the courts have jurisdiction over such offenses only because Congress has authorized them to do so.

In recent years, the courts have begun a more detailed examination of the meaning and the limits of the clause. The Offenses against the Law of Nations provision made a brief, but consequential, appearance in the Supreme Court's decision of *Hamdan v. Rumsfeld* (2006). Hamdan had been charged with conspiracy to commit acts of terrorism. The Court noted that Congress had not specifically defined "conspiracy" as an offense against the law of nations. Rather, through Article 21 of the Uniform Code of Military Justice, Congress has "'incorporated by reference' the common law of war, which may render triable by military commission certain offenses not defined by statute." But the Court indicated that, if Congress wishes to incorporate a rule from the law of nations, that precedent must be "plain and unambiguous" in international law. Conspiracy was not. The opinion left open the question of Congress's power to define expressly on its own an offense like conspiracy as an offense against the law of nations.

A number of federal circuit courts have been drawn into discussion of the allowable breadth of the Offenses Against the Law of Nations Clause, with differing conclusions. In 1980, Congress passed the Maritime Drug Law Enforcement Act (MDLEA). The law proscribes various drug-related offenses on board any vessel within the jurisdiction of the United States or any vessel if the individual is a citizen or resident alien of the United States. In *United States v. Davis* (9th Cir. 1990), the Ninth Circuit Court of Appeals found that Congress intended to give extraterritorial effect to the act under its power to define "piracies and felonies on the high seas."

In *United States v. Martinez-Hidalgo* (3d Cir. 1993), the Third Circuit determined that, under Article I, Section 8, Clause 10, Congress could constitutionally criminalize drug trafficking on the high seas even when the offense had no nexus with the United States, because "the trafficking of narcotics is condemned universally by law-abiding nations," which would only be relevant if the court was invoking the law of nations provision of the clause. Congress would not have such power, the court suggested, if the prohibited conduct "were generally lawful throughout the world."

In *United States v. Bellaizac-Hurtado* (11th Cir. 2012), however, the Eleventh Circuit went further. Differing from other circuits, it found that drug trafficking was not an offense against the law of nations either at the founding or at the present time. The clause limits Congress to defining only established offenses under the law of nations, which the court defined as "customary international law." The court declared, "The power to 'define' offenses against the law of nations does not grant Congress the authority to punish conduct that is not a violation of the law of nations."

Hamdan and *Bellaizac-Hurtado* represent the first times that acts of Congress were struck down as exceeding the law of nations provision. And with *Sosa* opening the door, albeit narrowly, to federal common law based on the customary international law, it is reasonable to expect more challenges to Congress's ability to define the law of nations based on the court's interpretation of customary international law.

The clause permits Congress not only to establish criminal sanctions but civil legislation as well. In any event, like the other delegated grants of power to Congress, the clause defining Offenses Against the Law of Nations is limited by other "constitutional limitations," *ex parte Quirin*, such as the First Amendment's free speech guarantees. *Boos v. Barry* (1988).

Lastly, an additional question raised by scholars is whether the clause grants Congress power to define offenses and prescribe remedies for violation of the rights of individuals, or whether it also allows Congress to "punish" foreign states for their transgressions of international law. The latter interpretation bears upon the relative war and foreign affairs powers of Congress and the President.

David F. Forte

See Also

Article I, Section 8, Clause 10 (Piracy and Felonies)

Suggestions for Further Research

1 Records of the Federal Convention of 1787, at 19, 25 (Max Farrand ed., 1911)

2 Records of the Federal Convention of 1787, at 614–615 (Max Farrand ed., 1911)

21 JOURNALS OF THE CONTINENTAL CONGRESS 1136 (1781)

29 JOURNALS OF THE CONTINENTAL CONGRESS 654–666 (1785)

Anthony J. Bellia, Jr., & Bradford R. Clark, *The Federal Common Law of Nations*, 109 COLUM. L. REV. 1 (2009)

J. Andrew Kent, *Congress's Under-Appreciated Power to Define and Punish Offenses Against the Law of Nations*, 85 TEX. L. REV. 843 (2007)

Eugene Kontorovich, *The "Define and Punish Clause" and the Limits of Universal Jurisdiction*, 103 Nw. U. L. REV. 1 (2008)

Eugene Kontorovich, *Beyond the Article I Horizon: Congress's Enumerated Powers and Universal Jurisdiction Over Drug Crimes*, 93 MINN. L. REV. 1191 (2009)

Eugene Kontorovich, *Discretion, Delegation, and Defining in the Constitution's Law of Nations Clause*, 106 Nw. U. L. REV. 1675 (2012)

Mark K. Moller, *Old Puzzles, Puzzling Answers: The Alien Tort Statute and Federal Common Law in* Sosa v. Alvarez-Machain, 2004 CATO SUP. CT. REV. 209 (2004)

Charles D. Siegal, *Deference and Its Dangers: Congress' Power to "Define... Offenses Against the Law of Nations*, 21 VAND. J. TRANSNAT'L L. 865, 874–879 (1988)

Beth Stephens, *Federalism and Foreign Affairs: Congress's Power to "Define and Punish... Offenses Against the Law of Nations,"* 42 WM. & MARY L. REV. 447 (2000)

Ernest A. Young, *Historical Practice and the Contemporary Debate Over Customary International Law*, 109 COLUM. L. REV. SIDEBAR 31 (2009)

Significant Cases

United States v. Palmer, 16 U.S. (3 Wheat.) 610 (1818)

United States v. Smith, 18 U.S. (5 Wheat.) 153 (1820)

United States v. Furlong, 18 U.S. (5 Wheat.) 184 (1820)

United States v. Arjona, 120 U.S. 479 (1887)

Erie R.R. Co. v. Tompkins, 304 U.S. 64 (1938)

Ex parte Quirin, 317 U.S. 1 (1942)

Reid v. Covert, 354 U.S. 1 (1957)

Boos v. Barry, 485 U.S. 312 (1988)

United States v. Davis, 905 F.2d 245 (9th Cir. 1990)

United States v. Martinez-Hidalgo, 993 F.2d 1052 (3d Cir. 1993)

Sosa v. Alvarez-Machain, 542 U.S. 692 (2004)

Hamdan v. Rumsfeld, 548 U.S. 557 (2006)

U.S. v. Bellaizac-Hurtado, 700 F.3d 1245 (11th Cir. 2012)

Declare War

The Congress shall have Power... To declare War....
(**ARTICLE I, SECTION 8, CLAUSE 11**)

~

*F*ew constitutional issues have been so consistently and heatedly debated by legal scholars and politicians in recent years as the distribution of war powers between Congress and the President. As a matter of history and policy, it is generally accepted that the executive takes the lead in the actual conduct of war. A single, energetic actor is better able to prosecute war successfully than a committee; the enemy will not wait for deliberation and consensus. At the same time, the Founders plainly intended to establish congressional checks on the executive's war power. Between these guideposts is a question of considerable importance: Does the Constitution require the President to obtain specific authorization from Congress before initiating hostilities?

Presidential power advocates argue that Article II, Section 1 (which vests the "executive Power" in the President of the United States) and Article II, Section 2 (which designates the President as "Commander in Chief of the Army and Navy of the United States...") confer substantive constitutional power upon the President to initiate military hostilities with foreign nations. The leading political thinkers to influence the Framers, such as Machiavelli, Thomas Hobbes, John Locke, William Blackstone, and Montesquieu, understood the executive power to arise from the need for a part of government to act quickly, vigorously, and decisively in response to unforeseen dangers and events—the most serious of which was war. Executives throughout British history as well as in the colonial governments and several of the states prior to the Constitution generally enjoyed such power.

The Declare War Clause, in this view, was not addressed to the power to begin actual hostilities. Instead, declarations of war altered legal relationships between subjects of warring nations and triggered certain rights, privileges, and protections under the laws of war. According to Hugo Grotius, declarations gave notice of the legal grounds for the war and the opportunity for enemy nations to make amends. They served notice on the enemy's allies that they would be regarded as cobelligerents and their shipping would be subject to capture. Under a declaration of war, one's own navy and privateers could not be treated as pirates by the enemy, but on the other hand one's own citizens were subject to prosecution if they dealt with the enemy. Additionally, declarations of war triggered legal actions, such as the internment or expulsion of enemy aliens, the breaking of diplomatic relations, and the confiscation of the enemy's property. In short, in this view, the power to declare war was understood as a power to affect legal rights and duties in times of hostilities. It was not a check on executive power to engage in hostilities in the first place.

The check on executive war power, it is argued, instead comes from Congress's power over appropriations. Any power to initiate hostilities would be useless, of course, without the resources necessary to engage in hostilities. Under our Constitution, the power to provide those resources is unequivocally vested with Congress. Under Article I, it is Congress, not the President, that has the power to "lay and collect Taxes" and to "borrow Money," to make "Appropriations" and "provide for the common Defence," to "raise and support Armies" and "provide and maintain a Navy," and

to "provide for calling forth the Militia." The President is Commander in Chief, but he has nothing to command except what Congress provides. As a result of Congress's authority over the purse, the President is unable as a practical (if not constitutional) matter to engage in hostilities alone. Based on these provisions of the Constitution, some scholars have concluded that Congress's war power is limited to its control over funding and its power to impeach executive officers. They contend that the President is constitutionally empowered to engage in hostilities with whatever resources Congress has made available to the executive.

In contrast, many scholars contend that the Declare War Clause limits presidential war power by giving the legislature the sole authority to begin an offensive war. In one reading, the clause requires Congress to issue a formal declaration of war before the United States may begin hostilities. The more common view among these scholars, however, is that the clause requires congressional authorization of hostilities, which may be done by formal declaration or otherwise. The latter interpretation is often textually grounded in the observation that in eighteenth-century terminology "declaring" could be done by a formal proclamation or simply by initiating hostilities. As Emmerich de Vattel wrote in 1758, "when one nation takes up arms against another, she from that moment declares herself an enemy to all the individuals of the latter." Thus the Declare War Clause is read to give Congress power to initiate war either by issuing a formal declaration or by directing actions (such as hostile attacks) that have the effect of signaling—declaring informally—the start of a war.

Advocates of congressional power also point to numerous statements during and after the drafting process saying or heavily implying that the President alone cannot initiate war. For example, James Madison wrote to Thomas Jefferson in 1798, "The constitution supposes, what the History of all Governments demonstrates, that the Executive is the branch of power most interested in war, and most prone to it. It has accordingly with studied care, vested the question of war in the Legislature." Alexander Hamilton, though generally a strong proponent of presidential power, wrote in his 1793 *Pacificus* essay: "It is the province and duty of the executive to preserve to the nation the blessings of peace. The Legislature alone can interrupt those blessings by placing the nation in a state of war." Defenders of presidential power discount these post-ratification statements and respond that the records of the ratification debates show no Federalists or Anti-Federalists identifying the clause as a significant check on executive activity. If anything, they say, the debates looked to Congress's power over the establishment and funding of the military as the critical legislative tool for restraining the executive.

Advocates of presidential power further argue that the text distinguishes between "declaring" and beginning war. Article I, Section 10, Clause 3 forbids states from "engaging in" war without the consent of Congress. Article III, Section 3, Clause 1 defines treason as "levying" war. The Articles of Confederation also suggested that declaring war is but a subset of the broader power over war. Article IX of the Articles gave to Congress "the sole and exclusive right and power of determining on peace and war," and Article VI similarly declared that "no state shall engage in any war" without "the consent of Congress." If "declare" war held the meaning attributed to it by supporters of congressional power, it is argued, the Framers should have used the same phrases in these other constitutional provisions instead of "engage" or "levy."

History casts some doubt on the idea that the Framers would have thought a formal declaration was prerequisite to initiating armed conflict. In the one hundred years preceding the ratification of the Constitution, the British rarely declared war formally before the outbreak of hostilities. The Founders, who drew the language in the Declare War Clause directly from British constitutional practice (as they were British citizens for much of their lives), were well aware of the long practice of undeclared wars, as Hamilton noted in *The Federalist* No. 25: "the ceremony of a formal denunciation of war has of late fallen into disuse." They also would have been well aware of the nation's first declaration of war—the Declaration of Independence—which issued a year *after* hostilities broke out between the colonists and the British at Lexington and Concord. Since the ratification of the Constitution, there have been only five wars formally declared by Congress in the history of

the United States. Of those, only the first, the War of 1812, was formally declared before the start of hostilities. In the remaining four, the Mexican-American War of 1846, the Spanish-American War of 1898, World War I, and World War II, Congress merely declared the prior existence of a state of war. Notably, those declarations were accompanied by express authorizations of the use of force, suggesting a distinction in practice between the two.

Congress has, however, specifically authorized numerous other conflicts using instruments other than formal declarations of war; and particularly in the early post-ratification period there appeared to have been broad consensus that such authorizations were constitutionally required in the case of offensive war. For example, offensive actions taken by the United States during its first real "war"—against Tripoli beginning in 1801—were statutorily authorized but not accompanied by a formal declaration. Although the President arguably directed some offensive action against Tripoli prior to congressional authorization, this was defended (including by Hamilton) only on the ground that Tripoli had itself begun the war. Congress also expressly authorized the use of force in the Quasi-War with France in 1798, and it was assumed at the time that such authorization was needed.

In much of American history, limited budgets and a small peacetime military led Presidents to defer to Congress. If Presidents wanted to wage a war, they had to ask Congress to build them the armed forces with which to fight it. After World War II, however, the creation of a large standing military dramatically altered the balance of war powers between the two branches. Beginning with Franklin D. Roosevelt, modern Presidents have been more aggressive in asserting unilateral authority to use force abroad without a declaration of war or other congressional authorization. The United States intervention in Korea in 1950 received congressional support but no formal approval. When the war stalemated, executive power was challenged. President Harry S. Truman responded by claiming independent constitutional authority to commit troops without congressional authorization. Presidents Lyndon B. Johnson and Richard M. Nixon undertook military operations in Vietnam, armed with only the vaguely worded congressional approval in the Gulf of Tonkin Resolution. Congressional criticism of that protracted campaign led not only to funding restrictions that forced the end of U.S. participation in the war, but also to the 1973 enactment of the War Powers Resolution, over President Nixon's veto. The Resolution claims to limit the President's ability to engage U.S. forces in hostilities for more than sixty days, absent a declaration of war or specific congressional authorization, and requires the President to consult with Congress about military deployments.

The War Powers Resolution has proven impotent. No President has ever conceded its constitutionality, though many have acted "consistent with" its 60-day limit on foreign interventions. President James Earl Carter did not consult with Congress before attempting to rescue Iranian hostages. President Ronald Reagan unilaterally dispatched American military forces to Lebanon, Grenada, Libya, and the Persian Gulf. Before Desert Storm, President George H.W. Bush publicly declared that he had constitutional power to initiate war unilaterally, but sought an authorization from Congress, which he barely received. President William Jefferson Clinton followed these precedents in Somalia, Haiti, Bosnia, the Middle East, and Kosovo. Ironically, given the attacks on his exercise of executive power, President George W. Bush asked for and received congressional approval for wars in Afghanistan and Iraq. But President Barack Obama unilaterally ordered a limited intervention in the Libyan civil war in 2011, on the ground that the intervention did not involve sustained hostilities, did not include ground troops, was part of a multilateral coalition to implement a U.N. Security Council resolution, and the hostilities were too small to constitute a "war" under the Constitution.

Members of Congress have periodically filed suit to enforce the War Powers Resolution and the congressionalist interpretation of the Declare War Clause, but courts have generally avoided ruling on the merits by dismissing such cases on a variety of procedural grounds. In *Campbell v. Clinton* (2000), for example, the D.C. Circuit unanimously dismissed a congressional challenge to President Clinton's airstrikes campaign in the former Yugoslavia,

under a panoply of competing theories arising out of the legislative standing, mootness, and political question doctrines. In *O'Connor v. United States* (2003), the court dismissed a challenge to President George W. Bush's intention behind the war in Iraq because it posed a nonjusticiable political question and "there are no judicially discoverable standards that would permit a court to determine whether the intentions of the President in prosecuting a war are proper."

The Supreme Court has never intervened to stop a war, regardless of whether Congress had authorized it, although it did say (*in dicta*) in *The Prize Cases* (1863) that the President "has no power to initiate or declare a war." Some federal courts of appeals have held or implied that at least some level of congressional authorization is constitutionally required before the President may conduct military hostilities. *See, e.g., Orlando v. Laird* (1971). Other courts have found the issue nonjusticiable. *See, e.g., Mitchell v. Laird* (1973).

Even if the Declare War Clause is thought to limit the President's ability to initiate war, almost all scholars accept that it does not prevent the President from defending against attacks upon the United States. James Madison successfully advocated in the Constitutional Convention that Congress be given the power, not to "make" war but to "declare" war, so as to (as he said) "leav[e] to the Executive the power to repel sudden attacks." In *The Prize Cases*, the Supreme Court upheld President Abraham Lincoln's military actions against the Confederacy, although they occurred prior to congressional authorization, because "the President is not only authorized but bound to resist force by force…without waiting for any special legislative authority."

The scope of the President's defensive power remains debated, however. One key question is whether, once an attack on the United States occurs, the President may authorize counterattacks against the enemy without Congress's approval. Alexander Hamilton, for example, took this view in 1801 in connection with hostilities against Tripoli, and in *The Prize Cases* the Supreme Court approved President Lincoln's unauthorized blockade of the southern states, which was not purely a defensive measure. The opposing view is that the President may only act defensively; any offensive action, even in response to an attack, requires congressional approval under the Declare War Clause. Relatedly, there is debate over whether and to what extent the President may act against an anticipated attack without Congress's approval.

Whatever the domestic constitutional implications for the initiation of hostilities, the Declare War Clause gives Congress certain powers under international and domestic statutory law. Formally declaring war defines the legal relationship between the citizens of the United States and that of the enemy nation. It also expands the powers of the U.S. government vis-à-vis its own citizens at home. A particularly dramatic example is the Alien Enemies Act (1 Stat. 577 (1798), codified in 50 U.S.C. § 21 (2003)), which authorizes the President to detain and deport citizens of enemy nations, but only following either a declaration of war or an attack upon the United States. Nonetheless, the legal significance of formal declarations has declined. For example, the Geneva Conventions of 1949, which guarantee various enumerated rights to lawful combatants, prisoners of war, and civilians, explicitly apply to all armed conflicts between contracting nations and not just to formally declared wars.

John Yoo and Michael Ramsey

See Also

Article I, Section 10, Clause 3 (Compact Clause)
Article II, Section 2, Clause 1 (Commander in Chief)
Article III, Section 3, Clause 1 (Treason)

Suggestions for Further Research

Ellen C. Collier, Congressional Research Service, Instances of Use of United States Forces Abroad, 1798–1993 (1993)

Robert J. Delahunty and John C. Yoo, *Making War*, 93 Cornell L. Rev. 123 (2007)

Louis Fisher, Congressional Abdication on War & Spending (2000)

Louis Fisher, Presidential War Power (2d ed. 2004)

Louis Fisher, *Lost Constitutional Moorings: Recovering the War Power*, 81 Ind. L.J. 1199 (2006)

Louis Henkin, Foreign Affairs and the United States Constitution (2d ed. 1996)

Harold Hongju Koh, The National Security Constitution: Sharing Power After the Iran-Contra Affair (1990)

Michael Stokes Paulsen, *The War Power*, 33 Harv. J.L. & Pub. Pol'y 113 (2010)

Saikrishna Prakash, *Unleashing the Dogs of War: What the Constitution Means by "Declare War,"* 93 Cornell L. Rev. 45 (2007)

Saikrishna Prakash, *The Separation and Overlap of War and Military Powers*, 87 Tex. L. Rev. 299 (2008)

Michael D. Ramsey, The Constitution's Text in Foreign Affairs, Chs. 11-12 (2007)

Michael D. Ramsey, *The President's Power to Respond to Attacks*, 93 Cornell L. Rev. 169 (2007)

Michael D. Ramsey, *Textualism and War Powers*, 69 U. Chi. L. Rev. 1543 (2002)

Michael D. Ramsey, *Text and History in the War Powers Debate: A Reply to Professor Yoo*, 69 U. Chi. L. Rev. 1685 (2002)

Robert Turner, Repealing the War Powers Resolution: Restoring the Rule of Law in U.S. Foreign Policy (1991)

John C. Yoo, *The Continuation of Politics by Other Means: The Original Understanding of War Powers*, 84 Cal. L. Rev. 167 (1996)

John C. Yoo, *War and Constitutional Texts*, 69 U. Chi. L. Rev. 1639 (2002)

Significant Cases

Bas v. Tingy, 4 U.S. (4 Dall.) 37 (1800)
Brown v. United States, 12 U.S. (8 Cranch) 110 (1814)
The Prize Cases, 67 U.S. (2 Black) 635 (1863)
Orlando v. Laird, 443 F.2d 1039 (2d Cir. 1971)
Mitchell v. Laird, 488 F.2d 611 (D.C. Cir. 1973)
Campbell v. Clinton, 203 F.3d 19 (D.C. Cir. 2000)
Doe v. Bush, 322 F.3d 109 (1st Cir. 2003)
O'Connor v. United States, 72 Fed. Appx. 768 (2003)

Marque and Reprisal

The Congress shall have Power To . . . grant Letters of Marque and Reprisal. . . .

(Article I, Section 8, Clause 11)

~

$\mathcal{A}$t the time of the Founding, the sovereign of any nation could authorize holders of "letters of marque and reprisal" to engage in hostile actions against enemies of the state. The common understanding of "Reprisal" is a seizure of property (or sometimes persons) of a foreign state as redress for an injury committed by that state. Because the word "Marque" is the French equivalent of "Reprisal," the constitutional term "Marque and Reprisal" is best understood as a single phrase.

The only serious debate over the meaning of the Marque and Reprisal Clause is not whether it extends to authorizing private parties (known as "privateers") to engage in reprisals for private, commercial gain. Rather, it centers on whether the clause gives Congress authority over all forms of hostilities short of declared wars.

That debate mirrors the larger war powers debate over the Declare War Clause. Supporters of congressional power construe the Declare War Clause and the Marque and Reprisal Clause jointly to cover all forms of armed conflict, from covert action to a full and open armed conflict. Under this reading, the President lacks any power whatsoever to initiate hostilities (except perhaps defensively to repel invasions), no matter their scope. They contend that the Declare War Clause requires Congress to authorize wars, whereas the Marque and Reprisal Clause requires Congress to authorize lower level hostilities, whether by public forces or by privateers.

Supporters of presidential war powers on the other hand, maintain that the Marque and Reprisal Clause was originally understood as a narrower power to vest sovereign authority to use force against enemy nations with private parties. The argument is that Congress could authorize privateers to engage in military hostilities, with neither government funding nor oversight (other than after-the-fact judicial determinations of prizes by the prize courts). The Marque and Reprisal power allows Congress to "outsource" American warfighting capabilities to private parties, which would have held out great attraction to some revolutionary Americans who feared standing armies and navies.

Thus, the supporters of presidential war powers contend, the Marque and Reprisal Clause is best read in conjunction with Congress's power over the purse. Congress has exclusive authority over all funding of military hostilities, whether through public appropriations for a national military or letters of marque and reprisal for private actors. But Congress has no power to control directly the President's ability to initiate hostilities with whatever resources Congress has previously made available to him. Under this framework, locating the Marque and Reprisal Clause in Article I prevents the President from engaging in hostilities free from congressional control over resources, whether in the form of public appropriations or the issuance of letters of marque and reprisal to private actors. The clause thus helps fill a hole that would otherwise exist in Congress's control over the "sinews of war."

Outside of the law reviews and scholarly debates over the allocation of war powers, the Marque and Reprisal Clause has played little if any role in modern times. The United States has not issued letters of marque and reprisal since the War of 1812, and has not seriously considered doing so since Andrew Jackson's presidency. In addition, the 1856 Declaration of Paris prohibits privateering as a matter of international law. Although the United States has not ratified the Declaration, it has upheld the ban in practice.

During the Iran-Contra controversy of Ronald Reagan's administration, Members of Congress objected to the President's private financing of hostilities, absent prior congressional consent. Congress did not expressly invoke the Marque and Reprisal Clause, however, in objecting to executive branch action. The recent emergence of piracy has led some to propose a resurrection of letters of marque and reprisals, which would give private actors an incentive to protect commercial shipping while allowing the U.S. Navy to focus on more important missions.

John Yoo

See Also

Article III, Section 3, Clause 2 (Punishment of Treason)

Suggestions for Further Research

Ellen C. Collier, Congressional Research Service, Instances of Use of United States Forces Abroad, 1798–1993 (1993)

Robert J. Delahunty and John C. Yoo, *Making War*, 93 Cornell L. Rev. 123 (2007)

Louis Fisher, Congressional Abdication on War & Spending (2000)

Louis Henkin, Foreign Affairs and the United States Constitution (2d ed. 1996)

Harold Hongju Koh, The National Security Constitution: Sharing Power After the Iran-Contra Affair (1990)

C. Kevin Marshall, *Putting Privateers in Their Place: The Applicability of the Marque and Reprisal Clause to Undeclared Wars*, 64 U. Chi. L. Rev. 953 (1997)

Michael Stokes Paulsen, *The War Power*, 33 Harv. J.L. & Pub. Pol'y 113 (2010)

Saikrishna Prakash, *Unleashing the Dogs of War: What the Constitution Means by "Declare War,"* 93 Cornell L. Rev. 45 (2007)

Saikrishna Prakash, *The Separation and Overlap of War and Military Powers*, 87 Tex. L. Rev. 299 (2008)

Michael D. Ramsey, *Textualism and War Powers*, 69 U. Chi. L. Rev. 1543 (2002)

J. Gregory Sidak, *The Quasi War Cases—And Their Relevance to Whether "Letters of Marque and Reprisal" Constrain Presidential War Powers*, 28 Harv. J.L. & Pub. Pol'y 465 (2005)

John C. Yoo, *The Continuation of Politics by Other Means: The Original Understanding of War Powers*, 84 Cal. L. Rev. 167 (1996)

John C. Yoo, *War and Constitutional Texts*, 69 U. Chi. L. Rev. 1639 (2002)

Significant Case

Bas v. Tingy, 4 U.S. (4 Dall.) 37 (1800)

Captures Clause

The Congress shall have Power To…make Rules concerning Captures on Land and Water….

(Article I, Section 8, Clause 11)

~

*U*nder the Captures Clause, Congress has the power to make rules for the confiscation, disposition, and distribution of captured enemy property. Although the original understanding suggests that the clause covers the seizure of enemy shipping as prizes, the war against terrorism has spurred debate over whether it also includes enemy prisoners. Three main arguments have developed over the reach of the Captures Clause: (1) The clause does not apply to prisoners, and therefore the power over enemy prisoners rests with the President; (2) the clause applies only to property, not persons, but Congress can regulate the treatment of prisoners via its authority to regulate and govern the armed forces; and (3) the clause applies to prisoners, and moreover Congress has additional authority through the Offenses Against the Law of Nations and Declare War Clauses.

The roots of the Captures Clause can be traced to Article IX of the Articles of Confederation, which vested in Congress the power "of establishing rules for deciding in all cases, what captures on land or water shall be legal, and in what manner prizes taken by land or naval forces in the service of the united states shall be divided or appropriated." The original understanding of the clause appears to be that Congress alone has the power to establish rules governing the circumstances under which wartime "captures"—generally enemy ships or vessels aiding the enemy and their valuable goods—will be adjudged lawful "prizes," to which the captors are entitled at least partial title. This construction is supported by the practice that, during the Revolutionary War, captors could not claim lawful title to captured property until after a prize court had granted it.

Under this interpretation, the term "captures," as understood by the Framers of the Constitution, includes only enemy property. The term could not include captured enemy soldiers, as persons can neither be "divided" nor "appropriated," nor can they be treated as legally awarded prizes. This approach is bolstered by the fact that the term capture was understood under international law, as listed in *Bouvier's Law Dictionary* (1914), as "the taking of property by one belligerent from another or from an offending neutral."

There was little commentary among the Framers regarding the breadth of the notion of wartime captures, so scholars have resorted to discerning contemporaneous historical practice. Presidentialists argue that during the war for independence, the Continental Congress frequently issued letters of marque and reprisal exclusively to privateers "to make Captures of British Vessels and Cargoes," pursuant to rules established by Congress. Presidentialists conclude that the Captures Clause authorizes Congress to regulate captures by private parties only and not by the armed forces of the United States. But congressionalists note that although the bulk of congressional authorizations and concern related to the actions of private vessels outfitted against the British, early Continental Congress resolutions asserted the power to control captures by both private and public vessels. Thus Congress has some constitutional authority to prescribe rules for at least some elements of military conflict.

Although the executive's power to conduct war necessarily includes the power to seize persons and property on the battlefield, the Supreme Court has construed the Captures Clause to deny the executive constitutional power to seize enemy property off the battlefield. In *Brown v. United States* (1814), the Court concluded that, by virtue of the Captures Clause, the executive lacks inherent constitutional authority to confiscate property owned by subjects of enemy nations, and must seek congressional authorization in order to do so. Congress has long conferred such power upon the executive by enacting laws such as the Trading with the Enemy Act.

In recent cases arising from the War on Terror, the Court has generally avoided a discussion of the Captures Clause. Its only reference comes in *Hamdan v. Rumsfeld* (2006), where the Court referred to the Captures Clause as an example of congressional powers distinct from the President's powers in executing war, but did not clarify the powers included in the Captures Clause. Furthermore, five members of the Court found the detention of enemy combatants for the duration of the conflict to be "so fundamental and accepted an incident to war as to be an

exercise of the 'necessary and appropriate force' Congress has authorized the President to use," without clarifying whether Congress even needed to authorize the President to execute his war powers in areas "so fundamental and accepted."

John Yoo

See Also

Suggestions for Further Research

David J. Barron & Martin S. Lederman, *The Commander in Chief at the Lowest Ebb—Framing the Problem, Doctrine, and Original Understanding*, 121 Harv. L. Rev 689 (2008)

Ellen C. Collier, Congressional Research Service, Instances of Use of United States Forces Abroad, 1798–1993 (1993)

Robert J. Delahunty and John C. Yoo, *Making War*, 93 Cornell L. Rev. 123 (2007)

Louis Fisher, Congressional Abdication on War & Spending (2000)

Louis Henkin, Foreign Affairs and the United States Constitution (2d ed. 1996)

Harold Hongju Koh, The National Security Constitution: Sharing Power After the Iran-Contra Affair (1990)

C. Kevin Marshall, *Putting Privateers in Their Place: The Applicability of the Marque and Reprisal Clause to Undeclared Wars*, 64 U. Chi. L. Rev. 953 (1997)

Michael Stokes Paulsen, *The War Power*, 33 Harv. J.L. & Pub. Pol'y 113 (2010)

Saikrishna Prakash, *Unleashing the Dogs of War: What the Constitution Means by "Declare War,"* 93 Cornell L. Rev. 45 (2007)

Saikrishna Prakash, *The Separation and Overlap of War and Military Powers*, 87 Tex. L. Rev. 299 (2008)

Michael D. Ramsey, *Textualism and War Powers*, 69 U. Chi. L. Rev. 1543 (2002)

Ingrid Wuerth, *The Captures Clause*, 76 U. Chi. L.
   Rev. 1683 (2009)
John C. Yoo, *The Continuation of Politics by Other
   Means: The Original Understanding of War Powers*,
   84 Cal. L. Rev. 167 (1996)
John C. Yoo, *War and Constitutional Texts*, 69 U. Chi.
   L. Rev. 1639 (2002)

Significant Cases

Brown v. United States, 12 U.S. (8 Cranch) 110 (1814)
The Prize Cases, 67 U.S. (2 Black) 635 (1863)
Hamdan v. Rumsfeld, 548 U.S. 557 (2006)

Army Clause

The Congress shall have
Power...To raise and support
Armies, but no Appropriation of
Money to that Use shall be for a
longer Term than two Years....
(ARTICLE I, SECTION 8, CLAUSE 12)

*F*or most Americans after the Revolution, a
standing army was one of the most dangerous
threats to liberty. In thinking about the potential
dangers of a standing army, the Founding generation had before them the precedents of Rome and
England. In the first case, Julius Caesar marched
his provincial army into Rome, overthrowing the
power of the Senate, destroying the republic, and
laying the foundation of empire. In the second,
Oliver Cromwell used the army to abolish Parliament and to rule as dictator.

Under British practice, the King was not only
the commander in chief; he also asserted the right
to raise forces on his own. King James II, a Roman
Catholic, raised a peacetime standing army
and stationed it in small garrisons and camps
throughout England, including one alarmingly
near London. James was also suspected of building a "Catholic" army in Ireland. The threats that
James's standing armies were perceived to pose to
English and Protestant institutions was a prominent cause of the dissatisfaction with James that
led to the Glorious Revolution of 1688. The ensu-

ing Bill of Rights of 1689 accordingly declared
that "the raising or keeping a standing army
within the kingdom in time of peace, unless it be
with consent of Parliament, is against law."

In addition, in the period leading up to the
Revolution, the British Crown had forced the
American colonists to quarter and otherwise support its troops. The colonists regarded the British
action as being nothing other than imposing an
army of occupation. The Framers were determined not to lodge the power of raising an army
with the executive.

Many of the men who met in Philadelphia
to draft the Constitution, however, had the
experience of serving with the Continental Line,
the army that ultimately bested the British for
independence. Founders like George Washington, James Madison, and Alexander Hamilton
were also acutely aware of the dangers external
enemies posed to the new republic. The British
and Spanish were not only on the frontiers of the
new nation. In many cases they were within the
frontiers, allying with the Indians and attempting
to induce frontier settlements to split off from
the country. The recent Shays' Rebellion in Massachusetts had also impelled the Framers to consider the possibility of local rebellion.

The "raise and support Armies" clause was
the Framers' solution to the dilemma. The Constitutional Convention accepted the need for a
standing army but sought to maintain control
by the appropriations power of Congress, which
the Founders viewed as the branch of government
closest to the people.

The compromise, however, did not satisfy
the Anti-Federalists. They largely shared the
perspective of James Burgh, who, in his *Political
Disquisitions* (1774), called a "standing army in
times of peace, one of the most hurtful, and most
dangerous of abuses." The Anti-Federalist article
"A Democratic Federalist" called a standing army
"that great support of tyrants." And Brutus, the
most influential series of essays opposing ratification, argued that standing armies "are dangerous to the liberties of a people...not only because
the rulers may employ them for the purposes
of supporting themselves in any usurpation of
powers, which they may see proper to exercise,
but there is a great hazard, that any army will

subvert the forms of government, under whose authority, they are raised, and establish one, according to the pleasure of their leader." During the Virginia ratifying convention, George Mason exclaimed, "What havoc, desolation, and destruction, have been perpetrated by standing armies!" The Anti-Federalists would have preferred that the defense of the nation remain entirely with the state militias.

The Federalists disagreed. For them, the power of a government to raise an army was a dictate of prudence. Thus, during the Pennsylvania ratifying convention, James Wilson argued that "the power of raising and keeping up an army, in time of peace, is essential to every government. No government can secure its citizens against dangers, internal and external, without possessing it, and sometimes carrying it into execution." In *The Federalist* No. 23, Hamilton argued, "These powers [of the federal government to provide for the common defense] ought to exist without limitation, *because it is impossible to foresee or to define the extent and variety of national exigencies, and the correspondent extent and variety of the means which may be necessary to satisfy them.*"

Nonetheless, both Federalists and Anti-Federalists alike expressed concerns about a standing army, as opposed to a navy or the militia. Accordingly, this is the only clause related to military affairs that includes a time limit on appropriations. The appropriations power of Congress is a very powerful tool, and one that the Framers saw as particularly necessary in the case of a standing army. Indeed, some individuals argued that army appropriations should be made on a yearly basis. During the Constitutional Convention, Elbridge Gerry raised precisely this point. Roger Sherman replied that the appropriations were permitted, not required, for two years. The problem, he said, was that in a time of emergency, Congress might not be in session when an annual army appropriation was needed.

The Army Clause has subtle but significant connections with other clauses of the Constitution. The Framers did not envisage that Congress would authorize a large, permanent federal land force; they believed that for most defensive purposes, the federal navy and a federalized militia

would suffice. But without the availability of a standing army, presidential ambitions to win fame through military conquests in offensive wars would be checked. The Army Clause thus reinforces Congress's authority to declare war, magnifies its power over the purse, and tends to inhibit presidential war-making. Further, the expected absence of a caste of permanent military officers stationed inside the country and comparable to Europe's aristocracies helps sustain the "republican" nature of the American system. Finally, the Third Amendment, which requires an act of legislation before military personnel can be housed in private dwellings in wartime, raises additional hurdles for maintaining an army.

Since the time of the Constitution, legal developments based on the clause have been legislatively driven, and barely the subject of judicial interpretation. With the establishment of a federal department of defense in 1947, Army appropriations have been subsumed by a single department-wide appropriation that includes the Army, the Navy, and the Air Force (established in 1947 as part of the Army), as well as other agencies of the department. Despite periodic congressional efforts to move to a two-year appropriations cycle, the annual appropriations for the military are the rule, although not for the reasons that animated Elbridge Gerry during the Constitutional Convention. In addition, the Armed Services Committees of Congress have taken on the responsibility of authorizing almost all aspects of the defense budget as well as appropriating the funds for the services.

The character of the United States Army has changed significantly since the constitutional period in two fundamental ways. The first is its way of mobilizing. The second is its orientation and purpose.

With respect to wartime mobilization, Hamilton and later John C. Calhoun envisioned the United States Army as an "expansible" force. A small peacetime establishment would serve as the foundation for a greatly expanded force in times of emergency. The emergency ended, the citizen-soldiers would demobilize and return to their civilian occupations. With modifications, this was essentially the model for mobilization from the Mexican War through World War II.

During the Cold War, the United States for the first time in its history maintained a large military establishment during peacetime. Even so, the fact that soldiers were drafted meant that citizen-soldiers continued to be the foundation of the Army. But with the end of the draft in 1973, the citizen-soldier was superseded by the long-term professional.

The draft, of course, has been a controversial issue. Although compulsory military service can be traced to the colonial and revolutionary period in America, it usually involved the states obligating service in the militia. The United States did not have a national draft until the Civil War and did not resort to a peacetime draft until 1940. Opponents of a draft have used a number of constitutional arguments in support of their position. The Supreme Court has ruled, however, that a draft is constitutional. As Chief Justice Edward White declared in *The Selective Draft Law Cases* (1918), "It may not be doubted that the very conception of a just government and its duty to the citizen includes the reciprocal obligation of the citizen to render military service in case of need and the right to compel it."

The power to compel service includes a draft during peacetime, and the power to dispatch draftees overseas remains unsettled. The Seventh Circuit declared in *United States v. Holmes* (1967): "the power of Congress to raise armies and to take effective measures to preserve their efficiency, is not limited by the Thirteenth Amendment or the absence of a military emergency." But according to Justice William O. Douglas dissenting from denial of certiorari in *Holmes v. United States* (1968), "It is clear from our decisions that conscription is constitutionally permissible when there has been a declaration of war. But we have never decided whether there may be conscription in absence of a declaration of war. Our cases suggest (but do not decide) that there may not be."

Throughout the history of the draft, the Supreme Court has seconded Congress's broad power to protect the selective service system, even in the face of First Amendment objections. *Schenck v. United States* (1919), *United States v. O'Brien* (1968). The draft does not intrude on

the state's right to maintain a militia, but, as the Court pointed out in *The Selective Draft Law Cases*, the states' militia power can be restricted at any time by the constitutional grants of power to Congress.

Despite the Court's affirmation of Congress's power to institute a draft, the Court has, for some time now, been broadening exemptions to the draft, such as those with conscientious objections to war. One's beliefs must be "sincere and meaningful," but they do not have to be religiously based to qualify for conscientious objector status. *United States v. Seeger* (1965). *Welsh v. United States* (1970). In *Gillette v. United States* (1971), the Court allowed conscientious objector status to persons who had beliefs opposed to participating in armed conflict in general, but not to persons who objected only to a specific war.

In modern times, the questions of who can be a soldier and who can engage in combat have been controversial. In 1993, a Democrat-controlled Congress passed a law that codified regulations prohibiting military service for homosexuals that had been in effect before President Clinton's inauguration. This law (10 U.S.C. § 654, included in the *National Defense Authorization Act for Fiscal Year 1994, Public Law 103-160*, November 30, 1993, and accompanying Senate and House report language) made the historical ban a matter of statute law. The only modification of previous regulations codified in the 1993 law was suspension of the longstanding policy of asking recruit candidates if they were homosexuals before entering service, a policy that came to be called the "don't ask, don't tell" compromise. In fact, the law continued to require that homosexuals, identified on the basis of acts or self-admission, must be separated from the service.

In 2010, however, Congress repealed the 1993 law, pending certification by the President, the Secretary of Defense, and the Chairman of the Joint Chiefs of Staff that military readiness would not be compromised. The certification was issued in 2011, and the ban on service by homosexuals in the military was lifted.

The congressional policy of restricting women from performing combat-related functions, though upheld as constitutional, *see Rostker v. Goldberg* (1981), *Schlesinger v. Ballard* (1975), has been gradually done away with since 1990. In 2013, Secretary of Defense Leon Panetta and the Chairman of the Joint Chiefs of Staff issued a directive permitting women to serve in front-line combat positions.

The Supreme Court has recognized that Congress's powers to raise an army and maintain a navy extend to the military's recruiting efforts. In opposition to the military draft of the Vietnam War, many universities prohibited the presence of military recruiters. In addition, law schools "began restricting the access of military recruiters to their students" in opposition to the military's "don't ask, don't tell" policy. *Rumsfeld v. Forum for Academic and Institutional Rights, Inc.* (2006). In response, Congress passed and the Supreme Court upheld the Solomon Amendment, which denied federal funds to any school that refused military recruiters access.

In dicta in *Rumsfeld*, the Supreme Court affirmed that Congress has broad and sweeping power to raise armies and that "there is no dispute in this case that it includes the authority to require campus access for military recruiters." The Court ultimately held that the Solomon Amendment was not an impermissible restriction because it merely requires military recruiters to be "given access to students at least equal to that '*provided* to any other employer.'" Since the repeal of "don't ask, don't tell," military recruiters have largely returned to the campuses.

The purpose of the United States Army has not always been primarily to win the nation's wars, but also to act as a constabulary. Soldiers were often used during the antebellum period to enforce the fugitive slave laws and suppress domestic violence. The Fugitive Slave Act of 1850 permitted federal marshals to call on the posse comitatus to aid in returning a slave to his owner, and Attorney General Caleb Cushing issued an opinion that included the Army in the posse comitatus.

In response, Congress enacted the Posse Comitatus Act (1878), which prohibited the use of the military to aid civil authorities in enforcing the law or suppressing civil disturbances unless expressly ordered to do so by the Presi-

dent. The Army welcomed the legislation. The use of soldiers as a posse removed them from their own chain of command and placed them in the uncomfortable position of taking orders from local authorities who had an interest in the disputes that provoked the unrest in the first place. As a result, many officers came to believe that the involvement of the Army in domestic policing was corrupting the institution.

In 1904, Secretary of War Elihu Root reoriented the Army away from constabulary duties to a mission focused on defeating the conventional forces of other states. This view has shaped U.S. military culture since at least World War II and continues to this day. Whether the exigencies of a modern war against terrorism once again changes the military's mission towards domestic order is yet to be seen.

Mackubin Owens, David F. Forte, and
Robert Delahunty

See Also

Article I, Section 8, Clause 11 (Declare War)
Article I, Section 8, Clause 13 (Navy Clause)
Article I, Section 8, Clause 14 (Military Regulations)
Article I, Section 8, Clause 16 (Organizing the Militia)
Article II, Section 2, Clause 1 (Commander in Chief)
Amendment III (Quartering of Troops)

Suggestions for Further Research

Robert J. Delahunty, *Structuralism and the War Powers: The Army, Navy, and Militia Clauses*, 19 Ga. St. U. L. Rev. 1021 (2003)

Kenneth J. Hagan & William J. Roberts, eds., Against All Enemies: Interpretations of American Military History from Colonial Times to the Present (1986)

Richard H. Kohn, Eagle and Sword: The Federalists and the Creation of the Military Establishment in America, 1783–1802 (1975)

Allan R. Millett & Peter Maslowski, For the Common Defense: A Military History of the United States of America from 1607–2012 (2012)

Mackubin Thomas Owens, US Civil-Military Relations After 9/11: Renegotiating the Civil-Military Bargain, Ch. 4 (2011)

John Philip Reid, In Defiance of the Law: The Standing-Army Controversy, the Two Constitutions, and the Coming of the American Revolution (1981)

Lois G. Schwoerer, "No Standing Armies!": The Antiarmy Ideology in Seventeenth-Century England (1974)

The United States Military Under the Constitution of the United States, 1789–1989 (Richard H. Kohn ed., 1991)

Emory Upton, The Military Policy of the United States (1904)

Karl-Friedrich Walling, Republican Empire: Alexander Hamilton on War and Free Government (1999)

Significant Cases

The Selective Draft Law Cases, 245 U.S. 366 (1918)
Schenck v. United States, 249 U.S. 47 (1919)
Witmer v. United States, 348 U.S. 375 (1955)
United States v. Seeger, 380 U.S. 163 (1965)
United States v. Holmes, 387 F.2d 781 (7th Cir. 1967)
Holmes v. United States, 391 U.S. 936 (1968)
Hart v. United States, 391 U.S. 956 (1968)
United States v. O'Brien, 391 U.S. 367 (1968)
Welsh v. United States, 398 U.S. 333 (1970)
Gillette v. United States, 401 U.S. 437 (1971)
Schlesinger v. Ballard, 419 U.S. 498 (1975)
Rostker v. Goldberg, 453 U.S. 57 (1981)
Rumsfeld v. Forum for Academic and Institutional Rights, Inc., 547 U.S. 47 (2006)

Navy Clause

The Congress shall have Power...To provide and maintain a Navy....

(**Article I, Section 8, Clause 13**)

∼

*I*n 1641, an act of Parliament firmly overruled King Charles's assertion that he had a right under royal prerogative to appropriate funds to develop a navy. The Framers of the Constitution followed Parliament's example and lodged the power to provide a navy in the legislative branch.

But because the Founding generation considered navies to be less dangerous to republican liberty than standing armies, the Navy Clause did not elicit the same level of debate as did the Army Clause (*see* Article I, Section 8, Clause 12). Their experience taught them that armies, not navies, were the preferred tools of tyrants. Readers of Thucydides could view a navy as particularly compatible with democratic institutions. As Robert Delahunty has noted, the Framers were extremely well informed, not only about the politics and constitutions of the ancient world, but also about those of modern European history. Thus, they were well aware that the Venetian navy underpinned that city's republican institutions, much as the Athenian navy had protected rather than threatened the city's democracy; that the same was true of the navies of republican Holland; and that Britain, though in form a monarchy, was in truth a commercial republic whose liberty and prosperity depended on its fleet. It would not be going too far to say that the Founders came close to the insight of later students of history that the United States, like Britain, Holland, Venice, and Athens before it, is geopolitically an island, and that its insulation from land warfare which this afforded was an important factor in the emergence and survival of its liberal institutions.

The Framers were also aware of how much the economic prosperity and even the survival of the country depended upon sea-going trade. Consequently, the Framers imposed no time limit on naval appropriations as they did in the case of the army.

John Adams deserves credit as the great patron of the United States Navy. In October 1775 in the Second Continental Congress, Adams successfully overcame opposition and convinced Congress to begin outfitting ships to defend American interests in the war with Britain. In the 1780s, the United States possessed one of the principal merchant fleets in the world, but it was largely defenseless. In June 1785 Congress voted to sell the one remaining ship of the Continental Navy, a frigate, leaving the fledgling nation with only a fleet of small Treasury Department revenue cutters for defense.

During the contest over the Constitution, both Federalists and Anti-Federalists believed that maritime trade was necessary if the United States was to maintain its independence of action, but they disagreed over how to protect this trade. Federalists such as Alexander Hamilton argued for a federal navy, which "if it could not vie with those of the great maritime powers, would at least be of respectable weight if thrown into the scale of either of two contending parties." Hamilton maintained in *The Federalist* No. 11 that without a navy, "[a] nation, despicable by its weakness, forfeits even the privilege of being neutral." Anti-Federalists argued that instead of defending American commerce and guaranteeing American neutrality, creating a navy would provoke the European powers and invite war. They were also concerned about the expense of maintaining a navy and the distribution of that expense. In the Virginia ratifying convention, William Grayson argued that, despite the fact that a navy would not appreciably reduce the vulnerability of southern ports, the South would bear the main burden of naval appropriations.

The wisdom of granting Congress the power to provide and maintain a navy became evident during the two decades after the framing and ratification of the Constitution. As Europe once again erupted in war, American merchantmen increasingly found themselves at the mercy of British and French warships and the corsairs of the Barbary States. Only the rapid creation of a navy under John Adams's brilliant Secretary of the Navy, Benjamin Stoddert, permitted the United States to hold its own in the Quasi-War with France (1798–1800) and the War of 1812 with the British.

Though Adams and Hamilton disagreed vehemently on the need to raise an army during the Quasi-War with France, they were fully in accord on the value of a strong navy. Adams had long argued that the army was less necessary than the navy, for he believed that the United States was best protected by the "wooden walls" of a well-funded navy. Thomas Jefferson believed differently, however, and under his administration the navy floundered and remained largely unfunded. It was because of the War of 1812 and the extraordinary feats of older American frigates like the *U.S.S. Constitution* that the country came around, beginning with the administration of James Monroe, to an unbroken consensus that a strong navy was essential to preserving American liberty.

The Navy Clause has changed little, if at all, in practice. Neither have the arguments for and against naval power. Indeed, many of the major debates over foreign policy that have taken place since the middle of the nineteenth century were adumbrated by those between Federalists and Anti-Federalists during the framing of the Constitution.

Similarly, despite vast technological changes, the character of the Navy as a service, in contrast to the Army, has not altered much. While the "citizen soldier" envisioned by the Founders has virtually disappeared from the Army of today, today's sailor, both officer and enlisted, has much in common with his predecessor who manned the Navy of the Constitution, technical expertise excepted. Although service reforms beginning in the latter decades of the nineteenth century created a powerful Navy, the foundation of this Navy was laid by the likes of Hamilton, Adams, Benjamin Stoddert, and other Federalists who recognized the shortcomings of a navy limited to coastal defense alone.

The main changes affecting the Navy, if not the Navy Clause, have to do with defense organization, primarily the National Security Act of 1947 (and subsequent modifications). These include downgrading the Department of the Navy from a Cabinet department and the creation of the Air Force as a separate branch of the armed forces.

Mackubin Owens and David F. Forte

See Also

Article I, Section 8, Clause 11 (Declare War)
Article I, Section 8, Clause 12 (Army Clause)
Article I, Section 8, Clause 14 (Military Regulations)

Suggestions for Further Research

GEORGE W. BAER, ONE HUNDRED YEARS OF SEA POWER (1994)

Demetrios Caraley, The Politics of Military Unification: A Study of Conflict and the Policy Process (1966)

Robert J. Delahunty, *Structuralism and the War Powers: The Army, Navy, and Militia Clauses,* 19 Ga. St. U. L. Rev. 1021 (2003)

The Department of Defense: Documents on Establishment and Organization, 1944–1978 (Alice C. Cole et al., eds., 1978)

Marshall Smelser, The Congress Founds the Navy, 1787–1798 (1959, reprint 1973)

Craig L. Symonds, Navalists and Antinavalists: The Naval Policy Debate in the United States, 1785–1827 (1980)

Robert W. Tucker & David C. Hendrickson, Empire of Liberty: The Statecraft of Thomas Jefferson (1990)

Military Regulations

The Congress shall have Power . . . To make Rules for the Government and Regulation of the land and naval Forces. . . .

(**Article I, Section 8, Clause 14**)

*I*n his *Commentaries on the Constitution of the United States* (1833), Justice Joseph Story remarked that Congress's power to govern and regulate the land and naval forces is "a natural incident to the preceding powers to make war, to raise armies, and to provide and maintain a navy." Yet the Framers had overlooked this "natural incident" until after the Committee of Detail submitted its draft. Only then was a motion made from the floor to copy the language from the Articles of Confederation into the new Constitution, making explicit the grant of plenary power to Congress. It passed without controversy.

By placing the power in Congress, the Framers helped to define the respective roles of the legislature, the executive, and the judiciary over the Armed Forces and thus lessen the chances for serious conflict. Story explains: "The whole power is far more safe in the hands of congress,

than of the executive; since otherwise the most summary and severe punishments might be inflicted at the mere will of the executive." The central purpose of the clause is the establishment of a system of military law and justice outside of the ordinary jurisdiction of the civil courts. Tradition and experience taught the Framers that the necessities of military discipline require a system of jurisprudence separate from civilian society.

The American experience with military law predates the Constitution. In 1775, the Continental Congress adopted codes of military law for the Army and the Navy—largely based on corresponding British codes. John Adams, then a Massachusetts representative to the Continental Congress and chairman of its Naval Committee, wrote both *Rules for the Regulation of the Navy of the United Colonies* (1775) and the *American Articles of War* (1775). Following the adoption of the Constitution, the First Congress decided that both of these codes would continue in force. The *American Articles of War,* although revised several times, remained the basic code for the United States Army until 1917. Revisions included changes to punishments; rules governing the appointment of courts-martial; and, during the Civil War, the expansion of military jurisdiction over crimes and persons leading to major contests in the courts of law.

A common criticism of the Articles of War was that they were too harsh. This criticism remained even after the Articles were significantly modified in 1917 to deal with a mass army of citizen-soldiers. Critics charged that punishments were disproportionate to the crimes and that military authorities had too much discretion. For instance, following a race riot in Houston in 1917, the military hastily executed thirteen black enlisted soldiers. The same complaint arose during World War II, leading to the Elston Act of 1948, which modified the Articles. Such criticisms and the creation of a unified Department of Defense finally led Congress to enact the Uniform Code of Military Justice (UCMJ) in 1950. The Navy code followed a similar path.

The UCMJ is a compilation of federal statutes that establish uniform policies, procedures, and penalties within the military justice system. Congress's objective in creating the UCMJ was to eliminate disparities between the codes of the Army and Navy and to reduce, insofar as it was possible, "command influence," considered by critics to be the bane of a fair military justice system.

Throughout the history of the United States, the civil courts have been highly deferential to decisions of the military justice system. That is particularly true in the enforcement of military orders. The more difficult question is determining whether the military or civilian courts have jurisdiction over military personnel charged with "ordinary" or "civilian" crimes such as murder, robbery, or rape. Most civilian court reviews of courts-martial center on whether the military had proper jurisdiction over the cause.

Although commanders in the field have always possessed authority to punish infractions of military discipline, it was not until 1863 that Congress permitted the trial during wartime of soldiers who were charged with committing civil crimes such as murder. Until that time, soldiers had been turned over to state courts for trial. Subsequently, Congress expanded court-martial jurisdiction over civil offenses. After the Korean War, however, the Supreme Court and the federal appeals courts have limited the reach of the military's jurisdiction only to those acts that are "service connected."

There is no dispute that a civilian offense committed by a soldier on a military base, or in the theatre of war, or overseas is service connected and falls under military jurisdiction. Civilian dependents charged with crimes during peacetime, however, may not be tried by court-martial, *Reid v. Covert* (1957), *Grisham v. Hagan* (1960), at least while the civil courts are still in operation. *Ex parte Milligan* (1866). To avoid such civilians being charged by host nations abroad, in 2000 Congress passed the Military Extraterritorial Jurisdiction Act. That law imposes federal jurisdiction for crimes allegedly committed by civilians accompanying U.S. Armed Forces abroad, and also for military personnel charged with civil crimes but over whom the military has no further control.

Outside of these categories, federal courts consider a number of factors to determine if the act of the accused member of the military was service connected. *O'Callahan v. Parker* (1969). Among others, the factors considered include: (1) whether the victim of the crime was a member of the military; (2) whether the accused was properly off base when the crime occurred; (3) whether military property was involved; and (4) whether the act by the accused was within his military duties. When reviewing the jurisdiction of a military court, the federal courts utilized these and similar factors on a case-by-case basis. However, in *Solorio v. United States* (1987), the Supreme Court reversed *O'Callahan* and found that the military status of the defendant was sufficient by itself to establish the jurisdiction over the person irrespective of whether the offense was service connected. Subsequent to *Solorio*, military courts obtained greater jurisdiction over cases that previously had been tried by the civilian courts. Judicial deference toward military exigencies goes beyond respect for the different rules, procedures, and liabilities in the UCMJ. Deference also includes allowances for military orders and regulations that would hardly be constitutional in a civilian context.

The military courts and tribunals authorized by Congress are established pursuant to Congress's powers under Article I. They do not have the same protections and independence as Article III courts. Military courts fall into two jurisdictional categories: (1) martial and military courts of inquiry, which deal with military personnel; and (2) military commissions (or tribunals) and provost courts, which deal with civilians who have fallen under military jurisdiction. Depending on the degree of punishment attached to the offense, the military courts of first instance are the summary court-martial, the special court-martial, and the general court-martial, each of which may be convened by a successively more senior military authority. Following the decision of the court-martial, the convening authority reviews the decision and may revise it but only in favor of the defendant. The record is then further reviewed by a Judge Advocate General and, in cases of a serious sentence, is reviewed yet again by the Court of Military Review for the appropriate service. The UCMJ established a Court of Military Appeals (renamed in 1994 as the U.S. Court of Appeals for the Armed Forces), which, for the first time in United States history, created a civilian court with appellate jurisdiction over military justice. The U.S. Court of Appeals for the Armed Forces may review decisions of the Court of Military Review. Finally, upon a writ of certiorari, the Supreme Court can hear petitions from decisions by the U.S. Court of Appeals for the Armed Forces.

Collateral appeal to the federal courts is also available, normally through a writ of habeas corpus. They cannot review the factual basis of the decision, and their collateral review is limited to issues of jurisdiction, whether the proceeding denied fundamental constitutional rights, *Burns v. Wilson* (1953) (*see* the Fifth Amendment), and whether the military court gave full and fair consideration to the constitutional issue raised. Moreover, collateral review on a petition for habeas corpus is only available if the petitioner is in actual military custody, and he has exhausted all available military-justice remedies.

One controversial aspect of military justice is the establishment of military tribunals. Military tribunals established in an occupied territory are governed by international law. In *Dow v. Johnson* (1880), the Court ruled that the law governing an army invading an enemy's country is not the civil law of the invaded country or of the conquering country "but military law—the law of war."

After the events of 9/11, President George W. Bush signed a military order called the Detention, Treatment and Trial of Certain Non-Citizens in the War against Terrorism, 66 Fed. Reg. 57,833 (Nov. 13, 2011), in which he ordered the detention and trial by military tribunal of any non-citizens who were members of al Qaeda, conspired to commit terrorism, or harbored such terrorists. The Supreme Court had earlier upheld the authority of the President to try enemy aliens (and United States citizens working with them) by military tribunal in *Ex parte Quirin* (1942). There, the Court held that enemy aliens (in this case saboteurs, who had entered the United States in secret for the purpose of committing hostile acts) are not entitled to prisoner-of-war status, but are unlawful combatants who can be tried by military tribunal.

In 2004, the Court, relying on *Burns v. Wilson* and other cases, held in *Rasul v. Bush* that the federal habeas statute confers federal district court jurisdiction to hear challenges of alien detainees held at Guantanamo Bay. However, the Court explicitly did not decide the substance of those rights and limited the habeas extraterritorial reach to Guantanamo Bay, which it said had a unique relationship to the United States. At the same time, in *Rumsfeld v. Padilla* (2004), the Court, on jurisdictional grounds, avoided ruling on the extent of the President's power to keep a U.S. citizen in military custody as an enemy combatant; but in *Hamdi v. Rumsfeld* (2004) the Court decided, without a majority opinion, that the government must give a U.S. citizen held in the United States some type of hearing at which he may contest the facts on which the government decided to treat him as an enemy combatant.

In 2005, Congress passed the Detainee Treatment Act (Pub. L. No. 109-148, 119 Stat. 2680), which stated that "no court, justice, or judge shall have jurisdiction to hear" applications for writs of habeas corpus filed by aliens detained at Guantanamo Bay, Cuba, and that the D.C. Circuit Court of Appeals would have "exclusive jurisdiction to determine the validity" of a military tribunal's decision regarding the proper detention of the enemy combatant.

The Supreme Court, in *Hamdan v. Rumsfeld* (2006), held that the Act did not strip the federal courts of jurisdiction over pending cases. Justice John Paul Stevens, joined by Justices Stephen Breyer, Ruth Bader Ginsburg, and David Souter, argued that the Government must show that the detainee is accused of a crime that "is acknowledged to be an offense against the law of war." Ultimately, a majority of the Court held that military commissions lacked the power to try *Hamdan* because the rules governing the military commissions were different from those governing court martials, violating the UCMJ's requirement that all rules be "uniform." The Court also held that the commissions violated the Geneva Convention's guarantee of judgments "pronounced by a regularly constituted court."

In 2006, Congress passed the Military Commissions Act (Pub. L. No. 109-366, 120 Stat. 2600) to deny the federal courts jurisdiction over habeas actions filed by those detained aliens designated as enemy combatants. However, the Court held, in *Boumediene v. Bush* (2008), that "aliens designated as enemy combatants and detained at the United States Naval Station at Guantanamo Bay, Cuba...have the habeas corpus privilege." The Court also held that while Cuba maintained "de jure sovereignty" over Guantanamo Bay, the territory was under the U.S.'s "complete and total control."

David F. Forte and Mackubin Owens

See Also

Article I, Section 8, Clause 11 (Declare War)
Article I, Section 8, Clause 12 (Army Clause)
Article I, Section 8, Clause 15 (Militia Clause)
Article I, Section 8, Clause 16 (Organizing the Militia)
Article II, Section 2, Clause 1 (Commander in Chief)
Amendment V (Grand Jury Requirement)
Amendment VI (Jury Trial)

Suggestions for Further Research

Ronald D. Rotunda, *The Detainee Cases of 2004 and 2006 and Their Aftermath*, 57 Syracuse L. Rev.1 (2006)

1 Jonathan O. Lurie, Arming Military Justice: The Origins of the United States Court of Military Appeals, 1775–1950 (1992)

2 Jonathan O. Lurie, Pursuing Military Justice: The History of the United States Court of Appeals for the Armed Forces, 1951–1980 (1998)

Jonathan O. Lurie, *The Role of the Federal Judiciary in the Governance of the American Military: The United States Supreme Court and "Civil Rights and Supervision" Over the Armed Forces,* in The United States Military Under the Constitution of the United States, 1789–1989 (Richard H. Kohn ed., 1991)

David B. Rivkin & Lee Casey, *The Use of Military Commissions in the War on Terror*, 24 B.U. Int'l L.J. 123 (2006)

Glenn R. Schmitt, *Closing the Gap in Criminal Jurisdiction over Civilians Accompanying the Armed Forces Abroad—A First Person Account of the Creation of the Military Extraterritorial Jurisdiction Act of 2000*, 51 Cath. U. L. Rev. 55 (2001)

William Winthrop, Military Law and Precedents (2d ed.1979)

Significant Cases

Dynes v. Hoover, 61 U.S. (20 How.) 65 (1857)
Ex parte Vallandigham, 68 U.S. (1 Wall.) 243 (1864)
Ex parte Milligan, 71 U.S. (4 Wall.) 2 (1866)
Dow v. Johnson, 100 U.S. 158 (1880)
Ex parte Quirin, 317 U.S. 1 (1942)
Duncan v. Kahanamoku, 327 U.S. 304 (1946)
In re Yamashita, 327 U.S. 1 (1946)
United States v. Clay, 1 C.M.R. 74 (1951)
Burns v. Wilson, 346 U.S. 137 (1953)
Toth v. Quarles, 350 U.S. 11 (1955)
Reid v. Covert, 354 U.S. 1 (1957)
Grisham v. Hagan, 361 U.S. 278 (1960)
Kinsella v. United States *ex rel.* Singleton, 361 U.S. 234 (1960)
McElroy v. United States *ex rel.* Guagliardo, 361 U.S. 281 (1960)
United States v. Jacoby, 29 C.M.R. 244 (1960)
United States v. Tempia, 37 C.M.R. 249 (1967)
O'Callahan v. Parker, 395 U.S. 258 (1969)
Parker v. Levy, 417 U.S. 733 (1974)
Middendorf v. Henry, 425 U.S. 25 (1976)
Rostker v. Goldberg, 453 U.S. 57 (1981)
Solorio v. United States, 483 U.S. 435 (1987)
Hamdi v. Rumsfeld, 542 U.S. 507 (2004)
Rasul v. Bush, 542 U.S. 466 (2004)
Rumsfeld v. Padilla, 542 U.S. 426 (2004)
Hamdan v. Rumsfeld, 548 U.S. 557 (2006)
Boumediene v. Bush, 553 U.S. 723 (2008)

Militia Clause

The Congress shall have Power ... To provide for calling forth the Militia to execute the Laws of the Union, suppress Insurrections and repel Invasions...

(**Article I, Section 8, Clause 15**)

$\mathcal{F}$or the Founders, the militia arose from the posse comitatus, constituting the people as a whole and embodying the Anglo-American idea that the citizenry is the best enforcer of the law. "A militia when properly formed," wrote Richard Henry Lee in his *Letters From the Federal*

Farmer (1787–1788), "are in fact the people themselves . . . and include all men capable of bearing arms." From its origins in Britain, the posse comitatus (from medieval Latin meaning "the force of the country") was generally understood to constitute the constabulary of the shire. When order was threatened, the "shire reeve," or sheriff, would raise the "hue and cry," and all citizens who heard it were bound to render assistance in apprehending a criminal or maintaining order. The Framers transferred the power of calling out the militia from local authorities to the Congress.

The Anti-Federalists were not pleased. They wanted the militia to remain under state control as a check on the national government. Many feared that an institution intended for local defense could be dispatched far from home. As Luther Martin objected in *Genuine Information* (1788),

> As it now stands, the Congress will have the power, if they please, to march the whole militia of Maryland to the remotest part of the union, and keep them in service as long as they think proper, without being in any respect dependent upon the government of Maryland for this unlimited exercise of power over its citizens.

In the "Calling Forth" Act of 1792, Congress exercised its powers under the Militia Clause and delegated to the president the authority to call out the militia and issue it orders when invasion appeared imminent or to suppress insurrections. While the act gave the president a relatively free hand in case of invasion, it constrained his authority in the case of insurrections by requiring that a federal judge certify that the civil authority and the posse comitatus were powerless to meet the exigency. The president had also to order the insurgents to disband before he could mobilize the militia. This was the procedure that President George Washington followed during the Whiskey Rebellion of 1794.

Congress authorized the president to federalize the militia in the Militia Act of 1792 (reiterated in 1795):

> [W]henever the United States shall be invaded, or be in imminent danger of invasion from any foreign nation or Indian tribe, it shall be lawful for the President of the United States to call forth such number of the militia of the state, or states most convenient to the place of danger, or scene of action, as he may judge necessary to repel such invasion, and to issue his orders for that purpose to such officer or officers of the militia, as he shall think proper.

But even such clear language was insufficient to prevent a challenge to presidential authority during the War of 1812. At the outset of the conflict, President James Madison ordered the governors of Connecticut and Massachusetts to provide militia detachments for the defense of the maritime frontiers of the United States. These governors, however, were Federalists who opposed the war. They claimed that they, not the president, had the authority to determine whether an emergency existed. Governor Caleb Strong of Massachusetts requested an opinion of his state's Supreme Judicial Court, which concluded that this right was "vested in the commanders in chief of the militia of the several states." *Op. of Justices*, 8 Mass. 548 (1812).

The issue was finally resolved by the Supreme Court in 1827 in *Martin v. Mott*. Although the case explicitly concerned the validity of a court-martial of a militiaman, the decision rendered by Justice Joseph Story validated the claim that the president had the exclusive right to judge whether there was an exigency sufficient for calling forth the militia. State governors, however, retain concurrent authority to call out their respective militias to handle civil and military emergencies, as well as to repel invasions (Article I, Section 10, Clause 3). *Houston v. Moore* (1820).

Congress's authority to call out the militia is limited to three purposes: to execute the laws, stamp out domestic insurrections, and defeat foreign invasions. Absent from the list is the ability to call the militia for offensive use in foreign wars. In 1912, Attorney General George W. Wickersham authored an opinion contrasting the army with the militia, arguing that the militia's service should be domestic in nature. Historically, however, the militia was used across the Canadian border in 1812 and across the Florida border in the Seminole War of 1818.

Mackubin Owens

See Also

Article I, Section 8, Clause 11 (Declare War)
Article I, Section 8, Clause 12 (Army Clause)
Article I, Section 8, Clause 14 (Military Regulations)
Article I, Section 8, Clause 16 (Organizing the Militia)
Article I, Section 10, Clause 3 (Compact Clause)
Article II, Section 2, Clause 1 (Commander in Chief)
Amendment II (To Keep and Bear Arms)

Suggestions for Further Research

Op. of Justices, 8 Mass. 548 (1812)

Clarence A. Berdahl, War Powers of the Executive in the United States (1921)

Lawrence Delbert Cress, Citizens in Arms: The Army and Militia in American Society to the War of 1812 (1982)

Robert J. Delahunty, *Structuralism and the War Powers: The Army, Navy, and Militia Clauses*, 19 Ga. St. U. L. Rev. 1021 (2003)

Richard A. Epstein, *Executive Power, the Commander In Chief, and the Militia Clause*, 34 Hofstra L. Rev. 317 (2005)

Herbert Lawrence Fenster, *The Great War Powers Misconstruction*, 5 J. Nat'l Security L. & Pol'y 339 (2012)

J. Norman Heath, *Exposing the Second Amendment: Federal Preemption of State Militia Legislation*, 79 U. Detroit Mercy L. Rev. 39 (2001)

Richard H. Kohn, *The Constitution and National Security: The Founders' Intent*, in The United States Military Under the Constitution of the United States, 1789–1989 (Richard H. Kohn ed., 1991)

Military Laws of the United States from the Civil War Through the War Powers Act of 1973 (Richard H. Kohn ed., 1979)

Allan R. Millett & Peter Maslowski, For the Common Defense: A Military History of the United States of America, from 1607–2012 (2012)

Significant Cases

Meade v. Deputy Marshal, 16 F. Cas. 1291 (C.C.D. Va. 1815) (No. 9372)

Moore v. Houston, 3 S. & R. (Pa.) 169 (1817), *aff'd*, Houston v. Moore, 18 U.S. (5 Wheat.) 1 (1820)

Martin v. Mott, 25 U.S. (12 Wheat.) 19 (1827)

Texas v. White, 74 U.S. (7 Wall.) 700 (1869)

Tarble's Case, 80 U.S. (13 Wall.) 397 (1872)

Dunne v. People, 94 Ill. 120 (1879)

Cox v. Wood, 247 U.S. 3 (1918)

The Selective Draft Law Cases, 245 U.S. 366 (1918)

Perpich v. Department of Defense, 496 U.S. 334 (1990)

Organizing the Militia

The Congress shall have Power... To provide for organizing, arming, and disciplining, the Militia, and for governing such Part of them as may be employed in the Service of the United States, reserving to the States respectively, the Appointment of the Officers, and the Authority of training the Militia according to the discipline prescribed by Congress....

(Article I, Section 8, Clause 16)

~

*T*he militia, long a staple of republican thought, loomed large in the deliberations of the Framers, many of whom were troubled by the prospect of a standing army in times of peace. For the Founders, a militia, composed of a "people numerous and armed," was the ultimate guardian of liberty. It was a means to enable citizens not only to protect themselves against their fellows but also, particularly for the Anti-Federalists, to protect themselves from an oppressive government. "The militia...is our ultimate safety," said Patrick Henry during the Virginia ratifying convention. "We can have no security without it.... The great object is, that every man be armed.... Every one who is able may have a gun." Both the Pennsylvania and Vermont constitutions asserted that "the people have a right to bear arms for the defence of themselves and the state...."

The Anti-Federalists feared that Congress would permit the militia to atrophy, leaving the states defenseless against the central government. In the Virginia ratifying convention, George Mason, while advocating a stronger central control over the militia, nevertheless argued that there was a danger that Congress could render the militia useless "by disarming them. Under various pretences, Congress may neglect to provide for arming and disciplining the militia; and the state governments cannot do it, for Congress has an exclusive right to arm them &c [et cetera]." The desire to prevent enfeebling state militias, which provided a check to a standing army, prompted the ratifying conventions to call for an amendment guaranteeing the right of citizens to bear arms. The First Congress responded, but the Second Amendment did not remove national control over armed forces or the state militias.

Federal preemption of state-militia legislation commenced very early in the history of the Republic. In *Houston v. Moore* (1820), the Supreme Court stated that the federal government's power over the militia "may be exercised to any extent that may be deemed necessary by Congress."

Despite the generally poor performance of the militia during the Revolution, Federalists recognized that without a militia, there would be no United States military establishment. They believed, however, that they could minimize the weaknesses of the militia by creating a select militia corps in each state and establishing federal control over officership and training. The ultimate Federalist goal was to turn the militia into a national reserve of uniform, interchangeable units. In 1792, Congress passed the Uniform Militia Act, which remained the basic militia law of the United States until the twentieth century. This act established an "obligated" militia, based on universal military service. All able-bodied white men between the ages of eighteen and forty-five were required to enroll. But the act fell far short of Federalist goals. It did not create select state corps and, most importantly, did not impose penalties on the states or individuals for noncompliance. For the most part, the states ignored the provisions of the act. The abysmal performance

of the militia during the War of 1812 ensured the demise of the obligated reserve as established by the Founding generation.

The obligated militia was succeeded by the "uniformed" militia, local volunteer units generally equipped and supported by their own members. In addition, the states continued to provide volunteer citizen-soldiers when the regular U.S. Army had to be expanded, as was the case during the Mexican War and the Civil War. After the Civil War, the uniformed militia reemerged as the National Guard, but, unhappy with their largely domestic constabulary role, guardsmen lobbied for the mission of a national reserve. In the Militia Act of 1903 (the Dick Act), amended and expanded in 1908, Congress divided the eligible male population into an "organized militia" (the National Guard of the several states) and a "reserve," or "unorganized," militia.

In response to an opinion by the Attorney General that the Militia Clause and the Dick Act precluded the employment of guardsmen outside of United States borders, Congress included in the National Security Act of 1916 (amended in 1920 and 1933) provisions that explicitly "federalized" the National Guard. This act, as amended, has continued to govern federal-state military relations. By giving the United States Army extensive control of National Guard officers and units, and by making state forces available for duty overseas, the National Security Act of 1916 essentially stripped the states of all of their militia powers. It effectively repealed the power of the states to appoint officers by limiting such appointments to those who "shall have successfully passed such tests as to...physical, moral and professional fitness as the President shall prescribe." The law stated that the army of the United States now included both the regular army and "the National Guard while in the service of the United States." In *Cox v. Wood* (1918), the Supreme Court validated the action of Congress, holding that the plenary power to raise armies was "not qualified or restricted by the provisions of the Militia Clause."

The World War I draft completely preempted state sovereignty regarding the militia by drafting individual guardsmen directly into the United States Army. In *The Selective Draft Law*

Cases (1918), the Court held that the states held sway over the militia only "to the extent that such control was not taken away by the exercise by Congress of its power to raise armies." Congress was given power to "direct the organization and training of the militia...leaving the carrying out of such command to the states."

The transition of the National Guard into a national reserve reached its completion during the Cold War. Despite the existence of a large regular army, Guard units were included in most war plans. But with federal funding, which covered about ninety-five percent of the costs, came federal control. While governors continued to call up the Guard to quell domestic disturbances and to aid in disaster relief, they discovered that their control was trumped by federal demands. For instance, in protest against United States actions in Central America during the 1980s, several governors attempted to prevent units from their states from deploying to Honduras and El Salvador for training. In response, Congress passed the Montgomery Amendment (10 U.S.C. 672(f) (Supp. V 1987), a law "prohibiting a governor from withholding consent to a unit of the National Guard's being ordered to active duty outside the United States on the ground that the governor objects to the location, purpose, type, or schedule of that duty." In such cases as *Perpich v. Department of Defense* (1990), the Court supported Congress's position.

With the end of the Cold War, the National Guard's role as a national reserve was called into question. As a result of the terrorist attacks of September 11, 2001, some observers believed that the Guard could return to a domestic constabulary role. On the other hand, extensive military commitments abroad have required the Guard to remain an active element in the United States armed forces.

Mackubin Owens

See Also

Suggestions for Further Research

Lawrence Delbert Cress, Citizens in Arms: The Army and Militia in American Society to the War of 1812 (1982)

J. Norman Heath, *Exposing the Second Amendment: Federal Preemption of State Militia Legislation*, 79 U. Detroit Mercy L. Rev. 39 (2001)

Richard H. Kohn, *The Constitution and National Security: The Founders' Intent, in* The United States Military Under the Constitution of the United States, 1789–1989 (Richard H. Kohn ed., 1991)

Military Laws of the United States from the Civil War Through the War Powers Act of 1973 (Richard H. Kohn ed., 1979)

Allan R. Millett & Peter Maslowski, For the Common Defense: A Military History of the United States of America from 1607–2012 (2d ed. 1994)

Significant Cases

Meade v. Deputy Marshal, 16 F. Cas. 1291 (C.C.D. Va. 1815) (No. 9372)

Moore v. Houston, 3 S. & R. (Pa.) 169 (1817), *aff'd*, Houston v. Moore, 18 U.S. (5 Wheat.) 1 (1820)

Tarble's Case, 80 U.S. (13 Wall.) 397 (1872)

Dunne v. People, 94 Ill. 120 (1879)

Cox v. Wood, 247 U.S. 3 (1918)

The Selective Draft Law Cases, 245 U.S. 366 (1918)

Perpich v. Department of Defense, 496 U.S. 334 (1990)

Enclave Clause

The Congress shall have Power...To exercise exclusive Legislation in all Cases whatsoever, over such District (not exceeding ten Miles square) as may, by Cession of particular States, and the Acceptance of Congress, become the Seat of the Government of the United States....

(**Article I, Section 8, Clause 17**)

~

*I*n *The Federalist* No. 43, James Madison explained the need for a "federal district," subject to Congress's exclusive jurisdiction and separate from the territory, and authority, of any single state:

> The indispensable necessity of complete authority at the seat of government carries its own evidence with it. It is a power exercised by every legislature of the Union, I might say of the world, by virtue of its general supremacy. Without it, not only the public authority might be insulted and its proceedings interrupted with impunity, but a dependence of the members of the general government, on the State comprehending the seat of the government for protection in the exercise of their duty might bring on the national councils an imputation of awe or influence equally dishonorable to the government and dissatisfactory to the other members of the Confederacy.

Madison's concerns about insults to the "public authority" were not speculative. In June 1783, several hundred unpaid and angry Continental soldiers had marched on Philadelphia, menacing the Confederation Congress meeting in Independence Hall. Pennsylvania refused all requests for assistance and, after two days, Congress adjourned. Its Members fled into New Jersey.

The incident made a lasting impression. The Framers referenced it over and again in defending their provision for a "federal town," which Anti-Federalists persisted in visualizing as a sink of corruption and a potential nursery for tyrants. In fact, however, the Framers understood that the need for a territory in which the general government exercised full sovereignty, not beholden to any state, was an inherent necessity for the federal system itself.

Once the Constitution had come into effect in 1789, the location of the new capital inevitably became more contentious than its necessity. Both New York and Pennsylvania were desperate for the plum. In fact, Benjamin Franklin had earlier urged Pennsylvania's legislature to grant the land moments after the proposed Constitution was first read to that body. In 1790, the First Congress wrangled over the issue. The resultant "Compromise of 1790" provided for a "Southern" site, near the fall line of the Potomac River. In exchange, the Southern states agreed to Alexander Hamilton's proposal that the new federal government would assume the states' Revolutionary War debts. That arrangement was sealed in a meeting between Hamilton and Thomas Jefferson by which the South gained the capital (Philadelphia remaining the temporary capital for ten years), but also by which the federal government obtained practical control of national monetary policy. Maryland and Virginia ceded "ten miles square" on their respective sides of the river, and the government finally moved to its permanent, but still rude and undeveloped, seat in 1800.

The week before John Adams left the presidency in 1801, Congress established a government for the District of Columbia, dividing it into two counties, Washington and Alexandria. The law provided that the laws then existing in the two counties, deriving from Virginia and Maryland, respectively, would remain in force until modified by Congress. A realization that the original bill would have left the District without a judiciary prompted Congress to provide for justices of the peace to be appointed by the President. That act eventually led to the case of *Marbury v. Madison* (1803).

In 1846, the Virginia portion of the original territory of Columbia, encompassing Old Town Alexandria and Arlington County, was "retroceded" by Congress to the Commonwealth. The constitutionality of this act has never been determined. In 1875, the Supreme Court dismissed, for lack of standing, a case brought by a Virginia taxpayer who argued that he was properly subject to the District's then less-onerous tax burden. The Court noted that the plaintiff sought to "vicariously raise a question" that neither Virginia nor the federal government had "desire[d] to make." *Phillips v. Payne* (1875).

Over the last two centuries, Congress has experimented with varying methods of home rule, as well as with direct Congressional rule. The history is complex, including periods of county home rule, as well as city (Georgetown, Alexandria, and Washington) self-rule. Since 1973, the District enjoys substantial home rule, with an elected mayor and city council, though, under the Constitution Congress could revoke or alter the arrangement at any time.

Today, the most controversial aspect of Congress's authority over the District is the fact that Washington, D.C., residents cannot elect Members to Congress. The Twenty-third Amendment gave the District the right to participate in presidential elections but not in congressional elections. Instead, the residents elect a nonvoting "delegate" to the House of Representatives.

Because of the District's unique character as the federal city, neither the Framers nor Congress accorded the inhabitants the right to elect Members of the House of Representatives or the Senate. In exchange, however, the District's residents received the multifarious benefits of the national capital. As Justice Joseph Story noted in *Commentaries on the Constitution of the United States* (1833), "there can be little doubt, that the inhabitants composing [the District] would receive with thankfulness such a blessing, since their own importance would be thereby increased, their interests be subserved, and their rights be under the immediate protection of the representatives of the whole Union." In effect, the Framers believed that the residents were "virtually" represented in the federal interest for a strong, prosperous capital.

There have been a number of efforts to change this original design, including a proposed constitutional amendment (passed by Congress in 1977) that would have granted the District of Columbia congressional voting representation "as if it were a state." This amendment, however, was not ratified in the seven-year period established by Congress. Other proposals have included a retrocession of most or all of the District to Maryland—a plan that Attorney General Robert F. Kennedy in 1964 deemed impractical and unconstitutional—and the admission of Washington, D.C., to the Union as the fifty-first state.

In 2000, the courts rejected a series of arguments suggesting that the District's inhabitants were, on various constitutional and policy grounds, entitled to voting representation in Congress without an amendment. See *Adams v. Clinton* (2000). More recently, the courts have rejected efforts to invalidate a congressionally imposed limit on the District's ability to tax nonresident commuters. *Banner v. United States* (2004). In that case, the court noted that, "simply put...the District and its residents are the subjects of Congress' unique powers, exercised to address the unique circumstances of our nation's capital."

Statehood is now the clear preference of District of Columbia voting-rights advocates, but the proposal has never excited much support in Congress. It would, in any case, require a constitutional amendment, for an independent federal territory comprising the seat of government and subject to the ultimate authority of Congress was a critical part of the Framers' original notion of an indestructible federal union of indestructible states.

Lee Casey

See Also

Amendment XXIII (Electors for the District of Columbia)

Suggestions for Further Research

Bob Arnebeck, THROUGH A FIERY TRIAL: BUILDING WASHINGTON, 1790–1800 (1991)

WILHELMUS B. BRYAN, A HISTORY OF THE NATIONAL CAPITAL (1914)

OFFICE OF LEGAL POLICY, U.S. DEPARTMENT OF JUSTICE, REPORT TO THE ATTORNEY GENERAL ON THE QUESTION OF STATEHOOD FOR THE DISTRICT OF COLUMBIA (April 3, 1987)

Peter Raven-Hansen, *The Constitutionality of D.C. Statehood*, 60 Geo. Wash. L. Rev. 160 (1991)

Significant Cases

Marbury v. Madison, 5 U.S. (1 Cranch) 137 (1803)

Phillips v. Payne, 92 U.S. 130, 133 (1875)

Albaugh v. Tawes, 233 F. Supp. 576 (D. Md. 1964), *aff'd*, 379 U.S. 27 (1964) (per curiam)

Evans v. Cornman, 398 U.S. 419 (1970)

Adams v. Clinton, 90 F. Supp. 2d 27, 35 (D.D.C. 2000), *aff'd*, 531 U.S. 941 (2000)

Banner v. United States, 303 F. Supp. 2d 1 (D.D.C. 2004)

Seegars v. Ashcroft, 297 F. Supp. 2d 201 (D.D.C. 2004)

Military Installations

The Congress shall have Power To...exercise like Authority over all Places purchased by the Consent of the Legislature of the State in which the Same shall be, for the Erection of Forts, Magazines, Arsenals, dock-Yards, and other needful Buildings....

(ARTICLE I, SECTION 8, CLAUSE 17)

$\sim$

*I*n addition to the permanent seat of government, established by 1800 in the District of Columbia, the Constitution gave Congress exclusive legislative authority over certain federal installations. Like the federal district, the purpose of this grant was to accommodate and guarantee the independence of both federal and state sovereignties. As Justice Joseph Story noted in his *Commentaries on the Constitution of the United States*:

> The public money expended on such places, and the public property deposited in them, and the nature of the military duties, which may be required there, all demand, that they should be exempted from state authority. In truth, it would be wholly improper, that places, on which the security of the entire Union may depend, should be subjected to the control of any member of it. The power, indeed, is wholly unexceptionable; since it can only be exercised at the will of the state; and it is therefore placed beyond all reasonable scruple.

Federal "enclave" jurisdiction, obtained under this provision, must be distinguished from instances where the federal government has obtained only a "proprietarial" interest in a particular building or parcel of land through purchase—although federal authority over such areas may turn out to be nearly as broad under the Territories and Property Clauses (Article IV, Section 3, Clause 2).

Enclave jurisdiction may come into effect as a result of a federal reservation of legislative authority over an area at the time a state is admitted to the Union, or based upon a particular cession by the state to the federal government of that authority. Federal enclave jurisdiction may apply to individual buildings, or parts of buildings (such as the U.S. Customs House, and the northern portion of the U.S. Mint, located in Denver, Colorado), or to vast territories (such as the 200-square-mile Camp Pendleton in California). Federal enclaves include such varying installations as the National Institutes of Health in Bethesda, Maryland, and Cape Canaveral, Florida, while "other needful buildings" includes locks, dams, federal courts, customs houses, post offices, and "whatever [other] structures are found to be necessary in the performance of the functions of the Federal Government." *James v. Dravo Contracting Co.* (1937).

The federal government began regulating federal enclaves from the start with the Federal Crimes Act of 1790. Beginning in 1825, Congress began applying state law to crimes within federal enclaves where federal law was silent. These Assimilative Crimes Acts continue to the present day, including one passed in 1948 that adopted state laws not only then existing but any future state law that may be applicable. In 1958, the Supreme Court validated Congress's adoption of future state laws, reversing a lower court ruling holding that the 1948 Act was an improper delegation of Congressional authority to the states. *United States v. Sharpnack* (1958)

The case law dealing with federal enclaves is complex. Such areas are subject to the "special maritime and territorial jurisdiction of the United States," 18 U.S.C. § 2243; and criminal offenses committed within an enclave are subject to federal prosecution, although the substantive offense may well be grounded in the surrounding state's law pursuant to the Assimilative Crimes Act, 18 U.S.C. § 13(a). As noted, the 1948 Assimilative Crimes Act provides that where a criminal offense has been committed within a federal enclave and there is no federal law applicable, federal courts will instead apply applicable state law. The applicable state law becomes "absorbed" as federal law.

Outside of the provisions of the Assimilative Crimes Act, the ceding state retains no authority in a federal enclave unless it specifically reserved such rights at the time it consented to the purchase or made the cession. In fact, most states have reserved at least the right to serve state civil and criminal process in federal enclaves, and they may also retain certain regulatory authority. *Paul v. United States* (1963). At the same time, although a state's rights vis-à-vis a federal enclave depend upon the terms of the original cession, the Supreme Court has ruled that federal enclave residents are entitled to vote as residents of the surrounding state no matter what the terms of the original cession. *Evans v. Cornman* (1970).

Lee Casey

See Also

Article IV, Section 3, Clause 2 (Territories Clause; Property Clause)

Suggestions for Further Research

David E. Engdahl, *State and Federal Power over Federal Property*, 18 Ariz. L. Rev. 283 (1976)

Jurisdiction over Federal Areas Within the States: Report of the Interdepartmental Committee for the Study of Jurisdiction over Federal Areas Within the States (April 1956)

Significant Cases

Fort Leavenworth R.R. Co. v. Lowe, 114 U.S. 525 (1885)
James v. Dravo Contracting Co., 302 U.S. 134 (1937)
James Stewart & Co. v. Sadrakula, 309 U.S. 94 (1940)
United States v. Sharpnack, 355 U.S. 286 (1958)
Paul v. United States, 371 U.S. 245, 268 (1963)
Evans v. Cornman, 398 U.S. 419 (1970)
Lewis v. United States, 523 U.S. 155 (1998)

Necessary and Proper Clause

The Congress shall have Power... To make all Laws which shall be necessary and proper for carrying into Execution the foregoing Powers, and all other Powers vested by this Constitution in the Government of the United States, or in any Department or Officer thereof.

(Article I, Section 8, Clause 18)

～

*T*he delegates to the Constitutional Convention declared, by resolution, that Congress should possess power to legislate "in all Cases for the general Interests of the Union, and also in those Cases to which the States are separately incompetent, or in which the Harmony of the United States may be interrupted by the Exercise of individual Legislation." It was left to the Committee of Detail—a distinguished body consisting of four prominent lawyers (Oliver Ellsworth, Edmund Randolph, John Rutledge (chair), and James Wilson) and a prominent businessman (Nathaniel Gorham)—to translate that resolution into concrete form. At the Constitutional Convention, the Committee of Detail took the Convention's resolutions on national legislative authority and particularized them into a series of enumerated congressional powers. This formalized the principle of enumerated powers, under which federal law can govern only as to matters within the terms of some power-granting clause of the Constitution. By including the Necessary and Proper Clause at the conclusion of Article I, Section 8, the Framers set the criteria for laws that, even if they are not within the terms of other grants, serve to make other federal powers effective.

Although modern scholars often express bafflement at the Necessary and Proper Clause, the meaning and purpose of the clause would actually have been clear to an eighteenth-century citizen. The enumeration of congressional powers in Article I, Section 8 is similar to the enumeration of powers that one would find in an eighteenth-century private agency instrument or corporate charter. That is not surprising, as the Founders viewed the Constitution as, in the words of James Iredell, "a great power of attorney," in which the principals ("We the People") grant power to official agents (the government). Eighteenth-century agency law understood that grants of power to agents generally carried implied powers in their wake: the enumerated, or *principal*, granted powers were presumptively accompanied by implied, or *incidental*, powers that were needed to effectuate the principal powers. As William Blackstone wrote, "[a] subject's grant shall be construed to include many things, besides what are expressed, if necessary for the operation of the grant." Agency instruments accordingly often referred to "necessary," "proper," or (most restrictively) "necessary and proper" incidental powers of agents. A Committee of Detail composed of lawyers and a businessman would have written, and a public accustomed to serving as or employing agents in a wide range of everyday affairs would have recognized, the Necessary and Proper Clause as a provision clarifying the scope of incidental powers accompanying the grants of enumerated (or principal) congressional powers.

So understood, the Framers crafted the Necessary and Proper Clause to serve three great purposes. The first was to facilitate organization of the government, such as empowering Congress to organize the judicial department and to create executive offices. The second was to help effectuate the other enumerated powers of Congress. The third, and most general, was to define the limits of these implied or incidental powers.

As to the first purpose, the Constitution could not prescribe all points of government organization, so Detail Committee member Edmund Randolph proposed empowering Congress to "organize the government." James Wilson proposed the "necessary and proper" clause as a substitute, authorizing laws "for carrying into Execution" the "other" federal powers. The committee, and then the Convention, approved. The organizational function of this clause was recognized from the outset. Among Congress's first acts were establishing executive departments and staffs, determining the number of Justices of the Supreme Court, and allocating the judicial power among federal courts. The Supreme

Court has acknowledged the Necessary and Proper Clause as the source of Congress's power to legislate about judicial process and procedure.

As to the second and more significant purpose, the clause also supports laws for carrying into execution "the foregoing Powers," that is, those specified for the legislature itself in Article I, Section 8. It thus enhances the other powers given to Congress. During the ratification debates, opponents dubbed it the "sweeping clause" and the "general clause," arguing that it subverted the principle of enumerated powers by giving sweeping general legislative competence to Congress. The Anti-Federalist Brutus, for example, said it "leaves the national legislature at liberty, to do every thing, which in their judgment is best." Defenders of the Constitution strongly disagreed. At Pennsylvania's ratification convention, James Wilson, the author of the clause, explained that the words "necessary and proper" are "limited and defined by the following, 'for carrying into execution the foregoing powers.' It is saying no more than that the powers we have already particularly given, shall be effectually carried into execution." It authorizes what is "necessary to render effectual the particular powers that are granted." Congress thus can make laws about something otherwise outside the enumerated powers, insofar as those laws are "necessary and proper" to effectuate federal policy for something within an enumerated power.

The third purpose has the broadest implications for constitutional law. The Articles of Confederation expressly forbade any inference of incidental powers by specifying that "[e]ach state retains...every power, jurisdiction, and right, which is not by this Confederation *expressly* delegated to the United States, in Congress assembled" (emphasis added). The Constitution contains no such clause, and it is therefore appropriate to find some measure of implied congressional powers. Had the Constitution been silent about implied powers, the ordinary background rules of agency law would have mandated inferring some measure of such powers to effectuate the enumerated powers, but would have left uncertainty about how broadly or narrowly to construe the implied powers. By selecting a relatively restrictive phrase—"necessary and proper," in the conjunctive—to describe the range of implied congressional powers, the Constitution eliminated that uncertainty by limiting implied powers to those that bear a close relationship to the principal powers.

Accordingly, every law enacted under the Necessary and Proper Clause must meet four requirements: (1) it must be incidental to a principal power; (2) it must be "for carrying into Execution" a principal power; (3) it must be "necessary" for that purpose; and (4) it must be "proper" for that purpose. And, because the clause provides that all such laws "shall be" necessary and proper for executing federal powers, rather than prescribing that such laws "shall be deemed by Congress" to be necessary and proper, these inquiries are all objective, contrary to Brutus's suggestion of unreviewable congressional discretion.

In *McCulloch v. Maryland* (1819), Chief Justice John Marshall confirmed the original understanding of the clause. He noted that other grants of power by themselves "according to the dictates of reason" would "imply" a "means of execution." He went on, however, to declare that the Constitution "has not left the right of Congress to employ the necessary means for the execution of the powers conferred on the Government to general reasoning." For the Chief Justice, the Necessary and Proper Clause makes express a power that otherwise would only have been implied and thus might have been subject to cavil. By implanting the clause among the powers of Congress, the Framers confirmed that Congress may act to make the constitutional plan effective. In his parsing of the words of the clause, he concluded that the Necessary and Proper Clause authorizes laws enacted as means "really calculated to effect any of the objects intrusted to the government." Arguments for laws that lack this crucial means-to-end characteristic find no support in Marshall's opinion or in the Necessary and Proper Clause.

While modern case law does not fully reflect the original meaning of the Necessary and Proper Clause, it has moved significantly towards conformance with original meaning in recent years, at least with respect to several of the clause's requirements. Most notably, the modern Supreme Court

has recognized, after a long period of neglect, the requirement that laws under the Necessary and Proper Clause be incidental to a principal power, as Marshall emphasized in *McCulloch*. The *McCulloch* case concerned in large measure whether the Necessary and Proper Clause authorized Congress to incorporate a national bank, given that neither the power to create a corporation nor the power to create a bank is among the principal (enumerated) powers of Congress. The Chief Justice devoted the bulk of his opinion to explaining why the power to incorporate a bank was incidental, that is, not as great as a principal power. He said that incorporation was "not, like the power of making war, or levying taxes, or of regulating commerce, a great substantive and independent power, which cannot be implied as incidental to other powers," but rather "must be considered as a means not less usual, not of higher dignity." If a power is not incidental—if it is of the same "dignity" or (as founding-era agency lawyers would say) as "worthy" as the principal enumerated powers—then it cannot be implied under the Necessary and Proper Clause, no matter how convenient, useful, or even indispensable it might be to effectuation of a principal power. This basic idea played a key role nearly two centuries later in Chief Justice John Roberts' decisive opinion for the Court in *National Federation of Independent Business v. Sebelius* (2012), in which the Court upheld the Patient Protection and Affordable Care Act (PPACA) provision known as the "individual mandate" to purchase government-approved health insurance under the taxing power but found the mandate unsupportable by either the Commerce Clause or the Necessary and Proper Clause. In explaining why the mandate was not authorized by the Necessary and Proper Clause, Chief Justice Roberts wrote, extensively quoting *McCulloch*, that the clause "vests Congress with authority to enact provisions 'incidental to the [enumerated] power'.... Although the Clause gives Congress authority to 'legislate on that vast mass of incidental powers which must be involved in the constitution,' it does not license the exercise of any 'great substantive and independent power[s]' beyond those specifically enumerated." He concluded that a governmental power to force people to buy a product could not be " 'incidental' to the exercise of the commerce power.... Rather, such a conception of the Necessary and Proper Clause would work a substantial expansion of federal authority." Accordingly, it is now clear that any power claimed by Congress under the Necessary and Proper Clause must be incidental—meaning that it must *not* be the sort of power that an ordinary reader would assume must be enumerated as a principal power in order to exist.

In addition to being incidental to a principal power, any law enacted under the Necessary and Proper Clause must be "for carrying into Execution" some other federal power. The Necessary and Proper Clause allows Congress to decide whether, when, and how to legislate "for carrying into Execution" the powers of another branch; but it respects and even reinforces the principle of separation of powers. Unlike Randolph's authorization to "organize the government"—which the Committee of Detail replaced with Wilson's more exacting phrase—"laws . . . for carrying into Execution" the powers reposed in another branch—can only mean laws to help effectuate the discretion of that other branch, not laws to control or limit that discretion. It gives Congress no power to instruct or impede another branch in the performance of that branch's constitutional role. For example, Congress could not, under the guise of this clause, dictate to courts how to decide cases, *United States v. Klein* (1871), or tell the President whom to prosecute. Of course, when the clause is invoked to effectuate ends within Congress's own powers, it compounds Congress's discretion: not only the selection of means, but also the selection of policy ends, rests in Congress's own discretion.

Incidental laws that carry into execution federal powers must also be "necessary" for that purpose. The requirement of necessity entails some degree of causal connection between the implementing law and the implemented power. The degree of that required causal connection between the means chosen and the particular "end" sought, i.e., the specific enumerated power, has been a contentious issue for more than two centuries. Thomas Jefferson, and the State of Maryland in *McCulloch*, famously argued that a "necessary" law must be indispensable to the

achievement of a permissible governmental end. Alexander Hamilton equally famously argued that necessity in this context meant merely that a law "might be conceived to be conducive" to a permissible end. And somewhat less famously, but no less importantly, James Madison trod a middle ground, describing necessity as requiring "a definite connection between means and ends" in which the executory law and the executed power are linked "by some obvious and precise affinity."

In *McCulloch*, Chief Justice Marshall, writing for the Court, upheld the Second Bank of the United States, utilizing the very rationale that Secretary Hamilton, and James Wilson before him, had employed. Marshall rejected Jefferson's view that the clause limits Congress to "those means without which the grant of power would be nugatory." That would have precluded Congress from deliberating alternatives, and the Court read the clause instead as vesting "discretion, with respect to the means by which the powers it confers are to be carried into execution." *McCulloch* countenanced "any means calculated to produce the end," giving Congress "the capacity to avail itself of experience, to exercise its reason, and to accommodate its legislation to circumstances." According to *McCulloch*, unless otherwise inconsistent "with the letter and spirit of the constitution," any law that is "appropriate," "plainly adapted to that end," and "really calculated to effect any of the objects entrusted to the government" is valid under the Necessary and Proper Clause. For the judiciary "to inquire into the degree of its necessity," Marshall said, "would be . . . to tread on legislative ground."

So long as a law promotes an end within the scope of some enumerated power, extraneous objectives do not render it unconstitutional. Indeed, one means might be preferred over others precisely because it advances another objective as well. For example, besides helping Congress effectuate various enumerated powers, a bank could make private loans to augment business capital or to satisfy consumer wants; while these extraneous ends could provide no independent constitutional justification, Hamilton urged them as principal reasons why Congress should incorporate a bank.

Record-keeping and reporting requirements regarding drug transactions, if apt as means to enforce federal taxes on those transactions, are no less valid because crafted for police ends that are not within any enumerated power. Extraneous objectives are constitutionally immaterial; but to invoke the Necessary and Proper Clause, a sufficient link to some enumerated-power end is constitutionally indispensable.

McCulloch remains the classic elucidation of this clause, but it has been elaborated in many other cases, such as in the proceedings concerning the Legal Tender Act of 1862. Congress, in an effort to stabilize commerce and support military efforts during the Civil War, determined that new paper currency must be accepted at face value as legal tender. The Supreme Court, in the *Legal Tender Cases* (1871), affirmed Congress's discretion to choose among means it thought conducive to enumerated-power ends. The Court upheld Congress's choice, even though better means might have been chosen, and though the legal tender clause proved to be of little help: "The degree of the necessity for any Congressional enactment, or the relative degree of its appropriateness, if it have any appropriateness, is for consideration in Congress, not here," said the Court.

Modern cases have interpreted these precedents to require that laws under the Necessary and Proper Clause accomplish valid legislative ends "by rational means," *Sabri v. United States* (2004), or by "a means that is rationally related to the implementation of a constitutionally enumerated power," *United States v. Comstock* (2010). In *Comstock,* four Justices (Samuel Alito, Anthony Kennedy, Antonin Scalia, and Clarence Thomas) expressed—in three different opinions and three different forms—some measure of unease with this "rational basis" formulation of the required means-ends connection, though only Justice Thomas has specifically endorsed the Madisonian formulation as an alternative.

Finally, laws under the Necessary and Proper Clause must be "proper" for executing federal powers. It is textually clear—and five Justices in *NFIB v. Sebelius* have confirmed—that the requirement of propriety is separate from and in addition to the requirement of necessity. Given the agency-law origins of the Necessary and Proper Clause, it is evident that the term "proper" imports into the clause basic fiduciary principles, that is, the means must be true to the end of effectuating a principal power. As Chief Justice Marshall famously warned, "Should Congress, in the execution of its powers, adopt measures which are prohibited by the Constitution, or should Congress, under the pretext of executing its powers, pass laws for the accomplishment of objects not intrusted to the Government, it would become the painful duty of this tribunal, should a case requiring such a decision come before it, to say that such an act was not the law of the land."

The modern Supreme Court has not elaborated upon this requirement of propriety in detail, but a majority of Justices of the Court have endorsed some version of it in recent years. Several late twentieth-century cases held that laws failed to be "proper" if they violated principles of federalism by compelling state officials to enforce federal law, *Printz v. United States* (1997), or by wrongly using Article I powers to abrogate state sovereign immunity, *Alden v. Maine* (1999). In *NFIB v. Sebelius,* four Justices clarified that "the scope of the Necessary and Proper Clause is exceeded not only when the congressional action directly violates the sovereignty of the States but also when it violates the background principle of enumerated (and hence limited) federal power," and a fifth (Chief Justice Roberts) noted that laws are not "proper" when they "undermine the structure of government established by the Constitution" and specifically found that the individual mandate of the PPACA "is not a 'proper' means" for effectuating the statute's insurance reforms.

On the other hand, the Court has decided a number of recent cases involving the Necessary and Proper Clause, most notably *Sabri v. United States* (2004) and *United States v. Comstock* (2010), without conducting a separate inquiry into whether the challenged law is "proper." It remains to be seen how fully an analysis of propriety becomes integrated into modern doctrine.

The Necessary and Proper Clause, along with its in-built limitations, is the relevant source of congressional power in many contexts. For example, federal tax lien and collection laws; record-keeping, reporting, and filing requirements; and civil and criminal penalties for non-payment are not themselves exertions of Congress's power to tax, but are laws "necessary and proper for carrying into Execution" the federal taxing power. That is why "provisions extraneous to any tax need" are not rendered valid simply by inclusion in a tax statute. *United States v. Kahriger* (1953); see also *Linder v. United States* (1925). Similarly, with regard to federal condemnation of property, "the really important question to be determined" is whether "it is necessary or appropriate to use the land in the execution of any of the powers granted to it by the constitution." *United States v. Gettysburg Electric Railway Co.* (1896). Finally, some scholars believe that the Necessary and Proper Clause is the source of federal spending authority, though modern doctrine locates that power in the Article I, Section 1 Taxation Clause (while other scholars locate it in the Article IV, Section 3 (Territories and Property Clauses).

Perhaps the best-known use of the clause is to regulate matters that do not constitute commerce among the states (or with foreign nations or the Indian tribes) in order to effectuate exercises of Congress's power under the Commerce Clause. The Necessary and Proper Clause's enhancement of Congress's power over commerce among the states had been judicially recognized decades before Congress began to exercise that power extensively. See *Gilman v. Philadelphia* (1866). Its means-to-end logic underlay the Supreme Court's approval of antitrust prosecutions for local monopolies when the government could prove a purpose to restrain interstate trade, *Addyston Pipe & Steel v. United States* (1899), but not when the government omitted to prove such a purpose, *United States v. E.C. Knight Co.* (1895). The same rationale sustained an amendment to the Safety Appliance Act, which prescribed safety equipment for railcars used only within a state, because the amendment increased safety for interstate cars and cargos on the same rails. *Southern Railway v. United States* (1911). Likewise, the Interstate Commerce Commission could authorize carriers to disregard state limits on rates for trips within a state, as a means to eliminate price discrimination against interstate commerce. *Shreveport Rate Case* (1914). Upholding the wage and hour

provisions of the Fair Labor Standards Act on this ground in *United States v. Darby* (1941), the Court cited not only those older cases but also *NLRB v. Jones & Laughlin Steel Corp.* (1937) as illustrating the rationale of the Necessary and Proper Clause.

The Necessary and Proper Clause does not confer *general* authority over a matter simply because its regulation in some respects might serve an enumerated-power end; it only supports the *particular* regulations that have such an effect. For example, what mattered in *Jones & Laughlin* was not that steel manufacturing impacts interstate commerce, but rather that applying the particular National Labor Relations Act provisions prohibiting those factories' unfair labor practices would promote Congress's policy of uninterrupted interstate commerce in steel. Similarly, in *Heart of Atlanta Motel v. United States* (1964), Title II of the 1964 Civil Rights Act was held applicable, not because hotels affect interstate commerce, but because prohibiting racial discrimination by hotels promotes Congress's interstate commerce policy of unimpeded travel.

Often the Supreme Court has not articulated the Necessary and Proper Clause basis of its so-called "affecting commerce doctrine," but has instead written as though matters affecting commerce could be reached directly under the commerce power. This omission led to one of the most confused areas of all constitutional law. Justice Sandra Day O'Connor, however, did emphasize it: first in her dissent in *Garcia v. San Antonio Metropolitan Transit Authority* (1985), and then for the majority in *New York v. United States* (1992). Justice Scalia specifically articulated the role of the Necessary and Proper Clause in his concurring opinion in *Gonzalez v. Raich* (2005).

Gary Lawson and David Engdahl

See Also

Suggestions for Further Research

Randy E. Barnett, *Necessary and Proper*, 44 UCLA L. Rev. 745 (1997)

J. Randy Beck, *The New Jurisprudence of the Necessary and Proper Clause*, 2002 U. Ill. L. Rev. 581 (2002)

David E. Engdahl, *The Necessary and Proper Clause as an Intrinsic Restraint on Federal Lawmaking Power*, 22 Harv. J.L. & Pub. Pol'y 107 (1998)

David E. Engdahl, *Sense and Nonsense About State Immunity*, 2 Const. Comment. 93 (1985)

Stephen A. Gardbaum, *Rethinking Constitutional Federalism*, 74 Tex. L. Rev. 795 (1996)

Gary Lawson & Patricia B. Granger, *The "Proper" Scope of Federal Power: A Jurisdictional Interpretation of the Sweeping Clause*, 43 Duke L.J. 267 (1993)

Gary Lawson & David B. Kopel, *Bad News for Professor Koppelman: The Incidental Unconstitutionality of the Individual Mandate*, 121 Yale L.J. Online 267 (2011)

Gary Lawson, Geoffrey P. Miller, Robert G. Natelson, and Guy I. Seidman, The Origins of the Necessary and Proper Clause (2010)

Robert G. Natelson, *The Agency Law Origins of the Necessary and Proper Clause*, 55 Case W. Res. L. Rev 243 (2004)

Significant Cases

McCulloch v. Maryland, 17 U.S. (4 Wheat.) 316 (1819)

Gilman v. Philadelphia, 70 U.S. (3 Wall.) 713 (1865)

The Legal Tender Cases, 79 U.S. (12 Wall.) 457 (1871)

United States v. E.C. Knight Co., 156 U.S. 1 (1895)

United States v. Gettysburg Electric Ry. Co., 160 U.S. 668 (1896)

Addyston Pipe & Steel Co. v. United States, 175 U.S. 211 (1899)

Southern Ry. v. United States, 222 U.S. 20 (1911)

Shreveport Rate Case, 234 U.S. 342 (1914)

Linder v. United States, 268 U.S. 5 (1925)

NLRB v. Jones & Laughlin Steel Corp., 301 U.S. 1 (1937)

United States v. Darby, 312 U.S. 100 (1941)

United States v. Kahriger, 345 U.S. 22 (1953)

Heart of Atlanta Motel v. United States, 379 U.S. 241 (1964)

Garcia v. San Antonio Metropolitan Transit Auth., 469 U.S. 528 (1985)

New York v. United States, 505 U.S. 144 (1992)

Printz v. United States, 521 U.S. 898 (1997)

Alden v. Maine, 527 U.S. 706 (1999)

Sabri v. United States, 541 U.S. 600 (2004)

Gonzales v. Raich, 545 U.S. 1 (2005)

United States v. Comstock, 560 U.S. 126 (2010)

National Federation of Independent Business v. Sebelius, 132 S. Ct. 2566 (2012)

Migration or Importation Clause

The Migration or Importation of such Persons as any of the States now existing shall think proper to admit, shall not be prohibited by the Congress prior to the Year one thousand eight hundred and eight, but a Tax or duty may be imposed on such Importation, not exceeding ten dollars for each Person.

(**Article I, Section 9, Clause 1**)

      ~

*W*hile the first debate over slavery at the Constitutional Convention concerned representation (see Article I, Section 2, Clause 3), the second debate arose when Southern delegates objected that an unrestricted congressional power to regulate commerce could be used against Southern commercial interests to restrict or outlaw the slave trade. That the resulting provision was an important compromise is underscored by the fact that the clause stands as the first independent restraint on congressional powers, prior even to the restriction on the power to suspend the writ of habeas corpus.

Taking Southern concerns into consideration, the draft proposed by the Committee of Detail (chaired by John Rutledge of South Carolina) dealt with trade issues as well as those relating to slavery. The draft permanently forbade Congress to tax exports, to outlaw or tax the slave trade, or to pass navigation laws without two-thirds majorities in both houses of Congress. Several delegates strongly objected to the proposal, including Gouverneur Morris, who delivered one of the Convention's most spirited denunciations of slavery, calling it a "nefarious institution" and "the curse of heaven."

When the issue came up for a vote, the Southern delegates themselves were sharply divided. George Mason of Virginia condemned the "infernal traffic," and Luther Martin of Maryland saw the restriction on Congress's power over the slave trade as "inconsistent with the principles of the Revolution and dishonorable to the American character." But delegates from Georgia and South Carolina announced that they would not support the Constitution without the restriction, with Charles Pinckney arguing that failing to include the clause would trigger "an exclusion of South Carolina from the Union."

This same divide had also occurred in debating the Declaration of Independence. Though that document proclaimed the central principle of the Revolution that all men are created equal, a draft clause specifically condemning the slave trade was dropped based on Southern objections.

At the Constitutional Convention, the serious split caused by Southern insistence was referred to the Committee of Eleven (chaired by William Livingston of New Jersey), which took the opposite position from Rutledge and recognized a congressional power over the slave trade, but recommended that it be restricted for twelve years, though allowing a tax on slave importation. Although that was a significant change from the Committee of Detail's original proposal, Southern delegates accepted the new arrangement but with the extension of the time period to twenty years, from 1800 to 1808.

Agitation against the slave trade was the leading cause espoused by the antislavery movement at the time of the Constitutional Convention, so it is not surprising that this clause was the most immediately controversial of the so-called slave clauses of the proposed Constitution (see also Article I, Section 2, Clause 3; Article IV, Section 2, Clause 3; and Article V). Although some denounced the Migration or Importation Clause as a major concession to slavery interests, most begrudged it to be a necessary and prudent compromise. Roger Sherman of Connecticut stated "better to let the southern states import slaves than to part with those states." James Madison argued at the Convention that the twenty-year exemption was "dishonorable," but in *The Federalist* No. 42, he declared that it was "a great

point gained in favor of humanity that a period of twenty years may terminate forever, within these States" what he called an "unnatural traffic" that was "the barbarism of modern policy."

In the North Carolina ratifying convention, James Iredell (later Supreme Court Justice) explained the reasons for the clause.

> For my part, were it practicable to put an end to the importation of slaves immediately, it would give me the greatest pleasure; for it certainly is a trade utterly inconsistent with the rights of humanity, and under which great cruelties have been exercised. When the entire abolition of slavery takes place, it will be an event which must be pleasing to every generous mind, and every friend of human nature; but we often wish for things which are not attainable. It was the wish of a great majority of the Convention to put an end to the trade immediately; but the states of South Carolina and Georgia would not agree to it.

Even so, John Jay, later the first Chief Justice of the United States, thought that the clause had a limited geographical application, restricting Congress's authority over the slave trade to the *then existing* states, but not to new states that might be admitted after ratification but prior to 1808.

Meanwhile, the states were left free to deal with the slavery question on their own. A number of states before 1800 did abolish slavery or provide for gradual emancipation. New Jersey, Rhode Island, and Connecticut had already abolished the slave trade; and New York and Delaware did likewise after the Constitution went into effect. Virginia declared that those slaves brought illegally into the state were free.

Although Southern delegates at the Constitutional Convention had hoped opposition to the slave trade would weaken with time, the practical effect of the clause was to create a growing expectation of federal legislation against the practice. The Slave Trade Act of 1794 prohibited any citizen or resident of the United States from carrying on any trade or traffic in slaves from the United States to any foreign country. Legislation in 1800 likewise prohibited engaging in such trade or traffic from one foreign country or place to another. Congress passed, and President Thomas Jefferson signed into law, a federal prohibition of the importation of slaves to the United States, effective January 1, 1808, the first day that Article I, Section 9, Clause 1 allowed such a law to go into effect.

Some observers at the time claimed that the Commerce Clause gave Congress the power to regulate both the interstate and the foreign slave trade once the twenty-year period had lapsed. James Wilson of Pennsylvania optimistically argued, "yet the lapse of a few years, and Congress will have power to exterminate slavery from within our borders." Madison denied this interpretation during the First Congress. In *Groves v. Slaughter* (1841), the Supreme Court avoided the question whether slaves were articles of commerce for purposes of the Commerce Clause. Yet Abraham Lincoln did not claim that congressional power to regulate commerce could be used to restrict interstate commerce in slaves.

After 1808, the clause still had an effect on Supreme Court opinions. In *Smith v. Turner* (1849), Justice John McKinley opined (as James Iredell earlier declared in the North Carolina ratifying convention) that "migration" and "importation" referred to immigrants and slaves as distinct classes of people, and the clause therefore buttressed Congress's exclusive power over immigration after the year 1808.

In *Dred Scott v. Sandford* (1857), Chief Justice Roger B. Taney pointed to this clause, along with the Fugitive Slave Clause (Article IV, Section 2, Clause 3), as evidence that persons of African descent were not ever intended to be accorded citizenship. Nevertheless, observers are virtually unanimous that those clauses did not address the question of citizenship at all. Although protection of the slave trade was a major concession demanded by proslavery delegates, the final clause was not a permanent element of the constitutional structure, but a temporary restriction of a delegated federal power. Moreover the restriction applied only to states existing at the time, not to new states or territories, and it did not prevent states from restricting or outlawing the slave trade for themselves. As the dissent in *Dred Scott* points out, there were free blacks who were citizens in a number of Northern states and who had voted to ratify the new constitution.

It is significant that the words slave and slavery are not used in the Constitution of 1787, and that the Framers used the word person rather than property. This would assure, as Madison explained in *The Federalist* No. 54, that a slave would be regarded "as a moral person, not as a mere article of property." It was in the context of the slave trade debate at the Constitutional Convention that Madison argued that it was "wrong to admit in the Constitution the idea that there could be property in men."

Matthew Spalding

See Also

Article I, Section 2, Clause 3 (Three-fifths Clause)

Article I, Section 8, Clause 3 (Commerce with Foreign Nations)

Article I, Section 8, Clause 3 (Commerce Among the States)

Article IV, Section 2, Clause 3 (Fugitive Slave Clause)

Article V (Prohibition on Amendment: Slave Trade)

Suggestions for Further Research

RICHARD BEEMAN, PLAIN HONEST MEN: THE MAKING OF THE AMERICAN CONSTITUTION (2009)

Walter Berns, *The Constitution and the Migration of Slaves*, 78 Yale L.J. 198 (1968)

David P. Currie, *The Constitution in the Supreme Court: Contracts and Commerce, 1836–1864*, 1983 Duke L. J. 471 (1983)

DON E. FEHRENBACHER, THE SLAVEHOLDING REPUBLIC: AN ACCOUNT OF THE UNITED STATES GOVERNMENT'S RELATIONS TO SLAVERY (2001)

Michael Daly Hawkins, *John Quincy Adams and the Antebellum Maritime Slave Trade: The Politics of Slavery and the Slavery of Politics*, 25 Okla. City U. L. Rev. 1 (2000)

DONALD L. ROBINSON, SLAVERY IN THE STRUCTURE OF AMERICAN POLITICS, 1765–1820 (1971)

Ronald D. Rotunda & John E. Nowak, *Joseph Story: A Man for All Seasons*, in 1990 Yearbook of the Supreme Court Historical Society (1990)

David O. Stewart, The Summer of 1787: The Men Who Invented the Constitution (2008)

Herbert J. Storing, *Slavery and the Moral Foundations of the American Republic*, *in* The Moral Foundations of the American Republic 313 (Robert H. Horwitz ed., 1986)

Significant Cases

Groves v. Slaughter, 40 U.S. (15 Pet.) 449 (1841)

The Amistad, 40 U.S. (15 Pet.) 518 (1841)

Prigg v. Pennsylvania, 41 U.S. (16 Pet.) 539 (1842)

Jones v. Van Zandt, 46 U.S. (5 How.) 215 (1847)

Smith v. Turner, 48 U.S. 283 (1849)

Moore v. People of the State of Illinois, 55 U.S. (14 How.) 13 (1852)

Dred Scott v. Sandford, 60 U.S. (19 How.) 393 (1857)

Ableman v. Booth, 62 U.S. (21 How.) 506 (1859)

Osborn v. Nicholson, 80 U.S. (13 Wall.) 654 (1871)

Suspension of Habeas Corpus

The Privilege of the Writ of Habeas Corpus shall not be suspended, unless when in Cases of Rebellion or Invasion the public Safety may require it.

(Article I, Section 9, Clause 2)

~

*T*he Magna Carta (1215) established that no one could be "imprisoned or dispossessed, or outlawed, or banished, or in any way destroyed...except by the legal judgment of his peers or by the law of the land." But the Magna Carta provided no mechanism of enforcement. Ultimately, the writ of habeas corpus (the "Great Writ") came to be the means by which a court orders a person holding a prisoner to produce the legal grounds for the prisoner's detention. Habeas corpus (or *habeas corpus ad subjiciendum*)—translated "[We command] you shall have the body [of the detained person] delivered [to court]" for examination—was originally part of the early English kings' efforts to consolidate power. The King's courts issued the writ to non-royal authorities to release to the courts persons whom the King wished protected. Eventually, the King's courts evolved into the common law courts, and they entertained the writ against the King himself or against his officials. Parliament codified the writ's protections in The Habeas Corpus Act of 1679.

A century later, Sir William Blackstone could describe habeas corpus as "the great and efficacious writ." *Commentaries on the Laws of England* (1765–1769). In treating of it extensively, Blackstone summarized, "[T]he glory of the English law consists in clearly defining the times, the causes, and the extent, when, wherefore, and to what degree, the imprisonment of the subject may be lawful." Although the Crown successfully limited the reach of habeas corpus to some of the empire's colonies, it was not able to prevent its use in the American colonies prior to the Revolution. In 1774, the First Continental Congress featured it in its *Appeal to the Inhabitants of Quebec* as one of the "grand" rights available to Englishmen. It was available in common law in all thirteen colonies, and after independence, a number of states incorporated the right into their constitutions.

At the Constitutional Convention, the delegates simply assumed that habeas corpus was a preexisting and continuing right. Some delegates, such as John Rutledge, opposed any allowance in the Constitution for suspending the writ. But, in the end, there was agreement that in circumstances of war or invasion, it should be possible to suspend the writ, at least temporarily.

Yet for all that, the drafters failed to delineate in the text which part of the government possessed the legal power to suspend the writ. The original motion stated that the writ "shall not be suspended by the Legislature except upon the most urgent and pressing occasions." After some debate, the Convention approved the wording in the present passive form, omitting where the power lay, and placing the clause alongside others dealing with the judiciary.

In the Committee of Style, however, Gouverneur Morris may have resolved the ambiguity. In organizing the text along separation of powers lines, Morris shifted the clause from among those dealing with the courts to Article I, focused on Congress. It is true that Morris did not rewrite the clause to be an affirmative grant of power to

Congress, such as those listed in Article I, Section 8. But it may have been that the clause's wording as protective of a *right* could not readily or appropriately be translated into a *power*.

Nonetheless, the textual ambiguity remained, prompting President Abraham Lincoln's famous suspension of the writ during the Civil War and his refusal to obey Chief Justice Roger B. Taney's ruling, on circuit, that only Congress possessed the power to suspend. *Ex parte Merryman* (1861). Lincoln temporarily mooted the issue by ordering the release of militarily held civilian prisoners in late 1862, but the controversy that Lincoln's action engendered was not fully resolved until Congress passed the Habeas Corpus Suspension Act in 1863. A century and a half later, in *Hamdi v. Rumsfeld* (2004), the Supreme Court confirmed that only Congress possesses the constitutional power to suspend the writ.

Other perplexing questions remained, however. Did Congress need to codify the right and its procedures, as had Parliament in 1679, in positive law? To this, Chief Justice John Marshall seemed to give an unequivocal "yes" in *Ex parte Bollman* (1807). "[F]or the meaning of the term 'habeas corpus,'" he wrote, "resort may unquestionably be had to the common law; but the power to award the writ by any of the courts of the United States must be given by written law." He noted the moral obligation that must have moved the First Congress to provide for habeas corpus relief for persons held in federal custody: "they must have felt, with peculiar force, the obligation of providing efficient means by which this great constitutional privilege should receive life and activity; for if the means be not in existence, the privilege itself would be lost, although no law for its suspension should be enacted." A number of recent commentators have contested Marshall's position. They conclude that the Framers of the Constitution regarded habeas corpus as an implicit judicial power, which the courts could exercise in relation to persons held by either federal or state courts without need of congressional authorization. Under that interpretation, Congress could provide the forms for habeas relief through its use of the Necessary and Proper Clause (Article I, Section 8, Clause 18), or it could, under its Article I powers, employ its limited capacity to sus-

pend. Recently, Justice Clarence Thomas opined that habeas corpus was indeed a constitutional right, one that was a "privilege or immunity" of national citizenship and protected against state infringement by the Fourteenth Amendment. *McDonald v. City of Chicago* (2010)

Nonetheless, since 1789, Congress has continued to regulate the availability of habeas corpus through statute. In 1867, for example, to alleviate the problem of former slaves being arrested and jailed in the South, Congress expanded habeas protection to persons "restrained . . . in violation of the constitution, or any treaty or law of the United States," in the Habeus Corpus Act. In 1868, Congress amended the act to prevent the Supreme Court from hearing appeals from lower court decisions under the 1867 Act. In *Ex parte McCardle* (1869), the Court approved the validity of the Congress's removal of Supreme Court appellate jurisdiction.

The modern Supreme Court, however, has moved to limit Congress's discretion in removing habeas corpus jurisdiction from the federal courts. In *INS v. St. Cyr* (2001), Justice John Paul Stevens for a narrow majority of the Court declared: 1) that if Congress wishes to repeal a previous grant of habeas jurisdiction, it must do so clearly and unambiguously; 2) that habeas corpus was an available, i.e., pre-existing, remedy against unlawful executive action at the time the Constitution went into effect; and 3) that therefore, Congress may limit available recourse to habeas corpus only when there is an "adequate" procedure available to contest the legality of executive action. Otherwise, Congress, by going too far, could run afoul of the Suspension Clause. Justice Stevens also doubted whether Chief Justice Marshall in *Bollman* really intended to affirm that the only route to habeas relief was through congressional authorization. If that were true, Stevens observed, Congress could by inaction effect a permanent suspension of the writ when the Constitution allowed for only a temporary suspension during an emergency.

During the Warren Court era, the availability of habeas relief enlarged. Much of the growth occurred through the incorporation of many of the procedural protections of the Bill of Rights into the Fourteenth Amendment, which made them applicable to the states. In addition, the Court expanded the definition of "custody" to include more than arrest, allowed for successive habeas petitions in the same case, and permitted habeas actions even when defendants had failed to raise timely objections in the court below. The cascading amount of habeas petitions allowed by the courts soon engendered a reaction from the Supreme Court.

Beginning in the 1970s, the Supreme Court changed course and began to narrow the ready use of habeas actions. In *Stone v. Powell* (1976), the Court held that a habeas petition was not appropriate when the petitioner had the opportunity to adjudicate his substantive claim in the court below. In *Wainwright v. Sykes* (1977), the Court deferred to the state's "contemporaneous objection rule" to bar a habeas petition when the petitioner did not follow the state's requirements for lodging objections during a trial. The result is that federal courts are no longer hearing habeas claims as before, and most are lodged at the state level.

Congress also tried to narrow the opportunities for habeas petitions. After the World Trade Center bombing of 1993 and the Oklahoma City bombing of 1995, Congress passed the Antiterrorism and Effective Death Penalty Act of 1996, which prohibited prisoners held under state law from seeking habeas relief in federal court unless the state court's decision was contrary to clearly established federal law or was based on an "unreasonable determination of the facts." Further, the law prohibited successive habeas petitions by the same defendant and required all claims to be consolidated into one appeal. The Ninth Circuit agreed with other circuits that found that the Antiterrorism and Effective Death Penalty Act is not a violation of the Suspension of Habeus Corpus Clause as it "simply modifies the preconditions for habeas relief, and does not remove all habeas jurisdiction." *Crater v. Galaza* (9th Cir. 2007).

Congress and the Court came into collision following the attacks of September 11, 2001. In *Hamdi*, the Supreme Court heard a habeas petition and ruled that a detained United States citizen needed to be afforded the opportunity to contest the grounds of his detention. In response, Congress passed the Detainee Treatment Act of

2005, removing habeas jurisdiction from all federal courts regarding detained aliens, and vesting any appeal from the decisions of military tribunals in the U.S. Court of Appeals for the District of Columbia. But in *Hamdan v. Rumsfeld* (2006), the Court ruled that the Detainee Treatment Act did not apply to a pending case, and went on to accept the habeas petition and rule that the military tribunals established by executive action were unconstitutional. Congress reacted by passing the Military Commissions Act of 2006, establishing military commissions and explicitly removing the possibility of habeas corpus relief for alien detainees as stated in the Detainee Treatment Act of 2005.

In *Boumediene v. Bush* (2008), the Supreme Court squarely ruled that removal of habeas jurisdiction from federal courts was valid only if there were adequate and effective substitutes for protecting a defendant's procedural rights. Because those substitutes were lacking, the Court held that Congress had violated the Suspension of Habeas Corpus Clause. However, the federal circuit courts have decided many cases subsequently and based upon a finding that where Congress has provided an adequate and effective substitute for habeas review, the consistent rulings were that there was no violation of the Suspension Clause.

Federalism concerns have also influenced the interpretation of the Suspension Clause. In *Bollman,* Chief Justice Marshall drew a clear line between federal habeas authority and state courts. Some delegates at the Constitutional Convention had presumed that state courts could issue writs for prisoners under federal authority, and that therefore Congress could, in appropriate circumstances, suspend writs in state courts. That presumption was plausible, because the state courts were already in the business of hearing habeas petitions, and there was no guarantee that Congress would set up a federal court system anyway. (*See* Inferior Courts, Article I, Section 8, Clause 9; and Article III, Section 1). In fact, some state courts early on did exercise such authority over federal prisoners. But Justice Marshall rejected any such state authority. In *Bollman,* he held that the Suspension of Habeas Corpus Clause applied only to persons held under federal control. The

Supreme Court has consistently confirmed Marshall's interpretation. In 1859, for example, the Court unanimously rejected in *Ableman v. Booth* the authority of the Wisconsin courts to issue a writ for the release of an abolitionist who had been arrested for violating the federal Fugitive Slave Act. In 1953, the Court reaffirmed the authority of the federal courts over state courts in *Brown v. Allen*, albeit with its convoluted and much criticized opinions.

David F. Forte

See Also

Article I, Section 8, Clause 9 (Inferior Courts)
Article I, Section 8, Clause 18 (Necessary and Proper Clause)
Article VI, Clause 2 (Supremacy Clause)

Suggestions for Further Research

Paul M. Bator, *Finality in Criminal Law and Federal Habeas Corpus for State Prisoners*, 76 HARV. L. REV. 441 (1963)
WILLIAM F. DUKER, A CONSTITUTIONAL HISTORY OF HABEAS CORPUS (1980)
Richard H. Fallon Jr., *The Supreme Court, Habeas Corpus, and the War on Terror: As Essay on Law and Political Science*, 110 COLUM. L. REV. 352 (2010)
CARY FEDERMAN, THE BODY AND THE STATE: HABEAS CORPUS AND AMERICAN JURISPRUDENCE (2006)
ERIC M. FREEDMAN, HABEAS CORPUS: RETHINKING THE GREAT WRIT OF LIBERTY (2001)
ANTHONY GREGORY, THE POWER OF HABEAS CORPUS IN AMERICA: FROM THE KING'S PREROGATIVE TO THE WAR ON TERROR (2013)
PAUL D. HALLIDAY, HABEAS CORPUS: FROM ENGLAND TO EMPIRE (2010)
Lee B. Kovarsky, *A Constitutional Theory of Habeas Power*, 99 Va. L. Rev. 753 (2013)
A Native of Virginia, *Observations upon the Proposed Plan of Federal Government*, reprinted in 9 DOCUMENTARY HISTORY OF THE RATIFICATION OF THE CONSTITUTION 655 (John P. Kaminski & Gaspare J. Saldino, eds., 1984)
Saikrishna Bangalore Prakash, *The Great Suspender's Unconstitutional Suspension of the Great Writ*, 3 ALB. GOV'T L. REV. 575 (2010)

Martin H. Redish & Colleen McNamara, *Habeas Corpus, Due Process and the Suspension Clause: A Study in the Foundations of American Constitutionalism*, 96 VA. L. REV. 1361 (2010)
Ronald D. Rotunda, *The Detainee Cases of 2004 and 2006 and Their Aftermath*, 57 SYRACUSE L. REV. 1 (2006)
Stephen J. Vladeck, *The Suspension Clause as a Structural Right*, 62 U. MIAMI L. REV. 275 (2008)

Significant Cases

Ex parte Bollman, 8 U.S. (4 Cranch) 75 (1807)
Ableman v. Booth, 62 U.S. (21 How.) 506 (1859)
Ex parte Merryman, 17 F. Cas. 144 (C.C. Md. 1861) (No. 9487)
Ex parte McCardle, 74 U.S. (7 Wall.) 506 (1869)
Brown v. Allen, 344 U.S. 443 (1953)
Fay v. Noia, 372 U.S. 391 (1963)
Sanders v. United States, 373 U.S. 1 (1963)
Townsend v. Sain, 372 U.S. 293 (1963)
Stone v. Powell, 428 U.S. 465 (1976)
Wainwright v. Sykes, 433 U.S. 72 (1977)
INS v. Enrico St. Cyr, 533 U.S. 289 (2001)
Hamdi v. Rumsfeld, 542 U.S. 507 (2004)
Hamdan v. Rumsfeld, 548 U.S. 557 (2006)
Crater v. Galaza, 491 F.3d 1119 (9th Cir. 2007)
Munaf v. Geren, 553 U.S. 674 (2008)
Boumediene v. Bush, 553 U.S. 723 (2008)
Muka v. Baker, 559 F.3d 480 (6th Cir. 2009)
McDonald v. City of Chicago, 130 S. Ct. 3020 (2010)
Al Maqaleh v. Gates, 605 F.3d 84 (D.C. Cir. 2010)
Luna v. Holder, 637 F.3d 85 (2d Cir. 2011)

Bill of Attainder

No Bill of Attainder . . . shall be passed.
(ARTICLE I, SECTION 9, CLAUSE 3)

*T*he Constitution prohibits both the federal government (in this clause) and the states (in Article I, Section 10, Clause 1) from passing either bills of attainder or ex post facto laws. The Framers considered freedom from bills of attainder and ex post facto laws so important that these are the only two individual liberties that the original Constitution protects from both federal and state intrusion. In Philadelphia, the Constitutional Convention approved both provisions without debate. As James Madison said in *The Federalist* No. 44, "Bills of attainder, *ex post facto* laws, and laws impairing the obligation of contracts are contrary to the first principles of the social compact and to every principle of sound legislation."

In common law, bills of attainder were legislative acts that, without trial, condemned specifically designated persons or groups to death. Bills of attainder also required the "corruption of blood"; that is, they denied to the condemned's heirs the right to inherit his estate. Bills of pains and penalties, in contrast, singled out designated persons or groups for punishment less than death, such as banishment or disenfranchisement. Many states had enacted both kinds of statutes after the Revolution.

The Framers forbade bills of attainder as part of their strategy of undoing the English law of treason, and to contend with what they regarded as the most serious historical instances of legislative tyranny by state or national legislatures. Raoul Berger argues that the bill of attainder clauses protect only against legislative actions that affect the life of the individual, not his property, which was the province of bills of pains and penalties. Beginning with Chief Justice John Marshall, however, the Supreme Court has insisted that "a Bill of Attainder may affect the life of an individual, or may confiscate his property, or may do both," *Fletcher v. Peck* (1810), and that "[t]he term 'bill of attainder' in the National Constitution is generical, and embraces bills of both classes," *Drehman v. Stifle* (1869).

Marshall and his successors saw the Bill of Attainder Clause as an element of the separation of powers. As the decisions of the Court in *Marbury v. Madison* (1803) and *United States v. Klein* (1871) made clear, only a court can hold a trial, evaluate the evidence, and determine the merits of the claim or accusation. The Constitution forbade Congress from "exercis[ing] the power and office of judge." *Cummings v. Missouri* (1867). In *United States v. Brown* (1965), the Court specifically rejected a "narrow historical approach" to the clauses and characterized the Framers' pur-

pose as to prohibit "legislative punishment, of any form or severity, of specifically designated persons or groups." In *Ex parte Garland* (1867), for example, the Supreme Court struck down under the Attainder Clause a congressional statute directed against former Confederates that barred persons from practicing law before United States courts who had, among other things, merely given "encouragement" to rebels.

Bills of attainder can also operate conditionally, that is, the punishment may not only be for past acts, but it also may be triggered whenever the person engages in any future prohibited acts. Test oaths can be a type of attainder, and exclusion from employment can be a form of punishment. A Missouri test oath required one to affirm, among other things, that one had never indicated "disaffection to the government of the United States in its contest with the Rebellion." Those who failed to take the oath were prohibited from practicing the otherwise lawful occupation of clergyman. The Court found to oath to be a bill of attainder. *Cummings v. Missouri* (1867). In other instances, however, the Court has found a test oath "merely provides standards of qualification and eligibility for employment." *Garner v. Board of Public Works of City of Los Angeles* (1951).

After World War II, the Supreme Court dealt with laws limiting the activities of members of the Communist Party. The Court struck as violative of the Bill of Attainder Clause an appropriation act that barred payment of salaries to certain named individuals who were thought to be subversive. *United States v. Lovett* (1946). In *Communist Party of the United States v. Subversive Activities Control Board* (1961), a divided Court upheld the application of the Subversive Activities Control Act of 1950, which required the Communist Party and its officers to register with the Attorney General. The Court stated that the law did not restrict a class of individuals. Rather, it only regulated "designated activities." But in *United States v. Brown*, the Court invalidated a law that prohibited Communist Party members from serving as leaders of labor organizations.

Nonetheless, even with an expansive definition, the Bill of Attainder Clause provides only limited protection against retroactive civil legislation. The modern Court rarely invokes the clause's protection; it has not invalidated legislation on bill-of-attainder grounds since *Brown* in 1965. Moreover, the only laws that the Court has invalidated as bills of attainder have been bars on the employment of specific individuals or groups of individuals.

The Court has devised a three-part test to determine when a piece of legislation violates the Bill of Attainder Clause: (1) such legislation specifies the affected persons (even if not done in terms within the statute), (2) includes punishment, and (3) lacks a judicial trial. Because of the Court's relatively narrow definition of punishment, however, it rarely, if ever, invalidates legislation on this basis. For example, the Court has held that the denial of noncontractual government benefits such as financial aid was not punishment, *Selective Service System v. Minnesota Public Interest Research Group* (1984), nor did an act requisitioning the recordings and material of President Richard M. Nixon and several of his aides constitute punishment. *Nixon v. Administrator of General Services* (1977).

Daniel Troy

See Also

Article I, Section 9, Clause 3 (Ex Post Facto)
Article I, Section 10, Clause 1 (State Bill of Attainder and State Ex Post Facto)

Suggestions for Further Research

Raoul Berger, *Bills of Attainder: A Study of Amendment by the Court*, 63 Cornell L. Rev. 355 (1978)
Andrew Kim, *Falling from the Legislative Grace: The ACORN Defunding and the Proposed Restraint of Congress' Appropriations Power through the Bill of Attainder Clause*, 60 Am. U. L. Rev. 643 (2011)
Daniel E. Troy, Retroactive Legislation (1998)

Significant Cases

Marbury v. Madison, 5 U.S. (1 Cranch) 137 (1803)
Fletcher v. Peck, 10 U.S. (6 Cranch) 87 (1810)
Ex parte Garland 71 U.S. (4 Wall.) 333 (1867)
Cummings v. Missouri, 71 U.S. (4 Wall.) 277 (1867)
Drehman v. Stifle, 75 U.S. 595 (1869)

United States v. Klein, 80 U.S. (13 Wall.) 128 (1871)
United States v. Lovett, 328 U.S. 303 (1946)
Garner v. Bd. of Public Works of City of Los Angeles, 341 U.S. 716 (1951)
Communist Party of the United States v. Subversive Activities Control Bd., 367 U.S. 1 (1961)
United States v. Brown, 381 U.S. 437 (1965)
Nixon v. Administrator of General Services, 433 U.S. 425 (1977)
Selective Service System v. Minnesota Public Interest Research Group, 468 U.S. 841 (1984)

Ex Post Facto

No . . . ex post facto Law shall be passed.
(**Article I, Section 9, Clause 3**)

~

*A*s generally understood, a law that is ex post facto—literally, after the fact—is one that criminally punishes conduct that was lawful when it was done. It is an aspect of the fundamental maxim, *nulla poena sine lege*: there can be no punishment without law—in this case, without preexisting law. The presumption against retroactive legislation "embodies a legal doctrine centuries older than our Republic." *Landgraf v. USI Film Products* (1994). Despite the fact that the prohibition against such laws had worked its way into English law—as celebrated by Sir William Blackstone in his *Commentaries on the Laws of England* (1765–1769)—Parliament had, nonetheless, claimed the right to enact certain kinds of ex post facto laws in the form of bills of attainder against unpopular groups and persons. In addition, prior to the Constitutional Convention, some states themselves had passed ex post facto laws. (The prohibition of state ex post facto state laws is found in Article I, Section 10, Clause 1.)

Nevertheless, opposition to ex post facto laws was a bedrock principle among the Framers. In *The Federalist* No. 84, Alexander Hamilton noted that "the subjecting of men to punishment for things which, when they were done, were breaches of no law" is among "the favorite and most formidable instruments of tyranny." Thomas Jefferson noted in an 1813 letter to Isaac McPherson "the sentiment that ex post facto laws are against natural right."

In Philadelphia, the Framers debated the issue vigorously. Some thought an explicit ban on ex post facto laws an absolute necessity. Others, such as Oliver Ellsworth of Connecticut, echoed the natural law tradition and "contended that there was no lawyer, no civilian who would not say that ex post facto laws were void of themselves. It cannot then be necessary to prohibit them." James Wilson declared that the prohibition against ex post facto laws in the state constitutions had been ineffective and would be likewise "useless" in the national constitution. Hugh Williamson then pointed to North Carolina's prohibition of ex post facto laws. He acknowledged that the prohibition had been violated, but argued that "it has done good there & may do good here, because the Judges can take hold of it." The delegates then approved the clause, seven states to three.

Later, James Dickinson reported that, on examining Blackstone's *Commentaries on the Laws of England*, he found that "the terms 'ex post facto' related to criminal cases only; that they would not consequently restrain the states from retrospective laws in civil cases and that some further provision for this purpose would be requisite." After the Committee of Style had reported the ex post facto law clauses in their current form, George Mason of Virginia moved to strike the prohibition against ex post facto laws because the clause might apply to civil laws "and no Legislature ever did or can altogether avoid them in Civil cases." Elbridge Gerry seconded the motion because he wanted a clearer statement that the prohibition did in fact apply to "Civil cases." Mason's motion was unanimously rejected.

The Court addressed the issue of the scope of the clause in one of its earliest constitutional decisions. *Calder v. Bull*, decided in 1798, involved a determination by the Connecticut legislature that a judicial decree should be set aside and a new trial held regarding a contested will. Without dissent, the Court held that the Connecticut legislature's action was not an ex post facto law forbidden

under Article I, Section 10, Clause 1. Justice Samuel Chase defined ex post facto laws as:

> 1st. Every law that makes an action done before the passing of the law, and which was innocent when done, criminal; and punishes such action. 2d. Every law that aggravates a crime, or makes it greater than it was, when committed. 3d. Every law that changes the punishment, and inflicts a greater punishment, than the law annexed to the crime, when committed. 4th. Every law that alters the legal rules of evidence, and receives less, or different, testimony, than the law required at the time of the commission of the offence, in order to convict the offender. All these, and similar laws, are manifestly unjust and oppressive.

Chase also made the point that, had the ex post facto law clauses barred all retroactive civil laws, the prohibition on the impairment of contracts by states (Article I, Section 10, Clause1) and on uncompensated takings by the federal government (Amendment V) would have been unnecessary.

Although some believe that the question of the scope of the Ex Post Facto Clause had not been squarely presented in *Calder v. Bull*, the Supreme Court adopted and upheld Justice Chase's position in *Carpenter v. Pennsylvania* (1855). A few commentators and two Justices, William Johnson in *Satterlee v. Matthewson* (1829) and Clarence Thomas in *Eastern Enterprises v. Apfel* (1998), have voiced doubt over the accepted rule that the Ex Post Facto Clause applies only to criminal legislation. In *Apfel*, citing Justice Joseph Story, Thomas contended that the Ex Post Facto Clause, even more clearly than the Takings Clause, reflects the principle that retrospective laws are "generally unjust." He continued:

> Since *Calder v. Bull*…this Court has considered the Ex Post Facto Clause to apply only in the criminal context. I have never been convinced of the

soundness of this limitation, which in *Calder* was principally justified because a contrary interpretation would render the Takings Clause unnecessary.... In an appropriate case, therefore, I would be willing to reconsider *Calder* and its progeny to determine whether a retroactive civil law that passes muster under our current Takings Clause jurisprudence is nonetheless unconstitutional under the Ex Post Facto Clause.

The weight of precedent and scholarly opinion, however, supports Justice Chase's view. Nonetheless, the Court will not apply retroactive civil laws unless there is a clear congressional intent. *Landgraf v. USI Film Products.*

While the Supreme Court has hewn to the position that the Ex Post Facto Clause prohibits criminal penalties only, it still will apply the clause in civil cases where criminal penalties are disguised as civil disabilities. As the Court has said, "it is the effect, not the form, of the law that determines whether it is ex post facto." *Weaver v. Graham* (1981).

When undertaking this inquiry, courts assess whether the ostensibly civil fine or penalty is penal in nature. As Justice Felix Frankfurter articulated the inquiry in *De Veau v. Braisted* (1960):

> The mark of an ex post facto law is the imposition of what can fairly be designated punishment for past acts. The question in each case where unpleasant consequences are brought to bear upon an individual for prior conduct, is whether the legislative aim was to punish that individual for past activity, or whether the restriction of the individual comes about as a relevant incident to a regulation of a present situation, such as the proper qualifications for a profession.

The issue of what constitutes "punishment" involves other clauses of the Constitution as well. For example, recent interpretations of the Double Jeopardy Clause of the Fifth Amendment may have implications for the Ex Post Facto Clause. In *United States v. Halper* (1989), the Supreme Court said that if "civil proceedings ... advance punitive as well as remedial goals," they do not constitute punishment that is prohibited under the Double Jeopardy Clause. In *United States v. Ursery* (1996), the Court found that confiscating the home of an individual convicted for growing marijuana was a "civil remedial sanction" rather than a civil penalty. On the other hand, the Court has found that an imposed forfeiture constitutes a punitive sanction under the Eighth Amendment's excessive fines clause. *United States v. Bajakajian* (1998).

More recently, in *Smith v. Doe* (2003), the Court (by a 6–3 decision) rejected the claim that Alaska's sex offender registration and notification law constituted retroactive punishment forbidden by the Ex Post Facto Clause (of the analogue Article I, Section 10, Clause 1). The Court focused on the legislature's "intention" and applied the following analytical framework:

> If the intention of the legislature was to impose punishment, that ends the inquiry. If, however, the intention was to enact a regulatory scheme that is civil and nonpunitive, we must further examine whether the statutory scheme is "so punitive either in purpose or effect as to negate [the State's] intention to deem it 'civil.'" Because we ordinarily defer to the legislature's stated intent, only the clearest proof will suffice to override legislative intent and transform what has been denominated a civil remedy into a criminal penalty.

A possible problem with the Court's current interpretation of the Ex Post Facto Clause is the fact that many criminal laws could be rephrased as civil. As currently understood, the Ex Post Facto Clause thus guards against only the most severe use of the legislature's power to make laws retroactive. They do so effectively where personal liberty is at issue. But the clause is of little use to those who are aggrieved by most forms of retroactive civil legislation, which frequently affect property rights of one form or another.

The clause applies only to criminal statutes, not judicial decisions having a retroactive effect. Retroactive judicial decisions, however, can be challenged under the Due Process Clause. See *Rogers v. Tennessee* (2001). Retroactive procedural statutes that work to deny a defense, bar the practice of law, increase punishment, or increase the likelihood of conviction may violate the Ex Post Facto Clause. See *Cummings v. Missouri*; *Ex parte Garland* (1867); *Carmell v. Texas* (2000). In *Stogner v. California* (2003), the Court struck down a California law that revived prosecutions for sexual abuse of children after the statute of limitations had expired.

A statutory increase in punishment is also an impermissible ex post facto law, *Collins v. Youngblood* (1990), but not a statute that decreases punishment. *Dorsey v. United States* (2012). The clause prohibits canceling early-release credits after they have been awarded, *Lynce v. Mathis* (1997); but not a retroactive decrease in the availability of parole hearings, *California Department of Corrections v. Morales* (1995); nor a change in the place of trial, *Cook v. United States* (1891); nor deportation, *Mahler v. Eby* (1924). The Court found no increase in punishment in a change of method of execution from hanging to electrocution, *Malloy v. South Carolina* (1915); or in imposing civil commitment on a sexual predator after sentence, *Kansas v. Hendricks* (1997). There is much scholarly criticism of the Court's position on post-sentence civil commitment or registration of sex offenders.

The clause prohibits applying new mandatory sentencing guidelines to a defendant who committed the crime prior to their promulgation, *Miller v. Florida* (1987), although since the Court made those guidelines advisory in *United States v. Booker* (2005), there is a split among the federal circuit courts as to whether the now advisory guidelines implicate the Ex Post Facto Clause.

Daniel Troy

See Also

Article I, Section 9, Clause 3 (Bill of Attainder)
Article I, Section 10, Clause 1 (State Bill of Attainder and State Ex Post Facto)
Amendment V (Double Jeopardy Clause; Due Process Clause; Takings Clause)
Amendment VIII (Excessive Fines)
Amendment XIV, Section 1 (Due Process Clause)

Suggestions for Further Research

Wayne A. Logan, *"Democratic Despotism" and Constitutional Constraint: An Empirical Analysis of Ex Post Facto Claims in State Courts*, 12 WM. & MARY BILL RTS. J. 439 (2004)

Wayne A. Logan, *The Ex Post Facto Clause and the Jurisprudence of Punishment*, 35 AM. CRIM. L. REV. 1261 (1998)

Robert G. Natelson, *Statutory Retroactivity: The Founders' View*, 39 IDAHO L. REV. 489 (2003)

R. Brian Tanner, *A Legislative Miracle: Revival Prosecutions and the Ex Post Facto Clauses*, 50 EMORY L.J. 397 (2001)

DANIEL E. TROY, RETROACTIVE LEGISLATION (1998)

Daniel E. Troy, Symposium: *When Does Retroactivity Cross the Line? Winstar, Eastern Enterprises and Beyond: Toward a Definition and Critique of Retroactivity*, 51 ALA. L. REV. 1329 (2000)

Significant Cases

Calder v. Bull, 3 U.S. (3 Dall.) 386 (1798)
Society for the Propagation of the Gospel v. Wheeler, 22 F. Cas. 756 (C.C.N.H. 1814)
Satterlee v. Mathewson, 27 U.S. (2 Pet.) 380 (1829)
Carpenter v. Pennsylvania, 58 U.S. (17 How.) 456 (1855)
Cummings v. Missouri, 71 U.S. (4 Wall.) 277 (1867)
Ex parte Garland, 71 U.S. (4 Wall.) 333 (1867)
Cook v. United States, 138 U.S. 157 (1891)
Johannessen v. United States, 225 U.S. 227 (1912)
Frank v. Magnum, 237 U.S. 309 (1915)
Malloy v. South Carolina, 237 U.S. 180 (1915)
Mahler v. Eby, 264 U.S. 32 (1924)
Lindsey v. State of Washington, 301 U.S. 397 (1937)
Harisiades v. Shaughnessy, 342 U.S. 580 (1952)
De Veau v. Braisted, 363 U.S. 144, 160 (1960)
Dobbert v. Florida, 432 U.S. 282 (1977)
Weaver v. Graham, 450 U.S. 24 (1981)
Miller v. Florida, 482 U.S. 423 (1987)
United States v. Halper, 490 U.S. 435 (1989)

Collins v. Youngblood, 497 U.S. 37 (1990)

Landgraf v. USI Film Products, 511 U.S. 244 (1994)

California Department of Corrections v. Morales, 514 U.S. 499 (1995)

United States v. Ursery, 518 U.S. 267 (1996)

Kansas v. Hendricks, 521 U.S. 346 (1997)

Lynce v. Mathis, 519 U.S. 433 (1997)

Eastern Enterprises v. Apfel, 524 U.S. 498 (1998)

United States v. Bajakajian, 524 U.S. 321 (1998)

Carmell v. Texas, 529 U.S. 513 (2000)

Rogers v. Tennessee, 532 U.S. 451 (2001)

Smith v. Doe, 538 U.S. 84 (2003)

Stogner v. California, 539 U.S. 607 (2003)

United States v. Booker, 543 U.S. 220 (2005)

Vartelas v. Holder, 132 S.Ct.1486 (2012)

Dorsey v. United States, 132 S. Ct. 2321 (2012)

Direct Taxes

No Capitation, or other direct, Tax shall be laid, unless in Proportion to the Census or enumeration herein before directed to be taken.
(**ARTICLE I, SECTION 9, CLAUSE 4**)

∼

*T*he Constitution was intended to give the national government greater power to raise revenue—the Articles of Confederation had been a fiscal disaster—but many Framers remained fearful of taxation. Indirect taxes (generally understood as falling on articles of consumption) did not lend themselves to congressional abuse (for reasons that will be described presently), but the Framers believed that "direct taxes" needed to be cabined. The cumbersome apportionment rule, requiring that a direct tax be apportioned among the states on the basis of population (so that, for example, a state with twice the population of another state would have to pay twice the tax, even if the more populous state's share of the national tax base were smaller), made the more dangerous taxes politically difficult for Congress to impose.

The effectiveness of apportionment as a limitation on congressional power obviously depends on the levies to which it applies, and students of the Founding disagree on this point. At one extreme, some scholars, citing Rufus King's unanswered question at the Constitutional Convention ("Mr King asked what was the precise meaning of direct taxation? No one answd."), have argued that "direct taxes" had no agreed-upon meaning, or, much the same thing, that the Framers did not think through what they were doing. They created an apportionment scheme so unworkable that a cramped definition of "direct taxes" became necessary to prevent the collapse of the system.

Those views overstate the extent of the confusion in 1787. No interpretation of "direct taxes" can be consistent with all statements made at the time, but the Founding debates are full of references to two forms of taxation for which apportionment was clearly intended: capitation taxes (specifically denominated as direct in the Constitution) and taxes on land (generally including slaves as well). Although intended to be difficult, apportionment was not impossible. Between 1798 and 1861, Congress enacted several real-estate taxes, all with complex schemes for apportionment.

Does "direct taxes" include anything beyond capitation and taxes on property? The conventional wisdom is that it does not, based on dicta in *Hylton v. United States* (1796), which held that a tax on carriages was an excise rather than a direct tax. Justice William Paterson, for example, thought the provision was designed to allay Southern fears of a federal tax on their lands and slaves—nothing more. Because the Federalist justices were themselves among the Framers, these dicta are often accepted as evidence of original understanding. Not all significant Framers thought the concept of "direct taxes" was so limited—James Madison voted against the carriage tax in Congress because he thought it needed to be apportioned—but, based on the *Hylton* dicta, the Supreme Court in the nineteenth century upheld unapportioned federal taxes on insurance company receipts, *Pacific Insurance Co. v. Soule* (1869); on notes of state-chartered banks, *Veazie Bank v. Fenno* (1869); on inheritances of real estate, *Scholey v. Rew* (1875); and on the Civil War income tax, *Springer v. United States* (1881).

What looked to be a revolutionary change occurred in 1895, when, in *Pollock v. Farmers' Loan & Trust Co.* (1895), a divided Court accepted a broader conception of "direct taxes" and concluded that an unapportioned 1894 income tax—which largely reached income from property—was invalid. In rejecting the notion that nothing but a capitation or land tax could be direct, the Court stressed that a limitation on congressional power ought not to be interpreted in a way that destroys the limitation. Although the Court after *Pollock* continued to approve a large number of unapportioned federal taxes, calling them "excises," *Pollock* unquestionably hampered the government's ability to raise revenue. In 1913, the Sixteenth Amendment was ratified, exempting "taxes on incomes" from apportionment.

Over the years, until 2012 (see below), Supreme Court authority had provided little further guidance on the meaning of "direct taxes." That was understandable because the Sixteenth Amendment made worrying about new sources of revenue less pressing for the federal government. Nonetheless, it seems that any direct tax other than an income tax should still be subject to the apportionment rule today. At a minimum, that would include capitation and land taxes. (In 1934, the Supreme Court emphasized, in dictum, that a tax on the value of real estate would be direct. *Helvering v. Independent Life Insurance Co.* (1934).)

Furthermore, after *Pollock*, a broader interpretation of "direct taxes" was certainly possible. In fact, a broad interpretation of "direct taxes" can reconcile the clear original understanding that capitation and land taxes were direct with the equally clear intention that apportionment should have bite. The Constitution divided governmental levies into two mutually exclusive categories: indirect taxes subject to the uniformity requirement, and direct taxes subject to apportionment. Indirect taxes, which the Framers assumed would fund the national government in ordinary circumstances, were "Duties, Imposts, and Excises"—generally taxes on articles of consumption. These taxes were considered safe because, regardless of who collected them, the burden was thought to be shifted to consumers.

If Congress became greedy and raised rates too high, fewer taxed goods would be purchased and revenue would decrease. It was because taxes on articles of consumption "contain in their own nature a security against excess," wrote Alexander Hamilton in *The Federalist* No. 21, that further constitutional protection against congressional overreaching was unnecessary.

Direct taxes, which were expected to be used only in emergencies, did not have the built-in protections characteristic of indirect taxes. Direct taxes were imposed directly on individuals, who, it was assumed, could not shift the tax burden away from themselves. If a tax was not indirect, the Framers thought it should be apportioned. Capitation and land taxes (the eighteenth century form of a wealth tax) were direct under this understanding, but so might other taxes be, whether known in 1787 or not.

Recent scholarship has provided another reason to think that the phrase "direct taxes" has a much broader meaning than is generally understood today. James Campbell has demonstrated that the term "capitation" was understood in the late eighteenth century to encompass much more than a lump-sum head tax; it would, for example, have included an income tax.

With the exception of *Pollock*, however, the Supreme Court has not blessed an expansive conception of what constitutes a direct tax. For one brief moment in 2006, a panel of the U.S. Court of Appeals for the District of Columbia Circuit did just that. In *Murphy v. Internal Revenue Service*, the panel initially held that an unapportioned tax on a whistleblower's recovery, received because she was wrongly discharged from her governmental position and suffered emotional distress, was direct and was not exempted from apportionment by the Sixteenth Amendment. Facing criticism, however, the panel vacated that decision, reheard the case, and in 2007 made a 180-degree turn. As a matter of first principle, the panel seemed sympathetic to the notion of direct taxes outlined above, but it could find no support for that understanding in Supreme Court cases.

There continues to be no Supreme Court support for a broader conception of direct taxes. In 2012, in ruling on the constitutionality of the individual mandate in the Affordable Care Act (the requirement that individuals must purchase health insurance or pay a "penalty"), the Court held that the penalty provision was actually a tax. The opinion of Chief Justice John Roberts went further. It effectively held that the only "recognized" categories of direct taxes are capitations and taxes on the ownership of property, and that, as a result, the penalty for failure to acquire suitable health insurance, scheduled to come into effect in 2014, will not be a direct tax. *National Federation of Independent Business v. Sebelius* (2012). (To no avail, four dissenters complained that *NFIB* presented a case of first impression about the scope of direct taxes, and that that issue had been inadequately briefed and argued.) Moreover, writing for the majority, Chief Justice Roberts quoted Justice Samuel Chase's opinion in *Hylton* that "[c]apitations are taxes paid by every person 'without regard to property, profession, or *any other circumstance*'"—in effect, limiting capitations to lump-sum head taxes. With the Supreme Court's decision in *NFIB*, we are left with a narrow understanding of direct taxes, encompassing at most capitation taxes (itself narrowly construed) and taxes on property, even though the original understanding of direct taxes may have been far broader.

Erik M. Jensen

See Also

Article I, Section 2, Clause 3 (Allocation of Representatives)

Article I, Section 8, Clause 1 (Taxation; Spending Clause)

Article I, Section 8, Clause 1 (Uniformity Clause)

Amendment XVI (Income Tax)

Suggestions for Further Research

Bruce Ackerman, *Taxation and the Constitution*, 99 Colum. L. Rev. 1 (1999)

James Campbell, *Dispelling the Fog About Direct Taxation*, 1 Brit. J. Am. Legal Stud. 109 (2012)

Erik M. Jensen, *The Apportionment of "Direct Taxes": Are Consumption Taxes Constitutional?*, 97 Colum. L. Rev. 2334 (1997)

Erik M. Jensen, *Murphy v. Internal Revenue Service, the Meaning of "Income," and Sky-Is-Falling Tax Commentary*, 60 Case W. Res. L. Rev. 751 (2010)

Calvin H. Johnson, *Apportionment of Direct Taxes: The Foul-Up in the Core of the Constitution*, 7 Wm. & Mary Bill Rts. J. 1 (1998)

Significant Cases

Hylton v. United States, 3 U.S. (3 Dall.) 171 (1796)

Pacific Ins. Co. v. Soule, 74 U.S. (7 Wall.) 433 (1869)

Veazie Bank v. Fenno, 75 U.S. (8 Wall.) 533 (1869)

Scholey v. Rew, 90 U.S. (23 Wall.) 331 (1875)

Springer v. United States, 102 U.S. 586 (1881)

Pollock v. Farmers' Loan & Trust Co., 157 U.S. 429, *aff'd on reh'g,* 158 U.S. 601 (1895)

Helvering v. Independent Life Ins. Co., 292 U.S. 371 (1934)

Murphy v. Internal Revenue Service, 460 F.3d 79 (D.C. Cir. 2006), *vacated* (2006); *opinion on reh'g,* 493 F.3d 170 (D.C. Cir. 2007), *cert. denied,* 553 U.S. 1004 (2008)

National Federation of Independent Business v. Sebelius, 132 S. Ct. 2566 (2012)

Export Taxation Clause

No Tax or Duty shall be laid on Articles exported from any State.
(Article I, Section 9, Clause 5)

≈

*T*he Export Taxation Clause was one of the many accommodations that the Framers made to cement unity among the various sections of the union. Many of the Southern delegates at the Constitutional Convention regarded the clause as a prerequisite to gaining their approval of the Constitution. As the primary exporter of goods (particularly cotton) in the late eighteenth century, the South believed that it would have borne a disproportionate burden from export taxes. In addition to the disproportionate burden argument, George Mason voiced the South's fear that a tax on exports would create a mechanism through which the more numerous Northern states could overwhelm the Southern states' economies. They also worried that export taxes could be used indirectly to attack slavery (because slaves were then very important in harvesting cotton). The Southerners were joined by Northerners such as Oliver Ellsworth, who declared that export taxes would stifle industry.

In response, some of the most distinguished delegates at the Convention, including James Madison, Alexander Hamilton, George Washington, Gouverneur Morris, and James Wilson, favored export taxes. They argued variously that export taxes were a necessary source of revenue for the central government, that they were an important means for the federal government to regulate trade, and that the South's disproportionate need for naval protection justified its disproportionate share of export taxes. Attempts to limit the absolute prohibition on export taxes failed. James Madison's attempt to require a supermajority for passage of an export tax was barely defeated by a 6–5 vote. The absolute prohibition on export taxation then passed by a 7–4 vote. It provoked little discussion during the ratifying conventions.

Scholars point out that the Export Taxation Clause was part of a complex set of compromises related to the South's economic interest in slaves and in the products that slaves produced. They argue that inclusion of the clause was linked to the removal of a two-thirds voting requirement to pass a navigations act and the inclusion of a twenty-year limitation of Congress's power over the slave trade (Article V).

What the South did not realize until John C. Calhoun noted it in 1828 was that by taxing imports of goods that competed with Northern manufacture, Congress could increase the value of Northern goods relative to Southern ones, all without ever actually taxing exports. Calhoun stated, "To the growers of cotton, rice, and tobacco, it is the same, whether, the Government takes one-third of what they raise, for the liberty of sending the other two-thirds abroad, or one-third of the iron, salt, coffee, cloth, and other articles they may need in exchange, for the liberty of bringing them home."

Despite the position of Calhoun and the findings of contemporary economists that import duties are indirect export taxes, the federal courts have relied on a textual, not an economic, definition of the Export Taxation Clause. The Court will enforce the flat ban that the Framers placed into the Constitution's text, rather than seeking to measure an export tax's discriminatory effect.

Moreover, unlike its analysis of Commerce Clause cases, the Supreme Court has kept distinct what is intended for export and what remains available for local trade. Although a product may ultimately be intended for export, the Export Taxation Clause does not prohibit federal taxation of goods and services or of imports before they enter the course of exportation. *Nufarm America's Inc. v. United States* (2008). But the prohibition does extend to services and activities directly related to the export process. Thus, the Court has invalidated taxes on bills of lading, ship charters, and marine insurance; but it has upheld federal assessments on pre-export goods and services, such as an excise tax on manufactured tobacco, a tax on the manufacturing of cheese intended for export, and a corporate income tax on exporters. Congress does retain the power to regulate exports under the Commerce Clause, even to the extent of creating embargoes, but it may not utilize export taxes as a means of regulation.

Although the Export Taxation Clause was integral to the judicial evaluation of numerous levies between 1876 and 1923, the clause did not make its way back onto the Court's docket until 1996. After over seven decades of obscurity, the Court utilized the Export Taxation Clause twice between 1996 and 1998 to strike down federal tax statutes. In *United States v. IBM Corp.* (1996), the Court relied on the Export Taxation Clause to strike down a nondiscriminatory federal excise tax on insurance premiums paid to foreign insurers, but which were, in this case, paid for the purpose of insuring goods against loss during exportation. The Court also expressly rejected the government's arguments that the dormant Commerce Clause and Import-Export Clause jurisprudence altered or governed the interpretation of the Export Taxation Clause. In *United States v. United States Shoe Corp.* (1998), a unanimous Court relied on the Export Taxation Clause to strike down, to the extent it applied to exports, the Harbor Maintenance Tax. The tax was an excise imposed on any "port use." The Court rejected the government's contention that the charge was a valid user fee rather than a tax.

Congress may not tax exports, but under the Commerce Clause, it constitutionally may impose an *embargo* on goods for export, even though—in an economic sense—an embargo is functionally equivalent to an unlimited export tax.

In sum, cases interpreting the Export Taxation Clause have made clear that the clause "strictly prohibits any tax or duty, discriminatory or not, that falls on exports during the course of exportation," and that the protection extends to "services and activities closely related to the export process." *United States v. IBM Corp.* However, Congress may modify procedural remedies available for claims based on a violation of the Export Taxation Clause. So, for example, the Court recently held that Congress may place time limitations on export clause claims. *See United States v. Clintwood Elkhorn Min. Co.*, 553 U.S. 1 (2008).

David F. Forte

See Also
Article I, Section 8, Clause 3 (Commerce with Foreign Nations)

Article I, Section 8, Clause 3 (Commerce Among the States)

Article I, Section 10, Clause 2 (Import-Export Clause)

Suggestions for Further Research
Ben Baack et al., *Constitutional Agreement During the Drafting of the Constitution: A New Interpretation*, 38 J. Legal Stud. 533 (2009)

Erik M. Jensen, *The Export Clause*, 6 Fla. Tax. Rev. 1 (2003)

1 Ronald D. Rotunda & John E. Nowak, Treatise on Constitutional Law: Substance and Procedure §1.1(q)(v) (5th ed. 2012)

Significant Cases
Turpin v. Burgess, 117 U.S. 504 (1886)

Fairbank v. United States, 181 U.S. 283 (1901)

Cornell v. Coyne, 192 U.S. 418 (1904)

Thames & Mersey Marine Ins. Co. v. United States, 237 U.S. 19 (1915)

United States v. Hvoslef, 237 U.S. 1 (1915)

William E. Peck & Co. v. Lowe, 247 U.S. 165 (1918)

National Paper & Type Co. v. Bowers, 266 U.S. 373 (1924)

Mulford v. Smith, 307 U.S. 38 (1939)

United States v. IBM Corp., 517 U.S. 843 (1996)

United States v. United States Shoe Corp., 523 U.S. 360 (1998)

Nufarm America's Inc. v. United States, 521 F.3d 1366 (Fed Cir. 2008)

Consolidation Coal Co. v. United States, 528 F.3d 1344 (Fed. Cir. 2008)

United States v. Clintwood Elkhorn Mining Co., 553 U.S. 1 (2008)

Port Preference Clause

No Preference shall be given by any Regulation of Commerce or Revenue to the Ports of one State over those of another; nor shall Vessels bound to, or from, one State, be obliged to enter, clear, or pay Duties in another.

(**Article I, Section 9, Clause 6**)

~

*L*ike the Uniformity Clause, with which it was initially joined at the Constitutional Convention, and the Export Taxation Clause, the Port Preference Clause was meant to interfere with the natural tendency of legislatures to become instruments through which powerful commercial interests injure their politically weaker rivals.

The impetus for the Port Preference Clause came from the Maryland delegation, whose members were especially worried that vessels bound to or from the port of Baltimore might be required to stop in Virginia. Some other delegates objected that Congress should not have its hands tied, lest it be unable to deal adequately with problems such as smuggling on long rivers like the Delaware. The issue was referred to a committee, which included a delegate from each state, and which recommended language nearly identical to the final version now in the Constitution.

This was not sufficient for Maryland's Luther Martin, who became a leading Anti-Federalist. He objected that Congress might easily violate the spirit of the provision, perhaps by limiting Maryland to one inappropriate port of entry on the Potomac: this would effectively require Baltimore shipping to stop in Virginia.

The language of the Port Preference Clause sweeps beyond the specific concerns that motivated its proponents at the Convention. The Supreme Court, however, has construed the Port Preference Clause very narrowly, holding that Congress may grant enormous "incidental" preferences to the ports of certain states through devices such as making improvements (like dredging) or creating obstructions (like bridges) in one place rather than another. *Pennsylvania v. Wheeling & Belmont Bridge Co.* (1856) ("*Wheeling Bridge II*"); *South Carolina v. Georgia* (1876). The Court has indicated that the clause would be violated by naked discrimination between all the ports of one state and those of another. *Wheeling Bridge II.* But even this prohibition is essentially toothless: it has been read to allow Congress to impose a tax that affected all the ports of some states and no ports in some others. *Augusta Towing Co., Inc. v. United States* (1984).

A dissent in the seminal Supreme Court case complained that the majority's interpretation rendered the clause a dead letter. *Wheeling Bridge II* (McLean, J., dissenting). More recently, Justice Clarence Thomas suggested in a concurrence that a natural reading of the constitutional language "prohibits Congress from using its commerce power to channel commerce through certain favored ports." *United States v. Lopez* (1995) (Thomas, J., concurring). As the case law stands, however, Congress is only on its honor to comply with the spirit of the clause by refraining from politically motivated favoritism that distorts the natural economic competition among American ports.

Nelson Lund

See Also

Article I, Section 8, Clause 1 (Uniformity Clause)

Article I, Section 8, Clause 3 (Commerce Among the States)

Article I, Section 9, Clause 5 (Export Taxation Clause)

Suggestion for Further Research

3 The Founders' Constitution 370–73 (Philip B. Kurland & Ralph Lerner eds., 1987)

Significant Cases

Pennsylvania v. Wheeling & Belmont Bridge Co., 59 U.S. (18 How.) 421 (1856)

South Carolina v. Georgia, 93 U.S. 4 (1876)

Augusta Towing Co., Inc. v. United States, 5 Cl. Ct. 160 (1984)

United States v. Lopez, 514 U.S. 549 (1995) (Thomas, J., concurring)

Appropriations Clause

No Money shall be drawn from the Treasury, but in Consequence of Appropriations made by Law; and a regular Statement and Account of the Receipts and Expenditures of all public Money shall be published from time to time.

(**Article I, Section 9, Clause 7**)

$\sim$

*T*he Appropriations Clause is the cornerstone of Congress's "power of the purse." It assigns to Congress the role of final arbiter of the use of public funds. The source of Congress's power to spend derives from the Necessary and Proper Clause (Article I, Section 8, Clause 18) or, as some modern commentators aver, from Article I, Section 8, Clause 1 (Taxation and Spending Clauses), or possibly as an implication from the Appropriations Clause itself. The Appropriations Clause provides Congress with a mechanism to control or to limit spending by the federal government. The Framers chose the particular language of limitation, not authorization, for the first part of the clause and placed it in Section 9 of Article I, along with other restrictions on governmental actions to limit, most notably, executive action.

The Virginia Plan offered at the opening of the Constitutional Convention did not contain an appropriations clause, although the plan did refer, albeit indirectly, to Congress's authority under the Articles of Confederation to appropriate public funds. The Appropriations Clause first appeared at the Convention as part of a proposed division of authority between the House of Representatives and the Senate. A part of that proposal declared that all bills raising or appropriating money—"money bills"—were to originate in the House, and were not subject to alteration or amendment in the Senate. Further, no money could be drawn from the "public Treasury, but in pursuance of appropriations that shall originate in the House of Representatives." The Convention rejected both the provision vesting exclusive control of money bills in the House of Representatives (resolved in Article I, Section 7, Clause 2) and the associated appropriations clause. Late in the Convention, the Committee of Eleven, appointed to consider unresolved parts of the Constitution, offered a compromise to permit the Senate to amend or concur in amendments of money bills, provided that "no Money shall be drawn from the Treasury, but in Consequence of Appropriations made by Law." The Convention incorporated the proposal, resulting, with only minor changes made by the Committee of Style and Arrangement, in the final language of the first part of the Appropriations Clause.

In *The Federalist* No. 58, James Madison described the centrality of the power of the purse's role in the growth of representative government and its particular importance in the Constitution's governmental structure:

> The House of Representatives cannot only refuse, but they alone can propose the supplies requisite for the support of government. They, in a word, hold the purse—that powerful instrument by which we behold, in the history of the British Constitution, an infant and humble representation of the people gradually enlarging the sphere of its activity and importance, and finally reducing, as far as it seems to have wished,

all the overgrown prerogatives of the other branches of the government. This power over the purse may, in fact, be regarded as the most complete and effectual weapon with which any constitution can arm the immediate representatives of the people, for obtaining a redress of every grievance, and for carrying into effect every just and salutary measure.

Under the Articles of Confederation, under which Congress possessed the power to appropriate, there was no independent executive authority. With the creation of an executive under the Constitution, the Founders decided, in the words of Justice Joseph Story in *Commentaries on the Constitution of the United States* (1883), "to preserve in full vigour the constitutional barrier between each department...that each should possess equally...the means of self-protection." An important means of self-protection for the legislative department was its ability to restrict the executive's access to public resources "but in Consequence of Appropriations made by Law." Justice Story continues:

> And the [legislature] has, and must have, a controlling influence over the executive power, since it holds at its own command all the resources by which a chief magistrate could make himself formidable. It possesses the power over the purse of the nation and the property of the people. It can grant or withhold supplies; it can levy, or withdraw taxes; it can unnerve the power of the sword by striking down the arm which wields it.

The second part of the clause, the "Statement and Account" provision, resulted from an amendment offered by George Mason of Virginia in the final days of the Convention. Mason proposed that "an Account of the public expenditures should be annually published." Questions concerning the wisdom and practicality of this proposal led to the adoption of an amendment, offered by James Madison, to substitute the less-demanding "from time to time" for "annually." This "would enjoin the duty of frequent publications," Madison argued, "and leave enough to the discretion of the legislature." The requirement for a "Statement and Account," said Justice Story, makes Congress's responsibility as guardian of the public treasure "complete and perfect" by requiring an account of receipts and expenditures "that the people may know, what money is expended, for what purposes, and by what authority." Today, the "discretion of the legislature" is a "plenary power to exact any reporting and accounting [the Congress] considers appropriate in the public interest." *United States v. Richardson* (1974).

The courts have consistently recognized the primacy given to Congress by the Appropriations Clause in allocating the resources of the Treasury. As the Supreme Court declared in *Cincinnati Soap Co. v. United States* (1937), the Appropriations Clause "was intended as a restriction upon the disbursing authority of the Executive department." It means simply that "no money can be paid out of the Treasury unless it has been appropriated by an act of Congress." In *United States v. MacCollom* (1976), the Court articulated an "established rule" that "the expenditure of public funds is proper only when authorized by Congress, not that public funds may be expended unless prohibited by Congress."

The power reserved to Congress by the Appropriations Clause is, as Madison described it, "the most complete and effectual weapon," because, as one court determined, "any exercise of a power granted by the Constitution to one of the other Branches of Government is limited by a valid reservation of congressional control over funds in the Treasury." *Office of Personnel Management v. Richmond* (1990). *See also Knote v. United States* (1877). For example, because public funds may only be paid out of the Treasury "according to the letter of the difficult judgments reached by Congress," private litigants may not use equitable principles of estoppel to require the payment of benefits for which there is no appropriation. *Office of Pers. Mgmt. v. Richmond.* Similarly, a court may no more order the obli-

gation or a payment of funds for which there is no appropriation, *Reeside v. Walker* (1850), than it may make or order an appropriation. *Rochester Pure Water District v. United States Environmental Protection Agency* (1992); *National Ass'n of Regional Councils v. Costle* (1977). A possible exception may be the Consumer Financial Protection Bureau established by Congress in 2011. It is a regulatory agency that receives its funding from the Federal Reserve, which is itself self-funded and outside of the appropriations oversight of Congress, though Congress could change its manner of funding by revising the underlying law.

Congress has broad authority to give meaning to the Appropriations Clause. As a technical matter, Congress regularly enacts statutes, specifically styled as appropriations acts, of varying types, durations, and effect. To satisfy the Appropriations Clause, however, Congress need do no more than enact a law expressly directing a payment out of a designated fund or source in the Treasury. As the Court of Claims explained, an appropriation is "per se nothing more than the legislative authorization prescribed by the Constitution that money may be paid out at the Treasury." *Campagna v. United States* (1891).

Congress also may, and does, adjust, suspend, or repeal various provisions of law through appropriations acts. *United States v. Dickerson* (1940); *Robertson v. Seattle Audubon Society* (1992); *United States v. Bean* (2002). The Supreme Court has insisted, however, that Congress must clearly articulate its purposes when it uses the appropriations process to adjust, suspend, or repeal other provisions of law. *United States v. Will* (1980). Nevertheless, Congress has "wide discretion in . . . prescribing details of expenditures," *Cincinnati Soap Co. v. United States* (1937), and indeed has a long and consistent practice of setting conditions on the expenditure of appropriations. One particularly noteworthy example was the Boland Amendments of the 1980s, which limited the use of appropriated funds by any agency or entity of the United States involved in intelligence activities to support the Nicaraguan insurgency against the Sandinista regime.

There are limits to the length to which Congress may go in its exercise of the appropriations power. Congress's power, in this respect, like all of its other powers, is subject to the Bill of Rights and other structural constraints in the Constitution. Congress may not, for example, in the guise of appropriating, subject named individuals to bills of attainder explicitly prohibited by the Constitution. *United States v. Lovett* (1946). It may not preclude or direct an act in derogation of an individual's First Amendment rights. *Legal Service Corp. v. Velazquez* (2001). Similarly, just as a presidential pardon may not effect payment of a claim out of the Treasury barred by act of Congress, *Hart v. United States* (1886), or permit the recovery of the proceeds of confiscated property deposited in the Treasury, *Knote v. United States,* Congress cannot, through a rider in an appropriations act, impair the express and enumerated power of the President to grant pardons. *United States v. Klein* (1871).

Gary Kepplinger

See Also

Article I, Section 7, Clause 1 (Origination Clause)
Article I, Section 8, Clause 1 (Taxation; Spending Clause)
Article I, Section 8, Clause 12 (Army Clause)
Article I, Section 8, Clause 18 (Necessary and Proper Clause)

Suggestions for Further Research

2 Office of General Counsel, U.S. Gov't Accountability Office, GAO-06-382SP, Principles of Federal Appropriations Law (3d ed. 2004)
J. Gregory Sidak, *The President's Power of the Purse*, 1989 Duke L.J. 1162 (1989)
Kate Stith, *Congress' Power of the Purse*, 97 Yale L.J. 1343 (1988)
Charles Tiefer, Congressional Practice and Procedure (1989)

Significant Cases

Reeside v. Walker, 52 U.S. (11 How.) 272 (1850)
United States v. Klein, 80 U.S. (13 Wall.) 128 (1871)
Knote v. United States, 95 U.S. 149 (1877)
Hart v. United States, 118 U.S. 62, 67 (1886)
Campagna v. United States, 26 Ct. Cl. 316, 317 (1891)
Cincinnati Soap Co. v. United States, 301 U.S. 308 (1937)

United States v. Dickerson, 310 U.S. 554 (1940)
United States v. Lovett, 328 U.S. 303 (1946)
United States v. Richardson, 418 U.S. 166 (1974)
United States v. MacCollom, 426 U.S. 317 (1976)
National Ass'n of Regional Councils v. Costle, 564 F.2d 583 (D.C. Cir. 1977)
United States v. Will, 449 U.S. 200 (1980)
Office of Personnel Management v. Richmond, 496 U.S. 414 (1990)
Robertson v. Seattle Audubon Society, 503 U.S. 429 (1992)
Rochester Pure Water District v. United States Environmental Protection Agency, 960 F.2d 180 (D.C. Cir. 1992)
Legal Service Corp. v. Velazquez, 531 U.S. 533 (2001)
United States v. Bean, 537 U.S. 71 (2002)

Emoluments Clause

No Title of Nobility shall be granted by the United States: And no Person holding any Office of Profit or Trust under them, shall, without the Consent of the Congress, accept of any present, Emolument, Office, or Title, of any kind whatever, from any King, Prince, or foreign State.

(Article I, Section 9, Clause 8)

$\sim$

*A*rticle VI of the Articles of Confederation was the source of the Constitution's prohibition on federal titles of nobility and the so-called Emoluments Clause. The clause sought to shield the republican character of the United States against corrupting foreign influences.

The prohibition on federal titles of nobility—reinforced by the corresponding prohibition on state titles of nobility in Article I, Section 10 and more generally by the republican Guarantee Clause in Article IV, Section 4—was designed to underpin as well the republican character of the American government. In the ample sense James Madison gave the term in *The Federalist* No. 39, a "republic" was "a government which derives all its powers directly or indirectly from the great body of the people, and is administered by persons holding their offices during pleasure for a limited period, or during good behavior."

Republicanism so understood was the ground of the constitutional edifice. The prohibition on titles of nobility buttressed the structure by precluding the possibility of an aristocracy, whether hereditary or personal, whose members would inevitably assert a right to occupy the leading positions in the state.

Further, the prohibition on titles complemented the prohibition in Article III, Section 3, on the "Corruption of Blood" worked by "Attainder[s] of Treason" (i.e., the prohibition on creating a disability in the posterity of an attained person upon claiming an inheritance as his heir, or as heir to his ancestor). Together these prohibitions ruled out the creation of certain caste-specific legal privileges or disabilities arising solely from the accident of birth.

In addition to upholding republicanism in a political sense, the prohibition on titles also pointed to a durable American social ideal. This is the ideal of equality; it is what David Ramsay, the eighteenth-century historian of the American Revolution, called the "life and soul" of republicanism. The particular conception of equality denied a place in American life for hereditary distinctions of caste—slavery being the most glaring exception. At the same time, however, it also allowed free play for the "diversity in the faculties of men," the protection of which, as Madison insisted in *The Federalist* No. 10, was "the first object of government." The republican system established by the Founders, in other words, envisaged a society in which distinctions flowed from the unequal uses that its members made of equal opportunities: a society led by a natural aristocracy based on talent, virtue, and accomplishment, not by an hereditary aristocracy based on birth. "Capacity, Spirit and Zeal in the Cause," as John Adams said, would "supply the Place of Fortune, Family, and every other Consideration, which used to have Weight with Mankind." Or as the Jeffersonian St. George Tucker put it in 1803: "A Franklin, or a Washington, need not the pageantry of honours, the glare of titles, nor the pre-eminence of station to distinguish them...."

Equality of rights...precludes not that distinction which superiority in virtue introduces among the citizens of a republic."

Similarly, the Framers intended the Emoluments Clause to protect the republican character of American political institutions. "One of the weak sides of republics, among their numerous advantages, is that they afford too easy an inlet to foreign corruption," Alexander Hamilton wrote in *The Federalist* No. 22. And in *The Federalist* No. 84, he stated, "This may truly be denominated the cornerstone of republican government; for so long as they are excluded there can never be serious danger that the government will be any other than that of the people."

The delegates at the Constitutional Convention specifically designed the clause as an antidote to potentially corrupting foreign practices of a kind that the Framers had observed during the period of the Confederation. Louis XVI had the custom of presenting expensive gifts to departing ministers who had signed treaties with France, including American diplomats. In 1780, the King gave Arthur Lee a portrait of the King set in diamonds above a gold snuff box; and in 1785, he gave Benjamin Franklin a similar miniature portrait, also set in diamonds. Likewise, the King of Spain presented John Jay (during negotiations with Spain) with the gift of a horse. All these gifts were reported to Congress, which in each case accorded permission to the recipients to accept them. Wary, however, of the possibility that such gestures might unduly influence American officials in their dealings with foreign states, the Framers institutionalized the practice of requiring the consent of Congress before one could accept "any present, Emolument, Office, or Title, of any kind whatever, from... [a] foreign State."

Like several other provisions of the Constitution, the Emoluments Clause also embodies the memory of the epochal constitutional struggles in seventeenth-century Britain between the forces of Parliament and the Stuart dynasty. St. George Tucker's explanation of the clause noted that "in the reign of Charles the [S]econd of England, that prince, and almost all his officers of state were either actual pensioners of the court of France, or supposed to be under its influence, directly, or indirectly, from that cause. The reign of that monarch has been, accordingly, proverbially disgraceful to his memory." As these remarks imply, the clause was directed not merely at American diplomats serving abroad, but more generally at officials throughout the federal government.

The Emoluments Clause has rarely been litigated. The D.C. Circuit Court in *U.S. ex rel. New v. Rumsfeld* (2006) dismissed a claim by a U.S. soldier who alleged that the required wearing of a United Nations' patch and cap violated the clause. The appeals court upheld the District Court's decision in 2004 that Congress had exercised its power of "Consent" under the clause by enacting the Foreign Gifts and Decorations Act, which authorizes federal employees to accept foreign governmental benefits of various kinds in specific circumstances.

The Emoluments Clause has been interpreted and enforced through a long series of opinions of the Attorneys General and by less-frequent opinions of the Comptrollers General. A recent debate has emerged regarding the applicability of the clause to the Nobel Peace Prize, which is awarded by a committee elected by the Storting (the Norwegian Parliament). Three sitting Presidents have been awarded the prize: Theodore Roosevelt, Woodrow Wilson, and Barack Obama. President Roosevelt waited until he left office to accept the prize and even then submitted the monetary prize to Congress for consent. However, after President Obama was awarded the Nobel Prize in 2009, the Office of Legal Counsel argued that the Emoluments Clause was not a bar to acceptance of the prize because it was not awarded by a "foreign state." The Office argued that the Nobel Committee had grown politically independent from the Parliament over time. Additionally, the Office contended that historically all federal officeholders awarded the prize received it without congressional consent. President Obama accepted the award in 2009 and donated the monetary prize to various charities without seeking congressional consent.

It is also argued that the Emoluments Clause is implicated when U.S. officials take teaching or speaking positions at foreign universities. During the Clinton Administration, the Office of Legal Counsel reasoned that the clause was not violated when two scientists at NASA were employed at a foreign public university but the university made employment decisions independent of the foreign government (citing a similar 1986 opinion by then Deputy Assistant Attorney General Samuel Alito).

The Emoluments Clause has also been applied to private citizens who serve on federal advisory committees. The Office of Legal Counsel wrote in 1993 that professors serving on the Administrative Conference of the United States could not accept any payment from a foreign government or university. The Office subsequently wrote opinions that retreated from this expansive view, arguing that many federal committee members do not occupy "Offices of Profit or Trust."

It is also questioned whether the clause applies to Members of Congress. In 2009, Senator Edward Kennedy received an honorary knighthood from Queen Elizabeth II, and although there is no indication that he sought consent from Congress, he received a standing ovation from lawmakers when the announcement of his award was made.

Robert Delahunty and David F. Forte

See Also

Suggestions for Further Research

Applicability of Emoluments Clause to Employment of Government Employees by Foreign Public Universities, 18 Op. O.L.C. 13 (1994)

Applicability of the Emoluments Clause to Non-Government Members of ACUS, 17 Op. O.L.C. 114 (1993)

Gifts from Foreign Prince, 24 Op. Att'y Gen. 116 (1902)

Memorandum for the Counsel to the President, from David Barron, Assistant Attorney General, Office of Legal Counsel of the Department of Justice, *Applicability of the Emoluments Clause and the Foreign Gifts and Decorations Act to the President's*

Receipt of the Nobel Peace Prize (Dec. 7, 2009), http://www.justice.gov/olc/2009/emoluments-nobel-peace.pdf

Gary J. Edles, *Service on Federal Advisory Committees: A Case Study of OLC's Little-Known Emoluments Clause Jurisprudence*, 58 Admin. L. Rev. 1 (2006)

President Reagan's Ability to Receive Retirement Benefits from the State of California, 5 Op. O.L.C. 187 (1981)

2 Ronald D. Rotunda & John E. Nowak, Treatise on Constitutional Law: Substance and Procedure §9.18 (5th ed. 2012)

Zephyr Teachout, *Gifts, Offices, and Corruption*, 107 Nw. U. L. Rev. Colloquy 30 (2012)

Eugene Volokh, *Does Senator Kennedy Need Congressional Permission for His Knighthood?*, The Volokh Conspiracy (Blog) (Mar. 4, 2009 1:07 PM), at http://www.volokh.com/2009/03/04/does-senator-kennedy-need-congressional-permission-for-his-knighthood

Jay Wexler, The Odd Clauses (2011)

Significant Case

U.S. *ex rel.* New v. Rumsfeld, 448 F.3d 403 (D.C. Cir. 2006)

State Treaties

No State shall enter into any Treaty, Alliance, or Confederation; grant Letters of Marque and Reprisal....

(Article I, Section 10, Clause 1)

~

*I*n addition to granting the government powers to regulate trade and raise revenue that it either lacked or could not enforce under the Articles of Confederation, the Framers intended the Constitution to centralize much, if not all, power over foreign affairs. Many of the federal government's enumerated powers relate to foreign affairs and have corresponding restrictions on states in Article I, Section 10. Article VI of the Articles of Confederation had permitted the states to conclude treaties with foreign governments with the consent of Congress. States could also grant letters of marque and reprisal after Congress had declared war. While some of Article I, Section 10's proscriptions, such as the ability to levy tonnage duties or enter into "compacts or agreements," may be permitted by Congress, others, such as the prohibitions described here, are absolute.

Treaties, as well as alliances and confederations, are formal, binding agreements between nations that are the subjects of international law. "Compacts and agreements" are usually made by governmental officials, such as the executive, or by subsidiary governmental units, such as states or municipalities. In the late eighteenth century, governments issued letters of marque and reprisal to authorize private ships to attack certain foreign shipping and gain booty for their efforts. Issuing them was regarded as an act of war.

In *The Federalist* No. 44, James Madison noted that these proscriptions (like the prohibition on treaties) either "need[ed] no explanation" or (like the restrictions on letters of marque and reprisal) were "fully justified by the advantage of uniformity in all points which relate to foreign powers; and of immediate responsibility to the nation in all those for whose conduct the nation itself is to be responsible." Justice Joseph Story concurred, writing in his *Commentaries on the Constitution of the United States* (1833) that the power to issue letters of marque and reprisal "is appropriately confined to the national government" because "the protection of the whole Union is confided to the national arm, and the national power," and no state "should possess military means to overawe the Union, or to endanger the general safety." As noted foreign-affairs scholar Louis Henkin remarked, "these restrictions are as clear as words can make them and have raised no issues...."

The courts have had little occasion to deal with the clause, though in *Holmes v. Jennison* (1840), Justice Roger B. Taney, writing for himself and three other Justices, commented that the clause "positively and unconditionally" forbade states from entering into treaties, and that "even the consent of Congress could not authorize" them to do so. Taney, citing Emmerich de Vattel (1714–1767), also distinguished formal "treaties," which were expressly forbidden to states, from "agreements" and "compacts," which Congress could authorize.

The Supreme Court has not had an opportunity recently to distinguish between a "treaty" and a foreign "compact" or "agreement." In fact, in *U.S. Steel Corp. v. Multistate Tax Commission* (1978), the Supreme Court described the original understanding of the terms as historically "lost." It may be that Court would consider the distinction a political question. As one author has noted, states and municipalities have recently entered into a number of such compacts and agreements without the consent of Congress and have attempted to distinguish these compacts and agreements from treaties by inserting language that these agreements constitute political commitments with no legal effect. Another reason that many state-initiated compacts and agreements have not been challenged in court as violating the State Treaties Clause is that the executive branch has encouraged such agreements. Michael Ramsey argues that the founders did indeed distinguish between treaties and compacts, drawing upon ancient Roman distinctions maintained by authorities such as Hugo Grotius (1583–1645) and de Vattel. Ramsey also asserts that states reserve all foreign affairs powers not delegated to the federal government or prohibited to the states by the Constitution.

Brannon P. Denning

See Also

Article I, Section 8, Clause 11 (Marque and Reprisal)
Article I, Section 10, Clause 3 (Compact Clause)
Article II, Section 2, Clause 2 (Treaty Clause)

Suggestions for Further Research

Tess DeLiefde, *Filling in the Gaps: A New Approach to Treaty Implementation Reconciling the Supremacy Clause and Federalism Concerns*, 66 U. MIAMI L. REV. 567 (2012)

LOUIS HENKIN, FOREIGN AFFAIRS AND THE UNITED STATES CONSTITUTION (2d ed. 1996)

Duncan B. Hollis, *The Elusive Foreign Compact*, 73 Mo. L. REV. 1071 (2008)

MICHAEL RAMSEY, THE CONSTITUTION'S TEXT IN FOREIGN AFFAIRS (2007)

Significant Cases

Holmes v. Jennison, 39 U.S. (14 Pet.) 540 (1840)
U.S. Steel Corp. v. Multistate Tax Comm'n, 434 U.S. 452 (1978)

State Coinage

No State shall...coin Money; emit Bills of Credit; make any Thing but gold and silver Coin a Tender in Payment of Debts....
(**ARTICLE I, SECTION 10, CLAUSE 1**)

～

*T*he prohibition on the states to create any form of money signaled the shift of the power to make economic policy from the states to the federal government. In the late eighteenth century, money and trade were the prime mechanisms for regulating the economy, and the Constitution gave both exclusively to the new central government.

"Bills of Credit" was the generic name for various forms of paper money not backed by gold or silver (known as "specie"). Up until near the end of the Revolution, the states had managed, as they had when they were colonies, the issuance of paper money as a means of stimulating and cooling the economy, not unlike the practice of the modern Federal Reserve. After issuing a currency to increase investment, the colony or state would later call in, or "sink," the currency by levying taxes payable in that particular issue. The colony would then issue a new currency (sometimes overlapping with the collection of the previous one) to begin (or maintain) the cycle again. Inevitably, currencies became depreciated, and the complexities of determining who owed how much in which currency to whom confounded transactions and the courts. See *Deering v. Parker* (1760).

During the latter half of the eighteenth century, Parliament laid increasing monetary regulations on the colonies until 1764, when, as part of its program of centralizing control in London, it put a complete ban on making bills of credit legal tender. During the Revolution, the states began issuing paper currencies again, having a somewhat better record in financing the war than Congress had with its ultimately worthless paper "continentals." After 1783, however, specie dried up in a popular rush to purchase imported goods, and the states' currency issues exacerbated the serious depression of 1784. In early 1787, Massachusetts, which had resisted currency issues, was faced with Shays' Rebellion, whose partisans demanded new currency. In Philadelphia, the Framers were determined to put an end to the practice that they believed had contributed to so much economic and political dislocation. Rhode Island, a major issuer of paper money, refused to send delegates to the Constitutional Convention precisely because it feared monetary reform.

At the Convention, the delegates found a proposal to allow the states to issue bills of credit with the approval of Congress not stringent enough, and James Wilson and Roger Sherman successfully moved to insert the current language. In the ratifying conventions, the Anti-Federalists quickly saw what was afoot. The states could no longer debase the currency with new issues of paper tender. Luther Martin asserted that the states would no longer be able "to prevent the wealthy creditor and the monied man from totally destroying the poor though even industrious debtor." After ratification, the full force of the constitutional changes soon came to fruition; Alexander Hamilton pushed through a program by which the federal government absorbed all previous federal and state debt, established a national bank, and levied new tariffs and internal taxes.

The need for circulating currency, however, did not abate, for the prohibition on state currency did not apply to private entities. Soon, private and state chartered banks were issuing bank notes redeemable in specie. States still could not enter the monetary field directly. In *Craig v. Missouri* (1830), the Supreme Court struck down state loan offices that had issued loan-office certificates, but in *Briscoe v. Bank of Kentucky* (1837), the Court upheld the con-

stitutionality of bank notes issued from a state-chartered bank because they were not formally issued by the state. By the time of the Civil War, there were more than 1,600 state-chartered banks in the country. With never enough specie to back the notes, their value fluctuated widely. In order to control these problems and support the adoption of a federal currency, Congress levied a ten percent tax on state bank notes. After the Supreme Court upheld the tax in *Veazie Bank v. Fenno* (1869), state bank notes began their journey to extinction. State banks then turned to more modern financial devices, such as deposit accounts and checks, to stay in business.

While states are prohibited from coining money and emitting bills of credit, they are not barred from making "gold and silver Coin a Tender in Payment of debts." In recent years, legislators from no fewer than thirteen states have proposed that their state governments issue a gold and silver currency. How this might complicate the present legal and monetary structure is yet to be determined.

David F. Forte

See Also

Suggestions for Further Research
Gerald T. Dunne, Monetary Decisions of the Supreme Court (1960)

William Watts Folwell, *Evolution in Paper Money in the United States*, 8 Minn. L. Rev. 561 (1924)

Robert S. Getman, *The Right to Use Gold Clauses*, 42 Brook. L. Rev. 487 (1976)

John R. Hanson II, Small Notes in the American Colonies, 17 Explorations in Economic Hist. 411 (1980)

Ali Khan, *The Evolution of Money: A Story of Constitutional Nullification*, 67 U. Cin. L. Rev. 393 (1999)

Robert G. Natelson, *Paper Money and the Original Understanding of the Coinage Clause*, 31 Harv. J.L. & Pub. Pol'y 1017 (2008)

Lewis D. Solomon, *Legal Currency: A Legal and Policy Analysis*, 5 Kan. J.L. & Pub. Pol'y 59 (1996)

Significant Cases

Deering v. Parker, 4 Dall. App. xxiii (P.C. 1760)

Craig v. Missouri, 29 U.S. (4 Pet.) 410 (1830)

Byrne v. Missouri, 33 U.S. (8 Pet.) 40 (1834)

Briscoe v. Bank of Kentucky, 36 U.S. (11 Pet.) 257 (1837)

Griffin v. Thompson, 43 U.S. (2 How.) 244 (1844)

Gwin v. Breedlove, 43 U.S. (2 How.) 29 (1844)

Darrington v. Bank of Alabama, 54 U.S. (13 How.) 12 (1851)

Veazie Bank v. Fenno, 75 U.S. (8 Wall.) 533 (1869)

The Legal Tender Cases (Juilliard v. Greenman), 110 U.S. 421 (1884)

Poindexter v. Greenhow, 114 U.S. 270 (1885)

Chaffin v. Taylor, 116 U.S. 567 (1886)

Houston & Texas Central R.R. v. Texas, 177 U.S. 66 (1900)

State Bill of Attainder and State Ex Post Facto

No State shall . . . pass any Bill of Attainder, ex post facto Law. . . .
(ARTICLE I, SECTION 10, CLAUSE 1)

~

The Framers regarded bills of attainder and ex post facto laws as so offensive to liberty that they prohibited their use by both Congress (Article I, Section 9, Clause 3) and the states. The Framers had observed the use of bills of attainder by Parliament, particularly in cases of treason, and they were determined to deny the national legislature any such power. The Bill of Attainder Clause was part of the Framer's plan to limit and refine what they saw as the unacceptable English abuse of the law of treason. As Justice Samuel Chase noted in *Calder v. Bull* (1798), the Framers applied the prohibition to the states "[t]o prevent such and similar acts of violence and injustice." There is also

historical evidence that the clause was designed to prohibit what the Framers observed as recent abusive state practices in the taking of private property.

The issue of ex post facto laws was more nuanced. Many of the Founders regarded retroactive laws, both civil and criminal, as contrary to the principle of legality itself. Roman law as well as Henry de Bracton (1210–1268), Sir Edward Coke (1552–1634), and Sir William Blackstone (1723–1780) in English law, and the influential Baron de Montesquieu (1689–1755), condemned the practice. Thomas Jefferson noted in an 1813 letter to Isaac McPherson, "The sentiment that ex post facto laws are against natural right, is so strong in the United States, that few, if any, of the state constitutions have failed to proscribe them." At Philadelphia, some Framers, such as James Wilson, thought ex post facto laws so extra-legal that they were void *ab initio*; no textual prohibition was necessary. But a majority of the delegates wanted the prohibition stated in express terms.

All seemed to agree that ex post facto *criminal laws* were forbidden, but there was more ambiguity as to the validity of ex post facto *civil laws*. Part of the issue lay in the difference between a new law that changed preexisting legal obligations, and one that merely impacted (albeit severely) preexisting legal relationships. When Rhode Island, for example, issued a massive amount of paper money, it vitiated creditors' holdings even though the legislature had not changed the terms of the contracts. Yet even here, some observers termed the issuance of paper money an ex post facto law. More seriously, other states did change the terms of contracts that is, of legal relationships, tolling the period for repayment. These kinds of measures constituted the "fluctuating policy" and "legislative interferences" that James Madison decried in *The Federalist* No. 44.

At the Constitutional Convention, George Mason moved to remove the ex post facto prohibition from the states precisely because he believed it would prevent some state retroactive legislation in civil areas that he thought beneficial. Elbridge Gerry supported Mason, but apparently only because he wanted the clause rewritten to apply specifically to civil cases. Mason's motion was unanimously rejected. In the ratifying conventions, Anti-Federalists such as Patrick Henry also feared the impact of ex post facto prohibition on state economic legislation.

After the Convention, most Federalists believed the prohibition applied only to criminal statutes, a view adopted by the Supreme Court beginning with *Calder v. Bull* (1798). In *Calder,* Justice Samuel Chase noted that if the Ex Post Facto Clause (Article I, Section 9, Clause 3) applied to retroactive civil legislation, then the impairment of contracts clause (Article I, Section 10, Clause 1) would have been superfluous. As Robert Natelson has pointed out, in the end, the resulting prohibitions in the Constitution form a coherent pattern. The Ex Post Facto Clause prohibited retroactive criminal legislation, whereas the prohibition on the states from issuing paper money and from impairing the obligation of contracts covered the most objectionable forms of retroactive civil laws. Finally, the pattern was completed in the Fifth Amendment by the Takings Clause and the Due Process Clause, each of which limited the federal government's ability to enact certain kinds of retroactive civil laws.

In recent cases, federal courts have applied the understanding of the Ex Post Facto Clause as applicable to criminal but not civil matters. So, for example, the Tenth Circuit found that a state regulation imposing a $25 monthly supervision fee on parolees did not violate the Ex Post Facto and Bill of Attainder Clauses because it was not punitive in nature and had legitimate legislative purpose. *Taylor v. Sebelius* (2006). The First Circuit held that a state constitutional amendment preventing the imprisoned from voting in state elections did not violate the Ex Post Facto Clause because there was a non-excessive and "obvious rational nonpunitive purpose for disenfranchisement." *Simmons v. Galvin* (2009). In *In re DNA Ex Post Facto Issues* (2009), the Fourth Circuit found that requirements that prisoners must provide DNA samples and pay a $250 fee was not punitive enough to violate the Ex Post Facto Clause, but the requirement that the fee be paid before allowing a prisoner to be paroled or released did violate the Ex Post Facto Clause.

The substantive legal content of the Bill of Attainder and the Ex Post Facto Clauses in Sec-

tions 9 and 10 of Article I are fundamentally the same. Consult the entries on Article I, Section 9, Clause 3.

David F. Forte

See Also

Article I, Section 9, Clause 3 (Bill of Attainder)
Article I, Section 9, Clause 3 (Ex Post Facto)
Article I, Section 10, Clause 1 (State Coinage)
Article I, Section 10, Clause 1 (Obligation of Contract)
Amendment V (Due Process Clause)
Amendment V (Takings Clause)

Suggestions for Further Research

J. Richard Broughton, *On Straddle Crimes and the Ex Post Facto Clauses,* 18 Geo. Mason L. Rev. 719 (2011)

Joan Comparet-Cassani, *Extending the Statute of Limitations in Child Molestation Cases Does Not Violate the Ex Post Facto Clause of Stogner,* 5 Whittier J. Child & Fam. Advoc. 303 (2006)

Wayne A. Logan, *"Democratic Despotism" and Constitutional Constraint: An Empirical Analysis of Ex Post Facto Claims in State Courts,* 12 Wm. & Mary Bill Rts. J. 439 (2004)

Robert G. Natelson, *Statutory Retroactivity: The Founders' View,* 39 Idaho L. Rev. 489 (2003)

Duane L. Ostler, *The Forgotten Constitutional Spotlight: How Viewing the Ban on Bills of Attainder as a Takings Protection Clarifies Constitutional Principles,* 42 U. Tol. L. Rev. 395 (2011)

Daniel E. Troy, *Symposium: When Does Retroactivity Cross the Line? Winstar, Eastern Enterprises and Beyond: Toward a Definition and Critique of Retroactivity,* 51 Ala. L. Rev. 1329 (2000)

Significant Cases

Calder v. Bull, 3 U.S. (3 Dall.) 386 (1798)
Eastern Enterprises v. Apfel, 524 U.S. 498 (1998)
Taylor v. Sebelius, 189 Fed.Appx. 752, 756–58 (10th Cir. 2006)
Chan v. Gantner, 464 F.3d 289 (2d Cir. 2006)
Houston v. Williams, 547 F.3d 1357, 1364 (11th Cir. 2008)
In re DNA Ex Post Facto Issues, 561 F.3d 294, 299–301 (4th Cir. 2009)

Simmons v. Galvin, 575 F.3d 24, 45 (1st Cir. 2009)
ACORN v. United States, 618 F.3d 125 (2d Cir. 2010)
Dorsey v. United States, 132 S. Ct. 2321 (2012)

Obligation of Contract

No State shall . . . pass any . . . Law impairing the Obligation of Contracts. . . .

(ARTICLE I, SECTION 10, CLAUSE 1)

~

*A*rticle I, Section 10 contains a list of prohibitions concerning the role of the states in political, monetary, and economic affairs. As the Constitutional Convention was completing its work on prohibiting states from issuing paper money as legal tender, Rufus King of Massachusetts rose to propose "a prohibition on the States to interfere in private contracts." King relied on a central provision of the Northwest Ordinance:

> [I]n the just preservation of rights and property, it is understood and declared, that no law ought ever to be made, or have force in the said territory, that shall, in any manner whatever, interfere with or affect private contracts or engagements, bona fide, and without fraud, previously formed.

The Obligation of Contract Clause thus had its origins in earlier national policy, by extending to the states a prohibition that was already in effect in the Northwest Territory. In the brief debate that followed, George Mason feared the prohibition would prevent the states from establishing time limits on when actions could be brought on state-issued bonds. James Wilson responded that the clause would prevent "retrospective interferences only," that is, impairment of contracts already made. These comments suggest that the Framers may well have intended to limit states in their impairment of private contracts already made. But the issue is not com-

pletely free from doubt. The words "previously formed" were not carried over to the Obligation of Contract Clause, so that the text could read as though it has some prospective application.

The twin protections found in Article I, Section 10 prohibited the state from issuing paper money and, to some extent at least, from regulating economic affairs. That one-two combination troubled the Anti-Federalists, who feared that the two clauses operating in tandem would prevent the states from assisting the debtor classes. The states could no longer debase the currency with new issues of paper tender. In reporting why he had voted against the clause at the Constitutional Convention, Luther Martin asserted that the states would no longer be able "to prevent the wealthy creditor and the monied man from totally destroying the poor though even industrious debtor." In response to the Anti-Federalists, James Madison declared in *The Federalist* No. 44 that the Obligation of Contract Clause was essential to "banish speculations on public measures, inspire a general prudence and industry, and give a regular course to the business of society." Debtor relief was regarded as undermining the long-term stability of commercial expectations.

Support for the Obligation of Contract Clause was found in other quarters. In the South Carolina ratifying convention, Charles Pinckney argued that these two limitations on the states would help cement the union by barring the states from discriminating against out-of-state commercial interests. Edmund Randolph, in the Virginia ratifying convention, declared that the Obligation of Contract Clause was essential to enforcing the provision in the peace treaty with Great Britain guaranteeing private British debts. The Obligation of Contract Clause, therefore, served a double duty: it afforded both a protection to individuals against their states and a limitation on the states that prevented them from intruding on essential federal interests.

In tone, the clause reads as a stern imperative. Unlike the Import-Export Clause (Article I, Section 10, Clause 2) and the Compact Clause (Article I, Section 10, Clause 3), Congress cannot override the prohibition by giving its consent to any state action that violates this provision. The brief terms of the clause, however, cover more than the endless round of debtor-relief statutes the Framers had in mind, for the clause textually covers all types of contracts, not just debt instruments. Further, unlike the Commerce Clause (Article I, Section 8, Clause 3) the Obligation of Contract Clause applies not only to those contracts with interstate connections, but also to all contracts, even local contracts.

What is clear is that in the antebellum period, the Obligation of Contract Clause was the only open-ended federal constitutional guarantee that applied to the states. As such, the Obligation of Contract Clause came by default to be the focal point of litigation for those who sought to protect economic liberties against state intervention. The Supreme Court's interpretation of the clause, both before and after the Civil War, has been filled with odd turns and strange surprises.

Everyone conceded that the clause applied to ordinary contracts between private persons, including partnerships and corporations. That seemed to be the understanding at the Constitutional Convention. But did the Obligation of Contract Clause also reach actions by the state so as to prevent it from repudiating its own contracts, including those that granted legal title of state-owned lands to private persons, *Fletcher v. Peck* (1810), or sought to revoke state charters for private colleges, *Trustees of Dartmouth College v. Woodward* (1819)? In both of these cases, Chief Justice John Marshall opted strongly for the broader reading of the clause in order to restrain conduct by government—reneging on grants—that would be regarded as unacceptable if done by any private individual. In this instance, moreover, the broad reach of the Obligation of Contract Clause uneasily coexisted with the principle of sovereign immunity, which Alexander Hamilton had strongly defended in *The Federalist* Nos. 81 and 82. That principle prevented the state from being sued for breach of its own ordinary commercial contracts. But that immunity did not allow the state to undo its own contracts once their performance was completed. This reading fits so well with the Framers' antipathy to corrupt self-dealing as well as the general purpose of limited government that to this day no one has rejected the view that the Obligation of Contract Clause applies to state contracts. But there remains a spirited debate

as to how much protection it supplies in light of the doctrine of sovereign immunity.

Certainly much is to be said on behalf of the stability of titles to property obtained in grants from the states. And it has been universally held that the Contracts Clause does not authorize actions for money damages. But we cannot ignore the reciprocal problem: if the Obligation of Contract Clause is read so broadly so as to invite groups to lobby for sweetheart agreements, reformist governments would not be able to set such agreements aside.

Most of the interpretive questions regarding the clause, however, deal with the impact of the Obligation of Contract Clause on the state regulation of private agreements, where the issue of sovereign immunity does not arise. That issue, in turn, is divided into two parts. The first asks whether the Obligation of Contract Clause protects the rights that are vested in private party contracts that are in existence at the time the state legislates a new regulation that could apply to the contract. The second asks whether the Obligation of Contract Clause imposes limitations on the power of the state to regulate contracts not yet established.

The answer to the first question is relatively uncontroversial. The clause must apply to pre-existing contracts, for otherwise it would be a dead letter. Hence, early decisions held that state insolvency laws could not order the discharge of contracts that were formed before the state statute was passed. *Sturges v. Crowninshield* (1819). The legislature could not flip the background rules of the legal system to the prejudice of individuals who had advanced money on the faith of earlier arrangements. The clause also applied to a wide range of debtor-relief laws, wherein individuals sought to escape or defer the payment of interest, or to avoid foreclosure of their mortgages in hard economic times.

It was, however, one thing to say that the Obligation of Contract Clause applied, and quite another to say that all forms of debtor relief were regarded as beyond the power of the state. Many cases adopted the slippery distinction that the Obligation of Contract Clause preserved the *obligation* under contract, but did not prevent the state from limiting one or another *remedy* otherwise available. The result was that small erosions of contract rights came to be accepted, but large deviations were not, even though the clause speaks of all impairments (large or small) in the same breath. Still, in general, the prohibition against state intervention into the substance of existing contracts continues to hold today, unless (as will be discussed later) the state offers some police-power justification for its actions.

The Supreme Court reached a much more definitive conclusion on the second question in 1827, by holding in *Ogden v Saunders* (4–3, with Justices John Marshall and Joseph Story dissenting) that the Obligation of Contract Clause did not apply to those contracts that had not been formed as of the date of the passage of the regulatory legislation. In that case, Justice Bushrod Washington, for the majority, made a distinction between laws that affect contracts generally, such as statutes of limitations, and laws that affect the obligation of contracts. In one sense, Justice Washington's distinction is surely unexceptionable, for it would be odd if a revision of, say, the parol evidence rule in 2000 could not apply to any contracts signed before that date. The rule itself does not bias the case one way or another, but it is intended to improve the overall administration of justice. Individuals typically do not rely on these rules at formation, either. It would be contrary to its original design to read the Obligation of Contract Clause as blocking any improvements in the administration of commercial justice.

By the same token, the broad refusal to apply the Obligation of Contract Clause prospectively could go too far. For example, suppose a state just announced that from this day forward it reserved the right to nullify at will any contracts that were thereafter formed. At that point, it would take only a short generation after passage of this statute to gut the Obligation of Contract Clause making it "mere surplussage," something that is normally not permitted under standard rules of statutory interpretation. Thus, notwithstanding intimations in the Convention that it only had retroactive application, the courts have interpreted the clause to hold that its prohibitions are prospective but not absolute. The state may alter the rules governing future contracts in ways that offer greater security and stability to contractual obligations. Procedural legislative reforms that arose most frequently in

the early debates—a statute of frauds, a statute of limitations, and recording acts—are all measures that meet this standard.

Beyond allowing for procedural changes for future contracts (and modifications of remedy for existing contracts), the Court's refusal to give the clause any other prospective role opened the way to partisan legislation that limited the ability of some parties to contract without imposing similar restrictions on their economic competitors. In practice, *Ogden* meant that all general state economic regulation lay outside the scope of constitutional limitation. That gap in the system of constitutional regulation remained until after the Civil War, at which time some protection against state interference with future contracts was supplied under the so-called dormant Commerce Clause (with respect to interstate agreements only) and under the doctrine of liberty of contract as it developed under the Due Process Clause, and, in certain limited cases, under the equal protection clauses. But since *Ogden*, the Obligation of Contract Clause has been an observer, not a central player, in the constitutional struggle to limit prospective state economic regulation.

The Obligation of Contract Clause continued to have some traction with respect to contracts previously formed, but even in this context, two types of implied limitations on its use were introduced: the just-compensation exception (i.e., the Fifth Amendment's Takings Clause) and the police-power exception. In principle, the initial question is why any implied terms should be read into any constitutional provision, when no mention of them is made by the Framers. Here the simplest answer is that the logic of individual rights and liberties requires that adjustment. The Constitution thus creates presumptions and leaves it open to interpretation as to how these should be qualified in ways that do not gut the original guarantee.

Consider first the question of property takings with just compensation. Suppose that A buys land from B, which the government then wishes to condemn with payment of just compensation. Surely the government's right to condemn is not blocked by A's declaration that he received absolute title to the property from B in a contract that cannot now be impaired by the government. There is, however, a general principle deriving from the common law and Anglo-American constitutional history that the power to take property for public use is "inherent in government," so that the condemnation can go forward even when a person buys the land from the government. *West River Bridge Co. v. Dix* (1848). Thus, the Obligation of Contract Clause has to be read subject to a just-compensation exception, even though the condemnation can be seen to "impair" the contract right by denying the owner's right to hold out for an above-market price.

The second set of exceptions to the Obligation of Contract Clause involves the police power. Again, this power is nowhere mentioned explicitly in the Constitution, but it is read in connection with every substantive guarantee that it supplies against the exercise of federal or state power. The customary formulation allows the state to override (without compensation) private rights of property. It should, therefore, do so with ordinary contracts as well. Nonetheless, because no compensation is provided, logically, the class of justifications should be more stringent than the public-use requirement that allows the impairment of contracts with compensation. The canonical formulation defines the state police power as regulation in the name of safety, health, morals, and the general welfare. Stopping contracts to pollute, to bribe, or to fix prices has always been held to fall within the police-power exception.

The New Deal constitutional transformation of 1937, however, expanded the scope of the police power beyond these limited objectives, so that it no longer was possible to distinguish between general welfare and special interests. *Home Building & Loan Ass'n v. Blaisdell* (1934) vastly multiplied the police-power exceptions to the contractual guarantees offered by the Obligation of Contract Clause, even when no compensation was supplied. The actual decision, dealing with a state-imposed mortgage moratorium, could be explained in part as an effort to counter the ruinous effects of deflationary policies (which in effect increased, in constant dollars, the amount of the debts), but the decision itself was cast in broader terms and unleashed many other legislative initiatives that sought to neutralize the protections secured by individual contracts. Most notably, in *Exxon Corp.*

v. Eagerton (1983), the Court found that a "broad societal interest" was sufficient to justify a decision to prevent a company from asserting its explicit contractual right to pass on any increased severance tax to its consumers.

At present, therefore, it is virtually certain that the Supreme Court will find a police-power justification for any piece of special legislation with interest-group support, thereby gutting the clause insofar as it applies to broad classes of existing contracts. Ironically, however, the Court has remained more suspicious of government's efforts to use legislation to extricate itself from its own covenants, noting the obvious risk of self-dealing that this behavior represents. It thus struck down efforts of the Port Authority of New York and New Jersey to nullify bond covenants that prohibited it from using bond proceeds to support mass transit. *United States Trust Co. v. New Jersey* (1977). And in *Allied Structural Steel Co. v. Spannaus* (1978), the Court refused to allow Minnesota to impose retroactively more-stringent financial obligations on an employer in the winding up of its pension plan. Ironically, the most active use of the contracts clause today is over the unresolved issue of the power of state and local governments unilaterally to restrict pension benefits with public employees, both union and nonunion. Dealing with private contracts, however, the modern age often finds little intellectual respect for freedom of contract or for the sanctity of contracts validly formed. More than any fine point of the law, that initial intellectual predilection explains the lukewarm reception of Obligation of Contract Clause claims in dealing with these private arrangements.

Richard A. Epstein

See Also

Amendment V (Takings Clause)

Suggestions for Further Research

William Winslow Crosskey, Politics and the Constitution in the History of the United States (1953)

Richard A. Epstein, *Toward the Revitalization of the Contract Clause*, 51 U. Chi. L. Rev. 703 (1984)

Robert L. Hale, *The Supreme Court and the Contract Clause: I, II, III*, 57 Harv. L. Rev. 512, 621, 852 (1944)

Douglas W. Kmiec & John O. McGinnis, *The Contract Clause: A Return to the Original Understanding*, 14 Hastings Const. L. Q. 525 (1987)

Stanley I. Kutler, Privilege and Creative Destruction: The Charles River Bridge Case (1971)

Michael W. McConnell, *Contract Rights and Property Rights: A Case Study in the Relationship Between Individual Liberties and Constitutional Structure*, 76 Cal. L. Rev. 267 (1988)

Samuel R. Olken, *Charles Evans Hughes and the Blaisdell Decision: A Historical Study of Contract Clause Jurisprudence*, 72 Or. L. Rev. 513 (1993)

Stewart E. Sterk, *The Continuity of Legislatures: Of Contracts and the Contract Clause*, 88 Colum. L. Rev. 647 (1988)

Benjamin Fletcher Wright, Jr., The Contract Clause of the Constitution (1938)

Significant Cases

Fletcher v. Peck, 10 U.S. (6 Cranch) 87 (1810)

Sturges v. Crowninshield, 17 U.S. (4 Wheat.) 122 (1819)

Trustees of Dartmouth College v. Woodward, 17 U.S. (4 Wheat.) 518 (1819)

Ogden v. Saunders, 25 U.S. (12 Wheat.) 213 (1827)

Charles River Bridge v. Warren Bridge, 36 U.S. (11 Pet.) 420 (1837)

West River Bridge Co. v. Dix, 47 U.S. (6 How.) 507 (1848)

Home Building & Loan Ass'n v. Blaisdell, 290 U.S. 398 (1934)

United States Trust Co. v. New Jersey, 431 U.S. 1 (1977)

Allied Structural Steel Co. v. Spannaus, 438 U.S. 234 (1978)

Energy Reserves Group v. Kansas Power & Light Co., 459 U.S. 400 (1983)

Exxon Corp. v. Eagerton, 462 U.S. 176 (1983)

State Title of Nobility

No State shall . . . grant any Title of Nobility.

(Article I, Section 10, Clause 1)

*L*ike the corresponding prohibition on federal titles of nobility in Article I, Section 9, Clause 8, the prohibition on state titles of nobility was designed to affirm and protect the republican character of the American government. Both provisions were carried forward from Article VI of the Articles of Confederation, which had forbidden "the United States in Congress assembled," as well as "any of them," to "grant any title of nobility."

Even before the Articles, states had renounced the power to grant titles. David Ramsay, the eighteenth-century historian of the American Revolution, reported that at the time of independence the states "agreed in prohibiting all hereditary honours and distinction of ranks" in order to provide "farther security for the continuance of republican principles in the American constitution." *The History of the American Revolution* (1789). American state legislatures, he further observed, were "miniature pictures of the community," representing persons of all stations and classes rather than confining their membership to persons of noble rank. James Madison also found in *The Federalist* No. 39 that "the general form and aspect" of American governments could only be "strictly republican": "[i]t is evident that no other form would be reconcilable with the genius of the people of America; with the fundamental principles of the Revolution; or with that honorable determination . . . to rest all our political experiments on the capacity of mankind for self-government." Given the social and political circumstances of the United States at the time of the Founding, therefore, it is not surprising that the Constitution's prohibition on state titles of nobility was uncontroversial: as Madison wrote tersely in *The Federalist* No. 44, the prohibition "needs no comment." What is perhaps surprising, then, is that it was thought necessary at all.

The answer may be that the Founders feared that, without adequate precautions, the republican venture might fail. "[W]ho can say," Madison asked in *The Federalist* No. 43, "what experiments may be produced by the caprice of particular States, by the ambition of enterprising leaders, or by the intrigues and influence of foreign powers?" Before the

French Revolution, republican governments were rare: they existed only in such countries as Holland, Poland, or Venice, and even there only (as Madison argued in *The Federalist* No. 39) in attenuated or precarious forms. The existence of genuinely republican institutions, made possible by the absence of a hereditary aristocracy, was the hallmark of American exceptionalism. Conscious of that fact, the Founders sought to ensure, chiefly by the architectural features of the Constitution but also by such minor clauses as the prohibitions on titles, that the American political experiment that rested, as Madison said, "on the capacity of mankind for self-government" would succeed.

The defense of a republican polity led some of the state ratifying conventions in 1788 to propose amendments that would have stiffened the prohibition on titles, such as deleting the exception in the clause that allows Congress to consent to a state grant of a title of nobility. In addition, the fear that foreign immigrants already possessing titles might retain them led Congress in 1795 to forbid naturalization to a titled foreigner unless he formally renounced his title. 1 Stat. 414 (1795).

In 1810, Congress went further. In their long political and military contest, both Great Britain and Napoleonic France had sought to induce the United States to take sides. In response, Congress with near unanimity passed an amendment to the Constitution that would have revoked the citizenship of any person, whether natural born or naturalized, who accepted or retained a foreign title or emolument. The amendment had no congressional consent exception for titles although it did for emoluments. Eleven of the then required thirteen states ratified the amendment and, for a while, it was mistakenly listed as "The Thirteenth Amendment" in the United States Statutes at Large, prompting an 1817 House resolution and a follow-up presidential enquiry that corrected the error.

Robert Delahunty and David F. Forte

See Also
Article I, Section 9, Clause 8 (Emoluments Clause)

Import-Export Clause

No State shall, without the Consent of the Congress, lay any Imposts or Duties on Imports or Exports, except what may be absolutely necessary for executing its inspection Laws: and the net Produce of all Duties and Imposts, laid by any State on Imports or Exports, shall be for the Use of the Treasury of the United States; and all such Laws shall be subject to the Revision and Controul of the Congress.
(**ARTICLE I, SECTION 10, CLAUSE 2**)

~

A primary concern of the Framers of the Constitution was ending the interstate commercial depredations that had occurred during the Confederation period. Thus, the Constitution gave Congress the power to regulate interstate, foreign, and Indian commerce. The Framers also took care to place restrictions on state power under the new government. Often, the restrictions in Article I, Section 10 mirror the powers granted to Congress. Evidence from the Constitutional Convention and the ratification debates suggest that the Framers intended the Import-Export Clause to complement congressional power to raise revenue and regulate interstate commerce by restricting the states' ability to tax commerce entering and leaving their borders.

Indeed, the clause was likely understood originally to encompass domestic, as well as foreign, imports and exports. During the Convention, James Madison opposed allowing states to tax imports to protect native industries. Such protections would "[require] duties not only on imports directly from foreign Countries, but from the other States in the Union, which would revive all the mischiefs experienced from the want of a Gen[era]l Government over commerce." Opponents of ratification often complained of the restrictions placed on states by the new constitution and proposed that only their powers to tax and regulate foreign commerce be restricted.

The Supreme Court's early interpretations of the clause confirmed this interpretation. In *Brown v. Maryland* (1827), Chief Justice John Marshall assumed that the clause applied "equally to importations from a sister State" as well as to foreign imports. In *Almy v. California* (1861), the Court held that the clause prohibited California from taxing gold exported to New York. In *Woodruff v. Parham* (1869), however, the Court concluded that the "Imports or Exports" referred to in the clause referred only to foreign imports and exports. In reaching that conclusion, however, the Court made no analysis of the original understanding, and declared that Chief Justice John Marshall was in error in *Brown v. Maryland*. In fact, the *Woodruff* opinion recharacterized Chief Justice Roger B. Taney's *Almy* opinion as a "dormant" Commerce Clause opinion, though it clearly was not. Nonetheless, the Import-Export Clause has been almost completely subsumed by the Court's Dormant Foreign Commerce Clause doctrine.

The only issue in Supreme Court jurisprudence that sets the Import-Export Clause apart is whether the state tax "divert[s] import revenues from the federal government to the states," *Michelin Tire Corp. v. Wages* (1976). Subsequent cases addressed when domestic goods became "Exports" or when foreign goods ceased being "Imports" and thus subject to state taxation. *See, e.g., Kosydar v. National Cash Register* (1974) (discussing when goods become "exports"); *Low v. Austin* (1872) (holding that goods cease to be "Imports" when no longer in "original package"). In *Michelin*, the Supreme Court adopted a new analysis of the Import-Export Clause. A nondiscriminatory state tax would be invalidated only if it: (1) prevented the federal government from regulating foreign commerce uniformly; (2) diverted import revenue from the federal government to the states; or (3) risked interstate disharmony like that seen under the Confederation. See also *Itel Containers Int'l Corp. v. Huddleston* (1993) (applying *Michelin Tire*).

More recently, *Woodruff v. Parham* has been questioned. In 1997, Justice Clarence Thomas argued that the case was wrongly decided, that the historical evidence plainly showed that the Import-Export Clause did apply domestically,

and that the clause should be substituted for the Court's dormant Commerce Clause doctrine, which infers limits on a state's ability to regulate interstate commerce from the Commerce Clause. *Camps Newfound/Owatonna, Inc. v. Town of Harrison* (1997) (Thomas, J., dissenting). In addition, Justice Thomas noted that since the Supreme Court's narrowing of the Import-Export Clause in *Michelin Tire*, the fear expressed in *Woodruff* that applying the clause to domestic imports would unfairly exempt out-of-state goods from taxation was no longer credible.

Brannon P. Denning

See Also

Article I, Section 8, Clause 1 (Taxation; Spending Clause)

Article I, Section 8, Clause 3 (Commerce with Foreign Nations)

Article I, Section 8, Clause 3 (Commerce Among the States)

Article I, Section 9, Clause 6 (Port Preference Clause)

Article I, Section 10, Clause 3 (Compact Clause)

Suggestions for Further Research

Boris I. Bittker, Bittker on the Regulation of Interstate and Foreign Commerce §§ 12.01–12.09 (1999 & supp.)

Boris I. Bittker & Brannon P. Denning, *The Import-Export Clause*, 68 Miss. L.J. 521 (1998)

1 William Winslow Crosskey, Politics and the Constitution in the History of the United States 295–304, 316–17 (1953)

Brannon P. Denning, *Justice Thomas, the Import-Export Clause, and* Camps Newfound/Owatonna v. Harrison, 70 Colo. L. Rev. 155 (1999)

Walter Hellerstein, Michelin Tire Corp. v. Wages, *Enhanced State Power to Tax Imports*, 1976 Sup. Ct. Rev. 99 (1977)

Michael D. Ramsey, *The Power of the States in Foreign Affairs: The Original Understanding of Foreign Policy Federalism*, 75 Notre Dame L. Rev. 341 (1999)

Significant Cases

Brown v. Maryland, 25 U.S. (12 Wheat.) 419 (1827)

Almy v. California, 65 U.S. (24 How.) 169 (1861)

Woodruff v. Parham, 75 U.S. (8 Wall.) 123 (1869)

Low v. Austin, 80 U.S. (13 Wall.) 29 (1872)

Zschernig v. Miller, 389 U.S. 429 (1968)

Kosydar v. National Cash Register, 417 U.S. 62 (1974)

Michelin Tire Corp. v. Wages, 423 U.S. 276 (1976)

Itel Containers Int'l Corp. v. Huddleston, 507 U.S. 60 (1993)

Camps Newfound/Owatonna, Inc. v. Town of Harrison, 520 U.S. 564 (1997) (Thomas, J., dissenting)

Compact Clause

No State shall, without the Consent of Congress, lay any Duty of Tonnage, keep Troops, or Ships of War in time of Peace, enter into any Agreement or Compact with another State, or with a foreign Power, or engage in War, unless actually invaded, or in such imminent Danger as will not admit of delay.

(**Article I, Section 10, Clause 3**)

$\sim$

*T*he Framers of the Constitution had little difficulty seeing that combinations among the states, or any foreign-affairs activities undertaken by the states, were so fraught with danger to the union that none should be allowed unless Congress consented. Comparable prohibitions had already been contained in the Articles of Confederation, but the Framers chose somewhat stronger language in the Constitution to assure national supremacy in foreign affairs and in relations among the states. The provisions caused no significant debate at the Constitutional Convention, and James Madison described them in *The Federalist* No. 44 as "fall[ing] within reasonings which are either so obvious, or have been so fully developed, that they may be passed over without remark."

The constitutional logic of the provisions reflects a profound insight. Fearing that "factions," or interest groups, operating at the state level would endanger the Union and the legitimate interests of sister-states, Madison urged the Convention to include a congressio-

nal "negative" of "state laws in all cases whatsoever." Under his plan, no state law could go into effect without prior congressional approval. The Convention rejected Madison's proposal as unduly nationalistic and, moreover, unnecessarily broad, on the theory that most state laws would have little if any effect on the union or sister-states. The Convention instead subjected state laws to the operation of the Supremacy Clause: state laws become and remain in effect unless they are inconsistent with federal law or the Constitution.

Courts, however, cannot always be relied upon, and constitutional obstacles—in particular, the difficulty of mobilizing concurrent majorities in both houses of Congress and the executive's assent—may prevent Congress from counteracting dangerous state enactments. Thus, for classes of state activities that could be presumed to threaten the union or sister-states, the Convention supplemented federal supremacy with either an absolute prohibition on state action (*see* Article I, Section 10, Clause 1) or the Madisonian "negative" (*see* Article I, Section 10, Clauses 2 and 3). The congressional approval requirement ensures that each state will be informed of, and heard on, potentially threatening sister-state activities, thus reducing the states' costs in monitoring and countermanding such activities. Moreover, the requirement compels the proponents of presumptively problematic state activities to mobilize the requisite majorities at the federal level, thus affording an added measure of security.

Throughout the nineteenth century, the Compact Clause generated no more than a handful of cases, usually involving state border disputes. In the twentieth century, the Founders' fear of state compacts gave away to a more benign view of compacts as a useful instrument of state cooperation. Accordingly, the Supreme Court interpreted the clause in an explicitly nontextual fashion. While the foreign Compact Clause still applies (as a constitutional matter, if not always in practice) to a broad range of formal and informal agreements between a state and foreign countries, the Supreme Court has held that the domestic Compact Clause applies only to a narrow class of state agreements (those that establish binding obligations and, typically, multistate administrative agencies). Moreover, in *U.S. Steel Corp. v. Multistate Tax Commission* (1978), the Supreme Court declared that state compacts require congressional approval only if they "encroach upon the supremacy of the United States." Because states may not encroach upon federal supremacy in any event, a broad reading of the Court's decision effectively deprives the Compact Clause of any independent constitutional force.

The Supreme Court has never found a state compact void for want of congressional approval. Partly due to that permissiveness, states have seized on compacts to establish national tax and regulatory regimes of unprecedented complexity and consequence. Prominently, a 1998 agreement among states and tobacco producers created a permanent, nationwide regime for the taxation and regulation of tobacco sales. So far, however, this trend has failed to prompt a judicial reexamination and rediscovery of the nearly-forgotten Compact Clause.

Michael S. Greve

See Also

Article I, Section 10, Clause 1 (State Treaties)
Article I, Section 10, Clause 2 (Import-Export Clause)
Article I, Section 10, Clause 3 (Compact Clause)

Suggestions for Further Research

David E. Engdahl, *Characterization of Interstate Arrangements: When Is a Compact Not a Compact?* 64 Mich. L. Rev. 63 (1965)
Felix Frankfurter & James M. Landis, *The Compact Clause of the Constitution: A Study in Interstate Adjustments*, 34 Yale L.J. 685 (1925)
Michael S. Greve, *Compacts, Cartels, and Congressional Consent*, 68 Mo. L. Rev. 285 (2003)
Larry D. Kramer, *Madison's Audience*, 112 Harv. L. Rev. 611 (1999)

Significant Cases

Virginia v. Tennessee, 148 U.S. 503 (1893)
U.S. Steel Corp. v. Multistate Tax Comm'n, 434 U.S. 452 (1978)

A Note on the Separation of Powers

Separation of Powers is a fixture of the federal constitutional system even as its contours are uncertain and contested. The theory envisions three principal powers of government—legislative, executive, and judicial—and contemplates three distinct branches (the Founders often used the term "departments") to wield those powers. At the core, the legislative power makes laws, the executive power executes them, and the judicial power resolves disputes between parties.

While the theory does not dictate the ideal structure of the three branches, there were (and are) some patterns in governments that embodied the system. A multimember body typically wielded the legislative power, while numerous judges exercised the judicial power individually or in smaller units. The structure of the executive might vary in size from a small assembly to a single man.

The separation concept developed over time in England as Parliament acquired exclusive authority to make law (by limiting the king's "prerogative" to do the same), as the judicial power became the exclusive province of the courts (by gradually separating itself from the executive and by virtue of statutes ensuring a measure of independence), and as the executive became wedded to executing and enforcing the laws of Parliament and the judgments of courts. Writing in the mid-eighteenth century, Baron de Montesquieu argued that keeping the three core powers in separate hands helped prevent tyranny. If one branch acted tyrannically, the others might check it, something impossible when all three powers of government were in the hands of one entity. In other words, Montesquieu believed that the diffusion of power helped to secure liberty. Yet he did not believe in a strict separation, for he asserted that the executive ought to have a check on the legislative and that the latter ought to be able to disband the executive's army.

Shortly after the break with England, early American state constitutions sometimes paid lip service to the idea of separation of powers, containing provisions calling for separation. But quite often, state legislatures were too strong and their executives too weak. For instance, confronting a plural executive council that lacked a veto, the Pennsylvania unicameral assembly repeatedly assumed the powers of the other two branches. Some constitutions (New York and Massachusetts) created executives strong enough to withstand their legislatures and their vortex-like tendency to seize powers vested elsewhere. Meanwhile, the Articles of Confederation, crafted in 1777 and ratified in 1781, paid no heed to the idea of separation at all. It vested the Continental Congress with executive power as well as some legislative and judicial functions.

Most delegates to the Philadelphia convention were determined to avoid the mistakes that plagued the state constitutions. Others were content to have the legislature dominate the executive, conceiving of the latter as but the agent of the former. Even so, there always was a consensus that there would be three branches (legislative, executive, and judicial) vested with the three principal powers.

The introductory sections of the first three articles, shaped by the drafting skills of Gouverneur Morris and the Committee of Style, reflect that consensus. The implication is that only Congress can exercise legislative power (Article I). Only the president can exercise executive power (Article II). And only the federal courts can exercise judicial power (Article III). To make that separation more meaningful, the Incompatibility Clause (Article I, Section 6, Clause 2) bars legislators from simultaneously serving in the executive and judicial branch. The Constitution's salary and tenure protections for the president and the judges also help ensure that both have some measure of independence from a potentially overbearing Congress.

But the Framers also decided to grant to Congress and the president what James Madison termed "partial agency" (*The Federalist* No. 47) over certain acts of the other branches. There would, in other words, be some cross-branch checks. The Senate influences the exercise of two powers traditionally deemed executive: appointments and treaty-making. The legis-

lature has a judicial power over executive and judicial officers through impeachment. And the executive may check legislation, using his veto, as well as recommend measures to be law and (typically) enjoy some discretion in enforcing the law. During the ratification process, these cross-branch checks led some to complain that the Philadelphia convention had not fashioned a proper separation of powers. For instance, some Anti-Federalists protested that the Senate should not have a treaty or appointment role and that the Constitution ought to have relied upon a separate executive council instead. James Madison retorted that a well-functioning separation of powers required some cross-branch checks and that Montesquieu himself never favored a hermetic separation. Checks and balances had a role in ensuring a more meaningful separation of powers for they helped ensure that no one branch would dominate.

Once one recognizes that the Constitution does not neatly separate the three powers, some difficult questions arise. First, do the functions of the three powers overlap, meaning that more than one branch may exercise the same function? Second, are the Constitution's checks meant to be the only legal constraints on the exercise of federal powers or does the Constitution permit the imposition through legislation or custom of additional checks?

The first question arose during the Washington administration. James Madison and Alexander Hamilton debated the legality of President George Washington's Neutrality Proclamation (1793), which sought to assure non-involvement in the war between Great Britain and France. In a series of essays, writing as "Helvidius," and contradicting his earlier support of partial agency, Madison advanced the position of clear and defined separation. He insisted that only Congress could declare American neutrality in the war between France and England and that the Constitution would never permit more than one branch to have the same power. "A concurrent authority in two independent departments, to perform the same function... would be as awkward in practice, as it is unnatural in theory." Parallel power to declare neutrality, said Helvidius, would upend the "partition...so carefully made among the several branches" and throw the powers into "absolute hotchpot," exposing them to a "general scramble." Madison's scorn was directed at his erstwhile ally.

Alexander Hamilton (writing as "Pacificus") defended Washington's Neutrality Proclamation, arguing that in the course of executing the law of nations the executive could declare the nation neutral. The executive had such authority, Pacificus wrote, because it enjoyed a generic foreign affairs power and because the neutrality declaration helped to enforce the laws of neutrality, laws the president was duty-bound to enforce. Hamilton admitted that perhaps Congress also might decide whether the nation could remain neutral in light of its treaty obligations, but denied that this legislative authority excluded a "similar right of Judgment, in the execution of [the executive's] own functions."

Whether the Constitution permits the imposition of additional cross-branch constraints on the exercise of federal powers also arose in the early years. In *The Federalist* No. 48, Madison noted that legislatures were apt to usurp the powers of the other branches because they could "with the greater facility, mask, under complicated and indirect measures, the encroachments." Representative James Madison spoke to this matter in 1789, asserting that the president had an absolute power to remove executive officers and denying that Congress could by statute grant the Senate a check on the president's power. "If the constitution has invested all executive power in the president, I venture to assert, that the legislature has no right to diminish or modify his executive authority."

The Supreme Court has long recognized the core functions of the three departments and that these functions overlap to some extent. "The difference between the departments undoubtedly is, that the legislature makes, the executive executes, and the judiciary construes the law," said Chief Justice John Marshall in *Wayman v. Southard* (1825). The Court also acknowledged that Congress might leave some discretion to the other departments and in so doing suggested that the powers overlap. When Congress makes rules about commerce, it exer-

cises legislative power. But when it conveys limited discretion to the executive, the latter exercises executive power as it makes similar commercial rules.

The Supreme Court's "nondelegation doctrine" rests on the notion that the three powers overlap to some extent but that at some point, should Congress vest too much discretion with others (when a delegation lacks an "intelligible principle"), Congress unconstitutionally delegates its legislative powers. (*See* Article I, Section 1, Clause 1, Legislative Vesting Clause). Because the modern Court has been rather lax in policing delegations, it is clear that Congress can convey a great deal of discretion to the executive and judicial branches to fashion rules.

The question whether and how much Congress can *constrain* the functions of the other two branches is much more disputed. The Supreme Court itself has been inconsistent, particularly with respect to statutes affecting the executive. In *Ex Parte Garland* (1866), the Court declared that the president's pardon power was "not subject to legislative control." Similarly, in *Myers v. United States* (1926), the Court refused to allow the Senate to participate in the executive power of removal. Yet in a series of cases from *Humphreys' Executor v. United States* (1935) to *Morrison v. Olson* (1988), the Court sanctioned Congress's imposition of "for cause" removal restraints on the president's power to remove officials, both "quasi-judicial" and executive.

Some justices have suggested that the Court has strictly limited Congress's ability to restrain or curb "express" presidential powers but has been more tolerant with respect to implied powers, such as removal. But insofar as removal is part of the Vesting Clause's grant of executive power (as the Supreme Court held in *Myers*), it is no less express than the President's ability to commute sentences, a power that flows from the Pardon Power Clause.

Other justices have asserted that the Court's jurisprudence has turned on the whether Congress, in its statutes, has sought to aggrandize itself. When Congress has usurped powers, executive or judicial, the Court has struck it down. When Congress merely weakens the other branches without also aggrandizing itself, say by merely limiting when those branches may remove officers or by requiring public access to their records and meetings, the Courts have been far more forgiving. Yet one might suppose that any legislation that weakens or hampers the other two branches advantages Congress in interbranch struggles.

Needless to say, distinguishing what the Court believes to be permissible congressional regulation of executive power from impermissible encroachments remains a perplexing task. Indeed, the best explanation for the Court's case law might be that Court has been inconsistent, vacillating between a devotion to formalism and an embrace of functionalism.

Formalists tend to find bright-line, determinate rules in the Constitution's first three articles. They are drawn to the view that when the Constitution grants a power to one branch, no other branch may exercise it. And they have supposed that unless the Constitution expressly provides otherwise, Congress may not interfere with how another branch exercises its powers. For instance, many formalists are drawn to the view that Congress cannot limit the removal power, the power to appoint (Article II, Section 2, Clause 2), or the power to pardon (Article II, Section 2, Clause 1).

Functionalists favor flexibility in the separation of powers and are more comfortable with the idea that a function might simultaneously and constitutionally rest with more than one branch. Their reasoning sometimes rests less upon text, structure, and history and more on a sense that the Constitution fashions a flexible separation of powers. Generally, when functions or powers overlap, functionalists tend to believe that Congress's statutes should prevail over contrary executive and judicial conclusions, likely because the Supremacy Clause provides that federal statutes are supreme and because Congress is the most representative of the branches. Functionalists also are more apt to believe that Congress can properly regulate the exercise of executive and judicial powers. The source of this power to regulate is often said to be the Necessary and Proper Clause (Article I, Section 8, Clause 18).

When the Court embraces formalism, the majority opinion asks whether the Constitution contains a clear textual commitment of a function to one branch, or alternatively, whether one branch is seeking to perform a function properly the domain of another branch. In *INS v. Chadha* (1983), for example, the Court struck down the so-called "legislative veto" exercised by one house of the Congress because the Court believed that the veto permitted a chamber to make law outside the confines of the Presentment Clause (Article I, Section 7, Clause 2). And in *Bowsher v. Synar* (1976), the Court declared unconstitutional a law that gave the comptroller general, part of the legislative branch, the executive power of determining what kind of budget reductions should be made under a statute.

When the Court adopts functionalist standards, it asks whether one branch has *unduly* interfered with the *essential* functions of another branch, thus allowing for a wide range of variable overlap. In *Morrison v. Olson*, the Court declared that when Congress established the office of independent counsel, it did not unduly hamper the president's essential executive power of enforcing the laws, even though the president had little supervisory or removal power over the independent counsel. In dissent, Justice Antonin Scalia adopted formalist reasoning. He insisted that prosecution was wholly within the executive's domain and that Congress could not strip away that function and vest it in an independent officer.

Functionalist opinions have implicitly given the Court's imprimatur to the creation of what is often called a "fourth branch" of government. So-called independent agencies, not part of the executive branch, such as the Securities and Exchange Commission, the Federal Election Commission, etc., execute federal law through civil prosecutions. But because such agencies typically create rules and adjudicate violations, the agencies and their officers are sometimes seen as "quasi-legislative" and "quasi-judicial." Functionalists in the academy tend to welcome cases that have enlarged congressional flexibility to create new governmental structures. Formalists are more apt to lament the fourth branch as inconsistent with a Constitution that, in the first three articles and the Oaths Clause (Article VI, Clause 2), presupposes three branches and three governmental powers.

As hinted at above, functionalist opinions have permitted the concentration of the three powers within particular governmental sub-units, allowing one entity to make binding rules, adjudicate violations of the law, and prosecute legal violations before the courts. This concentration of the three powers, which displeases some formalists, is found in both executive and independent agencies. In contrast, many functionalists see wisdom in vesting the three powers of government in a body of experts able to change law more rapidly. (*See* essay "A Note on Administrative Agencies").

Lest too much be made of functionalism and formalism, it is important to recognize that they represent general approaches and do not inevitably yield conflicting answers. In *Clinton v. City of New York* (1998), the Court struck down the Line Item Veto Act, an act ceding the president the power to cancel certain newly enacted provisions of law. Both the majority and the dissenting groups of justices were composed of interesting amalgams of functionalist and formalist justices.

The Court's stance toward federal judicial power is equally complicated, with respect to both both what non-judicial authority Congress may convey and Congress's attempts to exercise judicial authority. In some laws, Congress has assigned rulemaking, law execution, and appointing authority to judges. The Court has approved such statutes when they concern tasks related to the judicial power, while reserving the right to strike down laws that assign tasks wholly alien to the exercise of the judicial power. Hence Congress can delegate to federal courts the powers to fix punishments and appoint prosecutors, as these are linked to the judicial function. Yet it likely cannot grant the courts authority to create rules of military discipline or to appoint a deputy secretary of state.

The Court also has limited Congress's ability to assume judicial power. The Constitution contains some hints that Congress cannot exercise judicial power itself. The Bill of Attainder Clause (Article I, Section 9, Clause 3) prohibits Congress from declaring that certain individuals are guilty of a crime or shall be punished. The Ex Post Facto Clause (Article I, Section 9, Clause 3) bars Congress from changing criminal law and punishment and applying those laws to prior acts, a prohibition that means that Congress cannot effectively dictate guilty verdicts in pending criminal cases.

Yet those rules apply only to punishment. Civil laws that affect exercises of judicial power face fewer such constraints. While Congress cannot declare who wins in an ongoing civil case nor revive a case in which a court has entered a final judgment, it may change the underlying substantive law applicable to an ongoing civil case and create new causes of action applicable to acts occurring in the past. In a sense there is a formal (if implied) rule against legislative usurpations of judicial power, a rule said to reflect the Founders distaste for the sorts of legislative aggrandizement that was all too common in the states. Nonetheless, if Congress is displeased with the result in a particular civil case, pending or otherwise, it can come close to dictating the outcome if it enacts new legislation changing the substantive law and creating a cause of action that reaches prior acts.

With respect to congressional regulation of exercises of judicial power, Congress has long dictated quorum rules, rules of procedure, and the like. It also has imposed rules about when courts must meet. These powers likely stem from Congress's power to create necessary and proper laws in order to carry federal powers into execution. The limits of congressional power remain uncertain, and it is unclear whether Congress could, for example, require a supermajority of a multi-member panel in order for a court to strike down laws as unconstitutional or whether it could require judges to write opinions in all cases.

The Supreme Court also has cited the Constitution's separation of powers as a basis for a number of implied branch privileges. In *United States v. Nixon* (1974), the Supreme Court said that executive privilege (like judicial privilege) was an implicit feature of the separation of powers, reading the Constitution as ceding to each branch a limited dominion over conversations and documents within it. In *Nixon v. Fitzgerald* (1982), the Court rooted its finding of absolute presidential immunity for official acts in the separation of powers. Obviously, not all immunity claims are successful, as *Clinton v. Jones* (1997) rejected the view that the separation of powers cedes the president a temporary immunity from civil suit while in office. Hence while the separation of powers shields the president from suits contesting his official acts, it poses no barrier to suits challenging his private conduct.

In modern times, some scholars have expressed skepticism about the extent to which the Constitution's system of separation of powers has actually prevented tyrannies and concentrations of federal power. Some scholars have said that for the separated powers system to work effectively, different political parties must control the various branches, for co-partisans are unlikely to check their allies in the other branches. Ambition does not much counteract ambition when one branch generally sees eye-to-eye with another. Others have asserted that courts will do little to check the political branches during crises and only rise to the occasion when an emergency has passed, meaning that temporary tyrannies are possible. Finally, some scholars have suggested that the separation of powers system is in shambles because Congress has delegated so much authority to the president that the courts cannot meaningfully check the latter. These scholars suggest that public opinion acts as the chief, if not the only, restraint on the executive.

Saikrishna Prakash

See Also

Suggestions for Further Research

Gerhard Casper, Separating Powers: Essays on the Founding Period (1997)

A Federalist Society Symposium, The Presidency and Congress: Constitutionally Separated and Shared Powers, 68 Wash. U. L.Q. 485 (1990)

W. B. Gwyn, The Meaning of the Separation of Powers (1965)

Gary Lawson, *The Rise and Rise of the Administrative State*, 107 Harv. L. Rev. 1231 (1994)

Daryl J. *Levinson* and Richard H. *Pildes, Separation of Parties, Not Powers*, 119 Harv. L. Rev. 2311 (2006)

John F. Manning, *Separation of Powers as Ordinary Interpretation*, 124 Harv. L. Rev. 1939 (2011)

Eric A. Posner & Adrian Vermeule, The Executive Unbound (2011)

Saikrishna Prakash, *Regulating Presidential Power*, 91 Cornell L. Rev. 215 (2005)

Peter L. Strauss, *Formal and Functional Approaches to Separation-of-Powers Questions—A Foolish Inconsistency?*, 72 Cornell L. Rev. 488 (1987)

M.J.C. Vile, Constitutionalism and the Separation of Powers (1998)

Significant Cases

Wayman v. Southard, *23 U.S. (10 Wheat.) 1 (1825)*

Ex parte Garland, 71 U.S. (4 Wall.) 333 (1867)

Myers v. United States, 272 U.S. 52 (1926)

Humphrey's Executor v. United States, 295 U.S. 602 (1935)

Wiener v. United States, 357 U.S. 349 (1958)

United States v. Nixon, 418 U.S. 683 (1974)

Buckley v. Valeo, 424 U.S. 1 (1976)

Nixon v. Fitzgerald, 457 U.S. 731 (1982)

INS v. Chadha, 462 U.S. 919 (1983)

Bowsher v. Synar, 478 U.S. 714 (1986)

Morrison v. Olson, 487 U.S. 654 (1988)

Plaut v. Spendthrift Farm, Inc., 514 U.S. 211, 218 (1995)

Clinton v. Jones, 520 U.S. 681 (1997)

Clinton v. City of New York, 524 U.S. 417 (1998)

ARTICLE II

Executive Vesting Clause

The executive Power shall be vested in a President of the United States of America.
(ARTICLE II, SECTION 1, CLAUSE 1)

The Executive Vesting Clause (or "Vesting Clause") grants the president the executive power traditionally associated with chief executives, subject to the many clarifications and constraints listed elsewhere in Article II. The Vesting Clause is best read as granting authority to direct and remove executive officers, a power to control the execution of federal law, and an interstitial power over foreign affairs.

The Articles of Confederation lacked an independent chief executive. Instead, the Continental Congress exercised the executive power, appointing and dominating the secretaries of the executive departments. Execution of the laws by a distracted, plural executive was hardly vigorous. Congress likewise proved a poor steward of foreign affairs, with American diplomats complaining that Congress could not act with the requisite speed or secrecy. Similar problems plagued the states. Though state constitutions formally created separate executives, most were nearly as weak as their federal counterparts. Some executive powers, such as appointments and pardons, were granted to the legislatures. Other constitutions subjected executive authority to statutory limitation, meaning that constitutional allocations of power were default rules. Finally, executive powers occasionally were shared with, or checked by, a council.

Resolving to avoid the problems plaguing state and national executives, the Founders rejected both a triumvirate and a powerful executive council. Instead, they crafted an energetic, responsible, and (largely) unified executive. A single executive could act with vigor and speed and avoid the dissension that might plague a plural executive. A unitary executive also would conduce towards responsibility, because all eyes would be drawn to the chief executive rather than to a plural executive, where each executive would claim credit and shift blame.

In discussing the need for a unitary executive, the Founders repeatedly confirmed the chief executive's law-enforcement power. James Wilson captured the spirit of the reform when he remarked that a "single magistrate" would supply the "most energy, dispatch, and responsibility" to the execution of the laws, a view echoed by Alexander Hamilton in *The Federalist* No. 70. Likewise, some Founders spoke of the president's significant role in foreign affairs, discussing the Senate's check on treaty-making as an exception to the grant of executive power. Early practices confirmed these readings of the Executive Vesting Clause. President George Washington took many actions not traceable to any specific foreign affairs clause in Article II, including issuing the Neutrality Proclamation, asking for the recall of French emissary, Citizen Genêt, and directing United States diplomats posted overseas. Similarly the first president directed federal law execution and executive officers of various sorts—soldiers, customs officials, the U.S. attorneys, and departmental secretaries, among others.

The Vesting Clause's rule that the president enjoys those powers traditionally vested with chief executives admits of two limitations. First, the president lacks executive authority explicitly granted to Congress. Hence he cannot declare war, grant letters of marque and reprisal, or regulate commerce, even though some chief executives had such authority. In these instances, Congress retained portions of the executive power that the Continental Congress had wielded under the Articles of Confederation. Second, specific constitutional provisions check customary executive authority. Despite his executive power, the president cannot make treaties or appointments without the Senate's advice and consent. In this regard, the Senate acts as a limited executive council. Likewise, the president cannot pardon impeachments or violations of state law.

From the Constitution's inception, some have doubted whether the Vesting Clause grants any power at all. Some have asserted that the "executive Power" merely refers to those specific powers enumerated elsewhere in Article II. Others have argued that the Vesting Clause does no more than designate the title and number of the apex of the executive. To claim more for the Vesting Clause supposedly would make the rest of Article II redundant. There are reasons to reject such claims. First, these arguments shunt aside the eighteenth-century understanding of executive power. The phrase "executive Power" was not an empty catchall encompassing any and all authority granted by a constitution to an executive. The phrase encompassed, at a minimum, control of the execution of laws, foreign affairs, and executive officers.

Second, traditional rules of interpretation require us to take seriously the differences across the three vesting clauses. Article I, Section 1 ("All legislative Powers herein granted shall be vested in a Congress of the United States...") makes clear that it vests no powers apart from those enumerated in the rest of Article I. In contrast, Article III, Section 1 ("The judicial Power of the United States, shall be vested in one supreme Court, and in such inferior Courts as the Congress may...establish.") clearly vests the federal courts with judicial authority. The Executive Vesting Clause reads like its Article III counterpart, in sharp contrast to the Article I introductory clause.

Third, although the title and number theory seeks to avoid redundant readings, it fails on its own terms. Because the rest of Article II makes clear that there would be only one executive styled the "president" (provisions in Article II repeatedly mention a "president" and use the singular pronoun "he"), the title and number theory would render the Executive Vesting Clause redundant. If every reading of the clause yields some redundancy, then arguments about redundancy cannot supply a reason for preferring one reading over another.

While the Vesting Clause is most often associated with execution of the laws, foreign affairs, and direction of executive officers, some imagine that it grants additional authority. For instance, many believe that the clause supports an executive privilege that enables the president to shield executive communications from Congress and the judiciary. Others contend that the clause grants the president certain immunities in court, such as immunity from suits challenging his official actions. Perhaps the clause conveys certain "emergency powers" to take extraordinary actions during exigencies, of the sort that Abraham Lincoln took during the Civil War.

The Vesting Clause has played a limited role in constitutional litigation. With some exceptions—including Justice Robert H. Jackson's concurring opinion in *Youngstown Sheet & Tube Co. v. Sawyer* (1952)—the Supreme Court has accepted that the clause grants powers beyond those specifically enumerated in Article II. In *Myers v. United States* (1926), the Court cited the Executive Vesting Clause as the source of removal and supervisory powers over executive officers. *Nixon v. Fitzgerald* (1982) cited the clause as a source of three powers (law enforcement, foreign affairs, and a supervisory power over the executive branch). In a 2003 case touching upon foreign affairs, the judiciary affirmed that the Vesting Clause grants foreign affairs authority. See *American Insurance Ass'n v. Garamendi* (2003). This marks a departure from prior case law, which had grounded the executive's foreign affairs powers in necessity and sovereignty. See *United States v. Curtiss-Wright Export Corp.* (1936). In a rather recent case, the Supreme Court repeatedly declared that multi-layered removal protections were inconsistent with the grant of executive power, thereby grounding the president's removal power in the Vesting Clause. See *Free Enterprise Fund v. Public Company Accounting Oversight Board* (2010). Yet the Court did not disturb the existing scheme of "for cause" removal restrictions that help grant the independent agencies their autonomy.

Indeed, despite the willingness to read the clause as granting power, judicial decisions have consistently limited its reach. Post-*Myers*, the Supreme Court essentially sanctioned the creation of a fourth branch of government in the form of numerous independent agencies that simultaneously exercise legislative, executive, and judicial powers. The most notable such case, *Morrison v. Olson* (1988), acknowledged that the Executive Vesting Clause granted the president control over prosecutions even as it upheld the constitutionality of the Independent Counsel Act. The *Morrison* Court concluded that the good-cause removal restriction protecting Independent Counsels did not "unduly trammel on executive authority." That framework well describes the Supreme Court's case law on the Vesting Clause: while the clause grants the president substantive power not found elsewhere in the Constitution, those powers are often subject to congressional regulation and modification.

Saikrishna Prakash

See Also

Article I, Section 1 (Legislative Vesting Clause)

Article II, Section 2, Clause 1 (Commander in Chief)

Article II, Section 2, Clause 2 (Treaty Clause; Appointments Clause)

Article II, Section 3 (Take Care Clause)

Article III, Section 1 (Judicial Vesting Clause)

Suggestions for Further Research

Steven G. Calabresi, *Some Normative Arguments for the Unitary Executive*, 48 Ark. L. Rev. 23 (1995)

Steven G. Calabresi & Saikrishna B. Prakash, *The President's Power to Execute the Laws*, 104 Yale L.J. 541 (1994)

Steven G. Calabresi & Kevin H. Rhodes, *The Structural Constitution: Unitary Executive, Plural Judiciary*, 105 Harv. L. Rev. 1153 (1992)

Harold Hongju Koh, The National Security Constitution: Sharing Power After the Iran-Contra Affair (1990)

Lawrence Lessig & Cass R. Sunstein, *The President and the Administration*, 94 Colum. L. Rev. 1, 4 (1994)

H. Jefferson Powell, *The Founders and the President's Authority over Foreign Affairs*, 40 Wm. & Mary L. Rev. 1471 (1999)

Saikrishna B. Prakash, *The Essential Meaning of Executive Power*, 2003 U. Ill. L. Rev. 701 (2003)

Saikrishna B. Prakash & Michael D. Ramsey, *The Executive Power over Foreign Affairs*, 111 Yale L.J. 231 (2001)

Abraham D. Sofaer, War, Foreign Affairs, and Constitutional Power (1984)

Significant Cases

Myers v. United States, 272 U.S. 52 (1926)

Humphrey's Executor v. United States, 295 U.S. 602 (1935)

United States v. Curtiss-Wright Export Corp., 299 U.S. 304 (1936)

Youngstown Sheet & Tube Co. v. Sawyer, 343 U.S. 579 (1952)

United States v. Nixon, 418 U.S. 683 (1974)

Nixon v. Fitzgerald, 457 U.S. 731 (1982)

Morrison v. Olson, 487 U.S. 654 (1988)

Clinton v. Jones, 520 U.S. 681 (1997)

American Ins. Ass'n v. Garamendi, 539 U.S. 396 (2003)

Free Enterprise Fund v. Public Co. Accounting Oversight Bd., 130 S. Ct. 3138 (2010)

Presidential Term

[The President] shall hold his Office during the Term of four Years ...

(**Article II, Section 1, Clause 1**)

～

*B*efore deciding on the length of the term of office for the president, the Framers of the Constitution debated whether, after a first term, the president was to be reappointed by the legislature or by the people. James Madison vehemently opposed reappointment by the legislature, arguing that the separation of powers was essential to the preservation of liberty: "The Executive could not be independent of the Legislature, if dependent on the pleasure of that branch for a re-appointment." If the president were thus beholden to the legislature, "tyrannical laws may be made that they may be executed in a tyrannical manner."

On the other hand, the proposal to allow "reappointment by Legislature for good-behavior" struck George Mason as allowing for too long a tenure. The phrase "good behavior" indicated protected life tenure for judges. Thus, Mason worried, "An Executive during good behavior [is] a softer name only for an executive for life."

While debating whether the president should be reappointed by the Legislature, the Framers also discussed whether a president should be eligible for a second term at all. George Mason wanted a single term of seven years in order to avoid "a temptation on the side of the executive to intrigue with the Legislature for a re-appointment." Some feared foreign intrigue in the reappointment of a president. But other Framers supported eligibility for more than one term. As Roger Sherman reasoned, there was no need of "throwing out of office the men best qualified to execute its duties." Gouverneur Morris argued that eligibility for more than one term would incite a president to merit public esteem with the hopes of reelection and would eliminate the risk of having a president use his short time in office to garner wealth and provide for friends. Alexander Hamilton adamantly argued that one of the keys to a successful executive is administrative stability, which would be best supported by a longer duration in office and would encourage a president to "act his part well."

After removing the exclusion from more than a single term, the Framers turned to determine how many years a given term would be (proposals ranged from three to twenty). Eventually, the Framers settled on four years. According to Justice Joseph Story in his *Commentaries on the Constitution of the United States* (1833), the period of four years is not long enough to risk any harm to the public safety. Although some Anti-Federalists thought that four years was sufficient time for a president "to ruin his country," Hamilton wrote in *The Federalist* No. 71 that duration in office is "requisite to the energy of the executive authority" and that a four-year term struck the proper balance, giving a president enough time "to make the community sensible of the propriety of the measures he might incline to pursue" and to not "justify any alarm for the public liberty."

It should be noted that the four-year limitation is absolute, and every president (no matter how disputed the election results may have been) has always turned the office over to his successor on the appointed day (January 20, after the ratification of the Twentieth Amendment). Nor has any president sought to have the election postponed because of a crisis. The election of 1864 went forward despite the Civil War, as did the election of 1944 despite World War II.

David F. Forte

See Also

Article II, Section 1, Clause 3 (Electoral College)
Amendment XII (Electoral College)
Amendment XX (Presidential Terms)
Amendment XXII (Presidential Term Limit)

Suggestion for Further Research

Jack M. Beerman & William P. Marshall, *The Constitutional Law of Presidential Transitions*, 84 N.C. L. Rev. 1253 (2006)

Vice President

... and, together with the Vice President, chosen for the same Term....
(**Article II, Section 1, Clause 1**)

∾

*I*n early September 1787, after the Constitutional Convention had received and debated the draft from the Committee of Detail, the delegates appointed a Committee of Eleven to resolve a number of issues that continued to stymie the convention. Among the committee's felicitous innovations was the office of vice president, derived from the model of the lieutenant governor in the New York state constitution of 1777. In this brief phrase, later approved by the convention, the Committee of Eleven accomplished two signal results. First, the vice president would be elected at the same time, for the same term, and by the same constituency as the president. The intent was to preserve the independence of the executive should the person who was vice president succeed to the duties of the presidency. Second, by separating this phrase from the previous sentence, the Framers made it clear that the vice president was not vested with any part of the constitutionally mandated executive power. There would be no plural executive.

The primary constitutional role of the vice president was to be available to become president (or acting president) should the office become vacant, or should a contingent election of a president fail in the House of Representatives. This is underscored by the original arrangement whereby presidential electors voted for two candidates; the one with the most votes (provided he carried a majority of the electors) would be president and the individual with the next greatest number of votes would be vice president. (Article II, Section 1, Clause 3.) Even when the Twelfth Amendment modified the method of electing a president and vice president, the purpose of the Framers remained: the person who was to hold the office of president or vice president should be chosen free of legislative control. Of course, should it happen that there was no person so chosen available to fill the presidency, the Constitution provides that Congress may by law provide for an officer to "act as President" until a president is elected. That contingency, however, has never occurred, and its need has been further obviated by the operation of the Twenty-fifth Amendment.

The other constitutional duty of the vice president (see Article I, Section 3, Clause 4), to be president of the Senate, had implications for succession as well. George Mason objected to the mixing of executive and legislative powers; he preferred that an executive council be established, the president of which would serve as vice president of the United States. But the Framers were opposed to an executive council. Further, were the Senate to have elected its own president, that person would almost certainly have been in line for succession. As James Madison stated, the question centered "on the appointment of the vice President [as] president of the Senate instead of making the President of the

Senate the vice president, which seemed to be the alternative."

As it occurred, for 140 years, the primary role of the vice president was legislative though without much influence. John Nance Garner, former Speaker of the House and vice president to Franklin D. Roosevelt, famously described the office (in a bowdlerized quote) as "not worth a bucket of warm spit." The vice president did not begin to have executive responsibilities until the twentieth century. Vice President Thomas R. Marshall chaired some of Woodrow Wilson's Cabinet meetings when the president was absent. President Warren G. Harding had his vice president, Calvin Coolidge, attend all Cabinet meetings, a practice that became institutionalized under Franklin D. Roosevelt, though Garner still felt excluded from any effective voice on policy. Harry Truman, through the National Security Act of 1947, made the vice president an *ex officio* member of the National Security Council. It was not until the 1950s, under President Dwight D. Eisenhower, that the vice president, Richard M. Nixon, became a fully functioning executive official, attending 193 cabinet meetings, 217 National Security Council sessions, and chairing important executive committees. In 1961, the offices of the vice president moved from Capitol Hill to executive offices nearer to the White House, and then in 1977 to the West Wing itself, completing the position's transformation into an integral part of executive governance.

The extent of the executive role of the vice president depends upon his relationship with the president. Similarly, since the middle of the twentieth century, candidates for vice president have been selected by the person running for president, rather than in and by the convention as had previously been the case. Recently, however, New Hampshire has instituted a separate vice-presidential primary.

Nine vice presidents have filled the presidency upon the death or resignation of the President: John Tyler, Millard Fillmore, Andrew Johnson, Chester A. Arthur, Theodore Roosevelt, Calvin Coolidge, Harry S. Truman, Lyndon B. Johnson, and Gerald R. Ford (Roosevelt, Coolidge, Truman, and Lyndon Johnson were subsequently re-elected as president). Five other vice presidents have attained the presidency by election in their own right: John Adams, Thomas Jefferson, Martin Van Buren, Richard M. Nixon, and George H.W. Bush. Thus, although a candidate for president often chooses a running mate for electoral reasons, the person elected as vice president has a significant chance to become president.

David F. Forte

See Also

Article I, Section 3, Clause 4 (Vice President as Presiding Officer)
Article II, Section 1, Clause 3 (Electoral College)
Article II, Section 1, Clause 6 (Presidential Succession)
Amendment XXII (Presidential Term Limit)
Amendment XXV (Presidential Succession)

Suggestions for Further Research

Richard Albert, *The Evolving Vice Presidency*, 78 Temp. L. Rev. 811 (2005)

Joel K. Goldstein, The Modern American Vice Presidency: The Transformation of a Political Institution (1982)

Joel K. Goldstein, *The New Constitutional Vice Presidency*, 30 Wake Forest L. Rev. 505 (1995)

Mark O. Hatfield, Vice Presidents of the United States, 1789–1993 (1997)

Paul C. Light, Vice-Presidential Power: Advice and Influence in the White House (1984)

Harold C. Relyea, The Vice-Presidency: Evolution of the Modern Office, 1933–2001, Congressional Research Service (2001)

Vice Presidents: A Biographical Dictionary (L. Edward Purcell ed., 4th ed., 2010)

Presidential Electors

[The President] shall ... together with the Vice President, chosen for the same Term, be elected, as follows: Each State shall appoint, in such Manner as the Legislature thereof may direct, a Number of Electors, equal to the whole Number of Senators and Representatives to which the State may be entitled in the Congress: but no Senator or Representative, or Person holding an Office of Trust or Profit under the United States, shall be appointed an Elector.

(Article II, Section 1, Clause 2)

~

*A*fter struggling with numerous proposals on the election of the president, the delegates to the Constitutional Convention settled on establishing a college of electors and apportioning the number according to the total of representatives and senators from each state. This method permitted the smaller states to have a somewhat greater proportionate share in the choosing of the president, though not as large an advantage as they had in the Senate. The Framers not only rejected the direct popular election of the president, but also left it to the state legislatures to determine how the states' electors were to be appointed.

This language in fact paralleled the provisions for state legislative appointment of congressional delegates in the Articles of Confederation and of U.S. Senators under Article I of the Constitution. With political parties widely disdained, this process was designed to pick not the candidate from the most popular political faction, but the wisest and most virtuous leader. The Framers rejected direct popular election of the president (and of senators) both because they believed that the populace would be ill-informed about national figures and because the Framers wanted to avoid interfering with state authority and depreciating the influence of small states. The Framers also rejected having Congress select the president because they feared that would make the president dependent on Congress. They hoped that the Electoral College would obviate these problems and would form a truly deliberative body on this single issue. The delegates to the Convention disagreed about whether electors should be popularly elected or appointed by state legislatures. They resolved that question by leaving the matter up to each state legislature.

Developments since then have changed much of the expected practice, but cases have confirmed the original understanding regarding electoral powers absent constitutional alteration. Our democratic ethos increasingly embraced popular elections, leading all state legislatures by 1880 to provide for popular election of presidential electors, and the Seventeenth Amendment in 1913 mandated the same for senators. This development, and the growing view that political party politics reflected rather than undermined democratic choice, made the notion of electors exercising their own independent judgment seem dubious by the early 1800s. Current case law such as *Ray v. Blair* (1952) allows the states to present voters with ballots that list only the presidential candidates (even though the votes for a candidate are really for his party's slate of electors), and also permits the states to pass laws requiring electors to pledge that, if chosen, they will vote for their party's candidate. Electors rarely do otherwise, though the enforceability of those pledges against a wayward elector remains unsettled.

Because these ballot and pledge requirements were directed by state legislatures, they came within those legislatures' federal constitutional power to direct the manner of selecting presidential electors. Although the Framers appear not to have considered whether this state legislative power could be constricted by state constitutions, subsequent cases adjudicating the question held that it could not because the federal Constitution's text vests this authority directly in the state legislatures rather than in the states. Indeed, although what a state legislature "is" might reasonably be thought to be determined by state constitutional procedures, *McPherson v. Blacker* (1892) stated that state legislatures need not (though they usually did) even follow normal state constitutional procedural requirements that legislatures vote bicamerally or present their decisions to the executive for possible veto. The Supreme Court's initial unanimous decision in the 2000 election dispute vacated the Florida supreme court's first decision for failing to take into account this doctrine prohibiting state constitutions from constricting state legislative directions about the appointment of presidential electors. *Bush v. Palm Beach County Canvassing Board* (2000).

State legislatures must, however, exercise their federal constitutional power to direct the manner of selecting presidential electors consistent with other provisions of the federal Constitution, including the First and Fourteenth Amendments. So have held a series of cases, from *McPherson, Williams v. Rhodes* (1968), and *Anderson v. Celebrezze* (1983), to the *Bush v. Gore* (2000) decision that invalidated a manual recount process for unconstitutionally allowing election officials' standardless discretion over how to count certain ballots. *McPherson* and *Williams* explicitly rejected the argument, sometimes cited by critics of *Bush v. Gore*, that the selection of presidential electors is a political question beyond any judicial review to assure compliance with the federal Constitution.

An unresolved question is whether a state legislature's determination that a state court deviated from state legislative directions would be judicially reviewable. This issue would have arisen had the Supreme Court not decided *Bush v. Gore* on December 12, 2000, because the Florida legislature was poised to complete its direct appointment of electors on December 13, citing its concern that the state supreme court had deviated from the state legislature's preelection directions and allowed the contest to exceed the federal statutory deadline for making contest determinations binding when Congress counted electoral votes. Had the Florida legislature proceeded with such a direct appointment, the courts might have concluded that such a state legislative decision was an unreviewable political question (as are state legislative ratifications of constitutional amendments) or that only Congress (when exercising its Twelfth Amendment counting powers) could review the validity of such state legislative action.

There has been a constant flow of attempts to change the Electoral College system. Prompted by the 2000 presidential election, in which George W. Bush won the presidency through the Electoral College despite Al Gore's having received a plurality of popular votes, several academics and reformers proposed the "National Popular Vote Compact" (NPVC), an attempt to nationalize the vote for president without a constitutional amendment. Each state entering the compact agrees to award its electoral votes to the person who received the most popular votes nationwide. The compact would not go into effect until states with a total of 270 electoral votes have joined the compact. In this way at least 270 electors would vote for the winner of the national popular vote, regardless of who won the popular vote in the electors' individual states. A number of states have approved the agreement but not enough to put it into effect, and there is a question whether Congress under the Compact Clause (Article I, Section 10, Clause 3) would have to approve the agreement.

Einer Elhauge

See Also

Article I, Section 3, Clause 1 (Senate)
Article V
Amendment XII (Electoral College)
Amendment XVII (Popular Election of Senators)

Significant Cases

McPherson v. Blacker, 146 U.S. 1 (1892)
Ohio *ex rel.* Davis v. Hildebrant, 241 U.S. 565 (1916)
Hawke v. Smith, 253 U.S. 221 (1920)
Burroughs v. United States, 290 U.S. 534 (1934)
Ray v. Blair, 343 U.S. 214 (1952)
Williams v. Rhodes, 393 U.S. 23 (1968)
Anderson v. Celebrezze, 460 U.S. 780 (1983)
Bush v. Palm Beach Cnty. Canvassing Bd., 531 U.S. 70 (2000)
Bush v. Gore, 531 U.S. 98 (2000)

Electoral College

The Electors shall meet in their respective States, and vote by Ballot for two Persons, of whom one at least shall not be an Inhabitant of the same State with themselves. And they shall make a List of all the Persons voted for, and of the Number of Votes for each; which List they shall sign and certify, and transmit sealed to the Seat of the Government of the United States, directed to the President of the Senate. The President of the Senate shall, in the Presence of the Senate and House of Representatives, open all the Certificates, and the Votes shall then be counted. The Person having the greatest Number of Votes shall be the President, if such Number be a Majority of the whole Number of Electors appointed; and if there be more than one who have such Majority, and have an equal Number of Votes, then the House of Representatives shall immediately chuse by Ballot one of them for President; and if no Person have a Majority, then from the five highest on the List the said House shall in like Manner chuse the President. But in chusing the President, the Votes shall be taken by States, the Representation from each State having one Vote; A quorum for this purpose shall consist of a Member or Members from two thirds of the States, and a Majority of all the States shall be necessary to a Choice. In every Case, after the Choice of the President, the Person having the greatest Number of Votes of the Electors shall be the Vice President. But if there should remain two or more who have equal Votes, the Senate shall chuse from them by Ballot the Vice President.

(ARTICLE II, SECTION 1, CLAUSE 3)

~

*A*t the Constitutional Convention in 1787, delegates had expressed concern that a meeting of a single body in the nation's capital to elect a president opened the door to intrigue and undue influence by special interests, foreign governments, and political factions. Meeting in their home states, electors would find it difficult to collude or buy and sell votes.

A more difficult problem was how to structure the voting within the Electoral College. During the debates at the Constitutional Convention, some delegates argued that the diversity and dispersal of the people over an expansive territory militated against direct popular election, for voters would be unable to form a majority behind any one candidate. In response, James Madison proposed that every individual voter cast three votes for president, at least two for persons from a state other than his own. Madison's idea later resurfaced, and the convention applied it in modified form to the presidential electors of the Electoral College. Requiring each elector to cast two votes for president increased the chances that electors could form a majority. Indeed, under the arithmetic, it was possible that as many as three candidates could have a majority of the votes of the electors. The provision did not prevent a New York elector from voting for two Virginians, but prohibited a Virginia elector from doing so. The Framers also accepted Madison's small but significant amendment to add the word "appointed" after the original text requiring a "Majority of the whole Number of Electors" for election. Thus the basis of what constitutes a majority changes if a state fails to appoint electors. As it turned out, in the first presidential election, New York failed to appoint electors, and George Washington won by the unanimous vote of the electors appointed.

If two or three persons received a majority vote and an equal vote, the House of Representatives must choose one of them for president. In deference to a suggestion by George Washington, the convention gave this responsibility to the popularly elected House, not the Senate, but representatives had to vote as state delegations, each state having one vote. If no candidate received a majority of the electoral vote, the House would choose from among the top five candidates. Because each state had one vote, regardless of population, the procedure gave proportionately more influence to the smaller states. The choice of five also gave to smaller states a greater chance of having one of their residents elected by the House, a concession to them that balanced the advantage that large states had in the electoral vote. The contingency election process also reassured delegates who had favored congressional

election of the president in the first instance. The Twelfth Amendment modified these provisions, following a crisis in 1800, when Thomas Jefferson and Aaron Burr each received an equal number of electoral votes.

The creation of the office of vice president appears to have been directly related to the mode of choosing the president. The Constitution gives to the vice president only two specific constitutional responsibilities: to act as president of the Senate and to receive and open the electoral votes. In 1789, the Senate elected John Langdon as president of the Senate "for the sole purpose of opening and counting the votes for President of the United States" (there being no sitting vice president). In 1793, the vice president, John Adams, "opened, read, and delivered" the certificates and votes of the electors to the tellers appointed by the respective houses. The tellers "ascertained the votes." By 1797, Vice President Adams only opened and delivered the certificates and reports of the electors to the tellers who counted the votes. Practice has generally followed that precedent. The issue of who counts the votes was particularly sensitive in 1876, during the contested election between Rutherford B. Hayes and Samuel Tilden. There were disputes in South Carolina, Louisiana, and Florida about which electors had been appointed (and one elector from Oregon was disqualified for being a government employee). The president of the Senate, Thomas W. Ferry, was a Republican; the Democratic Party controlled the House and the Republicans controlled the Senate. The Congress invented a novel solution to the problem of who would count the votes by creating an electoral commission, composed of five senators, five representatives, and five Supreme Court justices, to determine the results.

Finally, under this clause, whoever was runner-up in the electoral vote, with or without a majority vote, presumably a national figure competent to serve as president, became vice president. Clearly, the Founders did not anticipate rival national political parties whose top candidates could be the top two vote recipients. In the 1796 election, Federalist John Adams became president and Republican Thomas Jefferson (Adams's bitter political opponent) became vice president. Four years later, both Jefferson and his vice-presidential running mate, Aaron Burr, received an equal number of votes. The House ultimately voted in favor of Jefferson, but only after thirty-six ballots. Hence, the Twelfth Amendment, ratified in 1804, also changed this method of choosing the vice president. In the contingency election for vice president, the Senate makes the choice. Senators do not vote as state delegations; thus, disagreements between the two senators from a state do not lead to a stalemate. Only one time in U.S. history, in the 1836 election, did the Senate choose the vice president, Richard M. Johnson, who served under Martin Van Buren.

Tadahisa Kuroda

See Also

Article II, Section 1, Clause 2 (Presidential Electors)
Article II, Section 1, Clause 4 (Presidential Vote)
Amendment XII (Electoral College)
Amendment XXV, Section 2 (Presidential Succession)

Suggestions for Further Research

Joseph Jackson, Survey of the Electoral College in the Political System of the United States (1945)

Tadahisa Kuroda, The Origins of the Twelfth Amendment: The Electoral College in the Early Republic, 1787–1804 (1994)

David A. McKnight, The Electoral System of the United States (1878)

Jack N. Rakove, Original Meanings, Politics and Ideas in the Making of the Constitution (1996)

Shlomo Slonim, *The Electoral College at Philadelphia: The Evolution of an Ad Hoc Congress for the Selection of a President*, 73 J. Am. Hist. 35 (1986)

Presidential Vote

The Congress may determine the Time of chusing the Electors, and the Day on which they shall give their Votes; which Day shall be the same throughout the United States.

(**Article II, Section 1, Clause 4**)

~

*T*his clause requires that all electors vote on the same "Day" but allows Congress to set a multiday range of "Time" for when states choose their electors. Congress has exercised this authority to set a uniform day (the Tuesday after the first Monday in November) for states to appoint electors. But Congress has also provided in the same statute that, if a state's election "has failed to make a choice" on that day, then the state legislature can afterward appoint electors in any manner it deems fit, thus effectively extending the "Time" for choosing electors.

Unfortunately, the statutory text exercising this constitutional authority provides no criteria for deciding when an election "fails to make a choice" or who gets to decide when no choice was made. The historical record indicates that Congress thought this statutory language included cases where floods or inclement weather prevented "any considerable number" of voters from reaching the polls and that, in such cases, Congress wanted to confirm the power of the state's "legislature to authorize the continuance of the elections" past the congressionally prescribed election day. This legislative history indicates that an election might "fail to make a choice" even though there had been an election with a certifiable result, at least when that result was distorted by flooding or bad weather. It also makes clear that, at least in that circumstance, Congress contemplated that the state legislature was the entity that would decide whether the election had failed to make a choice. Unfortunately, the legislative history does not indicate what other circumstances Congress thought might mean an election failed to make a choice.

One interpretation is that Congress contemplated that each state legislature would have the power to decide when in its judgment other problems (including perhaps a state judicial failure to follow legislative directions or resolve election contests by congressional deadlines) meant the election failed to make a choice or was distorted. Alternatively, one might narrowly interpret the "failure to make a choice" language to prevent state legislatures from using dubious pretexts to reverse whatever presidentialelection outcomes they disliked. Arguing against the alternative interpretation is the fact that state legislative decisions (unlike judicial decisions) are political actions ultimately reviewable by the state electorate, which would be displeased if a state legislature tried to alter that electorate's presidential choice on mere pretext. Further, allowing state legislatures to make such judgments could be coupled with (possibly deferential) federal judicial review as to whether the state legislatures acted on mere pretext or with congressional review when it exercises its constitutional power to decide which electoral votes to count or both.

Another unresolved issue is whether Congress's Twelfth Amendment power to "count" electoral votes gives it discretion to refuse to count the votes of electors whom the state legislature has properly appointed. Such congressional refusal would seem to violate the Presidential Electors Clause (Article II, Section1, Clause 2). But the action might not be judicially reviewable, in which case only the national electorate would (at the next congressional election) be able to review any such congressional decision to exceed the proper scope of its counting power.

Einer Elhauge

See Also

Presidential Eligibility

No Person except a natural born Citizen, or a Citizen of the United States, at the time of the Adoption of this Constitution, shall be eligible to the Office of President; neither shall any Person be eligible to that Office who shall not have attained to the Age of thirty five Years, and been fourteen Years a Resident within the United States.
(**ARTICLE II, SECTION 1, CLAUSE 5**)

～

*T*he Constitution imposes three eligibility requirements on the presidency—based on the officeholder's age, residency, and citizenship—that must be satisfied at the time of taking office. By virtue of the Twelfth Amendment, the qualifications for vice president are the same. The Framers established these qualifications in order to increase the chances of electing a person of patriotism, judgment, and civic virtue.

First, presidents must be thirty-five years of age or older. In contrast, senators must be at least thirty years old, and representatives no less than twenty-five years old. As Justice Joseph Story has noted in his *Commentaries on the Constitution of the United States* (1833), the "character and talents" of a man in the middle age of life are "fully developed," and he has had the opportunity "for public service and for experience in the public councils."

Second, the president must have been a "resident" of the United States for fourteen years. By contrast, to be a member of Congress, one must be an "inhabitant" of the state one is representing. During the Constitutional Convention, James Madison contended that "both [terms] were vague, but the latter ['Inhabitant'] least so in common acceptation, and would not exclude persons absent occasionally for a considerable time on public or private business." Then as now, inhabitant meant being a legal domiciliary, but resident could mean either a domiciliary or a physical presence. Perhaps the Framers desired a person as president who had actually been present in the United States for the required period and had developed an attachment to and understanding of the country, rather than one who was legally an inhabitant, but who may have lived abroad for most of his life. On the other hand, the distinction may have been one of style rather than substance. As Justice Story later noted, "[b]y 'residence,' in the constitution, is to be understood, not an absolute inhabitancy within the United States during the whole period; but such an inhabitancy, as includes a permanent domicil in the United States."

There is some evidence that the Framers believed the fourteen-year residency requirement could be satisfied cumulatively, rather than consecutively. An earlier version of the clause excluded individuals who have "not been in the whole, at least fourteen years a resident within" the United States, and historical evidence suggests that deletion of the phrase "in the whole" was not intended to alter the provision's meaning. This might explain the election of Herbert Hoover, whose successful 1928 campaign for president came less than fourteen years after his return to the United States in 1917. Others may argue that Hoover had simply maintained a United States domicile throughout his tenure abroad.

The third qualification to be president is that one must be a "natural born Citizen" (or a citizen at the time of the adoption of the Constitution). Although any citizen may become a member of Congress so long as he has held citizenship for the requisite time period, to be president, one must be "a natural born Citizen." Undivided loyalty to the United States was a prime concern. During the Constitutional Convention, John Jay wrote to George Washington, urging "a strong check to the admission of Foreigners into the administration of our national Government; and to declare expressly that the Commander in Chief of the American army shall not be given to nor devolve on, any but a natural born Citizen." Justice Story later noted that the natural born citizenship requirement "cuts off all chances for ambitious foreigners, who might otherwise be intriguing for the office."

Under the longstanding English common law principle of *jus soli*, persons born within the territory of the sovereign (other than children of enemy aliens or foreign diplomats) are citizens from birth. Thus, persons born within the United States are plainly "natural born citizens" eligible to be president.

Being born on U.S. soil is not the only way for a person to be entitled to U.S. citizenship at birth, however. A person can be a citizen from birth based on the citizenship of one or both parents—under a British doctrine known as *jus sanguinis*. The First Congress codified that doctrine into U.S. law, declaring that "the children of citizens of the United States, that may be born beyond the sea, or out of the limits of the United States, shall be considered as natural born citizens." 1 Stat. 104 (1790).

For decades, constitutional scholars have debated whether a person is a natural born citizen eligible to serve as president, so long as he is a U.S. citizen at birth, regardless of the location of his birth. That debate ended as a practical matter in 2008, when the United States Senate unanimously approved a resolution deeming Senator John McCain eligible for the presidency. The resolution noted that "previous presidential candidates were born outside of the United States of America and were understood to be eligible to be President." S. Res. 511, 110th Cong. (2008). The resolution also added that any other view would be "inconsistent with the purpose and intent of the 'natural born Citizen' clause of the Constitution of the United States, as evidenced by the First Congress's own statute defining the term 'natural born Citizen.'"

The Presidential Eligibility Clause does not explicitly cover those who serve merely as acting president (*see* Twenty-fifth Amendment), a constitutionally distinct office. Although Congress has imposed by statute, 3 U.S.C. § 19(e), the same eligibility requirements for service as acting president, that provision may not be required as a constitutional matter.

James C. Ho

See Also

Suggestions for Further Research

Charles Gordon, *Who Can Be President of the United States: The Unresolved Enigma*, 28 Md. L. Rev. 1 (1968)

James C. Ho, *President Schwarzenegger—Or At Least Hughes?*, 7 Green Bag 2d 108 (2004)

James C. Ho, *Unnatural Born Citizens and Acting Presidents*, 17 Const. Comment. 575 (2000)

Randall Kennedy, *A Natural Aristocracy?*, 12 Const. Comment. 175 (1995)

Jordan Steiker, Sanford Levinson & J. M. Balkin, *Taking Text and Structure Really Seriously: Constitutional Interpretation and the Crisis of Presidential Eligibility*, 74 Tex. L. Rev. 237 (1995)

Significant Cases ´

United States v. Wong Kim Ark, 169 U.S. 649 (1898)

United States *ex rel.* Guest v. Perkins, 17 F. Supp. 177 (D.D.C. 1936)

Presidential Succession

In Case of the Removal of the President from Office, or of his Death, Resignation, or Inability to discharge the Powers and Duties of the said Office, the Same shall devolve on the Vice President, and the Congress may by Law provide for the Case of Removal, Death, Resignation or Inability, both of the President and Vice President, declaring what Officer shall then act as President, and such Officer shall act accordingly, until the Disability be removed, or a President shall be elected.

(**Article II, Section 1, Clause 6**)

~

*T*his provision, side by side with the Twentieth and Twenty-fifth Amendments, is a major anchor for presidential succession in the United States. It provides, as supplemented by the Twenty-fifth Amendment, for the vice president to take over in the event of the removal, death,

resignation, or inability of the president. It also authorizes Congress to establish a line of succession beyond the vice presidency. Left unclear by the clause was whether the vice president became president or simply acted as president in a case of succession.

Other ambiguities in the provision were noted at the Constitutional Convention by John Dickinson of Delaware, who asked, "[W]hat is the extent of the term 'disability' & who is to be the judge of it?" James Madison expressed concern that the provision would prevent the filling of a presidential vacancy by a special election, and he therefore successfully inserted the expression "until the Disability be removed, or a President shall be elected." It is not clear whether this change was intended to apply when the vice president succeeded or only when an officer designated by Congress was called upon to serve in the case of a double vacancy. Nor is it clear whether after a special election the winner(s) serves a full four-year term. In any event, there has never been a special election for president, although the provision allowing for its possibility was included in the country's early presidential succession laws.

A related question is whether "officers" when called on to serve were constitutionally required to retain their position during a period of service as acting president, as both James Madison and some current scholars opine. The 1792 statute seemed to indicate that when an "officer" became acting president, that officer retained his current position until a successor filled the presidential office. The current succession law of July 18, 1947, as amended, contemplates a resignation by statutory successors once they assume the powers of the presidency as acting president. That provision creates an issue as to whether in a case of presidential inability, it is appropriate to have an acting president who does not retain his or her existing office, and, in turn, whether legislative officers in line would violate the Incompatibility Clause of Article I, Section 6, Clause 2, which forbids a member of either House "during his Continuance in Office" from holding an "Office under the United States."

In addition, serious constitutional questions remain regarding the "bumping" provision of the succession statute, which requires a statutory successor, in the case of cabinet members, to step down once a Speaker or president pro tempore becomes available. The "bumping" provision may run afoul of the requirement of the Presidential Succession Clause that "such Officer shall act accordingly [as acting president], until the Disability be removed, or a President shall be elected."

Another ambiguity may be what kind of "officer" Congress can designate in a statute of presidential succession. The drafting history of Article II, Clause 1, Section 6 indicates that the Framers intended "officers of the United States" as the eligible category, but less clear is whether legislative leaders or legislators are included. Debate surrounding that issue has been a constant since the first succession law, with many scholars contending that neither the Speaker of the House of Representatives nor president pro tempore of the Senate is an officer in the sense contemplated by the Constitution. Proponents and opponents of this view cite provisions of the Constitution for support, such as Article I, Section 2, Clause 5 (Impeachment) and Article I, Section 6, Clause 2 (Sinecure Clause).

Both the First and Second Congresses debated who should be in the line of succession. The secretary of state, the chief justice, the president pro tempore of the senate, and the Speaker of the House of Representatives were all mentioned. On March 1, 1792, Congress resolved the issue by choosing the president pro tempore and the Speaker, respectively, prompting criticism from Madison and others that the congressional officers were not within the contemplation of the succession provision. No occasion called for the law to be implemented. Interestingly, at one point in history—when Chester A. Arthur succeeded to the presidency—there was no Speaker or president pro tempore, and therefore there was no one at all in the line of succession under the law of 1792. From 1886 until 1947, Congress included only cabinet members and not legislators in the line of succession, largely because of doubts whether legislators qualified as "officers." The current succession statute, however, contains the legislative offices, with the Speaker first and the president pro tem next, followed by a line of

cabinet officers in the order in which the executive departments were created.

In 1841, when President William Henry Harrison died in office, Vice President John Tyler assumed the presidency for the rest of the term. His claim to president, not simply vice president acting as president, drew criticism. The precedent he set, however, took and became the operating principle when other presidents died in office. These presidents were Zachary Taylor, Abraham Lincoln, James Garfield, William McKinley, Warren Harding, Franklin Roosevelt, and John Kennedy. On the other hand, Tyler's example became a major obstacle for situations involving the temporary inability of a president because, under the wording of this clause, the status of a vice president in a case of death would appear to be the same as in a case of inability or resignation or removal. As a consequence, on a number of occasions vice presidents declined to consider relieving a disabled president because of the Tyler precedent and also because of the ambiguities first raised by John Dickinson. This was the case in 1881 when President James A. Garfield lay dying and some suggested that Vice President Chester A. Arthur take charge, and again in 1919 after President Woodrow Wilson's stroke, when Vice President Thomas R. Marshall was urged to do the same. In 1967, the adoption of the Twenty-fifth Amendment eliminated much of the remaining uncertainties regarding presidential succession.

John Feerick

See Also

Article I, Section 2, Clause 5 (Impeachment)
Article I, Section 6, Clause 2 (Sinecure Clause)
Article I, Section 6, Clause 2 (Incompatibility Clause)
Amendment XXV (Presidential Succession)

Suggestions for Further Research

Akhil R. Amar & Vikram David Amar, *Is the Presidential Succession Law Constitutional?*, 48 Stan. L. Rev. 113 (1995)

Continuity of Gov't Comm'n, Preserving Our Institutions: The Continuity of the Presidency (Second Report 2009)

Steven G. Calabresi, *The Political Question of Presidential Succession*, 48 Stan. L. Rev. 155 (1995)

John D. Feerick, From Failing Hands: The Story of Presidential Succession (1965)

Joel K. Goldstein, *Akhil Reed Amar and Presidential Continuity*, 47 Houston L. Rev. 67 (2010)

Joel K. Goldstein, *Taking from the Twenty-Fifth Amendment: Lessons in Ensuring Presidential Continuity*, 79 Fordham L. Rev. 959 (2010)

John F. Manning, Response, *Not Proved: Some Lingering Questions About Legislative Succession to the Presidency*, 48 Stan. L. Rev. 141 (1995)

Ruth C. Silva, Presidential Succession (1968)

Symposium, The Adequacy of the Presidential Succession System in the 21st Century: Filling the Gaps and Clarifying the Ambiguities in Constitutional and Extraconstitutional Arrangements, 79 Fordham L. Rev. 775 (2010)

Seth Barrett Tillman, The Annals of Congress, the Original Public Meaning of the Succession Clause, and the Problem of Constitutional Memory (2011), available at http://papers.ssrn.com/sol3/papers.cfm?abstract_id=1524008

Compensation

The President shall, at stated Times, receive for his Services, a Compensation, which shall neither be increased nor diminished during the Period for which he shall have been elected, and he shall not receive within that Period any other Emolument from the United States, or any of them.

(Article II, Section 1, Clause 7)

∼

*T*his clause accomplishes two things: it establishes that the president is to receive a "compensation" that is unalterable during the period "for which he shall have been elected," and it prohibits him within that period from receiving "any other emolument" from either the federal government or the states.

The proposition that the president was to receive a fixed compensation for his service in office seems to have been derived from the Massachusetts constitution of 1780, which served as a model for the Framers in other respects as well. The Constitutional Convention hardly debated the issue, except to reject, politely but decisively, the elderly Benjamin Franklin's proposal that the president should receive no monetary compensation. Perhaps the Framers feared that if Franklin's proposal were accepted, only persons of great wealth would accept presidential office.

As Alexander Hamilton explained in *The Federalist* No. 73, the primary purpose of requiring that the president's compensation be fixed in advance of his service was to fortify the independence of the presidency, and thus to reinforce the larger constitutional design of separation of powers. "The legislature, with a discretionary power over the salary and emoluments of the Chief Magistrate, could render him as obsequious to their will as they might think proper to make him. They might in most cases either reduce him by famine, or tempt him by largesses, to surrender at discretion his judgment to their inclinations." For similar separation of powers reasons, Article III, Section 1, provides that federal judges "shall, at stated Times, receive for their Services, a Compensation," although that provision only forbids Congress from diminishing the judges' compensation, not from increasing it. The distinction, as Hamilton noted in *The Federalist* No. 79, "probably arose from the difference in the duration of the respective offices."

The prohibition on presidential "emoluments" is one of several constitutional provisions addressed to potential conflicts of interest. Further, the Compensation Clause eliminated one possible means of circumventing the requirement that the president's compensation be fixed: without this provision Congress might seek to augment the president's "compensation" by providing him with (what would purportedly differ) additional "emoluments." Significantly, the prohibition on presidential emoluments also extends to the states. That requirement helps to ensure presidential impartiality among particular members or regions of the Union.

A modern problem arose when President Ronald Reagan continued to receive retirement benefits as a retired governor of California while he was in the White House. He had been receiving benefits since the expiration of his second term in 1975. In a 1981 opinion, the Justice Department's Office of Legal Counsel focused on the purpose of the Compensation Clause, which was in its view "to prevent Congress or any of the states from attempting to influence the President through financial rewards or penalties." Given that President Reagan's retirement benefits were a vested right under California law rather than a gratuity that the state could withhold, the purpose of the clause would not be furthered by preventing him from receiving them.

The meaning of the Compensation Clause also arose in the context of President Richard M. Nixon's papers. As authorized by the Presidential Recordings and Materials Preservation Act of 1974, the government had taken or seized President Nixon's papers after he had left office. President Nixon (succeeded by his estate) sued for compensation for the taking of what he alleged to be his property under the Takings Clause of the Fifth Amendment. The government argued that the Compensation Clause precluded payment of compensation on the theory that the presidential materials were the product of President Nixon's exercise of powers conferred on him by the United States, and that therefore he could not sell them for his personal profit, even after his presidency, without impermissibly receiving an "Emolument" over and above the fixed compensation to which he was entitled. The district court rejected the government's argument, relying in part on a prior appellate determination that President Nixon was the owner of the materials in question. It found that President Nixon's entitlement to just compensation had vested when the government took his property (i.e., after he had left office), and therefore that "the plain language of the Emoluments Clause would not be violated because Mr. Nixon would receive compensation subsequent to the expiration of his term of office." The government argued that such a finding necessarily implied that a sitting president could sell his papers for profit during his tenure of office—to which the court demurred that "those are not the facts in this case." The court also found, however, that the papers "were not transferred to [President Nixon] by the government as compensation for his service in office," perhaps implying that a president could indeed sell his papers during his term. *Griffin v. United States* (1995). Under the Presidential Records Act of 1978, however, presidents no longer have title to their papers, 44 U.S.C. § 2202, and so cannot sell them, thus obviating the issue of whether such sales would be emoluments.

Robert Delahunty

See Also
Article I, Section 9, Clause 8 (Emoluments Clause)
Article III, Section 1 (Judicial Compensation Clause)

Suggestions for Further Research
The President and the Judges—Tax on Salaries of, 13 Op. Att'y Gen. 161 (1869)
President Reagan's Ability to Receive Retirement Benefits from the State of California, 5 Op. O.L.C. 187 (1981)
Adrian Vermeule, *The Constitutional Law of Official Compensation*, 102 Colum. L. Rev. 501 (2002)

Significant Case
Griffin v. United States, 935 F. Supp. 1 (D.D.C. 1995)

Presidential Oath of Office

Before he enter on the Execution of his Office, he shall take the following Oath or Affirmation:—"I do solemnly swear (or affirm) that I will faithfully execute the Office of President of the United States, and will to the best of my Ability, preserve, protect and defend the Constitution of the United States."

(Article II, Section 1, Clause 8)

~

*T*he Framers fittingly placed the Oath of Office Clause between preceding clauses that set forth the organization of the executive department and succeeding clauses that specify the contours of the president's executive power. The president takes the oath after he is to assume the office, but importantly before he executes it. The location and phrasing of the clause strongly suggest that it is not empowering, but that it is limiting—the clause limits how the president's "executive power" is to be exercised.

The clause is one of several that employ the oath concept, but it is the only clause that specifies the actual oath language for a constitutional actor. The clause does not specify who shall administer the oath, though it has been the common, but not universal, practice for the chief justice to do so. While Article VI's Oaths Clause simply requires the persons specified therein to "be bound by Oath or Affirmation, to support this Constitution," the Presidential Oath of Office Clause requires much more than this general oath of allegiance and fidelity. The clause, in notable part, enjoins the president to swear or affirm that he "will to the best of [his] Ability, preserve, protect and defend the Constitution of the United States."

The Framers undoubtedly drew upon similar provisions in a number of early state constitutions in drafting the clause, but they plainly believed that a special oath for the president was indispensable. At the Constitutional Convention, when George Mason and James Madison moved to add the "preserve, protect and defend" language, only James Wilson objected, on the ground that "the general provision for oaths of office, in a subsequent place, rendered the amendment unnecessary." The prospect of George Washington's becoming president cannot be discounted. The Framers perhaps desired an oath that would replicate the public values of the man who was presiding over the Convention. More significantly, because the presidency was unitary, there were no available internal checks, as there were in the other branches with their multiple members. A specially phrased internal check was therefore necessary, one that tied the president's duty to "preserve, protect and defend" to his obligations to God, which is how the Founders understood what was meant by an oath or affirmation. As Justice Joseph Story

noted in his *A Familiar Exposition of the Constitution of the United States* (1842):

> A President, who shall dare to violate the obligations of his solemn oath or affirmation of office, may escape human censure, nay, may even receive applause from the giddy multitude. But he will be compelled to learn, that there is a watchful Providence, that cannot be deceived; and a righteous Being, the searcher of all hearts, who will render unto all men according to their deserts. Considerations of this sort will necessarily make a conscientious man more scrupulous in the discharge of his duty; and will even make a man of looser principles pause, when he is about to enter upon a deliberate violation of his official oath.

Presidents have traditionally sworn the oath on a Bible (Washington kissed the Bible at his inaugural) and have ended with "So help me God," though the Constitution requires none of these gestures. A suit requesting a court order to prohibit the chief justice from prompting the "So help me God" phrase was dismissed for lack of standing. *Newdow v. Roberts* (2010).

The clause is tightly linked with Article II's Take Care Clause, which requires that the President "shall take Care that the Laws be faithfully executed." The duty faithfully to execute the laws under the Constitution might be thought to presuppose a power to interpret what is to be executed: "to say what the law is," to borrow a famous phrase from Chief Justice John Marshall. Indeed, some scholars—and presidents—have seized upon the clause as the font of the president's power of "executive review," the president's coordinate power to interpret the Constitution and what is to be "preserved, protected, and defended," even against conflicting interpretations by the legislative or judicial departments. The penultimate draft of the clause, referred by the Framers to the Committee of Style and Arrangement and reported by that committee, provides some support for this reading. That draft provided that the president act to the best of his "judgment and power," instead of to the best of his "ability." However, the Ninth Circuit has declared that the Presidential Oath of Office Clause does not allow the president to suspend the operation of laws that he believes are unconstitutional. *Lear Siegler, Inc. v. Lehman* (1988).

Finally, the "preserve, protect and defend" language of the Presidential Oath of Office Clause might be thought to place a special constitutional duty on the president to fight for the nation's survival, whether Congress has declared war or not. So thought President Abraham Lincoln during the Civil War.

Vasan Kesavan

See Also

Article II, Section 3 (Take Care Clause)
Article VI, Clause 3 (Oaths Clause)

Suggestions for Further Research

Robert F. Blomquist, *The Presidential Oath, the American National Interest and a Call for Presiprudence*, 73 UMKC L. Rev. 1 (2004)

Scott E. Gant & Bruce G. Peabody, *Musings on a Constitutional Mystery: Missing Presidents and "Headless Monsters"?*, 14 Const. Comment. 83 (1997)

Joel K. Goldstein, *The Presidency and the Rule of Law: Some Preliminary Explorations*, 43 St. Louis U. L.J. 791 (1999)

Paul Horwitz, *Honor's Constitutional Moment: The Oath and Presidential Transitions*, 103 Nw. U. L. Rev. 1067 (2009)

Frederick B. Jonassen, *Kiss the Book . . . You're President . . . : "So Help Me God" and Kissing the Book in the Presidential Oath of Office*, 20 Wm. & Mary Bill Rts. J. 853 (2012)

Henry P. Monaghan, *The Protective Power of the Presidency*, 93 Colum. L. Rev. 1 (1993)

Michael Stokes Paulsen, *The Most Dangerous Branch: Executive Power to Say What the Law Is*, 83 Geo. L.J. 217 (1994)

Saikrishna Bangalore Prakash, *The Executive's Duty to Disregard Unconstitutional Laws*, 96 Geo. L.J. 1613 (2008)

Significant Cases

Lear Siegler, Inc. v. Lehman, 842 F.2d. 1102 (9th Cir. 1988)

Newdow v. Roberts, 603 F. 3d1002 (D.C. Cir. 2010)

Commander in Chief

The President shall be Commander in Chief of the Army and Navy of the United States. . . .
(**Article II, Section 2, Clause 1**)

$\sim$

*T*he Commander in Chief Clause assures that there can be no military force beyond the president's control. The military cannot be made an independent force (thus guaranteeing civilian authority over it), and it cannot be made to report to an entity other than the president (such as Congress, as under the Articles of Confederation). Further, as commander in chief, the president has authority over the deployment and operations of the military in peacetime, and over the conduct of military strategy, tactics and objectives once war has begun. In his discussion of the president's powers in *The Federalist* No. 72, Hamilton observed that the "administration of government" falls "peculiarly within the province of the executive department." That power includes the conduct of foreign affairs, the preparation of the budget, the expenditure of appropriated funds, and the direction of the military and "the operations of war." As the Framers understood, success in the conduct of war demands the unique qualities of the president—unity, decisiveness, speed, secrecy, and energy.

Two substantial constitutional debates involve the Commander in Chief Clause. The first is whether the clause permits the president to initiate war without Congress's approval. As discussed in connection with the Declare War Clause (Article I, Section 8, Clause 11), some scholars believe the president does have this independent power, while others believe that the Declare War Clause gives war-initiation power exclusively to Congress. As further noted in connection with the Declare War Clause, almost all scholars believe that the Commander in Chief Clause gives the president power to respond to attacks on the United States.

The second debate is the extent to which Congress can by statute or appropriations direct the way that the president controls the military. For example, Congress enacted or considered enacting statutes or restrictions on appropriations directing the president to take or refrain from taking specific actions in the War on Terrorism and in the conflict in Iraq. Congress of course has authority over the creation and supply of the military under Article I, Section 8—the legislature has no constitutional obligation to provide the weapons that the president wants to carry out his chosen war plans. It is less clear, however, whether and when Congress can intervene to compel the president to take particular actions regarding military operations. To some scholars, the president's power under the Commander in Chief Clause is plenary, allowing no congressional intervention. Others believe that Congress's various powers over war and the military allow a full range of congressional interventions—thus finding the president's authority as commander in chief to be only residual, to be exercised in the absence of specific statutory direction. A third view holds that Congress has authority to restrict and direct the authority of the commander in chief in certain areas but not others.

Traditionally the courts treated decisions made by the president as commander in chief with great deference. Recent cases involving the War on Terrorism raised questions about the relationship between the commander in chief power and the courts. In *Hamdi v. Rumsfeld* (2004), the Supreme Court held that the writ of habeas corpus extended to the president's decision to declare a U.S.-born detainee in the War on Terrorism an "enemy combatant." *Hamdan v. Rumsfeld* (2006) found that the president's unilateral creation of military commissions (specialized war crimes tribunals used in most major American wars) violated the Uniform Code of Military Justice enacted by Congress. In 2008, in *Boumediene v. Bush*, the Court held that habeas corpus extended even to non-citizen detainees held outside the

United States at Guantanamo Bay, Cuba. In each case, strong dissents argued that the Court was interfering with the president's traditional power as commander in chief.

John Yoo and Michael D. Ramsey

See Also

Article I, Section 8, Clause 11 (Marque and Reprisal)
Article I, Section 8, Clause 12 (Army Clause)
Article I, Section 8, Clause 13 (Navy Clause)
Article I, Section 8, Clause 15 (Militia Clause)
Article I, Section 8, Clause 16 (Organizing the Militia)
Article II, Section 2, Clause 1 (Commander of Militia)

Suggestions for Further Research

David J. Barron & Martin S. Lederman, *The Commander in Chief at the Lowest Ebb—Framing the Problem, Doctrine, and Original Understanding*, 121 Harv. L. Rev. 689 (2008)

David J. Barron & Martin S. Lederman, *The Commander in Chief at the Lowest Ebb—A Constitutional History*, 121 Harv. L. Rev. 941 (2008)

Curtis A. Bradley & Jack L. Goldsmith, *Congressional Authorization and the War on Terrorism*, 118 Harv. L. Rev. 2047 (2005)

Robert J. Delahunty and John C. Yoo, *Making War*, 93 Cornell L. Rev. 123 (2007)

Louis Fisher, Presidential War Power (2d ed. 2004)

Louis Henkin, Foreign Affairs and the United States Constitution (2d ed. 1996)

H. Jefferson Powell, The President's Authority over Foreign Affairs: An Essay in Constitutional Interpretation (2002)

Saikrishna Prakash, *The Separation and Overlap of War and Military Powers*, 87 Tex. L. Rev. 299 (2008)

Michael D. Ramsey, *Response: Directing Military Operations*, 87 Tex. L. Rev. See Also 29 (2009)

John C. Yoo, *The Continuation of Politics by Other Means: The Original Understanding of War Powers*, 84 Cal. L. Rev. 167 (1996)

John C. Yoo, Crisis and Command: A History of Executive Power from George Washington to George W. Bush (2010)

John C. Yoo, The Powers of War and Peace: The Constitution and Foreign Affairs After 9/11 (2005)

Significant Cases

The Prize Cases, 67 U.S. (2 Black) 635 (1863)

Johnson v. Eisentrager, 339 U.S. 763 (1950)

Hamdi v. *Rumsfeld*, 542 U.S. 507 (2004)

Hamdan v. Rumsfeld, 548 U.S. 557 (2006)

Boumediene v. Bush, 553 U.S. 723 (2008)

Commander of Militia

The President shall be Commander in Chief... of the Militia of the several States, when called into the actual Service of the United States....

(ARTICLE II, SECTION 2, CLAUSE 1)

*T*he Framers of the Constitution crafted a complex network of provisions dealing with the militia. They believed that there should be a national army, but that resources and politics dictated that the militia would provide the bulk of the forces needed to defend the country. Although they were sensitive to the fear of a standing army and the political concerns of the states, there was one principle on which they agreed: when the states' militias were needed to defend the country, the President, and not the governors, would be in charge. The phrasing of the President's power changed over the months in Philadelphia, but the exclusivity of the President's power was never questioned. The most significant change came from Roger Sherman, who moved the addition "and of the Militia of the several States, when called into the actual service of the US." This assured that the president could not take the militia away from the states except when properly called forth by Congress under Article I, Section 8, Clause 15.

Yet there remained the question of what the president could do with the militia. William Blackstone, in his influential *Commen-taries on the Laws of England* (1765–1769), declared that the militia could not be deployed overseas. (The militia "are not compellable to march out of their counties, unless in case of invasion or actual rebellion within the realm, nor in any case compellable to march out of the kingdom.") A possible inference is that, in the context of the American Constitution, any tendency of the executive to wage aggressive war (as the English kings were wont to do) is stymied—not only, it is agued by some, by the Declare War Clause—but also by the fact that the principal land force, the militia, could not be sent to fight on foreign soil. For that purpose, the president would need an army; and Congress firmly held the reins over the army, if only by virtue of the need for a recurring appropriation in every congressional election cycle. Whether that was the original understanding has not yet been conclusively determined. In any event, modern practice has allowed the militia (in its form as the National Guard) to be deployed overseas.

In 1792, Congress passed the Uniform Militia Act, also known as the "Calling Forth" act, permitting the president to call out the militia to put down insurrections or rebellions. This power was initially limited to those events that could not be handled by judicial proceedings or by marshals in the exercise of their duties. The act also required a district judge to certify that circumstances were beyond the control of lawful authority and required the president to alert the insurrectionists to end their activities before the militia could be called out. In the meantime, the government launched three major campaigns against the Indians in the Ohio Territory in 1790, 1791, and 1794. In each case, federal forces were supplemented by large numbers of militia volunteers. But it was the Whiskey Rebellion in the summer of 1794 that impelled George Washington to issue the first formal call for the militia to put down the threatened insurrection. Washington took personal command of the force of 12,950 militiamen from Pennsylvania, New Jersey, Virginia, and Maryland. No president since Washington has taken personal control of the militia when called into the active service of the federal government.

In 1795, Congress passed another militia act, aimed at giving the president the power to call out the state forces in the event of insurrection. This law did away with the certification requirements (but retained the requirement of alerting the insurrectionists to disperse) of the 1792 law and granted the president the authority to call forth the militia when the nation was invaded, in imminent danger of invasion, or when faced with "combinations" against the nation. The key provision of that law was: "That whenever it may be necessary, in the judgment of the President, to use the military force hereby directed to be called forth...."

During the War of 1812, when President James Madison called up the militias, the New England states, opposed to the war and threatening secession, objected to the president's powers. In response to a request by the governor of Massachusetts, the Supreme Judicial Court of Massachusetts issued an advisory opinion declaring that the governors or commanders in chief of the several states had the exclusive right to determine whether exigent circumstances existed for the militia to be called out. This decision effectively recognized a veto power of governors over the use of their respective state's militia. It also stood the Constitution's enumerated powers on their head. Article I, Section 8, Clause 15 and Article II, Section 2, Clause 1 specifically granted to Congress and the president, respectively, the power to call out and command the militia when needed in active service to the United States.

In response to the argument for state control of the militia, Secretary of State James Monroe argued that when the militia is called into the actual service of the United States, all state authority over that militia ends. The militia assumes a position within the regular standing army and is paid by the federal government. Its members become, effectively, United States soldiers. They are subject to the same control as regular army personnel, including command by regular army officers.

In 1827 the U.S. Supreme Court supported the Monroe position. In *Martin v. Mott*, Justice Joseph Story stated, "We are all of opinion, that the authority to decide whether the exigency has arisen, belongs exclusively to the President, and

that his decision is conclusive upon all other persons." To cement further the right of the president to determine when to call forth the militia, Chief Justice Roger B. Taney declared in *Luther v. Borden* (1849) that not only is a decision by a president to call out the militia in response to an exigency not subject to state executive approval, but the decision is not subject to judicial review either.

Gubernatorial resistance to the president's call for the militia reemerged during the Civil War. On April 15, 1861, President Abraham Lincoln called for seventy-five thousand militiamen for three-month terms. The governors of Maryland, Kentucky, Missouri, Tennessee, Arkansas, and North Carolina (the last three of which states eventually seceded) refused, although volunteer units from all those states ultimately fought for the Union. As the war progressed, the bulk of the army came from requisitions from the states and the draft. The militias, relatively small and often not well trained, were marginal.

After the Civil War, the militia fell into desuetude (except for a brief and unsuccessful attempt to constitute a militia, based mostly on the freedmen in the reconstructed South) until it began a slow transition into the National Guard. The National Defense Act of 1916 made the National Guard a component of the regular army. During World War I, President Woodrow Wilson drafted members of the National Guard into the regular army.

In 1957, resisting a federal court order, Governor Orval Faubus ordered portions of the Arkansas National Guard to prevent the entrance of black students into Little Rock Central High School. In the first use of the guard to maintain internal order since the Civil War, President Dwight Eisenhower placed the entire Arkansas National Guard under presidential control and ordered the guard to obey the president and not the governor. The Arkansas National Guard complied.

In the 1980s, governors again resisted a presidential call for the militia (National Guard). Some of them objected to the deployment of their states' National Guard troops to Central America. Led by Minnesota governor Rudy Perpich, these governors withheld their consent to federally ordered

National Guard active duty training, as was their prerogative under then current federal law. In response, Congress enacted the Montgomery Amendment to the National Defense Authorization Act for Fiscal Year 1987, which prohibited governors from withholding consent for National Guard active duty service outside the United States. Perpich filed suit against the Department of Defense, arguing that the Montgomery Amendment was unconstitutional because it infringed on the militia training authority granted to the states under Article I, Section 8, Clause 16. Perpich also sought to enjoin the use of Minnesota National Guard troops in any training outside the United States that did not have the governor's consent. Ultimately, the Supreme Court upheld the supremacy of presidential control over the operations of the militia when called into actual service of the United States, even abroad, the example of Blackstone notwithstanding. Like James Monroe and Justice Joseph Story, the Court held that a state governor could not veto the use of a state militia when called upon by the nation in accordance with Congress's constitutional power and the president's constitutional authority.

Recent presidents have made more use of the National Guard as a reserve, calling units up for long periods of duty abroad in actions in the two Gulf Wars, Bosnia, and Afghanistan.

David F. Forte

See Also
Article I, Section 8, Clause 11 (Declare War)
Article I, Section 8, Clause 12 (Army Clause)
Article I, Section 8, Clause 14 (Military Regulations)
Article I, Section 8, Clause 15 (Militia Clause)
Article I, Section 8, Clause 16 (Organizing the Militia)
Article II, Section 2, Clause 1 (Commander in Chief)
Amendment II (To Keep and Bear Arms)

Suggestions for Further Research
Jerry Cooper, The Militia and the National Guard in America Since Colonial Times: A Research Guide (1993)

Lawrence Delbert Cress, Citizens in Arms: The Army and Militia in American Society to the War of 1812 (1982)

John K. Mahon, History of the Militia and the National Guard (1983)

William H. Riker, Soldiers of the States: The Role of the National Guard in American Democracy (1957)

Otis A. Singletary, Negro Militia and Reconstruction (1957)

C. Edward Skeen, Citizen Soldiers in the War of 1812 (1999)

Significant Cases
Martin v. Mott, 25 U.S. (12 Wheat.) 19 (1827)
Luther v. Borden, 48 U.S. (7 How.) 1 (1849)
Dukakis v. U.S. Dep't of Defense, 686 F. Supp. 30 (D. Mass. 1988), *aff'd* 859 F.2d 1066 (1st Cir. 1988)
Perpich v. Dep't of Defense, 496 U.S. 334 (1990)

Opinion Clause

The President . . . may require the Opinion, in writing, of the principal Officer in each of the executive Departments, upon any Subject relating to the Duties of their respective Offices. . . .
(ARTICLE II, SECTION 2, CLAUSE 1)

*T*he Opinion Clause arose out of the debates at the Constitutional Convention regarding whether the president would exercise executive authority singly or in concert with other officials or privy councilors. A brief review of English custom illuminates the choices made by the Framers. Formally, parliamentary "ministers" were ministers to the king. In addition, all British citizens were "subjects" of the king, and the king could require any nobleman, judge, or member of Parliament to serve in his privy council and provide him with personal or official advice. By the end of the eighteenth century, however, the ministerial offices had assumed such practical and administrative power that it diminished the king's responsibility for actions taken by the government. The king was increasingly expected to defer to his ministers' decisions. The state of the

English executive at the time of the framing was this: legally, the king could do no wrong; politically, the king was responsible for no administrative wrong.

At various stages during the convention, the Framers rejected proposals to divide or condition executive power. Their intent from contemporary records is clear: they wanted "[e]nergy in the executive," as Alexander Hamilton put it in *The Federalist* No. 70; and they wanted to maximize presidential responsibility for executive decisions. Some of the Framers, including James Madison, desired a single executive but supported a Council of Revision—composed of the president and judges—to exercise the veto power. Rufus King explained why the proposal was rejected: "If the Unity of the Executive was preferred for the sake of responsibility, the policy of it is as applicable to the revisionary [i.e., the veto] as to the Executive power." Yet vesting all executive power in one person was enough of a break with English tradition to cause unease. Several delegates supported a constitutional "Privy Council" or "Council of State," which could not bind the president but would provide him with advice.

One argument advanced against a privy council was that the department head most responsible for the matter that had been put to the council might evade his special share of responsibility for the decision. The Opinion Clause was born of this concern. The original version assumed the president would have a privy council but that he could "require the written opinions of any one or more of the [relevant] members [of the council] ... [and] every officer abovementioned shall be responsible for his opinion on the affairs relating to his particular Department." But the Framers rejected even a weak advisory council. Charles Pinckney concluded that: "The President shd. be authorized to call for advice or not as he might chuse. Give him an able Council and it will thwart him; a weak one and he will shelter himself under their sanction." Later, a committee headed by Gouverneur Morris was told to consider the matter further. The committee also rejected the idea. Morris explained: "The Presidt. by persuading his Council to concur in his wrong measures, would acquire their protection for them."

Instead, Morris proposed language that formed the basis of the current Opinion Clause, merely authorizing the president "to call for the opinions of the Heads of Departments, in writing." To distinguish this proposal even further from that of a collegial council, the clause was later revised to specify that written opinions could be obtained "upon any Subject relating to the Duties of their respective Offices." Thus modified, the clause does not encourage the president to seek a consensus from all department heads on any matter.

The resulting Opinion Clause prompted Alexander Hamilton to opine in *The Federalist* No. 74 that the clause added nothing to the president's executive power: "This I consider as a mere redundancy in the plan, as the right for which it provides would result of itself from the office." Some scholars think, however, that the Opinion Clause is not redundant, but rather an example of an enumerated executive power demonstrating that the president does not possess unenumerated powers through the Executive Vesting Clause (Article II, Section 1, Clause 1). Others assert that that the president's power in the Opinion Clause is limited to purely "executive departments" such as the early Departments of Foreign Affairs and War, and not to other congressionally created departments, such as Treasury, nor to so-called "independent" agencies. Although there is some evidence from congressional practice supporting the latter two interpretations, they conflict with drafting history that strongly reinforces the notion of a unitary executive, for there is more meaning in what the Framers rejected (i.e., limitations on the executive) than in what they settled on in the end.

The final version of the Opinion Clause adopted by the Convention, and confirmed through constitutional practice, reinforces the authority and accountability of an executive who is bound by law. The Framers' rejection of a formal cabinet independent of the president prevents department heads from exercising an independent sphere of influence over policy and denies them a forum in which to enlist others in debates over the president's policies. Instead, it was made explicit that the president possessed the typical management authority to require even department heads to prepare written reports for him on the performance of their official duties. In addition, the Opinion Clause contains a negative inference concerning a principal officer's independence, reinforced by the Recommendations Clause of Article II, Section 3, which allows the president to recommend to Congress such measures "as he shall judge necessary and expedient." The two clauses reflect the Constitution's separation of powers structure by preventing Congress from requiring presidential appointees to report directly to Congress rather than to the president. As Chief Justice John Marshall noted in *Marbury v. Madison* (1803), "[t]o aid [the president] in the performance of these duties, he is authorized to appoint certain officers, who act by his authority and in conformity with his orders." Congress can require reports from the respective departments, but Congress cannot interfere with prior presidential review of those reports and presidential control over what is transmitted to Congress.

As a result of the debates over the Opinion Clause and a privy council, the Constitution nowhere requires a formal cabinet. President George Washington found it prudent to organize his principal officers into a cabinet, and it has been part of the executive branch structure ever since. Nevertheless, no "prime minister" deflects the political accountability of the president. Presidents have used cabinet meetings of selected principal officers but to widely differing extents and for different purposes. Secretary of State William H. Seward and then-Professor Woodrow Wilson advocated use of a parliamentary-style cabinet government. But President Abraham Lincoln rebuffed Seward, and Woodrow Wilson would have none of it in his administration. Several twentieth-century presidents made pledges to use their "cabinets" as deliberative bodies, but Eisenhower was one of the few who did so.

Recent cabinets have grown unwieldy for effective deliberations, with up to twenty-five members including key White House staff, in addition to department and agency heads. President Ronald Reagan formed seven sub-cabinet councils to review many policy issues,

and subsequent presidents have followed that practice. But most recent presidents have met infrequently with their entire cabinets. In an age when the president relies heavily on White House staff for immediate advice and assistance, presidents often use cabinet meetings to make the cabinet members feel more a part of the president's inner circle or to increase their loyalty to the administration.

A cabinet that has no constitutional blessing may actually make it a more valuable tool than one constrained by constitutional design. There is more flexibility in the president's choice of which officers and councilors should be included. Moreover, a cabinet that meets at the pleasure of the president will naturally be more mindful to serve his interests rather than their own or those of their departments. Thus, the Framers increased the likelihood that the president will obtain useful advice from his principal officers by leaving the advice structure entirely to his discretion.

Todd Gaziano

See Also

Article I, Section 7, Clause 3 (Presentment of Resolutions)

Article II, Section 1, Clause 1 (Executive Vesting Clause)

Article II, Section 2, Clause 2 (Appointments Clause)

Article II, Section 2 (A Note on Administrative Agencies)

Article II, Section 3 (Recommendations Clause; Take Care Clause)

Suggestions for Further Research

Akhil Reed Amar, *Some Opinions on the Opinion Clause*, 82 Va. L. Rev. 647 (1996)

Curtis A. Bradley & Martin S. Flaherty, *Executive Power Essentialism and Foreign Affairs*, 102 Mich. L. Rev. 545 (2004)

Steven G. Calabresi & Kevin H. Rhodes, *The Structural Constitution: Unitary Executive, Plural Judiciary*, 105 Harv. L. Rev. 1153 (1992)

Lawrence Lessig & Cass R. Sunstein, *The President and the Administration*, 94 Colum. L. Rev. 1 (1994)

James P. Pfiffner, The Modern Presidency (3d ed. 2000)

Significant Cases

Marbury v. Madison, 5 U.S. (1 Cranch) 137 (1803)

United States v. Germaine, 99 U.S. 508 (1879)

Freytag v. Commissioner of Internal Revenue, 501 U.S. 868 (1991)

Pardon Power

The President . . . shall have Power to grant Reprieves and Pardons for Offences against the United States, except in Cases of Impeachment.

(ARTICLE II, SECTION 2, CLAUSE 1)

~

The power to pardon is one of the least limited powers granted to the president in the Constitution. It includes the power to commute sentences to a lesser penalty. The only limits mentioned in the Constitution are that pardons are limited to offenses against the United States (i.e., not civil or state cases) and that they cannot affect an impeachment process. A reprieve is the commutation or lessening of a sentence already imposed; it does not affect the legal guilt of a person. A pardon, however, completely wipes out the legal effects of a conviction. A pardon can be issued from the time an offense is committed, and can even be issued after the full sentence has been served. It cannot, however, be granted before an offense has been committed, which would give the president the power to waive the laws.

The presidential power to pardon was derived from the prerogative of the English king, which dated from before the Norman Conquest. The royal power was absolute, and the king often granted a pardon in exchange for money or military service. Parliament tried unsuccessfully to limit the king's pardon power, and it finally succeeded to some degree in 1701 when it passed the Act of Settlement, which exempted impeachment from the royal pardon power.

During the period of the Articles of Confederation, the state constitutions conferred pardon powers of varying scopes on their governors, but neither the New Jersey Plan nor the Virginia Plan presented at the Constitutional Convention included a pardon power for the chief executive. On May 29, 1787, Charles Pinckney introduced a proposal to give the chief executive the same pardon power as enjoyed by English monarchs, that is, complete power with the exception of impeachment. Some delegates argued that treason should be excluded from the pardon power. George Mason argued that the president's pardon power "may be sometimes exercised to screen from punishment those whom he had secretly instigated to commit the crime, and thereby prevent a discovery of his own guilt." James Wilson answered that pardons for treason should be available and successfully argued that the power would be best used by the president. Impeachment was available if the president himself were involved in the treason. A proposal for Senate approval of presidential pardons was also defeated.

The development of the use of the pardon power reflects its several purposes. One purpose is to temper justice with mercy in appropriate cases; another is to do justice if new or mitigating evidence comes to bear on a person who may have been wrongfully convicted. Alexander Hamilton reflects this in *The Federalist* No. 74, in which he argues that "[h]umanity and good policy" require that "the benign prerogative of pardoning" be available to mitigate the harsh justice of the criminal code. The pardon power would provide for "exceptions in favor of unfortunate guilt."

Chief Justice John Marshall in *United States v. Wilson* (1833) also commented on the benign aspects of the pardon power: "A pardon is an act of grace, proceeding from the power entrusted with the execution of the laws, which exempts the individual, on whom it is bestowed, from the punishment the law inflicts for a crime he has committed. It is the private, though official act of the executive magistrate . . ." Another purpose of the pardon power focuses not on obtaining justice for the person pardoned, but rather on the public policy purposes of the government. For instance, James Wilson argued during the convention that "pardon before conviction might be necessary, in order to obtain the testimony of accomplices." The public policy purposes of the pardon were echoed by Justice Oliver Wendell Holmes in *Biddle v. Perovich* (1927): "A pardon in our days is not a private act of grace from an individual happening to possess power. It is a part of the constitutional scheme."

Pardons have also been used for the broader public policy purpose of ensuring peace and tranquility in the case of uprisings and to bring peace after internal conflicts. Its use might be needed in such cases. As Alexander Hamilton argued in *The Federalist* No. 74, "in seasons of insurrection or rebellion there are often critical moments when a well-timed offer of pardon to the insurgents or rebels may restore the tranquility of the commonwealth; and which, if suffered to pass unimproved, it may never be possible afterwards to recall."

Presidents have sought to use the pardon power to overcome or mitigate the effects of major crises that afflicted the polity. President George Washington granted an amnesty to those who participated in the Whiskey Rebellion; Presidents Abraham Lincoln and Andrew Johnson issued amnesties to those involved with the Confederates during the Civil War; and Presidents Gerald R. Ford and James Earl Carter granted amnesties to Vietnam-era draft evaders.

The scope of the pardon power remains broad, if not plenary. As Justice Stephen Field wrote in *Ex parte Garland* (1867),

> If granted before conviction, it prevents any of the penalties and disabilities consequent upon conviction from attaching [thereto]; if granted after conviction, it removes the penalties and disabilities, and restores him to all his civil rights; it makes him, as it were, a new man, and gives him a new credit and capacity. . . . A pardon reaches both the punishment prescribed for the offence and the guilt of the offender . . . so that in the eye of the law the offender is as innocent as if he had never committed the offence.

Because its purposes are primarily public, a pardon is valid whether accepted or not, unless the president places conditions on the pardon or commutation. But a recipient of a pardon or commutation necessarily accepts the conditions

if he accepts the pardon or commutation itself. *Schick v. Reed* (1974).

A pardon is an official executive act. According to *United States v. Klein* (1871), Congress cannot limit the president's grant of an amnesty or pardon, but it can grant other or further amnesties itself. Though pardons have been litigated, the Court has consistently refused to limit the president's discretion, so long as the president has attached "conditions which do not in themselves offend the Constitution." *Schick v. Reed.*

The possibility of a president's pardoning himself for a crime is not precluded by the explicit language of the Constitution, and during the summer of 1974, some of President Richard M. Nixon's lawyers argued that it was constitutionally permissible. But a broader reading of the Constitution and the general principles of the traditions of United States law might lead to the conclusion that a self-pardon is constitutionally impermissible. It would seem to violate the principles that a man should not be a judge in his own case; that the rule of law is supreme and the United States is a nation of laws, not men; and that the president is not above the law.

The pardon power has been and will remain a powerful constitutional tool of the president. It can be an occasion for corruption. Yet, not only is the pardon power free of the normal checks and balances of the constitutional order, but even the political checks on the president in awarding pardons are limited. President Ford did pay a political price in pardoning Richard Nixon, but Presidents William J. Clinton and George W. Bush issued their most controversial pardons as they were leaving office, when they were immune from political accountability.

Only the wisdom and moral sense of the president can ensure its appropriate use.

James Pfiffner

See Also

Article I, Section 2, Clause 5 (Impeachment)

Suggestions for Further Research

David Gray Adler, *The President's Pardon Power, in* Inventing the American Presidency (Thomas E. Cronin ed., 1989)

Edward S. Corwin, The President: Office and
    Powers, 1787–1957 (5th ed. 1984)

William F. Duker, *The President's Power to Pardon:
    A Constitutional History*, 18 Wm. & Mary L. Rev.
    475 (1977)

Brian C. Kalt, *Pardon Me? The Constitutional Case
    Against Presidential Self-Pardons*, 106 Yale L.J. 779
    (1996)

Paul Rosenzweig, *Reflections on the Atrophying Pardon
    Power*, 102 J. Crim. L. & Criminology 593 (2012)

Significant Cases

United States v. Wilson, 32 U.S. (7 Pet.) 150 (1833)
Ex parte Garland, 71 U.S. (4 Wall.) 333 (1867)
United States v. Klein, 80 U.S. (13 Wall.) 128 (1871)
Biddle v. Perovich, 274 U.S. 480 (1927)
Schick v. Reed, 419 U.S. 256 (1974)

Treaty Clause

The President...shall have Power,
by and with the Advice and Consent of the Senate, to make Treaties, provided two thirds of the
Senators present concur....
(Article II, Section 2, Clause 2)

～

*T*he Treaty Clause has a number of striking
features. It gives the Senate, in James Madison's terms, a "partial agency" in the president's
foreign-relations power. The clause requires a
supermajority (two-thirds) of the Senate for
approval of a treaty, but it gives the House of
Representatives, representing the "people," no
role in the process.

Midway through the Constitutional Convention, a working draft had assigned the treaty-
making power to the Senate, but the Framers,
apparently considering the traditional role of
a nation-state's executive in making treaties,
changed direction and gave the power to the president, with the proviso of the Senate's "advice and
consent." In a formal sense, then, treaty-making
became a mixture of executive and legislative
power. Most people of the time recognized the
actual conduct of diplomacy as an executive
function, but under Article VI treaties were, like
statutes, part of the "supreme Law of the Land."
Thus, as Alexander Hamilton explained in *The
Federalist* No. 75, the two branches were appropriately combined:

> The qualities elsewhere detailed as
> indispensable in the management
> of foreign negotiations point out
> the executive as the most fit agent
> in those transactions; while the vast
> importance of the trust and the
> operation of treaties as laws plead
> strongly for the participation of the
> whole or a portion of the legislative
> body in the office of making them.

Another reason for involving both president and Senate was that the Framers thought
American interests might be undermined by treaties entered into without proper reflection. The
Framers believed that treaties should be strictly
honored, both as a matter of the law of nations
and as a practical matter, because the United
States could not afford to give the great powers
any cause for war. But this meant that the nation
should be doubly cautious in accepting treaty
obligations. As James Wilson said, "Neither the
President nor the Senate, solely, can complete a
treaty; they are checks upon each other, and are
so balanced as to produce security to the people."

The fear of disadvantageous treaties also
underlay the Framers' insistence on approval by
a two-thirds majority of the Senate. In particular,
the Framers worried that one region or interest
within the nation, constituting a bare majority,
would make a treaty advantageous to it but prejudicial to other parts of the country and to the
national interest. An important episode under
the Articles of Confederation had highlighted
the problem. The United States desired a trade
treaty with Spain and sought free access to the
Mississippi River through Spanish-controlled
New Orleans. Spain offered favorable trade terms,
but only if the United States would give up its
demands on the Mississippi. The Northern states,
which would have benefited most from the trade
treaty and cared little about New Orleans, had a

majority, but not a supermajority, in the Continental Congress. Under the Articles of Confederation, treaties required assent of a supermajority (nine out of thirteen) of the states, and the South was able to block the treaty. It was undoubtedly that experience that impelled the Framers to carry over the supermajority principle from the Articles of Confederation, as the Southern states (and many people in the North) concluded that the supermajority requirement had prevented an unwise treaty.

At the Convention, several prominent Framers argued unsuccessfully to have the House of Representatives included. But most delegates thought that the House had substantial disadvantages when it came to treaty-making. For example, as a large body, the House would have difficulty keeping secrets or acting quickly. The small states, wary of being disadvantaged, also preferred to keep the treaty-making power in the Senate, where they had proportionally greater power.

The ultimate purpose, then, of the Treaty Clause was to ensure that treaties would not be adopted unless most of the country stood to gain. True, treaties would be more difficult to adopt than statutes, but the Framers realized that an unwise statute could simply be repealed, while an unwise treaty remained a binding international commitment that would not be so easy to unwind.

Other questions, however, remained. First, are the provisions of the clause exclusive—that is, does it provide the only way that the United States may enter into international obligations?

While the clause does not say, in so many words, that it is exclusive, its very purpose—not to have any treaty disadvantage one part of the nation by a bare majority's approval—suggests that no other route is possible, whether through the president's acting alone or through ordinary legislation with the popularly elected House's having a role. Further, the drafting and ratifying debates reflect a broad consensus that the clause was the only constitutional avenue for treaty-making. Nonetheless, while it appears that the Treaty Clause was, in the original understanding, the exclusive way to make treaties, the Framers also apparently recognized a class of less-important international agreements, not

rising to the level of "treaties," which could be approved in some other way. Article I, Section 10, in describing restrictions upon the states, speaks of "Treat[ies]" and "Agreement[s]...with a foreign Power" as two distinct categories. Some scholars believe this shows that not all international agreements are treaties, and that these other agreements would not need to go through the procedures of the Treaty Clause. Instead, the president, in the exercise of his executive power, could conclude such agreements on his own. This exception for lesser agreements would have to be limited to "agreements" of minor importance, or else it would provide too great an avenue for evasion of the protections the Framers placed in the Treaty Clause.

A second question is how the president and Senate should interact in their joint exercise of the treaty power. Many Framers apparently thought that the president would oversee the actual conduct of diplomacy, but that the Senate would be involved from the outset as a sort of executive council advising the president. This was likely a reason that the Framers thought the smaller Senate was more suited than the House to play a key role in treaty-making. In the first effort at treaty-making under the Constitution, President George Washington attempted to operate in just this fashion. He went to the Senate in person to discuss a proposed treaty before he began negotiations. What is less clear, however, is whether the Constitution actually requires this process, or whether it is only what the Framers assumed would happen. The Senate, of course, is constitutionally authorized to offer "advice" to the president at any stage of the treaty-making process, but the president is not directed (in so many words) as to when advice must be solicited. The Appointments Clause, which appears in the same sentence of Article II, Section 2, as the Treaty Clause, also requires the "advice and consent of the Senate," but it seems evident (and post-ratification practice confirms) that this is satisfied by a Senate vote on a finalized presidential proposal and does not require the Senate's "advice" throughout the selection process. As we shall see, this uncertainty has led, in modern practice, to a very different procedure than some Framers envisioned. It seems clear, however, that the Framers expected that the Senate's "advice and consent" would be a close review and not a mere formality, as they thought of it as an important check upon presidential power.

A third difficult question is whether the Treaty Clause implies a Senate power or role in treaty termination. Scholarly opinion is divided, and few Framers appear to have discussed the question directly. One view sees the power to make a treaty as distinct from the power of termination, with the latter being more akin to a power of implementation. Since the Constitution does not directly address the termination power, this view would give it to the president as part of the president's executive powers to conduct foreign affairs and to execute the laws. When the termination question first arose in 1793, Washington and his cabinet, which included Hamilton and Thomas Jefferson, embraced this view. All of them thought Washington could, on his own authority, terminate the treaty with France if necessary to keep the United States neutral.

An alternative view holds that, as a matter of the general eighteenth-century understanding of the legal process, the power to take an action (such as passing a statute or making a treaty) implies the power to undo the action. This view would require the consent of the president and a supermajority of the Senate to undo a treaty. There is, however, not much historical evidence that many Framers actually held this view of treaty termination, and it is inconsistent with the common interpretation of the Appointments Clause (under which Senate approval is required to appoint but not to remove executive officers).

A third view is that Congress as a whole has the power to terminate treaties, based on an analogy between treaties and federal laws. When the United States first terminated a treaty in 1798 under President John Adams, this procedure was adopted, but there was little discussion of the constitutional ramifications. Moreover, when there is a conflict between a statute and a treaty, the Supreme Court has concluded that for purposes of U.S. law the last expression of the sovereign will controls, so that a later-enacted statute overrides an earlier-enacted treaty and vice versa. *The Cherokee Tobacco* (1870).

Finally, there is a question of the limits of the treaty power. A treaty presumably cannot alter the constitutional structure of government, and the Supreme Court has said that executive agreements—and so apparently treaties—are subject to the limits of the Bill of Rights just as ordinary laws are. *Reid v. Covert* (1957). In *Geofroy v. Riggs* (1890), the Court also declared that the treaty power extends only to topics that are "properly the subject of negotiation with a foreign country." However, at least in the modern world, one would think that few topics are so local that they could not, under some circumstances, be reached as part of the foreign-affairs interests of the nation. Some scholars have argued that treaties are limited by the federalism interests of the states. The Supreme Court rejected a version of that argument in *Missouri v. Holland* (1920), holding that the subject matter of treaties is not limited to the enumerated powers of Congress. The revival of interest in federalism limits on Congress in such areas as state sovereign immunity, see *Seminole Tribe of Florida v. Florida* (1996), and the Tenth Amendment, see *Printz v. United States* (1997), raises the question whether these limits also apply to the treaty power, but the Court has not yet taken up these matters.

Turning to modern practice, the Framers' vision of treaty-making has in some ways prevailed and in some ways been altered. First, it is not true—and has not been true since George Washington's administration—that the Senate serves as an executive council to advise the president in all stages of treaty-making. Rather, the usual modern course is that the president negotiates and signs treaties independently and then presents the proposed treaty to the Senate for its approval or disapproval. Washington himself found personal consultation with the Senate to be so awkward and unproductive that he abandoned it, and subsequent presidents have followed his example.

Moreover, the Senate frequently approves treaties with conditions and has done so beginning with the Washington administration. If the president makes clear to foreign nations that his signature on a treaty is only a preliminary commitment subject to serious Senate scrutiny, and if the Senate takes seriously its constitutional role of reviewing treaties (rather than merely deferring to the president), the check that the Framers sought to create remains in place. By going beyond a simple "up-or-down" vote, the Senate retains some of its power of "advice": the Senate not only disapproves the treaty proposed by the president but suggests how the president might craft a better treaty. As a practical matter, there is often consultation between the executive and members of the Senate before treaties are crafted and signed.

A more substantial departure from the Framers' vision may arise from the practice of executive agreements. Presidents have made minor agreements on their own authority since soon after ratification, and some scholars find this practice consistent with the original meaning of the Constitution. Article I, Section 10 indicates that the Framers recognized a category of "agreements" that did not rise to the level of "treaties," because individual states in the Union are prohibited from making the latter but can make the former with the consent of Congress. The president's Article II, Section 1, "executive power" thus might be understood to encompass the power to make agreements that are not treaties (although other scholars doubt that the grant of "executive power" was intended to convey this or any other substantive power).

Although initially a minor diplomatic tool, executive agreements increased enormously in their frequency and importance during the New Deal and World War II. After the Second World War, a number of important agreements were concluded by the president and approved by a majority of both houses of Congress without being submitted for the Senate's supermajority approval. According to the Restatement (Third) of the Foreign Relations Law of the United States, Section 303 (1987), the president may validly conclude executive agreements that: (1) cover matters that are solely within his executive power, or (2) are made pursuant to a treaty, or (3) are made pursuant to a legitimate act of Congress. Section 303 further states that treaties and congressional-executive agreements are generally regarded as

fully interchangeable as constitutional methods of agreement making, and many scholars continue to find this statement an accurate assessment.

When the president acts pursuant to a prior treaty, there seems to be little tension with the Framers' vision, as Senate approval has, in effect, been secured in advance. The modern practice of congressional-executive agreements, by which some international agreements have been made by the president and approved (either in advance or after the fact) by a simple majority of both houses of Congress, rather than two-thirds of the Senate, is more troubling. In modern times, post-signature approval by Congress has been especially common for trade agreements, such as the North American Free Trade Agreement (NAFTA), the agreement establishing the World Trade Organization, and other bilateral and regional free trade agreements. International trade, especially tariffs, is an area of Congress's particular constitutional interest, and congressional-executive agreements, at least with respect to trade matters, are now well established. Some scholars regard two cases from the late nineteenth and early twentieth centuries as indirectly approving congressional-executive agreements in the trade area, although the Court did not elaborate its rationale. *Field v. Clark* (1892); *B. Altman & Co. v. United States* (1912). More recently, one court of appeals found a prominent court challenge to NAFTA to be a non-justiciable "political question." *Made in the USA Foundation v. United States* (2001). The practice now appears so settled that it is unlikely to be overturned or even substantially questioned.

On the other hand, arguments for "complete interchangeability"—that is, claims that anything that can be done by treaty can be done by congressional-executive agreement—seem counter to the Framers' intent and unconfirmed by modern practice. The Framers carefully considered the supermajority rule for treaties and adopted it in response to specific threats to the Union; finding a complete alternative to the Treaty Clause would in effect eliminate the supermajority rule and make important international agreements easier to adopt than the Framers wished. Despite the rise of congressional-executive agreements, Article II, Section 2, treaties remain an important part of U.S. international agreement-making. Outside the trade area, in recent years the most important international agreements—including in critical areas such as arms control, human rights, the environment, tax, and extradition—have been submitted for the Senate's advice and consent under the Treaty Clause. The Senate has refused to approve several key high-profile agreements, including the Comprehensive Nuclear Test Ban Treaty and the Law of the Sea Treaty, and it has not been thought that these refusals could be avoided through an alternative means of agreement-making. At the same time, agreements made by the president on the basis of prior congressional approval (often indirect or implicit approval) remain the most numerous type of U.S. international agreement, although typically they involve less important matters. Recent scholarship has challenged the Restatement's claim of complete equivalence between treaties and congressional-executive agreements, but there has not been consensus upon the appropriate constitutional roles of the two forms of agreement-making.

The third type of executive agreement is one adopted by the president without formal approval by either the Senate or Congress as a whole. The Supreme Court and modern practice embrace the idea that the president may under some circumstances make these so-called sole executive agreements. *United States v. Belmont* (1937); *United States v. Pink* (1942). But the scope of this independent presidential power remains a serious question. The *Pink* and *Belmont* cases involved agreements relating to the recognition of a foreign government, a power closely tied to the president's textual power to receive ambassadors (Article II, Section 3). The courts have consistently permitted the president to settle foreign claims by sole executive agreement, but at the same time have emphasized that Congress has acquiesced in the practice. *Dames & Moore v. Regan* (1981); *American Insurance Ass'n v. Garamendi* (2003); *Medellin v. Texas* (2008).

The president is also widely believed to have some executive agreement-making power in military affairs flowing from his power as commander in chief. Beyond this, the modern limits of the president's ability to act independently in making international agreements have not been explored by the courts, although modern scholarship tends to be critical of an expansive presidential power to make sole executive agreements, and the Court in the *Medellin* case seemed to read it narrowly, at least where it would have implications for domestic U.S. law.

With respect to treaty termination, modern practice allows the president to terminate treaties on his own, at least where termination is permitted by a treaty's terms. In noteworthy episodes, President James Earl Carter terminated the Mutual Defense Treaty between the United States and the Republic of China (Taiwan) in 1980, and President George W. Bush terminated the Anti-Ballistic Missile Treaty with the Soviet Union in 2002, six months after announcing that the United States would withdraw from that treaty. Some senators objected to President Carter's actions, but the Supreme Court rebuffed their challenge in *Goldwater v. Carter* (1979), albeit without a clear explanation of its holding. President Bush's action was criticized by some scholars but received general acquiescence and some academic defense. In light of the consensus early in George Washington's administration, it is probably fair to say that this sort of presidential treaty termination does not obviously depart from the original understanding, inasmuch as the Framers were much more concerned about checks upon entering into treaties than they were about checks upon terminating them. On the other hand, the president's constitutional ability to terminate or suspend treaties in violation of their terms remains more contested because of the president's textual obligation to faithfully execute the laws (as treaties are declared to be laws by Article VI). A proposal early in the George W. Bush administration to "suspend" the Geneva Conventions on the treatment of prisoners of war, as applied to terrorism suspects determined to be "unlawful combatants" in the war on terror, was sharply criticized on this ground and ultimately not adopted by the president. Some scholars would say, however, that the president's treaty termination power extends even to violating treaties, especially treaties in core areas of presidential power such as the military and national defense.

Michael D. Ramsey

See Also

Article I, Section 10 (Compact Clause)

Article II, Section 1, Clause 1 (Executive Vesting Clause)

Article II, Section 2, Clause 2 (Appointments Clause)

Article VI, Clause 2 (Supremacy Clause)

Suggestions for Further Research

Bruce Ackerman & David Golove, *Is NAFTA Constitutional?*, 108 Harv. L. Rev. 799 (1995)

David Gray Adler, The Constitution and the Termination of Treaties (1986)

Arthur Bestor, Respective *Roles of the Senate and President in the Making and Abrogation of Treaties: The Original Intent of the Framers of the Constitution Historically Examined*, 55 Wash. L. Rev. 1 (1979)

Curtis A. Bradley, *The Treaty Power and American Federalism*, 97 Mich. L. Rev. 390 (1998)

Curtis A. Bradley & Jack L. Goldsmith, *Treaties, Human Rights, and Conditional Consent*, 149 U. Pa. L. Rev. 399 (2000)

Bradford R. Clark, *Domesticating Sole Executive Agreements*, 93 Va. L. Rev. 1573 (2007)

Brannon P. Denning & Michael D. Ramsey, American Insurance Association v. Garamendi *and Executive Preemption in Foreign Affairs*, 46 Wm. & Mary L. Rev. 825 (2004)

David F. Forte, *The Foreign Affairs Power: The Dames & Moore Case*, 31 Cleveland St. L. Rev. 43 (1982)

David Golove, *Treaty-Making and the Nation: The Historical Foundations of the Nationalist Conception of the Treaty Power*, 98 Mich. L. Rev. 1075 (2000)

Oona A. Hathaway, *Treaties' End: The Past, Present, and Future of International Lawmaking in the United States*, 117 Yale L.J. 1236 (2008)

Duncan B. Hollis & Joshua J. Newcomer, *"Political" Commitments and the Constitution*, 49 Va. J. Int'l L. 507 (2009)

Andrew T. Hyman, *The Unconstitutionality of Long-Term Nuclear Pacts that are Rejected by Over One-*

Third of the Senate, 23 Denv. J. Int'l L. & Pol'y 313 (1995)

Derek Jinks and David Sloss, *Is the President Bound by the Geneva Conventions?*, 90 Cornell L. Rev. 97 (2004)

Gary Lawson & Guy Seidman, *The Jeffersonian Treaty Clause*, 2006 U. Ill. L. Rev. 1 (2006)

Myres S. McDougal & Asher Lans, *Treaties and Congressional-Executive or Presidential Agreements: Interchangeable Instruments of National Policy*, 54 Yale L.J. 181 [Part I], & 534 [Part II] (1945)

John O. McGinnis & Michael B. Rappaport, *Our Supermajoritarian Constitution*, 80 Tex. L. Rev. 703 (2002)

Saikrishna B. Prakash & Michael D. Ramsey, *The Executive Power over Foreign Affairs*, 111 Yale L.J. 231 (2001)

Jack N. Rakove, *Solving a Constitutional Puzzle: The Treatymaking Clause as a Case Study*, 1 Persp. Am. Hist. (n.s.), 233–81 (1984)

Michael D. Ramsey, The Constitution's Text in Foreign Affairs, Chs. 8–10 & 15 (2007)

Michael D. Ramsey, *Executive Agreements and the (Non)Treaty Power*, 77 N.C. L. Rev. 133 (1999)

Michael D. Ramsey, *Missouri v. Holland and Historical Textualism*, 73 Missouri L . Rev. 969 (2008)

Restatement (Third) of the Foreign Relations Law of the United States, Section 303 (1987)

1 Ronald D. Rotunda & John E. Nowak, Treatise on Constitutional Law: Substance & Procedure §6.7 (5th ed. 2012)

Peter J. Spiro, *Treaties, Executive Agreements, and Constitutional Method*, 79 Tex. L. Rev. 961 (2001)

Edward T. Swaine, *Does Federalism Constrain the Treaty Power?*, 103 Colum. L. Rev. 403 (2003)

Laurence H. Tribe, *Taking Text and Structure Seriously: Reflections on Free-Form Method in Constitutional Interpretation*, 108 Harv. L. Rev. 1221 (1995)

John C. Yoo, *Laws as Treaties? The Constitutionality of Congressional-Executive Agreements*, 99 Mich. L. Rev. 757 (2001)

John C. Yoo, *Rational Treaties: Article II, Congressional-Executive Agreements, and International Bargaining*, 97 Cornell L. Rev. 1 (2011)

Significant Cases

The Cherokee Tobacco, 78 U.S. (11 Wall.) 616 (1870)

De Geofroy v. Riggs, 133 U.S. 258 (1890)

Field v. Clark, 143 U.S. 649 (1892)

B. Altman & Co. v. United States, 224 U.S. 583 (1912)

Missouri v. Holland, 252 U.S. 416 (1920)

United States v. Belmont, 301 U.S. 324 (1937)

United States v. Pink, 315 U.S. 203 (1942)

Reid v. Covert, 354 U.S. 1 (1957)

Goldwater v. Carter, 444 U.S. 996 (1979)

Dames & Moore v. Regan, 453 U.S. 654 (1981)

Seminole Tribe of Florida v. Florida, 517 U.S. 44 (1996)

Printz v. United States, 521 U.S. 898 (1997)

Made in the USA Foundation v. United States, 242 F.3d 1300 (11th Cir. 2001)

American Ins. Ass'n v. Garamendi, 539 U.S. 396 (2003)

Medellin v. Texas, 552 U.S. 491 (2008)

Appointments Clause

The President . . . shall nominate, and by and with the Advice and Consent of the Senate, shall appoint Ambassadors, other public Ministers and Consuls, Judges of the supreme Court, and all other Officers of the United States, whose Appointments are not herein otherwise provided for, and which shall be established by Law ...

(ARTICLE II, SECTION 2, CLAUSE 2)

~

*T*his clause contemplates three sequential acts for the appointment of principal officers—the nomination of the president, the advice and consent of the Senate, and the appointment of the official by the president.

The requirements of this part of Article II, Section 2, Clause 2, apply to principal officers, in contrast to inferior officers, whose appointments are addressed in the next part (Inferior Officers). Although the Senate must confirm principal officers, including ambassadors and Supreme Court justices, Congress may still require that any inferior officers whose office is "established by law" also be confirmed by the Senate.

There are a number of possibilities why the Framers chose the Senate (rather than Congress as a whole, or nobody) as the body that must approve the nominations of principal officers. Before the Revolution, many in the colonies had insisted on a "governor's council' to monitor and approve the royal governor's appointments, and some Framers may have seen the Senate as playing an analogous role. In addition, the small states designedly had proportionately greater power in the Senate, and could serve as a check on a president from a large state who might otherwise be able to make appointments of persons from his own state.

The important questions for principal officers and their confirmation are, first, whether the president has plenary power of nomination or whether the Constitution limits this power by requiring the president to seek pre-nomination "advice;" second, whether the president must nominate only those who meet qualifications set by Congress; and, third, whether the Senate has plenary power to reject nominees or whether that power is circumscribed by some standard.

Both the debates among the Framers and subsequent practice confirm that the president has plenary power to nominate. He is not obliged to take advice from the Senate on the identity of those whom he will nominate. On its part, the Senate possesses the plenary authority to reject or confirm the nominee, although its weaker structural position means that it is likely to confirm most nominees, absent compelling reasons to reject them.

The very grammar of the clause is telling: the act of nomination is separated from the act of appointment by a comma and a conjunction. Only the latter act is qualified by the phrase "advice and consent." Furthermore, it is not at all anomalous to use the word advice with respect to the action of the Senate in confirming an appointment. The Senate's consent is advisory because confirmation does not bind the president actually to appoint the confirmed nominee. Instead, after receiving the Senate's advice and consent, the president may deliberate again before appointing the nominee. After the president formally appoints, the appointee may, as was frequent in the early republic, then refuse the appointment, in which case the appointment is regarded as never having been made.

The principal concern of the Framers regarding the Appointments Clause, as in many of the other separation of powers provisions of the Constitution, was to ensure accountability while avoiding tyranny. Hence, following the suggestion of Nathaniel Gorham of Massachusetts and the example of the Massachusetts constitution drafted by John Adams, the Framers gave the power of nomination to the president so that the initiative of choice would be the president's responsibility, but provided the check of advice and consent to forestall the possibility of abuse of this power. Gouverneur Morris described the advantages of this multistage process: "As the President was to nominate, there would be responsibility, and as the Senate was to concur, there would be security."

The Federalist similarly recognizes the power of nomination to be an exclusively presidential prerogative. In fact, in *The Federalist* No. 76, Alexander Hamilton answered critics who would have preferred the whole power of appointment to be lodged in the president by asserting that the assignment of the power of nomination to the president alone assures sufficient accountability:

> [I]t is easy to show that every advantage to be expected from such an arrangement would, in substance, be derived from the power of *nomination* which is proposed to be conferred upon him; while several disadvantages which might attend the absolute power of appointment in the hands of that officer would be avoided. In the act of nomination, his judgment alone would be exercised; and as it would be his sole duty to point out the man who, with the approbation of the Senate, should fill an office, his responsibility would be as complete as if he were to make the final appointment.

Chief Justice John Marshall in *Marbury v. Madison* (1803), Justice Joseph Story in his *Commentaries on the Constitution of the United States* (1833), and the modern Supreme Court in

Edmond v. United States (1997) all confirm that understanding.

Congress establishes offices, and the president, at least in regard to principal officers, nominates office holders. Under the Necessary and Proper Clause (Article I, Section 8, Clause 18), Congress has often established qualifications for those who can serve in the offices it has created, thereby limiting the range of those the president can nominate. Andrew Jackson protested that such acts were an unconstitutional infringement of his appointing power, but Congress has continued the practice to this day. The Supreme Court has held that Congress may not provide itself with the power to make appointments, *Buckley v. Valeo* (1976), but it is unclear how far Congress may go in setting qualifications for principal officers without contravening the Framers' interest in assuring the president's accountability for the initial choice. President James Monroe declared that Congress had no right to intrude upon the president's appointing power. In *Myers v. United States* (1926), Chief Justice William Howard Taft declared that the qualifications set by Congress may not "so limit selection and so trench upon executive choice as to be in effect legislative designation." In *Public Citizen v. U.S. Department of Justice* (1989), Justice Anthony Kennedy, concurring, opined that the president's appointing power was exclusive, and that only the Incompatibility Clause (Article I, Section 6, Clause 2) limits the range of his choice.

There are a number of possibilities. Perhaps Congress may set whatever limited standards it wants to. Or, it may be that it may not set standards that are too limited (such as limiting the nomination to one of three approved by the House). Perhaps the legislative branch may not impose *any* standards, for that would allow the House to intrude on the Senate's confirmation process. And, even if the Senate confirms one who does not meet the standards, it may be that that would be a political question unreviewable by the courts. The Court, however, has yet to make a definitive statement on the issue.

Another related question is whether a new appointment is necessary if Congress expands the duties of an office after an appointment takes place. In *Weiss v. United States* (1994), the

Supreme Court held that military officers who served as judges in courts-martial did not need a separate act of appointment and Senate approval. The Court declared that serving as military judge was not "so different" from the duties of a military officer that a separate appointment was necessary. In fact, the Court went so far as to say that being a military judge was "germane" to being a military officer. Nor could the Court find that Congress had authorized a new appointment.

Closely related to the Framers' interest in assuring accountability was their interest in avoiding an appointment that would be the result of secret deals. In defending the clause's structure of presidential nomination and public confirmation, Hamilton in *The Federalist* No. 77 contrasted it with the appointments process by a multimember council in his own state of New York. Such a council acting in secret would be "a conclave in which cabal and intrigue will have their full scope. . . . [T]he desire of mutual gratification will beget a scandalous bartering of votes and bargaining for places." Delegates to the Constitutional Convention had expressed similar concerns. If the Senate had a formal pre-nomination advisory role, the Senate leaders and the president might well be tempted to make a deal that would serve their parochial interests and then be insulated from all but pro forma scrutiny. Other contemporaneous commentary on the Appointments Clause repudiates any special constitutional pre-nomination role for the Senate. James Iredell, a leading proponent of ratification in North Carolina and subsequently a Supreme Court justice, observed at his state's ratifying convention: "As to offices, the Senate has no other influence but a restraint on improper appointments. The President proposes such a man for such an office. The Senate has to consider upon it. If they think him improper, the President must nominate another, whose appointment ultimately again depends upon the Senate."

The practice of the first president and Senate supported the construction of the Appointments Clause that reserves the act of nomination exclusively to the president. In requesting confirmation of his first nominee, President Washington sent the Senate this message: "I nominate William Short, Esquire, and request your advice on the propriety of appointing him." The Senate then notified the president of Short's confirmation, which showed that they too regarded "advice" as a post-nomination rather than a pre-nomination function: "Resolved, that the President of the United States be informed, that the Senate advise and consent to his appointment of William Short Esquire. . . ." The Senate has continued to use this formulation to the present day. Washington wrote in his diary that Thomas Jefferson and John Jay agreed with him that the Senate's powers "extend no farther than to an approbation or disapprobation of the person nominated by the President, all the rest being Executive and vested in the President by the Constitution." Washington's construction of the Appointments Clause has been embraced by his successors. Some presidents have consulted with key Senators and a few with the Senate leadership, but they have done so out of comity or political prudence and never with the understanding that they were constitutionally obliged to do so. A law setting qualifications would not only invade the power of the president, it would also undermine the authority of the Senate as the sole authority to decide whether a principal officer should be confirmed.

The other principal controversy arising from the Appointments Clause has concerned the authority of the Senate to reject nominees. The Senate has independent authority in that it may constitutionally refuse to confirm a nominee for any reason. While ideology and jurisprudential "point of view" were not among the kinds of concerns listed by the Framers as justifying the requirement of advice and consent, nothing in the text of the clause appears to limit the kind of considerations the Senate can take up. It is thus reasonable to infer that the Framers located the process of advice and consent in the Senate as a check to prevent the president from appointing people who have unsound principles as well as blemished characters. As the president has complete discretion in the use of his veto power, the Senate has complete and final discretion in whether to accept or approve a nomination.

Given that the Senate was not to exercise choice itself, it appeared to Alexander Hamilton in *The Federalist* No. 76 that a nominee should be rejected only for "special and strong reasons." The president's power of repeated nomination provides a check on the Senate's ability to reject a nominee on something less than an articulable weighty reason. In fact, Hamilton argued that if the Senate fails to make that case and rejects the nominee for a pretextual reason, the president would generally be in a position to find a second candidate without these putative defects who generally shares the president's point of view. It is rare, however, for a president to renominate a person to a position once the Senate has declined to accept the nomination.

The president does possess an advantage in the unitary nature of the executive office as compared to the diffuse and variegated nature of the Senate—even when it is controlled by the opposition party. The president is a single individual, whereas the Senate is a body composed of many individuals with a wide range of views, including members with views like those of the president. When the president has a substantial basis of party support in the Senate and thus a nucleus of probable supporters, he has leverage for confirmation. Thus, the image of a divided government as a government in any sense equally divided when it comes to an analysis of the Appointments Clause and the confirmation process is a fundamentally false image, as George Mason recognized at the Philadelphia convention: "Notwithstanding the form of the proposition by which the appointment seemed to be divided between the Executive & Senate, the appointment was substantially vested in the former alone." Moreover, the president's advantage in the process is a considered feature of the Framers' design: they knew how to create a process by which the power of the executive and the Senate would be rendered more equal. Unlike the approval of treaties, it does not take a supermajority to approve a presidential nominee.

Because the president has the initiative of choice in appointments to the executive branch and the judiciary, the views of his prospective appointees are more likely to become a presidential campaign issue than in senatorial campaigns. Since he possesses the greatest discretion, the political process fastens upon him the greatest accountability. However, when a substantial

number of Senators assert that there are strong and compelling political reasons to reject a nominee (as opposed to rejecting one because of a flawed character), the Constitution's structure ensures a confirmation battle. As such, the Constitution contains mechanisms designed to contain conflict within the republican process in order to protect against the degeneration of the republic's original ideals and thus ensure the republic's stability. The Appointments Clause is a prime example of such a mechanism. It structures the confirmation process so that when two of the republic's national governing branches are in fundamental disagreement, there will be a struggle to persuade the people of the correctness of their respective positions. In the case of a struggle over constitutional interpretation as in a Supreme Court nomination, as has been more frequent in recent decades, the public will be forced to consider the first principles of the republic—in this case, the role of the judiciary and the proper method of interpreting its governing document. Citizens will thus vicariously enjoy some measure of the experience of the framing of the Constitution, thus contributing to the republic's self-regeneration.

John McGinnis

See Also

Article I, Section 6, Clause 2 (Incompatibility Clause)
Article I, Section 8, Clause 18 (Necessary and Proper Clause)
Article II, Section 2, Clause 2 (Inferior Officers)
Article II, Section 2, Clause 3 (Recess Appointments Clause)
Article II, Section 3 (Commissions)

Suggestions for Further Research

MICHAEL J. GERHARDT, THE FEDERAL APPOINTMENTS PROCESS: A CONSTITUTIONAL AND HISTORICAL ANALYSIS (2001)

John O. McGinnis, *The President, the Senate, the Constitution, and the Confirmation Process: A Reply to Professors Strauss and Sunstein*, 71 Tex. L. Rev. 633 (1993)

David A. Strauss & Cass R. Sunstein, *The Senate, the Constitution, and the Confirmation Process*, 101 Yale L.J. 1491 (1992)

Significant Cases

Marbury v. Madison, 5 U.S. (1 Cranch) 137 (1803)

Myers v. United States, 272 U.S. 52 (1926)

Buckley v. Valeo, 424 U.S. 1 (1976)

Morrison v. Olson, 487 U.S. 654 (1988)

Public Citizen v. U.S. Department of Justice, 491 U.S. 440 (1989)

Weiss v. United States, 510 U.S. 163 (1994)

Edmond v. United States, 520 U.S. 651 (1997)

Inferior Officers

... but the Congress may by Law vest the Appointment of such inferior Officers, as they think proper, in the President alone, in the Courts of Law, or in the Heads of Departments.

(ARTICLE II, SECTION 2, CLAUSE 2)

~

*T*he appointment power has become one of the chief powers of the president. The "by law" language concerning inferior officers—sometimes known as the Excepting Clause—authorizes the president in certain cases to exercise the appointment power alone, or through the heads of departments who are themselves his appointees. That greatly expands the scope of the appointment power beyond the mechanism of Senate consent.

The Appointments Clause divides constitutional officers into two classes: principal officers, who must be appointed through the advice and consent mechanism; and inferior officers, who may be appointed through advice and consent of the Senate, but whose appointment Congress may place instead in any of the "three repositories of the appointment power" in the Excepting Clause. *See Freytag v. Commissioner of Internal Revenue* (1991); *United States v. Germaine* (1879). These two methods are the only means of appointing government officers under the Constitution. Most officers are considered inferior officers; but, significantly, most government employees are not considered officers at all.

See Free Enterprise Fund v. Public Co. Accounting Oversight Board (2010).

Congress itself may not exercise the appointment power; its functions are limited to the Senate's role in advice and consent and to deciding whether to vest a direct appointment power over a given office in the president, a head of department, or the courts of law. The Framers were particularly concerned that Congress might seek to exercise the appointment power and fill offices with their supporters, to the derogation of the president's control over the executive branch. The Appointments Clause thus functions as a restraint on Congress and as an important structural element in the separation of powers. Attempts by Congress to circumvent the Appointments Clause, either by making appointments directly, or through devices such as "unilaterally appointing an incumbent to a new and distinct office" under the guise of legislating new duties for an existing office, have been rebuffed by the courts. *Buckley v. Valeo* (1976); *Weiss v. United States* (1994). Congress may attempt to define the qualifications for an office (particularly one that Congress creates) so restrictively that Congress effectively exercises the appointment power. The precise constraints on the ability of Congress to encroach on the appointment power in this way have not been established.

The final "by law" language emerged at the end of the Constitutional Convention, as a late addendum to the compromise over the device of presidential nomination and Senate advice and consent for principal officers. The language occasioned little debate. An earlier version of the language would have given the president a broader power to "appoint officers in all cases not otherwise provided for by this Constitution," but some delegates worried that this language would permit the president to create offices as well as to fill them, a classic case of institutional corruption. The requirement that the president can appoint inferior officers only when Congress has "by Law vest[ed]" that power in the president apparently sought to preclude that possibility.

Although separation of powers values lay behind the language of the Appointments Clause, early judicial interpretations struck a more practical note. Chief Justice John Marshall, sitting as a circuit justice, opined that the "by law" language was the Framers' means to ensure "that they had provided for all cases of offices" needing appointments. *United States v. Maurice* (1823). The Supreme Court in *United States v. Germaine* gave its explanation of the Framers' intent behind the "by law" language as anticipating that "when offices became numerous, and sudden removals necessary," the advice and consent process might prove too "inconvenient."

Two chief questions recur under the "by law" language: (1) Who are "inferior Officers," not subject to the requirement of advice and consent? and (2) Who qualifies as a head of department, when Congress seeks to place the appointment power away from the president?

As noted above, most government employees are not officers and thus are not subject to the Appointments Clause at all. In *Buckley v. Valeo*, the Supreme Court held that only those appointees "exercising significant authority pursuant to the laws of the United States" are "Officers of the United States," and consequently it is only those who exercise such "significant authority" who must be appointed by a mechanism set forth in the Appointments Clause. Employees not subject to the requirements of the Appointments Clause were described by the Court as "lesser functionaries subordinate to officers of the United States."

The Framers did not define the line between principal officers and inferior officers, and the Court has been content to approach the analysis on a case-by-case basis rather than through a definitive test. *See Morrison v. Olson* (1988). In *Morrison*, the Court listed certain factors as hallmarks of "inferior Officer" status, such as removability by a higher executive branch official other than the president, and limitations on the officer's duties, jurisdiction, and tenure. In *Edmond v. United States* (1997), the Court, while continuing to deny that it had recognized any definitive test, stated that "'inferior officers' are officers whose work is directed and supervised at some level by others who were appointed by Presidential nomination with the advice and consent of the Senate." Although the Court has not rejected consideration of the factors announced in *Morrison*, it has relied on the standard applied in *Edmond* to distinguish between principal and inferior officers. *See Free Enterprise Fund v. Public Co. Accounting Oversight*

Board. Among those officers recognized as "inferior" are district court clerks, federal supervisors of elections, the Watergate special prosecutor, and an independent counsel appointed under the Ethics in Government Act of 1978.

The phrase "heads of departments" also has not been defined precisely by the Court. Judicial interpretations of the phrase refer to the heads of departments that are within the executive branch, "or at least have some connection with that branch." *Buckley v. Valeo*. In *Freytag v. Commissioner of Internal Revenue*, the Court interpreted "heads of departments" to refer "to executive divisions like the Cabinet-level departments," but seemed to reserve the question whether the heads of non-cabinet executive-branch agencies could be deemed to be "heads of departments" for purposes of the Appointments Clause. In *Free Enterprise Fund*, the Court answered that question by adopting the reasoning of Justice Antonin Scalia's concurring opinion in *Freytag* and holding that the non-cabinet Securities and Exchange Commission constituted a department for purposes of the Appointments Clause because the commission "is a freestanding component of the Executive Branch, not subordinate to or contained within any other such component." Under this view, the heads of all freestanding agencies and departments exercising executive power under the president would seem to qualify as "heads of departments."

Douglas Cox

See Also

Suggestions for Further Research
Theodore Y. Blumoff, *Separation of Powers and the Origins of the Appointments Clause*, 37 Syracuse L. Rev. 1037 (1987)

Michael J. Gerhardt, *Toward a Comprehensive Understanding of the Federal Appointments Process*, 21 Harv. J.L. & Pub. Pol'y 479 (1998)

Memorandum for the General Counsels of the Executive Branch, from Steven G. Bradbury, Acting Assistant Attorney General, Office of Legal Counsel, *Officers of the United States Within the Meaning of the Appointments Clause* (Apr. 16, 2007), at http://www.justice.gov/olc/2007/appointmentsclausev10.pdf

Edward Susolik, *Separation of Powers and Liberty: The Appointments Clause,* Morrison v. Olson, *and the Rule of Law,* 63 S. Cal. L. Rev. 1515 (1990)

Significant Cases

United States v. Maurice, 26 F. Cas. 1211 (C.C.D. Va. 1823)

United States v. Germaine, 99 U.S. 508 (1879)

Buckley v. Valeo, 424 U.S. 1 (1976)

Morrison v. Olson, 487 U.S. 654 (1988)

Freytag v. Commissioner of Internal Revenue, 501 U.S. 868 (1991)

Weiss v. United States, 510 U.S. 163 (1994)

Edmond v. United States, 520 U.S. 651 (1997)

Free Enterprise Fund v. Public Co. Accounting Oversight Bd., 130 S. Ct. 3138 (2010)

Recess Appointments Clause

The President shall have Power to fill up all Vacancies that may happen during the Recess of the Senate, by granting Commissions which shall expire at the End of their next Session.

(Article II, Section 2, Clause 3)

~

*A*t the Constitutional Convention, the Framers adopted the Recess Appointments Clause, without debate, to prevent governmental paralysis that might occur during the long periods of the year when the Senate was not expected to be in session. In fact, early sessions of the Senate lasted only three to six months, with senators dispersing throughout the country during the six- to nine-month recesses. During these periods, they were unable to provide their advice and consent to executive nominations for positions that fell open when officeholders died or resigned. The

clause thus served as a "supplement" to the vigorously debated appointment power. Although the Anti-Federalists feared that a unilateral recess appointment power would give the president "monarchical" powers, Alexander Hamilton answered that the recess appointment power was necessary so that the Senate was not required "to be continually in session for the appointment of officers." *The Federalist* No. 67.

The Recess Appointments Clause presents two primary issues. The first concerns when the vacancy initially occurs. Under the *arise* view, the clause's language allowing the president to "fill up all vacancies that may happen during the recess of the Senate" requires that the vacancy first occur during a Senate recess. If the vacancy arises during a Senate session, then the clause assumes that the Senate had the opportunity to confirm a nominee and therefore a recess appointment is unnecessary. The *arise* view was adopted by Edmund Randolph, the first attorney general, in a legal opinion written in 1792 that constrained the power of the president.

Under the second view, a vacancy is eligible to be filled with a recess appointment, even if it arises during a recess, as long as it "happens to exist" during the recess. This *exist* view was articulated in 1823 in a legal opinion by Attorney General William Wirt. While Wirt acknowledged that the constitutional language supported the *arise* view, he concluded that the spirit of the Constitution supported the *exist* view, because an unanticipated occurrence, such as a public emergency, might cause the Senate to recess without confirming a nominee.

The *exist* view espoused by Wirt has reflected the executive branch's interpretation of the recess appointment power for the past two centuries. The executive, however, has not limited itself to the reasons that Wirt gave for his view, and has made recess appointments not only when an unanticipated circumstance has prevented confirmation, but also when the Senate has refused to approve a nominee. For a long period, the Senate resisted the executive's assertion of the *exist* view. In 1863, Senator Jacob Howard wrote a report for the Senate Judiciary Committee that supported the *arise* interpretation. S. Rep. No. 37-80 (3rd Sess. 1863). Almost simultaneously, Congress passed a statute that prohibited payment to officers who had been recess appointed to an office that had been vacant during the Senate session. 12 Stat. 646 (1863). It was only in 1940 that Congress amended the statute, allowing payment to recess appointees in three situations, including when the Senate had not acted on a nomination at the time of the recess. 54 Stat. 751 (1940).

The second basic issue regarding the interpretation of the Recess Appointments Clause involves the type of recess during which a recess appointment can be made. Under the *intersession* view, "the recess of the Senate" refers only to the intersession recess—in other words, the recess between the two annual sessions of the Senate. Intersession recesses of six to nine months occurred in the early years of the republic. By contrast, the *intrasession* view holds that "the recess" refers not only to intersession recesses, but also to intrasession recesses that occur during a session of the Senate.

The argument for the *intersession* view begins with the text of the Constitution itself. A review of the seven clauses in the Constitution using the terms "recess" and "adjournment" makes clear that the term recess refers only to intersession recesses while the word adjournment refers to all breaks in legislative business, both intersession and intrasession. This conclusion is supported by the meaning of these terms at the time the Constitution was enacted, as reflected in English and state practice.

The *intersession* view also draws support from the length of the appointment received by an official under the clause. A recess appointment lasts until the end of the "next session" of the Senate. Since sessions in the early twenty-first century typically last ten to twelve months, an appointment made during an intersession recess would last approximately one year, until the end of the next Senate session. On the other hand, an *intrasession* appointment could last as long as two years, through the end of the succeeding session.

The *intersession* interpretation was largely followed until 1921, with only a limited number of intrasession recess appointments being made during the presidency of Andrew Johnson. Attorney General Harry Daugherty's opinion to President Warren G. Harding in 1921 set the stage for the modern view of the recess appointment power. Daugherty asserted that the "real question" was not

"whether the Senate has adjourned or recessed" but "whether in a practical sense the Senate is in session so that its advice and consent can be obtained." Ever since the Daugherty opinion, the executive has followed the *intrasession* view. While the opinion did not specify the minimum length of intrasession recess that would allow a recess appointment—stating only that it had to be more than ten days and that twenty-eight days was long enough—the executive has made recess appointments during recesses as short as ten days and has implied that it could do so during recesses of more than three days. The *intrasession* view lacks a clear basis for determining the minimum length of a recess that would allow use of the power. In the post–World War II era, however, and especially since the mid-1980s, presidents have made recess appointments during relatively short intrasession recesses.

In an attempt to limit presidents' uses of recess appointments within Senate sessions, Congresses led by both parties have employed the device of a "pro forma" session. Such sessions generally are not marked by legislative business and can last less than a minute. In 2012, President Barack Obama appointed four officials during a three-day recess surrounded by two pro forma sessions. This recess appointment was supported by an opinion of the Office of Legal Counsel that relied on "practical" reasoning in concluding that "[t]he convening of periodic pro forma sessions in which no business is to be conducted does not have the legal effect of interrupting an intrasession recess otherwise long enough" to allow the president to make recess appointments.

Federal courts have disagreed about the scope of the recess appointment power. The Eleventh Circuit upheld President George W. Bush's appointment during an intrasession recess of William Pryor Jr. to the Eleventh Circuit Court of Appeals, relying on the *exist* view of vacancy and *intrasession* view of recess. *See Evans v. Stephens* (2004). In contrast, the D.C. Circuit held that President Obama's recess appointments to the National Labor Relations Board during a pro forma session were unconstitutional, relying on the *arise* view of vacancy and *intersession* view of recess. *See Noel Canning v. NLRB* (2013).

In *NLRB v. Canning* (2014), the Supreme Court held that the president can make recess appointments during intra-session recesses, but held that a three-day recess was too short to trigger the president's recess-appointment power.

A final issue involves the recess appointment of Article III judges. The recess appointment power, like the appointment power (Article II, Section 2, Clause 2), extends to all "officers of the United States," including federal judges. Some have argued that the short duration of the recess appointment is inconsistent with the life tenure provision of Article III. Others have responded that the Recess Appointments Clause represents an exception to the life tenure provision. In any event, more than three hundred judges have received recess appointments, including Supreme Court Justices William J. Brennan Jr. and Potter Stewart and Chief Justice Earl Warren (all appointed by President Dwight D. Eisenhower). Since 1980, only three judges have received recess appointments: Roger L. Gregory (appointed by President William J. Clinton to the Fourth Circuit), Charles W. Pickering Sr. (appointed by President George W. Bush to the Fifth Circuit), and William H. Pryor Jr. (appointed by President George W. Bush to the Eleventh Circuit).

Michael A. Carrier & Michael B. Rappaport

See Also

Article I, Section 3, Clause 2 (Senatorial Classes and Vacancies Clause)

Article I, Section 5, Clause 4 (Adjournment)

Article I, Section 7, Clause 2 (Pocket Veto)

Article II, Section 2, Clause 2 (Appointments Clause)

Suggestions for Further Research

Appointments of Officers—Holiday Recess, 23 Op. Att'y Gen. 599 (1901)

Executive Authority to Fill Vacancies, 1 Op. Att'y Gen. 631 (1823)

Executive Power—Recess Appointments, 33 Op. Att'y Gen. 20 (1921)

Lawfulness of Recess Appointments During a Recess of the Senate Notwithstanding Periodic Pro Forma Sessions, 36 Op. O.L.C. 5 (2012)

Recess Appointments—Compensation, 3 Op. O.L.C. 314 (1979)

Recess Appointments During an Intrasession Recess, 16 Op. O.L.C. 15 (1992)

Michael A. Carrier, Note, *When Is the Senate in Recess for Purposes of the Recess Appointments Clause?*, 92 Mich. L. Rev. 2204 (1994)

Stuart J. Chanen, *Constitutional Restrictions on the President's Power to Make Recess Appointments*, 79 Nw. U. L. Rev. 191 (1984)

Thomas A. Curtis, *Recess Appointments to Article III Courts: The Use of Historical Practice in Constitutional Interpretation*, 84 Colum. L. Rev. 1758 (1984)

Edward A. Hartnett, *Recess Appointments of Article III Judges: Three Constitutional Questions*, 26 Cardozo L. Rev. 377, 416 (2005)

Note, Recess Appointments to the Supreme Court—Constitutional but Unwise?, 10 Stan. L. Rev. 124 (1957)

Michael B. Rappaport, *The Original Meaning of the Recess Appointments Clause*, 52 UCLA L. Rev. 1487 (2005)

Virginia L. Richards, *Temporary Appointments to the Federal Judiciary: Article II Judges?*, 60 N.Y.U. L. Rev. 702 (1985)

Significant Cases

Gould v. United States, 19 Ct. Cl. 593 (1884)

United States v. Allocco, 305 F.2d 704 (2d Cir. 1962)

Staebler v. Carter, 464 F. Supp. 585 (D.D.C. 1979)

United States v. Woodley, 751 F.2d 1008 (9th Cir. 1985)

Mackie v. Clinton, 827 F. Supp. 56 (D.D.C. 1993), *vacated in part as moot,* 1994 WL 163761 (D.C. Cir. 1994)

Swan v. Clinton, 100 F.3d 973 (D.C. Cir. 1996)

Wilkinson v. Legal Services Corp., 865 F. Supp. 891 (D.D.C. 1994), *rev'd on other grounds,* 80 F.3d 535 (D.C. Cir. 1996)

Evans v. Stephens, 387 F.3d 1220 (11th Cir. 2004)

Noel Canning v. NLRB, 705 F.3d 490 (D.C. Cir. 2013)

NLRB v. Noel Canning, 573 U.S.___ (2014)

A Note on Administrative Agencies

*A*dministrative agencies, the hallmark institutions of the modern regulatory state, vary by form and function according to their statutory mandates. Some are relatively small entities executing narrowly specified duties; others are sizeable bureaucracies armed with large budgets and broad rulemaking authority. Some are sub-units of executive departments;

others are free-standing. The latter, in turn, fall into two categories: executive agencies (so called because they are accountable to the president) and "independent" agencies (which are wholly accountable neither to the president nor to Congress). The difference between the two generally inheres in the degree to which the president can unilaterally dismiss the head of the agency.

The legal status, powers, and purpose of administrative agencies are prescribed by acts of Congress, which differ considerably in their delegation of administrative discretion. Some statutes grant great leeway to agencies, e.g., the power to define and police "unfair methods of competition," or to promulgate rules based on "public interest, convenience, or necessity." Others seek to circumscribe the scope of agency autonomy. In either event, most agencies are authorized to make rules having the same force and effect as statutes. Many combine legislative, executive, and judicial powers: they not only make rules; they conduct trials to determine whether their rules have been violated and impose fines and penalties for infractions. Unless otherwise specified in their enabling acts or subsequent legislation, agency operations are governed by the Administrative Procedure Act (APA) of 1946, which distinguishes various kinds of proceedings, sets rules for each, and establishes criteria for obtaining judicial review following final agency action.

The APA requires—and general principles of administrative law dictate—that all agency regulations and rulings (1) constitute a valid delegation of legislative authority, (2) be based on an agency's factual findings, (3) be made with the goal of serving the public interest or meeting public necessity, and (4) conform to certain procedural requirements, such as "notice and comment."

The APA distinguishes between two general categories of agency action: rulemaking and adjudication. Each is normally preceded by investigation (though sometimes agencies adjudicate matters brought before them by private parties without any prior investigation). In many cases, the power to gather information can be quite plenary.

In terms of *rulemaking,* all procedural rules that bind agencies are found in legislation; *only* Congress can impose procedural limitations on agency rulemaking; courts are not free to do so

on their own authority, but must instead turn to enabling statutes. Agencies are free to add legally binding procedural requirements by regulation on their own. The public must have notice of an intended rulemaking so as to prepare meaningful comment and to consider the proffered facts supporting the intended rule.

Adjudications can take many forms, but generally can be grouped into law enforcement adjudications (such as those conducted by the Federal Trade Commission), benefits adjudications (such as those conducted by the Social Security Administration), and licensing and permit adjudications (such as those conducted by the Environmental Protection Agency). Many of these adjudications, known as "informal" adjudications, are effectively subject to no procedural requirements imposed by the APA, though the agencies' governing statutes, the agencies' own regulations, and due process constraints can all be sources of procedural law. Traditional common law rules, or those found in the Federal Rules of Civil Procedure, are unenforceable against federal administrative agencies.

Many administrative agencies with regulatory authority have been created to redress perceived or actual market failures—for example, to regulate monopoly power, "windfall" profits, or "unfair" methods of competition or to compensate for externalities, inadequate information, or unequal bargaining power. Others exist to administer benefits programs. Whatever might be said by way of justifying the purpose or behavior of particular agencies, their number and variety testify to the growth of federal authority during the past century. Expansive interpretations of Congress's powers under the Commerce Clause and the Fourteenth Amendment have broadened federal jurisdiction to the extent that few subjects now lie beyond its reach. And whereas earlier phases of federal regulation focused primarily on the economic activities of businesses, a new era of "social regulation" (beginning in the 1970s) expanded federal jurisdiction over matters that cut deeply into the personal lives of citizens, e.g., civil rights, workplace safety, environmental and consumer protection, and, most recently, doctor-patient relations.

Although politicians have long since accommodated themselves to administrative agencies as a necessary adjunct of modern government, the scope of agency powers continues to generate heated controversy. This is especially true of independent agencies, sometimes referred to as the "headless fourth branch of government," which are and remain a constitutional anomaly. In theory, independent agencies are subject to supervision by the constitutional branches in the sense that the president appoints agency leadership (subject to Senate confirmation), Congress authorizes agency budgets and conducts legislative oversight, and judicial review ensures agency compliance with statutory and constitutional requirements. But these controls, precisely because they are remote, indirect, and incomplete, strain the legal and political accountability that the separation of powers was designed to secure.

The anomalous constitutional character of independent agencies has prompted efforts by the political branches to exert greater political control over their behavior. President Franklin D. Roosevelt, for example, unsuccessfully sought to bring independent agency appointees within the ambit of the president's removal power. *Humphrey's Executor v. United States* (1935). Congress, in turn, has tried and failed to assert its authority over both the appointment and removal of independent agency officers. *Buckley v. Valeo* (1976); *Bowsher v. Synar* (1986).

Executive-congressional competition of this sort reflects unresolved ambiguities in the modern administrative state. Conceding that Congress cannot specify every detail of policy, some degree of legislative delegation is inevitable, especially when Congress tries to regulate many subjects extensively. The separation of powers, however, necessarily limits the extent to which Congress may delegate its legislative authority. What are the constitutional standards that distinguish valid and invalid delegations? When Congress delegates, does discretion then vest automatically and entirely in the executive? And once it delegates, may Congress nevertheless retain control over certain details of policy and, if so, by how much and by what means? What happens when congressional efforts to control details run up against the president's constitutional duty to execute the law?

These questions are difficult enough when applied to executive agencies, but they are particularly nettlesome when applied to independent agencies, which by their nature are neither congressional fish nor presidential fowl. As it constructed the administrative state, Congress slowly began to recognize a political dilemma. Congress was at first content to delegate broad rulemaking authority to administrative agencies, even while referring to them, somewhat incongruously, as "arms of Congress." As the number and authority of agencies expanded, Congress sought in diverse ways to limit executive control over agency policy and operations. Presidents, for their part, initially sought to maximize their authority over administrative agencies, but yielded over time to the palpable reality of congressional power. After much experimentation and conflict over many decades, as qualified from time to time by the instruction of the Supreme Court, independent agencies, despite their constitutional irregularity, became politically acceptable. They are, at bottom, the institutional embodiment of a congressional desire to delegate the details of governance while simultaneously seeking to retain some measure of control.

The short history of the administrative state is a tale of more or less continual struggle between the political branches for control of agency lawmaking, with the judiciary playing the occasional role of referee. Prior to the 1930s, the Supreme Court sustained piecemeal delegations of legislative authority on varying grounds. *Field v. Clark* (1892); *United States v. Grimaud* (1911); and *J. W. Hampton, Jr. & Co. v. United States* (1928). Later efforts to invest administrative agencies with essentially open-ended authority to make and enforce rules gave the Court pause. Accordingly, it invalidated a number of New Deal regulatory schemes, either because they lacked intelligible standards necessarily implied by the separation of powers (the nondelegation doctrine) or because they failed to meet the requirements of due process. *A.L.A. Schechter Poultry Corp. v. United States* (1935); *Panama Refining Co. v. Ryan* (1935); *Carter v. Carter Coal Co.* (1936).

In the late 1930s, the Court essentially abandoned its effort to police the growth of administrative lawmaking. See *United States v. Carolene Products Co.* (1938). Even so, judicial reservations about the scope of administrative discretion have retained a certain purchase. The enactment of the APA in 1946 quieted many procedural concerns, but the substantive scope of rulemaking authority (whether exercised by executive or independent agencies) remains a matter of continuing contro-versy. The judiciary originally granted agencies great freedom to interpret their statutory mandates. In the 1970s, the courts began to second-guess the interpretative license they had previously granted, but then reverted to a modified version of its earlier embrace of administrative deference. See *Chevron U.S.A. Inc. v. Natural Resources Defense Council, Inc.* (1984). Judges also seem to be of two minds concerning congressional delegation generally. In some instances, they have upheld vague or even conflicting delegations, but in others they have sought to place tighter reins on Congress. And in many cases, Supreme Court justices remain sharply divided. Compare *Industrial Union Dep't, AFL-CIO v. American Petroleum Institute* (1980); *Mistretta v. United States* (1989); *Whitman v. American Truck-ing Ass'ns, Inc.* (2001); and *Massachusetts v. EPA* (2007). This oscillation and conflict may reflect a continuing, though mostly unarticulated, ambiva-lence about the constitutionality of delegation.

Although administrative agencies are a given of modern industrial society, the political branches continue to battle for control of agency action. In the 1960s and 1970s, in an effort to curb regulatory excess and to tighten its control over administrative agencies, Congress imposed vari-ous forms of legislative veto, which the Supreme Court invalidated in *INS v. Chadha* (1983). Presi-dential efforts to control regulation have been relatively more successful. In 1981, President Ron-ald Reagan issued an executive order requiring executive agencies to apply cost-benefit analysis to proposed major rules and authorizing the Office of Management and Budget to police their efforts. Despite criticism by certain legislators and inter-est groups, the approach initiated by Reagan has continued, with relatively minor modification, under his successors in office.

The growth of administrative rulemaking is a dominant theme of American political develop-ment during the past century. It permeates virtually every aspect of economic and even social activity, and in recent decades has extended its reach into the lives of individuals in ways that would have been thought shocking only a generation ago. Whatever the virtues or vices of particular rules in terms of policy outcomes, the regulatory regime under which we now live has significantly altered the nation's constitutional structure. To under-score only the most obvious point, administrative rulemaking entails a massive shift of legislative authority from elected representatives to bureau-cratic officials who are for the most part neither known nor accountable to the citizens whose lives are increasingly subjected to their control.

This development is no accident. While American history from its early days has been replete with examples of administrative delega-tion, Congress and the courts once kept fairly tight control over the substance and many details of policy. Such is no longer the case. The adminis-trative state today differs not only in degree but in kind from prevalent practice prior to the New Deal. The intellectual godfathers of the modern administrative state—Woodrow Wilson and Her-bert Croly, to name but two of the most influential thinkers—believed that the Founders' Constitu-tion was hopelessly antiquated, inefficient, anti-democratic, and dogmatically committed to the idea of limited government. They evinced a dislike for the separation of powers, which they correctly identified as the principal structural obstacle to the growth of efficient federal regulatory power. Allied with this belief was a second conviction: that there was a group of men whose dedication to the commonweal was unsullied by the spirit of faction, and whose public-spirited, non-partisan expertise could be brought to bear against the most press-ing social and economic problems of the day. The objective was to reconstitute government in such a way as to vest these experts with power to devise rules and regulations that Congress, left to its own devices, would be reluctant to impose.

Though Congress was at first wary about the manner in which it delegated its legislative respon-sibilities, it has gradually and willingly surrendered a good deal of its authority to administrative agen-cies and has learned how to profit politically from its abdication. Members of Congress continue to insist, at least formally, that they remain in charge by controlling agency budgets and conducting over-sight hearings to ensure bureaucratic compliance with legislative mandates. These are indeed potent instruments of control, but they are infrequently deployed in a systemically efficacious manner. In truth, with episodic exceptions, Congress seems content to play ombudsman to the operations of the administrative state. Its members intervene on behalf of diverse factional interests that stand to gain or lose under extant or proposed regulations and, in return, receive campaign contributions and other forms of support from those whom they assist. Apart from this politically advantageous quid pro quo, however, Congress evinces little interest in defining or controlling many of the most important details of public policy. It may complain about bureaucratic malfeasance, excess, or neglect, but it continues to delegate vast discretionary authority to administrative agencies.

Two of the most significant additions to the administrative agency regime are the Patient Protection and Affordable Care Act (commonly called "Obamacare") and the Wall Street Reform and Consumer Protection Act (usually referred to as "Dodd-Frank"). Each statute will require hundreds of separate rulemakings, which will in turn produce many thousands of pages of new or revised regulations. The administrative regimes created by both acts are, and will continue to be for some time, the subject of litigation challenging various features of these laws, including their constitutionality. How all this will turn out cannot be predicted, but this much seems clear: the new regulations spawned by these and other recent enactments portend a quantum leap in the way the federal government can control the details of individual behavior.

At the height of the New Deal, President Roosevelt and Congress initiated such schemes as the National Industrial Recovery Act and the Agricultural Adjustment Act, which sought to regulate in minute detail virtually every aspect of economic behavior. The Supreme Court turned back that effort in the mid-1930s, but thereafter stopped trying to control the growth and reach of delegated regulatory authority. For many reasons, the Court is unable or unwilling to exercise a similar policing function today, whence it follows that remedies, if they are to be found, must originate in the political branches, and especially in Congress.

In recent years, a number of significant legislative plans have been advanced to limit the scope of administrative discretion. These include proposals that would narrow the scope of legislative delegations, delay the effective date of major rules until they are affirmatively approved by Congress, impose tighter restrictions on agency rulemaking

procedures, enhance the scope of judicial review, subject proposed regulations to cost-benefit analysis, and bring independent agencies under presidential control. For the most part, such reforming legislation has not passed both houses of Congress.

Michael M. Uhlmann

Suggestions for Further Research

Stephen Breyer, Regulation and Its Reform (1982)

Herbert Croly, The Promise of American Life (1909)

James O. Freedman, Crisis and Legitimacy (1978)

Richard A. Harris & Sidney M. Milkis, The Politics of Regulatory Change (1996)

Gary Lawson, Federal Administrative Law (6th ed. 2012)

Gary Lawson, *The Rise and Rise of the Administrative State*, 107 Harv. L. Rev. 1231 (1994)

Jerry L. Mashaw, Creating the Administrative Constitution (2012)

Matthew McCubbins, Roger Noll, & Barry Weingast, *The Political Origins of the Administrative Procedure Act*, 15 J.L. Econ. & Org. 180 (1999)

Ronald J. Pestritto, *The Birth of the Administrative State: Where It Came From and What It Means for Limited Government,* Heritage Foundation First Principles Report, November 20, 2007

Robert L. Rabin, *Federal Regulation in Historical Perspective,* 38 Stan. L. Rev. 1189 (1986)

Woodrow Wilson, *The Study of Administration*, 2 Pol. Sci. Q. 197 (1887)

Significant Cases

Field v. Clark, 143 U.S. 649 (1892)

United States v. Grimaud, 220 U.S. 506 (1911)

Bi-Metallic Inv. Co. v. State Bd. of Equalization of Colorado, 239 U.S. 441 (1915)

J. W. Hampton Jr. & Co. v. United States, 276 U.S. 394 (1928)

A. L. A. Schechter Poultry Corp. v. United States, 295 U.S. 495 (1935)

Humphrey's Executor v. United States, 295 U.S. 602 (1935)

Panama Refining Co. v. Ryan, 293 U.S. 388 (1935)

Carter v. Carter Coal Co., 298 U.S. 238 (1936)

United States v. Carolene Products Co., 304 U.S. 144 (1938)

United States v. Florida East Coast Ry., 410 U.S. 224 (1973)

Buckley v. Valeo, 424 U.S. 1 (1976)

Vermont Yankee Nuclear Power Corp. v. Natural Resources Defense Council, Inc., 435 U.S. 519 (1978)

Industrial Union Dep't, AFL-CIO v. American Petroleum Inst., 448 U.S. 607 (1980)

INS v. Chadha, 462 U.S. 919 (1983)

Chevron U.S.A. Inc. v. Natural Resources Defense Council, Inc., 467 U.S. 837 (1984)

Bowsher v. Synar, 478 U.S. 714 (1986)

Mistretta v. United States, 488 U.S. 361 (1989)

Whitman v. American Trucking Ass'ns, Inc., 531 U.S. 457 (2001)

Massachusetts v. EPA, 549 U.S. 497 (2007)

State of the Union

[The President] shall from time to time give to the Congress Information of the State of the Union....
(ARTICLE II, SECTION 3)

~

*A*s Chief Justice John Marshall pointed out in *Marbury v. Madison* (1803), much of the power of the executive is, in its nature, discretionary. Not so with the President's obligation to provide Congress with a report on the state of the Union. In his *Commentaries on the Constitution of the United States* (1833), Justice Joseph Story observed that because the President has more information of the complex workings of the government, "[t]here is great wisdom, therefore, in not merely allowing, but in requiring, the president to lay before congress all facts and information, which may assist their deliberations; and in enabling him at once to point out the evil, and to suggest the remedy." Only the president—who posseses unique knowledge of military operations, foreign affairs, and the day-to-day execution of the laws and is the only national representative of the whole people—can give a comprehensive assessment of the overall state of the nation and its relations with the world.

The Framers fastened this duty upon the president as a means of transparency and accountability. Justice Story noted, "He is thus justly made responsible, not merely for a due administration of the existing systems, but for due diligence and examination into the means of improving them." Other constitutionally defined communications, such as the president's veto message to Congress, his recommendation of measures to Congress, and the Senate's advice and consent of presidential nominations, represent what James Madison called the "partial agency" (*The Federalist* No. 47) of one department in the workings of another department. But like the Presidential Oath of Office Clause (Article II, Section 1, Clause 8), the State of the Union Clause requires the president to respect the legislative role of Congress while retaining executive discretion in the fulfillment of his role in enforcing the laws.

Unlike the British model of a "speech from the throne" to Parliament, which represents the sovereignty of the "king in parliament" of the British constitution, the American version, at least as written in the Constitution, presumes the vitality of the separation of powers and the ultimate accountability of each branch of government to the sovereign people. The modern practice of the State of the Union address, however, seems to borrow elements from the British form of the "speech from the throne."

The origins of the clause are in the early state constitutions, as well as Alexander Hamilton's unadopted draft language:

> The President at the beginning of every meeting of the Legislature as soon as they shall be ready to proceed to business, shall convene them together at the place where the Senate shall sit, and shall communicate to them all such matters as may be necessary for their information, or as may require their consideration.

George Washington gave the first "Annual Message" in the Senate chamber in January 1790, at the beginning of the second session of the First Congress. Subsequent messages came shortly after the convening of Congress, fulfilling the intended purpose of the Framers that the occasion was not for pomp but for practical content. Congress, for its part, does not need to respond, although it did so early in the republic through a formal resolution of each House and, in more recent times, by a reply by a member of the opposition party.

Historically, annual messages mostly focused on foreign relations and introduced the reports and recommendations of department heads. It was not until the twentieth century, with the ease of communications and access to information, as well as the president's increased public presence and role as political party leader, that the State of the Union became less reporting and assessment and more policy advocacy and political persuasion. Although it is not a requirement, there was an expectation that the president would deliver the message orally (as was done by Washington and John Adams). Thomas Jefferson thought the practice too royal and refused to do so personally; he had clerks read it to Congress. Woodrow Wilson revived the oral tradition in 1913, a practice that every president since Franklin D. Roosevelt has followed. With the advent of radio (first used by Calvin Coolidge in 1923) and television (first used by Harry S. Truman in 1947), the State of the Union address has become an important occasion for speaking directly to the American people.

Beginning with Lyndon Johnson, the presidents have delivered their addresses in the evening to obtain a wider television audience. Showmanship, partisanship, and pomp have increased in recent decades, raising the issue of whether it is appropriate for members of the Supreme Court to attend. Despite the intentions of the Framers, the State of the Union has evolved to something like the "speech from the throne" but with a signal difference. In England, the leader of governing party in Parliament writes the speech for the monarch, whereas in the United States, the president is the de facto national leader (regardless of party control by the legislature), and the State of the Union address now demonstrates how powerful an initiator of the legislative process the president has become.

Matthew Spalding

See Also

Suggestions for Further Research

Edward S. Corwin, The President: Office and Powers, 1787–1984 (5th ed. rev. 1984)

Vasan Kesavan & J. Gregory Sidak, *The Legislator-in-Chief*, 44 Wm. & Mary L. Rev. 1 (2002)

Colleen J. Shogan & Thomas H. Neale, "The President's State of the Union Address: Tradition, Function, and Policy Implications," Congressional Research Service 7-5700, December 17, 2012

Joseph Story, Commentaries on the Constitution of the United States (Constitutional Bicentennial Edition, Carolina Academic Press, Durham, N.C. 1987) (with introduction by Ronald D. Rotunda & John E. Nowak)

Recommendations Clause

[The President] shall from time to time . . . recommend to their Consideration such Measures as he shall judge necessary and expedient. . . .

(**Article II, Section 3**)

$\sim$

*D*espite the Article I provision that "All legislative Powers herein granted shall be vested in a Congress of the United States," the Constitution gives the president, as James Madison put it in *The Federalist* No. 47, a significant "partial agency" in the legislative process. Among his most important legislative functions is the duty to recommend measures to the Congress. Through this provision, the president has come to play an important, and often primary, role in the legislative process, though it took more than a century for the implications of the Recommendations Clause to be fully developed. One reading of the Constitution is that Congress proposes legislation, then the president signs or vetoes the bill. In practice, Congress often waits for the president to propose legislation, and it is common for legislators to criticize him if he does not make such proposals.

At the Constitutional Convention, the clause originally contained the word "matters," but the

Framers changed it to "measures," indicating that the president was to recommend specific legislation (including the improvement of existing legislation) and not simply put forth general ideas. On the motion of Gouverneur Morris, the convention also changed the word "may" to "shall," as Morris stated, "in order to make it the duty of the President to recommend, & thence prevent umbrage or cavil at his doing it." Beyond those changes, there was little discussion. In *The Federalist* No. 77, Alexander Hamilton listed the provision among several minor presidential powers, commenting that "no objection has been made to this class of authorities; nor could they possibly admit of any."

Explicitly, the clause imposes a duty, but its performance rests solely with the president. Congress possesses no power to compel the president to recommend. Unlike the Necessary and Proper Clause of Article I, which limits Congress's discretion in exercising its delegated powers, the phrase "he shall judge necessary and expedient" explicitly grants discretion to the president in fulfilling the clause's duty. Because this is a political question, there has been little judicial involvement with the president's actions under the clause. In *Youngstown Sheet & Tube Co. v. Sawyer* (1952), the Court noted that the Recommendations Clause serves as a reminder that the president cannot make law by himself: "The power to recommend legislation, granted to the president, serves only to emphasize that it is his function to recommend and that it is the function of the Congress to legislate." The Court made a similar point in striking down the line-item veto. *Clinton v. City of New York* (1998). When President William J. Clinton attempted to shield the records of the president's Task Force on Health Care Reform as essential to his functions under the Recommendations Clause, a federal circuit court rejected the argument and noted, "[T]he Recommendation Clause is less an obligation than a right. The President has the undisputed authority to recommend legislation, but he need not exercise that authority with respect to any particular subject or, for that matter, any subject." *Ass'n of American Physicians & Surgeons v. Clinton* (1993).

Questions regarding the scope of the Recommendations Clause remain. Congress often directs agencies to submit legislative recommendations. But President George W. Bush asserted not merely that all recommendations from executive agencies to Congress must be approved by him, but that Congress lacked the power altogether to compel recommendations from the president or any of the executive agencies.

The phrase "recommend to their Consideration" signifies the republican nature of the process. The president's recommendations are not royal edicts. They are suggestions to the people's and the states' representatives. His election is from a different constituency from either the House or the Senate, and his recommendations consequently provide a more national perspective for Congress to consider. Combined with the later addition of the Right of Assembly and Freedom of Petition clauses (in the First Amendment), the Recommendations Clause serves as an additional conduit for mediated public influence on the legislative process.

Except in times of emergency or war, early presidents were not actively involved in trying to influence Congress. George Washington sent only three proposals to Congress, and though Thomas Jefferson actively influenced the legislative process, he preferred to act behind the scenes rather than through formal recommendations. John Adams was more aloof than either. But as the national government became more involved in the economy (after the Interstate Commerce Act of 1887 and the development of the Industrial Revolution), presidents began to try to affect congressional action.

Active presidential involvement in pressing for legislation began with Theodore Roosevelt and expanded during the presidency of Woodrow Wilson. With the approach of World War I, the executive branch drafted legislation before working with Congress. With the return of Republican presidents in the 1920s, presidential activism decreased. The breakthrough of the modern presidency with respect to the legislative process came with Franklin D. Roosevelt's legendary Hundred Days. After calling the Seventy-Third Congress into special session on March 9, 1933, shortly after his inauguration, Roosevelt sent to Congress over the next one hundred days a flurry of proposed laws intended to help the nation cope with the economic disaster of the Great Depression. Most of the laws were actually drafted in the White House, and the Democrat-controlled Congress passed most without hearings or any careful legislative scrutiny.

After FDR, presidentially inspired programs became a mainstay of the legislative process. Though reluctant at first, President Dwight D. Eisenhower established the Office of Congressional Relations to assist him in dealing with Congress. The subsequent record of presidential administrations has been varied, though the role of the president in proposing legislation remains a core feature of the modern presidency.

Vasan Kesavan, James Pfiffner, and
J. Gregory Sidak

See Also

Article I, Section 1 (Legislative Vesting Clause)
Article I, Section 7, Clause 2 (Pocket Veto)
Article II, Section 2, Clause 2 (Treaty Clause)
Article II, Section 2, Clause 2 (Appointments Clause)
Article II, Section 3 (State of the Union)

Suggestions for Further Research

Edward S. Corwin, THE PRESIDENT: OFFICE AND POWERS, 1787–1984 (5th ed. rev. 1984)

George C. Edwards, AT THE MARGINS: PRESIDENTIAL LEADERSHIP OF CONGRESS (1989)

Vasan Kesavan & J. Gregory Sidak, *The Legislator-in-Chief*, 44 Wm. & Mary L. Rev. 1 (2002)

Harold J. Krent, *From a Unitary to a Unilateral Presidency*, 88 B.U. L. Rev. 523 (2008)

J. Gregory Sidak, *The Recommendation Clause*, 77 Geo. L.J. 2079 (1989)

James L. Sundquist, THE DECLINE AND RESURGENCE OF CONGRESS (1981)

Stephen J. Wayne, THE LEGISLATIVE PRESIDENCY (1978)

Significant Cases

Youngstown Sheet & Tube Co. v. Sawyer, 343 U.S. 579 (1952)

Ass'n of American Physicians & Surgeons v. Clinton, 997 F.2d 898 (D.C. Cir. 1993)

Clinton v. City of New York, 524 U.S. 417 (1998)

Convening of Congress

[The President] may, on extraordinary Occasions, convene both Houses, or either of them, and in Case of Disagreement between them, with Respect to the Time of Adjournment, he may adjourn them to such Time as he shall think proper....

(ARTICLE II, SECTION 3)

≈

*U*nder British practice, the king could convene or dissolve Parliament at will. This powerful right was naturally a source of tension between the crown and Parliament. Kings wielded this power as they wished but would have to re-convene Parliament when they wanted more money. The right to dissolve or convene Parliaments bred dangerous instability and was one of the driving forces of the English Civil War (1642–1651), which was, at bottom, a war of institutions: the Parliament against the crown.

The experience of England was fresh in the mind of the American founders when they issued the Declaration of Independence, for in many ways the Americans believed they were replicating the Glorious Revolution of 1688:

He has called together legislative bodies at places unusual, uncomfortable, and distant from the repository of their public records, for the sole purpose of fatiguing them into compliance with his measures. He has dissolved Representative Houses repeatedly, for, opposing with manly firmness his invasions on the rights of the people. He has refused for a long time, after such dissolutions, to cause others to be elected....

That American statesmen learned well from the experience of England can also be seen in the state constitutions that were drafted between the Declaration of Independence and Constitutional Convention. Under nine of the state constitutions adopted during that period, the governor had no power to "prorogue, dissolve, or adjourn" the legislature.

With the Framers' knowledge of English history, their experience with King George III, and the practice of the states, it is no surprise that the decision to give the executive of the United States little authority over when and where Congress should meet appeared to pass the Convention with no debate, following the proposal first made in the Committee of Detail. The Constitution insists that Congress's right to convene must be independent of the will of the executive. Article I, Section 4, Clause 2. "Each house," Thomas Jefferson wrote in 1790, had a "natural right to meet when and where it should think best."

Nonetheless, the Framers also understood that the government must be able to meet exigent circumstances and therefore gave the president the very limited power to convene Congress "on extraordinary occasions." Justice Joseph Story indicated in his *Commentaries on the Constitution of the United States* (1833) that the president's need to conduct foreign relations effectively would be the primary motive for convening Congress. He gave as examples the need "to repel foreign aggressions, depredations, and direct hostilities; to provide adequate means to mitigate, or overcome unexpected calamities; to suppress insurrections; and to provide for innumerable other important exigencies, arising out of the intercourse and revolutions among nations."

Beginning with John Adams in 1797, the president has convened both the House and the Senate twenty-seven times, normally for crises such as war, economic emergency, or critical legislation. In addition, the president has called the Senate to meet to confirm nominations. With the ratification of the Twentieth Amendment, which brought forward the date on which Congress convenes, and with the practice of Congress to remain in session twelve months out of the year, there is practically no need for the president to call extraordinary sessions anymore. President Harry S. Truman called the last special session on July 26, 1948.

Of course, even more important to the Framers was limiting the power of the executive to dissolve the legislature. They understood from English history that such power was among the quickest routes to tyranny. Under the Constitution, therefore, as Alexander Hamilton explained,

"[t]he President can only adjourn the national Legislature in the single case of disagreement about the time of adjournment." *The Federalist* No. 69. It is only an administrative power, one that the president has never had to exercise.

David F. Forte

See Also
Article I, Section 4, Clause 2 (Meetings of Congress Clause)
Article I, Section 5, Clause 4 (Adjournment)
Amendment XX (Presidential Terms)

Suggestions for Further Research
Bernard Bailyn, THE IDEOLOGICAL ORIGINS OF THE AMERICAN REVOLUTION (1967)
Curtis A. Bradley & Martin S. Flaherty, *Executive Power Essentialism and Foreign Affairs*, 102 Mich. L. Rev. 545 (2004)
Christopher Hibbert, THE STORY OF ENGLAND (1992)

Ambassadors

[The President] shall receive Ambassadors and other public Ministers....
(ARTICLE II, SECTION 3)

~

*T*he Articles of Confederation vested the powers "of sending and receiving ambassadors" in Congress, though they were delegated to the Committee of the States when Congress was not in session (Article IX). In the Constitutional Convention, the delegates at first followed the example of the Articles by vesting the appointment of American ambassadors as well as the treaty power in the Senate without executive participation. The Committee of Detail adopted Edmund Randolph's suggestion that the president be given the power to "receive" ambassadors. The Committee of Eleven later transferred to the president the treaty and appointment powers (subject to Senate approval), joining them to the independent power to receive ambassadors and other public ministers, such as consuls and other diplomats accredited to the United States by any foreign state. The convention approved the changes. In this light, it is difficult to say that the framers thought that the power to receive ambassadors was part of any larger executive branch responsibility for foreign affairs. In *The Federalist* No. 69, in fact, Alexander Hamilton described the president's power to receive ambassadors as merely the most "convenient" expedient, compared with the "necessity of convening the legislature" whenever a new ambassador arrived in the American capital.

Does the power to receive ambassadors necessarily imply a power to refuse their reception? And if it does, what degree of presidential control of foreign relations follows from such a power? In his 1829 book, *A View of the Constitution of the United States*, William Rawle declared, "Under the expression, he is to receive ambassadors, the president is charged with all transactions between the United States and foreign nations." The president can refuse to receive putative ambassadors whose credentials are in serious doubt. Where no such doubt exists, however, a presidential refusal to receive an ambassador amounts to a decision not to "recognize" a foreign government, or at least not to carry on diplomatic relations with it, with all the consequences in international law and diplomacy that may follow from such a rupture.

From an early date, the federal courts have held, until quite recently, that the clause raises only "political questions" to be decided by the other branches, not by the judiciary. Credentials as an ambassador may matter greatly in certain legal cases, but the courts will not inquire further than to assure themselves that the president has or has not received an ambassador as representing his government. *United States v. Ortega* (1825); *In re Baiz* (1890).

The historical debate over the deeper implications of the clause—namely, whether it accords the president an unfettered right to "recognize" another nation for diplomatic purposes—has accordingly taken place in the political arena, at least for the most part. Alexander Hamilton (as "Pacificus") and James Madison (as "Helvidius")

first discussed the question in their debate over President Washington's Proclamation of Neutrality of 1793. Madison characterized the power of reception as merely ministerial, carrying no discretion to accept or reject the legitimacy of a foreign government—a discretion he would have lodged in Congress. Hamilton, altering the position he expressed in *The Federalist*, held that the power "includes that of judging, in the case of a Revolution of Government in a foreign Country, whether the new rulers are competent organs of the National Will and ought to be recognised or not." He concluded that the clause touched on "an important instance of the right of the Executive to decide the obligations of the Nation with regard to foreign Nations."

As a practical matter, Hamilton's argument of 1793 has prevailed historically. As then Representative John Marshall put it in 1800, "[t]he President is the sole organ of the nation in its external relations, and its sole representative with foreign nations. Of consequence the demand of a foreign nation can only be made on him." Should a would-be ambassador arrive in the capital and be refused reception by the president, there is nowhere else under the Constitution that he can turn. Likewise, it is difficult to see how the reception of an ambassador, and the consequent opening of diplomatic relations with a previously unrecognized government, can be undone by the action of another branch of government. *United States v. Belmont* (1937). Congress possesses other formal powers over foreign affairs, but this clause has come to be widely understood as giving the president one of his considerable advantages in the conduct of American foreign policy. He has, for example, the power to make agreements incident to his act of receiving ambassadors. Thus, the Supreme Court relied upon the clause to validate President Franklin D. Roosevelt's signing of the Litvinov Assignment with the U.S.S.R. on the basis of his power to recognize foreign governments and receive ambassadors. *United States v. Pink* (1942).

The Supreme Court has recently held that the clause does not—at least not invariably—necessitate the invocation of the "political questions" doctrine. The case involved a statute arguably impinging on the conduct of our diplomatic relations. Congress had legislated an affirmative right of citizens born in Jerusalem to have "Israel" named as their place of birth in official United States documents. But the executive branch, resisting the mandate of the statute, argued that the courts must either treat the matter as nonjusticiable under the "receive Ambassadors" clause, or, if deciding the merits, hold that Congress may not invade the executive's control of foreign relations by legislating on the contents of documents issued by the United States where those documents affect our diplomacy. Lower courts took the first position, holding the dispute nonjusticiable as a political question. The Supreme Court disagreed, holding that the constitutionality of the statute was a fit subject for judicial review, and remanded for further proceedings on the merits of the controversy between Congress and the executive branch. *Zivotofsky v. Clinton* (2012).

Matthew Franck

See Also

Article I, Section 8, Clause 3 (Commerce with Foreign Nations)
Article I, Section 8, Clause 11 (Declare War)
Article I, Section 10, Clause 1
Article II, Section 2, Clause 2 (Treaty Clause)
Article II, Section 2, Clause 2 (Appointments Clause)
Article III, Section 2, Clause 1
Article III, Section 2, Clause 2

Suggestions for Further Research

Edward S. Corwin, THE PRESIDENT: OFFICE AND POW-ERS, 1787–1984 (5th ed., revised, 1984)

Alexander Hamilton, *Pacificus no. 1* (29 June 1793), *in* 15 The Papers of Alexander Hamilton 33 (Harold C. Syrett et al. eds., 1969)

Louis Henkin, FOREIGN AFFAIRS AND THE UNITED STATES CONSTITUTION (2d ed.1996)

James Madison, *Helvidius no. 3* (7 September 1793), *in* 15 The Papers of James Madison 95 (William T. Hutchinson et al. eds., 1985)

RESTATEMENT (THIRD) OF THE FOREIGN RELATIONS LAW OF THE UNITED STATES, Section 303, Comment g (1987)

Significant Cases

United States v. Ortega, 27 F. Cas. 359 (C.C.E.D. Pa. 1825) (No. 15,971)
In re Baiz, 135 U.S. 403 (1890)
United States v. Belmont, 301 U.S. 324 (1937)
Guaranty Trust Co. of New York v. United States, 304 U.S. 126 (1938)
United States v. Pink, 315 U.S. 203 (1942)
Goldwater v. Carter, 444 U.S. 996 (1979)
Zivotofsky v. Clinton, 132 S. Ct. 1421 (2012)

Take Care Clause

[The President] shall take Care that the Laws be faithfully executed....
(ARTICLE II, SECTION 3)

~

*T*he Take Care Clause imposes a duty that qualifies the Article II, Section 1, Clause 1 grant of executive power. By virtue of his executive power, the president may execute federal laws and control officers who execute those laws. The Take Care Clause modifies the grant of executive power, requiring the president to "take Care that the Laws be faithfully executed."

Though the clause's antecedents can be traced as far back as the late seventeenth century, its more immediate predecessors were found in the 1776 Pennsylvania constitution and in the 1777 New York constitution. Both not only granted their executives the "executive power," but also required them to execute the laws faithfully. These state executives understood that they had a power to execute the laws and a duty to ensure faithful execution.

The ratifying debates reflect these understandings. Dozens spoke of the president's power to execute the law. A few confused the power and the duty, as when Alexander Hamilton, in *The Federalist* No. 77, spoke of the unobjectionable "power" of "faithfully executing the laws." Once in office George Washington directed federal and state officers in their execution of federal law. In the midst of the Whiskey Rebellion, Washington observed, "it is my duty to see the Laws executed:

to permit them to be trampled upon with impunity would be repugnant to" that duty.

The Take Care Clause means that the president may neither breach federal law himself nor order his subordinates to do so, for defiance cannot be considered faithful execution. The Constitution also incorporates the 1689 English Bill of Rights' bars on dispensing with or suspending the laws. Hence the president can neither authorize private violations of the law (issue individualized dispensations) nor nullify statutes (wholly suspend their operation).

Despite these constraints, the president typically enjoys a great deal of enforcement discretion. To begin with, he may pardon (see Article II, Section 2, Clause 1) offenses even before trial or conviction, meaning that he need not investigate and prosecute every offender. Moreover, in the modern era, complete enforcement of every federal law is practically impossible. Resource constraints coupled with innumerable violations preclude such enforcement. Given the inevitable tradeoffs, the president may allocate scarce enforcement resources after weighing the costs and benefits of investigation, apprehension, and prosecution.

Those opposed to the claims that the president may execute federal law and control the federal law execution of others offer alternative constructions of the Take Care Clause. In one view, the clause does not assume that the president may control law execution, but merely requires that the president oversee those statutorily charged with executing law. In other words, the president is limited to the narrow power of ensuring faithful law execution by others. A more radical reading suggests that the president must obey even those statutes that forbid him from overseeing law execution. Thus, if a tax statute bars presidential oversight with respect to its execution, the president must heed that statutory constraint on presidential power.

These readings run afoul of historical evidence. The grant of executive power was widely understood at the Founding as encompassing authority to execute the laws and control the execution of others (see essay on Article II, Section 1, Clause 1). Given this sense of the Executive Vesting Clause, the Take Care Clause should not

be read to limit the president to a mere overseer of law execution. Indeed, early discussions emphasized the president's sweeping power over law execution; they did not suggest that the president could do no more than ensure faithful execution by others. Furthermore, there is no evidence supporting the notion that Congress can use the faithful execution duty as a means by which it may strip away every presidential prerogative, even the executive's law execution function. That reading of the Take Care Clause would undermine the Constitution's separation of powers and make the Executive Vesting Clause largely irrelevant. Again, the Take Care Clause is best read as constraining the otherwise broad law execution power that flows from the executive power.

The Take Care Clause has surfaced in Supreme Court opinions in myriad ways. Sometime case law confirms uncontroversial constraints. For instance, the president may not prevent an executive officer from performing a ministerial duty that Congress has lawfully imposed upon him. *Kendall v. United States ex rel. Stokes* (1838). Nor may the president take an action unauthorized either by the Constitution or by a lawful statute, for then he would not be faithfully executing the laws, so much as making them. *Youngstown Sheet & Tube Co. v. Sawyer* (1952).

Other times, the clause has played a more interesting role, authorizing presidential direction and control of executives. In 1831, the Supreme Court observed that in faithfully executing the law, "[the president] is bound to avail himself of every appropriate means not forbidden by law." *United States v. Tingey.* Based on this understanding, the Court concluded that the president could demand bonds from federal officers to ensure their faithful handling of federal funds.

Justices also have cited the clause as a reason for enforcing Article III's case or controversy requirement. These opinions note that unlike the executive, the judiciary lacks a roving commission to ensure faithful execution of the laws. Rather, the judiciary may vindicate the laws only when a proper case or controversy exists. If a court adjudicates cases where plaintiffs lack standing, it improperly assumes the president's

Take Care duty. Most recently, in *Medellin v. Texas* (2008) the Court continued the tradition, going back to Hamilton, of reading the clause as a grant of power, saying that it was the "authority [that] allows the President to execute the laws, not make them."

The clause has featured prominently in arguments about whether the president may impound (refuse to expend) appropriated funds. The practice traces back to President Thomas Jefferson's refusal to construct gunboats, saying that they were not immediately needed and that he was awaiting a better design. Beginning with President Franklin D. Roosevelt, the executive began to withhold spending for some objects altogether. President Richard M. Nixon expanded that practice, refusing to spend for budgetary and fiscal reasons. Sometimes the executive has argued that this impoundment power flows from the Executive Vesting Clause or the Take Care Clause or both. Other times, the executive has claimed that the appropriation statutes themselves granted discretion to impound sums appropriated. Impoundment opponents often have cited the Take Care Clause as a reason why impoundments are unconstitutional, at least where Congress indicates that the entire sums appropriated must be expended. In the wake of the impoundment controversies of the 1970s, when federal courts struck down President Nixon's impoundments, *see Train v. City of New York* (1975), Congress enacted a restrictive impoundment framework. To date, no successor president has argued that Congress's impoundment rules unconstitutionally limit executive power or infringe upon the Take Care Clause.

The clause is at the epicenter of several ongoing disputes involving law execution. First, there have long been controversies about statutory restrictions on the removal of officers. From the New Deal era on, the Supreme Court has sanctioned the creation of independent agencies, which operate as a fourth branch of government. Among other things, these independent agencies execute various federal laws (communications, banking, securities) by investigating and prosecuting alleged lawbreakers. "For cause" restrictions on removal (statutory restrictions requiring a reason for removal) and a tradition of independence make it difficult, if not impossible, for the president to ensure that these agencies faithfully execute the law. In a recent case, the Supreme Court recognized as much, when it invalidated a statutory removal restriction. *Free Enterprise Fund v. Public Company Accounting Oversight Board* (2011). The Court said the Constitution forbade multi-layered schemes where Congress makes one set of officers (in this case the commissioners of the Securities and Exchange Commission) removable for cause by the president and makes another set of officers (members of the Public Company Accounting Oversight Board) removable for cause only by the first set of officers (the Securities and Exchange Commission). Striking down the second layer of "for cause" restrictions (but leaving the first layer intact), the Court declared that "[t]he President cannot 'take Care that the Laws be faithfully executed' if he cannot oversee the faithfulness of the [PCAOB] officers who execute them." But the same could be said of a single layer of "for cause" restrictions. The "for cause" restrictions protecting the SEC commissioners lessen their responsibility to the chief executive, thereby making it more difficult for him to ensure that they are faithfully executing the law. Perhaps the Court will revisit cases, such as *Humphrey's Executor v. United States* (1935), that have upheld single-layer "for cause" restrictions.

Second, there are continuing disagreements about whether the president may, or perhaps must, abide by, defend, and enforce laws that he believes are unconstitutional. In "signing statements" (issued by the president when he signs a bill into law), presidents sometimes declare that they regard parts of a new law to be unconstitutional and that they will not honor or implement those provisions. Sometimes this stance reflects a narrow claim that when a provision of law trenches upon presidential power (e.g., the commander in chief authority or the pardon power), the president has a power to ignore such provisions. In other instances, the president claims a broad power to ignore any provision of law that he regards as unconstitutional, even if it relates to individual rights or federalism. Some scholars have argued that the Take Care Clause bars executive review. On this view, presentment is the only time where the president may act on constitutional objections. Once a bill becomes law, the president must enforce it. Other scholars disagree. They believe that unconstitutional laws are void *ab initio* and thus not laws at all within the meaning of the Take Care Clause. Moreover, consistent with his oath to preserve the Constitution, the president can take no action that would violate the Constitution, including enforcing laws that he believes are unconstitutional. Finally, the Constitution has been read from the beginning to authorize such review, with James Wilson noting that both the executive and the judiciary could refuse to enforce unconstitutional laws. Thomas Jefferson was the first president to refuse to enforce a law he believed was unconstitutional. He terminated ongoing Sedition Act prosecutions and pardoned those previously convicted. He argued that the Constitution barred the act's enforcement and that he could no more enforce it than he could a law requiring the worship of a golden calf.

Lastly, there are recurring clashes about whether the president may decline to enforce statutes on policy grounds. As noted earlier, the Constitution never conveys any power to decline to enforce (to suspend) a statute. If the president has power to decline to enforce a statute, it arises from the express or implicit terms of that statute and its interaction with the vast realm of federal law. Recognizing that it would be impolitic to assert a constitutional power to decline to enforce statutes, modern presidents carefully avoid embracing such a power. Instead, they argue that certain laws implicitly convey enforcement discretion or that new statutory provisions tacitly permit the executive to grant transition relief with respect to their implementation. Critics of these presidential measures deny that the statutes in question grant the discretion that the executive asserts and insist that in declining to enforce a law the president has violated his Faithful Execution duties.

Saikrishna B. Prakash

See Also

Article II, Section 1, Clause 1 (Executive Vesting Clause)

Article II, Section 2, Clause 1 (Pardon Power)

Article III, Section 1 (Judicial Vesting Clause)

Suggestions for Further Research

Steven G. Calabresi & Saikrishna B. Prakash, *The President's Power to Execute the Laws*, 104 Yale L.J. 541 (1994)

Steven G. Calabresi & Kevin H. Rhodes, *The Structural Constitution: Unitary Executive, Plural Judiciary*, 105 Harv. L. Rev. 1153 (1992)

Gary Lawson & Christopher D. Moore. *The Executive Power of Constitutional Interpretation*, 81 Iowa L. Rev. 1267 (1996)

Lawrence Lessig & Cass R. Sunstein, *The President and the Administration*, 94 Colum. L. Rev. 1 (1994)

Christopher N. May, Presidential Defiance of "Unconstitutional" Laws: Reviving the Royal Prerogative (1998)

Saikrishna B. Prakash, *The Essential Meaning of Executive Power*, 2003 U. Ill. L. Rev. 701 (2003)

Saikrishna Bangalore Prakash, *The Executive's Duty to Disregard Unconstitutional Laws*, 96 Geo. L.J. 1613 (2008)

Peter L. Strauss, *Presidential Rulemaking*, 72 Chi.-Kent L. Rev. 965 (1997)

Significant Cases

United States v. Tingey, 30 U.S. (5 Pet.) 115 (1831)

Kendall v. United States *ex rel*. Stokes, 37 U.S. (12 Pet.) 524 (1838)

United States *ex rel*. Goodrich v. Guthrie, 58 U.S. (17 How.) 284 (1854)

Mississippi v. Johnson, 71 U.S. (4 Wall.) 475 (1866)

Cunningham v. Neagle, 135 U.S. 1 (1890)

Myers v. United States, 272 U.S. 52 (1926)

Humphrey's Executor v. United States, 295 U.S. 602 (1935)

Youngstown Sheet & Tube Co. v. Sawyer, 343 U.S. 579 (1952)

Train v. City of New York, 420 U.S. 35 (1975)

Lujan v. Defenders of Wildlife, 504 U.S. 555 (1992)

Medellin v. Texas, 552 U.S. 491 (2008)

Free Enterprise Fund v. Public Co. Accounting Oversight Bd., 130 S. Ct. 3138 (2011)

Commissions

[The President] shall Commission all the Officers of the United States.
(Article II, Section 3)

~

*A*t the time of the Framing, every officer of the English government was an officer of the crown, commissioned in the king's name. In feudal Britain, the sovereign enjoyed an absolute prerogative to create and bestow fiefs, packages of rights and responsibilities that included titles, land grants, and offices. The grant of a fief would often be evidenced by a gift, which might be a banner, a sword, or a more formal charter. As the feudal system faded, the authority to create offices and to commission officers remained an attribute of monarchical power. The king took care to commission the royal governors of the colonies, listing their duties and their powers. But the king commissioned many more officers, prompting the complaint in the Declaration of Independence, "He has erected a multitude of New Offices, and sent hither swarms of Officers to harass our people, and eat out their substance." Many Americans considered the English system inherently flawed, consolidating too much power with the executive and thus begetting cronyism and abuse.

In the years following independence, the new state and national governments experimented with decentralized methods of selecting and empowering officials. The Articles of Confederation granted Congress the power to appoint civil officers and split the power to appoint military officers between Congress and the state legislatures. Regardless of the mode of selection, the Confederation Congress was to commission "all officers whatever in the service of the United States." The states experimented with numerous other mechanisms.

The delegates at the Constitutional Convention vigorously debated the appointment power, eventually arriving at the system described in Article II, Section 2. But the Commissions Clause was never subject to debate; the Framers apparently accepted that granting commissions was a natural duty for the executive. When the Committee of Detail issued the first draft of the Constitution, the clause was already in its present form. The one person vested with the executive power (the president) would commission every officer of the national government.

The Framers structured the appointment power as follows. Congress creates the office (except for those solely under the president in his exercise of the foreign affairs power). The president "appoints" (actually, nominates) principal officers, but Congress may by law vest the appointment of inferior officers in other persons or departments but not in Congress itself. The Senate approves the nominee, and the president completes the appointment by commissioning the officer. Delivery of the commission is not necessary to effectuate the appointment. *Marbury v. Madison* (1803).

Where the president has either constitutional or statutory authority to appoint (nominate) an officer, and the Senate has approved the nomination, the president may still decide not to commission the officer, which effectually kills the appointment. On the other hand, when an inferior officer has been appointed by someone other than the president, the president's duty is then ministerial: he is obliged to commission that person once the nomination has been approved.

While Justice Robert H. Jackson once called this duty "trifling," Chief Justice John Marshall pointed out in *Marbury* that granting a commission is the distinct act, done in the name of the president, which empowers an officer. Marshall also noted the important evidentiary value of commissions to officers in asserting their authority to citizens and in courts of law.

The placement of the Commissions Clause is also instructive. Rather than being nestled in the discussion on appointments in Article II, Section 2, the clause is attached with a comma to the Take Care Clause. The two together contemplate that the president will supervise others in their enforcement of the law. Solicitor General James Beck, successfully defending the president's removal power in *Myers v. United States* (1926), argued that "the commission of every high federal official comes to him not from Congress, which created the office, but from the President." Although the executive power is vested in the president alone, he necessarily exercises this power through government officers, and thus the clause focuses accountability for the execution of the laws in the unitary executive. Beck argued that the president can only "take Care that the Laws be faithfully executed" if he is responsible for (and can remove) the officers who exercise his executive authority.

Trent England

Suggestions for Further Research

Robert G. Natelson, *The Original Meaning of the Constitution's "Executive Vesting Clause"—Evidence from Eighteenth-Century Drafting Practice*, 31 WHITTIER L. REV. 1 (2009)

Peter L. Strauss, *The Constitution Under Clinton, A Critical Assessment: The President and Choices Not to Enforce*, 63 L. & CONTEMP. PROBS. 107 (2000)

Significant Cases

Marbury v. Madison, 5 U.S. (1 Cranch) 137 (1803)

Myers v. United States, 272 U.S. 52 (1926)

Youngstown Sheet & Tube Co. v. Sawyer, 343 U.S. 579 (1952)

Buckley v. Valeo, 424 U.S. 1 (1976)

Standards for Impeachment

The President, Vice President and all civil Officers of the United States, shall be removed from Office on Impeachment for, and Conviction of, Treason, Bribery, or other high Crimes and Misdemeanors.

(ARTICLE II, SECTION 4)

≈

Impeachment is the constitutionally specified means by which an official of the executive or judicial branch may be removed from office for misconduct. There has been considerable controversy about what constitutes an impeachable offense. At the Constitutional Convention, the delegates early on voted for "mal-practice and neglect of duty" as grounds for impeachment, but the Committee of Detail narrowed the basis to treason, bribery, and corruption, then deleting the last point. George Mason, who wanted the grounds much broader and similar to the earlier formulation, suggested "maladministration," but James Madison pointed out that this would destroy the president's independence and make him dependent on the Senate. Mason then suggested "high Crimes and Misdemeanors," which the Convention accepted.

Because "high Crimes and Misdemeanors" was a term of art used in English impeachments, a plausible reading supported by many scholars is that the grounds for impeachment can be not only the defined crimes of treason and bribery, but also other criminal or even noncriminal behavior amounting to a serious dereliction of duty. That interpretation is disputed, but it is agreed by virtually all that the impeachment remedy was to be used in only the most extreme situations, a position confirmed by the relatively few instances in which Congress has used the device.

The word "impeachment" is popularly used to indicate both the bringing of charges in the House and the Senate vote on removal from office. In the Constitution, however, the term refers only to the former. At the convention, the delegates experimented with differing impeachment proceedings. As finally agreed, a majority vote of the House of Representatives is required to bring impeachment charges (Article I, Section 2, Clause 5), which are then tried before the Senate (Article I, Section 3, Clause 6). Two-thirds of the Senate must vote to convict before an official can be removed. The president may not pardon a person who has been impeached (Article II, Section 2, Clause 1). If an official is impeached by the House and convicted by the requisite vote in the Senate, then Article I, Section 3, Clause 7, provides that the person convicted is further barred from any "Office of honor, Trust or Profit under the United States." The convicted official also loses any possible federal pensions. With a few exceptions, those impeached and removed have generally faded into obscurity.

In *The Federalist* No. 64, John Jay argued that the threat of impeachment would encourage executive officers to perform their duties with honor, and, used as a last resort, impeachment itself would be effective to remove those who betray the interests of their country. Like the limitations on the offense of treason, the Framers placed particular grounds of impeachment in the Constitution because they wished to prevent impeachment from becoming politicized, as it had in England. Nonetheless, Alexander Hamilton, in *The Federalist* No. 65, also warned that during impeachment proceedings, it would be difficult for Congress to act solely in the interests of the nation and resist political pressure to remove a popular official. The Framers believed that the Senate, elected by the state legislatures, would have the requisite independence needed to try impeachments. The Framers also mandated a supermajority requirement to militate against impeachments brought by the House for purely political reasons.

There have been several impeachment proceedings initiated since the adoption of the Constitution, principally against judges in the lower federal courts. The most important impeachments were those brought against Justice Samuel Chase of the Supreme Court in 1805, against President Andrew Johnson in 1867, and against President William Jefferson Clinton in 1999. None of these three resulted in removal from office, and all three stand for the principle that impeachment should not be perceived as a device simply to remove a political opponent. In that regard, the caution of the Framers has been fulfilled.

President George Washington appointed Samuel Chase to the Supreme Court in 1796. Washington had been warned of Chase's mercurial behavior, but Chase had written the president that, if he were appointed, he would do nothing to embarrass the administration. In his early years on the Court, Chase kept his pledge and did render some fine decisions clarifying the powers of the federal government. In the election of 1800, however, when Thomas Jefferson ran against Washington's vice president and successor, John Adams, Chase earned the ire of Jefferson's emerging Republican party. For one thing, Chase actively took to the hustings to campaign for Adams (a move rare for sitting judges even then). What finally brought President Jefferson to approve of efforts by his party's representatives in Congress to remove the justice was a grand jury charge Chase made in Baltimore in 1803. There Chase lamented the Jeffersonian restructuring of

the federal judiciary in order to abolish the circuit court judgeships that the Adams administration had created and the Maryland Jeffersonians' abolition of a state court and the establishment of universal male suffrage in that state. Chase argued that all of this was plunging the country into "mobocracy." Chase voiced sentiments common to a wing of the party of Washington and Adams, but Jefferson and his men believed that to have a federal judge publicly articulating such views was harmful to the government, and they moved against Chase. In addition to citing his behavior in Baltimore, the impeachment charges included several counts based on Chase's conduct during controversial trials in 1800 against Jeffersonian writers who had been prosecuted under the Alien and Sedition Act of 1798 (a temporary measure that punished libels against the government).

The proceeding against Chase was part of a broader Jeffersonian assault on the judiciary, and it was widely believed, at least among Federalists, that if it were successful, Chief Justice John Marshall might be the next target. None of the charges brought against Chase involved any criminal conduct, and their thrust seemed to be that his legal rulings were simply not in accordance with Jeffersonian theory on how trials ought to be conducted or how juries should function. There was substantial legal precedent behind each of Chase's rulings, however, and although he may have been guilty of having a hair-trigger temper, it was also clear that to permit his removal would seriously, perhaps permanently, compromise the independence of the judiciary. The requisite two-thirds majority of Senators could not be cobbled together to remove Chase, and, in fact, even members of Jefferson's own party voted for acquittal. From that time to this, the Chase acquittal has been understood to bar the removal of a Supreme Court justice on the ground of his political preferences. Subsequently, there have been several attempts to begin impeachment proceedings against particular justices, but none has ever prevailed in the House.

Andrew Johnson, who succeeded to the presidency following Abraham Lincoln's assassination in 1865, was impeached because of his failure to follow procedures specified in federal legislation (passed over his veto) that prohibited the firing of cabinet officials without the permission of Congress. The legislation, known as the Tenure of Office Act, was arguably unconstitutional because it compromised the independence of the executive. Nevertheless, the radical Republicans, who then controlled Congress and who recoiled at President Johnson's active hostility to their plans to protect the newly freed slaves, sought to keep the sympathetic members of Abraham Lincoln's cabinet in office. When Johnson fired Secretary of War Edwin Stanton, the gauntlet was thrown down, and impeachment was voted by the House. Though Johnson's impeachment was just as political as Chase's, there was some support for the Tenure of Office Act (Alexander Hamilton, writing in the *The Federalist* No. 77, had suggested that the consent of the Senate would be necessary "to displace as well as to appoint" officials). As it turned out, the conviction of Johnson failed in the Senate by only one vote.

The administration of President William Jefferson Clinton was beset by assorted scandals, many of which resulted in the appointment of special federal prosecutors, and several of which resulted in the convictions of lesser officials. One of the special prosecutors, the former federal judge Kenneth Starr, recommended to Congress in 1998 that it consider evidence that the president had obstructed justice, tampered with witnesses, lied to a grand jury, and sought to conceal evidence in connection with a civil proceeding brought against him involving claims of sexual harassment. President Clinton denied the charges, but the Arkansas federal judge who presided in that civil proceeding eventually cited and fined Clinton for contempt based on his untruthful testimony.

A majority of the Republican-controlled House of Representatives voted in early 1999 to impeach the president based upon Judge Starr's referral. The House managers argued that what the president had done was inconsistent with his sworn duty to take care that the laws of the nation be faithfully executed. When the matter was tried in the Senate, in February 1999, however, the president's defenders prevailed, and no more than fifty Senators (all Republicans) could be found to vote for conviction on any of the charges.

The only other time a president came close to being impeached was the case of Richard M. Nixon.

He resigned from office in 1974 after a House committee had voted to put before the full House a number of impeachment charges, the most serious of which was that he had wrongly used the FBI and the CIA in order to conceal evidence that persons connected to the White House had participated in a burglary at the Democratic Party's offices at the Watergate complex in Washington, D.C. Nixon avoided impeachment though not disgrace.

There is no authoritative pronouncement, other than the text of the Constitution itself, regarding what constitutes an impeachable offense and what meaning to accord to the phrase "other high Crimes and Misdemeanors." When he was a member of Congress, Gerald R. Ford advocated the ultimately unsuccessful impeachment of a Supreme Court justice by defining an impeachable offense as anything on which a majority of the House of Representatives can agree. As impeachment is understood to be a political question, Ford's statement correctly centers responsibility for the definition of "high Crimes and Misdemeanors" in the House. The federal courts have thus far treated appeals from impeachment convictions to be nonjusticiable. *Nixon v. United States* (1993). Even if the issue of impeachment is nonjusticiable, it does not mean that there are no appropriate standards that the House should observe.

Some scholarly commentary at the time of the Nixon impeachment proceedings argued that the actual commission of a crime was necessary to serve as a basis for an impeachment proceeding. However, the historical record of impeachments in England, which furnished the Constitution's Framers with the term "high Crimes and Misdemeanors," does not support such a limitation. In the late eighteenth century, the word "misdemeanors" meant simply "misdeeds," rather than "petty crimes," as it now does. The issue was revisited at the time of the Clinton impeachment, when those who sought to remove the president from office, basing their arguments principally on the English experience and *The Federalist* No. 64, claimed that a president could be removed for any misconduct that indicated that he did not possess the requisite honor, integrity, and character to be trusted to carry out his functions in a manner free from corruption. As James Iredell (later an associate justice of the Supreme Court) opined in the

North Carolina ratifying convention, impeachment should be used to remedy harm "aris[ing] from acts of great injury to the community."

On the other hand, some have argued that a president should not be impeached unless he has actually engaged in a major abuse of power flowing from his office as president (although judges, who serve during "good behavior," have been impeached for conduct occurring outside of their official duties). In the end, because it is unlikely that a court would ever exercise judicial review over impeachment and removal proceedings, the definitional responsibility to carry them out with fidelity to the Constitution's text remains that of the House of Representatives and the Senate.

There is always a risk that the impeachment power will be invoked whenever Congressional opponents of the president seek to undo what he has done or to criticize policies he has implemented. For example, on July 25, 2008, Chairman John Conyers of the Judiciary Committee convened a hearing on the subject "Executive Power and its Constitutional Limitations," in order to examine charges (some of which involved calls for impeachment by some Democrats) that President George W. Bush had engaged in "(1) improper politicization of the Justice Department and the U.S. Attorneys offices, including potential misuse of authority with regard to election and voting controversies; (2) misuse of executive branch authority and the adoption and implementation of the so-called unitary executive theory, including in the areas of presidential signing statements and regulatory authority; (3) misuse of investigatory and detention authority with regard to U.S. citizens and foreign nationals, including questions regarding the legality of the administration's surveillance, detention, interrogation, and rendition programs; (4) manipulation of intelligence and misuse of war powers, including possible misrepresentations to Congress related thereto; (5) improper retaliation against administration critics, including disclosing information concerning CIA operative Valerie Plame, and obstruction of justice related thereto; and (6) misuse of authority in denying Congress and the American people the ability to oversee and scrutinize conduct within the administration, including through the use of various asserted privileges and immunities." While some Democrats on the committee were sympathetic to

bringing impeachment charges against President Bush, all the Republicans on the committee denied that any conduct of the president was impeachable. As often occurs in these situations, scholars testified in support of both political positions. No impeachment articles were filed against President Bush, but the hearing was a reminder of the intensely political character of impeachment.

Stephen B. Presser

See Also

Article I, Section 2, Clause 5 (Impeachment)

Article I, Section 3, Clause 6 (Trial of Impeachment)

Article I, Section 3, Clause 7 (Punishment for Impeachment)

Article I, Section 5, Clause 2 (Rules and Expulsion Clause)

Article I, Section 9, Clause 2 (Habeas Corpus)

Article II, Section 2, Clause 1 (Pardon Power)

Article III, Section 2, Clause 3 (Criminal Trials)

Suggestions for Further Research

RAOUL BERGER, IMPEACHMENT: THE CONSTITUTIONAL PROBLEMS (1974)

Committee on the Judiciary, U.S. House of Representatives, Hearing held on July 25, 2008, "Executive Power and its Constitutional Limitations," available at http://judiciary.house.gov/hearings/hear_072508.html

MICHAEL J. GERHARDT, THE FEDERAL IMPEACHMENT PROCESS: A CONSTITUTIONAL AND HISTORICAL ANALYSIS (2D ED. 2000)

PETER CHARLES HOFFER & N. E. H. HULL, IMPEACHMENT IN AMERICA, 1635–1805 (1984)

STANLEY I. KUTLER, THE WARS OF WATERGATE: THE LAST CRISIS OF RICHARD NIXON (1990)

RICHARD A. POSNER, AN AFFAIR OF STATE: THE INVESTIGATION, IMPEACHMENT, AND TRIAL OF PRESIDENT CLINTON (1999)

Stephen B. Presser, *Would George Washington Have Wanted Bill Clinton Impeached?*, 67 GEO. WASH. L. REV. 666 (1999)

WILLIAM H. REHNQUIST, GRAND INQUESTS: THE HISTORIC IMPEACHMENTS OF JUSTICE SAMUEL CHASE AND PRESIDENT ANDREW JOHNSON (1992)

Cass R. Sunstein, *Impeachment and Stability*, 67 GEO. WASH. L. REV. 699 (1999)

Keith E. Whittington, Constitutional Construction: Divided Powers and Constitutional Meaning (1999)

Significant Cases

United States v. Nixon, 418 U.S. 683 (1974)

Nixon v. United States, 506 U.S. 224 (1993)

Clinton v. Jones, 520 U.S. 681 (1997)

A Note on the Foreign Affairs Power

*T*he Constitution's text does not mention a general power over foreign affairs. Nonetheless, some courts and commentators have suggested a foreign affairs power of the federal government arising either from a combination of the text's specific foreign affairs–related powers, from the structural implications of the federal system, or from the inherent powers of sovereignty all nations possess under international law.

The foreign affairs power might have three distinct implications. First, it might give Congress foreign affairs powers beyond those listed in Article I, Section 8, or elsewhere in the text. Second, it might mean that the president has foreign affairs powers that do not arise from Article II or from grants of power from Congress. Third, it might preclude the states from acting in ways that interfere with the federal government's exercise of the foreign affairs power (in addition to the express or implied preclusions in the Constitution's text or in preemptive treaties or statutes).

As to the first category, consider for example the power to restrict immigration. To many people, this seems an obvious power of Congress. However, no clause of the text grants it directly, and while it might be implied from Congress's express power over naturalization, that does not seem an obvious conclusion. Another possibility is that it arises outside the text. In *Chae Chan Ping v. United States* (1889), the Supreme Court found that Congress's immigration power arose from the federal government's possession of external sovereignty, being a power that all sovereign governments necessarily have. As recently as 2012, Justice Antonin Scalia in a dissenting opinion in

Arizona v. United States, referred to the immigration power as an inherent power of the national government.

Another nineteenth-century example of Congress's foreign affairs power is the power to acquire territory. Though he signed the treaty by which the United States obtained the Louisiana Territory, Thomas Jefferson had serious misgivings about its constitutionality. He would have preferred a constitutional amendment allowing the United States to acquire territory. That right could, nonetheless, be derived from the Treaty Clause (Article II, Section 2, Clause 2) or the Property Clause (Article IV, Section 3, Clause 2). But in *Jones v. United States* (1890), the Court found acquisition of territory to be an inherent power of sovereignty derived from international law that Congress could exercise without tying it to a specific constitutional power. An example nearer the framing might be the 1799 Logan Act, which prohibited private persons from conducting diplomacy; it is not obvious what enumerated power might support Congress's action. The distinguished commentator Louis Henkin described a "Foreign Affairs Power" exercised by Congress in cases such as *Jones* and *Chae Chan Ping* and resting on "the powers of the United States inherent in its sovereignty and nationhood." Henkin thought that, in addition, it would support, for example, Congress's power to enact the Foreign Sovereign Immunities Act (regulating when a foreign government may be sued in United States courts), to regulate conduct of U.S. citizens that occurred abroad or otherwise affected foreign relations, and indeed to regulate any activity with international implications.

The president's non-textual foreign affairs power is most strongly associated with Justice George Sutherland's opinion for the Court in *United States v. Curtiss-Wright Export Corp.* (1936). According to Sutherland, powers of "external sovereignty" (foreign affairs powers) vested inherently in the national government at the moment of independence; thus they were never possessed by the states and so are not subject to the delegated powers rule of the Tenth Amendment. Further, according to Sutherland's opinion, the president is the "sole organ" of the United States in foreign affairs (Sutherland did not say on what basis) and therefore the president alone exercises many of the federal government's foreign affairs powers. Sutherland concluded on this basis that Congress can make very broad delegations to the president in foreign affairs without implicating the doctrine that Congress may not delegate or give away its law-making powers to the president. However, the case has been interpreted—especially by the executive branch—to mean that the president can exercise broad independent authority in foreign affairs without tracing it to a statutory or constitutional delegation. For example, *Curtiss-Wright* might be the basis of the President's independent power to conduct diplomacy, to make international executive agreements, and to terminate treaties. In addition, the foreign affairs power might be invoked to assert that Congress acts unconstitutionally when it attempts to restrict or interfere with the president's role as the nation's "sole organ" in foreign affairs.

The third implication of the foreign affairs power is that states may be constitutionally prevented from participating in foreign affairs. Of course, states are precluded from certain foreign affairs–related activities by the prohibitions in Article I, Section 10, by the negative implication of other specific clauses, and often by statutes or treaties. But in *Zschernig v. Miller* (1968), the Supreme Court found a state law relating to foreign affairs invalid even absent a statute, treaty, or specific constitutional provision. In that case, decided against the backdrop of the Cold War, Oregon law prohibited citizens of communist countries from inheriting property from Oregon estates on the ground that such inheritances aided enemy nations. This rule (and similar ones in other states) had provoked diplomatic protests to the U.S. government. The Supreme Court found the Oregon law unconstitutional as "an intrusion by the State into the field of foreign affairs which the Constitution entrusts to the President and the Congress." Later commentary began referring to this idea as the "dormant foreign affairs doctrine," associating it with the dormant commerce clause doctrine that prohibits states from interfering with interstate commerce even in the absence of federal regulation.

The foreign affairs power may also support a related federal common law of foreign affairs, developed by federal courts, that displaces state law in certain instances. In *Banco Nacional de Cuba v. Sabbatino* (1964), the Court held that the act of state doctrine (which prohibits courts from holding invalid acts of foreign sovereigns done in their own territory) is part of federal common law and overrides state law to the contrary. Although subsequent opinions have referred to foreign affairs as an area in which federal courts can determine when federal common law displaces state legislation, the Court has not explained the boundaries of the field nor directly revisited the issue since *Sabbatino*. Nonetheless, lower courts have invoked the doctrine in various ways to set aside state law. At a minimum, the federal common law of foreign affairs presumably includes various common law doctrines of foreign sovereign immunity (to the extent they are not codified by statute or treaty), as well as the act of state doctrine.

It is unclear how much force the foreign affairs power has in modern law. After the mid–twentieth-century expansion of Congress's power under the Commerce Clause and other enumerated powers, the need for Congress to rely on inherent or structural sources of foreign affairs powers has declined, and inherent congressional powers in foreign affairs have not played a material role in the modern Court's holdings. Although the executive branch continues to rely on arguments based on *Curtiss-Wright*, the Court moved sharply away from the idea of inherent presidential powers in *Youngstown Sheet and Tube Co. v. Sawyer* (1952) (limiting the domestic impact of the president's foreign affairs power), and the modern Court has approached questions of executive power more through the lens of *Youngstown* than *Curtiss-Wright*. For example, *Dames & Moore v. Regan* (1981), upholding the president's power to settle the Iran hostage crisis, relied on congressional acquiescence in the longstanding presidential practice of claims settlement rather than on inherent presidential powers in foreign affairs. Similarly, the Court's war-on-terror cases, such as *Hamdi v. Rumsfeld* (2004), have focused on congressional authorization rather than inherent presidential power. The Court has cited *Curtiss-Wright* in some modern cases, but it is not clear that it was important to the outcomes.

The foreign affairs power has the most potential for modern relevance in connection with the foreign affairs of the states. Globalization of commerce, transportation, and communications has brought state activities increasingly into the international spotlight. As a result, the states' potential to interfere with national foreign policies—and, correspondingly, to have their laws challenged on that ground—seems substantial. But the Constitution's express preclusions of the states from foreign affairs are narrow (chiefly relating to war, treaties, and import and export taxes). Thus preclusion of states from interference in foreign affairs may need to come, if at all, from the dormant foreign affairs power or federal common law or both.

Nonetheless, the Supreme Court has not rendered a definitive ruling in this area since *Zschernig*. On several occasions the issue seemed to be presented, but the Court's ruling took a different route. For example, in *Crosby v. National Foreign Trade Council* (2000), a business group challenged a Massachusetts statute that prohibited companies doing business in Burma (Myanmar) from bidding on state contracts, a law passed in response to that nation's poor human rights record. A lower court enjoined the state law, in part under the dormant foreign affairs power. The Supreme Court affirmed that judgment but did not reach the foreign affairs power, as it found the state law preempted by a federal statute relating to trade with Burma. In *American Insurance Association v. Garamendi* (2003), insurers challenged a California law relating to insurance contracts issued in Europe prior to the Holocaust; the law was apparently an effort to assist recovery by Holocaust victims and their beneficiaries, some of whom were California residents. The court of appeals rejected a *Zschernig*-based argument by the insurers. The Supreme Court reversed, invalidating the state law, but expressly declined to rely on *Zschernig*. Instead, the Court found that the California law conflicted with an executive branch policy of

settling Holocaust claims through an international settlement body, established under various executive agreements, rather than by litigation in national courts. The Court did not clearly explain the constitutional basis of this preclusion. In a later case, *Medellin v. Texas* (2008), the Court described *Garamendi* as based on the president's ability to settle international claims by executive agreement, a power recognized as deriving from Congress's consent in *Dames & Moore*. *Medellin* refused to extend *Garamendi* to allow the president to override Texas's decision to execute a Mexican citizen convicted of murder in Texas, even though the president argued (and the Court conceded) that the matter had substantial foreign policy implications.

The existence and operation of a non-textual foreign affairs power remains sharply contested in academic commentary. Modern scholarship has been highly critical of the historical underpinnings of the *Curtiss-Wright* opinion, while the Court's federalism revival in domestic matters beginning in the 1990s caused scholars to devote more attention to the structural significance of the Tenth Amendment. Renewed interest in formalist and textualist approaches to the Constitution, including in foreign affairs, has cast doubt on the idea of inherent or structural powers not linked to constitutional grants. At the same time, some modern executive power scholarship supports a broad reading of the president's constitutional foreign affairs power under the Executive Vesting Clause (Article II, Section 1) and the Commander in Chief Clause (Article II, Section 2) that would lessen the need to rely on non-textual sources of presidential power in foreign affairs.

As in the courts, the debate over the foreign affairs power in academic commentary is most significant in the area of restrictions on the states. The idea that states are restricted by non-textual sources of national foreign affairs power has been broadly challenged as inconsistent with the express exclusions of the states from some foreign affairs powers (which implies that powers not listed are not excluded). Moreover, some modern scholarship indicates that pre- and post-ratification history does not support the idea of non-textual exclusions of the states. On the other hand, the structural need for a unified national foreign policy continues to persuade some scholars of the importance of "dormant" limits on the states. Although *Zschernig* itself has relatively few committed defenders, various forms of non-textual preclusion continue to be strongly advocated.

Michael D. Ramsey

See Also

Article I, Section 8
Article I, Section 10
Article II, Sections 1–3
Article VI, Clause 2 (Supremacy Clause)
Amendment X (Reserved Powers of the States)

Suggestions for Further Research

Anthony J. Bellia, Jr., & Bradford R. Clark, *The Federal Common Law of Nations*, 109 COLUM. L. REV. 1 (2009)

Anthony J. Bellia, Jr., & Bradford R. Clark, *The Law of Nations as Constitutional Law*, 98 VA. L. REV. 729 (2012)

Sarah H. Cleveland, *Powers Inherent in Sovereignty: Indians, Aliens, Territories, and the Nineteenth Century Origins of Plenary Power over Foreign Affairs*, 81 TEX. L. REV. 1 (2002)

Brannon P. Denning & Michael D. Ramsey, American Insurance Association v. Garamendi *and Executive Preemption in Foreign Affairs*, 46 Wm. & Mary L. Rev. 825 (2004)

Jack L. Goldsmith, *Federal Courts, Foreign Affairs, and Federalism*, 83 VA. L. REV. 1617 (1997)

Jack L. Goldsmith, *The New Formalism in United States Foreign Relations Law*, 70 U. COLO. L. REV. 1395 (1999)

LOUIS HENKIN, FOREIGN AFFAIRS AND THE UNITED STATES CONSTITUTION, Chs. 1– 3, 6 (2nd ed. 1996)

HAROLD HONGJU KOH, THE NATIONAL SECURITY CONSTITUTION: SHARING POWER AFTER THE IRAN-CONTRA AFFAIR (1990)

GARY LAWSON & GUY SEIDMAN, THE CONSTITUTION OF EMPIRE: TERRITORIAL EXPANSION AND AMERICAN LEGAL HISTORY 21–85 (2004)

Charles A. Lofgren, *United States v. Curtiss-Wright Export Corporation: An Historical Reassessment*, 83 YALE L.J. 1 (1973)

Harold G. Maier, *Preemption of State Law: A Recommended Analysis*, 83 AM. J. INT'L L. 832 (1989)

Saikrishna B. Prakash & Michael D. Ramsey, *The Executive Power over Foreign Affairs*, 111 YALE L.J. 231 (2001)

Garrick B. Pursley, *Dormancy*, 100 GEO. L.J. 497 (2012)

MICHAEL D. RAMSEY, THE CONSTITUTION'S TEXT IN FOREIGN AFFAIRS, Chs. 1–6, 10, 13–14 (2007)

Michael D. Ramsey, *The Power of the States in Foreign Affairs: The Original Understanding of Foreign Policy Federalism*, 75 NOTRE DAME L. REV. 341 (1999)

Michael D. Ramsey, *The Myth of Extraconstitutional Foreign Affairs Power*, 42 WM. & MARY L. REV. 379 (2000)

Michael D. Ramsey, *International Wrongs, State Law Remedies, and Presidential Policies*, 32 LOY. L.A. INT'L & COMP. L. REV. 19 (2010)

Michael D. Ramsey, *The Textual Basis of the President's Foreign Affairs Power*, 30 HARV. J.L. & P. POL'Y 141 (2006)

Peter J. Spiro, *Foreign Relations Federalism*, 70 U. COLO. L. REV. 1223 (1999)

Edward T. Swaine, *Negotiating Federalism: State Bargaining and the Dormant Treaty Power*, 49 DUKE L.J. 1127 (2000)

Carlos Manuel Vazquez, *W(h)ither Zschernig?*, 46 VILL. L. REV. 1259 (2001)

Significant Cases

Chae Chan Ping v. United States, 130 U.S. 581 (1889)
Jones v. United States, 137 U.S. 202 (1890)
United States v. Curtiss-Wright Export Corp., 299 U.S. 304 (1936)
Youngstown Sheet & Tube Co. v. Sawyer, 343 U.S. 579 (1952)
Banco Nacional de Cuba v. Sabbatino, 376 U.S. 398 (1964)
Zschernig v. Miller, 389 U.S. 429 (1968)
Dames & Moore v. Regan, 453 U.S. 654 (1981)
Crosby v. National Foreign Trade Council, 530 U.S. 363 (2000)
American Ins. Ass'n v. Garamendi, 539 U.S. 396 (2003)
United States v. Lara, 541 U.S. 193 (2004)
Hamdi v. *Rumsfeld*, 542 U.S. 507 (2004)
Pasquantino v. United States, 544 U.S. 349 (2005)
Medellín v. Texas, 552 U.S. 491 (2008)
Arizona v. United States, 567 U.S. __ (2012)

ARTICLE III

Judicial Vesting Clause

The judicial Power of the United States shall be vested in one supreme Court, and in such inferior Courts as the Congress may from time to time ordain and establish.

(ARTICLE III, SECTION 1)

~

*T*he Constitution's first three articles contain symmetrical introductory language. Each provides that a basic type of governmental "power"—"legislative" (making laws), "executive" (administering the laws), and "judicial" (expounding laws to decide particular cases)— "shall be vested" in a corresponding institution: "Congress," the "President," and "Courts," respectively. As originally conceived, the Constitution embodied the sovereign will of "We the People," who delegated power to three independent yet coordinate branches of government.

This separation-of-powers structure incorporated two novel Federalist ideas. First, "judicial power" became a distinct part of government, whereas in England it had been treated as an aspect of executive authority (although the English recognized adjudication as a discrete function). Second, like Congress and the president, federal judges ultimately derived their power from "the People," even though they were unelected and given tenure and salary guarantees to ensure their impartiality and prestige. This separate and independent judiciary consisted of a Supreme Court and any lower federal tribunals Congress chose to create. The powers of federal courts can most usefully be divided into three components: judicial review, justiciability, and equitable authority.

Since 1787, the central meaning of "judicial power" has remained remarkably consistent: neutrally deciding a case by interpreting the law and applying it to the facts, then rendering a final and binding judgment. The most important cases in Article III are those "arising under th[e] Constitution [and] Laws of the United States." This clause complements Article VI, which provides that "[t]his Constitution, and the Laws of the United States which shall be made in Pursuance thereof...shall be the supreme Law of the Land." There was a general understanding that this language, and the very nature of a written Constitution ordained by "the People," authorized judicial review of the constitutional validity of government actions. For example, in *The Federalist* No. 78, Alexander Hamilton reasoned as follows: (1) courts have a duty to resolve cases impartially according to the law, (2) the Constitution is the fundamental and supreme law in which "the People" explicitly limited the political branches, and (3) therefore, judges must follow the Constitution instead of a clearly contrary ordinary law. Hamilton's Anti-Federalist rival "Brutus," however, expressed the fear that federal judges would naturally aggrandize their power and that of the central government. "In their decisions," he said, "they will not confine themselves to any fixed or established rules." "This power," he concluded, "will enable them to mold the government into almost any shape they please."

The early Supreme Court operated on a restricted notion of judicial review, although it did not strike down any statute until *Marbury v. Madison* (1803). In that case, Chief Justice John Marshall repeated Hamilton's analysis and then held that Congress, by forcing the Court to assume original jurisdiction over an action involving a writ of mandamus (an order compelling action by an executive official), had plainly violated limitations on such jurisdiction prescribed in Article III. The Court expressly cabined its power to examining "judicial" issues of law rather than "political" questions committed by the Constitution to the executive branch's discretion.

This relatively constrained view of the judicial function continued until 1857, when the Court next invalidated a federal law—the critical and politically delicate Missouri Compromise—in *Dred Scott v. Sandford*. This disastrous attempt to transform judicial review into a mandate to substitute the justices' policy preferences on slavery for those of political officials crippled the Court's prestige for a generation.

By the late nineteenth century, however, the Court began to interpret the judicial power as allowing it to overturn legislation that did not transgress any explicit constitutional command. Most famously, in *Lochner v. New York* (1905), it held that a state law restricting workers' hours violated the Fourteenth Amendment by depriving employers and employees of "liberty" and "property" without "due process of law." The Court construed this language, which originally had been intended to guarantee procedural protections, as creating a substantive right to contract freely. In 1937, the Court abandoned this approach and announced that economic legislation would be upheld if it had any rational basis. Subsequently, however, the Court has not shown similar deference to social legislation. Instead, it has struck down laws dealing with issues like education, crime, voting, and abortion—areas previously thought to have been left by the Constitution to the political process.

Judicial review can be exercised only over cases that are "justiciable" (i.e., presented in a form suitable for judicial resolution). The Supreme Court has developed many justiciability doctrines, which reflect both Article III requirements and self-imposed prudential limitations.

The Federalist justices swiftly established three bedrock justiciability rules. First, federal court judgments expounding the law are final and cannot be reexamined or revised by Congress or the president. Second, judges will not render legal advice to political officials outside the context of a contested case. Third, even if a federal court possesses Article III jurisdiction over a case, it will decline to issue a decision if the underlying question presented is "political" in the sense of being entrusted by the Constitution exclusively to the president or Congress. Long-recognized examples of such political questions include the conduct of war and foreign affairs and the appointment of executive and judicial officials.

Gradually, several other justiciability doctrines evolved. Most importantly, a plaintiff must establish "standing" to sue by demonstrating the existence of an individualized injury caused by an adverse defendant. Furthermore, courts avoid premature adjudication, especially challenges to administrative agency proceedings, by insisting that claims be "ripe" for review (i.e., sufficiently developed both factually and legally). Finally, cases are usually dismissed as "moot" if the parties' dispute has ended.

Although the Court has never deviated from its bans on nonfinal judgments and advisory opinions, it has not taken a similarly consistent approach to standing, ripeness, mootness, and the political question doctrine during the modern era. The justices appointed by Franklin D. Roosevelt strengthened all of these doctrines to minimize litigation attacking regulatory and social welfare legislation, which mushroomed during the New Deal. By contrast, the Warren Court relaxed justiciability requirements to broaden access to the federal judiciary, particularly where necessary to vindicate constitutional rights. Perhaps most significantly, the Court interpreted the Constitution as allowing judicial review of several questions formerly viewed as "political," such as the apportionment of state legislatures, *Baker v. Carr* (1962), and Congress's power to judge the qualifications of its Members, *Powell v. McCormack* (1969).

The Burger, Rehnquist, and Roberts Courts likewise have rejected "political question" defenses in controversial cases involving gerrymandering, the apportionment of congressional districts, procedures for enacting statutes, Indian tribal affairs, assertions of executive privilege, the 2000 presidential election deadlock, and executive branch determinations regarding treaty compliance. Indeed, since the *Baker* decision, only two issues, impeachment and military training, have been deemed beyond the scope of judicial review. Although the Burger and Rehnquist Courts continued the loose approach to the political question doctrine, they generally strengthened rules of standing, ripeness, and mootness.

In short, the justiciability doctrines have changed over the years and have been employed with varying degrees of rigor. Nonetheless, their purpose has remained constant: to assure the appropriate exercise of judicial power, especially the decision of constitutional cases.

Article III has long been construed as implicitly conferring all auxiliary "inherent" authority necessary for courts to exercise judicial power competently. For instance, because adjudication depends on finding accurate and relevant facts, federal judges inherently have the ability to manage pretrial discovery, make evidentiary rulings, compel witnesses to testify, and appoint experts. Similarly, issuing a judgment is a key component of judicial power, and therefore courts can independently enter and correct their judgments. Finally, courts by their very nature must be able to maintain their authority and supervise the judicial process—for example, by sanctioning disobedience of their orders and courtroom misconduct. Over the past century, the scope of inherent judicial powers has grown dramatically to cope with the vast increase in the amount and complexity of litigation.

Likewise, the judiciary's equitable discretion has expanded greatly since *Brown v. Board of Education* (1954), which countenanced broad decrees to remedy unconstitutional discrimination in public schools. *Brown* and other desegregation cases encouraged federal courts to fashion complex remedies in other major public policy areas, such as prison reform. Congress, however, can limit the range of the federal judiciary's injunctive powers.

In sum, Article III's introductory language has always been read as granting federal courts the "judicial power" of deciding cases and any inherent and equitable authority needed to do so properly. The Court has continually adapted the contours of judicial power, however, to address broader legal and political changes.

Robert J. Pushaw Jr.

See Also

Preamble

Article I, Section 1 (Legislative Vesting Clause)

Article I, Section 8, Clause 9 (Inferior Courts)

Article II, Section 1, Clause 1 (Executive Vesting Clause)

Article II, Section 2, Clause 2 (Appointments Clause)

Article VI, Clause 2 (Supremacy Clause)

Suggestions for Further Research

Evan Caminker, *Allocating the Judicial Power in a "Unified Judiciary*," 78 Tex. L. Rev. 1513 (2000)

Letter from the Justices of the Supreme Court to President George Washington (Aug. 8, 1793), reprinted in Stewart Jay, Most Humble Servants: The Advisory Role of Early Judges, at 179–80 (1997)

James S. Liebman & William F. Ryan, *"Some Effectual Power": The Quantity and Quality of Decisionmaking Required of Article III Courts*, 98 Colum. L. Rev. 696 (1998)

Robert J. Pushaw, Jr., *The Inherent Powers of Federal Courts and the Structural Constitution*, 86 Iowa L. Rev. 735 (2001)

Robert J. Pushaw, Jr., *Justiciability and Separation of Powers: A Neo-Federalist Approach*, 81 Cornell L. Rev. 393 (1996)

Significant Cases

Hayburn's Case, 2 U.S. (2 Dall.) 409 (1792)

Marbury v. Madison, 5 U.S. (1 Cranch) 137 (1803)

United States v. Hudson & Goodwin, 11 U.S. (7 Cranch) 32 (1812)

Martin v. Hunter's Lessee, 14 U.S. (1 Wheat.) 304 (1816)

Cohens v. Virginia, 19 U.S. (6 Wheat.) 264 (1821)

Osborn v. Bank of the United States, 22 U.S. (9 Wheat.) 738 (1824)

Wayman v. Southard, 23 U.S. (10 Wheat.) 1 (1825)

Dred Scott v. Sandford, 60 U.S. (19 How.) 393 (1857)

United States v. Klein, 80 U.S. (13 Wall.) 128 (1871)

Murdock v. City of Memphis, 87 U.S. (20 Wall.) 590 (1875)

Lochner v. New York, 198 U.S. 45 (1905)

West Coast Hotel Co. v. Parrish, 300 U.S. 379 (1937)

Coleman v. Miller, 307 U.S. 433 (1939)

Brown v. Board of Education, 347 U.S. 483 (1954)

Baker v. Carr, 369 U.S. 186 (1962)

United Mine Workers v. Gibbs, 383 U.S. 715 (1966)

Abbott Laboratories v. Gardner, 387 U.S. 136 (1967)

Powell v. McCormack, 395 U.S. 486 (1969)

United States Parole Commission v. Geraghty, 445 U.S. 388 (1980)

Lujan v. Defenders of Wildlife, 504 U.S. 555 (1992)

Bush v. Gore, 531 U.S. 98 (2000)

Hollingsworth v. Perry, 133 S.Ct. 2652 (2013)

Supreme Court

The judicial Power of the United States shall be vested in one supreme Court....

(ARTICLE III, SECTION 1)

~

*W*hen the Constitutional Convention opened in Philadelphia, the very existence of a national judiciary was at issue. Delegates who favored state power argued that national laws could be enforced by state courts, whereas others, such as James Madison, foresaw the need for national judicial power. The "one supreme Court" created by the Constitution reflected ambivalence over the nature and scope of this power, and the Framers left to Congress significant discretion to determine the number of Supreme Court justices; the establishment, structure and jurisdiction of a lower federal judiciary; and the ability to make exceptions to the Court's appellate jurisdiction.

While considering the question of a unitary executive, the delegates to the Constitutional Convention concluded that the judiciary was to be a legal rather than a political body. The Convention rejected the notion that the judicial branch should be any part of a proposed "council of revision," which would have overseen the executive power to exercise a veto or to revise laws. Elbridge Gerry remarked that it was foreign to the nature of the judicial office to judge the policy of public measures. Rufus King argued that judges have to consider laws afresh, without having participated in making them.

Following the implicit command of the Constitution, Congress created a Supreme Court in the Judiciary Act of 1789 and set the number of justices at six. The Judiciary Act also established a subordinate federal judicial structure of several district and three circuit courts, each of the latter including two "riding" Supreme Court justices

(reduced to one in 1793). The act also gave the Supreme Court appellate jurisdiction over federal questions growing out of litigation in state courts, thus cementing national power, while at the same time allowing state courts to make determinations on federal questions prior to final appeal. However, the act also confined the Supreme Court to questions of law rather than fact—an appellate limitation unusual for the time. This innovation was aimed at calming residual fears of national judicial power overturning local jury findings.

The first chief justice, John Jay, confirmed the intention of the Framers by insisting on the legal, rather than political, function of the Court and its justices. In *Hayburn's Case* (1792), he wrote on circuit that Congress could assign only properly judicial tasks to the judiciary, thus upholding federal judges' refusal to act as pensions claims adjudicators. Jay, speaking for the Court in a letter to President George Washington, also declined to render an advisory opinion Washington had requested concerning treaty interpretation.

In *Marbury v. Madison* (1803), Chief Justice John Marshall deftly reinforced both federal judicial power and the notion of the Court as a legal body. He did so by refusing to enter into a political dispute on the grounds that Congress could not constitutionally grant to the Court powers not authorized by the Constitution—in this case, original jurisdiction to issue a writ of mandamus. Underlying Marshall's reasoning is the idea that the Constitution itself is a law to be interpreted by courts, and that courts cannot decide "questions, in their nature political," or force coequal branches to perform political or discretionary acts.

The Federalist Congress reduced the number of justices sitting on the Supreme Court to five by the Judiciary Act of 1801, hoping to prevent incoming President Thomas Jefferson from appointing a justice when the sixth sitting justice retired. The 1801 act also established separate circuit court judgeships, obviating the need for Supreme Court justices to ride circuit. But such riding—and a Supreme Court of six—were quickly reinstituted in the Judiciary Act of 1802 under Jefferson, who was suspicious of national judicial power and desirous of keeping justices in contact with local mores. As the nation expanded, so did the number of circuits and the number of Supreme Court justices to sit on them. The number of justices also expanded and contracted because of the politics of the Civil War and its aftermath, first from nine to ten to support President Abraham Lincoln's war policies, then to seven to deprive President Andrew Johnson of several appointments. Since 1869, Congress has set the number of justices at nine, despite an unsuccessful effort by President Franklin D. Roosevelt to increase the Court's size to suit his political agenda.

There has been a vigorous debate among scholars whether the vesting of judicial power in "one supreme Court" creates a "unitary judiciary" analogous to the idea of a "unitary executive" under Article II, Section 1, Clause 1 (Executive Vesting Clause). The "unitary judiciary" concept has two parts. The first is related to the Supreme Court's jurisdiction and the extent of its ability to have the final word on all federal question matters. The second part relates to the Supreme Court's supervisory authority over inferior courts.

Regarding the range of the Supreme Court's jurisdiction, David Engdahl has argued that the use of the terms "supreme" and "inferior" in relation to courts, unlike the use of "inferior officers" in Article II, does not carry any connotation of hierarchy of authority. At the time of the founding, the terms "supreme" and "inferior" described the breadth of a tribunal's jurisdiction, geographic scope, or some other status. A "supreme" court did not necessarily have appellate review or ultimate authority to have a final say concerning legal interpretations.

In contrast, Laurence Claus finds it important that the Framers used the lower-case "supreme" instead of the upper-case "Supreme" and that they included only one, instead of several supreme courts. The word "supreme," he argues, is used as a description, not a title, signifying that the Court has the "last word" on all matters concerning "the judicial Power of the United States." In the same way that the Constitution, federal law, and national treaties are "the supreme Law of the Land" taking precedence over state constitutions and state laws, the Supreme Court is "supreme" and its rulings take precedence over all "inferior" courts.

James Pfander also declares that the term "supreme" relates to the Supreme Court's ability to review the decisions of courts "inferior" to it in the federal judicial hierarchy, but he asserts that "inferior" courts may include state courts that Congress may constitute as "inferior tribunals" under Article I, Section 8, Clause 9 (Inferior Courts). But Jason Mazzone notes that under the Judiciary Act of 1789, both inferior federal courts and, to some extent, state courts could reach decisions independent of and unappealable to the Supreme Court.

Steven Calabresi and Gary Lawson also argue, on the basis of the Constitution's text and structure, that the Supreme Court has ultimate authority over any inferior courts. Significant is the fact that the word "inferior" is only used elsewhere in the Constitution in relation to "inferior officers," and they conclude that the Supreme Court has authority over inferior courts in the same way the president has authority over inferior officers.

But Amy Barrett counters that the Constitution does not grant the Supreme Court nomination or appointment powers over inferior courts in the way that the president can nominate and appoint inferior officers in the executive branch. Moreover, the Constitution explicitly protects all judges with life tenure during period of good behavior, removing the possibility of Supreme Court judges removing or otherwise punishing inferior judges. Thus, "[i]nferior courts are capable of exercising judicial power wholly independently of the Supreme Court's direction. They do not depend on the Supreme Court to give them the power, and the Supreme Court cannot take it away."

The second part of the unitary judiciary concept relates to the supervisory authority of the Supreme Court—not only its ability to have appellate review of decisions of inferior courts, but also to issue procedural, evidentiary, and other types of rules that inferior courts must follow. Congress has granted the Supreme Court some rule-making authority by statute, but the Supreme Court has issued supervisory rules on inferior courts outside of these statutory bounds on the basis of its "inherent authority" that stems from "the judicial Power." The issue and the history are complex. Scholars similarly argue whether the Court has either explicit or implicit power to make rules for lower federal courts, and to what extent Congress, under the Necessary and Proper Clause, can displace the Supreme Court in making such procedural or evidentiary rules.

Bradley C. S. Watson

See Also

Article I, Section 8, Clause 9 (Inferior Courts)
Article II, Section 1, Clause 1 (Executive Vesting Clause)
Article III, Section 1 (Judicial Vesting Clause)

Suggestions for Further Research

Amy Coney Barrett, *The Supervisory Power of the Supreme Court*, 106 COLUM. L. REV. 324 (2006)

Steven G. Calabresi & Gary Lawson, *The Unitary Executive, Jurisdiction Stripping, and the* Hamdan *Opinions: A Textualist Response to Justice Scalia*, 107 COLUM. L. REV. 1002 (2007)

Laurence Claus, *The One Court That Congress Cannot Take Away: Singularity, Supremacy, and Article III*, 96 GEO. L.J. 59 (2007)

DAVID P. CURRIE, THE CONSTITUTION IN THE SUPREME COURT: THE FIRST HUNDRED YEARS, 1789–1888 (1985)

THE DOCUMENTARY HISTORY OF THE SUPREME COURT OF THE UNITED STATES, 1789–1800, (Maeva Marcus et al. eds., 1985)

David E. Engdahl, *What's in a Name? The Constitutionality of Multiple "Supreme" Courts*, 66 IND. L.J. 457 (1991)

1 JULIUS GOEBEL JR., HISTORY OF THE SUPREME COURT OF THE UNITED STATES: ANTECEDENTS AND BEGINNINGS TO 1801 (1971)

Jason Mazzone, *When the Supreme Court Is Not Supreme*, 104 NW. U. L. REV. 979 (2010)

ORIGINS OF THE FEDERAL JUDICIARY: ESSAYS ON THE JUDICIARY ACT OF 1789 (Maeva Marcus ed., 1992)

James E. Pfander, *Federal Supremacy, State Court Inferiority, and the Constitutionality of Jurisdiction-Stripping Legislation*, 101 NW. U. L. REV. 191 (2007)

Charles Warren, *New Light on the History of the Federal Judiciary Act of 1789*, 37 HARV. L. REV. 49 (1923)

Significant Cases

Hayburn's Case, 2 U.S. (2 Dall.) 409 (1792)
Marbury v. Madison, 5 U.S. (1 Cranch) 137 (1803)
Ex parte Bollman, 8 U.S. (4 Cranch) 75 (1807)
United States v. Palmer, 16 U.S. (3 Wheat.) 610 (1818)
United States v. Furlong, 18 U.S. (5 Wheat.) 184 (1820)
Eakin v. Raub, 12 Serg. & Rawle 330 (Pa. 1825)
United States v. Gooding, 25 U.S. (12 Wheat.) 460 (1827)
United States v. Wood, 39 U.S. (14 Pet.) 430 (1840)
United States v. Murphy, 41 U.S. (16 Pet.) 203 (1842)
Skelly v. Jefferson Branch of the State Bank of Ohio, 9 Ohio St. 606 (1859)
Funk v. United States, 290 U.S. 371 (1933)
Wolfle v. United States, 291 U.S. 7 (1934)
McNabb v. United States, 318 U.S. 332 (1943)
Edmond v. United States, 520 U.S. 651 (1997)

Inferior Courts

The judicial Power of the United States shall be vested in one supreme Court, and in such inferior Courts as the Congress may from time to time ordain and establish.

(ARTICLE III, SECTION 1)

~

*T*he clause is discussed in David Engdahl's essay on the Inferior Courts Clause (Article I, Section 8, Clause 9) on page 155.

Good Behavior Clause

The Judges, both of the supreme and inferior Courts, shall hold their Offices during good Behaviour....

(ARTICLE III, SECTION 1)

The Framers firmly believed that republican liberty could be secured only under the rule of law, and that the rule of law could not be guaranteed without an independent judiciary. The Good Behavior Clause of Article III anchors judicial independence by protecting judges from being removed at the whim of the other branches.

Guaranteed life-tenure for judges had become the rule in England after the Act of Settlement in 1701, though it did not come fully into effect until 1760. Prior to that time, many (including the crown) regarded the "king's courts" as attached to the executive branch. But as William Blackstone summarized the law in his *Commentaries on the Laws of England* (1765–1769), "In this distinct and separate existence of the judicial power, in a peculiar body of men, nominated indeed, but not removeable at pleasure, by the crown, consists one main preservative of the public liberty."

It was different in the colonies. Judges did not have same independence from the crown as they were coming to have in England, leading to the complaint in the Declaration of Independence, "He has made Judges dependent on his Will alone, for the tenure of their offices. . . ." John Adams, wielding great influence during the Second Continental Congress, had pressed for judicial independence. In his *Thoughts on Government* (April 1776), he urged that judges "should hold estates for life in their offices; or, in other words, their commissions should be during good behavior."

After independence, the "good behavior" standard appeared in some state constitutions, and in Philadelphia, the Framers approved the phrase with no comment. During ratification, Hamilton defended the clause in *The Federalist* No. 78, stating:

> In a monarchy it is an excellent barrier to the despotism of the prince; in a republic it is a no less excellent barrier to the encroachments and oppressions of the representative body. And it is the best expedient which can be devised in any government to secure a steady, upright, and impartial administration of the laws.

The question that arises is whether "good behavior" is simply a code phrase for life-tenure or whether it also establishes a standard for removal of judges different from "high crimes and misdemeanors" in the Standards for Impeachment Clause (Article II, Section 4). In his *Thoughts on Government*, Adams had suggested that only "misbehavior" should be the cause for impeachment.

Under English law, there remained two methods of removing life-tenured judges, one by joint action of the executive and legislature, and one by the judiciary. The Act of Settlement provided a removal procedure through a formal request by the crown to both houses of Parliament for one who, in the words of Blackstone, had "breach[ed] . . . good behavior." Additionally, a judge's misbehavior could still lead to his removal from the bench by means of a writ of scire facias issued by a court of equity by which a patent, charter, or land grant—or in the case of judges, an appointment—could be annulled for "misbehavior." Prior to independence, some states had similar procedures for the removal of judges.

At the Constitutional Convention, the Framers rejected the first English method of removal. John Dickinson moved to add, after the words "good Behaviour," the words "Provided that they may be removed by the Executive on the application by the Senate and House of Representatives." There ensued a vigorous debate, Gouverneur Morris arguing that it would be "a contradiction in terms to say that the Judges should hold their offices during good behavior, and yet be removeable without a trial." The Dickenson proposal lost by a vote of seven to one, but no mechanism for "trial" was added to the Good Behavior Clause. Instead, two weeks later, the convention settled on the "high crimes and misdemeanors" language for removal of the president, and then, by separate motion, extended the process for impeachment to "all civil officers of the United States," presumably including judges.

Impeachment is not mentioned in Article III, dealing with the judiciary, though it is in Article I, setting the powers of Congress, and in Article II, dealing with the executive. Nonetheless textually, impeachment is the only method mentioned in the Constitution for the removal of executive officers and of judges.

Hamilton pronounced in *The Federalist* No. 79 that impeachment was the only method of removing a judge and that any other cause would "be liable to abuse" and would "give scope to personal and party attachments and enmities." Hamilton did opine that insanity would be a "virtual disqualification," though he did not speculate on the method by which a judge could be removed for mental incapacity. He made no reference to the common law writ of scire facias.

Thomas Jefferson, perhaps from frustration at not being able to remove Federalist judges, pronounced the "high crimes and misdemeanors" standard a "bungling way of removing Judges . . . an impracticable thing—a mere scarecrow." But Justice Joseph Story, in his *Commentaries on the Constitution of the United States* (1833), agreed with Hamilton. "[I]nstances of absolute imbecility would be too rare," he wrote, "to justify the introduction of so dangerous a provision" of removal other than impeachment.

Except in one instance, Thomas Jefferson's attempt to attack the federal judiciary through impeachment failed, but he was able to remove the whole cohort of federal circuit judges simply by having Congress legislate their courts out of existence in the Judiciary Act of 1802, an act upheld by the Supreme Court in *Stuart v. Laird* (1803).

Over the history of the republic, judges have been impeached and removed for a variety of misdeeds, not all of them actual crimes. There have been fifteen cases of judicial impeachment tried before the Senate. Among these fifteen officials were one associate justice of the Supreme Court, one commerce court judge, and thirteen district judges. Their charges ranged from "mental instability and drunkenness on the bench" to "improper business relationship with litigants," and from "favoritism in the appointment of bankruptcy receivers" to "sexual assault."

The first judge removed was John Pickering of the federal district court in New Hampshire, whose trial in 1804 was a precursor to Jefferson's campaign to remove Samuel Chase from the Supreme Court. Pickering was charged with being biased in some of his decisions and for "being a man of loose morals and intemperate habits," who appeared in court "in a total state of intoxication" and "in a most profane and indecent manner, invoke[d] the name of the Supreme Being," said actions amounting to "high misdemeanors." The Senate heard evidence that showed convincingly that Pickering suffered from a debilitating insanity that voided any imputation of criminal intent. It was politically necessary, however, for the Democrats in Congress to convict Pickering so that they could go on to the impeachment of Justice Chase. To avoid the problem of Pickering's lack of criminal liability, the Democrats agreed to have the question changed from whether Pickering was guilty of "high crimes and misdemeanors" to whether he was "guilty as charged." By a vote of nineteen to seven, Pickering was convicted and removed from office.

The Pickering case raised the continuing problem of whether impeachment is the only mechanism for removing a judge who has not actually committed a crime. In the impeachment trial of President William Clinton, his counsel affirmed that judges were subject to impeachment, but he argued that the "good Behavior" clause sets a lower standard for the impeachment of judges than does "high crimes and misdemeanors" for a president. A number of scholars, on the other hand, have asserted that Congress, through the Necessary and Proper Clause, can provide the judiciary with a mechanism, analogous to the old common law writ of scire facias, to police themselves and remove a judge incapable of carrying out his duties, without having to have recourse to impeachment.

Throughout the debate, Congress has insisted that (1) the Good Behavior Clause means merely no fixed term (i.e., for life), (2) only Congress can remove federal judges using impeachment, and (3) "high crimes and misdemeanors" does not require the offensive conduct to be a crime. In 1993, the congressionally authorized National Commission on Judicial Discipline and Removal declared that the Good Behavior Clause defines life tenure and is not a separate basis for what constitutes an impeachable offense for judges.

There have been instances where the judiciary itself sought the removal of a judge from office. In 1989, for example, the Judicial Conference of the

United States (composed of the senior judges of the federal circuits and the chief justice of the Supreme Court) recommended to the Speaker of the House of Representatives that Judge Alcee Hastings be impeached, even though Hastings had been acquitted of charges of conspiracy to solicit and accept a bribe. The Judicial Conference deferred to the power of Congress to impeach and convict. The House went forward to impeach Hastings and the Senate convicted him.

In 1980, Congress passed the Judicial Councils Reform and Judicial Conduct and Disability Act, empowering Judicial Councils (disciplinary bodies of the circuit courts) to suspend case assignments from judges who were mentally or physically unable to discharge their duties or who had engaged in inappropriate conduct. But, Congress declared, "in no circumstances may the council order removal from office of any judge appointed to hold office during good behavior."

In *Chandler v. Judicial Council of the Tenth Circuit of the United States* (1970), the Supreme Court considered the constitutionality of a judicial council's decision to bar a federal judge, who had been a civil and criminal defendant in a number of proceedings, from hearing cases to which he was assigned, and to prevent further assignment of cases to his docket. In effect, the judicial council had removed the judge from performing his office. The judge asserted that the judicial council had usurped the power of the House of Representatives and of the Senate to impeach and to convict. The Court dismissed the suit on jurisdictional grounds. Justice John M. Harlan, concurring, opined that the Court did have jurisdiction, but on reaching the merits, found that the circuit courts possessed disciplinary authority to prevent a judge from hearing cases. Justices William Douglas and Hugo L. Black vigorously dissented asserting that the judicial council had gone too far and that the only constitutionally permissible method of a removing a judge from his duties was through impeachment.

David F. Forte

See Also

Article I, Section 2, Clause 5 (Impeachment)

Article I, Section 3, Clause 7 (Punishment for Impeachment)

Article I, Section 8, Clause 9 (Inferior Courts)

Article II, Section 4 (Standards for Impeachment)

Suggestions for Further Research

Raoul Berger, *Impeachment of Judges and "Good Behavior" Tenure*, 79 Yale L.J. 1475 (1970)

William S. Carpenter, *Repeal of the Judiciary Act of 1801*, 9 Am. Pol. Sci. Rev. 519 (1915)

History of the Federal Judiciary: Impeachments of Federal Judges, Federal Judicial Center, at http://www.fjc.gov/history/home.nsf/page/judges_impeachments.html (accessed January 7, 2014)

Robert Kramer & Jerome A. Barron, *The Constitutionality of Removal and Mandatory Retirement Procedures for the Federal Judiciary: The Meaning of "During Good Behavior,"* 35 Geo. Wash. L. Rev. 455, 458 (1967)

Saikrishna Prakash and Steven D. Smith, *How to Remove a Federal Judge*, 116 Yale L.J. 72 (2006)

Martin H. Redish, *Response: Good Behavior, Judicial Independence, and the Foundations of American Constitutionalism*, 116 Yale L.J. 139 (2006)

G. W. C. Ross, *"Good Behavior" of Federal Judges*, 12 U. Kan. City L. Rev. 119 (1944)

Ronald D. Rotunda, *An Essay on the Constitutional Parameters of Federal Impeachment*, 76 Ky. L.J. 707 (1988)

Jeff Sessions & Andrew Sigler, Judicial Independence: *Did the Clinton Impeachment Trial Erode the Principle?*, 29 Cumb. L. Rev. 489 (1999)

Burke Shartel, *Federal Judges—Appointment, Supervision, and Removal—Some Possibilities Under the Constitution*, 28 Mich. L. Rev. 870 (1930)

Jonathan Turley, *The Executive Function Theory, The Hamilton Affair, and Other Constitutional Mythologies*, 77 N.C. L. Rev. 1791 (1999)

Martha Andes Ziskind, *Judicial Tenure in the American Constitution: English and American Precedents*, 1969 Sup. Ct. Rev. 135 (1969)

Significant Cases

Stuart v. Laird, 5 U.S. 299 (1803)

Chandler v. Judicial Council of the Tenth Circuit of the United States, 398 U.S. 74 (1970)

Nixon v. United States, 506 U.S. 224 (1993)

Judicial Compensation Clause

The Judges, both of the supreme and inferior Courts... shall, at stated Times, receive for their Services a Compensation, which shall not be diminished during their Continuance in Office.

(ARTICLE III, SECTION 1)

~

*A*long with the Good Behavior Clause, the Judicial Compensation Clause is a guarantee of judicial independence within the Constitution's separation of powers system. Montesquieu, held in the highest esteem by the Framers, had declared, "[T]here is no liberty, if the judiciary power be not separated from the legislative and executive." *L'Esprit des Lois* (1748). In his influential *Thoughts on Government* (April 1776), John Adams called for an independent judiciary.

> [The judges'] minds should not be distracted with jarring interests; they should not be dependent upon any man, or body of men. To these ends, they should hold estates for life in their offices;... and their salaries ascertained and established by law.

Three months later, the Declaration of Independence would have as one of its bill of complaints against the king: "He has made Judges dependent on his Will alone, for the tenure of their offices, and the amount and payment of their salaries."

Justice Joseph Story in his *Commentaries on the Constitution of the United States* (1833) expressed the same principle: "Without this provision [the Judicial Compensation Clause] the other, as to the tenure of office [the Good Behavior Clause], would have been utterly nugatory, and indeed a mere mockery." Alexander Hamilton had already made the point in *The Federalist* No. 79: "Next to permanency in office, nothing can contribute more to the independence of the judges than a fixed provision for their support." A century and a half after, the Supreme Court would affirm that the purpose of the judicial compensation clause was to preserve judicial "independence of action and judgment" essential to maintaining the Constitution. *Evans v. Gore* (1920).

The issue at the Constitutional Convention was whether judges' salaries, like the president's, should be fixed during their tenures, or whether Congress could allow for increases. The Convention considered James Madison's resolution that judges receive "fixed compensation for their services, in which no increase or diminution shall be made." When Gouverneur Morris moved to strike "no increase," Madison objected that judges would fall under the blandishments of the legislature, which could offer them raises. But Morris retorted that the fluctuations in the value of money, the increase in judicial business, and the evolving style of living might create a necessity for raising judges' salaries. On the motion to strike the phrase, Morris, supported by Benjamin Franklin, won. Congress may not reduce judges' salaries, but it may increase them.

Though Congress may not directly diminish a judge's salary, what of indirect or collateral reductions? What of taxes, or the effect of inflation? There is no question that the Framers were concerned about collateral reductions. Although there was no income tax or cost of living adjustments at the time, the concept of inflation adjustment was not unfamiliar in the 1780s. For example, Hamilton noted in *The Federalist* No. 79, "It will readily be understood that the fluctuations in the value of money and in the state of society rendered a fixed rate of compensation in the Constitution inadmissible."

The question of the validity of taxes did not arise until the adoption of the Sixteenth Amendment, providing for a federal income tax, and the subsequent social safety net programs. In *Evans v. Gore* and *Miles v. Graham* (1925), the Court held that Congress had no power to tax a federal judge's salary, stating in *Miles* that "his compensation is protected from diminution in any form."

However, in *O'Malley v. Woodrough* (1939), dealing with the income tax, and *United States v. Hatter* (2001), addressing the Medicare tax, the Court overruled *Miles* and *Evans* respectively. The Court held that the judiciary's independence was not impaired by congressionally enacted taxation. In *Hatter*, the Court held that the Judicial

Compensation Clause was not a barrier to a "generally applicable, nondiscriminatory tax" to the salaries of federal judges, stating that there "is no good reason why a judge should not share the tax burdens borne by all citizens." Thus, whether or not a judge was appointed before enactment of the tax did not matter. The Social Security taxes, however, were a different matter, for the law at issue was discriminatory: it had allowed most federal employees to opt out of paying for Social Security, but not federal judges.

In *United States v. Will* (1980) and *Williams v. United States* (2002), judges challenged the repeal or the denial of annual cost-of-living adjustments (COLAs) for judicial salaries. In *Will*, the Court found that some repeals of the COLA were invalid depending upon when they took effect. A similar issue arose in *Williams*, which dealt with the Ethics Reform Act. That Act had allowed for salary supplements to take account of inflation. However, Congress blocked salary adjustments in 1995, 1996, 1997, and 1999 for federal judges. Though a district court found that Congress could not rescind the adjustments, the United States Court of Appeals for the Second Circuit reversed. The case was appealed, but in *Williams*, the Supreme Court denied a writ of certiorari, though Justices Stephen Breyer, Antonin Scalia, and Anthony Kennedy found merit in the challenge.

The issue of the adequacy of judicial compensation remains. Chief Justice John Roberts has argued that Congress's failure to increase judicial compensation "has now reached the level of a constitutional crisis that threatens to undermine the strength and independence of the federal judiciary." Under his view, "judges are no longer drawn primarily from among the best lawyers in the practicing bar." However, studies have not established a quantifiable relationship between judicial performance and compensation.

Retirement of judges has also been also part of the question of compensation. At the time of the Constitutional Convention, the state of New York had required its judges to retire at age sixty, which Alexander Hamilton termed "inhumane," as it left the retired judge with no income. In *The Federalist* No. 79, Hamilton argued against mandatory retirement: "[F]ew there are who outlive the season of intellectual vigor." After the Civil War, the question of whether retired judges could receive a salary began to be debated. The Judiciary Act of 1869 provided for judicial retirement and a pension equal to their salary. In 1919, Congress allowed federal judges (excepting those on the Supreme Court) to retire from active service at their salary, but continue to serve where needed, an arrangement that came to be termed "senior status." When Congress attempted in 1933 to reduce the salary of retired judges, the Supreme Court voided the legislation, holding that when a judge retired from active service, he still retained his "office" and the constitutional guarantee of no diminution of salary. *Booth v. United States* (1934). Congress extended the option of senior status to Supreme Court justices in 1937.

David F. Forte

See Also
Article III, Section 1 (Good Behavior Clause)
Amendment XVI (Income Tax)

Suggestions for Further Research
James M. Anderson & Eric Helland, *How Much Should Judges Be Paid?*, 64 Stan. L. Rev. 1277 (2012)

Scott Baker, *Should We Pay Federal Circuit Judges More?*, 88 B.U. L. Rev. 63 (2008)

Stephen B. Burbank, et al., *Leaving the Bench, 1970–2009: The Choices Federal Judges Make, What Influences Those Choices, and Their Consequences,* 161 U. Pa. L. Rev. 1 (2012)

Jonathan L. Entin, *Getting What You Pay For: Judicial Compensation and Judicial Independence,* 2011 Utah L. Rev. 25 (2011)

1 Chief Justice John Roberts, 2006 Year-End Report on the Federal Judiciary (Jan. 1, 2007)

Ronald D. Rotunda, *A Few Modest Proposals to Reform the Law Governing Federal Judicial Salaries,* 12 The Professional Lawyer 1 (A.B.A., Fall 2000)

Adrian Vermeule, *The Constitutional Law of Official Compensation,* 102 Colum. L. Rev. 501 (2002)

Albert Yoon, *Love's Labor's Lost? Judicial Tenure Among Federal Court Judges: 1945–2000,* 91 Cal. L. Rev. 1029 (2003)

Significant Cases
Evans v. Gore, 253 U.S. 245, 247 (1920)

Miles v. Graham, 268 U.S. 501 (1925)
Booth v. United States, 291 U.S. 339 (1934)
O'Malley v. Woodrough, 307 U.S. 277 (1939)
United States v. Will, 449 U.S. 200 (1980)
United States v. Hatter, 532 U.S. 557 (2001)
Williams v. United States, 535 U.S. 911 (2002)

A Note on Non–Article III Courts

*A*rticle III vests the "judicial Power of the United States" in judges of the supreme and inferior federal courts. It then specifies that all of those judges "shall hold their Offices during good Behaviour, and shall, at stated Times, receive for their Services a Compensation, which shall not be diminished during their Continuance in Office." The "judicial Power" is quintessentially the power to adjudicate disputes in accordance with governing law. Nonetheless, most federal adjudications are conducted by persons who are not Article III federal judges. Determining whether and how federal adjudication by nonjudges is constitutionally permissible is one of the longest-lived and most perplexing questions in all of constitutional law.

There are three categories of federal adjudication that occur under the Constitution. First, under Article III, life-tenured judges, on both the Supreme Court and the inferior federal courts, exercise the judicial power of the United States as defined in Article III.

The second category of adjudications is conducted by "judges" and "courts," created under either Article I or Article IV, who do not satisfy the criteria specified in Article III. These judges are often appointed and confirmed in the same manner as Article III judges but do not enjoy constitutional protections of life tenure or guarantees against diminishment in salary, though Congress by statute generally provides some measure of (revocable) tenure in office and salary protection. In addition, the work of Article III judges is often supplemented by federal magistrates, who are appointed by federal district judges to eight-year terms and who preside over many pre-trial matters. The four national Article I courts—the

Court of Federal Claims, the Tax Court, the Court of Appeals for the Armed Forces, and the Court of Veterans Appeals—and the local courts for the District of Columbia derive their authority from various powers given by Article I to Congress: the payment of money owed by the United States, taxation, regulation of the armed forces, and the governance of the District of Columbia. The Article IV territorial courts—for Guam, the Virgin Islands, the Northern Mariana Islands, and American Samoa—derive their authority from Congress's power to govern federal territories.

The third category of adjudicators is career employees of the executive branch; immigration judges, for example, are employees of the United States Department of Justice. This is by far the largest group, consisting of around four thousand individuals organized into hundreds of categories. Some have special career tenure protection. Others have no tenure protection other than civil service. And some are political appointees with no career protection. Most of these executive-branch adjudicators are subject to review by political appointees, either in departments or by independent regulatory commissions. In turn, the political appointees' decisions can be reviewed in Article I or Article III courts.

Territorial judges (including in this category judges for the District of Columbia) have been around since the founding. These judges have never had life tenure or salary guarantees. William Marbury, for instance, held his commission by John Adams as a justice of the peace for the District of Columbia under a five-year term of office; and judges today in Guam, the Virgin Islands, and the Northern Mariana Islands have ten-year terms of office and no constitutional salary guarantees. Judges in American Samoa, who are appointed by the secretary of the interior, have indefinite terms of office. Although a lower court in 1803 held unconstitutional the absence of salary guarantees for these judges, the Supreme Court, in *American Insurance Co. v. 356 Bales of Cotton, Canter* (1828), broadly approved the use of non–Article III tribunals in federally governed territory on the ground that their jurisdiction "is not a part of that judicial power" described in Article III. Accordingly, tribunals in federal territories may determine all kinds of cases, including criminal cases, without necessarily conforming to the requirements of Article III. Some originalists (and non-originalists) find this jurisdiction incompatible with Article III's declaration that federal judicial power can only be exercised by Article III judges, but the authority of territorial judges has been settled by history established contemporaneously with the Constitution.

Military courts-martial also exercise essentially criminal jurisdiction, though in a limited sphere. The members of courts-martial need not have Article III tenure and salary guarantees; their authority stems instead from the president's Article II executive power as commander in chief and from Congress's Article I powers to "make rules for the government and regulation of the land and naval forces" and to "provide for . . . disciplining, the militia." As the Supreme Court held in *Dynes v. Hoover* (1857),

> [t]hese provisions show that Congress has the power to provide for the trial and punishment of military and naval offences in the manner then and now practiced by civilized nations; and that the power to do so is given without any connection between it and the 3d article of the Constitution defining the judicial power. . . .

Military justice, in other words, is an exercise of executive and legislative rather than judicial power.

Sovereign immunity provided the rationale for the creation of the first major non–Article III court under Congress's Article I powers: the Court of Claims. For the first seventy-nine years of the Republic, there was no legally enforceable remedy against the federal government for takings of property, breaches of contract, or governmental torts. Relief against virtually any legal wrong, except imprisonment, was at the whim of the federal government. The only remedy was to implore Congress for a private bill of relief. By the 1850s, more than twenty thousand such bills were pending. Few were dealt with, and corruption in the passage of some resulted in scandal. In 1855, Congress created the Court of Claims to deal with the claims that had led to private bills. In 1887, Congress passed

the Tucker Act, creating a life-tenured panel of five judges who heard any claim for money against the United States based on the Constitution, statute, regulation, or contract. Only tort claims were left to congressional discretion. In 1947, Congress also waived sovereign immunity for (at least some) torts and gave to Article III courts jurisdiction over tort claims, subject to certain procedural limitations such as the denial of a jury trial.

Modern statutes permit tax-refund actions, tort actions, and some contract or takings claims involving small amounts to be brought in Article III courts, but many statutory waivers of sovereign immunity require suit to be brought in non–Article III tribunals. Because Congress does not have to permit suit at all, it can set conditions on those suits to which it has consented, including having the "suit" heard by a non–Article III "judge." *United States v. Sherwood* (1941). Today, the principal non–Article III tribunals that hear such cases include the Court of Federal Claims, which adjudicates claims against the United States founded in contracts, statutes, regulations, or takings; the Tax Court, which allows taxpayers to challenge their tax liability without first paying the tax and then filing for a refund; and the Court of Veterans Appeals, which determines claims by veterans under relevant benefits statutes. The United States Court of Appeals for the Armed Forces was established to provide a civilian court for the review of court-martial criminal sentences.

All of the national Article I courts are subject to Article III appellate review. The Court of Federal Claims and the Court of Veterans Appeals are subject to appellate review by the Court of Appeals for the Federal Circuit. The Tax Court is subject to appellate review by the circuit in which the taxpayer resides. The United States Court of Appeals for the Armed Forces is subject to Supreme Court review. All Article I judges are appointed by the president with Senate confirmation. They are thus officers of the United States, unlike administrative judges, who the lower courts have held can be appointed without compliance with the Appointments Clause. Their salaries are statutorily tied to district or circuit judge salaries. They all have lengthy tenure by statute, as well as senior status systems, which in the case of the Tax Court and Court of Federal Claims are similar to those of Article III judges.

The federal bankruptcy courts merit special mention. Congress has Article I power to establish uniform bankruptcy rules. Most claims by and against estates in bankruptcy are determined—with finality if there is no appeal—by non–Article III bankruptcy judges, subject to limited appellate review by Article III district judges. The Supreme Court has determined on several occasions that the bankruptcy judges cannot decide common-law contract or tort actions that arise independently from the regulatory regime constructed by the bankruptcy laws. *See*, e.g, *Stern v. Marshall* (2011). These cases assume, however, that Congress can allow bankruptcy judges to address in the first instance all non-collateral matters that concern the bankruptcy proceeding.

The most sweeping rationale for non–Article III tribunals is the so-called public rights doctrine. This doctrine originated in 1856 in *Murray's Lessee v. Hoboken Land & Improvement Co.*, in which the Supreme Court permitted the government to adjudicate deficiencies against its own tax collectors without full judicial process. "Public rights" in that context meant rights of the public against certain government officials. More broadly, public rights were understood in 1932 to involve matters "between the Government and persons subject to its authority in connection with the performance of the constitutional functions of the executive or legislative departments." *Crowell v. Benson*. This broader notion of "public rights" could arguably permit non–Article III adjudication in any cases in which the government is a party pursuant to a regulatory scheme (which, as a matter of original meaning, might seem to be precisely the cases in which requiring an independent Article III judge and a jury would be most appropriate). Modern cases, however, have permitted ordinary administrative agencies to adjudicate even purely private common law rights on the theory that such rights are "public" whenever they are ancillary to a regulatory scheme. Thus, for example, the Commodity Futures Exchange Commission has been allowed to adjudicate common law counterclaims resulting from transactions within its enforcement jurisdiction. *Commodity Futures Trading Commission v. Schor* (1986). This rationale obviously validates as well ordinary agency adjudication in the administration of regulatory programs. The limits, if any, of Congress's power to entrust adjudication to non–Article III decision-makers is uncertain. Nor is it clear to what extent the decisions of non–Article III tribunals must be subject to appellate review in Article III courts, although Congress by statute has generally made such review available.

As a matter of original understanding, executive adjudication of any kind may seem problematic, but matters are actually more complicated. Not all adjudication—understood as the application of legal standards to particular facts—requires an exercise of the judicial power. Many exercises of Article II "executive power" are functionally indistinguishable from exercises of the "judicial power," which is not surprising given the close historical and conceptual connections between executive and judicial power. So long as a particular exercise of power, such as a court-martial or a benefit determination, meets the constitutional definition of "executive power," it need not be performed by an Article III judge, even if could be performed by such a judge. There can be areas of overlap between the executive and judicial powers, which gives Congress a measure of freedom as to which department to charge with particular adjudicative tasks.

The task of figuring out which adjudicative functions, if any, must be performed only by Article III courts has perplexed originalists and non-originalists alike for more than two centuries. It has also perplexed the courts—the Supreme Court divided four-one-four on the proper approach to these questions in 2011. *See Stern v. Marshall* (in which the Court held unconstitutional a congressional delegation of jurisdiction to the bankruptcy court to determine an issue that was a matter of state common law).

Loren Smith and Gary Lawson

Suggestions for Further Research

Richard H. Fallon Jr., *Of Legislative Courts, Administrative Agencies, and Article III*, 101 Harv. L. Rev. 915 (1988)

Gary Lawson & Guy Seidman, The Constitution of Empire: Territorial Expansion and American Legal History, 139–50 (2004)

James E. Pfander, *Article I Tribunals, Article III Courts, and the Judicial Power of the United States*, 118 Harv. L. Rev. 643–776 (2004)

Martin H. Redish, *Legislative Courts, Administrative Agencies, and the Northern Pipeline Decision*, 1983 Duke L.J. 197 (1983)

Craig A. Stern, *What's a Constitution Among Friends?—Unbalancing Article III*, 146 U. Penn. L. Rev. 1043 (1998)

Significant Cases

United States v. More, 7 U.S. (3 Cranch) 159 (1805)

American Ins. Co. v. 356 Bales of Cotton, Canter, 26 U.S. (1 Pet.) 511 (1828)

Murray's Lessee v. Hoboken Land & Improvement Co., 59 U.S. (18 How.) 272 (1856)

Dynes v. Hoover, 61 U.S. (20 How.) 65 (1857)

Crowell v. Benson, 285 U.S. 22 (1932)

United States v. Sherwood, 312 U.S. 584 (1941)

Palmore v. United States, 411 U.S. 389 (1973)

Northern Pipeline Construction Co. v. Marathon Pipe Line Co., 458 U.S. 50 (1982)

Commodity Futures Trading Comm'n v. Schor, 478 U.S. 833 (1986)

Stern v. Marshall, 131 S. Ct. 2594 (2011)

Judicial Power

The judicial Power shall extend to all Cases, in Law and Equity, arising under this Constitution, the Laws of the United States....
(**Article III, Section 2, Clause 1**)

⁓

*A*rticle III, Section 2 delineates the scope of the federal judicial power by listing nine kinds of "cases" and "controversies" to which the "judicial power" of the United States may extend. By far the most important is the category encompassing "all Cases, in Law and Equity, arising under this Constitution, the Laws of the United States, and Treaties made, or which shall be made, under

their Authority." This is often referred to as the "federal question" jurisdiction, and, although that is something of a misnomer, it is a convenient label.

From the beginning, the Framers intended the scope of the jurisdiction to be broad. The federal question jurisdiction made its first appearance at the Constitutional Convention in the Virginia Plan, which would have authorized federal courts to hear "questions which may involve the national peace and harmony." By the time the Committee of Detail began its work, the convention had added to this language a grant of jurisdiction over "Cases arising under the Laws passed by the general Legislature." When the Committee of Detail reported to the convention, the reference to "national peace and harmony" had disappeared, but the "arising under" language remained.

There was little discussion of this provision at the convention. In the course of a single day, the convention made three important changes. It replaced the reference to "laws passed by the Legislature" with "laws of the United States." And, on separate motions, it extended the judicial power first to cases arising under the Constitution and then to cases arising under treaties, in addition to the cases arising under federal laws. When the Committee of Style reported to the convention in September, the provision read substantially as it does today: the federal judicial power extends "to all cases, both in law and equity, arising under this constitution, the laws of the United States, and treaties made, or which shall be made, under their authority."

The potential breadth of this language prompted criticism by opponents of the proposed Constitution during the debates over ratification in the key state of Virginia. George Mason, for example, could find no "limitation whatsoever, with respect to the nature or jurisdiction of [the federal] courts." James Madison, a supporter of ratification, did not dispute this assertion; rather, he asserted that "the judicial power [of the national government] should correspond with the legislative."

When does a case "arise under" federal law, so that it falls within the judicial power of the United States? The authoritative answer to this question is found largely in two decisions by

Chief Justice John Marshall in the early years of the republic.

The better-known of the two decisions is *Osborn v. Bank of the United States* (1824). Marshall's delineation of the constitutional scope of the jurisdictional grant proceeds in two steps. First, he declares that a "question" is "federal" if "the title or right set up by the party, may be defeated by one construction of the Constitution or law of the United States, and sustained by the opposite construction, provided the facts necessary to support the action be made out." In other words, a federal question is a question whose answer depends in some way on federal law. Marshall then says that a case "arises under" the Constitution or laws of the United States if a federal question "forms an ingredient of the original cause"—that is, is an element of the plaintiff's claim.

The breadth of this definition is made clear by a companion case in which the Court upheld federal jurisdiction over a suit by the Bank of the United States to recover on negotiable notes issued by a state bank. *Bank of the United States v. Planters' Bank of Georgia* (1824). The liability of the defendant state bank would appear to have depended solely on state law. How, then, could Marshall have concluded that a federal question formed an element of the "original cause"? Marshall's answer is that there are some federal questions—for example, the federal bank's capacity to sue—that necessarily exist in every case brought by the bank, even though the particular proposition is not questioned. *Osborn* thus establishes that, so long as a proposition of federal law is a logical antecedent of the plaintiff's claim, it is sufficient as a constitutional matter to support federal judicial power over the case.

Three years before *Osborn*, in *Cohens v. Virginia* (1821), the Court considered a challenge to its own authority to exercise appellate jurisdiction over a case originating in state court. The defendants, convicted of a crime under state law, invoked what we would today call a defense of preemption: they "claimed the protection of an act of Congress." They also asserted that the Supreme Court could consider their appeal because it was a case "arising under" federal law. The state of Virginia disagreed, taking the posi-

tion that a case could "arise under" the federal Constitution or federal law only if the Constitution or law was the basis for the claim of the party who had initiated the lawsuit.

The state's interpretation is a plausible reading of the language of Article III, but the Supreme Court rejected it as "too narrow." The Court said that cases are defined by the rights of both parties, and a case "may truly be said to arise under the constitution or a law of the United States, whenever its correct decision depends on the construction of either." The *Cohens* definition thus supports the Supreme Court's jurisdiction to hear appeals from state courts when those courts have decided federal questions.

Capacious though they are, neither the *Osborn* definition nor the one in *Cohens* would necessarily cover all of the cases in which Congress has authorized the *removal* of actions from state to federal court. But in a series of nineteenth-century decisions the Court made plain that Article III authorizes removal of any case in which a defense under federal law has been invoked, even though the federal issue may prove not to be dispositive.

The leading case is *Tennessee v. Davis* (1880). James Davis was a federal revenue officer whose duties included seizing illicit distilleries. In the course of one such effort "he was assaulted and fired upon by a number of armed men." He fired back, killing one of the men, and was prosecuted in state court for murder. Davis removed the case to federal court under an act of Congress that allowed removal of any suit brought against a federal revenue officer on account of any act done "under color of" any revenue law. The state challenged the constitutionality of the removal statute, but the Supreme Court held that the statute was valid. The Court relied heavily on Marshall's opinion in *Cohens*. It emphasized that in order to preserve the supremacy of federal judicial power, it is essential that the national government be able to "take control" "whenever and wherever a case arises under the Constitution and laws or treaties of the United States...whether it be civil or criminal, *in any stage of its progress*" (emphasis added).

The Supreme Court's decisions have thus established that Congress can authorize federal courts to hear cases in which a federal question is (1) a logical antecedent of the plaintiff's claim (whether or not contested), or (2) the basis of a defense actually raised (even though it may not be dispositive), or (3) the basis of the decision actually made (typically by a state court). The area of uncertainty involves Congress's power to authorize jurisdiction over cases in which a federal question is an element neither of the original cause nor of the defense, but in which a litigant is a member of a class that Congress seeks to protect (e.g., federal employees sued in state court) or the area is one in which Congress has taken an interest under an Article I grant of power (e.g., consumer protection or nuclear accidents).

Until recently, Supreme Court case law cast little doubt on the breadth of Congress's authority to vest federal question jurisdiction in federal courts. However, the decision in *Mesa v. California* (1989) makes clear that the power is not unlimited. In *Mesa*, the Court construed the statute that allows removal to federal court of suits brought against federal officers for acts done under color of their federal office (a modern-day version of the statute involved in *Tennessee v. Davis*). The Court held that the statute allows removal only if the officer alleges a federal defense to the state-law claim. The Court explained that if the statute were construed to grant federal jurisdiction simply because a federal officer is a defendant, it would "unnecessarily present grave constitutional problems." The opinion thus implies that to support "arising under" jurisdiction, a federal question must be present somewhere in the case. However, the Court did not rule out the possibility that, under some circumstances, Congress might be able to vest "arising under" jurisdiction to protect federal interests even in the absence of a federal question.

It is important to emphasize that the broad construction of the "arising under" language of Article III has no bearing on the scope of the statutory grant of federal question jurisdiction, even though the statute uses language identical to that of the Constitution. The Court has read the statutory jurisdiction not to extend as far as it could under the Constitution. Full discussion is beyond the scope of this essay; it is sufficient to note that neither a federal defense (as in *Cohens*) nor a "logical antecedent" provides a basis for

district court jurisdiction under 28 U.S.C. § 1331. Rather, the federal question must be, at a minimum, a necessary element of a "well pleaded complaint"—the plaintiff's claim for relief.

Finally, it should be made clear that federal jurisdiction extends to cases, not issues. When a federal court has jurisdiction over a case that arises under federal law, the jurisdiction extends to the whole case, and the court will often have power to consider other issues in the case whether state or federal.

The Court defined the boundaries of the constitutional "case" in *United Mine Workers v. Gibbs* (1966). Under *Gibbs*, if a federal court has jurisdiction over a case based on the plaintiff's federal claims, it can also hear non-federal claims as long as the federal and non-federal claims "derive from a common nucleus of operative fact" and are sufficiently related that the plaintiff "would ordinarily be expected to try them all in one judicial proceeding." Congress codified the substance of the *Gibbs* decision in 1990 when it recognized "supplemental jurisdiction" in section 1367 of the Judicial Code.

Until 2011, the removal chapter of the Judicial Code included a provision—section 1441(c)—that appeared to go beyond the limits of judicial power as defined in *Gibbs*. Congress cured this infirmity in the Federal Courts Jurisdiction and Venue Clarification Act of 2011, when it rewrote section 1441(c) to require the district court, upon removal, to sever and remand all claims not within its jurisdiction.

Arthur Hellman

See Also
Article III, Section 2

Suggestions for Further Research
Ray Forrester, *The Nature of a "Federal Question,"* 16 Tulane L. Rev. 362 (1942)

Paul J. Mishkin, *The Federal "Question" in the District Courts,* 53 Colum. L. Rev. 157 (1953)

G. Edward White, The Marshall Court and Cultural Change 1814–1835, Ch. 8 (Oxford 1991)

Significant Cases
Cohens v. Virginia, 19 U.S. (6 Wheat.) 264 (1821)

Bank of the United States v. Planters' Bank of Georgia, 22 U.S. (9 Wheat.) 904 (1824)

Osborn v. Bank of the United States, 22 U.S. (9 Wheat.) 738 (1824)

Tennessee v. Davis, 100 U.S. 257 (1880)

Mesa v. California, 489 U.S. 121 (1989)

United Mine Workers v. Gibbs, 383 U.S. 715 (1966)

Treaties

The judicial Power shall extend to all Cases, in Law and Equity, arising under this Constitution, the Laws of the United States, and Treaties made, or which shall be made, under their Authority....

(**Article III, Section 2, Clause 1**)

~

*T*hroughout the Constitutional Convention, the Framers consistently expressed the desire that a national judiciary have jurisdiction over legal issues arising from the nation's international rights and obligations. Nevertheless, while such a proposition was part of both the Virginia and New Jersey Plans, the delegates were unable to reach a consensus, putting forward numerous alternative formulations. They wanted, in Edmund Randolph's words, to protect "the security of foreigners" and "the harmony of states and the citizens thereof."

It was not until August 27, 1787, when the delegates were refining the Committee of Detail's jurisdictional language, that John Rutledge of South Carolina moved to include the words "and treaties made or which shall be made under their authority" after the "United States" in the first clause of what would become Article III, Section 2. That language guaranteed the federal judiciary jurisdiction over all treaties entered into by the United States from the moment of its independence. The proposal was unanimously approved. During ratification, Alexander Hamilton explained the provision in *The Federalist* No. 80, reasoning that because "the peace of the whole ought not to be left at the disposal of a part ... the federal judiciary ought to have cognizance of all

causes in which the citizens of other countries are concerned," which "have an evident connection with the preservation of the national peace."

The Judiciary Act of 1789 granted limited jurisdiction, and limited rights of appeal, to the newly created federal court system. Under Section 25, the Supreme Court was allowed to hear appeals from the states' highest courts when such decisions touched on the "validity of a ... treaty ... or against any title, right, privilege, or exemption set up or claimed under any ... treaty." Outside of the appeals permitted by the Judiciary Act, the Court would not go. It refused to offer advisory opinions on the construction of treaties, as President George Washington had asked it to do in 1793, or to review veterans' pension claims at congressional request. In the latter instance, the Court claimed that such review would exceed the judicial function and was contrary to the separation of powers.

Chief Justice John Marshall provided the earliest construction of the Article III Treaties Clause in *Owings v. Norwood's Lessee* (1809), a case concerning the property claims of British subjects whose lands had been confiscated during the Revolution. The Treaty of Paris of 1783 had explicitly preserved the "just rights" of such persons to reclaim lands in certain instances. Marshall, explaining the origin of the Treaties Clause, and enforcing the application of the Treaty's provisions, explained:

> The reason for inserting that clause in the constitution was, that all persons who have real claims under a treaty should have their causes decided by the national tribunals. It was to avoid the apprehension as well as the danger of state prejudices.... Each treaty stipulates something respecting the citizens of the two nations, and gives them rights. Whenever a right grows out of, or is protected by, a treaty, it is sanctioned against all the laws and judicial decisions of the States; and whoever may have this right, it is to be protected. But if the person's title is not affected by the treaty, if he claims nothing under a treaty, his title cannot be protected by the treaty.

The mere existence of a treaty, and its application to any one party in a dispute, however, does not assure federal jurisdiction. *Mayor, Alderman and Inhabitants of the City of New Orleans v. De Armas* (1835). While jurisdiction may extend "without regard to the character of the parties" involved in any dispute, *Cohens v. Virginia* (1821), the legal rights asserted by the parties must in fact flow from an enforceable treaty.

Federal jurisdiction also requires that the legal right claimed under any treaty actually be contested. For example, in *Martin v. Hunter's Lessee* (1816), Justice Joseph Story noted that a claimant must have relied on a treaty provision to his detriment, with such error evident from the record. At the same time, Story declared that the record need not refer to the disputed interpretation of a treaty in specific terms, for treaties are part of "the supreme law of the land of which all courts must take notice."

As far as the relationship between treaties and the "laws of Congress" is concerned, the Court has made a clear distinction between those cases involving claims that "grow directly out of [a] treaty" and are "thus clearly dependent upon it," and those cases where Congress has acted upon a treaty and created legislation to effect its obligations thereunder. In the latter case, the claim must be founded on the act of Congress. *United States v. Weld* (1888).

Historically, the construction of treaties, especially when they are applied as domestic law, has been understood as the "peculiar province of the judiciary," except in "cases purely political." *Jones v. Meehan* (1899). But under the political-question doctrine, the courts will not determine whether a treaty obligation with another nation has been broken. *Clark v. Allen* (1947). And while treaties can have the force of domestic law, the Constitution remains the supreme law of the land; neither a statute nor a treaty can override the Constitution where specific constitutional guarantees are in issue. *Reid v. Covert* (1957).

Over the years, the Court has crafted a number of prudential rules in its interpretation of treaties. Assuming that a treaty's text is self-executing (i.e., enforceable as domestic law without need for implementing legislation), all interpretations begin with the explicit meaning of its text.

Medellin v. Texas (2008). Unambiguous textual provisions are controlling unless their plain meaning would be clearly "inconsistent with the intent or expectations" of the treaty's signatories. *Maximov v. United States* (1963). The question of signatory "intent" is especially controversial. The courts will rely on clarifications, interpretations, and understandings of a treaty formulated by the executive branch. But the courts will not infer an obligation from a treaty that has not been articulated in clear terms. *Society for the Propagation of the Gospel in Foreign Parts v. New Haven* (1823).

Where ambiguities do exist, courts can turn to any number of other sources: (1) ratification history, *Air France v. Saks* (1985); (2) the understanding entertained by the political branches, *Charlton v. Kelly* (1913); (3) the interpretations held by administrative agencies typically charged with a treaty's enforcement, *Kolovrat v. Oregon* (1961); or (4) the opinions of "sister signatories," or those nations with which the United States has entered into the treaty, *Abbott v. Abbott* (2010).

Traditionally, the courts were less likely to accord the legislative branches a say in the interpretation of a treaty. *Jones v. Meehan*. The text would govern, *Maximov v. United States*, unless an ambiguity caused recourse to ratification history for clarification. *See Air France v. Saks*. In *Sumitomo Shoji America, Inc. v. Avagliano* (1982), the Court went so far as to suggest that the parties' intent would control even over the text. Justice Antonin Scalia vigorously objected to this proposition in *United States v. Stuart* (1989), where the majority had limited its investigation of treaty intent to Senate floor debates. Scalia condemned the "unprecedented" use of such materials: "The question before us in a treaty case is what the two or more sovereigns agreed to, rather than what a single one of them, or the legislature of a single one of them, thought it agreed to."

As a rule, courts will only recognize the legal validity of a treaty, and legal claims arising therefrom, if it has been "executed" into federal law. This can be accomplished in two ways. In the first instance, a treaty may convey an intention that it be "self-executing," and acknowledged as such during congressional ratification. *Foster v. Neilson* (1829). In the second, the treaty may require "legislation to carry [it] into effect."

Whitney v. Robertson (1888). The courts will not enforce "non–self-executing treaties" until they are carried into law by an act of Congress. (*See* Article VI, Clause 2). Whether a given treaty is self-executing or requires special implementing legislation to give force and effect to its provisions is generally understood as a question for the courts. *Diggs v. Richardson* (1976).

Federal statutes and properly executed treaties have equal status in law, the later in time taking precedence. Therefore, if Congress passes a statute that contradicts earlier treaty obligations of the United States, the courts will enforce the statute over the treaty. In order to avoid such a conflict, however, the courts will construe a law not to be in conflict with extant treaty obligations if such a construction is at all reasonable.

The jurisdictional statute regulating treaty review is currently 28 U.S.C. § 1257. It allows appeal by writ of certiorari to the Supreme Court if the validity of a treaty or of a state statute under a treaty is questioned or if "any title, right, privilege, or immunity is specially set up or claimed" under a treaty. Furthermore, under 28 U.S.C. § 1331, "district courts shall have original jurisdiction of all civil actions arising under ... treaties of the United States." District courts may also take jurisdiction over cases brought in state court involving treaties under the complicated rules of pendent jurisdiction.

Dennis W. Arrow

See Also

Article I, Section 10, Clause 1 (State Treaties)
Article II, Section 2, Clause 2 (Treaty Clause)
Article VI, Clause 2 (Supremacy Clause)

Suggestions for Further Research

Dennis W. Arrow, *Federal Question Doctrines and American Indian Law*, 14 Okla. City U. L. Rev. 263 (1989)

Martin S. Flaherty, *History Right? Historical Scholarship, Original Understanding, and Treaties as "Supreme Law of the Land,"* 99 Colum. L. Rev. 2095 (1999)

Julian G. Ku, *Treaties as Laws: A Defense of the Last-in-Time Rule for Treaties and Federal Statutes*, 80 Ind. L.J. 319 (2005)

John Norton Moore, *Treaty Interpretation, the Constitution and the Rule of Law*, 42 Va. J. Int'l. L. 163 (2001)

Peter J. Spiro, *Treaties, International Law, and Constitutional Rights*, 55 Stan. L. Rev. 1999 (2003)

Michael P. Van Alstine, *The Judicial Power and Treaty Delegation*, 90 Cal. L. Rev. 1305 (2002)

John C. Yoo, *Globalism and the Constitution: Treaties, Non-Self-Execution, and the Original Understanding*, 99 Colum. L. Rev. 1955 (1999)

John C. Yoo, *Treaty Interpretation and the False Sirens of Delegation*, 90 Cal. L. Rev. 1305 (2002)

Ernest A. Young, *Treaties as "Part of Our Law,"* 88 Tex. L. Rev. 91 (2009)

Significant Cases

Owings v. Norwood's Lessee, 9 U.S. (5 Cranch) 344 (1809)
Smith v. Maryland, 10 U.S. (6 Cranch) 286 (1810)
Martin v. Hunter's Lessee, 14 U.S. (1 Wheat.) 304 (1816)
Cohens v. Virginia, 19 U.S. (6 Wheat.) 264 (1821)
Society for the Propagation of the Gospel in Foreign Parts v. New Haven, 21 U.S. (8 Wheat.) 464 (1823)
Foster v. Neilson, 27 (2 Pet.) 253 (1829)
United States v. Arredondo, 31 U.S. (6 Pet.) 691 (1832)
Mayor, Alderman and Inhabitants of the City of New Orleans v. De Armas, 34 U.S. 224 (1835)
Gill v. Oliver's Executors, 52 U.S. (11 How.) 529 (1850)
United States v. Weld, 127 U.S. 51 (1888)
Whitney v. Robertson, 124 U.S. 190 (1888)
De Geofroy v. Riggs, 133 U.S. 258 (1890)
New York Indians v. United States, 170 U.S. 1 (1898)
Jones v. Meehan, 175 U.S. 1 (1899)
Devine v. City of Los Angeles, 202 U.S. 313 (1906)
Muskrat v. United States, 219 U.S. 346 (1911)
Charlton v. Kelly, 229 U.S. 447 (1913)
Gully v. First National Bank in Meridian, 299 U.S. 109 (1936)
Bacardi Corp. of America v. Domenech, 311 U.S. 150 (1940)
Clark v. Allen, 331 U.S. 503 (1947)
Reid v. Covert, 354 U.S. 1 (1957)
Kolovrat v. Oregon, 366 U.S. 187 (1961)
Maximov v. United States, 373 U.S. 49 (1963)
Oneida Indian Nation of New York State v. Cnty. of Oneida, 414 U.S. 661 (1974)
Phillips Petroleum Co. v. Texaco, Inc., 415 U.S. 125 (1974)
Diggs v. Richardson, 555 F.2d 848 (D.C. Cir. 1976)

British Caledonian Airways Ltd. v. Bond, 665 F.2d 1153 (D.C. Cir. 1981)

Sumitomo Shoji America, Inc. v. Avagliano, 457 U.S. 176 (1982)

Air France v. Saks, 470 U.S. 392 (1985)

United States v. Stuart, 489 U.S. 353 (1989)

Medellin v. Texas, 552 U.S. 491 (2008)

Abbott v. Abbott, 130 S. Ct. 1983 (2010)

Ambassadors

The judicial Power shall extend...to all Cases affecting Ambassadors, other public Ministers and Consuls....

(ARTICLE III, SECTION 2, CLAUSE 1)

~

*A*t the Constitutional Convention, William Paterson put forward the New Jersey Plan designed to counter the more nationalist plan set out by Virginia. Despite its focus on the rights of the states, Paterson's plan nonetheless acknowledged the necessity of national competency and supremacy in a number of areas. It proposed to authorize, for example, the federal judiciary to hear appeals from state courts in "all cases touching the rights of Ambassadors." The provision excited no discussion, and the Committee of Detail penned the final version, including placing the subject within the original jurisdiction of the Supreme Court. (See Article III, Section 2, Clause 2.)

All, including the Anti-Federalist Brutus, seemed to agree with the sentiments of Alexander Hamilton that placing the jurisdiction of cases dealing with foreign ministers had "an evident connection with the preservation of the national peace." *The Federalist* No. 80. Justice Joseph Story in his *Commentaries on the Constitution of the United States* (1833) thought that every question involving the "rights, powers, duties, and privileges" of public ministers was "so intimately connected with the public peace, and policy, and diplomacy of the nation, and touches the dignity and interest of the sovereigns of the ministers concerned so deeply, that it would be unsafe, that they should be submitted to any other, than the highest judicature of the nation."

In *Osborn v. Bank of the United States* (1824), the Supreme Court declared that the foreign diplomat need not be a party to the case to trigger federal jurisdiction, although original jurisdiction is not mandated when the diplomat is merely a victim of a crime. *United States v. Ortega* (1826). Federal jurisdiction under this clause applies to foreign, not United States, diplomats, *Ex parte Gruber* (1925). It does not apply to divorce suits involving foreign diplomats, *Ohio ex rel. Popovici v. Agler* (1930), or to suits involving former foreign diplomatic agents or those whose tours of duty in the United States have ended, *Farnsworth v. Sanford* (1941). Furthermore, although the Ambassadors Clause speaks of "Ambassadors, other public Ministers and Consuls," as early as 1890 the Supreme Court held that consuls representing foreign countries but who are United States citizens invested with only commercial duties are not subject to this provision. *In re Baiz* (1890). Under modern practice, consuls in general are not normally regarded as diplomatic agents.

The fact that the Constitution lodges these cases in the federal judiciary does not preclude the foreign diplomatic agent from pleading diplomatic immunity. Under traditional international law principles, codified in the Vienna Convention on Diplomatic Relations (1961), accredited foreign ambassadors and other ministers may plead immunity from suits in the courts of the host country. The United States became a party to the Convention in 1972, and in 1978 Congress passed the Diplomatic Relations Act implementing the Vienna Convention. In addition, Congress decided that there was no justification for continuing to vest original jurisdiction solely in the Supreme Court and gave district courts concurrent original jurisdiction over civil actions brought against members of diplomatic missions and their families. Actions initiated by foreign diplomats or their families, however, remain solely under the original jurisdiction of the Supreme Court.

David F. Forte

Admiralty

**The judicial Power shall extend ... to
all Cases of admiralty and maritime
Jurisdiction....**

(**ARTICLE III, SECTION 2, CLAUSE 1**)

≈

*I*n England, a separate system of courts that
dated to the reign of Edward III dealt with maritime and admiralty issues. "Maritime" originally applied to the high seas, while "admiralty"
applied to areas such as harbors and inlets,
though the two terms eventually became synonymous. The substance of traditional admiralty law lay in the civil law, in opposition to
and competition with the common law. It covered activities in the country's territorial sea,
and beyond, as permitted by international law.
According to Sir William Blackstone in *Commentaries on the Laws of England*, these courts
had jurisdiction "to determine all maritime
injuries, arising upon the seas, or in parts out
of the reach of the common law." In the English
tradition, then, admiralty jurisdiction did not
reach land or inland waters, which were subject to the common law. Thus, when England
enforced the Stamp Act (1765) through the
admiralty courts, the colonists rebelled against
losing their "inestimable" common law right
of trial by jury (admiralty and maritime cases
typically involve bench trials).

During the Revolution, maritime states
exercised their own admiralty jurisdiction. But
state prize courts often violated international
law by condemning prizes belonging to sister
states or nations that were neutral or even allies
of the United States. The Articles of Confederation divided admiralty jurisdiction between the
states and the United States, but the Constitution
gave the national government exclusive admiralty
and maritime jurisdiction. In Philadelphia, the
only debate among the Framers of the Constitution was whether to lodge admiralty questions
in a separate court or, as they finally decided,
in the federal judiciary. There was unanimity,
even among the Anti-Federalists, that this power
should be national.

Admiralty law covers (1) damages to ships
and cargo on the high seas as well as torts, injuries, and crimes and (2) contracts and activities
bearing on shipping, transport, and cargoes on
the sea. It was obvious to the founding generation that the federal courts would be applying
a pre-existing body of maritime law that was
observed by most maritime nations. Both John
Adams and Alexander Hamilton practiced
admiralty law. According to Chief Justice John
Marshall, maritime cases before federal courts
do not "arise under the Constitution or laws of
the United States" but "are as old as navigation
itself." *American Ins. Co. v. 356 Bales of Cotton,
Canter* (1828).

Though there is no grant of power in the
Constitution to Congress to regulate maritime
law as such, Congress has in fact modified its
content. Some Supreme Court decisions assume
that the Commerce Clause provides Congress
that power. Justice Joseph Bradley, however, held
that the Commerce Power was neither a source
nor a limitation of Congress's power to regulate
maritime affairs. Rather, because maritime law
is national law, "the power to make such amendments [to maritime law] is coextensive with that
law. It is not confined to the boundaries or class of
subjects which limit and characterize the power
to regulate commerce; but, in maritime matters,
it extends to all matters and places to which the
maritime law extends." *In re Garnett* (1891).

Congress, under the Judiciary Act of 1789,
gave the district courts exclusive jurisdiction over

admiralty and maritime cases, now codified in 28 U.S.C. § 1333. The Admiralty Clause also accords exclusive federal jurisdiction to captures and prize cases, codified in 28 U.S.C. § 1333(2). See *Glass v. The Sloop Betsey* (1794); *The Paquete Habana* (1900). Until 1875, maritime states continued to pass laws regulating activities in their adjacent waters, and federal courts often applied such state law. But in *The Lottawanna* (1874), the Supreme Court declared that the substance of admiralty law was exclusively federal. In fact, the Court has insisted that Congress's broad power to alter traditional admiralty and maritime rules does not include the capacity to delegate such power to the states (in contrast to Congress's power under the Commerce Clause). *Knickerbocker Ice Co. v. Stewart* (1920).

In 1845, breaking from English precedent that had limited admiralty jurisdiction to the seas and the ebb and flow of the tides, Congress extended admiralty jurisdiction to include inland navigable lakes and rivers. In an approving response, the Supreme Court held that English statutes restricting admiralty jurisdiction from inland waters were not part of American law at the time of the Constitution. *Waring v. Clarke* (1847); *Genessee Chief v. Fitzhugh* (1852).

Admiralty jurisdiction in England also did not cover acts committed on land. But in 1815, Justice Joseph Story declared in *DeLovio v. Boit* that admiralty jurisdiction includes "all contracts, (wheresoever they may be made or executed, or whatsoever may be the form of the stipulations,) which relate to the navigation, business or commerce of the sea." *See also United States v. Wiltberger* (1820); *Waring v. Clarke*.

In *DeLovio*, the Court had broken new ground by extending admiralty jurisdiction to maritime insurance contracts. But this only created a new problem: when was a contract truly maritime? Whether a contract is "purely maritime" has been a central question in determining the extent of admiralty jurisdiction. For example, in *People's Ferry Co. v. Beers* (1858), the Court held that a construction contract to build a ship, as opposed to a repair contract, was not under maritime jurisdiction.

Until recently, the Court has held that contracts that had to be performed on both land and sea were cognizable in admiralty only if the application of the contract to land was "merely incidental." But in 2004, the Supreme Court found that where the primary purpose of the contract is to ship something over water, even if the goods are also shipped over land, the contract is a maritime contract and the federal courts have admiralty jurisdiction. *Norfolk Southern Ry. Co. v. James N. Kirby, Pty Ltd.* (2004).

Much of admiralty jurisdiction deals with torts, injuries, and prize cases, including shipwrecks and the like. In 1948, Congress expanded admiralty jurisdiction to "include all cases of damage or injury, to person or property, caused by a vessel on navigable water, notwithstanding that such damage or injury be done or consummated on land." At first, the Court, in *Gutierrez v. Waterman Steamship Corp.* (1963), held that this act covered injuries that occur to a person while on a dock loading or unloading a vessel; but in *Victory Carriers, Inc. v. Law* (1971), the Court limited *Gutierrez* only to situations where the injury is "caused by an appurtenance of a ship."

Even though the federal courts have expanded the reach of admiralty jurisdiction, nonetheless, Congress has often sought to preserve the states' jurisdiction wherever possible. States retain jurisdiction over maritime matters in two ways: geographically and substantively. Thus, although federal maritime law now extends to the interior navigable waters of a state, the state courts still have territorial jurisdiction over actions that occur there. When a case involving maritime law is heard in state court, the state judge must apply federal maritime law over state law.

Substantively, Congress has tried to make room for the application of the states' common law. This has created line-drawing difficulties for the courts. The Judiciary Act of 1789 created an exception known as the savings clause, which defers to the states' common law jurisdiction. The savings clause reads, "saving to suitors, in all cases, the right of a common law remedy, where the common law is competent to give it." It is currently codified in 28 U.S.C. § 1333(1). In *Waring v. Clarke*, the Court stated that the purpose behind the savings clause was to preserve a right to trial by jury (a common law right) whenever possible.

In *The Moses Taylor* (1866), the Court made the distinction that federal courts have exclusive jurisdiction over *in rem* suits and concurrent jurisdiction with the states over *in personam* suits, but only insofar as *in personam* jurisdiction is part of the state's traditional common law jurisdiction. The great majority of cases, however, are *in personam*, and thus in fact state courts and federal courts have concurrent jurisdiction over most maritime actions. A later Supreme Court case allowed a state to obtain jurisdiction even over an *in rem* proceeding if the state is seeking the common law remedy of forfeiture. *C. J. Hendry Co. v. Moore* (1943).

A state's concurrent jurisdiction over *in personam* suits is not without limits, however. The scope of those limits has been a highly disputed subject in the Supreme Court's jurisprudence. For many decades, the Supreme Court held, for example, that state worker's compensation laws as applied to maritime injuries invaded the exclusive jurisdiction of Congress. *Southern Pacific Co. v. Jensen* (1917). In response, Congress tried to allow some range of state jurisdiction in the Longshore and Harbor Workers' Compensation Act in 1927, which reserved application of the federal act only after a remedy under state law had been held to be inapplicable. The post-1938 Court upheld the act. *Parker v. Motor Boat Sales, Inc.* (1941). But Congress's attempt to protect the concurrent jurisdiction of the states was dealt a blow by the Court in *Calbeck v. Travelers Insurance Co.* (1962). Justice William J. Brennan Jr., writing for the majority, essentially deleted recourse to state jurisdiction from the statute. As a result, the federal statute now applies regardless of whether an appropriate state remedy is available. Justices Potter Stewart and John M. Harlan dissented on the ground that the majority was rewriting the clear language and undoing the legislative history of the statute. Since that time, both Congress and the Court have continued to try to define the appropriate limits to state jurisdiction in statutes and cases. See *United States v. Locke* (2000); *Lewis v. Lewis & Clark Marine, Inc.* (2001).

Prior to 1875, the Supreme Court exercised appellate review over both the facts and the law in admiralty and maritime suits. In fact, Justice Joseph Story has argued that the real goal of the controversial Appellate Jurisdiction Clause (Article III, Section 2, Clause 2) "was to retain the power of reviewing the fact, as well as the law, in cases of admiralty and maritime jurisdiction." But in an effort to relieve the Supreme Court of a rather cumbersome caseload, Congress has limited appellate review over admiralty and maritime disputes to issues of law.

David F. Forte

See Also

Article III, Section 2, Clause 2 (Appellate Jurisdiction Clause)

Amendment XI (Suits Against a State)

Suggestions for Further Research

David J. Bederman, *Admiralty and the Eleventh Amendment*, 72 Notre Dame L. Rev. 935 (1997)

Henry J. Bourguignon, The First Federal Court: The Federal Appellate Prize Court of the American Revolution, 1775–1787 (1977)

William R. Casto, *The Origins of Federal Admiralty Jurisdiction in an Age of Privateers, Smugglers, and Pirates*, 37 Am. J. Legal Hist. 117 (1993)

Jonathan M. Gutoff, *Original Understandings and the Private Law Origins of the Federal Admiralty Jurisdiction: A Reply to Professor Casto*, 30 J. Mar. L. & Com. 361 (1999)

Matthew J. Harrington, *The Legacy of the Colonial Vice-Admiralty Courts*, 26 J. Mar. L. & Com. 581 (1995) and 27 J. Mar. L. & Com. 323 (1996)

Gerald J. Mangone, United States Admiralty Law (1997)

Thomas J. Schoenbaum, Admiralty and Maritime Law (2004)

Graydon S. Staring, *The Lingering Influence of Richard II and Lord Coke in the American Admiralty*, 41 J. Mar. L. & Com. 239 (2010)

Significant Cases

Chisholm v. Georgia, 2 U.S. (2 Dall.) 419 (1793)

Glass v. The Sloop Betsey, 3 U.S. (3 Dall.) 6 (1794)

United States v. McGill, 4 U.S. (4 Dall.) 426 (C.C.D. Pa. 1806)

DeLovio v. Boit, 7 F. Cas. 418 (C.C.D. Mass. 1815) (No. 3776)

United States v. Wiltberger, 18 U.S. (5 Wheat.) 76 (1820)

American Ins. Co. v. 356 Bales of Cotton, Canter, 26 U.S. (1 Pet.) 511 (1828)

Waring v. Clarke, 46 U.S. (5 How.) 441 (1847)

New Jersey Steam Nav. Co. v. Merchants' Bank of Boston, 47 U.S. (6 How.) 344 (1848)

Genesee Chief v. Fitzhugh, 53 U.S. (12 How.) 443 (1852)

People's Ferry Co. v. Beers, 61 U.S. (20 How.) 393 (1858)

The Moses Taylor, 71 U.S. (4 Wall.) 411 (1866)

The Daniel Ball, 77 U.S. (10 Wall.) 557 (1870)

The Lottawanna, 88 U.S. (21 Wall.) 558 (1874)

Ex parte Easton, 95 U.S. 68 (1877)

The Abbotsford, 98 U.S. 440 (1878)

In re Garnett, 141 U.S. 1 (1891)

The Paquete Habana, 175 U.S. 677 (1900)

Martin v. West, 222 U.S. 191 (1911)

Southern Pacific Co. v. Jensen, 244 U.S. 205 (1917)

North Pacific Steamship Co. v. Hall Bros. Marine Ry. & Shipbuilding Co., 249 U.S. 119 (1919)

Knickerbocker Ice Co. v. Stewart, 253 U.S. 149 (1920)

Western Fuel Co. v. Garcia, 257 U.S. 233 (1921)

Grant Smith-Porter Ship Co. v. Rohde, 257 U.S. 469 (1922)

Panama R. Co. v. Johnson, 264 U.S. 375 (1924)

Red Cross Line v. Atlantic Fruit Co., 264 U.S. 109 (1924)

Washington v. W. C. Dawson & Co., 264 U.S. 219 (1924)

Langnes v. Green, 282 U.S. 531 (1931)

Marine Transit Corp. v. Dreyfus, 284 U.S. 263 (1932)

United States v. Flores, 289 U.S. 137 (1933)

Parker v. Motor Boat Sales, Inc., 314 U.S. 244 (1941)

Davis v. Dep't of Labor & Industries, 317 U.S. 249 (1942)

C. J. Hendry Co. v. Moore, 318 U.S. 133 (1943)

O'Donnell v. Great Lakes Dredge & Dock Co., 318 U.S. 36 (1943)

Madruga v. Superior Court of California, 346 U.S. 556 (1954)

Romero v. International Terminal Operating Co., 358 U.S. 354 (1959)

Kossick v. United Fruit Co., 365 U.S. 731 (1961)

Calbeck v. Travelers Ins. Co., 370 U.S. 114 (1962)

Gutierrez v. Waterman Steamship Corp., 373 U.S. 206 (1963)

Nacirema Operating Co. v. Johnson, 396 U.S. 212 (1969)

Victory Carriers, Inc. v. Law, 404 U.S. 202 (1971)

Executive Jet Aviation, Inc. v. Cleveland, 409 U.S. 249 (1972)

Sun Ship v. Pennsylvania, 447 U.S. 715 (1980)

Foremost Ins. Co. v. Richardson, 457 U.S. 668 (1982)

Sisson v. Ruby, 497 U.S. 358 (1990)

Exxon Corp. v. Central Gulf Lines, 500 U.S. 603 (1991)

American Dredging Co. v. Miller, 510 U.S. 443 (1994)

Jerome B. Grubart, Inc. v. Great Lakes Dredge & Dock Co., 513 U.S. 527 (1995)

United States v. Locke, 529 U.S. 89 (2000)

Lewis v. Lewis & Clark Marine, Inc., 531 U.S. 438 (2001)

Norfolk Southern Ry. Co. v. James N. Kirby, Pty Ltd., 543 U.S. 14 (2004)

Federal Party

The judicial Power shall extend...to Controversies to which the United States shall be a Party....
(ARTICLE III, SECTION 2, CLAUSE 1)

~

*A*mong the numerous jurisdictional grants to the new federal court system, one of the least controversial was the proposition that the federal courts should have jurisdiction over any case to which the United States was a party. The provision for jurisdiction over cases to which the United States is a party was a comparatively late addition to the Constitution, adopted long after the Committee of Detail had completed its work. It seemed to reflect nothing more than a correction of an oversight. As Alexander Hamilton said of this jurisdictional grant in *The Federalist* No. 80, "any other plan would be contrary to reason." Even the Constitution's most vigorous opponents in the Anti-Federalist camp acknowledged the logic of this position. Later, Chief Justice John Jay noted in *Chisholm* *v. Georgia* (1793) that federal jurisdiction over cases involving the United States was necessary "because in cases in which the whole people are interested, it would not be equal or wise to let any one state decide and measure out the justice due to others."

Today, the interesting legal questions about this clause involve determinations of precisely what entity is the "United States" and when the United States has consented to be a party to a lawsuit.

The text of the Federal Party Clause, of course, allows for jurisdiction when the United States acts as a plaintiff, but that circumstance (in which the affirmative act of filing a suit is, effectively, also a consent to the jurisdiction of the court) is far less problematic or controversial than when the United States has been named as a party defendant. The Supreme Court early on held that the United States, as a legal entity, had an inherent right to bring suit without authorization from Congress, *Dugan v. United States* (1818), although the Judiciary Act of 1789 channeled civil suits brought by the United States to federal district courts.

The more difficult issue relates to the United States' status as a defendant in a suit. The clause, while providing for federal jurisdiction over suits to which the United States is a party, does not specify the situations in which such suits are in fact permitted. When the United States is named as a defendant, the general rule has become that, absent a waiver, sovereign immunity shields the federal government and its agencies from suit. As Alexander Hamilton said, "It is inherent in the nature of sovereignty not to be amenable to the suit of an individual *without its consent*." *The Federalist* No. 81. Early Supreme Courts cases affirmed the doctrine. *Cohens v. Virginia* (1821); *United States v. Clarke* (1834). Consent can only be manifested when Congress passes a statute expressly waiving the United States' claim of sovereign immunity from suit for a particular case or class of cases. The waiver must be unequivocal. *FAA v. Cooper* (2012). Further, "when Congress attaches conditions to legislation waiving the sovereign immunity of the United States, those conditions must be strictly observed, and exceptions thereto are not to be lightly implied." *Block*

v. North Dakota ex rel. Board of Univ. and School Lands (1983).

Many examples of these waivers exist in the law today. Agencies, such as the Federal Deposit Insurance Corporation, are often created with the power to "sue or be sued." And the United States frequently consents to subject itself to generally applicable laws, as it has done in permitting itself to be sued by private parties for alleged environmental violations. A most frequent source of suits against the United States, however, is the Federal Tort Claims Act of 1948, which waives the sovereign immunity of the United States for certain torts committed by federal employees "under circumstances where the United States, if a private person, would be liable to the claimant in accordance with the law of the place where the act or omission occurred." This provision captures a large host of conduct, ranging from medical malpractice of army doctors to traffic accidents of federal employees. Then, in 1976, an amendment to the Administrative Procedure Act waived sovereign immunity for suits against the United States that do not involve monetary damages. As a result of these various waivers, the Federal Party Clause has become a significant source of litigation in the federal courts.

Finally, it bears noting that the United States, as a distinct entity, may in many circumstances be distinguished from either federal officers acting in their official capacity or distinct federal entities and instrumentalities. The law regarding this distinction is complex. In some instances, for example, the United States may be substituted as a party for a federal official sued in his official capacity. In that situation the suit becomes grounded in the constitutional grant of jurisdiction over "controversies to which the United States is a party." In other cases, the official or the instrumentality stands apart from the United States, and suits in federal court must rely on different jurisdictional grants, such as the statutory grant of federal-question jurisdiction.

Paul Rosenzweig

Significant Cases

Chisholm v. Georgia, 2 U.S. (2 Dall.) 419 (1793)

Dugan v. United States, 16 U.S. (3 Wheat.) 172 (1818)

Cohens v. Virginia, 19 U.S. (6 Wheat.) 264 (1821)

United States v. Clarke, 33 U.S. (8 Pet.) 436, 444 (1834)

Federal Housing Administration v. Burr, 309 U.S. 244 (1940)

United States v. Sherwood, 312 U.S. 584 (1941)

Block v. North Dakota *ex rel.* Bd. of Univ. and School Lands, 461 U.S. 273 (1983)

FAA v. Cooper, 132 S. Ct. 1441 (2012)

Interstate Disputes

The judicial Power shall extend...to Controversies between two or more States....

(**Article III, Section 2, Clause 1**)

~

*T*hough of modest jurisprudential importance today, the clause providing for federal-court jurisdiction over disputes between two states is emblematic of the issues at the heart of the constitutional founding. The movement to adopt a Constitution grew out of substantial dissatisfaction with the operation of the Articles of Confederation, including the Confederation's difficulty in settling disputes between states over economic policies and territorial claims. Establishing federal jurisdiction to resolve such disputes reflects the political sea change involved in the movement from a confederation to a federal union.

Under Article IX of the Articles of Confederation, disputes between the states (which mostly involved the settlement of land claims to the west) were settled in a convoluted manner: Congress would name thirty-nine individuals (three from each state) as potential commissioners to resolve the dispute. The opposing states would then each alternately strike names from the list until thirteen names remained, from which seven or nine names would be drawn by lot. Those selected were to determine the dispute. This process had some success. Article IX courts, advancing the conception that the states could be subjected to a higher authority, resolved

a few land disputes between states. However, as might be imagined, this cumbersome process often proved to be an impediment to dispute resolution.

Initially, the Committee of Detail retained this method for adjudicating interstate disputes in the draft of the Constitution. After further consideration, the Framers provided for federal court jurisdiction over interstate disputes generally, but retained the Confederation Article IX method for resolving territorial and jurisdictional questions. It was not until rather late in the process, on August 24, 1787, that the Convention chose to adopt the simpler system of federal court jurisdiction for arbitrating all disputes between two or more states. As John Rutledge of South Carolina said in making the proposal, the provision of a national judiciary made the Article IX–type provisions for resolving interstate disputes "unnecessary."

As the Supreme Court noted in the modern case of *New York v. United States* (1992), "[i]n the end, the Convention opted for a Constitution in which Congress would exercise its legislative authority directly over individuals rather than over States." Nonetheless, providing for federal jurisdiction to monitor disputes between states is an unavoidable exception to that general principle. As Alexander Hamilton explained, "The reasonableness of the agency of the national courts in cases in which the State tribunals cannot be supposed to be impartial speaks for itself. No man ought certainly to be a judge in his own cause, or in any cause in respect to which he has the least interest or bias." *The Federalist* No. 80.

The logic of this position was such that even Anti-Federalists, such as "Brutus," conceded the utility of the provision, and there is little or no recorded opposition to this grant of federal jurisdiction in the ratifying debates. Thus, the Convention had come to the view that, as Justice Joseph Story later summarized in his *Commentaries on the Constitution of the United States* (1833), federal jurisdiction over interstate disputes was appropriate "because domestic tranquility requires, that the contentions of states should be peaceably terminated by a common judicatory; and, because, in a free country, justice ought not to depend on the will of either of the litigants."

The Constitution neither compels nor limits the Supreme Court in deciding what kinds of disputes between states it will hear. *Rhode Island v. Massachusetts* (1838). In the early years of the republic, boundary cases constituted the principal source of disputes that states brought before the Supreme Court, but subsequently the Court has heard, among others, cases dealing with water rights, natural gas, and contractual and other financial conflicts. The predominant contemporary application of this clause is that, in conjunction with the Original Jurisdiction provisions of Clause 2 (*see* Article III, Section 2, Clause 2), it provides a mechanism for resolving border and water-resource disputes between neighboring states. Two recent examples of such suits are the dispute between New York and New Jersey to settle title to Ellis Island, *New Jersey v. New York* (1998), and the dispute among several states allocating the water flowing in the North Platte River. *Nebraska v. Wyoming and Colorado* (2001). Typically, such cases are resolved by the Supreme Court directly, after extensive factual inquiry and a report from an appointed special master. When it is appropriate, the Court has permitted private parties whose rights may also be affected to intervene in and participate in these disputes, though this is a relatively rare occurrence. *South Carolina v. North Carolina* (2010).

Paul Rosenzweig

See Also

Article I, Section 10, Clause 3 (Compact Clause)
Article III, Section 2, Clause 2 (Original Jurisdiction)

Suggestion for Further Research

Vincent L. McKusick, *Discretionary Gatekeeping: The Supreme Court's Management of Its Original Jurisdiction Docket Since 1961*, 45 Me. L. Rev. 185 (1993)

Significant Cases

Martin v. Hunter's Lessee, 14 U.S. (1 Wheat.) 304 (1816)
New Jersey v. New York, 30 U.S. (5 Pet.) 284 (1831)

Rhode Island v. Massachusetts, 37 U.S. (12 Pet.) 657 (1838)
New York v. United States, 505 U.S. 144 (1992)
New Jersey v. New York, 523 U.S. 767 (1998)
Nebraska v. Wyoming & Colorado, 534 U.S. 40 (2001)
South Carolina v. North Carolina, 130 S. Ct. 854 (2010)

Citizen-State Diversity

The judicial Power shall extend...to Controversies...between a State and Citizens of another State...and between a State...and foreign States, Citizens or Subjects.
(**Article III, Section 2, Clause 1**)

~

*A*rticle III's provisions extending the federal judicial power "to Controversies between a State and Citizens of another State" and "between a State...and foreign States, Citizens or Subjects" are generally known as the Citizen-State Diversity Clauses. Although these clauses have a variety of applications, they have played a primary role in enduring controversies over the scope of state sovereign immunity in suits by private parties.

The Founding generation seems generally to have accepted the notion that the states enjoyed some form of sovereign immunity, derived from the common law that shielded them against suits by private individuals. Article III's express provision for federal court jurisdiction over suits between individuals and state governments thus raised the possibility that ratification of the Constitution would override this common law immunity. Some Framers, such as Edmund Randolph and James Wilson, seemed to embrace this possibility as a means for ensuring that state governments would honor their debts; Randolph, for example, asked, "Are we to say that we shall discard this government because it would make us all honest?" Anti-Federalists, on the other hand, opposed Article III based on the same expectation. George Mason emphasized the threat of private lawsuits to a state's dignity, inquiring, "Is this state to be brought to the bar of justice like a delinquent individual?" Others stressed the practical consequences of state suability, given the financially precarious position of the states following the Revolutionary War. In particular, many feared that suits by private parties to enforce the states' war debts in federal courts might bankrupt the nascent state governments. The Anti-Federalist writer Brutus, for example, warned that Article III would "produce the utmost confusion, and in its progress, will crush the states beneath its weight."

James Madison, Alexander Hamilton, and other Federalists reacted to these concerns by insisting that Article III left the states' preexisting immunities intact. At the Virginia ratifying convention, Madison explained that the Citizen-State Diversity Clauses were designed to allow state governments to come into federal court as plaintiffs, not to allow private citizens to overcome a state's immunity as a defendant. John Marshall agreed: "The intent is, to enable states to recover claims of individuals residing in other states." And Hamilton acknowledged the states' fundamental immunity from such suits in *The Federalist* No. 81, stating that "[i]t is inherent in the nature of sovereignty not to be amenable to the suit of an individual *without its consent*.... [T]he exemption...is now enjoyed by the government of every State in the Union. Unless, therefore, there is a surrender of this immunity in the plan of the convention, it will remain with the States."

The Supreme Court rejected Madison's and Hamilton's reading, however, in *Chisholm v. Georgia* (1793). That case involved a suit by a South Carolina citizen to recover Revolutionary War debts owed by the State of Georgia. The state insisted that it was immune from such suits, but the Court upheld its jurisdiction. While Justice James Wilson rejected the very notion of state sovereign immunity on the broad ground that it was antithetical to republican government, Justices John Jay, John Blair, and William Cushing relied primarily on the Citizen-State Diversity Clauses. They argued that those clauses had in fact done precisely what the Anti-Federalists feared—that is, overridden the common law immunity that the states would otherwise have enjoyed in a suit by a private individual. Only Justice James Iredell dissented, primarily on the

ground that Congress had not passed any statute that clearly authorized private suits against state governments in the federal courts.

The Court would later say, in *Hans v. State of Louisiana* (1890), that *Chisholm* "created such a shock of surprise throughout the country that, at the first meeting of Congress thereafter, the Eleventh Amendment to the Constitution was almost unanimously proposed, and was in due course adopted by the legislatures of the States." That amendment provided that "[t]he Judicial power of the United States shall not be construed to extend to any suit in law or equity, commenced or prosecuted against one of the United States by Citizens of another State, or by Citizens or Subjects of any Foreign State." Several commentators have noted the extent to which the latter part of the amendment tracks the language of the Citizen-State Diversity Clauses; the "diversity theory" of the amendment thus infers that it was intended simply to "repeal" the Citizen-State Diversity Clauses in all cases in which a nonconsenting state is the defendant. Others have advanced somewhat different interpretations of the amendment's text and intent; the important point for present purposes is simply that the proper reading of the Eleventh Amendment—and the scope of state sovereign immunity generally—remains bound up with disputes about what the Framers intended to accomplish with the Citizen-State Diversity Clauses.

Ernest A. Young

See Also
Amendment XI (Suits Against a State)

Suggestions for Further Research
William A. Fletcher, *A Historical Interpretation of the Eleventh Amendment: A Narrow Construction of an Affirmative Grant of Jurisdiction Rather Than a Prohibition Against Jurisdiction*, 35 Stan. L. Rev. 1033 (1983)

Clyde Jacobs, The Eleventh Amendment and Sovereign Immunity (1972)

Caleb Nelson, *Sovereign Immunity as a Doctrine of Personal Jurisdiction*, 115 Harv. L. Rev. 1559 (2002)

Ann Woolhandler & Michael G. Collins, *State Standing*, 81 Va. L. Rev. 387 (1995)

Significant Cases

Chisholm v. Georgia, 2 U.S. (2 Dall.) 419 (1793)

Cohens v. Virginia, 19 U.S. (6 Wheat.) 264 (1821)

Hans v. Louisiana, 134 U.S. 1 (1890)

Atascadero State Hospital v. Scanlon, 473 U.S. 234 (1985)

Seminole Tribe of Florida v. Florida, 517 U.S. 44 (1996)

Alden v. Maine, 527 U.S. 706 (1999)

Diversity Clause

The judicial Power shall extend...
to Controversies...between Citizens of different States....
(**Article III, Section 2, Clause 1**)

∽

*T*he clause authorizing diversity of citizenship jurisdiction was intended to protect out-of-state litigants from local bias in state courts. The records of the Constitutional Convention contain surprisingly little discussion of the clause. The reason for this silence, however, may have been that most delegates shared Alexander Hamilton's belief that "the reasonableness of the agency of the national courts in cases in which the state tribunals cannot be supposed to be impartial speaks for itself." *The Federalist* No. 80. Some of the Framers appear to have been less worried about state court partiality. In the Virginia ratification debates, James Madison is said to have conceded that diversity jurisdiction might well have been left to the state courts; and Chief Justice John Marshall is reported to have given only half-hearted support to the Diversity Clause. But as Marshall later remarked in the classic statement of the purpose of the clause, however impartial the state courts may be in fact, "the Constitution itself either entertains apprehensions on this subject, or views with such indulgence the possible fears and apprehensions" of potential out-of-state litigants that it authorizes the extension of the federal judicial power to controversies between citizens of different states. *Bank of the United States v. Deveaux* (1809).

Although the Diversity Clause authorizes such extension, the actual grant of power to try diversity cases is conferred by statute. Congress has never conferred this power to the full extent authorized by the clause. For example, it has always limited the federal courts' jurisdiction over diversity cases to those in which the amount in controversy between the parties exceeds a certain sum; and it has refused to allow a defendant to invoke diversity jurisdiction for the purpose of removing a case from a state court to the federal system when the defendant is a citizen of the state in which the suit was brought (and when, consequently, he would generally have nothing to fear from any local bias on the part of a state court).

Chief Justice Marshall interpreted the clause as not applying to residents of the District of Columbia, *Hepburn v. Ellzey* (1805), but Congress later extended federal diversity jurisdiction to the district's residents by statute. 28 U.S.C. §1332. In *National Mutual Insurance Co. of the District of Columbia v. Tidewater Transfer Co.* (1949), the Supreme Court upheld Congress's authority to accord the District of Columbia the status of a state for diversity purposes, but the Court did so with shifting majorities and conflicting rationales.

Chief Justice Marshall also excluded corporations from qualifying as parties under the clause, *Bank of the United States v. Deveaux*, but later Court decisions allowed corporations to be parties under the fiction that their shareholders were citizens of the state of incorporation. *See Marshall v. Baltimore & Ohio Railroad Co.* (1853).

More recently, Congress specified that a corporation is deemed to be a citizen not only of the state in which it is incorporated but also the state of its principal place of business; the effect was to make it more difficult for defendant corporations to remove cases to federal court. However, in 2010, the Supreme Court made diversity removal easier for corporate defendants by specifying that a corporation's "principal place of business" means its "nerve center," or the place where the officers direct, control, and coordinate the corporation's activities. *Hertz Corp. v. Friend* (2010). *Hertz* enables a corporation to utilize diversity removal from state court even in states where it does a plurality of its business, so long as that state is not its "nerve center."

The Supreme Court has recognized certain limitations on the federal courts' diversity jurisdiction. Most importantly, the Court has required (with a few exceptions) that parties to a lawsuit based on diversity jurisdiction be "completely" diverse: that is, no party on one side of the dispute may be a citizen of the same state as any party on the other side. To qualify under the clause, the parties must actually be domiciled in different states. Differential residency alone is not sufficient.

For many years, the substantive law that federal courts applied in diversity cases was its own federal common law. *Swift v. Tyson* (1842). Through statute, however, the courts applied the procedural law of the state in which the court sat. That formula was reversed in *Erie Railroad Co. v. Tompkins* (1938). Subsequently, a complex body of law has developed governing which law the federal court will apply. In the main, a federal court will apply the substantive law of the state in which the court sits, including the state's conflict-of-laws rules, but the federal court will follow federal procedural practice, unless the state's procedure would be material in determining the outcome of the case. *See Guaranty Trust Co. v. York* (1945). In most cases, the federal court is bound to apply state law as determined by the state's highest court. Although drastically reduced by the *Erie* decision, federal common law still governs in some areas of peculiar federal concern, such as relations with other nations. *Banco Nacional de Cuba v. Sabbatino* (1964).

Despite a longstanding prejudice against diversity jurisdiction by legal academics and jurists, Congress has significantly broadened it over the last two decades. In the early 1990s, Congress enlarged the class of claims and parties that a federal court must entertain as part of a single diversity "case" to include both related state law claims ("pendent" jurisdiction) as well as claims relating to third parties that would otherwise defeat diversity of citizenship ("ancillary" claims). The Supreme Court has expanded diversity jurisdiction even beyond what Congress apparently intended. *See Exxon Mobil v. Allapattah Servs., Inc.* (2005), which held that federal courts can entertain diversity jurisdiction even in cases where not all the claimants assert claims over the dollar minimum specified by statute.

In 2002, Congress eliminated the requirement that all plaintiffs and defendants be citizens of different states ("complete diversity") for mass torts involving the deaths of at least seventy-five individuals in an accident in one location (the Multiparty, Multiforum Trial Jurisdiction Act). In 2005, Congress further provided that so long as there was diversity of citizenship between any two plaintiffs and defendants, a class action lawsuit could be removed to federal court no matter how large was the class (the Class Action Fairness Act of 2005). In neither case was Congress concerned with bias against out-of-state defendants. Rather, it acted simply to further judicial efficiency (MMTJA) and to address the lack of uniformity that would occur when multiple state courts handled large consumer-oriented class action suits against national corporations (Class Action Fairness Act).

Not only did Congress's expansion of the availability of diversity jurisdiction in the early 2000s arguably go beyond the original purpose for diversity jurisdiction, which was to remedy state court bias, but it amounted to a significant transfer of judicial authority from the state courts to the federal courts. For this reason, some commentators have suggested the new, expansive rules distort the federalist structure envisioned by the Framers.

Many academics and federal judges continue to believe that diversity jurisdiction should be curtailed or abolished. They argue that it is anachronistic because there is little danger today of bias against out-of-state litigants, that it encourages forum-shopping, that it has an innate bias against the states, and that it results in an inefficient use of judicial resources. On the other side, a widespread belief that federal judges are better qualified than their state court counterparts leads many practitioners to oppose further restrictions. Moreover, many practitioners continue to insist that local bias persists, especially in rural areas (where state courts are somewhat more likely to be located); and they counsel against departing from the precaution of the Framers.

Terence J. Pell

Suggestion for Further Research

C. Douglas Floyd, *The Limits of Minimal Diversity*, 55 Hastings L.J. 613 (2004)

Henry J. Friendly, *The Historical Basis of Diversity Jurisdiction*, 41 Harv. L. Rev. 483 (1928)

James M. Underwood, *The Late, Great Diversity Jurisdiction*, 57 Case W. Res. L. Rev. 179 (2006)

Significant Cases

Hepburn v. Ellzey, 6 U.S. (2 Cranch) 445 (1805)

Strawbridge v. Curtiss, 7 U.S. (3 Cranch) 267 (1806)

Bank of the United States v. Deveaux, 9 U.S. (5 Cranch) 61 (1809)

Swift v. Tyson, 41 U.S. (16 Pet.) 1 (1842)

Marshall v. Baltimore & Ohio R.R. Co., 57 U.S. (16 How.) 314 (1853)

Dodge v. Woolsey, 59 U.S. (18 How.) 331 (1856)

Erie R.R. Co. v. Tompkins, 304 U.S. 64 (1938)

Klaxon Co. v. Stentor Electric Manufacturing Co., 313 U.S. 487 (1941)

Guaranty Trust Co. v. York, 326 U.S. 99 (1945)

National Mutual Ins. Co. of the District of Columbia v. Tidewater Transfer Co., 337 U.S. 582 (1949)

Lumbermen's Mutual Casualty Co. v. Elbert, 348 U.S. 48 (1954)

Banco Nacional de Cuba v. Sabbatino, 376 U.S. 398 (1964)

Finley v. United States, 490 U.S. 545 (1989)

Carden v. Arkoma Assocs., 494 U.S. 185 (1990)

Dole Food Co. v. Patrickson, 538 U.S. 468 (2003)

Grupo Dataflux v. Atlas Global Group, L.P., 541 U.S. 567 (2004)

Lincoln Property Co. v. Roche, 546 U.S. 81 (2005)

Exxon Mobil Corp. v. Allapattah Servs., Inc., 545 U.S. 546 (2005)

Wachovia Bank N.A. v. Schmidt, 546 U.S. 303 (2006)

Hertz Corp. v. Friend, 130 S. Ct. 1181 (2010)

Land Grant Jurisdiction Clause

The judicial Power shall extend...
to Controversies...between Citizens
of the same State claiming Lands
under Grants of different States....
(Article III, Section 2, Clause 1)

~

Derived from Article IX of the Articles of Confederation, the Land Grant Jurisdiction Clause was included with the Citizen-State Diversity Clause in order to promote "peace and harmony" among the states. The clauses provide, as Justice Joseph Story put it, an impartial federal tribunal in matters where "a state tribunal might not stand indifferent in a controversy where the claims of its own sovereign were in conflict with those of another sovereign." *Town of Pawlet v. Clark* (1815).

The Framers were mindful of the possibility of serious disputes over the western lands among the states and between citizens of the several states and of the same state. It was the same concern that had led to the predecessor clause in the Articles of Confederation. Maryland refused to ratify the Articles of Confederation until 1781—four years after the Continental Congress had approved the document—because of conflicting land claims. Maryland's primary concern was that Virginia would be able to dominate the national congress should it prevail in its extensive claim to all the lands west "to the South Sea," as conveyed in its initial royal charter. Moreover, several other states—Massachusetts, Connecticut, North Carolina, South Carolina, and Georgia—had similar, overlapping claims, derived from their own royal charters, and New York, as "suzerain of the Iroquois Indians," also laid claim to vast expanses of land west of the Delaware River. These conflicting claims threatened to embroil the states in a series of border disputes that were significant enough to place the new union itself at risk.

Virginia's cession of the lands northwest of the Ohio River in 1783, the parallel cessions of the western lands by the other states over the following decade, and the passage of the Northwest Ordinance while the Constitutional Convention was meeting all defused much potential conflict. These often-overlooked cessions demonstrated the commitment and the sacrifice that the states made for the sake of the future stability of the union. Nonetheless, boundary disputes among ten of the states convinced the Framers of the need of a federal forum to settle such conflicts. The convention rejected a proposal to lodge jurisdiction in the Senate in favor of making it a judicial concern. Further agreements and compromises by the states have largely rendered the Land Grant Jurisdiction Clause obsolete.

A few minor border disputes have occasionally arisen involving citizens of the same state. *Schroeder v. Freeland* (1951) dealt with a private dispute over ownership of land between Iowa and Nebraska affected by accretion of the Missouri River. The more serious land disputes, over which the Supreme Court has original jurisdiction, typically involve the states themselves. For example, in 1998, the Supreme Court resolved a dispute over portions of Ellis Island in favor of New Jersey over New York. *New Jersey v. New York* (1998).

The Land Grant Jurisdiction Clause is currently implemented by 28 U.S.C. § 1354, which gives federal district courts jurisdiction without regard to the amount in controversy, *United States v. Sayward* (1895). Unlike the general diversity jurisdiction clause (Article III, Section 2, Clause 1), which the Court has strictly interpreted to require complete diversity of citizenship between the parties, a lower court has held that jurisdiction under this Clause is not destroyed by the fact that the dispute also extends to citizens of other states, as long as there is at least one defendant who is a citizen of the "same state" claiming under a grant from another state than the plaintiff's claim. *Port of Portland v. Tri-Club Islands, Inc.* (1970).

Disputes entirely between citizens of different states, claiming land under grants from different states, can have their cause heard in federal court only under the Citizen-State Diversity Clause. *Stevenson v. Fain* (1904). Nevertheless, the Land Grant Jurisdiction Clause stands for two important propositions: the federal courts should decide cases in which the state courts would have an apparent bias, and too great a geographic imbalance between members of the union was a threat to the body politic.

John C. Eastman

See Also

Article III, Section 2, Clause 1 (Citizen-State Diversity Clause)

Suggestions for Further Research

Charles Moore, The Northwest Under Three Flags: 1635–1796 (1900, reprint 1989)

Shosuke Sato, History of the Land Question in the United States (1886)

Payson Jackson Treat, The National Land System, 1785–1820 (1910)

Significant Cases

Town of Pawlet v. Clark, 13 U.S. (9 Cranch) 292 (1815)

United States v. Sayward, 160 U.S. 493 (1895)

Stevenson v. Fain, 195 U.S. 165 (1904)

Schroeder v. Freeland, 188 F.2d 517 (8th Cir. 1951)

Port of Portland v. Tri-Club Islands, Inc., 315 F. Supp. 1160 (D. Or. 1970)

New Jersey v. New York, 523 U.S. 767 (1998)

Citizen-State Diversity

The judicial Power shall extend... to Controversies...between a State and Citizens of another State... and between a State...and foreign States, Citizens or Subjects.
(**ARTICLE III, SECTION 2, CLAUSE 1**)

~

*T*his clause is discussed in Ernest A. Young's essay on the Citizen-State Diversity Clause on page 328.

Original Jurisdiction

In all Cases affecting Ambassadors, other public Ministers and Consuls, and those in which a State shall be Party, the supreme Court shall have original Jurisdiction.
(**ARTICLE III, SECTION 2, CLAUSE 2**)

≈

*T*he Supreme Court's original jurisdiction is limited to a narrow but important range of cases. The grant of appellate jurisdiction under Article III is far broader, although Congress has some discretion to modify it. However, the Court has been assiduous in protecting the Constitution's core grant of original jurisdiction from congressional expansion. The Court declared in *Marbury v. Madison* (1803) that Congress cannot add to the Supreme Court's original jurisdiction. Under Section 13 of the Judiciary Act of 1789, Congress had granted the Court mandamus power (the power to order lower courts or executive officials to perform duties required by law). In *Marbury*, Chief Justice John Marshall held that the mandamus power as applied to executive officials was actually a grant of original jurisdiction, and that Congress could not constitutionally expand the original jurisdiction of the Supreme Court. Writing for the Court, the chief justice declared Section 13 unconstitutional and denied the relief sought. Marshall's carefully crafted opinion reinforced the significance of original jurisdiction by (1) limiting its scope to the categories of cases contained in the text and, as a consequence, (2) shifting its focus from executive matters to suits between states. Similarly, in *Hodgson v. Bowerbank* (1809), Marshall, invalidated Section 11 of the Judiciary Act of 1789 because it provided for federal jurisdiction "in all suits in which an alien is a party," and that section also unconstitutionally extended Article III jurisdiction.

The Original Jurisdiction Clause has both theoretical and practical importance. Although Marshall's opinion is an example of textual interpretation, it also made practical sense that Article III should limit the power of Congress to add to the Court's original jurisdiction. If Congress could have expanded the Court's original docket, citizens would have been forced to litigate in the national capital, which was often inconvenient and distant. But even as narrowly written and construed, in state-versus-state cases original jurisdiction still played an indispensable role in eliminating the bias and parochialism of state courts and lower federal courts (where judges were likely to be drawn from the same pool of local lawyers). The need for original federal power in state-versus-state cases had been a concern of the Constitution's drafters: "Whatever practices may have a tendency to disturb the harmony between the States are proper objects of federal superintendence and control." *The Federalist* No. 80.

While Congress cannot add to the Supreme Court's original jurisdiction, the Court has accepted a reduction of the power through Congress's creation of concurrent jurisdiction with lower federal courts over some kinds of original matters (suits against ambassadors and consuls and suits between the United States and a state, for example). Parochial biases are less prevalent in these cases and, in any event, when filed in the lower federal courts, these cases can later be transferred to the Court's appellate docket. The current jurisdictional statute, 28 U.S.C. § 1251, sends controversies between two or more states exclusively to the Supreme Court and provides for concurrent jurisdiction over all other categories of original cases.

From the beginning, the most important suits between states were disputes over boundaries. These suits presented precisely those situations where the forces of provincialism and self-interest were most likely to compromise a state or lower federal court. Between 1790 and 1900, boundary disputes were the only suits between states the Court heard on its original docket. By the twentieth century, the category of original disputes expanded to include other important matters, such as water-rights cases and Commerce Clause claims (related to the use of state economic, regulatory, or tax powers). These kinds of cases continue to this day. *See, e.g., Maryland v. Louisiana* (1981), which deals with Louisiana's severance tax on natural gas. On occasion, when purely legal and urgent constitutional challenges are raised, the Court has also permitted suits to be filed on an original basis by states against the United States. *See South Carolina v. Katzenbach* (1966) (the Voting Rights Act of 1965).

Original cases are not heard before the Supreme Court as of right, even though its jurisdiction is exclusive. Original cases are commenced by a petition for leave to file a complaint. Such petitions are frequently denied, sometimes because the Court believes that a matter between states is too trivial (e.g., whether state universities breached a contract to play football) or, conversely, when the Court considers that the subject matter is too broad or unmanageable (e.g., issues of interstate water or air pollution) or simply because the Court is not ready to hear the matter.

Once the Court grants the states' petitions to file a complaint, it usually appoints a special master to make factual and legal recommendations. The special master, in turn, holds hearings and takes testimony, guided in a general way by the Federal Rules of Civil Procedure and the Federal Rules of Evidence. *See* Rule 17 of the *Rules of the Supreme Court of the United States* (2010). Unlike appeals of district court decisions under the Federal Rules of Civil Procedure, the master is given no formal deference on findings of fact by the Supreme Court, although such findings are often accepted by the Court. The parties also present briefs, arguments, and proposed recommendations, after which the special master issues a final report. The parties can take exceptions to that report to the Supreme Court, where it is briefed and argued and proceeds much like a traditional appellate or certiorari case. One issue of continuing interest is whether non-state entities, ranging from water districts to cities to private parties, are allowed to intervene in original cases. The Court monitors such requests closely. *See South Carolina v. North Carolina* (2010).

There have been fewer than two hundred state-versus-state original cases in the history of the republic, less than one per year of the Constitution's life. There have been only two original cases under the "affecting Ambassadors" section of the clause. Despite these relatively modest numbers, original jurisdiction continues to serve an indispensable purpose in resolving matters of high moment between states. No forum other than the Supreme Court can act with the authority and dignity necessary to resolve what are in effect diplomatic encounters between contending sovereigns under our constitutional system.

Paul R. Verkuil

Suggestions for Further Research

Vincent L. McKusick, *Discretionary Gatekeeping: The Supreme Court's Management of Its Original Jurisdiction Docket Since 1961*, 45 Me. L. Rev. 185 (1993)

James E. Pfander, *Marbury, Original Jurisdiction, and the Supreme Court's Supervisory Powers*, 101 Colum. L. Rev. 1515 (2001)

Significant Cases

Marbury v. Madison, 5 U.S. (1 Cranch) 137 (1803)

Hodgson v. Bowerbank, 9 U.S. (5 Cranch) 303 (1809)

Cohens v. Virginia, 19 U.S. (6 Wheat.) 264 (1821)

Ames v. Kansas *ex rel.* Johnston, 111 U.S. 449 (1884)

Kansas v. Colorado, 185 U.S. 125 (1902)

South Carolina v. Katzenbach, 383 U.S. 301 (1966)

Maryland v. Louisiana, 451 U.S. 725 (1981)

New Jersey v. New York, 523 U.S. 767 (1998)

Nebraska v. Wyoming & Colorado, 534 U.S. 40 (2001)

Alaska v. United States, 546 U.S. 413 (2006)

New Jersey v. Delaware, 552 U.S. 597 (2008)

South Carolina v. North Carolina, 558 U.S. 256 (2010)

Appellate Jurisdiction Clause

In all the other Cases before mentioned, the supreme Court shall have appellate Jurisdiction, both as to Law and Fact, with such Exceptions, and under such Regulations as the Congress shall make.
(**Article III, Section 2, Clause 2**)

~

*T*he phrase in the Appellate Jurisdiction Clause that raised the most serious concerns was the grant to the Supreme Court of appellate jurisdiction "both as to Law and Fact." The Anti-Federalist opposition was certain it meant the end of the civil jury and allowed a second trial of those criminally charged at the appellate level.

The Anti-Federalist Brutus argued:

> Who are the supreme court? Does it not consist of the judges? and they

are to have the same jurisdiction of the fact as they are to have of the law. They will therefore have the same authority to determine the fact as they will have to determine the law, and no room is left for a jury on appeals to the supreme court.

Alexander Hamilton responded in *The Federalist* No. 81, arguing that for common law cases "revision of the law only" would be proper for the Supreme Court, but for civil law cases, such as prize cases, review of facts "might be essential to the preservation of the public peace." Hamilton added that the grant of appellate jurisdiction would not abolish the right to trial by jury and that Congress possessed the power to restrict the Supreme Court in this area: "The legislature of the United States would certainly have full power to provide that in appeals to the Supreme Court there should be no re-examination of facts where they had been tried in the original causes by juries."

Following Hamilton's lead, Justice Joseph Story suggested in his *Commentaries on the Constitution of the United States* (1833) that the object of the clause's reference to jurisdiction over "law and fact" was to allow for the review of law and fact in cases of admiralty and maritime jurisdiction. Ultimately, the Seventh Amendment and the Double Jeopardy Clause of the Fifth Amendment mollified the Anti-Federalists' concerns by removing jury findings of fact from appellate review. *See* Amendment VII, Reexamination Clause; Amendment V, Double Jeopardy.

The Appellate Jurisdiction Clause also seemingly grants Congress unbounded authority to make "exceptions" to the appellate jurisdiction. The convention delegates at first rejected a clause providing that "the Judicial power shall be exercised in such manner as the Legislature shall direct"; but later, after the judicial power was defined in what eventually became Article III, the Framers appended this clause, permitting, as Federalists like John Marshall claimed, a broad power of Congress to regulate the appeals process to the Supreme Court. Justice Story later opined that Congress possessed "the utmost latitude" in limiting classes of cases that could

reach the Supreme Court, so long as "the whole judicial power" was "vested either in an original or appellate form, in some courts created under [Congress's] authority." *Martin v. Hunter's Lessee* (1816).

Early on, Chief Justice Oliver Ellsworth had gone further and suggested that "If Congress has provided no rule to regulate our proceedings, we cannot exercise an appellate jurisdiction." *Wiscart v. D'Auchy* (1796). In dissent, Justice James Wilson maintained that the Supreme Court's appellate jurisdiction flowed directly from the Constitution until Congress took steps to make exceptions to it. Justice Wilson's dissenting view in *Wiscart* prevailed unanimously in *Durousseau v. United States* (1810). Chief Justice John Marshall's opinion in the latter case recognized that the appellate jurisdiction is created by the Constitution, not by the Judiciary Act of 1789. Nevertheless, applying standard rules for statutory interpretation, Marshall explained that Congress had described particular aspects of the Court's jurisdiction in that statute, "and this affirmative description has been understood to imply a negative on the exercise of such appellate power as is not comprehended within it." In other words, by providing for certain classes of appeals to reach the Supreme Court, Congress tacitly intended to "except" all others from Supreme Court review. In fact, then, the Judiciary Act of 1789 withdrew almost all federal questions from the Supreme Court's jurisdiction by not providing an appeal mechanism to the Court.

In *Martin v. Hunter's Lessee* and in *Ableman v. Booth* (1859), Justice Story and Chief Justice Roger B. Taney each described the need to provide for Supreme Court review of decisions of the states' highest courts, in order, as Taney put it, "to secure the independence and supremacy of the General Government in the sphere of action assigned to it; [and] to make the Constitution and laws of the United States uniform, and the same in every State."

The seminal decision on jurisdiction-stripping statutes under the Appellate Jurisdiction Clause came shortly after the Civil War. *Ex parte McCardle* (1869) involved a newspaper editor in military custody, who had appealed a lower federal court's denial of habeas corpus relief to the

United States Supreme Court, pursuant to the Habeas Corpus Act of 1867. After the Supreme Court heard oral argument, Congress repealed the provisions of the statute that had authorized Supreme Court review. The Court concluded that, pursuant to Congress's power under the Appellate Jurisdiction Clause, it had no jurisdiction to decide the case. The Court also expressed a deferential view toward legislative acts in this context, noting: "We are not at liberty to inquire into the motives of the legislature. We can only examine into its power under the Constitution; and the power to make exceptions to the appellate jurisdiction of this court is given by express words."

Shortly thereafter, the Supreme Court found that a different jurisdiction-stripping statute did not fall within Congress's Appellate Jurisdiction Clause power. In *United States v. Klein* (1871), Congress had enacted a statute which provided that persons whose property had been seized during the Civil War could recover proceeds of their property if they proved they had not given aid to the rebellion during the war. The Supreme Court had previously held that a presidential pardon for such activities was proof that a person had not given aid to the rebellion. *United States v. Padelford* (1870). In *Klein*, the claimant had succeeded in the lower court, but the government had appealed. While the case was pending in the Supreme Court, Congress passed a law that attempted to reverse the holding in *Padelford*. The new law required courts to treat the pardon as proof of disloyalty, and on proof of such pardon, the jurisdiction of the court would cease and the suit be dismissed.

The *Klein* Court noted that, if Congress had "simply denied the right of appeal in a particular class of cases," the act would have been a valid exercise of legislative power under the Appellate Jurisdiction Clause. However, the Court determined that the statute withheld jurisdiction only as a means to an end, and that its purpose was to negate the legal effect of a presidential pardon, which was exclusively in the president's hands. Congress did have the power, the Court averred, to change underlying substantive law upon which the claim had been litigated, *Pennsylvania v. Wheeling & Belmont Bridge Co.* (1856), but

Congress could not do so by invading the president's power to pardon, nor to direct a particular decision in a pending case. Nor could Congress dictate to a Court how to decide the substance of a case before it under the guise of regulating its appellate jurisdiction.

Klein was a rare case. Although it showed that Congress cannot use its powers over jurisdiction to override a constitutional provision (such as the president's pardon power, or, by extension, a provision of the bill of rights), the Supreme Court has affirmed Congress's broad power to make exceptions to its jurisdiction, *The Francis Wright* (1881), and its equally broad power to change underlying substantive law even if that change affects the outcome in a pending case. *Robertson v. Seattle Audubon Society* (1992). Congress, however, may not by legislation reopen a case already decided and finalized, that is, when the time for appeal has passed. *Plaut v. Spendthrift Farm, Inc.* (1995).

Recent debate over the Appellate Jurisdiction Clause has centered on proposals for legislation that would remove parts of existing Supreme Court jurisdiction. Constitutional scholars strongly disagree as to how far Congress may go in removing Supreme Court jurisdiction under the clause. The traditional view, exemplified by Gerald Gunther, is that the text gives Congress power to remove the Supreme Court's appellate jurisdiction with little or no internal Article III limitation. Gunther and Ronald Rotunda argue that extrinsic restraints, such as those found in the Bill of Rights and elsewhere in the Constitution, could be applied. However, Gunther notes that under *McCardle*, the Court must still avoid looking into Congress's "motivations" except where an extrinsic restraint (such as those found in the Bill of Rights) so requires.

Henry Hart and others have suggested that the Appellate Jurisdiction Clause may not be used to "destroy the essential role of the Supreme Court in the constitutional plan." As Gunther noted, however, there is no "essential functions" limit on the face of the Appellate Jurisdiction Clause, and *McCardle* provides precedent for judicial deference to congressional limitations of appellate jurisdiction.

Ira Mickenberg and Robert Clinton distinguish between the words "exceptions" and "regulations" in the Constitution. Clinton argues that the phrase "such exceptions" refers to the class of cases assigned to the original, not appellate, jurisdiction of the Supreme Court under Article III. Mickenberg suggests that an "exception" could not abolish all appellate jurisdiction, and supports limits to the exception power as a matter of original intent. David Engdahl, Gary Lawson, and Steven Calabresi argue that the Appellate Jurisdiction Clause is not an express grant of power, but rather a cross-reference to Congress's enumerated powers under Article I, specifically, the Necessary and Proper Clause (Article I, Section 8, Clause 18). They hold that Congress can only divide federal jurisdiction among the federal courts and the Supreme Court, but not remove any Article III grant of jurisdiction entirely. Their view, however, would contradict the assumptions behind the Judiciary Act of 1789 and the holding of Chief Justice Marshall in *Marbury v. Madison* (1803). Paul Bator recognizes Congress's power to strip the Court of its appellate jurisdiction, but, as a matter of policy and in light of intended constitutional structure, argues that such an act would violate "the spirit of the Constitution."

Lawrence Sager takes the view that although Congress has broad authority to regulate appellate jurisdiction, Congress cannot remove jurisdiction with regard to a federal constitutional question from both the lower courts and the Supreme Court. In a variation, Akhil Amar has argued that Article III provides for two tiers of jurisdiction. Those grants of jurisdiction phrased with the emphatic "shall" must be left somewhere in the federal judicial system; the remaining grants may be removed or excepted by Congress. Justice Joseph Story, in dictum, made a similar claim in *Martin v. Hunter's Lessee*. John Harrison disputes Amar's thesis on the basis of a careful textual analysis of Article III.

For almost a century, Congress has rarely attempted to take away a whole swath of subject matter from the appellate jurisdiction of the Court. However, over the past decade, due to the government's response to the terrorist attacks of September 11, 2001, the Court has perforce become an actor in a constitutional contest between the executive, legislative, and judiciary branches. The "jurisdiction-stripping" power of the Appellate Jurisdiction Clause has played its part in this contest, and the way in which the Court has handled it (or the way in which the Court has worked itself around it) has only increased the scholarly debate on the issue.

In *Rasul v. Bush* (2004), the Supreme Court interpreted the federal habeas corpus statute to extend to the detainees at Guantanamo Bay. Congress responded by passing the Detainee Treatment Act of 2005. The DTA limited jurisdiction over habeas corpus petitions originating from detainees at Guantanamo Bay exclusively to the U.S. Court of Appeals for the District of Colombia Circuit, thereby making an exception to the Supreme Court's appellate jurisdiction over the matter. But in *Hamdan v. Rumsfeld* (2006), the Supreme Court avoided the issue of Congress's removal of its appellate jurisdiction by stating that the statute had not yet come into effect regarding habeas petitions.

Congress once again responded to the Supreme Court by passing a new statute, the Military Commissions Act of 2006, affirmatively making the limitation of the Court's appellate jurisdiction come into effect. In *Boumediene v. Bush* (2008), the Court held that that statute was actually an invalid suspension of the writ of habeas corpus under Article I, Section 9, Clause 2, because it did not provide an adequate substitute for the writ. The question of the extent to which Congress can remove the appellate jurisdiction of the Court was left unanswered.

Scholars have different opinions of what *Boumediene* means for future Supreme Court jurisprudence and Congress's power over federal jurisdiction. Some have argued that *Boumediene* will result in Congress's retaining power over the Court's jurisdiction while others have argued that *Boumediene* will result in a limit on Congress's powers.

Steven Calabresi and Gary Lawson argue that a proper textual and structural analysis of Article III would result in the conclusion that there is one judicial power vested in the Supreme Court, signifying that the Supreme Court *must* have the last word on any federal or constitutional question. Laurence Claus makes a similar case and concludes that, the idea of a "unitary judiciary" is not only apparent from the text of the Constitution, but it is what the Framers originally intended based on the convention's proceedings. Paul Taylor disagrees, and concludes that the Appellate Jurisdiction Clause was originally understood as a constraint on the federal courts.

Thus far, the Supreme Court has remained aloof from the scholarly contest, leaving its precedents to stand at present for broad congressional authority to limit the appellate jurisdiction of the Supreme Court. Thus far, the Court has followed the lead of John Marshall, who stated in the Virginia ratifying convention, "Congress is empowered to make exceptions to the appellate jurisdiction, as to law and fact, of the Supreme Court. These exceptions certainly go as far as the legislature may think proper for the interest and liberty of the people."

Andrew S. Gold and David F. Forte

See Also

Article III, Section 2, Clause 1 (Judicial Power)
Amendment V (Double Jeopardy)
Amendment VII (Reexamination Clause)

Suggestions for Further Research

Akhil R. Amar, *A Neo-Federalist View of Article III: Separating the Two Tiers of Federal Jurisdiction*, 65 B.U. L. Rev. 205 (1985)

Paul M. Bator, *Congressional Power Over the Jurisdiction of the Federal Courts*, 27 Villanova L. Rev. 1030 (1982)

Steven G. Calabresi & Gary Lawson, *The Unitary Executive, Jurisdiction Stripping, and the Hamdan Opinions: A Textualist Response to Justice Scalia*, 107 Colum. L. Rev. 1002 (2007)

Laurence Claus, *The One Court That Congress Cannot Take Away: Singularity, Supremacy, and Article III*, 96 Geo. L.J. 59 (2007)

Robert N. Clinton, *A Mandatory View of Federal Court Jurisdiction: A Guided Quest for the Original Understanding of Article III*, 132 U. Pa. L. Rev. 741 (1984)

David E. Engdahl, *Intrinsic Limits of Congress' Power Regarding the Judicial Branch*, 1999 BYU L. Rev. 75 (1999)

Richard H. Fallon, Jr., *Jurisdiction-Stripping Reconsidered*, 96 Va. L. Rev. 1043, 1088 (2010)

Brian T. Fitzpatrick, *The Constitutionality of Federal Jurisdiction-Stripping Legislation and the History of State Judicial Selection and Tenure*, 98 Va. L. Rev. 839 (2012)

Alex Glashausser, *A Return to Form for the Exceptions Clause*, 51 B.C. L. Rev. 1383 (2010)

Gerald Gunther, *Congressional Power to Curtail Federal Court Jurisdiction: An Opinionated Guide to the Ongoing Debate*, 36 Stan. L. Rev. 895 (1984)

John Harrison, *The Power of Congress to Limit the Jurisdiction of Federal Courts and the Text of Article III*, 64 U. Chi. L. Rev. 203 (1997)

Henry M. Hart, Jr., *The Power of Congress to Limit the Jurisdiction of Federal Courts: An Exercise in Dialectic*, 66 Harv. L. Rev. 1362 (1953)

Martin J. Katz, *Guantanamo, Boumediene, and Jurisdiction-Stripping: The Imperial President Meets the Imperial Court*, 25 Const. Comment. 377, 400 (2009)

Ira Mickenberg, *Abusing the Exceptions and Regulations Clause: Legislative Attempts to Divest the Supreme Court of Appellate Jurisdiction*, 32 Am. U. L. Rev. 497 (1983)

Robert J. Pushaw, Jr., *Creating Legal Rights for Suspected Terrorists: Is the Court Being Courageous or Politically Pragmatic?* 84 Notre Dame L. Rev. 1975 (2009)

Martin H. Redish, *Constitutional Limitations on Congressional Power to Control Federal Jurisdiction: A Reaction to Professor Sager*, 77 Nw. U. L. Rev. 143 (1982)

Ronald D. Rotunda, *Congressional Power to Restrict the Jurisdiction of the Lower Federal Courts and the Problem of School Busing*, 64 Geo. L.J. 839 (1976)

Lawrence G. Sager, *Constitutional Limitations on Congress' Authority to Regulate the Jurisdiction of the Federal Courts*, 95 Harv. L. Rev. 17 (1981)

Heather P. Scribner, *A Fundamental Misconception of Separation of Powers*: Boumediene v. Bush, 14 Tex. Rev. Law & Pol. 90 (2009)

Mark Strasser, *Taking Exception to Traditional Exceptions Clause Jurisprudence: On Congress's Power to Limit the Court's Jurisdiction*, 2001 Utah L. Rev. 125 (2001)

Paul Taylor, *Congress's Power to Regulate the Federal Judiciary: What the First Congress and the First Federal Courts Can Teach Today's Congress and Courts*, 37 Pepp. L. Rev. 847 (2010)

William W. Van Alstyne, *A Critical Guide to* Ex Parte McCardle, 15 Ariz. L. Rev. 229 (1973)

Julian Velasco, *Congressional Control Over Federal Court Jurisdiction: A Defense of the Traditional View*, 46 Cath. U. L. Rev. 671 (1997)

Significant Cases

Wiscart v. D'Auchy, 3 U.S. (3 Dall.) 321 (1796)

Marbury v. Madison, 5 U.S. (1 Cranch) 137 (1803)

United States v. More, 7 U.S. (3 Cranch) 159 (1805)

Durousseau v. United States, 10 U.S. (6 Cranch) 307 (1810)

Martin v. Hunter's Lessee, 14 U.S. (1 Wheat.) 304 (1816)

Pennsylvania v. Wheeling & Belmont Bridge Co., 59 U.S. (18 How.) 421 (1856)

Ableman v. Booth, 62 U.S. (21 How.) 506 (1859)

Ex parte McCardle, 74 U.S. (7 Wall.) 506 (1869)

Ex parte Yerger, 75 U.S. (8 Wall.) 85 (1869)

United States v. Padelford, 76 U.S. (9 Wall.) 531 (1870)

United States v. Klein, 80 U.S. (13 Wall.) 128 (1871)

The Francis Wright, 105 U.S. 381 (1881)

United States v. Sioux Nation of Indians, 448 U.S. 371 (1980)

Morrison v. Olson, 487 U.S. 654 (1988)

Robertson v. Seattle Audubon Society, 503 U.S. 429 (1992)

Plaut v. Spendthrift Farm, Inc., 514 U.S. 211 (1995)

Felker v. Turpin, 518 U.S. 651 (1996)

Edmond v. United States, 520 U.S. 651 (1997)

Miller v. French, 530 U.S. 327 (2000)

Rasul v. Bush, 542 U.S. 466 (2004)

Hamdan v. Rumsfeld, 548 U.S. 557 (2006)

Boumediene v. Bush, 553 U.S. 723 (2008)

Criminal Trials

The Trial of all Crimes, except in Cases of Impeachment, shall be by Jury; and such Trial shall be held in the State where the said Crimes shall have been committed; but when not committed within any State, the Trial shall be at such Place or Places as the Congress may by Law have directed.

(Article III, Section 2, Clause 3)

*T*he American right to a trial by a jury of one's peers traces its lineage back to 1297 and the Magna Carta. By the mid-sixteenth century, the jury (known as the petit jury as opposed to the grand jury) had already taken on the form it retains to this day in federal courts and some state courts—twelve citizens were summoned to sit in sworn judgment of the criminal allegations against one of their peers.

The English practice of using juries continued in America from the very first settlements. The Charter of the Virginia Company in 1606 declared that the colonists who were to settle there would enjoy all the rights of Englishmen, which included the right to jury trial. Juries played a vital role in the mid-eighteenth century in resisting English authority in the contest that ultimately led up to the American Revolution. The most noted of the colonial cases was the trial of John Peter Zenger, a New York printer whom the jury acquitted on charges of seditious libel, forty-one years before the drafting of the Declaration of Independence.

King George III responded to such jury nullification of English laws by expanding the jurisdiction of non-jury courts, such as the admiralty courts, and increasingly using those courts as the vehicles for enforcement. Thus it was that in 1776 the Declaration of Independence listed as a grievance against George III his "depriving us…of the benefits of trial by jury." As a consequence, Article III—the portion of the Constitution governing the role of the judiciary—makes clear that judges are not the only judicial actors of constitutional significance. It provides a crucial role for the jury.

There was little debate about this portion of the Constitution, because the need for the criminal jury was one of the few subjects of agreement between Federalists and Anti-Federalists. Alexander Hamilton observed in *The Federalist* No. 83 that "[t]he friends and adversaries of the plan of the convention, if they agree in nothing else, concur at least in the value they set upon the trial by jury." The only distinction to be drawn, in his view, was between the Federalist view that it is "a valuable safeguard to liberty" and the Anti-Federalist view that it is "the very palladium of free government."

Indeed, Thomas Jefferson believed so strongly in the jury that he noted, "[w]ere I called upon to decide whether the people had best be omitted in the Legislative or Judiciary department, I would say it is better to leave them out of the Legislative." John Adams shared Jefferson's praise of the jury, observing that "the common people...should have as complete a control, as decisive a negative, in every judgment of a court of judicature" as they have in the legislature.

Because judges themselves were part of the government, many Framers feared they would not be an adequate check on government abuse of the criminal process. The jury, therefore, was made part of the original structure of government in order to provide a mechanism for ensuring that individuals would not lose their liberty under a criminal law until the people themselves concurred.

In many criminal cases in the nation's early history, the jury not only applied the law to the facts it found, but decided questions of law themselves. Thus, many judges refused to tell jurors that they were obliged to accept the judge's view of the law, and lawyers argued questions of law before the jury in some cases.

Over time, however, this power eroded. In 1895, the Supreme Court concluded in *Sparf and Hansen v. United States* that the jury did not have the "right" to decide legal questions. As a result, today judges can—and do—instruct juries that they must accept the judge's view of the law, and lawyers are no longer allowed to argue the merits of the law to the jury. Because the jury possesses authority to issue an unreviewable general verdict of acquittal, the jury nevertheless retains the raw power to check general laws with which it disagrees in individual cases. But because the trial judge does not instruct the jury that it has this authority, the jurors may not know that they have it. In addition, even if the jurors are aware of this power, they must exercise it knowing it is contrary to the judge's instructions. Hence, there are many cases in which the jury does not exercise that power and instead follows the judge's instructions, even when the jury itself disagrees with the law in question, with the judge's interpretation of the law, or with the law's application in the case before it.

The jury's power has eroded in a second respect. Prior to 1930, jury trials in federal court, like jurisdictional provisions, could not be waived, reflecting the mandatory language in Article III that the trial of all crimes "shall" be by jury. In *Patton v. United States* (1930), however, the Supreme Court concluded that a defendant could waive a jury trial in favor of a bench trial. Nonetheless, the prosecutor may still insist upon, and the court must grant, a jury trial.

There are two additional trends in criminal justice that have further diminished the jury's ability to check the government in criminal cases. First, the vast majority of cases never reach the jury because of the increase in the number of cases resolved by plea bargain.

The second major trend involves the changing nature of sentencing. Congress and many state legislatures have shifted from a model that vested broad sentencing discretion with judges to a regime in which the legislature (or a sentencing commission) specifies in generally applicable laws how particular findings of fact must affect the defendant's sentence. Thus, these laws are indistinguishable from other criminal laws: they identify blameworthy behavior and specify the criminal punishment for that behavior. But there is a crucial exception: the legislature insists that judges, not juries, apply these laws.

But there are limits to what the legislature can prescribe. In *Apprendi v. New Jersey* (2000), the Supreme Court held that the legislature does not have unbounded authority to label criminally blameworthy facts as *sentencing* factors (instead of substantive elements of the criminal offense itself), because such authority could undercut the jury's constitutional role. The Court in *Apprendi* therefore held that it is unconstitutional for the legislature to remove from the jury the assessment of facts (other than recidivism) that increase the statutorily prescribed range of penalties to which a defendant is exposed. In *Blakely v. Washington* (2004), the Court made clear that "the 'statutory maximum' for *Apprendi* purposes is the maximum sentence a judge may impose *solely on the basis of the facts reflected in the jury verdict or admitted by the defendant...without any additional findings*." This subsequently led the Supreme Court to conclude that the federal sentencing guidelines in their mandatory form ran afoul of the Constitution's jury guarantee because they required judges, as opposed to jurors, to find facts that "the law makes essential" to a defendant's punishment by mandating that they must increase a sentence in a particular way. *United States v. Booker* (2005). As a remedy, the Court made the federal guidelines "advisory" instead of mandatory.

Article III (and the Sixth Amendment) also contain provisions relating to venue, the place where a case is to be tried, and vicinage, the place from which the members of the jury pool trying the case are to be drawn. The Declaration of Independence condemned the English practice of transporting colonial defendants overseas to England for trial by juries of Englishmen. In response, the Constitution guarantees a criminal defendant both the right to be tried in the state where his alleged crime was committed and by a jury drawn from the population of the state and district where the alleged crime occurred.

Rachel E. Barkow

See Also

Amendment V (Double Jeopardy)
Amendment VI (Jury Trial)
Amendment VII (Right to Jury in Civil Cases)

Suggestions for Further Research

Jeffrey B. Abramson, We, the Jury: The Jury System and the Ideal of Democracy (1994)

Albert W. Alschuler & Andrew G. Deiss, *A Brief History of the Criminal Jury in the United States*, 61 U. Chi. L. Rev. 867 (1994)

Andrew J. Gildea, *The Right to Trial by Jury*, 26 Am. Crim. L. Rev. 1507 (1989)

Matthew P. Harrington, *The Law-Finding Function of the American Jury*, 1999 Wisc. L. Rev. 377 (1999)

Mark DeWolfe Howe, *Juries as Judges of Criminal Law*, 52 Harv. L. Rev. 582 (1939)

Stanton D. Krauss, *An Inquiry into the Right of Criminal Juries to Determine the Law in Colonial America*, 89 J. Crim. L. & Criminology 111, 123 (1998)

Significant Cases

Sparf and Hansen v. United States, 156 U.S. 51 (1895)

Patton v. United States, 281 U.S. 276 (1930)
Duncan v. Louisiana, 391 U.S. 145 (1968)
Apprendi v. New Jersey, 530 U.S. 466 (2000)
Blakely v. Washington, 542 U.S. 296, 303 (2004)
United States v. Booker, 543 U.S. 220, 232 (2005)

Treason

Treason against the United States, shall consist only in levying War against them, or in adhering to their Enemies, giving them Aid and Comfort. No Person shall be convicted of Treason unless on the Testimony of two Witnesses to the same overt Act, or on Confession in open Court.

(**Article III, Section 3, Clause 1**)

$\sim$

*T*he word treason, as transmitted to the English language from the Latin through the French, means "giving or delivering up." The common law understood treason as treachery or breach of faith. It was therefore a crime committed between parties who enjoyed an established relationship of mutual benefit and trust. Petit treason referred to a wife's killing her husband, or a servant's or ecclesiastic's killing his lord or master. High treason involved a breach between subject and sovereign, a betrayal of (or neglect of duty or renunciation of allegiance to, in word or deed) a sovereign to whom a subject owed allegiance by birth or residence. Sir Edward Coke, Baron de Montesquieu, Sir Matthew Hale, and Sir William Blackstone considered treason the highest of crimes and declared that it must be precisely defined to prevent its abuse by governmental authorities. In England, commencing during the reign of Edward III, Parliament narrowed the definition of treason but later widened it according to political exigencies.

The laws of the American colonies reflected the broad outlines of the common law of England, both as to breadth of the offense and severity of punishment, though sometimes the definitions of treason in the colonies were broader than the definition in England. By the eighteenth century, laws began more consistently to reflect the

English law of treason, and eventually, during the Revolutionary period, came to require more precise definitions, more exacting standards of proof, and more lenient punishments. During the Revolution, many states adopted language recommended by the Continental Congress and its "Committee on Spies," defining treason as adherence to the king of Great Britain (including accepting commissions from him) or to other "Enemies," giving them "Aid and Comfort."

Reflecting the American Founders' concern with protecting individual rights and their fear of arbitrary governmental power, the Framers of the Constitution sought a precise and permanent definition of treason, the permissible means of proving it, and the limitations on the punishment for it. The drafters of the Constitution reached back (as had the Continental Congress) to language in the Statute of Treasons, 25 Edw. 3, 1351, ch. 2, stat. 5, which limited treason, among other things, to compassing or imagining the death of the king, levying war against the king, or adhering to the king's enemies, giving them aid and comfort. But the Framers' definition was even narrower. It did not include the language of "compassing or imagining," which had been the basis of the English doctrine of "constructive treason," an effective and easily abused method for dealing with political opponents. Thus, in the Constitution, treason consists only in levying war against the United States or adhering to its enemies by giving them aid and comfort. It may be proved only by confession in open court or on the testimony of no fewer than two witnesses to the same overt act.

The debates in the Constitutional Convention show an awareness of English common law and legislative history. James Madison suggested that the proposed definition reported by the Committee of Detail—limiting treason to the levying of war and adherence to enemies—was imprudently narrow and would effectively disallow the wisdom of experience. Others, such as John Dickinson, argued in favor of narrow wording. In the end, the phrase "giving them aid and comfort" was added to restrict even further the definition of the crime, and evidentiary requirements were tightened by the addition of the phrase "overt act." Furthermore, as James

Wilson noted in his 1791 *Lectures on Law*, treason requires generalized grievances and aims against the United States or its government as a whole, rather than particularized, essentially private grievances or aims. Respecting the federal nature of the union, the constitutional definition leaves open the possibility of concurrent state laws for treasons against them in their respective sovereign capacities.

When it came time to defend the Constitution, Madison left behind his earlier aversion to a narrow definition of treason and, in *The Federalist* No. 43, lauded the Convention's wisdom as raising a constitutional bar to "new-fangled and artificial treasons" (understood as the results and instruments of faction), and as limiting the consequences of guilt. In *The Federalist* No. 84, Alexander Hamilton mentions the definition of treason as one of the guarantors of rights that make a separate bill of rights unnecessary.

The Supreme Court has had occasion to pronounce on treason, albeit infrequently. In *Ex parte Bollman* (1807), Chief Justice John Marshall rejected the idea of "constructive treason" and held that for treason to be established on the ground of levying war against the United States, an accused must be part of an actual assemblage of men for a treasonable purpose. Conspiracy short of the actual levying of war is insufficient. But in the related case of *United States v. Burr* (1807), Marshall tacked slightly. He again rejected constructive treason, but did so by holding that Aaron Burr, if not physically present in an assemblage of men, could still be convicted of treason on the testimony of two witnesses that he actively helped effect or aid such an assemblage—in effect, aided in the levying of war. Together, these cases made a treason conviction exceedingly difficult for anything other than manifest participation in a treasonable act.

After *Burr*, the leading treason cases grew out of World War II, for adherence to enemies. In *Cramer v. United States* (1945), the Supreme Court held that a specific intent—adherence to the enemy, and therefore to harm the United States— is necessary, rather than the simple rendition of aid. Further, the majority came close to holding that such adherence requires proof, not just of an act that on its face is "commonplace" (such as a meeting) but a manifestly treasonable overt act, evidenced by the testimony of at least two witnesses. But in *Haupt v. United States* (1947)—the Court's first affirmation of a treason conviction—the Court effectively relaxed the standard of proof in *Cramer* by holding that the testimony of two witnesses to overt acts might be supported by other evidence as to the accused's treasonable intent, including out-of-court confessions and admissions. In a concurring opinion, Justice William O. Douglas (who dissented in *Cramer*) affirmed that the separate elements of intent and overt act are amenable to different modes of proof, and only the latter triggers the constitutional requirement of testimony by two witnesses.

In *Kawakita v. United States* (1952), the Supreme Court held that dual citizenship does not diminish a citizen's allegiance to the United States, and, in a treason prosecution, whether someone intends to renounce American citizenship hinges on particular facts and may be a question for a jury.

Lower courts have had occasion to enter verdicts of treason, commencing with the Whiskey Rebellion, some of them arguably on broader grounds than what the Supreme Court would later countenance. For example, courts held that armed resistance to the collection of taxes constituted constructive treason. A number of cases arising out of the Civil War also suggested, without directly interpreting the Constitution, that Confederate activities amounted to treason (although the general amnesty of December 25, 1868, pardoned all Confederates). Because of the particular and high constitutional standards associated with the definition and proof of treason, hostile or subversive acts falling short of treason but directed toward the whole polity have been prosecuted under various laws of Congress, including those dealing with espionage (for example, the conviction and execution of Ethel and Julius Rosenberg in 1953) and, more recently, terrorism. The exercise of federal prosecutorial discretion has also led to the prosecution on other grounds of individuals for acts that arguably amount to treason (for example, John Walker Lindh captured in Afghanistan in 2001), or to failure to prosecute at all.

In 2006, Adam Yahiye Gadahn—who, like Lindh, was a convert to Islam—became the first American to be charged with treason since Tomoya Kawakita in 1952. He remains at large but is accused of treason by knowingly adhering to and giving aid and comfort to an enemy of the United States by appearing in al Qaeda videos threatening Americans and the United States with violence. He is also accused of aiding and abetting al Qaeda through the provision of material support and resources.

Bradley C. S. Watson

Suggestions for Further Research
Henry Mark Holzer, *Why Not Call It Treason? From Korea to Afghanistan*, 29 S.U. L. Rev. 181 (2002)

James Willard Hurst, The Law of Treason in the United States: Collected Essays (1971)

Significant Cases
Ex parte Bollman, 8 U.S. (4 Cranch) 75 (1807)

United States v. Burr, 25 F. Cas. 55 (C.C.D. Va. 1807) (No. 14,693)

Cramer v. United States, 325 U.S. 1 (1945)

Haupt v. United States, 330 U.S. 631 (1947)

Kawakita v. United States, 343 U.S. 717 (1952)

Punishment of Treason

The Congress shall have Power to declare the Punishment of Treason, but no Attainder of Treason shall work Corruption of Blood, or Forfeiture except during the Life of the Person attainted.

(Article III, Section 3, Clause 2)

~

*U*nder English common law, punishment for treason generally included drawing, hanging, beheading, and quartering. As with other crimes carrying sentence of death, those adjudged guilty of treason and finally sentenced were considered attaint, or stained, meaning dead in the eyes of the law—even before execution. Once attainder was established, the attainted forfeited his real estate to the crown—a requirement symbolizing lack of entitlement to the benefits of society.

Attainder also worked corruption of blood, preventing the attainted from inheriting or transmitting property and preventing any person from deriving title through the attainted. Forfeitures and corruption of blood worked hardship on dependents and relatives in order to provide maximum deterrence. Eventually, Parliament modified the laws of forfeiture and corruption of blood to protect the innocent.

According to the Constitution, punishment can be set by Congress, but cannot include corruption of blood or forfeiture extending beyond the offender's life. Quite apart from this limitation, Justice Joseph Story notes in his *Commentaries on the Constitution of the United States* (1833) that the explicit grant of congressional power over punishment was intended as a leniency, to preclude the assumption of the common law punishment's harshest elements. The First Congress used its constitutional power of declaring the punishment for treason by establishing the penalty of death, with seven years' imprisonment for misprision of treason.

The actual punishments for those convicted of the federal crime of treason have generally been more lenient than the statutory maximums. President George Washington pardoned those convicted for their part in the Whiskey Rebellion. The United States government regarded Confederate activity as a levying of war, but all Confederates were pardoned by presidential amnesty. Max Haupt, convicted for giving aid and comfort to his alien son, was spared death and sentenced to life imprisonment. (His son, Herbert, was convicted by a military tribunal for his role as saboteur and executed in 1942.) Tomoyo Kawakita, convicted of treason for abusing American prisoners of war, was sentenced to death but had his sentence commuted to life imprisonment by President Dwight D. Eisenhower. By contrast, the Ethel and Julius Rosenbergs' espionage convictions brought death sentences.

Of the two successful prosecutions for treason at the state level—Thomas Dorr in Rhode Island in 1844 and John Brown in Virginia in 1859—only Brown was executed. Dorr was pardoned, and elements of the political agitations for which he was convicted were soon adopted into law in Rhode Island.

Bradley C. S. Watson

See Also

Article I, Section 9, Clause 3 (Bill of Attainder)

ARTICLE IV

Full Faith and Credit Clause

Full Faith and Credit shall be given in each State to the public Acts, Records, and judicial Proceedings of every other State. And the Congress may by general Laws prescribe the Manner in which such Acts, Records and Proceedings shall be proved, and the Effect thereof.

(**ARTICLE IV, SECTION 1**)

*A*n essential purpose of the Full Faith and Credit Clause is to assure that the courts of one state will honor the judgments of the courts of another state without the need to retry the whole cause of action. It was an essential mechanism for creating a "union" out of multiple sovereigns. The first sentence of the Full Faith and Credit Clause appeared almost verbatim in Article IV of the Articles of Confederation, which read: "Full faith and credit shall be given in each of these States to the records, acts and judicial proceedings of the courts and magistrats of every other State." But while "faith and credit" was a familiar evidentiary term, early courts disagreed on whether the Articles obliged states merely to receive each other's documents in evidence, or also to treat such documents, once admitted, as conclusive on the merits. In 1781, a committee of the Confederation Congress tried to obtain clarification from the states on how they treated other states' official documents and judgments.

At the Constitutional Convention, the Framers rejected a proposal that would have required each state to enforce the other states' judgments regarding debts. Instead, it adopted the Confederation clause almost verbatim but added a second sentence giving Congress power over the "manner of authentication" and the documents' "effect." Moreover, the "public Acts" requirement was apparently added to force state courts to enforce each other's insolvency laws.

Because the clause was drawn from the Articles of Confederation, there is very little discussion of it in the *The Federalist Papers*, although James Madison asserted in No. 42 that its clarity was a great improvement over the version in the Articles. He listed the clause as one of several that "provide for the harmony and proper intercourse among the States."

It seems clear that a major purpose of the clause was to prevent a judgment debtor (i.e., someone who had been found financially liable by a court) from evading his creditors by crossing into other states. In the colonial courts, a judgment creditor from another colony would have to prove the other colony's court's judgment as an issue of fact—and might even have to relitigate the merits, with the old judgment given only *prima facie* effect.

While it is possible to read the clause's first sentence (and the word "full") to require conclusive effect for all state records, the dominant view at the Founding was that any additional substan-

tive effect was for Congress to determine. In *The Federalist* No. 42, James Madison emphasized Congress's power, describing the Article's language (and thus the new clause's first sentence) as "extremely indeterminate" and "of little importance under any interpretation which it will bear." This echoed James Wilson's argument at the Constitutional Convention, that the clause would be largely useless "if the Legislature were not allowed to declare the effect," as it "would amount to nothing more than what now takes place among all Independent Nations."

Congress first exercised its power in 1790, specifying the mode of authentication in the Full Faith and Credit Statute (1 Stat. 122). That statute gave properly authenticated court records, in particular, "such faith and credit" in other states as they had at home. But this only produced disputes over whether "such faith and credit" referred to evidentiary admissibility, or whether it made each state's court records equally conclusive in other states. The Supreme Court adopted the equally-conclusive view in *Mills v. Duryee* (1813), but as a construction of the act of Congress, not of the Constitution.

Over time, the Court began to merge the statutory and constitutional inquiries—treating the substantive effect of judgments as determined by the Constitution itself, following a suggestion made by Justice Joseph Story in his *Commentaries on the Constitution of the United States* (1833). The Court eventually read the Constitution to extend conclusive effect to state laws, which the 1790 statute had pointedly not required. *Chicago & Alton Railroad v. Wiggins Ferry Co.* (1887). When Congress recodified the statute in 1948, it amended its language to accord with the Supreme Court's view.

The Supreme Court has continued to use the broad view of the clause's effect to develop a detailed jurisprudence, policing state court proceedings in three contexts: (1) determining when a state must take jurisdiction over claims that arise in other states, (2) limiting the application of local state law over another state's law in multistate disputes, and (3) recognizing and enforcing judgments rendered in sister-state courts.

First, the Court has obliged state courts to hear claims that arise under sister-state laws, at least where the courts recognize the equivalent claim is based on local law. *Hughes v. Fetter* (1951). A state may also not attempt to monopolize litigation by requiring that enforcement actions be heard solely in its own local courts. *Tennessee Coal, Iron & Railroad Co. v. George* (1914); *Crider v. Zurich Insurance Co.* (1965).

Second, the Supreme Court has also restricted state courts' ability to apply their own laws to multistate disputes. State courts may almost always apply their own procedural rules, including their own statutes of limitations, but there are times when a state's substantive law should give way to the substantive law of another state, under what is called "choice of law." It was Justice Story who first seriously explored this issue in his *Commentaries on the Conflict of Laws, Foreign and Domestic* (1834). In the early twentieth century, the Court began to treat these doctrines as mandated by the Constitution. Initially, the Court required the states to adhere to the traditional territorial principles (*lex loci*) in the choice of law. Thus, if particular legally designated events of a dispute happened in a particular state, say Massachusetts, but the dispute came to trial in Pennsylvania, the Pennsylvania court had to apply Massachusetts law. *Western Union Telegraph Co. v. Brown* (1914); *New York Life Insurance Co. v. Dodge* (1918). Later, the Court allowed a state to apply its own substantive law whenever it had a legitimate interest in the outcome of the case. *Pacific Employers Insurance Co. v. Industrial Accident Commission* (1939). The most recent Supreme Court cases have collapsed Due Process Clause and Full Faith and Credit Clause inquiries into a single requirement for the application of "forum law" (the law of the state where the case is being heard): "that state must have a significant contact or significant aggregation of contacts, creating state interests, such that choice of its law is neither arbitrary nor fundamentally unfair." *Allstate Insurance Co. v. Hague* (1981).

With this shift in tests, the Court has backed away from constitutional scrutiny of state court choice-of-law decisions. In fact, the Court has even allowed one state to sue another state in the first state's courts despite the defendant state's sovereign immunity laws. *State of Nevada v. Hall* (1979); *Franchise Tax Board of California v. Hyatt* (2003). Moreover, the Court has only once in the last fifty years limited a state's ability to apply its own law. *Phillips Petroleum Co. v. Shutts* (1985).

Third, although the Court has largely backed away from policing state choice-of-law decisions, it has imposed stringent requirements regarding recognition and enforcement of sister-state judgments. Practical interests usually require each state to recognize and enforce almost all final court judgments rendered by sister states, even those that offend the public policy of the enforcing state. Pursuant to Congress's implementing statute of the Full Faith and Credit Clause, the enforcing state's courts must give judgments at least as much effect as the rendering state would. Nonetheless, states can still apply their own statutes of limitations when enforcing judgments by other states' courts, and state administrative decisions that are not reviewed by a court are not entitled to respect in other states.

The Court has recognized a few relatively narrow policy-based exceptions to the states' obligations to enforce the judgments of other states' courts. First, a defendant who did not appear in the first proceeding can collaterally attack a judgment against him on the grounds that the first state's courts lacked personal jurisdiction over the defendant. Second, states are not permitted directly to affect land titles in other states by, for example, issuing a deed to land located in another state. Third, judgments based on purely penal claims (i.e., criminal or administrative fines) need not be enforced by other states. To fall into this penal exception, the judgment must be for the purpose of punishment rather than compensation, and the recovery must be in favor of the state, not a private individual. But tax judgments, judgments for punitive damages in favor of private plaintiffs, and compensatory tort judgments in favor of the state all fail to qualify for this penal exception. Fourth, state courts enforcing an out-of-state court judgment can apply their own evidentiary rules. For example, the enforcing state may accept testimony that would have been illegal under the other state's law. Finally, if a state court issues a divorce decree in an *ex parte* proceeding (where only one spouse appears), the absent spouse can collaterally attack the validity of the present spouse's domicile within the rendering state.

Congress has invoked its full faith and credit authority in certain specific contexts related to marriage, divorce, and children. When it acts, Congress presumably displaces Supreme Court Full Faith and Credit precedents in these areas. Under the congressional acts, a state court may modify a sister-state court's child-custody and support orders to suit "the best interests of the child." The Parental Kidnapping Prevention Act of 1980 (28 U.S.C. § 1738A) attempts to fix jurisdiction over child-custody determinations and requires states that lack jurisdiction under the act to enforce valid custody orders. The Full Faith and Credit for Child Support Orders Act of 1995 (28 U.S.C. § 1738B) allocates jurisdiction over the rendering of child-support orders and specifies states' enforcement obligations.

Finally, when it appeared that Hawaii might recognize the validity of same-sex marriages, Congress responded in 1996 with the Defense of Marriage Act (DOMA) (28 U.S.C. § 1738C). Section 2 of DOMA permits each state to refuse to give effect to other states' acts, records, and judicial proceedings respecting same-sex marriages. Moreover, the act specifically enables each state to deny rights and claims arising from same-sex marriages created in other states. Section 3 of DOMA, which defines marriage as consisting only of unions between a man and a woman for purposes of federal law and federal benefits, does not implicate the Full Faith and Credit Clause. Nonetheless, in *United States v. Windsor* (2013), the Court struck down section 3 as violative of the Due Process Clause of the Fifth Amendment on the grounds that it was based on an animus against those persons whose same-sex marriages had been validated by state law. However, section 2 (pertaining to full faith and credit) has not been the subject of constitutional attack by any branch of the federal government.

Erin O'Connor and Stephen E. Sachs

See Also

Amendment XIV, Section 1 (Due Process Clause)

Suggestions for Further Research

David E. Engdahl, *The Classic Rule of Faith and Credit*, 118 YALE L.J. 1584 (2009)

Robert H. Jackson, *Full Faith and Credit: The Lawyer's Clause of the Constitution*, 45 COLUM. L. REV. 1 (1945)

Frederic L. Kirgis, Jr., *The Roles of Due Process and Full Faith and Credit in Choice of Law*, 62 CORNELL L. REV. 94 (1976)

Douglas Laycock, *Equal Citizens of Equal and Territorial States: The Constitutional Foundations of Choice of Law*, 92 COLUM. L. REV. 249 (1992)

James R. Pielemeier, *Why We Should Worry About Full Faith and Credit to Laws*, 60 S. CAL. L. REV. 1299 (1987)

Polly J. Price, *Full Faith and Credit and the Equity Conflict*, 84 VA. L. REV. 747 (1998)

William L. Reynolds, *The Iron Law of Full Faith and Credit*, 53 MD. L. REV. 412 (1994)

Stephen E. Sachs, *Full Faith and Credit in the Early Congress*, 95 VA. L. REV. 1201 (2009)

Stewart E. Sterk, *The Muddy Boundaries Between Res Judicata and Full Faith and Credit*, 58 WASH. & LEE L. REV. 47 (2001)

Russell J. Weintraub, *Due Process and Full Faith and Credit Limitations on a State's Choice of Law*, 44 IOWA L. REV. 449 (1959)

Ralph U. Whitten, *The Constitutional Limitations on State Choice of Law: Full Faith and Credit*, 12 MEM. ST. U. L. REV. 1 (1981)

Ralph U. Whitten, *The Original Understanding of the Full Faith and Credit Clause and the Defense of Marriage Act*, 32 CREIGHTON L. REV. 255 (1998)

Significant Cases

Phelps v. Holker, 1 Dall. 261 (Pa. 1788)

Mills v. Duryee, 11 U.S. (7 Cranch) 481 (1813)

Chicago & Alton R.R. v. Wiggins Ferry Co., 119 U.S. 615 (1887)

Huntington v. Attrill, 146 U.S. 657 (1892)

Fauntleroy v. Lum, 210 U.S. 230 (1908)

Fall v. Eastin, 215 U.S. 1 (1909)

Tennessee Coal, Iron & R.R. Co. v. George, 233 U.S. 354 (1914)

Western Union Telegraph Co. v. Brown, 234 U.S. 542 (1914)

New York Life Ins. Co. v. Dodge, 246 U.S. 357 (1918)

Pacific Employers Ins. Co. v. Industrial Accident Comm., 306 U.S. 493 (1939)

Williams v. North Carolina, 325 U.S. 226 (1945)

Hughes v. Fetter, 341 U.S. 609 (1951)

Crider v. Zurich Ins. Co., 380 U.S. 39 (1965)

Nevada v. Hall, 440 U.S. 410 (1979)

Allstate Ins. Co. v. Hague, 449 U.S. 302 (1981)

Phillips Petroleum Co. v. Shutts, 472 U.S. 797 (1985)

University of Tennessee v. Elliott, 478 U.S. 788 (1986)

Sun Oil Co. v. Wortman, 486 U.S. 717 (1988)

Baker v. General Motors Corp., 522 U.S. 222 (1998)

Franchise Tax Bd. of California v. Hyatt, 123 S. Ct. 1683 (2003)

In re Golinski, 587 F.3d 901 (9th Cir. 2009)

In re Levenson, 560 F.3d 1145 (9th Cir. 2009)

Massachusetts v. U.S. Dept. of Health & Human Servs., 682 F.3d 1 (1st Cir. 2012)

United States v. Windsor 133 S. Ct. 2675 (2013)

Privileges and Immunities Clause

The Citizens of each State shall be entitled to all Privileges and Immunities of Citizens in the several States.

(**Article IV, Section 2, Clause 1**)

"*P*rivileges and immunities" constituted a critical element of the ancient rights of Englishmen that the colonists fought to maintain during the struggle against the mother country. Founding documents, such as the Declarations and Resolves of the First Continental Congress and the Articles of Confederation, championed and, in the Articles' case, protected these rights. At the Constitutional Convention in Philadelphia, the Committee of Detail proposed the text of the Privileges and Immunities Clause, and the Framers approved it with no debate.

In many of the charters of the original colonies, the crown guaranteed some variation of franchises, privileges, immunities, or liberties to "free and natural subjects...as if they and every of them were born within the realm of England." Ultimately deriving from privileged grants of land in medieval England, the privileges, immunities, franchises, and liberties summed up the legal rights of freemen, which were inestimably greater than those afforded to the serf, the indentured servant, or the foreigner. The crown

granted them to the colonists in the New World to the same extent as to freemen in England itself, thereby creating a common subject status among freeborn Englishmen.

The package of rights granted to the colonists had distinct components. "Liberties" were not rights of individuals, but the right of a guild (and later a corporation) or manor or monastery to make and enforce laws within its jurisdiction. A formal grant of liberty from the king was a "franchise." It was, in effect, a partial transfer of the king's prerogative to declare the law. Thus, when the king allowed a colony the right "from Time to Time to Make, Ordain, and Establish all manner of wholesome and reasonable Laws, Statutes, Ordinances, Directions, and Instructions, not Contrary to the Laws of this Realm of England," the king was legally granting a franchise to the colonists to exercise the liberty of self-governance. The phrase "to exercise the franchise," meaning to vote, ultimate derives from this older notion of the "liberty" to make laws.

"Liberties" and "franchises" constituted the power of a governing unit to make rules. In contrast, "immunities" were exceptions that the king granted from the force of the law. Immunities gave individuals, towns, or other entities freedom from having to abide by a legal obligation. The king frequently gave villages and guilds immunity from having to pay tolls on merchandise produced within their precincts. From the protected guild later developed the notion of a protected "common calling." The king also granted certain individuals immunity from compulsory public service.

The courts were the entities that enforced "privileges," which included trial by jury; the initiation of suits against freemen by summons, not arrest; freedom from civil process while a witness or an attorney was at court or while a clergyman was performing divine service; the exclusion of essential personal property, like plows or the tools of one's trade, from distraint; the benefit of clergy in capital cases (which meant that first-time offenders received more lenient sentences for certain crimes); the rights of possession and inheritance of land; the right to use deadly force to defend one's abode; the privilege of members of Parliament to be free from arrest while on duty; the writ of habeas corpus, and the right of merchants in certain towns to trade freely. Conceptually, "privileges" and "immunities" refer to exemptions from otherwise applicable law, and thus they came to be seen as logically interchangeable.

In America, there were specific practical effects to the guarantees of privileges and immunities. First, despite the significant differences among the colonies, the granting of common privileges and immunities made all colonists common subjects under a single crown. Second, any freeman had the right to travel and take up residence within any of the English colonies. No colonist could be held to be a foreigner in any other colony. Benjamin Franklin, born in Boston, became a Pennsylvanian simply by moving to Philadelphia. Third, as has been described, privileges and immunities referred to a specific set of legal entitlements, individual as well as communitarian.

Finally, the grants of privileges and immunities operated as a kind of equal-protection guarantee, particularly for merchants. It meant that temporary travelers in a colony, not just those who moved in to take up residence, could buy and sell and have the protection of the law without the need for a special grant or charter from the host colony. Even under the umbrella of mercantilism, then, common privileges and immunities allowed for a robust exchange of goods and commercial paper.

The privilege to be free from economic discrimination was based on the underlying right to carry on a lawful trade. The government could pass generally applicable laws and commercial regulations, but it could not discriminate against visitors in their lawful mercantile activities. Corporations, as creations of the state, were a special case; but if a governmental agent prevented a freeman from participating in mercantile endeavors on equal legal grounds with others, the freeman could justly claim a violation of his rights as a freeborn English subject. As a corollary, many regarded monopolies as "odious" and violative of the right to a lawful calling. The prohibition of monopolies, however, never quite gelled into a fundamental privilege.

In sum, the colonial experience of privileges and immunities meant (1) membership in a common political community, (2) a right to travel, (3) a series of particularly defined rights centering around access to the courts, and (4) equal protection of the laws for commercial activities based upon the right of every freeman to a lawful calling.

In his *Commentaries on the Laws of England* (1765–1769), Sir William Blackstone had written that immunities were the natural rights that a citizen continued to enjoy after a government had been formed, and privileges were the substitutes that the government gave to citizens for the rights that he had given up when entering society. But the American colonists came to think differently. Along the path to independence, "Privileges and Immunities" began to be set alongside ideas of natural rights as mutual supports for the patriot cause, but the colonists defined them as different categories of rights. The notion of privileges and immunities referred to a set of historically obtained rights and not to general natural rights, though the two categories were seen to be in harmony. The First Continental Congress made that distinction in its Declarations and Resolves of 1774. The delegates asserted some rights as natural, that is, that the colonists "are entitled to life, liberty, and property, and they have never ceded to any sovereign power whatever, a right to dispose of either without their consent." But when the delegates came to describing the privileges and immunities of the colonists, they pointed to specific English grants: "That these, His Majesty's Colonies, are likewise entitled to all the immunities and privileges granted and confirmed to them by royal charters, or secured by their several codes of provincial laws."

After independence, a clause protecting privileges and immunities went through a number of drafts before its final formulation in the Articles of Confederation. The Privileges and Immunities Clause of the Articles of Confederation deals explicitly with three rights: (1) a ban on discrimination against persons from other states (as for example in access to judicial procedures), (2) a right to travel, and (3) a ban on discrimination on the "privileges of trade and commerce" (or, as would be later formulated, a common or lawful calling).

Robert Natelson has suggested that the first guarantee of no discrimination against out-of-state persons derived from the fact that the states (as had the colonies) possessed the right of internal self-governance, and it was therefore necessary to limit its abuse against residents of other states. On the other hand, in colonial times, the legislative authority of the British empire controlled the right to travel and to conduct business. However, because the drafters of the Articles of Confederation refused to place such powers in the Confederation Congress, it was necessary to establish additionally the right to travel and to conduct business as a separate textual guarantee. When the drafters of the Constitution established the power of Congress to control interstate commerce, there was no need for a separate guarantee for travel and business, as that would be, as it had been under the empire, in the hands of the central government. Thus, the Privileges and Immunities Clause of Article IV only guarantees protection against discrimination of out-of-staters by host states in their exercise of their internal police power.

But the interpretation by other observers finds no substantive difference between the lengthier guarantees in the Articles of Confederation and the text of Article IV of the Constitution. Historically, the right to travel as a freeborn British subject had already been established in colonial times, subject to the empire's limited regulation of trade between colonies, it was still a privilege of freeborn Englishmen to be able to travel and to exercise one's trade in any way that was lawful in any host colony. Thus, the simpler summary of the Constitution's Privileges and Immunities Clause carries the traditional understanding of no discrimination, the right to travel, and the right to carry on a lawful trade, subject only to whatever regulations Congress might impose on commerce between states. In summary, the drafters based the guarantee of privileges and immunities on the same principles as were in the colonial charters. As finally approved, Article IV (including a full faith and credit clause) sought to create a common citizenship, a right to travel, and equal protection for commercial activities.

In *The Federalist* No. 42, James Madison bluntly declared that the privileges and immunities clause in the Articles of Confederation was repetitive and confusing and stood in the way of Congress's power to regulate naturalization. As a result, the Constitution's Article IV became simpler and direct. It created a common citizenship, but Congress would determine who could become citizens. It also prohibited states from discriminating against residents of other states in judicial process and in economic activities.

The clause is self-executing. Congress possesses no independent power to enforce the clause. *United States v. Harris* (1883). As Alexander Hamilton noted in *The Federalist* No. 80, the federal courts would be the agency of enforcement.

As the colonists had insisted during the struggle with England, the Privileges and Immunities guarantee did not refer to a set of independent natural rights; in fact, many of the new state constitutions distinguished between natural rights and privileges and immunities. Privileges and immunities remained positive, not natural, rights and subject to the tradition of liberty as self-government. Consequently, after the Revolution, the states stood in the place that Parliament had occupied in the 1760s: privileges and immunities existed, and some certainly were longstanding and fundamental, but the "people" through their legislature could alter them.

Despite the presumed common corpus of privileges and immunities derived from tradition, Article IV of the Constitution does not compel a state to provide for the privileges and immunities of its own citizens, but only to treat out-of-state residents equally in the enjoyment of whatever privileges and immunities obtained within the state.

Thus, a state could revise or repeal a traditional privilege or immunity, and the nonresident had no right to claim it for himself. In 1821, William Cranch, chief judge of the circuit court of the District of Columbia, was called upon to decide the constitutionality of a federal law prohibiting free blacks from residing in the district without first obtaining a surety from a white person guaranteeing their good behavior. The purpose of the act was to prevent poor blacks from immigrating into the district and burdening the distribution of services under the poor laws. Gaining a white surety was expected to be impossible.

Cranch found no obstacle to the law in the Privileges and Immunities Clause of Article IV (which treats the District of Columbia as a state). "A citizen of one state," he wrote, "coming into another state, can claim only those privileges and immunities which belong to citizens of the latter state, in like circumstances." *Costin v. Corp. of Washington* (1821). Free blacks lost (prospectively, Cranch found) the effective right to travel to the District of Columbia, and Article IV afforded them no protection.

Two years later, however, a judge equated privileges and immunities with natural rights. In *Corfield v. Coryell* (1823), Justice Bushrod Washington, on circuit, declared,

> The inquiry is, what are the privileges and immunities of citizens in the several states? We feel no hesitation in confining these expressions to those privileges and immunities which are, in their nature, fundamental; which belong, of right, to the citizens of all free governments; and which have, at all times, been enjoyed by the citizens of the several states which compose this Union, from the time of their becoming free, independent, and sovereign.

Justice Washington's statement was dictum. In the actual holding, he decided that New Jersey could discriminate against out-of-state citizens in the harvesting of oysters because the citizens of New Jersey "owned" oysters as a natural resource. A number of courts cited *Corfield v. Coryell* before the Civil War, but only for its holding and never for its dictum.

The Supreme Court rejected a natural-rights content to Article IV's Privileges and Immunities Clause in *Paul v. Virginia* (1869). Thus, although Justice Samuel F. Miller confusingly quoted Justice Washington's dictum in the famous *Slaughter-House Cases* (1873), his summary of the meaning of the clause was correct as a matter of law: the "sole purpose" of Article IV's Privileges and Immunities Clause, he wrote,

> was to declare to the several States, that whatever those rights, as you grant or establish them to your own citizens, or as you limit or qualify, or impose restrictions on their exercise, the same, neither more nor less, shall be the measure of the rights of citizens of other States within your jurisdiction.

Bushrod Washington's dictum, however, had taken on a life of its own. It figured in abolitionist ideology and had much to do with the debate over the Privileges or Immunities Clause of the Fourteenth Amendment. But the Supreme Court continued to reject it as defining the Privileges and Immunities Clause of Article IV. *See McKane v. Durston* (1894).

The application of most of the procedural protections of the Bill of Rights to the states by way of the Fourteenth Amendment limited the traditional scope of the Privileges and Immunities Clause of Article IV to access to courts, travel, and equal treatment for nonresidents. The courts have affirmed a right of the nonresident to have "reasonable and adequate" access to the courts of a host state. *Canadian Northern Railway Co. v. Eggen* (1920). The Supreme Court has recognized a right to travel, but it has had difficulty in finding a secure constitutional locus for the right. Recently in *Saenz v. Roe* (1999), the Court noted that there are three components to the right to travel: the right to enter and leave a state, the right of visitors to a state to be treated like residents, and the right of visitors wishing to become permanent residents to be treated like residents. The Court held that the second component was protected by the Privileges and Immunities Clause of Article IV and that the third component was protected by the Privileges or Immunities Clause of the Fourteenth Amendment. The Court declined to state the constitutional source of the first component of the right to travel because it was not implicated in that case.

In terms of equal treatment for visitors, however, the modern Court's application of the Privileges and Immunities Clause of Article IV has been generally consistent with legal tradition and the views of the Framers. The clause protects nonresident citizens, not corporations. *Bank of Augusta v. Earle* (1839); *Paul v. Virginia*. The clause protects visitors only in regard to their enjoyment of a "fundamental right," which is almost invariably defined as a right to a lawful or common calling, which, in turn, can be regulated by generally applicable legislation by the host state.

Lawful callings include the practice of law, *Supreme Court of New Hampshire v. Piper* (1985); fishing (the Court has abandoned the fiction that a state's citizens own its natural resources), *Toomer v. Witsell* (1948); construction work, *United Building & Construction Trades Council v. Mayor and Council of Camden* (1984); merchant activities, *Ward v. Maryland* (1871); and journalism, *Lee v. Minner* (2006); but not recreational hunting, *Baldwin v. Fish and Game Commission* (1978) or volunteer political advocacy, *Jones v. City of Memphis* (2012).

Once the Court determines that there is a lawful calling, it applies a form of intermediate scrutiny, asking (1) whether "noncitizens constitute a peculiar source of the evil at which the [discriminatory] statute is aimed" and (2) whether there is a "reasonable relationship between the danger represented by noncitizens, as a class, and the ... discrimination practiced upon them." *Hicklin v. Orbeck* (1978).

The Court has also applied the clause to discriminatory taxation, *Lunding v. New York Tax Appeals Tribunal* (1998), but, controversially, it has found that the clause was not violated when a state requires a higher tuition at a state university for nonresident students. *Vlandis v. Kline* (1973). Justice Antonin Scalia would substitute the nondiscriminatory imperative of the Privileges and Immunities Clause for the Court's traditional use of the dormant commerce power, even though the Privileges and Immunities Clause does not apply to corporations. *Tyler Pipe Industries v. Washington State Department of Revenue* (1987). Finally, the suspicion against monopolies is treated as it was historically: not as a fundamental immunity, but as an activity regulated by legislation.

David F. Forte and Ronald D. Rotunda

See Also

Article I, Section 8, Clause 3 (Commerce Among the States)

Article I, Section 8, Clause 4 (Naturalization)

Amendment XIV, Section 1 (Privileges or Immunities)

Amendment XIV, Section 1 (Due Process Clause)

Suggestions for Further Research

David S. Bogen, *The Privileges and Immunities Clause of Article IV*, 37 Case W. Res. L. Rev. 794 (1987)

Thomas H. Burrell, *A Story of Privileges and Immunities: From Medieval Concept to the Colonies and United States Constitution*, 34 Campbell L. Rev. 7 (2011)

Michael Conant, *Antimonopoly Tradition Under the Ninth and Fourteenth Amendments: Slaughter-House Cases Re-examined*, 31 Emory L.J. 785 (1982)

Gillian E. Metzger, *Congress, Article IV, and Interstate Relations*, 120 Harv. L. Rev. 1468 (2007)

Robert G. Natelson, *The Original Meaning of the Privileges and Immunities Clause*, 43 Ga. L. Rev. 1117 (2009)

Bryce Nixon, *"Rational Basis with a Bite": A Retreat from the Constitutional Right to Travel*, 18 Law & Ineq. 209 (2000)

Andrew M. Perlman, *A Bar Against Competition: The Unconstitutionality of Admission Rules for Out-of-State Lawyers*, 18 Geo. J. Legal Ethics 135 (2004)

Douglas G. Smith, *Natural Law, Article IV, and Section One of the Fourteenth Amendment*, 47 Am. U. L. Rev. 351 (1997)

David R. Upham, *Corfield v. Coryell and the Privileges and Immunities of American Citizenship*, 83 Tex. L. Rev. 1483 (2005)

Significant Cases

Costin v. Washington, 6 F. Cas. 612 (C.C.D.C. 1821) (No. 3266)

Corfield v. Coryell, 6 F. Cas. 546 (C.C.E.D. Pa. 1823) (No. 3230)

Bank of Augusta v. Earle, 38 U.S. (13 Pet.) 519 (1839)

Paul v. Virginia, 75 U.S. (8 Wall.) 168 (1869)

Ward v. Maryland, 79 U.S. (12 Wall.) 418 (1871)

Slaughter-House Cases, 83 U.S. (16 Wall.) 36 (1873)

United States v. Harris, 106 U.S. 629 (1883)

McKane v. Durston, 153 U.S. 684 (1894)

Chalker v. Birmingham & Northwestern Ry. Co., 249 U.S. 522 (1919)

Canadian Northern Ry. Co. v. Eggen, 252 U.S. 553 (1920)

Toomer v. Witsell, 334 U.S. 385 (1948)

Mullaney v. Anderson, 342 U.S. 415 (1952)

United States v. Guest, 383 U.S. 745 (1966)

Vlandis v. Kline, 412 U.S. 441 (1973)

Baldwin v. Montana Fish and Game Comm'n, 436 U.S. 371 (1978)

Hicklin v. Orbeck, 437 U.S. 518 (1978)

United Building & Construction Trades Council v. Mayor and Council of Camden, 465 U.S. 208 (1984)

Supreme Court of New Hampshire v. Piper, 470 U.S. 274 (1985)

Tyler Pipe Industries v. Washington State Dep't of Revenue, 483 U.S. 232 (1987)

Supreme Court of Virginia v. Friedman, 487 U.S. 59 (1988)

Barnard v. Thorstenn, 489 U.S. 546 (1989)

Lunding v. New York Tax Appeals Tribunal, 522 U.S. 287 (1998)

Saenz v. Roe, 526 U.S. 489, 500 (1999)

Ponderosa Dairy v. Lyons, 259 F.3d 1148, 1156 (9th Cir. 2003)

Hillside Dairy, Inc. v. Lyons, 539 U.S. 59 (2003)

Bach v. Pataki, 408 F.3d 75 (2d Cir. 2005)

Lee v. Minner, 458 F.3d 194 (3d Cir. 2006)

Young v. Hawaii, 548 F. Supp. 2d 1151 (D. Haw. 2008)

Branch v. Franklin, 285 Fed. Appx. 573 (11th Cir. 2008)

Council of Ins. Agents & Brokers v. Molasky-Arman, 522 F.3d 925 (9th Cir. 2008)

Kleinsmith v. Shurtleff, 571 F.3d 1033 (10th Cir. 2009)

McDonald v. City of Chicago, 130 S. Ct. 3020 (2010)

Yerger v. Mass. Turnpike Auth., 395 Fed. Appx. 878 (3d Cir. 2010)

Peruta v. County of San Diego, 758 F. Supp. 2d 1106 (S.D. Calif.2010)

Peterson v. LaCabe, 783 F. Supp. 2d 1167 (D. Colo. 2011)

Osterweil v. Bartlett, 819 F. Supp. 2d 72 (N.D.N.Y. 2011)

McBurney v. Young, 667 F.3d 454 (4th Cir. 2012)

Jones v. City of Memphis, 2012 WL 1228181 (W.D. Tenn. April 11, 2012)

Interstate Rendition Clause

A Person charged in any State with Treason, Felony, or other Crime, who shall flee from Justice, and be found in another State, shall on Demand of the executive Authority of the State from which he fled, be delivered up, to be removed to the State having Jurisdiction of the Crime.

(**Article IV, Section 2, Clause 2**)

~

*T*he Interstate Rendition or extradition clause derives from similar language in the Articles of Confederation, but the principle of extradition between governments dates to antiquity. The Framers' purpose was to foster comity between states and to prevent criminals from evading law enforcement. The Framers regarded interstate rendition, despite its classical roots, as distinct from international extradition. In 1793, Congress passed the first rendition act—today, 18 U.S.C. § 3182—for fear that the clause was not self-executing. The statute governed rendition from territories as well as states. Although there is no express power granted to Congress to govern rendition, Justice Joseph Story regarded it as implied from the moral duty of Congress to carry into execution the duties imposed on the federal government by the Constitution. *Prigg v. Pennsylvania* (1842).

On its face, the clause requires: (1) a facially valid criminal charge in a demanding state, (2) a flight to an asylum state, and (3) an executive demand for return. The Framers specified the offenses of treason and felony to show that political crimes warrant rendition, as well as "other crimes" to comprehend all crimes, regardless of gravity. *Taylor v. Taintor* (1872); *Kentucky v. Dennison* (1860). Exempted from the scope of the clause are civil liabilities and private debts. As to what constitutes a criminal charge, the 1793 rendition act requires formal indictment or affidavit, but it does not mention a method known as "criminal information," generally, a unilateral accusation by the government. This omission likely was deliberate, as such information was a known device abused by the British.

The Interstate Rendition Clause suggests that deliberate and voluntary flight is required. Thus, early scholars speculated, for example, that a person involuntarily removed from one state to a second state (by another person or even by court order) could not be rendered back or rendered forward to a third state. But consistently with the clause's law-enforcement purpose, flight has been construed without regard to intent, requiring only that the state seeking rendition allege that the person sought had committed an overt criminal act in the demanding state. *Strassheim v. Daily* (1911); *Appleyard v. Massachusetts* (1906). That the person sought was present in an asylum state before the indictment issued does not insulate him from rendition. *Roberts v. Reilly* (1885).

In the antebellum period, a crisis of executive demands and compliance arose, as some Northern governors refused to return fugitives charged with slavery-related crimes to Southern states. Since the Civil War, the Supreme Court has clarified and limited the scope of the executive power in the asylum state to decline rendition. A state's governor may determine only (1) whether the person sought is charged with a crime under the demanding state's law and (2) whether that person is a fugitive, that is, was present in the demanding state when the alleged overt act occurred. *Munsey v. Clough* (1905). Upon a habeas corpus petition, a court also may make inquiries only on those two questions. *Michigan v. Doran* (1978). Other questions—for example, guilt or innocence, sufficiency of evidence, construction of state law, or adequacy of justice in the demanding state—are triable only in the demanding state. *New Mexico ex rel. Ortiz v. Reed* (1998); *Lascelles v. Georgia* (1893). In 1987, the Supreme Court resolved the last vestige of antebellum indecision on whether governors had to return fugitives. It ruled in *Puerto Rico v. Branstad* (1987) that federal courts may compel state executives to render fugitives who have been properly demanded by the requesting state.

Rendition particulars today are controlled chiefly by the Uniform Extradition and Rendition Act adopted in some form in every state. State rendition laws have been upheld insofar as they are consistent with the Constitution and federal statutes. Furthermore, states today can provide for rendition outside the scope of the clause. For example, states may agree to render subpoenaed witnesses and charged persons who were never present in the demanding state. It is unclear whether the original conception of the Interstate Rendition Clause contemplated an exclusive process of rendition. If so, then ancillary agreements between two states to allow rendition even if there are procedural deficiencies in the demand for rendition may contravene the Due Process Clause of the Fourteenth Amendment.

Richard Peltz-Steele

See Also

Article IV, Section 1 (Full Faith and Credit Clause)

Article IV, Section 2, Clause 1 (Privileges and Immunities Clause)

Article IV, Section 2, Clause 3 (Fugitive Slave Clause)

Article IV, Section 3, Clause 2 (Territories Clause; Property Clause)

Amendment X (Reserved Powers of the States)

Amendment XIV, Section 1 (Due Process Clause)

Suggestions for Further Research

Leslie W. Abramson, *Extradition in America: Of Uniform Acts and Governmental Discretion*, 33 Baylor L. Rev. 793 (1981)

John G. Hawley, Inter-State Extradition (1890)

Rollin C. Hurd, A Treatise on the Right of Personal Liberty, and on the Writ of Habeas Corpus (1858)

James M. Kerr, Interstate Extradition (1880)

2 John Bassett Moore, A Treatise on Extradition and Interstate Rendition (1891)

John J. Murphy, *Revising Domestic Extradition Law*, 131 U. Pa. L. Rev. 1063 (1983)

James A. Scott, The Law of Interstate Rendition (1917)

Dale Patrick Smith, Interstate Extradition: A Case Study in Constitutional Interpretation (1984) (unpublished Ph.D. dissertation, University of Georgia) (on file with University of Georgia)

Samuel T. Spear, The Law of Extradition, International and Inter-State (3d ed. 1885)

Joseph Francis Zimmerman, Horizontal Federalism: Interstate Relations (2011)

Significant Cases

Prigg v. Pennsylvania, 41 U.S. (16 Pet.) 539 (1842)

Kentucky v. Dennison, 65 U.S. (24 How.) 66 (1861)

Taylor v. Taintor, 83 U.S. (16 Wall.) 366 (1873)

Roberts v. Reilly, 116 U.S. 80 (1885)

Lascelles v. Georgia, 148 U.S. 537 (1893)

Munsey v. Clough, 196 U.S. 364 (1905)

Appleyard v. Massachusetts, 203 U.S. 222 (1906)

Strassheim v. Daily, 221 U.S. 280 (1911)

Michigan v. Doran, 439 U.S. 282 (1978)

Puerto Rico v. Branstad, 483 U.S. 219 (1987)

New Mexico *ex rel.* Ortiz v. Reed, 524 U.S. 151 (1998)

Fugitive Slave

No Person held to Service or Labour in one State, under the Laws thereof, escaping into another, shall, in Consequence of any Law or Regulation therein, be discharged from such Service or Labour, but shall be delivered up on Claim of the Party to whom such Service or Labour may be due.

(ARTICLE IV, SECTION 2, CLAUSE 3)

≈

*T*oward the end of the Constitutional Convention, during the debate over the Privileges and Immunities Clause (Article IV, Section 2, Clause 1), Charles Pinckney of South Carolina remarked that "some provision should be included in favor of property in slaves." The Articles of Confederation contained an extradition clause for escaped criminals, but Pinckney wanted something more specifically directed to the return of slaves. He and his fellow South Carolinian Pierce Butler moved "to require fugitive slaves and servants to be delivered up like criminals." The motion was withdrawn after James Wilson and Roger Sherman objected, Wilson because the states would be required to track down slaves "at public expense," and Sherman more pointedly wondered why there was "more propriety in the public seizing and surrendering a slave or servant, than a horse." The next day, however, the motion was renewed as a formal addition to what would become this clause of Article IV. It passed unanimously and

without debate. This was probably because there was a strong precedent in the Northwest Ordinance of 1787 (passed six weeks earlier by Congress), which included a fugitive-slave provision along with its declaration (presaging the Thirteenth Amendment) that "neither slavery nor involuntary servitude" would exist in that territory.

In addition, the English case of *Somerset v. Stewart* (1772) had concerned Southern slave owners. The master of a fugitive slave from Virginia petitioned for his return. The lord chief justice of the King's Bench, Lord Mansfield (William Murray), ruled:

The state of slavery is of such a nature that it is incapable of being introduced on any reasons, moral or political, but only by positive law, which preserves its force long after the reasons, occasions, and time itself from whence it was created, is erased from memory. It is so odious, that nothing can be suffered to support it, but positive law. Whatever inconveniences, therefore, may follow from the decision, I cannot say this case is allowed or approved by the law of England; and therefore the black must be discharged.

So the slave was not returned, and news of the case spread through the colonies. The principle that the slave shed his status in a realm free of the positive law of slavery caused alarm in the South. The phrasing of the clause responded directly to Lord Mansfield's ruling.

Mansfield's reasoning was grounded in the Western natural law tradition—one held by Chief Justice John Marshall and Justice Joseph Story. Slavery was not a natural condition, but a positive act *of law*. Indeed, prior to *Dred Scott v. Sandford* (1857), Missouri law had held that when a master moves a slave into a state prohibiting slavery, the very act "thereby emancipates his slave." *Scott v. Emerson* (1852).

A model of circumlocution, the resulting clause is the closest of the so-called Slave Clauses

(Article I, Section 2, Clause 3; Article I, Section 9, Clause 1; and Article V) to recognizing slavery as a protected institution. It also became the most controversial of the clauses and was at the center of many constitutional disputes in the 1840s and 1850s.

As initially proposed in the Convention, the language spoke of persons "bound to service or labor" being delivered up to the person "justly claiming their service or labor." The Committee of Style revised the language to refer to persons "legally held to service or labour" being delivered up to "the party to whom such service or labour may be due," thereby removing the implication that the claim to the property may be "just."

At the last moment, the phrase "Person legally held to Service or Labour in one state" was amended to read "Person held to Service or Labour in one state, under the Laws thereof" to make the clause comply, according to James Madison's notes, "with the wish of some who thought the term legal equivocal, and favoring the idea that slavery was legal in a moral view." The revision emphasized as well that slaves were held according to the laws of individual states, and that slaveholding was not based either upon natural law or the common law, avoiding the implication that the Constitution itself legally sanctioned the practice. The section also leaves a clear implication, contrary to the holding in *Dred Scott v. Sandford*, that the slave owner's property claim did not apply in federal territories, if Congress chose to prohibit slavery there.

Unlike the other three sections of Article IV, Section 2 is written in the passive voice and confers no powers on the federal government. It simply limits state authority, giving rise to the argument that the clause is only declaratory. In 1793, however, Congress passed the Fugitive Slave Act to enforce the clause, but left the mechanism of enforcement primarily with the states. In *Prigg v. Pennsylvania* (1842), however, Justice Joseph Story effectively nationalized the fugitive slave regime by declaring that a state law that penalized the seizure of fugitive slaves was unconstitutional. Story did note, in an obiter dictum, that the federal government could not compel state officials to enforce the act. This led to numerous states passing personal-liberty laws (prohibiting state officials from enforcing the federal statute).

In one famous case in 1842, Salmon P. Chase (who in 1864 would become chief justice of the Supreme Court) argued that natural law did not recognize the state of slavery and that, on this basis, the 1793 Fugitive Slave Act was unconstitutional. Justice John McLean (who would later dissent in *Dred Scott v. Sandford*), was on circuit presiding over the trial. He firmly rejected Chase's argument. Chase and co-counsel William Seward took the case to the Supreme Court, which unanimously found against them. *Jones v. Van Zandt* (1847).

In response to state reluctance to enforce the 1793 act, the South pressed for and gained a new federal Fugitive Slave Act enacted as part of the Compromise of 1850. That act forbade state officials from interfering with the return of slaves. Further, in *Moore v. Illinois* (1852), the Supreme Court held that states could impose penalties on their citizens for harboring fugitive slaves.

The Fugitive Slave Act of 1850 engendered vigorous popular and legal opposition across the North. Local conventions passed resolutions declaring the act unconstitutional, such as happened in New York and Cleveland. Rescues of slaves who were to be returned caught the public eye in Massachusetts, New York, and Pennsylvania. Juries often refused to convict rescuers. After the Wisconsin Supreme Court set two slave rescuers (John Ryecraft and Sherman Booth) free declaring the Fugitive Slave Act unconstitutional, the United States Supreme Court unanimously reversed the state court in *Abelman v. Booth* (1859), but the Wisconsin high court refused to acknowledge the decision.

In *Dred Scott*, Chief Justice Roger B. Taney attempted to use this clause, along with the so-called Migration or Importation Clause (Article I, Section 9, Clause1), as evidence that slaves were not citizens but were to be considered property according to the Constitution. By this clause, Taney argued, "the States pledge themselves to each other to maintain the right of property of the master, by delivering up to him any slave who may have escaped from his service."

The more generally accepted interpretation, however, is that this clause did not speak to the issue of citizenship at all, but was a necessary accommodation to existing slavery interests in particular states, required for the sake of establishing the Constitution— "scaffolding to the magnificent structure," Frederick Douglass called it, "to be removed as soon as the building was completed." This point is underscored by the fact that, although slavery was abolished by constitutional amendment (Thirteenth Amendment), not one word of the original text on the subject had to be amended or deleted.

Matthew Spalding

See Also

Article I, Section 2, Clause 3 (Three-fifths Clause)
Article I, Section 8, Clause 3 (Commerce Among the States)
Article I, Section 9, Clause 1 (Migration or Importation Clause)
Article V (Prohibition on Amendment: Slave Trade)

Suggestions for Further Research

H. Robert Baker, *The Fugitive Slave Clause and the Antebellum Constitution*, 30 Law & Hist. Rev. 1133 (2012)

Richard Beeman, Plain, Honest Men: The Making of the American Constitution (2009)

Don E. Fehrenbacher, The Slaveholding Republic: An Account of the United States Government's Relations to Slavery (2001)

Matthew J. Grow, *Fugitive Slaves, the Higher Law, and the Coming of the Civil War*, 40 Revs. in Am. Hist. 68–72 (2012)

Steven Lubet, Fugitive Justice: Runaways, Rescuers, and Slavery on Trial (2010)

Earl M. Maltz, *Slavery, Federalism, and the Constitution:* Ableman v. Booth *and the Struggle Over Fugitive Slaves*, 56 Clev. St. L. Rev. 83 (2008)

Donald L. Robinson, Slavery in the Structure of American Politics, 1765–1820 (1971)

Herbert J. Storing, *Slavery and the Moral Foundations of the American Republic*, in The Moral Foundations of the American Republic (Robert H. Horwitz, ed., 1986)

Stephen Usherwood, "The Black Must be Discharged—The Abolitionists' Debt to Lord Mansfield," in 31 History Today (1982) at http://www.historytoday.com/stephen-usherwood/black-must-be-discharged-abolitionists-debt-lord-mansfield

George William Van Cleve, *Race in America: Slavery, the Rule of Law, and the Civil War*, 47 Tulsa L. Rev. 257 (2011) (book review)

Significant Cases

Prigg v. Pennsylvania, 41 U.S. (16 Pet.) 539 (1842)
Jones v. Van Zandt 46 U.S. 5 How. 215 (1847)
Moore v. People of the State of Illinois, 55 U.S. (14 How.) 13 (1852)
Scott v. Emerson, 15 Mo. Rpts. 576 (1852)
Dred Scott v. Sandford, 60 U.S. (19 How.) 393 (1857)
Ableman v. Booth, 62 U.S. (21 How.) 506 (1859)

Admissions Clause

New States may be admitted by the Congress into this Union; but no new States shall be formed or erected within the Jurisdiction of any other State; nor any State be formed by the Junction of two or more States, or Parts of States, without the Consent of the Legislatures of the States concerned as well as of the Congress.

(Article IV, Section 3, Clause 1)

~

*A*t the Constitutional Convention, the Committee of Detail proposed that "new States shall be admitted on the same terms with the original States." That proposal would have taken the policy behind the Northwest Ordinance of 1787 and made it a constitutional imperative. But Gouverneur Morris wanted the equality of admitted states to be struck because he feared the political power of the Western states would "overwhelm" the East. Over the objections of James Madison, his motion to strike out the requirement of equality won by a vote of seven to two. He then moved to make sure that no state could be formed out of a previous state without the consent of the previous state as well as the "general legislature" (i.e., Congress). In this case as well, he wanted the Eastern states that still had claims to Western lands (viz., Virginia and North Carolina) to have a veto over whether their western counties (which eventually became Kentucky and Tennessee) could become states. This motion passed by a vote of six to five. Like the question of the establishment of lower federal courts, the Convention effectively passed the issue of the status of newly admitted states over to the political process.

Once the new Constitution went into effect, however, Congress admitted Vermont and Kentucky on equal terms with the original thirteen states and thereafter formalized the condition in its acts of admission for subsequent states, declaring that the new state enters "on an equal footing with the original States in all respects whatever." Thus Congress, exercising the discretion allowed it by the Framers, adopted a policy of equal status for newly admitted states.

A number of observers, however, including Gouverneur Morris, had contended that Congress could admit states only from territory that the United States possessed at the time of the Constitution's formation. That position was echoed by New England Federalists upset with Thomas Jefferson over the purchase of Louisiana. There is no indication of any such limitation, however, in the text or in the view of most of the Framers. Further, time and the admission of new states have made that argument irrelevant. Exercising its discretion, Congress admitted new states from newly acquired territory and opted to give equal status to each.

The Supreme Court adopted the view of Congress regarding the "equal footing" of new states and made it a constitutional requirement. In doing so, the Court chose to impose the very constitutional rule that the Framers had rejected. *Pollard's Lessee v. Hagan* (1845) ("There can be no distinction between those states which acquired their independence by force of arms and those which acquired it by the peaceful consent of older states. The Constitution says, the latter must be admitted into the union on an

equal footing with the rest."). By its terms, the Admissions Clause sets the exclusive method by which territories may become states. Thus, Puerto Rico has no right to elect members to the House of Representatives (nor may Congress by statute create such a right), for it is not legally a "state," no matter what "functional equivalents" to a state Puerto Rico may possess. *Igartúa v. United States* (2010). Congress may, however, create new Indian enclaves within a state without needing the consent of the host state because such enclaves are not on "equal footing" with the state from which they were formed. *Carcieri v. Kempthorne* (2007).

The "equal footing" doctrine remains constant to this day but has engendered problems in construing the legal effect of conditions that Congress has placed on the admission of a number of states.

According to traditional historical practice, Congress passes an enabling act prescribing the process by which the people of a United States territory may draft and adopt a state constitution. Many enabling acts contain restrictions, such as the prohibition of bigamy in the Utah, Arizona, New Mexico, and Oklahoma acts. The applicant state then submits its proposed constitution to Congress, which either accepts it or requires changes. For example, in 1866, Congress refused the proposed Nebraska constitution because it limited suffrage to white males. Upon approval of the new state constitution, Congress may direct the president to issue a proclamation certifying the entry of the new state into the United States. A number of states, however, drafted constitutions for submission to Congress absent enabling acts and were subsequently admitted.

Texas is a special case: it was an independent republic and, under the Resolution of Annexation, has the option of creating up to four additional states out of its territory. Some commentators have wondered whether, under the Admissions Clause, Texas can constitutionally exercise that option unilaterally, or whether those would-be additional states would have to petition Congress independently as well.

Although Congress's enabling act becomes a "fundamental law" of the state, its provisions must give way to the "equal footing" rights of other states once the new state becomes a member of the Union. In *Pollard's Lessee*, the Supreme Court held that an enabling act could not divest Alabama of its sovereign ownership rights to land under internal navigable waters, and in *Coyle v. Smith* (1911), the Court invalidated a provision in Oklahoma's enabling act that constrained where the state could place its capital. The rule the Court has fashioned is that Congress can regulate the state through the enabling act only insofar as Congress could do so under one of its enumerated powers. Thus, under its power to regulate territories, Congress could, in its enabling act, require Utah to deny the franchise to women in the election of delegates to the state's constitutional convention (at a time when the U.S. Constitution did not guarantee women's suffrage), but that restriction could not bind Utah once it had become a state. *Anderson v. Tyree* (1895). More typically, enforceable provisions in enabling acts have included exemption of federal property from state taxation, the method of regulating public lands, and the rules of commerce among the Indians.

Finally, despite the ambiguous second semicolon in the clause, new states may be formed out of an existing state provided all parties consent: the new state, the existing state, and Congress. In that way, Kentucky, Tennessee, Maine, West Virginia, and arguably Vermont came into the Union. It is doubtful, however, whether a state could reassign territory (in a swap with another state for example), or whether Congress could "de-annex" to another sovereign any territory that was part of a state without the consent of the affected state.

David F. Forte

See Also

Article IV, Section 3, Clause 2 (Territories Clause; Property Clause)

Suggestions for Further Research

Ralph H. Brock, *The Ultimate Gerrymander: Dividing Texas Into Four New States*, 6 CARDOZO PUB. L. POL'Y & ETHICS J. 651 (2008)

Frank W. DiCastri, Comment: *Are All States Really Equal? The "Equal Footing" Doctrine and Indian Claims to Submerged Lands*, 1997 WIS. L. REV. 179 (1997)

Allan Erbsen, *Constitutional Spaces*, 95 MINN. L. REV. 1168 (2011)

Vasan Kesavan & Michael Stokes Paulsen, *Is West Virginia Unconstitutional?*, 90 CAL. L. REV. 291 (2002)

Vasan Kesavan & Michael Stokes Paulsen, *Let's Mess with Texas*, 82 TEX. L. REV. 1587 (2004)

Carolyn M. Landever, *Whose Home on the Range? Equal Footing, the New Federalism and State Jurisdiction on Public Lands*, 47 FLA. L. REV. 557 (1995)

GARY LAWSON & GUY SEIDMAN, THE CONSTITUTION OF EMPIRE: TERRITORIAL EXPANSION AND AMERICAN LEGAL HISTORY (2004)

Stephen E. Sachs, *Constitutional Backdrops*, 80 GEO. WASH. L. REV. 1813 (2012)

Significant Cases

Pollard's Lessee v. Hagan, 44 U.S. (3 How.) 212 (1845)

Anderson v. Tyree, 12 Utah 129 (1895)

Stearns v. Minnesota, 179 U.S. 223 (1900)

Coyle v. Smith, 221 U.S. 559 (1911)

United States v. Sandoval, 231 U.S. 28 (1913)

Carcieri v. Kempthorne, 497 F. 3d 15 (1st Cir. 2007)

Igartúa v. United States, 626 F.3d 592 (1st Cir. 2010)

Territories Clause

The Congress shall have Power to dispose of and make all needful Rules and Regulations respecting the Territory ... belonging to the United States....

(ARTICLE IV, SECTION 3, CLAUSE 2)

~

*A*fter the Constitution was ratified in 1788, the new United States government assumed ownership of the vast Northwest Territory that had been ceded to the pre-constitutional confederation by states with (real or potential) claims to the land. Further cessions from states were expected, and various founding-era figures hoped to acquire additional territory ranging from

Canada to Cuba. The Northwest Ordinance of 1787 promised that the Northwest Territory would eventually be formed into states, and Article VI, Clause 1, of the Constitution (guaranteeing the "engagements" of the government) carried that promise forward after ratification. Still, some provision needed to be made for the governance of this federally-held territory until states were formed—and provision made as well for the governance of any later-acquired federal territory. Accordingly, the Constitution gave Congress "power to dispose of and make all needful rules and regulations respecting the territory or other property belonging to the United States...."

As with the Enclave Clause (Article I, Section 8, Clause 17), which gives Congress the power of "exclusive legislation" over both the nation's capital and federal lands acquired from and within states, the Territories Clause appears to be a plenary grant of power to Congress to govern territory as a general government, without having to trace each act of legislation to an enumeration of power beyond the Territories Clause itself. On this understanding, Congress can pass a general criminal code, regulate the private law of torts and contracts, provide for rules of marriage and descent, and behave within territories as could any state government within its own jurisdiction. This view emerges naturally from the text, which places territories in the same phrase as, and gives Congress the same power over, "other property," such as inkwells and wagons (see Property Clause). It was surely the view of the clause's author, Gouverneur Morris, who explained in 1803, "I always thought that when we should acquire Canada and Louisiana, it would be proper to govern them as provinces and allow them no voice in our councils. In wording the third section of the fourth article, I went as far as circumstances would permit to establish the exclusion." And it is the view that has prevailed in the case law, where the Supreme Court has repeatedly declared that Congress has "general and plenary" power over federal territory. *Late Corp. of the Church of Jesus Christ of Latter-Day Saints v. United States* (1890).

To be sure, at various times, the Court has sought to ground federal power to govern territories in sources other than the Territories Clause, such as the treaty power or general notions of sovereignty. *See Sere v. Pitot* (1810). Others, including Gouverneur Morris and the plurality in *Dred Scott v. Sandford* (1857), have occasionally argued that the Territories Clause applies only to territory held at the time of ratification, essentially reading the clause to say "territory... belonging to the United States [as of June 21, 1788]." With all due respect to the author of the Territories Clause (and all due disrespect to the author of the plurality opinion in *Dred Scott*), it is textually very difficult to limit the Territories Clause to territory held at the time of ratification. As Albert Gallatin pointed out in 1803, this would also limit the clause to "other property" held at the time of ratification, as the constitutional power over "territory" and "other property" is identical. The Territories Clause applies to after-acquired territory as surely as it applies to after-acquired inkwells and wagons. In any event, little has turned on these disputes, as the claimed scope of the power of territorial governance has not seemed to vary significantly with the claimed source. As the Court noted in *National Bank v. County of Yankton* in 1880, "There have been some differences of opinion as to the particular clause of the Constitution from which the power [to govern territory] is derived, but that it exists has always been conceded."

The broad consensus that Congress can rule federal territory as a general government has not prevented the Territories Clause from becoming among the most contentious sentences in the Constitution. Debates about territorial governance have been at the heart of disputes as heated and violent as the Civil War and the debates over imperialism at the outset of the twentieth century.

The Territories Clause is a self-contained grant of power, in the sense that it gives (or confirms in) Congress the powers of a general government over federal territories. But does that mean that the Constitution imposes no limits on territorial legislation? The answer to that question is obviously no; Congress, for example, cannot pass territorial legislation without complying with the formalities of Article I, Section 7, for lawmaking. If that is true, however, one must then ask what other parts of the Constitution might also limit the reach of the Territories Clause.

The simple answer would be that *all* parts of the Constitution that impose general limitations on the scope and form of federal power, other than the principle of enumerated congressional powers, would apply to action involving federal territories as surely as they apply to other federal action. That simple answer, however, while it might well be correct as a matter of original meaning, has never been the law, and it is emphatically not the law today.

From the founding onward, Congress has entrusted the inhabitants of federal territories with as much power of self-governance as has seemed prudent at the time, as a matter of democratic theory and to lay the groundwork for statehood (or nationhood if the territory eventually assumes independence), primarily by authorizing elected territorial legislatures with broad authority. If the Constitution's general separation-of-powers principles apply to territorial governance, this arrangement seems to violate even the weakest form of the nondelegation doctrine by creating autonomous lawmaking bodies that act with no "intelligible principle" to guide them. See Note on Separation of Powers. Courts have nonetheless repeatedly and consistently upheld (albeit with little reasoning) territorial legislatures against such challenges. *See, e.g., District of Columbia v. John R. Thompson Co.* (1953); *Cincinnati Soap Co. v. United States* (1937).

Judges in federal territories do not have the tenure and salary guarantees that Article III, Section 1, requires of federal judges, an anomaly that has been consistently upheld by the courts since 1828. *See American Insurance Co. v. 356 Bales of Cotton, Canter* (1828). Since the middle of the twentieth century, many federal territories have been allowed to elect their own executive officers, such as governors, in apparent violation of the Appointments Clause (Article II, Section 2, Clause 2), which requires federal officers (and territorial governors rather clearly meet this description) to be appointed by the president, executive department heads, or federal courts. The constitutionality of this arrangement actually remains an open question, and high-ranking U.S. Department of Justice officials on more than

one occasion in modern times have expressed doubts about it. And in the early years of the twentieth century, the Supreme Court held that the Constitution's provisions regarding the uniformity of duties and tariffs (Article I, Section 8, Clause 1) throughout the United States did not apply to territories. *See Downes v. Bidwell* (1901). The bottom line is that, for more than two centuries, territorial governance has stood largely, though not quite entirely, outside the Constitution's normal structural rules.

Even larger anomalies plague the question whether protections of individual rights, such as the Bill of Rights, apply to federal governance of territories. This was perhaps the nation's most pressing constitutional question in the first quarter of the twentieth century when, as the United States became a global empire, the federal government had to decide whether to impose American legal institutions, such as trial by jury, on cultures that were unfamiliar with the practices. In a series of cases over two decades, the Court developed the so-called "doctrine of territorial incorporation" to address this issue. The doctrine defies easy description, but in essence it distinguishes territories that are likely candidates for future statehood from those that are not. For the former, all provisions of the Constitution apply of their own force to territorial inhabitants. For the latter, those provisions that are "fundamental"—and the requirements of criminal juries and grand jury indictment have been specifically deemed *not* to be fundamental in this sense—apply of their own force to territorial inhabitants, while "nonfundamental" constitutional rights apply only if and how Congress chooses to extend them. This doctrine has been universally criticized by scholars, but it has never been overruled, and indeed was cited approvingly by the Court in *Boumediene v. Bush* (2008), which wrote that this "century-old doctrine informs our analysis in the present matter."

Furthermore, federal equal protection principles have consistently been held to apply differently to inhabitants of territories than to inhabitants of states. Courts have upheld, for example, race-based employment preferences and restrictions on land sales in territories that would be dubious if imposed in states. *See Wabol v. Villacrusis* (1992).

Thus, under current doctrine, the Constitution does not apply to territorial governance in a straightforward, uniform, easily understood fashion.

Even larger conceptual problems lurk in the interplay between congressional and presidential authority over territory. During times of war, American forces will sometimes occupy foreign land. Under international law principles, an occupying force has both the power and duty to govern the occupied territory. Because that occupied territory does not "belong" to the United States, the Territories Clause does not authorize congressional legislation to govern it. Instead, the power to govern occupied territory during wartime stems from the president's "executive power" and role as commander in chief of the military (Article II, Section 2, Clause 1). Territorial governance in that setting is part of, and is limited by, the international laws of war. *See Fleming v. Page* (1850). (Whether Congress could take part in that governance pursuant to its own war powers or the Necessary and Proper Clause or both is unsettled.) If the occupied territory is eventually ceded to the United States by a treaty of peace, as has happened on several occasions, then it becomes "territory . . . belonging to the United States," the president's wartime powers of governance seem to end, and Congress's power to govern under the Territories Clause seems to begin. But what if Congress does not get around to governing?

This precise sequence of events occurred with respect to California in 1848 following the Mexican-American War. Congress, largely because of gridlock over slavery, did not pass a statute for the governance of California—not even a general statute delegating authority to executive officials. Military officials in California nonetheless set up, with no congressional authorization, a peacetime military government, including customs offices to collect tariffs. In the historically obscure but theoretically important case of *Cross v. Harrison* (1854), the Supreme Court upheld the constitutionality of a peacetime military government in federal territory. The precedent was extended following the Spanish-

American War. *See Santiago v. Nogueras* (1909). The precise scope of this presidential authority to erect military governments during peacetime has yet to be fully explored.

Gary Lawson

See Also

Article I, Section 8, Clause 1 (Taxation)
Article I, Section 8, Clause 17 (Enclave Clause)
Article II, Section 2, Clause 1 (Commander in Chief)
Article II, Section 2, Clause 2 (Appointments Clause)
Article IV, Section 3, Clause 2 (Property Clause)
Article VI, Clause 1 (Debt Assumption)

Suggestions for Further Research

Frederic R. Coudert, *The Evolution of the Doctrine of Territorial Incorporation*, 26 Colum. L. Rev. 823 (1926)

Gary Lawson & Guy Seidman, The Constitution of Empire: Territorial Expansion and American Legal History (2004)

Gary Lawson & Robert D. Sloane, *The Constitutionality of Decolonization by Associated Statehood: Puerto Rico's Legal Status Reconsidered*, 50 B.C. L. Rev. 1123 (2009)

Arnold H. Leibowitz, Defining Status: A Comprehensive Analysis of United States—Territorial Relations (1989)

Gerald L. Neuman, *Anomalous Zones*, 48 Stan. L. Rev. 1197 (1996)

Significant Cases

Sere v. Pitot, 10 U.S. (6 Cranch) 332 (1810)
American Ins. Co. v. 356 Bales of Cotton, Canter, 26 U.S. (1 Pet.) 511 (1828)
Fleming v. Page, 50 U.S. (9 How.) 603 (1850)
Cross v. Harrison, 57 U.S. (16 How.) 164 (1854)
Dred Scott v. Sandford, 60 U.S. (19 How.) 393 (1857)
National Bank v. County of Yankton, 101 U.S. 129 (1880)
Late Corp. of the Church of Jesus Christ of Latter-Day Saints v. United States, 136 U.S. 1 (1890)
Downes v. Bidwell, 182 U.S. 244 (1901)
Santiago v. Nogueras, 214 U.S. 260 (1909)
Balzac v. Porto Rico, 258 U.S. 298 (1922)
Cincinnati Soap Co. v. United States, 301 U.S. 308 (1937)

District of Columbia v. John R. Thompson Co., 346
U.S. 100 (1953)

Wabol v. Villacrusis, 958 F.2d 1450 (9th Cir. 1992)

Boumediene v. Bush, 553 U.S. 723 (2008)

Property Clause

**The Congress shall have Power to
dispose of and make all needful Rules
and Regulations respecting… other
Property belonging to the United
States …**

(ARTICLE IV, SECTION 3, CLAUSE 2)

*T*he federal government owns or controls about
30 percent of the land in the United States. These
holdings include national parks, national forests,
recreation areas, wildlife refuges, vast tracts of range
and wasteland managed by the Bureau of Land
Management, reservations held in trust for Native
American tribes, military bases, and ordinary federal buildings and installations. Although federal
property can be found in every state, the largest
concentrations are in the west, where, for example,
the federal government owns over 80 percent of the
land within Nevada.

The primary constitutional authority for the
management and control of this vast real estate
empire is the Property Clause. The exact scope
of this clause has long been a matter of debate.
Broadly speaking, three different theories have been
advanced.

The narrowest conception, which can be called
the proprietary theory, maintains that the Property
Clause simply allows Congress to act as an ordinary
owner of land. It can set policy regarding whether
such lands will be sold or retained and, if they are
retained, who may enter these lands and for what
purposes. Under this conception, the clause confers
no political sovereignty over federal landholdings.
Unless one of the enumerated powers of Article I
applies, such as the power to raise armies or establish a post office, political sovereignty over federal
lands remains with the several states in which the
land is located.

An intermediate conception of the Property
Clause can be labeled the protective theory. This
conception would go beyond the proprietary theory
by allowing the federal government to adopt certain
"needful rules and regulations" of a governmental
nature in order to protect its interest in property.
Under this intermediate conception, for example,
the clause would permit Congress to pass federal
legislation regulating the sale of federal land, protecting federal land from trespasses and nuisances,
or exempting federal land from state taxation. On
the other hand, the clause would not permit Congress to exercise general sovereign authority on federal lands. For example, it would not allow Congress
to enact a general code of criminal law or family
law on federal lands, nor would it permit Congress
to exempt persons residing on federal land from
general rules of state taxation.

The broadest conception, which can be called
the police power theory, regards the clause as conferring not only the powers of ownership but also
general sovereign authority to regulate private
conduct that occurs on federal land or that affects
federal land. In default of any federal rule, state
law applies. But if Congress determines that a federal rule "respecting" federal land is "needful," it
may adopt federal legislation that supersedes state
law. Thus, the Property Clause gives Congress the
authority to adopt any type of legislation for federal lands, including codes of criminal law, family
law, and exemptions from state taxation for persons
residing on federal lands. The police-power theory
would mean that Congress would not even need
the Necessary and Proper Clause to pass detailed
legislation governing the territory. Nor would other
structural constitutional constraints apply, such as
the nondelegation doctrine, which ordinarily means
that Congress cannot devolve its lawmaking power
on the president.

It is not certain which of these three theories
corresponds with the original understanding of the
Framers, inasmuch as the debates from the Constitutional Convention and the ratification process
have little to say about the Property Clause. One
clue is provided by the structure of the Constitution.
Article I, which sets forth the enumerated powers of
Congress, includes a specific grant of power over the
governance of federal property. Article I, Section 8,
Clause 17, the Enclave Clause, is plainly a grant of

sovereign authority—indeed, exclusive sovereign authority—over the District of Columbia and other federal enclaves acquired with the consent of the state in which they are located.

Article I is the place where one would expect to find a grant of power to Congress to exercise political sovereignty over federal lands. Article IV, in contrast, which generally deals with state-to-state relations (full faith and credit, privileges and immunities, extradition, repatriation of slaves, admission of new states, protection of states against invasion), would be an odd place to put such a power. Moreover, it is inconsistent with the careful drafting of the Constitution to assume that the Framers included two overlapping grants of sovereign political authority over federal lands. These structural considerations make it doubtful that the broad police power theory is consistent with the original understanding.

Another important piece of evidence is the Northwest Ordinance, which the Congress under the Articles of Confederation enacted as the Constitutional Convention was meeting, and which the First Congress reenacted after the Constitution was ratified. This statute established the territorial government for the land comprising what is today the states of Ohio, Indiana, Michigan, Illinois, and Wisconsin. James Madison and other leaders at the Convention thought that the Articles of Confederation did not contain an adequate source of power to sustain the Northwest Ordinance. The Property Clause presumably was designed to remedy that defect. This suggests that the Framers intended the Property Clause to be broad enough at least to constitutionalize the provisions of the Northwest Ordinance.

The Northwest Ordinance included a number of provisions respecting the governance of the new territory that would have to be described as pure police power measures. These include clauses preserving the freedom of religion, prohibiting uncompensated takings of property, and outlawing slavery. Other provisions of the ordinance addressed the status of federal land once new states were formed from the territory and admitted to the Union. Such states were prospectively prohibited from interfering with the disposal of lands by the United States or with regulations adopted by Congress to secure

title to bona fide purchasers, and they were barred from imposing any tax on federal lands.

Taking the structural and historical evidence together, we can infer what may plausibly have been the original understanding of the Property Clause. The Property Clause authorized Congress to exercise a general police power within the territories before they were formed into states. Once states were admitted to the Union, however, Congress could exercise full police powers over federal land located in a state only in accordance with the Enclave Clause, that is, only when the land was acquired with the consent of the state in question. As to what "needful rules and regulations" Congress could enact respecting federal lands other than enclaves in a state, the Northwest Ordinance suggests that at least some preemptive federal legislation was contemplated, but only if designed to protect the proprietary interests of the United States. In short, the Framers plausibly intended that the police power theory would apply to federal land located in territories, but that the protective theory would apply to non-enclave federal land located in states.

The judicial vision of how much power the Property Clause confers on the federal government has hardly remained constant. To the contrary, it has evolved significantly over time. In the first half of the nineteenth century, the clause was understood to be primarily a source of authority for establishing territorial governments. Once new states were admitted to the Union, the federal government became a mere trustee of any remaining federal lands, holding and protecting them, pending their sale to private persons. *Pollard's Lessee v. Hagan* (1845). With the infamous decision of *Dred Scott v. Sandford* (1857) the Court went further, holding that the Property Clause does not permit the exercise of police powers by the federal government in territory acquired after the founding, and in particular that it does not permit the federal government to prohibit slavery in such territory. Because the Northwest Ordinance had included a similar prohibition, and the Property Clause was designed to constitutionalize the Northwest Ordinance, *Dred Scott* is contrary to the original understanding in this respect.

By the end of the nineteenth century, the interpretation of the clause shifted decisively toward the protective theory. A leading nineteenth-century exposition of the constitutional authority of the federal government over federal lands, *Fort Leavenworth Railroad Co. v. Lowe* (1885), is generally consistent with this conclusion. There, Justice Stephen J. Field wrote that the authority of the federal government over territories is "necessarily paramount." But once a territory is organized as a state and admitted to the Union on equal footing with other states, the state government assumes general sovereignty over federal lands, and the federal government has the rights only of an "individual proprietor." The federal government can exercise rights of general sovereignty over property only if there has been a formal cession of sovereignty by the state under the Enclave Clause. Justice Field qualified this vision of separated sovereignty, however, by noting that if the federal government acquires land outside the Enclave Clause, any federal forts, buildings, or other installations erected on such land "will be free from any such interference and jurisdiction of the State as would destroy or impair their effective use for the purposes designed."

Other decisions built on the *Fort Leavenworth* framework. Thus, the Court held that Congress could prohibit persons from putting up fences on private land if this would block access to public lands, *Camfield v. United States* (1897); it could protect federal lands by prohibiting fires on neighboring property, *United States v. Alford* (1927); and it could authorize exterminating state-protected deer to prevent overbrowsing of federal lands, *Hunt v. United States* (1928). As the Court stated in *Camfield*:

> While we do not undertake to say that Congress has the unlimited power to legislate against nuisances within a State, which it would have within a Territory, we do not think the admission of a Territory as a State deprives it of the power of legislating for the protection of the public lands, though it may thereby involve the exercise of what is ordinarily known as the police power, so long as such power is directed solely to its own protection. A different rule would place the public domain of the United States completely at the mercy of state legislation.

The leading modern decision, *Kleppe v. New Mexico* (1976), reflects a further evolution in judicial understanding, as it in effect embraces the full-blown police power theory. At issue was the constitutionality of the Wild, Free-Roaming Horses and Burros Act of 1971, which prohibits capturing, killing, or harassing wild horses and burros that range on public lands. Writing for the Court, Justice Thurgood Marshall specifically rejected the contention that the Property Clause includes only "(1) the power to dispose of and make incidental rules regarding the use of federal property; and (2) the power to protect federal property." He concluded that "Congress exercises the powers both of a proprietor and of a legislature over the public domain." Thus, without regard to whether wild animals are the property of the United States, or whether the act could be justified as a form of protection of the public lands, Congress was said to have power to legislate with respect to federal lands "without limitations."

The *Kleppe* Court made no effort to justify this interpretation of the Property Clause in terms of original understanding. This plenary police power theory is in tension with the reference to "needful" rules and regulations "respecting" the "property belonging to the United States." This language seems to require some nexus between the exercise of power and the preservation of federal property. And as we have seen, the general police power interpretation probably goes beyond the original understanding of the clause. To date, Congress has generally refrained from drawing upon *Kleppe*'s expansive notion of federal power under the Property Clause. Consequently, the courts have had little occasion to follow up on *Kleppe*'s extravagant conception of the powers conferred by the clause.

Another issue that has simmered ever since the decision in *Pollard's Lessee*, and occasionally boils over, is whether the Property Clause (and Territories Clause) authorizes the indefinite retention of federal lands. The clauses mention disposal of territory and other property belonging to the United States, and authorizes needful rules and regulations of such property. But it says nothing about retention of such lands. The Enclave Clause, for its part, clearly contemplates indefinite retention of lands, but only for designated purposes and with the consent of the state in which the land is located. From the juxtaposition of these clauses, a number of commentators, especially those frustrated by the federal land bureaucracies in the western states, have argued that if the federal government fails to dispose of lands other than those acquired under the Enclave Clause, it must turn the land over to the states.

There is no clear original understanding about indefinite federal retention of lands outside the Enclave Clause. The issue probably did not occur to anyone at the time of the framing. The lands immediately subject to the Territories and Property Clauses, in the territories just west of the original thirteen colonies, were quickly sold or claimed and very little was retained by the federal government. Only much later, in the arid lands west of the 100th Meridian, did the federal government find that it held vast tracts of land that no one wanted. Whatever the original understanding, established practice has long been that the federal government may "reserve" vast tracts of these lands from disposition or sale. This is the origin of the many Indian reservations and military reservations in the west, not to mention the national parks, national forests, wildlife preserves, and wilderness areas that dot the landscape.

Other than the "sagebrush rebels" who want to throw off the yoke of the federal bureaucracies, general public sentiment has gradually turned against further private disposition of the federal public domain. The Federal Land Policy and Management Act of 1976 now declares it national policy that "the public lands be retained in federal ownership." The Property Clause is broad enough to support such a policy in any of its three possible interpretations. Only if we read the silence of the Constitution about retention (outside the Enclave Clause) to be an implied prohibition can it be maintained that retention of lands by the federal government is unconstitutional.

Thomas W. Merrill

See Also
Article I, Section 8, Clause 3 (Commerce Among the States)

Article I, Section 8, Clause 17 (Enclave Clause)
Article IV, Section 3, Clause 2 (Territories Clause)

Suggestions for Further Research
Peter A. Appel, *The Power of Congress "Without Limitation": The Property Clause and Federal Regulation of Private Property*, 86 Minn. L. Rev. 1 (2001)

David E. Engdahl, *State and Federal Power Over Federal Property*, 18 Ariz. L. Rev. 283 (1976)

Robert G. Natelson, *Federal Land Retention and the Constitution's Property Clause: The Original Understanding*, 76 Colo. L. Rev. 327 (2005)

Significant Cases
Pollard's Lessee v. Hagan, 44 U.S. (3 How.) 212 (1845)
Dred Scott v. Sandford, 60 U.S. (19 How.) 393 (1857)
Fort Leavenworth R.R.Co. v. Lowe, 114 U.S. 525 (1885)
Camfield v. United States, 167 U.S. 518 (1897)
United States v. Alford, 274 U.S. 264 (1927)
Hunt v. United States, 278 U.S. 96 (1928)
Kleppe v. New Mexico, 426 U.S. 529 (1976)

Claims

… [A]nd nothing in this Constitution shall be so construed as to Prejudice any Claims of the United States, or of any particular State.
(Article IV, Section 3, Clause 2)

~

*S*hortly after the Constitutional Convention had adopted a constitutional provision that required the consent of affected state legislatures if Congress tried to create a state out of the territory of any existing ones (Article IV, Section 3, Clause 1), the Framers faced a potentially divisive problem that arose from that provision. The Framers feared that states might weaken federal power by preventing Congress from making "needful rules and regulations" for admission to the Union of the western territory ceded to the United States during and after the American Revolution. The western land claims of many states were still unresolved, and the convention had adopted a provision that required the consent of state legislatures in order to create new states out of existing states; for these reasons, the Framers feared that some states might argue that any territory for which Congress would try to make "needful rules and regulations" was in fact their territory and so could not be prepared for admission to the Union by the United States.

To prevent such a misconstruction and protect the legitimate claims of the new federal government, Daniel Carroll of Maryland proposed at the convention that "nothing in this Constitution shall be construed to affect the claim of the U.S. to vacant lands ceded to them by the Treaty of peace." While holding that states were not sovereign nations and thus could not in principle claim land ceded by one nation (Britain) to another, James Madison recognized (as Justice Joseph Story later wrote in his *Commentaries on the Constitution of the United States*) that the question of "to whom of right belonged the vacant territory appertaining to the crown at the time of the revolution, whether to the states, within whose charter territory it was situated, or to the Union in its federative capacity" was "a subject of long and ardent controversy, and ... threatened to disturb the peace, if not to overthrow the government of the Union." To avert a potential crisis, Madison successfully proposed that the Convention should be "neutral and fair" and "ought to go farther and declare that the claims of particular States also should not be affected."

Since its adoption in the Constitution, this clause has spawned very little constitutional controversy and has functioned largely as its author hoped: by giving the same protection to both state and federal land claims, it diffused potential conflict over whose claims in the western territories would have constitutional preeminence. Potential conflicts were put over for decision by the political branches, which successfully handled the disposition of the western territories.

Jeffrey Sikkenga

See Also

Article IV, Section 3, Clause 1 (Admissions Clause)

Article IV, Section 3, Clause 2 (Territories Clause; Property Clause)

Suggestion for Further Research

Dale van Every, Ark of Empire: The American Frontier, 1784–1803 (1963)

Guarantee Clause

The United States shall guarantee to every State in this Union a Republican Form of Government, and shall protect each of them against Invasion; and on Application of the Legislature, or of the Executive (when the Legislature cannot be convened), against domestic Violence.

(Article IV, Section 4)

~

*T*his section is called the Guarantee Clause, because by its terms the federal government makes certain guarantees to the states. One of these—protection from foreign invasion—continued Congress's prior obligation under the Articles of Confederation. This guarantee is related to the principle that although the federation may be decentralized internally, it is to have a substantially common foreign policy and be seen as a unified sovereign in international law.

The other principal guarantee in Article IV, Section 4 is that the federal government will assure the states "a republican form of government." This assurance did not appear in the Articles of Confederation. The guarantee of protection from domestic violence can also be seen as part of the republican guarantee.

Founding-era dictionaries defined a "republic" as a "commonwealth," a "free state," and "a state or government in which the supreme power is lodged in more than one." In other words, a republic was a state governed by those citizens who enjoyed the franchise rather than by a monarch or autocrat. Accordingly, founding-era dictionaries often defined "republican" as "placing the government in the people."

Despite some shades of difference, the views of those participating in the constitutional debates of 1787–1789 were broadly consistent with the dictionary definitions. There was, moreover, a consensus as to three criteria of republicanism, the lack of any of which would render a government un-republican.

The first of these criteria was popular rule, broadly understood. The Founders believed that for government to be republican, political decisions had to be made by a majority (or in some cases, a plurality) of voting citizens. The citizenry might act either directly or through elected representatives. Either way, republican government was government accountable to the citizenry. To a generation immersed in Latin learning and looking to pre-imperial Rome for inspiration, a republic was very much *res publica*—the people's affair.

The second required element of republican government was that there be no monarch. The participants in the constitutional debates believed that monarchy, even constitutional monarchy, was inconsistent with republican government. When Alexander Hamilton proposed a president with lifetime tenure, the delegates disagreed so strongly that they did not even take the time to respond.

The third criterion for a republic was the rule of law, a concept deemed fundamental to a free state. The Framers believed that ex post facto laws, bills of attainder, extreme debtor-relief measures—most kinds of retroactive legislation, for example—were inconsistent with the rule of law, and therefore un-republican.

Some participants in the ratification debates (such as James Iredell of North Carolina) suggested an additional criterion of republicanism: absence of a titled aristocracy. This criterion was not part of the consensus, however, because other participants observed that some previous republics (e.g., pre-imperial Rome) and some contemporary republics (e.g., Holland) featured titled aristocracies. Indeed, the most influential contemporary foreign political writer, Baron de Montesquieu, divided republics into aristocracies and democracies. To assure, therefore, that the American states remained more purely democratic republics, the drafters

of the Constitution inserted Article I, Section 10, which forbids states from conferring titles of nobility.

It is sometimes claimed that the Founders wanted American governments to be "republics rather than democracies," but this claim is not quite accurate. As noted above, some dictionaries defined "republican" as "placing the government in the people" and writers such as Montesquieu and Ephraim Chambers considered a democracy as merely one form of republic. Leading Founders similarly employed the terms "democracy" and "republic" with overlapping or even interchangeable meanings. Although it is true that many of the Framers recoiled against the excesses of legislative democracy during the period prior to the Constitutional Convention, nonetheless in principle, only one species of democracy was deemed inconsistent with republicanism. This was "pure democracy" or "simple and perfect democracy," a theoretical constitution *identified* by Aristotle and mentioned by John Adams and James Madison, among others. A pure democracy had no magistrates, because the "mob" made all decisions, including all executive and judicial decisions. The Founders saw this kind of democracy as inconsistent with republicanism, because it did not honor the rule of law. The Guarantee Clause's protection against domestic violence assures orderly government and the rule of law, and protects the states' legitimate magistracy against mob rule.

The primary purpose of the Guarantee Clause, however, was not protection against pure democracy but against monarchy. Based on precedents in ancient Greece, the drafters feared that kings in one or more of the states would attempt to expand their power in ways that would destabilize the entire federation. They believed that having a republican government in each state was necessary to protect republican government throughout the United States.

There is not much federal case law on the Guarantee Clause, primarily because in the 1849 case of *Luther v. Borden*, the Supreme Court declared in dictum that enforcement of the clause is a political question for Congress and not a justiciable issue for the courts. With one minor deviation, the Court has continued to adhere to this doctrine. Examples are the Court's decisions in *Pacific States Telephone & Telegraph Co. v. Oregon* (1912) and *Baker v. Carr* (1962). Thus, citizens of a state who believe their state government is no longer republican should apply to Congress for relief rather than to the courts. Congressional control over what is a "republican form" is seen in the congressional admission of a state to the union, which legally implies that the state's then-existing constitution satisfies the Guarantee Clause. Yet the clause does not freeze that state constitution into place, but allows states wide latitude to innovate, so long as they retain the three basic elements of the republican form.

There has been somewhat more Guarantee Clause activity in state courts. Most have arisen when opponents of direct citizen lawmaking (initiative and referendum) argued that it violated the "republican form" for voters to legislate directly rather than through representatives, even though early in our history states often passed resolutions instructing their representatives on how to vote on certain issues. The Delaware Supreme Court accepted that argument in *Rice v. Foster* (1847). However, numerous citations from the founding era indicate that this argument is erroneous, and it has been rejected entirely or in part by all other state courts considering the issue. Examples include the supreme courts of Colorado, *Bernzen v. City of Boulder* (1974) and other cases; of Washington, *Hartig v. City of Seattle* (1909); and of Oregon, *Kadderly v. City of Portland* (1903).

The other portion of the clause declaring that the United States shall protect each state "against invasion" was designed by the Framers to prevent a sectional president from refusing to defend certain parts of the nation from foreign attack. As St. George Tucker noted in his *Blackstone's Commentaries* (1803), the provision guarded against "[t]he possibility of an undue partiality in the federal government in affording it's [sic] protection to one part of the union in preference to another, which may be invaded at the same time." There has been, however, no occasion when that section has been invoked.

Robert G. Natelson

See Also

Article I, Section 10, Clause 1 (State Title of Nobility)

Suggestions for Further Research

Akhil Reed Amar, America's Constitution: A Biography (2005), 276–81.

George M. Dennison, The Dorr War: Republicanism on Trial, 1831–1861 (1976)

Robert G. Natelson, *A Republic, Not a Democracy? Initiative, Referendum, and the Constitution's Guarantee Clause*, 80 Tex. L. Rev. 807 (2002)

M. N. S. Sellers, The Sacred Fire of Liberty: Republicanism, Liberalism, and the Law (1998)

St. George Tucker, Blackstone's Commentaries (1803)

William M. Wiecek, The Guarantee Clause of the U.S. Constitution (1972)

Founding-era Dictionaries:

Francis Allen, A Complete English Dictionary (1765)

John Ash, The New and Complete Dictionary of the English Language (1775)

Nicholas Bailey, An Universal Etymological English Dictionary (25th ed. 1783)

Ephraim Chambers, Cyclopaedia, or An Universal Dictionary of Arts and Sciences (1778–1781)

Samuel Johnson, A Dictionary of the English Language (8th ed. 1786)

Thomas Sheridan, A Complete Dictionary of the English Language (2d ed. 1789)

Significant Cases

Rice v. Foster, 4 Harr. 479 (De. 1847)

Luther v. Borden, 48 U.S. (7 How.) 1 (1849)

Minor v. Happersett, 88 U.S. (21 Wall.) 162 (1874)

Kadderly v. City of Portland, 44 Or. 118, 74 P. 710 (1903)

Hartig v. City of Seattle, 53 Wash. 432, 102 P. 408 (1909)

Pacific States Telephone & Telegraph Co. v. Oregon, 223 U.S. 118 (1912)

Baker v. Carr, 369 U.S. 186 (1962)

Bernzen v. City of Boulder, 186 Colo. 81, 525 P.2d 416 (1974)

ARTICLE V

Amendments

The Congress, whenever two thirds of both Houses shall deem it necessary, shall propose Amendments to this Constitution, or, on the Application of the Legislatures of two thirds of the several States, shall call a Convention for proposing Amendments, which, in either Case, shall be valid to all Intents and Purposes, as Part of this Constitution, when ratified by the Legislatures of three fourths of the several States, or by Conventions in three fourths thereof, as the one or the other Mode of Ratification may be proposed by the Congress..."

(ARTICLE V)

The process of amendment developed hand in hand with the emergence of written constitutions that established popular government. The charters established by William Penn in 1682 and 1683 provided for amending, as did eight of the state constitutions in effect in 1787. Three state constitutions provided for amendment through the legislature, and the other five gave the power to specially elected conventions.

The Articles of Confederation provided for amendments to be proposed by Congress and ratified by the unanimous vote of all thirteen state legislatures. This proved to be a major flaw in the Articles, as it created an insuperable obstacle to constitutional reform. The amendment process in the Constitution, as James Madison explained in *The Federalist* No. 43, was meant to establish a balance between the excesses of constant change and inflexibility: "It guards equally against that extreme facility which would render the Constitution too mutable; and that extreme difficulty, which might perpetuate its discovered faults."

In his *Commentaries on the Constitution of the United States* (1833), Justice Joseph Story wrote that a government that provides

> no means of change, but assumes to be fixed and unalterable, must, after a while, become wholly unsuited to the circumstances of the nation; and it will either degenerate into a despotism, or by the pressure of its inequalities bring on a revolution.... The great principle to be sought is to make the changes practicable, but not too easy; to secure due deliberation, and caution; and to follow experience, rather than to open a way for experiments, suggested by mere speculation or theory.

In its final form, Article V creates two ways to propose amendments to the Constitution: through Congress or by a special convention called by the states for the purpose of proposing amendments (Article V, Convention for Proposing Amendments). In either case, the proposed amendment or amendments must then be ratified by the states, either (as determined by Congress) by state legislatures or by ratifying conventions in the states.

More significantly, the double supermajority requirements—two-thirds of both houses of Congress and three-quarters of the states—create extensive deliberation and stability in the amendment process and restrain factions and special interests. It helps to maintain the Constitution as a "constitution" and not an assemblage of legislative enactments. It also roots the amending process in the Founders' unique concept of structural federalism based on the dual sovereignty of the state and national governments.

The Virginia Plan introduced at the start of the Constitutional Convention called only in a general way for an amendment process that would allow but not require amendment by the national legislature "whensoever it shall seem necessary." The Committee of Detail proposed a process whereby Congress would call for an amendments convention on the request of two-thirds of the state legislatures. After further debate, the delegates passed language, proposed by Madison (and seconded by Alexander Hamilton), that the national legislature would propose amendments when two-thirds of each house of Congress deem it necessary, or on the application of two-thirds of the state legislatures. Proposed amendments were to be ratified by three-fourths of the states in their legislatures or by state convention. Just before the end of the Convention, George Mason objected that the amendment proposal would allow Congress to block as well as propose amendments, and the method was changed once again to require Congress to call a convention to propose amendments on the application of two-thirds of the states.

The Constitutional Convention made two specific exceptions to the Amendments Clause of Article V, one concerning the slave trade (Prohibition on Amendment: Migration or Importation) and another on voting in the Senate (Prohibition on Amendment: Equal Suffrage in the Senate), but defeated a motion to prevent amendments that affected internal police powers in the states.

The advantage of the Amendments Clause was immediately apparent. The lack of a bill of rights—the Convention had considered and rejected this option—became a rallying cry during the ratification debate. Partly to head off an attempt to call for another general convention or a formal amendments convention under Article V, but mostly to legitimize the Constitution among patriots who were Anti-Federalists, the advocates of the Constitution (led by Madison) agreed to add amendments in the first session of Congress. North Carolina and Rhode Island acceded to the Constitution, and further disagreements were cabined within the constitutional structure.

Madison had wanted the amendments that became the Bill of Rights to be interwoven into the relevant sections of the Constitution. More for stylistic rather than substantive reasons, though, Congress proposed (and set the precedent for) amendments appended separately at the end of the document. Some have argued that this method makes amendments more susceptible to an activist interpretation than they would be otherwise.

Since 1789, well over five thousand bills proposing to amend the Constitution have been introduced in Congress; thirty-three amendments have been sent to the states for ratification. Of those sent to the states, two have been defeated, four are still pending, and twenty-seven have been ratified. Because of the national distribution of representation in Congress, most amendment proposals are defeated by a lack of general support and those amendments that are proposed to the states by Congress are likely to be ratified.

In a challenge to the Eleventh Amendment, the Supreme Court waved aside the suggestion that amendments proposed by Congress must be submitted to the president according to the Presentment Clause (Article I, Section 7, Clause 2). *Hollingsworth v. Virginia* (1798). In *The National Prohibition Cases* (1920), the Court held that the "two-thirds of both Houses" requirement applies to a present quorum, not the total membership of each body. One year later, in *Dillon v. Gloss* (1921), the Court allowed Congress, when proposing an amendment, to set a reasonable time limit for ratification by the states. Since 1924, no amendment has been proposed without a ratification time limit, although the Twenty-seventh Amendment, proposed by Madison in the First Congress more than two hundred years ago, was finally ratified in 1992.

Regardless of how an amendment is proposed, Article V gives Congress authority to direct the mode of ratification. *United States v. Sprague* (1931). Of the ratified amendments, all but the Twenty-first Amendment, which was ratified by state conventions, have been ratified by state legislatures. In *Hawke v. Smith* (1920), the Court struck down an attempt by Ohio to make that state's ratification of constitutional amendments subject to a vote of the people, holding that where Article V gives authority to state legislatures, these bodies are exercising a federal function.

Although some scholars have asserted that certain kinds of constitutional amendments might be "unconstitutional," actual substantive challenges to amendments have so far been unsuccessful. *National Prohibition Cases*; *Leser v. Garnett* (1922). The Supreme Court's consideration of procedural challenges thus far does not extend beyond the decision of *Coleman v. Miller* (1939), dealing with Kansas's ratification of a child labor amendment. The Court split on whether state ratification disputes are nonjusticiable political questions, but then held that Congress, "in controlling the promulgation of the adoption of constitutional amendment[s]," should have final authority over ratification controversies.

The careful consideration of the amending power calls into question theories claiming the right of the Supreme Court to superintend a "living" or "evolving" Constitution outside of the amendment process. Non-originalist versions of this argument are those of Akhil Amar, who contends that Article V limits only government and that the people can propose and ratify amendments by popular vote, and Bruce Ackerman, who posits that extra-constitutional "constitutional moments" (such as the period after the Civil War or the New Deal) effectively amend the Constitution through politics (e.g., the election of 1936) followed by judicial codification (e.g., Supreme Court decisions upholding New Deal legislation).

In the end, the Framers believed that the amendment process would protect the Constitution from undue change at the same time that it would strengthen the authority of the Constitution with the people by allowing its deliberate reform while elevating it above immediate political passions. "The basis of our political systems is the right of the people to make and to alter their Constitutions of Government," George Washington wrote in his Farewell Address of 1796. "But the Constitution which at any time exists, 'till changed by an explicit and authentic act of the whole People, is sacredly obligatory upon all."

Matthew Spalding and Trent England

See Also
Article I, Section 7, Clause 2 (Presentment Clause)
Article V (Convention for Proposing Amendments)
Article V (Prohibition on Amendment: Migration or Importation)

Article V (Prohibition on Amendment Equal Suffrage in the Senate)

Suggestions for Further Research
Richard B. Bernstein, Amending America: If We Love the Constitution So Much, Why Do We Keep Trying to Change It? (1993)

Richard B. Bernstein, *The Sleeper Wakes: The History and Legacy of the Twenty-seventh Amendment*, 61 Fordham L. Rev. 497 (1992)

Robert A. Goldwin, From Parchment to Power: How James Madison Used the Bill of Rights to Save the Constitution (1997)

Edward A. Hartnett, *A "Uniform and Entire" Constitution; Or, What If Madison Had Won?*, 15 Const. Comment. 251 (1998)

Seth Barrett Tillman, *A Textualist Defense of Article I, Section 7, Clause 3: Why* Hollingsworth v. Virginia *Was Rightly Decided, and Why* INS v. Chadha *Was Wrongly Reasoned* 83 Tex. L. Rev. 1265 (2005)

John R. Vile, The Constitutional Amending Process in American Political Thought (1992)

Significant Cases
Hollingsworth v. Virginia, 3 U.S. (3 Dall.) 378 (1798)
Hawke v. Smith, 253 U.S. 221 (1920)
National Prohibition Cases, 253 U.S. 350 (1920)
Dillon v. Gloss, 256 U.S. 368 (1921)
Leser v. Garnett, 258 U.S. 130 (1922)
United States v. Sprague, 282 U.S. 716 (1931)
Coleman v. Miller, 307 U.S. 433 (1939)

Convention for Proposing Amendments

The Congress,...on the Application of the Legislatures of two thirds of the several States, shall call a Convention for proposing Amendments,..."

(ARTICLE V)

~

*A*fter the Virginia Plan introduced at the start of the Constitutional Convention called in a general way for an amendment process that would allow but not require amendment by the national legislature "whensoever it shall seem necessary," the Committee of Detail proposed a process whereby Congress would call for an amendments convention on the request of two-thirds of the state legislatures. George Mason feared this method was insufficient to protect the states, while Alexander Hamilton thought that Congress should be able to propose amendments independent of the states. Madison (as recorded in his *Notes of Debates in the Federal Convention of 1787*) thought the vagueness of an amendments convention sufficiently problematic to reject the provision: "How was a Convention to be formed? By what rule decide? What the force of its acts?" After further debate, the delegates passed language proposed by Madison (and seconded by Alexander Hamilton) that combined the two ideas without an amendments convention: the national legislature would propose amendments when two-thirds of each house of Congress deemed it necessary, or on the application of two-thirds of the state legislatures. Proposed amendments were to be ratified by three-fourths of the states in their legislatures or by state convention.

Just before the end of the convention, George Mason objected that the amendment proposal would allow Congress to block as well as propose amendments, and the method was changed once again to require Congress to call a convention to propose amendments on the application of two-thirds of the states. Madison did not see why Congress would not be equally bound by two-thirds of the states' directly proposing amendments (his original proposal for the states' initiation of amendments) as opposed to the same number calling for an amendments convention, especially when the proposed Article V convention process left so many unresolved questions. In the end, Madison accepted the compromise to include an amendments convention but consistent with his earlier comments warned "that difficulties might arise as to the form, the quorum etc. which in constitutional regulations ought to be as much as possible avoided."

As Madison predicted, the numerous unanswered questions inherent in the Article V amendments convention process have prevented

its use. A first set of questions concerns calling the convention. The language here is "peremptory" according to Alexander Hamilton in *The Federalist* No. 85: "The Congress '*shall* call a convention.' Nothing in this particular is left to the discretion of that body." Nevertheless, there is dispute about the tabulation of applications in triggering that call. There have been hundreds of applications for an amending convention over the years from virtually every state; some argue that there are currently more than enough applications to require Congress to call a convention. While various organizations have tabulated state applications, Congress has never officially tabulated or listed applications and has established no process for doing so. It is unclear, despite Hamilton's confidence, whether Congress could be compelled to call an Article V convention if it chose not to.

A second set of questions concerns whether such a convention can be limited in scope, either to a particular proposal or within a particular subject. While most calls for amendments conventions in the nineteenth century were general, the modern trend is to call (and thus count applications) for conventions limited to considering a single amendment. There seems to be a consensus that a convention cannot be limited to considering a specific amendment, as merely confirming a particular amendment already written, approved, and proposed by state legislatures would effectively turn the convention for *proposing* amendments into a *ratifying* convention. The debate focuses rather on whether a convention must be general and without limits or whether the convention can or even must be limited to a subject or subject areas based on state applications.

Still, some scholars, such as Michael Rappaport, do suggest that a "ratifying convention" is not outside the scope of Article V. As evidence, they cite James Madison's initial suggestion (that two thirds of the states should be able to propose amendments directly) and argue that the addition of a convention was merely to facilitate communication amongst the states in order to develop proposed amendments. If, however, two-thirds of the states were able to agree on the text of an amendment beforehand, then restricting the convention to an affirmation of that amendment would be appropriate.

Michael Stokes Paulsen makes an originalist argument that a convention properly understood holds broad powers as a deliberative political body. Other scholars argue from an originalist view that the states determine through their applications whether a convention is general or limited, and that an Article V convention is an agent of and responsible to the states. Robert G. Natelson has made a case for this view based on the history of interstate meetings prior to the Constitutional Convention. Nevertheless, it is not at all clear as a matter of constitutional construction that the power of two-thirds of the states to make applications for a convention restricts, supersedes, or overrides the power of all the states assembled in that convention to propose amendments to the Constitution. *The Federalist Papers*, unfortunately, offer little guidance on this matter. Madison refers to amendments conventions in *The Federalist* No. 43 only in general terms, noting that Article V "equally enables the general and the State governments to originate the amendment of errors." And in *The Federalist* No. 85, while discussing how Congress cannot limit the scope of an Article V convention, Hamilton says nothing as to whether states can or cannot do so.

A third set of questions concerns the many practical aspects of how an amendments convention would operate (time, place, duration, voting procedure, etc.) and whether authority over some or all of these questions belongs to the states or is implied in Congress's power to call the convention. Congress has historically understood its authority to "call" a convention as a broad mandate to establish procedures for such a convention, and in the last forty years has considered (but not passed) numerous bills to that effect. These procedural issues (along with limiting the subject matter of the convention) raise a further question as to whether Congress can refuse to forward amendments for ratification if those amendments are deemed to be beyond the scope of the convention.

Lastly, there is the general question whether and to what extent aspects of such a convention (including going beyond its instructions) would be subject to judicial review. A suit asserting that existing applications require Congress to call an Article V convention, for instance, was denied at the district court level (and later denied certiorari) as without standing and because it raised political questions more properly the province of Congress. *Walker v. United States* (2001).

While a valid method created and available under the Constitution, "a Convention for proposing Amendments" has never been viewed as a tool for reform as much as an option to be deployed in extremis for the sake of maintaining the Constitution. Hence, the only time Madison proposed an amendments convention was during the Nullification Crisis of 1832, seeing it as a last ditch effort to prevent the unconstitutional alternatives of nullification and secession that then threatened the continued existence of the United States. Likewise, when Abraham Lincoln looked to constitutional reforms to resolve disputed questions in the midst of the Civil War, he noted that "under existing circumstances" the convention mode "seems preferable" precisely because it "allows amendments to originate with the people themselves, instead of only permitting them to take or reject propositions originated by others, not especially chosen for the purpose." Yet when the immediate crisis was over, Lincoln strongly advocated what became the Thirteenth Amendment by congressional proposal and did not pursue an amendments convention, despite the amendment's initial failure in the House of Representatives. It should be noted that in both cases an amendments convention was understood to be free to propose whatever amendments thought necessary to address the problems at issue.

The requirement that amendments proposed by such a convention must be ratified by three-fourths of the states is a significant limit on the process and likely prevents a true "runaway" convention from fundamentally altering the Constitution. It is worth noting, however, that of the amendments that have been proposed to the states the vast majority (twenty-seven out of thirty-three) have been ratified. Because of the lack of clear intentions or constitutional precedent, scholars will undoubtedly continue to debate the historical record and speculate about the possibility of an amendments convention under Article V.

Precisely because of the potential chaos of the process, the very threat of an amendments convention can be used to pressure Congress to act rather than risk an amendments convention.

The movement favoring direct election of senators was just one state away from an amending convention when Congress proposed the Seventeenth Amendment in 1911. There was also an effort to overturn the Supreme Court's 1964 one man, one vote decisions (*Wesberry v. Sanders* and *Reynolds v. Sims*). By 1969, the proponents obtained thirty-three state applications for a convention to consider amendments regarding legislative apportionment in the states; one vote short of the two-thirds necessary for Congress to call an amendments convention. Most recently, in the 1980s, state applications for a convention to propose a balanced budget amendment led Congress to vote on such an amendment and pass the Gramm-Rudman-Hollings Act (later declared unconstitutional in part by the Supreme Court) requiring the federal budget to be balanced.

Following the 2010 elections, renewed efforts on both sides of the political spectrum have looked to an Article V amendments convention as a way for the states to circumvent Congress in order to achieve various policy outcomes, in particular to propose a balanced budget amendment. More recently, some scholars, recognizing the many unknowns of an Article V amendments convention, have suggested that an agreement among two-thirds of the states under the Compact Clause (Article I, Section 10, Clause 3) could be used to address many of the procedural questions involved in that process.

Matthew Spalding

See Also

Article V (Amendments)
Article V (Prohibition on Amendment: Migration or Importation)
Article V (Prohibition on Amendment Equal Suffrage in the Senate)

Suggestions for Further Research

Russell L. Caplan, Constitutional Brinksmanship: Amending the Constitution by National Convention (1988)

John O. McGinnis & Michael B. Rappaport, *Our Supermajoritarian Constitution*, 80 Tex. L. Rev. 703 (2002)

Henry P. Monaghan, *We the People[s], Original Understanding, and Constitutional Amendment*, 96 Colum. L. Rev. 121 (1996)

Robert G. Natelson, *Proposing Constitutional Amendments by Convention: Rules Governing the Process*, 78 Tenn. L. Rev. 693 (2011)

Michael Stokes Paulsen, *How to Count to Thirty-Four: The Constitutional Case for a Constitutional Convention*, 34 Harv. J.L. & Pub. Pol'y 837 (2011)

Michael B. Rappaport, *The Constitutionality of a Limited Convention: An Originalist Analysis* 28 Const. Comment. 53 (2012)

Michael B. Rappaport, *Reforming Article V: The Problems Created by the National Convention Amendment Method and How to Fix Them*, 96 Va. L. Rev. 1511 (2010)

James Kenneth Rogers, *The Other Way to Amend the Constitution: The Article V Constitutional Convention Amendment Process*, 30 Harv. J.L. & Pub. Pol'y 1005 (2007)

Significant Cases

Wesberry v. Sanders, 376 U.S. 1 (1964)
Reynolds v. Sims, 377 U.S. 533 (1964)
Walker v. United States (W.D. Wash., C00-2125C, March 21, 2001)

Prohibition on Amendment: Migration or Importation

...no Amendment which may be made prior to the Year One thousand eight hundred and eight shall in any Manner affect the first and fourth Clauses in the Ninth Section of the first Article ...

(Article V)

~

*T*oward the end of the Constitutional Convention, after previous clauses concerning slavery had been settled, and in the midst of the discussion about the process of amending the Constitution, John Rutledge of South Carolina declared that "he never could agree to give a power by which the articles relating to slaves might be altered by the States not interested in that property and prejudiced against it." An addition to the clause was immediately agreed to that forbade amending the Migration or Importation Clause (Article I, Section 9, Clause 1) and the Direct Taxes Clause (Article I, Section 9, Clause 4) prior to 1808, after which Congress could regulate the slave trade.

This provision calls attention to the delicacy and precariousness of the compromises involved in these two clauses. Even though only a few states had begun to move toward abolition or gradual emancipation at the time, the tide of anti-slavery opinion seemed so strong as to excite the demands of Georgia and South Carolina in particular to preserve the institution at least within their own states. Taking a mid-summer break from the convention and knowing Southern opinion on the matter, Alexander Hamilton—without breaking his pledge of secrecy—prevailed upon John Jay and the New York Manumission Society not to submit a proposed petition to the Constitutional Convention to abolish slavery. At Hamilton's request, Jay even destroyed his draft of the petition.

Protecting the slave trade in the Migration or Importation Clause revealed Southern concerns about the strength of antislavery opinion (which was at that time focused on stopping the slave trade). In fact, in 1787, only North Carolina and Georgia permitted the importation of slaves, and so the slave states thought that it might be difficult to prevent a coalition of Northern and upper Southern states from changing the Constitution on this question by amendment. Likewise, shielding the Direct Taxes Clause was an indirect way to emphasize the "Three-fifths Compromise" (Article I, Section 2, Clause 3) concerning the apportionment of direct taxes, as well as adding "other taxes" to that ratio, reflecting significant fears that the power to tax could be used to undermine the institution of slavery. Earlier, Gouverneur Morris, the most outspoken opponent of slavery at the convention, nonetheless conceded that "he did not believe that those [southern] States would ever confederate on terms that would deprive them of that trade."

Underscoring the temporary nature of the compromise, language in Article V ties the Direct Taxes Clause to this clause's "implied invitation" to legislate on the slave trade after 1808. By that time, the internal production of slaves would be sufficient to supply the growing market so that economic self-interest did not stand in the way of legislation based on the moral revulsion to the slave trade. Congress accepted the invitation, and although the law underwent several modifications in subsequent years, on March 2, 1807, it passed a federal prohibition of the slave trade, effective January 1, 1808. The vote in the Senate had been eighteen to nine (with seven abstentions) and, in the House, 113 to five (with twenty-two not voting). A few weeks later, on March 25, 1807, following decades of agitation by William Wilberforce, the British Parliament also banned the trade.

Interestingly, reference to the Fugitive Slave Clause (Article IV, Section 2, Clause 3) is not included here among the clauses protected from amendment. The omission signifies the broad consensus supporting the Fugitive Slave Clause and the fact that it was not at the time thought to be controversial.

Matthew Spalding

See Also

Article I, Section 2, Clause 3 (Three-fifths Clause)

Article I, Section 9, Clause 1 (Migration or Importation Clause)

Article I, Section 9, Clause 4 (Direct Taxes)

Article IV, Section 2, Clause 3 (Fugitive Slave Clause)

Suggestions for Further Research

Paul Finkelman, *The American Suppression of the African Slave Trade: Lessons on Legal Change, Social Policy, and Legislation*, 42 Akron L. Rev. 431 (2009)

Henry P. Monaghan, *We the People[s], Original Understanding, and Constitutional Amendment*, 96 Colum. L. Rev. 121 (1996)

Prohibition on Amendment: Equal Suffrage in the Senate

...no State, without its consent, shall be deprived of its equal Suffrage in the Senate.

(Article V)

*A*rticle V specifies the means by which the Constitution can be amended. It ends by forbidding amendments that would repeal the language in Article I, Section 9, which prohibits a ban on the importation of slaves prior to 1808, or the language in Article I, Section 3, which provides for equal representation of the states in the Senate. These are the only textually entrenched provisions of the Constitution. The first prohibition was absolute but of limited duration—it was to be in force for only twenty years; the second was less absolute—"no state, without its consent, shall be deprived of its equal Suffrage in the Senate"—but permanent.

The first unamendable provision of the Constitution was part of what Frederick Douglass called the "scaffolding" necessary for the construction and adoption of the Constitution's "magnificent structure, to be removed as soon as the building was completed." The second unamendable provision shows how seriously the smaller states were committed to protecting the "original federal design." Its sponsor was Roger Sherman of Connecticut, architect of what is often called the Connecticut Compromise or "the Great Compromise," whereby states were to be represented proportionally in the House and equally in the Senate. Two days before the convention ended, on September 15, Sherman "expressed his fears that three fourths of the States might be brought to do things fatal to particular States, as abolishing them altogether or depriving them of their equality in the Senate." He therefore proposed language barring amending the Constitution to deprive states of their equal suffrage. When his motion failed, Sherman indicated how profoundly concerned he was by proposing the elimination of Article V altogether. This motion also failed, but it prompted Gouverneur Morris to propose the language ultimately adopted by the Constitutional Convention. As James Madison wrote in his notes, "This motion being dictated by the circulating murmurs of the small States was agreed to without debate, no one opposing it, or on the question saying no."

The provision does more than protect the equal representation of small states. As Madison noted in *The Federalist* No. 39, it ensures a polity of mixed sovereignty, one in which the states are an integral part of the federal government. This, of course, is precisely why those who do not think the Constitution "democratic" enough would wish to remove that portion of the Constitution. They argue variously that Article V can be amended through the convention mechanism; or by the people as a whole as stated in the Preamble; or, more brazenly, by first amending out the provision of the Fifth Article, and then requiring the Senate to be apportioned by population. Henry Monaghan points out that such proposals are inconsistent with the vision of the Framers and would undermine the structural plan of the Constitution. That plan is an integrated and dynamic federalism.

As Chief Justice Salmon Chase declared in *Texas v. White* (1869):

> Not only, therefore, can there be no loss of separate and independent autonomy to the States, through their union under the Constitution, but it may be not unreasonably said that the preservation of the States, and the maintenance of their governments, are as much within the design and care of the Constitution as the preservation of the Union and the maintenance of the National government. The Constitution, in all its provisions, looks to an indestructible Union, composed of indestructible States.

Denying the states their intended role in the federal government by abolishing their equality in the Senate would destroy the grounding of the Union: "without the States in union, there could be no such political body as the United States," *Texas v. White*, citing *Lane County v. Oregon* (1869). Moreover, as the text itself stands, at most the provision could only technically be voided by the unanimous consent of all the states.

This provision has been seldom invoked. Most recently, it has been employed by those opposed to proposed constitutional amendments that would give the District of Columbia full representation in Congress. Their argument is that an amendment that would allow the district—a nonstate—to have two senators would deprive the states of their equal suffrage in the Senate and would therefore require unanimous ratification by all the states. Others have suggested that the provision would void a constitutional amendment requiring a superma-jority to pass tax increases.

Ralph Rossum

See Also

Article I, Section 3, Clause 1 (Senate)
Article V

Suggestions for Further Research

Akhil R. Amar, *The Consent of the Governed: Consti-tutional Amendment Outside Article V*, 94 COLUM. L. REV. 457 (1994)

Lynn A. Baker, *Federalism: The Argument from Article V*, 13 GA. ST. U. L. REV. 923 (1997)

Henry P. Monaghan, *We the People[s], Original Understanding, and Constitutional Amendment*, 96 COLUM. L. REV. 121 (1996)

Eric A. Posner & Adrian Vermeule, *Legislative Entrenchment: A Reappraisal*, 111 YALE L.J. 1665 (2002)

John O. McGinnis & Michael B. Rappaport, *Symmetric Entrenchment: A Constitutional and Normative Theory*, 89 VA. L. REV. 385 (2003)

Stewart E. Sterk, *Retrenchment on Entrenchment*, 71 GEO. WASH. L. REV. 231 (2003)

Significant Cases

Lane County v. Oregon, 74 U.S. (7 Wall.) 71 (1869)
Texas v. White, 74 U.S. (7 Wall.) 700 (1869)

ARTICLE VI

Debt Assumption

All Debts contracted and Engage-ments entered into, before the Adoption of this Constitution, shall be as valid against the United States under this Constitution, as under the Confederation.

(ARTICLE VI, CLAUSE 1)

~

To finance the War of Independence, the American states and the Continental Con-gress sold millions of dollars in public bonds to soldiers, ordinary Americans, and investors both within America and abroad. The Consti-tutional Convention first addressed the debt issue during its debates on the proposed powers of Congress. On August 21, 1787, the Conven-tion considered this proposal: "The Legislature

of the U.S. shall have the power to fulfil the engagements which have been entered into by Congress, and to discharge as well the debts of the U-S: as the debts incurred by the sev-eral States during the late war, for the common defence and general welfare."

Whether Congress could discharge the state debts was left unsettled because the ensu-ing debate centered on a different question: Would the new federal government necessarily inherit the debt obligations of the old Conti-nental and Confederation Congresses? There was precedent for such an action in Article XII of the Articles of Confederation, which declared that the Confederation Congress was liable for "monies borrowed and debts contracted by" the old Continental Congress.

Nor was this the only support. Writers on the law of nations, such as Dutch jurist Hugo Grotius, held that the various forms of government were only different means by which political societies achieved the same basic ends. In their view, political societies existed prior to and separate from their particular forms of government (e.g., monarchy or aristocracy), and they could change that form without destroying their existence or altering their fundamental obligations to other countries.

Elbridge Gerry objected that the August 21 proposal only gave the new Congress the "power" rather than the obligation to pay back the debt. He feared that this wording would allow Congress to neglect the rightful return on bonds due to the creditor "class of citizens." To Oliver Ellsworth and Roger Sherman, such a concern was misplaced because the "U-S heretofore entered into Engagements" by Congresses "who were their agents" and "will hereafter be bound to fulfil them by their new agents."

While Edmund Randolph agreed that the United States was still liable for its obligations, he maintained that the "new Govt" was one of enumerated powers and thus would have only the power given to it by the Constitution. Without an explicit grant of constitutional power, the federal government would be in the strange position of not having the authority to pay off the debts still owed by the country. Unlike Randolph, James Madison held that the obligation to pay debts necessarily conferred the power to pay debts whether or not the Constitution gave the new government such a specific power. Madison argued that the new federal government would receive its constitutional power in domestic matters through enumerated grants from the people of the states; but the states themselves "never possessed the essential rights of sovereignty," which were "war, peace, treaties," and other powers over external affairs. Thus, in matters relating to repayment of debts to foreign bondholders, the new national government would inherit its powers directly from the Articles. Thus, Congress did not need an explicit grant of power from the new Constitution. In defending the clause against Anti-Federalist criticism, Madison maintained that its insertion was not a legal or constitutional necessity but was done only "for the satisfaction of the foreign creditors of the United States." *The Federalist* No. 43.

Following a motion by Gouverneur Morris on August 25, the convention changed the clause from a grant of power to Congress to an obligation of the United States. The change was then accepted by the convention, which split the power to "pay the Debts," leaving it in Article I, Section 8, from the obligation to uphold "debts" and "Engagements," moving the latter to Article VI. A few commentators later thought that "engagements" also referred to the central government's obligations to the people of the Northwest Territory under the Northwest Ordinance (1787), but none of the Framers in Philadelphia made that connection while debating the clause.

After some political struggles in the early 1790s, the new federal government made good on the bond obligations inherited from the Articles of Confederation, thus vitiating the possibility for serious constitutional controversy. Subsequently, early Supreme Court cases like *Ware v. Hylton* (1796) and *Terrett v. Taylor* (1815) settled constitutional issues of contracts and property rights from the pre-Constitution era, not by interpreting the Debt Assumption Clause, but by invoking the Supremacy Clause of Article VI.

The clause's purpose, therefore, was less legal than it was to reaffirm the Grotian principle that the nation as a juridical entity maintained its international obligations even through changes in the form of government. Inasmuch as a primary motivation for the calling the Constitutional Convention was to create a solid financial basis for the country to honor its foreign debts, the Debt Assumption Clause had a salutary effect on the United States' standing in the international community.

Jeffrey Sikkenga

See Also
Article I, Section 8, Clause 1 (Spending Clause)

Suggestions for Further Research
David P. Currie, *The Constitution in Congress: Substantive Issues in the First Congress, 1789–1791*, 61 U. Chi. L. Rev. 775 (1994)

Peter Onuf, Statehood and Union: A History of the Northwest Ordinance (1987)

Significant Cases

Ware v. Hylton, 3 U.S. (3 Dall.) 199 (1796)

Terrett v. Taylor, 13 U.S. (9 Cranch) 43 (1815)

Supremacy Clause

This Constitution, and the Laws of the United States which shall be made in Pursuance thereof; and all Treaties made, or which shall be made, under the Authority of the United States, shall be the supreme Law of the Land; and the Judges in every State shall be bound thereby, any Thing in the Constitution or Laws of any State to the Contrary notwithstanding.

(ARTICLE VI, CLAUSE 2)

~

*A*ny federal system needs a strategy for dealing with potential conflicts between the national and local governments. There are at least three strategies available. First, each government could be given exclusive jurisdiction over its respective sphere, which would avoid altogether the possibility of direct conflict. Second, the governments could have concurrent jurisdiction, but one government could be given power to veto actions of the other, either in the event of actual conflict or in general classes of cases. Third, both governments could be allowed to act without mutual interference, but one government's acts could be given primacy over the other's acts in the event of actual conflict.

The Supremacy Clause embodies the third strategy. It is a conflict-of-laws rule specifying that certain national acts take priority over any state act that conflicts with national law. In this respect, the Supremacy Clause follows the lead of Article XIII of the Articles of Confederation, which provided that "[e]very state shall abide by the determinations of the united states in congress assembled, on all questions which by this confederation are submitted to them." While the last portion of the Supremacy Clause specifically

singles out only state court judges as bound by federal law, the declaration of federal supremacy in the clause's opening portion is general and binds all legal actors, ranging from federal officials to state jurors. In fact, Article VI, Clause 3, the Oaths Clause, requires all legislative, executive, and judicial officers of both state and federal governments to swear to support the U.S. Constitution.

The Supremacy Clause does not distinguish among the three named sources of federal law: the Constitution, the laws of the United States, and treaties. All are equally supreme over competing sources of state law or other sources of federal law (such as federal common law). Thus, the Supremacy Clause does not itself establish the supremacy of the Constitution over federal statutes or treaties. Rather, constitutional primacy over other sources of "supreme" federal law is a structural inference from the nature of the Constitution—as elaborated by Chief Justice John Marshall in *Marbury v Madison* (1803). The sequencing of sources of federal law in the Supremacy Clause, with the Constitution coming first, is some modest evidence in favor of constitutional primacy, which is precisely how Marshall's argument in *Marbury* employed the clause. One could use similar intra-textual and structural considerations to argue that federal statutes must always take precedence over federal treaties, but standard law has long been that federal statutes and treaties are equally supreme, with the latest enactment controlling in the event of conflict between them.

Modern law also treats federal administrative regulations as supreme over competing sources of state law. *See Geier v. American Honda Motor Co., Inc.* (2000). This conclusion rests more uneasily with the language of the Supremacy Clause, which names only the Constitution, the laws of the United States made pursuant thereto, and treaties as supreme federal instruments. Normally, one thinks of the "Laws of the United States...made in Pursuance" of the Constitution as statutes enacted in accordance with the lawmaking procedures of Article I, Section 7, and administrative regulations do not fit that description. But the courts have attempted to resolve the possible contradiction by holding that administrative regulations are made pursuant to a delegation of law from Congress. Thus, they take on the character of federal "laws." Whatever the correct answer may be as a matter of original meaning, the principle of federal regulatory supremacy over state law is now firmly established. Indeed, federal regulations have emerged as the most frequent source of federal-state conflicts.

The Supremacy Clause does not grant power to any federal actor, such as Congress. It is an interpretative rule that deals with resolving conflicts between the federal and state governments once federal power has been validly exercised. It does not preclude other strategies for dealing with potential national and state conflicts, nor does it allocate power between the national and state governments. Other parts of the Constitution do that.

There was support at the Constitutional Convention for a supremacy clause that would adopt other conflict-resolving strategies. James Madison, among others, favored a direct congressional power to veto state laws, and he even seconded the strong proposal of Charles Pinckney "that the National Legislature shd. have authority to negative all [state] Laws which they shd. judge to be improper." The Convention repeatedly rejected all such proposals for a federal veto power over state laws. The objective of the Framers throughout was to devise strategies that would reduce occasions for national and state conflict.

The Supremacy Clause in its final form was adopted by the Convention without serious dissent. Indeed, the essence of its final form was proposed by the Anti-Federalist Luther Martin. While some Anti-Federalists subsequently objected in broad terms to the prospect of federal supremacy, nothing in those debates negated the general understanding that the Supremacy Clause was a straightforward conflict-of-laws rule designed to resolve conflicts between state and federal law touching on the same subject.

The clause's language, context, and history leave some important questions unanswered. For example, what constitutes a conflict? Must it be literally impossible to comply with both the state and federal rules, or is it enough that a state's law will in some fashion alter or stand as an obstacle to the operation of the federal rule?

Properly applied as a conflict-of-laws provision, the Supremacy Clause would lead a common law court to acknowledge that a conflict does not always occur simply because two sovereigns have legislated on a common subject; both Congress and the courts recognize that principle today.

Consequently, the modern Court has fashioned subsidiary rules to try to determine when there is a genuine conflict between a state and federal law on the same subject, or, in modern parlance, whether the federal law has "preempted" the state law. Modern doctrine generally holds that preemption occurs whenever it is intended by Congress. That intent, of course, can most directly be demonstrated by an express provision in a federal statute declaring the statute's preemptive effect (or lack thereof). Even in the absence of an express preemption provision, however, state law is preempted "[w]hen Congress intends federal law to 'occupy the field'" or "to the extent of any conflict with a federal statute." *Crosby v. National Foreign Trade Council* (2000). Conflicts can also result either when it is literally impossible to comply with both state and federal law, *Pliva, Inc. v. Mensing* (2011), or, much more commonly, when a state law "stands as an obstacle to the accomplishment and execution of the full purposes and objectives of Congress." *Hines v. Davidowitz* (1941). Determining whether a state law sufficiently obstructs federal purposes and is thus preempted "is a matter of judgment, to be informed by examining the federal statute as a whole and identifying its purpose and intended effects." *Crosby.* There is, however, an interpretative presumption against preemption in areas of traditional state concern. As the Court stated in *Rice v. Santa Fe Elevator Corp.* (1947), "[W]e start with the assumption that the historic police powers of the States were not to be superseded by the Federal Act unless that was the clear and manifest purpose of Congress."

The preemption doctrine in its current form is a twentieth-century development. No state statute was invalidated for anything other than a straightforward conflict with a specific federal enactment until 1912, and the focus on congressional intent as the touchstone of preemption did not emerge until the New Deal, when the locus of reformist legislation shifted from the states to the federal government.

In addition to serving a central role in preemption analysis, the Supremacy Clause is often seen as the source of the principle that states cannot regulate, interfere with, or control dera ... instrumentalities. This principle is generally traced to *McCulloch v. Maryland* (1819), in which the Court held that Maryland could not constitutionally tax the operations of the Bank of the United States. Chief Justice Marshall declared in *McCulloch* that

> [i]t is of the very essence of supremacy to remove all obstacles to its action within its own sphere, and so to modify every power vested in subordinate governments, as to exempt its own operations from their own influence. This effect need not be stated in terms. It is so involved in the declaration of supremacy, so necessarily implied in it, that the expression of it could not make it more certain.

Modern law has to some extent qualified the broadest implications of this early formulation of the supremacy principle. If federal supremacy indeed "remove[s] all obstacles" to federal action that might be posed by state regulation, states could be constitutionally forbidden even from taxing the salaries of federal employees. The Court indeed embraced such an idea for some time before specifically rejecting it in *Graves v. New York ex rel. O'Keefe* (1939). Modern law maintains instead that "[a] state regulation is invalid only if it regulates the United States directly or discriminates against the Federal Government or those with whom it deals." *North Dakota v. United States* (1990) (plurality opinion).

While the federal government can prevent states from interfering with federal operations, whether through taxes or otherwise, that does not necessarily mean that the Supremacy Clause is the basis upon which Congress exercises its power to protect federal operations, for the Supremacy Clause is not a grant of power to Congress. Rather, the valid exercise of any one of

Congress's enumerated powers can constitute the constitutional source of a statute that effectively preempts a state law. In particular, the Necessary and Proper Clause would be a vehicle for a statute that explicitly disables state law from operating in an area of federal concern. Thus, for an explicitly preemptive statute to be constitutional, it must be "necessary and proper for carrying into execution" some enumerated federal power, subject, of course, to the constitutional limits of the Necessary and Proper Clause itself.

For example, Congress could decide (explicitly or implicitly) that it alone should regulate the radiological-safety aspects involved in the construction and operation of a nuclear plant and thus preempt the field from any state regulation of nuclear power safety. *Pacific Gas & Electric v. Energy Resources Commission* (1983). Congress could decide (explicitly or implicitly) that it wanted gradually to phase in passive restraints in automobiles, thus preempting a local tort law that required airbags to be installed in all new cars. *Geier v. American Honda Motor Co., Inc.* Congress might decide that it wanted an area in interstate commerce to be regulated only by the free market and not by the states, thus precluding state legislation in this particular area altogether.

Inasmuch as any state statute that regulates federal activities in ways forbidden by a congressional statute would conflict with valid federal law, Congress is thus logically free to permit state regulation of federal instrumentalities through a sufficient expression of intent. For example, the Supreme Court has allowed Congress either to authorize or to limit state taxation of federal banks. *Carson v. Roane-Anderson Co.* (1952). In any event, the sequence is this: Congress, under its delegated powers, or a state, under its police power, may establish legal rules dealing with the same subject. It then falls to the courts to determine, under the Supremacy Clause, whether the state and federal rules are in conflict.

Article VI, Section 2, has separate provisions for treaties and federal laws. There is a textual distinction in the clause between laws "made in pursuance [of the Constitution]" and treaties "made under the authority of the United States." See *Missouri v. Holland* (1920). The effectiveness of national treaties was a special concern of the

Founding generation. This language ensured that treaties entered into by the United States prior to ratification of the Constitution—most notably, the 1783 treaty of peace with Great Britain and its guarantees against confiscations of loyalist property—took precedence over conflicting state laws, and the language in the Supremacy Clause targeting state court judges no doubt reflected the concern about treaty enforcement. The phrasing does not in any way imply that treaties are "supreme" even if they conflict with other constitutional provisions. The Supreme Court has declared that neither a treaty approved by the Senate nor an executive agreement made under the president's authority can create obligations that violate constitutional guarantees such as found in the Bill of Rights. *Reid v. Covert* (1957).

Like federal statutes, treaties are "supreme" only when they are effective as domestic law. Thus, the manner in which treaties become legally effective is important for determining when they take priority over state law. "Self-executing treaties" become part of the law of the United States directly. On the other hand, the courts will not enforce "non-self-executing treaties" until they are carried into law by an act of Congress. Determining whether a treaty is self-executing or non-self-executing is a complex and confusing task, as lower courts have readily averred. In general, the courts will regard a treaty as non-self-executing if it requires any governmental funding to accomplish its purposes, or if there is any expressed intent by the terms of the treaty, the president, the Senate, or even the record of negotiation that indicates that the government desired that the treaty be non-self-executing.

In addition, there is a vigorous debate among scholars over what was the Framers' original understanding on this point. One group holds that the Framers intended that most treaties were to be self-executing (unless the terms of the treaty indicate otherwise). Another group of commentators argues that any treaty that impinges upon Congress's Article I powers is non-self-executing. Otherwise, the Framers' careful system of protecting the people from onerous legislation through the separation of powers could be outflanked by the president and the Senate alone.

However a treaty becomes part of the law of the United States, it is on a par with other federal laws and can be repealed by Congress, though the United States' obligations under international law remain. Under Supreme Court precedents, the last expression of the sovereign will controls what will be enforced, so an act of Congress that is in conflict with a treaty will control if the act became law after the Senate ratified the treaty, and vice versa. To avoid such conflicts, the courts have fashioned a prudential rule whereby laws will be interpreted to be in harmony with United States treaty obligations if at all possible.

Gary Lawson

See Also

Article I, Section 8, Clause 18 (Necessary and Proper Clause)

Article VI, Clause 3 (Oaths Clause)

Suggestions for Further Research

David E. Engdahl, Constitutional Federalism in a Nutshell (1987)

Stephen A. Gardbaum, *The Nature of Preemption*, 79 Cornell L. Rev. 767 (1994)

S. Candice Hoke, *Transcending Conventional Supremacy: A Reconstruction of the Supremacy Clause*, 24 Conn. L. Rev. 829 (1992)

Vasan Kesavan, *The Three Tiers of Federal Law*, 100 Nw. U. L. Rev. 1479 (2006)

Gary Lawson, *Rebel Without a Clause: The Irrelevance of Article VI to Constitutional Supremacy*, 110 Mich. L. Rev. First Impressions 33 (2011)

Thomas W. Merrill, *Preemption and Institutional Choice*, 102 Nw. U. L. Rev. 727 (2008)

Jonathan F. Mitchell, *Stare Decisis and Constitutional Text*, 110 Mich. L. Rev. 1 (2011)

Caleb Nelson, *Preemption*, 86 Va. L. Rev. 225 (2000)

Jordan J. Paust, *Self-Executing Treaties*, 82 Am. J. Int'l L. 760 (1988)

Catherine M. Sharkey, *Inside Agency Preemption*, 110 Mich. L. Rev. 521 (2012)

John C. Yoo, *Globalism and the Constitution: Treaties, Non-Self-Execution, and the Original Understanding*, 99 Colum. L. Rev. 1955 (1999)

Significant Cases

Marbury v. Madison, 5 U.S. (1 Cranch) 137 (1803)

McCulloch v. Maryland, 17 U.S. (4 Wheat.) 316 (1819)

Gibbons v. Ogden, 22 U.S. (9 Wheat.) 1 (1824)

Cooley v. Bd. of Wardens, 53 U.S. (12 How.) 299 (1851)

Missouri v. Holland, 252 U.S. 416 (1920)

Graves v. New York *ex rel.* O'Keefe, 306 U.S. 466 (1939)

Hines v. Davidowitz, 312 U.S. 52 (1941)

Rice v. Santa Fe Elevator Corp., 331 U.S. 218 (1947)

Carson v. Roane-Anderson Co., 342 U.S. 232 (1952)

Reid v. Covert, 354 U.S. 1 (1957)

Pacific Gas & Electric Co. v. Energy Resources Conservation & Development Comm'n, 461 U.S. 190 (1983)

North Dakota v. United States, 495 U.S. 423 (1990)

Crosby v. National Foreign Trade Council, 530 U.S. 363 (2000)

Geier v. American Honda Motor Co., 529 U.S 861 (2000)

PLIVA, Inc. v. Mensing, 132 S. Ct. 55 (2011)

Arizona v. Inter Tribal Council of Ariz., 133 S. Ct. 2247 (2013)

Oaths Clause

The Senators and Representatives before mentioned, and the Members of the several State Legislatures, and all executive and judicial Officers, both of the United States and of the several States, shall be bound by Oath or Affirmation, to support this Constitution....

(ARTICLE VI, CLAUSE 3)

~

*A*lthough the practical application of the Constitution is largely in the hands of state judges, the primacy of the Constitution ultimately depends on officers of the law—in particular, officers of each branch of government—being equally bound to its support. In this sense, the Oaths Clause is the completion of the Supremacy Clause. Stated more precisely, the Oaths Clause, along with the president's oath of office prescribed in Article II, Section 1, Clause 8, is the practiced mechanism to uphold the Constitution's supremacy as invoked in the Supremacy Clause of Article VI, Clause 2.

In England, subjects were required to swear loyalty to the reigning monarch; many early American documents included oaths of allegiance to the British king. During the American Revolution, General George Washington required all officers to subscribe to an oath renouncing any allegiance to King George III and pledging their fidelity to the United States. Most of the new state constitutions included elaborate oaths that tied allegiance to and provided a summary of the basic constitutional principles animating American constitutionalism. There was no oath in the Articles of Confederation.

At the Constitutional Convention, Edmund Randolph proposed, as part of the Virginia Plan, "that the Legislative Executive & Judiciary powers within the several States ought to be bound by oath to support the articles of Union." When it was objected that this would unnecessarily intrude on state jurisdiction, Randolph responded that he

considered it as necessary to prevent that competition between the National Constitution & laws & those of the particular States, which had already been felt. The officers of the States are already under oath to the States. To preserve a due impartiality they ought to be equally bound to the Natl. Govt. The Natl. authority needs every support we can give it.

The Oaths Clause helps to fulfill the Framers' plan to integrate the states into the electoral, policymaking, and executory functions of the federal union, subject to the limits of the Tenth Amendment. For example, the Supreme Court has held that Congress may not "conscript" the legislatures or executive officers of a state directly into federal service. *New York v. United States* (1992); *Printz v. United States* (1997). In *The Federalist* No. 27, Alexander Hamilton offered a careful and nuanced description of the Oaths Clause: "[t]hus the legislatures, courts, and magistrates, of the respective members, will be incorporated into the operations of the national government *as far as its just and constitutional authority extends*; and will be rendered auxiliary to the enforcement of its laws."

For the sake of consistency and unity, the delegates amended the Oaths Clause to cover officers of the national government as well. Later, the delegates added the words "or affirmation" (to oblige the Quakers and other sects that refused oaths as a matter of religious doctrine) as well as the ban on federal religious tests (Article VI, Clause 3).

The simple declaration to "support the Constitution" has constitutional significance at all levels of government. An opinion of the attorney general in 1875 declared that members of Congress do not assume office until the completion of the oath, but that a state may not question a state representative's motives and refuse to allow him to take the oath and his seat. *Bond v. Floyd* (1966). The oath was at the heart of Chief Justice John Marshall's opinion in *Marbury v. Madison* (1803), obliging judges to give priority to the Constitution over ordinary legislative acts. Justice Joseph Story likewise stated in his *Commentaries on the Constitution of the United States* (1833) that officers sworn to support the Constitution are "conscientiously bound to abstain from all acts, which are inconsistent with it," and that in cases of doubt they must "decide each for himself, whether, consistently with the Constitution, the act can be done." But taking the oath does not relieve a judge from obedience to higher judicial authority, even if he thinks the higher court is acting contrary to the Constitution. *Glassroth v. Moore* (2003). Beyond the mechanism of the separation of powers, the Oaths Clause places an independent obligation on officeholders to observe the limits of their authority.

The Framers' general understanding was that proscribing religious tests did not necessarily remove the religious significance of the general oath. "The Constitution enjoins an oath upon all the officers of the United States," Oliver Wolcott noted at the Connecticut ratifying convention. "This is a direct appeal to that God who is the avenger of perjury." Customarily, officeholders add the words "so help me God" at the completion of their oaths.

The very first law passed by the first session of the House of Representatives was "An Act to regulate the Time and Manner of administering certain Oaths." Two days later, the chief justice

of New York administered to the representatives an oath to "solemnly swear or affirm (as the case may be) that I will support the Constitution of the United States." The Senate amended the legislation to apply to state officers, who are also subject to Article VI. When Representative Elbridge Gerry objected that Congress had no authority to specify the oath of state officers, the response was that Congress was implicitly authorized by Article VI itself, if not by the Necessary and Proper Clause, to prescribe oaths for the states.

Congress's argument was that the Constitution, by requiring public officials to be "bound by Oath or Affirmation" to support it, also empowered the Congress to decide on when such oath would be taken and what the oath would be. This understanding carried a broad interpretation of implied congressional power that was later used as justification for the Fugitive Slave Act in 1793—another instance of Congress legislating specific rules for states to follow the much broader Fugitive Slave Clause (Article IV, Section 2, Clause 3). The breadth of Congress's authority would later be upheld, on similar grounds, by the Supreme Court in *Prigg v. Pennsylvania* (1842). There is some doubt, however, whether Congress could constitutionally require an oath of state officials, because Article VI is not a grant of power to Congress and therefore cannot be implemented by the Necessary and Proper Clause (Article I, Section 8, Clause 18), though Congress can use the Necessary and Proper Clause to prescribe the oath for federal officers.

During the Civil War, Congress promulgated an oath to require civil servants and military officers not only to swear allegiance to the United States but also to affirm that they had not engaged in any previous disloyal conduct. Congress repealed the latter condition in 1884, leaving wording that is nearly identical to the current oath taken by members and federal employees.

Under current law any individual elected or appointed to an office of honor or profit in the civil service or uniformed services, except the president, shall take the following oath: "I, [name], do solemnly swear (or affirm) that I will support and defend the Constitution of the United States against all enemies, foreign and domestic; that I will bear true faith and allegiance to the same; that I take this obligation freely, without any mental reservation or purpose of evasion; and that I will well and faithfully discharge the duties of the office on which I am about to enter." (5 U.S.C. § 3331.) By federal statute, all state officers shall take an oath in the simple form first promulgated in 1789. (4 U.S.C. § 101.)

Matthew Spalding

See Also

Article I, Section 3, Clause 6 (Trial of Impeachment)

Article I, Section 8, Clause 18 (Necessary and Proper Clause)

Article II, Section 1, Clause 8 (Presidential Oath of Office)

Article VI, Clause 2 (Supremacy Clause)

Article VI, Clause 3 (Religious Test)

Suggestions for Further Research

14 Op. Att'y Gen. 406 (1874)

Patrick O. Gudridge, *The Office of the Oath*, 20 Const. Comment. 387 (2003)

Harold M. Hyman, To Try Men's Souls: Loyalty Tests in American History (1981)

Gary Lawson, *The Constitution's Congress*, 89 B.U. L. Rev. 399 (2009)

Gary Lawson, *Rebel Without a Clause: The Irrelevance of Article VI to Constitutional Supremacy*, 110 Mich. L. Rev. First Impressions 33 (2011)

Nash E. Long, *The "Constitutional Remand": Judicial Review of Constitutionally Dubious Statutes,* 14 J.L. & Pol. 667 (1998)

Matthew A. Pauley, I Do Solemnly Swear: The President's Constitutional Oath (1999)

Vic Snyder, *You've Taken an Oath to Support the Constitution, Now What? The Constitutional Requirement for a Congressional Oath of Office*, 23 U. Ark. Little Rock L. Rev. 897 (2001)

Significant Cases

Marbury v. Madison, 5 U.S. (1 Cranch) 137 (1803)

Prigg v. Pennsylvania, 41 U.S. (16 Pet.) 539 (1842)

Bond v. Floyd, 385 U.S. 116 (1966)

New York v. United States, 505 U.S. 144 (1992)

Printz v. United States, 521 U.S. 898 (1997)

Glassroth v. Moore, 335 F.3d 1282 (11th Cir. 2003)

Religious Test

…no religious Test shall ever be required as a Qualification to any Office or public Trust under the United States.

(Article VI, Clause 3)

~

*T*he Constitution contained one explicit reference to religion: the Article VI ban on religious tests for "any office or public trust under the United States." Despite much constitutional litigation over the boundary between church and state in the years since—most of it since World War II—there are no judicial decisions construing the religious test ban. This is not to suggest that the clause has been ineffectual. On the contrary: no federal official has ever been subjected to a formal religious test for holding office. The Article VI religious test clause, because it is relatively clear, is a self-executing success.

By its plain terms, the ban extended only to federal officeholders. States were free at the time of the Founding to impose religious tests as they saw fit. And they did. State tests generally limited public offices to Christians or, in some states, only to Protestants. National offices were, on the other hand, open to everyone. While today this freedom from religious tests seems obvious, this clause was remarkably progressive for its time.

The surviving accounts of the Constitutional Convention indicate that the Article VI ban "was adopted by a great majority of the convention, and without much debate." Only North Carolina opposed the prohibition; the Connecticut and Maryland delegations were divided. All the other delegates were in favor. But even some "nay" voters did not favor religious tests for federal office. Connecticut's Roger Sherman, for example, thought the ban unnecessary, because "the prevailing liberality" provided sufficient security against restrictive tests.

The "prevailing liberality" was not, however, as prevailing as Sherman believed. In fact, the clause was hotly disputed in some states during the 1788–1789 struggles over ratification of the Constitution. The main objection was that "Jews," "Turks," "infidels," "heathens," and even "Roman Catholics" might hold national office under the proposed Constitution. The times were such that the force of this objection was, for many, substantial and self-evident. Pennsylvania's Benjamin Rush expressed the more restrained view that "many pious people wish the name of the Supreme Being had been introduced somewhere in the new Constitution." The Religious Test Clause was thus a focal point for reservations about the Constitution's entirely secular language.

Some defenders of the Constitution argued, in response, that a belief in God and a future state of reward and punishment *could*, notwithstanding the test ban, be required of public officers. On this interpretation, Article VI would rule out only sectarian tests, such as would exclude some Christians (but not others) from office. Others asserted that the constitutional requirement that officers take an oath to support and defend the Constitution necessarily implied that officers had to affirm at least some tenets of natural religion. *See* Oaths Clause, Article VI, Clause 3.

Defenders of the Constitution put forward two reasons for the religious test ban. First, various Christian sects feared that, if any test were permitted, one might be designed to their disadvantage. No single sect could hope to dominate national councils. But any sect could imagine itself the victim of a combination of the others. Oliver Ellsworth noted that if a religious oath "were in favour of either congregationalists, presbyterians, episcopalions, baptists, or quakers, it would incapacitate more than three-fourths of the American citizens for any publick office; and thus degrade them from the rank of freemen." More importantly, they argued that the Constitution wisely declined to exclude some of the best minds and the least parochial personalities to serve in the national government. In his 1787 pamphlet, "An Examination of the Constitution," Tench Coxe said of the religious test ban: "The people may employ any wise or good citizen in the execution of the various duties of the government."

The limitation of Article VI, Clause 3, to *federal* officeholders was effectively eliminated by the Supreme Court in the 1961 case, *Torcaso v. Watkins*. Relying upon the First Amendment religion clauses, the Court struck down religious tests for any public office in the United States. *Torcaso* means that not even a simple profession of belief in God—as was required of Roy Torcaso, an aspiring notary public—may now be required.

The scope of anyone's immunity from disqualification from office on religious bases now depends upon the meaning of the Establishment and Free Exercise of Religion Clauses, not upon Article VI. At present, the central rule enunciated by the Supreme Court for Establishment Clause jurisprudence is the "endorsement" test. It stipulates all public authority—from state and federal to the most local municipal body—must never do or say anything that a reasonable person could understand to be an "endorsement" of religion, i.e., that favors adherents over non-adherents. Nothing in the neighborhood of a religious test for office could survive application of this norm.

The Establishment Clause thus totally eclipses the Religious Test Clause. Questions about the precise scope of the sort of "religious test" banned, and about whether "office[s] of public trust" include members of Congress as well as the most junior postal worker, no longer matter—save, perhaps, to historians.

Gerard V. Bradley

See Also

Amendment I

Suggestions for Further Research

Morton Borden, Jews, Turks, and Infidels (1984)

Gerard V. Bradley, *The No Religious Test Clause and the Constitution of Religious Liberty: A Machine That Has Gone of Itself*, 37 Case W. Res. L. Rev. 674 (1987)

Significant Case

Torcaso v. Watkins, 367 U.S. 488 (1961)

ARTICLE VII

Ratification Clause

The Ratification of the Conventions of nine States, shall be sufficient for the Establishment of this Constitution between the States so ratifying the Same.

(ARTICLE VII, CLAUSE 1)

*T*his laconic sentence, in the last and shortest of the Constitution's articles, was the key to the legal and political process that replaced the Articles of Confederation with the Constitution of the United States. In one stroke, Article VII expressed the Constitution's view of the Union and echoed the Declaration of Independence's view of the relation between positive and natural law. Seldom has so much political import been conveyed in so few words.

Behind the provision lay the delicate political problem confronting the Framers of the new Constitution: what to do about the Articles of Confederation. In 1786, the abortive Annapolis convention had issued a summons (drafted by Alexander Hamilton) requesting a new meeting of the states to consider all measures that would "render the constitution of the Federal Government adequate to the exigencies of the Union." The Confederation Congress had renewed but narrowed that call, charging the delegates to the Constitutional Convention with "the sole and express purpose of revising the Articles of Confederation and reporting to Congress and the several legislatures such alterations and provisions therein as shall...render the federal constitution adequate to the exigencies of Government & the preservation of the Union." Eight of the twelve state delegations to the Convention arrived under the former terms, and four under the latter, less elastic ones.

But now the convention was proposing to replace, not renovate, the Articles. And it was appealing not to "Congress and the state legislatures," but over and around their heads to special ratification conventions to be elected by the people in each state. And to add insult to injury, the Framers were setting the threshold for ratification at nine states, not the thirteen necessary for constitutional revision under the Articles.

Article VII thus announced a bold new ratification procedure. It was needed because there was no chance that the one specified in the Articles would result in the Constitution's passage. The Confederation Congress, which under the Articles had to approve amendments before sending them to the state legislatures, could not be expected to rejoice at its own extinction. The state legislatures, which would be stripped of considerable powers by the proposed plan of government (see Article I, Section 10), could not be expected to concur in their own diminishment. Experience supported these conjectures: no amendment, however minor its attempt to strengthen the general government, had ever survived the ratification process dictated by the Articles.

It was not that Article VII's procedures were wholly unheard of: The Massachusetts Constitution of 1780, largely written by John Adams, had already pioneered the use of the popularly elected ratifying convention. Nor did Article VII entirely bypass Congress and the state legislatures. The Constitutional Convention sent its handiwork to the Confederation Congress and, in a separate resolution, requested (1) that Congress forward the proposed Constitution to the state legislatures and (2) that the legislatures call special elections for the ratifying conventions. Congress unanimously went along and the thirteen legislatures eventually complied, and their actions, historian Forrest McDonald has argued, constituted in effect "an amendment to the Articles' amending process," thus serving to legalize or at least regularize the Constitution's departures from the Articles' writ. Nevertheless, the Framers went out of their way to remove any suggestion from

Article VII that the Congress (never mentioned therein) was being asked to give its approbation to the Constitution, much less that it and the legislatures were invited to debate it line by line. On the contrary, the implication was that the Congress and the state legislatures were middlemen, intended to transmit the plan to the real authorities, the popular conventions.

The political necessity of circumventing the established procedure was apparent to almost everyone. The Virginia Plan at the Constitutional Convention had called for the ultimate decision on ratification to be made by popular conventions, not by the state legislatures. James Wilson, early in the Convention, had urged that a "partial union" of consenting states not be held hostage to "the inconsiderate or selfish opposition" of a few states. Nonetheless, the plan's opponents objected, in Elbridge Gerry's words, to "the indecency and pernicious tendency of dissolving in so slight a manner, the solemn obligations of the Articles of Confederation."

Yet the case for superseding the Articles' strictures was not so "slight." There were important republican principles at stake. As James Madison argued in *The Federalist* No. 40, "in all great changes of established governments forms ought to give way to substance" because "a rigid adherence...to the former, would render nominal and nugatory the transcendent and precious right of the people to 'abolish or alter their governments as to them shall seem most likely to effect their safety and happiness....'" In *The Federalist* No. 43, Madison noted that the Framers were "recurring to the absolute necessity of the case; to the great principle of self-preservation; to the transcendent law of nature and of nature's God, which declares that the safety and happiness of society are the objects at which all political institutions aim and to which all such institutions must be sacrificed."

In short, to save the Revolution and its principles, and to vindicate the Declaration of Independence, it was necessary to set aside the Articles of Confederation. The way from a flawed confederation to "a more perfect Union" involved a return to first principles. This was the very sort of return and renewal—of "revolution," in the sense of coming back around to the starting point—

contemplated in the Virginia and Massachusetts bills of rights. During the ratification debates, the Constitution's advocates focused their arguments, therefore, on the defects of the Confederation. The more numerous and deep-seated its flaws, the less it deserved the veneration it was manifestly not receiving.

Among its shortcomings, none was more telling than its departure from the republican standard in respect of its own ratification. In many states, the Articles had been ratified by the legislature only; the people themselves had not been consulted. In conflicts between acts of the states and Congress, the republican presumption thus often went to the former. To repeat the mistake by asking the state legislatures to ratify the proposed Constitution would vitiate the new government before it had begun. At the Convention, James Madison admitted that the new plan would make "essential inroads on the State Constitutions," but pointed out that asking state legislatures to ratify the new Constitution would in effect promulgate "a novel and dangerous doctrine" that a legislature could change the constitution "under which it held its existence."

To the Anti-Federalists, these objections were beside the point. In their view, the Articles had not needed full-blown popular ratification because they were precisely not a constitution. The Articles were more like a treaty among sovereign powers. The Federalists regarded this point as a confession of the Confederation's "imbecility." Madison, in a striking passage at the convention, explained that "the difference between a system founded on the Legislatures only, and one founded on the people, [is] the true difference between a league or treaty, and a Constitution." In the former, there were no real questions of constitutionality; only in the latter case, when a law violated "a constitution established by the people themselves," would judges consider an "unwise or perfidious" measure "null & void."

In a treaty under the law of nations, Madison continued, "a breach of any one article by any of the parties, frees the other parties from their engagements." He implied that the state governments' frequent violations of their obligations to the Confederation had already come close to dissolving (in the Articles' words) their "firm league of friendship," and with it the obligation to abide scrupulously by its amendment provisions. In "a union of people under one Constitution," by contrast, "the nature of the pact always has been understood to exclude such an interpretation." As the supreme law of the land, ordained and established by "We the People," the Constitution would be obligatory on the states.

Article VII's bold dismissal of the Confederation's rule of unanimity emphasized the break still further. The number nine had been proposed in the convention by Edmund Randolph. It was, he said, a "respectable majority of the whole" and had the advantage of being familiar from "the constitution of the existing Congress," which required nine votes (a traditional supermajority of two-thirds, rounded up) in order to approve any important question. Other numbers had been considered, but anything short of thirteen signified the same thing, that the United States was no longer a treaty organization of sovereign or virtually sovereign states, but a people with a government in which constitutional majorities would be empowered actually to govern. The republican cause would be rescued from embarrassment and paralysis: twelve states could no longer be denied by a thirteenth, the majority would not be ruled by the minority, and the virtuous would not be beholden to the vicious.

At the same time, however, the Constitution's ratification by conventions in at least nine states would establish the new government only "between the states so ratifying the Same." There were limits to the nationalism contemplated by the plan. The people of the United States could not compel constitutional change on the states choosing to be disunited. In this respect, as in others, the Constitution recognized and granted to the states considerable sovereignty or jurisdiction in their own spheres. Once the people of a state agreed to ratify the Constitution, it agreed in effect to amend its own state constitution to align it with the supreme law's new distribution of powers and duties, and henceforth to subordinate itself to that supreme law. The best description of the new arrangement is probably Madison's, who in *The Federalist* No. 39 famously pronounced it "neither a national nor a federal Constitution, but a composition of both."

The number of nine states to ratify was also emblematic of the Constitution's requirement that three-quarters of the states were needed to approve amendments. The high supermajority number in each case allowed for each generation to develop a wide consensus on what the fundamental compact of the Union should become.

In the event, New Hampshire became the ninth state to ratify, and the Confederation Congress, still very much in existence, began to take steps to put the new Constitution into operation. This was in keeping with the resolutions of the Constitutional Convention that had accompanied the proposed Constitution to Congress. Virginia and New York quickly ratified as well, creating a union of eleven states. In September 1788, the Congress passed a resolution authorizing the appointment of presidential electors in the ratifying states by January 1789, the first presidential vote by the electors in February, and the commencement of proceedings under the new Constitution on March 4, 1789. North Carolina rejected the Constitution and did not reverse itself until November 1789. Rhode Island, which did not participate in the Constitutional Convention and refused at first to call a ratifying convention, held out until May 1790.

One effect of Article VII, which allowed the Constitution to proceed despite the holdout states, was to induce those states to come aboard. They, least of all, wished to confront the delicate question of what would become of them if they remained permanently outside the Union. In its wake, Article VII left a minor controversy over when exactly the Articles of Confederation had expired, which the Supreme Court addressed in *Owings v. Speed* (1820). The Court ruled that Congress had effectively dissolved "by the successive disappearance of its members" in November 1788, and that, legally speaking, it had breathed its last on March 2, 1789, the day before the new Congress had been directed to assemble. Some scholars dispute the accuracy of the Court's holding in *Owings* and suggest that the Constitution came into effect in stages after the ratification. But all agree that the nature of the new federal Congress was entirely different from what had gone before. Unlike the old Congress, essentially the meeting place of a league based on states' rights, the new Congress was a creature of the Constitution, based on what Madison called "the supreme authority of the people themselves." That is the ultimate significance of Article VII.

Charles Kesler

See Also

Preamble

Article I, Section 10

Suggestions for Further Research

Vasan Kesavan, *When Did the Articles of Confederation Cease to Be Law?*, 78 NOTRE DAME L. REV. 35 (2002)

Gary Lawson & Guy Seidman, *The First 'Establishment' Clause: Article VII and the Post-Constitutional Confederation*, 78 NOTRE DAME L. REV. 83 (2002)

Gary Lawson & Guy Seidman, *When Did the Constitution Become Law?*, 77 NOTRE DAME L. REV. 1 (2001)

John O. McGinnis & Michael B. Rappaport, *Originalism and the Good Constitution*, 98 GEO. L.J. 1693 (2010)

Significant Case

Owings v. Speed, 18 U.S. (5 Wheat.) 420 (1820)

Attestation Clause

Done in Convention by the Unanimous Consent of the States present the Seventeenth Day of September in the Year of our Lord one thousand seven hundred and Eighty seven and of the Independence of the United States of America the Twelfth In witness whereof We have hereunto subscribed our Names....

(ARTICLE VII, CLAUSE 2)

~

*T*wo days before the end of the Constitutional Convention, just before the final vote on the completed document, three delegates voiced objections to the new Constitution. Edmund

Randolph of Virginia (who had introduced the Virginia Plan) thought the Constitution was not sufficiently republican, and moved that there should be another convention to address amendments to be proposed by the states. George Mason, also of Virginia, seconded the motion, arguing that without significant changes the new government would end in either monarchy or a tyrannical aristocracy. Elbridge Gerry of Massachusetts feared the powers of Congress were too broad; he thought the best that could be done was to provide for a second general convention. When the two questions were put to a vote, the eleven states present (Rhode Island had not sent a delegation, and New York's had left) all voted against a second convention and then all voted in favor of the final text of the Constitution. The document was then ordered engrossed, or formally written, in preparation for endorsement.

When the convention reconvened on September 17, after the final reading of the document, Benjamin Franklin delivered an address (read by James Wilson) strongly endorsing the Constitution despite any perceived imperfections. Hoping to gain the support of critics and create a sense of common accord, Franklin then proposed, and the Convention agreed, that the Constitution be signed by the delegates as individual witnesses of "the unanimous consent of the states present."

Thus the signers subscribed their names "In witness" to what was "Done in Convention," and, with the exception of George Washington, who signed first and separately (as president and deputy from Virginia), the names are grouped by state. As a result, the document suggests the unanimity of the Declaration of Independence: delegates did not sign "on the part and behalf of" particular states, as they had in the Articles of Confederation. The states are listed (as in Article I, Section 2, and the draft of the Preamble, as well as in the Declaration of Independence and the Articles of Confederation) in geographical order, from New Hampshire in the north to Georgia in the south.

In the end, Randolph, Mason, and Gerry did not sign the Constitution; as Madison wrote in his notes, they "declined to give it the sanction of their names." The arrangement did allow Alexander Hamilton to sign as a witness for New

York, even though the rest of his delegation had already departed.

At least sixty-five individuals had received appointments to the convention, fifty-five attended at various times over the course of the sessions, and thirty-nine delegates signed the final document. George Read of Delaware signed twice: once for himself, then again for John Dickinson (who had left due to illness, and had authorized Read to sign his name). Although he was not a delegate, William Jackson, the secretary of the convention, signed to attest, or authenticate, the delegates' signatures.

Also of note is the method by which the Constitution is dated: "the Seventeenth Day of September in the Year of our Lord" 1787, and "of the Independence of the United States of America the Twelfth." Dating documents to "the Year of our Lord" had become more unusual; the Declaration of Independence, for instance, simply states "In Congress, July 4, 1776." Dating important documents in American political history to the Declaration of Independence was at that point relatively frequent. The dual reference, which was used by the Continental Congress in the late 1770s and early 1780s on various documents and declarations, can be found in two other important national documents: the Articles of Confederation and the Northwest Ordinance (considered, along with the Declaration, to be the "organic documents" of the nation). The language here is not insignificant. The dates serve to place the document in the context of the Christian religious traditions of Western civilization. At the same time, the dates formally link the document to the regime principles proclaimed in the Declaration of Independence, the Constitution having been written in the twelfth year after July 1776. The usage stands in contrast to both the contemporary British tradition, in which documents were dated to the reign of the sitting monarch (see, for example, the Magna Carta of 1215 and the Petition of Right of 1628), and the French decision in 1793 to reject the Gregorian calendar altogether and begin measuring time starting with the French Revolution.

Akhil Amar suggests that attestations and signatures are not normally regarded as part of the substance of a legal document. Nonetheless, the Attestation Clause has traditionally been included in reprintings of the Constitution.

Matthew Spalding

See also
Article 6, Clause 3 (Religious Test Clause)
Amendment I (Establishment Clause)
Amendment I (Free Exercise Clause)

Suggestion for Further Research
Akhil Reed Amar, Commentary: "The Constitution and the Candidates: Race, Religion, Romney, and Ryan," *The Daily Beast*, August 19, 2012, at http://www.law.yale.edu/news/15960.htm

AMENDMENTS

Establishment of Religion

Congress shall make no law respecting an establishment of religion....
(AMENDMENT I)

*I*n recent years the U.S. Supreme Court's rulings have placed the First Amendment's Establishment and Free Exercise of Religion Clauses in tension, but it was not so for the Framers. None of the Framers believed that a public role for religion was an evil in itself. Rather, many opposed an established church like the established Anglican Church in England because they believed that it was a threat to the free exercise of religion. Their primary goal was to protect free exercise. That was the main thrust of James Madison's famous *Memorial and Remonstrance Against Religious Assessments* (1785), in which he argued that the state of Virginia ought not to pay the salaries of the Anglican clergy because that practice was an impediment to a person's free connection to whatever religion his conscience directed him.

Nor did most of the founding generation believe that government ought to be "untainted" by religion, or ought not to take an interest in furthering the people's connection to religion. The Northwest Ordinance (1787), which the First Congress reenacted, stated: "Religion, morality, and knowledge, being necessary to good government and the happiness of mankind, schools and the means of education shall forever be encouraged." As President, George Washington put into practice the understanding of most of his contemporaries regarding religion's place in public life. In his first inaugural address (1789), Washington declared as his "first official act" his "fervent supplications to that Almighty Being who rules over the universe" that He might bless the new government. Addressing his compatriots, Washington said:

> In tendering this homage to the Great Author of every public and private good, I assure myself that it expresses your sentiments not less than my own; nor those of my fellow citizens at large less than either. No people can be bound to acknowledge and adore the invisible hand which conducts the affairs of men more than those of the United States.

Washington bracketed his years as President with similar sentiments in his Farewell Address (1796):

> Of all the dispositions and habits which lead to political prosperity,

Religion and morality are indispensable supports. In vain would that man claim the tribute of Patriotism, who should labor to subvert these great Pillars of human happiness, these firmest props of the duties of Men and citizens. The mere Politician, equally with the pious man, ought to respect and to cherish them.

He then added: "And let us with caution indulge the supposition, that morality can be maintained without religion.... [R]eason and experience both forbid us to expect that National morality can prevail in exclusion of religious principle."

There is nothing in the legislative history of the First Amendment that contradicts Washington's understanding of the appropriate relationship between government and religion. In the First Congress, which drafted the First Amendment, a House committee proposed the following language: "no religion shall be established by law, nor shall the equal rights of conscience be infringed." But some representatives evinced concern that the proposal might put in doubt the legitimacy of some of the states' own religious establishments, or at least make it questionable whether taxes could still be earmarked for clergy.

In fact, by the time independence was secured, there was no consensus as to what constituted an "establishment of religion." Most of the newly independent states retained laws, policies, or practices that would be regarded as religious establishments by twenty-first–century legal standards. There was general agreement that exclusive legal preference for one church or religion over all others—as was the prevailing arrangement in Europe—constituted an establishment of religion. So, too, was an arrangement where the civil government imposed articles of faith and forms of worship on all those under its authority. Although this definition was widely accepted, there were disputes about whether or not specific state policies and practices constituted an establishment. The use of general assessments, which taxed all residents for the support of religion, was an especially contentious policy. Although regarded as an odious establishment by some, others denied that such tax-supported clergy constituted an "establishment" at all.

In reply to the expressed concerns, Representative James Madison of Virginia believed modifying the proposal to prohibit a "national religion" would be sufficient to allay that apprehension and would make clear that the new government was not to impinge on the rights of conscience by establishing a governmental connection to a church. Representative Samuel Livermore of New Hampshire suggested this formulation: "Congress shall make no laws touching religion, or infringing the rights of conscience." After some debate, the House finally settled on this language: "Congress shall make no law establishing religion, or prohibiting the free exercise thereof, nor shall the rights of Conscience be infringed."

The Senate, however, wanted more specificity. After a number of attempted formulations, the Senate agreed upon the formula: "Congress shall make no law establishing articles of faith or a mode of worship, or prohibiting the free exercise of religion," which would prohibit a European-type establishment, but likely would have permitted direct financial support to a sect. Settling the difference in a conference committee (of which Madison was a member) between the House and the Senate, all agreed on the final version: "Congress shall make no law respecting an establishment of religion, or prohibiting the free exercise thereof." The addition of the word "respecting" may be significant. Its meaning seems to signify that Congress may not legislate either to establish a national religion or to disestablish a state religion. As Laurence Tribe has observed, "[a] growing body of evidence suggests that the Framers principally intended the Establishment of Religion Clause to perform two functions: to protect state religious establishments from national displacement, and to prevent the national government from aiding some, but not all, religions."

Leaving the question of establishment to the states does not entail the absence of religious liberty. Even before the incorporation of the religion clauses and without intervention by the federal courts, religious freedom and tolerance had spread throughout the United States. To be sure, religious conflicts occurred at the local level where discrimination, particularly against Catholics and Jews,

existed. The framework established by the Constitution, however, made it possible for religious minorities to gain protection through political representation.

Contemporaneous history strongly indicates that most Framers supported religion, not for credal purposes, but because it promoted civic virtue among the people, which they thought was a necessary element for the maintenance of republican self-government. Nonetheless, when, many decades later and far removed from the Founding, the Supreme Court chose to base its conception of the original understanding of the Establishment of Religion Clause on a phrase from a letter by Thomas Jefferson to the Danbury Baptist Association of Connecticut (1802). Although Jefferson was not directly involved in framing the Constitution or First Amendment, his metaphor of a "wall of separation between church and state" was accepted by the Court as an authoritative expression of the Establishment Clause. This "wall," the Court said, "must be kept high and impregnable," even though Jefferson's own practice as President was inconsistent with a "high and impregnable" barrier. *Everson v. Board of Education of Ewing Township* (1947); *see also Reynolds v. United States* (1879).

The modern view of the Establishment of Religion Clause began with *Everson v. Board of Education*, where the Court adopted a separationist interpretation of the Clause. "The 'establishment of religion' clause of the First Amendment," the Court said, "means at least this: neither a state nor the Federal Government can set up a church. Neither can pass laws which aid one religion, aid all religions, or prefer one religion over another.... No person can be punished for entertaining or professing religious beliefs or disbeliefs, for church attendance or non-attendance. No tax in any amount, large or small, can be levied to support any religious activities or institutions, whatever they may be called, or whatever form they may adopt to teach or practice religion." In this ruling, the Supreme Court also held that the Due Process Clause of the Fourteenth Amendment applied the First Amendment's proscriptions against establishment to the states.

Although there is vigorous debate as to whether the provisions of the Fourteenth Amendment "incorporate," or replicate, the guarantees of the Bill of Rights and fasten them on the states, most commentators opine that the Establishment of Religion Clause is the least likely candidate for incorporation. It was designed as a protection of the states against the federal government. It seems anomalous to many scholars, even to some who support incorporation generally, that the Establishment of Religion Clause could be called an individual right for purposes of incorporation into the Fourteenth Amendment. Notwithstanding the historians' doubts, the Supreme Court has firmly adhered to the incorporation of the Establishment of Religion Clause against the states.

One point on which most church-state scholars agree is that Establishment Clause jurisprudence lacks coherence and consistency. A "moment of silence for meditation and prayer" in public schools is contrary to the Constitution (only if the *motive* is religious), *Wallace v. Jaffree* (1985), but a paid chaplain in state legislatures is not, *Marsh v. Chambers* (1983). For a time, the Supreme Court permitted states to provide religious schools with textbooks on secular subjects, *Board of Education v. Allen* (1968), but disallowed states to provide religious schools with instructional equipment like maps, *Meek v. Pittenger* (1975) (modified by *Mitchell v. Helms* (2000). Religious schools may not receive funds for maintenance expenses, *Committee for Public Education & Religious Liberty v. Nyquist* (1973), but places of worship can enjoy a tax exemption, *Walz v. Tax Commission of City of New York* (1970). Prayers at high school football games are invalid, *Santa Fe Independent School District v. Doe* (2000), but the bailiff's call, "God Save this Honorable Court," may be heard within the chambers of the Supreme Court.

Since *Everson*, the Supreme Court has developed a number of different and conflicting approaches to interpreting the Establishment of Religion Clause, namely: (1) separationism, (2) coercion, and (3) endorsement.

The separationist view of *Everson* led to the banning of state-sponsored prayer and Bible reading in public schools. *Engel v. Vitale* (1962); *School District of Abington Township v. Schempp* (1963). To enforce separationism, the Court settled on a three-part test in *Lemon v. Kurtzman* (1971). In order to withstand an Establishment Clause challenge, the *Lemon* test requires a court to find that a law, practice, or policy in question has: (1) a secular purpose, (2) a primary effect that neither advances nor inhibits religion, and (3) does not create excessive entanglement with religion. The strict separationists on the Court did allow for a few exceptions to the *Lemon* test under the rubric of "ceremonial deism," whereby particular customary practices may be protected from Establishment Clause scrutiny if "they have lost through rote repetition any significant religious content." *Lynch v. Donnelly* (1984).

A major historical challenge to the separationist position emerged in the dissent written by (then) Justice William H. Rehnquist in *Wallace v. Jaffree*. Rehnquist argued that the original meaning of the Establishment of Religion Clause only "forbade establishment of a national religion, and forbade preference among religious sects or denominations." In defending this "no denominational preference" position and criticizing strict separationism, Rehnquist observed that Thomas Jefferson is "a less than ideal source of contemporary history as to the meaning of the Religion Clauses of the First Amendment." Absent from the country when the Constitution and Bill of Rights were written, Jefferson was not involved in the drafting of the First Amendment. Although Jefferson, along with James Madison, had earlier played prominent roles in the legislative battles to promote religious liberty in revolutionary Virginia, Rehnquist disputed that the views they had expressed in the Virginia debates found equivalent expression in the First Amendment.

Rehnquist offered several other pieces of evidence to contradict the notion that the "wall of separation" metaphor accurately represents First Amendment principles, including numerous Thanksgiving proclamations and other actions by Presidents and Congress, as well as the Northwest Ordinance, which Congress took up on the same day the proposed amendments crafted into the Bill of Rights were introduced. The Northwest Ordinance is generally known for providing land grants for public schools in the new states and territories, but it also allowed grants for religious schools, until Congress limited grants to nonsectarian institutions in 1845.

Although these various pieces of historical evidence support the proposition that the Establishment of Religion Clause merely requires "no preference between denominations," others criticize that view on originalist grounds. For instance, Douglas Laycock has noted that the Congress that drafted the First Amendment rejected several preliminary drafts that would have clearly stated the "no preference" principle—for example, one draft stated that "Congress shall make no law establishing One Religious Sect or Society in preference to others." Instead, Congress adopted the arguably broader language forbidding any law "respecting an establishment of religion." The "no preference" position, whatever its originalist merits, has not figured in Supreme Court opinions since the 1985 Rehnquist dissent in *Wallace v. Jaffree*.

As another alternative to separationism, some Justices assert that the Establishment of Religion Clause was originally meant only to prohibit the government from coercing individuals to practice religion or support it. It is often associated with Justices who believe the government has the power to "accommodate" the diverse religious practices of the people. This principle, to which the Court has given attention in decisions such as *Lee v. Weisman* (1992), would allow government to support religion in ways that do not coerce individuals. For example, states could permit the erection of religious symbols in public places or issue proclamations of thanksgiving to God. This position likewise finds some support in Founding-era statements, such as James Madison's 1789 explanation to the House that the goal was to prevent a sect or combination of sects from "establish[ing] a religion to which they would compel others to conform," or from "enforc[ing] the legal observation of it by law." The "no coercion" principle likewise is consistent with the long line of religious expressions by government, running from the Founding period to the present; government may express religious sentiments as long as it does not force anyone to agree with such expressions or participate in such ceremonies. As applied by the Court, however, particularly in the opinions of Justice Anthony Kennedy, the "no coercion principle" is broad enough to prohibit even student-led nonsectarian prayers at school assemblies (such as graduations or sporting events) if the state, in some way, selected the student for that purpose.

Finally, Justice Sandra Day O'Connor offered an alternative to both the strict separationist view (usually articulated in the *Lemon* test) and the "no coercion" principle. According to Justice O'Connor, the Establishment Clause prohibits a state from "endorsing" a religion. She defines the test for "endorsement" as whether an objective, reasonable observer would see the state action as sending "a message to nonadherents that they are outsiders, not full members of the political community." *Lynch v. Donnelly*. Justice Antonin Scalia, along with several other current members of the Court, have criticized the test, though some of the strict separationists have adopted Justice O'Connor's wording as supporting their interpretation of the clause. *See County of Allegheny v. American Civil Liberties Union, Greater Pittsburgh Chapter* (1989).

Establishment of Religion Clause jurisprudence remains unsettled as Justices form shifting majorities around one or the other of these different approaches to interpreting the clause. The coercion test was the basis for invalidating prayers in public school settings, *Lee v. Weisman*; *Santa Fe Independent School District v. Doe*. Concerning the question whether the phrase "under God" can be part of the Pledge of Allegiance public-school children are allowed (but not required) to recite, the Supreme Court refused to rule in a case because the plaintiff lacked standing (and was not directly injured by the practice). *Elk Grove Unified School District v. Newdow* (2004).

The *Lemon* test, or a form of it, was invoked to invalidate the teaching of creationism, *Edwards v. Aquillard* (1987), and state-sponsored posting of the Ten Commandments in public schools, *Stone v. Graham* (1980). The endorsement test has provided the formula that a number of Justices have used to decide the constitutionality of religious displays on public property, such as a Nativity scene, *County of Allegheny v. American Civil Liberties Union, Greater Pittsburgh Chapter*, and a cross, *Capitol Square Review and Advisory Board v. Pinette* (1995). In two cases decided the same day in June 2005, the Court added to the doctrinal confusion surrounding the constitutionality of public displays of the Ten Commandments. In *McCreary County, Kentucky v.*

ACLU of Kentucky, the Court, invoking the *Lemon* test, ruled that a Ten Commandments display in a county courthouse communicated a religious purpose, thus violating the Establishment of Religion Clause. In the companion case, *Van Orden v. Perry*, a plurality of the Justices held that a Ten Commandments monument erected on the grounds of a state capitol surrounded by other monuments did not violate the clause because the challenged display, when viewed in the light of its history, purpose, and context, did not convey a message of endorsement of religion. The Court, it should be noted, has frequently approved religious expression or symbols on public property as protected by the Freedom of Speech Clause of the First Amendment, *Good News Club v. Milford Central School* (2001).

After a long series of cases dealing with aid to religious schools, a majority of the Court has embraced the principle that there is no Establishment Clause violation if the state gives tuition aid (e.g., tuition vouchers) directly to the parents who can decide which schools their children will attend, whether religiously affiliated or not, rather than giving the aid directly to the religious school. *Zelman v. Simmons-Harris* (2002). Finally, the Court has approved "exceptions" based on tradition, such as tax exemptions, *Walz v. Tax Commission of City of New York*, and legislative chaplains, *Marsh v. Chambers*, even though the Framers of the Establishment of Religion Clause did not find a provision of a chaplain to be an "exception" but in harmony with a governmental policy of encouraging religious expression and exercise.

In a major ruling for religious autonomy from government interference, the Supreme Court held unanimously in 2012 that the Establishment and Free Exercise of Religion Clauses bar lawsuits brought on behalf of ministers against their churches alleging termination in violation of employment anti-discrimination laws. The case involved a teacher and "commissioned minister" at a church-run school who had claimed that she was fired from her job in violation of the Americans with Disabilities Act. The church and school sought to dismiss a subsequent suit brought by the Equal Employment Opportunity Commission on behalf of the terminated employee, invoking a "ministerial exception" rooted in the First Amendment, which the employer argued prohibited the government's interference in the employment relationship between a religious institution and its ministers. Chief Justice John Roberts, writing for a unanimous Court, found that the teacher was a "minister" for purposes of the exception and then noted: "The Establishment Clause prevents the Government from appointing ministers, and the Free Exercise Clause prevents it from interfering with the freedom of religious groups to select their own." "Requiring a church to accept or retain an unwanted minister, or punishing a church for failing to do so," Roberts continued, "intrudes upon more than a mere employment decision. Such action interferes with the internal governance of the church, depriving the church of control over the selection of those who will personify its beliefs." Nothing less than "the interest of religious groups in choosing who will preach their beliefs, teach their faith, and carry out their mission" was at stake in this case, the Court concluded. *Hosanna-Tabor Evangelical Lutheran Church and School v. EEOC* (2012).

John S. Baker, Jr. and Daniel Dreisbach

See Also

Article VI, Clause 3 (Oaths Clause)
Amendment I (Free Exercise of Religion)

Suggestions for Further Research

John S. Baker, Jr., *The Establishment Clause as Intended: No Preference Among Sects and Pluralism in a Large Commercial Republic*, in THE BILL OF RIGHTS: ORIGINAL MEANING AND CURRENT UNDERSTANDING (Eugene W. Hickok, Jr., ed., 1991)

GERARD V. BRADLEY, CHURCH–STATE RELATIONSHIPS IN AMERICA (1987)

DONALD L. DRAKEMAN, CHURCH, STATE, AND ORIGINAL INTENT (2009)

DANIEL L. DREISBACH, THOMAS JEFFERSON AND THE WALL OF SEPARATION BETWEEN CHURCH AND STATE (2002)

PHILIP A. HAMBURGER, SEPARATION OF CHURCH AND STATE (2002)

Douglas Laycock, *"Noncoercive" Support for Religion: Another False Claim About the Establishment Clause*, 26 VAL. U. L. REV. 37 (1991)

Douglas Laycock, *"Nonpreferential" Aid to Religion: A False Claim About Original Intent*, 27 Wm. & Mary L. Rev. 875 (1986)

Douglas Laycock, *The Underlying Unity of Separation and Neutrality*, 46 Emory L.J. 43 (1997)

Michael W. McConnell, *Establishment and Disestablishment at the Founding, Part I: Establishment of Religion*, 44 Wm. & Mary L. Rev. 2105 (2003)

Significant Cases

Reynolds v. United States, 98 U.S. 145 (1879)

Everson v. Bd. of Education of Ewing Twp., 330 U.S. 1 (1947)

Illinois *ex rel.* McCollum v. Bd. of Education, 333 U.S. 203 (1948)

Zorach v. Clauson, 343 U.S. 306 (1952)

Engel v. Vitale, 370 U.S. 421 (1962)

School Dist. of Abington Twp. v. Schempp, 374 U.S. 203 (1963)

Epperson v. Arkansas, 393 U.S. 97 (1968)

Bd. of Education v. Allen, 392 U.S. 236 (1968)

Walz v. Tax Comm'n of City of New York, 397 U.S. 664 (1970)

Lemon v. Kurtzman, 403 U.S. 602 (1971)

Committee for Public Education & Religious Liberty v. Nyquist, 413 U.S. 756 (1973)

Meek v. Pittenger, 421 U.S. 349 (1975)

Stone v. Graham, 449 U.S. 39 (1980)

Marsh v. Chambers, 463 U.S. 783 (1983)

Mueller v. Allen, 463 U.S. 388 (1983)

Lynch v. Donnelly, 465 U.S. 668 (1984)

Wallace v. Jaffree, 472 U.S. 38 (1985)

Witters v. Washington Dept. of Services for Blind, 474 U.S. 481 (1986)

Edwards v. Aguillard, 482 U.S. 578 (1987)

Bowen v. Kendrick, 487 U.S. 589 (1988)

Cnty. of Allegheny v. ACLU, Greater Pittsburgh Chapter, 492 U.S. 573 (1989)

Lee v. Weisman, 505 U.S. 577 (1992)

Zobrest v. Catalina Foothills School Dist., 509 U.S. 1 (1993)

Capitol Square Review and Advisory Bd. v. Pinette, 515 U.S. 753 (1995)

Rosenberger v. Rector and Visitors of the University of Virginia, 515 U.S. 819 (1995)

Agostini v. Felton, 521 U.S. 203 (1997)

Santa Fe Independent School Dist. v. Doe, 530 U.S. 290 (2000)

Mitchell v. Helms, 530 U.S. 793 (2000)

Good News Club v. Milford Central School, 533 U.S. 98 (2001)

Zelman v. Simmons-Harris, 536 U.S. 639 (2002)

Elk Grove Unified School Dist. v. Newdow, 542 U.S. 1 (2004)

Van Orden v. Perry, 545 U.S. 677 (2005)

McCreary Cnty. v. ACLU of Kentucky, 545 U.S. 844 (2005)

Hein v. Freedom From Religion Foundation, 551 U.S. 587 (2007)

Salazar v. Buono, 559 U.S. 700 (2010)

Hosanna-Tabor Evangelical Lutheran Church and School v. EEOC, 132 S. Ct. 694 (2012)

Free Exercise of Religion

Congress shall make no law…prohibiting the free exercise thereof….

(Amendment I)

~

*E*stablishing freedom of religion as both constitutional principle and social reality is among America's greatest contributions to the world. Nevertheless, the concept of free exercise of religion is not self-defining. The boundaries of free exercise, like those of other rights, must be delineated as against the claims of society and of other individuals. The history of the Free Exercise of Religion Clause, in both its original understanding and modern interpretations, reveals two recurring impulses, one giving free exercise a broad, the other a narrow, scope. The narrower view sometimes collapses free exercise into other constitutional rights, for example treating religious activity as no more than a variety of speech or expression. The broader view sees the right of choice in religious practice as independently valuable. The tension between broad and narrow rights has played out in five sets of issues under the Free Exercise of Religion Clause: belief vs. conduct; discriminatory vs. generally applicable laws; institutional free exercise and internal vs. outward acts; religion vs. secular conscience; and the scope of "prohibiting" vs. "burdening."

The first key issue concerns the meaning of the protected "exercise" of religion: does it encompass only the belief and profession of a religion, or does it also protect conduct that stems from religious tenets or motivations; for example, wearing a head covering or religious garb, or refusing to accept blood transfusions or other medical treatment?

The great weight of the original understanding controverts the narrowest interpretation of the text, that is, that belief alone is protected. At the Founding, as today, dictionaries defined "exercise" to include action, not just internal belief. Thomas Jefferson, in his famous 1802 "wall of separation" letter to the Danbury Baptist Association, drew a sharp distinction between protected belief and unprotected action: "the legitimate powers of government reach actions only, and not opinions" and "[man] has no natural right in opposition to his social duties." But a number of statements from other leading figures support the broader view—from James Madison's statement that religion includes "the manner of discharging" duties to God, to William Penn's statement that "liberty of conscience [means] not only a meer liberty of the mind, in believing or disbelieving…but the exercise of ourselves in a visible way of worship."

In its first interpretation of the Free Exercise of Religion Clause, *Reynolds v. United States* (1879), the Supreme Court drew a sharp line between belief and action, relying on Jefferson's letter to the Danbury Baptists, in holding that the Mormon practice of polygamy was not protected. Since then, however, the Court has ruled more frequently in line with the original meaning, protecting certain religiously motivated actions such as proselytization, *Cantwell v. Connecticut* (1940), refusing work on one's Sabbath, *Sherbert v. Verner* (1963), choosing the education of one's children, *Wisconsin v. Yoder* (1972), and sacrificing animals at a worship service, *Church of Lukumi Babalu Aye v. City of Hialeah* (1993). Action inevitably receives less protection than belief, but it is not unprotected.

Reynolds, which involved federal and territorial laws against polygamy, was the Court's only free exercise decision on the merits until the middle of the twentieth century, since the clause applied only to acts by the federal government. During that time, the significance of the Free Exercise of Religion Clause lay less in its legal effect than in its affirmation of the value of religion in American culture. In 1940, however, in *Cantwell*, the Court "incorporated" the Free Exercise of Religion Clause into the Due Process Clause of the Fourteenth Amendment and applied it to the states. Subsequently, most contests over free exercise have involved state laws.

A second key issue involves discriminatory vs. generally applicable laws. Because it is now accepted that the Free Exercise of Religion Clause protects religiously motivated conduct as well as belief, the most important modern issue has been whether the clause only prohibits laws that target religion itself for restriction, or more broadly requires an exemption in some cases even from a generally applicable law that happens to conflict with a particular religious practice. To take just one of many examples, must an Orthodox Jewish military officer, who is religiously obligated to wear a yarmulke, be exempted from a general rule forbidding all servicemen to wear anything other than official headgear?

On this issue, the text of the clause can support either the narrow or the broad reading. A law could well be said to be "*prohibiting* the free exercise [of religion]" if it in fact prohibits a religious practice, even if it does so incidentally, rather than overtly or intentionally. On the other hand, one might argue that the legislature does not "*make [a] law* prohibiting the free exercise" unless the prohibition or restriction on religion is part of the law's very terms or is the legislature's intent, as opposed to simply the effect of the law in a particular application.

This issue therefore requires examination of the legal background and the Founding generation's attitude toward conflicts between law and religious conscience. By 1789, all but one of the states had free-exercise–type provisions in their constitutions. Many of these state guarantees included provisos that such freedom would not justify, or could be denied for, practices that "disturb[ed] the public peace" or were "inconsistent with the peace and safety of the State." Michael McConnell has argued that the provisos reflect the broader, pro-exemptions conception of free exercise, because if religious practices were subject to all general laws, there would be no reason to identify a subset of laws that protected the peace of the state. In response, Philip Hamburger has asserted that in eighteenth-century legal terminology, "every breach of law [was] against the peace [of the state]," so that the provisos would have been triggered by any secular law of general applicability.

The legal background also includes accommodations made by colonial and state legislatures for specific religious practices. Virtually all states by 1789 allowed Quakers to testify or vote by an affirmation rather than an oath; several colonies had exempted Quakers and Mennonites from service in the militia; and there was a patchwork of other exemptions throughout the states. Supporters of the narrower view of the Free Exercise of Religion Clause, such as Professor Hamburger, argue that these examples imply only that specific statutory exemptions may be granted by legislative grace. But advocates of the broader interpretation, such as Professor McConnell, infer that the Founding generation thought that exemption from the law was the appropriate response to conflicts between legal and religious duties, that is, an exemption was part of the meaning of "free exercise" so long as the religious activity did not harm public peace or others' rights.

More deeply, the question of exemptions from generally applicable laws implicates ideological differences over the relationship between civil government and religion. One important philosophical influence on the Founders, the Enlightenment liberalism stemming from the writings of John Locke, does not lend itself easily to exempting religious practice from general secular laws. In his famous *Letter Concerning Toleration* (1689), Locke argued that the proper domains of government and religion were largely separate; "the power of civil government...is confined to the care of the things of this world," whereas "churches have [no] jurisdiction in worldly matters." Although this limit on government control over belief and doctrine was liberal for its time, just as central to Locke's understanding was the limit on religion's role in worldly matters. And in those cases where both religion and government claimed jurisdiction—that is where

religious duties clashed with general laws, and an exemption is sought—Locke gave the nod to the government on the ground that "the private judgment of any person concerning a law enacted in political matters...does not take away the obligation of that law, nor deserve a dispensation."

The Enlightenment view, however, was hardly the dominant impetus for religious freedom in America. Popular support for religious freedom came most heavily from the newer evangelical Protestant sects, especially the Baptists and Presbyterians. These religious "enthusiasts," who helped defeat religious taxes in Virginia and elect James Madison to Congress, began from a different premise: that religion was a matter of duties to God, and that God, in the words of Massachusetts Baptist leader Isaac Backus, "is to be obeyed rather than any man." Madison echoed these ideas in his *Memorial and Remonstrance Against Religious Assessments* (1785), arguing that the duty to the Creator "is precedent, both in order of time and in degree of obligation, to the claims of Civil Society"; thus, everyone who joins a civil society must "do it with a saving of his allegiance to the Universal Sovereign." This view logically suggests that the proper governmental response to conflicts between legal and religious duties is, at least sometimes, exemption from legal duties.

Whether religious exemptions from generally applicable laws are ever constitutionally mandated has been the central question in this area for many years. After rejecting mandated exemptions for many years, the Supreme Court switched course and exempted religious claimants from laws in *Sherbert v. Verner* and *Wisconsin v. Yoder*. In *Sherbert*, the Court struck down a state law that denied unemployment benefits to a Seventh-Day Adventist on the basis that she had refused "available" work, when her religion forbade her from working or being available for work on Saturday. Because a different provision of state law specifically barred employers from firing or penalizing employees who objected to Sunday work, the state's laws overall discriminated against Saturday sabbatarians. However, much of the *Sherbert* opinion's language cut more broadly, and subsequent decisions interpreted *Sherbert* as a protection for religiously based objections to laws that were clearly generally applicable. Thus, in *Yoder* the Court held that the Free Exercise of Religion Clause protected members of the Amish faith from having to abide by a compulsory school attendance law.

The pro-exemptions approach, however, was often applied half-heartedly in the next two decades, and in *Employment Division, Department of Human Resources of Oregon v. Smith* (1990) the Court declared that the Free Exercise of Religion Clause did not grant an exemption from generally applicable drug law to members of a Native American religion who used peyote in its religious services. The Court abandoned the pro-exemptions approach in most cases, holding that exemptions are not required from a "neutral law of general applicability." Because most restrictions on religious conduct today come from the application of general laws rather than from laws targeting religion, *Smith* greatly limited the protections accorded religiously motivated actions.

In response to *Smith*, Congress passed the Religious Freedom Restoration Act of 1993 (RFRA), reinstating the *Sherbert-Yoder* test that laws that "substantially burden" religion, even if they are neutral and generally applicable, must be justified as the "least restrictive means" of achieving a "compelling governmental interest." Nonetheless, in *City of Boerne v. Flores* (1997), the Supreme Court struck down RFRA as applied to state and local laws, on the ground that Congress exceeded its power to enforce the Fourteenth Amendment in attempting to define the constitutional parameters of the (incorporated) Free Exercise of Religion Clause. RFRA, however, remains applicable to federal laws and regulations, and a number of states have passed their own versions of RFRA. Thus, the rule concerning exemptions from general laws remains divided under modern law, just as there is division and ambivalence in the original understanding of the Free Exercise of Religion Clause.

Questions also remain over what makes a law fail the "neutral, generally applicable" test. In *Lukumi*, the Court held that ordinances prohibiting the killing of animals fell "far below" the standard because they contained so many exceptions that they effectively targeted only the ritual sacrifices of the Santeria religion. Many laws, however, contain some secular exceptions but not so many as to target religion. In *Fraternal Order of Police v. City of Newark* (1999), the Third Circuit, through then-Judge Samuel Alito, held that a police department's rule against officers wearing beards violated a Muslim officer's free exercise rights because the rule contained an exception for officers with medical conditions requiring beards. In the court's view, the department's willingness to accommodate a secular interest but not a religious need "devalued" religion, triggering strict scrutiny. But other lower courts have required that a law contain more than one secular exception in order to find it not "generally applicable."

The question whether the provision of secular accommodations triggers a duty to accommodate religious objectors also arises in lawsuits over the Obama administration's rule requiring employers to include contraception, including some "emergency contraception" medicines that may act as abortifacients, in their employees' health-insurance coverage. The rule exempts churches, but many other religious organizations (social services, hospitals, and schools), along with commercial businesses run by religious individuals, have objected that it would force them to support acts they believe are sinful, including abortions of new embryos. Suing under both the Free Exercise of Religion Clause and RFRA, the organizations argue that the government must exempt them because it has already recognized numerous exceptions for small businesses, "grandfathered" plans, and businesses receiving case-by-case waivers on ground of hardship.

A third key issue regards the institutional free exercise of religion and internal vs. outward acts. Although many Free Exercise of Religion Clause cases involve the religious practices of individuals, questions also arise whether religious institutions enjoy distinctive protection, especially for their internal governance. Several Supreme Court decisions affirm institutional rights, beginning with *Watson v. Jones* (1872), the first in a line of disputes over property ownership in the wake of schisms within denominations. *Watson* held that courts should resolve such disputes by accepting the decision of the body's highest authority: for a hierarchically organized church, the highest tribunal, and for a congregationally organized church, the congregation in question. *Watson's* principles rested on general common law, but the Court adopted them for the Free Exercise of Religion Clause in *Kedroff v. St. Nicholas Cathedral* (1952). *Kedroff* affirmed a religious organization's "power to decide for themselves, free from state interference, matters of church government as well as those of faith and doctrine." It held that a state statute transferring control of church property from one Russian Orthodox bishop to another intruded on what was "strictly a matter of ecclesiastical government": the power of the church's highest authority to appoint the ruling bishop for North America.

However, in *Jones v. Wolf* (1979), the Court determined that courts deciding church-property disputes could apply "neutral principles" of property, trust, or contract law applicable to organizations in general. *Jones*, coupled with the ruling a few years later in *Employment Division v. Smith*, led many to question whether special free exercise protection for religious organizations survived.

Even after *Jones* and *Smith*, however, lower courts continued to recognize the "ministerial exception" to Title VII and other anti-discrimination laws. Under that exception, a court cannot hear a lawsuit by a minister challenging a religious employer's decision to dismiss him, refuse to hire him, or control the terms of his employment. The lower courts pointed out that *Smith* had continued to prohibit the government from intervening in "controversies over religious dogma or authority." And in *Hosanna-Tabor Evangelical Lutheran Church and School v. EEOC* (2012), the Court unanimously affirmed the ministerial exception, holding that the Free Exercise of Religion Clause guarantees an organization "the authority to select and control who will minister to the faithful."

In *Hosanna-Tabor*, the federal government argued that *Smith's* rejection of exemptions had undermined the ministerial exception, and that protection for churches' decisions concerning ministers rested largely on the First Amendment's freedom of expressive association. The government's position in *Hosanna-Tabor* thus epitomized the narrow view of religious freedom, all but reducing it to expressive rights held equally by secular organizations. *Hosanna-Tabor* resoundingly rejected the narrow position, calling it "hard to square with the text of the First Amendment itself, which gives special solicitude to the rights of religious organizations"; it rejected "the remarkable view that the Religion Clauses have nothing to say about a religious organization's freedom to select its own ministers."

The Court held that *Smith's* rejection of exemptions extended only to "outward physical acts," such as the ingestion of peyote in that case, and not to "internal decisions" concerning a religious organization's governance or doctrine. Future cases will surely explore this line. One principle should be clear: a religious organization does not lose distinctive free-exercise protection simply because it turns "outward" to the broader society by running schools or social services. This principle is implicated in several recent controversies; the contraception mandate, for example, initially denied protection entirely to a religious organization if it served persons outside its own faith, *or* if it served anyone through health or social services, rather than preaching or teaching ("inculcat[ing] religious values"). Such a provision confines free-exercise protection to the narrowest category of the house of worship—reflecting the view of many proponents that once religion enters any area that might be possibly be described as "public," it must follow all the rules of the regulatory state. But *Hosanna-Tabor* rejects this narrow approach, confirming that a non-church organization such as a school has institutional religious-freedom rights. The question remains, however, what acts of a school, hospital, or social service count as "internal" matters of doctrine and governance.

The original understanding supports the freedom of religious organizations to decide certain matters of internal governance without state interference—especially to select and control religious leaders. The clergy-selection question has been sensitive in Western history for almost a thousand years, at least since the medieval controversy between popes and Holy Roman Emperors over who had the power to appoint bishops. Although that dispute involved a fundamental clash between two authorities seeking predominance, the rough compromise that ultimately emerged—popes appointed bishops, emperors appointed civil officials—reflected a solution of separating certain core powers of the church and of the state.

Early Protestantism, in struggling with the Catholic Church, often sought assistance from civil rulers, sometimes to the point of letting them control clergy selection and other important religious functions. In the Church of England, the most familiar example of an establishment to the American Founders, the government appointed leading clerics, the monarch was official head of the church, and Parliament approved the Thirty-Nine Articles (the church's doctrinal tenets) and the Book of Common Prayer.

The First Amendment, in its non-establishment as well as its free exercise provision, confirms that Americans rejected any role for the federal government in choosing church leaders. In 1783 the Vatican proposed an agreement with Congress to approve a Bishop-Apostolic for America now that the new states were outside English authority; but Congress responded that it had "no authority to permit or refuse" the appointment, and the Pope could appoint whomever he wished, because "[t]he subject . . . being purely spiritual, it is without the jurisdiction and powers of Congress." James Madison, as secretary of state in 1806, reaffirmed that the civil government had no power over the purely "ecclesiastical" matters of choosing a Catholic leader for the Louisiana Territory.

Leading Founding-era proponents of the First Amendment understood it to protect religious institutions' autonomy, especially concerning clergy selection. Isaac Backus, the leader of Massachusetts Baptists, wrote in 1773 that, "God has appointed two kinds of government in the world which are distinct in their nature and ought never to be confounded together"—civil and ecclesiastical government—and therefore it was solely a church prerogative to determine what [God's] worship shall be, who shall minister in it, and how they shall be supported." The same sentiments were expressed by Enlightenment statesmen such as Madison, who as President vetoed a bill incorporating a church in the District of Columbia on the ground, in part, that the bill enacted rules "relative purely to the organiza-

tion and polity of the church incorporated, and comprehending even the election and removal of the Minister of the same, so that no change could be made therein by" the congregation or the denomination. After the U.S. took control of the Louisiana Territory, President Jefferson, responding to a letter from Ursuline nuns who ran a school in New Orleans, assured them that "the principles of the Constitution of the United States" guarantee that "your institution will be permitted to govern itself according to its own voluntary rules, without interference from the civil authority."

Civil involvement in clergy selection, a feature of several colonial arrangements, disappeared during the Founding and early republic. In New England and the Southern colonies, civil authorities regulated the conduct of clergy in the established church and at first prohibited, then licensed, religious teachers from dissenting sects. Such measures triggered massive resistance from Baptists and other dissenters, and they disappeared as part of the commitment both to disestablishment and to free exercise. Clergy-selection issues also led to the demise in 1833 of the Massachusetts religious establishment under which a majority of a town's voters determined which clergyman would presumptively receive tax-funded subsidies and occupy the town's "First Church." When Unitarians began to control some towns, and courts awarded them control of the First Church and of tax funds, support for the tax system collapsed. This was disestablishment, but it was also a victory for a congregation's free exercise of religion against civil (town) interference.

In *Hosanna-Tabor*, the Court refused to limit the ministerial exception to cases where the government explicitly second-guessed a church's religious criteria for selecting its minister. The original understanding supports this holding; it shows that government can trigger the harms that the Religion clauses seek to avoid—coercion, divisiveness, government overreaching—simply by overriding a church's decision on who is suitable to be its minister. Under the Massachusetts scheme for clergy taxes, the majority of town voters needed no theological rationale for selecting one clergyman for the "First" church; they could choose based on any factor. Other restrictions—Virginia's limit on the number of places where a minister could be licensed to speak, and Massachusetts' requirement that all ministers have college degrees—were formally neutral among theologies and called for no doctrinal determination by civil authorities. Nevertheless these restrictions provoked intense resistance and eventually were repealed.

A fourth key issue addresses religion vs. secular conscience. Related to the question whether religious exercise should be exempted from generally applicable laws is the question whether the exercise "of religion" extends to behavior motivated by norms of secular conscience, as opposed to beliefs in God or other traditional features of religion. For example, should the exemption from school-attendance laws for the Amish in *Yoder* extend to followers of Henry Thoreau who rejected traditional schooling for their children? (*Yoder* itself answered no.)

The word "religion" might be understood in direct contrast to a broader idea of "conscience" that includes secular-based norms. Both terms were used during the Founding period—indeed, during the debates on the language of the First Amendment, which began with Madison's proposal to protect "the full and equal rights of conscience" but eventually changed to "the free exercise of religion." The change may have meant little substantively, because during the Founding period "conscience" was often used as synonymous with "religion." Or possibly the change may have meant a narrowing from all deep moral convictions to theistic ones.

In a pair of cases involving challenges to military conscription during the Vietnam War, the Supreme Court read the statutory phrase "religious training and belief" to encompass objections based on any secular conscientious belief "which occupies in the life of its possessor a place parallel to that filled by the God of those" who are traditionally religious. *United States v. Seeger* (1965); *Welsh v. United States* (1970). Those expansive definitions, however, were adopted under the language of the draft-exemption statute. For the Free Exercise of Religion Clause itself, the Court has been more cautious in construing "religion" in cases like *Yoder*. And

Hosanna-Tabor confirms that the clause gives "special solicitude to the rights of religious organizations" in distinction to secular ideological organizations.

The fifth key issue involves the Scope of "prohibiting" vs. "burdening." Another question bedeviling courts in Free Exercise of Religion Clause cases has been just what sort of effects on religious exercise trigger protection. Are Free Exercise rights violated only when one is put in jail or fined for religious practice, or are some less serious burdens also unconstitutional?

The term "prohibiting" in the Free Exercise of Religion Clause may suggest the narrower scope of the right, covering only the affirmative imposition of sanctions such as imprisonment or a fine. Indeed, "prohibiting" might be contrasted directly with "infringing," the term used in an earlier draft, and with its broader counterpart in other First Amendment Clauses: "no law abridging" the freedom of speech, press, assembly, or petition. Madison rejected a parallel argument during the 1798 debate over the Alien and Sedition Acts. In response to the claim that Congress could regulate freedom of the press without "abridging" it, he argued against such a semantic distinction because "the liberty of conscience and the freedom of the press were equally and completely exempted from all [congressional] authority whatever."

In *Sherbert*, the Court adopted a broad understanding of unconstitutional "burdens" on religion, holding that the state violated Free Exercise by withholding unemployment benefits on the basis of the claimant's religiously motivated refusal to work on Saturdays. Later, however, the Court took a more narrow approach, pointing to the term "prohibiting" in holding that the government did not violate Free Exercise by building a road that disrupted forest areas sacred to Native American believers, because the project did not "coerce individuals into acting contrary to their religious beliefs." *Lyng v. Northwest Indian Cemetery Protective Ass'n* (1988). *Sherbert*, however, though now limited in its application, has never been directly overruled by the Court. The Court has never questioned *Sherbert*'s holding that the government can "prohibit" free exercise by withholding important benefits from the individual because of a religious practice, not only by imprisoning or fining him.

Thomas Berg

See Also

Amendment I (Establishment of Religion Clause)

Amendment XIV, Section 1 (Due Process Clause)

Suggestions for Further Research

Thomas C. Berg et al., _Religious Freedom, Church-State Separation, and the Ministerial Exception_, 106 Nw. L. Rev. Colloquy 175 (2011)

Walter Berns, The First Amendment and the Future of American Democracy (Regnery Publishing, Inc., 1985)

Philip A. Hamburger, _A Constitutional Right of Religious Exemption: An Historical Perspective_, 60 Geo. Wash. L. Rev. 915 (1992)

Kurt T. Lash, _The Second Adoption of the Free Exercise Clause: Religious Exemptions Under the Fourteenth Amendment_, 88 Nw. U. L. Rev. 1106 (1994)

Ira C. Lupu, _Where Rights Begin: The Problem of Burdens on the Free Exercise of Religion_, 102 Harv. L. Rev. 933 (1989)

Michael J. Malbin, Religion and Politics: The Intentions of the Authors of the First Amendment (1978)

Michael W. McConnell, _The Origins and Historical Understanding of Free Exercise of Religion_, 103 Harv. L. Rev. 1409 (1990)

John Witte, Jr., _The Essential Rights and Liberties of Religion in the American Constitutional Experiment_, 71 Notre Dame L. Rev. 371 (1996)

Significant Cases

Watson v. Jones, 80 U.S. 679 (1872)

Reynolds v. United States, 98 U.S. 145 (1879)

Cantwell v. Connecticut, 310 U.S. 296 (1940)

Kedroff v. St. Nicholas Cathedral, 344 U.S. 94 (1952)

Sherbert v. Verner, 374 U.S. 398 (1963)

United States v. Seeger, 380 U.S. 163 (1965)

Welsh v. United States, 398 U.S. 333 (1970)

Wisconsin v. Yoder, 406 U.S. 205 (1972)

Jones v. Wolf, 443 U.S. 595 (1979)

Lyng v. Northwest Indian Cemetery Protective Ass'n, 485 U.S. 439 (1988)

Employment Div., Dept. of Human Resources of Oregon v. Smith, 494 U.S. 872 (1990)

Church of Lukumi Babalu Aye v. City of Hialeah, 508 U.S. 520 (1993)

City of Boerne v. Flores, 521 U.S. 507 (1997)

Fraternal Order of Police v. City of Newark, 170 F.3d 359 (3d Cir. 1999)

Cutter v. Wilkinson, 544 U.S. 709 (2005)

Hosanna-Tabor Evangelical Lutheran Church and School v. EEOC, 132 S. Ct. 694 (2012)

Freedom of Speech and of the Press

Congress shall make no law ... abridging the freedom of speech, or of the press....

(Amendment I)

~

_W_hat exactly did the Framers mean by "freedom of speech, or of the press"? Little is definitively known about the subject. The debates in the First Congress, which proposed the Bill of Rights, are brief and unilluminating. Early state constitutions generally included similar provisions, but there is no record of detailed debate about what those state provisions meant. The Framers cared a good deal about the freedom of the press, as the _Appeal to the Inhabitants of Quebec_, written by the First Continental Congress in 1774, shows:

> The last right we shall mention regards the freedom of the press. The importance of this consists, besides the advancement of truth, science, morality, and arts in general, in its diffusion of liberal sentiments on the administration of Government, its ready communication of thoughts between subjects, and its consequential promotion of union among them, whereby oppressive officers are shamed or intimidated into more honorable and just modes of conducting affairs.

The statement mentions some of the values that the Founders saw as inherent in the principle of freedom of the press: the search and attainment of truth, scientific progress, cultural development, the increase of virtue among the people, the holding of governmental officials to republican values, the strengthening of community, and a check upon self-aggrandizing politicians. But broad statements such as this tell us less than we would like to know about what "the freedom of the press" meant to the Founders as a rule of law, when the freedom would yield to competing concerns, or whether the freedom prohibited only prior restraints or also subsequent punishments.

There were few reported Founding-era court cases that interpreted the federal and state Free Speech and Free Press Clauses, and few Founding-era political controversies excited detailed discussion of what the clauses meant. The governments of the time were small, and the statute books thin. Not many states passed laws restricting commercial advertising. Only one state law banned pornography, and that ban appears to have been unenforced until 1821. Some states had blasphemy laws, but they were largely unenforced from the early 1700s until the 1810s. No laws banned flag-burning, campaign spending, or anonymous speech.

This may but does not necessarily mean that such speech was broadly believed to be constitutionally protected; then, as today, the government did not ban all that it had the power to ban. But the paucity of such bans meant that few people in that era had occasion to define carefully what the constitutional boundaries of speech and press protection might be.

In fact, the most prominent free press debate of the years immediately following the Framing—the Sedition Act controversy—illustrated that there was little consensus on even as central an issue as whether the free press guarantee only prohibited prior restraints on publications critical of the government, or whether it also forbade punishment for "seditious" speech once it was made.

In 1798, the country was fighting the Quasi-War with France. The Federalist Party controlled all three branches of the federal government, and its members suspected many Republican party stalwarts of sympathizing with France and the French Revolution and thus of fomenting disloyalty. Congress consequently made it a crime to publish "any false, scandalous and malicious writing or writings...with intent to defame" the government, Congress, or the President, "or to stir up sedition within the United States, or to excite any unlawful combinations...for opposing or resisting any law of the United States...or to aid, encourage or abet any hostile designs of any foreign nation against the United States, their people or government." Several publishers were in fact convicted under the law, often under rather biased applications of the falsity requirement.

The Federalists' actions likely represented a serious constitutional judgment, and not just political expediency. True, malicious falsehoods about the Vice President—Thomas Jefferson, who was a leading Republican—were not covered by the law, and the law was scheduled to expire on March 3, 1801, the day before Federalist President John Adams's term was to end. But shortly before the law expired, and after the Federalists lost the 1800 election, Federalist Representatives nonetheless tried to renew the Act; had they succeeded, the Act would have punished libels against President Jefferson and the new Democratic-Republican Congressional majority. The bill was defeated in the House by a 53–49 vote, with all but four Federalists voting for it and all Republicans voting against it.

Indeed, in 1799 Federalist Congressman John Marshall (who would soon become Chief Justice), expressed doubts that the Sedition Act was wise but nonetheless argued that the free press guarantee meant only "liberty to publish, free from previous restraint"—free of requirements that printers be licensed, or that their material be approved before publication. Under this view, which echoed the British law as expounded by Sir William Blackstone, criminal punishment after publication was constitutional, at least if the punishment was consistent with the traditional rules of the common law. Other early American political leaders, such as James Madison, the principal drafter of the Bill of Rights, argued the opposite: "[T]his idea of the freedom of the press can never be admitted to be the American idea of it; since a law inflicting penalties on printed publications would have a similar effect with a law authorizing a previous restraint on them."

Likewise, Marshall and other Federalists argued that the freedom of the press must necessarily be limited, because "government cannot be…secured, if by falsehood and malicious slander, it is to be deprived of the confidence and affection of the people." Not so, reasoned Madison and other Republicans: even speech that creates "a contempt, a disrepute, or hatred [of the government] among the people" should be tolerated because the only way of determining whether such contempt is justified is "by a free examination [of the government's actions], and a free communication among the people thereon." It was as if half the country read the constitutional guarantee one way, and the other half, the other way.

The Founding generation undoubtedly believed deeply in the freedom of speech and of the press, but then, as now, these general terms were understood differently by different people. Many people did not think about their precise meaning until a concrete controversy arose; and when a controversy did arise, people disagreed sharply on that meaning.

A Supreme Court case, *McIntyre v. Ohio Elections Commission* (1995), illustrates the continuing debate over the original meaning of the clause. The question in *McIntyre* was whether the government could outlaw anonymous electioneering. The majority dealt with the question based on the Court's twentieth-century case law and twentieth-century First Amendment theories. Justices Clarence Thomas and Antonin Scalia, the Court's most devoted originalists, however, did focus on the original meaning discussion but reached different results.

Both Justices recognized that there was "no record of discussions of anonymous political expression either in the First Congress, which drafted the Bill of Rights, or in the state ratifying conventions." They both recognized that much political speech in the time of the Framers (such as *The Federalist Papers* itself) was anonymous. Indeed, much political speech justifying resis-

tance to Parliament before the Revolution was also anonymous.

To Justice Thomas, the experience of the Founders in their own use of anonymous speech—*The Federalist Papers* being a classic example—was dispositive of what they would have regarded as a vital part of the freedom of speech, particularly where political speech was at issue. Justice Scalia, however, who has a narrower view of what can be accepted as evidence of original intent apart from the text of the provision itself, argued that "to prove that anonymous electioneering was used frequently is not to establish that it is a constitutional right"; perhaps the legislatures simply chose not to prohibit the speech, even though they had the constitutional power to do so.

Justice Thomas did produce evidence that some Founding-era commentators saw anonymous commentary as protected by "the Liberty of the Press," but Justice Scalia replied that many of these were mere "partisan cr[ies]" that said little about any generally accepted understanding. Justice Thomas found the evidence sufficient to justify reading the First Amendment as protecting anonymous speech. Justice Scalia did not think the historical evidence of what people did necessarily shows much about what people believed they had a constitutional right to do. Instead, Scalia turned to American practices of the 1800s and the 1900s, a source that he considers authoritative where the original meaning is uncertain. A consensus on the original meaning on this subject thus remains elusive.

This having been said, on some questions it is possible to have a good idea of what the Framers thought, based on a combination of pre-Framing, Framing-era, and shortly post-Framing evidence. First, traditional libel law was seen as permissible. Several state constitutions also secured the "freedom of the press" and the "liberty of the press," and under them, defaming another person was understood to be constitutionally unprotected.

Second, the Free Press Clause was seen as covering the press as technology—all who used printing presses to try to communicate to the public at large—and not the press in the sense of a specific industry or occupation. Professional publishers and journalists were not seen as having any additional constitutional rights beyond those that everyone else had.

Third, Framing-era law treated conventionally symbolic expression, such as paintings, effigies (whether just being displayed or being burnt), liberty poles, and the like as tantamount to verbal expression. Both would be equally punishable as libel, if they conveyed false and defamatory messages about someone. But both would also be equally covered by the freedom of speech or of the press.

Fourth, Framing-era sources treat civil tort liability for speech the same as criminal liability for constitutional purposes. Indeed, the very first court cases setting aside government action on constitutional freedom of expression grounds, an 1802 Vermont case and an 1806 South Carolina case, involved civil libel verdicts set aside because of the state constitutions' Petition Clauses. Similar cases from that era applied the same principle to state Free Speech and Free Press Clauses.

As noted above, there was considerable controversy about how broad the constitutional protections were, and what the scope of the exceptions to protection might be. But the constitutional protections, whatever their substantive breadth, applied equally without regard to whether the speaker was a professional publisher, whether the communication was symbolic expression or verbal expression, and whether the case involved tort liability or criminal punishment.

Notwithstanding occasional references to originalist debates—such as the originalist debate between Justices Thomas and Scalia in *McIntyre*—today's free speech and free press law is not much influenced by original meaning. It mostly stems from the experience and thinking of the twentieth century, as the Court first began to hear a wide range of free speech cases only in the late 1910s. This approach has produced the following general free speech rules:

1. As with all of the Bill of Rights, the free speech/free press guarantee restricts only government action, not action by private employers, property owners, householders, churches, universities, and the like.

2. As with most of the Bill of Rights, the free speech/free press guarantee applies equally to federal and state governments, which includes local governments as well as all branches of each government. In particular, the civil courts are subject to the First Amendment, which is why libel law and other tort law rules must comply with free speech/press principles. *New York Times Co. v. Sullivan* (1964).

3. The Free Speech and Free Press Clauses have been read as providing essentially equal protection to speakers and writers, whether or not they are members of the institutional press, and largely regardless of the medium—books, newspapers, movies, the Internet—in which they communicate. Newspapers enjoy no more and no fewer constitutional rights than individuals. The one exception is over-the-airwaves radio and television broadcasting, which has for historical reasons been given less constitutional protection. *Reno v. ACLU* (1997).

4. The free speech/free press guarantee also extends to any conduct that is conventionally understood as expressive—for instance, waving a flag, wearing an armband, or burning a flag. It also extends to conduct that is necessary in order to speak effectively, as, for example, using money to buy a public address system or to buy advertising. Restrictions on independent campaign expenditures, for instance, raise First Amendment problems because restricting the use of money for speech purposes is a speech restriction. *Stromberg v. California* (1931); *Buckley v. Valeo* (1976); *Citizens United v. FEC* (2010).

5. The free speech/free press guarantee extends not just to political speech but also to speech about

religion, science, morality, social conditions, and daily life, as well as to art and entertainment. In the words of a 1948 case, "The line between the informing and the entertaining is too elusive for the protection of that basic right. Everyone is familiar with instances of propaganda through fiction. What is one man's amusement, teaches another's doctrine." And the guarantee extends to low-brow expression (such as jokes or even profanity) as well as high-brow expression. *Winters v. New York* (1948); *Cohen v. California* (1971).

6. The free speech/free press guarantee extends to all viewpoints, good or evil. There is no exception, for instance, for Communism, Nazism, Islamic radicalism, sexist speech, or "hate speech," whatever that term may mean. "Under the First Amendment there is no such thing as a false idea. However pernicious an opinion may seem, we depend for its correction not on the conscience of judges and juries but on the competition of other ideas." *Gertz v. Robert Welch, Inc.* (1974); *New York Times Co. v. Sullivan.*

7. There is, however, a small set of rather narrow exceptions to free speech protection:

   a. *Incitement:* Speech may be restricted if it is: (i) intended to persuade people to engage in (ii) imminent unlawful conduct, and (iii) likely to cause such imminent unlawful conduct. Outside this narrow zone, even speech that advocates lawbreaking is constitutionally protected. *Brandenburg v. Ohio* (1969).

   b. *Libel, fraud,* and *perjury:* Libel, fraud, and perjury may generally be punished if they consist of knowing lies, though generally not if they are honest mistakes (even unreasonable mistakes). There are, however, some situations where even honest mistakes can be punished. *United States v. Alvarez* (2012); *Gertz v. Robert Welch, Inc.*

   c. *Obscenity:* Hard-core pornography is punishable if: (i) the average person, applying contemporary community standards, would find that the work, taken as a whole, appeals to a shameful or morbid interest in sex or excretion; (ii) the work depicts or describes, in a way that is patently offensive under contemporary community standards, sexual conduct specifically defined by the applicable state law; and (iii) the work, taken as a whole, lacks serious literary, artistic, political, or scientific value. *Miller v. California* (1973).

   d. *Child pornography:* Sexually themed live performances, photographs, and movies that were made using actual children may be punished even if they do not fit within the obscenity test. This does not cover digitized pictures, drawings, or text materials, which are constitutionally protected unless they are obscene. The Court has reasoned that child pornography is unprotected because it hurts the children involved in its making, so the exception only covers cases where actual children were indeed involved. *Ashcroft v. Free Speech Coalition* (2002).

   e. *Threats:* Speech that is reasonably perceived as a threat of violence (and not just rhetorical hyperbole) can be punished. *Virginia v. Black* (2003).

f. *Fighting words*: Face-to-face insults that are addressed to a particular person and are likely to cause an imminent fight can be punished. More generalized offensive speech that is not addressed to a particular person cannot be punished even if it is profane or deeply insulting. *Cohen v. California.*

g. *Speech owned by others*: Intellectual property laws, such as copyright law, may restrict people from using particular expression that is owned by someone else; but the law may not let anyone monopolize facts or ideas. *Harper & Row, Publishers, Inc. v. Nation Enterprises* (1985).

h. *Commercial advertising*: Commercial advertising is constitutionally protected, but less so than other speech (political, scientific, artistic, and the like). Misleading commercial advertising may be barred, whereas misleading political speech cannot be. Commercial advertising may also be required to include disclaimers to keep it from being misleading; such disclaimers can't be required for political speech. Recent cases hold that commercial advertising may not be restricted for paternalistic reasons, because of a fear that people will learn accurate information but will do bad things based on that information—for example, buy more alcohol, smoke more, or prescribe more expensive pharmaceuticals than the government thinks wise. This rule applies only to speech that proposes a commercial transaction between the speaker and the listener; it does not apply to speech that is merely sold in commerce, such as books, videos, and databases. *Sorrell v. IMS Health Inc.* (2011).

8. All of the preceding rules apply to restrictions that relate to what the speech communicates—to the tendency of the speech to persuade people, offend them, or make them feel unsafe. Content-neutral restrictions that relate to the noncommunicative impact of speech—for instance, noise, obstruction of traffic, and so on—are easier to justify. The test for content-neutral restrictions is complicated, but the key point is that the government may generally impose content-neutral "time, place, and manner restrictions" so long as those restrictions leave open ample alternative channels for communication. All such restrictions, however, must be neutral as to content: if they treat speech differently based on content, they are generally unconstitutional even if they focus only on the time, place, and manner of the speech. *Ward v. Rock Against Racism* (1989).

9. Finally, the preceding rules apply to restrictions that are imposed by the government acting as sovereign and backed by the threat of jail terms, fines, or civil liability. They also apply to the government controlling what is said in "traditional public fora," such as parks, streets, sidewalks, or the post office. But when the government is acting as, for instance, (a) employer, (b) K–12 educator, (c) proprietor of government property other than traditional public fora, (d) subsidizer, (e) speaker, or (f) regulator of the airwaves, it has broader (though not unlimited) authority. The rules for that, unfortunately,

are too elaborate to set forth here. *Connick v. Myers* (1983); *Tinker v. Des Moines Independent Community School District* (1969); *ISKCON v. Lee* (1992); *Rosenberger v. Rector and Visitors of the University of Virginia* (1995); *FCC v. League of Women Voters of California* (1984).

Free speech/free press law is sometimes called the tax code of constitutional law. The discussion above suggests how complex the law is, but while some of the complexity may be needless, much of it is inevitable. Communication is in many ways the most complicated of human activities, and no simple rule can properly deal with all the different kinds of harms that it can cause—or all the different kinds of harms that restricting communication can cause.

Eugene Volokh

See Also

Article I, Section 6, Clause 1 (Speech and Debate Clause)

Suggestions for Further Research

Michael Kent Curtis, Free Speech, "The People's Darling Privilege" (2000)

Leonard W. Levy, Emergence of a Free Press (1995)

David M. Rabban, Free Speech in Its Forgotten Years, 1870–1920 (1997)

Rodney A. Smolla, Smolla and Nimmer on Freedom of Speech (1996)

Eugene Volokh, *Freedom for the Press as an Industry, or for the Press as a Technology? From the Framing to Today*, 160 U. Pa. L. Rev. 459 (2012)

Eugene Volokh, *Tort Liability and the Original Meaning of the Freedom of Speech, Press, and Petition*, 96 Iowa L. Rev. 249 (2010)

Eugene Volokh, *Symbolic Expression and the Original Meaning of the First Amendment*, 97 Geo. L.J. 1057 (2009)

Thomas G. West, *Freedom of Speech in the American Founding and in Modern Liberalism*, 21 Soc. Phil. & Pol'y 310 (2004)

Significant Cases

Stromberg v. California, 283 U.S. 359 (1931)

Winters v. New York, 333 U.S. 507 (1948)

New York Times Co. v. Sullivan, 376 U.S. 254 (1964)

Brandenburg v. Ohio, 395 U.S. 444 (1969)

Tinker v. Des Moines Independent Community School Dist., 393 U.S. 503 (1969)

Cohen v. California, 403 U.S. 15 (1971)

Miller v. California, 413 U.S. 15 (1973)

Gertz v. Robert Welch, Inc., 418 U.S. 323 (1974)

Buckley v. Valeo, 424 U.S. 1 (1976)

Connick v. Myers, 461 U.S. 138 (1983)

FCC v. League of Women Voters of California, 468 U.S. 364 (1984)

Harper & Row, Publishers, Inc. v. Nation Enterprises, 471 U.S. 539 (1985)

Ward v. Rock Against Racism, 491 U.S. 781 (1989)

ISKCON v. Lee, 505 U.S. 672 (1992)

McIntyre v. Ohio Elections Comm'n, 514 U.S. 334 (1995)

Rosenberger v. Rector and Visitors of the University of Virginia, 515 U.S. 819 (1995)

44 Liquormart, Inc. v. Rhode Island, 517 U.S. 484 (1996)

Reno v. ACLU, 521 U.S. 844 (1997)

Ashcroft v. Free Speech Coalition, 535 U.S. 234 (2002)

Virginia v. Black, 538 U.S. 343 (2003)

Johanns v. Livestock Marketing Ass'n, 544 U.S. 550 (2005)

Citizens United v. Federal Elections Comm'n, 558 U.S. 310 (2010)

Sorrell v. IMS Health Inc., 131 S. Ct. 2653 (2011)

United States v. Alvarez, 132 S. Ct. 2537 (2012)

Right of Assembly

Congress shall make no law... abridging... the right of the people peaceably to assemble....

(Amendment I)

~

*T*here has been some debate as to whether "the right of the people peaceably to assemble, and to petition the government for a redress of grievances" in the First Amendment recognizes a unitary right to assemble for the purpose of petitioning the government, or whether it establishes both an unencumbered right of assembly and a separate right of petition. Though the issue continues to be disputed, the text of the First Amendment and the corresponding debates over the Bill of Rights suggest that the Framers understood assembly to encompass more than petition. There are two reasons supporting this viewpoint. First, while punctuation at the Framing did not carry the same significance as it does today, the comma after "assemble" appears to be residual from proposed language for the Bill of Rights forwarded by the several states. Those drafts included separate clauses for assembly and petition.

A second reason against construing the right of assembly as limited to the purpose of petition comes from a debate between Theodore Sedgwick of Massachusetts and John Page of Virginia during the House of Representatives' consideration of the language that would become the Bill of Rights. Sedgwick criticized the proposed right of assembly as redundant in light of the freedom of speech: "If people freely converse together, they must assemble for that purpose; it is a self-evident, unalienable right which the people possess; it is certainly a thing that never would be called in question; it is derogatory to the dignity of the House to descend to such minutiae." Page countered Sedgwick's proposal with a pointed reference to the trial of William Penn to illustrate the importance of the right of assembly. Penn had been arrested and tried in London for unlawful assembly following his preaching on the streets—an act of religious worship that had nothing to do with petitioning the government. After Page spoke, the House defeated Sedgwick's motion to strike assembly from the draft amendment by a "considerable majority."

The first groups to rely upon the freedom of assembly also construed it broadly. At the end of the eighteenth century, the Democratic-Republican Societies repeatedly invoked the right of assembly against Federalist challenges to their gatherings and activities. During the antebellum era, slaves and free blacks contested the denial of free assembly by Southern legislatures. Meanwhile, female abolitionists and suffragists in the North organized and asserted the right of assembly in conjunction with their political conventions.

In *Presser v. Illinois* (1886), the Supreme Court narrowly construed the text of the First Amendment by suggesting that the right of assembly was limited to the purposes of petitioning for a redress of grievances. *Presser* is the only time that the Court has expressly limited the right of assembly in this way, and the Court has since indirectly contradicted the view that assembly and petition compose one right.

While some commentators accepted the Supreme Court's narrow interpretation in *Presser*, state courts interpreting parallel state constitutional provisions of assembly articulated far broader protections that extended to religious groups and social activities. This more expansive sense of assembly was also asserted by the women's movement and labor protesters during the Progressive Era.

Nineteenth-century legal commentators applied the right of assembly to a broad array of gatherings. In 1867, a treatise by John Alexander Jameson referred to "wholly unofficial" gatherings and "spontaneous assemblies" that were protected by the right of peaceable assembly, a "common and most invaluable provision of our constitutions, State and Federal." These assemblies were "at once the effects and the causes of social life and activity, doing for the state what the waves do for the sea: they prevent stagnation, the precursor of decay and death." Albert Wright's 1883 *Exposition of the Constitution of the United States* observed that under the right of assembly, "any number of people may come together in any sort of societies, religious, social or political, or even in treasonous conspiracies, and, so long as they behave themselves and do not hurt anybody or make any great disturbance, they may express themselves in public meetings by speeches and resolutions as they choose."

The Supreme Court made the federal right of assembly applicable to the states in *De Jonge v. Oregon* (1937). After speaking before a group of 150 people at a meeting that occurred under the auspices of the Communist Party, Dirk De Jonge had been convicted under Oregon's criminal syndicalism statute, which prohibited "the organization of a society or assemblage" that "advocate[d] crime, physical violence, sabotage or any unlawful acts or methods as a means of accomplishing or effecting industrial or political change or revolution." A unanimous Supreme Court reversed the conviction. Chief Justice Charles Evans Hughes underscored the significance of applying the right of assembly to state action by observing that "the right of peaceable assembly is a right cognate to those of free speech and free press and is equally fundamental."

In 1939, assembly joined religion, speech, and press as one of the "Four Freedoms" celebrated at the New York World's Fair. Speeches, newspaper editorials, and other tributes surrounding the Fair heralded the singular importance of assembly to American freedom. When later that year the Supreme Court issued its decision in *Hague v. Committee for Industrial Organization* (an assembly case that first recognized the concept of the public forum, which now plays a central role in free speech doctrine), the editors of the *New York Times* pronounced that "with the right of assembly reasserted, all 'four freedoms' of [the] Constitution are well established."

In 1941, festivities around the country marked the sesquicentennial anniversary of the Bill of Rights. In Washington, D.C.'s Post Square, organizers of a celebration displayed an oversized copy of the Bill of Rights next to the four phrases: "Freedom of Speech, Freedom of Assembly, Freedom of Religion, Freedom of the Press." The Sesquicentennial Committee, with President Franklin D. Roosevelt as its chair, issued a proclamation describing the four freedoms as "the pillars which sustain the temple of liberty under law." Days before the attack on Pearl Harbor, the President heralded the "immeasurable privileges" of the First Amendment and signed a proclamation for Bill of Rights Day against the backdrop of a mural listing the four freedoms. (Roosevelt's 1941 State of the Union Address posited a different four freedoms. Rather than refer to the freedoms of speech, religion, assembly, and press that had formed the centerpiece of the World's Fair, Roosevelt's "Four Freedoms Speech" called for freedom of speech and expression, freedom of religion, freedom from want, and freedom from fear. The new formulation—absent assembly—quickly overtook the old.

In *Thomas v. Collins* (1945), the Supreme Court emphasized that because of the "preferred place given in our scheme to the great, the indispensable democratic freedoms secured by the First Amendment," only "the gravest abuses, endangering paramount interests, give occasion for permissible limitation." Justice Wiley Blount Rutledge's opinion noted that the right of assembly guarded "not solely religious or political" causes but also "secular causes," great and small. Rutledge also observed that the rights of the speaker and the audience were "necessarily correlative."

The attention to assembly in the 1940s quickly receded. Although the right remained important in several decisions overturning convictions of African Americans who participated in peaceful civil rights demonstrations, courts had largely ignored the right by the close of the Civil Rights Era. The Supreme Court has not addressed a right of assembly claim in thirty years.

At least part of the reason for the neglect of assembly has been the Court's recognition of a non-textual right of association, beginning in *NAACP v. Alabama* (1958). Justice John M. Harlan's opinion for a unanimous Court cited *De Jonge* and *Thomas* for the principle that: "Effective advocacy of both public and private points of view, particularly controversial ones, is undeniably enhanced by group association, as this Court has more than once recognized by remarking upon the close nexus between the freedoms of speech and assembly." Based on these precedents, Harlan could have resolved the case under the freedom of assembly. But he instead shifted away from assembly, finding it "beyond debate that freedom to engage in association for the advancement of beliefs and ideas is an inseparable aspect of the 'liberty' assured by the Due Process Clause of the Fourteenth Amendment, which embraces freedom of speech." The members of the petitioner NAACP had a "constitutionally protected right of association" that meant they could "pursue their lawful private interests privately" and "associate freely with others in doing so."

Later, the Court split the right of association into two component parts in *Roberts v. United States Jaycees* (1984). Justice William J. Brennan's majority opinion asserted that previous decisions had identified two separate constitutional sources for the right of association. One line of decisions protected "intimate association" as "a fundamental element of personal liberty." Another set of decisions guarded "expressive association," which was "a right to associate for the purpose of engaging in those activities protected by the First Amendment—speech, assembly, petition for the redress of grievances, and the exercise of religion." Expressive association to pursue "a wide variety of political, social, economic, educational, religious, and cultural ends" was "implicit in the right to engage in activities protected by the First Amendment."

Subsequent decisions have suggested that few groups outside of the family qualify for protection under the right of intimate association. Other decisions have revealed a deep incoherence in the doctrine of expressive association that has led to less robust protections than those envisioned by the right of assembly. For example, in *Christian Legal Society v. Martinez* (2010), the Court concluded that a Christian group's right of association claim "merged" with the group's free speech claim. In other words, the Court found no value in association apart from speech.

John Inazu

See Also

Amendment I (Freedom of Speech and of the Press; Right to Petition)

Amendment XIV, Section 1 (Due Process Clause)

Suggestions for Further Research

M. Glenn Abernathy, The Right of Assembly and Association (2d ed. 1981, 1961)

Akhil Reed Amar, The Bill of Rights: Creation and Reconstruction (1998)

Ashutosh Bhagwat, *Associational Speech*, 120 Yale L.J. 978 (2011)

Tabatha Abu El-Haj, *The Neglected Right of Assembly*, 56 UCLA L. Rev. 543 (2009)

Richard A. Epstein, *Forgotten No More, A Review of Liberty's Refuge: The Forgotten Freedom of Assembly*, 13 Engage (March 2012)

John D. Inazu, Liberty's Refuge: The Forgotten Freedom of Assembly (2012)

John D. Inazu, *The Unsettling "Well-Settled" Law of Freedom of Association*, 43 Conn. L. Rev. 149 (2010)

Linda J. Lumsden, Rampant Women: Suffragists and the Right of Assembly (1997)

Jason Mazzone, *Freedom's Associations*, 77 Wash. L. Rev. 639 (2002)

Michael W. McConnell, *Freedom By Association*, First Things (August/September 2012)

Significant Cases

United States v. Cruikshank, 92 U.S. 542 (1876)

Presser v. Illinois, 116 U.S. 252, 267 (1886)

De Jonge v. Oregon, 299 U.S. 353 (1937)

Herndon v. Lowry, 301 U.S. 242 (1937)

Hague v. Committee for Industrial Organization, 307 U.S. 496 (1939)

Thomas v. Collins, 323 U.S. 516 (1945)

NAACP v. Alabama *ex rel* Patterson, 357 U.S. 449 (1958)

Roberts v. United States Jaycees, 468 U.S. 609 (1984)

Boy Scouts of America v. Dale, 530 U.S. 640 (2000)

Christian Legal Society v. Martinez, 130 S. Ct. 2971 (2010)

Freedom of Petition

> Congress shall make no law...abridging...the right of the people...to petition the Government for a redress of grievances.
>
> (Amendment I)

*U*nder modern Supreme Court jurisprudence, the right to petition has been almost completely collapsed into freedom of speech. Yet an analysis of the text and background of the First Amendment suggests that the petition right has independent scope.

Before it was explicitly recognized in the Constitution, the right to petition had a longstanding Anglo-American pedigree as a right independent of general free speech and press rights. The Magna Carta first formally recognized the right to petition the King. Initially, the right applied only to certain nobles. Later,

Parliament claimed the right to petition as a quid pro quo for its approval of royal requests for new taxes. In 1669, Parliament recognized the right of every British subject to petition Parliament, and in 1689 the Declaration of Rights established that not only is it "the right of the subjects to petition the king," but that "all commitments and prosecutions for such petitioning are illegal." At a time when the King was considered above the law, petitions were the only method (short of revolt) to seek redress for illegal royal action.

By the late seventeenth century, petitions were the public's primary means of communicating with government officials and were directed to all levels of government, including the royal bureaucracy and parliament. Moreover, the King and Parliament generally treated petitions seriously and worked to resolve legitimate grievances raised by petitions. Much of the legislation passed by Parliament over a period of centuries was introduced in response to petitions from the public.

Petitioning naturally spread to the American colonies. In 1641, the Massachusetts Body of Liberties became the first colonial charter to provide explicit protection for the right to petition. By the time of the American Revolution, five other colonies—Delaware, New Hampshire, North Carolina, Pennsylvania, and Vermont—had followed suit. The remaining colonies recognized the right informally. Throughout British North America, petitioning was an important way for individuals to express their views to the local governing bodies, especially colonial assemblies. The assemblies, following English tradition, treated petitions seriously and often referred them to committees for further action. Petitions were not always granted, but they were always answered.

In 1774, the Declarations and Resolves of the First Continental Congress proclaimed that the colonists "have a right peaceably to assemble, consider of their grievances, and petition the King; and that all prosecutions, prohibitory proclamations, and commitments for the same, are illegal." The emphasis on the government's lack of power to punish a citizen for petitioning made the right to petition more robust in the Revolutionary era than the more general right to freedom of speech. Colonial governments gener-

ally recognized the right to freedom of speech and of the press, but whatever the right's extent, there is little evidence that it included the right to petition. Rather, the right to petition had its own legal pedigree. When considering the Bill of Rights, Congress approved the right to petition with little controversy and differentiated it in the text of the Amendment from the freedom of speech and press.

The right to petition guarantees only that citizens can communicate with the sovereign through petitions. It does not guarantee or require that the sovereign will respond in any particular way, or indeed, at all. Parliament and colonial legislatures nevertheless regarded themselves as obligated to respond to every petition, but that may have been because those bodies had judicial as well as legislative functions. In the American constitutional scheme, judicial power rests solely in the judicial branch, and the judiciary is the only branch of government that is always obligated to consider and respond to "petitions," i.e., suits and complaints submitted to it.

The Supreme Court recently stated that the Petition Clause "protects the right of individuals to appeal to courts...established by the government for resolution of legal disputes." *Borough of Duryea, Pennsylvania v. Guarnieri* (2011). In a vigorous dissent, Justice Antonin Scalia argued that the Petition Clause applied only to Congress and the Executive, and that the idea that it also applied to the courts came solely from dicta from late twentieth-century Supreme Court cases. The executive branch (including for these purposes the independent regulatory agencies), which traditionally would have had the option of replying to petitions, may arguably also have the obligation to respond to petitions when, in the modern administrative era, it is exercising judicial-like functions.

Congress initially took petitions very seriously, following the tradition of its colonial forebears. Most petitions were private claims, asking for a special bill as a means of settlement. The House of Representatives scheduled time into its regular business in order to hear petitions on the floor. Typically, the Representative of the petitioner's state would assume the role of referring the petition to a special committee for consideration.

The committee considered petitions and reported to Congress, resulting either in a consideration of a bill or rejection of the petition. The exception was in petitions regarding slavery. A pattern developed by which Congress responded to petitions by sending them to committee, where they ultimately died without being answered, rejected, or denied.

In 1836, the House adopted a rule that "all petitions relating . . . to the subject of slavery or the abolition of slavery shall, without being either printed or referred, be laid upon the table and that no further action whatever by had thereon." In 1840, the House ruled that it would not receive abolitionist petitions at all. After a fierce debate over the right to petition, led in part by Representative John Quincy Adams, the House repealed the "gag rule" in 1844; but thereafter anti-slavery petitions simply died in committee as before. Unlike those from the abolitionist movement, petitions regarding such issues as the National Bank, expulsion of Cherokees from Georgia, and the Alien and Sedition Acts, among many others, were duly considered by Congress.

The right to petition became less important as modern democratic politics gradually replaced petitioning and public protests as the primary means for constituents to express their views to their representatives. Today, Congress treats most petitions in a pro forma way. A Representative may present a petition on behalf of a private party to the Clerk of the House who enters it in the Journal. Normally, the House takes no formal action.

The right to petition has become somewhat anachronistic in modern times and has largely been subsumed in the right to freedom of speech. Indeed, in *Borough of Duryea, Pennsylvania v. Guarnieri*, the Supreme Court not only held, as noted above, that suits in court are a form of petition, but also that the right to petition provides no greater or different protection to government employees beyond what such employees have from the right to freedom of speech. Thus, the Court concluded, a government employee who criticizes his agency or superiors has protection against retaliatory action only if his criticism concerned a "matter of public concern" under both the free speech clause and the petition clause.

Here too Justice Scalia dissented. He would have allowed a suit based on the Petition Clause depending on whom the petitioner was suing: "[T]he Petition Clause protects public employees against retaliation for filing petitions unless those petitions are addressed to the government in its capacity as the petitioners' employer, rather than its capacity as their sovereign."

Nevertheless, the longstanding tradition of a right to petition does influence First Amendment jurisprudence. Under the *Noerr-Pennington* doctrine, for example, an effort to influence the exercise of government power, even for the purpose of gaining an anti-competitive advantage, may not create liability under the antitrust laws. *Eastern Railroad Presidents Conference v. Noerr Motor Freight, Inc.* (1961), *United Mine Workers v. Pennington* (1965). The Supreme Court initially adopted this doctrine under the right to freedom of speech, but it more precisely finds its constitutional source in the right to petition. Unlike speech, which can often be punished in the antitrust context, as when corporate officers verbally agree to collude, the right to petition confers absolute immunity on efforts to influence government policy in a non-corrupt way. *Noerr-Pennington* has been expanded beyond its original antitrust context to all situations in which plaintiffs claim a defendant's lobbying activity or a lawsuit it filed (provided the lawsuit was not a sham) as evidence of illegal conduct. For example, trade associations cannot be held liable in tort for lobbying the government for lenient safety standards for their industry.

The Supreme Court first confronted the right to petition and its cognate, the right of assembly, in *United States v. Cruikshank* (1876), declaring that the right was "an attribute of national citizenship." In *Hague v. Committee for Industrial Organization* (1939), members of the Court debated whether the right as applied against states resided in the Fourteenth Amendment's Privileges or Immunities Clause or, as later cases concluded, in the Amendment's Due Process Clause. The rights to petition and to peaceable assembly were also crucial in persuading the Supreme Court to hold that the First Amendment implicitly contains a right to expressive association, that is, a right to associate to engage in the activities protected by the First Amendment. The right of expressive association protected civil rights protestors from hostile state action in the 1950s and 1960s, and, after the Court's decision in *Boy Scouts of America v. Dale* (2000), also protects groups that wish to promote ideals and values that conflict with the goals of modern antidiscrimination laws. To a large extent, then, the right to petition has found its modern home as an aspect of the right of expressive association.

David E. Bernstein

See Also

Amendment I (Freedom of Speech and Freedom of the Press; Freedom of Assembly)

Amendment XIV, Section 1 (Due Process Clause)

Suggestions for Further Research

Akhil Reed Amar, The Bill of Rights: Creation and Reconstruction (1998)

Freedom of Assembly and Petition: Its Constitutional History and the Contemporary Debate (Margaret M. Russell ed., 2010)

Stephen A. Higginson, *Note, A Short History of the Right to Petition Government for the Redress of Grievances*, 96 Yale L.J. 142, 145 (1986)

Gary Lawson & Guy Seidman, *Downsizing the Right to Petition*, 93 Nw. U. L. Rev. 739 (1996)

Gregory A. Mark, *The Vestigial Constitution: The History and Significance of the Right to Petition*, 66 Fordham L. Rev. 2153 (1998)

Jason Mazzone, *Freedom's Associations*, 77 Wash. L. Rev. 639 (2002)

James E. Pfander, *Sovereign Immunity and the Right to Petition: Toward a First Amendment Right to Pursue Judicial Claims Against the Government*, 91 Nw. U. L. Rev. 899 (1997)

Don L. Smith, The Right to Petition for the Redress of Grievances: Constitutional Development and Interpretations (1971)

Significant Cases

United States v. Cruikshank, 92 U.S. 542 (1876)

Hague v. Committee for Industrial Organization, 307 U.S. 496 (1939)

Eastern Railroad Presidents Conference v. Noerr Motor Freight, Inc., 365 U.S. 127 (1961)

United Mine Workers v. Pennington, 381 U.S. 657 (1965)

Boy Scouts of America v. Dale, 530 U.S. 640 (2000)

Borough of Duryea, Pennsylvania v. Guarnieri, 131 S. Ct. 2488 (2011)

To Keep and Bear Arms

A well regulated Militia, being necessary to the security of a free State, the right of the people to keep and bear Arms, shall not be infringed.

(Amendment II)

*M*odern debates about the meaning of the Second Amendment have focused on whether it protects a private right of individuals to keep and bear arms, or a right that can only be exercised through militia organizations like the National Guard. This question, however, was apparently never even raised until long after the Bill of Rights was adopted. The early discussions took the basic meaning of the Amendment for granted and focused instead on whether it added anything significant to the original Constitution. The debate later shifted because of changes in the Constitution and in constitutional law, and because legislatures began regulating firearms in ways undreamed of in our early history.

The Founding generation mistrusted standing armies. Many Americans believed, on the basis of English history and their colonial experience, that governments of large nations are prone to use soldiers to oppress the people. One way to reduce that danger would be to permit the government to raise armies (consisting of full-time paid troops) only when needed to fight foreign adversaries. For other purposes, such as responding to sudden invasions or similar emergencies, the government might be restricted to using a militia, consisting of ordinary civilians who supply their own weapons and receive a bit of part-time, unpaid military training.

Using a militia as an alternative to standing armies had deep roots in English history, and possessed considerable appeal, but it also had some serious problems. Alexander Hamilton, for example, thought the militia system could never provide a satisfactory substitute for a national army. And even those who treasured the militia recognized that it was fragile. The cause of the militia's fragility was just what made Hamilton disparage it: citizens were always going to resist undergoing unpaid military training, and governments were always going to want more professional—and therefore more efficient and tractable—forces.

This led to a dilemma at the Constitutional Convention. Experience during the Revolutionary War had demonstrated convincingly that militia forces could not be relied on for national defense, and the onset of war is not always followed by a pause during which an army can be raised and trained. The Convention therefore decided to give the federal government almost unfettered authority to establish armies, including peacetime standing armies. But that decision created a threat to liberty, especially in light of the fact that the proposed Constitution also forbade the states from keeping troops without the consent of Congress.

One solution might have been to *require* Congress to establish and maintain a well-disciplined militia. Such a militia would have to comprise a large percentage of the population, in order to prevent it from becoming a federal army under another name, like our modern National Guard. This might have deprived the federal government of the excuse that it needed peacetime standing armies, and it might have established a meaningful counterweight to any rogue army that the federal government might create. That possibility was never taken seriously, and for good reason. How could a constitution define a well-regulated or well-disciplined militia with the requisite precision and detail, and with the necessary regard for unforeseeable changes in the nation's circumstances? It would almost certainly have been impossible.

Another approach might have been to forbid Congress from interfering with the states' control over their militias. This might have been possible, but it would have been self-defeating. Fragmented control over the militia would inevitably have resulted in an absence of uniformity in training, equipment, and command, and no really effective national fighting force could have been created.

Thus, the Convention faced a choice between entrenching a multiplicity of militias controlled by the individual states—which would likely be too weak and divided to protect the nation—or authorizing a unified militia under federal control—which almost by definition could not be expected to prevent federal tyranny. The conundrum could not be solved, and the Convention did not purport to solve it. Instead, the Constitution presumes that a militia will exist, but it gives Congress almost unfettered authority to regulate that militia, just as it gives the federal government almost unfettered authority to keep up an army.

This massive shift of power from the states to the federal government generated one of the chief objections to the proposed Constitution. Anti-Federalists argued that federal control over the militia would take away from the states their principal means of defense against federal oppression and usurpation, and that European history demonstrated how serious the danger was. James Madison, for one, responded that such fears of federal oppression were overblown, in part because the new federal government was to be structured differently from European governments. But he also pointed out another decisive difference between Europe's situation and ours: the American people were armed and would therefore be almost impossible to subdue through military force, even if one assumed that the federal government would try to use an army to do so. In *The Federalist* No. 46, he wrote:

> Besides the advantage of being armed, which the Americans possess over the people of almost every other nation, the existence of subordinate governments, to which the people are attached and by which the militia officers are appointed, forms a barrier against the enterprises of ambition, more insurmountable than any which a simple government of any form can admit of. Notwithstanding

the military establishments in the several kingdoms of Europe, which are carried as far as the public resources will bear, the governments are afraid to trust the people with arms. And it is not certain that with this aid alone they would not be able to shake off their yokes.

Implicit in the debate between the Federalists and Anti-Federalists were two *shared* assumptions: first, that the proposed new constitution gave the federal government almost total legal authority over the army and the militia; and second, that the federal government should not have any authority at all to disarm the citizenry. The disagreement between Federalists and Anti-Federalists was only over the narrower question of whether an armed populace could adequately assure the preservation of liberty.

The Second Amendment conceded nothing to the Anti-Federalists' desire to sharply curtail the military power that the Constitution gave the federal government. But that very fact prevented the Second Amendment from generating any opposition. Attempting to satisfy the Anti-Federalists would have been hugely controversial, and it would have required substantial changes to the original Constitution. Nobody suggested that the Second Amendment could have any such effect, but neither did anyone suggest that the federal government needed or rightfully possessed the power to disarm American citizens.

As a political gesture to the Anti-Federalists—a gesture highlighted by the Second Amendment's prefatory reference to the value of a well-regulated militia—express recognition of the people's right to arms was something of a sop. But the provision was easily accepted because *everyone* agreed that the federal government should not have the power to infringe the right of the people to keep and bear arms, any more than it should have the power to abridge the freedom of speech or prohibit the free exercise of religion.

A great deal has changed since the Second Amendment was adopted. The traditional militia fairly quickly fell into desuetude, and the state-based militia organizations were eventually incorporated into the federal military structure.

For its part, the federal military establishment has become enormously more powerful than eighteenth-century armies, and Americans have largely lost their fear that the federal government will use that power to oppress them politically. Furthermore, eighteenth-century civilians routinely kept at home the very same weapons they would need if called to serve in the militia, while modern soldiers are equipped with weapons that differ significantly from those that are commonly thought appropriate for civilian uses. These changes have raised new questions about the value of an armed citizenry, and many people today reject the assumptions that almost everyone accepted when the Second Amendment was adopted.

The law has also changed. At the time of the Framing, gun control laws were virtually nonexistent, and there was no reason for anyone to discuss what kinds of regulations would be permitted by the Second Amendment. The animating concern behind the Amendment was fear that the new federal government might try to disarm the citizenry in order to prevent armed resistance to political usurpations. That has never occurred, but a great many new legal restrictions on the right to arms have since been adopted. Nearly all of these laws are aimed at preventing the misuse of firearms by irresponsible civilians, but many of them also interfere with the ability of law-abiding citizens to defend themselves against violent criminals.

Another important legal development was the adoption of the Fourteenth Amendment. The Second Amendment originally applied only to the federal government, leaving the states to regulate weapons as they saw fit. During the twentieth century, the Supreme Court invoked the Fourteenth Amendment's Due Process Clause to apply most provisions of the Bill of Rights to the states and their political subdivisions. The vast majority of gun control laws have been adopted at the state and local level, and the potential applicability of the Second Amendment at this level raised serious issues that the Founding generation had no occasion to consider. It is one thing to decide that authority over the regulation of weapons will largely be reserved to the states. It is quite another to decide that all regulations will be subjected to judicial review under a vaguely worded constitutional provision like the Second Amendment.

Until recently, the judiciary treated the Second Amendment almost as a dead letter. Many courts concluded that citizens have no constitutionally protected right to arms at all, and the federal courts never invalidated a single gun control law. In the late twentieth century, however, the judicial consensus was challenged by a large body of new scholarship. Through analysis of the text and history of the Second Amendment, these commentators sought to establish that the Constitution does protect an individual right to have weapons for self-defense, including defense against criminal violence that the government cannot or will not prevent.

In *District of Columbia v. Heller* (2008), the Supreme Court finally did strike down a gun control regulation, in this case a federal law that forbade nearly all civilians to possess a handgun in the District of Columbia. A narrow 5-4 majority adopted the main conclusions and many of the arguments advanced by the revisionist commentators, ruling that the original meaning of the Second Amendment protects a private right of individuals to keep and bear arms for the purpose of self-defense. The dissenters interpreted the original meaning differently. In an opinion that all four of them joined, Justice John Paul Stevens concluded that the Second Amendment's nominally individual right actually protects only "the right of the people of each of the several States to maintain a well-regulated militia." In a separate opinion, also joined by all four dissenters, Justice Stephen Breyer argued that even if the Second Amendment did protect an individual right to have arms for self-defense, it should be interpreted to allow the government to ban handguns in high-crime urban areas.

Two years later, in *McDonald v. City of Chicago* (2010), the Court struck down a similar law at the state level, again by a vote of 5-4. The four-Justice *McDonald* plurality relied largely on substantive due process precedents that had applied other provisions of the Bill of Rights to the states. Justice Clarence Thomas concurred in the judgment, but he rejected the Court's longstanding doctrine of substantive due process, which he concluded is inconsistent with the original mean-

ing of the Constitution. Instead, he set forth a detailed analysis of the original meaning of the Fourteenth Amendment's Privileges or Immunities Clause, and concluded that it protects the same individual right that is protected from federal infringement by the Second Amendment.

Notwithstanding the lengthy opinions in *Heller* and *McDonald*, their holdings are narrowly confined to invalidating bans on the possession of handguns by civilians in their own homes. Neither case provides clear guidance on the constitutionality of less restrictive forms of gun control, although *Heller* did suggest a non-exclusive list of "presumptively lawful" regulations. These include bans on the possession of firearms by felons and the mentally ill; bans on carrying firearms in "sensitive places such as schools and government buildings"; laws restricting the commercial sale of arms; bans on the concealed carry of firearms; and bans on weapons "not typically possessed by law-abiding citizens for lawful purposes."

In the short period of time since *Heller* was decided, the lower courts have struggled to divine how it applies to regulations the Court did not address, such as bans on carrying weapons in public and bans on the possession of firearms by violent misdemeanants. At the moment, the dominant approach in the federal courts of appeals can be roughly summarized as follows:

1. Some regulations, primarily those that are "longstanding," are presumed not to infringe the right protected by the Second Amendment. Thus, for example, the D.C. Circuit upheld a regulation requiring gun owners to register each of their weapons with the government. *Heller v. District of Columbia* ("*Heller II*") (2011).

2. Regulations that substantially restrict the core right of self-defense are scrutinized under a demanding test, which generally permits only regulations that are narrowly tailored to accomplish a compelling government purpose. Applying a

test of this kind, the Seventh Circuit found that a city had failed to provide an adequate justification for its ban on firing ranges. *Ezell v. City of Chicago* (2011).

3. Regulations that do not severely restrict the core right are subject to a more deferential form of scrutiny, which generally requires that the regulation be substantially related to an important government objective. The Third Circuit, for example, held that a ban on possessing a handgun with an obliterated serial number was valid under this standard. *United States v. Marzzarella* (2010).

The application of this framework has varied somewhat among the courts, and *Heller* left room for other approaches to develop. One important outstanding issue is the scope of the right to carry firearms in public. *Heller* laid great stress on the text of the Second Amendment, which protects the right to keep *and bear* arms, while also giving provisional approval to bans on the concealed carry of firearms. A ban (or severe restrictions) on both concealed and open carry would seem to conflict with the constitutional text. It would also seem hard to reconcile with the Court's emphasis on the importance of the right to self-defense against violent criminals, who are at least as likely to be encountered outside the home as within it. *Heller*, however, did not unambiguously recognize any right to carry weapons in public. Some lower courts have concluded that no such right exists, while others have disagreed. The Supreme Court may eventually have to address the issue.

A more general question concerns the scope of the government's power to inhibit the possession and use of firearms through regulations that impose onerous conditions and qualifications on gun owners. In the analogous area of free speech, courts have struggled endlessly to draw lines that allow governments to serve what they see as the public interest without allowing undue suppression of individual liberties. If the Supreme Court is serious about treating the right to arms as an important part of the constitutional

fabric, we should expect the Justices to encounter similar challenges in its emerging gun control jurisprudence.

Nelson Lund

See Also

Article I, Section 8, Clauses 11–16

Article I, Section 10, Clause 3 (Compact Clause)

Amendment XIV, Section 1 (Privileges or Immunities; Due Process Clause)

Suggestions for Further Research

STEPHEN P. HALBROOK, THE FOUNDERS' SECOND AMENDMENT: ORIGINS OF THE RIGHT TO BEAR ARMS (2008)

Don B. Kates, Jr., Handgun *Prohibition and the Original Meaning of the Second Amendment*, 82 Mich. L. Rev. 204 (1983)

Nelson Lund, *The Past and Future of the Individual's Right to Arms*, 31 Ga. L. Rev. 1 (1996)

Nelson Lund, *The Second Amendment,* Heller, *and Originalist Jurisprudence*, 56 UCLA L. Rev. 1343 (2009)

Jack N. Rakove, *The Second Amendment: The Highest Stage of Originalism*, 76 Chi.-Kent L. Rev. 103 (2000)

Eugene Volokh, *Implementing the Right to Keep and Bear Arms for Self-Defense: An Analytical Framework and a Research Agenda*, 56 UCLA L. Rev. 1443 (2009)

Significant Cases

United States v. Miller, 307 U.S. 174 (1939)

District of Columbia v. Heller, 554 U.S. 570 (2008)

McDonald v. City of Chicago, 130 S. Ct. 3020 (2010)

United States v. Mazzarella, 614. F.3d 85 (3d Cir. (2010)

Ezell v. City of Chicago, 651 F.3d 684 (7th Cir. 2011)

Heller v. District of Columbia, 670 F.3d 1244 (D.C. Cir. 2011) ("Heller II")

Quartering of Troops

No Soldier shall, in time of peace be quartered in any house, without

the consent of the Owner, nor in time of war, but in a manner prescribed by law.

(AMENDMENT III)

~

*T*he Third Amendment combines a straightforward ban on nonconsensual, peacetime quartering of soldiers in citizens' houses with a requirement that wartime quartering be done by means approved by the legislature. The brief congressional debates on the text make clear that the amendment reflects an effort to balance private property rights and the potential wartime need for military quarters.

The Anti-Federalists used the absence of a ban on quartering as an argument against ratification. Once the concept of a Bill of Rights was agreed upon, however, there was little controversy over the inclusion of a ban on quartering. Six of the original thirteen states also adopted constitutional provisions banning the quartering of soldiers.

The British practice of quartering soldiers in America grew out of the lack of regular army bases, unclear legislative authority for British army quartering in America, and the need to move large bodies of troops about the country during conflicts with the French and Indians. Although there were numerous conflicts over quartering in both Britain and America before the 1770s, the most significant episodes concerned the British quartering of soldiers in private homes to punish the people of Boston under the Intolerable Acts of 1774.

Because of its clear text, there have been few court opinions discussing the Third Amendment. Recently, the Supreme Court declared that the Amendment has not been "fully incorporated" by the Due Process Clause of the Fourteenth Amendment and therefore, by implication, it is not applicable to the states, *McDonald v. City of Chicago* (2010). The Court ignored an earlier federal circuit court opinion that had found the Amendment was indeed incorporated. *Engblom v. Carey* (1982). In *Engblom*, the federal circuit court also determined that residences of all types would be subject to Third Amendment protection. The case had arisen when New York State correctional officers on strike

were evicted from their state-provided residences, which were then provided to National Guardsman. Upon remand, the district court dismissed the state correctional officers' suit without reaching the substance of the Third Amendment claim.

Other courts have not been receptive to Third Amendment claims. One federal court dismissed as bordering on the "frivolous" the assertion that federal approval of military flights through the airspace over one's home violated the Amendment. *Custer County Action Ass'n v. Garvey* (2001).

Earlier, the Supreme Court had cited the Third Amendment as part of non-originalist interpretations that list it as one of the sources of "penumbras, formed by emanations" that create a zone of privacy in no specific clause of the Constitution. For example, the Court cited it in the name of marital privacy as support for constitutional restrictions on state governments' abilities to regulate the sale of contraceptives in *Griswold v. Connecticut* (1965).

Court action has been rare because the quartering problem is largely solved today by the government's paying communities to host military bases.

Andrew P. Morriss

See Also

Declaration of Independence, Para. 16

Suggestions for Further Research

Tom W. Bell, *The Third Amendment: Forgotten but Not Gone*, 2 WM. & MARY BILL RTS. J. 117 (1993)

Andrew P. Morriss and Richard L. Stroup, *Quartering Species: The "Living Constitution," the Third Amendment, and the Endangered Species Act*, 30 ENVTL. L. 769 (2000)

Significant Cases

Griswold v. Connecticut, 381 U.S. 479 (1965)

Engblom v. Carey, 677 F.2d 957 (2d Cir. 1982), *on remand*. 572 F. Supp. 44 (S.D.N.Y.), *aff'd per curiam*, 724 F.2d 28 (2d Cir. 1983)

Custer County Action Ass'n v. Garvey, 256 F.3d 1024 (10th Cir. 2001)

McDonald v. City of Chicago, 130 S. Ct. 3020 (2010)

Searches and Seizures

The right of the people to be secure in their persons, houses, papers, and effects, against unreasonable searches and seizures, shall not be violated ...

(Amendment IV)

~

*L*eading up to the Revolution, a series of abuses by King George III and his representatives led to the widespread recognition in the colonies of a right against unreasonable searches and seizures by the government. Several state constitutions adopted such protections soon after the Declaration of Independence was proclaimed. In 1780, for example, the Constitution of Massachusetts announced that every individual has "a right to be secure from all unreasonable searches and seizures of his person, his house, his papers, and all his possessions." The Fourth Amendment text ratified in 1791 closely resembled these state provisions in its recognition of the "right of the people to be secure in their persons, houses, papers, and effects, against unreasonable searches and seizures."

The most significant abuse that had led to the adoption of the Fourth Amendment was the execution of general warrants in the colonies. General warrants were court orders authorizing government officials to search and seize evidence with few if any limitations on where the officials could search and what they could seize. Opposition to general warrants had derived in part from two famous English cases, *Entick v. Carrington* (1765) and *Wilkes v. Wood* (1763). Both cases involved pamphleteers who were critics of the government. They were arrested and their books and papers were seized (including, in John Wilkes' case, all the papers of forty-nine of his friends) using warrants that named neither the suspects nor the places to be searched. Both defendants sued the seizing agents for trespass and won judgments in their favor. The latter half of the text of the Fourth Amendment is directly addressed to abolishing the general warrant used in cases like *Entick* and *Wilkes*. Its plain language requires warrants to be narrow, as "no Warrants shall issue, but upon

probable cause, supported by Oath or affirmation, and particularly describing the place to be searched, and the persons or things to be seized."

The Fourth Amendment was also inspired by colonial opposition to the writs of assistance, which permitted the customs agents to search any place in which smuggled goods might be concealed, even if there was no particular suspicion the goods were there. In a famous case, known as *Paxton's Case* (1761), widely known among the Framers of the Constitution, James Otis defended several colonial smugglers against seizures made through the use of these writs. Although Otis lost the case, no less an authority than John Adams—who watched Otis in court—saw the dispute as the spark of the American Revolution.

Despite the general agreement among Supreme Court decisions and legal historians that one major purpose of the Fourth Amendment was to abolish general warrants and writs of assistance, there is widespread disagreement about the original understanding of the specific terms and purposes of the Fourth Amendment. For example, Thomas Davies argues that the Fourth Amendment was largely focused on abolishing general warrants, and that it is wrong to see the text of the Fourth Amendment as imposing a more general requirement of reasonable police practices. William Cuddihy argues that the Fourth Amendment was originally understood both to prohibit general warrants and more generally to guard against abusive law enforcement practices. On the other hand, Akhil Amar argues that the original understanding of the Fourth Amendment was to require reasonableness in government investigations.

The Fourth Amendment lay largely dormant until the twentieth century. That was true for three major reasons. First, the Fourth Amendment applied only to the federal government, which at the time was both relatively small and had few resources devoted to law enforcement. Second, the concept of modern police officers hired by the government to investigate crime did not emerge until the middle of the nineteenth century. Third, the remedies for violations of the Fourth Amendment remained uncertain until the introduction of the exclusionary rule in *Weeks v. United States* (1914) (evidence unlawfully seized may not be introduced into evidence). Before the prohibition era in the 1920s, the lack of a clear remedy, the absence of modern police forces, and the narrow role of the federal government ensured that Fourth Amendment issues arose only rarely.

The opposite is true today. Fourth Amendment questions now arise in an extraordinary number of cases, and they are litigated with unusual frequency. The inversion of the three reasons above explains why. First, since *Wolf v. Colorado* (1949) and *Mapp v. Ohio* (1961), the Supreme Court applied the Fourth Amendment (and later the exclusionary rule) to state and local police officers under the theory that they were "incorporated" by the Fourteenth Amendment. Second, federal and state law enforcement has become a remarkably vast enterprise: there are more than 750,000 state and local officers with the power to make arrests, and upwards of 100,000 federal officers with that power. Third, Fourth Amendment remedies now include both a modified exclusionary rule and civil remedies in federal court. The result is an extremely large body of modern Fourth Amendment case law.

The threshold question under the Fourth Amendment is whether a government search or seizure has occurred. A person's property is "seized" when the government meaningfully interferes with a person's possessory interest in their property. *United States v. Jacobsen* (1984). This occurs when the government takes a suspect's property away; when the government forces a person out of their home; or when the government takes a package or letter out of the course of delivery. Similarly, a person is "seized" under the Fourth Amendment when the government terminates or restrains his freedom of movement through means intentionally applied. *Brendlin v. California* (2007). This happens when a government official places a suspect under arrest or temporarily detains a person in circumstances where a reasonable person would not feel free to terminate the encounter and leave.

The question of when government conduct is a Fourth Amendment "search" has received a enormous amount of judicial attention. The doctrine recognizes two tests. First, government conduct is a search if it is a trespass onto a person, his house, his papers, or his effects with the intent to obtain information. *United States v. Jones* (2012). Second, under the test first announced in a concurring opinion in *Katz v. United States* (1967), government conduct is a search if it violates a subjective expectation of privacy, and society is prepared to recognize that expectation as objectively reasonable. For the most part, government conduct usually ends up being labeled a search if it is an invasion into a private space such as a home, a car, a package, a letter, or a person's pockets. On the other hand, government conduct is not labeled a search if it involves surveillance in public.

Once courts recognize a search or seizure, the next question is whether the search or seizure is constitutionally "reasonable" or "unreasonable." Likewise, a person can be searched without a warrant incident to his arrest, but absent exigent circumstances a warrant is required to search the digital contents of an arrestee's cell phone. *United States v. Robinson* (1973); *Riley v. California* (2014). In the case of persons, brief seizures are reasonable with specific and articulable facts, while arrests are reasonable based on probable cause to believe a crime has been committed and that person has committed it. *United States v. Watson* (1976); *Terry v. Ohio* (1968). After a person has been arrested, he can be searched fully without a warrant incident to arrest. *United States v. Robinson* (1973).

The rules for searching homes tend to be somewhat more restrictive than the rules for seizing and searching individuals. In the case of homes, entrance is constitutionally reasonable (and therefore legal) only pursuant to a valid warrant or an exception to the warrant requirement. The exceptions to the warrant requirement include exigent circumstances or consent by a party who has authority over the space to be searched. If the police are lawfully in a position to view evidence outside the scope of a warrant but its incriminating nature is immediately apparent, the police can seize that evidence under the "plain view" exception. *Horton v. California* (1990).

The rules for searching and seizing cars tend to give the government significantly broader powers than the rules for homes. A police officer can order a driver to pull over a car, seizing the car and its occupants, based on any traffic violation. *Whren v. United States* (1996). The officer can then arrest the driver based on only a minor violation, even if the crime of arrest does not provide for any jail time. *Atwater v. City of Lago Vista* (2001). Once the person has been arrested, he can be searched incident to arrest even if the arrest violates state law. *Virginia v. Moore* (2008). Further, the car can be searched without a warrant if there is probable cause to believe that contraband or evidence is located inside it. *Carroll v. United States* (1925).

After a Fourth Amendment violation has been established, the remaining question is whether there is a remedy for the violation in a court of law. The exclusionary rule remains one remedy, although it is subject to many exceptions and those exceptions appear to be expanding over time. In general, a defendant can successfully invoke the exclusionary rule only if his own rights were violated and the constitutional violation was the direct cause of the evidence being discovered. Also, the Supreme Court has recently developed the so-called "good faith" exception to the exclusionary rule. Under the most recent precedents, the exclusionary rule is a last resort available only when the officer who conducted the search acted in a personally culpable manner, such as in the case of a knowing or intentional violation. *Davis v. United States* (2011). Civil suits against officers who conducted unconstitutional searches or seizures have similar limits. Under the doctrine of qualified immunity, an officer is immune from suit unless the violation was clearly established at the time and a reasonable officer would have recognized that the act violated the Constitution. *Anderson v. Creighton* (1987).

Orin S. Kerr

See Also
Amendment IV (Warrant Clause)
Amendment V (Self-Incrimination Clause)

Suggestions for Further Research
Gerard V. Bradley, *The Constitutional Theory of the Fourth Amendment*, 38 DePaul L. Rev. 817 (1988)

William J. Cuddihy, The Fourth Amendment: Origins and Original Meaning 602–1791 (2009)

Thomas Y. Davies, *Recovering the Original Fourth Amendment*, 98 Mich. L. Rev. 547 (1999)

Wayne R. LaFave, Search and Seizure: A Treatise on the Fourth Amendment (4th ed. 2004)

Nelson B. Lasson, The History and Development of the Fourth Amendment to the United States Constitution (1937)

Wesley M. Oliver, *The Neglected History of Criminal Procedure, 1850–1940*, 62 Rutgers L. Rev. 447 (2010)

William J. Stuntz, *The Uneasy Relationship Between Criminal Procedure and Criminal Justice*, 107 Yale L.J. 1 (1997)

Significant Cases
Writs of Assistance Case, 1 Quincy 51 (Mass. 1761) (Paxton's Case)

Wilkes v. Wood, 19 How. St. Tr. 1153 (C.P. 1763)

Entick v. Carrington, 19 How. St. Tr. 1029 (C.P. 1765)

Weeks v. United States, 232 U.S. 383 (1914)

Carroll v. United States, 267 U.S. 132 (1925)

Wolf v. Colorado, 338 U.S. 25 (1949)

Mapp v. Ohio, 367 U.S. 643 (1961)

Katz v. United States, 389 U.S. 347 (1967)

Terry v. Ohio, 392 U.S. 1 (1968)

United States v. Robinson, 414 U.S. 218 (1973)

United States v. Watson, 423 U.S. 411 (1976)

United States v. Jacobsen, 466 U.S. 109, 113 (1984)

Anderson v. Creighton, 483 U.S. 635 (1987)

Horton v. California, 496 U.S. 128 (1990)

Whren v. United States, 517 U.S. 806 (1996)

Atwater v. City of Lago Vista, 532 U.S. 318 (2001)

Brendlin v. California, 551 U.S. 249 (2007)

Virginia v. Moore, 553 U.S. 164 (2008)

Davis v. United States, 131 S. Ct. 2419 (2011)

United States v. Jones, 132 S. Ct. 945 (2012)

Riley v. California, 573 U.S. ___ (2014)

Warrant Clause

... no Warrants shall issue, but upon probable cause, supported by Oath or affirmation, and par-

ticularly describing the place to be
searched, and the persons or things
to be seized.

(AMENDMENT IV)

~

The first half of the Fourth Amendment
bans "unreasonable searches and seizures." The
second half, known as the Warrant Clause, states
a set of basic requirements for search and arrest
warrants—that they must be supported by an
affidavit that establishes probable cause, and that
they must describe both the location and objects
of the search or the person to be seized.

On its face, the Warrant Clause would appear
to be one of the most clearly written clauses in the
Constitution. It requires that warrants be supported by probable cause, that the police officer
seeking the warrant swear to the truth of the facts
used to support the application for the warrant, and
that, once issued, the warrant describe who is to be
arrested, where the search is to take place and what
the officer is allowed to look for. All this is plain
from the text. Perhaps because they are so plain, the
rules have been relatively easy for courts to apply,
although close questions can arise on how specific
a search warrant must be in describing the place
to search and the items the police are looking for.

There are, though, two important questions the text does not answer, or at least does
not answer clearly. Those questions have been
the subject of a great deal of litigation and commentary: First, what does "probable cause"
mean? Second, a trickier question, are officers
ever required to obtain warrants in order to carry
out a search or make an arrest, and if so, in what
circumstances? The text leaves the question open,
but it implies that the answer is that warrants are
not required: the phrasing of the Warrant Clause
limits warrants but does not mandate their use.

The first of these questions can be quickly
answered. In *Brinegar v. United States* (1949),
the Supreme Court defined "probable cause" as
information that would lead "a man of reasonable
caution" to believe "that an offense has been or is
being committed." In *Illinois v. Gates* (1983), the
Court put it more succinctly, describing probable
cause as "a fair probability" that evidence will be
found in the place searched or that the person

arrested committed a crime. Those definitions
may sound too vague to be useful, but in practice the standard seems clear enough. In most
cases "probable cause" means what the ordinary
definition of "probable" would suggest: more
likely than not. That "51 percent" standard does
not always apply: in practice, courts seem to give
the police a little more leeway when the crime
being investigated is especially serious, and a little
less when the crime seems minor. The Supreme
Court itself has refused to quantify the degree
of certainty needed to establish probable cause.

As with any vague standard, the phrase
"probable cause" has occasioned a great deal of
litigation and commentary, but the contested
territory is small. All sides agree that the phrase
means more than just a possibility, and less than
a near-certainty. A clearer definition than that
may be impossible.

The second question, whether warrants are
ever required, is more complex. At first blush the
question seems nonsensical. Of course, warrants
are sometimes required; otherwise, why would
the Fourth Amendment mention them? When the
Fourth Amendment was written, the sole remedy
for an illegal search or seizure was a lawsuit for
money damages. Government officials used warrants as a defense against such lawsuits. Today a
warrant seems the police officer's foe—one more
hoop to jump through—but at the time of the
Founding, it was the constable's friend, a legal
defense against any subsequent claim. Thus it was
perfectly reasonable to specify limits on warrants
(probable cause, particular description of the
places to be searched and the things to be seized)
but never to require their use.

That is probably (though not clearly—some
historians disagree) how the clause was understood when it was written. Like the state constitutional provisions on which it was modeled,
the Fourth Amendment arose as a response to
three famous cases decided in the 1760s. In each
of those cases, agents of the Crown conducted
very broad searches; in each, the agents had warrants authorizing the searches; finally, in none of
the three searches did those warrants meet the
requirements that were later spelled out in the
Fourth Amendment. The point of the text was
to forbid the kind of behavior seen in the three

cases—not to require warrants, but to prevent the government from using them to justify overly broad searches.

The first of the three cases was *Wilkes v. Wood* (1763). John Wilkes was a London pamphleteer critical of the king's ministers; he was also a Member of Parliament and perhaps the most popular man in England. One of the King's secretaries issued a sweeping warrant, ordering the arrest of Wilkes and those associated with a pamphlet he had authored, as well as the seizure of all Wilkes's books and papers. Wilkes sued, and won the then-staggering total of five thousand pounds. *Wilkes v. Wood* was a famous and celebrated case in the colonies, so much so that several towns were named after John Wilkes (as was Abraham Lincoln's assassin).

The second case, *Entick v. Carrington* (1765), was similar. Like Wilkes, John Entick wrote pamphlets criticizing the government. As with Wilkes, one of the King's underlings issued a warrant commanding officers to seize Entick and all his papers. As with Wilkes, the warrant extended to all Entick's papers, not merely to those that might offer evidence of a crime. Entick also sued and won; the case was likewise famous in the colonies, prompting local officials to name several towns after the judge in Entick's case—Lord Camden.

The third case is the famous *Writs of Assistance Case* (1761) in Boston. The warrant in that case authorized the search of any place in which the Crown's agents thought smuggled goods might be hidden. The things to be seized were described, but the places to be searched were not. A number of Boston merchants challenged these "writs of assistance." James Otis, representing the merchants, argued that the common law banned such "general warrants." Otis lost his case, but his argument struck a chord in the increasingly rebellious colonies.

Historians generally agree that the Warrant Clause was written to adopt the decisions in *Wilkes* and *Entick* and the losing argument in the Writs of Assistance Case. General warrants, meaning both warrants not supported by probable cause and warrants that failed to describe the places or objects of the search, were banned. But the police (at that time, constables) were probably free to not use warrants at all. The reason that this last point is not entirely clear is that no one seems to have thought much about the question. When the Fourth Amendment was adopted, police forces did not yet exist (they arose in America beginning in the 1830s). A good deal of criminal investigation was conducted by private parties, with evidence turned over to the local constable or magistrate after the suspect was charged. Constables became involved only when it was time to make an arrest (and sometimes not even then), at which time they typically searched the arrestee's person and home. It is clear that those actions did not require a warrant in 1791.

Thus the original understanding of the Warrant Clause was in one sense clear, and in one sense not. It was clear what the conditions were for a valid warrant—those conditions are spelled out in the Fourth Amendment's text. It was not clear whether warrants were ever required (though they probably were not), because the issue had not arisen with any regularity.

Today's Warrant Clause doctrine differs from the historical understanding in some important respects. That doctrine can be divided into two parts. The first deals with the conditions of a valid warrant. The second deals with when warrants are required.

The conditions of a valid warrant are relatively straightforward, because Warrant Clause doctrine continues to track the Fourth Amendment's text. Probable cause and particular description are required, and the application for a warrant must be made under oath, as the text says. Another requirement is not mentioned in the text: early on, American courts decided that warrants should be issued only by judicial officers (usually, that means magistrates) and not by anyone in the prosecutor's office or the executive branch of government more generally.

One important qualification to the Fourth Amendment language concerns probable cause. The Supreme Court has approved warrants not based on probable cause in some regulatory settings. Thus, in *Camara v. Municipal Court* (1967), housing inspectors were allowed to use what the Court called "administrative warrants"—orders authorizing the random selection of some buildings for code inspection. Such administrative warrants are sometimes used, as in *Camara*, to enforce building and fire codes, but not for much else.

The police are not allowed to use administrative warrants to investigate and enforce the criminal law, although information uncovered when executing these warrants may be used in a criminal prosecution. The justification of this state of affairs is that police officers investigating crime tend to have more power than other government officials: the police can break down doors, use force to subdue suspects, and, in some cases, they may destroy suspects' property if that is a necessary consequence of the search for evidence. Other government officials tend not to have those powers. Consequently ordinary citizens tend not to find a building code inspection as frightening as a police search or arrest. The distinct legal requirements reflect those differences in official power and in the fear that such power inspires.

The second issue, when are warrants required, is more complicated. In summary, warrants are required when the police search a home or an office, unless the search must happen immediately, and there is no opportunity to obtain a warrant. Containers such as luggage that are not found in cars or at airport security checkpoints may be seized without a warrant, but normally cannot be searched without one. Warrants are also required for wiretaps and some computer searches—a special category covered by federal statute. And while the scope of the rule is not entirely clear, the Court has said that before the police can attach a GPS unit to a suspect's car that will allow them to continuously track the car's movement, a warrant is needed. Outside those categories warrants are almost never required.

There is a slightly more elaborate way to put the point. Until recently the Supreme Court said that warrants were required for all searches and seizures, save those that fell within some exception to that requirement. The classic statement of this rule, and the classic defense of a broad warrant requirement, was penned by Justice Robert H. Jackson in *Johnson v. United States* (1948). Today, the Court uses different language, emphasizing not the second half of the Fourth Amendment's text, but the first (the ban on "unreasonable searches and seizures"). See *Indianapolis v. Edmond* (2000). Notwithstanding this change in legal rhetoric, the old categories, a warrant requirement with a list of exceptions, still exist. The scope of the requirement is defined by the many exceptions to it. The major ones are these:

1. *Exigent circumstances.* The police need not get a warrant when doing so is practically impossible, because of, for example, the risk that the evidence will be destroyed or moved, the risk that the suspect will flee, or if there is some danger created if the police do not act immediately.

2. *Arrests outside the home.* The police must have probable cause to justify the arrest, but they need not have a warrant.

3. *Searches incident to arrest.* This means a search of the arrestee's person and any baggage he or she may be carrying; if the person is arrested in his car, the police may search the car if they have reason to believe that evidence related to the crime of arrest may be found there.

4. *Inventory searches.* The police may seize any belongings the arrestee has in his possession at the time of arrest (including his car), bring those items back to the police station, and make a record of them and their contents. So long as the police conduct the inventory according to standard procedures, they do not need to have any suspicion that the inventoried items contain evidence, but may use any such evidence that they find.

5. *Automobiles.* Cars, including their trunks, may be searched without warrants, as long as the searching officers have probable cause to believe that the car contains evidence of a crime or contraband.

6. *Street stops and frisks.* Officers are allowed to detain a suspect for a brief period, and to frisk him for weapons, given "reasonable

suspicion" of criminal activity, a standard that is easier for the police to satisfy than probable cause.

In addition to these exceptions, there are several categories of searches that involve government officials other than police officers (e.g., searches of lockers by school principals, and government employers searching employees' desks), or government interests separate from the interest in criminal law enforcement (e.g., searches of vehicles at the nation's borders, searches of persons and baggage at airports). Such searches generally do not require warrants, and often do not require probable cause.

That list of exceptions and special categories aside, other searches and seizures do require warrants. Notice, however, that the major categories of searches and seizures that do not appear on the above list are searches of homes, arrests within homes, searches of private offices or other privately owned buildings (other than for fire inspection and the like), and wiretaps. The overwhelming majority of search and arrest warrants are issued in such cases.

A generation ago those propositions were widely contested; the scope of the warrant requirement was the subject of a great deal of litigation, including a number of Supreme Court decisions. That is no longer the case. Today Fourth Amendment litigation focuses on warrantless searches and seizures. The Searches and Seizures Clause—the first half of the Fourth Amendment's text—is now the primary source of Fourth Amendment litigation and commentary.

William J. Stuntz and Andrew D. Leipold

See Also
Amendment IV (Searches and Seizures)

Suggestions for Further Research
Thomas Y. Davies, *Recovering the Original Fourth Amendment*, 98 MICH. L. REV. 547 (1999)

Orin S. Kerr, *The Modest Role of the Warrant Clause in National Security Investigations*, 88 TEX. L. REV. 1669 (2010)

WAYNE R. LaFAVE, SEARCH AND SEIZURE: A TREATISE ON THE FOURTH AMENDMENT (4th ed. 2004)

MAURICE H. SMITH, THE WRITS OF ASSISTANCE CASE (1978)

Carol S. Steiker, *Second Thoughts About First Principles*, 107 HARV. L. REV. 820 (1994)

William J. Stuntz, *The Substantive Origins of Criminal Procedure*, 105 YALE L.J. 393 (1995)

William J. Stuntz, *Warrants and Fourth Amendment Remedies*, 77 VA. L. REV. 881 (1991)

TELFORD TAYLOR, TWO STUDIES IN CONSTITUTIONAL INTERPRETATION (1969)

Significant Cases
Writs of Assistance Case, 1 Quincy 51 (Mass. 1761) (Paxton's Case)

Wilkes v. Wood, 19 How. St. Tr. 1153 (C.P. 1763)

Entick v. Carrington, 19 How. St. Tr. 1029 (C.P. 1765)

Johnson v. United States, 333 U.S. 10 (1948)

Brinegar v. United States, 338 U.S. 160 (1949)

Camara v. Municipal Court, 387 U.S. 523 (1967)

Illinois v. Gates, 462 U.S. 213 (1983)

Indianapolis v. Edmond, 531 U.S. 32 (2000)

United States v. Jones, 132 S. Ct. 945 (2012)

Grand Jury Requirement

No person shall be held to answer for a capital, or otherwise infamous crime, unless on a presentment or indictment of a Grand Jury....

(AMENDMENT V)

~

*G*rand juries have historically served two functions: accusatory and protective. The accusatory function has roots in the English common law. The Founders' motivation for adding this provision to the U.S. Constitution was principally to protect those accused of crimes from prosecutorial overreaching. Contemporary practice, however, limits the extent to which grand juries are capable of performing this second aspect of their traditional role.

A typical federal grand jury consists of twenty-three citizens drawn from the community.

The jurors meet in a closed courtroom, with no judge, no accused, no press, and no lawyer except the prosecutor present. The prosecution presents evidence that a particular suspect committed a crime; the prosecutor is then excused, and the jurors deliberate and vote on whether there is enough evidence to justify the filing of criminal charges against this suspect and sending the case forward to trial. If a majority of jurors believe that there is sufficient evidence, the jurors return a "true bill," which when signed by the prosecutor becomes the indictment: the formal criminal charge that the government must prove beyond a reasonable doubt at trial.

The evidence that is considered by the grand jurors may have been gathered by law enforcement, but also may have been gathered by the grand jury itself. Normally under the direction of the prosecutor, the grand jury may subpoena witnesses to come before them to testify, and those who refuse may be held in contempt. Although the subpoena power is a powerful investigative tool for the prosecutor, a witness may not be required to provide information that is protected by the Fifth Amendment privilege against self-incrimination or other privileges. The grand jury also may issues subpoenas *duces tecum*, requiring a witness or entity to produce documents and other tangible objects for review.

The most distinctive feature of federal grand juries is their secrecy. Even though a transcript is made of the proceedings, matters occurring before the grand jury may not be revealed by the jurors or by the government, on pain of contempt, subject to certain exceptions set forth in the Federal Rules of Criminal Procedure. This requirement is taken very seriously by the courts, and grand jury materials remain secret even after the case is finally resolved. Grand jury witnesses, however, are not subject to the secrecy requirement, and they are free to disclose information they learn to anyone they wish.

Grand juries originated in England, probably in the twelfth century, and began as an effort to increase the King's power. Their original purpose was strictly accusatory—grand jurors were expected to bring to the proceedings any information or suspicions they had about their neighbors' involvement in crimes. By the mid-seventeenth century, however, the jurors also assumed the responsibility to investigate and protect citizens against unfounded charges. This dual role of accuser and protector was the model that settlers brought with them to this country. The first grand-jury session was held in Virginia in 1625, and the practice soon spread to the other English colonies.

Prior to the American Revolution, the grand jury's role as a shield took on increasing importance. The most famous such case involved John Peter Zenger, accused of seditious libel in 1734 for publishing material that was critical of the governor of New York. The evidence against Zenger was strong, but three grand juries refused to indict, impressing on colonists their power to frustrate the enforcement of unpopular laws. As the Revolution drew closer, royal prosecutors who tried to enforce English tax and import laws at times found themselves stymied by local grand juries, who at times refused to let even meritorious cases go forward to trial. These experiences, coupled with the writings of influential legal thinkers (particularly Sir William Blackstone, Henry Care, and John Adams), convinced the colonists of the need for grand-jury review as a restraint on government power. When there was no mention of grand juries in the original Constitution, the criticism was swift; so in December 1791, the Fifth Amendment to the Constitution, containing the Grand Jury Clause, was ratified.

The Supreme Court has not, however, given the Clause a robust interpretation. The Court has concluded, for example, that unlike nearly all of the other provisions of the Bill of Rights, the Grand Jury Requirement Clause is not "incorporated" against the states through the Due Process Clause of the Fourteenth Amendment. That is, the federal Constitution does not require that states use grand juries at all. If states do use grand juries, they are not required to follow the federal procedures. *Hurtado v. California* (1884). The result is that many states use grand juries sparingly, and, when they do, they follow significantly different procedures than is used in federal criminal cases. Given that states are still the primary enforcers of the criminal law, this interpretation severely limits the importance of this part of the Fifth Amendment.

The Supreme Court's current interpretation of the Fifth Amendment also restricts the ability of a grand jury to serve as a significant shield against prosecutorial overreach. There are several reasons for this. First, the Court has greatly limited the ability of criminal suspects to challenge federal grand-jury procedures. Because the proceedings are secret, a suspect has no way of knowing if the evidence presented by the prosecution is complete or accurate. Even if a suspect can determine what evidence the jury hears, his ability to attack the indictment based on this information is small. Federal courts have not required prosecutors to disclose evidence to the grand jurors that is favorable to the accused. *See United States v. Williams* (1992). In addition, a suspect has no ability to challenge an indictment even if the jurors only considered evidence (such as hearsay) that would not be admissible in a later trial; "[a]n indictment returned by a legally constituted and unbiased grand jury," the Court has said, "if valid on its face, is enough to call for a trial of the charge on the merits. The Fifth Amendment requires nothing more." *Costello v. United States* (1956).

Second, criminal law enforcement has changed dramatically since the Bill of Rights was ratified. Prosecutors are now highly professional and specialized, and federal criminal laws have become more complex. One result of this change is that grand jurors lack the ability to decide whether the prosecutor has presented "enough" evidence to justify an indictment. The question that jurors are asked is ultimately a legal one concerning the sufficiency of the evidence, a question that is posed after the only lawyer in the room—the prosecutor—has recommended that the defendant be indicted. Because the prosecutor has complete control over the evidence the grand jurors hear, and because the jurors have no benchmark against which to measure that evidence, it is rare for jurors to second-guess a prosecutor's recommendation to indict. Consequently, grand jurors agree with the prosecutor's recommendation and return a true bill in nearly every case where they are asked to do so.

So despite the original purpose of the Fifth Amendment, most observers now agree that the grand jury has returned to its accusatory roots and is now used as an investigative tool that is much more of a benefit to the prosecutor than to criminal suspects. Perhaps as a consequence, suspects often waive the right to grand-jury review of their case; they may prefer to forgo the minimal protection that comes from this review and avoid the potential for a more searching investigation of their conduct.

Andrew D. Leipold

See Also

Article III, Section 2, Clause 3 (Criminal Trials)
Amendment V (Grand Jury Exception)
Amendment VI (Jury Trial)

Suggestions for Further Research

Sara Sun Beale et al., Grand Jury Law and Practice (2d ed. 1997)

R. Michael Cassidy, *Toward a More Independent Grand Jury: Recasting and Enforcing the Prosecutor's Duty to Disclose Exculpatory Evidence*, 13 Geo. J. Legal Ethics 361 (2000)

Roger A. Fairfax, Jr., *Grand Jury Discretion and Constitutional Design*, 93 Cornell L. Rev. 703, 703–763 (2008)

Grand Jury 2.0: Modern Perspectives on the Grand Jury (Roger Fairfax, Jr., ed., 2010)

Mark Kadish, *Behind the Locked Door of an American Grand Jury: Its History, Its Secrecy, and Its Process*, 24 Fla. St. U. L. Rev. 1 (1996)

Wayne R. LaFave, Jerold H. Israel, & Nancy J. King, Criminal Procedure, 8.1–8.15, 15.1–15.7 (2d ed. 1999)

Andrew D. Leipold, *Why Grand Juries Do Not (and Cannot) Protect the Accused*, 80 Cornell L. Rev. 260 (1995)

Ric Simmons, *Re-Examining the Grand Jury: Is There Room for Democracy in the Criminal Justice System?*, 82 B.U. L. Rev. 1 (2002)

Richard D. Younger, The People's Panel: The Grand Jury in the United States 1634–1941 (1963)

Significant Cases

Hurtado v. California, 110 U.S. 516 (1884)
Costello v. United States, 350 U.S. 359 (1956)
United States v. Williams, 504 U.S. 36 (1992)

Grand Jury Exception

No person shall be held to answer
for a capital, or otherwise infamous
crime, unless on a presentment or
indictment of a Grand Jury, except
in cases arising in the land or naval
forces, or in the Militia, when in
actual service in time of War or
public danger....

(AMENDMENT V)

~

Since the time of the drafting of the Fifth
Amendment, there has been a debate over which
constitutional protections are applicable to courts-
martial. The text of the amendment exempts
only the requirement of a grand jury indictment.
Though it was universally understood at the time
of the Founding that jury trials did not apply to
courts-martial, there is no such textual exception
in the Sixth Amendment. An earlier draft presented
to Congress did specifically exclude military trials from the jury guarantee, but that version was
rejected. Perhaps the Framers believed that the
exemption to jury trials was so universally recognized that it would have been redundant to have
specified it.

During the Virginia ratifying convention,
Anti-Federalists Patrick Henry and George Mason
feared that the lack of a bill of rights would permit Congress, as Henry stated, to "inflict the most
cruel and ignominious punishments on the militia,"
implying that there was a danger of establishing a
national standing army. But it does not necessarily follow that the Fifth Amendment was intended
to apply to military defendants, although in contemporaneous British practice, the protections
against double jeopardy and self-incrimination were
accorded to defendants in military trials. Early in
the eighteenth century, Sir Matthew Hale declared
that members of the military should not be subject
to courts-martial during peacetime, a principle Sir
William Blackstone confirmed in his *Commentaries
on the Laws of England* (1765–1769). How much of
British practice was to be carried over into the legal
obligations of the American Constitution is difficult
to discern. The Framers and ratifiers are virtually
silent on the matter.

It seems clear enough that the Framers
intended Congress to have plenary authority to
define the rules regulating the armed forces (Article
I, Section 8, Clause 14), at least in relation to what
the executive is permitted to do, and perhaps to the
judiciary as well.

In fact, subsequent to the ratification of the
Fifth Amendment, the courts left it to Congress to
define offenses against the military and the manner of their being adjudicated. Judicial review of
decisions of military tribunals was very limited. In
1950, the Supreme Court, in *Johnson v. Eisentrager*,
held that German nationals in U.S. Army custody in
Germany after their conviction by a military commission of violating the laws of war had no right to
the writ of habeas corpus to test the legality of their
detention. In the course of reaching that conclusion,
the majority reasoned that enemy aliens have no
greater rights than Americans, and that "American
citizens conscripted into the military service are
thereby stripped of their Fifth Amendment rights
and as members of the military establishment are
subject to its discipline, including military trials for
offenses against aliens or Americans." The Court
further emphasized that the military has "well-
established...power...to exercise jurisdiction over
members of the armed forces...." If the military
tribunals acquire "lawful authority to hear, decide
and condemn, [then] their action is not subject to
judicial review merely because they have made a
wrong decision on disputed facts."

On the other hand, the Uniform Code of Military Justice (1950), supplemented by the Manual for
Courts-Martial, affirmatively grants due process
rights essentially comparable to those in a civilian court, such as the guarantee of counsel, protection from self-incrimination and double jeopardy,
and being advised of rights before interrogation;
and the Court of Military Appeals (renamed the
United States Court of Appeals for the Armed
Forces in 1994) has held that service members are
entitled to all constitutional rights except those that
are expressly or by implication inapplicable to the
military. *United States v. Clay* (1951); *United States
v. Jacoby* (1960).

The only appeal to an Article III court permitted by the Uniform Code of Military Justice is to the
Supreme Court by writ of certiorari from a decision
of the United States Court of Appeals for the Armed

Forces. Nonetheless, federal courts will review cases collaterally, primarily through the writ of habeas corpus. Until 1953, such collateral review centered on the question of whether the military tribunal possessed proper jurisdiction. *Hiatt v. Brown* (1950). Review remained highly deferential. For the civilian courts to entertain a petition on a writ of habeas corpus, the petitioner must be in actual military custody, and he must have exhausted all available legal remedies within the military justice system.

In 1953, the Supreme Court opened a new avenue of appeal. In *Burns v. Wilson* (1953), a decision that remains highly controversial, a plurality of the justices declared that military courts had the same responsibility as civilian courts "to protect a person from a violation of his constitutional rights." But the justices also stated that the requirements of military discipline may result in an application of constitutional rights different from those accorded to civilian defendants. Finally, the justices stated that civilian courts could review claims de novo, but only if the military courts had "manifestly refused to consider" the petitioners' assertions of error.

Rasul v. Bush (2004), relying on *Burns* and other cases, read *Eisentrager* narrowly and held that the federal habeas statute now confers federal district court jurisdiction to hear challenges of alien detainees held at Guantanamo Bay. However, the Court explicitly did not decide the substance of those rights and limited the habeas extraterritorial reach to Guantanamo Bay, which it said had a unique relationship to the United States. At the same time, in *Rumsfeld v. Padilla* (2004), the Court, on jurisdictional grounds, avoided ruling on the extent of the president's power to keep a U.S. citizen in military custody as an enemy combatant; but in *Hamdi v. Rumsfeld* (2004) the Court decided, without a majority opinion, that the government must give a U.S. citizen held in the United States some type of hearing at which he can contest the facts on which the government decided to treat him as an enemy combatant.

Subsequently, the Court held in *Hamdan v. Rumsfeld* (2006) that a presidential order that directed the trying of alien combatants by military commission exceeded procedural protections afforded by the Uniform Code of Military Justice and the Geneva Conventions (1949). The Court would allow the executive to create deviations from the required procedures only to the extent that "the exigencies . . . necessitate" it. The Court had also held that the Detainee Treatment Act of 2005 did not strip the Court of jurisdiction to hear habeas corpus petitions in cases begun before the Act went into effect.

In response, Congress passed the Military Commissions Act of 2006 applying the restriction of habeas corpus petitions even to ongoing cases. In *Boumediene v. Bush* (2008), the Court held that the procedures established in the Detainee Treatment Act and the Military Commission Act were "not an adequate and effective substitute for habeas corpus" that was available to aliens held in Guantanamo Bay. Subsequently, by July 2010, nineteen of thirty-four detainees won release from Guantanamo on the grounds of insufficient evidence. However, in *Al-Adahi v. Obama* (2010) and *Latif v. Obama* (2011), the D.C. Circuit regularized the methods for evaluating evidence for the lower federal courts, and far fewer detainees succeeded in their habeas corpus petitions.

David F. Forte

See Also

Article I, Section 8, Clause 11
Article I, Section 8, Clause 12 (Army Clause)
Article I, Section 8, Clause 14 (Military Regulations)
Article I, Section 8, Clause 15 (Militia Clause)
Article I, Section 8, Clause 16 (Organizing the Militia)
Article II, Section 2, Clause 1 (Commander in Chief)
Amendment VI (Jury Trial)

Suggestions for Further Research

Joshua Alexander Geltzer, *Of Suspension, Due Process, and Guantanamo: The Reach of the Fifth Amendment after Boumediene and the Relationship between Habeas Corpus and Due Process*, 14 U. Pa. J. Const. L. 719 (2012)

Gordon D. Henderson, *Courts-Martial and the Constitution: The Original Understanding*, 71 Harv. L. Rev. 293 (1957)

Jonathan O. Lurie, *The Role of the Federal Judiciary in the Governance of the American Military: The United States Supreme Court and "Civil Rights and Supervision" Over the Armed Forces*, in The United States Military Under the Constitution of

THE UNITED STATES, 1789–1989 (Richard Kohn ed., 1991)

Significant Cases

Hiatt v. Brown, 339 U.S. 103 (1950)

Johnson v. Eisentrager, 339 U.S. 763 (1950)

United States v. Clay, 1 C.M.R. 74 (1951)

Burns v. Wilson, 346 U.S. 137 (1953)

United States v. Jacoby, 29 C.M.R. 244 (1960)

Rumsfeld v. Padilla, 542 U.S. 426 (2004)

Rasul v. Bush, 542 U.S. 466 (2004)

Hamdi v. Rumsfeld, 542 U.S. 507 (2004)

Hamdan v. Rumsfeld, 548 U.S. 557 (2006)

Boumediene v. Bush, 553 U.S. 723 (2008)

Al-Adahi v. Obama, 613 F.3d 1102 (D.C. Cir. 2010)

Latif v. Obama, 666 F.3d 746 (D.C. Cir. 2011)

Double Jeopardy

… nor shall any person be subject
for the same offence to be twice put
in jeopardy of life or limb.…

(AMENDMENT V)

~

*A*lthough the principle can be found in Greek, Roman, and canon law, the prohibition against double jeopardy came into the United States Constitution from English common law. According to Sir William Blackstone's *Commentaries on the Laws of England*, it was a "universal maxim of the common law of England, that no man is to be brought into jeopardy more than once of the same offence." A defendant to a criminal charge could plead either a former conviction or a former acquittal to the same offense and have the charges dismissed.

All state constitutions drafted prior to the Bill of Rights contained a double jeopardy provision. The principle was so universal that when James Madison proposed on the floor of the First Congress that "No person shall be subject, except in cases of impeachment, to more than one punishment, or trial for the same offence," members rose to object that the language was not strong enough. Representatives Egbert Benson

and Roger Sherman declared that the wording would prevent a new trial for a person who had been improperly convicted. Others argued that it should stand as drafted, because it was merely "declaratory of the law as it now stood." The House defeated an attempt to remove the words "or trial," but the Senate revised the language to its present form, which the House accepted.

The history of the interpretation of the Double Jeopardy Clause by the Supreme Court is complex, and, as the Court itself confessed, it is not a "model of consistency and clarity." *Burks v. United States* (1978). Over time, however, the Court identified the clause as embodying three protections of the individual against the government: (1) no second prosecution for the same offense after an acquittal (2) no second prosecution for the same offense after a guilty verdict and (3) no multiple punishments for the same offense. *See Monge v. California* (1998). The Court recognized early on that the clause could not be read literally; it refers only to "jeopardy of life or limb," a reference that made sense when most serious offenses were sanctioned by capital punishment but hardly makes sense today, when most sanctions are merely a fine or imprisonment. Despite the wording of the clause, the Court applies it to any indictment or information charging a person with any statutory or common law felony or misdemeanor sanctioned by death, imprisonment, or fine. Of course, the Double Jeopardy Clause originally applied only to the federal government, *Palko v. Connecticut* (1937), but in *Benton v. Maryland* (1969), the Court held that the Double Jeopardy Clause of the Fifth Amendment applied to the states as well as to the federal government.

Current double jeopardy jurisprudence falls under five basic headings: sovereign, sanction, trial, retrial, and offense.

First, the Court reads the Double Jeopardy Clause as a protection against conduct by the same "sovereign." Accordingly, since the federal government is, like each state, a separate "sovereign," the Double Jeopardy Clause does not prohibit a federal prosecution after a state prosecution. Despite the doctrine, the federal government as a matter of policy will not prosecute a matter first prosecuted at the state level, absent unusual circumstances. The clause does not prohibit a state prosecution following a federal prosecution or successive prosecutions by different states. But it does prohibit successive prosecutions by the state and a local government under it or by two local governments in the same state, because each derives its sovereign authority from a common source, the state constitution. Indian entities are separate sovereigns.

Second, a sanction counts for double jeopardy purposes only if it is a criminal "punishment." What counts as a punishment for double jeopardy purposes depends on the nature of the sanction imposed. Based on identical conduct, a civil forfeiture of property may follow a criminal acquittal of the owner of the property. Civil fines are not a form of criminal punishment. But a tax may not be specially imposed on criminal conduct. The retention of a sexual predator in civil confinement after his criminal term of imprisonment ends is constitutional: the Court holds that the confinement is punishment under neither the Double Jeopardy nor the Ex Post Facto Clause.

Third, determining when a "lawful trial" begins and ends is crucial to the application of the concept of double jeopardy. Accordingly, the court must have jurisdiction over the offense. Jeopardy attaches in a bench trial when the first witness is sworn; it begins in a jury trial when the jury is sworn. The trial ends with an acquittal, that is, a decision of not guilty on the facts, whether the decision is legally right or legally wrong, even if the acquittal is "based upon an egregiously erroneous foundation." *Fong Foo v. United States (1962).* An appellate court may also grant an acquittal.

Fourth, the Double Jeopardy Clause does not absolutely prohibit retrials. Because a defendant who bribed a court to attain an acquittal was never in jeopardy, his retrial is constitutional. The clause is no bar to a new trial when the defendant successfully appeals his conviction, but a successful appeal of a lesser charge (manslaughter) by a defendant precludes a retrial on a greater charge (murder). Nor may a new trial be held if an appellate court finds that the conviction was not based on sufficient evidence. On the other hand, retrials may be held when a defendant requests a mistrial or when a "manifest necessity" is present. Manifest necessity is present, for example, if the jury deadlocks or is unduly influenced by the misconduct of the defense counsel. Because an appeal review of a trial court's finding of manifest necessity is highly deferential, the appeal court seldom reverses it.

Fifth, a crucial issue turns on the definition of "offense." Modern criminal law is characterized by "specificity in draftsmanship"; it is also characterized, as a result, by an "extraordinary proliferation of overlapping and related statutory offenses." *Ashe v. Swenson* (1970). Double jeopardy protections depend, therefore, on a careful ascertaining of what constitutes an "offense," that is, what is the "allowable unit of prosecution." However, few limits, if any, are imposed by the Double Jeopardy Clause on the legislative power to define offenses. But once a legislature defines that proscription, it "determines the scope of protection afforded by a prior conviction or acquittal." To ascertain whether two statutory offenses constitute two "offenses" for double jeopardy, prohibiting successive prosecutions, the Court follows a multiple-element test to determine whether each "offense" contains an element that is not common to the other. *Blockburger v. United States* (1932). Under the *Blockburger* test, the Double Jeopardy Clause prevents successive prosecutions for both greater and lesser included offenses. The focus of the test is on statutory elements rather than evidence or conduct. Nevertheless, a prosecution of a lesser offense (e.g., assault and battery) does not preclude the prosecution of a greater offense (murder) if all of the elements of the greater offense (e.g., death) were not present at the time of the prosecution of the lesser offense. On the other hand, a distinction is drawn between successive prosecutions and multiple punishments. Even if individual offenses are not separate under the *Blockburger* test, the Double Jeopardy Clause does not prevent multiple punishments for them when the courts try them together, when the legislature intended the higher level of punishment.

G. Robert Blakey

See Also
Amendment XIV (Due Process Clause)

Suggestions for Further Research

Roscoe Pound, The Development of Constitutional Guarantees of Liberty (1957)

Thirty-Ninth Annual Review of Criminal Procedure, 39 Geo. L.J. Ann. Rev. Crim. Proc. 856 (2010)

Significant Cases

United States v. Perez, 22 U.S. (9 Wheat.) 579 (1824)

Ex parte Lange, 85 U.S. (18 Wall.) 163 (1874)

United States v. Ball, 163 U.S. 662 (1896)

Blockburger v. United States, 284 U.S. 299 (1932)

Palko v. Connecticut, 302 U.S. 319 (1937)

United States v. Green, 355 U.S. 184 (1957)

Petite v. United States, 361 U.S. 529 (1960)

Fong Foo v. United States, 369 U.S. 141 (1962)

Benton v. Maryland, 395 U.S. 784 (1969)

Waller v. Florida, 397 U.S. 387 (1970)

Brown v. Ohio, 432 U.S. 161 (1977)

Burks v. United States, 437 U.S. 1 (1978)

Sanabria v. United States, 437 U.S. 54 (1978)

Missouri v. Hunter, 459 U.S. 359 (1983)

Heath v. Alabama, 474 U.S. 82 (1985)

Kansas v. Hendricks, 521 U.S. 346 (1997)

Monge v. California, 524 U.S. 721 (1998)

Smith v. Massachusetts, 543 U.S. 426 (2005)

Renico v. Lett, 130 S. Ct. 1855 (2010)

Self-Incrimination

No person...shall be compelled in any criminal case to be a witness against himself....

(AMENDMENT V)

~

Scholars such as John Wigmore and Leonard Levy have suggested that the privilege against self-incrimination reflects the Framers' antipathy to two specific abuses. One abuse was the European practice of judicial torture, and the other was the questioning of witnesses sworn to the oath ex officio before the notorious courts of the High Commission and the Star Chamber in England. The oath ex officio pledged the witness to answer any and all questions truthfully, without any indication of the subject matter. The oath was used to persecute political and religious dissenters and had the obnoxious effect of forcing devout individuals to choose between admitting offenses, to be followed by hanging, or denying offenses, to be followed by damnation. Some recent scholarship has offered an alternative to this account. It suggests that the privilege against self-incrimination arose mainly from American practice rather than as a reaction against European or English royal abuses.

In America, the privilege arose against the background of the particular practice of self-representation by defendants. Consistent with the practice of English common law, the accused could not be forced to be sworn as a witness in the late eighteenth and early nineteenth centuries in America. The reason for the rule was fear that the guilty would be tempted to swear falsely and be damned by God. The accused representing himself, therefore, literally could not be called to be a witness against himself. This rule was also congenial with a law, which prevailed in England well into the nineteenth century, that parties to the litigation were themselves incompetent to testify, either on their own behalf or if examined by their adversaries. In effect, the Fifth Amendment codified this practice.

The defendant typically represented himself and could speak for himself throughout the trial, both by making unsworn statements heard by the jury and by examining witnesses. Such statements were, of course, voluntary. On the other hand, early American practice involved pretrial questioning of the accused by a magistrate or justice of the peace where the defendant could be pressed to admit wrongdoing.

The Founders, then, regarded the privilege as valuable enough to include in the Constitution, but their own practice put considerable pressure on defendants to surrender incriminating information before trial. The assertion of the privilege at trial became more common as the advent of modern police forces had the effect of replacing pretrial judicial questioning with custodial interrogation by the police, particularly when defendants availed themselves of professional attorneys.

Judicial interpretations of the Self-Incrimination Clause were slow in coming. John Marshall, both in *Marbury v. Madison* (1803) and in the treason trial of Aaron Burr (1807), permitted third-party witnesses to claim the privilege. The federal government prosecuted relatively few cases, and the Court held that the privilege, like the rest of the Bill of Rights, did not apply to the states, a situation that did not change until after the Civil War, when the Supreme Court, over a period of many years, read the Due Process Clause of the Fourteenth Amendment to incorporate most of the Bill of Rights.

In the 1880s, the Supreme Court took the view that the privilege protected private books and papers. With antecedents in the common law, the privilege protected an individual against a subpoena demanding incriminating private documents. Indeed, even if the government obtained the papers without a subpoena, the use of private papers as evidence against their owner was equated with compelled testimony. During this same period, the Supreme Court upheld a congressional statute providing for compelled testimony under the grant of transactional immunity, but rejected the claim that corporations could assert the privilege.

In 1964, the Supreme Court held that the privilege applies against the states as a matter of Fourteenth Amendment due process and that testimony compelled in state court could not be used against the witness in a federal prosecution (and vice versa). *Malloy v. Hogan* (1964); *Murphy v. Waterfront Commission* (1964).

Subsequently, Fifth Amendment doctrine changed significantly. The most dramatic change was the decision in *Miranda v. Arizona* (1966), holding that information received from the interrogation of arrested persons by the police was presumptively the product of unconstitutional compulsion in the absence of the specific warnings. The *Miranda* doctrine prohibits custodial interrogation without a knowing and voluntary waiver of the rights to silence and counsel.

Subsequent cases have developed in detail the meaning of custody, interrogation, waiver, and the consequences of invoking silence or counsel. For example, in *Berghuis v. Thompkins* (2010) the Court ruled that a suspect who said nothing in response to the warning and next to nothing in response to police questions for three

hours made a voluntary waiver by eventually responding to one of the questions. Another line of cases limits the scope of the *Miranda* exclusionary rule, permitting admission of evidence derived form *Miranda* violations that would be suppressed if derived from a Fourth Amendment violation. If the defendant elects to testify at trial, statements tainted by *Miranda* violations may be admitted to impeach. In *Dickerson v. United States* (2000), the Supreme Court reaffirmed *Miranda* and struck down a congressional statute that had purported to return to pre-*Miranda* practice, although the majority appeared to concede that the Constitution itself did not require the *Miranda* rule.

Outside the police-interrogation context, the privilege protects against compelled testimonial evidence tending to incriminate the witness. Compulsion is not limited to court order, but includes such pressures as the threatened loss of government employment or public contracts, or an inference of guilt from silence at a criminal trial. Testimonial evidence means a communication of information from the target's memory or knowledge. Thus fingerprints, tissue samples, and physical evidence are not testimonial: the government can compel their production. In a reversal of its earlier position, the modern Court has held that the Fifth Amendment does not protect physical evidence like private papers unless official compulsion forced the defendant to create the document. In the case of private papers, the Fourth Amendment and not the Fifth Amendment normally governs the government's power to seize papers, just as the Fourth Amendment limits the government's powers to seize conversations by wiretap. The privilege applies when the evidence sought is incriminating, that is, it provides a link in a chain of proof that might be useful, and the risk of prosecution is more than fanciful. Where a violation of the Self-Incrimination Clause is the product of a directly coerced or compelled confession, the government may not use in a later case that confession or any evidence that is the fruit of such coercion. If, however, the original illegality is a violation of the *Miranda* rule, rather than actual coercion, the government may use in a later prosecution evidence that was discovered as a fruit of that confession.

Evidence is not incriminating, however, and the privilege cannot be asserted if it is produced under an immunity order by the court, that is, a promise not to use the compelled information against the defendant. The government may grant the witness "transactional immunity" or "use and derivative use immunity." Transactional immunity bars any prosecution for the conduct to which the testimony relates. Use and derivative use immunity, the only type of immunity constitutionally required, permits the government to prosecute the witness, but only after proving that it, the prosecution, has made no use of the compelled testimony or any evidence derived from it. Typically, the prosecution will exhaust all other avenues of investigation before applying for a use immunity order, and the supporting affidavit will describe in detail all of the evidence the prosecution has prior to the compelled testimony. Nonetheless, the risk that immunized testimony may aid the prosecution indirectly is thought sufficiently serious that many states still authorize only transactional immunity above and beyond the Fifth Amendment's protections.

Leaving the *Miranda* situation aside, the witness must claim the privilege, or it will be deemed waived. Of course, direct physical or psychological coercion or compulsion by the police that produces a "confession" is inadmissible whether or not a "waiver" is asserted by the police. In addition, the government may not coercively obtain a waiver by, for example, threatening the loss of public employment or government contracts. A criminal defendant who elects to take the stand waives the privilege with respect to questions asked on cross-examination that are reasonably related to the direct examination.

Donald Dripps

See Also
Amendment IV (Searches and Seizures)
Amendment XIV, Section 1 (Due Process Clause)

Suggestions for Further Research
R. H. Helmholz, et al., The Privilege Against Self-Incrimination: Its Origins and Development (1997)

Wayne R. LaFave, Jerold H. Israel, & Nancy J. King, Criminal Procedure (2d ed.1999)

Leonard W. Levy, Origins of the Fifth Amendment (1968)

Leonard W. Levy, *Origins of the Fifth Amendment and Its Critics,* 19 Cardozo L. Rev. 821 (1997)

John Henry Wigmore, A Treatise on the System of Evidence in Trials at Common Law 2250 (1904)

Significant Cases
Marbury v. Madison, 5 U.S. (1 Cranch) 137 (1803)
Malloy v. Hogan, 378 U.S. 1 (1964)
Murphy v. Waterfront Comm'n, 378 U.S. 52 (1964)
Miranda v. Arizona, 384 U.S. 436 (1966)
Schmerber v. California, 384 U.S. 757 (1966)
Kastigar v. United States, 406 U.S. 441 (1972)
Pennsylvania v. Muniz, 496 U.S. 582 (1990)
Dickerson v. United States, 530 U.S. 428 (2000)
Berghuis v. Thompkins, 130 S. Ct. 2250 (2010)

Due Process Clause

No person shall…be deprived of life, liberty, or property, without due process of law.…

(Amendment V)

～

$\mathscr{A}$rticle Thirty-nine of the Magna Carta (1215) proclaimed that "no free man shall be taken or imprisoned or disseised or outlawed or exiled or in any way ruined, nor will we go or send against him, except by the lawful judgment of his peers or by the law of the land." This "law of the land" requirement, which is often called the principle of legality, prohibited unilateral, arbitrary action by the king against certain protected private interests. Executive and judicial deprivations of such interests could take place only pursuant to valid legal authority.

The phrase "due process of law" made its first appearance in a statute of 1354 concerning court procedures. "Due process of law" meant that judgments could issue only when the defendant was personally given the opportunity to appear in court pursuant to an appropriate writ (i.e., was served process). The phrase retained this technical meaning in English law into the eighteenth century.

At the time of the drafting of the Bill of Rights, at least eight state constitutions contained clauses restraining government from depriving persons of life, liberty, or property except pursuant to the law of the land. The Fifth Amendment, which otherwise tracked the form of these state provisions, used the phrase "due process of law" instead of "law of the land." The reasons for this change in terminology are uncertain, but it is likely that the founding generation was misled by some seventeenth-century statements of Sir Edward Coke (familiar to virtually all the Founders), who in 1642 had declared—wrongly, in the judgment of modern historians—that the phrases "law of the land" and "due process of law" were essentially equivalent. Accordingly, the constitutional meaning of "due process of law," as understood in America in the late eighteenth century, almost certainly refers to the principle of legality rather than to pleading technicalities.

Until very close to the time of the framing, the judicial power was generally viewed as an aspect of executive power. In eighteenth-century America, therefore, the phrase "without due process of law" meant something like "executive or judicial action taken without lawful authorization or not in accordance with traditional procedural forms of justice." The Supreme Court modestly extended the principle to Congress in *Murray's Lessee v. Hoboken Land & Improvement Co.* (1856)—the first Supreme Court case that turned on the meaning of the Due Process Clause. There the Court determined that the Due Process Clause limited the power of Congress to authorize novel forms of adjudication. The case involved a constitutional challenge to a statutory procedure in which the government collected deficiencies from tax collectors without first having a court determine whether the tax collector really owed the money to the government. The Court found that the clause "is a restraint on the legislative as well as on the executive and judicial powers of the government, and cannot be so construed as to leave congress free to make any process 'due process of law,' by its mere will." In order to determine whether leg-

islatively prescribed forms of adjudication violated due process of law, the Court looked to "those settled usages and modes of proceeding existing in the common and statute law of England." The Court found a long tradition in English and American law of auditing tax collectors without prior hearings and accordingly upheld the practice.

The Due Process Clause requires that deprivations of "life, liberty, or property" be accompanied by due process of law. The deprivation of other interests not enumerated here need not be accompanied by due process of law. When the Due Process Clause was ratified in 1791, the meaning of "liberty" as a personal right was clear. Sir William Blackstone, whose influence on the founding generation was enormous, wrote in his *Commentaries on the Laws of England* (1765–1769) that the right to liberty meant "the power of locomotion, of changing situation, or removing one's person to whatsoever place one's own inclination may direct; without imprisonment or restraint, unless by due course of law." That definition is quite narrow and focused, and it excludes such matters as bodily integrity and reputation. Those interests, however, were encompassed by Blackstone's (expansive to modern ears) definition of "life," which referred to an array of rights lumped together under the general heading of personal security: "a person's legal and uninterrupted enjoyment of his life, his limbs, his body, his health, and his reputation." The term "property" in 1791 was more ambiguous. It could have referred to land, to land plus chattels, to anything of exchangeable value, or (what seems most likely) to whatever interests common law courts would have recognized as property entitled to legal protection. None of these understandings would include as property future enjoyment of government benefits, such as jobs or licenses. The law sharply distinguished between property rights and mere privileges that the government could continue or terminate at its pleasure.

The eighteenth-century lawyer trying to define the phrase "life, liberty, or property" would have faced a sticky problem that could not be answered by reference to Blackstone, tradition, or any other authority: Do these terms draw their meaning from federal law, state law, or both? Does the Constitution contain its own internal definitions of those terms, so that the Constitution itself determines whether a particular interest is property? Are they defined by reference to the laws of the states, so that a particular interest might be constitutional "property" in Pennsylvania but not in New York? Or must the universe of constitutionally protected interests be determined by some combination of federal and state law?

Perhaps the best answer, though it is impossible to say decisively, is that federal law sets the outer boundaries of "life, liberty, and property" and state law fixes the details. Surely the Constitution does not itself determine whether a particular estate in land, such as a surface estate on mining land, is or is not "property" for purposes of the Due Process Clause or whether water rights must be appropriative or riparian; either answer is permissible and, accordingly, can vary from one jurisdiction to another. But if a state decided that land itself was henceforth no longer to be considered "property," that would pass the boundaries of acceptability. Federal law thus establishes for each term a "core" of meaning that no jurisdiction can alter, but beyond that core, governments are free to expand or contract the range of constitutionally protected interests.

Accordingly, the original meaning of the Due Process Clause was essentially that the federal government could not take people's lives, health, reputation, freedom of movement, or common law property without prior legal authorization and without following traditional judicial procedures. Describing modern doctrine is considerably more difficult.

Modern doctrine has significantly modified the original understanding of how one determines compliance with "due process of law." Instead of reference to traditionally accepted procedural forms, contemporary law dating back more than a century has judged the adequacy of procedures by a mélange of practical factors that resist easy reduction. Late nineteenth-century and early twentieth-century cases described due process as procedures "appropriate to the case, and just to the parties to be affected," *Hagar v. Reclamation Dist. No. 108* (1884), and the absence of due process as procedures that are "inadequate or manifestly unfair." *ICC v. Louisville & Nashville R.R. Co.* (1913). As Justice Felix Frankfurter summarized matters in a famous concurring opinion in *Joint Anti-Fascist*

Refugee Committee v. McGrath (1951), due process "is compounded of history, reason, the past course of decisions, and stout confidence in the strength of the democratic faith which we profess.... It is a delicate process of judgment by those whom the Constitution entrusted with the unfolding of the process."

In *Mathews v. Eldridge* (1976), the Court clarified that this "delicate process of judgment" generally requires consideration of

> first, the [significance of the] private interest that will be affected by the official action; second, the risk of an erroneous deprivation of such interest through the procedures used, and the probable value, if any, of additional or substitute procedural safeguards; and finally, the [weight of the] Government's interest, including the function involved and the fiscal and administrative burdens that the additional or substitute procedural requirement would entail.

While there is no indication that the Court in *Mathews* thought that it was changing or limiting the previous century's focus on fundamental fairness as determined by all-things-considered reasoning, within a few years this formulation from *Mathews* took on a life of its own, and today it serves as the near-exclusive frame of reference for analyzing procedural adequacy under the Due Process Clause. This modern balancing-of-factors approach is universally criticized as unpredictable. Many observers also object to the Court's optimistic goal of accurate decision-making, and there is considerable disagreement about which other possible goals of procedure should be factored into the mix. For example, if one limits the due process analysis to the concerns identified in *Mathews*, then the interests of children and custodial parents would not seem to be relevant to determining the procedures for enforcement of child support, which struck the Court's originalist-leaning justices in 2011 as implausible. *See Turner v. Rogers* (2011). Nonetheless, a relatively rote application of the *Mathews* factors is the standard modern approach to establishing the constitutional adequacy of procedures.

One of the trickiest questions in modern law concerns the timing of procedures: which procedures (if any) must come *before* the government deprives people of protected interests? The law in this area remains unsettled in many important respects and defies simple description. Perhaps the most that can be said—and can be said only as a rough generalization—is that there is a presumption in favor of pre-deprivation procedures that can be overcome when the value of such procedures would be low, the potential risks to the government or public from delaying the deprivation would be high, or the person deprived would have an adequate remedy after the deprivation.

The most dramatic transformations in modern due process have concerned the range of interests encompassed by the phrase "life, liberty, or property." As late as 1950, the original meaning still largely held sway, though Blackstone's broad understanding of "life" as including bodily integrity and reputation mysteriously vanished in favor of a much narrower meaning. No doubt this development, which was never expressly acknowledged, put pressure on the other terms in the enumeration ("liberty" and "property") to include such worthy interests as physical integrity and reputation. More importantly, the rise of the post–New Deal administrative state vastly expanded the range of circumstances under which official action could affect people's lives; and the concomitant expansion of government benefits, jobs, and licenses raised the stakes of excluding such interests from procedural protection. By the early 1960s, a majority of the Court was prepared to treat the phrase "life, liberty, or property" as a convenient shorthand for any interest whose loss would be grievous rather than as a list of three distinct terms with distinct, ascertainable meanings—a development that some commentators half-jokingly described as the emergence of "lifelibertyproperty." On this new understanding, government benefits could easily constitute an interest whose loss would be grievous and whose deprivation therefore required some measure of procedure.

In 1970, the Court formalized this understanding in *Goldberg v. Kelly*, where the State of New York, in its argument to the Supreme Court concerning hearings prior to termination of benefits under the Aid to Families with Dependent Children Act, did not even argue that expected future receipt of AFDC benefits was not a constitutionally protected interest. Subsequent cases quickly extended constitutional protection to such interests as government licenses and reputation.

In 1972, the Supreme Court established the framework of modern law in *Board of Regents of State Colleges v. Roth*. That case reestablished some differentiations among the three enumerated categories of protected interests. The Court held that "liberty" and "property" were distinct terms with ascertainable meanings, though "life" continues to be conspicuously absent from modern recitations of the range of protected interests in anything other than its narrowest and most literal application. The Court explicitly stated, however, that these terms would not be construed in accordance with their original meaning, but would have to be construed to include the extended range of interests recognized in prior case law, including government benefits.

Accordingly, the Court has expanded the definition of the term "liberty," drawing upon *Meyer v. Nebraska* (1923), in which it declared that "liberty" includes "not merely freedom from bodily restraint but also the right of the individual to contract, to engage in any of the common occupations of life, to acquire useful knowledge, to marry, establish a home and bring up children, to worship God according to the dictates of his own conscience, and generally to enjoy those privileges long recognized...as essential to the orderly pursuit of happiness by free men." The Court's extraordinary expansion of the concept of "liberty" reached its apogee in the famous (some critics say infamous) declaration by Justice Anthony Kennedy: "At the heart of liberty is the right to define one's own concept of existence, of meaning, of the universe, and of the mystery of human life." *Planned Parenthood of Southeastern Pennsylvania v. Casey* (1992). He quoted this passage a decade later, holding in *Lawrence v. Texas* (2003) that the state could not prohibit homosexual sodomy, and in *United States v. Windsor* (2013), that the federal government could not deny federal benefits to legally married same-sex couples.

Although one may have the right to define reality in any way that one may please, acting upon those beliefs is another story. So despite Justice Kennedy's sweeping language, the constitutional meaning of liberty has been held not to include, at least under some circumstances, a right to government employment, an interest in reputation, or many interests claimed by prisoners. The government is free to construct these excluded interests to be constitutionally protected through statutes and regulations by specifying a clear causal connection between satisfaction of criteria of eligibility and receipt of a benefit, but they are not automatically protected as a matter of constitutional command.

Today, it is state law that primarily defines the term "property." Interests within the traditional common-law understanding of property are generally still considered to be property. Different states can, for example, prescribe different kinds of estates in land as "property," but a state could not by statutory or judicial fiat declare land per se (or money in a bank account) not to be private property for purposes of the Constitution. Interests beyond the traditional common law understanding, such as government benefits and licenses, are constitutionally protected if statutory or regulatory provisions draw a clear causal line from the satisfaction of eligibility criteria to the receipt of benefits. The case law distinguishes the substance of the created interest from the procedures for its termination. The latter is what the Due Process Clause protects. Within the zone beyond the constitutional core of "liberty" and "property," government can determine which substantive interests shall receive due process protection, but once that substantive decision is made, the constitutional law of due process assesses the adequacy of the procedures. In other words, the government may not make acceptance of "unconstitutional" termination procedures a condition of receiving government benefits.

If an interest does not fall within the meaning of the phrase "life, liberty, or property,"

the Due Process Clause does not mandate any particular procedures for its deprivation. Other sources of law, whether constitutional or statutory, may well do so, but the Due Process Clause is, so to speak, "turned off." There are several other "on-off switches" that also determine the applicability of the Due Process Clause.

First, the clause applies only to government action; private entities are not bound by the Fifth Amendment or, indeed, by anything in the Constitution except the Thirteenth Amendment. This can pose difficult questions when the acting entity is nominally private but is involved in some fashion with the government. *See* State Action Clause (Amendment XIV, Section 1). Second, modern law holds that the word "deprived" in the Due Process Clause means an intentional (or, at a minimum, a reckless) taking of a protected interest. Losses inflicted by government negligence do not implicate the Due Process Clause.

Third, and most importantly, administrative agencies are responsible for the vast bulk of governmental actions that work deprivations of interests within the compass of the Due Process Clause, but large classes of agency action have been held to fall outside the clause's protection. Agencies engage in two forms of official action: rule-making, which strongly resembles in form and function the promulgation of a statute by the legislature, and adjudication, which strongly resembles in form and function the decision of a case by a court. The Due Process Clause has never been understood to impose procedural requirements on legislatures (though it does, under modern understandings, regulate the content of legislation that authorizes executive or judicial procedures). For almost a century, courts have held that agency rule-making shares in this legislative immunity from due-process analysis; agency rule-making is subject to no constitutional procedural requirements. *Bi-Metallic Investment Co. v. State Board of Equalization of Colorado* (1915). Agency adjudication, however, is subject to due process analysis, but agencies do not stand in the same shoes as courts. Procedures that would be obviously inadequate in judicial proceedings are considered constitutionally adequate for agency adjudication. The size of the gap is uncertain, which typifies the complexity of the modern law of procedural due process.

Gary Lawson

See Also

Amendment XIV, Section 1 (State Action)
Amendment XIV, Section 1 (Due Process Clause)

Suggestions for Further Research

Frank H. Easterbrook, *Substance and Due Process*, 1982 SUP. CT. REV. 85 (1982)

John C. Harrison, *Substantive Due Process and the Constitutional Text*, 83 VA. L. REV. 493 (1997)

Keith Jurow, *Untimely Thoughts: A Reconsideration of the Origins of Due Process of Law*, 19 AM. J. LEGAL HIST. 265 (1975)

GARY LAWSON, FEDERAL ADMINISTRATIVE LAW 670–798 (5th ed. 2009)

Gary Lawson, Katharine Ferguson & Guillermo A. Montero, *"Oh Lord, Please Don't Le Me Be Misunderstood!": Rediscovering the* Mathews v. Eldridge *and* Penn Central *Frameworks*, 81 NOTRE DAME L. REV. 1 (2005)

JERRY L. MASHAW, DUE PROCESS IN THE ADMINISTRATIVE STATE (1985)

Ryan C. Williams, *The One and Only Substantive Due Process Clause*, 120 YALE L.J. 408 (2010)

Significant Cases

Murray's Lessee v. Hoboken Land & Improvement Co., 59 U.S. (18 How.) 272 (1856)

Hagar v. Reclamation Dist. No. 108, 111 U.S. 701 (1884)

ICC v. Louisville & Nashville R.R. Co., 227 U.S. 88 (1913)

Bi-Metallic Inv. Co. v. State Bd. of Equalization of Colorado, 239 U.S. 441 (1915)

Meyer v. Nebraska, 262 U.S. 390 (1923)

Joint Anti-Fascist Refugee Committee v. McGrath, 341 U.S. 123 (1951)

Goldberg v. Kelly, 397 U.S. 254 (1970)

Bd. of Regents of State Colleges v. Roth, 408 U.S. 564 (1972)

Mathews v. Eldridge, 424 U.S. 319 (1976)

Planned Parenthood of Southeastern Pennsylvania v. Casey, 505 U.S. 833 (1992)

Lawrence v. Texas, 539 U.S. 558 (2003)

Turner v. Rogers, 131 S. Ct. 2507 (2011)

United States v. Windsor, 133 S. Ct. 2675 (2013)

Takings Clause

... nor shall private property be taken for public use, without just compensation.

(AMENDMENT V)

~

Considering its modern importance, the original purpose of the Takings Clause is surprisingly obscure. Most provisions of the Bill of Rights were requested in some form as the states ratified the original Constitution. The Takings Clause was not. Representative James Madison added it for unexplained reasons as he sifted through the requested amendments to propose a slate of them. There were a few historical precedents for the clause. The Northwest Ordinance contained a just-compensation requirement. Two colonial charters and two state constitutions had such a requirement as well. Other states sometimes provided just compensation by custom or due process. But there was virtually no recorded discussion about the Takings Clause itself.

The origins of the clause are still more enigmatic in light of the background of limited federal power. It has been argued that the original Constitution did not grant Congress the power of eminent domain within the boundaries of a state. Indeed, in 1845, the Supreme Court declared that "the United States have no constitutional capacity to exercise ... eminent domain" in the states. *Pollard's Lessee v. Hagan* (1845). Under this theory, neither Congress's enumerated powers nor the Necessary and Proper Clause grants a general power of eminent domain.

Whether or not that is so, Congress did not generally exercise such a power. For the first seventy-five years of the republic, when Congress authorized federal roads, lighthouses, fortifications, or military bases, it relied upon the *states* to exercise eminent domain over land for the federal project. Congress did exercise eminent domain in areas where it had plenary power under the Constitution, such as the District of Columbia and occasionally the territories. It also may have occasionally taken property in other ways, such as the temporary impressment of personal property for military purposes. But neither of these methods was commonplace. Hence, the clause's purpose and original scope can sometimes be difficult to discern.

Under modern doctrine, the Takings Clause is of much greater importance and its zone of application is much broader. Beginning with its decision in *Kohl v. United States* (1875), the Supreme Court has recognized a federal power of eminent domain. The Court has alternately suggested that the power is granted by the Necessary and Proper Clause, *United States v. Gettysburg Electric Railway Co.* (1896), that it is granted by implication of the Takings Clause itself (despite the Ninth Amendment), or that it is an inherent power of sovereignty whose specific enumeration is unnecessary, *United States v. Jones* (1883). Whatever its source, the power is seated in Congress, not the executive. Furthermore, the clause, like most of the Bill of Rights, has been held to be incorporated by the Fourteenth Amendment and thus applicable to the states. In fact, a requirement of just compensation was the first element of the Bill of Rights held to be part of the Fourteenth Amendment's Due Process requirement. *Chicago, Burlington & Quincy Railroad Co. v. Chicago* (1897). Thus, the clause applies today to takings by any government—federal, state, or local. A state's power to exercise eminent domain derives, like the police power, from the state's inherent sovereignty.

The Fifth Amendment's protections are triggered only when the property at issue is "taken" and when it is "property" as defined by applicable state or federal law. For purposes of the clause, property need not be land (real property), but can be personal property, such as bank accounts, *Webb's Fabulous Pharmacies v. Beckwith* (1980) or intangible property, such as trade secrets. *Ruckelshaus v. Monsanto Co.* (1984).

There are a range of government actions that affect the value or use of property—some of which are clearly takings, some of which are more subject to doubt. It is easiest to see that there has been a taking when the government formally "condemns" property and takes legal title to it. Such an exercise of eminent domain is the paradigmatic example of a taking. But as noted above, the federal government rarely exercised eminent domain in the generations after the Founding,

and today the hard takings questions occur when there is no formal condemnation.

Even when there has been no formal condemnation, the courts have held that there is a taking any time the government authorizes a "permanent physical occupation," even of only part of the property. *Loretto v. Teleprompter Manhattan CATV Corp.* (1982). The Supreme Court made a similar ruling as early as 1871, concluding that a government-authorized flooding was a taking of property. *Pumpelly v. Green Bay & Mississippi Canal Co.* (1871). There is some historical basis for this rule: state courts frequently confronted similar problems in the nineteenth century under state "mill acts," which let one landowner dam a river for a mill, permanently flooding neighboring properties.

Temporary physical occupations can also be takings for purposes of the clause, *First English Evangelical Lutheran Church v. Los Angeles County* (1987), but temporary occupations are judged by a less categorical analysis. Recent Supreme Court decisions have said that they "are subject to a more complex balancing process to determine whether they are a taking," and that there is no "magic formula" for evaluating them. *Arkansas Game & Fish Comm'n v. United States* (2012).

Regulations of land pose even harder questions. There were regulations of land at the Founding, but there is no evidence that landowners were compensated during this period. At the Founding, regulations of land generally did not give rise to claims for compensation. But in the early twentieth century, the Supreme Court created a doctrine of so-called "regulatory takings." Justice Oliver Wendell Holmes wrote for the Court that "while property may be regulated to a certain extent, if regulation goes too far it will be recognized as a taking." *Pennsylvania Coal Co. v. Mahon* (1922). The doctrine has been criticized for lacking a historical basis, especially in light of the Founding-era practice of uncompensated regulations, and an opinion for the Court by Justice Antonin Scalia has conceded that "early constitutional theorists did not believe the Takings Clause embraced regulations of property at all." *Lucas v. South Carolina Coastal Council* (1992).

On the other hand, some scholars have suggested that the implications from the history are not so clear cut. It is possible, for example, that the early regulations were consistent with a background theory that still prohibited some regulatory takings. In particular, it has been argued that early uncompensated regulations were limited to those consistent with the owners' natural rights, whereas regulations that violate natural rights require compensation. Alternatively, it has been argued that the purpose and structure of the Fourteenth Amendment, as well as judicial decisions between the Founding and the ratification of that amendment, justify a doctrine of regulatory takings against state governments under the Fourteenth Amendment, even if none was originally established against the federal government under the Fifth Amendment.

At any rate, under modern doctrine, regulations of property are sometimes, but not frequently, held to be takings. The general principle is that the government is forbidden "from forcing some people alone to bear public burdens which, in all fairness and justice, should be borne by the public as a whole." *Armstrong v. United States* (1960). In making this "essentially ad hoc" determination, the Court has particularly emphasized "the economic impact of the regulation on the claimant," the interference with "distinct investment-backed expectations," and "the character of the government action." *Penn Central Transportation Co. v. City of New York* (1978).

In practice, courts rarely find that a regulation qualifies as a taking under this test. Zoning regulations, for example, are almost never held to be takings. *Village of Euclid v. Ambler Realty Co.* (1926). However, there are a few specific types of regulation that are categorically considered takings—for example, a regulation that deprives an owner of all economically viable use of the land, *Lucas v. South Carolina Coastal Council*, or a regulation that unfairly conditions the grant of a governmental permit upon the forfeiture of a physical property interest or the exaction of inappropriate fees. *Nollan v. California Coastal Comm'n* (1987); *Dolan v. City of Tigard* (1994); *Koontz v. St. Johns River Water Management District* (2013).

The Takings Clause has also long been held to require that the taking be "for public use." In other words, it must not take property from one person and give it to another for purely private

gain. As a purely textual matter, the clause is ambiguous about such a requirement. It is possible to read the clause as simply *describing* the conditions under which property will be taken. Indeed, one might say that the enumerated powers doctrine independently requires all federal takings to be for a public use, and hence that any federal taking that is within the enumerated powers is necessarily one for public use. One could also read the clause as *limiting* compensation to takings for public use, while providing no compensation if the taking is for private use.

The conventional reading of the Takings Clause, however, infers an independent public use requirement. This avoids rendering the "public use" phrase redundant and avoids the strange result of leaving takings for private interest without compensation. It is also the view taken by many state courts throughout the nineteenth century in the course of interpreting their own state constitutional law. As with the regulatory takings doctrine, it is possible that the original meaning of the Fourteenth Amendment incorporates a public use requirement against the states even if the Fifth Amendment was not originally understood to apply it against the federal government.

There has been controversy over how to define a "public use." As an original matter, given the text's focus on "use," one might have thought that the property taken must be usable by the public—either by a government entity or a private entity obligated to grant access on broad and neutral terms, like a common carrier. Again, many nineteenth-century state courts interpreted the requirement in this fashion, as when the courts allowed eminent domain for railroads to claim a right-of-way or for flooding under the "mill acts" mentioned above.

Throughout the twentieth century, however, the Supreme Court has only required the taking to have a public *purpose* rather than requiring that the property be used by the public, and it has gradually adopted a more relaxed view of that public-purpose requirement. In *Berman v. Parker* (1954), it upheld the use of eminent domain to condemn blighted property for urban renewal, saying that "the legislature, not the judiciary, is the main guardian of the public needs to be served by social legislation." In *Hawaii Housing Authority v. Midkiff,* (1984), the Court unanimously approved the State of Hawaii's breaking up of large landed estates to transfer titles from the landowners to smaller lessees on the principle that the people of Hawaii were breaking up a "land oligopoly traceable to their monarchs."

Most recently, the Court invoked the "diverse and always evolving needs of society" to conclude that governments have "broad latitude in determining what public needs justify the use of the takings power." *Kelo v. City of New London* (2005). In *Kelo,* the Court allowed a local government to take a private home and give it to a private corporation for purposes of economic development. It was a closely divided and extremely controversial decision, prompting Justice Sandra Day O'Connor to write in dissent, "The specter of condemnation hangs over all property." The unfavorable reaction to the five-to-four decision in *Kelo* resulted in state laws designed to increase protection for property holders throughout much of the country.

When property has been taken for public use, the Takings Clause mandates "just compensation." At bottom, the exercise of eminent domain is a forced sale. Obviously, the amount of this compensation requires a case-specific inquiry. In principle, the Court has said, just compensation means that the owner "is entitled to be put in as good a position pecuniarily as if his property had not been taken." *Olson v. United States* (1934). It has also said, however, that "serious practical difficulties" preclude giving "this principle of indemnity…its full and literal force." Instead, the owner is awarded the "fair market value" of his property, even if that is less than his true loss. *United States v. 564.54 Acres of Land, More or Less* (1979).

A few kinds of takings, as a matter of law, are non-compensable. The confiscation or destruction of property during military hostilities, for example, is normally non-compensable. *United States v. Caltex* (1952). But when compensation is due, in normal takings situations, the amount awarded may well depend on who awards it, judge or jury. Early eminent domain proceedings varied as to whether juries, judges, or other officials were in charge of determining just compensa-

tion. More recently, the Supreme Court has said that "there is no constitutional right to a jury in eminent domain proceedings," *United States v. Reynolds* (1970), but in the different context of a "regulatory taking," landowners do have the right to a jury trial. *City of Monterey v. Del Monte Dunes at Monterey* (1999).

William Baude

See Also
Article I, Section 10, Clause 1 (Obligation of Contract)
Amendment V (Due Process Clause)
Amendment XIV, Section 1 (Due Process Clause)

Suggestions for Further Research
Akhil Reed Amar, The Bill of Rights: Creation and Reconstruction (1998)

William Baude, *Rethinking the Federal Eminent Domain Power*, 122 Yale L.J. 1738 (2013)

Paxton Blair, *Federal Condemnation Proceedings and the Seventh Amendment*, 41 Harv. L. Rev. 29 (1927)

Eric R. Claeys, *Takings, Regulations, and Natural Property Rights*, 88 Cornell L. Rev. 1549 (2003)

Richard A. Epstein, Takings: Private Property And The Power Of Eminent Domain (1985)

Matthew P. Harrington, *"Public Use" and the Original Understanding of the So-Called "Takings" Clause*, 53 Hastings L.J. 1245, 1263 (2002)

John F. Hart, *Land Use Law in the Early Republic and the Original Meaning of the Takings Clause*, 94 Nw. U. L. Rev. 1099 (2000)

Michael B. Rappaport, *Originalism and Regulatory Takings: Why the Fifth Amendment May Not Protect Against Regulatory Takings, but the Fourteenth Amendment May*, 45 San Diego L. Rev. 729 (2008)

William Michael Treanor, *The Original Understanding of the Takings Clause and the Political Process*, 95 Colum. L. Rev. 782 (1995)

Significant Cases
Pollard's Lessee v. Hagan, 44 U.S. (3 How.) 212 (1845)

United States v. Gettysburg Electric Ry. Co., 160 U.S. 668 (1896)

Pumpelly v. Green Bay & Mississippi Canal Co., 80 U.S. 166 (1871)

Kohl v. United States, 91 U.S. 367 (1876)

United States v. Jones, 109 U.S. 513 (1883)

Chicago, Burlington & Qunicy. R.R. Co. v. City of Chicago, 166 U.S. 226 (1897)

Pennsylvania Coal Co. v. Mahon, 260 U.S. 393 (1922)

Village of Euclid v. Ambler Realty Co., 272 US 365 (1926)

Olson v. United States, 292 U.S. 246 (1934)

Youngstown Sheet & Tube Co. v. Sawyer, 343 U.S. 579 (1952)

United States v. Caltex, 344 U.S. 149 (1952)

Berman v. Parker, 348 U.S. 26 (1954)

Armstrong v. United States, 364 U.S. 40 (1960)

United States v. Reynolds, 397 U.S. 14 (1970)

Penn Central Transportation Co. v. City of New York, 438 U.S. 104 (1978)

United States v. 564.54 Acres of Land, More or Less, 441 U.S. 506 (1979)

Webb's Fabulous Pharmacies, Inc. v. Beckwith, 449 U.S. 155 (1980)

Loretto v. Teleprompter Manhattan CATV Corp., 458 U.S. 419 (1982)

Hawaii Housing Auth. v. Midkiff, 467 U.S. 229 (1984)

Ruckelshaus v. Monsanto Co., 467 U.S. 986 (1984)

First English Evangelical Lutheran Church v. Los Angeles County, 482 U.S. 304 (1987)

Nollan v. California Coastal Comm'n, 483 U.S. 825 (1987)

Lucas v. South Carolina Coastal Council, 505 U.S. 1003 (1992)

Dolan v. City of Tigard, 512 U.S. 374 (1994)

City of Monterey v. Del Monte Dunes at Monterey, Ltd., 526 U.S. 687 (1999)

Palazollo v. Rhode Island, 533 U.S. 606 (2001)

Tahoe-Sierra Preservation Council, Inc. v. Tahoe Regional Planning Agency, 535 U.S. 302 (2002)

Kelo v. City of New London, 545 U.S. 469 (2005)

Arkansas Game & Fish Comm'n v. United States, 133 S. Ct. 511 (2012)

Koontz v. St. Johns River Water Management District, 133 S. Ct. 2586 (2013)

Speedy Trial Clause

In all criminal prosecutions, the accused shall enjoy the right to a speedy...trial....

(Amendment VI)

~

The right to a speedy trial is an ancient common law right that is linked to the writ of habeas corpus. These protections emerged in response to monarchs who imprisoned enemies of the crown in the Tower of London without permitting them access to courts. By 1642, Sir Edward Coke was able to conclude that English judges "have not suffered the prisoner to be long detained, but...have given the prisoner full and speedy justice.... " The Framers of the Constitution understood that preventing lengthy pre-trial detention was critical to a justice system. Indeed, the Constitution contains three inter-related rights that are designed to ensure that prisoners cannot be detained in an American version of the Tower of London: the rights to habeas corpus (Article I, Section 9, Clause 2), to non-excessive bail (Amendment VIII), and to a speedy trial (Amendment VI). Early American cases sometimes decided the issue of pre-trial detention simply through the application of state habeas corpus without even referring to the right to a speedy trial.

But the speedy trial right has a role to play beyond avoiding pre-trial detention. In 1804, a South Carolina court held that a defendant who was out on bail could *not* use the state habeas corpus act to obtain discharge from an indictment. *State v. Buyck* (1804). The court noted, however, that "it was the duty of the court to take care that criminal causes should not be unreasonably protracted or delayed." The speedy trial right became an exclusive remedy for defendants who were on bail and thus did not suffer pre-trial detention.

The modern court views the right to a speedy trial as preventing both the harm of pretrial detention and the harm to the defense caused by delay—for example, fading memories or the deaths of witnesses. The right is triggered only if the delay is caused by the prosecution, not by the defense attorney's actions. *Vermont v. Brillon* (2009). The defendant must also show that the unreasonable delay caused by the state prejudiced his case. *Reed v. Farley* (1994). Delays between arrest and indictment and between indictment and trial, as well as continuances at trial and an unduly lengthy appellate process, are relevant to a court's determination if there has been a constitutional violation.

The seminal case on speedy trial, *Barker v. Wingo* (1972), held that courts should consider (1) whether and how the defendant asserts his right to a speedy trial, (2) the length of the delay, (3) the reason the state offers to excuse the delay, and (4) the harm that the defendant suffered because of the delay. As with any balancing test, greater levels of harm in one or two categories will compensate for lesser harms in other categories. So, for example, the court held in 1992 that a delay of more than eight years, with no legitimate excuse for the delay, was sufficient to show a speedy trial violation even though the defendant was unaware of his indictment and thus suffered no pre-trial detention or anxiety. *Doggett v. United States* (1992).

When measuring the length of the delay, the Court has held that the period begins from the time of arrest or indictment, not from the moment an investigation begins. *United States v. MacDonald* (1982). It is left to statutes of limitations and the Due Process Clause to cure the abuse of too long an investigation before charges are brought. *United States v. Loud Hawk* (1986).

Most constitutional violations are cured by ordering a trial that is free of the error. But the harm that delay would normally cause the defense cannot be remedied by a new trial, which would take place after even further delay. The Court's response to this conundrum is to forbid the prosecution of a defendant who has proven that his speedy trial rights were violated. *Strunk v. United States* (1973).

To make a conviction impossible to obtain when the trial is held too late is logical but extreme. As a result, courts are loath to find speedy trial violations. Perhaps not coincidentally, the *Barker* test gives lower courts great discretion in deciding speedy-trial claims. The facts of *Barker* itself demonstrate how much discretion courts have to decide whether a trial is speedy. Willie Barker stood convicted of the brutal murder of an elderly couple. Even though the trial occurred more than five years after indictment, the court unanimously held that it did not violate Barker's right to a speedy trial. Critical to the court's reasoning is that Barker did not demand a trial until very late in the five-year period. Though the court denied making demand the

most important of the four factors, it would appear that it viewed Barker's failure to demand a trial as acquiescence in the delay.

If demanding a trial is the most important factor in the *Barker* test, then it seems likely that there will be few speedy trial violations. Defendants who demand a trial will in most cases get one. And, if the defendant is happy being free on bail and does not demand a trial, it will probably be difficult to prove a speedy trial violation.

George Thomas

See Also

Article I, Section 9, Clause 2 (Habeas Corpus)
Amendment V (Due Process Clause)
Amendment VIII (Cruel and Unusual Punishment)

Suggestions for Further Research

Akhil Reed Amar, *Sixth Amendment First Principles*, 84 Geo. L.J. 641 (1996)
Anthony G. Amsterdam, *Speedy Criminal Trial Rights and Remedies*, 27 Stan. L. Rev. 525 (1975)
Brian P. Brooks, Comment, *A New Speedy Trial Standard for* Barker v. Wingo: *Reviving a Constitutional Remedy in an Age of Statutes*, 61 U. Chi. L. Rev. 587 (1994)
Brook Dooley, *Thirty First Annual Review of Criminal Procedure: Speedy Trial*, 90 Geo. L.J. 1454 (2002)
Alfredo Garcia, *Speedy Trial, Swift Justice: Full-Fledged Right or "Second-Class" Citizen?*, 21 Sw. U. L. Rev. 31 (1992)
H. Richard Uviller, *Barker v. Wingo: Speedy Trial Gets a Fast Shuffle*, 72 Colum. L. Rev. 1376 (1972)

Significant Cases

State v. Buyck, 2 S.C.L. 563 (2 Bay) (Const. Ct. App. 1804)
Beavers v. Haubert, 198 U.S. 77 (1905)
Klopfer v. North Carolina, 386 U.S. 213 (1967)
Barker v. Wingo, 407 U.S. 514 (1972)
Strunk v. United States, 412 U.S. 434 (1973)
United States v. MacDonald, 456 U.S. 1 (1982)
United States v. Loud Hawk, 474 U.S. 302 (1986)
Doggett v. United States, 505 U.S. 647 (1992)
Reed v. Farley, 512 U.S. 339 (1994)
Cutter v. Wilkinson, 544 U.S. 709 (2005)
Vermont v. Brillon, 556 U.S. 81 (2009)

Public Trial

In all criminal prosecutions, the accused shall enjoy the right to a...public trial....

(AMENDMENT VI)

~

The right to a public trial in the Sixth Amendment is deeply rooted in Anglo-American history, tradition, and values. It reflects, among other things, the Founders' hostility toward secret proceedings reaching back to the Star Chamber, which pre-dated the Glorious Revolution in England (1688). There was widespread agreement with Sir Edward Coke's view, expressed in 1607, that a trial is almost by definition open and public. Thus, Justice Joseph Story, in his *Commentaries on the Constitution of the United States* (1833), emphasized that in "the established course of the common law...trials for crimes" are "always public." The Supreme Court has echoed this view, stating, "By immemorial usage, wherever the common law prevails, all trials are in open court, to which spectators are admitted." *In re Oliver* (1948).

Like most other provisions of the Bill of Rights, the guarantee of a public trial has been construed by the Supreme Court to constrain both federal and state governments. Although deeply rooted and fundamental, the right is not absolute. Although the Sixth Amendment's public-trial right belongs to the criminal defendant, the public and the press also have a First Amendment interest in open proceedings. Therefore, "a defendant can, under some circumstances, waive his constitutional right to a public trial, [but] he has no absolute right to compel a private trial." *Singer v. United States* (1965). In addition, when the "dignity, order and decorum" that are and must be "the hallmarks of all court proceedings in our country," are flagrantly disregarded, *Illinois v. Allen* (1970), the proceedings may, if necessary, be closed temporarily. *Waller v. Georgia* (1984). For example, judges will occasionally close portions of trials to protect minor victims in sex-offense trials or when necessary to preserve the confidentiality of sensitive information, such as the identity of undercover witnesses. Though

the Sixth Amendment's guarantee of a public "trial" includes the impaneling of the jury and return of the verdict, as well as certain pretrial proceedings, it does not require that all stages and phases of criminal prosecutions be open to the public. Grand jury proceedings, for example, are secret. *United States v. Procter & Gamble Co.* (1958). Still, the Court's most recent treatment of the matter confirms the existence of a strong presumption in favor of public criminal trials, including juror *voir dire* proceedings. *Presley v. Georgia* (2010).

For individual defendants, as Justice Hugo L. Black observed in the *Oliver* case, a public trial serves as a "safeguard against any attempt to employ our courts as instruments of persecution." As Justice John M. Harlan later put it, "the public-trial guarantee embodies a view of human nature, true as a general rule, that judges, lawyers, witnesses, and jurors will perform their respective functions more responsibly in an open court than in secret proceedings." *Estes v. Texas* (1965). Public trials also make proceedings known to potential witnesses and help to deter untruthful testimony. As Sir William Blackstone wrote in his *Commentaries on the Laws of England* (1765–1769), the "open examination of witnesses...in the presence of all mankind, is much more conducive to the clearing up of truth, than private and secret examination.... [A] witness may frequently depose that in private which he will be ashamed to testify in a public and solemn tribunal."

Thus, any closure of a criminal trial implicates not only the defendant's Sixth Amendment rights but also the First Amendment freedoms of the press and citizens generally. Open trials not only protect the innocent from wrongful conviction, they also serve the public interest in maintaining confidence in the criminal justice system and its officers. As the Supreme Court has observed, "the First Amendment right of access to criminal trials" reflects the "common understanding" that "a major purpose of that Amendment was to protect the free discussion of governmental affairs." *Globe Newspaper Co. v. Superior Court* (1982). Our constitutionalized preference for open trials, in other words, reflects our democratic commitment to "the ultimate right of the public to change policy and policymakers." *Gannett Co. v. DePasquale* (1979). The Court has also relied upon the First Amendment to guarantee a presumption of public trials in civil cases. *Richmond Newspapers, Inc. v. Virginia* (1980). Nonetheless, a lawyer may be disciplined for statements to the press about a pending case he is involved in for "speech that is substantially likely to have a materially prejudicial effect." *Gentile v. State Bar of Nevada* (1991).

Richard W. Garnett

See Also

Amendment I (Freedom of Speech and of the Press)
Amendment VI (Jury Trial)
Amendment VI (Confrontation Clause)

Suggestions for Further Research

Akhil Reed Amar, *Sixth Amendment First Principles*, 84 Geo. L.J. 641 (1996)

Annual Review of Criminal Procedure: Sixth Amendment at Trial, 32 Geo. L.J. 584 (2003)

Thomas M. Fleming, Annotation, *Exclusion of Public from State Criminal Trial in Order to Prevent Disturbance by Spectators or Defendant*, 55 A.L.R. 4TH 1170 (1998)

Alfredo Garcia, *Clash of the Titans: The Difficult Reconciliation of a Fair Trial and a Free Press in Modern American Society*, 32 Santa Clara L. Rev. 1107 (1992)

John H. Langbein, *Shaping the Eighteenth Century Criminal Trial: A View from the Ryder Sources*, 50 U. Chi. L. Rev. 1 (1983)

Thomas F. Liotti, *Closing the Courtroom to the Public: Whose Rights Are Violated?*, 63 Brook. L. Rev. 501 (1997)

Max Radin, *The Right to a Public Trial*, 6 Temp. L. Q. 381 (1932)

Significant Cases

In re Oliver, 333 U.S. 257 (1948)
United States v. Procter & Gamble Co., 356 U.S. 677 (1958)
Estes v. Texas, 381 U.S. 532 (1965)
Singer v. United States, 380 U.S. 24 (1965)
Illinois v. Allen, 397 U.S. 337 (1970)

Gannett Co. v. DePasquale, 443 U.S. 368 (1979)
Richmond Newspapers, Inc. v. Virginia, 448 U.S. 555 (1980)
Globe Newspaper Co. v. Superior Court, 457 U.S. 596 (1982)
Press-Enterprise Co. v. Superior Court of California, 464 U.S. 501 (1984)
Waller v. Georgia, 467 U.S. 39 (1984)
Press-Enterprise Co. v. Superior Court of California, 478 U.S. 1 (1986)
Arizona v. Fulminante, 499 U.S. 279 (1991)
Gentile v. State Bar of Nevada, 501 U.S. 1030 (1991)
Presley v. Georgia, 130 S. Ct. 721 (2010)

Jury Trial

In all criminal prosecutions, the accused shall enjoy the right to a . . . trial, by an impartial jury of the State and district wherein the crime shall have been committed, which district shall have been previously ascertained by law. . . .

(AMENDMENT VI)

~

*T*he Framers of the Constitution and of the Bill of Rights revered trial by jury—a right that Sir William Blackstone had described as "the palladium of English liberty." By the time of the Framing, common law juries had a more than five-century history in England, and they had been part of the American experience from the start. Although juries then were considerably less representative of the adult population than they are today, they were the most democratic of the governmental institutions in the colonies. Most Americans cheered their resistance to repressive colonial measures, especially British revenue laws and seditious libel laws.

In some colonies, juries had the power to judge questions of law as well as fact. They consisted of twelve people who always acted by unanimous vote. In felony cases, nonjury trials were unknown and guilty pleas infrequent. Trials were expeditious and routine.

The period since the Framing has seen notable changes in the general understanding of the right to jury trial.

As originally understood, the Sixth Amendment guaranteed the right to jury trial only in the federal courts, although each of the states also guaranteed trial by jury. The ratification of the Fourteenth Amendment in 1868 did not alter this understanding. One hundred years after the approval of the Fourteenth Amendment, however, the Supreme Court held in *Duncan v. Louisiana* (1968) that the amendment's Due Process Clause "incorporated" the right to jury trial and made it applicable to the states. The Court said that although juries were not essential to fairness in every legal system, they were essential to the U.S. system. It wrote, "Providing an accused with the right to be tried by a jury of his peers gave him an inestimable safeguard against the corrupt or overzealous prosecutor and against the compliant, biased, or eccentric judge."

The federal courts initially followed the jury selection rules of the states in which they sat, and all of the states limited jury service to men. All except Vermont also limited jury service to property owners or taxpayers. Only a few states formally disqualified blacks.

The Sixth Amendment was not thought to preclude the expansion of the right to serve on juries, but neither was it thought to require any expansion. Moreover, the Fourteenth Amendment's Equal Protection Clause was not initially thought to extend "political" rights, including the right to serve on juries, to either African-Americans or women.

In 1880, however, the Supreme Court held in *Strauder v. West Virginia* that a statute disqualifying blacks from jury service violated the equal protection rights of black litigants. It was only in 1991 that the Court concluded that the Equal Protection Clause protected prospective jurors themselves from discrimination.

The Court has read the Sixth Amendment as well as the Equal Protection Clause to eliminate jury disqualifications of the sort the Framers approved. It held in 1975 that a "fair cross-section requirement" implicit in the amendment precluded the "systematic" exclusion of a "distinctive group in the community." Because "systematic" exclusion need not be purposeful, the Sixth Amendment prohibits some forms of exclusion the Equal Protection Clause does not reach. Racial minorities and women qualify as "distinctive groups," and under the Sixth Amendment, the exclusion of a distinctive group need not be purposeful and need not be total; it must merely be regular and foreseeable.

At the time of the Framing, litigants could challenge a limited number of prospective jurors peremptorily. In a series of cases beginning in 1986, however, the Court held that litigants may not use peremptory challenges to discriminate on the basis of race, sex, or any other classification subject to heightened scrutiny.

Although the Supreme Court previously had said that the Sixth Amendment required juries of twelve (a number that had more than half a millennium of history behind it), the Court concluded in 1970 that the amendment allows juries of six. In 1978, however, it held five-person juries impermissible. A great many states now use six-person juries, especially in misdemeanor cases.

In *Apodaca v. Oregon* in 1972, four Supreme Court justices concluded that conviction by a vote of ten to two did not violate the Sixth Amendment. Four justices dissented, arguing that the amendment preserved the historical requirement of unanimity. The remaining justice agreed with the dissenters on the construction of the Sixth Amendment but rejected the view that "all of the elements of jury trial within the meaning of the Sixth Amendment are necessarily embodied in or incorporated into the Due Process Clause of the Fourteenth." As a result, non-unanimous verdicts are permissible in state but not federal courts. In a companion case, the Court upheld a state court conviction by a jury vote of nine to three. Later, the Court held conviction by a vote of five to one unconstitutional; convictions by six-person juries must be unanimous.

Although juries sometimes disregarded the legal instructions of judges in England, they never acquired formal authority to do so. As early as 1628, Chief Justice Edward Coke declared that judges do not decide questions of fact and juries do not decide issues of law.

The American practice, however, was different. In 1735 in New York, Andrew Hamilton told the court trying his client, publisher John Peter Zenger, that the authority of juries "to determine both the law and the fact" was "beyond all dispute." The jury's acquittal of Zenger, despite his apparent guilt of seditious libel, helped shape the American understanding of the role and duties of jurors. Some, but not all, American colonies permitted juries to decide issues of law, and in 1771 John Adams called it "an Absurdity to suppose that the Law would oblige [jurors] to find a Verdict according to the Direction of the Court, against their own Opinion, Judgment, and Conscience."

The authority of juries to decide issues of law was contested throughout the nineteenth century, but the opponents of jury authority gained the clear upper hand in the century's second half. Although three state constitutions still declare that juries may decide legal issues, the Supreme Court's 1895 decision in *Sparf and Hansen v. United States* effectively ended the battle and held that federal juries may not decide questions of law.

In the late 1960s and early 1970s, defendants charged with unlawful resistance to the war in Vietnam sought to revive the issue. They argued that judges should inform jurors of their right to acquit whenever conviction would be unjust (or at least permit defense attorneys to argue in favor of jury nullification). Although appellate courts rejected the defendants' arguments, the courts did not deny in all circumstances the appropriateness of jury nullification. If, as a matter of conscience, jurors decided to disregard the court's instruction, their disobedience might be justified. More recently, however, many courts have denied the legitimacy of nullification altogether. Several have held that, even after jury deliberations have begun, a trial judge may remove a juror who has revealed "beyond doubt" an intention to violate the court's instructions on the law.

The Anti-Federalists who opposed ratification of the Constitution protested that the right to jury trial guaranteed by Article III was inadequate. Their objections led to the Sixth Amendment's requirement that juries must be drawn from "the State and district wherein the crime shall have been committed." Although the Sixth Amendment also declared that juries must be impartial, the requirement of impartiality did not imply that jurors should arrive at the courtroom unaware of the circumstances of the case before them. George Mason and Patrick Henry insisted that local juries would protect the defendant's right to be judged on the basis of "his character and reputation." Courts now voice greater concern about information obtained prior to trial, especially in cases of widespread pretrial publicity. The Supreme Court has said that although a juror need not "be totally ignorant of the facts and issues," he must be able to "lay aside his impression or opinion and render a verdict based on the evidence presented in court." *Irvin v. Dowd* (1961).

Since the Framing, a defendant has been entitled to a jury determination of every fact necessary to constitute the crime with which he has been charged. When finding a particular element would make the defendant guilty of a more serious crime rather than a lesser one, the effect was to increase his punishment. A defendant found guilty of murder, for example, was punished more severely than one found guilty of manslaughter.

In 2000, the Supreme Court held that a defendant is entitled to a jury determination of every fact necessary to increase the punishment to which he is exposed even when this fact is not formally called an element of a crime. Although a legislature might have called such a fact a sentencing aggravator, the Court concluded that it was functionally an element. *Apprendi v. New Jersey* (2000). *Apprendi* requires a jury to determine beyond a reasonable doubt every fact other than conviction of a prior offense that increases the *maximum* sentence a defendant faces. At the same time, the Supreme Court has said that the *Apprendi* principle does not require a jury to determine every fact necessary to impose a mandatory *minimum* sentence. In 2013, the Supreme Court decided that under the Sixth Amendment, any fact that increases the mandatory sentence is an "element" that must be submitted to the jury. *Alleyne v. United States* (2013).

The Supreme Court has applied *Apprendi* in a number of subsequent cases—notably in *United States v. Booker* (2005), which held mandatory federal sentencing guidelines unconstitutional.

Under these guidelines, a judicial determination of fact automatically increased the sentence to which a defendant was exposed.

There were two majority opinions in *Booker*—one holding the guidelines unconstitutional and the other prescribing the remedy for this violation. Both majority opinions were by five to four votes, and only one justice joined both of them. The remedy approved by the Court was not to require a jury determination of every fact that would increase the maximum guideline sentence. It was to make the federal sentencing guidelines advisory. In other words, the Court's remedy for a violation of the right to jury trial did not provide jury trials.

Every justice recognized, however, that discretionary sentencing by judges is constitutional, and the majority reasoned that Congress would have preferred advisory guidelines to guidelines administered by juries. In fact, discretionary sentencing was familiar to the Framers. The Crimes Act of 1790, for example, authorized judges to impose such punishments as maximum imprisonment of one, three, or seven years, or death, depending on the crime; a fine of up to "one thousand dollars," and public whipping "not exceeding thirty-nine stripes." It was only when finding a material fact automatically increased the punishment to which a defendant was exposed that the Sixth Amendment entrusted this finding to a jury.

At the time of the Sixth Amendment, all trials in serious criminal cases were jury trials. In 1874, the Supreme Court declared that a defendant could not "be tried in any other manner than by a jury of twelve men, although he consent in open court to be tried by a jury of eleven men." *Home Insurance Co. of New York v. Morse* (1874). Nevertheless, the Court held in *Patton v. United States* (1930) that a defendant could waive the right to jury trial and agree to be tried by the court alone.

Today about half of all convictions in the felony cases that are resolved by trials occur in trials without juries. Moreover, only a small minority of felony cases go to trial. Ninety-seven percent of the felony convictions in federal courts and 94 percent of those in state courts are by guilty plea. Behind these figures lies the practice of bargaining with defendants to waive the Sixth Amendment right to jury trial.

Far from encouraging guilty pleas in felony cases, courts at the time of the Bill of Rights actively discouraged them. Sir William Blackstone's *Commentaries on the Laws of England* (1765–1769) observed that courts were "very backward in receiving and recording [a guilty plea] . . . and will generally advise the prisoner to retract it." Similar statements appeared in American treatises throughout the nineteenth century. When instances of plea bargaining began to appear in appellate reports in the decades following the Civil War, lower courts generally denounced the practice and often declared it unconstitutional. The Supreme Court did not uphold the constitutionality of plea-bargained waivers of the right to jury trial until 1970.

When jury trial was routine, it was a reasonably summary procedure. As recently as the 1890s, a felony court apparently could conduct a half-dozen jury trials in a single day. The intervening decades have seen a proliferation of procedures in contested cases and, as a result, an inability to contest many cases. Prolonged jury-selection procedures, cumbersome rules of evidence, repetitive cross-examination of witnesses, courtroom battles of experts, jury instructions that many empirical studies tell us jurors do not understand, and other complications have made trials inaccessible for all but a small minority of defendants. Only a shadow of the communitarian institution the Framers wished to preserve has survived into the twenty-first century. Although the Sixth Amendment declares, "In all criminal prosecutions, the accused shall enjoy the right to a speedy and public trial, by an impartial jury," one commentator has said that Americans could replace the word "all" in this Amendment with the words "virtually none."

Albert W. Alschuler

See Also

Suggestions for Further Research

Jeffrey B. Abramson, We, the Jury: The Jury System and the Ideal of Democracy (1994)

Stephen J. Adler, The Jury: Trial and Error in the American Courtroom (1994)

Albert W. Alschuler, *Plea Bargaining and Its History*, 79 Colum. L. Rev. 1 (1979)

Albert W. Alschuler, *The Supreme Court and the Jury: Voir Dire, Peremptory Challenges, and the Review of Jury Verdicts*, 56 U. Chi. L. Rev. 153 (1989)

Albert W. Alschuler & Andrew G. Deiss, *A Brief History of the Criminal Jury in the United States*, 61 U. Chi. L. Rev. 867 (1994)

Steve Bogira, Courtroom 302: A Year Behind the Scenes in an American Criminal Courthouse (2006)

Randolph N. Jonakait, The American Jury System (2003)

Harry Kalven Jr. & Hans Zeisel, The American Jury (1966)

Linda K. Kerber, No Constitutional Right to Be Ladies: Women and the Obligations of Citizenship (1998)

Benno C. Schmidt, *Juries, Jurisdiction, and Race Discrimination: The Lost Promise of* Strauder v. West Virginia, 61 Tex. L. Rev. 1401 (1983)

Signifcant Cases

Home Ins. Co. of New York v. Morse, 87 U.S. (20 Wall.) 445 (1874)

Strauder v. West Virginia, 100 U.S. 303 (1880)

Sparf and Hansen v. United States, 156 U.S. 51 (1895)

Patton v. United States, 281 U.S. 276 (1930)

Hoyt v. Florida, 368 U.S. 57 (1961)

Irvin v. Dowd, 366 U.S. 717 (1961)

Swain v. Alabama, 380 U.S. 202 (1965)

Duncan v. Louisiana, 391 U.S. 145 (1968)

Williams v. Florida, 399 U.S. 78 (1970)

Apodaca v. Oregon, 406 U.S. 404 (1972)

Johnson v. Louisiana, 406 U.S. 356 (1972)

United States v. Dougherty, 473 F.2d 1113 (D.C. Cir. 1972)

Taylor v. Louisiana, 419 U.S. 522 (1975)

Ballew v. Georgia, 435 U.S. 223 (1978)

Burch v. Louisiana, 441 U.S. 130 (1979)

Duren v. Missouri, 439 U.S. 357 (1979)

Batson v. Kentucky, 476 U.S. 79 (1986)

Tanner v. United States, 483 U.S. 107 (1987)

Powers v. Ohio, 499 U.S. 400 (1991)

Georgia v. McCollum, 505 U.S. 42 (1992)

J.E.B. v. Alabama *ex rel.* T.B., 511 U.S. 127 (1994)

United States v. Thomas, 116 F.3d 606 (2d Cir. 1997)

Apprendi v. New Jersey, 530 U.S. 466 (2000)

Blakely v. Washington, 542 U.S. 296 (2004)

Miller-El v. Dretke, 545 U.S. 231 (2005)

United States v. Booker, 543 U.S. 220 (2005)

Skilling v. United States, 561 U.S. 40 (2010)

Southern Union Co. v. United States, 132 S. Ct. 2344 (2012)

Alleyne v. United States, 133 S. Ct. 2151 (2013)

Arraignment Clause

In all criminal prosecutions, the accused shall enjoy the right…to be informed of the nature and cause of the accusation.…

(Amendment VI)

~

*T*he Constitution requires that an accused criminal defendant be informed of the nature of the charges against him. As Justice Hugo L. Black wrote in *Cole v. Arkansas* (1948):

> No principle of procedural due process is more clearly established than that notice of the specific charge, and a chance to be heard in a trial of the issues raised by that charge, if desired, are among the constitutional rights of every accused in a criminal proceeding in all courts, state or federal.

The requirement of fair notice derives from early English common law, it was generally recognized at the time of the adoption of the Constitution, and it is today largely a ministerial matter of routine criminal procedure.

The accused's right to be informed of the charges against him originated at least as far back as the twelfth century. English law required a precise and properly substantiated accusation, initiated either by individual complaint (called an appeal) or by an accusing jury (the predecessor of our grand jury), and specifying particular charges. In twelfth century England, however, the Church administered a separate judicial system, one based on an inquisitorial process derived from Roman law. For example, one could be called to answer charges of heresy upon the mere unsworn suggestion of "ill fame" without the need for greater specificity.

In 1164, seeking to restrict the power of the ecclesiastical courts, King Henry II issued the Constitutions of Clarendon, which required Church courts to identify a definite accusation before calling a layman to answer a charge. The development of an accusatorial system based on specific charges continued with the Magna Carta in 1215, only to founder in the sixteenth century, as the inquisitorial system of justice returned to prominence. The High Commission and Star Chamber revived the practice of questioning a subject without specifying the nature of the accusation against him. As a result, the practice of refusing to inform one being questioned of the nature of the charges against him became intertwined with the right (now embodied in the Fifth Amendment) against self-incrimination (which the English courts of this era applied only prior to the presentation of formal charges). Those called to answer in the Star Chamber refused to do so on the dual grounds that they did not know what they were accused of and that they could not be compelled to answer, thereby condemning themselves from their own mouths.

Thus in 1637, when Freeborn John Lilburne, a Puritan, was examined by the Star Chamber on unspecified charges, his response was twofold:

> I am not willing to answer you to any more of these questions, because I see you go about by this examination to ensnare me; for, seeing the things for which I am imprisoned cannot be proved against me, you will get other matter out of my examination; and therefore, if you will not ask me about the thing laid to my charge, I shall answer no more.

In 1641, on the eve of the English Civil War, the Long Parliament passed the Act for the Abolition of the Court of Star Chamber, which provided:

> [N]one shall be taken by petition or suggestion made to the King or to his Council, unless it be by indictment or presentment of good and lawful people of the same neighbourhood where such deeds be done, in due manner or by process made by writ original at the common law....

It is unsurprising, then, that the American legal tradition, born of the English common law and informed by the history of persecution that motivated many religious dissenters to emigrate, reflects an early and consistent adoption of the common law accusatorial requirement for specificity. Requirements that an accused be informed of the nature of the charges against him can be found, for example, in the Virginia Declaration of Rights and in the constitutions of many (though not all) of the original states.

When the Bill of Rights was drafted in 1789, the right to be informed of the nature and cause of the accusation was included in James Madison's draft and, without recorded comment, became a part of the Sixth Amendment.

Initially, the function of the constitutional requirement was to provide the accused with adequate notice of the charges against him so that he could prepare a defense. As the concept of double jeopardy developed, the notice requirement came to serve the secondary purpose of allowing the accused to plead a prior acquittal as a bar to a second prosecution for the "same offense." It also came to serve as a means of informing the court of the nature of the charges so that the court might determine their legal sufficiency. One illustration of the early enforcement of this requirement was *United States v. Cruikshank* (1876), where the Supreme Court concluded that an indictment charging a defendant with having hindered certain citizens in their "free exercise and enjoyment of...the several rights and privileges granted and secured to them by the constitution" was insufficiently specific to satisfy the constitutional standard.

In contemporary American law, the notice and specificity requirement has taken on a largely ministerial character. Although indictments are required to state clearly the statutory offense being charged, the courts routinely refuse to enforce the requirement by requiring hypertechnical specificity. Generally, a charging instrument will be sufficient if it recites the offense in the terms of the statute allegedly violated (including all the elements of the crime) and identifies the date of the offense and the individuals alleged to have violated the law. *Hamling v. United States* (1974).

Thus, though no longer a practical basis for a defendant's challenge to his indictment, the Arraignment Clause has enduring practical effects on the administration of justice. It is the constitutional foundation, for example, of the continuing requirement that every defendant be arraigned on charges and have the indictment read to him; it lies behind every defendant's request for a bill of particulars, providing more specification for the charges; and it is the underlying basis for every challenge to the sufficiency of an indictment as vague or containing multiple charges in a single count. If arraignment is unreasonably delayed, that delay may even form a basis for suppressing a defendant's pre-arraignment confession. *Corley v. United States* (2009). Thus, the constitutional requirement to be "informed of the nature and cause of the accusation" has become internalized by the judicial system and is interwoven into the fabric of daily procedure.

Paul Rosenzweig

Suggestions for Further Research

Laurence A. Benner, *Requiem for Miranda: The Rehnquist Court's Voluntariness Doctrine in Historical Perspective*, 67 Wash. U. L. Q. 59 (1989)

Leonard W. Levy, The Origins of the Fifth Amendment (1968)

Frederick Pollock & Frederic William Maitland, The History of English Law Before the Time of Edward I (1895) (2d ed. 1951)

James Fitzjames Stephen, History of the Criminal Law of England (1883)

Significant Cases

United States v. Cruikshank, 92 U.S. 542 (1876)

Seven Cases of Eckman's Alternative v. United States, 239 U.S. 510 (1916)

Hagner v. United States, 285 U.S. 427 (1932)

Cole v. Arkansas, 333 U.S. 196 (1948)

Hamling v. United States, 419 U.S. 885 (1974)

Corley v. United States, 556 U.S. 303 (2009)

Confrontation Clause

In all criminal prosecutions, the accused shall enjoy the right ... to be confronted with the witnesses against him....

(Amendment VI)

~

*T*he Confrontation Clause guarantees an essential element of the adversarial trial process. The clause envisions a trial where the accused sees and hears prosecution witnesses testify in person, in open court, in his presence, and subject to cross-examination. But that basic starting point still leaves difficult questions about the scope and limits of these rights. Is face-to-face confrontation always required? Or, given modern technology, can we substitute a rough equivalent—a video camera connection for example—where necessary to obtain a witness's testimony? What limits can a court place on cross-examination? And when does the clause allow prosecutors to use hearsay from an out-of court declarant who cannot be cross-examined?

The text of the clause suggests some basic limits, and some ambiguity. The verb "confront" has always been understood to mean more than just a right to see and listen. It includes the right to challenge the witness and to test his credibility through cross-examination. The clause applies to "witnesses against" the accused, but a satisfactory definition of that term has proved elusive. Clearly it includes someone called by the prosecution to testify at trial. Whether it includes, as mentioned above, a hearsay declarant—a person whose out-of-court statement is offered in evidence against the accused, though that person never appears in court to testify (and thus is not subject to cross-examination)—is a question that continues to challenge the courts.

There is no record of any debate over the Confrontation Clause in the First Congress. Nevertheless, history offers some guidance to understanding the purpose of the clause. By the time the American Constitution was drafted, trials featuring live testimony in open court were typical in English and American criminal courts, though few defendants were represented by counsel, and the practice of cross-examination was in its infancy. The Framers likely were familiar with the very different procedure in a series of early seventeenth-century "State Trials," where British prosecutors or examining magistrates obtained affidavits or depositions in private, then presented them as evidence in trials for treason against the crown. Defendants futilely demanded to have their accusers brought before them face to face. The American colonists themselves faced similar abuses in the 1760s, when Parliament allowed the colonial vice-admiralty courts to try certain offenses using a "civil law" model of trial based on written interrogatories instead of live testimony. Both George Mason and John Adams publicly condemned that practice. As the Supreme Court declared in its first major Confrontation Clause opinion, "The primary object of [the clause] was to prevent depositions or *ex parte* affidavits, such as were sometimes admitted in civil cases, being used against the prisoner in lieu of a personal examination and cross-examination of the witness." *Mattox v. United States* (1895).

Under the current state of the law, in most circumstances, basic confrontation rights are well settled. The clause gives a defendant the right to be present in the courtroom when prosecution witnesses testify. *Kentucky v. Stincer* (1987). The clause guarantees an "adequate opportunity" for "effective" cross-examination. *Pointer v. Texas* (1965).

Applying these basic principles has proved especially difficult in two circumstances, (1) confrontation and hearsay, and (2) child witnesses and face-to-face confrontation.

When a witness at trial merely repeats "hearsay," a statement made out of court by someone else (the declarant), and when that declarant does not testify at trial, the defendant cannot "confront"

or cross-examine him. Yet recognizing that British and American courts admitted some forms of hearsay both before and after 1791, the Supreme Court has not gone so far as to hold that all incriminating hearsay is inadmissible when the declarant cannot be confronted. After a series of cases that had sought to establish "exceptions" to the confrontation right based on the "reliability" of some forms of hearsay, the Court changed its course in *Crawford v. Washington* (2004). There the Court held that the prosecutor's use of "testimonial" hearsay violates the Confrontation Clause unless the declarant is unavailable and the defendant had a prior opportunity to cross-examine the declarant. Looking at the text of the clause, the Court found that a "witness against" an "accused" is someone who "bears testimony," a definition that does not apply to everyone who utters hearsay. Drawing on history, the Court found that the principal concern of the Confrontation Clause was the use of *ex parte* "testimony"—such as depositions, affidavits, or statements made by witnesses under government interrogation—against an accused. Hence, the Court held that "testimonial" hearsay is inadmissible against a criminal defendant who has no opportunity to confront and cross-examine the declarant, while the use of other hearsay is not affected by the Confrontation Clause.

Since *Crawford*, in a series of cases, the Court has defined "testimonial" hearsay to include formal testimony under oath (like depositions and affidavits), "structured" police interrogation, and other statements made for the "primary purpose" of providing evidence for criminal prosecution. Hearsay statements made for other purposes, like 911 calls for emergency assistance, are not "testimonial" and therefore not excluded from evidence by the Confrontation Clause. In *Melendez-Diaz v. Massachusetts* (2009), the Court held that certificates of analysis reporting the results of forensic laboratory tests were testimonial statements made for the purpose of providing evidence for criminal prosecution. The practical effect of the Melendez ruling has been to require live testimony from laboratory analysts regarding drug, blood, DNA, and other forensic testing. Several recent cases suggest that the justices have developed differing views on the breadth of the clause. Justice Clarence Thomas would apply the clause narrowly to reach only "formal" testimony (like depositions or affidavits) or its equivalent. Justice Samuel Alito has suggested that "testimonial hearsay" includes only statements made with a primary purpose of accusing a "targeted individual," rather than the broader range of statements made to police investigating a crime. The majority of the Court continues to apply the clause to any hearsay statement made for the "primary purpose" of criminal prosecution.

The Court has limited the right to face-to-face confrontation in extraordinary cases. In *Maryland v. Craig* (1990), the Court allowed a child witness to testify by closed-circuit television without physically entering the courtroom because the child was emotionally unable to testify in the defendant's presence. The Court found that the process nevertheless satisfied the Confrontation Clause because it allowed for cross-examination and for the jury, defendant, and counsel to observe the demeanor of the child while she testified.

John G. Douglass

See Also
Amendment VI (Compulsory Process Clause)

Suggestions for Further Research
Akhil Reed Amar, *Foreword: Sixth Amendment First Principles*, 84 Geo. L.J. 641 (1996)

Margaret A. Berger, *The Deconstitutionalization of the Confrontation Clause: A Proposal for a Prosecutorial Restraint Model*, 76 Minn. L. Rev. 557 (1992)

John G. Douglass, *Beyond Admissibility: Real Confrontation, Virtual Cross-Examination, and the Right to Confront Hearsay*, 67 Geo. Wash. L. Rev. 191 (1999)

John G. Douglass, *Confronting Death: Sixth Amendment Rights at Capital Sentencing*, 105 Colum. L. Rev. 1967 (2005)

Richard D. Friedman, *Confrontation: The Search for Basic Principles*, 86 Geo. L.J. 1011 (1998)

Randolph N. Jonakait, *Restoring the Confrontation Clause to the Sixth Amendment*, 35 UCLA L. Rev. 557 (1988)

Graham C. Lilly, *Notes on the Confrontation Clause and* Ohio v. Roberts, 36 U. Fla. L. Rev. 207 (1984)

Peter Westen, *Confrontation and Compulsory Process: A Unified Theory of Evidence for Criminal Cases*, 91 Harv. L. Rev. 567 (1978)

Significant Cases
Mattox v. United States, 156 U.S. 237 (1895)

Pointer v. Texas, 380 U.S. 400 (1965)

Bruton v. United States, 391 U.S. 123 (1968)

Davis v. Alaska, 415 U.S. 308 (1974)

Ohio v. Roberts, 448 U.S. 56 (1980)

Delaware v. Fensterer, 474 U.S. 15 (1985)

Kentucky v. Stincer, 482 U.S. 730 (1987)

Maryland v. Craig, 497 U.S. 836 (1990)

White v. Illinois, 502 U.S. 346 (1992)

Lilly v. Virginia, 527 U.S. 116 (1999) (concurring opinions)

Crawford v. Washington, 541 U.S. 36 (2004)

Davis v. Washington, 547 U.S. 813 (2006)

Giles v. California, 554 U.S. 353 (2008)

Melendez-Diaz v. Massachusetts, 557 U.S. 305 (2009)

Michigan v. Bryant, 131 S. Ct. 1143 (2011)

Williams v. Illinois, 132 S. Ct. 2221 (2012)

Compulsory Process Clause

In all criminal prosecutions, the accused shall enjoy the right ... to have compulsory process for obtaining witnesses in his favor....
(Amendment VI)

~

*F*or centuries, the common law forbade an accused person from calling witnesses in his defense in cases of treason or felony or forbade the defense witnesses, if called, to testify under oath. The English remedied that injustice for treason trials in a 1695 statute and for all cases in 1702. Sir William Blackstone in his *Commentaries on the Laws of England* (1765–1769) summarized the right by declaring, "[the defendant] shall have the same compulsive process to bring in his witnesses for him, as was usual to compel their appearance against him."

Before he came to America, William Penn had been the victim of the old common law rule. In 1670, he was arrested for preaching his dissenting religious views to a group of Quakers in London, that is, to an "unlawful assembly." Penn attempted to put on his own defense without having counsel and without the right to compel the testimony of witnesses on his behalf. The presiding judge ultimately silenced and removed Penn from the proceedings. Later in America, when Penn wrote Pennsylvania's Charter of Privileges (1701), he included: "THAT all Criminals shall have the same Privileges of Witnesses and Council as their Prosecutors."

After the Revolution, nine of the new state constitutions established in one form or another the right to call defense witnesses. Two of them, Massachusetts and New Hampshire, added the subpoena power. When James Madison, in the First Congress, formulated what would become the Compulsory Process Clause, he opted for including not only the right to call witnesses, but the stronger privilege of being able to subpoena them as well. Congress considered Madison's draft language with little debate, and it became part of the Sixth Amendment without opposition. As written, the clause assures that the accused in a criminal case enjoys the right to call or subpoena witnesses, so that evidence available to the defense can be evaluated by a jury or, in a nonjury criminal case, by a judge. It became, in sum, an essential part of the right of an accused to present a defense.

Issues that surrounded the clause centered on (1) whether the right to call witnesses included the right to documentary evidence, (2) whether the right was available before as well as after indictment, and (3) whether the defense enjoyed the same degree of subpoena power as did the prosecution. Chief Justice John Marshall answered these questions when he presided over the treason trial of Aaron Burr in 1807. *United States v. Burr* (1807). Burr's lawyers had requested a subpoena for documents in the possession of the president, and the government opposed the request. Marshall approved the request to obtain documents and ruled that an indictment was not needed to trigger the right to compulsory process. In upholding a 1790 federal statute that he regarded as declaratory of the constitutional right to compulsory process, Marshall also found that there was parity between the defense and the prosecution in the enjoyment of the right: "[the defense] shall have the like process of the court where he or they shall be tried, to compel his or

their witnesses to appear at his or their trial as is usually granted to compel witnesses to appear on the prosecution against them."

He further allowed the defense to obtain any relevant documents before having to decide which ones might be material at trial, and that the subpoena right allowed the defense to obtain original documents, not mere copies.

Though John Marshall had explicated the contours of the clause in the Aaron Burr trial, the Supreme Court itself had little opportunity to interpret the Compulsory Process Clause and explain its meaning prior to 1967, when the Court ruled in *Washington v. Texas* that the clause was so fundamental to a fair trial that it was part of the Fourteenth Amendment's Due Process Clause and therefore binding on the states as well as on the federal government. *Washington v. Texas* also expanded the reach of the clause by holding unconstitutional a Texas penal statute that permitted the government to offer the testimony of one charged as a principal, accomplice, or accessory, but barred a defendant from calling the same person unless that person had been previously acquitted of the charges. The rationale for the disadvantage imposed upon defendants was that defendants would attempt to exculpate each other, and thus their testimony would be inherently biased and untrustworthy. The Supreme Court had upheld a similar rule in federal trials in *United States v. Reid* (1852) before changing its mind and rejecting the rule for federal trials in *Rosen v. United States* (1918). Although *Rosen* was not a constitutional ruling, the Court adopted its position in *Washington v. Texas* as binding under the Compulsory Process Clause, reasoning that "it could hardly be argued that a State would not violate the clause if it made all defense testimony inadmissible as a matter of procedural law." Furthermore, the Court declared that "[i]t is difficult to see how the Constitution is any less violated by arbitrary rules that prevent whole categories of defense witnesses from testifying on the basis of a priori categories that presume them unworthy of belief."

The Court has had few occasions since to deal with the clause. *Green v. Georgia* (1979) held that it was an error for a state court to exclude a codefendant's confession offered by a defendant in a capital sentencing proceeding where the prosecution had relied on a codefendant's confession at his own trial. In *United States v. Valenzuela-Bernal* (1982), the defendant complained that the government had violated his rights under the clause when it deported potential alien witnesses; the Court ruled that the defendant must show that the testimony of the deported aliens would have been favorable and material. Similarly, in *Pennsylvania v. Ritchie* (1987), the Court modified John Marshall's position in the Aaron Burr case by declaring that the Compulsory Process Clause does not permit a defendant free rein to peruse files that are confidential under state law. Rather, the defendant is entitled to have access only to material evidence, a right that is in fact also guaranteed by the Due Process Clause. In *Rock v. Arkansas* (1987), the Court held that a *per se* rule excluding all hypnotically refreshed testimony impermissibly infringed on a criminal defendant's right to call "witnesses in his own favor," including the right to testify on one's own behalf.

Unlike other Sixth Amendment guarantees, the right to call witnesses is at the defendant's initiative. It is not unlimited, but subject to reasonable restrictions. *Taylor v. Illinois* (1988). The ordinary rules of evidence apply to the exercise of the right. The Compulsory Process Clause, for example, does not guarantee a defendant the right to use polygraph evidence in a jurisdiction that forbids such evidence. *United States v. Scheffer* (1998).

It should also be noted that the Supreme Court has declared that the word "witnesses" in the Compulsory Process Clause has a different meaning than the same term in the Confrontation Clause. In the Compulsory Process Clause, it refers to those who have relevant information that the defense might present at trial. In the Confrontation Clause, it refers to all witnesses who provide "testimony" against the accused, including hearsay declarants whose testimonial statements are offered by the government. *Crawford v. Washington* (2004).

The federal courts faced the invocation of the Compulsory Process Clause in the trial of Zacarias Moussaoui, accused of acts of terrorism in connection with the 9/11 attacks. Moussaoui requested access to al Qaeda members in United States custody in order to gain exculpatory evidence. The government wanted to deny

him access to other al Qaeda members, citing national security concerns. To resolve the dispute, the Fourth Circuit balanced the interests of Moussaoui and the government. The court, as Megan Healy has written, held that "although the production of these witnesses imposed substantial burdens on the government, such burdens could not outweigh the finding that the witnesses possessed information material to the defense." Nonetheless, in an effort to protect the government's interest in national security, the court did not allow the defendant direct access to witnesses, but ordered the government to produce summaries of classified information compiled from interrogations of witnesses. *United States v. Moussaoui*, (2004).

Stephen Saltzburg

See Also

Suggestions for Further Research
Robert N. Clinton, *The Right to Present a Defense, An Emergent Constitutional Guarantee in Criminal Trials*, 9 IND. L. REV. 713 (1976)

Megan A. Healy, Note, *Compulsory Process and the War on Terror: A Proposed Framework*, 90 MINN. L. REV. 1821 (2006)

Randolph N. Jonakait, *"Witnesses" in the Confrontation Clause:* Crawford v. Washington, *Noah Webster, and Compulsory Process*, 79 TEMP. L. REV. 155 (2006)

Peter Westen, *The Compulsory Process Clause*, 73 MICH. L. REV. 71 (1974)

Peter Westen, *Compulsory Process II*, 74 MICH. L. REV. 191 (1975)

Peter Westen, *Confrontation and Compulsory Process: A Unified Theory of Evidence for Criminal Cases*, 91 HARV. L. REV. 567 (1978)

Significant Cases
United States v. Burr, 25 F. Cas. 30 (C.C.D. Va. 1807)
United States v. Reid, 53 U.S. (12 How.) 361 (1852)
Rosen v. United States, 245 U.S. 467 (1918)
Washington v. Texas, 388 U.S. 14 (1967)
Green v. Georgia, 442 U.S. 95 (1979)

United States v. Valenzuela-Bernal, 458 U.S. 858 (1982)

Pennsylvania v. Ritchie, 480 U.S. 39 (1987)

Rock v. Arkansas, 483 U.S. 44 (1987)

Taylor v. Illinois, 484 U.S. 400 (1988)

United States v. Scheffer, 523 U.S. 303 (1998)

Crawford v. Washington, 541 U.S. 36 (2004)

United States v. Moussaoui, 382 F.3d 453 (4th Cir. 2004), *cert. denied,* 544 U.S. 931 (2005)

Holmes v. South Carolina, 547 U.S. 319 (2006)

Clark v. Arizona, 548 U.S. 735 (2006)

Melendez-Diaz v. Massachusetts, 557 U.S. 305 (2009)

Right-to-Counsel Clause

In all criminal prosecutions, the accused shall enjoy the right...to have the Assistance of Counsel for his defence.

(**AMENDMENT VI**)

~

*B*y affording a right to assistance of counsel, the Founders specifically meant to reject the English practice of prohibiting felony defendants from appearing through counsel except upon debatable points of law that arose during trial. After the Glorious Revolution in England (1688), Parliament passed a statute allowing those accused of treason to appear through counsel. The Framers clearly meant to extend the right to be heard through counsel to cases of felony as well as treason.

History does not speak so clearly to the related but distinct question of whether a defendant who is too poor to retain private counsel should have a right to a lawyer paid at public expense. Self-representation appears to have been common at the time of the Founding, but representation by professional lawyers became more frequent during the first half of the nineteenth century. Some of the nineteenth-century treatise writers assumed that the legal profession would offer voluntary legal assistance to indigent defendants in serious cases. There were some instances of litigation over the question of whether volunteer lawyers for the poor would have an action for fees against the public authorities. The common practice thus seems to have been that members of the bar would represent indigent criminal defendants, motivated by public spirit, a thirst for trial experience, or the attendant publicity. In some places such lawyers were compensated at public expense.

While there can be no doubt that the Framers valued the right to counsel, their primary purpose lay in removing legal obstacles to representation by lawyers privately retained by defendants who could afford lawyers. Not until 1938 did the Supreme Court hold that the Sixth Amendment required court-appointed counsel for defendants too poor to afford private counsel, or a knowing and intelligent waiver of court-appointed counsel by the accused. *Johnson v. Zerbst* (1938). The Sixth Amendment, however, applied only in federal cases. As late as 1963, several poorer states, all in the South, refused to provide appointed counsel for all indigent felony defendants, many, if not most, of whom were black. Prior to 1963, the Supreme Court had addressed the question of counsel for the indigent accused persons in state cases under the Due Process Clause of the Fourteenth Amendment, rather than under the Sixth Amendment, which deals specifically with the right to counsel. In the state cases, beginning with *Powell v. Alabama* (1932), the Court read due process to require appointed counsel in capital cases, and in felony cases when they presented special needs for legal advice.

The modern law interpreting the Right to Counsel Clause really begins with the 1963 decision in *Gideon v. Wainwright,* holding that the Fourteenth Amendment incorporates Sixth Amendment's guarantee of the right to counsel, making it applicable in state as well as federal cases. *Gideon* left open at least three important questions: First, when does the right to counsel arise? Second, are there offenses so minor that the government need not provide appointed counsel? Third, how competently must defense counsel perform to satisfy constitutional standards?

In the years since *Gideon,* the Court has held that the right to counsel arises with the institution of formal proceedings by way of indictment, information, complaint, or arraignment.

Thus, whatever rights to counsel a suspect enjoys after arrest but before the filing of the charge (a timing decision largely within the control of the authorities) come not from the Sixth Amendment but from other sources, such as the *Miranda* rights derived from the Fifth Amendment Self-Incrimination Clause. Once the Sixth Amendment right to counsel has attached, the accused has the right to the presence of counsel during all subsequent critical stages of the case, including the preliminary hearing, pretrial motions, interrogation, plea negotiations, and of course the trial itself. The right to counsel ends with a final judgment of the trial court. The Supreme Court has declared that the right to counsel on appeal arises from the Equal Protection Clause, not the Sixth Amendment.

As to the level of criminal charge that triggers the right to counsel, the courts have never complied with the literal meaning of the Sixth Amendment. In this instance, at least, "all" does not mean "all criminal prosecutions"; it means some. Petty offenses have been adjudicated without counsel from the time of the Founding to this day. The traditional understanding of petty offenses included misdemeanors punishable by less than six months in jail. The modern Supreme Court has held that no offense can be deemed petty for purposes of the exception to the right to counsel if the accused does in fact receive a sentence that includes incarceration, however brief.

As for the standard of representation, the Supreme Court in *Strickland v. Washington* (1984) adopted a two-step test for ineffective assistance of counsel claims. To set aside a plea, verdict, or sentence on account of defective lawyering, the defendant must show that defense counsel's performance fell outside the range of professional competence and that counsel's performance prejudiced the defendant so as to call the reliability of the proceedings into question. In the first prong of the test, the courts indulge a presumption of competence; many vital decisions (e.g., whether to accept a plea bargain, whether to call the defendant as a witness) are so problematic that they are classified as unreviewable tactical choices. In the second prong, the burden lies on the defendant to show that, but for counsel's unprofessional

errors, there is a fair probability that the results of the proceedings might have been different. Prejudice against the right to effective assistance of counsel is presumed only from the actual or constructive denial of counsel, an actual conflict of interest that impairs counsel's performance, or arbitrary interference by court ruling or statute with counsel's presentation of the defense. Lack of sufficient resources for indigent defense, in and of itself, does not constitute a violation of the Sixth Amendment. That question is left to Congress and the state legislatures to address.

Recent cases suggest the Court is looking more closely at the performance of counsel for the great majority of defendants whose convictions result from pleas. Under these cases, a guilty plea may be vacated when defense counsel fails to advise the client of adverse immigration consequences, or fails to communicate to the defendant a prosecution offer. A trial conviction may be set aside if counsel gave negligent advice that exaggerates the defendant's chances at trial.

Donald Dripps

See Also

Amendment V (Self-Incrimination)

Amendment XIV, Section 1 (Due Process Clause; Equal Protection)

Suggestions for Further Research

William M. Beaney, The Right to Counsel in American Courts (1955)

Richard Klein & Robert L. Spangenberg, The Indigent Defense Crisis (1993)

Wayne R. LaFave, Jerold H. Israel, & Nancy J. King, Criminal Procedure (2D ED. 1999)

Anthony Lewis, Gideon's Trumpet (1964)

Significant Cases

Powell v. Alabama, 287 U.S. 45 (1932)

Johnson v. Zerbst, 304 U.S. 458 (1938)

Gideon v. Wainwright, 372 U.S. 335 (1963)

Strickland v. Washington, 466 U.S. 668 (1984)

Alabama v. Shelton, 535 U.S. 654 (2002)

Padilla v. Kentucky, 559 U.S. 356 (2010)

Lafler v. Cooper, 132 S. Ct. 1376 (2012)

Missouri v. Frye, 132 S. Ct. 1399 (2012)

Right to Jury in Civil Cases

In Suits at common law, where the value in controversy shall exceed twenty dollars, the right of trial by jury shall be preserved....
                      (AMENDMENT VII)

~

*T*oward the end of the Constitutional Convention, Hugh Williamson of North Carolina noted that "no provision was yet made for juries in civil cases and suggested the necessity of it." Elbridge Gerry agreed, while George Mason further argued that the omission demonstrated that the Constitution needed a Bill of Rights. Nathaniel Gorham of Massachusetts responded that the question should be left to Congress because of complexities in determining what kind of civil cases should be given to a jury. A few days later, when Gerry and Charles Pinckney moved to insert "And a trial by jury shall be preserved as usual in civil cases," Gorham argued that there was no usual form, because the structure of civil juries varied among the states. Apparently sensing the difficulty in phrasing the guarantee, the convention unanimously defeated the motion.

It was a costly oversight, for the omission of a guarantee of civil juries occasioned the greatest opposition to the Constitution in the ratifying conventions, as Alexander Hamilton candidly admitted in *The Federalist* No. 83. Hamilton tried to minimize the differences by arguing that the only difference between the supporters and detractors of the Constitution on this issue was that "the former regard it as a valuable safeguard to liberty; the latter represent it as the very palladium of free government." Mason and Gerry had themselves refused to sign the Constitution, citing the absence of the guarantee among their other concerns. In the ratification debates, the Anti-Federalists argued that the provision in the Constitution for juries in criminal cases necessarily implied their abolition in civil cases. The Anti-Federalists tied this argument to their objections to the power of the Supreme Court in Article III to hear appeals "both as to law and fact," suggesting that the Constitution would effectively abolish juries in the states as well.

In response, the Federalists continued to argue that defining in the Constitution the appropriate cases for civil juries was too difficult a task and that the Congress could be trusted to make provision for civil juries. This was a weak argument, as twelve of the states themselves protected civil juries in their constitutions. Of the six ratifying conventions that proposed amendments to the Constitution, five included a right to a jury in civil cases.

The history of the revolutionary struggle also counted against the Federalists. The colonists had had no objection to trials without juries in traditional admiralty and maritime cases. But when Parliament extended the jurisdiction of the admiralty courts to other cases, the colonists' opposition to England crystallized around the deprivation of their right to trial by jury. In the *Declaration of the Causes and Necessity of Taking up Arms* (1775), the Second Continental Congress declared: "[S]tatutes have been passed for extending the jurisdiction of courts of Admiralty and Vice-Admiralty beyond their ancient limits; for depriving us of the accustomed and inestimable privilege of trial by jury, in cases affecting both life and property." The complaint was also among the bill of particulars in the Declaration of Independence.

The Seventh Amendment, passed by the First Congress without debate, cured the omission by declaring that the right to a jury trial shall be preserved in common law cases, thus leaving the traditional distinction between cases at law and those in equity or admiralty, where there normally was no jury. The implied distinction parallels the explicit division of federal judicial authority in Article III to cases (1) in law, (2) in equity, and (3) in admiralty and maritime jurisdiction. The contemporaneously passed Judiciary Act of 1789 similarly provided that "the trial of issues in fact, in the district courts, in all causes except civil causes of admiralty and maritime jurisdiction, shall be by jury." As Justice Joseph Story later explained in *Parsons v. Bedford* (1830) "In a just sense, the amendment then may well be construed to embrace all suits which are not of equity and admiralty jurisdiction, whatever may be the peculiar form which they may assume to settle legal rights."

The Supreme Court has, however, arrived at a more limited interpretation. It applies the amendment's guarantee to the kinds of cases that "existed under the English common law when the amendment was adopted," *Baltimore & Carolina Line v. Redman* (1935), or to newly developed rights that can be analogized to what existed at that time, *Luria v. United States* (1913), *Curtis v. Loether* (1974). Accordingly, in a series of decisions in the second half of the twentieth century, the Supreme Court ruled that the Seventh Amendment guarantees the right to trial by jury in procedurally novel settings, like declaratory judgment actions, *Beacon Theatres v. Westover* (1959), and shareholder derivative suits, *Ross v. Bernhard* (1970). The Court also applied the amendment to cases adjudicating newly created statutory rights, *Curtis v. Loether, Pernell v. Southall Realty* (1974). In addition, the Supreme Court has ruled unanimously that when factually overlapping "legal" and "equitable" claims are joined together in the same action, the Seventh Amendment requires that the former be adjudicated first (by a jury), and that when legal claims triable to a jury are erroneously dismissed, relitigation of the entire action is "essential to vindicating [the plaintiff's] Seventh Amendment rights." *Lytle v. Household Manufacturing, Inc.* (1990).

The right to trial by jury is not constitutionally guaranteed in certain classes of civil cases that are concededly "suits at common law," particularly when "public" or governmental rights are at issue and if one cannot find eighteenth-century precedent for jury participation in those cases. *Atlas Roofing Co. v. Occupational Safety & Health Review Commission* (1977). Thus, Congress can direct Article III courts to resolve personal and property claims against the United States without the aid of a jury, or simply divert such claims to non–Article III courts with no jury component. *Osborn v. Haley* (2007). In addition, where practice as it existed in 1791 "provides no clear answer," the rule is that "[o]nly those incidents which are regarded as fundamental, as inherent in and of the essence of the system of trial by jury, are placed beyond the reach of the legislature." *Markman v. Westview Instruments, Inc.* (1996). In those situations, too, the Seventh Amendment does not restrain congressional choice.

In contrast to the near-universal support for the civil jury trial in the eighteenth and early nineteenth centuries, modern jurists consider civil jury trial neither "implicit in the concept of ordered liberty," *Palko v. Connecticut* (1937), nor "fundamental to the American scheme of justice," *Duncan v. Louisiana* (1968). Accordingly, in solitary company with the Grand Jury Requirement Clause of the Fifth Amendment, the Seventh Amendment is not "incorporated" against the states; it applies only in the federal courts. In the federal courts, the parties can waive the right, but there is no longer a requirement, as there was in 1791, that civil juries be composed of twelve persons and must reach a unanimous verdict. *Colgrove v. Battin* (1973).

Eric Grant

See Also

Article III, Section 2, Clause 1 (Federal Party)
Article III, Section 2, Clause 2 (Original Jurisdiction)
Amendment V (Grand Jury Requirement)
Amendment VI (Jury Trial)

Suggestions for Further Research

George E. Butler II, Compensable Liberty: A Historical and Political Model of the Seventh Amendment Public Law Jury, 1 Notre Dame J.L. Ethics & Pub. Pol'y 595 (1985)

Eric Grant, A Revolutionary View of the Seventh Amendment and the Just Compensation Clause, 91 Nw. U. L. Rev. 144 (1996)

Kenneth S. Klein, Is Ashcroft v. Iqbal the Death (Finally) of the "Historical Test" for Interpreting the Seventh Amendment?, 88 Neb. L. Rev. 467 (2010)

Stanton D. Krauss, The Original Understanding of the Seventh Amendment Right to Jury Trial, 33 U. Rich. L. Rev. 407 (1999)

1 John Phillip Reid, Constitutional History of the American Revolution: The Authority of Rights (1986)

Symposium, Originalism and the Jury, 71 Ohio St. L.J. 883 (2010)

Charles W. Wolfram, The Constitutional History of the Seventh Amendment, 57 Minn. L. Rev. 639 (1973)

Significant Cases

Parsons v. Bedford, 28 U.S. (3 Pet.) 433 (1830)
Kohl v. United States, 91 U.S. 367 (1876)
Luria v. United States, 231 U.S. 9 (1913)

Baltimore & Carolina Line, Inc. v. Redman, 295 U.S. 654 (1935)

Palko v. Connecticut, 302 U.S. 319 (1937)

Beacon Theatres, Inc. v. Westover, 359 U.S. 500 (1959)

Duncan v. Louisiana, 391 U.S. 145 (1968)

Ross v. Bernhard, 396 U.S. 531 (1970)

Colgrove v. Battin, 413 U.S. 149 (1973)

Curtis v. Loether, 415 U.S. 189 (1974)

Pernell v. Southall Realty, 416 U.S. 363 (1974)

Atlas Roofing Co. v. Occupational Safety & Health Review Comm'n, 430 U.S. 442 (1977)

Tull v. United States, 481 U.S. 412 (1987)

Granfinanciera, S.A. v. Nordberg, 492 U.S. 33 (1989)

Lytle v. Household Manufacturing, Inc., 494 U.S. 545 (1990)

Markman v. Westview Instruments, Inc., 517 U.S. 370 (1996)

Monterey v. Del Monte Dunes at Monterey, Ltd., 526 U.S. 687 (1999)

Osborn v. Haley, 549 U.S. 225 (2007)

Reexamination Clause

In Suits at common law...no fact tried by a jury, shall be otherwise re-examined in any Court of the United States, than according to the rules of the common law....

(AMENDMENT VII)

~

*T*he principle that juries determine questions of fact is a fundamental underpinning of the American legal system. The Seventh Amendment was drafted in response to complaints raised during the ratification process that the Constitution failed to protect the institution of the civil jury. The Reexamination Clause, in particular, answered the chorus of objections in the ratifying conventions that the Supreme Court's appellate power "both as to Law and Fact" would effectively abolish the civil jury by allowing the Supreme Court to retry facts on appeal. It is for this reason that Justice Joseph Story characterized the Reexamination Clause as "more important" than the initial phrase of the amendment

guaranteeing juries in civil trials. *Parsons v. Bedford* (1830).

The "law and facts" provision in Article III, combined with the lack of express protection for civil juries in the Constitution, caused Anti-Federalists to fear that the right to juries in civil matters would be abolished upon the Constitution's ratification. Both George Mason and Richard Henry Lee of Virginia argued that the Constitution abolished juries in all civil cases. As *The Federal Farmer* (thought to be Lee) noted, "By Article 3, section 2,...the Supreme Court shall have appellate jurisdiction, both as to law and fact.... By court is understood a court consisting of judges; and the idea of a jury is excluded."

In *The Federalist* No. 83, Alexander Hamilton denied that the Constitution's silence regarding civil juries amounted to an abolition of civil juries. Reexaminations of facts, he said, would only result in a remand for another jury trial. He declared that under the Constitution, Congress had the power to protect the right to a jury trial in civil cases. Hamilton's disclaimer did not silence the Anti-Federalist demands for constitutional guarantees, and the ratifying conventions of New York, Virginia, Massachusetts, and New Hampshire proposed adding a protection for civil juries in the Constitution. Thus, although the Anti-Federalists were unsuccessful in preventing the ratification of the Constitution, they made it clear that their demand for a right to a civil jury trial would have to be acceded to.

The Seventh Amendment's Reexamination Clause prohibits reviewing courts from reexamining any fact tried by a jury in any manner other than according to the common law (juries are not required in equitable or admiralty actions). Congress codified the distinction in the Judiciary Act of 1789, prior to the ratification of the Seventh Amendment. Under common law, appellate courts could review judgments only on writ of error, which limited review to questions of law. For example, in *Parsons v. Bedford*, Justice Story held that reviewing courts have no power to grant new trials based on a reexamination of the facts tried by a jury. The court can consider only those facts that "bear upon any question of law arising at the trial," and if there is error, the reviewing court's only option is to grant a new trial. Earlier, while on circuit in *United States v. Wonson* (1812), Story noted that a writ of error allows examination of "general errors of law only," and appellate courts "never can re-try the issues already settled by a jury, where the judgment of the inferior court is affirmed." Trial courts could order a new trial for good cause, but reviewing courts could examine only alleged errors of law. Story's opinion encapsulates the traditional meaning of the Reexamination Clause.

The advent of the Federal Rules of Civil Procedure, along with other procedural devices allowing courts to weigh evidence, has cut into the traditional interpretation of the Reexamination Clause. Specifically, procedures such as summary judgment and directed verdicts, which greatly affect the substantive power enjoyed by juries, call into question the traditional view that appellate courts are allowed to review only questions of law, not fact. Dissenting in *Parklane Hosiery Co. v. Shore* (1979), Justice William H. Rehnquist declared, "[T]o sanction creation of procedural devices which limit the province of the jury to a greater degree than permitted at common law in 1791 is in direct contravention of the Seventh Amendment."

The Supreme Court had, until recently, consistently held that the calculation of damages, including punitive damages, "involves only a question of fact." *St. Louis, Iron Mountain & Southern Railway Co. v. Craft* (1915); *Barry v. Edmunds* (1886). However, in *Cooper Industries, Inc. v. Leatherman Tool Group, Inc.* (2001), the Court characterized punitive damages as a question of law and therefore not subject to the reexamination clause, permitting a de novo review by the appeals court of excessive jury awards under the Cruel and Unusual Punishment Clause of the Eighth Amendment.

A parallel trend is present in the handling of ordinary or compensable damages. The Court's decision in *Gasperini v. Center for Humanities, Inc.* (1996) specifically rejected the common law standard of review in place in 1791 and validated review of the jury's fact-finding power by permitting appellate consideration of a jury award

on the ground of excessiveness. The Court in *Gasperini* validated the practice, in which federal appellate courts had set aside jury verdicts only for "gross error," or if the result "shocked the conscience," or, later, if there was an "abuse of discretion" by the jury. None of these, the Court held, was contrary to the Reexamination Clause. It characterized such actions as "questions of law." In dissent, Justice Antonin Scalia stated, "It is not for us, much less for the Courts of Appeals, to decide that the Seventh Amendment's restriction on federal-court review of jury findings has outlived its usefulness."

The general rule, as articulated by the United States Court of Appeals for the Federal Circuit, remains that when an appellate court reduces a jury award on grounds on excessiveness, the "'Seventh Amendment [ordinarily] requires that a plaintiff be given the option of a new trial in lieu of remitting a portion of the jury award[,]'" unless the award is reduced because of legal error. *Minks v. Polaris Industries, Inc.* (2008). Thus, when a district court imposed a cap on an asbestos settlement that limited a jury award, the court declared the Reexamination Clause inapplicable, because it was merely effectuating what the legislature deemed reasonable. *In re W. R. Grace & Co.* (D. Del.).

Similarly, in *Weisgram v. Marly Co.* (2000), the Supreme Court rejected the argument that a reviewing court's striking of evidence from the record required remand to the lower court to consider whether a new trial was warranted. Instead, the Court found that a federal appellate court can direct the entry of judgment as a matter of law when, after "excis[ing] testimony erroneously admitted," there remains insufficient evidence to support the jury's verdict." A federal district court subsequently extended *Weisgram* to hold that in granting a motion for a new trial, the court is entitled to reject jury findings when the court determines that certain testimony is "not credible in light of the manifest weight of the evidence." *Galvan v. Norberg* (2011).

The continuing erosion of the jury function exemplified in *Gasperini* and *Weisgram* seems therefore to confirm at least partially what the Anti-Federalists' suspicion, which the Framers of the Seventh Amendment sought to allay that jury findings would become vulnerable to judicial reexamination.

David F. Forte

See Also
Article III, Section 2, Clause 2 (Appellate Jurisdiction Clause)
Amendment VII (Right to Jury in Civil Cases)

Suggestions for Further Research
Debra Lyn Bassett, *"I Lost at Trial—In the Court of Appeals!": The Expanding Power of the Federal Appellate Courts to Reexamine Facts*, 38 Hous. L. Rev. 1129 (2001)

Ellen E. Sward, *The Seventh Amendment and the Alchemy of Fact and Law*, 33 Seton Hall L. Rev. 573 (2003)

Rachael E. Swartz, *"Everything Depends on How You Draw the Lines": An Alternative Interpretation of the Seventh Amendment*, 6 Seton Hall Const. L.J. 599 (1996)

Patrick Woolley, *Mass Tort Litigation and the Seventh Amendment Reexamination Clause*, 83 Iowa L. Rev. 499 (1998)

Significant Cases
United States v. Wonson, 28 F. Cas. 745 (C.C.D. Mass. 1812) (No. 16,750)

Blunt v. Little, 3 F. Cas. 760 (C.C.D. Mass. 1822) (No. 1578)

Parsons v. Bedford, 28 U.S. (3 Pet.) 433 (1830)

Barry v. Edmunds, 116 U.S. 550 (1886)

Metropolitan Ry. Co. v. Moore, 121 U.S. 558 (1887)

Aetna Life Ins. Co. v. Ward, 140 U.S. 76 (1891)

St. Louis, Iron Mountain, & Southern Ry. Co. v. Craft, 237 U.S. 648 (1915)

United States v. Jefferson Electric Mfg. Co., 291 U.S. 386 (1934)

Parklane Hosiery Co. v. Shore, 439 U.S. 322 (1979)

Pullman-Standard v. Swint, 456 U.S. 273 (1982)

Gasperini v. Center for Humanities, Inc., 518 U.S. 415 (1996)

Weisgram v. Marley Co., 528 U.S. 440 (2000)

Cooper Industries, Inc. v. Leatherman Tool Group, Inc., 532 U.S. 424 (2001)

Minks v. Polaris Indus., Inc., 546 F.3d 1364 (Fed. Cir. 2008)

Galvan v. Norberg, 2011 U.S. Dist. LEXIS 53208 (N.D. IL May 18, 2011); upheld 678 F.3d 581, 589 (7th Cir. 2012)

In re W.R. Grace & Co., 475 B.R. 34, (D. Del. July 23, 2012)

Excessive Bail

Excessive bail shall not be required…
(Amendment VIII)

~

*T*he text of the Eighth Amendment Excessive Bail Clause derives from the 1689 English Bill of Rights, redacted in the Virginia Declaration of Rights and recommended by the Virginia ratifying convention. The English version used the words "excessive bail ought not to be required" as opposed to the amendment's "excessive bail shall not be required," the latter reflecting James Madison's insistence that the amendments be legally enforceable and not merely hortatory. When considering the amendment, one member of Congress stated that he thought the wording unclear. Nevertheless, Congress approved the language by a strong majority, perhaps because its phrasing had such a solid pedigree.

The excessive bail clause of the 1689 English Bill of Rights had been a response to the judicial practice of setting bails high in particular instances to avoid having to release defendants on writs of habeas corpus (*see* Article I, Section 9, Clause 2), an abuse, like the Parliamentary bill of attainder, that targeted certain defendants because of their political leanings.

In both English and American practice, the level of bail is determined on a case-by-case basis. The court often takes into account the character of the charged offense and the previous behavior of the defendant. The Supreme Court has declared that a bail amount would be "excessive" under the Eighth Amendment if it were "a figure higher than is reasonably calculated" to ensure the defendant's appearance at trial. *Stack v. Boyle* (1951); *see also United States v. Salerno* (1987). Procedurally, the defendant must file a motion for reduction in order to contest a bail as excessive.

The wording of the Excessive Bail Clause seems to point to a preexisting right to bail. In fact, absent weighty circumstances, American courts have generally presumed that each defendant has a right to liberty pending trial by payment of bail. But that right turns out not to be particularly fundamental as the courts have been deferential to legislative exceptions. *Carlson v. Landon* (1952). In British practice, most serious crimes were in fact nonbailable. *See Hunt v. Roth* (1981). In America, many colonial charters and state constitutions, as well as the Northwest Ordinance of 1787 and the Judiciary Act of 1789, guaranteed a right to bail but made exception for capital offenses. More recently, the Supreme Court has approved a state statute allowing pretrial detention of some juveniles. *Schall v. Martin* (1984). In *Salerno*, the Court upheld the pretrial detention provisions in the Bail Reform Act of 1984 that applied to persons who were arrested for serious crimes and who might pose a danger to the community, allowing for a more personalized judgment of who is entitled to bail that is arguably contrary to the original understanding of the Excessive Bail Clause. Based on the Bail Reform Act, a federal district court has upheld detention without bail of persons with alleged terrorist connections. *United States v. Goba* (2003).

Scholars have debated the extent to which the clause restricts Congress as well as the judiciary. In *Salerno*, the Court declared that the government may pursue particular "compelling interests through regulation of pre-trial release," but it expressly left open the question of "whether the Cruel and Unusual Punishment Clause speaks at all to Congress's power to define the classes of criminal arrestees who shall be admitted to bail."

Up until the case of *McDonald v. City of Chicago* (2010), the Supreme Court had not authoritatively applied the prohibitions on excessive bail to the states through the Due Process Clause of the Fourteenth Amendment, although in *Schilb v. Kuebel* (1971), Justice Harry Blackmun for the majority noted that the Court has "assumed" that the prohibition has been incorporated. In *McDonald*, Justice Samuel Alito left no doubt. After finding that "almost all of the provisions

of the Bill of Rights" have been incorporated, Justice Alito, who delivered the opinion of the Court, included the Eighth Amendment's prohibition against excessive bail in a list of those rights that have been affirmed as judicially enforceable against the states. Perhaps because there may have been uncertainty whether the Excessive Fines Clause had been fully incorporated, earlier federal courts found that a state judge had imposed an excessive fine only if it had been arbitrary, a standard that would have been applicable in any event under the Fourteenth Amendment's Due Process Clause. *See, e.g., United States ex rel. Savitz v. Gallagher* (1992). Other federal courts, on the assumption of incorporation, have limited the right against excessive bail to *pretrial* situations. Thus, the denial of bail pending appeal, for example, would not be in violation of the Excessive Bail Clause. *See Garson v. Perlman* (2008).

David F. Forte

See Also

Article I, Section 9, Clause 2 (Habeas Corpus)
Amendment XIV, Section 1 (Due Process Clause)

Suggestions for Further Research

William F. Duker, *The Right to Bail: A Historical Inquiry*, 42 ALA. L. REV. 33 (1977)

Joseph L. Lester, *Presumed Innocent, Feared Dangerous: The Eighth Amendment's Right to Bail*, 32 N. KY. L. REV. 1·(2005)

Hermine Herta Meyer, *Constitutionality of Pretrial Detention*, 60 GEO. L.J. 1139 (1972)

Samuel Wiseman, *Discrimination, Coercion, and the Bail Reform Act of 1984: The Loss of Core Constitutional Protections of the Excessive Bail Clause*, 36 FORDHAM URB. L.J. 121 (2009)

Significant Cases

Stack v. Boyle, 342 U.S. 1 (1951)
Carlson v. Landon, 342 U.S. 524 (1952)
Schilb v. Kuebel, 404 U.S. 357 (1971)
Hunt v. Roth, 648 F.2d 1148 (8th Cir. 1981)
Schall v. Martin, 467 U.S. 253 (1984)
United States v. Salerno, 481 U.S. 739 (1987)
United States *ex rel.* Savitz v. Gallagher, 800 F. Supp. 228 (E.D. Pa. 1992)

United States v. Goba, 240 F. Supp. 2d 242 (W.D.N.Y. 2003)

Garson v. Perlman, 541 F. Supp. 2d 515 (E.D.N.Y. 2008)

McDonald v. City of Chicago, 130 S. Ct. 3020 (2010)

Excessive Fines

… nor excessive fines imposed …
(Amendment VIII)

∽

*T*he English Bill of Rights of 1689 also sought to undo the practice of the judges who, favoring the Stuarts, levied fines against the king's enemies, thus allowing them to be jailed for nonpayment. At the time of the drafting of the Eighth Amendment, a majority of states included the prohibition of excessive fines in their constitutions, and the provision in the amendment induced no debate on the floor of Congress.

In *United States v. Bajakajian* (1998), the Supreme Court found little in the history of the clause to determine what would constitute an "excessive" fine. It declared that, within the context of judicial deference to the legislature's power to set punishments, a fine would not offend the Eighth Amendment unless it were "grossly disproportional to the gravity of a defendant's offense."

Applying the standard, the Court, through Justice Clarence Thomas, found that a $357,144 civil forfeiture penalty for failing to report a currency transfer of more than ten thousand dollars was grossly disproportionate to the fine for conviction, which would have been only five thousand dollars. In dissent, Justice Anthony Kennedy found the scale of forfeiture quite common and would have deferred to Congress's determination of the need for and the appropriateness of the forfeiture. But the "grossly disproportionate" standard has also led courts to permit substantial fines. *See, e.g., United States v. Blackwell* (2006) (upholding a fine of one million dollars for insider trading, in addition to seventy-two months' imprisonment).

Although the Court had held in *Austin v. United States* (1993) that a civil forfeiture penalty was included within the protections of the Excessive Fines Clause, it had also declared that a punitive damage award in a purely civil case is not covered by the clause, holding that there must be "a payment to a sovereign as punishment for some offense" for the clause to apply. *Browning-Ferris Industries v. Kelco Disposal, Inc.* (1989). Thus, in *Exxon Shipping Co. v. Baker* (2008), the Court ruled that the Excessive Fines Clause does not constrain an award of money damages in a civil suit when the government has neither prosecuted the action nor has any right to receive a share of the damages awarded. The Court, in some highly contested decisions, now reviews punitive damage awards under the Due Process Clause of the Fourteenth Amendment. *See, e.g., BMW of North America, Inc. v. Gore* (1996).

In *Cooper Industries, Inc. v. Leatherman Tool Group, Inc.* (2001), the Court determined that the Fourteenth Amendment's Due Process Clause had essentially incorporated the Excessive Fines Clause and made it applicable to the states.

David F. Forte

See Also

Article I, Section 9, Clause 2 (Habeas Corpus)

Amendment XIV, Section 1 (Due Process Clause)

Suggestions for Further Research

Barry L. Johnson, *Purging the Cruel and Unusual: The Autonomous Excessive Fines Clause and Desert-Based Constitutional Limits on Forfeiture after United States v. Bajakajian*, 2000 U. Ill. L. Rev. 461 (2000)

Calvin R. Massey, *The Excessive Fines Clause and Punitive Damages: Some Lessons from History*, 40 Vand. L. Rev. 1233 (1987)

Brent Skorup, *Ensuring Eighth Amendment Protection from Excessive Fines in Civil Asset Forfeiture Cases*, 22 Geo. Mason U. C.R. L.J. 427 (2012)

Significant Cases

Browning-Ferris Industries v. Kelco Disposal, Inc., 492 U.S. 257 (1989)

Austin v. United States, 509 U.S. 602 (1993)

BMW of North America, Inc. v. Gore, 517 U.S. 559 (1996)

United States v. Bajakajian, 524 U.S. 321 (1998)

Cooper Industries, Inc. v. Leatherman Tool Group, Inc., 532 U.S. 424 (2001)

United States v. Blackwell, 459 F.3d 739 (6th Cir. 2006)

Exxon Shipping Co. v. Baker, 554 U.S. 471 (2008)

Cruel and Unusual Punishment

... nor cruel and unusual punishment inflicted.

(AMENDMENT VIII)

~

*T*here is little in the historical record to suggest that the Cruel and Unusual Punishment Clause was the subject of much discussion during the drafting and ratification of the Bill of Rights. Consequently, there has been a continuing controversy over the particular meanings of "cruel" and "unusual" and the categories of punishments that the clause prohibits.

Three categories of punishments are at issue: (1) punishments not prescribed by the legislature, (2) torturous punishments, and (3) disproportionate and excessive punishments.

The declaration in the English Bill of Rights that "cruel and unusual punishments [ought not to be] inflicted" was commonly understood to apply only to those punishments not authorized by Parliament, that is to say, the form of punishment could no longer be the king's prerogative. The Magna Carta (1215) had prohibited arrest and other like actions unless carried out according to "the law of the land," and the 1689 Bill of Rights extended the principle to punishments as well. But though the king was limited, Parliament could, at least in theory, devise new punishments. Some scholars, however, have suggested that the proscription of "cruel and unusual punishments" included any novel punishment devised by Parliament that conflicted with longstanding tradition.

The second category, which arguably reflects the understanding that prevailed in America before the drafting of the Eighth Amendment, would prohibit torturous punishments such as pillorying, disemboweling, decapitation, and drawing and quartering. Inasmuch as such punishments were virtually absent in colonial America, Justice Joseph Story in his *Commentaries on the Constitution of the United States* (1833) believed that "[t]he provision would seem to be wholly unnecessary in a free government, since it is scarcely possible, that any department of such a government should authorize, or justify such atrocious conduct."

Early Supreme Court interpretations subscribed to the view that the clause curbed only torturous punishments as defined at the time of the amendment's ratification. See *Pervear v. Commonwealth of Massachusetts* (1866). Based on that understanding, the Court subsequently upheld execution by public shooting, *Wilkerson v. Utah* (1879), and electrocution, *In re Kemmler* (1890). Some scholarly opinion, however, holds that "unusual" referred not only to punishments that were illegal at the time of the Founding but to punishments that did not conform to longstanding practice. In this sense, "unusual" would also include the third category of proscribed punishments, those that are disproportionate or excessive.

The notion that "unusual" requires respect to ongoing tradition and to the humane treatment of criminals was first raised in dissent in *O'Neil v. Vermont* (1892). The Court adopted the dissent's view in *Weems v. United States* (1910) and reconfirmed that holding in *Louisiana ex rel. Francis v. Resweber* (1947). In *Trop v. Dulles* (1958), Chief Justice Earl Warren rejected the notion of reliance on the original understanding as the appropriate standard in favor of the aforementioned "evolving standards of decency that mark the progress of a maturing society." Since that time, the Supreme Court's views on the amendment have been confused, and the current Court appears divided and unable to agree on a common interpretive standard.

The Court first considered the question of incorporating the Cruel and Unusual Punishment Clause into the Due Process Clause of the Fourteenth Amendment in *Resweber*, but it did not resolve it definitively until *Robinson v. California* (1962).

In *Furman v. Georgia* (1972), the Court held in a five-to-four decision that the Eighth Amendment banned the arbitrary infliction of the death penalty, requiring states to rewrite their laws to give judges and juries standards according to which the penalty could be imposed. In the majority, three justices opined that the intent of the clause was to ban "arbitrary" punishments. Two other justices rejected an originalist approach to reach the same result. In toto, the majority believed that the penalty had been applied in a discriminatory or arbitrary manner, and the decision inspired some expectation that the Court would ban the death penalty altogether. In dissent in *Furman*, Chief Justice Warren E. Burger clung to the view that the Framers meant to ban only punishments not prescribed by law as well as torturous punishments.

In *Gregg v. Georgia* (1976), the Court flatly held that the death penalty was not a per se violation of the Eighth Amendment. The majority opinion agreed with Chief Justice Burger's historical view of the original intent of the Eighth Amendment, but nonetheless adopted Chief Justice Warren's added "evolving standards of decency" standard. The Court declared that the decision to impose capital punishment requires separate phases in a trial for the determination of guilt and the imposition of the death sentence. In the punishment phase, the law must leave the jury with discretion. *Woodson v. North Carolina* (1976).

The meandering history of Supreme Court opinions continued. In *Solem v. Helm* (1983), Justice Lewis F. Powell's majority opinion held that the ban on disproportionate punishments was part of the 1689 English Bill of Rights, even if the Framers' view was different. *Harmelin v. Michigan* (1991), however, reversed *Solem*, and Chief Justice William Rehnquist rejected Justice Powell's analysis. Chief Justice Rehnquist and Justice Antonin Scalia reiterated that the primary purpose of the amendment was to void judge-imposed punishments that were not prescribed in the law. Concurring, Justice Anthony Kennedy nonetheless argued that disproportionality is also forbidden by the amendment. Justice Kennedy's views were accepted by the majority in *Atkins v. Virginia* (2002) in an opinion written by Justice John Paul Stevens. Nonetheless, Stevens refused to base his decision on the original meaning and relied on Warren's "evolving standards of decency" to hold that it is cruel and unusual to execute the mentally ill.

Generally speaking, we can now conclude that there is a proportionality requirement at least in the Court's death-penalty cases. In back-to-back cases, *Ewing v. California* (2003) and *Lockyer v. Andrade* (2003), the Court continued to follow Justice Kennedy's interpretation of the Eighth Amendment but held that the life sentence in California's three-strikes law did not offend the principle of proportionality. In Ewing, Justice Scalia, joined by Justice Thomas, concurred, but asserted that the clause lacks a proportionality requirement.

Over the past few decades, the Court has held that rape may not be punished by death, *Coker v. Georgia* (1977), because the state should not be able to take away the perpetrator's life if he did not take away the life of his victim. In line with this argument, the Court later held that only major accomplices in a felony murder conviction may be sentenced to death. *Enmund v. Florida* (1982), *Tison v. Arizona* (1987). In *Kennedy v. Louisiana* (2008), the Supreme Court determined that the Cruel and Unusual Punishment Clause prohibited the use of capital punishment against a convicted child rapist. In so doing, the Court also seemed to suggest that the death penalty would violate the Eighth Amendment in all instances where it was imposed on non-homicide offenders, except for those who commit "offenses against the State," namely, "treason, espionage, terrorism, and drug kingpin activity."

Based on the standard of disproportionality, the Court has also held that Congress may not take away a person's citizenship for desertion from the army. *Trop v. Dulles*. Nor are inhumane prison conditions permissible under the Eighth Amendment, *Estelle v. Gamble* (1976), *Rhodes v. Chapman* (1981). Further, the amendment forbids serious or malicious harm caused by prison officials. *Wilson v. Seiter* (1991), *Hudson v. McMillian* (1992). But in order to succeed on an Eighth Amendment claim against prison officers for excessive use of force, an inmate must show (1) that the alleged wrongdoing was objectively harmful and (2) that the officers acted with a sufficiently culpable state of mind. *Norton v. City of Marietta* (2005).

Nor may a state execute a person under eighteen years of age, *Roper v. Simmons* (2005). In *Graham v. Florida* (2010), the Supreme Court extended *Roper* and held that juvenile offenders, and now even those convicted of murder, *Miller v. Alabama* (2012), could not be sentenced to life imprisonment without possibility of parole for non-homicide offenses. A state may not punish a person for a "status offense," such as being a drug addict, *Robinson v. California*, though the amendment does not, of course, bar prosecution for the buying and selling of drugs. The amendment, however, does not prohibit corporal punishment in public schools, *Ingraham v. Wright* (1977). In addition, a mandatory life sentence after three convictions is constitutional. *Rummel v. Estelle* (1980).

The disproportionality rule has not seemed overly restrictive in recent lower federal court rulings. The imposition of two concurrent sixty-year prison sentences, with the last thirty years suspended for supervised release, was determined to be permissible for a defendant convicted of two counts of unlawful sale of a controlled substance next to a church. *Brooks v. Kelly* (2009). Given the nature of the offense, and the type of harm it causes, a statutory minimum sentence of five years for the receipt of child pornography was determined not to be grossly disproportionate to the offense. *United States v. Woods* (2010). In *Gherebi v. Bush* (2003), the federal appeals court did not reach the merits of the assertion by plaintiffs that the detention of persons at Guantanamo Bay was a violation of the Cruel and Unusual Punishment Clause.

In sum, the current law is that punishments do not violate the clause if they involve no "unnecessary and wanton infliction of pain" and if they are not "grossly out of proportion to the severity of the crime." *Gregg v. Georgia.* The clause also proscribes "all excessive punishments, as well as cruel and unusual punishments that may or may not be excessive." *Atkins v. Virginia.* More recently, the Court has grounded the clause's protection in "the basic 'precept of justice that punishment for [a] crime should be

graduated and proportioned to [the] offense.'" In adopting this approach, courts ought to consider contemporary and "evolving standards of decency," rather than those conceptions of "cruel" or "unusual" punishment that prevailed at the time of the Eighth Amendment's adoption. Today, this would specifically include consideration for the "respect for the dignity of the person." *Kennedy v. Louisiana.*

David F. Forte

See Also
Article I, Section 9, Clause 2 (Habeas Corpus)
Amendment XIV, Section 1 (Due Process Clause)

Suggestions for Further Research
Richard S. Frase, *Limiting Excessive Prison Sentences Under Federal and State Constitutions*, 11 U. Pa. J. Const. L. 39 (2008)

Megan J. Ryan, *Does the Eighth Amendment Punishments Clause Prohibit Only Punishments That Are Both Cruel and Unusual?*, 87 Wash. U. L. Rev. 567 (2010)

John F. Stinneford, *The Original Meaning of "Unusual": The Eighth Amendment as a Bar to Cruel Innovation*, 102 Nw. U. L. Rev. 1739 (2008)

Significant Cases
Pervear v. Commonwealth of Massachusetts, 72 U.S. (5 Wall.) 475 (1866)
Wilkerson v. Utah, 99 U.S. 130 (1879)
In re Kemmler, 136 U.S. 436 (1890)
O'Neil v. Vermont, 144 U.S. 323 (1892)
Weems v. United States, 217 U.S. 349 (1910)
Louisiana *ex rel.* Francis v. Resweber, 329 U.S. 459 (1947)
Trop v. Dulles, 356 U.S. 86 (1958)
Robinson v. California, 370 U.S. 660 (1962)
Furman v. Georgia, 408 U.S. 238 (1972)
Gregg v. Georgia, 428 U.S. 153 (1976)
Estelle v. Gamble, 429 U.S. 97 (1976)
Woodson v. North Carolina, 428 U.S. 280 (1976)
Ingraham v. Wright, 430 U.S. 651 (1977)
Coker v. Georgia, 433 U.S. 584 (1977)
Lockett v. Ohio, 438 U.S. 586 (1978)
Rummel v. Estelle, 445 U.S. 263 (1980)
Rhodes v. Chapman, 452 U.S. 337 (1981)

Enmund v. Florida, 458 U.S. 782 (1982)

Solem v. Helm, 463 U.S. 277 (1983)

Ford v. Wainwright, 477 U.S. 399 (1986)

Tison v. Arizona, 481 U.S. 137 (1987)

Thompson v. Oklahoma, 487 U.S. 815 (1988)

Penry v. Lynaugh, 492 U.S. 302 (1989)

Stanford v. Kentucky, 492 U.S. 361 (1989)

Wilson v. Seiter, 501 U.S. 294 (1991)

Harmelin v. Michigan, 501 U.S. 957 (1991)

Hudson v. McMillian, 503 U.S. 1 (1992)

Atkins v. Virginia, 536 U.S. 304 (2002)

Ewing v. California, 538 U.S. 11 (2003)

Lockyer v. Andrade, 538 U.S. 63 (2003)

Gherebi v. Bush, 352 F.3d 1278 (9th Cir. 2003)

Roper v. Simmons, 543 U.S. 551 (2005)

Norton v. City of Marietta, 432 F.3d 1145 (10th Cir. 2005)

Kennedy v. Louisiana, 554 U.S. 407 (2008)

Brooks v. Kelly, 579 F.3d 521 (5th Cir. 2009)

United States v. Woods, 730 F. Supp. 2d 1354 (S.D. Ga. 2010)

Graham v. Florida, 130 S. Ct. 2011 (2010)

Miller v. Alabama, 132 S. Ct. 2455 (2012)

Rights Retained by the People

The enumeration in the Constitution, of certain rights, shall not be construed to deny or disparage others retained by the people.

(AMENDMENT IX)

~

During the much-publicized Senate hearings on his nomination to the U.S. Supreme Court in 1987, Judge Robert Bork famously analogized the Ninth Amendment to a constitutional "inkblot," arguing that judges could not use the amendment to decide cases "without knowing something of what it means." Judge Bork's inkblot analogy provoked a wave of criticism from self-described "noninterpretivists," who argued that the Ninth Amendment's recognition of unenumerated "rights retained by the people" demonstrated the Founders' rejection of Bork's jurisprudential approach.

This controversy also inspired a number of originalist scholars to undertake their own historical investigations to provide a more satisfactory answer to the question of how originalist judges should go about interpreting and applying the Ninth Amendment. These investigations have uncovered a wealth of information regarding the circumstances that led to the amendment's inclusion in the Bill of Rights and the specific concerns it was designed to address. But these impressive historical excavations have not led to a consensus view among originalists regarding the amendment's proper interpretation. Instead, there are presently three very different originalist theories of the Ninth Amendment's original meaning and modern significance.

Before discussing the leading originalist theories of the Ninth Amendment, it will be useful to briefly summarize the circumstances that led to its inclusion in the Bill of Rights. The story of the Ninth Amendment's adoption begins with the decision by the Philadelphia convention to omit a bill of rights from the original Constitution of 1787. The absence of a bill of rights was among the most controversial features of the original constitutional design and provided a rallying point for Anti-Federalist opposition during the state ratification debates. Supporters of ratification quickly converged on a defense of the decision to omit a bill of rights that was first articulated by Philadelphia Framer James Wilson. Wilson defended the Framers' decision to leave even very popular rights, such as freedom of the press, unprotected because the "very declaration" of such a right in the Constitution "might have been construed to imply that some degree of power was given" to the federal government with respect to the press "since we undertook to define its extent."

Wilson's argument drew upon the interpretive canon *inclusio unius est exclusio alterius* (the inclusion of one thing necessarily excludes all others), which was widely accepted by courts at the time. Federalists in other states quickly rallied to Wilson's argument, contending that if a bill of rights had been included in the Constitution, courts might construe the limited enumeration of rights to deny the existence of other rights and to constructively enlarge the scope of federal powers. As Alexander Hamilton warned in *The Federalist*

No. 84, a bill of rights that "contain[ed] various exceptions to powers which are not granted" would "afford a colorable pretext to claim more than were granted." Instead of relying on a limited and almost certainly incomplete enumeration of particular rights that the people would retain after the Constitution's adoption, Federalists argued that such rights would be better protected by the limited enumeration of federal powers.

But this defense of the Philadelphia convention's decision to omit a bill of rights left Federalists open to a devastating rejoinder. Because the Constitution that emerged from Philadelphia already protected a very limited set of rights, including the right of habeas corpus and the right to trial by jury in criminal cases, Anti-Federalists argued that the Constitution *already* posed the threat of expansive interpretation that Federalists claimed would result from enumerating rights. Federalists never settled on a satisfactory response to this objection. Nonetheless, ratification in the states proceeded apace, though increasingly supported by a tacit understanding that additional rights would be constitutionally protected through the Article V amendment process following ratification.

Several state ratifying conventions proposed lists of amendments that they wished to see adopted following ratification. Although none of these proposals perfectly mirrored the language that was ultimately included in the Ninth Amendment, two sets of such proposed amendments have been identified by modern originalists as potentially relevant to the amendment's original meaning. The first set of proposals called for an amendment that would expressly recognize the existence of "retained" individual natural rights. A characteristic example of such a proposal, suggested by Virginia's ratifying convention, acknowledged the existence of "certain natural rights, of which men, when they form a social compact, cannot deprive or divest their posterity," including "the enjoyment of life and liberty, with the means of acquiring, possessing, and protecting property, and pursuing and obtaining happiness and safety." The second set of amendment proposals, which were targeted more directly at the Federalists' concerns regarding the *inclusio unius* canon, called for a rule of

construction providing that provisions expressly withholding particular powers from Congress should not be read to imply the existence of unenumerated federal powers.

Following ratification, James Madison became the leading champion of a federal bill of rights as a representative from Virginia in the First Congress. Madison synthesized several of the state ratifying conventions' proposals into a list of proposed amendments that provided an important template for the first ten amendments to the Constitution. One of Madison's proposed amendments, which eventually evolved into the current Ninth Amendment, combined aspects of both the "retained" natural rights provisions proposed by various state conventions and the separate set of proposals calling for an interpretive rule prohibiting the constructive enlargement of federal powers. Madison's proposal declared that "exceptions" of constitutional powers "made in favor of particular rights" should "not be so construed as to diminish the just importance of other rights retained by the people, or as to enlarge the powers delegated by the Constitution...."

In a speech introducing the proposed amendments in the House, Madison explained the significance of this provision in the following terms:

> It has been objected ... against a bill of rights, that, by enumerating particular exceptions to the grant of power, it would disparage those rights which were not placed in that enumeration, and it might follow by implication, that those rights which were not singled out, were intended to be assigned into the hands of the general government, and were consequently insecure. This is one of the most plausible arguments I have ever heard urged against the admission of a bill of rights into this system; but, I conceive, that it may be guarded against.

Madison specifically identified his proto–Ninth Amendment as reflecting his effort to guard against such arguments.

Following this speech, Madison's proposals were referred to a Select Committee of the House on which he served. Unfortunately, this Select Committee kept no formal record of its proceedings, leaving modern interpreters with limited information regarding the considerations that influenced the amendment's final wording. A possible clue to the Select Committee's internal deliberations is provided by a handwritten list of proposed amendments penned by one of its members, Roger Sherman of Connecticut. The second amendment listed on the Sherman draft declared that "[t]he people have certain natural rights which are retained by them when they enter into Society," including "rights of Conscience in matters of religion," "of acquiring property and of pursuing happiness & Safety" and "of Speaking, writing and publishing their Sentiments," and barring the federal government from "depriv[ing]" them of such rights. A separate amendment in the Sherman draft contains a somewhat garbled provision that bears some resemblance to the rule-of-construction proposals urged by several of the state ratifying conventions: "nor shall...the exercise of power by the Government of the united States particular instances here in enumerated by way of caution be construed to imply the contrary."

In the end, the Select Committee settled on new language that departed from both Madison's initial proposal and the language reflected in the Sherman draft. This new language closely tracked the language that ultimately was included in the Ninth Amendment. For reasons that are not known, the reference to constructive enlargement of federal powers, which had appeared in both Madison's initial proposal and in proposals submitted by the state ratifying conventions, was dropped from the final version, limiting the Ninth Amendment's rule of construction to a prohibition on "constru[ing]" the "enumeration in the Constitution of certain rights to deny or disparage others retained by the people."

In considering the disagreement among modern originalists regarding the Ninth Amendment's original meaning, it is useful to note a distinction between what the amendment says explicitly and what might be implied by or inferred from its reference to other rights "retained by the people." When read literally, the only thing the Ninth Amendment does is state a rule about how other provisions in the Constitution should be read. The Ninth Amendment thus stands as one of only a handful of provisions, along with the Eleventh Amendment and Article IV, Section 3, Clause 2, that speak to how the Constitution itself should be interpreted. The Ninth Amendment's explicit command does not directly confer rights or limit the scope of federal powers. Rather, the Amendment simply instructs interpreters to reject arguments that seek to use the existence of particular enumerated rights in the Constitution to "deny or disparage" other "retained" rights.

This rule of construction function is at the center of the traditional originalist view of the Ninth Amendment; it views the amendment as a direct response to the *inclusio unius* concerns expressed during the ratification debates of 1787 and 1788. This traditional view was defended by Justice Hugo Black in his dissenting opinion in *Griswold v. Connecticut* (1965): quoting Madison's Bill of Rights speech, Black described the Ninth Amendment as having been "intended to protect against the idea that 'by enumerating particular exceptions to the grant of power' to the Federal Government 'those rights which were not singled out, were intended to be assigned into the hands of the General Government.... '"

Proponents of this traditional view have expressed subtly different understandings of what the Ninth Amendment's "retained rights" language was originally understood to encompass. But they agree that its prohibition on "denying or disparaging" such retained rights only comes into play when the basis for denial or disparagement is premised on the fact that the Constitution contains an enumeration of rights. Proponents of this view further agree that the amendment's interpretive command does not raise the "retained" rights referred to in the amendment to the status of constitutional rights and does not directly authorize courts to invalidate laws that infringe upon such rights. Instead, such "retained" rights are simply left with whatever legal status they would have possessed if an enumeration of rights had not been included in the Constitution. The traditional view thus interprets the Ninth Amendment as a "hold harmless" provision that functions much like the similarly phrased provision in Article IV instructing that the Constitution should not be "so construed as to Prejudice any Claims of the United States, or of any particular State."

While the traditional view is supported by a number of originalist scholars, this understanding of the provision has been called into question by two broader originalist theories. Though each of these competing theories recognizes the amendment's function as a rule of construction, both argue that a normal speaker of English at the time of enactment would have understood the amendment's text as implying both that the "retained" rights it refers to actually exist and that the federal government is prohibited from "denying or disparaging" those rights. Thus, according to these theories, the Ninth Amendment's original meaning (including both its explicit meaning and the implications that would have been understood by an ordinary reader) prohibits all denial or disparagement of "retained rights," even if such denial or disparagement is not premised on the misconstruction of some enumerated right.

The first of these competing theories is closely associated with the work of Randy Barnett. Much like the "noninterpretivists" of earlier decades, Barnett argues that the Ninth Amendment's reference to "retained" rights refers to unenumerated individual rights and that the amendment should be construed to empower courts to enforce such rights directly in the same manner as enumerated rights. But unlike those nonoriginalists who view the Amendment as an open-ended invitation for judges to protect only those unenumerated rights they find appealing, Barnett argues that the amendment's retained rights language points to a historically defined standard. According to Barnett, the "retained" rights to which the Ninth Amendment refers are individual natural rights that individuals possessed before the Constitution's adoption and that they "retained" to themselves upon forming their government. Barnett draws support for this interpretation from a variety of sources, including the natural rights language contained in Roger Sherman's draft bill of rights, early American legal treatises, and Madison's public statements regarding the amendment,

as well as Madison's private, handwritten notes for his bill of rights speech. Barnett contends that the "retained" natural rights to which the amendment refers may be protected by adopting a judicially enforced "presumption of liberty" that would require the federal government to demonstrate that its regulations are truly necessary to protect the liberties of others and not merely a pretense to impose undue burdens on the rightful exercise of natural rights by individuals.

More recently, Kurt Lash has defended a competing originalist interpretation of the Ninth Amendment that is distinct from both the traditional view and Barnett's individual natural rights interpretation. Lash emphasizes the similarity between the Ninth Amendment and the calls from numerous state ratifying conventions for a rule of construction that would limit the constructive enlargement of federal powers. Lash acknowledges the linguistic distinction between the states' rule-of-construction proposals and the final text of the Ninth Amendment, but argues that the Ninth Amendment's focus on preserving retained rights is properly viewed as responding to the state ratifying conventions' focus on constraining federal power. Lash argues that the amendment's reference to "retained rights" is best understood as encompassing *both* individual natural rights and the peoples' collective right to local self government within their respective states. Like Barnett, Lash views the Ninth Amendment's textual recognition of other retained rights as supporting judicial protection of such rights even in situations where the danger to such rights does not arise from arguments premised on the fact that other rights have been enumerated. But unlike Barnett, Lash sees the primary significance of the Ninth Amendment as a limitation on federal interference with collective self-governance in the states.

One point on which proponents of all three of the principal originalist theories regarding the Ninth Amendment tend to agree is that the amendment, like other provisions of the Bill of Rights, was originally designed to limit the power of the federal government alone and not that of the states. Thus, for example, under Barnett's individual natural rights interpretation, the amendment prohibits the federal government from infringing individual natural rights but does not impose any similar restriction on the states. An important corollary of this limitation is that the Ninth Amendment confers no power on the federal government, including the federal courts, to protect individual natural rights against state infringement. If any such power exists, it must be found in some other source, such as the Fourteenth Amendment's Privileges or Immunities Clause.

The scholarly attention lavished on the Ninth Amendment in recent decades has not been matched by a similar level of interest in the amendment among the judiciary. When it comes to Supreme Court decisions, it is much easier to identify instances where the potential interpretive significance of the Ninth Amendment was overlooked than it is to find instances where the amendment exerted a clear influence on the Court's ultimate decision. For example, Justice Samuel Chase's well-known paean to unwritten constitutionalism in *Calder v. Bull* (1798) contained no mention of the Ninth Amendment or that amendment's suggestion that non-enumerated rights had been "retained" by the American people. Likewise, Chief Justice Marshall's famous opinions in *McCulloch v. Maryland* (1819) and *Gibbons v. Ogden* (1824) made no effort to grapple with the possible tension between the expansive interpretations of federal power articulated in those cases and the Ninth Amendment's possible role as a limit on constructive enlargement of federal powers. And in *The Legal Tender Cases* (1871), the Court seemed to validate the worst fears of Wilson and other Federalists regarding the misapplication of the *inclusio unius* canon by asserting that the inclusion of a Bill of Rights in the Constitution "tend[ed] plainly to show" that the enactors expected the federal government would possess unenumerated powers. The Ninth Amendment, which had been adopted for the specific purpose of guarding against such reasoning, went unmentioned by the Court.

The earliest mention of the Ninth Amendment in a Supreme Court opinion came in Justice Joseph Story's dissent in *Houston v. Moore* (1820), where Story associated the amendment primarily with limiting the constructive enlargement of federal powers. This was by far the predominant judicial application of the amendment throughout the nineteenth century and the early portion of the twentieth century. Following the New Deal expansion of federal regulatory power, this interpretation faded in significance, and the Ninth Amendment largely fell into judicial disuse.

Justice Arthur Goldberg's concurring opinion in *Griswold* in 1965 signaled a possible revival of judicial interest in the Ninth Amendment. In that opinion, Goldberg pointed to the amendment as "reveal[ing] that the Framers of the Constitution believed that there are additional fundamental rights, protected from governmental infringement, which exist alongside those fundamental rights specifically mentioned in the first eight constitutional amendments" and as supporting the Court's decision to strike down state laws that infringed the unenumerated right to marital privacy. But Goldberg's suggestion that a jurisprudence of unenumerated rights be grounded in the Ninth Amendment went unheeded. Justice William Douglas's majority opinion in *Griswold* briefly mentioned the Ninth Amendment as part of a laundry list of textually specified individual rights, the "emanations" from which formed "penumbras" that allowed the Court to infer the existence of an unenumerated right to privacy.

In subsequent unenumerated rights cases like *Roe v. Wade* (1973), *Planned Parenthood of Southeastern Pennsylvania v. Casey* (1992), and *Lawrence v. Texas* (2003), the Court has moved away from this type of "penumbral" reasoning, as well as the Ninth Amendment, preferring instead to ground its fundamental rights jurisprudence in the "substantive" dimensions of the Fifth and Fourteenth Amendments' Due Process Clauses. The Supreme Court has never held the Ninth Amendment to be incorporated against the states through the Fourteenth Amendment, making it one of only a handful of Bill of Rights provisions that have not been so incorporated.

Ryan Williams

See Also

Article I, Section 8, Clause 18 (Necessary and Proper Clause)

Article IV, Section 3, Clause 2 (Claims)

Article VI, Clause 2 (Supremacy Clause)

Amendment X (Reserved Powers of the States)

Amendment XI (Suits Against a State)

Suggestions for Further Research

Randy E. Barnett, *The Ninth Amendment: It Means What It Says*, 85 Tex. L. Rev. 1 (2006)

Randy E. Barnett, Restoring the Lost Constitution: The Presumption of Liberty (2004)

Randy E. Barnett, The Rights Retained by the People: The History and Meaning of the Ninth Amendment (2004)

Raoul Berger, *The Ninth Amendment*, 66 Cornell L. Rev. 1 (1980)

Laurence Claus, *Protecting Rights from Rights: Enumeration, Disparagement, and the Ninth Amendment*, 79 Notre Dame L. Rev. 585 (2004)

Kurt T. Lash, The Lost History of the Ninth Amendment (2009)

Calvin R. Massey, Silent Rights: The Ninth Amendment and the Constitution's Unenumerated Rights (1995)

Thomas B. McAffee, Inherent Rights, the Written Constitution, and Popular Sovereignty: The Founders' Understanding (2000)

Thomas B. McAffee, *A Critical Guide to the Ninth Amendment*, 69 Temp. L. Rev. 61 (1996)

Thomas B. McAffee, *The Original Meaning of the Ninth Amendment*, 90 Colum. L. Rev. 1215 (1990)

Michael W. McConnell, *Natural Rights and the Ninth Amendment: How Does Lockean Legal Theory Assist in Interpretation?*, 5 N.Y.U. J.L. & Liberty 1 (2010)

Ryan C. Williams, *The Ninth Amendment as a Rule of Construction*, 111 Colum. L. Rev. 498 (2011)

John C. Yoo, *Our Declaratory Ninth Amendment*, 42 Emory L.J. 967 (1993)

Significant Cases

McCulloch v. Maryland, 17 U.S. (4 Wheat.) 316 (1819)

Houston v. Moore, 18 U.S. (5 Wheat.) 1 (1820)

The Legal Tender Cases, 79 U.S. (12 Wall.) 457 (1871)

Griswold v. Connecticut, 381 U.S. 479 (1965)

Roe v. Wade, 410 U.S. 113 (1973)

Planned Parenthood of Southeastern Pennsylvania v. Casey, 505 U.S. 833 (1992)

Lawrence v. Texas, 539 U.S. 558 (2003)

Reserved Powers of the States

The powers not delegated to the United States by the Constitution, nor prohibited by it to the States, are reserved to the States respectively, or to the people.

(Amendment X)

~

The Tenth Amendment expresses the principle that undergirds the entire plan of the original Constitution: the national government possesses only those powers delegated to it, and "leaves to the several States a residuary and inviolable sovereignty over all other objects." *The Federalist* No. 39. The Framers of the Tenth Amendment had two purposes in mind when they drafted it. The first was a necessary rule of construction. The second was to reaffirm the nature of the federal system.

Because the Constitution created a government of limited and enumerated powers, the Framers initially believed that a bill of rights was not only unnecessary, but also potentially dangerous. State constitutions recognized a general legislative power in the state governments; hence, limits in the form of state bills of rights were necessary to guard individual rights against the danger of plenary governmental power. The Constitution, however, conferred only the limited powers that were listed or enumerated in the federal Constitution. Because the federal government could not reach objects not granted to it, the Federalists originally argued, there was no need for a federal bill of rights. Further, the Federalists insisted that, under the normal rules of statutory construction, by forbidding the government from acting in certain areas, a bill of rights necessarily implied that the government could act in all other areas not forbidden to it. That would change the federal government from one of limited powers to one, like the states, of general legislative powers.

The Federalists relented and passed the Bill of Rights in the First Congress only after making certain that no such implication could arise from the prohibitions of the Bill of Rights. Hence, the Tenth Amendment (as well as the Ninth) enunciates a rule of construction that warns against interpreting the Bill of Rights to imply the existence of powers in the national government that were not granted by the original document.

That interpretative rule was vital because some of the provisions of the Bill of Rights purport to limit federal powers that are not actually granted by the original Constitution and thus might give rise to a (faulty) inference that the Bill of Rights implied the existence of such powers. The First Amendment, for instance, states that "Congress shall make no law…abridging the freedom of speech, or of the press." Did that mean that the original Constitution had therefore granted Congress power to abridge those freedoms? The Federalists did not think so, which is why they initially opposed inclusion of a bill of rights. As Alexander Hamilton observed of the unamended constitutional text in *The Federalist* No. 84: "Here, in strictness, the people surrender nothing; and as they retain everything they have no need of particular reservations.… Why, for instance, should it be said that the liberty of the press shall not be restrained, when no power is given by which restrictions may be imposed?" Numerous other important figures made similar statements during the ratification debates. Obviously, the nation chose to include the Bill of Rights, but only with the Tenth Amendment as a bulwark against implying any alteration in the original scheme of enumerated powers. If Congress was not originally delegated power to regulate speech or the press, no such power is granted or implied by adoption of the Bill of Rights.

Despite the Framers' concerns and the clear text of the Tenth Amendment, the Supreme Court indulged precisely this form of reasoning. In *The Legal Tender Cases* (1871), declining to locate the power to issue paper money in any enumerated power, the Court wrote:

> And, that important powers were understood by the people who adopted the Constitution to have been created by it, powers not enumerated, and not included incidentally in any one of those enumerated, is shown by the amendments.… They tend plainly to show that, in the

judgment of those who adopted the Constitution, there were powers created by it, neither expressly specified nor deducible from any one specified power, or ancillary to it alone, but which grew out of the aggregate of powers conferred upon the government, or out of the sovereignty instituted. Most of these amendments are denials of power which had not been expressly granted, and which cannot be said to have been necessary and proper for carrying into execution any other powers. Such, for example, is the prohibition of any laws respecting the establishment of religion, prohibiting the free exercise thereof, or abridging the freedom of speech or of the press.

This is precisely the kind of reasoning that the Tenth Amendment was designed to prohibit.

While providing a rule of construction for the relationship between the Bill of Rights and the scheme of enumerated powers, the Tenth Amendment also affirms the Constitution's basic scheme of defining the relationship between the national and state governments. The Founders were wary of centralized government and were protective of the sovereignty of their individual states. At the same time, the failure of the Articles of Confederation revealed the necessity of vesting some authority independent of the states in a national government. The Constitution therefore created a novel system of mixed sovereignty. Each government possessed direct authority over citizens: the states generally over their citizens, and the federal government under its assigned powers. In addition, the states qua states were made a constituency within the national government's structure. The state legislatures chose senators, determined how presidential electors should be chosen, and defined who would be eligible to vote for members of the House of Representatives. As noted in *The Federalist* No. 39, the new government was "in strictness, neither a national nor a federal Constitution, but a composition of both." Critical to this mixed system were the limitations on the national government inherent in the scheme of enumerated federal powers, which allow the federal government to operate only within defined spheres of jurisdiction where it is acknowledged to be supreme. As Chief Justice John Marshall wrote in *Marbury v. Madison* (1803), "the powers of the [national] legislature are defined, and limited; and that those limits may not be mistaken or forgotten, the constitution is written."

James Madison captured the essence of federalism in *The Federalist* No. 45:

> The powers delegated by the proposed Constitution to the federal government are few and defined. Those which are to remain in the State governments are numerous and indefinite. The former will be exercised principally on external objects, as war, peace, negotiation, and foreign commerce...The powers reserved to the several States will extend to all the objects which, in the ordinary course of affairs, concern the lives, liberties, and properties of the people, and the internal order, improvement, and prosperity of the state.

The Tenth Amendment memorialized this constitutional solution of carefully enumerated, and thus limited, federal powers. Alexander Hamilton, urging ratification in New York, recognized in *The Federalist* No. 33 that congressional acts beyond its enumerated powers are "merely acts of usurpation" which "deserve to be treated as such." And the Framers placed responsibility for resolving "controversies relating to the boundary" of the federal government's enumerated powers squarely on the Supreme Court, for as Hamilton put it in the *The Federalist* No. 39, "[s]ome such tribunal is clearly essential to prevent an appeal to the sword and a dissolution of the compact." Contrary to the command of the Tenth Amendment, the Supreme Court has not strictly confined the federal government to its enumerated powers.

The Tenth Amendment had limited judicial application in the nation's first half century. No decision turned upon it, and in *McCulloch v. Maryland* (1819), Chief Justice Marshall declined an invitation to use it as a vehicle for narrowly construing federal powers. In the middle of the nineteenth century, the Tenth Amendment was cited in support of the doctrine of "dual federalism," which maintained that the national and state governments were "separate and distinct sovereignties, acting separately and independently of each other, within their respective spheres." *Tarble's Case* (1872). Beginning with the New Deal Court, the Supreme Court has countenanced an expansion of federal powers far beyond the expectations of those who framed and ratified the Constitution. Because the Tenth Amendment is a textual reaffirmation of the scheme of enumerated powers, the modern expansion of the federal government's role in national life has shaped, and diminished, the role of the Tenth Amendment in modern jurisprudence.

Modern Supreme Court decisions recognize few limits on the scope of Congress's enumerated powers. Under current law, Congress may regulate, among other things, manufacturing, agriculture, labor relations, and many other purely intrastate activities and transactions. Indeed, in one case the Supreme Court upheld the power of Congress to regulate a single farmer's production of wheat intended for consumption on his own farm. *Wickard v. Filburn* (1942). This expansive interpretation of Congress's regulatory power under the Commerce Clause was based on the theory that because many farmers produce wheat for consumption on their own farms, such personal use, when viewed in the aggregate, has a substantial effect on interstate commerce in that commodity. The theory was applied more recently to uphold federal regulation of the home production and use of marijuana. *Gonzalez v. Raich* (2005).

The expansion of Congress's commerce powers has generated federal-state conflicts that were not contemplated by the founding generation, such as federal regulation of state-government employment relations, federal use of state officials to enforce federal regulatory regimes, and direct federal commands to state agencies or legislatures. These conflicts call for interpretation of the relevant grants of federal power, most significantly the Commerce Clause, the Spending

Clause, and the Necessary and Proper Clause (see Article I, Section 8). If the Constitution truly grants such expansive power to Congress, the Tenth Amendment's terms are satisfied; if it does not, the Tenth Amendment is violated. That is the meaning of the often repeated statement of Chief Justice Harlan F. Stone in *United States v. Darby* (1941) that the Tenth Amendment is "but a truism that all is retained which has not been surrendered."

In *National League of Cities v. Usery* (1976), however, the Supreme Court indicated that the Tenth Amendment carries some substantive protection of the states. In that case, the Court invoked the Tenth Amendment to prevent application of the Fair Labor Standards Act to state employees. Justice William H. Rehnquist's opinion barred the federal government from transgressing upon the "functions essential to [a state's] separate and independent existence," activities taken as state qua state, which he regarded as protected by the Tenth Amendment's reservation of powers to the states. *National League of Cities* overruled *Maryland v. Wirtz* (1968), an earlier case in which Justice William O. Douglas, joined by Justice Potter Stewart, had dissented because "what is done here is nonetheless such a serious invasion of state sovereignty protected by the Tenth Amendment that it is in my view not consistent with our constitutional federalism."

The Court, in *National League of Cities*, embraced Justice William O. Douglas's earlier dissent, but nine years later, in *Garcia v. San Antonio Metropolitan Transit Authority* (1985), the Court overruled *National League of Cities*. The language and reasoning of *Garcia* led many observers to think that the federal judiciary would no longer entertain federalism challenges to congressional exercises of power and that the states' participation in the national political process would be their only protection against federal encroachments.

During the 1990s, that perception began to change, as the Supreme Court revived the Tenth Amendment to enforce discrete limits on congressional attempts to extend enumerated powers to state operations. The Rehnquist Court, for example, repeatedly curtailed Congress's ability

to "commandeer" the machinery of state government. In *New York v. United States* (1992), the Court prevented Congress from requiring a state legislature either to take care of the disposal of low-level radioactive waste or to take title to this hazardous material and be responsible for its safe disposal. In *Gregory v. Ashcroft* (1991), the Court noted the serious Tenth Amendment implications that would be raised by a congressional attempt to regulate the employment of state judges. And in *Printz v. United States* (1997), the Court barred Congress from requiring state executive officials to implement a federal scheme of firearms regulation. Outside of this context of direct federal control of state operations, however, the Court has made little direct use of the Tenth Amendment.

In two more recent decisions, in opinions written by Chief Justice John Roberts, the Supreme Court reaffirmed the sovereign dignity of the states. In *United Haulers Ass'n v. Oneida-Herkimer Solid Waste Management Authority* (2007), the Court held that the dormant Commerce Clause did not prevent a state from favoring its own waste treatment facility (even though it could not favor local *private* facilities) over out-of-state competitors. The Court held that trash disposal is the kind of "traditional governmental activity" that is immune from the restrictions of the dormant Commerce Clause. And in *Shelby County v. Holder* (2013), the Court struck down Section 4 of the Voting Rights Act of 1965, which operated to require certain states and voting districts to obtain preclearance from the Department of Justice before putting changes in voting procedures or districting into effect. Chief Justice Roberts opined that the federal government may not discriminate against the equal sovereignty of the states absent current evidence of a violation of federal law. Such discrimination against certain states was no longer warranted under current conditions.

Several other recent cases recognize minor limits on the scope of federal power without expressly relying upon the Tenth Amendment. *United States v. Lopez* (1995) and *United States v. Morrison* (2000) both struck down federal laws premised on an expansive application of the Commerce Clause—the regulation of guns in school zones (*Lopez*) and the creation of a federal civil remedy under the Violence Against Women Act (*Morrison*). The Court concluded that these statutes regulated activity that had nothing to do with "commerce" or any sort of economic enterprise, however broadly defined. In neither case (possessing a gun or committing "criminal acts motivated by gender bias") was Congress regulating a commercial act. Possessing a gun may affect commerce but mere possession is not in itself a *commercial* act.

More recently, the Court recognized another limit on the scope of Congress's power: the power to regulate commerce does not include the power to *compel* commerce. In *National Federation of Independent Business v. Sebelius* (2012), the Court (although it upheld the individual mandate as a tax) held that Congress exceeded its commerce power in enacting a statute requiring most Americans to purchase health insurance. Not buying something may affect commerce, but it is not a commercial *act*. The requirement, as the Court emphasized, "does not regulate existing commercial activity. It instead compels individuals to *become* active in commerce by purchasing a product." To countenance such an exercise of congressional power would "fundamentally chang[e] the relation between the citizen and the Federal Government." The "police power to regulate individuals as such, as opposed to their activities, remains vested in the States." Given that the Tenth Amendment is a codification of the principle of enumerated federal power, those decisions implicate the Tenth Amendment, as does every decision involving the scope of federal power.

The recent decisions recognizing the Tenth-Amendment limitations on congressional power have been enormously controversial. But even assuming that our modern national economy permits (or requires) expansion of congressional authority well beyond its eighteenth-century limits, such expansion cannot extinguish the "retained" role of the states as limited but independent sovereigns. Thus, although Congress has broad power to regulate, and even to subject states to generally applicable federal laws, that power ends when it reaches too far into the retained dominion of state autonomy.

Charles Cooper

See Also

Article I, Section 8, Clause 1 (Spending Clause)

Article I, Section 8, Clause 3 (Commerce Among the States)

Article I, Section 8, Clause 18 (Necessary and Proper Clause)

Article VI, Clause 2 (Supremacy Clause)

Amendment IX (Rights Retained by the People)

Amendment XI (Suits Against a State)

Amendment XIV, Section 1 (State Action)

Suggestions for Further Research

Advisory Commission on Intergovernmental Relations, Intergovernmental Perspective, Vol. 17, No. 4 (Fall 1991)

Robert H. Bork, The Tempting of America: The Political Seduction of the Law (1990)

Gary Lawson, *A Truism with Attitude: The Tenth Amendment in Constitutional Context*, 83 Notre Dame L. Rev. 469 (2008)

Alexis de Toqueville, Democracy in America (1832)

Significant Cases

Marbury v. Madison, 5 U.S. (1 Cranch) 137 (1803)

McCulloch v. Maryland, 17 U.S. (4 Wheat.) 316 (1819)

Collector v. Day, 78 U.S. (11 Wall.) 113 (1871)

The Legal Tender Cases, 79 U.S. (12 Wall.) 457 (1871)

Tarble's Case, 80 U.S. (13 Wall.) 397 (1872)

United States v. Darby, 312 U.S. 100 (1941)

Wickard v. Filburn, 317 U.S. 111 (1942)

Maryland v. Wirtz, 392 U.S. 183 (1968)

National League of Cities v. Usery, 426 U.S. 833 (1976)

Garcia v. San Antonio Metropolitan Transit Auth., 469 U.S. 528 (1985)

Gregory v. Ashcroft, 501 U.S. 452 (1991)

New York v. United States, 505 U.S. 144 (1992)

United States v. Lopez, 514 U.S. 549 (1995)

Printz v. United States, 521 U.S. 898 (1997)

United States v. Morrison, 529 U.S 598 (2000)

Gonzales v. Raich, 545 U.S. 1 (2005)

United Haulers Ass'n v. Oneida-Herkimer Solid Waste Management Auth., 550 U.S. 330 (2007)

National Federation of Independent Business v. Sebelius, 132 S. Ct. 2566 (2012)

Shelby Cnty. v. Holder, 570 U.S. ___ (2013)

Suits Against a State

The Judicial power of the United States shall not be construed to extend to any suit in law or equity, commenced or prosecuted against one of the United States by Citizens of another State, or by Citizens or Subjects of any Foreign State.

(AMENDMENT XI)

~

*T*he Eleventh Amendment was ratified in 1795 as a response to the Supreme Court's decision in *Chisholm v. Georgia* (1793). *Chisholm* had held that the federal courts could hear suits by individuals against state governments for money damages, notwithstanding the sovereign immunity that the states had traditionally enjoyed at common law. The resulting furor—based largely on concerns that the states would be held accountable for their Revolutionary War debts—gave rise to the Eleventh Amendment, which established a fairly narrow textual bar to jurisdiction in cases like *Chisholm* itself. *Chisholm* was the first major constitutional decision of the new Court, and the Eleventh Amendment reversed it, eight years before *Marbury v. Madison* (1803).

The notion of sovereign immunity predates the Eleventh Amendment, having its origins in the English common law as well as notions of unitary sovereignty associated with thinkers like Thomas Hobbes and Jean Bodin. The Framers were aware of the traditional doctrine that the states were immune from private lawsuits as sovereign entities, and some Anti-Federalists feared that Article III, Section 2, of the Constitution—which declares that the federal judicial power extends to suits "between a State and Citizens of another State"—would override that doctrine. Several key Framers—including Alexander Hamilton, James Madison, and John Marshall—are on record denying that the Constitution would, of its own force, deprive the states of this immunity. The more difficult questions are ones that the Framers did not confront directly: Did the states' immunity apply in suits based on federal law, as opposed to the state common law claim relied upon in *Chisholm*? And was that immu-

nity constitutional in stature, or could Congress abrogate it by statute?

The Supreme Court answered the first question in *Hans v. Louisiana* (1890), holding that the Eleventh Amendment bars private suits against the states even where federal jurisdiction is based on a federal question rather than diversity. The Court reached this conclusion even though the amendment's text appears to bar jurisdiction only in suits "by Citizens of another State, or by Citizens or Subjects of any Foreign State." The Court reasoned that it would be anomalous to allow Hans—a Louisiana native—to sue in circumstances where out-of-staters would be barred. The best explanation of this holding, relied upon in more recent cases, is that the sovereign immunity enjoyed by the states at the Founding was broadly applicable to all sorts of suits, and the Eleventh Amendment was intended only to fill the gap in that preexisting immunity created by the Court's decision in *Chisholm*. After *Hans*, the Court extended the states' immunity in a number of other ways inconsistent with the amendment's text, holding that the immunity applies in admiralty (notwithstanding the textual limitation to "suit[s] in law or equity") and in suits by foreign sovereigns and Indian tribes (notwithstanding the textual limitation to "Citizens" of a "State" or "Foreign State").

The second question—whether Congress may abrogate the states' sovereign immunity—has preoccupied the Court more recently. There is little doubt that the states enjoyed, at the founding, the sort of sovereign immunity recognized in common law. Most common law doctrines, however, are subject to legislative override. Debates at the Constitutional and ratification conventions focused on whether Article III was itself intended to override this traditional immunity; they did not address, however, whether Congress could do so by later legislative enactment. The Court's decision in *Seminole Tribe of Florida v. Florida* (1996) held that Congress may not abrogate state sovereign immunity, at least when it acts pursuant to its enumerated powers in Article I of the Constitution. *Seminole Tribe* determined that the states' traditional immunity was not a mere holdover from the common law but rather a basic principle of the constitutional structure.

Three years later, in *Alden v. Maine* (1999), the Court held that, notwithstanding the amendment's limited application to "[t]he Judicial power of the United States," Congress also lacked power to override state sovereign immunity for suits in state court. *Alden* frankly acknowledged that no such principle could be gleaned from the amendment's text; the Court relied, however, on a structural principle that predated the text and applied much more broadly. The phrase "Eleventh Amendment immunity," Justice Anthony Kennedy said, is "something of a misnomer." He went on: "Sovereign immunity derives not from the Eleventh Amendment but from the structure of the original Constitution itself."

Notwithstanding *Seminole Tribe* and *Alden*, however, Congress retains power to abrogate state sovereign immunity when it acts pursuant to its power to enforce the Reconstruction Amendments (i.e., the Thirteenth, Fourteenth, and Fifteenth). Several reasons have been given for this: those amendments postdate the Eleventh, they were designed by the Civil War victors to cut back on state sovereignty, and their textual grant of power to Congress to "enforce" their provisions may extend to subjecting the states to monetary remedies for violations. Although the Court decided the leading case on the enforcement power—*Fitzpatrick v. Bitzer*—in 1976, its more recent decisions have all reaffirmed that precedent.

In order to take advantage of the *Fitzpatrick* exception, Congress and private litigants have sought to rethink a number of federal statutory schemes originally enacted under the Commerce Clause as efforts to enforce the Fourteenth Amendment. The *Florida Prepaid Postsecondary Education Expense Board v. College Savings Bank* (1999) decision rejected Congress's attempt to use Section 5 of the Fourteenth Amendment to abrogate state sovereign immunity in patent and false-advertising suits as a means of preventing deprivations of property without due process of law. More recently, *Kimel v. Florida Board of Regents* (2000) and *Board of Trustees of the University of Alabama v. Garrett* (2001) rejected claims that state liability under the Age Discrimination in Employment Act (ADEA) and Americans with Disabilities Act (ADA) would

validly remedy violations of the Equal Protection Clause. Nonetheless, abrogation under the enforcement power is appropriate when a high proportion of statutory violations are also constitutional violations of rights protected by Section 1 of the Fourteenth Amendment. Thus, *Nevada Department of Human Resources v. Hibbs* (2003) held that Congress may subject a state to suits for money damages by state employees in the event of the state's failure to comply with the family-care provision of the Family and Medical Leave Act. *Hibbs* and similar cases suggest that narrowly drawn abrogation statutes can pass muster under Section 5 of the Fourteenth Amendment, particularly where the rights being enforced call for heightened judicial scrutiny.

More recently, the Court has suggested that Congress may abrogate state sovereign immunity pursuant to some of its other enumerated powers. In *Central Virginia Community College v. Katz* (2006), the Court held that state sovereign immunity did not bar a bankruptcy trustee's suit, under the federal bankruptcy statute, to set aside a preferential transfer to a state agency. Much of the Court's opinion was devoted to the unique history, purpose, and nature of the Bankruptcy Clause in Article I, and it is difficult to know whether *Katz*'s reasoning can be extended to other enumerated powers.

In addition to abrogating state immunities under Section 5 of Amendment XIV, Congress retains other important tools for holding state actors accountable for violations of federal law. Congress can, for example, require the states to waive their immunities as a condition for receipt of federal grants under the Spending Clause (Article I, Section 8, Clause 1). Furthermore, state sovereign immunity has never been understood to bar suits by the United States itself. Federal enforcement agencies thus may continue to enforce the ADEA and ADA against state governments. Nor does state immunity bar claims against state officers for injunctive relief under the doctrine of *Ex parte Young* (1908) or (when the officer is sued in his personal capacity) for money damages. So long as these options exist, the sovereign immunity embodied in the Eleventh Amendment and its extratextual background principles will tend to force suits against the states into certain channels without entirely eliminating the possibility of relief.

Ernest A. Young

See Also

Suggestions for Further Research

Bradford R. Clark, *The Eleventh Amendment and the Nature of the Union*, 123 HARV. L. REV. 1817 (2010)

William A. Fletcher, *A Historical Interpretation of the Eleventh Amendment: A Narrow Construction of an Affirmative Grant of Jurisdiction Rather Than a Prohibition Against Jurisdiction*, 35 STAN. L. REV. 1033 (1983)

Alfred Hill, *In Defense of Our Law of Sovereign Immunity*, 42 B.C. L. REV. 485 (2001)

Vicki C. Jackson, *The Supreme Court, the Eleventh Amendment, and State Sovereign Immunity*, 98 YALE L.J. 1 (1988)

Daniel J. Meltzer, *The Seminole Decision and State Sovereign Immunity*, 1996 SUP. CT. REV. 1 (1996)

John E. Nowak, *The Scope of Congressional Power to Create Causes of Action Against State Governments and the History of the Eleventh and Fourteenth Amendments*, 75 COLUM.L.REV. 1413 (1975)

JOHN V. ORTH, THE JUDICIAL POWER OF THE UNITED STATES: THE ELEVENTH AMENDMENT IN AMERICAN HISTORY (1987)

Ernest A. Young, *Its Hour Come Round at Last? State Sovereign Immunity and the Great State Debt Crisis of the Early Twenty-First Century*, 35 HARV. J.L. & PUB. POL'Y 593 (2012)

Significant Cases

Chisholm v. Georgia, 2 U.S. (2 Dall.) 419 (1793)

Marbury v. Madison, 5 U.S. (1 Cranch) 137 (1803)

Hans v. Louisiana, 134 U.S. 1 (1890)

Ex parte Young, 209 U.S. 123 (1908)

Fitzpatrick v. Bitzer, 427 U.S. 445 (1976)

Seminole Tribe of Florida v. Florida, 517 U.S. 44 (1996)

Alden v. Maine, 527 U.S. 706 (1999)

College Savings Bank v. Florida Prepaid Postsecondary Education Expense Bd., 527 U.S. 666 (1999)

Florida Prepaid Postsecondary Education Expense Bd. v. College Savings Bank, 527 U.S. 627 (1999)

Kimel v. Florida Bd. of Regents, 528 U.S. 62 (2000)

Bd. of Trustees of the University of Alabama v. Garrett, 531 U.S. 356 (2001)

Nevada Dept. of Human Resources v. Hibbs, 538 U.S. 721 (2003)

Central Virginia Community College v. Katz, 546 U.S. 356 (2006)

Electoral College

The Electors shall meet in their respective states and vote by ballot for President and Vice-President, one of whom, at least, shall not be an inhabitant of the same state with themselves; they shall name in their ballots the person voted for as President, and in distinct ballots the person voted for as Vice-President, and they shall make distinct lists of all persons voted for as President, and of all persons voted for as Vice-President, and of the number of votes for each, which lists they shall sign and certify, and transmit sealed to the seat of the government of the United States, directed to the President of the Senate;—the President of the Senate shall, in the presence of the Senate and House of Representatives, open all the certificates and the votes shall then be counted;—The person having the greatest number of votes for President, shall be the President, if such number be a majority of the whole number of Electors appointed; and if no person have such majority, then from the persons having the highest numbers not exceeding three on the list of those voted for as President, the House of Representatives shall choose immediately, by ballot, the President. But in choosing the President, the votes shall be taken by states, the representation from each state having one vote; a quorum for this purpose shall consist of a member or members from two-thirds of the states, and a majority of all the states shall be necessary to a choice. And if the House of Representatives shall not choose a President whenever the right of choice shall devolve upon them, before the fourth day of March next following, then the Vice-President shall act as President, as in case of the death or other constitutional disability of the President.—The person having the greatest number of votes as Vice-President, shall be the Vice-President, if such number be a majority of the whole number of Electors appointed, and if no person have a majority, then from the two highest numbers on the list, the Senate shall choose the Vice-President; a quorum for the purpose shall consist of two-thirds of the whole number of Senators, and a majority of the whole number shall be necessary to a choice. But no person constitutionally ineligible to the office of President shall be eligible to that of Vice-President of the United States.

(Amendment XII)

~

*T*he Twelfth Amendment sets out the procedures for the election of the president and vice president. Electors cast one vote for each office in their respective states, and the candidate having the majority of votes cast for a particular office is elected. If no person has a majority for president, the House of Representatives votes from among the top three candidates, with each state delegation casting one vote. In the case of a failure of any vice presidential candidate to gain a majority of electoral votes, the Senate chooses between the top two candidates. The procedure for choosing the president and vice president is set out in Article

II, Section 1, Clause 2 through Clause 6, of the Constitution. This amendment replaces the third clause of that section, which had called for only a single set of votes for president and vice president, so that the vice presidency would go to the presidential runner-up. In the unamended Constitution, the choice in the case of a non-majority in the Electoral College fell to the House of Representatives, as it does under the amendment, and the runner-up there would be chosen as vice president.

The Twelfth Amendment, the last to be proposed by the founding generation, was proposed for ratification in December 1803 and was ratified in 1804, in time for the presidential election that year. The previous system had yielded, in 1796, Federalist John Adams's election as president, while his bitter rival and sometimes close friend, Republican Thomas Jefferson, was elected vice president. In the election of 1800, Republican electors, though they clearly preferred Jefferson, sought to guarantee that Republicans won both offices, and cast seventy-three electoral votes for both Thomas Jefferson and Aaron Burr. This threw the election into the House of Representatives, where it was only resolved (in Jefferson's favor) on the thirty-sixth ballot. The hardening of party lines, concomitant voting by party slates (which the Framers had not contemplated), and some dissatisfaction with the way in which electors were chosen in the states led to proposals for change, including a proposal that electors be chosen in separate electoral districts in each state. However, the only change successfully accomplished was that of separate voting for president and vice president.

Although it remains theoretically possible for the vice president to be someone other than the person designated by the president and his party, the Adams-Jefferson scenario, in which the top two presidential candidates must perforce form a partnership, is now much more unlikely. In fact, Jefferson refused to assist Adams in his administration and actively sought to frustrate the president's policies. In *Ray v. Blair* (1952), the Supreme Court held that a state could constitutionally impose a pledge from elector candidates to vote for their party's nominees in the Electoral College. However, electors have defected from time to time. In 1988, one elector voted for Lloyd

Bentsen as president rather than the Democratic nominee, Michael Dukakis. In 2000, Al Gore electors from the District of Columbia did not cast a vote, in protest of the fact that the district is not treated as a state under the Constitution. The extent to which the electors are bound to vote for the candidate of the party under whose designation they were elected as electors and whether all electors from a state are bound to vote as a bloc remain matters for each state to determine "in such manner as the legislature thereof shall direct." Article II, Section 1, Clause 2. At the present time, electors in all but two states (Maine and Nebraska) do vote as a bloc, effectively ensuring a two-party system, though other states are considering choosing electors by congressional district.

Most presidential elections have not generated Twelfth Amendment controversy. However, the provisions of the amendment have surfaced from time to time, most commonly when a third-party candidate threatens to take a substantial percentage of the vote. In 1824, the failure of either Andrew Jackson or John Quincy Adams to garner a majority of electoral votes threw the election into the House of Representatives, where Adams won the presidency despite having fewer electoral votes than Jackson. In 1876, similar circumstances were resolved differently, when neither Rutherford B. Hayes nor Samuel J. Tilden received a majority of electoral votes because of disputed votes in three Southern states. In that instance, Hayes won the presidency when a congressional commission awarded him all disputed electoral votes (and thus a one-vote majority).

The Twelfth Amendment also effected a less significant change by providing that if the House does not complete its selection by Inauguration Day, the vice president shall act as president. The Constitution had already set out in Article II, Section 1, Clause 6, as was repeated in the amendment, that the powers and duties of the presidency would devolve on the vice president in case of the president's death or disability. The procedure to be followed in the event of a failure to designate a president and related matters are now regulated by the Twentieth and Twenty-fifth Amendments.

The procedures for the selection of the president and vice president set out in this amendment have been more closely specified by 3 U.S.C. §§ 1–21. These provisions address the certification, delivery, and counting of the electoral ballots and the procedure to be followed if that count does not result in clear winners. Those procedures, as when there is controversy about the certification of Electoral College votes, are complex, and their constitutionality has never been tested. They were the subject of considerable discussion in *Bush v. Gore* (2000), although the decision in that case did not turn upon them.

Charles Fried

See Also

Amendment XX (Presidential Terms)
Amendment XXV (Presidential Succession)

Suggestions for Further Research

David P. Currie, The Constitution in Congress: The Jeffersonians, 1801–1829 (2001)

William Josephson & Beverly J. Ross, *Repairing the Electoral College*, 22 J. Legis. 145 (1996)

Tadahisa Kuroda, The Origins of the Twelfth Amendment: The Electoral College in the Early Republic, 1787–1804 (1994)

Sanford Levinson & Ernest A. Young, *Who's Afraid of the Twelfth Amendment?*, 29 Fla. St. U. L. Rev. 925 (2001)

Note: Rethinking the Electoral College Debate: The Framers, Federalism, and One Person, One Vote, 114 Harv. L. Rev. 2526 (2001)

Neal R. Pierce & Lawrence D. Longley, The People's President: The Electoral College in American History and the Direct Vote Alternative (1981)

Victor Williams & Alison M. Macdonald, *Rethinking Article II, Section 1 and its Twelfth Amendment Restatement: Challenging Our Nation's Malapportioned, Undemocratic Presidential Election Systems*, 77 Marq. L. Rev. 201 (1994)

Significant Cases

Ray v. Blair, 343 U.S. 214 (1952)
Bush v. Gore, 531 U.S. 98 (2000)

Abolition of Slavery

Section 1. Neither slavery nor involuntary servitude, except as a punishment for crime whereof the party shall have been duly convicted, shall exist within the United States, or any place subject to their jurisdiction.

Section 2. Congress shall have power to enforce this article by appropriate legislation.

(Amendment XIII)

~

*T*he Thirteenth Amendment was intended to complete the destruction of slavery begun by the U.S. government during the Civil War in its policy of military emancipation. The official aim of the war was to preserve the Union and the Constitution against the attempt of eleven Southern states to secede from the Union by armed force. In an attempt to keep the peace and prevent further secession, Congress proposed a constitutional amendment on March 2, 1861, stating that the Constitution should never be amended to give Congress power to abolish or interfere with slavery within any state. But once the South had seceded, the status of slavery in the rebellious states was subject to change. Union policy recognized that emancipation of slaves employed in support of the rebellion was a legitimate war measure. The Emancipation Proclamation, issued by President Abraham Lincoln on January 1, 1863, signaled the transformation of an expedient military strategy into a settled executive policy for maintaining the freedom of slaves, emancipated by military means or through enforcement of confiscation and treason statutes enacted by Congress.

On the assumption that slavery was a state rather than national institution, antislavery advocates at first anticipated that military defeat of the Confederacy would result in its abolition through amendment of state constitutions. The Emancipation Proclamation shifted the focus of antislavery strategy to the national government. Lincoln's proclamation stated that "the Executive government of the United States, including the military and naval authorities thereof, will recognize and maintain the freedom" of emancipated slaves. The legal effect of the executive order on individual slaves was uncertain, however, and it was generally agreed that the proclamation did not repeal state constitutions and laws establishing slavery. To place slave emancipation on a secure constitutional footing, Congress proposed on January 31, 1865, to abolish slavery by constitutional amendment. Ratification of the Thirteenth Amendment, including approval by reconstructed governments in the former Confederate states, was completed on December 6, 1865.

The text of the Thirteenth Amendment reflects its historical character as the culmination of a movement that began during the American Revolution. Eschewing originality, the authors of the amendment relied on the language of the Northwest Ordinance of 1787, intended to keep slavery from being taken into national territory, to abolish it in lands where it had been established for over two centuries. This demonstration of textual fidelity to an historic antislavery act of the national government expressed the desire of Congress to complete Lincoln's understanding of the Founders' system of constitutional liberty.

There has been some scholarly debate over the meaning of slavery at the time of the Revolution and the framing of the Constitution. Some suggest that the term had a broader meaning than merely ownership of another person's body and labor. But the prohibition of slavery in the Northwest Ordinance in the very year of the Constitutional Convention was clearly limited to chattel slavery. Moreover, the rhetorical references to "slavery" prior to the Revolution by luminaries such as James Otis and John Dickinson related more to preserving the liberty to the fruits of one's labor from British taxation, rather than a general French Enlightenment kind of claim to autonomous freedom.

The Thirteenth Amendment, then, was congruent with both meanings of slavery at the time of founding. Chattel slavery was prohibited, but the natural right to "free labor" was also protected. Thus, both slavery and involuntary servitude were proscribed.

As a guarantee of personal liberty for all persons in the United States, the amendment established a minimum national standard of equality founded on personal liberty, expressed by a proscription of slavery and involuntary servitude. Congress had rejected a more far-reaching proposal, which stated: "All persons are equal before the law, so that no person can hold another as a slave; and the Congress shall have the power to make all laws necessary and proper to carry this declaration into effect everywhere within the United States."

By conferring power on Congress to enforce the prohibition of slavery throughout the United States, the Thirteenth Amendment altered the relationship between the states and the federal government. State power to recognize or establish slavery as a legal institution was withdrawn; to that extent, at least, state authority to regulate the personal liberty and civil rights of individuals within their jurisdiction was restricted beyond the limits imposed by the original Constitution. Unlike most other parts of the Constitution, which are designed only to limit governmental action, enforcement of the Thirteenth Amendment is not limited by the requirement that it apply only to actions by states or state officials. The amendment establishes a rule of action for private individuals as well as for state governments. In the language of constitutional law, enforcement of the amendment is not limited by the requirement that the amendment's prohibitions apply only to state action. The U.S. Constitution, for the most part, does not apply to individuals except when they act under color of law (e.g., the policeman who searches your house). The Thirteenth Amendment is different because it also applies to private individuals acting in their private capacities. A person violates the Thirteenth Amendment if he keeps a slave. Where the fundamental right of personal liberty is concerned, the distinction between public and private spheres, which otherwise serves as a limitation on government power in the United States, is not recognized under the Thirteenth Amendment.

In the view of its congressional framers, the comprehensive sweep of the abolition amendment was balanced by its libertarian purpose.

The scope of the enforcement power delegated to Congress thus depends on the meaning of slavery and involuntary servitude. Explicit definition of these terms in the text of the Thirteenth Amendment was considered unnecessary because slavery was universally understood, and legally defined, as the right of a person to hold another human being as chattel. Slavery was appropriating the work of another person by irresistible power and not by his consent.

In legislative debate there was disagreement over the anticipated force and effect of the prohibition of slavery. The narrowest interpretation of the amendment viewed it as conferring only an individual right not to be held as the property of another. Except for this limitation, states otherwise retained authority to regulate the civil rights of persons within their jurisdiction, and private individuals enjoyed freedom of association, including the right to discriminate as they pleased in commercial and social interactions. This restrictive view of the abolition amendment was challenged by its congressional authors. They believed that prohibition of slavery and involuntary servitude necessarily implied the conferral of basic civil rights reasonably required to exercise the right of personal liberty guaranteed by the Thirteenth Amendment. Preeminent in their view were the rights to labor and enjoy the fruits thereof; to enter into marriage and establish family relationships; to make and enforce contracts; to bring suit and testify in court; and generally to receive the benefit of common law protections of person and property. Content to rely on the Northwest Ordinance and reluctant further to engage the contentious issue of the effect of the abolition of slavery on the federal system, congressional authors refrained from writing specific civil rights guarantees into the text of the Thirteenth Amendment.

A year later, faced with restrictive laws (the "Black Codes") enacted by reconstructed state governments regulating the status and rights of blacks within their jurisdictions, Congress enacted civil rights protections that it believed necessary to vindicate the right of personal liberty conferred by the Thirteenth Amendment. This legislative response forms an important part of the framing of the amendment because it can be viewed as an authoritative congressional construction of the national government's enforcement power.

The Civil Rights Act of 1866 declared that all persons born in the United States, except Indians not taxed, were citizens of the United States. Regardless of race, color, or previous condition of servitude, citizens had the same right to make and enforce contracts; to sue, be parties, and give evidence in court; to inherit, lease, or own property; and to have the full and equal benefit of all laws for the security of person and property as was enjoyed by white persons. The Civil Rights Act authorized the courts to protect persons denied the enumerated rights because of their race against anyone acting under color of state authority.

The constitutional basis for national civil rights legislation of this magnitude was a matter of dispute. Many Members of Congress were convinced that the classification and unequal treatment of black citizens under state laws in the reconstructed South were an infringement of liberty and a badge of servitude subject to legislative correction by Congress under Section 2 of the Thirteenth Amendment. Other lawmakers, objecting to the "Black Codes," doubted that the abolition amendment gave Congress power to displace the states in civil rights matters and impose criminal sanctions on their officers in the manner of the Civil Rights Act. To supply any supposed defect in constitutional authority to legislate on civil rights under the Thirteenth Amendment, Congress therefore proposed a constitutional amendment that expressly authorized national legislation against state civil rights infringement. Affirming the rule of citizenship adopted by the Civil Rights Act, the Fourteenth Amendment prohibited states from abridging the privileges and immunities of citizens of the United States, depriving persons of life, liberty, and property without due process of law, or denying persons equal protection of the laws.

Judicial and legislative construction has, in substantial measure, conformed to the original understanding of the Thirteenth Amendment. Slavery and involuntary servitude have been defined in personal libertarian terms with respect to conditions of enforced compulsory service, rather than in social egalitarian terms based on a subjective and metaphorical view of slavery that focuses on social and cultural systems of dominance and subordination.

The most serious challenge to the Thirteenth Amendment was presented by labor arrangements in the post-Reconstruction South intended to restrict the mobility of black citizens. In the first half of the twentieth century, the Supreme Court invalidated as forms of involuntary servitude state laws restricting employment and contract liberty and authorizing compulsory labor for indebtedness. *Bailey v. Alabama* (1911), *United States v. Reynolds* (1914), *Taylor v. Georgia* (1942), *Pollock v. Williams* (1944). In a wide variety of cases concerning, among other things, military conscription, public work laws, discrimination in contracts, social security benefits, deportation of aliens, treatment of the criminally insane, labor union activities, and duties required of public school students, courts generally rejected claims of involuntary servitude in violation of the Thirteenth Amendment.

In a second line of cases, dealing with the enforcement power of Congress under Section 2, a broader interpretation appears that suggests a more social egalitarian view of the Thirteenth Amendment.

In *The Civil Rights Cases* (1883), the Supreme Court stated that Congress's enforcement authority under Section 2 extended to the "badges and incidents of slavery." However, the Court adopted a narrow view of this concept, rejecting a claim that exclusion of black citizens from privately operated places of public accommodation was a badge of slavery. The Court declared that "compulsory service of the slave for the benefit of the master, restraint of his movements except by the master's will, disability to hold property, to make contracts, to have a standing in court, to be a witness against a white person, and such like burdens and incapacities, were the inseparable incidents of slavery."

Through most of the twentieth century, the Thirteenth Amendment was not utilized to try to dismantle state-sponsored racial discrimination. Federal civil rights enforcement policy in the 1950s and 1960s was principally based on the Fourteenth and Fifteenth Amendments. In 1968, however, the Supreme Court approved a dramatic expansion of the meaning of the "badges and incidents" of slavery in *Jones v. Alfred H. Mayer Co.* The Supreme Court decided that racial discrimination in the sale of housing, in the form of a property owner's refusal to sell to a Negro buyer, was a "relic of slavery" prohibited under the Civil Rights Act of 1866. Avoiding the requirements of the state-action doctrine under the Fourteenth Amendment, which made prohibition of private discrimination problematic, the Court relied on the antislavery amendment and permitted Congress to define for itself what the "badges and incidents" of slavery were. The Court declared: "Surely Congress has the power under the Thirteenth Amendment rationally to determine what are the badges and incidents of slavery, and the authority to translate that determination into effective legislation." The Court did not describe what limits Congress must observe in enforcing the amendment by "appropriate" legislation as required in Section 2. Again in *Runyon v. McCrary* (1976), the Court avoided the distinction between public and private required of legislation pursuant to the Fourteenth Amendment and held that exclusion of a black student from a private school was a denial of the right to make and enforce contracts guaranteed by the Civil Rights Act of 1866 and prohibited by the Thirteenth Amendment.

On the other hand, in cases outside of Congress's Section 2 enforcement power, the Court was more careful to limit the "badges and incident of slavery" doctrine to its historical context. For example, the Supreme Court found that a city's closing of its swimming pools, rather than operating them on a desegregated basis, was not a badge of slavery. *Palmer v. Thompson* (1971). In *City of Memphis v. Greene* (1981), the Court decided that the closing of a street in a white neighborhood, even if it had a disparate impact on blacks outside the neighborhood, was not a badge or incident of slavery in violation of the Thirteenth Amendment.

The most significant recent judicial exploration of the meaning of the Thirteenth Amendment reaffirms a narrow definition of involuntary servitude under federal statutes. In *United States v. Kozminski* (1988), the Supreme Court unanimously decided that private employers of two mentally retarded men, forced to labor in squalid conditions, violated statutes based on the Thirteenth Amendment. Controversy in the Court focused on the criteria used to determine the existence of involuntary servitude. The opinion of the Court stated that involuntary servitude is compulsory servitude by the use of physical restraint or injury or by the use or threat of coercion through legal process. Disputing a concurring opinion, the majority declared that compulsion by psychological coercion is not involuntary servitude under the Thirteenth Amendment.

Slavery and involuntary servitude in constitutional law retain the essential meaning intended by the framers of the Thirteenth Amendment, and congressional legislation under its enforcement clause remains limited. Since the reappearance of the Thirteenth Amendment in civil rights litigation in 1968, Congress has chosen not to enact any further legislation identifying and proscribing "badges and incidents of slavery."

Herman Belz

See Also
Amendment XIV
Amendment XV (Suffrage—Race)

Suggestions for Further Research
Herman Belz, A New Birth of Freedom: The Republican Party and Freedmen's Rights, 1861–1866 (2000)

G. Sidney Buchanan, *The Quest for Freedom: A Legal History of the Thirteenth Amendment,* 12 Hous. L. Rev. 12 (1976)

1 Charles Fairman, Reconstruction and Reunion, 1864–1888 (2010)

Robert L. Kohl, *The Civil Rights Act of 1866, Its Hour Come Round at Last:* Jones v. Alfred J. Mayer Co., 55 Va. L. Rev. 272 (1969)

Earl M. Maltz, Civil Rights, the Constitution, and Congress, 1863–1869 (1990)

Ronald D. Rotunda, *Congressional Power to Restrict the Jurisdiction of the Lower Federal Courts and the Problem of School Busing,* 64 Geo. L.J. 839 (1976)

Michael Vorenberg, Final Freedom: The Civil War, the Abolition of Slavery, and the Thirteenth Amendment (2001)

Michael P. Zuckert, *Completing the Constitution: The Thirteenth Amendment,* 4 Const. Comment. 259 (1987)

Significant Cases

The Civil Rights Cases, 109 U.S. 3 (1883)

Bailey v. Alabama, 219 U.S. 219 (1911)

United States v. Reynolds, 235 U.S. 133 (1914)

Taylor v. Georgia, 315 U.S. 25 (1942)

Pollock v. Williams, 322 U.S. 4 (1944)

Jones v. Alfred H. Mayer Co., 392 U.S. 409 (1968)

Palmer v. Thompson, 403 U.S. 217 (1971)

Runyon v. McCrary, 427 U.S. 160 (1976)

City of Memphis v. Greene, 451 U.S. 100 (1981)

United States v. Kozminski, 487 U.S. 931 (1988)

Citizenship

All persons born or naturalized in the United States, and subject to the jurisdiction thereof, are citizens of the United States and of the State wherein they reside.

(Amendment XIV, Section 1)

~

*B*efore the adoption of the Fourteenth Amendment, citizens of the states were automatically considered citizens of the United States. In 1857, the *Dred Scott v. Sandford* decision had held that no black of African descent (free or slave) could be a citizen of the United States. The Fourteenth Amendment was thus necessary to overturn *Dred Scott* and to settle the question of the citizenship of the newly freed slaves. The Fourteenth Amendment made United States citizenship primary and state citizenship derivative. The primacy of federal citizenship made it impossible for states to prevent former slaves from becoming United States citizens by withholding state citizenship. States could no longer bar any black from United States citizenship or from state citizenship either. The primacy of federal citizenship thus extended "the privileges or immunities" of United States citizenship to the newly freed slaves.

When first introduced, the Fourteenth Amendment stated, "No State shall make or enforce any law which shall abridge the privileges and immunities of citizens of the United States." Senator Benjamin Wade of Ohio suggested that a definition of United States citizenship was necessary and proposed that the first sentence of Section 1 should read, "No State shall make or enforce any law which shall abridge the privileges or immunities of persons born in the United States or naturalized by the laws thereof." The final version of section one that emerged from the Joint Committee on Reconstruction accepted Wade's suggestion but added the "jurisdiction" clause. Thus, there were two requirements for citizenship: born or naturalized in the United States *and* "subject to the jurisdiction" of the United States.

Today, we understand the Citizenship Clause as if the Wade proposal had been accepted without the jurisdiction clause, and assume that everyone born within the territorial limits of the United States is automatically subject to the jurisdiction of the United States and thus automatically a citizen of the United States. This renders the "jurisdiction" requirement superfluous, despite a principle of construction that no interpretation can render any provision without force or effect. If the framers of the Fourteenth Amendment had intended that everyone born within the geographical limits of the United States were automatically subject to its jurisdiction, they would simply have omitted this phrase and accepted Wade's proposal without it.

Hence the key question is what does it mean to be "subject to the jurisdiction" of the United States? Debate has focused on three groups of persons: Native Americans, children born in the United States of foreign diplomats, and children born in the United States of unnaturalized aliens.

Senator Jacob Howard of Michigan was a member of the Joint Committee on Reconstruction and a strong supporter of the Citizenship Clause. During Senate debate, he defended his handiwork against the charge that it would make Native Americans citizens of the United States.

"Indians born within the limits of the United States, and who maintain their tribal relations," he assured a skeptical Senate on May 30, 1866, "are not, in the sense of this amendment, born subject to the jurisdiction of the United States." Senator Lyman Trumbull of Illinois, chairman of the Senate Judiciary Committee, supported Howard, contending that "subject to the jurisdiction thereof" meant "not owing allegiance to anybody else…subject to the complete jurisdiction of the United States." Indians, he concluded, were not "subject to the jurisdiction" of the United States because they owed allegiance—even if only partial allegiance—to their tribes.

The United States has "treaties" with various Indian tribes and the Supreme Court has treated Indians as having a unique constitutional status. The Court treated Indian tribes as "dependent sovereigns" within the United States, and "domestic dependent nations." *Cherokee Nation v. Georgia* (1831). "Their relations to the United States resemble that of a ward to his guardian." Hence, an Indian born in the United States who was a member of a recognized Indian tribe within the United States was not considered "subject to the jurisdiction" of the United States but to the jurisdiction of his tribe. *Elk v. Wilkins* (1884).

Beginning in 1870, Congress began extending offers of citizenship to various Indian tribes. Any member of a specified tribe could become an American citizen if he so desired. The Indian Citizenship Act of 1924 granted full U.S. citizenship to American Indians. 8 U.S.C. § 1401(b).

Senator Howard also argued that the requirement of "jurisdiction," understood in the sense of "allegiance," would not include certain types of aliens, that is, it will not "include persons born in the United States who are foreigners, aliens, who belong to the families of ambassadors or foreign ministers accredited to the Government of the United States." Senator Howard's view regarding the children of foreign diplomats has been confirmed subsequently by the Supreme Court. Diplomatic immunity is only the other side of the coin that a foreign diplomat does not owe his allegiance to the United States.

The most contested issue is the status of children born in the United States of aliens residing here. Commentators supporting the notion of "birth right citizenship" for such persons point primarily to British practice, manifested in the common law, and supported by the Supreme Court in *United States v. Wong Kim Ark* (1898).

Birthright citizenship had been the basis of British citizenship (i.e., being a British "subject") ever since it was first articulated in *Calvin's Case* in 1608. Sir William Blackstone, in his *Commentaries on the Laws of England* (1765–1769), had argued that the idea of birthright citizenship was an inheritance from the "foedal system"— it derives from the "mutual trust or confidence subsisting between the lord and vassal." "Natural allegiance," says Blackstone, is "due from all men born within the king's dominion immediately upon their birth. [It] is a debt of gratitude which cannot be forfeited, cancelled, or altered, by any change of time, place or circumstance…. [T]he natural-born subject of one prince cannot by any act of his own, no, not by swearing allegiance to another put off or discharge his natural allegiance."

In 1898, the Supreme Court in *United States v. Wong Kim Ark*, Justice Horace Gray, writing for a five-to-four majority, agreed with Blackstone's view and held that a child born in the United States of alien parents of Chinese descent became, at the time of his birth, a citizen of the United States by virtue of Clause 1 of the Fourteenth Amendment. The alien parents were subjects of the emperor of China, but the parents had a permanent domicile and residence in the United States. They were carrying on business in the United States and were not employed in any diplomatic or official capacity under the emperor of China. Justice Gray conceded that children of an invading army would not become citizens, but the parents in *Wong Kim Ark* were not here illegally. (The United States did not have the complex immigration laws that we have today, with its concept of illegal or undocumented aliens.)

Subsequent courts have simply assumed that the any child born within the United States is automatically a U.S. citizen. *E.g., INS v. Rios-Pineda* (1985), *dicta* referring to the respondent and his wife, who illegally entered the U.S. By the time of his deportation, "respondent wife had given birth to a child, who, born in the United States, was a citizen of this country." However, there is also no case where the Supreme Court has explicitly held that birthright citizenship for the children of *illegal* aliens is the unambiguous command of the Fourteenth Amendment. It is hard to conclude that the framers of the Fourteenth Amendment intended to confer citizenship on the children of aliens illegally present when they explicitly denied that boon to Native Americans legally present but subject to a foreign jurisdiction.

Commentators contesting the notion of automatic "birthright citizenship" for children of aliens find highly significant Senator Howard's contention that "every person born within the limits of the United States, and subject to their jurisdiction, is by virtue of natural law and national law a citizen of the United States." Most contemporary observers would have understood "natural law" to refer to the social compact basis of citizenship, grounded in consent and adumbrated in the Declaration of Independence. Neither *Calvin's Case* nor Blackstone ever used the word "citizen." It remained for the Declaration to transform subjects into citizens by the requirement that republican government rest on the active consent of the governed.

In *A Summary View of the Rights of British America* (1774), Thomas Jefferson argued that it was a natural right possessed by all men to leave the country where "chance and not choice" had placed them. The notion of a natural right to expatriation is incongruent with a scheme of an indefeasible birthright citizenship. In 1868, the Reconstruction Congress passed an Expatriation Act that provided, in pertinent part, that "the right of expatriation is a natural and inherent right of all people, indispensable to the enjoyment of the rights of life, liberty, and the pursuit of happiness." Senator Howard was an enthusiastic supporter of the bill, describing the right of expatriation as the necessary counterpart of citizenship based on consent. During debate, commentators frequently described Blackstone's view of birthright citizenship as an "indefensible feudal doctrine of indefeasible allegiance" that was incompatible with republican government. One member remarked that "the old feudal doctrine stated by Blackstone and adopted as part of the common law of England...is not only at war with our institutions, but is equally at war with every principle of justice and of sound public law." By this argument, consent-based citizenship repudiated Blackstone's common law view.

Moreover, in *Elk v. Wilkins*, the Supreme Court decided that an Indian who had renounced allegiance to his tribe did not become "subject to the jurisdiction" of the United States by virtue of the renunciation. "The alien and dependent condition of the members of the Indian Tribes could not be put off at their own will, without the action or assent of the United States" signified either by treaty or legislation. Neither the "Indian Tribes" nor "individual members of those Tribes," no more than "other foreigners," can "become citizens of their own will." In the frequently cited case of *United States v. Wong Kim Ark*, Chief Justice Melville Fuller in dissent argued that birthright citizenship had been repealed by the principles of the American Revolution and rejected by the framers of the Fourteenth Amendment.

When Congress began extending offers of citizenship to various Indian tribes, it permitted any member of a specified tribe to become an American citizen if he so desired. Congress thus demonstrated that, using its Section 5 powers to enforce the provisions of the Fourteenth Amendment, it could define who was properly within the jurisdiction of the United States. Based on the intent of the framers of the Fourteenth Amendment, some believe that Congress could exercise its Section 5 powers to prevent the children of illegal aliens from automatically becoming citizens of the United States. An effort in 1997 failed in the face of intense political opposition from immigrant rights groups. Apparently, the question remains open to the determination of the political and legal processes.

Edward Erler

Suggestions for Further Research

Edward J. Erler, *From Subjects to Citizens: The Social Compact Origins of American Citizenship, in* THE AMERICAN FOUNDING AND THE SOCIAL COMPACT (Thomas G. West & Ronald J. Pestritto eds., 2003)

EDWARD J. ERLER, THOMAS G. WEST, AND JOHN MARINI, THE FOUNDERS ON CITIZENSHIP AND IMMIGRATION (2007)

ROBERT J. KACZOROWSKI, THE NATIONALIZATION OF
    CIVIL RIGHTS: CONSTITUTIONAL THEORY AND
    PRACTICE IN A RACIST SOCIETY, 1866–1883 (1987)
JAMES H. KETTNER, THE DEVELOPMENT OF AMERICAN
    CITIZENSHIP, 1608–1870 (1978)

Significant Cases

Calvin's Case, 77 Eng. Rep. 377 (1608)
Cherokee Nation v. Georgia, 30 U.S. 1 (1831)
Dred Scott v. Sandford, 60 U.S. (19 How.) 393 (1857)
Elk v. Wilkins, 112 U.S. 94 (1884)
United States v. Wong Kim Ark, 169 U.S. 649 (1898)
INS v. Rios-Pineda, 471 U.S. 444 (1985)

State Action

No State shall make or enforce any
law which shall abridge the privileges or immunities of citizens of
the United States; nor shall any
State deprive any person of life,
liberty, or property, without due
process of law; nor deny to any person within its jurisdiction the equal
protection of the laws.

(AMENDMENT XIV, SECTION 1)

~

"State action" is a general term used to
describe the kinds of actions specifically prohibited by Section 1 of the Fourteenth Amendment,
and by extension, the kinds of state or federal
actions prohibited by other provisions of the
Constitution. Since each prohibition in Section
1 is addressed directly to states, the generalization of "state action" makes logical sense, but it
leaves unanswered two questions of interpretation: First, are the directives in Section 1 aimed
only at states and those acting under state authority? Second, is Congress's power under Section
5 to enforce Section 1 limited to enacting laws
aimed *only* at states and those acting under state
authority?

The words of the provision identify three
kinds of prohibited conduct: (1) a state's making or enforcing any law "which shall abridge

the privileges or immunities of citizens of the
United States", (2) a state's depriving "any person
of life, liberty, or property, without due process
of law", and (3) a state's denying "to any person
within its jurisdiction the equal protection of the
laws." Although each prohibition seems to forbid
a different kind of conduct, all three seem aimed
at state action or conduct attributable to a state.

Soon after Congress had overturned President Andrew Johnson's veto of the Civil Rights
Act of 1866, it passed the Fourteenth Amendment
and sent it to the states for approval. This was to
counter President Andrew Johnson's claim when
he vetoed the Civil Rights Act that it was beyond
Congress's constitutional powers. The drafters of
Sections 1 and 5 of the Fourteenth Amendment
understood Section 5 as providing an unques-
tionable constitutional base for the 1866 Civil
Rights Act, and Section 1 as embedding the substantive proscriptions of that act in the Constitution itself, safe from subsequent repeal by mere
legislative action.

In fact, Congress had enacted the 1866 Civil
Rights Act to overturn the effects of the "Black
Codes" enacted by the reconstituted Southern
state governments in 1865 and 1866 under President Johnson's Reconstruction policies. Those
codes limited the basic civil rights of freed slaves
to contract, to own property, and to sue. Republicans in Congress viewed the Black Codes as
reducing freed slaves to an inferior legal status,
close to slavery, so they believed the Civil Rights
Act was constitutionally authorized by the Thirteenth Amendment, which abolished slavery
throughout the United States and gave Congress
power to enforce that prohibition.

Reading the words of Section 1 against this
history, the contemporary reader would likely
have concluded that they were aimed at the state
actions that the Civil Rights Act of 1866 intended
to prohibit: state laws or actions by state officials
that treated freed slaves differently from whites
with respect to basic litigation, contract, and
property rights, or that imposed on freed slaves
different punishments, pains, or penalties than
would be imposed on whites for the same conduct. Section 5 gave Congress the important but
limited power to pass legislation enforcing the
protections of Section 1.

The Fourteenth Amendment was integral to the Reconstruction policies of Republicans in the election of 1866: constitutional limitations on state power to withhold basic civil rights from the newly freed slaves; recognition and restoration of the fundamental features of the federal union, in which states hold primary lawmaking authority and Congress is given defined, limited powers; and restoration of the secessionist states to their full powers in a federal union only after they ratified the Fourteenth Amendment. Limiting the prohibitions in Section 1 to state actions was thus not mere happenstance. The limitation had an overriding *constitutional* aim: to preserve the federal system in which states had broad authority to legislate and act for the common good and the federal government had limited, defined powers.

However, a broad interpretation of Congress's power under Section 5 was proposed not long after its ratification. Section 1 forbids a state to deny a person the "equal protection of the laws." The "laws" in that directive should include the long-established common law that protected the right of any member of the public to be served by those private entities that hold themselves out to provide a service to the public: public accommodations, public transportation, and public places of amusement. For the courts of a state to refuse to enforce this common law right when asserted by a newly freed slave (while enforcing the law for a white customer) would be to deny the former slave the equal protection of the laws. One way for Congress to prevent this kind of violation of Section 1 would be to enact a general law under Section 5 protecting everyone's common law right of access to public accommodations, conveyances, and places of amusement. This could reasonably be understood as Congress's "enforcing" the right to equal protection of the laws recognized in Section 1. Congress did exactly that in the Civil Rights Act of 1875, which mandated equal access to public accommodations, common carriers, and places of amusement.

Nonetheless, the Supreme Court in *The Civil Rights Cases* (1883) held the Civil Rights Act of 1875 to be unconstitutional. In holding that Congress had no power under Section 1 and Section 5 of the Fourteenth Amendment to enact that legislation, the Court declared,

> The prohibitions of the amendment are against State laws and acts done under State authority. [But the Civil Rights Act of 1875] makes no reference to any supposed or apprehended violation of the Fourteenth Amendment on the part of the State.... [It] lays down rules for the conduct of individuals in society towards each other, and imposes sanctions for the enforcement of those rules, without referring in any manner to any supposed action of the State or its authorities.

The Court turned the "state common law" argument against its proponents. If private actors deprive anyone of their traditional common law rights of access to public accommodations, transportation, or places of amusement, those deprived should enforce their rights in the state courts.

Dicta in later cases have questioned the central holding of *The Civil Rights Cases* but never overruled it. In *United States v. Guest* (1966), the Supreme Court held that Congress under Section 5 could regulate the conduct of private individuals who conspired with state officials to deprive persons of their rights under Section 1, because a private individual's conspiracy with state officials brought his conduct within the state-action prohibition. Justices in two concurring opinions suggested that Congress could use its Section 5 powers to reach purely private conduct. But in no case since then has the Court embraced the *Guest* concurrences. In *United States v. Morrison* (2000), the Supreme Court reaffirmed the holding of *The Civil Rights Cases*, explicitly rejected the *Guest* dicta, and struck down the part of the federal Violence Against Women Act of 1994 that had provided a federal civil remedy for victims of "gender-motivated" violence. The Court reasoned that the act exceeded Congress's power under Section 5 of the Fourteenth Amendment because it was "directed not at any state or state actor, but at individuals who have committed criminal acts motivated by gender bias."

The Supreme Court has thus consistently held that some sort of state action is a prerequisite to judicial enforcement of the prohibitions in Section 1 of the Fourteenth Amendment. The remaining question, then, is what counts as state action. Of course, there are easy cases: "state action" clearly includes state legislative, judicial, and executive actions, as well as actions by entities expressly vested with governmental powers, such as municipalities and administrative agencies. The hard cases arise because it is difficult to discover clear standards for determining when conduct of a private entity may constitute "state action" under Section 1 of the Fourteenth Amendment.

The courts have determined that the question is whether, on all the facts and circumstances, including the private entity's relationship to the state and any of the state's acts, it is fair to say that the private entity's conduct is "state action" and thus attributable to the state. *Blum v. Yaretsky* (1982). Over the years, the Supreme Court has found that a private entity can be a "state actor" if it is acting *for* the state, acting *like* a state, or becoming too involved *with* the state.

Early on, the Court found that whether a person acts *for* the state is determined by the common law principles of vicarious responsibility for the conduct of others, embedded in the common law of agency, apparent agency, conspiracy, and joint venture.

At common law, for example, a principal is legally responsible for the actions of an agent even outside the scope of his express authority if the agent was clothed by the principal with "apparent" authority. After one false start, the Court concluded in 1912 that a state official who violated a state law or the Constitution and hence exceeded his actual authority nevertheless engaged in state action within the Fourteenth Amendment when the exercise of his apparent authority caused the harm that the Fourteenth Amendment intended to prevent. *Home Telephone & Telegraph Co. v. City of Los Angeles* (1913). *See also Monroe v. Pape* (1961). Also, at common law, each member of a conspiracy is responsible for the actions of his co-conspirators. So if a state

official conspires with a private person to deprive another of a constitutional right, the action of the private person is "state action" under the Fourteenth Amendment. *United States v. Guest. See also Dennis v. Sparks* (1980).

The Court after *Home Telephone* relied on explicit or implied delegation to act for the state in finding state action without requiring that all the technical requirements of agency be met. In the first of two "white primary" cases, the Court held that the allegedly private Democratic Party's primary elections were held using authority delegated by the state, so the party's exclusion of black voters was state action in violation of the Fifteenth Amendment, which forbids a state to deny or abridge the rights of citizens of the United States to vote "on account of race, color, or previous condition of servitude." *Nixon v. Condon* (1932); *Smith v. Allwright* (1944).

In the other white primary case, an all-white club held a pre-primary vote of its members, whose approved candidates usually won the subsequent Democratic Party primary. The Court held that this private, segregated pre-primary was state action because it effectively chose the Democratic Party's candidate for the general election. In conducting that primary, therefore, the club exercised a public function. *Terry v. Adams* (1953).

When a private party acts *like* a state, the Court determines that it is performing a "public function." In *Marsh v. Alabama* (1946), the Court held that a company town that prohibited the distribution of religious flyers in public violated the First Amendment of the Constitution, (applicable to the states through the Fourteenth Amendment's due process clause). *Marsh* held that the company's exercise of traditional public functions on property that it owned and developed, which appeared to be a town, was subject to the Fourteenth Amendment's restrictions on state action.

The public function test reached its high-water mark in *Evans v. Newton* (1966). The Court held that a private entity (a testamentary trust with private trustees) operating a park open to white members of the public was engaged in a public function—it looked like a public park except that it excluded all blacks. This holding was narrowed by a subsequent case, *Evans v.*

Abney (1970), which held that once the park had reverted to private heirs, they could thereafter exclude blacks from park.

The public function test was further restricted by subsequent cases distinguishing *Marsh v. Alabama*. The Court held that an owner of a private shopping mall was not exercising a public function. A mall is not an entire city, said *Hudgens v. National Labor Relations Board* (1976). The Court also held that a privately owned utility was not exercising a public function in providing electric power to the public, even though the utility was publicly licensed and regulated, and even though some local governments also provided electricity to the public. *Jackson v. Metropolitan Edison Co.* (1974). In the course of whittling away at the public function test, the *Jackson* Court explicitly limited its application to cases in which a private entity performs a necessary public function or exercises powers traditionally exercised exclusively by the state.

The key case for determining when a private entity has become too *involved* with the state is *Burton v. Wilmington Parking Authority* (1961). There, a privately owned restaurant and bar, the Eagle Coffee Shoppe, refused to serve a black prospective customer because of his race. The Eagle leased its space from the public parking garage authority and located its restaurant within the parking garage owned and operated by the authority. The Court, in reaching its conclusion, listed many factors, even that a flag was flying from the building. It found that the Eagle's yearly lease payments and that of other tenants were an indispensable part of the state's plan to operate the parking garage as a self-sustaining unit, that the parking garage benefitted from patronage by the Eagle's customers, and that the Eagle's profits earned through its discriminatory practice were important for its financial success, so that profits "earned by discrimination [were] indispensable elements in the financial success of the governmental agency." The Court concluded that the state through its public parking authority had become a "joint participant" in the discriminatory practice. The Court explicitly denied, however, that government leasing of property to a private entity always made the government lessor a joint participant in the lessee's conduct.

Often, private entities act pursuant to a license issued by the state or one of its regulatory agencies. The general rule seems relatively clear: a private entity acting pursuant to a state license is not engaged in state action unless the licensing authority specifically requires, approves, or encourages the licensee to infringe the constitutional rights of others. In *Moose Lodge No. 107 v. Irvis* (1972), the Court found that a state liquor license granted to a private club that discriminated against blacks did not make that discrimination state action.

The Court has yet to fashion a clear line of analysis in cases in which close involvement by the state makes private action into state action.

For example, the *Burton* case was thought to stand either for a "reciprocal benefit" test (symbiotic between the state and the private entity) or a test of whether the state was "inextricably entwined" with the private conduct. In *Brentwood Academy v. Tennessee Secondary School Athletic Association* (2001), the Court found state action by focusing on the inextricable connections between state secondary schools and a private association voluntarily formed by agreement among public and private secondary schools to regulate interscholastic athletic contests. At the same time, the Court also applied the reciprocal benefit test, relying on the nominal dues paid by public high schools to the association and the portion of the ticket sales the schools received attributable to membership in the association, all of which seemed to be de minimis.

Earlier, in *Shelley v. Kraemer* (1948), the Supreme Court held that judicial enforcement of a private restrictive covenant barring occupancy by "any person not of the Caucasian race" was state action denying equal protection of the laws to the black buyer of the property. The Court held that the lower court's application of the law of restrictive covenants was state action. Commentators quickly pointed out that the implications of *Shelley* were too broad: any private contract would become state action, for instance, when enforced by a court. To avoid this overbreadth, later commentators suggested that *Shelley* should be limited to its facts: a court's action in enforcing a racially discriminatory agreement would be in violation of the Equal Protection Clause only if it coerced someone to discriminate when he did not choose to do so. In fact, that is what the case said. It referred to a willing buyer (the black purchaser) and the willing seller (the while property owner). The state court sought to prevent that sale, and it was that judicial action to prevent a sale that constituted the state action.

In *Reitman v. Mulkey* (1967), California had repealed a fair housing act by adopting a constitutional amendment that barred the enactment of any law limiting the right of any property owner to refuse to sell his or her property to any buyer for any reason. The Court held the amendment unconstitutional even though the Fourteenth Amendment did not require the state to enact fair housing legislation. A simple legislative repeal of the California fair housing act, therefore, probably would have been constitutional, and the California amendment was on its face racially neutral. The Court justified its holding by arguing that the amendment would *forbid* a city or the legislature from enacting laws allowing open housing or forbidding private racial discrimination in the sale or rental of property. The California amendment did more than simply repeal an open housing act; it prohibited passage of another such act in the absence of another amendment to the state constitution. Emphasizing this difference, the constitutional scholar Charles Black subsequently explained the *Reitman* case as follows: the amendment was unconstitutional because it placed a larger, discriminatory burden on those seeking to obtain legislation that would remove racial discrimination from the housing market. Before obtaining a fair housing act they first had to obtain a constitutional amendment repealing this constitutional amendment. The Court adopted this argument in the subsequent case of *Romer v. Evans* (1996).

The Court emphasized this point in *James v. Valtierra* (1971). Justice Hugo Black, for the Court, upheld a California constitutional amendment that forbade the construction of any low-rent housing project unless a majority of those voting in the relevant area approved the low-rent housing. This amendment, unlike the one at issue in *Reitman*, did not rest "on distinctions based on race." *Reitman* imposed a special hurdle on black citizens who sought open housing, and the Court reviews such laws applying strict scrutiny. In contrast, *Valtierra* imposed a special hurdle on

poorer people. The Court applies strict scrutiny to racial distinctions but evaluates wealth distinctions using a rational basis test.

Two cases decided in the last thirty years present puzzling questions of consistency with seemingly settled state action doctrine. In *Lugar v. Edmondson Oil Co.* (1982), a creditor sought to attach a debtor's property. Pursuant to state law, the county clerk of the court issued a writ of attachment, which the sheriff served on the debtor. The Court held that the creditor's petition for a writ of attachment was "state action" because the creditor "jointly participated" with the sheriff in seizing the debtor's assets without due process of law. Some argue that the *Lugar* holding seems inconsistent with prior state action cases, which had held a private litigant's actions to be state action only when the litigant corruptly conspired with a state official in a jointly beneficial scheme to deprive another litigant of his right to a fair trial. *Dennis v. Sparks*. Without the elements of corruption and conspiracy, the *Lugar* holding seems to subject any litigant, acting in good faith under presumptively valid laws, to a successful federal civil rights action for damages if a court subsequently determines that the requested judicial action violated the Constitution. One way of looking at this case is that, in general, only the state can use violence to seize property. If the creditor uses the state powers to seize the debtor's property, that is state action. In some cases, the creditor can use self-help that does not involve violence, such as seizing the car without the help of a sheriff when the debtor is in default of a loan secured by the car. In such a case, there is no state action.

The Court followed *Lugar* nine years later in *Edmonson v. Leesville Concrete Co., Inc.* (1991), holding that a private litigant's racially discriminatory use of peremptory challenges to remove potential jurors in a civil trial constituted "state action." Reading *Lugar* as holding that a private litigant's extensive use of state procedures with the overt and significant assistance of state officials constitutes state action, the Court found significant assistance here by the judge in implementing the litigant's racially discriminatory peremptory challenges. The Court went on to conclude that the private litigant's exercise of peremptory challenges was the exercise of a public function. This seems to contradict the *Jackson* Court's limitation of the public function test to "activities that have traditionally been undertaken exclusively by the government," because unhindered choice by private litigants had always been the hallmark of the peremptory challenge procedure in civil cases, justified on grounds of fairness to both litigants. On the other hand, the Court majority said that it is the trial judge who removes the juror, and what a judge does is state action.

Patrick Kelley

See Also

Amendment XIV, Section 1 (Privileges or Immunities)
Amendment XIV, Section 1 (Due Process)
Amendment XIV, Section 1 (Equal Protection)
Amendment XIV, Section 5 (Enforcement)

Suggestions for Further Research

Charles L. Black, *The Supreme Court, 1966 Term— Foreword: "State Action," Equal Protection, and California's Proposition 14*, 81 Harv. L. Rev. 69 (1967)

Erwin Chemerinsky, *Rethinking State Action*, 80 Nw. U. L. Rev. 503 (1985)

1 Charles Fairman, Reconstruction and Reunion 1864–1888 (2010)

Eric Foner, Reconstruction: America's Unfinished Revolution, 1863–1877 (1988)

Robert J. Kaczorowski, The Politics of Judicial Interpretation: The Federal Courts, Department of Justice and Civil Rights, 1866–1876 (1985)

Earl M. Maltz, Civil Rights, the Constitution, and Congress, 1863–1869 (1990)

William E. Nelson, The Fourteenth Amendment: From Political Principle to Judicial Doctrine (1988)

Significant Cases

The Civil Rights Cases, 109 U.S. 3 (1883)
Home Telephone & Telegraph Co. v. City of Los Angeles, 227 U.S. 278 (1913)
Nixon v. Condon, 286 U.S. 73 (1932)
Smith v. Allwright, 321 U.S. 649 (1944)
Marsh v. Alabama, 326 U.S. 501 (1946)
Shelley v. Kraemer, 334 U.S. 1 (1948)
Terry v. Adams, 345 U.S. 461 (1953)

Burton v. Wilmington Parking Authority, 365 U.S. 715 (1961)
Monroe v. Pape, 365 U.S. 167 (1961)
Evans v. Newton, 382 U.S. 296 (1966)
Katzenbach v. Morgan, 384 U.S. 641 (1966)
Romer v. Evans, 517 U.S. 620 (1996)
United States v. Guest, 383 U.S. 745 (1966)
Reitman v. Mulkey, 387 U.S. 369 (1967)
Evans v. Abney, 396 U.S. 435 (1970)
James v. Valtierra, 402 U.S. 137 (1971)
Moose Lodge No. 107 v. Irvis, 407 U.S. 163 (1972)
Jackson v. Metropolitan Edison Co., 419 U.S. 345 (1974)
Hudgens v. National Labor Relations Bd., 424 U.S. 507 (1976)
Flagg Bros., Inc. v. Brooks, 436 U.S. 149 (1978)
Dennis v. Sparks, 449 U.S. 24 (1980)
Blum v. Yaretsky, 457 U.S. 991 (1982)
Lugar v. Edmondson Oil Co., 457 U.S. 922 (1982)
San Francisco Arts & Athletics v. United States Olympic Committee, 483 U.S. 522 (1987)
National Collegiate Athletic Ass'n v. Tarkanian, 488 U.S. 179 (1988)
Edmonson v. Leesville Concrete Co., Inc., 500 U.S. 614 (1991)
United States v. Morrison, 529 U.S. 598 (2000)
Brentwood Academy v. Tennessee Secondary School Athletic Ass'n, 531 U.S. 288 (2001)

Privileges or Immunities

No State shall make or enforce any law which shall abridge the privileges or immunities of citizens of the United States ...
(Amendment XIV, Section 1)

$\sim$

*A*lthough there is no agreement concerning a single original meaning of the Privileges or Immunities Clause, it is possible to identify three distinct, plausible, and credible original understandings. This essay first describes in general terms the nature of the disagreement, and then discusses in more detail the contending interpretations.

The initial division of opinion is whether the Privileges or Immunities Clause was intended simply to require the states to make their laws apply equally to all their citizens or to mandate a certain substantive content to state law. The equality argument reads the clause to say nothing about the content of a state's law; rather, it simply says that whatever the content of a state's law, it must be the same for all citizens. The substantive argument reads the clause to mandate certain content in state law—to prescribe a substantive package of entitlements under state law known as the privileges or immunities attaching to federal citizenship.

The substantive view is subdivided into two versions of the substance of the privileges and immunities of federal citizenship. The first view holds that these privileges or immunities consist of all of the rights and liberties contained in the Constitution, a category that includes such enumerated rights as habeas corpus and the protection against ex post facto legislation or bills of attainder, but, more importantly, the Bill of Rights, that is to say, the first eight amendments. Under this view, the principal, but not exclusive, function of the Privileges or Immunities Clause was to make the entire Bill of Rights binding on the states. This view is influenced by John Locke's view of natural rights and holds that the privileges and immunities of national citizenship are the natural rights of property and liberty possessed by free persons upon creation of government but never ceded to government. A variant of this view is the contention that the clause was intended to do nothing more than to make the Bill of Rights, and only the Bill of Rights, applicable to the states. The reason that it is so difficult to determine with confidence the original meaning of the Privileges or Immunities Clause is that the statements of proponents of the clause in the Thirty-ninth Congress, particularly Representative John A. Bingham of Ohio, were vague and sometimes inconsistent regarding the intended effect of the clause. Historical evidence outside the congressional debates is also inconclusive. Although each of the three plausible original understandings will be discussed, it is useful to begin with some common historical background.

A central focus of the Thirty-ninth Congress, the body that drafted and proposed the Fourteenth Amendment, was to protect newly emancipated slaves from discriminatory state laws, especially the "Black Codes," which severely limited the civil and political rights of African-Americans. The first effort in that direction was the Civil Rights Act of 1866, Section 1, which declared "all persons born in the United States and not subject to any foreign power, excluding Indians not taxed," to be United States citizens and provided that all

> citizens, of every race and color, without regard to previous condition of slavery...shall have the same right, in every State or Territory in the United States, to make and enforce contracts, to sue, be parties, and give evidence, to inherit, purchase, lease, sell, hold, and convey real and personal property, and to full and equal benefit of all laws...for the security of persons and property, as is enjoyed by white citizens...

Because some supporters of the Civil Rights Act were concerned that Congress lacked constitutional authority to enact the law, Representative Bingham proposed a constitutional amendment that was a precursor to the Fourteenth Amendment. Bingham's proposed amendment gave Congress "power to make all laws which shall be necessary and proper to secure to the citizens of each State all privileges and immunities of citizens in the several States." Bingham's proposal was tabled because it did not go far enough. All it purported to do was to give Congress the power to provide by federal law "that no State shall discriminate between its citizens and give one class of citizens greater rights than it confers upon another," but it failed to bar the states directly (without such federal legislation) from excluding "any class of citizens in any State from the privileges which other classes enjoy." In its stead, the Fourteenth Amendment was proposed, but the Fourteenth Amendment addressed a number of important practical problems associated with Reconstruction, only one of which was the absence of authority for the 1866 Civil Rights Act.

Even though the text of the clause suggests substantive content to the privileges or immunities of national citizenship, the historical context credibly suggests that the clause may have been intended to require the states to make their laws, whatever their content, apply equally to all their citizens, rather than to proscribe or prescribe state law in any particular substantive manner.

The argument for the equality view is partly historical and partly textual and makes the following contentions. First, the Citizenship Clause of Section 1, which immediately precedes the Privileges or Immunities Clause, defines both national and state citizenship. Because a citizen of the nation is a citizen of a state (unless he resides abroad), the privileges or immunities of national citizenship necessarily include the privileges or immunities of state citizenship. Second, because both the Equal Protection and Due Process Clauses extend protection to all persons within a state's jurisdiction (rather than just citizens), the reference to "citizens" in the Privileges or Immunities Clause is best understood as a reference to a particular group of individuals rather than a reference to a particular set of rights. Third, although the debate in the Thirty-ninth Congress is not a model of clarity, it contains ample suggestions that many members of Congress thought abridgement of a citizen's privileges or immunities consisted of state "legislation discriminating against classes of citizens" or that gave "one man...more rights upon the face of the laws than another man." Fourth, as a result of prior interpretation of the Privileges and Immunities Clause of Article IV, Section 2, the drafters of the Fourteenth Amendment understood that the privileges and immunities of state citizenship were rights derived from state law, and understood that the function of the Privileges and Immunities Clause of Article IV was to ensure that states treated citizens of other states equally with their own citizens with respect to the privileges and immunities of state citizenship. Finally, when Congress debated adoption of what ultimately became the Civil Rights Act of 1875, which forbade private racial discrimination by persons already subject to a legal duty to serve the public indiscriminately, members of Congress grounded that proposed legislation in the Privileges or Immunities Clause of the Fourteenth Amendment.

The idea that the privileges or immunities of national citizenship included substantive rights secured by the Constitution, especially those contained in the Bill of Rights, was partly grounded in the text of the clause, and partly in the comments of certain proponents of the Privileges or Immunities Clause, particularly Bingham, who repeatedly declared that "the privileges and immunities of citizens of the United States...are chiefly defined in the first eight amendments to the Constitution." To be sure, Bingham was, in the words of one modern commentator, a "gasbag" who frequently failed to articulate the constitutional analysis underlying his pronouncements, and that failing has led many subsequent commentators to deride Bingham as "befuddled," "confused," and "distinguished for elocution but not for hard thinking."

This point of view was most notably expressed by historian Charles Fairman and by Justice Felix Frankfurter in his concurring opinion in *Adamson v. California* (1947). Fairman and Frankfurter argued that incorporation of the Bill of Rights would have immediately invalidated numerous practices of the states and that there was neither any indication that the framers of the clause expected this to happen nor any movement, after ratification of the Fourteenth Amendment, to alter such local practices to comply with the Bill of Rights.

Yet despite this dissonance and Bingham's failings as an articulate analyst, later interpreters of the record have argued that it was, indeed, the intention of the framers of the clause to make the Bill of Rights, along with all other rights associated with national citizenship, binding on the states. These commentators argue that such an intention was entirely consistent with the antebellum antislavery view of the Constitution, comports with the clause's textual suggestion of substantive content, and reflects the framers' lack of concern with or ignorance of incipient conflict between local practices and the demands of the Bill of Rights. On the other hand, subsequent to ratification, Congress approved new state constitutions from the reconstructed states that contained provisions that conflicted with the federal Bill of Rights.

The other substantive conception of the Privileges or Immunities Clause is that it secures a bundle of natural rights of property and liberty, rights possessed by people in the abstract state of nature prior to their voluntary cession of some of these rights to secure the order and stability afforded by government. This reading is based primarily on the fact that, at the time the Privileges or Immunities Clause was proposed and ratified, the Privileges and Immunities Clause of Article IV, which requires states to afford the citizens of other states the same privileges and immunities they extend to their own citizens, had been read in a dictum by Justice Bushrod Washington as securing "those privileges and immunities which are, in their nature, fundamental; which belong, of right, to the citizens of all free governments; and which have, at all times, been enjoyed by the citizens of the several states . . . from the time of their becoming free, independent, and sovereign." *Corfield v. Coryell* (1823). Justice Washington had summarized those rights as "[p]rotection by the government; the enjoyment of life and liberty, with the right to acquire and possess property of every kind, and to pursue and obtain happiness and safety; subject nevertheless to such restraints as the government may justly prescribe for the general good of the whole." This reading of the Privileges or Immunities Clause is consistent with the framers' concern, manifested in the 1866 Civil Rights Act, to secure important fundamental rights for all citizens on a racially nondiscriminatory basis, but this reading goes well beyond that immediate objective by suggesting that states lack the power to enact laws that offend the fundamental rights identified by Justice Washington. This view was echoed most forcefully by Justice Stephen J. Field in his dissent to *The Slaughter-House Cases* (1873), and, to a lesser extent, by Justice Joseph P. Bradley in his dissent to the same decision. For these two justices, the Privileges and Immunities Clause of Article IV contained substantive protections that were carried over into the Privileges or Immunities Clause of the

Fourteenth Amendment. (*See* Article IV, Section 2, Clause 1.) Field also adopted the equality rationale of the clause as well, and Bradley an incorporationist view.

Nonetheless, the clause was effectively stripped of any meaningful substance by the Supreme Court's decision in *The Slaughter-House Cases*. The majority, in an opinion written by Justice Samuel F. Miller, concluded that the privileges or immunities of national citizenship were, indeed, substantive, but that they consisted of rights "which owe their existence to the Federal government, its National character, its Constitution, or its laws." The Court offered examples of these rights: the right "to come to the seat of government . . . the right of free access to its seaports . . . to the subtreasuries, land offices, and courts of justice in the several States . . . to demand the care and protection of the Federal government . . . when on the high seas or within the jurisdiction of a foreign government . . . to peaceably assemble and petition for redress of grievances, the privilege of the writ of habeas corpus . . . [t]he right to use the navigable waters, [and the right to] become a Citizen of any State of the Union by a bona fide residence therein, with the same rights as other citizens of that State."

Notably absent from these distinctively national rights were the fundamental natural rights identified by Justice Washington in *Corfield v. Coryell* and the rights secured by the Bill of Rights. Because each state has its own bill of rights in its state constitution, the Court found it unthinkable that the Privileges or Immunities Clause could have been intended "to transfer the security and protection of . . . civil rights . . . from the States to the Federal government," or "to bring within the power of Congress the entire domain of civil rights heretofore belonging exclusively to the States." Such a change, said the Court, "would constitute this court a perpetual censor upon all legislation of the States," and "[w]e are convinced that no such results were intended."

It should be noted that whatever might have been the true original meaning of the clause, no scholar has accepted Justice Miller's crabbed notion of privileges or immunities as reflecting its original understanding.

After *Slaughter-House*, the Privileges or Immunities Clause became a virtual dead letter. The equality function of the clause, much altered in character, was assumed by the Equal Protection Clause, and the substantive functions, again altered, were assumed by the Due Process Clause. Both of these clauses of the Fourteenth Amendment applies to "persons," whereas the Privileges or Immunities Clause is limited to "citizens." Indeed, except for *Colgate v. Harvey* (1935), overruled five years later in *Madden v. Commonwealth of Kentucky* (1940), the Supreme Court did not rely on that clause as the basis for any decision until 1999, when it decided *Saenz v. Roe* (1999). In *Saenz*, the Court struck down a California law that set welfare benefits for new residents and citizens of California at the level provided by their former state for the first year of their California residency. The Court concluded that one aspect of the right of travel, the right of new state citizens "to be treated like other citizens of that State," is one of the privileges or immunities of national citizenship.

In 2010, four justices of the Supreme Court ruled, in *McDonald v. City of Chicago*, that the Second Amendment right to possess a firearm for purposes of self-defense was so fundamental and deeply rooted in our national history and tradition that it was incorporated into the Fourteenth Amendment's due process clause, thus making the right applicable to the states. Justice Clarence Thomas provided the crucial fifth vote by his concurrence in the judgment, but his rationale was that the privileges and immunities of American citizens included the rights identified in the Bill of Rights. Justice Thomas marshaled historical evidence to conclude that "the most likely public understanding" of the Fourteenth Amendment's Privileges or Immunities Clause "at the time it was adopted" was that it protected "constitutionally enumerated rights, including the right to keep and bear arms." Justice Thomas has thus endorsed the more limited substantive view of the clause—that it protects the rights guaranteed by the Bill of Rights and other explicitly enumerated constitutional rights. As yet, he is the only justice to embrace this view.

Calvin Massey

See Also

Article IV, Section 2, Clause 1 (Privileges and Immunities)

Amendment XIV, Section 1 (Due Process)

Amendment XIV, Section 1 (Equal Protection)

Suggestions for Further Research

Akhil Reed Amar, The Bill of Rights: Creation and Reconstruction (1998)

Raoul Berger, Government by Judiciary: The Transformation of the Fourteenth Amendment (1997)

James E. Bond, No Easy Walk to Freedom: Reconstruction and the Ratification of the Fourteenth Amendment (1997)

Steven G. Calabresi & Sarah E. Agudo, *Individual Rights Under State Constitutions When the Fourteenth Amendment Was Ratified in 1868: What Rights Are Deeply Rooted in American History and Tradition?* 87 Texas L. Rev. 7 (2008)

2 William Crosskey, Politics and the Constitution in the History of the United States (1953)

David P. Currie, The Constitution in the Supreme Court: The First Hundred Years, 1789–1888 (1985)

Michael Kent Curtis, No State Shall Abridge: The Fourteenth Amendment and the Bill of Rights (1986)

Charles Fairman, *Does the Fourteenth Amendment Incorporate the Bill of Rights?*, 2 Stan. L. Rev. 5 (1949)

John Harrison, *Reconstructing the Privileges or Immunities Clause*, 101 Yale L.J. 1385 (1992)

Kurt T. Lash, *The Fourteenth Amendment and the Bill of Rights: Beyond Incorporation*, 18 J. Contemp. Legal Issues 447 (2009)

Kurt T. Lash, *The Origins of the Privileges or Immunities Clause, Part I: "Privileges and Immunities" as an Antebellum Term of Art*, 98 Geo. L.J. 1241 (2010)

Kurt T. Lash, *The Origins of the Privileges or Immunities Clause, Part II: John Bingham and the Second Draft of the Fourteenth Amendment*, 99 Geo. L. J. 329 (2011)

Kurt T. Lash, *The Origins of the Privileges or Immunities Clause, Part III: Andrew Johnson and the Constitutional Referendum of 1866*, 101 Geo. L.J. 1275 (2013)

Earl M. Maltz, Civil Rights, the Constitution, and Congress, 1863–1869 (1990)

Bernard H. Siegan, The Supreme Court's Constitution: An Inquiry into Judicial Review and Its Impact on Society (1987)

Significant Cases

Corfield v. Coryell, 6 F. Cas. 546 (C.C.E.D. Pa. 1823) (No. 3230)

The Slaughter-House Cases, 83 U.S. (16 Wall.) 36 (1873)

Colgate v. Harvey, 296 U.S. 404 (1935)

Madden v. Commonwealth of Kentucky, 309 U.S. 83 (1940)

Adamson v. California, 332 U.S. 46 (1947)

Saenz v. Roe, 526 U.S. 489 (1999)

McDonald v. City of Chicago, 130 S. Ct. 3020 (2010)

Due Process Clause

…nor shall any State deprive any person of life, liberty, or property, without due process of law….
(Amendment XIV, Section 1)

~

*B*oth the Fifth Amendment and the Fourteenth Amendment to the Constitution prohibit governmental deprivations of "life, liberty, or property, without due process of law." The Due Process Clause of the Fourteenth Amendment serves three distinct functions in modern constitutional doctrine, in the words of the Supreme Court in 1986: "First, it incorporates [against the States] specific protections defined in the Bill of Rights…Second, it contains a substantive component, sometimes referred to as 'substantive due process'…Third, it is a guarantee of fair procedure, sometimes referred to as 'procedural due process'…" *Daniels v. Williams* (1986) (Stevens, J., concurring).

Modern law interprets the Fifth and Fourteenth Amendments to impose the same substantive due process and procedural due process requirements on the federal and state governments. The doctrine of procedural due process under both amendments, as well as the definition of "life, liberty, or property" as the range of

interests protected by the respective Due Process Clauses, is addressed in more detail in the essay on Due Process in the Fifth Amendment. This essay will address substantive due process and the use of the Fourteenth Amendment's Due Process Clause as a vehicle for incorporating selected provisions of the Bill of Rights against the states.

To understand the Fourteenth Amendment's Due Process Clause, one must start with the Fifth Amendment's Due Process Clause, from which the language of the Fourteenth Amendment's provision was drawn nearly verbatim. Although the phrase "due process of law" first appeared in the fourteenth century with a very narrow and technical meaning involving the service of appropriate writs, the American Founding generation likely identified the Fifth Amendment's Due Process Clause with the clauses, prevalent in state constitutions in 1791, that required governmental deprivations of life, liberty, or property to conform to "the law of the land," as well as appropriate notice and ability to defend oneself in court.

There are certain respects in which "due process of law," understood as equivalent to "the law of the land," uncontroversially regulates the substance of governmental action. Most obviously, the core meaning of "law of the land" provisions, dating back to the Magna Carta, is to secure the principle of legality by ensuring that executive and judicial deprivations are grounded in valid legal authority. In this respect, the Fifth Amendment's Due Process Clause limits the substance of executive or judicial action by requiring it to be grounded in law.

The term "substantive due process" as used in modern discourse conventionally does not refer to the principle of legality or limitations on Congress's power to prescribe novel adjudicatory procedures for the deprivation of life, liberty, or property. Instead, it generally refers to limitations on the substance of legislation (other than legislation that seeks to alter the procedural aspect of "due process of law"). Few constitutional doctrines generate more heat than substantive due process. Many scholars doubt whether there is any legitimate doctrine of substantive due process, and there is a dispute among those who advocate some form of substantive due process about the scope and content of that doctrine.

Many advocates of substantive due process openly eschew any reliance on original meaning as support for their position, but some do find an originalist warrant in the doctrine. Originalist defenders of substantive due process emphasize the Due Process Clause's links to "law of the land" provisions and the likely eighteenth-century American understanding of those provisions. Americans were familiar with, and influenced by, the writings of English judges and legal scholars such as Sir Edward Coke and Sir William Blackstone. In the seventeenth century, Coke sought to check the arbitrary rule of the Stuart monarchs by emphasizing that the "law of the land" clause in the Magna Carta encompassed both procedural safeguards and substantive limitations on the power of government; monopoly grants, according to Coke, were invalid as contrary to "the law of the land." Scholars have debated whether Coke's understanding of the Magna Carta was correct, but there is no doubt that his views markedly influenced constitutional development in the American colonies. Blackstone, in his widely read and influential *Commentaries on the Laws of England* (1765–1769), also discussed the Magna Carta's "law of the land" provision in terms of both procedure and substance. Thus, some have argued, founding-era persons conversant with Blackstone and Coke would be disposed to a broad reading of "law of the land" provisions so as to place certain fundamental rights beyond the reach of government, and the Fifth Amendment's Due Process Clause, and therefore the Fourteenth Amendment's Due Process Clause, are best understood as part of this "law of the land" tradition.

Skeptics of substantive due process counter on several levels. First, they respond that British traditions of restraints on royal power do not readily translate into American constitutional restraints on congressional power. Second, they say that most of the substantive concerns voiced by pre-1791 writers are addressed by provisions written into the Constitution rather than the Due Process Clause, such as the Fifth Amendment's Takings Clause and the original Constitution's Ex Post Facto, Bill of Attainder, and Necessary and Proper Clauses. The skeptics maintain that there is no reason to force those substantive concerns into the unpromising language of "due process of law." Third, they argue that attempts to draw too close a linkage between the Due Process Clause and broadly and substantively construed "law of the land" provisions run headlong into the Supremacy Clause, which declares that all valid congressional statutes are, in fact, the "supreme Law of the Land." On balance, say the critics of substantive due process, the phrase "due process of law" is best read as compelling the government to act according to traditional modes of procedure ("due process") and pursuant to valid legal authorization ("of law").

The scope of the Due Process Clause was not a serious topic of discussion in the decades immediately after the Founding. The Supreme Court did not decide a case squarely involving the Fifth Amendment due process guarantee until the infamous *Dred Scott v. Sandford* decision in 1857. Even so, the use of the Due Process Clause in that case was brief and cryptic: the Court said only that a statute that effectively frees any slave brought by his or her master into federal territory "could hardly be dignified with the name of due process of law."

State courts in the pre–Civil War era dealt more actively with issues of due process. Some courts equated due process with procedural requirements only, whereas others in the antebellum era wrestled with substantive interpretations of due process. State courts early established the principle that transfer of property from one person to another by legislative fiat violated due process. Further, in the landmark case of *Wynehamer v. People* (1856), the New York Court of Appeals struck down a prohibition statute as applied to the sale of liquor owned when the law became effective. Holding that the act constituted a deprivation of property without due process, the Wynehamer court anticipated later doctrinal development by invalidating a generally applicable regulation on due process grounds. Thomas M. Cooley, in his influential work, *A Treatise on the Constitutional Limitations Which Rest Upon the Legislative Power of the States of the American Union* (1868), insisted that due process was not satisfied merely by any duly enacted legislation.

Rather, he argued that due process was not simply procedural but limited the legislature from violating fundamental constitutional values.

In 1868, the Fourteenth Amendment was added to the Constitution, and since that time, historians have debated what the intentions of the framers and ratifiers of the amendment were. Clearly the amendment was designed to extend protection to the newly freed slaves against mistreatment by the states. Some thought that the Bill of Rights' guarantees would now limit the states through the Privileges or Immunities Clause. A few, like Justice Joseph P. Bradley, thought that whatever "due process of law" meant in 1791, by 1868 it clearly signaled substantive restraints on legislation. Yet others no doubt believed that the Fourteenth Amendment's Due Process Clause had precisely the same meaning as the Fifth Amendment's Due Process Clause, so that if there was no legitimate doctrine of substantive due process under the latter, there could not be any such doctrine under the former either.

The Supreme Court at first construed narrowly the due process requirement of the Fourteenth Amendment. It adhered to the view that the Bill of Rights was not extended to the states by virtue of that amendment. It further held that the Due Process Clauses in the Fifth and Fourteenth Amendments had the same meaning, so that substantive due process under the two provisions had to stand or fall together. Disagreeing with the majority, Justice John M. Harlan argued that the Due Process Clause of the Fourteenth Amendment created a national standard of rights. And Justice Stephen J. Field forcefully maintained that the Due Process Clause protected the right to pursue lawful trades and contractual freedom from abridgement by the states. Field's understanding of the Fourteenth Amendment gained ground on the Supreme Court in the late nineteenth century.

Under Chief Justice Melville W. Fuller, the Court relied on substantive due process to uphold a variety of economic rights. In a line of cases, the Court held that under due process, regulated industries were entitled to charge reasonable rates. The justices ruled in *Allgeyer v. Louisiana* (1897) that the right to make contracts was a liberty interest protected by the Due Process Clause, thereby establishing the liberty of contract doctrine. In the seminal case of *Lochner v. New York* (1905), the Court invoked due process to strike down a state law regulating the hours of work in bakeries as an interference with contractual freedom. Building on the liberty of contract principle, the Court later determined in *Adkins v. Children's Hospital of D.C.* (1923) that a minimum wage law for women violated due process. The Court also relied on substantive due process to safeguard other types of fundamental rights not enumerated in the Constitution. For example, *Pierce v. Society of Sisters* (1925) affirmed the right of parents to control the education of their children.

The political triumph of the New Deal and the resulting constitutional revolution of 1937 transformed the interpretation of the Due Process Clause. The Supreme Court signaled its rejection of substantive due process as a basis on which to review economic legislation in *West Coast Hotel Co. v. Parrish* (1937). Until this point state and federal courts had not carefully differentiated between the procedural and substantive components of due process. As the unitary understanding of due process shattered, judges began in the 1940s to employ the term "substantive due process" for the first time.

The Court further downplayed the rights of property owners in *United States v. Carolene Products Co.* (1938) by holding that economic regulations would not be found to violate the Due Process Clause so long as they satisfied a minimal "rational basis" test. Conversely, the Court indicated that other rights deemed fundamental would receive heightened scrutiny. It is difficult to reconcile *Carolene Products* with the language of the Due Process Clause, which draws no distinction between the right to property and other personal rights, especially because the Framers of the Constitution and Bill of Rights closely identified security of private property with political freedom. The opinion also ranked rights into categories not expressed in the Constitution. Nonetheless, *Carolene Products* virtually eliminated due process review of economic regulations. In any event, scholars and justices steeped in Progressive–New Deal jurisprudence exaggerated the impact of the earlier substantive due process decisions and pictured these cases as examples of unwarranted judicial policy-making. After the mid-1930s, the Supreme Court did not invalidate a regulatory statute on grounds of due process until *BMW of North America, Inc. v. Gore* (1996), which concluded that there was a due process right not to be charged excessive punitive damages. Scholars debate whether the decision is grounded in substantive due process or in the procedural due process principle requiring one to be given fair notice of possible punishment.

Recent scholarship among originalists has sought to rehabilitate the bona fides of the *Lochner* line of cases, noting, for example, that the so-called substantive due process cases sought only to protect property owners from arbitrary deprivations by applying the traditional due process principle of legality.

More controversial has been the Supreme Court's revival of substantive due process to safeguard noneconomic rights that are not set out in the written text of the Constitution. Some modern critics, such as Robert H. Bork, have insisted that due process pertains entirely to matters of procedure, and the Court has gone beyond its function in finding that due process protects certain substantive liberties. Justice Antonin Scalia, in particular, has criticized the inconsistent picking among rights to receive substantive due process protection. In the discovery of new liberties protected by due process, the Court has more recently left behind both the text of the Constitution and historical tradition. These substantive personal rights include the right to marry and a right of privacy that encompasses the right of married couples to use birth-control devices. In *Roe v. Wade* (1973) the Court extended the concept of privacy to cover the right to obtain an abortion. In *Planned Parenthood of Southeastern Pennsylvania v. Casey* (1992), the Court grounded the abortion right in a highly subjective theory of the individual, extending, some observers believe, the principle to protect private homosexual acts in *Lawrence v. Texas* (2003). In striking down part of the federal Defense of Marriage Act that had denied federal benefits to "married" same-sex couples, the Court seemed to extend the principle from *Lawrence*. Justice Anthony Kennedy declared that the federal law violated "basic due process…principles" in that it

was "motivated by an improper animus" against homosexual persons lawfully married under state law. *United States v. Windsor* (2013). On the other hand, earlier in *Washington v. Glucksberg* (1997), the justices held that the Due Process Clause does not encompass an asserted individual liberty to commit an assisted suicide.

Until the ratification of the Fourteenth Amendment, the accepted opinion was that the Bill of Rights restricted only the federal government, a principle affirmed in *Barron v. City of Baltimore* (1833). Some abolitionists thought otherwise, and some think that the Privileges or Immunities Clause of the Fourteenth Amendment was meant to undo *Barron* and apply the Bill of Rights protections (and perhaps others in the Constitution) to the states. In *The Slaughter-House Cases* (1873), the Supreme Court sheared the Privileges or Immunities Clause of any real strength. If there were to be any application to the states of the guarantees found within the Bill of Rights, it would have to come through some other route.

At first, the Court did not "incorporate" rights within the Bill of Rights into the Fourteenth Amendment. Rather, the Court determined that the same right that was protected by the Bill of Rights against federal infringement was also protected against state infringement by the Due Process Clause of the Fourteenth Amendment. Later, Justice Felix Frankfurter would state that the clause had an "independent potency" separate from that of the Bill of Rights.

In *Chicago, Burlington & Quincey Railroad Co. v. Chicago* (1897), the justices unanimously determined that the Due Process Clause required the states to provide just compensation when they acquired private property for public use. Thus, the just compensation principle of the Fifth Amendment became in effect the first provision of the Bill of Rights to be federalized. In *Gitlow v. New York* (1925), the Court similarly suggested that principles of free speech basically identical to those contained in the First Amendment applied to the states by virtue of the Fourteenth Amendment. From the 1940s onward, however, the view that the Fourteenth Amendment's Due Process Clause literally "incorporates" the text of various provisions of the Bill of Rights rapidly gained steam. By the 1960s, what we know today as the "incorporation doctrine" was complete. Under current law, most provisions of the Bill of Rights are deemed applicable to the states in precisely the same manner that they are applicable to the federal government. Notable exceptions to the rule of incorporation are the Fifth Amendment's requirement of indictment by grand jury, the Seventh Amendment's guarantee of jury trial in civil cases, and, perhaps, the Third Amendment. (Similarly, ever since *Bolling v. Sharpe* in 1954, the Fifth Amendment's Due Process Clause has been held to "reverse-incorporate" the Fourteenth Amendment's Equal Protection Clause against the federal government.)

The incorporation doctrine, although settled as law, remains controversial in a number of respects. During the doctrine's formative years in the mid-twentieth century, Justice Hugo L. Black consistently maintained that all of the provisions in the first eight amendments should be deemed incorporated against the states, not simply those that the Court considers to be sufficiently fundamental. *Adamson v. California* (1947). Justice Frankfurter, as noted above, believed that the fundamental rights protected by the Due Process Clause were independent of those in the Bill of Rights, though they may coincide in some instances. The route the Court chose was "selective incorporation," often attributed to Justice Benjamin N. Cardozo's opinion in *Palko v. Connecticut* (1937). Through selective incorporation, the Warren Court brought most of the Bill of Rights into the Fourteenth Amendment, though the selective incorporation doctrine did not restrain some justices from finding additional rights to add that were not in the Bill of Rights.

More recently, in *McDonald v. City of Chicago* (2010), a plurality of the Supreme Court concluded that the Due Process Clause of the Fourteenth Amendment made the Second Amendment right to keep and bear arms applicable to the states. It reasoned that self-defense was a fundamental right entitled to substantive protection. Justice Clarence Thomas, concurring, favored overruling *Slaughter-House* and insisted that the right to bear arms is a privilege of citizenship protected under the Privileges or Immunities Clause.

James W. Ely Jr.

See Also

Amendment V (Due Process)
Amendment XIV, Section 1 (Privileges or Immunities)
Amendment XIV, Section 1 (Equal Protection)

Suggestions for Further Research

Akhil Reed Amar, The Bill of Rights: Creation and Reconstruction (1998)

David E. Bernstein, Rehabilitating Lochner: Defending Individual Rights Against Progressive Reform (2011)

Edward S. Corwin, *The Doctrine of Due Process of Law Before the Civil War*, 24 Harv. L. Rev. 366 (1911)

Barry Cushman, Rethinking the New Deal Court: The Structure of a Constitutional Revolution (1998)

James W. Ely Jr., *The Oxymoron Reconsidered: Myth and Reality in the Origins of Substantive Due Process*, 16 Const. Comm. 315 (1999)

James W. Ely Jr., *The Progressive Era Assault on Individualism and Property Rights*, 29 Soc. Phil. & Pol'y 255 (2012)

Howard Gillman, The Constitution Besieged: The Rise and Demise of Lochner Era Police Powers Jurisprudence (1993)

Herbert Hovenkamp, *The Political Economy of Substantive Due Process*, 40 Stan. L. Rev. 379 (1988)

Kurt T. Lash, *The Origins of the Privileges or Immunities Clause, Part I: "Privileges and Immunities" as an Antebellum Term of Art*, 98 Geo. L.J. 1241 (2010)

Kurt T. Lash, *The Origins of the Privileges or Immunities Clause, Part II: John Bingham and the Second Draft of the Fourteenth Amendment*, 99 Geo. L.J. 329 (2011)

Kurt T. Lash, *The Origins of the Privileges or Immunities Clause, Part III: Andrew Johnson and the Constitutional Referendum of 1866*, 101 Geo. L.J. 1275 (2013)

Earl M. Maltz, *Fourteenth Amendment Concepts in the Antebellum Era*, 32 Am. J. Legal Hist. 305 (1988)

David N. Mayer, Liberty of Contract: Rediscovering A Lost Constitutional Right (2011)

Rodney L. Mott, Due Process of Law (1926)

Michael J. Phillips, *The Slow Return of Economic Substantive Due Process*, 49 Syracuse L. Rev. 917 (1999)

Robert E. Riggs, *Substantive Due Process in 1791*, 1990 Wis. L. Rev. 941 (1990)

Ryan C. Williams, *The One and Only Substantive Due Process Clause*, 120 Yale L.J. 408 (2010)

Significant Cases

Calder v. Bull, 3 U.S. (3 Dall.) 386 (1798)

Barron v. City of Baltimore, 32 U.S. (7 Pet.) 243 (1833)

Murray's Lessee v. Hoboken Land & Improvement Co., 59 U.S. (18 How.) 272 (1856)

Wynehamer v. People, 13 N.Y. 378 (1856)

Dred Scott v. Sandford, 60 U.S. (19 How.) 393 (1857)

The Slaughter-House Cases, 83 U.S. (16 Wall.) 36 (1873)

Munn v. Illinois, 94 U.S. 113 (1877)

Hurtado v. California, 110 U.S. 516 (1884)

Mugler v. Kansas, 123 U.S. 623 (1887)

Allgeyer v. Louisiana, 165 U.S. 578 (1897)

Chicago, Burlington & Quincey R.R. Co. v. Chicago, 166 U.S. 226 (1897)

Lochner v. New York, 198 U.S. 45 (1905)

Muller v. Oregon, 208 U.S. 412 (1908)

Bunting v. Oregon, 243 U.S. 426 (1917)

Adkins v. Children's Hospital of D.C., 261 U.S. 525 (1923)

Meyer v. State of Nebraska, 262 U.S. 390 (1923)

Gitlow v. New York, 268 U.S. 652 (1925)

Pierce v. Society of Sisters, 268 U.S. 510 (1925)

Nebbia v. New York, 291 U.S. 502 (1934)

Palko v. Connecticut, 302 U.S. 319 (1937)

West Coast Hotel Co. v. Parrish, 300 U.S. 379 (1937)

United States v. Carolene Products Co., 304 U.S. 144 (1938)

Adamson v. California, 332 U.S. 46 (1947)

In re Oliver, 333 U.S. 257 (1948)

Rochin v. California, 342 U.S. 165 (1952)

Bolling v. Sharpe, 347 U.S. 497 (1954)

Williamson v. Lee Optical Co., 348 U.S. 483 (1955)

Mapp v. Ohio, 367 U.S. 643 (1961)

Gideon v. Wainwright, 372 U.S. 335 (1963)

Malloy v. Hogan, 378 U.S. 1 (1964)

Griswold v. Connecticut, 381 U.S. 479 (1965)

Pointer v. Texas, 380 U.S. 400 (1965)

Klopfer v. North Carolina, 386 U.S. 213 (1967)

Duncan v. Louisiana, 391 U.S. 145 (1968)

Benton v. Maryland, 395 U.S. 784 (1969)

Roe v. Wade, 410 U.S. 113 (1973)

Daniels v. Williams, 474 U.S. 327 (1986)

Planned Parenthood of Southeastern Pennsylvania v. Casey, 505 U.S. 833 (1992)

BMW of North America, Inc. v. Gore, 517 U.S. 559 (1996)

Washington v. Glucksberg, 521 U.S. 702 (1997)

Lawrence v. Texas, 539 U.S. 558 (2003)

Johnson v. California, 543 U.S. 499 (2005)

McDonald v. City of Chicago, 130 S. Ct. 3020 (2010)

United States v. Windsor, 133 S. Ct. 2675 (2013)

Equal Protection

No State shall . . . deny to any person within its jurisdiction the equal protection of the laws.

(**Amendment XIV, Section 1**)

~

*T*he Equal Protection Clause is one of the most litigated and significant provisions in contemporary constitutional law. The meaning of the clause is bound up with the entire drama of the Civil War and Reconstruction and, in particular, with slavery and emancipation. Thus, the Equal Protection Clause can be understood only as an organic part of the Fourteenth Amendment and in the broader context of all the Reconstruction amendments.

Debate on the original understanding of the Equal Protection Clause became intense in modern times after the Supreme Court ordered briefing and re-argument on the question in *Brown v. Board of Education* (1954), the school desegregation case. Scholarly debate on the original intention of the Equal Protection Clause and, more broadly, on Section 1 of the Fourteenth Amendment, continues to the present day. Controversy centers on two primary questions. The first is how far, or in relation to what rights, did the framers of the amendment intend the command of equality to apply? In other words, equal as to *what*? The second is what does it mean to treat persons equally? In other words, what is *equal* treatment?

Under current Supreme Court doctrine, the scope of equal protection is as broad as governmental action under the State Action doctrine. The command to treat persons equally extends to all actions by the government. Most commentators agree, however, that the intended scope of the Equal Protection Clause was not as broad.

The framers of the Fourteenth Amendment focused primarily on the status of the freed slaves, and debated the command of equal protection primarily in racial terms. Congress had enacted the Civil Rights Act of 1866 largely in response to perceived Southern oppression of the freed slaves, particularly in the form of "Black Codes" enacted in the former Confederate states. John A. Bingham, the primary author of Section 1 of the Fourteenth Amendment, did not believe that Congress had the constitutional authority to enact the Civil Rights Act of 1866, and he therefore intended to provide congressional authority for that enactment by constitutional amendment. When Bingham's version of Section 1 emerged from committee for consideration by the full Congress, it was received primarily as a means of legitimizing the 1866 Civil Rights Act. At a minimum, the framers intended that the command of equal protection apply to the rights protected by the Civil Rights Act of 1866, which provided for the "same right":

> [T]o make and enforce contracts, to sue, be parties, and give evidence, to inherit, purchase, lease, sell, hold, and convey real and personal property, and to full and equal benefit of all laws and proceedings for the security of person and property...and shall be subject to like punishment, pains, and penalties, and to none other....

The methodology of the first section of the Civil Rights Act was to define national citizenship and to declare that all citizens, "of every race and color," should have the same benefit of the listed rights "as is enjoyed by white citizens." The language of Section 1 of the Fourteenth Amendment, by contrast, can be read to distinguish between citizenship rights protected by the Privileges or Immunities Clause and personhood rights protected by the Due Process and Equal Protection Clauses. Once the Supreme Court gutted the Privileges or Immunities Clause of the Fourteenth Amendment in *The Slaughter-House Cases*, the Equal Protection Clause became the primary bulwark supporting the constitutionality of the Civil Rights Act and providing for the enforcement of its listed rights.

The framers' jurisprudence tended to lump together rights flowing from citizenship and personhood under the rubric of "civil rights," and to speak of them in religious or natural law and natural rights terms. In Section 1 of the Fourteenth Amendment, the framers attempted to create a legal bridge between their understanding of the Declaration of Independence, with its declarations of universal equality and rights endowed by a Creator God, and constitutional jurisprudence. However, the framers also prized federalism—although not in the absolutist sense of the Southern secessionists. Antislavery activists themselves had at times relied on state authority to resist federal policies protective of slavery and so shared that era's common mistrust of centralized authority. The Fourteenth Amendment's compromise between federal enforcement of civil rights and the maintenance of significant state authority has remained in tension since the amendment's ratification.

The rhetoric of the time distinguished civil equality from two other kinds of possible equality: political and social. The framers of the Fourteenth Amendment chose not to include political rights (such as the right to vote, which the Fifteenth Amendment would later address) and social rights within the protections of the Fourteenth Amendment. The Fourteenth Amendment, including its then more prominent sections regarding representation and the political exclusion of certain former Confederates, was part of the Republican Party's Reconstruction program during the critical 1866 election. The program was popular because of its perceived moderation by Northern opinion of the time, which was generally negative or ambivalent in regard to political and social equality for African-Americans. After achieving political success in the 1866 election, Republicans became bolder, enacting the Fifteenth Amendment, explicitly protecting the right to vote. However, the very passage of the Fifteenth Amendment indicates that voting rights were insufficiently protected by the Fourteenth Amendment.

The Equal Protection Clause burst into new prominence in the mid-twentieth century with the Court's decision in *Brown v. Board of Education*, invalidating segregated public education and signaling the end of the "separate but equal" doctrine of *Plessy v. Ferguson* (1896). The question of whether *Brown* was consonant with the original intent of the framers of the clause is the subject of much debate. Some scholars view the provision (and integration) of education as local, social, or political in nature, and hence as beyond the original scope of the Fourteenth Amendment. Others would point to post-1866 Republican efforts to desegregate schools as evidence that *Brown* is a plausible interpretation of the framers' intent. Antislavery rhetoric had been critical of Southern laws that outlawed basic education for slaves, and thus provision of education for the freed slaves would have been important to the framers. Arguably, then, education was neither a political nor a social right, but rather was related to a person's right to the pursuit of happiness, or was a right equipping citizens for their civic responsibilities.

Even if the framers had viewed public accommodations and education as local or social rights not directly protected by the Equal Protection Clause, their sense of racial justice would have opposed the systematic, legally enforced racial caste system that emerged in the 1890s. In fact, in the so-called Ku Klux Klan Act (1871), Congress did attempt to thwart the violent racism that was the harbinger of Jim Crow. In any event, by the time segregation swept the South, it was part of the Jim Crow program to reduce blacks to a status not unlike that imposed by the "Black Codes," which the Fourteenth Amendment was clearly intended to efface. The framers undoubtedly would have recognized that government and private institutions had coalesced to enforce a racial caste system that oppressed African-Americans in a manner inconsistent with the fundamental principle of civil equality. As Justice John M. Harlan famously declared in his dissent in *Plessy v. Ferguson*, "In view of the Constitution, in the eye of the law, there is in this country no superior, dominant, ruling class of citizens. There is no caste here." The comprehensiveness of the racial caste system developed under Jim Crow made the original distinctions between civil, political, and social equality irrelevant, justifying the Court's broad interpretation of the Equal Protection Clause in racial areas as necessary in order to effectuate the clause's comprehensive guarantee of the "equal protection of the laws."

During the era of "separate but equal" jurisprudence, the application of the clause to laws that discriminated on the basis of race was severely, although not entirely, eliminated. At the same time the Court had found the clause applicable to little else beyond race. Although the Equal Protection Clause textually restricted only the states, the principle behind it was also applied to the federal government in *Korematsu v. United States* (1944). Even though the Court used heightened scrutiny when it reviewed governmental action that discriminated against any race, not just African-Americans, the Court did not deem the principle sufficient to stop the internment of Japanese-Americans during World War II. With the clause generally ineffective as to racial matters and applicable to little else, the Equal Protection Clause became, in Justice Oliver Wendell Holmes's words, the "usual last resort of constitutional arguments ...." *Buck v. Bell* (1927).

After the Court resurrected the Equal Protection Clause in regard to racial classifications, it was inevitable that questions would arise as to how the clause would be applied to nonracial classifications. While the history of the clause is focused on race, the language is after all general. This presents a conceptual and practical problem: All laws classify, and all laws make distinctions, leading to a virtually unlimited number of potential Equal Protection challenges. Close judicial review of all classifications to ensure "equal protection of the laws" is a practical impossibility. Although the clause protects all persons, the Court, as a practical matter, cannot give close scrutiny to all classifications that governmental action may create among persons.

Thus, the modern Court developed a two-tiered system of review: (1) strict scrutiny and (2) rational basis. All classifications based on race were subjected to "strict judicial review," and they were thus subjected to a means-end test: the classification must be narrowly tailored to effectuate a compelling governmental interest. The Court determined which governmental interests (ends) were significant enough to be "compelling." As a practical matter, in many cases the government could at least claim to be implementing an end or purpose deemed compelling under the Court's precedents. Therefore the heart of strict scrutiny often rests in the means test.

Means-end testing involves essentially two questions: First, does the governmental action work, meaning does the governmental action actually serve the claimed interest? Second, if it does work, is there an alternative and less "suspect" (i.e., nonracial) classification that would work approximately as well, making use of the racial classification unnecessary to achievement of this goal? Under strict scrutiny, means-end testing involves a kind of public policy "second-guessing" of the legislative branch by the courts. By contrast, non-suspect classifications are presumptively constitutional, and they are therefore reviewed under the very lenient rational basis test, which asks whether the classification is rationally related to a legitimate government interest. Under rational basis review there is generally little second-guessing as to whether the law works, and the analysis of alternatives is irrelevant. The burden is on the complaining party to show that the only purpose of the legislation was entirely arbitrary, irrational, or invidiously discriminatory. *See Railway Express Agency, Inc. v. New York* (1949). Rational basis review has understandably developed into a virtual rubber stamp.

The group of classifications subject to strict scrutiny is very limited: race and its corollaries, such as national origin or ethnic group, and legal alienage, except where the classification is either created by the federal government (which has plenary control over immigration) or excludes aliens from political functions "intimately related to the process of democratic self-government," such as serving as police and probation officers or public school teachers. Alienage classifications operating within the two exceptions are generally reviewed under the lenient rational basis test. Laws that classify based on religion are also subject to strict scrutiny, but that is typically done under the Religion Clauses of the First Amendment.

Beginning in the 1970s, the Court developed a third, intermediate standard of review for two classifications: sex and legitimacy (the distinction between marital and nonmarital children). The test for intermediary scrutiny asks whether the law is substantially related to an important government interest. As to sex, a number of decisions have emphasized that there must be "an exceedingly persuasive justification" for any sex classification. *United States v. Virginia* (1996). Although some interpret this language as implying a creep toward strict scrutiny for sex classifications, officially sex remains subject to intermediary scrutiny.

The Supreme Court has thus far refused to extend "heightened" scrutiny (that is, either strict or intermediary scrutiny) to any other classifications, even though some, such as age, disability, and sexual orientation, are frequently included in antidiscrimination legislation. The Court's occasional decision to invalidate laws employing sensitive classifications, purportedly under the rational basis test, as in *City of Cleburne v. Cleburne Living Center, Inc.* (1985) (mental retardation) and *Romer v. Evans* (1996) (sexual orientation), underscores the Court's reluctance to expand the classifications officially subject to heightened scrutiny. In fact a majority of the Court thus far prefers to rest the protection of same-sex relationships on the basis of due process rather than on equal protection. *Lawrence v. Texas* (2003).

The methodology by which the Court determines which classifications receive heightened scrutiny, beyond that of race, is unclear. Commentators have invoked the classification of "discrete and insular minorities" from the famous footnote four of *United States v. Carolene Products Co.* (1938), but the relevance of that footnote in modern times is hardly certain. Women, for example, are neither minorities nor insular. Justices and commentators have sometimes compared the historical discrimination experienced by African-Americans to that experienced by women, the mentally retarded, the poor, and those with a same-sex sexual orientation, but it is unclear whether there is commensurable scale for measuring tragic histories. In addition, once a classification is made suspect, under current precedents the Court will protect members of the historically favored, as well as historically disfavored, group. For example, the equal protection cases protect "sex," not the female sex. Thus, the Court has invalidated a law that limited a nursing school to women, *Mississippi University for Women v. Hogan* (1982), and a law that allowed women, but not men, to buy alcohol at age 18, *Craig v. Boren*

(1976). Given these difficulties, the Court has not yet developed a single methodology for determining the critical question of which classifications receive heightened scrutiny, nor for choosing between strict and intermediary scrutiny.

The question of affirmative action has spawned much litigation. Under current precedents, all legislative racial classifications are evaluated under strict scrutiny, even if they purport to be positive affirmative action programs favoring racial minorities. Although the primary impetus behind the Fourteenth Amendment (and its Equal Protection Clause) was to protect African-Americans, the framers of the amendment, as noted above, phrased the protection in general terms, and the courts have applied it in that fashion. Thus today, even classifications favoring African-Americans are presumptively unconstitutional absent sufficiently weighty reasons. The courts have held that the protection of all races against discrimination effectuates the broader original purpose of the Equal Protection Clause, which constitutionalized the core concept of personal equality as described in the Declaration of Independence. Thus, the apparent tension between active efforts to promote the progress of racial minority groups and the promise of personal equality for each individual, regardless of race, has been resolved in favor of the latter.

Nonetheless, the Supreme Court has upheld some forms of race-based affirmative action despite the application of strict scrutiny. Thus, the Court has said that racially conscious acts by legislatures, courts, or other state actors will meet strict scrutiny if the racially conscious act rectifies, in a narrowly tailored fashion, a previous governmental violation of equal protection, or—more controversially—if it furthers the compelling interest of racial diversity in a student body in higher education by including race as a positive element in an applicant's profile. *Grutter v. Bollinger* (2003), *Gratz v. Bollinger* (2003). In 2007, however, the Court struck down two secondary school integration programs, voluntarily implemented by school districts, that assigned students to schools partially on the basis of race. *Parents Involved in Community Schools v. Seattle Sch. Dist.* (2007). In 2013, the Court refined its holding in *Grutter*, holding that although a court may show deference to a university's assertion that the *purpose* of its diversity admissions program was "essential to its educational mission," a court may not accord such deference to the *means* the university chose to implement its program. Rather, strict scrutiny requires that the university demonstrate "that each applicant is evaluated as an individual and not in a way that makes an applicant's race or ethnicity the defining feature of his or her application." Further, "the reviewing court must ultimately be satisfied that no workable race-neutral alternative would provide the educational benefits of diversity." *Fisher v. University of Texas at Austin* (2013).

The Equal Protection Clause textually limits only state governments, hence it is literally inapplicable to the federal government. However, the Court has developed the doctrine that the Due Process Clause of the Fifth Amendment has an "equal protection component" with requirements equivalent to those of the Equal Protection Clause of the Fourteenth Amendment. *See, e.g., Bolling v. Sharpe* (1954). Equal protection doctrine (if not literally the Equal Protection Clause) has thus become applicable to all governmental action, whether state, local, or federal. Justice Sandra Day O'Connor summarized the Court's current view in *Adarand Constructors v. Pena* (1995). First, she said, there is skepticism: "[A]ny official action that treats a person differently on account of his race or ethnic origin is inherently suspect." Second, there is consistency: "the standard of review under the Equal Protection Clause is not dependent on the race of those burdened or benefited...." Third, there is congruence: equal protection standards and analysis is the same as applied to both states and the federal government.

David Smolin

See Also

Amendment XIV, Section 1 (Privileges or Immunities)
Amendment XIV, Section 1 (Due Process)
Amendment XV (Suffrage—Race)

Suggestions for Further Research

Raoul Berger, Government by Judiciary: The Transformation of the Fourteenth Amendment (2d ed. 1997)

Alexander M. Bickel, *The Original Understanding and the Segregation Decision*, 69 Harv. L. Rev. 1 (1955)

James E. Bond, No Easy Walk to Freedom: Reconstruction and the Ratification of the Fourteenth Amendment (1997)

John Harrison, *Reconstructing the Privileges or Immunities Clause,* 101 Yale L.J. 1385 (1992)

Harold M. Hyman & William M. Wiecek, Equal Justice Under Law: Constitutional Development, 1835–1875 (1982)

Patrick J. Kelley, *An Alternative Originalist Opinion for* Brown v. Board of Education, 20 S. Ill. U. L.J. 75 (1995)

Michael J. Klarman, *An Interpretive History of Modern Equal Protection,* 90 Mich. L. Rev. 213 (1991)

Earl M. Maltz, Civil Rights, The Constitution, and Congress, 1863–1869 (1990)

Michael W. McConnell, *Originalism and the Desegregation Decisions,* 81 Va. L. Rev. 947 (1995)

William E. Nelson, The Fourteenth Amendment: From Political Principle to Judicial Doctrine (1988)

Significant Cases

Dred Scott v. Sandford, 60 U.S. (19 How.) 393 (1857)

The Slaughter-House Cases, 83 U.S. (16 Wall.) 36 (1873)

Yick Wo v. Hopkins, 118 U.S. 356 (1886)

Plessy v. Ferguson, 163 U.S. 537 (1896)

Buck v. Bell, 274 U.S. 200 (1927)

United States v. Carolene Products Co., 304 U.S. 144 (1938)

Korematsu v. United States, 323 U.S. 214 (1944)

Railway Express Agency, Inc. v. New York, 336 U.S. 106 (1949)

Sweatt v. Painter, 339 U.S. 629 (1950)

Bolling v. Sharpe, 347 U.S. 497 (1954)

Brown v. Board of Education, 347 U.S. 483 (1954)

Williamson v. Lee Optical Co., 348 U.S. 483 (1955)

Craig v. Boren, 429 U.S. 190 (1976)

Mathews v. Diaz, 426 U.S. 67 (1976)

Washington v. Davis, 426 U.S. 229 (1976)

Foley v. Connelie, 435 U.S. 291 (1978)

Regents of the University of California v. Bakke, 438 U.S. 265 (1978)

Mississippi University for Women v. Hogan, 458 U.S. 718 (1982)

Plyler v. Doe, 457 U.S. 202 (1982)

City of Cleburne v. Cleburne Living Center, Inc., 473 U.S. 432 (1985)

City of Richmond v. J. A. Croson, Co., 488 U.S. 469 (1989)

Adarand Constructors, Inc. v. Pena, 515 U.S. 200 (1995)

Romer v. Evans, 517 U.S. 620 (1996)

United States v. Virginia, 518 U.S. 515 (1996)

Vacco v. Quill, 521 U.S. 793 (1997)

Gratz v. Bollinger, 539 U.S. 244 (2003)

Grutter v. Bollinger, 539 U.S. 306 (2003)

Lawrence v. Texas, 539 U.S. 558 (2003)

Parents Involved in Community Schools v. Seattle Sch. Dist., 551 U.S. 701 (2007)

Fisher v. University of Texas at Austin, 133 S. Ct. 2411 (2013)

Apportionment of Representatives

Representatives shall be apportioned among the several States according to their respective numbers, counting the whole number of persons in each State, excluding Indians not taxed. But when the right to vote at any election for the choice of electors for President and Vice-President of the United States, Representatives in Congress, the Executive and Judicial officers of a State, or the members of the Legislature thereof, is denied to any of the male inhabitants of such State, being twenty-one years of age, and citizens of the United States, or in any way abridged, except for participation in rebellion, or other crime, the basis of representation therein shall be reduced in the proportion which the number of such male citizens shall bear to the whole number of male citizens twenty-one years of age in such State.

(Amendment XIV, Section 2)

~

*I*n his speech of April 11, 1865, President Abraham Lincoln described the Southern states that had rebelled in the Civil War as being "out of their proper practical relation with the Union." In setting the terms for the reintegration of those states with the Union, the Reconstruction Congress had to deal with several issues in addition to that of the status of the freedmen: representation in Congress, the political status of high-ranking rebels, and the debts of the United States and Confederate States.

The abolition of slavery increased the political power of the former slave states in the House of Representatives. Under the Three-fifths Clause of the original Constitution (Article I, Section 2, Clause 3), five slaves had counted as three persons; now they would be counted as five persons, though none of the Southern states would have permitted them to vote. Section 2 was a major concern in the South. Paper after paper carried charts showing its impact on Southern representation in Congress. The framers of the Fourteenth Amendment intended Section 2 to encourage the Southern states to enfranchise blacks, without directly compelling them to do so—for few Northern states allowed blacks to vote. Democrats condemned any congressional interference in the traditionally state-controlled matter of voting, and radical Republicans objected to the implicit approval of racial qualifications for voting. Section 2 was, therefore, a compromise position acceptable to the moderate Republicans who held the balance of power in Congress. A state like South Carolina or Mississippi, with a 50 percent black population, would lose half of its seats in the House if Section 2 were invoked. A state like New Hampshire or Michigan, with almost no blacks, would not lose any seats.

Although Section 2 allowed the disenfranchisement of persons who had engaged in the rebellion, none was denied the vote on those grounds. Neither did Congress reduce the representation of any Southern state that restricted the franchise on the basis of race.

The Fifteenth Amendment made Section 2 superfluous concerning "race, color or previous condition of servitude," and Congress never seriously attempted to apply it when Southern states began to disfranchise blacks—largely because such disfranchisement was cast in racially neutral terms. As it turned out, the inability or unwillingness to enforce either Section 2 of the Fourteenth Amendment or the provisions of the Fifteenth Amendment was the Achilles' heel of emancipation in the Reconstruction period and the years that followed because without federal enforcement, blacks were unable to protect themselves through the political

process. In one federal case, a putative candidate for Congress from Virginia sued under Section 2 of the Fourteenth Amendment to compel the state to adopt an at-large electoral system, because the state, by the poll tax, was not entitled to the nine seats that Congress had apportioned to it after the 1940 census. The Court dismissed the suit as a "political question." *Saunders v. Wilkins* (1945).

Despite being written in a particular historical context, Section 2 is still in operation and would apply in future cases of rebellion. By referring to "rebellion, or other crime," it recognizes and makes an exception for purposes of apportionment for states' traditional disfranchisement based on non-race-based criminal conduct. The Supreme Court has inferred from Section 2 that states may disenfranchise convicted felons subsequent to their prison sentences. *Richardson v. Ramirez* (1974).

In *Reynolds v. Sims* (1964), Justice John M. Harlan decried the Court's continuing disregard of Section 2. In dissenting from the Court's adoption of the one person, one vote rule, he stated,

> I am unable to understand the Court's utter disregard of the second section which expressly recognizes the States' power to deny "or in any way" abridge the right of their inhabitants to vote for "the members of the [state] legislature," and its express provision of a remedy for such denial or abridgment.

Justice Harlan was pointing out that there are sufficient political checks available to Congress to correct malapportionment at the state level without the need of judicial intervention.

Nonetheless, the failure of Congress to impose remedies for the South's disenfranchisement of black voters resulted in a larger number of representatives and hence electoral votes than otherwise would have been the case, giving Democratic presidential candidates some advantage.

Paul Moreno

See Also

Suggestions for Further Research

James E. Bond, No Easy Walk to Freedom: Reconstruction and the Ratification of the Fourteenth Amendment (1997)

Horace E. Flack, The Adoption of the Fourteenth Amendment (1908)

Joseph B. James, The Framing of the Fourteenth Amendment (1956)

Virginia Commission on Constitutional Government, The Reconstruction Amendments' Debates: The Legislative History and Contemporary Debates in Congress on the Thirteenth, Fourteenth, and Fifteenth Amendments (Alfred Avins ed., 1967)

Significant Cases

Saunders v. Wilkins, 152 F.2d 235 (4th Cir. 1945)

Reynolds v. Sims, 377 U.S. 533 (1964)

Richardson v. Ramirez, 418 U.S. 24 (1974)

Disqualification for Rebellion

No person shall be a Senator or Representative in Congress, or elector of President and Vice-President, or hold any office, civil or military, under the United States, or under any state, who, having previously taken an oath, as a member of Congress, or as an officer of the United States, or as a member of any State legislature, or as an executive or judicial officer of any state, to support the Constitution of the United States, shall have engaged in insurrection or rebellion against the same, or given aid or comfort to the enemies thereof. But Congress may by a vote of two-thirds of each House, remove such disability.

(Amendment XIV, Section 3)

~

*T*he disqualification of former rebels for federal and state office was the most controversial of the sections of the Fourteenth Amendment. Some called it vindictive. On the other hand, those who had taken a solemn oath to support the United States and had reneged on the oath could, it was argued, justifiably be prevented from simply reassuming positions of authority in the government. Moreover, many former U.S. officials who had joined the Confederacy led the resistance to the passage of Reconstruction legislation and had supported the imposition of the onerous Black Codes on the freedmen. Other objections to the Disqualification Clause asserted that it intruded on the president's pardon power, but obviously a constitutional amendment could modify that previously unlimited power. In any event, Congress might well have thought it prudent to limit President Andrew Johnson's pro-Southern actions.

An earlier draft of the section would have disqualified all who had voluntarily aided the Confederacy until 1870, but the Senate adopted Senator Jacob Howard's less severe but potentially more permanent version. When Jefferson Davis was indicted for treason, his lawyers argued that this provision foreclosed any other punishment. But President Johnson's blanket pardon for all crimes related to the rebellion, on Christmas Day 1868, mooted this point. Congress lifted the disqualification of many individuals, and in 1872 it did so for "all persons whomsoever, except Senators and Representatives of Thirty-sixth [1859–1861] and Thirty-seventh [1861–1863] Congresses, officers in the judicial, military and naval service of the United States, heads of Departments, and foreign ministers of the United States." Act of May 22, 1872, ch. 193, 194, 16 Stat. 142 (1872). In 1898, Congress removed all disqualifications for previous disloyal conduct.

Despite being written in a particular historical context, the clause is still in operation and would still apply in the case of government officers who may participate in insurrection or rebellion, including perhaps terrorist activities.

Paul Moreno

Suggestions for Further Research

James E. Bond, No Easy Walk to Freedom: Reconstruction and the Ratification of the Fourteenth Amendment (1997)

Horace E. Flack, The Adoption of the Fourteenth Amendment (1908)

Joseph B. James, The Framing of the Fourteenth Amendment (1956)

Virginia Commission on Constitutional Government, The Reconstruction Amendments' Debates: The Legislative History and Contemporary Debates in Congress on the Thirteenth, Fourteenth, and Fifteenth Amendments (Alfred Avins ed., 1967)

Debts Incurred During Rebellion

The validity of the public debt of the United States, authorized by law, including debts incurred for payment of pensions and bounties for services in suppressing insurrection or rebellion, shall not be questioned. But neither the United States nor any State shall assume or pay any debt or obligation incurred in aid of insurrection or rebellion against the United States, or any claim for the loss or emancipation of any slave; but all such debts, obligations and claims shall be held illegal and void.

(Amendment XIV, Section 4)

～

*T*he effort to make the national debt sacrosanct and to repudiate the Confederate debt was the least controversial of the sections of the Fourteenth Amendment, at least in the North. As Representative Thaddeus Stevens of Pennsylvania put it, "I need say nothing of the fourth section, for none dare object to it who is not himself a rebel." The only objection to it was from owners of slaves in the loyal slave states who thought they should be compensated.

In applying the section, federal courts held that no contracts involving Confederate bonds could be enforced and that "a court of the United States must hesitate to give them any recognition whatever." Contracts involving Confederate currency, on the other hand, were enforceable "to prevent injustice to people who, when war was

flagrant, had no other currency in which to make the exchanges required in the ordinary business of life." *Branch v. Haas* (1883).

The issue of the repudiation of the United States debt again emerged when Congress took the United States off the gold standard, and some of *The Gold Clause Cases* (1935) involved United States bonds. The Supreme Court did hold that Congress had exceeded its power under the Constitution in refusing to repay the bonds in gold, but it concluded that the bondholders had suffered only nominal damages and could not recover. Although Section 4 "was undoubtedly inspired by the desire to put beyond question the obligations of the Government issued during the Civil War, its language indicates a broader connotation [that embraces] whatever concerns the integrity of the public obligations." *The Gold Clause Cases.*

In fact, scholarly research indicates that the original purpose of the framers of the clause was to place a constitutional bar to any attempt by Congress to repudiate or undo debt obligations that Congress itself has incurred. Default, in others words, is constitutionally prohibited by this clause. Yet in 2011, former President William J. Clinton asserted that the clause had an entirely different meaning. As the Treasury approached its congressionally set debt ceiling, he and other commentators argued that the Fourteenth Amendment's debt clause means that the Treasury does not need congressional authorization to continue to borrow. This clause, they argued, mandates any and all means to avoid defaulting on the public debt. In other words, the president could unilaterally borrow without congressional authorization.

Others responded that Congress's power under the Spending Clause (Article I, Section 8, Clause 1) could not be circumvented in that way. Rather, they asserted that this clause prevents the president and the Congress from threatening default. The clause affirmatively requires that the federal government pay its debts, even if that means that it has to take extraordinary measures to reduce expenditures and borrowing to do so. President Barack Obama indicated that he did not support Clinton's view.

Outside of the Supreme Court's brief consideration of the issue in *The Gold Clause Cases,* the federal courts have shown little interest in fashioning a judicial method for enforcing the limitations required by the clause. At the present time, this clause remains but an historical artifact of the post–Civil War era.

Paul Moreno

See Also

Article I, Section 8, Clause 1 (Spending Clause)
Article VI, Clause 1 (Debt Assumption)

Suggestions for Further Research

Michael Abramowicz, *Beyond Balanced Budgets, Fourteenth Amendment Style*, 33 Tulsa L.J. 561 (1997)

James E. Bond, No Easy Walk to Freedom: Reconstruction and the Ratification of the Fourteenth Amendment (1997)

Horace E. Flack, The Adoption of the Fourteenth Amendment (1908)

Joseph B. James, The Framing of the Fourteenth Amendment (1956)

Virginia Commission on Constitutional Government, The Reconstruction Amendments' Debates: The Legislative History and Contemporary Debates in Congress on the Thirteenth, Fourteenth, and Fifteenth Amendments (Alfred Avins ed., 1967)

Significant Cases

Branch v. Haas, 16 F. 53 (C.C.M.D. Ala. 1883)
The Gold Clause Cases, 294 U.S. 330 (1935)

Enforcement Clause

The Congress shall have the power to enforce, by appropriate legislation, the provisions of this article.
(Amendment XIV, Section 5)

~

*F*ollowing the pattern of the Necessary and Proper Clause of Article I, Section 8, the enforcement clause of the Fourteenth Amendment grants to Congress the power to pass legislation directed at effectuating the provisions of Sections 1 through 4 of the amendment. Like the enforcement clauses of the two other Reconstruction Amendments (the Thirteenth and the Fifteenth), as well as those found in the Nineteenth, Twenty-third, Twenty-fourth, and Twenty-sixth Amendments, Section 5 delegates to Congress a power in addition to those listed in Article I, Section 8, of the Constitution.

One specific purpose of the Fourteenth Amendment when Congress proposed it in 1866 was to ensure that Congress had adequate power to adopt the Civil Rights Act of that year, of which the current 42 U.S.C. § 1981 is a descendant. That act prohibited state legislation—specifically, the notorious "Black Codes"—that denied blacks certain rights afforded to whites, including the power to make and enforce contracts.

A significant limitation in the text of Section 5 is that Congress is authorized only to "enforce, by appropriate legislation" the provisions of the Fourteenth Amendment. Justice William J. Brennan Jr.'s opinion in *Katzenbach v. Morgan* (1966) suggested that Section 5 might also give Congress authority to define the substantive scope of the rest of the Fourteenth Amendment, but this interpretation seems at odds with the text and history of Section 5, and more recent opinions of the Supreme Court have rejected it. As early as 1883 in *The Civil Rights Cases*, the Court declared that because the prohibitions of Section 1 of the amendment reached only actions committed by the state or its agents, Congress was not empowered to legislate against the discriminatory actions of private individuals. More recently, in *City of Boerne v. Flores* (1997), the Court struck down as unconstitutional the Religious Freedom Restoration Act, in which Congress tried to use Section 5 to overturn an earlier Supreme Court decision defining the scope of the Free Exercise Clause with respect to the states. In doing so, the Court explicitly rejected Justice Brennan's suggestion in *Morgan* that Section 5 allows Congress to expand the meaning of the rest of the amendment. Thus, for Congress to invoke its power under Section 5, the proposed legislation must be aimed at remedying or preventing actions that would violate some prohibition within the Fourteenth Amendment.

The legislation cannot be aimed at changing the scope of the amendment.

On the other hand, the Supreme Court has declared that Congress may, as a prophylactic matter, ban state actions that it has found generally to violate the Fourteenth Amendment, even if in some instances they might not. A classic example is the literacy test for voting. *See Oregon v. Mitchell* (1970). In theory, a state could use such a test in a constitutional way, but Congress determined that these tests were so commonly abused that they should be banned across the board, and the Court upheld this ban. The law was aimed at preventing actual and potential violations of the Constitution; it did not change the Constitution's substantive meaning and guarantees.

In *City of Boerne*, the Supreme Court declared that there must be a "proportionality" and "congruence" between the statute "and the legitimate end to be achieved." It follows that, before Congress invokes its Section 5 authority, it must ascertain that the actions it is concerned about do in fact violate the protections within the Fourteenth Amendment and that legislation remedying such violations has a "proportionality" and a "congruence" in accomplishing the remedy. This, in turn, requires a careful analysis of the rest of the Fourteenth Amendment and the scope of its guarantees.

For instance, there must be "state action." Section 5 gives Congress no authority to legislate with respect to the private sector because, the Court has held, there can be no Section 1 violation without state action. *The Civil Rights Cases.* Likewise, with respect to religious discrimination, the state action must amount to intentional discrimination. The Court found in *City of Boerne* that laws that are neutral in text and intention and that have only a disproportionate effect on a religious group are beyond Congress's authority to prohibit. The same kinds of distinctions and limitations apply with respect to other antidiscrimination legislation. For example, because the disabled are not "a suspect classification," state discrimination against the disabled violates the Fourteenth Amendment only if it is "irrational." Thus, the Court has held in *Board of Trustees of the Uni-*

versity of Alabama v. Garrett (2001) that Section 5 gives Congress authority only to ban irrational state employment discrimination against the disabled, although in the closely disputed case of *Tennessee v. Lane* (2004), the Court upheld Congressional abrogation of state sovereign immunity in actions brought under the Americans with Disabilities Act where Congress was seeking to ensure the right of access to the courts for persons with disabilities.

Roger Clegg

See also

Article I, Section 8, Clause 18 (Necessary and Proper Clause)

Amendment XIII, Section 2 (Abolition of Slavery)

Amendment XIV, Sections 1–4

Amendment XV (Suffrage—Race)

Amendment XIX (Suffrage—Sex)

Amendment XXIII (Electors for the District of Columbia)

Amendment XXIV (Poll Taxes)

Amendment XXVI (Suffrage—Age)

Suggestions for Further Research

Alexander M. Bickel, *The Voting Rights Cases*, 1966 Sup. Ct. Rev. 79 (1966)

Robert A. Burt, *Miranda and Title II: A Morganatic Marriage*, 1969 Sup. Ct. Rev. 81 (1969)

Ronald D. Rotunda, *The Powers of Congress Under Section 5 of the Fourteenth Amendment After* City of Boerne v. Flores, 32 Ind. L. Rev. 163 (1998)

J. TenBroek, Equal Under Law (1965)

The Human Life Bill: Hearings on S. 158 before the Subcommittee on Separation of Powers of the Committee on the Judiciary, United States Senate, 97th Cong., 1st Sess. 310 (1982) (statement of Professor Robert H. Bork)

Significant Cases

The Civil Rights Cases, 109 U.S. 3 (1883)

Katzenbach v. Morgan, 384 U.S. 641 (1966)

Oregon v. Mitchell, 400 U.S. 112 (1970)

City of Boerne v. Flores, 521 U.S. 507 (1997)

United States v. Morrison, 529 U.S. 598 (2000)

Bd. of Trustees of the University of Alabama v. Garrett, 531 U.S. 356 (2001)

Tennessee v. Lane, 541 U.S. 509 (2004)

Suffrage—Race

Section 1. The right of citizens of the United States to vote shall not be denied or abridged by the United States or by any State on account of race, color, or previous condition of servitude—
Section 2. The Congress shall have power to enforce this article by appropriate legislation.
(AMENDMENT XV)

~

*P*assed by Congress on March 3, 1869, and ratified in 1870, the Fifteenth Amendment was the last of the three Reconstruction Amendments. Though the language of the Fifteenth Amendment prohibits all race-based discrimination in qualifications for voting, the framers were primarily concerned with the enfranchisement of African-Americans. As early as 1866, many of the Republicans were convinced of the need for a constitutional amendment that would require the states to allow African-Americans to vote. Indeed, at one point the Joint Committee on Reconstruction voted to report a version of the Fourteenth Amendment that explicitly embraced the principle of race-blind suffrage. However, many Northerners continued to oppose black suffrage in principle, and fears of a political backlash led the committee to abandon the issue before the proposed amendment came to the floor. By 1869, the situation had changed. Although the outcome of referenda on black suffrage in the North continued to reflect the opposition of critical swing voters, other factors persuaded mainstream Republicans in Congress of the need for a federal constitutional amendment to deal with the issue.

Republicans had a variety of different reasons for supporting such an amendment. In the Reconstruction Act of 1867, Congress had forced black suffrage on the ex-Confederate states by

statute, and Republicans faced the charge that they were hypocritical in not imposing the same requirement on Northern states. Some also believed that if blacks were enfranchised in the states that had remained in the Union, they would provide critical support for Republican candidates in those states. Still others argued that, even in the South, black suffrage would be insecure without a constitutional amendment and that the governments of the ex-Confederate states could not be returned to local control until the political power of the freed slaves was guaranteed.

By 1869, these considerations, combined with the conviction that allowing blacks to vote was right in itself, convinced virtually all mainstream congressional Republicans that a constitutional amendment was desirable. Republicans were, nevertheless, deeply divided over the question of what precise language should be adopted. Initially, the House of Representatives adopted a proposal quite similar to the current Fifteenth Amendment. However, a number of prominent Republicans complained that this narrow language would allow states intentionally to disfranchise most African-Americans by adopting qualifications that, although neutral on their face, would in practice be impossible for most freed slaves to satisfy. Responding to these and other concerns, the Senate proposed to eliminate not only discrimination on the basis of race, color, and previous condition of servitude but also discrimination on the basis of nativity, property, education, or creed in both the right to vote and the right to hold elective office. In ordinary circumstances, one might have expected a conference committee to have been convened at this point. However, in the complex parliamentary maneuvering that followed, the Senate did not vote to enter into conference; instead, the entire drafting process began again in both houses. The House then produced a draft that tracked the original Senate version, except that it deleted the reference to discrimination on the basis of education. The Senate, by contrast, now passed a simple prohibition on racial discrimination with respect to the rights to vote and hold office. A conference committee was convened, and it produced the current language of the Fifteenth Amendment, which embraced only the prohibition on racial discrimination in voting, omitting any reference to the right to hold office.

In short, because of the difficulty of agreeing to the precise language, the framers adopted a simple prohibition on discrimination on the basis of race, color, and previous condition of servitude even though there was a risk that a court could interpret the language narrowly and thereby allow deliberate evasion by facially neutral statutes. At first, the Supreme Court did exactly that and refused to inquire into the motives of those who adopted facially neutral statutes, such as literacy tests. *Williams v. Mississippi* (1898). Subsequently, the Court took a slightly broader view and voided a grandfather clause, the effect of which was to allow illiterate whites to vote, on the ground that it could have no conceivable purpose other than racial discrimination. *Guinn v. United States* (1915). More recently, the Court has invoked both the Fourteenth and Fifteenth Amendments to invalidate facially neutral restrictions on voting rights where the legislative history reveals an intention to exclude or hinder African-Americans. *Rogers v. Lodge* (1982), *Hunter v. Underwood* (1985). The Court also invoked the amendments in cases where there was evident racial gerrymandering designed to disenfranchise blacks. *Gomillion v. Lightfoot* (1960). On the other hand, the Court has held that race may be considered in the redistricting process only so long as racial considerations do not predominate and there is no effort to dilute the voting strength of minorities. *Bush v. Vera* (1996).

Similarly, the Court adopted variable views on the sweep of congressional authority under the enforcement clause. One critical issue was whether the amendment armed Congress with the power to regulate purely private action. Many of the congressional Republicans, who were responsible for passing the Fifteenth Amendment, apparently believed they had such authority: a section in a statute passed in 1870 made private, racially motivated interference with voting a federal crime. Nonetheless, although *Ex parte Yarbrough* (1884) suggested that this statute was constitutional, in 1903 the

Supreme Court reversed course and held that the Fifteenth Amendment did not allow Congress to regulate purely private activity. *James v. Bowman* (1903). This basic principle was maintained until at least 1941, *United States v. Classic*, although the Court preferred to take the route of expansively defining nongovernmental activity as state action for purposes of the Fifteenth Amendment, applied particularly to the institution of the white primary. *Smith v. Allwright* (1944), *Terry v. Adams* (1953).

Although the legislative history of the Fifteenth Amendment provides little direct guidance on the precise scope of the enforcement authority under Section 2, recent decisions have upheld the constitutionality of sweeping remedial measures adopted to combat government-imposed racial discrimination. For example, when Congress had evidence of widespread racial discrimination in state elections, the Court allowed Congress to place the entire state and local electoral apparatus under federal supervision and to forbid the adoption of measures that had even the effect of diluting the voting power of racial minorities. *Thornburg v. Gingles* (1986). The Court, asserting that enforcement power had the same breadth as a necessary and proper clause, has also upheld the power of Congress to forbid literacy tests. *South Carolina v. Katzenbach* (1966). However in 2009, a majority of the justices suggested that Congress could no longer subject state electoral processes to such intrusive federal supervision unless there was evidence of continuing widespread racial discrimination in those practices. *Northwest Austin Municipal Utility District No. 1 v. Holder* (2009). Morover, in *Shelby County v. Holder* (2013), the Court struck down Section 4 of the Voting Rights Act of 1965, which had required certain states and voting districts to obtain preclearance from the U.S. Department of Justice before putting changes in voting procedures or districting into effect. Chief Justice John Roberts opined that the federal government may not discriminate against the equal sovereignty of the states absent evidence of a violation of federal law. He concluded that the formula that had been established in 1965 to determine which states should be subject to preclearance was outdated and could no longer justify the imposition of that burden on the designated state in the year 2013.

Earl Maltz

See Also

Amendment XIII (Abolition of Slavery)
Amendment XIV, Section 1
Amendment XIX (Suffrage—Sex)
Amendment XXIV (Poll Taxes)
Amendment XXVI (Suffrage—Age)

Suggestions for Further Research

Michael Les Benedict, A Compromise of Principle: Congressional Republicans and Reconstruction 1863–1869 (1974)

James G. Blaine, Twenty Years of Congress: From Lincoln to Garfield with a Review of the Events Which Led to the Political Revolution of 1860 (1884–1886)

LaWanda Cox & John H. Cox, *Negro Suffrage and Republican Politics: The Problem of Motivation in Reconstruction Historiography*, 33 J. S. Hist. 303 (1967)

William Gillette, The Right to Vote: Politics and the Passage of the Fifteenth Amendment (1965)

Earl M. Maltz, Civil Rights, the Constitution, and Congress, 1863–1869 (1990)

Xi Wang, The Trial of Democracy: Black Suffrage and Northern Republicans, 1860–1910 (1997)

Significant Cases

Ex parte Yarbrough, 110 U.S. 651 (1884)
Williams v. Mississippi, 170 U.S. 213 (1898)
James v. Bowman, 190 U.S. 127 (1903)
Guinn v. United States, 238 U.S. 347 (1915)
United States v. Classic, 313 U.S. 299 (1941)
Smith v. Allwright, 321 U.S. 649 (1944)
Terry v. Adams, 345 U.S. 461 (1953)
Gomillion v. Lightfoot, 364 U.S. 339 (1960)
South Carolina v. Katzenbach, 383 U.S. 301 (1966)
City of Rome v. United States, 446 U.S. 156 (1980)
Rogers v. Lodge, 458 U.S. 613 (1982)

Hunter v. Underwood, 471 U.S. 222 (1985)
Thornburg v. Gingles, 478 U.S. 30 (1986)
Bush v. Vera, 517 U.S. 952 (1996)
Johnson v. California, 543 U.S. 499 (2005)
Northwest Austin Municipal Utility District No. 1 v. Holder, 557 U.S. 193 (2009)
Shelby County v. Holder, 133 S. Ct. 2675 (2013)

Income Tax

The Congress shall have power to lay and collect taxes on incomes, from whatever source derived, without apportionment among the several States, and without regard to any census or enumeration.

(Amendment XVI)

~

*T*he Sixteenth Amendment, approved by Congress in 1909 and ratified in 1913, made it possible for Congress to enact an income tax without having to worry about whether, under the rules applicable to direct taxes, the tax had to be apportioned among the states on the basis of population.

Congress has the "power to lay and collect taxes," including an income tax, but, under two constitutional provisions (Article I, Section 2, Clause 3; Article I, Section 9, Clause 4), direct taxes must be apportioned—a difficult requirement to satisfy. If an income tax were subject to apportionment, a state with one-tenth of the nation's population, for example, would have to bear one-tenth of the aggregate tax liability, regardless of the state's financial condition. Suppose the populations of Iowa and Maine were equal, but Iowa's per capita income were twice that of Maine. The rates for an apportioned income tax would have to be twice as high in Maine, the poorer state, as in Iowa. Such geographic variability would make it difficult, if not impossible, for anyone in Congress to support that kind of tax.

National real estate taxes were enacted in antebellum America, with complex rules for apportionment—the Founders intended direct taxes to be difficult, not impossible—but, at the Founding, no one was thinking about an income tax. When this idea emerged and became politically possible, an income tax was assumed to be indirect, largely because justices in *Hylton v. United States* (1796) had intimated, in dicta, that the term "direct taxes" was limited to capitation and real estate taxes. Congress accordingly enacted an unapportioned income tax during the Civil War, and the Court, citing *Hylton*, upheld the tax in 1881. *Springer v. United States* (1881).

In 1894, with little attention to constitutional issues, Congress again enacted an unapportioned income tax with the clear goal of shifting the tax burden from regressive tariffs and excises to a levy based on ability of the individual to pay. Congressional debates were full of statements about how the well-to-do had not been paying their fair share. The sponsors of the income tax intended to accomplish what consumption taxes had not, and, to that end, the 1894 tax reached only the wealthiest 1 percent of the population.

This time the Supreme Court refused to approve the idea. In *Pollock v. Farmers' Loan & Trust Co.* (1895), a closely divided Court reinvigorated the direct-tax clauses, holding that the 1894 tax was direct and, because not apportioned, unconstitutional. With *Pollock* on the books, something had to be done if there was to be an unapportioned income tax.

Not every income tax proponent thought a constitutional amendment was necessary after *Pollock*. Many believed the decision was so clearly wrong that the Court would decide differently if given another chance. In addition, supporters feared that if a campaign to amend the Constitution failed, the income tax would be doomed for years. In fact, some Congressmen "backed" the amendment precisely because they expected it to die in state legislatures.

Whether *Pollock* was wrongly decided was, however, almost beside the point. Enacting a new tax to challenge a recent Supreme Court decision was politically risky. Even if wrong, the Court might not change its mind, particularly if Congress seemed to be questioning judicial authority. By 1909, it had become apparent there would be no income tax until the apportionment issue had been resolved.

The Sixteenth Amendment did that for "taxes on incomes." By its terms, it exempted only such taxes from apportionment, leaving apportionment to apply to other direct taxes (including capitation and real estate taxes, and, given *Pollock's* expanded conception of direct taxation, maybe more, like a direct consumption tax). The sponsor, Senator Norris Brown of Nebraska, said he intended to limit the amendment's application in this way, to make an unapportioned income tax possible, and he rejected changes that would have eliminated the direct-tax clauses.

Despite heated opposition, the amendment passed Congress with huge majorities. During ratification, Governor Charles Evans Hughes of New York raised a concern that the phrase "from whatever source derived" could be interpreted to permit national taxation of state and local bond interest, something the *Pollock* Court had said was inconsistent with intergovernmental immunity. Assured that the amendment was not intended to overturn that doctrine, New York signed on and ratification proceeded swiftly.

Facilitating an unapportioned income tax was hardly trivial, but some say the amendment did even more. Bruce Ackerman, for example, argues it was intended to repudiate all of *Pollock*, to contract the notion of "direct taxes," and to revive the plenary taxing power. That interpretation gives more weight to the amendment than the "taxes on incomes" language comfortably bears, however, and it relies on the questionable assumption, derived from *Hylton* dicta, that modern forms of taxation are immune from limitation simply because the Court did not mention them in 1796.

Except in tax protester cases, where ineffectual arguments about the amendment's legitimacy are made, the amendment is generally not involved in litigation today. The Supreme Court has had no recent occasion to articulate the meaning of the amendment or to consider whether the amendment, which broadened congressional power, also contains restrictions on that power.

The general understanding among contemporary scholars is that the taxing power is so broad that Congress alone determines what can be reached by an income tax. This view of unbounded congressional power conflicts with the original, limited role of the amendment, however, and it requires rejecting several old Supreme Court decisions that took the language of the amendment seriously: for an unapportioned tax to be authorized by the Sixteenth Amendment, it must be on "incomes."

In *Eisner v. Macomber* (1920), for example, the Court struck down an income tax as it applied to a stock dividend (a distribution not of money, but of additional shares), the receipt of which, said the Court, was not income. Even if the Court misunderstood stock dividends, as some have argued, the case remains significant for what it says about how the amendment should be interpreted. Throughout the 1920s, the Court assumed the term "incomes" had content, stressing that Congress could not circumvent apportionment by simply labeling a levy an income tax. These cases have not been overruled, and the Court has cited *Macomber* favorably, on nonconstitutional matters, as recently as 1991.

In one respect, the Court has revised the understanding of 1913. Although Congress, by statute, continues not to tax most interest on state and local bonds, the doctrine of intergovernmental immunity advanced by Governor Hughes has been discarded in this context (although not because of the Sixteenth Amendment). *See South Carolina v. Baker* (1988) (state bond interest is not immune from nondiscriminatory federal tax; *Pollock v. Farmers' Loan & Trust Co.* overruled). Thus, interest on state and local bonds is no longer constitutionally exempt from income taxation.

The Supreme Court has not considered the meaning of "incomes" for decades, but a panel of the U.S. Court of Appeals for the District of Columbia Circuit did just that in 2006, probably to its regret. In *Murphy v. Internal Revenue Service* (2006), the panel initially concluded that a whistleblower's recovery, received because she had been wrongfully discharged from her governmental position and had suffered emotional distress, was not income within the meaning of the Sixteenth Amendment (a conclusion that baffled commentators but was defensible in terms of 1913 understandings), and that a tax on the recovery was a direct tax not protected from apportionment by the Amendment. In the face of intense criticism, the panel subsequently vacated that decision and, in 2007, concluded that, given the Supreme Court's cramped conception of direct taxation the tax on the recovery was not direct to begin with. That conclusion rendered the Sixteenth Amendment

issue irrelevant. The Supreme Court did not grant certiorari, and, as a result, we are left with no guidance from *Murphy* on the meaning of "income."

Erik M. Jensen

See Also

Article I, Section 2, Clause 3 (Three-fifths Clause)
Article I, Section 8, Clause 1 (Taxation Clause; Spending Clause; Uniformity Clause)
Article I, Section 9, Clause 4 (Direct Taxes)

Suggestions for Further Research

Bruce Ackerman, *Taxation and the Constitution*, 99 COLUM. L. REV. 1 (1999)

Erik M. Jensen, *The Apportionment of "Direct Taxes": Are Consumption Taxes Constitutional?*, 97 COLUM. L. REV. 2334 (1997)

Erik M. Jensen, *The Taxing Power, the Sixteenth Amendment, and the Meaning of "Incomes,"* 33 ARIZ. ST. L.J. 1057 (2001)

Erik M. Jensen, Murphy v. Internal Revenue Service, *the Meaning of "Income," and Sky-Is-Falling Tax Commentary*, 60 CASE. W. RES. L. REV. 751 (2010)

Marjorie E. Kornhauser, *The Morality of Money: American Attitudes Toward Wealth and the Income Tax*, 70 IND. L.J. 119 (1994)

EDWIN R. A. SELIGMAN, THE INCOME TAX (1914)

Significant Cases

Hylton v. United States, 3 U.S. (3 Dall.) 171 (1796)
Springer v. United States, 102 U.S. 586 (1881)
Pollock v. Farmers' Loan & Trust Co., 157 U.S. 429 (1894), *att'd on reh'g*, 158 U.S. 601 (1895)
Eisner v. Macomber, 252 U.S. 189 (1920)
South Carolina v. Baker, 485 U.S. 505 (1988)
Murphy v. Internal Revenue Service, 460 F.3d 79 (D.C. Cir. 2006), *vacated* (2006); *opinion on reh'g*: 493 F.3d 170 (D.C. Cir. 2007), *cert. denied*, 553 U.S. 1004 (2008)

Popular Election of Senators

The Senate of the United States shall be composed of two Senators

from each State, elected by the people thereof, for six years; and each Senator shall have one vote. The electors in each State shall have the qualifications requisite for electors of the most numerous branch of the State legislatures.

(AMENDMENT XVII, CLAUSE 1)

~

*O*n May 12, 1912, the Seventeenth Amendment, providing for direct popular election of the Senate, was approved by Congress; the requisite three-fourths of the state legislatures ratified it in less than eleven months. Not only was it ratified quickly, but it was also ratified by overwhelming numbers. In fifty-two of the seventy-two state legislative chambers that voted to ratify the Seventeenth Amendment, the vote was unanimous, and in all thirty-six of the ratifying states the total number of votes cast in opposition to ratification was only 191, with 152 of these votes coming from the lower chambers of Vermont and Connecticut.

Although state ratification of the Seventeenth Amendment came quickly and easily, congressional approval of the idea of popular election of the Senate did not. The first resolution calling for direct election of the Senate was introduced in the House of Representatives on February 14, 1826. From that date, until the adoption of the Seventeenth Amendment eighty-six years later, 187 subsequent resolutions of a similar nature were also introduced before Congress, 167 of them after 1880. The House approved six of these proposals before the Senate gave its consent. By 1912, senators were already picked by direct election in twenty-nine of the forty-eight states. As Senator William E. Borah said in 1911, "I should not have been here [in the U.S. Senate] if it [direct election] has not been practiced, and I have great affection [for this system]." Most states had gradually turned to nonbinding primary elections to select their senators; state legislators promised to vote for the candidate that the people had selected in this "advisory" election. This "advisory" election had real teeth because many state laws provided that candidates for state legislator had to sign pledges (which were placed on the ballot) that they would promise (or refuse to promise) to vote for the U.S. Senate candidate that the people had selected in their nonbinding election.

If the state legislative candidate refused to sign the pledge, the people would vote against him, and so the Senate gradually became populated with people who were, in effect, selected by popular, direct election.

The Seventeenth Amendment was approved and ratified to make the Constitution more democratic. Progressives argued forcefully, persistently, and ultimately successfully that the democratic principle required the Senate to be elected directly by the people rather than indirectly through their state legislatures. By altering the manner of election, however, they also altered the principal mechanism employed by the Framers to protect federalism. The Framers understood that the mode of electing (and especially reelecting) senators by state legislatures made it in the self-interest of senators to preserve the original federal design and to protect the interests of states as states (see Article I, Section 3, Clause 1). This understanding was perfectly encapsulated in a July 1789 letter to John Adams, in which Roger Sherman emphasized that "[t]he senators, being eligible by the legislatures of the several states, and dependent on them for re-election, will be vigilant in supporting their rights against infringement by the legislative or executive of the United States."

In practice, the state legislatures' election of senators became more complicated. The members of the state legislators were often divided over whom to elect as senator. Many state legislators simply voted for themselves, and their deadlock would result in no senator's being chosen, which then deprived the state of any representation in the Senate for a year or more.

In addition to its effect on federalism, the ratification of the Seventeenth Amendment has also had demographic, behavioral, and institutional consequences on the Senate itself. Demographically, popularly elected senators are more likely to be born in the states they represent, are more likely to have an Ivy League education, and are likely to have had a higher level of prior governmental service. Institutionally, the states are now more likely to have a split Senate delegation, and the Senate now more closely matches the partisan composition of the House. Additionally, the amendment makes problematic the assertion in *Garcia v. San Antonio Metropolitan Transit Authority* (1985) that the political process in the Senate is sufficient to protect the states' sovereign interests against expansive federal legislation.

Ralph Rossum

See Also

Article I, Section 3, Clause 1 (Senate)

Article V (Prohibition on Amendment: Equal Suffrage in the Senate)

Suggestions for Further Research

Vikram David Amar, *Indirect Effects of Direct Election: A Structural Examination of the Seventeenth Amendment*, 49 Vand. L. Rev. 1347 (1996)

Jay S. Bybee, *Ulysses at the Mast: Democracy, Federalism, and the Sirens' Song of the Seventeenth Amendment*, 91 Nw. U. L. Rev. 500 (1997)

Sara Brandes Crook & John R. Hibbing, *A Not-So-Distant Mirror: The 17th Amendment and Congressional Change*, 91 Am. Pol. Sci. Rev. 845 (1997)

C. H. Hoebeke, The Road to Mass Democracy: Original Intent and the Seventeenth Amendment (1995)

Ralph A. Rossum, Federalism, the Supreme Court, and the Seventeenth Amendment: The Irony of Constitutional Democracy (2001)

Herbert Wechsler, *The Political Safeguards of Federalism: The Role of the States in the Composition and Selection of the National Government*, 54 Colum. L. Rev. 543 (1954)

Todd J. Zywicki, *Beyond the Shell and Husk of History: The History of the Seventeenth Amendment and Its Implications for Current Reform Proposals*, 45 Clev. St. L. Rev. 165 (1997)

Significant Cases

Garcia v. San Antonio Metropolitan Transit Auth., 469 U.S. 528 (1985)

Vacancies in the Senate

When vacancies happen in the representation of any State in the Senate, the executive authority of such State shall issue writs of election to fill such vacancies: Provided, That the legislature of any State may empower the executive thereof to make temporary appointments until the people fill the vacancies by election as the legislature may direct.

This amendment shall not be so construed as to effect the election or term of any Senator chosen before it becomes valid as part of the Constitution.

(Amendment XVII, Clauses 2 and 3)

~

*T*he Seventeenth Amendment, ratified in 1913, provided for the direct election of United States senators, replacing the original method that had left the choice to state legislatures. Previously, state legislatures could choose senators and fill vacancies at any time during a regular or special legislative session. After the ratification of the Seventeenth Amendment, it was recognized that the expense and inconvenience of election by popular vote made it necessary to schedule elections for senators at regular intervals. To avoid the hardship to a state's suffering a lack of representation pending a regular election, the Seventeenth Amendment also provided for methods of election or appointment to fill any unexpired term.

The language and history of the clause indicate that the states have the power to balance conflicting goals of a speedy popular election against the states' interests in conducting elections on a regularized basis so as to maximize voter participation and minimize administrative expense. Thus, when the death of Robert F. Kennedy created a vacancy in New York's Senate delegation in June 1968, New York was permitted to postpone the election of his replacement until 1970, rather than being required to hold both a primary and general election by the fall of 1968. *Valenti v. Rockefeller* (1969). Following the death of Senator John Heinz in 1991, Pennsylvania was permitted to fill the vacancy by a special election, with the candidates to be chosen by party conventions of the state's two major parties. The Court held that the Seventeenth Amendment did not mandate that party nominees be chosen by popular vote, so long as the actual election was by popular vote. *Trinsey v. Pennsylvania* (1991). In 2008, Roland Burris was appointed by the governor of Illinois, Rod Blagojevich, to fill President-elect Barack Obama's Senate seat. (Blagojevich was later impeached and imprisoned for bribery and corruption charges related to his activities in connection with filling the vacancy.) Echoing *Valenti*, the Court found no violation of the Seventeenth Amendment when a special election was not called before a regularly scheduled general election, but it found that a writ of election must be issued. *Judge v. Quinn* (2010). *See also* S. J. Res. 7, 111th Cong., "A Joint Resolution Proposing an Amendment to the Constitution of the United States Relative to the Election of Senators" (2009) and H.R. 899, the Ethical and Legal Elections for Congressional Transitions Act (2009).

The clause does not define when a vacancy exists. During the 2000 election, the people of Missouri knowingly voted for the deceased Mel Carnahan. The governor declared this election to have created a vacancy, which he filled by appointing Carnahan's widow, Jean Carnahan, and he then issued a writ of election for 2002. It remains an open question, however, whether the voters can create a Senate "vacancy" by knowingly voting for an ineligible candidate and allowing the governor to fill the position with an individual of his choice, as opposed to simply declaring the votes to be improper or "spoiled" ballots.

Renewed interest in the Senate vacancy clause has arisen because of the controversy surrounding the appointment of Roland Burris and the Massachusetts legislature's political machinations to assure a Democratic appointee after the death of longtime Senator Edward Kennedy. Bills were considered that would have seated only senators who were elected by the people. One commentator has argued that the original understanding of the Seventeenth Amendment would not have led to the result in *Quinn* that required a writ of election to be issued when it was inconsistent with procedures set up by a state legislature. Others have debated whether Congress has the authority to require states to establish uniform procedures to fill vacancies or whether a constitutional amendment is necessary.

Todd Zywicki

See Also

Article I, Section 3
Article I, Section 4
Amendment XVII (Popular Election of Senators)

Suggestions for Further Research

ROBERT C. BYRD, THE SENATE, 1789–1989 (4 vols. 1989-1994)

GEORGE H. HAYNES, THE SENATE OF THE UNITED STATES: ITS HISTORY AND PRACTICE (2 vols. 1938)

Furqan Mohammed, *Extracting Lessons from Illinois' 2010 Special Election Fiasco: A Closer Look at the Seventh Circuit's Decision in* Judge v. Quinn *and the Special Election Requirement of the Seventeenth Amendment*, 32 N. Ill. U. L. Rev. 295 (2012)

Election of Senators by Popular Vote, S. Rep. No. 961, 61st Cong., 3d Sess. 4–5 (1911)

Todd J. Zywicki, *Beyond the Shell and Husk of History: The History of the Seventeenth Amendment and Its Implications for Current Reform Proposals*, 45 Clev. St. L. Rev. 165 (1997)

Todd J. Zywicki, *The Law of Presidential Transitions and the 2000 Election*, 2001 BYU L. Rev. 1573 (2001)

Todd J. Zywicki, *Senators and Special Interests: A Public Choice Analysis of the Seventeenth Amendment*, 73 Or. L. Rev. 1007 (1994)

Significant Cases

Valenti v. Rockefeller, 292 F. Supp. 851 (S.D.N.Y. 1968), *aff'd* 393 U.S. 405 (1969)

Trinsey v. Pennsylvania, 941 F.2d 224 (1992)

Judge v. Quinn, 612 F.3d 537 (7th Cir. 2010), *amended on denial of reh'g*, 387 Fed. Appx. 629 (7th Cir. 2010), *cert. denied*, 131 S. Ct. 2958 (2011)

Prohibition

Section 1. After one year from the ratification of this article the manufacture, sale, or transportation of intoxicating liquors within, the importation thereof into, or the exportation thereof from the United States and all territory subject to the jurisdiction thereof for beverage purposes is hereby prohibited.

Section 2. The Congress and the several States shall have concurrent power to enforce this article by appropriate legislation.

Section 3. This article shall be inoperative unless it shall have been ratified as an amendment to the Constitution by the legislatures of the several States, as provided in the Constitution, within seven years from the date of the submission hereof to the States by the Congress.

(AMENDMENT XVIII)

~

*T*he Eighteenth Amendment, enacted in 1919, was one of four "Progressive" amendments passed and ratified in quick succession. Although the American involvement with alcohol and with temperance movements had been present from the beginning of the country's history, Prohibition rode to easy victory in an alliance with other elements of the Progressive Movement in the early twentieth century. The Sixteenth Amendment, permitting the income tax, freed the government from dependence on the tax on liquor. The direct election of senators, through the Seventeenth Amendment, made the Senate more amenable to electoral pressure for temperance. Although the Nineteenth Amendment, guaranteeing women the right to vote, was ratified in 1920, it reflected a general acceptance of woman suffrage (and temperance support) already present in the states, many of which allowed women to vote even before the Nineteenth Amendment came into effect.

Businesses supported the amendment to ensure a more reliable workforce, while prejudice against German-Americans and their breweries during World War I helped make Prohibition a patriotic cause. The amendment passed through both Congress and the states with amazing speed. There were no committee hearings in Congress, and debate took less than six hours, most of it centering on the time limit for ratification. The states ratified the amendment within a month.

The only problematic element of the amendment was Section 2, granting Congress and the states concurrent enforcement powers. Under its Section 2 powers, Congress enacted the Volstead Act in 1919 over President Woodrow Wilson's veto. The act defined "intoxicating liquors" as any drink with an alcohol content higher than .05 percent, a strict definition that prohibited even the intake of beer. It permitted exemptions for industrial, medicinal, and sacramental uses, and the act also contained a possession exemption for personal use within one's own private dwelling.

In the 1920 *National Prohibition Cases*, the Supreme Court ruled that, under the Supremacy Clause, states could not enact legislation that conflicted with congressional enactments regarding Prohibition. Because the states had been the engines of much Progressive legislation, the Progressive Movement assumed that the states would actively enforce the amendment, federal law, and their own state laws. The unexpected and widespread reluctance among the states to enforce Prohibition, along with the concomitant development of organized crime and the loss of tax revenues after the start of the Depression, led to a national scandal that undid Prohibition in little more than a decade. Prohibition was repealed in 1933 by the Twenty-first Amendment.

David Wagner

See Also
Amendment XXI (Repeal of Prohibition)

Suggestions for Further Research
EDWARD BEHR, PROHIBITION: THIRTEEN YEARS THAT CHANGED AMERICA (2011)

RICHARD F. HAMM, SHAPING THE EIGHTEENTH AMENDMENT: TEMPERANCE REFORM, LEGAL CULTURE, AND THE POLITY, 1880–1920 (1995)

JOHN KOBLER, ARDENT SPIRITS: THE RISE AND FALL OF PROHIBITION (reprint 1993)

THOMAS R. PEGRAM, BATTLING DEMON RUM: THE STRUGGLE FOR A DRY AMERICA, 1800–1933 (1998)

Significant Case
National Prohibition Cases, 253 U.S. 350 (1920)

Suffrage—Sex

The right of citizens of the United States to vote shall not be denied or abridged by the United States or by any State on account of sex.
Congress shall have power to enforce this article by appropriate legislation.

(AMENDMENT XIX)

~

*C*ontrary to popular belief, the United States Constitution of 1789 is a gender-neutral document. Throughout the original text, the Framers referred to "persons"—as opposed to "male persons"—and used the pronoun "he" only in the generic sense. The word "male" did not even appear in the Constitution until the Fourteenth Amendment was ratified in 1868.

Nothing in the original Constitution bars women from voting. Instead, the Framers left the matter of determining who was eligible to participate in the election of House members and presidential electors almost entirely to the discretion of the states. Article I, Section 2, minimally requires that each state's congressional electors "shall have the Qualifications requisite for Electors of the most numerous Branch of the State Legislature," and Article II, Section 1 simply directs each state legislature to appoint its presidential electors in whatever manner it chooses. Although it is true that almost every state opted to restrict the vote to men, New Jersey did not. Accordingly, between the late 1780s and 1807, when that state's legislature restricted the vote to men, many women participated in federal elections. Under the Constitution, in short, no change was needed to enable women to vote. This fact was ultimately reflected in the different strategies used by the advocates of woman suffrage to remove sexual qualifications for voting.

Although scholars typically trace the origins of the organized woman's rights movement generally, and the drive for woman suffrage particularly, to a famous 1848 gathering in Seneca Falls, New York, the woman suffrage movement began to affect policy only during Reconstruction. In this period, the advocates of woman suffrage began pursuing three main strategies. The first was a judicial strategy involving the Fourteenth Amendment. From the standpoint of the woman suffrage movement, the Fourteenth Amendment represented both a setback and an opportunity. It was a setback insofar as its second section introduced the word "male" into the Constitution and did so in a clause penalizing any state that abridged the right of its "male inhabitants" to vote in state or federal elections for reasons other than crime or rebellion. In so doing, woman suffrage advocates worried, the second section lent credibility to the idea that the Constitution restricted the right to vote to men. Nevertheless, they also viewed the amendment as an opportunity, because they believed the first section of the amendment contradicted the implication of the second. When the Citizenship Clause was read in combination with the Privileges or Immunities Clause, they argued, the Fourteenth Amendment barred states from denying a woman's right to vote in federal elections. In its 1874 decision of *Minor v. Happersett*, however, the Supreme Court unequivocally disagreed, holding that voting was not one of the privileges or immunities of citizens of the United States.

At the same time, various elements of the woman suffrage movement began pursuing other strategies. Consistent with the Framers' arrangements in Articles I and II, the first such strategy involved persuading individual states and territories to eliminate sexual qualifications for voting. In 1869, the Wyoming territory became the first territorial government to do so. Upon obtaining statehood in 1890, Wyoming became the first state since New Jersey to allow women to participate in federal elections on an equal basis with men. Although success was often slow in coming, by the time the Nineteenth Amendment was ratified in 1920, thirty states and one territory already permitted women to vote in at least some aspect in the selection of members of the House (and by then the Senate) or presidential electors.

The other strategy begun in this period involved amending the federal Constitution in a way that would render such state action unnecessary. More precisely, the advocates of woman suffrage sought to reduce the power conferred upon the states in Article I, Section 2; Article

II, Section 1; and eventually in the Seventeenth Amendment (which was ratified in 1913)—as well as by their own constitutions—by explicitly barring the states from making sex a qualification for voting in federal and state elections. The first such amendment was introduced in Congress in 1869. In 1878, California Senator Aaron A. Sargent introduced the proposal that would, without any change in wording, be approved by Congress in 1919 and ratified by three-fourths of the states in 1920. Sargent's proposal simply repeated the language of the Fifteenth Amendment save for one change: whereas the Fifteenth Amendment forbids both the U.S. and state governments from denying or abridging their citizens' right to vote "on account of race, color, or previous condition of servitude," the Nineteenth forbids the same "on account of sex."

Unlike so many other clauses of the Constitution—including the Fifteenth Amendment itself—the Nineteenth Amendment has generated a remarkably small body of case law. In the first decade or so following ratification, a relatively small number of state courts implemented its restriction on the power of the states by striking down constitutional or statutory provisions that restricted the vote to men, made it more difficult for women than men to qualify, or otherwise treated male and female ballots differently. The amendment has generated even fewer federal cases. Although the Court has obliquely commented on the meaning of the amendment in various cases, it has confronted this question squarely on only one occasion. In *Breedlove v. Suttles* (1937), a Georgia law exempted payment of a one-dollar poll tax for unregistered female voters, but required male voters to pay the tax before registering to vote. In its decision, the Court stated that the amendment's restriction on the power of the federal and state governments to deny or abridge their citizens' right to vote "on account of sex" applied to men and women equally, and superseded all federal or state measures to the contrary. The Court concluded, however, that the amendment was not designed to restrict the state's ability to tax.

Tiffany J. Miller

See Also

Article I, Section 2, Clause 1 (Elector Qualifications)
Article II, Section 1, Clause 2 (Presidential Electors)
Amendment XVII (Popular Election of Senators)

Suggestions for Further Research

Eleanor Flexner & Ellen Fitzpatrick, Century of Struggle: The Woman's Rights Movement in the United States (1996)

Judith Apter Klinghoffer & Lois Elkis, *"The Petticoat Electors": Women's Suffrage in New Jersey, 1776–1807,* 12 J. Early Rep. 159 (1992)

One Woman, One Vote: Rediscovering the Woman Suffrage Movement (Marjorie Spruill Wheeler ed., 1995)

Thomas G. West, Vindicating the Founders: Race, Sex, Class, and Justice in the Origins of America (1997)

Significant Cases

Minor v. Happersett, 88 U.S. (21 Wall.) 162 (1874)
Leser v. Garnett, 258 U.S. 130 (1922)
Breedlove v. Suttles, 302 U.S. 277 (1937)

Presidential Terms

Section 1. The terms of the President and Vice President shall end at noon on the 20th day of January, and the terms of Senators and Representatives at noon on the 3d day of January, of the years in which such terms would have ended if this article had not been ratified; and the terms of their successors shall then begin.

Section 2. The Congress shall assemble at least once in every year, and such meeting shall begin at noon on the 3d day of January, unless they shall by law appoint a different day.

Section 3. If, at the time fixed for the beginning of the term of the President, the President elect shall have died, the Vice President elect shall become President. If a President shall not have been chosen before the time fixed for the beginning of his term, or if the President elect shall have failed to qualify, then the Vice President elect shall act as President until a President shall have qualified; and the Congress may by law provide for the case wherein neither a President elect nor a Vice President shall have qualified, declaring who shall then act as President, or the manner in which one who is to act shall be selected, and such person shall act accordingly until a President or Vice President shall have qualified.

Section 4. The Congress may by law provide for the case of the death of any of the persons from whom the House of Representatives may choose a President whenever the right of choice shall have devolved upon them, and for the case of the death of any of the persons from whom the Senate may choose a Vice President whenever the right of choice shall have devolved upon them.

Section 5. Sections 1 and 2 shall take effect on the 15th day of October following the ratification of this article.

Section 6. This article shall be inoperative unless it shall have been ratified as an amendment to the Constitution by the legislatures of three-fourths of the several States within seven years from the date of its submission.

(Amendment XX)

~

*T*he Twentieth Amendment appears simply to embody minor structural changes to the Constitution. That the amendment was ratified by the states more quickly than any other constitutional amendment before or since supports this impression of an uncontroversial technical revision. So does the absence of litigation surrounding the meaning of the amendment. But the Twentieth Amendment became part of the Constitution only

after decades of congressional debate, and its meaning was debated as recently as the impeachment of President William Jefferson Clinton by the United States House of Representatives in December 1998.

The six sections of the Twentieth Amendment are readily divided into three pairs. The first two sections shorten the "lame-duck" period after an election and before the newly elected president, vice president, and members of Congress take office. The next two sections govern various presidential succession questions. The final two provisions are standard provisions specifying the manner of approval and the date of its coming into effect. The amendment was, in large part, the creation of Nebraska Senator George W. Norris, who championed it for over a decade until Congress approved it in March 1932 and three-fourths of the states ratified it by January 1933. Throughout its consideration by Congress and the states, it was known as "the lame-duck amendment."

The first two sections respond to the initial purpose for the amendment, which was the concern about lame-duck sessions of Congress. Prior to the passage of the amendment, a Congress would normally not assemble for its first session until thirteen months (December of the following year) after it was elected, and its second session would not begin until after the next Congress had been elected. Legislation enacted by lame-duck Congresses had been roundly criticized as undemocratic because the people had already selected the successors of the representatives who were enacting bills during lame-duck sessions. The question whether the framers of the Twentieth Amendment wanted to eliminate such lame-duck sessions of Congress altogether or just shorten them has been debated ever since the ratification of the amendment. Scholars on both sides of the question have drawn on the long and complex history of the passage of the amendment to discern its true intent.

As finally formulated, the text of the amendment failed to prohibit future lame-duck sessions, and, if the purpose had been to eliminate them, it was forgotten soon after the states ratified the amendment in 1933. As of this writing, Congress has met in lame-duck sessions fourteen times since the Twentieth Amendment became law. In recent years, a lame-duck Senate confirmed Stephen G. Breyer to a federal appeals court judgeship in 1980, and the House of Representatives impeached President Clinton after the 1998 election, despite calls from a number of scholars that such an action contradicted the spirit of the Twentieth Amendment. The Congress that met in the lame-duck session after the 2010 election enacted more legislation than any lame-duck Congress since the ratification of the Twentieth Amendment. No one has asked the courts to declare that the original understanding of the Twentieth Amendment was to prohibit lame-duck sessions, and it is likely that the courts would regard any issue arising out of a lame-duck session as nonjusticiable (i.e., not capable of a judicial resolution).

There is another question that the framers of the Twentieth Amendment anticipated but which the language of the amendment fails to resolve. According to the Twelfth Amendment, the House of Representatives chooses the president if no candidate receives a majority of the electoral votes. Thomas Jefferson, John Quincy Adams, and Rutherford B. Hayes were all elected by the House—more specifically, the lame-duck House, not the newly elected House. The supporters of the Twentieth Amendment indicated that they wanted to ensure that any future selections of the president would be made by the new members of the House. The text of the amendment does not express that purpose, however, and the question of which House (the lame-duck or the newly elected) could act was one of many unanswered constitutional questions discussed while the presidential election of 2000 was still in dispute.

Sections 3 and 4 address an issue unrelated to the concern about lame-duck Congresses, namely, the circumstances in which the president or the president-elect dies. In the words of Senator Norris, Sections 3 and 4 ensure that "there can never arise a contingency where the country will be without a chief magistrate or without the method of selecting a chief magistrate." The nation has never had the occasion to put Senator Norris's confidence to the test. A number of scholars, however, have imagined circumstances in which the selection of a new president would remain unclear, notwithstanding Sections 3 and 4. For example, Akhil Amar has asked,

What happens if, God forbid, the person who wins the general election in November and the Electoral College tally in December dies before the Electoral College votes are officially counted in Congress in January? If the decedent can be considered 'the President elect' within the meaning of the Twentieth Amendment, then the rules would be clear, but it is not self-evident that a person who dies before the official counting of electoral votes in Congress is formally the 'President elect.'

The solution, proposes Amar, is for Congress to enact a statute that would (1) postpone the election if a major candidate dies or becomes incapacitated shortly before election day and (2) authorize the counting of electoral votes for candidates who died on or after election day. Thus far, Congress has failed to heed such advice.

John Copeland Nagle

See Also
Article I, Section 4, Clause 1 (Election Regulations)
Article II, Section 1, Clause 4 (Presidential Vote)
Amendment XII (Electoral College)

Suggestions for Further Research
Bruce Ackerman, The Case Against Lameduck Impeachment (1999)

Akhil Reed Amar, *Presidents, Vice Presidents, and Death: Closing the Constitution's Succession Gap,* 48 Ark. L. Rev. 215 (1995)

Richard S. Beth & Richard C. Sachs, *Lame Duck Sessions, 74th–106th Congress* (1935–2000) (2000) (Congressional Research Service report)

Edward J. Larson, *The Constitutionality of Lame Duck Lawmaking: The Text, History, Intent, and Original Meaning of the Twentieth Amendment,* 2012 Utah l. Rev.707 (2012)

John Copeland Nagle, *Lame Duck Logic,* 45 U.C. Davis L. Rev. 1177 (2012)

John Copeland Nagle, *A Twentieth Amendment Parable,* 72 N.Y.U. L. Rev. 470 (1997)

George W. Norris, Fighting Liberal: The Autobiography of George W. Norris (1946)

Repeal of Prohibition

Section 1. The eighteenth article of amendment to the Constitution of the United States is hereby repealed.
Section 2. The transportation or importation into any State, Territory, or Possession of the United States for delivery or use therein of intoxicating liquors, in violation of the laws thereof, is hereby prohibited.
Section 3. This article shall be inoperative unless it shall have been ratified as an amendment to the Constitution by conventions in the several States, as provided in the Constitution, within seven years from the date of the submission hereof to the States by the Congress.

(AMENDMENT XXI)

$\sim$

*W*hen the nation repealed Prohibition by means of the Twenty-first Amendment in 1933, it vested primary control over alcoholic beverages in the states. The common understanding of the framers of the Twenty-first Amendment was that it grants each state the power to regulate alcoholic beverages within its borders without intrusion by federal law or regulation. The question remains, however, as to how much and what kind of federal intrusion the amendment blocks.

The Twenty-first Amendment has three parts. Section 1 explicitly repealed the Eighteenth Amendment and brought an end to Prohibition. Accordingly, because many saw the Twenty-first Amendment as nothing but a repeal of the Eighteenth Amendment, Congress passed the resolution without much substantive debate. Most of the legislative debate centered on the issue of saloons and the ratification process codified in

Section 3 of the amendment, which mandated the use of state conventions. The amendment was passed by the Senate on February 16, 1933, and by the House four days later. It was the only amendment to have been ratified by conventions in the several states, rather than by the state legislatures. Reportedly, Congress feared that rurally dominated state legislatures might be more likely to reject the repeal of Prohibition. The method resulted in a quick ratification, and it became part of the Constitution on December 5, 1933.

In the original resolution there was an additional section that granted Congress and the states "concurrent power to regulate or prohibit the sale of intoxicating liquors to be drunk on the premises where sold." This provision was designed primarily to authorize the prohibition of saloons. But members of Congress finally agreed that such regulation belonged with the states, and the section was removed.

Section 2 became the Twenty-first Amendment's primary source of judicial conflict. The question was whether the amendment gave the states absolute control over alcohol, notwithstanding the Commerce Clause and the Import-Export Clause, or whether the amendment permitted the states only enough autonomy to be dry without infringing on the scope of the rest of the Constitution. The amendment tracks very closely the language of a pre-Prohibition federal statute, the Webb-Kenyon Act (1913), current version at 27 U.S.C. § 122 (1994), which gave states power to tax alcoholic beverages not only when sold in the state, but also when sold through the mail in interstate commerce.

After repeal of Prohibition, many states enacted a three-tier distribution system in which each tier is permitted only to sell its product to the next licensed tier, requiring separate licensing for each tier. Discrimination against out-of-state liquor was often routed through the requirements of the three-tier system.

In *State Board of Equalization v. Young's Market Co.* (1936) and in *Ziffrin, Inc. v. Reeves* (1939), the Supreme Court originally interpreted the Twenty-first Amendment as an absolute exception to the Commerce Clause. However, this changed in 1964 with a string of Twenty-first Amendment cases. In *Hostetter v. Idlewild Bon*

Voyage Liquor Corp. (1964), Justice Potter Stewart, writing for the majority, argued forcefully that the Twenty-first Amendment was not an absolute exception to the Commerce Clause as far as liquor was concerned. Likewise, in *Department of Revenue v. James B. Beam Distilling Co.* (1964), the Court held that Kentucky's tax on imported whiskey violated the Import-Export Clause. Justice Stewart, again writing for the majority, stated:

> To sustain the tax which Kentucky has imposed in this case would require nothing short of squarely holding that the Twenty-first Amendment has completely repealed the Export-Import Clause so far as intoxicants are concerned. Nothing in the language of the Amendment nor in its history leads to such an extraordinary conclusion. This Court has never intimated such a view, and now that the claim for the first time is squarely presented, we expressly reject it.

Similarly, in *Wisconsin v. Constantineau* (1971), the Court held that a Wisconsin statute that empowered a police chief to post in all local retail liquor outlets a notice forbidding the sale of alcohol to the plaintiff because of his excessive drinking, without giving the plaintiff any advance notice or opportunity to contest it, violated the due process requirements of the Fourteenth Amendment.

Throughout the 1970s and early 1980s, the Supreme Court continued to chip away at the Twenty-first Amendment. *See, e.g., United States v. Tax Commission of Mississippi* (1975) (holding that the states could not tax the sale of liquor on military bases within their borders because the United States has concurrent jurisdiction over military bases); *Craig v. Boren* (1976) (noting that the Twenty-first Amendment does not override the equal-protection requirements of the Fourteenth Amendment); *California Retail Liquor Dealers Ass'n v. Midcal Aluminum, Inc.* (1980) (finding that the Twenty-first Amendment does not protect a state regulation that vio-

lates the Sherman Act because of the Supremacy Clause); *Larkin v. Grendel's Den, Inc.* (1982) (stating that the state may not exercise its powers under the Twenty-first Amendment in a way that impinges on the rights protected under the Establishment Clause). In *New York State Liquor Authority v. Bellanca* (1981), the Court allowed a state a greater range of freedom to regulate adult speech in connection with its power to regulate the sale of liquor within its boundaries, because "[w]hatever artistic or communicative value may attach to topless dancing is overcome by the State's exercise of its broad power under the Twenty-first Amendment"). But in *44 Liquormart, Inc. v. Rhode Island* (1996), the Court held that Rhode Island's prohibition against certain advertisements stating the prices of liquor was an abridgment of the First Amendment's protection of free speech. Although the lengthy decision contained several concurring opinions, all nine justices agreed that the Rhode Island law was not saved by the Twenty-first Amendment. For the majority, Justice John Paul Stevens stated, "[W]e now hold that the Twenty-First Amendment does not qualify the constitutional prohibition against laws abridging the freedom of speech embodied in the First Amendment."

In *Capital Cities Cable, Inc. v. Crisp* (1984), the Court finally articulated a balancing test to determine when the state's powers under the Twenty-first Amendment trump the Commerce Clause:

> In such a case, the central question is whether the interests implicated by a state regulation are so closely related to the powers reserved by the Amendment that the regulation may prevail, even though its requirements directly conflict with express federal policies.

Applying this balancing test in *Bacchus Imports, Ltd. v. Dias* (1984), the Court struck down a Hawaiian tax law that favored certain liquors that were only manufactured locally because "[s]tate laws that constitute mere economic protectionism are . . . not entitled to the same deference as laws enacted to combat the perceived evils of an unrestricted traffic in liquor."

In *324 Liquor Corp. v. Duffy* (1987), the Court balanced the state's virtually complete control over the liquor distribution system within its borders against the policy behind the Sherman Antitrust Act and found the latter of more weight. In a sharp dissent, Justice Sandra Day O'Connor, joined by Chief Justice William H. Rehnquist, rejected the majority's conclusion. The dissent described in detail the legislative history and the subsequent state practices to show that the amendment was designed to give the states absolute control over the manufacturing and distribution of liquor within their borders. The "Senate discussions," she wrote, "clearly demonstrate an intent to confer on States complete and exclusive control over the commerce of liquor." The states understood the meaning as well. Immediately after the ratification of the Twenty-first Amendment, states enacted strong price-control measures, "the very type of statute that this Court strikes down today." The majority opinion answered Justice O'Connor's argument with a one-paragraph footnote that focused on maintaining federal economic power through the Commerce Clause and the Antitrust Laws.

That same year in *South Dakota v. Dole* (1987), the Court held that Congress could use its spending power to regulate interstate commerce indirectly with regard to intoxicating liquors. In *Dole*, Congress made certain highway funding contingent upon a state's acceptance of a minimum drinking age of twenty-one years. Justice O'Connor and Justice William J. Brennan Jr. each filed dissents, with Brennan arguing that the Twenty-first Amendment limited the spending power.

The Supreme Court last addressed the Twenty-first Amendment in the case *Granholm v. Heald* (2005). The Court reiterated its prior holdings that the Twenty-first Amendment does not protect state laws that violate the First Amendment's Free Speech Clause, the Establishment Clause, the Equal Protection Clause, the Due Process Clause, and the Import-Export Clause. The Court also reaffirmed its decision in *Bacchus* that "forecloses any contention that § 2 of the

Twenty-first Amendment immunizes discriminatory direct-shipment laws from Commerce Clause scrutiny." Justice Clarence Thomas wrote a detailed dissent, arguing that the text and history of the Twenty-first Amendment make clear that there is no "negative Commerce Clause barrier to state regulation of liquor sales to in-state consumers."

After a number of years in which the Supreme Court pruned state powers under the Twenty-first Amendment, the amendment now leaves a state with the power to become dry if it chooses and to control to some extent the distribution and sales system of alcohol within its borders. The three-tier system remains intact in many states, and *Granholm* affirmed its legitimacy. But lower courts have divided on the extent to which state licensing requirements among the tiers can constitutionally restrict interstate trade in liquor and wine.

David Wagner and David F. Forte

See Also

Article I, Section 8, Clause 3 (Commerce with Foreign Nations)

Article I, Section 8, Clause 3 (Commerce Among the States)

Article I, Section 10, Clause 2 (Import-Export Clause)

Suggestions for Further Research

Edward Behr, Prohibition: Thirteen Years that Changed America (2011)

Duncan Baird Douglass, *Constitutional Crossroads: Reconciling the Twenty-first Amendment and the Commerce Clause to Evaluate State Regulation of Interstate Commerce in Alcoholic Beverages*, 49 Duke L.J. 1619 (2000)

John Foust, *State Power to Regulate Alcohol Under the Twenty-first Amendment: The Constitutional Implications of the Twenty-first Amendment Enforcement Act*, 41 B.C. L. Rev. 659 (2000)

Elyse Grossman and James F. Mosher, *Public Health, State Alcohol Pricing Policies, and the Dismantling of the 21st Amendment: A Legal Analysis*, 15 Mich. St. U. J. Med. & Law 177 (2011)

John Kobler, Ardent Spirits: The Rise and Fall of Prohibition (reprint 1993)

Susan Lorde Martin, *Wine Wars—Direct Shipment of Wine: The Twenty-first Amendment, the Commerce Clause, and Consumers' Rights*, 38 Am. Bus. L.J. 1 (2000)

Russ Miller, *The Wine Is in the Mail: the Twenty-first Amendment and State Laws Against the Direct Shipment of Alcoholic Beverages*, 54 Vand. L. Rev. 2495 (2001)

Thomas R. Pegram, Battling Demon Rum: The Struggle for a Dry America, 1800–1933 (1998)

Jonathan M. Rotter & Joshua S. Stambaugh, *What's Left of the Twenty-First Amendment?*, 6 Cardozo Pub. L. Pol'y & Ethics J. 601 (2008)

James Alexander Tanford, *E-Commerce in Wine*, 3 J. L. Econ. & Pol'y 275 (2007)

Significant Cases

State Bd. of Equalization of California v. Young's Market Co., 299 U.S. 59 (1936)

Joseph S. Finch & Co. v. McKittrick, 305 U.S. 395 (1939)

Ziffrin, Inc. v. Reeves, 308 U.S. 132 (1939)

United States v. Frankfort Distilleries, Inc., 324 U.S. 293 (1945)

Dep't of Revenue v. James B. Beam Distilling Co., 377 U.S. 341 (1964)

Hostetter v. Idlewild Bon Voyage Liquor Corp., 377 U.S. 324 (1964)

Wisconsin v. Constantineau, 400 U.S. 433 (1971)

California v. LaRue, 409 U.S. 109 (1972)

United States v. Tax Comm'n of Mississippi, 421 U.S. 599 (1975)

Craig v. Boren, 429 U.S. 190 (1976)

California Retail Liquor Dealers Ass'n v. Midcal Aluminum, Inc., 445 U.S. 97 (1980)

New York State Liquor Authority v. Bellanca, 452 U.S. 714 (1981)

Larkin v. Grendel's Den, Inc., 459 U.S. 116 (1982)

Capital Cities Cable, Inc. v. Crisp, 467 U.S. 691 (1984)

Bacchus Imports, Ltd. v. Dias, 468 U.S. 263 (1984)

324 Liquor Corp. v. Duffy, 479 U.S. 335 (1987)

South Dakota v. Dole, 483 U.S. 203 (1987)

North Dakota v. United States, 495 U.S. 423 (1990)

44 Liquormart, Inc. v. Rhode Island, 517 U.S. 484 (1996)

Granholm v. Heald, 544 U.S. 460 (2005)

Brooks v. Vassar, 462 F.3d 341 (4th Cir. 2006)

Arnold's Wines, Inc. v. Boyle, 571 F.3d 185 (2d Cir. 2009)

Presidential Term Limit

Section 1. No person shall be elected to the office of the President more than twice, and no person who has held the office of President, or acted as President, for more than two years of a term to which some other person was elected President shall be elected to the office of President more than once. But this Article shall not apply to any person holding the office of President when this Article was proposed by Congress, and shall not prevent any person who may be holding the office of President, or acting as President, during the term within which this Article becomes operative from holding the office of President or acting as President during the remainder of such term.

Section 2. This article shall be inoperative unless it shall have been ratified as an amendment to the Constitution by the legislatures of three-fourths of the several States within seven years from the date of its submission to the States by the Congress.

(Amendment XXII)

⁓

*T*he Twenty-second Amendment, proposed by Congress in 1947 when President Harry S. Truman was completing Franklin Delano Roosevelt's fourth term, was a reaction to FDR's unprecedented four consecutive elections to the presidency. But support for (and opposition to) presidential term limits had a lengthy and complex history prior to the amendment's becoming law.

Participants in the Constitutional Convention of 1787 extensively debated the idea of restricting the amount of time a person could serve as president, but ultimately included no such limits in the Constitution proposed to the states. *The Federalist Papers* explicitly defended this decision to leave presidents with unlimited eligibility, contending that the alternative would be "pernicious," depriving the nation of its best leaders and undermining "stability in the administration" of government. Other thinkers in the Founding era came to different conclusions, with Thomas Jefferson and George Mason, for example, arguing that limits on the number of times a person could serve as president would help sustain the republic.

George Washington, who famously declined to be considered for a third presidential term in 1796, is cited as the father of a two-term tradition that culminated in the Twenty-second Amendment. But Washington did not favor limits on eligibility, and he wrote that the decision to exclude such restrictions was "fairly discussed in the Convention."

Nevertheless, following Washington's retirement after his second elected term, numerous public figures subsequently argued that the nation should follow his example of limited service to create a check against any one person, or the presidency as a whole, accumulating too much power. While a number of presidents considered attempting a third term, no one successfully did so until Franklin Roosevelt's 1940 electoral victory.

Congress expressed its interest in presidential term limits by introducing 270 measures restricting the terms of office of the president prior to proposing the Twenty-second Amendment. Nonetheless, sustained attention to turning this legislative sentiment into law developed only with the Roosevelt presidency. The Republican Party's platforms of 1940 and 1944 called for a constitutional amendment that would limit a person from being president "for more than two terms" and campaign literature from this era warned of the dangers of entrenching executive power through years of successive service.

In 1946, congressional lawmakers made the president's four terms an issue in their election campaigns, pledging to support a constitutional amendment that would bar such lengthy presidencies in the future. In January 1947, prominent House leaders acted on these pledges, introducing an initiative that ultimately became the Twenty-second Amendment. Despite the arguments of some that the amendment was a posthumous rebuke of Roosevelt, it is notable that both houses

that proposed the amendment were controlled by the Democratic Party.

The turning point in the debates on the measure occurred when Democratic Senator Warren Magnuson argued for an amendment that would simply bar someone from being "elected to the office of President more than twice." Magnuson claimed that other proposals being considered were too "complicated" and might unfairly restrict a person who assumed the office of president "through circumstances beyond his control, and with no deliberation on his part...but because of an emergency," such as the death of an elected president.

When some legislators countered that Magnuson's proposal provided insufficient controls on those who assumed the presidency through these "unfortunate circumstance[s]," a compromise was struck. The final proposal provided a general prohibition against a person's being elected to the office of president more than twice while imposing additional restrictions on those who attained the office of president through nonelectoral means, such as succession. The resulting language is what is now the Twenty-second Amendment.

It can safely be concluded that those who drafted the amendment sought to prevent the emergence of a president who would serve for as many years as FDR. Some proponents of the measure further argued that they were seeking to codify the "two-term tradition" associated with Washington. But while these observations point to the general aspirations of the amendment's authors, they do not establish a specific picture of how they intended their proposal to apply.

Congressional deliberations about the amendment were curtailed, with the House restricting debate to two hours. Furthermore, the discussions leading up to the congressional vote did not obviously articulate a consistent, clear legislative purpose. Lawmakers expressed, at various times, their interest in limiting a president's "service," "terms," "tenure," and "[eligibility for] reelection," without elaborating exactly how these different terms should be understood. Moreover, when Congress discarded initial proposals foreclosing a person's eligibility for office if he or she had served in two prior terms, and instead adopted the current text that focuses on limiting elections to the presidency, it provided little explanation for this important shift beyond needing "compromise" as part of the lawmaking process.

One should also note that the immediate framers of the amendment did not obviously intend to create a two-term tradition in any narrow sense. They specifically discussed how the amendment would allow someone who became president through an "emergency" within the first two years of a presidential term to pursue the White House through election for two additional terms. Thus, despite the assumption of many that the Twenty-second Amendment codified Washington's two-term example, we are left with some genuine uncertainty about its creators' precise goals.

The ratification debates over the amendment do not provide much additional insight into the wishes of those who supported the proposal in the states. The amendment does not appear to have prompted a great deal of public or legislative discussion once approved by Congress.

Although numerous court opinions make passing reference to the Twenty-second Amendment, its implications have not been systematically examined by the judiciary. No doubt the low profile of the amendment in the courts reflects limited interest in and opportunity for testing the provision. Since the amendment was ratified, only six presidents have been technically limited by it (Dwight D. Eisenhower, Richard M. Nixon, Ronald Reagan, William Jefferson Clinton, George W. Bush, and Barack Obama were all twice elected), and none of them seriously considered challenging the amendment's legal restrictions or meaning.

These facts should not lead one to conclude that the Twenty-second Amendment is so straightforward that it requires no further interpretation. Among other unresolved questions, the amendment seems to leave open the possibility that a twice-elected president could still become president through nonelectoral means. For example, such a person might still be elevated to the presidency after serving as vice president, or, if authorized, to act as president through a presidential-succession statute. Indeed, many of today's scholarly and policy debates about the amendment speculate on how it could be interpreted or altered to give the nation greater options in dealing with problems related to terrorism, emergency rule, and presidential succession. Critics have urged repeal of the amendment on the grounds that it makes executive leadership more difficult and limits popular choice.

Bruce Peabody

See Also

Article II, Section 1, Clause 5 (Presidential Eligibility)
Article II, Section 1, Clause 6 (Presidential Succession)
Amendment XII (Electoral College)
Amendment XX (Presidential Terms)
Amendment XXV (Presidential Succession)

Suggestions for Further Research

David A. Crockett, *"An Excess of Refinement": Lame Duck Presidents in Constitutional and Historical Context*, 38 PRESIDENTIAL STUD. Q. 707 (2008)

Bruce G. Peabody & Scott E. Gant, *The Twice and Future President: Constitutional Interstices and the Twenty-second Amendment*, 83 MINN. L. REV. 565 (1999)

Stephen W. Stathis, *The Twenty-second Amendment: A Practical Remedy or Partisan Maneuver?*, 7 CONST. COMM. 61 (1990)

UNINTENDED CONSEQUENCES OF CONSTITUTIONAL AMENDMENT (David E. Kyvig ed., 2000)

Electors for the District of Columbia

Section 1. The District constituting the seat of Government of the United States shall appoint in such manner as the Congress may direct: A number of electors of President and Vice President equal to the whole number of Senators and Representatives in Congress to which the District would be entitled if it were a State, but in no event more than the least populous State; they shall be in addition to those appointed by the States, but they shall be considered, for the purposes of the election of President and Vice President, to be electors appointed by a State; and they shall meet in the District and perform such duties as provided by the twelfth article of amendment. Section 2. The Congress shall have power to enforce this article by appropriate legislation.

(Amendment XXIII)

~

The inability of the citizens of the District of Columbia to participate in federal elections has been controversial since the federal seat of government of the United States came into existence in 1800. In 1960, Congress rectified the situation concerning the district's participation in presidential elections by passing the Twenty-third Amendment. It enables the district to participate in presidential and vice-presidential elections in the same manner in which the states participate in those elections. The states swiftly ratified the proposed amendment in time for the district to cast electoral votes in the presidential election of 1964. The amendment did not address the district's lack of representation in Congress.

The legislative history of the amendment makes clear that the drafters sought to provide the seat of government of the United States, the District of Columbia, with the same method of selecting presidential electors in the Electoral College as the states employed to select their presidential electors. The legislative history also reveals that some of the key drafters were ignorant of the relevant constitutional history concerning the manner in which the states had selected their presidential electors. Early in U.S. history, some states chose electors by district, others by the state legislature, and others by a "winner-take-all" system. Despite this confusion, the Twenty-third Amendment clearly provides Congress the same leeway as the state legislatures in enacting the electoral vote selection procedures for the district.

The amendment contains some sui generis provisions. The amendment expressly caps the district's electoral votes at the number equal to the least populous state. This, in effect, provides the district with three electoral votes regardless of the population of the district. In addition,

because the parallel constitutional provisions grant the respective state legislatures with plenary power over the method of selection of the presidential electors, a like power was necessarily given to Congress. The House report accompanying the amendment notes that "[t]he language follows closely the language of article II of the Constitution."

Although not constitutionally required, Congress, by statute, has adopted a winner-take-all system, in which the winner of the plurality of votes receives all of the district's presidential electors. Such winner-take-all systems have been enacted in all the states except for Maine and Nebraska. Recently, controversies over the Twenty-third Amendment have arisen as part of efforts for district statehood or to provide the district with representation in the federal legislature. For example, if Congress, by statute, accepted the District of Columbia as the State of New Columbia, and the present "seat of government of the United States" was not eliminated but reduced to a small federal enclave containing the White House and the federal Mall, what would become of the Twenty-third Amendment?

Many district-statehood and district–voting-rights proponents generally seek to avoid amending the Constitution because of the difficulties of obtaining congressional approval and state ratification. They contend that the Twenty-third Amendment would become a "dead letter" without the necessity of formal repeal by constitutional amendment, because there would be virtually no residents left in the federal enclave. On the other hand, "the Seat of Government of the United States," the entity designated in the amendment to receive electoral votes, would still exist in its geographically reduced form. That constitutional entity, absent constitutional repeal, would still be constitutionally entitled to the electoral votes under the Twenty-third Amendment. Any congressional effort to repeal the enabling legislation without repealing the Twenty-third Amendment would likely face constitutional difficulty. For example, the concept that any constitutional provision can be deemed a "dead letter" by legislation runs contrary to basic principles of the American constitutional structure. Additionally, such a scenario could imply that a state legislature could exercise like authority and act to disenfranchise its citizens from participation in the Electoral College.

For decades, these concerns seemed academic and hypothetical. However, the 2000 presidential election and the controversy over Florida's electoral votes renewed focus on a state's constitutional prerogatives concerning the manner and selection of presidential electors. Those constitutional developments necessarily inform Congress's parallel obligations under the Twenty-third Amendment.

In addition, in an effort to assure that the popular vote winner is elected president, but without amending the Constitution, a National Popular Vote bill has been proposed. This bill, in the form of an interstate compact, would take effect only when enacted, in identical form, by states possessing at least 270 electoral votes—enough to elect the president. The bill would award each enacting state's electoral votes to the presidential candidate who has received the most popular votes. The bill has been enacted by nine jurisdictions, including the District of Columbia, that possess 132 electoral votes. The District's enactment may be problematic. Ultimately, based on the express terms of the Twenty-third Amendment, Congress, not the D.C. City Council, has the final word on the electoral vote selection procedure for the District of Columbia.

Adam Kurland

See Also Article I, Section 8, Clause 17 (Enclave Clause)
Article II, Section I, Clause 2 (Presidential Electors)
Amendment XII (Electoral College)

Suggestions for Further Research
After the People Vote: A Guide to the Electoral College (Walter Berns ed., rev. 1992)

Adam H. Kurland, *Partisan Rhetoric, Constitutional Reality, and Political Responsibility: The Troubling Constitutional Consequences of Achieving D.C. Statehood by Simple Legislation,* 60 Geo. Wash. L. Rev. 475 (1992)

Office of Legal Policy, U.S. Department of Justice, Report to the Attorney General on the Question of Statehood for the District of Columbia (April 3, 1987)

1 Ronald D. Rotunda & John E. Nowak, Treatise on Constitutional Law: Substance and Procedure § 3.6(c) (5th ed. 2012)

Explanation of National Popular Vote Bill, at http://nationalpopularvote.com/pages/explanation.php

Significant Cases
McPherson v. Blacker, 146 U.S. 1 (1892)
Williams v. Rhodes, 393 U.S. 23 (1968)
Adams v. Clinton, 90 F. Supp. 2d 35 (D.D.C. 2000), *aff'd,* 531 U.S. 941 (2000)
Bush v. Gore, 531 U.S. 98 (2000)
Bush v. Palm Beach Cnty. Canvassing Bd., 531 U.S. 70 (2000)

Poll Taxes

Section 1. The right of citizens of the United States to vote in any primary or other election for President or Vice President, for electors for President or Vice President, or for Senator or Representative in Congress, shall not be denied or abridged by the United States or any State by reason of failure to pay poll tax or other tax.
Section 2. The Congress shall have power to enforce this article by appropriate legislation.
(Amendment XXIV)

≈

Southern states enacted poll taxes of one or two dollars per year between 1889 and 1966 as a prerequisite to voting. A citizen paid the tax when registering and then annually thereafter; some laws required payment up to nine months before an election. Furthermore, many states had a cumulative feature that required an individual to pay all previous years' poll taxes before he could vote in the instant year.

Prior to the enactment of poll taxes, property ownership was frequently a prerequisite to voting. States instituted the poll tax early in the nineteenth century as a device to grant voting rights to individuals who did not own real property. Although most states had dispensed with both property qualifications and the poll tax by the time of the Civil War, the tax resurfaced in the South to dilute the effect of race-neutral voting provisions required in Southern states' constitutions as a condition for readmission to the Union following the Civil War.

Beginning in 1889, Southern states reintroduced the poll tax as a method of disenfranchising black voters. As delegate Carter Glass declared during the Virginia constitutional convention of 1902, the tax was designed "with a view to the elimination of every negro voter who can be gotten rid of, legally, without materially impairing the numerical strength of the white electorate." Additionally, poll taxes had the effect of disenfranchising the poor in general, including whites; later, it fell upon some women after the passage of the Nineteenth Amendment.

Legislation to eliminate poll taxes in federal elections was introduced in every Congress beginning in 1939, but no bill made it into law. By the time of the Twenty-fourth Amendment's ratification in 1964, only five states retained a poll tax. Nevertheless, Congress deemed the amendment necessary inasmuch as poll taxes had previously survived constitutional challenges in the courts, *Breedlove v. Suttles* (1937), and they had become a notorious symbol of black disenfranchisement.

During the debates, some members of Congress argued that because poll taxes were racially discriminatory, Congress should outlaw them directly under the enforcement powers of the Fourteenth and Fifteenth Amendments. However, Congress eventually decided against using its Fifteenth Amendment enforcement power because it did not directly reach the disenfranchisement of the poor. Early drafts of the Fifteenth Amendment had, in fact, sought to proscribe devices like poll taxes. Ultimately, however, the Fifteenth Amendment's drafters had settled on language forbidding only racial discrimination in the enjoyment of the franchise. A specific poll tax amendment would be both more sweeping and have greater symbolic status. In addition, the amendment's supporters attacked the poll tax as a vehicle for fraud because the tax facilitated political corruption through vote buying by political machines that had made block payments of the tax. Some states allowed third parties to pay an individual's poll tax, so some businesses interested in the repeal of the Eighteenth Amendment were able to pay the poll tax for their patrons. Similarly, unions, frustrated with the resistance to unionization in the South, encouraged registration of their members in some cases by paying their poll taxes. Defenders of states' rights, however, fended off any attempt to extend the amendment's application to local elections. Nonetheless, not long after the ratification of the amendment, Congress enacted the Voting Rights Act of 1965, which made problematic the continuing validity of the poll tax as a qualification in state elections.

In *Harman v. Forssenius* (1965), the Supreme Court for the first time construed the Twenty-fourth Amendment, giving broad effect to its prohibition. In anticipation of the amendment's adoption, Virginia had enacted a statute amending its election laws to provide that a qualified citizen might vote in federal elections only if, at least six months prior to each election, he had either paid a poll tax or filed a certificate of residence. In declaring the new Virginia voting law unconstitutional, the Court stressed the broad language of the Twenty-fourth Amendment, which prohibits not only the denial but also the abridgement of the right to vote. The Court noted that the Twenty-fourth Amendment, like the Fifteenth, "nullifies sophisticated as well as simple-minded modes of impairing the right guaranteed." Continuing, the Court also found that the Twenty-fourth Amendment applies to "onerous procedural requirements" that effectively handicap, impede, or impair the "exercise of the franchise by those claiming the constitutional immunity."

The drafters of the amendment carefully limited its scope to federal elections. Two years after its ratification, the Supreme Court announced that the use of poll taxes as a prerequisite to voting in state elections violated the Equal Protection Clause of the Fourteenth Amendment, even though it was evident that the conclusion was at odds with the original understanding of the framers of the Fourteenth Amendment, a position emphasized in the dissents of Justices Hugo L. Black and John M. Harlan. *Harper v. Virginia State Board of Elections* (1966). In *Harper*, the Court dealt with a Virginia statute requiring the payment of a poll tax not to exceed $1.50 as a precondition for voting, an amount that Virginia argued was minimal and thus not a significant burden on the right to vote. Admitting "the right to vote in state elections is nowhere expressly mentioned," the Court nevertheless invalidated the statute because "it is enough to say that once the franchise is granted to the electorate, lines may not be drawn which are inconsistent with the Equal Protection Clause of the Fourteenth Amendment." Justice William O. Douglas, writing for the Court, explained: "[A] state violates the Equal Protection Clause...whenever it makes the affluence of the voter or payment of any fee an electoral standard. Voter qualifications have no relation to wealth nor to paying or not paying this or any other tax." The logic of the Court's opinion has made the Twenty-fourth Amendment superfluous, as Justice John M. Harlan observed in his dissent in *Harper*.

Recent attempts to extend the Twenty-fourth Amendment to other contexts have failed. Federal courts have turned aside arguments that the amendment forbids re-enfranchisement of felons contingent upon payment of child support, *Johnson v. Bredesen* (2010), or payment of past due fines, *Harvey v. Brewer* (2012), or even a fee to cover the process for reinstatement of voting rights, *Howard v. Gilmore* (2000). Neither does voter identification laws constitute a poll tax, *Gonzalez v. Arizona* (2010). Voting disenfranchisement claims receive a better hearing from the courts under the Equal Protection Clause of the Fourteenth Amendment.

David F. Forte

See Also

Article I, Section 2, Clause 1 (Elector Qualifications)

Amendment XIV, Section 1 (Equal Protection)
Amendment XV (Suffrage—Race)
Amendment XIX (Suffrage—Sex)

Suggestions for Further Research

Bruce Ackerman & Jennifer Nou, *Canonizing the Civil Rights Revolution: The People and the Poll Tax*, 103 Nw. U. L. Rev. 63 (2009)

Steven F. Lawson, Black Ballots: Voting Rights in the South, 1944–1969 (1976)

Frederic D. Ogden, The Poll Tax in the South (1958)

Ronnie L. Podolefsky, *The Illusion of Suffrage: Female Voting Rights and the Women's Poll Tax Repeal Movement After the Nineteenth Amendment*, 7 Colum. J. Gender & L. 185 (1998)

Significant Cases

Breedlove v. Suttles, 302 U.S. 277 (1937)
Harman v. Forssenius, 380 U.S. 528 (1965)
Harper v. Virginia State Bd. of Elections, 383 U.S. 663 (1966)
Howard v. Gilmore, 2000 U.S. App. LEXIS 2680 (4th Cir., February 23, 2000)Johnson v. Bredesen, 624 F.3d 742 (6th Cir. 2010)
Gonzalez v. Arizona, 624 F.3d 1162 (9th Cir. 2010)
Harvey v. Brewer, 605 F.3d 1067 (9th Cir. 2010)

Presidential Succession

Section 1. In case of the removal of the President from office or of his death or resignation, the Vice President shall become President.

Section 2. Whenever there is a vacancy in the office of the Vice President, the President shall nominate a Vice President who shall take office upon confirmation by a majority vote of both Houses of Congress.

Section 3. Whenever the President transmits to the President pro tempore of the Senate and the Speaker of the House of Representatives his written declaration that he is

unable to discharge the powers and duties of his office, and until he transmits to them a written declaration to the contrary, such powers and duties shall be discharged by the Vice President as Acting President.

Section 4. Whenever the Vice President and a majority of either the principal officers of the executive departments or of such other body as Congress may by law provide, transmit to the President pro tempore of the Senate and the Speaker of the House of Representatives their written declaration that the President is unable to discharge the powers and duties of his office, the Vice President shall immediately assume the powers and duties of the office as Acting President.

Thereafter, when the President transmits to the President pro tempore of the Senate and the Speaker of the House of Representatives his written declaration that no inability exists, he shall resume the powers and duties of his office unless the Vice President and a majority of either the principal officers of the executive department or of such other body as Congress may by law provide, transmit within four days to the President pro tempore of the Senate and the Speaker of the House of Representatives their written declaration that the President is unable to discharge the powers and duties of his office. Thereupon Congress shall decide the issue, assembling within forty-eight hours for that purpose if not in session. If the Congress, within twenty-one days after receipt of the latter written declaration, or, if Congress is not in session, within twenty-one days after Congress is required to assemble, determines by two-thirds vote of both Houses

that the President is unable to discharge the powers and duties of his office, the Vice President shall continue to discharge the same as Acting President; otherwise, the President shall resume the powers and duties of his office.

(Amendment XXV)

~

*T*he original Presidential Succession Clause of the Constitution (Article II, Section 1, Clause 6) appeared to be relatively simple in providing for succession to the presidency. There were, however, troubling ambiguities. What was the meaning of "inability" of a president "to discharge the Powers and Duties of said Office"? Who determined the existence of an "inability"? Did a vice president become president for the rest of the presidential term in the case of an inability or in the event of death, resignation, or removal; or was he merely "acting as President"? It was clear that there was no procedure for filling a vacancy in the office of vice president, although the Constitution authorized Congress to legislate a line of succession to cover situations involving the death, resignation, removal, or inability of both the president and vice president.

Until the Twenty-fifth Amendment was adopted, the nation confronted a number of deaths in office of presidents and vice presidents, as well as periods when presidents were disabled. When President William Henry Harrison died in 1841, Vice President John Tyler, asserting that he was fully the president, ascended to the presidency for the rest of the term, claiming that was the proper interpretation of the clause. He insisted that he was "President," not "Acting President." The precedent he established by assumption of the presidency was followed by other vice presidents when presidents died in office. These presidents were Zachary Taylor, Abraham Lincoln, James A. Garfield, William McKinley, Warren G. Harding, Franklin D. Roosevelt, and John F. Kennedy. The vice presidents who succeeded to the office were Tyler, Millard Fillmore, Andrew Johnson, Chester A. Arthur, Theodore Roosevelt, Calvin Coolidge, Harry S. Truman, and Lyndon B. Johnson, respectively.

Although the Tyler precedent was helpful in providing for continuity and stability, it caused future vice presidents to hesitate in asserting any role in a case of presidential inability as opposed to the death of the president. There was the question of whether the vice president succeeded to the presidency for the rest of the term, even in a case of temporary inability, as well as the problem of the vice president's being seen as a usurper because of the constitutional silence about his role in determining whether there was an inability. This hesitancy occurred during the eighty days when President Garfield lay dying after being shot by an assassin in 1881, in the period after President Woodrow Wilson suffered a stroke in 1919, and when President Dwight D. Eisenhower suffered a heart attack, an attack of ileitis, and then a stroke. To cope with any future inability, President Eisenhower and Vice President Richard M. Nixon developed an informal protocol. Although it did not have the force of law, it gave assurance that a case of inability would be handled with due regard for stability. It provided for the president to declare his own inability and, if unable to do so, enabled the vice president, with appropriate consultation, to make the decision. In either event, the vice president served as acting president until the president recovered his powers and duties upon his own declaration of recovery. This protocol was followed in turn by President Kennedy and Vice President Johnson and then by President Johnson and Speaker John McCormack. President Johnson and Vice President Hubert Humphrey orally agreed to a similar arrangement, though they executed no written letter of agreement.

Compounding the problem of presidential inability was the problem of vice presidential vacancy. Such a vacancy occurred whenever a president died in office, on the seven occasions when vice presidents died in office, and when Vice President John C. Calhoun resigned in 1832. In the absence of a mechanism for filling a vacancy, a statutory line of succession provided the necessary backup. This line changed twice in the country's history. The original line, reflected in a law of 1792, placed the president pro tempore of the Senate next in line after the vice president.

In 1886 the secretary of state was made first in line, followed by other members of the cabinet. Then, in 1947, the Speaker of the House of Representatives and president pro tempore of the Senate, respectively, were placed ahead of the secretary of state and all the other cabinet officers in line, now ending with the secretary of homeland security.

After President John F. Kennedy was assassinated in 1963, there was a movement to constitutionalize these practices and to provide more certainty. The Twenty-fifth Amendment reflects the history of succession in its provisions providing for the vice president to become president in the event of the death, resignation, or removal of the president and to serve as acting president for the duration of any inability. It allows a president to declare his own inability and resume his powers and duties when it has ended. This provision has been used when presidents underwent surgery—in 1985 by President Ronald Reagan and in 2002 and 2007 by President George W. Bush. The transfer of presidential power to their vice presidents was of short duration in each case. On other occasions in the administrations of both President George H. W. Bush and William J. Clinton, when the president underwent a medical procedure, consideration among the presidential staff was given to whether he should invoke Section 3 of the Amendment, but as neither president underwent general anesthesia, the need did not arise.

The president's discretion in determining his own inability under Section 3 is broad. The discretion of those other officials whom Section 4 empowers to declare the president disabled, however, is more constrained. Section 4 was designed to cover cases where the president was unable to make or communicate a decision as to his competency. In those situations, the vice president with a majority of the cabinet, could declare the president unable to execute his office, whereupon the vice president would become acting president. However, if the president disagrees with the vice president and a majority of the cabinet, and the vice president and the cabinet renew their assertion of his inability, then Congress resolves the issue. The amendment also gives Congress the power to replace the cabinet and substitute another body to function with the vice president under Section 4.

It was not an accident that the amendment did not define "inability." It was intended principally to cover cases of both physical and mental inability, such as when a president undergoes surgery, is kidnapped, or becomes infirm. It does not cover political and policy differences or poor judgment, incompetence, laziness, and the like.

The amendment, recognizing the importance of the vice presidency, added a Section 2 procedure for filling a vacancy in that office, namely, nomination by the president and confirmation by both houses of Congress. This procedure was used when Vice President Spiro T. Agnew resigned and was replaced by Gerald R. Ford and again after Richard M. Nixon resigned as president. Ford became president and Nelson A. Rockefeller became vice president by the same process. President Ford's succession to the presidency was by virtue of Section 1 of the amendment and not based on the Tyler precedent.

Since 1967, there have been many meetings and studies to consider proposals to improve the system of presidential succession including the following: Congressional hearings in 1994, 2003, and 2004; a commission on presidential disability, the Miller Commission of the University of Virginia, which in 1988 proposed guidelines for advance planning by presidents; a Working Group on Presidential Disability, hosted by The Carter Center of Emory University and Wake Forest University, which focused on the role of doctors in cases of presidential inability; and studies and recommendations by the Continuity in Government Commission and a Presidential Succession Clinic at Fordham Law School with respect to gaps and ambiguities in the system, such as where there was no vice president, or the president and vice president were disabled at the same time, or a statutory successor acting as president became disabled.

John Feerick

See Also

Article II, Section 1, Clause 6 (Presidential Succession)

Amendment XX (Presidential Terms)

Suggestions for Further Research

Birch Evans Bayh, One Heartbeat Away: Presidential Disability and Succession (1968)

Continuity of Gov't Comm'n, Preserving Our Institutions: The Continuity of the Presidency (Second Report 2009)

Ensuring the Stability of Presidential Succession in the Modern Era: Report of the Fordham University School of Law's Clinic on Presidential Succession, 81 Fordham L. Rev. (2012)

John D. Feerick, *The Proposed Twenty-Fifth Amendment to the Constitution*, 34 Fordham L. Rev. 173 (1965)

John D. Feerick, The Twenty-Fifth Amendment: Its Complete History and Applications (1976, 2013)

Joel K. Goldstein, The Modern American Vice Presidency: The Transformation of a Political Institution (1982)

Managing Crisis: Presidential Disability and the Twenty-Fifth Amendment (Robert E. Gilbert ed., 2000)

Rose McDermott, Presidential Leadership, Illness, and Decision Making (2008)

Presidential Disability: Papers, Discussions, and Recommendations on the Twenty-Fifth Amendment and Issues of Inability and Disability in Presidents of the United States (James F. Toole and Robert J. Joynt eds., 2001)

Report of the Commission on Presidential Disability and the Twenty-Fifth Amendment (1988), by the fourth Miller Center Commission, at http://web1.millercenter.org/commissions/comm_1988.pdf

Suffrage—Age

Section 1. The right of citizens of the United States, who are eighteen years of age or older, to vote shall not be denied or abridged by the United States or by any State on account of age.

Section 2. The Congress shall have power to enforce this article by appropriate legislation.

(Amendment XXVI)

~

*T*he Vietnam War provoked many draft-age youngsters and like-minded adults to proclaim, "If eighteen- to twenty-year-olds are old enough to die for their country, they're old enough to vote." That slogan is commonly cited as the impetus for the Twenty-sixth Amendment. The truth is somewhat less colorful. The amendment was crafted primarily to overturn the holding of a fractured Supreme Court in *Oregon v. Mitchell* (1970). That case had invalidated an attempt by Congress to regulate voting age in state and local elections. Essentially, the Twenty-sixth Amendment did what Congress could not constitutionally do.

Earlier in 1970, Congress had amended the Voting Rights Act of 1965 (*see* P.L. 91–285, 84 Stat. 314), lowering the minimum voting age to eighteen in all federal, state, and local elections. When the revised law was challenged, primarily on federalism grounds, Justice Hugo L. Black wrote that Congress had no power to change the voting age in either state or local elections. Four justices in two separate opinions agreed with Black's conclusion regarding voting age, although they disagreed about other issues in the case (literacy tests and residency requirements). *See* also 42 U.S.C. 1971 *et seq.* The remaining four justices argued that Congress could change the minimum voting age in both state and local elections using its enforcement power under Section 5 of the Fourteenth Amendment.

Thus, Black's opinion, which no other justice joined in full, left us with the rule that Congress had the authority to extend the vote to eighteen-year-olds in federal elections but not in state or local contests. The Twenty-sixth Amendment changes that.

After *Oregon v. Mitchell*, states unwilling to set their minimum voting age at eighteen would have to maintain separate voting systems for federal and nonfederal elections. The great majority of people thought that eighteen-year-olds should have the right to vote, and the states ratified the Twenty-sixth Amendment in record time—a mere 107 days after Congress proposed it.

Almost immediately, the courts had to resolve issues peripheral to the new amendment. For example, did the right to vote for a candidate include eligibility to sign and vote for initiative petitions? In *Colorado Project-Common Cause v. Anderson* (1972), a state court found that enactment of the Twenty-sixth Amendment entailed participation by young voters in the entire political process—initiatives included.

Could states restrict voting by minors by denying them residency at schools or other places away from their parents? In *Jolicoeur v. Mihaly* (1971), the California Supreme Court found that denying minors voting residence where they actually lived—whether at school or elsewhere—violated the Twenty-sixth Amendment; the Court held that the amendment emancipated minors for all purposes related to voting. In the same vein, a New Jersey court added that the Twenty-sixth Amendment secured the rights of bona fide campus residents to register in the counties where their campuses were located. *Worden v. Mercer County Board of Elections* (1972).

On the other hand, a state constitution could, without offending the Twenty-sixth Amendment, institute twenty-one as the minimum age for holding elective public office. *Opatz v. City of St. Cloud* (1972). The amendment does not mandate that persons under twenty-one years of age be seated as jurors under state law. *Johnson v. State* (1972); *Commonwealth v. Cobbs* (1973); *State ex rel. McNary v. Stussie* (1974). Nor does the amendment cover an Indian tribal election, unless the secretary of the interior called the election to ratify or amend a tribal constitution, in which case the election is federal and the amendment applies. *Wounded Head v. Tribal Council of Oglala Sioux Tribe of Pine Ridge Reservation* (1975); *Cheyenne River Sioux Tribe v. Andrus* (1977).

Robert Levy

See Also

Amendment XIV, Section 2 (Apportionment of Representatives)

Amendment XV (Suffrage—Race)

Amendment XVII (Popular Election of Senators)

Amendment XIX (Suffrage—Sex)

Amendment XXIV (Poll Taxes)

Suggestions for Further Research

William H. Danne Jr., Annotation: Residence of Students for Voting Purposes, 44 A.L.R. 3d. 797 (1972)

Kenneth J. Guido, Student Voting and Residency Qualifications: The Aftermath of the Twenty-Sixth Amendment, 47 N.Y.U. L. Rev. 32 (1972)

Significant Cases

Oregon v. Mitchell, 400 U.S. 112 (1970)

Jolicoeur v. Mihaly, 5 Cal.3d 565 (1971)

Colorado Project-Common Cause v. Anderson, 178 Colo. 1, 495 P.2d 220 (1972)

Johnson v. State, 260 So.2d 436 (Miss. 1972)

Opatz v. City of St. Cloud, 293 Minn. 379, 196 N.W.2d 298 (1972)

Worden v. Mercer Cnty. Bd. of Elections, 61 N.J. 325, 294 A.2d 233 (1972)

Commonwealth v. Cobbs, 452 Pa. 397, 305 A.2d 25 (1973)

State *ex rel.* McNary v. Stussie, 518 S.W.2d 630 (Mo. 1974)

Wounded Head v. Tribal Council of Oglala Sioux Tribe of Pine Ridge Reservation, 507 F.2d 1079 (8th Cir. 1975)

Cheyenne River Sioux Tribe v. Andrus, 566 F.2d 1085 (8th Cir. 1977)

Congressional Compensation

No law, varying the compensation for the services of the Senators and Representatives, shall take effect, until an election of representatives shall have intervened.

(**Amendment XXVII**)

~

On June 8, 1789, James Madison proposed the Congressional Compensation Amendment as one of many that he presented to the House of Representatives that day. After debate, the House of Representatives and the Senate approved the proposed amendment and forwarded it and eleven others to the states. Only six states ratified it, well short of the three-quarters requirement, however, and thus it did not become part of the Bill of Rights. The proposed amendment languished for almost two hundred years before becoming the object of a successful ratification campaign in the 1980s, ultimately resulting in its formal acceptance by Congress as the Twenty-seventh Amendment on May 20, 1992.

At the Constitutional Convention, the Framers heatedly debated the question of whether individual states or the new national government would compensate elected representatives. The Compensation Clause of Article I, Section 6, was the result, providing that the central government would pay the representatives from the federal treasury as established by federal law.

The Anti-Federalists and others at state ratifying conventions found this compensation arrangement deeply worrisome; because members of Congress would enact the very law that set their salaries, there would be no check on Congress's ability to enrich itself. It was a classic case of the danger of self-dealing corruption. Madison responded to that criticism with the proposed Compensation Amendment, which would prevent representatives from granting themselves a pay raise that would take effect during the term in which they sat. Instead, Congress would be able to pass the pay raise only prospectively and would thereby face the electorate before it could take effect. Madison believed the amendment was necessary because of the "seeming impropriety in leaving any set of men without controul to put their hand into the public coffers, to take out money to put in their pockets."

Some legal scholars have speculated that the amendment failed at the time it was first proposed because state legislators, to whom the ratification question was presented, might have feared that, once ratified, a similar initiative might be pushed regarding their own compensation. Anti-Federalists who had proposed the idea during the Constitution's ratification debates were not so troubled, however, easily distinguishing the local legislator from the national. The former, the Anti-Federalist Cornelius wrote, was chosen annually, in small districts, and "sent but a small distance" from his home, whereas the latter was "far removed, and long detained, from the view of their constituents."

The issue of congressional compensation was the subject of periodic legislation and attendant political maneuvering in succeeding years. Particularly unpopular with the electorate was the notorious "Salary Grab" Act of 1873, which not only granted a pay raise to legislators but also made it retroactive. One of the Ohio General Assembly's responses to the act was ratification of the dormant Compensation Amendment, thus becoming the seventh state to do so, eighty-four years after Maryland, which was the first state to ratify.

Over a century later, the amendment became the object of a grassroots ratification campaign initiated by a college undergraduate who had authored a term paper on the subject in 1982. Despite widespread doubt about the propriety of actually adopting the long-dormant amendment should it ever be fully ratified, the ratification campaign gathered momentum. On May 7, 1992, Michigan became the thirty-eighth state to ratify the Compensation Amendment, completing the process initiated over two hundred years earlier by the First Congress in 1789.

The unique history of the Compensation Amendment raised initial questions about the validity of its ratification. In *Coleman v. Miller* (1939), the Supreme Court declared that disputes about ratification procedures and the time within which an amendment could be ratified were political questions assigned to the province of the legislative branch under Article V of the Constitution and, therefore, not subject to adjudication by the federal courts. *Coleman* seemed to envision some sort of formal congressional review of the constitutional validity of a fully ratified amendment prior to its official addition to the Constitution. Despite initial comments about formal review by rather stunned federal legislators following Michigan's ratifying vote on May 7, 1992, Congress, sensing the public mood, scheduled no formal hearings on the Compensation Amendment. On May 18, 1992, the National Archivist certified the amendment. Two days

later, overwhelming majorities in both chambers of Congress confirmed the Twenty-seventh Amendment. The Office of Legal Counsel of the Department of Justice also issued an opinion declaring that, despite the long passage in time, the ratification of the amendment was valid.

The first challenge arising under the amendment was brought by Representative John Boehner, who claimed that the automatic Cost of Living Adjustments (COLAs) provided to Congress under the Ethics Reform Act of 1989 amounted to an increase in compensation without an intervening election. Assuming that the Twenty-seventh Amendment applied to laws adopted before it was ratified, the Court of Appeals for the District of Columbia Circuit nevertheless rejected the claim, noting that "the COLA provision of the Ethics Reform Act of 1989 is constitutional because it did not cause any adjustment to congressional compensation until after the election of 1990 and the seating of the new Congress." *Boehner v. Anderson* (D.C. Cir. 1994).

Another challenge to the COLA provision in federal court centered on the question of standing. *Schaffer v. Clinton* (2001). Outside of Establishment Clause cases, *see Flast v. Cohen* (1968), the federal courts almost never recognize a taxpayer's standing to contest a spending provision of a law. Consequently, the district court denied standing to three of the plaintiffs, who came to the court as taxpayers. However, the district court reached the merits for the remaining plaintiff, Representative Bob Schaffer, whose salary had been increased under the statute (to the detriment, he asserted, of his anti-tax reputation).

On appeal, the Tenth Circuit declined to reach the merits, finding instead that Representative Schaffer also lacked standing, noting that "the standing inquiry must be 'especially rigorous'" when the dispute involves two branches of government. The circuit court held that the congressman "was not injured for standing purposes simply because he received a higher salary." If followed by later courts—the Supreme Court denied the petition for a writ of certiorari in the case—the Tenth Circuit's reasoning would appear to foreclose standing to any plaintiff challenging a statute under the Twenty-seventh

Amendment. Ironically, after lying dormant for two hundred years, this amendment may now have been put back to sleep. Nevertheless, it is clear that Congress still has the option of voluntarily abiding by the amendment.

John C. Eastman

See Also

Article I, Section 6, Clause 1 (Compensation Clause)
Article I, Section 9, Clause 7 (Appropriations Clause)
Article III, Section 2 (Judicial Power)

Suggestions for Further Research

Richard B. Bernstein, *The Sleeper Wakes: The History and Legacy of the Twenty-seventh Amendment*, 61 FORDHAM L. REV. 497 (1992)

Gary Lawson, *The Constitution's Congress*, 89 B.U. L. Rev. 399 (2009)

Office of Legal Counsel, Department of Justice, *Memorandum Opinion: Congressional Pay Amendment*, November 2, 1992, at http://www.justice.gov/olc/congress.17.htm

Ronald D. Rotunda, *Running Out of Time: Can the E.R.A. Be Saved?*, 64 A.B.A. J. 1507 (1978)

Adrian Vermeule, *The Constitutional Law of Official Compensation*, 102 COLUM. L. REV. 501 (2002)

Significant Cases

Coleman v. Miller, 307 U.S. 433 (1939)
Flast v. Cohen, 392 U.S. 83 (1968)
Boehner v. Anderson, 30 F.3d 156 (D.C. Cir. 1994)
Schaffer v. Clinton, 240 F.3d 878 (10th Cir. 2001), *cert. denied sub nom.* Schaffer v. O'Neill, 122 S. Ct. 458 (2001)

TABLE OF CASES

The Heritage Guide to the Constitution Additional Recommended Reading

Primary Sources and Collected Documents

The Essential Antifederalist
Edited by William B. Allen and Gordon Lloyd (University Press of America, 1985)

An accessible selection of leading anti-Federalist opinion. After an interpretative essay by the editors, the selections are grouped to focus on the origins of anti-Federalist thought, then later views on federalism, republicanism, capitalism, and democracy.

Debates on the Constitution
Edited by Bernard Bailyn (The Library of America, 1993)

A two-volume collection of Federalist and anti-Federalist speeches, articles, and letters during the struggle over ratification of the Constitution, focusing on debates in the press and correspondence between September 1787 and August 1788, as well as on the debates in the state ratifying conventions of Pennsylvania, Connecticut, Massachusetts, South Carolina, Virginia, New York, and North Carolina.

Commentaries on the Laws of England
William Blackstone (University of Chicago Press, 1991)

Originally lecture notes designed as a general introduction to the law, these volumes of British legal thinking and common law analysis were significant in England and the American colonies in the century after their initial publication in 1765 and were thus especially influential during the formation of the American legal system.

The Records of the Federal Convention of 1787
Edited by Max Farrand (Yale University Press, 1986)

This definitive work, originally published in 1937, gathers into three volumes all the written records left by participants of the Constitutional Convention of 1787, including James Madison's extensive official notes.

The Federalist Papers
Alexander Hamilton, John Jay, and James Madison (Mentor Books edition, 1999)

Published as a series of newspaper articles intended to sway New Yorkers in the debate over ratification, this famous collection of essays in defense of the Constitution remains the greatest work of American political philosophy. The classic edition, edited by the late Clinton Rossiter, has now been published with an introduction by Charles Kesler, as well as an historical glossary and other supplementary materials.

The U.S. Constitution: A Reader
Edited by the Hillsdale College Politics Faculty (Hillsdale College Press, 2012)

This reader features 113 primary source documents covering the principles of the American founding, the framing and structure of the Constitution, the secession crisis and the Civil War, the Progressive rejection of the Constitution, and the building of the administrative state based on Progressive principles. Each section has a full introduction and each entry is prefaced by an introductory note, thus placing all the documents in a coherent framework.

American Political Writing During the Founding Era
Edited by Charles Hyneman and Donald Lutz (Liberty Press, 1983)

This two-volume set includes pamphlets, articles, sermons and essays written by various political authors between 1762 and 1805. Each of the seventy-six entries is introduced by a brief note on the author.

The Founders' Constitution
Edited by Philip B. Kurland and Ralph Lerner (Liberty Fund, 2000)

Originally published by the University of Chicago Press to commemorate the bicentennial of the Constitution, this extensive work consists of extracts from the leading works on political theory, history, law, and constitutional arguments on which the Framers and their contemporaries drew and which they themselves produced. Liberty Fund has prepared a paperback edition of the entire work in five volumes. It is also available online at *http://press-pubs. uchicago.edu/founders*.

Commentaries on the Constitution
Joseph Story (Carolina Academic Press, 1987)

A classic work on the meaning of the U.S. Constitution by one of its early scholars and one of the greatest justices of the Supreme Court. A reprint of the 1833 edition includes histories of various colonies and of the Revolutionary and Confederation periods; it also includes straight-forward commentaries on most clauses of the Constitution.

Secondary Sources and Collected Documents

Taking the Constitution Seriously
Walter Berns (Simon and Schuster, 1987)

This brief work makes a defense of the original intent of the Framers by relating the Constitution back to the principles of the Declaration of Independence and considering how the Founding dealt with various challenges to the idea of constitutionalism.

Originalism: A Quarter-Century of Debate
Edited by Steven G. Calabresi (Regnery, 2007)

A collection of speeches, panel discussions, and debates, this book chronicles the development and growth of originalism as a judicial philosophy, compiling a variety of viewpoints on originalism from leading legal scholars. The volume includes Attorney General Edwin Meese's 1985 speech to the American Bar Association and his speech to the Federalist Society twenty years later.

The Age of Federalism: The Early American Republic, 1788–1800
Stanley Elkins and Eric McKitrick (Oxford University Press, 1993)

This lengthy work traces the development of the new nation from the time after the Constitutional Convention through its first three presidents. A comprehensive analysis of the early national period, including all the achievements and fights of the chief figures.

The Slaveholding Republic: An Account of the United States Government's Relations to Slavery
Don E. Fehrenbacher (Oxford University Press, 2001)

This detailed study, stretching from the First Continental Congress to the Civil War, argues persuasively that early trends in the colonies were against slavery and that the U.S. Constitution is not a pro-slavery document, despite later policies that supported the institution.

From Parchment to Power: How James Madison Used the Bill of Rights to Save the Constitution
Robert Goldwin (American Enterprise Institute, 1997)

A clear and convincing historical study of the constitutional issues surrounding the creation of the Bill of Rights, looking at the philosophical arguments behind these guarantees and how Madison crafted the first ten amendments and shepherded them through the First Congress.

Saving the Revolution: The Federalist Papers and the American Founding
Edited by Charles Kesler (New York: Free Press, 1987)

An approachable collection of fourteen essays by leading scholars explaining and interpreting the Federalist Papers on topics such as republicanism, federalism, foreign policy, the separation of powers, executive power, and the original purposes of the Constitution.

Ratification: The People Debate the Constitution 1787–1788
Pauline Maier (Simon and Schuster, 2010)

A well-researched, well-written history of what came after the convention in Philadelphia based on the wealth of historical sources surrounding the state ratification conventions.

Principles of Constitutional Law
John E. Nowak and Ronald D. Rotunda (West, 2010)

This concise treatise on American constitutional law (condensed from a five-volume legal text) provides law students and non-students with a basic understanding of the most fundamental principles of constitutional law. The text is designed to explain and analyze those principles, and it provides a guide as to how judges and legal practitioners apply them in the world outside the classroom, thus forming the foundation used to develop new precedents.

Originalism in American Law and Politics: A Constitutional History
Johnathan O'Neill (Johns Hopkins University Press, 2005)

This work chronicles the development of originalism from its beginning in Anglo-American constitutionalism to its reemergence as a prominent facet of post-war American political life, demonstrating that originalism derives from the core principles of the Anglo-American constitutional tradition.

The Beginnings of National Politics: An Interpretive History of the Continental Congress
Jack N. Rakove (Alfred Knopf, 1979)

Rakove follows the flow of events to reconstruct the circumstances and decisions of the First Continental Congress of 1774 and the Second Continental Congress (which began in 1775 and became the Congress of the Confederation in 1781), including the administration of the Revolutionary War, the framing (and breakdown) of the Articles of Confederation, and the reform movement that culminated in the Constitutional Convention of 1787.

1787: The Grand Convention
Clinton Rossiter (MacMillan Company, 1966)

Rossiter, the editor of the most widely read edition of *The Federalist Papers*, examines the meeting that created the Constitution in this very readable work, focusing on the setting, men, events, and consequences of the federal convention through the early years of the new republic. A number of related documents are also included.

What the Anti-Federalists Were For: The Political Thought of the Opponents of the Constitution
Herbert J. Storing (The University of Chicago, 1981)

A brief introduction to the thought of the Anti-Federalists, who opposed the ratification of the Constitution and wanted a small republic, more federalism, and a bill of rights, among other things. It also considers their effect on enduring themes of American political life, such as a concern for big government and the infringement of personal liberty.

Living Constitution, Dying Faith: Progressivism and the New Science of Jurisprudence
Bradley C. S. Watson (ISI Books, 2009)

This work explains how modern legal thinking began with the progressive rejection of America's principles and its creation of a new theory of the "living Constitution."

About the Editors

Senior Editor David F. Forte is Professor of Law at Cleveland State University. Forte is a graduate of Harvard College and holds an M.A. from the University of Manchester, a Ph.D. from the University of Toronto, and a law degree from Columbia University. A former Chief Counsel to the United States delegation to the United Nations, a National Endowment for the Humanities Fellow, and a Fulbright Scholar, Dr. Forte writes and lectures on a wide range of topics, including international law, constitutional law, natural law, and jurisprudence. He served as book review editor for the *American Journal of Jurisprudence* and is editor of *Natural Law and Contemporary Public Policy*.

Executive Editor Matthew Spalding is Associate Vice President and Dean of Educational Programs for Hillsdale College in Washington, D.C., and the Henry Salvatori Visiting Fellow at The Heritage Foundation. Spalding is a graduate of Claremont McKenna College and holds a Ph.D. from The Claremont Graduate School. An Associate Professor of Politics at Hillsdale College and a Senior Fellow of the Claremont Institute, he is the author of *We Still Hold These Truths: Rediscovering Our Principles, Reclaiming Our Future*, co-author of *A Sacred Union of Citizens: Washington's Farewell Address and the American Character*, and editor of *The Founders' Almanac: A Practical Guide to the Notable Events, Greatest Leaders & Most Eloquent Words of the American Founding*.

INDEX

*F*or page references to specific cases, please refer to the Table of Cases